WITHDRAWN

WILLIAM FAULKNER

PS
3511
.A86
F85
v. 1

WILLIAM FAULKNER

⌜NOVELS 1930–1935⌟

As I Lay Dying

Sanctuary

Light in August

Pylon

THE LIBRARY OF AMERICA

Salem College
Gramley Library
Winston-Salem, NC 27108

Volume arrangement, notes, and chronology copyright © 1985 by
Literary Classics of the United States, Inc., New York, N.Y.
All rights reserved.
No part of this book may be reproduced commercially
by offset-lithographic or equivalent copying devices without
the permission of the publisher.

As I Lay Dying copyright © 1930, renewed 1957; *Sanctuary* copyright © 1931,
renewed 1958; *Light in August* copyright © 1932, renewed 1959;
and *Pylon* copyright © 1935, renewed 1962, by William Faulkner.
Published by arrangement with Random House, Inc.

Published outside the United States and Canada by
arrangement with Chatto & Windus and the Hogarth Press.

The paper used in this publication meets the
minimum requirements of the American National Standard
for Information Sciences—Permanence of Paper for
Printed Library Materials, ANSI Z39.48-1984.

Distributed to the trade in the United States
and Canada by the Viking Press.

Published outside North America by the Press Syndicate
of the University of Cambridge,
The Pitt Building, Trumpington Street, Cambridge CB2IRP, England
ISBN 0 521 30094 0

Library of Congress Catalog Card Number: 84–23424
For cataloging information, see end of *Notes* section.
ISBN 0–940450–26–7

First Printing

Manufactured in the United States of America

Salem College
Gramley Library
Winston-Salem, NC 27108

JOSEPH BLOTNER AND NOEL POLK
WROTE THE NOTES AND SELECTED AND EDITED
THE TEXTS FOR THIS VOLUME

The texts of *As I Lay Dying, Sanctuary, Light in August,* and *Pylon* have been established by Noel Polk for publication by Faulkner's publisher.

Grateful acknowledgement is made to the National Endowment for the Humanities and the Ford Foundation for their generous financial support of this series.

The publishers wish to thank Mrs. Paul D. Summers, Jr., the Humanities Research Library of the University of Texas at Austin, the Alderman Library of the University of Virginia, and the John Davis Williams Library of the University of Mississippi for the use of archival materials.

Contents

AS I LAY DYING

To Hal Smith

Darl

J EWEL AND I come up from the field, following the path in
single file. Although I am fifteen feet ahead of him, anyone
watching us from the cottonhouse can see Jewel's frayed and
broken straw hat a full head above my own.

The path runs straight as a plumb-line, worn smooth by
feet and baked brick-hard by July, between the green rows of
laidby cotton, to the cottonhouse in the center of the field,
where it turns and circles the cottonhouse at four soft right
angles and goes on across the field again, worn so by feet in
fading precision.

The cottonhouse is of rough logs, from between which the
chinking has long fallen. Square, with a broken roof set at a
single pitch, it leans in empty and shimmering dilapidation in
the sunlight, a single broad window in two opposite walls
giving onto the approaches of the path. When we reach it I
turn and follow the path which circles the house. Jewel, fifteen feet behind me, looking straight ahead, steps in a single
stride through the window. Still staring straight ahead, his
pale eyes like wood set into his wooden face, he crosses the
floor in four strides with the rigid gravity of a cigar store
Indian dressed in patched overalls and endued with life from
the hips down, and steps in a single stride through the opposite window and into the path again just as I come around
the corner. In single file and five feet apart and Jewel now in
front, we go on up the path toward the foot of the bluff.

Tull's wagon stands beside the spring, hitched to the rail,
the reins wrapped about the seat stanchion. In the wagon bed
are two chairs. Jewel stops at the spring and takes the gourd
from the willow branch and drinks. I pass him and mount the
path, beginning to hear Cash's saw.

When I reach the top he has quit sawing. Standing in a
litter of chips, he is fitting two of the boards together. Between the shadow spaces they are yellow as gold, like soft
gold, bearing on their flanks in smooth undulations the marks
of the adze blade: a good carpenter, Cash is. He holds the
two planks on the trestle, fitted along the edges in a quarter
of the finished box. He kneels and squints along the edge of

them, then he lowers them and takes up the adze. A good carpenter. Addie Bundren could not want a better one, a better box to lie in. It will give her confidence and comfort. I go on to the house, followed by the

                         Chuck.   Chuck.   Chuck.

of the adze.

Cora

S O I SAVED OUT the eggs and baked yesterday. The cakes turned out right well. We depend a lot on our chickens. They are good layers, what few we have left after the possums and such. Snakes too, in the summer. A snake will break up a hen-house quicker than anything. So after they were going to cost so much more than Mr Tull thought, and after I promised that the difference in the number of eggs would make it up, I had to be more careful than ever because it was on my final say-so we took them. We could have stocked cheaper chickens, but I gave my promise as Miss Lawington said when she advised me to get a good breed, because Mr Tull himself admits that a good breed of cows or hogs pays in the long run. So when we lost so many of them we couldn't afford to use the eggs ourselves, because I could not have had Mr Tull chide me when it was on my say-so we took them. So when Miss Lawington told me about the cakes I thought that I could bake them and earn enough at one time to increase the net value of the flock the equivalent of two head. And that by saving the eggs out one at a time, even the eggs wouldn't be costing anything. And that week they laid so well that I not only saved out enough eggs above what we had engaged to sell, to bake the cakes with, I had saved enough so that the flour and the sugar and the stove wood would not be costing anything. So I baked yesterday, more careful than ever I baked in my life, and the cakes turned out right well. But when we got to town this morning Miss Lawington told me the lady had changed her mind and was not going to have the party after all.

"She ought to taken those cakes anyway," Kate says.

"Well," I say, "I reckon she never had no use for them now."

"She ought to taken them," Kate says. "But those rich town ladies can change their minds. Poor folks cant."

Riches is nothing in the face of the Lord, for He can see into the heart. "Maybe I can sell them at the bazaar Saturday," I say. They turned out real well.

"You cant get two dollars a piece for them," Kate says.

"Well, it isn't like they cost me anything," I say. I saved them out and swapped a dozen of them for the sugar and flour. It isn't like the cakes cost me anything, as Mr Tull himself realises that the eggs I saved were over and beyond what we had engaged to sell, so it was like we had found the eggs or they had been given to us.

"She ought to taken those cakes when she same as gave you her word," Kate says. The Lord can see into the heart. If it is His will that some folks has different ideas of honesty from other folks, it is not my place to question His decree.

"I reckon she never had any use for them," I say. They turned out real well, too.

The quilt is drawn up to her chin, hot as it is, with only her two hands and her face outside. She is propped on the pillow, with her head raised so she can see out the window, and we can hear him every time he takes up the adze or the saw. If we were deaf we could almost watch her face and hear him, see him. Her face is wasted away so that the bones draw just under the skin in white lines. Her eyes are like two candles when you watch them gutter down into the sockets of iron candle-sticks. But the eternal and the everlasting salvation and grace is not upon her.

"They turned out real nice," I say. "But not like the cakes Addie used to bake." You can see that girl's washing and ironing in the pillow-slip, if ironed it ever was. Maybe it will reveal her blindness to her, laying there at the mercy and the ministration of four men and a tom-boy girl. "There's not a woman in this section could ever bake with Addie Bundren," I say. "First thing we know she'll be up and baking again, and then we wont have any sale for ours at all." Under the quilt she makes no more of a hump than a rail would, and the only way you can tell she is breathing is by the sound of the mattress shucks. Even the hair at her cheek does not move, even with that girl standing right over her, fanning her with the fan. While we watch she swaps the fan to the other hand without stopping it.

"Is she sleeping?" Kate whispers.

"She's just watching Cash yonder," the girl says. We can hear the saw in the board. It sounds like snoring. Eula turns on the trunk and looks out the window. Her necklace looks real nice with her red hat. You wouldn't think it only cost twenty-five cents.

"She ought to taken those cakes," Kate says.

I could have used the money real well. But it's not like they cost me anything except the baking. I can tell him that anybody is likely to make a miscue, but it's not all of them that can get out of it without loss, I can tell him. It's not everybody can eat their mistakes, I can tell him.

Someone comes through the hall. It is Darl. He does not look in as he passes the door. Eula watches him as he goes on and passes from sight again toward the back. Her hand rises and touches her beads lightly, and then her hair. When she finds me watching her, her eyes go blank.

Darl

P A AND VERNON are sitting on the back porch. Pa is tilting snuff from the lid of his snuff-box into his lower lip, holding the lip outdrawn between thumb and finger. They look around as I cross the porch and dip the gourd into the water bucket and drink.

"Where's Jewel?" pa says. When I was a boy I first learned how much better water tastes when it has set a while in a cedar bucket. Warmish-cool, with a faint taste like the hot July wind in cedar trees smells. It has to set at least six hours, and be drunk from a gourd. Water should never be drunk from metal.

And at night it is better still. I used to lie on the pallet in the hall, waiting until I could hear them all asleep, so I could get up and go back to the bucket. It would be black, the shelf black, the still surface of the water a round orifice in nothingness, where before I stirred it awake with the dipper I could see maybe a star or two in the bucket, and maybe in the dipper a star or two before I drank. After that I was bigger, older. Then I would wait until they all went to sleep so I could lie with my shirt-tail up, hearing them asleep, feeling myself without touching myself, feeling the cool silence blowing upon my parts and wondering if Cash was yonder in the darkness doing it too, had been doing it perhaps for the last two years before I could have wanted to or could have.

Pa's feet are badly splayed, his toes cramped and bent and warped, with no toenail at all on his little toes, from working so hard in the wet in homemade shoes when he was a boy. Beside his chair his brogans sit. They look as though they had been hacked with a blunt axe out of pig-iron. Vernon has been to town. I have never seen him go to town in overalls. His wife, they say. She taught school too, once.

I fling the dipper dregs to the ground and wipe my mouth on my sleeve. It is going to rain before morning. Maybe before dark. "Down to the barn," I say. "Harnessing the team."

Down there fooling with that horse. He will go on through the barn, into the pasture. The horse will not be in sight: he is up there among the pine seedlings, in the cool.

8

Jewel whistles, once and shrill. The horse snorts, then Jewel sees him, glinting for a gaudy instant among the blue shadows. Jewel whistles again; the horse comes dropping down the slope, stiff-legged, his ears cocking and flicking, his mismatched eyes rolling, and fetches up twenty feet away, broadside on, watching Jewel over his shoulder in an attitude kittenish and alert.

"Come here, sir," Jewel says. He moves. Moving that quick his coat, bunching, tongues swirling like so many flames. With tossing mane and tail and rolling eye the horse makes another short curvetting rush and stops again, feet bunched, watching Jewel. Jewel walks steadily toward him, his hands at his sides. Save for Jewel's legs they are like two figures carved for a tableau savage in the sun.

When Jewel can almost touch him, the horse stands on his hind legs and slashes down at Jewel. Then Jewel is enclosed by a glittering maze of hooves as by an illusion of wings; among them, beneath the upreared chest, he moves with the flashing limberness of a snake. For an instant before the jerk comes onto his arms he sees his whole body earth-free, horizontal, whipping snake-limber, until he finds the horse's nostrils and touches earth again. Then they are rigid, motionless, terrific, the horse back-thrust on stiffened, quivering legs, with lowered head; Jewel with dug heels, shutting off the horse's wind with one hand, with the other patting the horse's neck in short strokes myriad and caressing, cursing the horse with obscene ferocity.

They stand in rigid terrific hiatus, the horse trembling and groaning. Then Jewel is on the horse's back. He flows upward in a stooping swirl like the lash of a whip, his body in midair shaped to the horse. For another moment the horse stands spraddled, with lowered head, before it bursts into motion. They descend the hill in a series of spine-jolting jumps, Jewel high, leech-like on the withers, to the fence where the horse bunches to a scuttering halt again.

"Well," Jewel says, "you can quit now, if you got a-plenty."

Inside the barn Jewel slides running to the ground before the horse stops. The horse enters the stall, Jewel following. Without looking back the horse kicks at him, slamming a single hoof into the wall with a pistol-like report. Jewel kicks him in the stomach; the horse arches his neck back, crop-toothed; Jewel strikes him across the face with his fist and slides on to the trough and mounts upon it. Clinging to the hay-rack he lowers his head and peers out across the stall tops and through the doorway. The path is empty; from here he cannot even hear Cash sawing. He reaches up and drags down hay in hurried armsful and crams it into the rack.

"Eat," he says. "Get the goddamn stuff out of sight while you got a chance, you pussel-gutted bastard. You sweet son of a bitch," he says.

Jewel

IT'S BECAUSE he stays out there, right under the window, hammering and sawing on that goddamn box. Where she's got to see him. Where every breath she draws is full of his knocking and sawing where she can see him saying See. See what a good one I am making for you. I told him to go somewhere else. I said Good God do you want to see her in it. It's like when he was a little boy and she says if she had some fertilizer she would try to raise some flowers and he taken the bread pan and brought it back from the barn full of dung.

And now them others sitting there, like buzzards. Waiting, fanning themselves. Because I said If you wouldn't keep on sawing and nailing at it until a man cant sleep even and her hands laying on the quilt like two of them roots dug up and tried to wash and you couldn't get them clean. I can see the fan and Dewey Dell's arm. I said if you'd just let her alone. Sawing and knocking, and keeping the air always moving so fast on her face that when you're tired you cant breathe it, and that goddamn adze going One lick less. One lick less. One lick less until everybody that passes in the road will have to stop and see it and say what a fine carpenter he is. If it had just been me when Cash fell off of that church and if it had just been me when pa laid sick with that load of wood fell on him, it would not be happening with every bastard in the county coming in to stare at her because if there is a God what the hell is He for. It would just be me and her on a high hill and me rolling the rocks down the hill at their faces, picking them up and throwing them down the hill faces and teeth and all by God until she was quiet and not that goddamn adze going One lick less. One lick less and we could be quiet.

Salem College
Gramley Library
Winston-Salem, NC 27108

Darl

WE WATCH HIM come around the corner and mount the steps. He does not look at us. "You ready?" he says.

"If you're hitched up," I say. I say "Wait." He stops, looking at pa. Vernon spits, without moving. He spits with decorous and deliberate precision into the pocked dust below the porch. Pa rubs his hands slowly on his knees. He is gazing out beyond the crest of the bluff, out across the land. Jewel watches him a moment, then he goes on to the pail and drinks again.

"I mislike undecision as much as ere a man," pa says.

"It means three dollars," I say. The shirt across pa's hump is faded lighter than the rest of it. There is no sweat stain on his shirt. I have never seen a sweat stain on his shirt. He was sick once from working in the sun when he was twenty-two years old, and he tells people that if he ever sweats, he will die. I suppose he believes it.

"But if she dont last until you get back," he says. "She will be disappointed."

Vernon spits into the dust. But it will rain before morning.

"She's counted on it," pa says. "She'll want to start right away. I know her. I promised her I'd keep the team here and ready, and she's counting on it."

"We'll need that three dollars then, sure," I say. He gazes out over the land, rubbing his hands on his knees. Since he lost his teeth his mouth collapses in slow repetition when he dips. The stubble gives his lower face that appearance that old dogs have. "You'd better make up your mind soon, so we can get there and get a load on before dark," I say.

"Ma aint that sick," Jewel says. "Shut up, Darl."

"That's right," Vernon says. "She seems more like herself today than she has in a week. Time you and Jewel get back, she'll be setting up."

"You ought to know," Jewel says. "You been here often enough looking at her. You or your folks." Vernon looks at him. Jewel's eyes look like pale wood in his high-blooded face. He is a head taller than any of the rest of us, always was. I told them that's why ma always whipped him and petted

12

Salem College
Gramley Library
Winston-Salem, NC 27108

him more. Because he was peakling around the house more. That's why she named him Jewel I told them.

"Shut up, Jewel," pa says, but as though he is not listening much. He gazes out across the land, rubbing his knees.

"You could borrow the loan of Vernon's team and we could catch up with you," I say. "If she didn't wait for us."

"Ah, shut your goddamn mouth," Jewel says.

"She'll want to go in ourn," pa says. He rubs his knees. "Dont ere a man mislike it more."

"It's laying there, watching Cash whittle on that damn. . . . . . ." Jewel says. He says it harshly, savagely, but he does not say the word. Like a little boy in the dark to flail his courage and suddenly aghast into silence by his own noise.

"She wanted that like she wants to go in our own wagon," pa says. "She'll rest easier for knowing it's a good one, and private. She was ever a private woman. You know it well."

"Then let it be private," Jewel says. "But how the hell can you expect it to be——" he looks at the back of pa's head, his eyes like pale wooden eyes.

"Sho," Vernon says, "she'll hold on till it's finished. She'll hold on till everything's ready, till her own good time. And with the roads like they are now, it wont take you no time to get her to town."

"It's fixing up to rain," pa says. "I am a luckless man. I have ever been." He rubs his hands on his knees. "It's that durn doctor, liable to come at any time. I couldn't get word to him till so late. If he was to come tomorrow and tell her the time was nigh, she wouldn't wait. I know her. Wagon or no wagon, she wouldn't wait. Then she'd be upset, and I wouldn't upset her for the living world. With that family burying-ground in Jefferson and them of her blood waiting for her there, she'll be impatient. I promised my word me and the boys would get her there quick as mules could walk it, so she could rest quiet." He rubs his hands on his knees. "No man ever misliked it more."

"If everybody wasn't burning hell to get her there," Jewel says in that harsh, savage voice. "With Cash all day long right under the window, hammering and sawing at that——"

"It was her wish," pa says. "You got no affection nor gentleness for her. You never had. We would be beholden to no man," he says, "me and her. We have never yet been, and she will rest quieter for knowing it and that it was her own blood sawed out the boards and drove the nails. She was ever one to clean up after herself."

"It means three dollars," I say. "Do you want us to go, or not?" Pa rubs his knees. "We'll be back by tomorrow sundown."

"Well. . . . . . ." pa says. He looks out over the land, awry-haired, mouthing the snuff slowly against his gums.

"Come on," Jewel says. He goes down the steps. Vernon spits neatly into the dust.

"By sundown, now," pa says. "I would not keep her waiting."

Jewel glances back, then he goes on around the house. I enter the hall, hearing the voices before I reach the door. Tilting a little down the hill, as our house does, a breeze draws through the hall all the time, upslanting. A feather dropped near the front door will rise and brush along the ceiling, slanting backward, until it reaches the down-turning current at the back door: so with voices. As you enter the hall, they sound as though they were speaking out of the air about your head.

Cora

It was the sweetest thing I ever saw. It was like he knew he would never see her again, that Anse Bundren was driving him from his mother's death bed, never to see her in this world again. I always said Darl was different from those others. I always said he was the only one of them that had his mother's nature, had any natural affection. Not that Jewel, the one she labored so to bear and coddled and petted so and him flinging into tantrums or sulking spells, inventing devilment to devil her until I would have frailed him time and time. Not him to come and tell her goodbye. Not him to miss a chance to make that extra three dollars at the price of his mother's goodbye kiss. A Bundren through and through, loving nobody, caring for nothing except how to get something with the least amount of work. Mr Tull says Darl asked them to wait. He said Darl almost begged them on his knees not to force him to leave her in her condition. But nothing would do but Anse and Jewel must make that three dollars. Nobody that knows Anse could have expected different, but to think of that boy, that Jewel, selling all those years of self-denial and down-right partiality—they couldn't fool me: Mr Tull says Mrs Bundren liked Jewel the least of all, but I knew better. I knew she was partial to him, to the same quality in him that let her put up with Anse Bundren when Mr Tull said she ought to poisoned him—for three dollars, denying his dying mother the goodbye kiss.

Why, for the last three weeks I have been coming over every time I could, coming sometimes when I shouldn't have, neglecting my own family and duties so that somebody would be with her in her last moments and she would not have to face the Great Unknown without one familiar face to give her courage. Not that I deserve credit for it: I will expect the same for myself. But thank God it will be the faces of my loved kin, my blood and flesh, for in my husband and children I have been more blessed than most, trials though they have been at times.

She lived, a lonely woman, lonely with her pride, trying to make folks believe different, hiding the fact that they just suffered her, because she was not cold in the coffin before they were carting her forty miles away to bury her, flouting the will of God to do it. Refusing to let her lie in the same earth with those Bundrens.

"But she wanted to go," Mr Tull said. "It was her own wish to lie among her own people."

"Then why didn't she go alive?" I said. "Not one of them would have stopped her, with even that little one almost old enough now to be selfish and stone-hearted like the rest of them."

"It was her own wish," Mr Tull said. "I heard Anse say it was."

"And you would believe Anse, of course," I said. "A man like you would. Dont tell me."

"I'd believe him about something he couldn't expect to make anything off of me by not telling," Mr Tull said.

"Dont tell me," I said. "A woman's place is with her husband and children, alive or dead. Would you expect me to want to go back to Alabama and leave you and the girls when my time comes, that I left of my own will to cast my lot with yours for better and worse, until death and after?"

"Well, folks are different," he said.

I should hope so. I have tried to live right in the sight of God and man, for the honor and comfort of my Christian husband and the love and respect of my Christian children. So that when I lay me down in the consciousness of my duty and reward I will be surrounded by loving faces, carrying the farewell kiss of each of my loved ones into my reward. Not like Addie Bundren dying alone, hiding her pride and her broken heart. Glad to go. Lying there with her head propped up so she could watch Cash building the coffin, having to watch him so he would not skimp on it, like as not, with those men not worrying about anything except if there was time to earn another three dollars before the rain come and the river got too high to get across it. Like as not, if they hadn't decided to make that last load, they would have loaded her into the wagon on a quilt and crossed the river first and then stopped and give her time to die what Christian death they would let her.

Except Darl. It was the sweetest thing I ever saw. Sometimes I lose faith in human nature for a time; I am assailed by doubt. But always the Lord restores my faith and reveals to me His bounteous love for His creatures. Not Jewel, the one she had always cherished, not him. He was after that three extra dollars. It was Darl, the one that folks say is queer, lazy, pottering about the place no better than Anse, with Cash a good carpenter and always more building than he can get around to, and Jewel always doing something that made him some money or got him talked about, and that near-naked girl always standing over Addie with a fan so that every time a body tried to talk to her and cheer her up, would answer for her right quick, like she was trying to keep anybody from coming near her at all.

It was Darl. He come to the door and stood there, looking at his dying mother. He just looked at her, and I felt the bounteous love of the Lord again and His mercy. I saw that with Jewel she had just been pretending, but that it was between her and Darl that the understanding and the true love was. He just looked at her, not even coming in where she could see him and get upset, knowing that Anse was driving him away and he would never see her again. He said nothing, just looking at her.

"What you want, Darl?" Dewey Dell said, not stopping the fan, speaking up quick, keeping even him from her. He didn't answer. He just stood and looked at his dying mother, his heart too full for words.

Dewey Dell

THE FIRST TIME me and Lafe picked on down the row. Pa dassent sweat because he will catch his death from the sickness so everybody that comes to help us. And Jewel dont care about anything he is not kin to us in caring, not care-kin. And Cash like sawing the long hot sad yellow days up into planks and nailing them to something. And pa thinks because neighbors will always treat one another that way because he has always been too busy letting neighbors do for him to find out. And I did not think that Darl would, that sits at the supper table with his eyes gone further than the food and the lamp, full of the land dug out of his skull and the holes filled with distance beyond the land.

We picked on down the row, the woods getting closer and closer and the secret shade, picking on into the secret shade with my sack and Lafe's sack. Because I said will I or wont I when the sack was half full because I said if the sack is full when we get to the woods it wont be me. I said if it dont mean for me to do it the sack will not be full and I will turn up the next row but if the sack is full, I cannot help it. It will be that I had to do it all the time and I cannot help it. And we picked on toward the secret shade and our eyes would drown together touching on his hands and my hands and I didn't say anything. I said "What are you doing?" and he said "I am picking into your sack." And so it was full when we came to the end of the row and I could not help it.

And so it was because I could not help it. It was then, and then I saw Darl and he knew. He said he knew without the words like he told me that ma is going to die without words, and I knew he knew because if he had said he knew with the words I would not have believed that he had been there and saw us. But he said he did know and I said "Are you going to tell pa are you going to kill him?" without the words I said it and he said "Why?" without the words. And that's why I can talk to him with knowing with hating because he knows.

He stands in the door, looking at her.

"What you want, Darl?" I say.

18

"She is going to die," he says. And old turkey-buzzard Tull coming to watch her die but I can fool them.

"When is she going to die?" I say.

"Before we get back," he says.

"Then why are you taking Jewel?" I say.

"I want him to help me load," he says.

Tull

Anse keeps on rubbing his knees. His overalls are faded; on one knee a serge patch cut out of a pair of Sunday pants, wore iron-slick. "No man mislikes it more than me," he says.

"A fellow's got to guess ahead now and then," I say. "But, come long and short, it wont be no harm done neither way."

"She'll want to get started right off," he says. "It's far enough to Jefferson at best."

"But the roads is good now," I say. It's fixing to rain to-night, too. His folks buries at New Hope, too, not three miles away. But it's just like him to marry a woman born a day's hard ride away and have her die on him.

He looks out over the land, rubbing his knees. "No man so mislikes it," he says.

"They'll get back in plenty of time," I say. "I wouldn't worry none."

"It means three dollars," he says.

"Might be it wont be no need for them to rush back, no ways," I say. "I hope it."

"She's a-going," he says. "Her mind is set on it."

It's a hard life on women, for a fact. Some women. I mind my mammy lived to be seventy and more. Worked every day, rain or shine; never a sick day since her last chap was born until one day she kind of looked around her and then she went and taken that lace-trimmed night gown she had had forty-five years and never wore out of the chest and put it on and laid down on the bed and pulled the covers up and shut her eyes. "You all will have to look out for pa the best you can," she said. "I'm tired."

Anse rubs his hands on his knees. "The Lord giveth," he says. We can hear Cash a-hammering and sawing beyond the corner.

It's true. Never a truer breath was ever breathed. "The Lord giveth," I say.

That boy comes up the hill. He is carrying a fish nigh long as he is. He slings it to the ground and grunts "Hah" and spits over his shoulder like a man. Durn nigh long as he is.

"What's that?" I say. "A hog? Where'd you get it?"

"Down to the bridge," he says. He turns it over, the under side caked over with dust where it is wet, the eye coated over, humped under the dirt.

"Are you aiming to leave it laying there?" Anse says.

"I aim to show it to ma," Vardaman says. He looks toward the door. We can hear the talking, coming out on the draft. Cash too, knocking and hammering at the boards. "There's company in there," he says.

"Just my folks," I say. "They'd enjoy to see it too."

He says nothing, watching the door. Then he looks down at the fish laying in the dust. He turns it over with his foot and prods at the eye-bump with his toe, gouging at it. Anse is looking out over the land. Vardaman looks at Anse's face, then at the door. He turns, going toward the corner of the house, when Anse calls him without looking around.

"You clean that fish," Anse says.

Vardaman stops. "Why cant Dewey Dell clean it?" he says.

"You clean that fish," Anse says.

"Aw, pa," Vardaman says.

"You clean it," Anse says. He dont look around. Vardaman comes back and picks up the fish. It slides out of his hands, smearing wet dirt onto him, and flops down, dirtying itself again, gapmouthed, goggle-eyed, hiding into the dust like it was ashamed of being dead, like it was in a hurry to get back hid again. Vardaman cusses it. He cusses it like a grown man, standing a-straddle of it. Anse dont look around. Vardaman picks it up again. He goes on around the house, toting it in both arms like a armful of wood, it overlapping him on both ends, head and tail. Durn nigh big as he is.

Anse's wrists dangle out of his sleeves: I never see him with a shirt on that looked like it was his in all my life. They all looked like Jewel might have give him his old ones. Not Jewel, though. He's long-armed, even if he is spindling. Except for the lack of sweat. You could tell they aint been nobody else's but Anse's that way without no mistake. His eyes look like pieces of burnt-out cinder fixed in his face, looking out over the land.

When the shadow touches the steps he says "It's five oclock."

Just as I get up Cora comes to the door and says it's time to get on. Anse reaches for his shoes. "Now, Mr Bundren," Cora says, "dont you get up now." He puts his shoes on, stomping into them, like he does everything, like he is hoping all the time he really cant do it and can quit trying to. When we go up the hall we can hear them clumping on the floor like they was iron shoes. He comes toward the door where she is, blinking his eyes, kind of looking ahead of hisself before he sees, like he is hoping to find her setting up, in a chair maybe or maybe sweeping, and looks into the door in that surprised way like he looks in and finds her still in bed every time and Dewey Dell still a-fanning her with the fan. He stands there, like he dont aim to move again nor nothing else.

"Well, I reckon we better get on," Cora says. "I got to feed the chickens." It's fixing to rain, too. Clouds like that dont lie, and the cotton making every day the Lord sends. That'll be something else for him. Cash is still trimming at the boards. "If there's ere a thing we can do," Cora says.

"Anse'll let us know," I say.

Anse dont look at us. He looks around, blinking, in that surprised way, like he had wore hisself down being surprised and was even surprised at that. If Cash just works that careful on my barn.

"I told Anse it likely wont be no need," I say. "I so hope it."

"Her mind is set on it," he says. "I reckon she's bound to go."

"It comes to all of us," Cora says. "Let the Lord comfort you."

"About that corn," I say. I tell him again I will help him out if he gets into a tight, with her sick and all. Like most folks around here, I done holp him so much already I cant quit now.

"I aimed to get to it today," he says. "Seems like I cant get my mind on nothing."

"Maybe she'll hold out till you are laid-by," I say.

"If God wills it," he says.

"Let Him comfort you," Cora says.

If Cash just works that careful on my barn. He looks up

when we pass. "Dont reckon I'll get to you this week," he says.

" 'Taint no rush," I say. "Whenever you get around to it."

We get into the wagon. Cora sets the cake box on her lap. It's fixing to rain, sho.

"I dont know what he'll do," Cora says. "I just dont know."

"Poor Anse," I say. "She kept him at work for thirty-odd years. I reckon she is tired."

"And I reckon she'll be behind him for thirty years more," Kate says. "Or if it aint her, he'll get another one before cotton-picking."

"I reckon Cash and Darl can get married now," Eula says.

"That poor boy," Cora says. "The poor little tyke."

"What about Jewel?" Kate says.

"He can, too," Eula says.

"Hmph," Kate says. "I reckon he will. I reckon so. I reckon there's more gals than one around here that dont want to see Jewel tied down. Well, they needn't to worry."

"Why, Kate!" Cora says. The wagon begins to rattle. "The poor little tyke," Cora says.

It's fixing to rain this night. Yes, sir. A rattling wagon is mighty dry weather, for a Birdsell. But that'll be cured. It will for a fact.

"She ought to taken them cakes after she said she would," Kate says.

Anse

DURN that road. And it fixing to rain, too. I can stand here and same as see it with second-sight, a-shutting down behind them like a wall, shutting down betwixt them and my given promise. I do the best I can, much as I can get my mind on anything, but durn them boys.

A-laying there, right up to my door, where every bad luck that comes and goes is bound to find it. I told Addie it want any luck living on a road when it come by here, and she said, for the world like a woman, "Get up and move, then." But I told her it want no luck in it, because the Lord put roads for travelling: why He laid them down flat on the earth. When He aims for something to be always a-moving, He makes it long ways, like a road or a horse or a wagon, but when He aims for something to stay put, He makes it up-and-down ways, like a tree or a man. And so He never aimed for folks to live on a road, because which gets there first, I says, the road or the house? Did you ever know Him to set a road down by a house? I says. No you never, I says, because it's always men cant rest till they gets the house set where everybody that passes in a wagon can spit in the doorway, keeping the folks restless and wanting to get up and go somewheres else when He aimed for them to stay put like a tree or a stand of corn. Because if He'd a aimed for man to be always a-moving and going somewheres else, wouldn't He a put him longways on his belly, like a snake? It stands to reason He would.

Putting it where every bad luck prowling can find it and come straight to my door, charging me taxes on top of it. Making me pay for Cash having to get them carpenter notions when if it hadn't been no road come there, he wouldn't a got them; falling off of churches and lifting no hand in six months and me and Addie slaving and a-slaving, when there's plenty of sawing on this place he could do if he's got to saw.

And Darl too. Talking me out of him, durn them. It aint that I am afraid of work; I always is fed me and mine and kept a roof above us: it's that they would short-hand me just because he tends to his own business, just because he's got

24

his eyes full of the land all the time. I says to them, he was alright at first, with his eyes full of the land, because the land laid up-and-down ways then; it wasn't till that ere road come and switched the land around longways and his eyes still full of the land, that they begun to threaten me out of him, trying to short-hand me with the law.

Making me pay for it. She was well and hale as ere a woman ever were, except for that road. Just laying down, resting herself in her own bed, asking naught of none. "Are you sick, Addie?" I said.

"I am not sick," she said.

"You lay you down and rest you," I said. "I knowed you are not sick. You're just tired. You lay you down and rest."

"I am not sick," she said. "I will get up."

"Lay still and rest," I said. "You are just tired. You can get up tomorrow." And she was laying there, well and hale as ere a woman ever were, except for that road.

"I never sent for you," I said. "I take you to witness I never sent for you."

"I know you didn't," Peabody said. "I bound that. Where is she?"

"She's a-laying down," I said. "She's just a little tired, but she'll——"

"Get outen here, Anse," he said. "Go set on the porch a while."

And now I got to pay for it, me without a tooth in my head, hoping to get ahead enough so I could get my mouth fixed where I could eat God's own victuals as a man should, and her hale and well as ere a woman in the land until that day. Got to pay for being put to the need of that three dollars. Got to pay for the way for them boys to have to go away to earn it. And now I can see same as second sight the rain shutting down betwixt us, a-coming up that road like a durn man, like it want ere a other house to rain on in all the living land.

I have heard men cuss their luck, and right, for they were sinful men. But I do not say it's a curse on me, because I have done no wrong to be cussed by. I am not religious, I reckon. But peace is in my heart: I know it is. I have done things but neither better nor worse than them that pretend otherlike, and I know that Old Marster will care for me as for ere a sparrow that falls. But it seems hard that a man in his need could be so flouted by a road.

Vardaman comes around the house, bloody as a hog to his knees, and that ere fish chopped up with the axe like as not, or maybe throwed away for him to lie about the dogs et it. Well, I reckon I aint no call to expect no more of him than of his man-growed brothers. He comes along, watching the house, quiet, and sits on the steps. "Whew," he says, "I'm pure tired."

"Go wash them hands," I say. But couldn't no woman strove harder than Addie to make them right, man and boy: I'll say that for her.

"It was full of blood and guts as a hog," he says. But I just cant seem to get no heart into anything, with this here weather sapping me, too. "Pa," he says, "is ma sick some more?"

"Go wash them hands," I say. But I just cant seem to get no heart into it.

Darl

HE HAS BEEN to town this week: the back of his neck is trimmed close, with a white line between hair and sunburn like a joint of white bone. He has not once looked back.

"Jewel," I say. Back running, tunnelled between the two sets of bobbing mule ears, the road vanishes beneath the wagon as though it were a ribbon and the front axle were a spool. "Do you know she is going to die, Jewel?"

It takes two people to make you, and one people to die. That's how the world is going to end.

I said to Dewey Dell: "You want her to die so you can get to town: is that it?" She wouldn't say what we both knew. "The reason you will not say it is, when you say it, even to yourself, you will know it is true: is that it? But you know it is true now. I can almost tell you the day when you knew it is true. Why wont you say it, even to yourself?" She will not say it. She just keeps on saying Are you going to tell pa? Are you going to kill him? "You cannot believe it is true because you cannot believe that Dewey Dell, Dewey Dell Bundren, could have such bad luck: is that it?"

The sun, an hour above the horizon, is poised like a bloody egg upon a crest of thunderheads; the light has turned copper: in the eye portentous, in the nose sulphurous, smelling of lightning. When Peabody comes, they will have to use the rope. He has pussel-gutted himself eating cold greens. With the rope they will haul him up the path, balloon-like up the sulphurous air.

"Jewel," I say, "do you know that Addie Bundren is going to die? Addie Bundren is going to die?"

Peabody

WHEN ANSE FINALLY sent for me of his own accord, I said "He has wore her out at last." And I said a damn good thing, and at first I would not go because there might be something I could do and I would have to haul her back, by God. I thought maybe they have the same sort of fool ethics in heaven they have in the Medical College and that it was maybe Vernon Tull sending for me again, getting me there in the nick of time, as Vernon always does things, getting the most for Anse's money like he does for his own. But when it got far enough into the day for me to read weather sign I knew it couldn't have been anybody but Anse that sent. I knew that nobody but a luckless man could ever need a doctor in the face of a cyclone. And I knew that if it had finally occurred to Anse himself that he needed one, it was already too late.

When I reach the spring and get down and hitch the team, the sun has gone down behind a bank of black cloud like a topheavy mountain range, like a load of cinders dumped over there, and there is no wind. I could hear Cash sawing for a mile before I got there. Anse is standing at the top of the bluff above the path.

"Where's the horse?" I say.

"Jewel's taken and gone," he says. "Cant nobody else ketch hit. You'll have to walk up, I reckon."

"Me, walk up, weighing two hundred and twenty-five pounds?" I say. "Walk up that durn wall?" He stands there beside a tree. Too bad the Lord made the mistake of giving trees roots and giving the Anse Bundrens He makes feet and legs. If He'd just swapped them, there wouldn't ever be a worry about this country being deforested someday. Or any other country. "What do you aim for me to do?" I say. "Stay here and get blowed clean out of the county when that cloud breaks?" Even with the horse it would take me fifteen minutes to ride up across the pasture to the top of the ridge and reach the house. The path looks like a crooked limb blown against the bluff. Anse has not been in town in twelve years. And how his mother ever got up there to bear him, he being his mother's son.

"Vardaman's gittin the rope," he says.

After a while Vardaman appears with the plowline. He gives the end of it to Anse and comes down the path, uncoiling it.

"You hold it tight," I say. "I done already wrote this visit onto my books, so I'm going to charge you just the same, whether I get there or not."

"I got hit," Anse says. "You kin come on up."

I'll be damned if I can see why I dont quit. A man seventy years old, weighing two hundred and odd pounds, being hauled up and down a damn mountain on a rope. I reckon it's because I must reach the fifty thousand dollar mark of dead accounts on my books before I can quit. "What the hell does your wife mean," I say, "taking sick on top of a durn mountain?"

"I'm right sorry," he says. He let the rope go, just dropped it, and he has turned toward the house. There is a little daylight up here still, of the color of sulphur matches. The boards look like strips of sulphur. Cash does not look back. Vernon Tull says he brings each board up to the window for her to see it and say it is all right. The boy overtakes us. Anse looks back at him. "Wher's the rope?" he says.

"It's where you left it," I say. "But never you mind that rope. I got to get back down that bluff. I dont aim for that storm to catch me up here. I'd blow too durn far once I got started."

The girl is standing by the bed, fanning her. When we enter she turns her head and looks at us. She has been dead these ten days. I suppose it's having been a part of Anse for so long that she cannot even make that change, if change it be. I can remember how when I was young I believed death to be a phenomenon of the body; now I know it to be merely a function of the mind—and that of the minds of the ones who suffer the bereavement. The nihilists say it is the end; the fundamentalists, the beginning; when in reality it is no more than a single tenant or family moving out of a tenement or a town.

She looks at us. Only her eyes seem to move. It's like they touch us, not with sight or sense, but like the stream from a hose touches you, the stream at the instant of impact as dissociated from the nozzle as though it had never been there. She does not look at Anse at all. She looks at me, then at the boy. Beneath the quilt she is no more than a bundle of rotten sticks.

"Well, Miss Addie," I say. The girl does not stop the fan. "How are you, sister?" I say. Her head lies gaunt on the pillow, looking at the boy. "You picked out a fine time to get me out here and bring up a storm." Then I send Anse and the boy out. She watches the boy as he leaves the room. She has not moved save her eyes.

He and Anse are on the porch when I come out, the boy sitting on the steps, Anse standing by a post, not even leaning against it, his arms dangling, the hair pushed and matted up on his head like a dipped rooster. He turns his head, blinking at me.

"Why didn't you send for me sooner?" I say.

"Hit was jest one thing and then another," he says. "That ere corn me and the boys was aimin to git up with, and Dewey Dell a-takin good keer of her, and folks comin in, a-offerin to help and sich, till I jest thought. . . . . . ."

"Damn the money," I say. "Did you ever hear of me worrying a fellow before he was ready to pay?"

"Hit aint begrudgin the money," he says. "I jest kept a-thinkin. . . . . . . She's goin, is she?" The durn little tyke is sitting on the top step, looking smaller than ever in the sulphur-colored light. That's the one trouble with this country: everything, weather, all, hangs on too long. Like our rivers, our land: opaque, slow, violent; shaping and creating the life of man in its implacable and brooding image. "I knowed hit," Anse says. "All the while I made sho. Her mind is sot on hit."

"And a damn good thing, too," I say. "With a trifling——" He sits on the top step, small, motionless in faded overalls. When I came out he looked up at me, then at Anse. But now he has stopped looking at us. He just sits there.

"Have you told her yit?" Anse says.

"What for?" I say. "What the devil for?"

"She'll know hit. I knowed that when she see you she would know hit, same as writing. You wouldn't need to tell her. Her mind——"

Behind us the girl says, "Paw." I look at her, at her face.

"You better go quick," I say.

When we enter the room she is watching the door. She looks at me. Her eyes look like lamps blaring up just before the oil is gone. "She wants you to go out," the girl says.

"Now, Addie," Anse says, " when he come all the way from Jefferson to git you well?" She watches me: I can feel her eyes. It's like she was shoving at me with them. I have seen it before in women. Seen them drive from the room them coming with sympathy and pity, with actual help, and clinging to some trifling animal to whom they never were more than pack-horses. That's what they mean by the love that passeth understanding: that pride, that furious desire to hide that abject nakedness which we bring here with us, carry with us into operating rooms, carry stubbornly and furiously with us into the earth again. I leave the room. Beyond the porch Cash's saw snores steadily into the board. A minute later she calls his name, her voice harsh and strong.

"Cash," she says; "you, Cash!"

Darl

P A STANDS beside the bed. From behind his leg Vardaman peers, with his round head and his eyes round and his mouth beginning to open. She looks at pa; all her failing life appears to drain into her eyes, urgent, irremediable. "It's Jewel she wants," Dewey Dell says.

"Why, Addie," pa says, "him and Darl went to make one more load. They thought there was time. That you would wait for them, and that three dollars and all. . . . . . ." He stoops laying his hand on hers. For a while yet she looks at him, without reproach, without anything at all, as if her eyes alone are listening to the irrevocable cessation of his voice. Then she raises herself, who has not moved in ten days. Dewey Dell leans down, trying to press her back.

"Ma," she says; "ma."

She is looking out the window, at Cash stooping steadily at the board in the failing light, laboring on toward darkness and into it as though the stroking of the saw illumined its own motion, board and saw engendered.

"You, Cash," she shouts, her voice harsh, strong, and un-impaired. "You, Cash!"

He looks up at the gaunt face framed by the window in the twilight. It is a composite picture of all time since he was a child. He drops the saw and lifts the board for her to see, watching the window in which the face has not moved. He drags a second plank into position and slants the two of them into their final juxtaposition, gesturing toward the ones yet on the ground, shaping with his empty hand in pantomime the finished box. For a while still she looks down at him from the composite picture, neither with censure nor approbation. Then the face disappears.

She lies back and turns her head without so much as glancing at pa. She looks at Vardaman; her eyes, the life in them, rushing suddenly upon them; the two flames glare up for a steady instant. Then they go out as though someone had leaned down and blown upon them.

"Ma," Dewey Dell says; "ma!" Leaning above the bed, her hands lifted a little, the fan still moving like it has for ten days, she begins to keen. Her voice is strong, young, tremulous and clear, rapt with its own timbre and volume, the fan still moving steadily up and down, whispering the useless air. Then she flings herself across Addie Bundren's knees, clutching her, shaking her with the furious strength of the young before sprawling suddenly across the handful of rotten bones that Addie Bundren left, jarring the whole bed into a chattering sibilance of mattress shucks, her arms outflung and the fan in one hand still beating with expiring breath into the quilt.

From behind pa's leg Vardaman peers, his mouth full open and all color draining from his face into his mouth, as though he has by some means fleshed his own teeth in himself, sucking. He begins to move slowly backward from the bed, his eyes round, his pale face fading into the dusk like a piece of paper pasted on a failing wall, and so out of the door.

Pa leans above the bed in the twilight, his humped silhouette partaking of that owl-like quality of awry-feathered, disgruntled outrage within which lurks a wisdom too profound or too inert for even thought.

"Durn them boys," he says.

Jewel, I say. Overhead the day drives level and gray, hiding the sun by a flight of gray spears. In the rain the mules smoke a little, splashed yellow with mud, the off one clinging in sliding lunges to the side of the road above the ditch. The tilted lumber gleams dull yellow, water-soaked and heavy as lead, tilted at a steep angle into the ditch above the broken wheel; about the shattered spokes and about Jewel's ankles a runnel of yellow neither water nor earth swirls, curving with the yellow road neither of earth nor water, down the hill dissolving into a streaming mass of dark green neither of earth nor sky. Jewel, I say

Cash comes to the door, carrying the saw. Pa stands beside the bed, humped, his arms dangling. He turns his head, his shabby profile, his chin collapsing slowly as he works the snuff against his gums.

"She's gone," Cash says.

"She taken and left us," pa says. Cash does not look at him. "How nigh are you done?" pa says. Cash does not answer. He enters, carrying the saw. "I reckon you better get at it," pa says. "You'll have to do the best you can, with them boys gone off that-a-way." Cash looks down at her face. He is not listening to pa at all. He does not approach the bed. He stops in the middle of the floor, the saw against his leg, his sweating arms powdered lightly with sawdust, his face composed. "If you get in a tight, maybe some of them'll get here tomorrow and help you," pa says. "Vernon could." Cash is not listening. He is looking down at her peaceful, rigid face fading into the dusk as though darkness were a precursor of the ultimate earth, until at last the face seems to float detached upon it, lightly as the reflection of a dead leaf. "There is Christians enough to help you," pa says. Cash is not listening. After a while he turns without looking at pa and leaves the room. Then the saw begins to snore again. "They will help us in our sorrow," pa says.

The sound of the saw is steady, competent, unhurried, stirring the dying light so that at each stroke her face seems to wake a little into an expression of listening and of waiting, as though she were counting the strokes. Pa looks down at the face, at the black sprawl of Dewey Dell's hair, the outflung arms, the clutched fan now motionless on the fading quilt. "I reckon you better get supper on," he says.

Dewey Dell does not move.

"Git up, now, and put supper on," pa says. "We got to keep our strength up. I reckon Doctor Peabody's right hungry, coming all this way. And Cash'll need to eat quick and get back to work so he can finish it in time."

Dewey Dell rises, heaving to her feet. She looks down at the face. It is like a casting of fading bronze upon the pillow, the hands alone still with any semblance of life: a curled, gnarled inertness; a spent yet alert quality from which weariness, exhaustion, travail has not yet departed, as though they doubted even yet the actuality of rest, guarding with horned and penurious alertness the cessation which they know cannot last.

Dewey Dell stoops and slides the quilt from beneath them and draws it up over them to the chin, smoothing it down, drawing it smooth. Then without looking at pa she goes around the bed and leaves the room.

She will go out where Peabody is, where she can stand in the twilight and look at his back with such an expression that, feeling

her eyes and turning, he will say: I would not let it grieve me,
now. She was old, and sick too. Suffering more than we knew. She
couldn't have got well. Vardaman's getting big now, and with you
to take good care of them all. I would try not to let it grieve me. I
expect you'd better go and get some supper ready. It dont have to
be much. But they'll need to eat, and she looking at him, saying
You could do so much for me if you just would. If you just knew.
I am I and you are you and I know it and you dont know it and
you could do so much for me if you just would and if you just
would then I could tell you and then nobody would have to know
it except you and me and Darl

Pa stands over the bed, dangle-armed, humped, motionless.
He raises his hand to his head, scouring his hair, listening to
the saw. He comes nearer and rubs his hand, palm and back,
on his thigh and lays it on her face and then on the hump of
quilt where her hands are. He touches the quilt as he saw
Dewey Dell do, trying to smoothe it up to the chin, but disarranging it instead. He tries to smoothe it again, clumsily,
his hand awkward as a claw, smoothing at the wrinkles which
he made and which continue to emerge beneath his hand
with perverse ubiquity, so that at last he desists, his hand falling to his side and stroking itself again, palm and back, on
his thigh. The sound of the saw snores steadily into the room.
Pa breathes with a quiet, rasping sound, mouthing the snuff
against his gums. "God's will be done," he says. "Now I can
get them teeth."

Jewel's hat droops limp about his neck, channelling water onto
the soaked towsack tied about his shoulders as, ankle-deep in the
running ditch, he pries with a slipping two-by-four, with a piece of
rotting log for fulcrum, at the axle. Jewel, I say, she is dead, Jewel.
Addie Bundren is dead

Vardaman

THEN I BEGIN to run. I run toward the back and come to the edge of the porch and stop. Then I begin to cry. I can feel where the fish was in the dust. It is cut up into pieces of not-fish now, not-blood on my hands and overalls. Then it wasn't so. It hadn't happened then. And now she is getting so far ahead I cannot catch her.

The trees look like chickens when they ruffle out into the cool dust on the hot days. If I jump off the porch I will be where the fish was, and it all cut up into not-fish now. I can hear the bed and her face and them and I can feel the floor shake when he walks on it that came and did it. That came and did it when she was all right but he came and did it.

"The fat son of a bitch."

I jump from the porch, running. The top of the barn comes swooping up out of the twilight. If I jump I can go through it like the pink lady in the circus, into the warm smelling, without having to wait. My hands grab at the bushes; beneath my feet the rocks and dirt go rubbling down.

Then I can breathe again, in the warm smelling. I enter the stall, trying to touch him, and then I can cry then I vomit the crying. As soon as he gets through kicking I can and then I can cry, the crying can.

"He kilt her. He kilt her."

The life in him runs under the skin, under my hand, running through the splotches, smelling up into my nose where the sickness is beginning to cry, vomiting the crying, and then I can breathe, vomiting it. It makes a lot of noise. I can smell the life running up from under my hands, up my arms, and then I can leave the stall.

I cannot find it. In the dark, along the dust, the walls I cannot find it. The crying makes a lot of noise. I wish it wouldn't make so much noise. Then I find it in the wagon shed, in the dust, and I run across the lot and into the road, the stick jouncing on my shoulder.

They watch me as I run up, beginning to jerk back, their eyes rolling, snorting, jerking back on the hitch-rein. I strike. I can hear the stick striking; I can see it hitting their heads, the breast-yoke, missing altogether sometimes as they rear and plunge, but I am glad.

"You kilt my maw!"

The stick breaks, they rearing and snorting, their feet popping loud on the ground; loud because it is going to rain and the air is empty for the rain. But it is still long enough. I run this way and that as they rear and jerk at the hitch-rein, striking.

"You kilt her!"

I strike at them, striking, they wheeling in a long lunge, the buggy wheeling onto two wheels and motionless like it is nailed to the ground and the horses motionless like they are nailed by the hind feet to the center of a whirling plate.

I run in the dust. I cannot see, running in the sucking dust where the buggy vanishes tilted on two wheels. I strike, the stick hitting into the ground, bouncing, striking into the dust and then into the air again and the dust sucking on down the road faster than if a car was in it. And then I can cry, looking at the stick. It is broken down to my hand, not longer than stove wood that was a long stick. I throw it away and I can cry. It does not make so much noise now.

The cow is standing in the barn door, chewing. When she sees me come into the lot she lows, her mouth full of flopping green, her tongue flopping.

"I aint a-goin to milk you. I aint a-goin to do nothing for them."

I hear her turn when I pass. When I turn she is just behind me with her sweet, hot, hard breath.

"Didn't I tell you I wouldn't?"

She nudges me, snuffing. She moans deep inside, her mouth closed. I jerk my hand, cursing her like Jewel does.

"Git, now."

I stoop my hand to the ground and run at her. She jumps back and whirls away and stops, watching me. She moans. She goes on to the path and stands there, looking up the path.

It is dark in the barn, warm, smelling, silent. I can cry quietly, watching the top of the hill.

Cash comes to the hill, limping where he fell off of the church. He looks down at the spring, then up the road and back toward the barn. He comes down the path stiffly and looks at the broken hitch-rein and at the dust in the road and then up the road, where the dust is gone.

"I hope they've got clean past Tull's by now. I so hope hit."

Cash turns and limps up the path.

"Durn him. I showed him. Durn him."

I am not crying now. I am not anything. Dewey Dell comes to the hill and calls me. Vardaman. I am not anything. I am quiet. You, Vardaman. I can cry quiet now, feeling and hearing my tears.

"Then hit want. Hit hadn't happened then. Hit was a-layin right there on the ground. And now she's gittin ready to cook hit."

It is dark. I can hear wood, silence: I know them. But not living sounds, not even him. It is as though the dark were resolving him out of his integrity, into an unrelated scattering of components—snuffings and stampings; smells of cooling flesh and ammoniac hair; an illusion of a co-ordinated whole of splotched hide and strong bones within which, detached and secret and familiar, an *is* different from my *is*. I see him dissolve—legs, a rolling eye, a gaudy splotching like cold flames—and float upon the dark in fading solution; all one yet neither; all either yet none. I can see hearing coil toward him, caressing, shaping his hard shape—fetlock, hip, shoulder and head; smell and sound. I am not afraid.

"Cooked and et. Cooked and et."

Dewey Dell

H E COULD DO so much for me if he just would. He could
do everything for me. It's like everything in the world
for me is inside a tub full of guts, so that you wonder how
there can be any room in it for anything else very important.
He is a big tub of guts and I am a little tub of guts and if
there is not any room for anything else important in a big tub
of guts, how can it be room in a little tub of guts. But I know
it is there because God gave women a sign when something
has happened bad.

It's because I am alone. If I could just feel it, it would be
different, because I would not be alone. But if I were not
alone, everybody would know it. And he could do so much
for me, and then I would not be alone. Then I could be all
right alone.

I would let him come in between me and Lafe, like Darl
came in between me and Lafe, and so Lafe is alone too. He
is Lafe and I am Dewey Dell, and when mother died I had
to go beyond and outside of me and Lafe and Darl to grieve
because he could do so much for me and he dont know it.
He dont even know it.

From the back porch I cannot see the barn. Then the sound
of Cash's sawing comes in from that way. It is like a dog
outside the house, going back and forth around the house to
whatever door you come to, waiting to come in. He said I
worry more than you do and I said You dont know what
worry is so I cant worry. I try to but I cant think long enough
to worry.

I light the kitchen lamp. The fish, cut into jagged pieces,
bleeds quietly in the pan. I put it into the cupboard quick,
listening into the hall, hearing. It took her ten days to die;
maybe she dont know it is yet. Maybe she wont go until
Cash. Or maybe until Jewel. I take the dish of greens from
the cupboard and the bread pan from the cold stove, and I
stop, watching the door.

"Where's Vardaman?" Cash says. In the lamp his sawdusted
arms look like sand.

"I dont know. I aint seen him."

"Peabody's team run away. See if you can find Vardaman. The horse will let him catch him."

"Well. Tell them to come to supper."

I cannot see the barn. I said, I dont know how to worry. I dont know how to cry. I tried, but I cant. After a while the sound of the saw comes around, coming dark along the ground in the dust-dark. Then I can see him, going up and down above the plank.

"You come in to supper," I say. "Tell him." He could do everything for me. And he dont know it. He is his guts and I am my guts. And I am Lafe's guts. That's it. I dont see why he didn't stay in town. We are country people, not as good as town people. I dont see why he didn't. Then I can see the top of the barn. The cow stands at the foot of the path, lowing. When I turn back, Cash is gone.

I carry the buttermilk in. Pa and Cash and he are at the table.

"Where's that big fish Bud caught, sister?" he says.

I set the milk on the table. "I never had no time to cook it."

"Plain turnip greens is mighty spindling eating for a man my size," he says. Cash is eating. About his head the print of his hat is sweated into his hair. His shirt is blotched with sweat. He has not washed his hands and arms.

"You ought to took time," pa says. "Where's Vardaman?"

I go toward the door. "I cant find him."

"Here, sister," he says; "never mind about the fish. It'll save, I reckon. Come on and sit down."

"I aint minding it," I say. "I'm going to milk before it sets in to rain."

Pa helps himself and pushes the dish on. But he does not begin to eat. His hands are halfclosed on either side of his plate, his head bowed a little, his awry hair standing into the lamplight. He looks like right after the maul hits the steer and it no longer alive and dont yet know that it is dead.

But Cash is eating, and he is too. "You better eat something," he says. He is looking at pa. "Like Cash and me. You'll need it."

"Ay," pa says. He rouses up, like a steer that's been kneeling in a pond and you run at it. "She would not begrudge me it."

When I am out of sight of the house, I go fast. The cow lows at the foot of the bluff. She nuzzles at me, snuffing, blowing her breath in a sweet, hot blast, through my dress, against my hot nakedness, moaning. "You got to wait a little while. Then I'll tend to you." She follows me into the barn where I set the bucket down. She breathes into the bucket, moaning. "I told you. You just got to wait, now. I got more to do than I can tend to." The barn is dark. When I pass, he kicks the wall a single blow. I go on. The broken plank is like a pale plank standing on end. Then I can see the slope, feel the air moving on my face again, slow, pale with lesser dark and with empty seeing, the pine clumps blotched up the tilted slope, secret and waiting.

The cow in silhouette against the door nuzzles at the silhouette of the bucket, moaning.

Then I pass the stall. I have almost passed it. I listen to it saying for a long time before it can say the word and the listening part is afraid that there may not be time to say it. I feel my body, my bones and flesh beginning to part and open upon the alone, and the process of coming unalone is terrible. Lafe. Lafe. "Lafe" Lafe. Lafe. I lean a little forward, one foot advanced with dead walking. I feel the darkness rushing past my breast, past the cow; I begin to rush upon the darkness but the cow stops me and the darkness rushes on upon the sweet blast of her moaning breath, filled with wood and with silence.

"Vardaman. You, Vardaman."

He comes out of the stall. "You durn little sneak! You durn little sneak!"

He does not resist; the last of rushing darkness flees whistling away. "What? I aint done nothing."

"You durn little sneak!" My hands shake him, hard. Maybe I couldn't stop them. I didn't know they could shake so hard. They shake both of us, shaking.

"I never done it," he says. "I never touched them."

My hands stop shaking him, but I still hold him. "What are you doing here? Why didn't you answer when I called you?"

"I aint doing nothing."

"You go on to the house and get your supper."

He draws back. I hold him. "You quit now. You leave me be."

"What were you doing down here? You didn't come down here to sneak after me?"

"I never. I never. You quit, now. I didn't even know you was down here. You leave me be."

I hold him, leaning down to see his face, feel it with my eyes. He is about to cry. "Go on, now. I done put supper on and I'll be there soon as I milk. You better go on before he eats everything up. I hope that team runs clean back to Jefferson."

"He kilt her," he says. He begins to cry.

"Hush."

"She never hurt him and he come and kilt her."

"Hush." He struggles. I hold him. "Hush."

"He kilt her." The cow comes up behind us, moaning. I shake him again.

"You stop it, now. Right this minute. You're fixing to make yourself sick and then you cant go to town. You go on to the house and eat your supper."

"I dont want no supper. I dont want to go to town."

"We'll leave you here, then. Lessen you behave, we will leave you. Go on, now, before that old green-eating tub of guts eats everything up from you." He goes on, disappearing slowly into the hill. The crest, the trees, the roof of the house stand against the sky. The cow nuzzles at me, moaning. "You'll just have to wait. What you got in you aint nothing to what I got in me, even if you are a woman too." She follows me, moaning. Then the dead, hot, pale air breathes on my face again. He could fix it all right, if he just would. And he dont even know it. He could do everything for me if he just knowed it. The cow breathes upon my hips and back, her breath warm, sweet, stertorous, moaning. The sky lies flat down the slope, upon the secret clumps. Beyond the hill sheet-lightning stains upward and fades. The dead air shapes the dead earth in the dead darkness, further away than seeing shapes the dead earth. It lies dead and warm upon me, touching me naked through my clothes. I said You dont know what worry is. I dont know what it is. I dont know whether I am worrying or not. Whether I can or not. I dont know whether I can cry or not. I dont know whether I have tried to or not. I feel like a wet seed wild in the hot blind earth.

Vardaman

WHEN THEY get it finished they are going to put her in it and then for a long time I couldn't say it. I saw the dark stand up and go whirling away and I said "Are you going to nail her up in it, Cash? Cash? Cash?" I got shut up in the crib the new door it was too heavy for me it went shut I couldn't breathe because the rat was breathing up all the air. I said "Are you going to nail it shut, Cash? Nail it? *Nail* it?"

Pa walks around. His shadow walks around, over Cash going up and down above the saw, at the bleeding plank.

Dewey Dell said we will get some bananas. The train is behind the glass, red on the track. When it runs the track shines on and off. Pa said flour and sugar and coffee costs so much. Because I am a country boy because boys in town. Bicycles. Why do flour and sugar and coffee cost so much when he is a country boy. "Wouldn't you ruther have some bananas instead?" Bananas are gone, eaten. Gone. When it runs on the track shines again. "Why aint I a town boy, pa?" I said. God made me. I did not said to God to made me in the country. If He can make the train, why cant He make them all in the town because flour and sugar and coffee. "Wouldn't you ruther have bananas?"

He walks around. His shadow walks around.

It was not her. I was there, looking. I saw. I thought it was her, but it was not. It was not my mother. She went away when the other one laid down in her bed and drew the quilt up. She went away. "Did she go as far as town?" "She went further than town." "Did all those rabbits and possums go further than town?" God made the rabbits and possums. He made the train. Why must He make a different place for them to go if she is just like the rabbit.

Pa walks around. His shadow does. The saw sounds like it is asleep.

And so if Cash nails the box up, she is not a rabbit. And so if she is not a rabbit I couldn't breathe in the crib and Cash is going to nail it up. And so if she lets him it is not her. I know. I was there. I saw when it did not be her. I saw. They think it is and Cash is going to nail it up.

It was not her because it was laying right yonder in the dirt. And now it's all chopped up. I chopped it up. It's laying in the kitchen in the bleeding pan, waiting to be cooked and et. Then it wasn't and she was, and now it is and she wasn't. And tomorrow it will be cooked and et and she will be him and pa and Cash and Dewey Dell and there wont be anything in the box and so she can breathe. It was laying right yonder on the ground. I can get Vernon. He was there and he seen it, and with both of us it will be and then it will not be.

Tull

I T WAS nigh to midnight and it had set in to rain when he woke us. It had been a misdoubtful night, with the storm making; a night when a fellow looks for most anything to happen before he can get the stock fed and himself to the house and supper et and in bed with the rain starting, and when Peabody's team come up, lathered, with the broke harness dragging and the neck-yoke betwixt the off critter's legs, Cora says "It's Addie Bundren. She's gone at last."

"Peabody mought have been to ere a one of a dozen houses hereabouts," I says. "Besides, how do you know it's Peabody's team?"

"Well, aint it?" she says. "You hitch up, now."

"What for?" I says. "If she is gone, we cant do nothing till morning. And it fixing to storm, too."

"It's my duty," she says. "You put the team in."

But I wouldn't do it. "It stands to reason they'd send for us if they needed us. You dont even know she's gone yet."

"Why, dont you know that's Peabody's team? Do you claim it aint? Well, then." But I wouldn't go. When folks wants a fellow, it's best to wait till they sends for him, I've found. "It's my Christian duty," Cora says. "Will you stand between me and my Christian duty?"

"You can stay there all day tomorrow, if you want," I says.

So when Cora waked me it had set in to rain. Even while I was going to the door with the lamp and it shining on the glass so he could see I am coming, it kept on knocking. Not loud, but steady, like he might have gone to sleep thumping, but I never noticed how low down on the door the knocking was till I opened it and never seen nothing. I held the lamp up, with the rain sparkling across it and Cora back in the hall saying "Who is it, Vernon?" but I couldn't see nobody a-tall at first until I looked down and around the door, lowering the lamp.

He looked like a drownded puppy, in them overalls, without no hat, splashed up to his knees where he had walked them four miles in the mud. "Well, I'll be durned," I says.

"Who is it, Vernon?" Cora says.

He looked at me, his eyes round and black in the middle like when you throw a light in a owl's face. "You mind that ere fish," he says.

"Come in the house," I says. "What is it? Is your maw——"

"Vernon," Cora says.

He stood kind of around behind the door, in the dark. The rain was blowing onto the lamp, hissing on it so I am scared every minute it'll break. "You was there," he says. "You seen it."

Then Cora come to the door. "You come right in outen the rain," she says, pulling him in and him watching me. He looked just like a drownded puppy. "I told you," Cora says. "I told you it was a-happening. You go and hitch."

"But he aint said——" I says.

He looked at me, dripping onto the floor. "He's a-ruining the rug," Cora says. "You go get the team while I take him to the kitchen."

But he hung back, dripping, watching me with them eyes. "You was there. You seen it laying there. Cash is fixing to nail her up, and it was a-laying right there on the ground. You seen it. You seen the mark in the dirt. The rain never come up till after I was a-coming here. So we can get back in time."

I be durn if it didn't give me the creeps, even when I didn't know yet. But Cora did. "You get that team quick as you can," she says. "He's outen his head with grief and worry."

I be durn if it didn't give me the creeps. Now and then a fellow gets to thinking. About all the sorrow and afflictions in this world; how it's liable to strike anywhere, like lightning. I reckon it does take a powerful trust in the Lord to guard a fellow, though sometimes I think that Cora's a mite over-cautious, like she was trying to crowd the other folks away and get in closer than anybody else. But then, when something like this happens, I reckon she is right and you got to keep after it and I reckon I am blessed in having a wife that ever strives for sanctity and well-doing like she says I am.

Now and then a fellow gets to thinking about it. Not often, though. Which is a good thing. For the Lord aimed for him to do and not to spend too much time thinking, because his brain it's like a piece of machinery: it wont stand a whole lot of racking. It's best when it all runs along the same, doing the day's work and not no one part used no more than needful. I have said and I say again, that's ever living thing the matter with Darl: he just thinks by himself too much. Cora's right when she says all he needs is a wife to straighten him out. And when I think about that, I think that if nothing but being married will help a man, he's durn nigh hopeless. But I reckon Cora's right when she says the reason the Lord had to create women is because man dont know his own good when he sees it.

When I come back to the house with the team, they was in the kitchen. She was dressed on top of her nightgownd, with a shawl over her head and her umbrella and her bible wrapped up in the oilcloth, and him sitting on a up-turned bucket on the stove-zinc where she had put him, dripping onto the floor. "I cant get nothing outen him except about a fish," she says. "It's a judgment on them. I see the hand of the Lord upon this boy for Anse Bundren's judgment and warning."

"The rain never come up till after I left," he says. "I had done left. I was on the way. And so it was there in the dust. You seen it. Cash is fixing to nail her, but you seen it."

When we got there it was raining hard, and him sitting on the seat between us, wrapped up in Cora's shawl. He hadn't said nothing else, just sitting there with Cora holding the umbrella over him. Now and then Cora would stop singing long enough to say "It's a judgment on Anse Bundren. May it show him the path of sin he is a-trodding." Then she would sing again, and him sitting there between us, leaning forward a little like the mules couldn't go fast enough to suit him.

"It was laying right yonder," he says, "but the rain come up after I taken and left. So I can go and open the windows, because Cash aint nailed her yet."

It was long a-past midnight when we drove the last nail, and almost dust-dawn when I got back home and taken the team out and got back in bed, with Cora's nightcap laying on the other pillow. And be durned if even then it wasn't like I could still hear Cora singing and feel that boy leaning forward between us like he was ahead of the mules, and still see Cash going up and down with that saw, and Anse standing there like a scarecrow, like he was a steer standing knee-deep in a

pond and somebody come by and set the pond up on edge
and he aint missed it yet.

It was nigh toward daybreak when we drove the last nail
and toted it into the house, where she was laying on the bed
with the window open and the rain blowing on her again.
Twice he did it, and him so dead for sleep that Cora says his
face looked like one of these here Christmas masts that had
done been buried a while and then dug up, until at last they
put her into it and nailed it down so he couldn't open the
window on her no more. And the next morning they found
him in his shirt tail, laying asleep on the floor like a felled
steer, and the top of the box bored clean full of holes and
Cash's new auger broke off in the last one. When they taken
the lid off they found that two of them had bored on into
her face.

If it's a judgment, it aint right. Because the Lord's got
more to do than that. He's bound to have. Because the only
burden Anse Bundren's ever had is himself. And when folks
talks him low, I think to myself he aint that less of a man or
he couldn't a bore himself this long.

It aint right. I be durn if it is. Because He said Suffer little
children to come unto Me dont make it right, neither. Cora
said, "I have bore you what the Lord God sent me. I faced it
without fear nor terror because my faith was strong in the
Lord, a-bolstering and sustaining me. If you have no son, it's
because the Lord has decreed otherwise in His wisdom. And
my life is and has ever been a open book to ere a man or
woman among His creatures because I trust in my God and
my reward."

I reckon she's right. I reckon if there's ere a man or woman
anywhere that He could turn it all over to and go away with
His mind at rest, it would be Cora. And I reckon she would
make a few changes, no matter how He was running it. And
I reckon they would be for man's good. Leastways, we would
have to like them. Leastways, we might as well go on and
make like we did.

Darl

THE LANTERN SITS on a stump. Rusted, grease-fouled, its cracked chimney smeared on one side with a soaring smudge of soot, it sheds a feeble and sultry glare upon the trestles and the boards and the adjacent earth. Upon the dark ground the chips look like random smears of soft pale paint on a black canvas. The boards look like long smooth tatters torn from the flat darkness and turned backside out.

Cash labors about the trestles, moving back and forth, lifting and placing the planks with long clattering reverberations in the dead air as though he were lifting and dropping them at the bottom of an invisible well, the sounds ceasing without departing, as if any movement might dislodge them from the immediate air in reverberant repetition. He saws again, his elbow flashing slowly, a thin thread of fire running along the edge of the saw, lost and recovered at the top and bottom of each stroke in unbroken elongation, so that the saw appears to be six feet long, into and out of pa's shabby and aimless silhouette. "Give me that plank," Cash says. "No; the other one." He puts the saw down and comes and picks up the plank he wants, sweeping pa away with the long swinging gleam of the balanced board.

The air smells like sulphur. Upon the impalpable plane of it their shadows form as upon a wall, as though like sound they had not gone very far away in falling but had merely congealed for a moment, immediate and musing. Cash works on, half turned into the feeble light, one thigh and one pole-thin arm braced, his face sloped into the light with a rapt, dynamic immobility above his tireless elbow. Below the sky sheet-lightning slumbers lightly; against it the trees, motionless, are ruffled out to the last twig, swollen, increased as though quick with young.

It begins to rain. The first harsh, sparse, swift drops rush through the leaves and across the ground in a long sigh, as though of relief from intolerable suspense. They are big as buckshot, warm as though fired from a gun; they sweep across the lantern in a vicious hissing. Pa lifts his face, slack-mouthed, the wet black rim of snuff plastered close along the

base of his gums; from behind his slack-faced astonishment
he muses as though from beyond time, upon the ultimate
outrage. Cash looks once at the sky, then at the lantern. The
saw has not faltered, the running gleam of its pistoning edge
unbroken. "Get something to cover the lantern," he says.

Pa goes to the house. The rain rushes suddenly down, without thunder, without warning of any sort; he is swept onto
the porch upon the edge of it and in an instant Cash is wet
to the skin. Yet the motion of the saw has not faltered, as
though it and the arm functioned in a tranquil conviction that
rain was an illusion of the mind. Then he puts down the saw
and goes and crouches above the lantern, shielding it with his
body, his back shaped lean and scrawny by his wet shirt as
though he had been abruptly turned wrong-side out, shirt
and all.

Pa returns. He is wearing Jewel's raincoat and carrying
Dewey Dell's. Squatting over the lantern, Cash reaches back
and picks up four sticks and drives them into the earth and
takes Dewey Dell's raincoat from pa and spreads it over the
sticks, forming a roof above the lantern. Pa watches him. "I
dont know what you'll do," he says. "Darl taken his coat with
him."

"Get wet," Cash says. He takes up the saw again; again it
moves up and down, in and out of that unhurried imperviousness as a piston moves in the oil; soaked, scrawny, tireless, with the lean light body of a boy or an old man. Pa
watches him, blinking, his face streaming; again he looks up
at the sky with that expression of dumb and brooding outrage
and yet of vindication, as though he had expected no less;
now and then he stirs, moves, gaunt and streaming, picking
up a board or a tool and then laying it down. Vernon Tull is
there now, and Cash is wearing Mrs Tull's raincoat and he
and Vernon are hunting the saw. After a while they find it in
pa's hand.

"Why dont you go on to the house, out of the rain?" Cash
says. Pa looks at him, his face streaming slowly. It is as
though upon a face carved by a savage caricaturist a monstrous burlesque of all bereavement flowed. "You go on in,"
Cash says. "Me and Vernon can finish it."

Pa looks at them. The sleeves of Jewel's coat are too short

for him. Upon his face the rain streams, slow as cold glycerin. "I dont begrudge her the wetting," he says. He moves again and falls to shifting the planks, picking them up, laying them down again carefully, as though they are glass. He goes to the lantern and pulls at the propped raincoat until he knocks it down and Cash comes and fixes it back.

"You get on to the house," Cash says. He leads pa to the house and returns with the raincoat and folds it and places it beneath the shelter where the lantern sits. Vernon has not stopped. He looks up, still sawing.

"You ought to done that at first," he says. "You knowed it was fixing to rain."

"It's his fever," Cash says. He looks at the board.

"Ay," Vernon says. "He'd a come, anyway."

Cash squints at the board. On the long flank of it the rain crashes steadily, myriad, fluctuant. "I'm going to bevel it," he says.

"It'll take more time," Vernon says. Cash sets the plank on edge; a moment longer Vernon watches him, then he hands him the plane.

Vernon holds the board steady while Cash bevels the edge of it with the tedious and minute care of a jeweler. Mrs Tull comes to the edge of the porch and calls Vernon. "How near are you done?" she says.

Vernon does not look up. "Not long. Some, yet."

She watches Cash stooping at the plank, the turgid savage gleam of the lantern slicking on the raincoat as he moves. "You go down and get some planks off the barn and finish it and come in out of the rain," she says. "You'll both catch your death." Vernon does not move. "Vernon," she says.

"We wont be long," he says. "We'll be done after a spell." Mrs Tull watches them a while. Then she reenters the house.

"If we get in a tight, we could take some of them planks," Vernon says. "I'll help you put them back."

Cash ceases the plane and squints along the plank, wiping it with his palm. "Give me the next one," he says.

Some time toward dawn the rain ceases. But it is not yet day when Cash drives the last nail and stands stiffly up and looks down at the finished coffin, the others watching him. In the lantern light his face is calm, musing; slowly he strokes his hands on his raincoated thighs in a gesture deliberate, final and composed. Then the four of them—Cash and pa and Vernon and Peabody—raise the coffin to their shoulders and turn toward the house. It is light, yet they move slowly; empty, yet they carry it carefully; lifeless, yet they move with hushed precautionary words to one another, speaking of it as though, complete, it now slumbered lightly alive, waiting to come awake. On the dark floor their feet clump awkwardly, as though for a long time they have not walked on floors.

They set it down by the bed. Peabody says quietly: "Let's eat a snack. It's almost daylight. Where's Cash?"

He has returned to the trestles, stooped again in the lantern's feeble glare as he gathers up his tools and wipes them on a cloth carefully and puts them into the box with its leather sling to go over the shoulder. Then he takes up box, lantern and raincoat and returns to the house, mounting the steps into faint silhouette against the paling east.

In a strange room you must empty yourself for sleep. And before you are emptied for sleep, what are you. And when you are emptied for sleep, you are not. And when you are filled with sleep, you never were. I dont know what I am. I dont know if I am or not. Jewel knows he is, because he does not know that he does not know whether he is or not. He cannot empty himself for sleep because he is not what he is and he is what he is not. Beyond the unlamped wall I can hear the rain shaping the wagon that is ours, the load that is no longer theirs that felled and sawed it nor yet theirs that bought it and which is not ours either, lie on our wagon though it does, since only the wind and the rain shape it only to Jewel and me, that are not asleep. And since sleep is is-not and rain and wind are *was*, it is not. Yet the wagon *is*, because when the wagon is *was*, Addie Bundren will not be. And Jewel *is*, so Addie Bundren must be. And then I must be, or I could not empty myself for sleep in a strange room. And so if I am not emptied yet, I am *is*.

How often have I lain beneath rain on a strange roof, thinking of home.

Cash

I MADE it on the bevel.

1. There is more surface for the nails to grip.
2. There is twice the gripping-surface to each seam.
3. The water will have to seep into it on a slant. Water moves easiest up and down or straight across.
4. In a house people are upright two thirds of the time. So the seams and joints are made up-and-down. Because the stress is up-and-down.
5. In a bed where people lie down all the time, the joints and seams are made sideways, because the stress is sideways.
6. Except.
7. A body is not square like a crosstie.
8. Animal magnetism.
9. The animal magnetism of a dead body makes the stress come slanting, so the seams and joints of a coffin are made on the bevel.
10. You can see by an old grave that the earth sinks down on the bevel.
11. While in a natural hole it sinks by the center, the stress being up-and-down.
12. So I made it on the bevel.
13. It makes a neater job.

Vardaman

My mother is a fish.

Tull

IT WAS ten oclock when I got back, with Peabody's team hitched on to the back of the wagon. They had already dragged the buckboard back from where Quick found it upside down straddle of the ditch about a mile from the spring. It was pulled out of the road at the spring, and about a dozen wagons was already there. It was Quick found it. He said the river was up and still rising. He said it had already covered the highest water-mark on the bridge-piling he had ever seen. "That bridge wont stand a whole lot of water," I said. "Has somebody told Anse about it?"

"I told him," Quick said. "He says he reckons them boys has heard and unloaded and are on the way back by now. He says they can load up and get across."

"He better go on and bury her at New Hope," Armstid said. "That bridge is old. I wouldn't monkey with it."

"His mind is set on taking her to Jefferson," Quick said.

"Then he better get at it soon as he can," Armstid said.

Anse meets us at the door. He has shaved, but not good. There is a long cut on his jaw, and he is wearing his Sunday pants and a white shirt with the neckband buttoned. It is drawn smooth over his hump, making it look bigger than ever, like a white shirt will, and his face is different too. He looks folks in the eye now, dignified, his face tragic and composed, shaking us by the hand as we walk up onto the porch and scrape our shoes, a little stiff in our Sunday clothes, our Sunday clothes rustling, not looking full at him as he meets us.

"The Lord giveth," we say.

"The Lord giveth."

That boy is not there. Peabody told about how he come into the kitchen, hollering, swarming and clawing at Cora when he found her cooking that fish, and how Dewey Dell taken him down to the barn. "My team all right?" Peabody says.

"All right," I tell him. "I give them a bait this morning. Your buggy seems all right too. It aint hurt."

"And no fault of somebody's," he says. "I'd give a nickel

to know where that boy was when that team broke away."

"If it's broke anywhere, I'll fix it," I say.

The women folks go on into the house. We can hear them, talking and fanning. The fans go whish. whish. whish and them talking, the talking sounding kind of like bees murmuring in a water bucket. The men stop on the porch, talking some, not looking at one another.

"Howdy, Vernon," they say. "Howdy, Tull."

"Looks like more rain."

"It does for a fact."

"Yes, sir. It will rain some more."

"It come up quick."

"And going away slow. It dont fail."

I go around to the back. Cash is filling up the holes he bored in the top of it. He is trimming out plugs for them, one at a time, the wood wet and hard to work. He could cut up a tin can and hide the holes and nobody wouldn't know the difference. Wouldn't mind, anyway. I have seen him spend a hour trimming out a wedge like it was glass he was working, when he could have reached around and picked up a dozen sticks and drove them into the joint and made it do.

When we finished I go back to the front. The men have gone a little piece from the house, sitting on the ends of the boards and on the saw-horses where we made it last night, some sitting and some squatting. Whitfield aint come yet.

They look up at me, their eyes asking.

"It's about," I say. "He's ready to nail."

While they are getting up Anse comes to the door and looks at us and we return to the porch. We scrape our shoes again, careful, waiting for one another to go in first, milling a little at the door. Anse stands inside the door, dignified, composed. He waves us in and leads the way into the room.

They had laid her in it reversed. Cash made it clock-shape, like this ⌐‾‾‾‾‾⌐ with every joint and seam bevelled and scrubbed ⌐____⌐ with the plane, tight as a drum and neat as a sewing basket, and they had laid her in it head to foot so it wouldn't crush her dress. It was her wedding dress and it had a flare-out bottom, and they had laid her head to foot in it so the dress could spread out, and they had made her a veil out of a mosquito bar so the auger holes in her face wouldn't show.

When we are going out, Whitfield comes. He is wet and muddy to the waist, coming in. "The Lord comfort this house," he says. "I was late because the bridge has gone. I went down to the old ford and swum my horse over, the Lord protecting me. His grace be upon this house."

We go back to the trestles and plank-ends and sit or squat.

"I knowed it would go," Armstid says.

"It's been there a long time, that ere bridge," Quick says.

"The Lord has kept it there, you mean," Uncle Billy says. "I dont know ere a man that's touched hammer to it in twenty-five years."

"How long has it been there, Uncle Billy?" Quick says.

"It was built in. . . . . . .let me see. . . . . . . It was in the year 1888," Uncle Billy says. "I mind it because the first man to cross it was Peabody coming to my house when Jody was born."

"If I'd a crossed it every time your wife littered since, it'd a been wore out long before this, Billy," Peabody says.

We laugh, suddenly loud, then suddenly quiet again. We look a little aside at one another.

"Lots of folks has crossed it that wont cross no more bridges," Houston says.

"It's a fact," Littlejohn says. "It's so."

"One more aint, no ways," Armstid says. "It'd taken them two-three days to got her to town in the wagon. They'd be gone a week, getting her to Jefferson and back."

"What's Anse so itching to take her to Jefferson for, anyway?" Houston says.

"He promised her," I say. "She wanted it. She come from there. Her mind was set on it."

"And Anse is set on it, too," Quick says.

"Ay," Uncle Billy says. "It's like a man that's let everything slide all his life to get set on something that will make the most trouble for everybody he knows."

"Well, it'll take the Lord to get her over that river now," Peabody says. "Anse cant do it."

"And I reckon He will," Quick says. "He's took care of Anse a long time, now."

"It's a fact," Littlejohn says.

"Too long to quit now," Armstid says.

"I reckon He's like everybody else around here," Uncle Billy says. "He's done it so long now He cant quit."

Cash comes out. He has put on a clean shirt; his hair, wet, is combed smooth down on his brow, smooth and black as if he had painted it onto his head. He squats stiffly among us, we watching him.

"You feeling this weather, aint you?" Armstid says.

Cash says nothing.

"A broke bone always feels it," Littlejohn says. "A fellow with a broke bone can tell it a-coming."

"Lucky Cash got off with just a broke leg," Armstid says. "He might have hurt himself bed-rid. How far'd you fall, Cash?"

"Twenty-eight foot, four and a half inches, about," Cash says. I move over beside him.

"A fellow can sho slip quick on wet planks," Quick says.

"It's too bad," I say. "But you couldn't a holp it."

"It's them durn women," he says. "I made it to balance with her. I made it to her measure and weight."

If it takes wet boards for folks to fall, it's fixing to be lots of falling before this spell is done.

"You couldn't have holp it," I say.

I dont mind the folks falling. It's the cotton and corn I mind.

Neither does Peabody mind the folks falling. How bout it, Doc?

It's a fact. Washed clean outen the ground it will be. Seems like something is always happening to it.

Course it does. That's why it's worth anything. If nothing didn't happen and everybody made a big crop, do you reckon it would be worth the raising?

Well, I be durn if I like to see my work washed outen the ground, work I sweat over.

It's a fact. A fellow wouldn't mind seeing it washed up if he could just turn on the rain himself.

Who is that man can do that? Where is the color of his eyes?

Ay. The Lord made it to grow. It's Hisn to wash up if He sees it fitten so.

"You couldn't have holp it," I say.

"It's them durn women," he says.

In the house the women begin to sing. We hear the first line commence, beginning to swell as they take hold, and we rise and move toward the door, taking off our hats and throwing our chews away. We do not go in. We stop at the steps, clumped, holding our hats between our lax hands in front or behind, standing with one foot advanced and our heads lowered, looking aside, down at our hats in our hands and at the earth or now and then at the sky and at one another's grave, composed face.

The song ends; the voices quaver away with a rich and dying fall. Whitfield begins. His voice is bigger than him. It's like they are not the same. It's like he is one, and his voice is one, swimming on two horses side by side across the ford and coming into the house, the mud-splashed one and the one that never even got wet, triumphant and sad. Somebody in the house begins to cry. It sounds like her eyes and her voice were turned back inside her, listening; we move, shifting to the other leg, meeting one another's eye and making like they hadn't touched.

Whitfield stops at last. The women sing again. In the thick air it's like their voices come out of the air, flowing together and on in the sad, comforting tunes. When they cease it's like they hadn't gone away. It's like they had just disappeared into the air and when we moved we would loose them again out of the air around us, sad and comforting. Then they finish and we put on our hats, our movements stiff, like we hadn't never wore hats before.

On the way home Cora is still singing. "I am bounding toward my God and my reward," she sings, sitting on the wagon, the shawl around her shoulders and the umbrella open over her, though it is not raining.

"She has hern," I say. "Wherever she went, she has her reward in being free of Anse Bundren." *She laid there three days in that box, waiting for Darl and Jewel to come clean back home and get a new wheel and go back to where the wagon was in the ditch. Take my team, Anse, I said.*

We'll wait for ourn, he said. She'll want it so. She was ever a particular woman.

On the third day they got back and they loaded her into the wagon and started and it already too late. You'll have to go all the way round by Samson's bridge. It'll take you a day to get there. Then you'll be forty miles from Jefferson. Take my team, Anse.

We'll wait for ourn. She'll want it so.

It was about a mile from the house we saw him, sitting on the edge of the slough. It hadn't had a fish in it never that I knowed. He looked around at us, his eyes round and calm, his face dirty, the pole across his knees. Cora was still singing.

"This aint no good day to fish," I said. "You come on home with us and me and you'll go down to the river first thing in the morning and catch some fish."

"It's one in here," he said. "Dewey Dell seen it."

"You come on with us. The river's the best place."

"It's in here," he said. "Dewey Dell seen it."

"I'm bounding toward my God and my reward," Cora sung.

Darl

I T'S NOT your horse that's dead, Jewel," I say. He sits erect on the seat, leaning a little forward, wooden-backed. The brim of his hat has soaked free of the crown in two places, drooping across his wooden face so that, head lowered, he looks through it like through the visor of a helmet, looking long across the valley to where the barn leans against the bluff, shaping the invisible horse. "See them?" I say. High above the house, against the quick thick sky, they hang in narrowing circles. From here they are no more than specks, implacable, patient, portentous. "But it's not your horse that's dead."

"Goddamn you," he says. "Goddamn you."

I cannot love my mother because I have no mother. Jewel's mother is a horse.

Motionless, the tall buzzards hang in soaring circles, the clouds giving them an illusion of retrograde.

Motionless, wooden-backed, wooden-faced, he shapes the horse in a rigid stoop like a hawk, hook-winged. They are waiting for us, ready for the moving of it, waiting for him. He enters the stall and waits until it kicks at him so that he can slip past and mount onto the trough and pause, peering out across the intervening stall-tops toward the empty path, before he reaches into the loft.

"Goddamn him. Goddamn him."

Cash

IT WONT BALANCE. If you want it to tote and ride on a balance, we will have——"

"Pick up. Goddamn you, pick up."

"I'm telling you it wont tote and it wont ride on a balance unless——"

"Pick up! Pick up, goddamn your thick-nosed soul to hell, pick up!"

It wont balance. If they want it to tote and ride on a balance, they will have

Darl

H E STOOPS among us above it, two of the eight hands. In his face the blood goes in waves. In between them his flesh is greenish looking, about that smooth, thick, pale green of cow's cud; his face suffocated, furious, his lip lifted upon his teeth. "Pick up!" he says. "Pick up, goddamn your thick-nosed soul!"

He heaves, lifting one whole side so suddenly that we all spring into the lift to catch and balance it before he hurls it completely over. For an instant it resists, as though volitional, as though within it her pole-thin body clings furiously, even though dead, to a sort of modesty, as she would have tried to conceal a soiled garment that she could not prevent her body soiling. Then it breaks free, rising suddenly as though the emaciation of her body had added buoyancy to the planks or as though, seeing that the garment was about to be torn from her, she rushes suddenly after it in a passionate reversal that flouts its own desire and need. Jewel's face goes completely green and I can hear teeth in his breath.

We carry it down the hall, our feet harsh and clumsy on the floor, moving with shuffling steps, and through the door.

"Steady it a minute, now," pa says, letting go. He turns back to shut and lock the door, but Jewel will not wait.

"Come on," he says in that suffocating voice. "Come on."

We lower it carefully down the steps. We move, balancing it as though it were something infinitely precious, our faces averted, breathing through our teeth to keep our nostrils closed. We go down the path, toward the slope.

"We better wait," Cash says. "I tell you it aint balanced now. We'll need another hand on that hill."

"Then turn loose," Jewel says. He will not stop. Cash begins to fall behind, hobbling to keep up, breathing harshly; then he is distanced and Jewel carries the entire front end alone, so that, tilting as the path begins to slant, it begins to rush away from me and slip down the air like a sled upon invisible snow, smoothly evacuating atmosphere in which the sense of it is still shaped.

"Wait, Jewel," I say. But he will not wait. He is almost

running now and Cash is left behind. It seems to me that the end which I now carry alone has no weight, as though it coasts like a rushing straw upon the furious tide of Jewel's despair. I am not even touching it when, turning, he lets it overshoot him, swinging, and stops it and sloughs it into the wagon bed in the same motion and looks back at me, his face suffused with fury and despair.

"Goddamn you. Goddamn you."

Vardaman

WE ARE GOING to town. Dewey Dell says it wont be sold because it belongs to Santa Claus and he taken it back with him until next Christmas. Then it will be behind the glass again, shining with waiting.

Pa and Cash are coming down the hill, but Jewel is going to the barn. "Jewel," pa says. Jewel does not stop. "Where you going?" pa says. But Jewel does not stop. "You leave that horse here," pa says. Jewel stops and looks at pa. Jewel's eyes look like marbles. "You leave that horse here," pa says. "We'll all go in the wagon with ma, like she wanted."

But my mother is a fish. Vernon seen it. He was there.

"Jewel's mother is a horse," Darl said.

"Then mine can be a fish, cant it, Darl?" I said.

Jewel is my brother.

"Then mine will have to be a horse, too," I said.

"Why?" Darl said. "If pa is your pa, why does your ma have to be a horse just because Jewel's is?"

"Why does it?" I said. "Why does it, Darl?"

Darl is my brother.

"Then what is your ma, Darl?" I said.

"I haven't got ere one," Darl said. "Because if I had one, it is *was*. And if it is was, it cant be *is*. Can it?"

"No," I said.

"Then I am not," Darl said. "Am I?"

"No," I said.

I am. Darl is my brother.

"But you *are*, Darl," I said.

"I know it," Darl said. "That's why I am not *is*. *Are* is too many for one woman to foal."

Cash is carrying his tool box. Pa looks at him. "I'll stop at Tull's on the way back," Cash says. "Get on that barn roof."

"It aint respectful," pa says. "It's a deliberate flouting of her and of me."

"Do you want him to come all the way back here and carry them up to Tull's afoot?" Darl says. Pa looks at Darl, his mouth chewing. Pa shaves every day now because my mother is a fish.

"It aint right," pa says.

Dewey Dell has the package in her hand. She has the basket with our dinner too.

"What's that?" pa says.

"Mrs Tull's cakes," Dewey Dell says, getting into the wagon. "I'm taking them to town for her."

"It aint right," pa says. "It's a flouting of the dead."

It'll be there. It'll be there come Christmas, she says, shining on the track. She says he wont sell it to no town boys.

Darl

H E GOES ON toward the barn, entering the lot, wooden-backed.

Dewey Dell carries the basket on one arm, in the other hand something wrapped square in a newspaper. Her face is calm and sullen, her eyes brooding and alert; within them I can see Peabody's back like two round peas in two thimbles: perhaps in Peabody's back two of those worms which work surreptitious and steady through you and out the other side and you waking suddenly from sleep or from waking, with on your face an expression sudden, intent, and concerned. She sets the basket into the wagon and climbs in, her leg coming long from beneath her tightening dress: that lever which moves the world; one of that caliper which measures the length and breadth of life. She sits on the seat beside Vardaman and sets the parcel on her lap.

Then he enters the barn. He has not looked back.

"It aint right," pa says. "It's little enough for him to do for her."

"Go on," Cash says. "Leave him stay if he wants. He'll be all right here. Maybe he'll go up to Tull's and stay."

"He'll catch us," I say. "He'll cut across and meet us at Tull's lane."

"He would have rid that horse, too," pa says, "if I hadn't a stopped him. A durn spotted critter wilder than a catty-mount. A deliberate flouting of her and of me."

The wagon moves; the mules' ears begin to bob. Behind us, above the house, motionless in tall and soaring circles, they diminish and disappear.

Anse

I TOLD HIM not to bring that horse out of respect for his dead ma, because it wouldn't look right, him prancing along on a durn circus animal and her wanting us all to be in the wagon with her that sprung from her flesh and blood, but we hadn't no more than passed Tull's lane when Darl begun to laugh. Setting back there on the plank seat with Cash, with his dead ma laying in her coffin at his feet, laughing. How many times I told him it's doing such things as that that makes folks talk about him, I dont know. I says I got some regard for what folks says about my flesh and blood even if you haven't, even if I have raised such a durn passel of boys, and when you fixes it so folks can say such about you, it's a reflection on your ma, I says, not me: I am a man and I can stand it; it's on your womenfolks, your ma and sister that you should care for, and I turned and looked back at him and him setting there, laughing.

"I dont expect you to have no respect for me," I says. "But with your own ma not cold in her coffin yet."

"Yonder," Cash says, jerking his head toward the lane. The horse is still a right smart piece away, coming up at a good pace, but I dont have to be told who it is. I just looked back at Darl, setting there laughing.

"I done my best," I says. "I tried to do as she would wish it. The Lord will pardon me and excuse the conduct of them He sent me." And Darl setting on the plank seat right above her where she was laying, laughing.

Darl

H E COMES UP the lane fast, yet we are three hundred yards beyond the mouth of it when he turns into the road, the mud flying beneath the flicking drive of the hooves. Then he slows a little, light and erect in the saddle, the horse mincing through the mud.

Tull is in his lot. He looks at us, lifts his hand. We go on, the wagon creaking, the mud whispering on the wheels. Vernon still stands there. He watches Jewel as he passes, the horse moving with a light, high-kneed driving gait, three hundred yards back. We go on, with a motion so soporific, so dreamlike as to be uninferant of progress, as though time and not space were decreasing between us and it.

It turns off at right angles, the wheel-marks of last Sunday healed away now: a smooth, red scoriation curving away into the pines; a white signboard with faded lettering: New Hope Church. 3 mi. It wheels up like a motionless hand lifted above the profound desolation of the ocean; beyond it the red road lies like a spoke of which Addie Bundren is the rim. It wheels past, empty, unscarred, the white signboard turns away its fading and tranquil assertion. Cash looks up the road quietly, his head turning as we pass it like an owl's head, his face composed. Pa looks straight ahead, humped. Dewey Dell looks at the road too, then she looks back at me, her eyes watchful and repudiant, not like that question which was in those of Cash, for a smoldering while. The signboard passes; the unscarred road wheels on. Then Dewey Dell turns her head. The wagon creaks on.

Cash spits over the wheel. "In a couple of days now it'll be smelling," he says.

"You might tell Jewel that," I say.

He is motionless now, sitting the horse at the junction, upright, watching us, no less still than the signboard that lifts its fading capitulation opposite him.

"It aint balanced right for no long ride," Cash says.

"Tell him that, too," I say. The wagon creaks on.

A mile further along he passes us, the horse, archnecked, reined back to a swift singlefoot. He sits lightly, poised, upright, wooden-faced in the saddle, the broken hat raked at a swaggering angle. He passes us swiftly, without looking at us, the horse driving, its hooves hissing in the mud. A gout of mud, backflung, plops onto the box. Cash leans forward and takes a tool from his box and removes it carefully. When the road crosses Whiteleaf, the willows leaning near enough, he breaks off a branch and scours at the stain with the wet leaves.

Anse

I<small>T'S A HARD COUNTRY</small> on man; it's hard. Eight miles of the sweat of his body washed up outen the Lord's earth, where the Lord Himself told him to put it. Nowhere in this sinful world can a honest, hardworking man profit. It takes them that runs the stores in the towns, doing no sweating, living off of them that sweats. It aint the hardworking man, the farmer. Sometimes I wonder why we keep at it. It's because there is a reward for us above, where they cant take their autos and such. Every man will be equal there and it will be taken from them that have and give to them that have not by the Lord.

But it's a long wait, seems like. It's bad that a fellow must earn the reward of his right-doing by flouting hisself and his dead. We drove all the rest of the day and got to Samson's at dust-dark and then that bridge was gone, too. They hadn't never see the river so high, and it not done raining yet. There was old men that hadn't never see nor hear of it being so in the memory of man. I am the chosen of the Lord, for who He loveth, so doeth He chastiseth. But I be durn if He dont take some curious ways to show it, seems like.

But now I can get them teeth. That will be a comfort. It will.

Samson

I<small>T WAS JUST</small> before sundown. We were sitting on the porch when the wagon came up the road with the five of them in it and the other one on the horse behind. One of them raised his hand, but they was going on past the store without stopping.

"Who's that?" MacCallum says: I cant think of his name: Rafe's twin; that one it was.

"It's Bundren, from down beyond New Hope," Quick says. "There's one of them Snopes horses Jewel's riding."

"I didn't know there was ere a one of them horses left," MacCallum says. "I thought you folks down there finally contrived to give them all away."

"Try and get that one," Quick says. The wagon went on.

"I bet old man Lon never gave it to him," I says.

"No," Quick says. "He bought it from pappy." The wagon went on. "They must not a heard about the bridge," he says.

"What're they doing up here, anyway?" MacCallum says.

"Taking a holiday since he got his wife buried, I reckon," Quick says. "Heading for town, I reckon, with Tull's bridge gone too. I wonder if they aint heard about the bridge."

"They'll have to fly, then," I says. "I dont reckon there's ere a bridge between here and Mouth of Ishatawa."

They had something in the wagon. But Quick had been to the funeral three days ago and we naturally never thought anything about it except that they were heading away from home mighty late and that they hadn't heard about the bridge. "You better holler at them," MacCallum says. Durn it, the name is right on the tip of my tongue. So Quick hollered and they stopped and he went to the wagon and told them.

He come back with them. "They're going to Jefferson," he says. "The bridge at Tull's is gone, too." Like we didn't know it, and his face looked funny, around the nostrils, but they just sat there, Bundren and the girl and the chap on the seat, and Cash and the second one, the one folks talks about, on a plank across the tail-gate, and the other one on that spotted horse. But I reckon they was used to it by then, because when

72

I said to Cash that they'd have to pass by New Hope again and what they'd better do, he just says,

"I reckon we can get there."

I aint much for meddling. Let every man run his own business to suit himself, I say. But after I talked to Rachel about them not having a regular man to fix her and it being July and all, I went back down to the barn and tried to talk to Bundren about it.

"I give her my promise," he says. "Her mind was set on it."

I notice how it takes a lazy man, a man that hates moving, to get set on moving once he does get started off, the same as he was set on staying still, like it aint the moving he hates so much as the starting and the stopping. And like he would be kind of proud of whatever come up to make the moving or the setting still look hard. He set there on the wagon, hunched up, blinking, listening to us tell about how quick the bridge went and how high the water was, and I be durn if he didn't act like he was proud of it, like he had made the river rise himself.

"You say it's higher than you ever see it before?" he says. "God's will be done," he says. "I reckon it wont go down much by morning, neither," he says.

"You better stay here tonight," I says, "and get a early start for New Hope tomorrow morning." I was just sorry for them bone-gaunted mules. I told Rachel, I says, "Well, would you have had me turn them away at dark, eight miles from home? What else could I do," I says. "It wont be but one night, and they'll keep it in the barn, and they'll sholy get started by daylight." And so I says, "You stay here tonight and early tomorrow you can go back to New Hope. I got tools enough, and the boys can go on right after supper and have it dug and ready if they want" and then I found that girl watching me. If her eyes had a been pistols, I wouldn't be talking now. I be dog if they didn't blaze at me. And so when I went down to the barn I come on them, her talking so she never noticed when I come up.

"You promised her," she says. "She wouldn't go until you promised. She thought she could depend on you. If you dont do it, it will be a curse on you."

"Cant no man say I dont aim to keep my word," Bundren says. "My heart is open to ere a man."

"I dont care what your heart is," she says. She was whispering, kind of, talking fast. "You promised her. You've got to. You——" then she seen me and quit, standing there. If they'd been pistols, I wouldn't be talking now. So when I talked to him about it, he says,

"I give her my promise. Her mind is set on it."

"But seems to me she'd rather have her ma buried close by, so she could——"

"It's Addie I give the promise to," he says. "Her mind is set on it."

So I told them to drive it into the barn, because it was threatening rain again, and that supper was about ready. Only they didn't want to come in.

"I thank you," Bundren says. "We wouldn't discommode you. We got a little something in the basket. We can make out."

"Well," I says, "since you are so particular about your womenfolks, I am too. And when folks stops with us at meal time and wont come to the table, my wife takes it as a insult."

So the girl went on to the kitchen to help Rachel. And then Jewel come to me.

"Sho," I says. "Help yourself outen the loft. Feed him when you bait the mules."

"I rather pay you for him," he says.

"What for?" I says. "I wouldn't begrudge no man a bait for his horse."

"I rather pay you," he says; I thought he said extra.

"Extra for what?" I says. "Wont he eat hay and corn?"

"Extra feed," he says. "I feed him a little extra and I dont want him beholden to no man."

"You cant buy no feed from me, boy," I says. "And if he can eat that loft clean, I'll help you load the barn onto the wagon in the morning."

"He aint never been beholden to no man," he says. "I rather pay you for it."

And if I had my rathers, you wouldn't be here a-tall, I wanted to say. But I just says, "Then it's high time he commenced. You cant buy no feed from me."

When Rachel put supper on, her and the girl went and fixed some beds. But wouldn't any of them come in. "She's been dead long enough to get over that sort of foolishness," I says. Because I got just as much respect for the dead as ere a man, but you've got to respect the dead themselves, and a woman that's been dead in a box four days, the best way to respect her is to get her into the ground as quick as you can. But they wouldn't do it.

"It wouldn't be right," Bundren says. "Course, if the boys wants to go to bed, I reckon I can set up with her. I dont begrudge her it."

So when I went back down there they were squatting on the ground around the wagon, all of them. "Let that chap come to the house and get some sleep, anyway," I says. "And you better come too," I says to the girl. I wasn't aiming to interfere with them. And I sholy hadn't done nothing to her that I knowed.

"He's done already asleep," Bundren says. They had done put him to bed in the trough in a empty stall.

"Well, you come on, then," I says to her. But still she never said nothing. They just squatted there. You couldn't hardly see them. "How about you boys?" I says. "You got a full day tomorrow." After a while Cash says,

"I thank you. We can make out."

"We wouldn't be beholden," Bundren says. "I thank you kindly."

So I left them squatting there. I reckon after four days they was used to it. But Rachel wasn't.

"It's a outrage," she says. "A outrage."

"What could he a done?" I says. "He give her his promised word."

"Who's talking about him?" she says. "Who cares about him?" she says, crying. "I just wish that you and him and all the men in the world that torture us alive and flout us dead, dragging us up and down the country——"

"Now, now," I says. "You're upset."

"Dont you touch me!" she says. "Dont you touch me!"

A man cant tell nothing about them. I lived with the same one fifteen years and I be durn if I can. And I imagined a lot of things coming up between us, but I be durn if I ever

thought it would be a body four days dead and that a woman.
But they make life hard on them, not taking it as it comes up,
like a man does.

So I laid there, hearing it commence to rain, thinking
about them down there, squatting around the wagon and the
rain on the roof, and thinking about Rachel crying there until
after a while it was like I could still hear her crying even after
she was asleep, and smelling it even when I knowed I
couldn't. I couldn't decide even then whether I could or not,
or if it wasn't just knowing it was what it was.

So next morning I never went down there. I heard them
hitching up and then when I knowed they must be about
ready to take out, I went out the front and went down the
road toward the bridge until I heard the wagon come out of
the lot and go back toward New Hope. And then when I
come back to the house, Rachel jumped on me because I
wasn't there to make them come in to breakfast. You cant tell
about them. Just about when you decide they mean one
thing, I be durn if you not only haven't got to change your
mind, like as not you got to take a rawhiding for thinking
they meant it.

But it was still like I could smell it. And so I decided then
that it wasn't smelling it, but it was just knowing it was there,
like you will get fooled now and then. But when I went to
the barn I knew different. When I walked into the hallway I
saw something. It kind of hunkered up when I come in and
I thought at first it was one of them got left, then I saw what
it was. It was a buzzard. It looked around and saw me and
went on down the hall, spraddle-legged, with its wings kind
of hunkered out, watching me first over one shoulder and
then over the other, like a old baldheaded man. When it got
outdoors it begun to fly. It had to fly a long time before it
ever got up into the air, with it thick and heavy and full of
rain like it was.

If they was bent on going to Jefferson, I reckon they could
have gone around up by Mount Vernon, like MacCallum did.
He'll get home about day after tomorrow, horseback. Then
they'd be just eighteen miles from town. But maybe this
bridge being gone too has learned him the Lord's sense and
judgment.

That MacCallum. He's been trading with me off and on for twelve years. I have known him from a boy up; know his name as well as I do my own. But be durn if I can say it.

Dewey Dell

THE SIGNBOARD comes in sight. It is looking out at the road now, because it can wait. New Hope. 3 mi. it will say. New Hope. 3 mi. New Hope. 3 mi. And then the road will begin, curving away into the trees, empty with waiting, saying New Hope three miles.

I heard that my mother is dead. I wish I had time to let her die. I wish I had time to wish I had. It is because in the wild and outraged earth too soon too soon too soon. It's not that I wouldn't and will not it's that it is too soon too soon too soon.

Now it begins to say it. New Hope three miles. New Hope three miles. *That's what they mean by the womb of time: the agony and the despair of spreading bones, the hard girdle in which lie the outraged entrails of events* Cash's head turns slowly as we approach, his pale empty sad composed and questioning face following the red and empty curve; beside the back wheel Jewel sits the horse, gazing straight ahead.

The land runs out of Darl's eyes; they swim to pin points. They begin at my feet and rise along my body to my face, and then my dress is gone: I sit naked on the seat above the unhurrying mules, above the travail. *Suppose I tell him to turn. He will do what I say. Dont you know he will do what I say?* Once I waked with a black void rushing under me. I could not see. I saw Vardaman rise and go to the window and strike the knife into the fish, the blood gushing, hissing like steam but I could not see. *He'll do as I say. He always does. I can persuade him to anything. You know I can. Suppose I say Turn here.* That was when I died that time. *Suppose I do. We'll go to New Hope. We wont have to go to town.* I rose and took the knife from the streaming fish still hissing and I killed Darl.

When I used to sleep with Vardaman I had a nightmare once I thought I was awake but I couldn't see and couldn't feel I couldn't feel the bed under me and I couldn't think what I was I couldn't think of my name I couldn't even think I am a girl I couldn't even think I nor even think I want to wake up nor remember what was opposite to awake so I could do that I knew that something was passing but I couldn't even think of time then all of a sudden I knew that something was it was wind blowing over me it was like the wind came and blew me back from where it was I was not blowing the room and Vardaman asleep and all of them back under me again and going on like a piece of cool silk dragging across my naked legs

It blows cool out of the pines, a sad steady sound. New Hope. Was 3 mi. Was 3 mi. I believe in God I believe in God.

"Why didn't we go to New Hope, pa?" Vardaman says. "Mr Samson said we was, but we done passed the road."

Darl says, "Look, Jewel." But he is not looking at me. He is looking at the sky. The buzzard is as still as if he were nailed to it.

We turn into Tull's lane. We pass the barn and go on, the wheels whispering in the mud, passing the green rows of cotton in the wild earth, and Vernon little across the field behind the plow. He lifts his hand as we pass and stands there looking after us for a long while.

"Look, Jewel," Darl says. Jewel sits on his horse like they were both made out of wood, looking straight ahead.

I believe in God, God. God, I believe in God.

Tull

AFTER THEY PASSED I taken the mule out and looped up the trace chains and followed. They was setting in the wagon at the end of the levee. Anse was setting there, looking at the bridge where it was swagged down into the river with just the two ends in sight. He was looking at it like he had believed all the time that folks had been lying to him about it being gone, but like he was hoping all the time it really was. Kind of pleased astonishment he looked, setting on the wagon in his Sunday pants, mumbling his mouth. Looking like a uncurried horse dressed up: I dont know.

The boy was watching the bridge where it was mid-sunk and logs and such drifted up over it and it swagging and shivering like the whole thing would go any minute, big-eyed he was watching it, like he was to a circus. And the gal too. When I come up she looked around at me, her eyes kind of blaring up and going hard like I had made to touch her. Then she looked at Anse again and then back at the water again.

It was nigh up to the levee on both sides, the earth hid except for the tongue of it we was on going out to the bridge and then down into the water, and except for knowing how the road and the bridge used to look, a fellow couldn't tell where was the river and where the land. It was just a tangle of yellow and the levee not less wider than a knife-back kind of, with us setting in the wagon and on the horse and the mule.

Darl was looking at me, and then Cash turned and looked at me with that look in his eyes like when he was figuring on whether the planks would fit her that night, like he was measuring them inside of him and not asking you to say what you thought and not even letting on he was listening if you did say it, but listening all right. Jewel hadn't moved. He sat there on the horse, leaning a little forward, with that same look on his face when him and Darl passed the house yesterday, coming back to get her.

"If it was just up, we could drive across," Anse says. "We could drive right on across it."

Sometimes a log would get shoved over the jam and float

on, rolling and turning, and we could watch it go on to where the ford used to be. It would slow up and whirl cross-ways and hang out of water for a minute, and you could tell by that that the ford used to be there.

"But that dont show nothing," I say. "It could be a bar of quicksand built up there." We watch the log. Then the gal is looking at me again.

"Mr Whitfield crossed it," she says.

"He was a horse-back," I say. "And three days ago. It's riz five foot since."

"If the bridge was just up," Anse says.

The log bobs up and goes on again. There is a lot of trash and foam, and you can hear the water.

"But it's down," Anse says.

Cash says, "A careful fellow could walk across yonder on the planks and logs."

"But you couldn't tote nothing," I say. "Likely time you set foot on that mess, it'll all go, too. What you think, Darl?"

He is looking at me. He dont say nothing; just looks at me with them queer eyes of hisn that makes folks talk. I always say it aint never been what he done so much or said or any-thing so much as how he looks at you. It's like he had got into the inside of you, someway. Like somehow you was looking at yourself and your doings outen his eyes. Then I can feel that gal watching me like I had made to touch her. She says something to Anse. ". . . . . . Mr Whit-field. . . ." she says.

"I give her my promised word in the presence of the Lord," Anse says. "I reckon it aint no need to worry."

But still he does not start the mules. We set there above the water. Another log bobs up over the jam and goes on; we watch it check up and swing slow for a minute where the ford used to be. Then it goes on.

"It might start falling tonight," I say. "You could lay over one more day."

Then Jewel turns sideways on the horse. He has not moved until then, and he turns and looks at me. His face is kind of green, then it would go red and then green again. "Get to hell on back to your damn plowing," he says. "Who the hell asked you to follow us here?"

"I never meant no harm," I say.

"Shut up, Jewel," Cash says. Jewel looks back at the water, his face gritted, going red and green and then red. "Well," Cash says after a while, " what you want to do?"

Anse dont say nothing. He sets humped up, mumbling his mouth. "If it was just up, we could drive across it," he says.

"Come on," Jewel says, moving the horse.

"Wait," Cash says. He looks at the bridge. We look at him, except Anse and the gal. They are looking at the water. "Dewey Dell and Vardaman and pa better walk across on the bridge," Cash says.

"Vernon can help them," Jewel says. "And we can hitch his mule ahead of ourn."

"You aint going to take my mule into that water," I say.

Jewel looks at me. His eyes look like pieces of a broken plate. "I'll pay for your damn mule. I'll buy it from you right now."

"My mule aint going into that water," I say.

"Jewel's going to use his horse," Darl says. "Why wont you risk your mule, Vernon?"

"Shut up, Darl," Cash says. "You and Jewel both."

"My mule aint going into that water," I say.

Darl

H E SITS THE HORSE, glaring at Vernon, his lean face suffused up to and beyond the pale rigidity of his eyes. The summer when he was fifteen, he took a spell of sleeping. One morning when I went to feed the mules the cows were still in the tie-up and then I heard pa go back to the house and call him. When we came on back to the house for breakfast he passed us, carrying the milk buckets, stumbling along like he was drunk, and he was milking when we put the mules in and went on to the field without him. We had been there an hour and still he never showed up. When Dewey Dell came with our lunch, pa sent her back to find Jewel. They found him in the tie-up, sitting on the stool, asleep.

After that, every morning pa would go in and wake him. He would go to sleep at the supper table and soon as supper was finished he would go to bed, and when I came in to bed he would be lying there like a dead man. Yet still pa would have to wake him in the morning. He would get up, but he wouldn't hardly have half sense: he would stand for pa's jawing and complaining without a word and take the milk buckets and go to the barn, and once I found him asleep at the cow, the bucket in place and half full and his hands up to the wrists in the milk and his head against the cow's flank.

After that Dewey Dell had to do the milking. He still got up when pa waked him, going about what we told him to do in that dazed way. It was like he was trying hard to do them; that he was as puzzled as anyone else.

"Are you sick?" ma said. "Dont you feel all right?"

"Yes," Jewel said. "I feel all right."

"He's just lazy, trying me," pa said, and Jewel standing there, asleep on his feet like as not. "Aint you?" he said, waking Jewel up again to answer.

"No," Jewel said.

"You take off and stay in the house today," ma said.

"With that whole bottom piece to be busted out?" pa said. "If you aint sick, what's the matter with you?"

"Nothing," Jewel said. "I'm all right."

"All right?" pa said. "You're asleep on your feet this minute."

"No," Jewel said. "I'm all right."

"I want him to stay at home today," ma said.

"I'll need him," pa said. "It's tight enough, with all of us to do it."

"You'll just have to do the best you can with Cash and Darl," ma said. "I want him to stay in today."

But he wouldn't do it. "I'm all right," he said, going on. But he wasn't all right. Anybody could see it. He was losing flesh, and I have seen him go to sleep chopping; watched the hoe going slower and slower up and down, with less and less of an arc, until it stopped and he leaning on it motionless in the hot shimmer of the sun.

Ma wanted to get the doctor, but pa didn't want to spend the money without it was needful, and Jewel did seem all right except for his thinness and his way of dropping off to sleep at any moment. He ate hearty enough, except for his way of going to sleep in his plate, with a piece of bread half way to his mouth and his jaws still chewing. But he swore he was all right.

It was ma that got Dewey Dell to do his milking, paid her somehow, and the other jobs around the house that Jewel had been doing before supper she found some way for Dewey Dell and Vardaman to do them. And doing them herself when pa wasn't there. She would fix him special things to eat and hide them for him. And that may have been when I first found it out, that Addie Bundren should be hiding anything she did, who had tried to teach us that deceit was such that, in a world where it was, nothing else could be very bad or very important, not even poverty. And at times when I went in to go to bed she would be sitting in the dark by Jewel where he was asleep. And I knew that she was hating herself for that deceit and hating Jewel because she had to love him so that she had to act the deceit.

One night she was taken sick and when I went to the barn to put the team in and drive to Tull's, I couldn't find the lantern. I remembered noticing it on the nail the night before, but it wasn't there now at midnight. So I hitched in the dark and went on and came back with Mrs Tull just after daylight.

And there the lantern was, hanging on the nail where I remembered it and couldn't find it before. And then one morning while Dewey Dell was milking just before sunup, Jewel came into the barn from the back, through the hole in the back wall, with the lantern in his hand.

I told Cash, and Cash and I looked at one another.

"Rutting," Cash said.

"Yes," I said. "But why the lantern? And every night, too. No wonder he's losing flesh. Are you going to say anything to him?"

"Wont do any good," Cash said.

"What he's doing now wont do any good, either."

"I know. But he'll have to learn that himself. Give him time to realise that it'll save, that there'll be just as much more tomorrow, and he'll be all right. I wouldn't tell anybody, I reckon."

"No," I said. "I told Dewey Dell not to. Not ma, anyway."

"No. Not ma."

After that I thought it was right comical: he acting so bewildered and willing and dead for sleep and gaunt as a beanpole, and thinking he was so smart with it. And I wondered who the girl was. I thought of all I knew that it might be, but I couldn't say for sure.

"'Taint any girl," Cash said. "It's a married woman somewhere. Aint any young girl got that much daring and staying power. That's what I dont like about it."

"Why?" I said. "She'll be safer for him than a girl would. More judgment."

He looked at me, his eyes fumbling, the words fumbling at what he was trying to say. "It aint always the safe things in this world that a fellow. . . . . . ."

"You mean, the safe things are not always the best things?"

"Ay; best," he said, fumbling again. "It aint the best things, the things that are good for him. . . . . . A young boy. A fellow kind of hates to see. . . . . . .wallowing in somebody else's mire. . . . . . ." That's what he was trying to say. When something is new and hard and bright, there ought to be something a little better for it than just being safe, since the safe things are just the things that folks have been doing so long they have worn the edges off and there's nothing to the doing of them that leaves a man to say, That was not done before and it cannot be done again.

So we didn't tell, not even when after a while he'd appear suddenly in the field beside us and go to work, without having had time to get home and make out he had been in bed all night. He would tell ma that he hadn't been hungry at breakfast or that he had eaten a piece of bread while he was hitching up the team. But Cash and I knew that he hadn't been home at all on those nights and he had come up out of the woods when we got to the field. But we didn't tell. Summer was almost over then; we knew that when the nights began to get cool, she would be done if he wasn't.

But when fall came and the nights began to get longer, the only difference was that he would always be in bed for pa to wake him, getting him up at last in that first state of semi-idiocy like when it first started, worse than when he had stayed out all night.

"She's sure a stayer," I told Cash. "I used to admire her, but I downright respect her now."

"It aint a woman," he said.

"You know," I said. But he was watching me. "What is it, then?"

"That's what I aim to find out," he said.

"You can trail him through the woods all night if you want to," I said. "I'm not."

"I aint trailing him," he said.

"What do you call it, then?"

"I aint trailing him," he said. "I dont mean it that way."

And so a few nights later I heard Jewel get up and climb out the window, and then I heard Cash get up and follow him. The next morning when I went to the barn, Cash was already there, the mules fed, and he was helping Dewey Dell milk. And when I saw him I knew that he knew what it was. Now and then I would catch him watching Jewel with a queer look, like having found out where Jewel went and what he was doing had given him something to really think about at last. But it was not a worried look; it was the kind of look I would see on him when I would find him doing some of Jewel's work around the house, work that pa still thought Jewel was doing and that ma thought Dewey Dell was doing. So I said nothing to him, believing that when he got done digesting it in his mind, he would tell me. But he never did.

One morning—it was November then, five months since it started—Jewel was not in bed and he didn't join us in the field. That was the first time ma learned anything about what had been going on. She sent Vardaman down to find where Jewel was, and after a while she came down too. It was as though, so long as the deceit ran along quiet and monotonous, all of us let ourselves be deceived, abetting it unawares or maybe through cowardice, since all people are cowards and naturally prefer any kind of treachery because it has a bland outside. But now it was like we had all—and by a kind of telepathic agreement of admitted fear—flung the whole thing back like covers on the bed and we all sitting bolt upright in our nakedness, staring at one another and saying "Now is the truth. He hasn't come home. Something has happened to him. We let something happen to him."

Then we saw him. He came up along the ditch and then turned straight across the field, riding the horse. Its mane and tail were going, as though in motion they were carrying out the splotchy pattern of its coat: he looked like he was riding on a big pinwheel, barebacked, with a rope bridle, and no hat on his head. It was a descendant of those Texas ponies Flem Snopes brought here twenty-five years ago and auctioned off for two dollars a head and nobody but old Lon Quick ever caught his and still owned some of the blood because he could never give it away.

He galloped up and stopped, his heels in the horse's ribs and it dancing and swirling like the shape of its mane and tail and the splotches of its coat had nothing whatever to do with the flesh-and-bone horse inside them, and he sat there, looking at us.

"Where did you get that horse?" pa said.

"Bought it," Jewel said. "From Mr Quick."

"Bought it?" pa said. "With what? Did you buy that thing on my word?"

"It was my money," Jewel said. "I earned it. You wont need to worry about it."

"Jewel," ma said; "Jewel."

"It's all right," Cash said. "He earned the money. He cleaned up that forty acres of new ground Quick laid out last spring. He did it single handed, working at night by lantern. I saw him. So I dont reckon that horse cost anybody anything except Jewel. I dont reckon we need worry."

"Jewel," ma said. "Jewel——" Then she said: "You come right to the house and go to bed."

"Not yet," Jewel said. "I aint got time. I got to get me a saddle and bridle. Mr Quick says he——"

"Jewel," ma said, looking at him. "I'll give——I'll give—— give——" Then she began to cry. She cried hard, not hiding her face, standing there in her faded wrapper, looking at him and him on the horse, looking down at her, his face growing cold and a little sick looking, until he looked away quick and Cash came and touched her.

"You go on to the house," Cash said. "This here ground is too wet for you. You go on, now." She put her hands to her face then and after a while she went on, stumbling a little on the plow-marks. But pretty soon she straightened up and went on. She didn't look back. When she reached the ditch she stopped and called Vardaman. He was looking at the horse, kind of dancing up and down by it.

"Let me ride, Jewel," he said. "Let me ride, Jewel."

Jewel looked at him, then he looked away again, holding the horse reined back. Pa watched him, mumbling his lip.

"So you bought a horse," he said. "You went behind my back and bought a horse. You never consulted me; you know how tight it is for us to make by, yet you bought a horse for me to feed. Taken the work from your flesh and blood and bought a horse with it."

Jewel looked at pa, his eyes paler than ever. "He wont never eat a mouthful of yours," he said. "Not a mouthful. I'll kill him first. Dont you never think it. Dont you never."

"Let me ride, Jewel," Vardaman said. "Let me ride, Jewel." He sounded like a cricket in the grass, a little one. "Let me ride, Jewel."

That night I found ma sitting beside the bed where he was sleeping, in the dark. She cried hard, maybe because she had to cry so quiet; maybe because she felt the same way about

tears she did about deceit, hating herself for doing it, hating
him because she had to. And then I knew that I knew. I knew
that as plain on that day as I knew about Dewey Dell on that
day.

Tull

S O THEY FINALLY got Anse to say what he wanted to do, and him and the gal and the boy got out of the wagon. But even when we were on the bridge Anse kept on looking back, like he thought maybe, once he was outen the wagon, the whole thing would kind of blow up and he would find himself back yonder in the field again and her laying up there in the house, waiting to die and it to do all over again.

"You ought to let them taken your mule," he says, and the bridge shaking and swaying under us, going down into the moiling water like it went clean through to the other side of the earth, and the other end coming up outen the water like it wasn't the same bridge a-tall and that them that would walk up outen the water on that side must come from the bottom of the earth. But it was still whole; you could tell that by the way when this end swagged, it didn't look like the other end swagged at all: just like the other trees and the bank yonder were swinging back and forth slow like on a big clock. And them logs scraping and bumping at the sunk part and tilting end-up and shooting clean outen the water and tumbling on toward the ford and the waiting, slick, whirling, and foamy.

"What good would that a done?" I says. "If your team cant find the ford and haul it across, what good would three mules or even ten mules do?"

"I aint asking it of you," he says. "I can always do for me and mine. I aint asking you to risk your mule. It aint your dead; I am not blaming you."

"They ought to went back and laid over until tomorrow," I says. The water was cold. It was thick, like slush ice. Only it kind of lived. One part of you knowed it was just water, the same thing that had been running under this same bridge for a long time, yet when them logs would come spewing up outen it, you were not surprised, like they was a part of water, of the waiting and the threat.

It was like when we was across, up out of the water again and the hard earth under us, that I was surprised. It was like we hadn't expected the bridge to end on the other bank, on something tame like the hard earth again that we had tromped on before this time and knowed well. Like it couldn't be me here, because I'd have had better sense than to done what I just done. And when I looked back and saw the other bank and saw my mule standing there where I used to be and knew that I'd have to get back there someway, I knew it couldn't be, because I just couldn't think of anything that could make me cross that bridge ever even once. Yet here I was, and the fellow that could make himself cross it twice, couldn't be me, not even if Cora told him to.

It was that boy. I said "Here; you better take a holt of my hand" and he waited and held to me. I be durn if it wasn't like he come back and got me; like he was saying They wont nothing hurt you. Like he was saying about a fine place he knowed where Christmas come twice with Thanksgiving and lasts on through the winter and the spring and the summer, and if I just stayed with him I'd be all right too.

When I looked back at my mule it was like he was one of these here spy-glasses and I could look at him standing there and see all the broad land and my house sweated outen it like it was the more the sweat, the broader the land; the more the sweat, the tighter the house because it would take a tight house for Cora, to hold Cora like a jar of milk in the spring: you've got to have a tight jar or you'll need a powerful spring, so if you have a big spring, why then you have the incentive to have tight, wellmade jars, because it is your milk, sour or not, because you would rather have milk that will sour than to have milk that wont, because you are a man.

And him holding to my hand, his hand that hot and confident, so that I was like to say: Look-a-here. Cant you see that mule yonder? He never had no business over here, so he never come, not being nothing but a mule. Because a fellow can see ever now and then that children have more sense than him. But he dont like to admit it to them until they have beards. After they have a beard, they are too busy because they dont know if they'll ever quite make it back to where they were in sense before they was haired, so you dont mind admitting then to folks that are worrying about the same thing that aint worth the worry that you are yourself.

Then we was over and we stood there, looking at Cash turning the wagon around. We watched them drive back down the road to where the trail turned off into the bottom. After a while the wagon was out of sight.

"We better get on down to the ford and git ready to help," I said.

"I give her my word," Anse says. "It is sacred on me. I know you begrudge it, but she will bless you in heaven."

"Well, they got to finish circumventing the land before they can dare the water," I said. "Come on."

"It's the turning back," he said. "It aint no luck in turning back."

He was standing there, humped, mournful, looking at the empty road beyond the swagging and swaying bridge. And that gal, too, with the lunch basket on one arm and that package under the other. Just going to town. Bent on it. They would risk the fire and the earth and the water and all just to eat a sack of bananas. "You ought to laid over a day," I said. "It would a fell some by morning. It mought not a rained tonight. And it cant get no higher."

"I give my promise," he says. "She is counting on it."

Darl

BEFORE US the thick dark current runs. It talks up to us in a murmur become ceaseless and myriad, the yellow surface dimpled monstrously into fading swirls travelling along the surface for an instant, silent, impermanent and profoundly significant, as though just beneath the surface something huge and alive waked for a moment of lazy alertness out of and into light slumber again.

It clucks and murmurs among the spokes and about the mules' knees, yellow, skummed with flotsam and with thick soiled gouts of foam as though it had sweat, lathering, like a driven horse. Through the undergrowth it goes with a plaintive sound, a musing sound; in it the unwinded cane and saplings lean as before a little gale, swaying without reflections as though suspended on invisible wires from the branches overhead. Above the ceaseless surface they stand—trees, cane, vines—rootless, severed from the earth, spectral above a scene of immense yet circumscribed desolation filled with the voice of the waste and mournful water.

Cash and I sit in the wagon; Jewel sits the horse at the off rear wheel. The horse is trembling, its eye rolling wild and baby-blue in its long pink face, its breathing stertorous like groaning. He sits erect, poised, looking quietly and steadily and quickly this way and that, his face calm, a little pale, alert. Cash's face is also gravely composed; he and I look at one another with long probing looks, looks that plunge unimpeded through one another's eyes and into the ultimate secret place where for an instant Cash and Darl crouch flagrant and unabashed in all the old terror and the old foreboding, alert and secret and without shame. When we speak our voices are quiet, detached.

"I reckon we're still in the road, all right."

"Tull taken and cut them two big whiteoaks. I heard tell how at high water in the old days they used to line up the ford by them trees."

"I reckon he did that two years ago when he was logging down here. I reckon he never thought that anybody would ever use this ford again."

"I reckon not. Yes, it must have been then. He cut a sight of timber outen here then. Payed off that mortgage with it, I hear tell."

"Yes. Yes, I reckon so. I reckon Vernon could have done that."

"That's a fact. Most folks that logs in this here country, they need a durn good farm to support the sawmill. Or maybe a store. But I reckon Vernon could."

"I reckon so. He's a sight."

"Ay. Vernon is. Yes, it must still be here. He never would have got that timber out of here if he hadn't cleaned out that old road. I reckon we are still on it." He looks about quietly, at the position of the trees, leaning this way and that, looking back along the floorless road shaped vaguely high in air by the position of the lopped and felled trees, as if the road too had been soaked free of earth and floated upward, to leave in its spectral tracing a monument to a still more profound desolation than this above which we now sit, talking quietly of old security and old trivial things. Jewel looks at him, then at me, then his face turns in in that quiet, constant, questing about the scene, the horse trembling quietly and steadily between his knees.

"He could go on ahead slow and sort of feel it out," I say.

"Yes," Cash says, not looking at me. His face is in profile as he looks forward where Jewel has moved on ahead.

"He cant miss the river," I say. "He couldn't miss seeing it fifty yards ahead."

Cash does not look at me, his face in profile. "If I'd just suspicioned it, I could a come down last week and taken a sight on it."

"The bridge was up then," I say. He does not look at me. "Whitfield crossed it a-horseback."

Jewel looks at us again, his expression sober and alert and subdued. His voice is quiet. "What you want me to do?"

"I ought to come down last week and taken a sight on it," Cash says.

"We couldn't have known," I say. "There wasn't any way for us to know."

"I'll ride on ahead," Jewel says. "You can follow where I am." He lifts the horse. It shrinks, bowed; he leans to it, speaking to it, lifting it forward almost bodily, it setting its feet down with gingerly splashings, trembling, breathing harshly. He speaks to it, murmurs to it. "Go on," he says. "I aint going to let nothing hurt you. Go on, now."

"Jewel," Cash says. Jewel does not look back. He lifts the horse on.

"He can swim," I say. "If he'll just give the horse time, anyhow. . . . . . ." When he was born, he had a bad time of it. Ma would sit in the lamp-light, holding him on a pillow on her lap. We would wake and find her so. There would be no sound from them.

"That pillow was longer than him," Cash says. He is leaning a little forward. "I ought to come down last week and sighted. I ought to done it."

"That's right," I say. "Neither his feet nor his head would reach the end of it. You couldn't have known," I say.

"I ought to done it," he says. He lifts the reins. The mules move, into the traces; the wheels murmur alive in the water. He looks back and down at Addie. "It aint on a balance," he says.

At last the trees open; against the open river Jewel sits the horse, half turned, it belly deep now. Across the river we can see Vernon and pa and Vardaman and Dewey Dell. Vernon is waving at us, waving us further down stream.

"We are too high up," Cash says. Vernon is shouting too, but we cannot make out what he says for the noise of the water. It runs steady and deep now, unbroken, without sense of motion until a log comes along, turning slowly. "Watch it," Cash says. We watch it and see it falter and hang for a moment, the current building up behind it in a thick wave, submerging it for an instant before it shoots up and tumbles on.

"There it is," I say.

"Ay," Cash says. "It's there." We look at Vernon again. He is now flapping his arms up and down. We move on down stream, slowly and carefully, watching Vernon. He drops his hands. "This is the place," Cash says.

"Well, goddamn it, let's get across, then," Jewel says. He moves the horse on.

"You wait," Cash says. Jewel stops again.

"Well, by God——" he says. Cash looks at the water, then he looks back at Addie. "It aint on a balance," he says.

"Then go on back to the goddamn bridge and walk across," Jewel says. "You and Darl both. Let me on that wagon."

Cash does not pay him any attention. "It aint on a balance," he says. "Yes, sir. We got to watch it."

"Watch it, hell," Jewel says. "You get out of that wagon and let me have it. By God, if you're afraid to drive it over. . . . . . ." His eyes are pale as two bleached chips in his face. Cash is looking at him.

"We'll get it over," he says. "I tell you what you do. You ride on back and walk across the bridge and come down the other bank and meet us with the rope. Vernon'll take your horse home with him and keep it till we get back."

"You go to hell," Jewel says.

"You take the rope and come down the bank and be ready with it," Cash says. "Three cant do no more than two can— one to drive and one to steady it."

"Goddamn you," Jewel says.

"Let Jewel take the end of the rope and cross upstream of us and brace it," I say. "Will you do that, Jewel?"

Jewel watches me, hard. He looks quick at Cash, then back at me, his eyes alert and hard. "I dont give a damn. Just so we do something. Setting here, not lifting a goddamn hand. . . ."

"Let's do that, Cash," I say.

"I reckon we'll have to," Cash says.

The river itself is not a hundred yards across, and pa and Vernon and Vardaman and Dewey Dell are the only things in sight not of that single monotony of desolation leaning with that terrific quality a little from right to left, as though we had reached the place where the motion of the wasted world accelerates just before the final precipice. Yet they appear dwarfed. It is as though the space between us were time: an irrevocable quality. It is as though time, no longer running straight before us in a diminishing line, now runs parallel between us like a looping string, the distance being the doubling accretion of the thread and not the interval between. The mules stand, their fore quarters already sloped a little, their rumps high. They too are breathing now with a deep groaning sound; looking back once, their gaze sweeps across us with in their eyes a wild, sad, profound and despairing quality as though they had already seen in the thick water the shape of the disaster which they could not speak and we could not see.

Cash turns back into the wagon. He lays his hands flat on Addie, rocking her a little. His face is calm, down-sloped, calculant, concerned. He lifts his box of tools and wedges it forward under the seat; together we shove Addie forward, wedging her between the tools and the wagon bed. Then he looks at me.

"No," I say. "I reckon I'll stay. Might take both of us."

From the tool box he takes his coiled rope and carries the end twice around the seat stanchion and passes the end to me without tying it. The other end he pays out to Jewel, who takes a turn about his saddle horn.

He must force the horse down into the current. It moves, highkneed, archnecked, boring and chafing. Jewel sits lightly forward, his knees lifted a little; again his swift alert calm gaze sweeps upon us and on. He lowers the horse into the stream, speaking to it in a soothing murmur. The horse slips, goes under to the saddle, surges to its feet again, the current building up against Jewel's thighs.

"Watch yourself," Cash says.

"I'm on it now," Jewel says. "You can come ahead now."

Cash takes the reins and lowers the team carefully and skillfully into the stream.

I felt the current take us and I knew we were on the ford by that reason, since it was only by means of that slipping contact that we could tell that we were in motion at all. What had once been a flat surface was now a succession of troughs and hillocks lifting and falling about us, shoving at us, teasing at us with light lazy touches in the vain instants of solidity underfoot. Cash looked back at me, and then I knew that we were gone. But I did not realise the reason for the rope until I saw the log. It surged up out of the water and stood for an instant upright upon that surging and heaving desolation like Christ. Get out and let the current take you down to the bend, Cash said, You can make it all right. No, I said, I'd get just as wet that way as this

The log appears suddenly between two hills, as if it had rocketed suddenly from the bottom of the river. Upon the end of it a long gout of foam hangs like the beard of an old man or a goat. When Cash speaks to me I know that he has been watching it all the time, watching it and watching Jewel ten feet ahead of us. "Let the rope go," he says. With his other hand he reaches down and reeves the two turns from the stanchion. "Ride on, Jewel," he says; "see if you can pull us ahead of the log."

Jewel shouts at the horse; again he appears to lift it bodily between his knees. He is just above the top of the ford and the horse has a purchase of some sort for it surges forward, shining wetly half out of water, crashing on in a succession of lunges. It moves unbelievably fast; by that token Jewel realises at last that the rope is free, for I can see him sawing back on the reins, his head turned, as the log rears in a long sluggish lunge between us, bearing down upon the team. They see it too; for a moment they also shine black out of water. Then the downstream one vanishes, dragging the other with him; the wagon sheers crosswise, poised on the crest of the ford as the log strikes it, tilting it up and on. Cash is half turned, the reins running taut from his hand and disappearing into the water, the other hand reached back upon Addie, holding her jammed over against the high side of the wagon. "Jump clear," he says quietly. "Stay away from the team and dont try to fight it. It'll swing you into the bend all right."

"You come too," I say. Vernon and Vardaman are running along the bank, pa and Dewey Dell stand watching us, Dewey Dell with the basket and the package in her arms. Jewel is trying to fight the horse back. The head of one mule appears, its eyes wide; it looks back at us for an instant, making a sound almost human. The head vanishes again.

"Back, Jewel," Cash shouts. "Back, Jewel." For another instant I see him leaning to the tilting wagon, his arm braced back against Addie and his tools; I see the bearded head of the rearing log strike up again, and beyond it Jewel holding the horse upreared, its head wrenched around, hammering its head with his fist. I jump from the wagon on the downstream side. Between two hills I see the mules once more. They roll up out of the water in succession, turning completely over, their legs stiffly extended as when they had lost contact with the earth.

Vardaman

CASH TRIED but she fell off and Darl jumped going under he went under and Cash hollering to catch her and I hollering running and hollering and Dewey Dell hollering at me Vardaman you vardaman you vardaman and Vernon passed me because he was seeing her come up and she jumped into the water again and Darl hadn't caught her yet

He came up to see and I hollering catch her Darl catch her and he didn't come back because she was too heavy he had to go on catching at her and I hollering catch her darl catch her darl because in the water she could go faster than a man and Darl had to grabble for her so I knew he could catch her because he is the best grabbler even with the mules in the way again they dived up rolling their feet stiff rolling down again and their backs up now and Darl had to again because in the water she could go faster than a man or a woman and I passed Vernon and he wouldn't get in the water and help Darl he wouldn't grabble for her with Darl he knew but he wouldn't help

The mules dived up again diving their legs stiff their stiff legs rolling slow and then Darl again and I hollering catch her darl catch her head her into the bank darl and Vernon wouldn't help and then Darl dodged past the mules where he could he had her under the water coming in to the bank coming in slow because in the water she fought to stay under the water but Darl is strong and he was coming in slow and so I knew he had her because he came slow and I ran down into the water to help and I couldn't stop hollering because Darl was strong and steady holding her under the water even if she did fight he would not let her go he was seeing me and he would hold her and it was all right now it was all right now it was all right

Then he comes up out of the water. He comes a long way up slow before his hands do but he's got to have her got to so I can bear it. Then his hands come up and all of him above the water. I cant stop. I have not got time to try. I will try to when I can but his hands came empty out of the water emptying the water emptying away

"Where is ma, Darl?" I said. "You never got her. You knew she is a fish but you let her get away. You never got her. Darl. Darl. Darl." I began to run along the bank, watching the mules dive up slow again and then down again.

Tull

WHEN I TOLD Cora how Darl jumped out of the wagon and left Cash sitting there trying to save it and the wagon turning over, and Jewel that was almost to the bank fighting that horse back where it had more sense than to go, she says "And you're one of the folks that says Darl is the queer one, the one that aint bright, and him the only one of them that had sense enough to get off that wagon. I notice Anse was too smart to been on it a-tall."

"He couldn't a done no good, if he'd been there," I said. "They was going about it right and they would have made it if it hadn't a been for that log."

"Log, fiddlesticks," Cora said. "It was the hand of God."

"Then how can you say it was foolish?" I said. "Nobody cant guard against the hand of God. It would be sacrilege to try to."

"Then why dare it?" Cora says. "Tell me that."

"Anse didn't," I said. "That's just what you faulted him for."

"His place was there," Cora said. "If he had been a man, he would a been there instead of making his sons do what he dursn't."

"I dont know what you want, then," I said. "One breath you say they was daring the hand of God to try it, and the next breath you jump on Anse because he wasn't with them." Then she begun to sing again, working at the washtub, with that singing look in her face like she had done give up folks and all their foolishness and had done went on ahead of them, marching up the sky, singing.

The wagon hung for a long time while the current built up under it, shoving it off the ford, and Cash leaning more and more, trying to keep the coffin braced so it wouldn't slip down and finish tilting the wagon over. Soon as the wagon got tilted good, to where the current could finish it, the log went on. It headed around the wagon and went on good as a swimming man could have done. It was like it had been sent there to do a job and done it and went on.

When the mules finally kicked loose, it looked for a minute

like maybe Cash would get the wagon back. It looked like him and the wagon wasn't moving at all, and just Jewel fighting that horse back to the wagon. Then that boy passed me, running and hollering at Darl and the gal trying to catch him, and then I see the mules come rolling slow up out of the water, their legs spraddled stiff like they had balked upside down, and roll on into the water again.

Then the wagon tilted over and then it and Jewel and the horse was all mixed up together. Cash went outen sight, still holding the coffin braced, and then I couldn't tell anything for the horse lunging and splashing. I thought that Cash had give up then and was swimming for it and I was yelling at Jewel to come on back and then all of a sudden him and the horse went under too and I thought they was all going. I knew that the horse had got dragged off the ford too, and with that wild drowning horse and that wagon and that loose box, it was going to be pretty bad, and there I was, standing knee deep in the water, yelling at Anse behind me: "See what you done now? See what you done now?"

The horse come up again. It was headed for the bank now, throwing its head up, and then I saw one of them holding to the saddle on the downstream side, so I started running along the bank, trying to catch sight of Cash because he couldn't swim, yelling at Jewel where Cash was like a durn fool, bad as that boy that was on down the bank still hollering at Darl.

So I went down into the water so I could still keep some kind of a grip in the mud, when I saw Jewel. He was middle deep, so I knew he was on the ford, anyway, leaning hard upstream, and then I see the rope, and then I see the water building up where he was holding the wagon snubbed just below the ford.

So it was Cash holding to the horse when it come splashing and scrambling up the bank, moaning and groaning like a natural man. When I come to it it was just kicking Cash loose from his holt on the saddle. His face turned up a second when he was sliding back into the water. It was gray, with his eyes closed and a long swipe of mud across his face. Then he let go and turned over in the water. He looked just like a old bundle of clothes kind of washing up and down against the bank. He looked like he was laying there in the water on his face, rocking up and down a little, looking at something on the bottom.

We could watch the rope cutting down into the water, and we could feel the weight of the wagon kind of blump and lunge lazy like, like it just as soon as not, and that rope cutting down into the water hard as a iron bar. We could hear the water hissing on it like it was red hot. Like it was a straight iron bar stuck into the bottom and us holding the end of it, and the wagon lazing up and down, kind of pushing and prodding at us like it had come around and got behind us, lazy like, like it just as soon as not when it made up its mind. There was a shoat come by, blowed up like a balloon: one of them spotted shoats of Lon Quick's. It bumped against the rope like it was a iron bar and bumped off and went on, and us watching that rope slanting down into the water. We watched it.

Darl

CASH LIES on his back on the earth, his head raised on a rolled garment. His eyes are closed, his face is gray, his hair plastered in a smooth smear across his forehead as though done with a paint brush. His face appears sunken a little, sagging from the bony ridges of eye sockets, nose, gums, as though the wetting had slacked the firmness which had held the skin full; his teeth, set in pale gums, are parted a little as if he had been laughing quietly. He lies pole-thin in his wet clothes, a little pool of vomit at his head and a thread of it running from the corner of his mouth and down his cheek where he couldn't turn his head quick or far enough, until Dewey Dell stoops and wipes it away with the hem of her dress.

Jewel approaches. He has the plane. "Vernon just found the square," he says. He looks down at Cash, dripping too. "Aint he talked none yet?"

"He had his saw and hammer and chalk-line and rule," I say. "I know that."

Jewel lays the square down. Pa watches him. "They cant be far away," pa says. "It all went together. Was there ere a such misfortunate man."

Jewel does not look at pa. "You better call Vardaman back here," he says. He looks at Cash. Then he turns and goes away. "Get him to talk soon as he can," he says, "so he can tell us what else there was."

We return to the river. The wagon is hauled clear, the wheels chocked (carefully: we all helped; it is as though upon the shabby, familiar, inert shape of the wagon there lingered somehow, latent yet still immediate, that violence which had slain the mules that drew it not an hour since) above the edge of the flood. In the wagon bed it lies profoundly, the long pale planks hushed a little with wetting yet still yellow, like gold seen through water, save for two long muddy smears. We pass it and go on to the bank.

One end of the rope is made fast to a tree. At the edge of the stream, knee-deep, Vardaman stands, bent forward a little, watching Vernon with rapt absorption. He has stopped yelling and he is wet to the armpits. Vernon is at the other end of the rope, shoulder-deep in the river, looking back at Vardaman. "Further back than that," he says. "You git back by the tree and hold the rope for me, so it cant slip."

Vardaman backs along the rope, to the tree, moving blindly, watching Vernon. When we come up he looks at us once, his eyes round and a little dazed. Then he looks at Vernon again in that posture of rapt alertness.

"I got the hammer too," Vernon says. "Looks like we ought to done already got that chalk-line. It ought to floated."

"Floated clean away," Jewel says. "We wont get it. We ought to find the saw, though."

"I reckon so," Vernon says. He looks at the water. "That chalk-line, too. What else did he have?"

"He aint talked yet," Jewel says, entering the water. He looks back at me. "You go back and get him roused up to talk," he says.

"Pa's there," I say. I follow Jewel into the water, along the rope. It feels alive in my hand, bellied faintly in a prolonged and resonant arc. Vernon is watching me.

"You better go," he says. "You better be there."

"Let's see what else we can get before it washes on down," I say.

We hold to the rope, the current curling and dimpling about our shoulders. But beneath that false blandness the true force of it leans against us lazily. I had not thought that water in July could be so cold. It is like hands molding and prodding at the very bones. Vernon is still looking back toward the bank.

"Reckon it'll hold us all?" he says. We too look back, following the rigid bar of the rope as it rises from the water to the tree and Vardaman crouched a little beside it, watching us. "Wish my mule wouldn't strike out for home," Vernon says.

"Come on," Jewel says. "Let's get outen here."

We submerge in turn, holding to the rope, being clutched by one another while the cold wall of the water sucks the slanting mud backward and upstream from beneath our feet and we are suspended so, groping along the cold bottom.

Even the mud there is not still. It has a chill, scouring quality, as though the earth under us were in motion too. We touch and fumble at one another's extended arms, letting ourselves go cautiously against the rope; or, erect in turn, watch the water suck and boil where one of the other two gropes beneath the surface. Pa has come down to the shore, watching us.

Vernon comes up, streaming, his face sloped down into his pursed blowing mouth. His mouth is bluish, like a circle of weathered rubber. He has the rule.

"He'll be glad of that," I say. "It's right new. He bought it just last month out of the catalogue."

"If we just knowed for sho what else," Vernon says, looking over his shoulder and then turning to face where Jewel had disappeared. "Didn't he go down fore me?" Vernon says.

"I dont know," I say. "I think so. Yes. Yes, he did."

We watch the thick curling surface, streaming away from us in slow whorls.

"Give him a pull on the rope," Vernon says.

"He's on your end of it," I say.

"Aint nobody on my end of it," he says.

"Pull it in," I say. But he has already done that, holding the end above the water; and then we see Jewel. He is ten yards away; he comes up, blowing, and looks at us, tossing his long hair back with a jerk of his head, then he looks toward the bank; we can see him filling his lungs.

"Jewel," Vernon says, not loud, but his voice going full and clear along the water, peremptory yet tactful. "It'll be back here. Better come back."

Jewel dives again. We stand there, leaning back against the current, watching the water where he disappeared, holding the dead rope between us like two men holding the nozzle of a fire hose, waiting for the water. Suddenly Dewey Dell is behind us in the water. "You make him come back," she says. "Jewel!" she says. He comes up again, tossing his hair back from his eyes. He is swimming now, toward the bank, the current sweeping him downstream quartering. "You, Jewel!" Dewey Dell says. We stand holding the rope and see him gain the bank and climb out. As he rises from the water, he stoops and picks up something. He comes back along the bank. He has found the chalk-line. He comes opposite us and stands there, looking about as if he were seeking something. Pa goes on down the bank. He is going back to look at the mules again where their round bodies float and rub quietly together in the slack water within the bend.

"What did you do with the hammer, Vernon?" Jewel says.

"I give it to him," Vernon says, jerking his head at Vardaman. Vardaman is looking after pa. Then he looks at Jewel. "With the square." Vernon is watching Jewel. He moves toward the bank, passing Dewey Dell and me.

"You get on out of here," I say. She says nothing, looking at Jewel and Vernon.

"Where's the hammer?" Jewel says. Vardaman scuttles up the bank and fetches it.

"It's heavier than the saw," Vernon says. Jewel is tying the end of the chalk-line about the hammer shaft.

"Hammer's got the most wood in it," Jewel says. He and Vernon face one another, watching Jewel's hands.

"And flatter, too," Vernon says. "It'd float three to one, almost. Try the plane."

Jewel looks at Vernon. Vernon is tall, too; long and lean, eye to eye they stand in their close wet clothes. Lon Quick could look even at a cloudy sky and tell the time to ten minutes. Big Lon I mean, not little Lon.

"Why dont you get out of the water?" I say.

"It wont float like a saw," Jewel says.

"It'll float nigher to a saw than a hammer will," Vernon says.

"Bet you," Jewel says.

"I wont bet," Vernon says.

They stand there, watching Jewel's still hands.

"Hell," Jewel says. "Get the plane, then."

So they get the plane and tie it to the chalk-line and enter the water again. Pa comes back along the bank. He stops for a while and looks at us, hunched, mournful, like a failing steer or an old tall bird.

Vernon and Jewel return, leaning against the current. "Get out of the way," Jewel says to Dewey Dell. "Get out of the water."

She crowds against me a little so they can pass, Jewel

holding the plane high as though it were perishable, the blue string trailing back over his shoulder. They pass us and stop; they fall to arguing quietly about just where the wagon went over.

"Darl ought to know," Vernon says. They look at me.

"I dont know," I says. "I wasn't there that long."

"Hell," Jewel says. They move on, gingerly, leaning against the current, reading the ford with their feet.

"Have you got a holt of the rope?" Vernon says. Jewel does not answer. He glances back at the shore, calculant, then at the water. He flings the plane outward, letting the string run through his fingers, his fingers turning blue where it runs over them. When the line stops, he hands it back to Vernon.

"Better let me go this time," Vernon says. Again Jewel does not answer; we watch him duck beneath the surface.

"Jewel," Dewey Dell whimpers.

"It aint so deep there," Vernon says. He does not look back. He is watching the water where Jewel went under.

When Jewel comes up he has the saw.

When we pass the wagon pa is standing beside it, scrubbing at the two mud smears with a handful of leaves. Against the jungle Jewel's horse looks like a patchwork quilt hung on a line.

Cash has not moved. We stand above him, holding the plane, the saw, the hammer, the square, the rule, the chalkline, while Dewey Dell squats and lifts Cash's head. "Cash," she says; "Cash."

He opens his eyes, staring profoundly up at our inverted faces.

"If ever was such a misfortunate man," pa says.

"Look, Cash," we say, holding the tools up so he can see; "what else did you have?"

He tries to speak, rolling his head, shutting his eyes.

"Cash," we say; "Cash."

It is to vomit he is turning his head. Dewey Dell wipes his mouth on the wet hem of her dress; then he can speak.

"It's his saw-set," Jewel says. "The new one he bought when he bought the rule." He moves, turning away. Vernon looks up after him, still squatting. Then he rises and follows Jewel down to the water.

"If ever was such a misfortunate man," pa says. He looms tall above us as we squat; he looks like a figure carved clumsily from tough wood by a drunken caricaturist. "It's a trial," he says. "But I dont begrudge her it. No man can say I begrudge her it." Dewey Dell has laid Cash's head back on the folded coat, twisting his head a little to avoid the vomit. Beside him his tools lie. "A fellow might call it lucky it was the same leg he broke when he fell offen that church," pa says. "But I dont begrudge her it."

Jewel and Vernon are in the river again. From here they do not appear to violate the surface at all; it is as though it had severed them both at a single blow, the two torsos moving with infinitesimal and ludicrous care upon the surface. It looks peaceful, like machinery does after you have watched it and listened to it for a long time. As though the clotting which is you had dissolved into the myriad original motion, and seeing and hearing in themselves blind and deaf; fury in itself quiet with stagnation. Squatting, Dewey Dell's wet dress shapes for the dead eyes of three blind men those mammalian ludicrosities which are the horizons and the valleys of the earth.

Cash

IT WASN'T on a balance. I told them that if they wanted it to tote and ride on a balance, they would have to

Cora

ONE DAY we were talking. She had never been pure religious, not even after that summer at the camp meeting when Brother Whitfield wrestled with her spirit, singled her out and strove with the vanity in her mortal heart, and I said to her many a time, "God gave you children to comfort your hard human lot and for a token of His own suffering and love, for in love you conceived and bore them." I said that because she took God's love and her duty to Him too much as a matter of course, and such conduct is not pleasing to Him. I said, "He gave us the gift to raise our voices in His undying praise" because I said there is more rejoicing in heaven over one sinner than over a hundred that never sinned. And she said "My daily life is an acknowledgment and expiation of my sin" and I said "Who are you, to say what is sin and what is not sin? It is the Lord's part to judge; ours to praise His mercy and His holy name in the hearing of our fellow mortals" because He alone can see into the heart, and just because a woman's life is right in the sight of man, she cant know if there is no sin in her heart without she opens her heart to the Lord and receives His grace. I said, "Just because you have been a faithful wife is no sign that there is no sin in your heart, and just because your life is hard is no sign that the Lord's grace is absolving you." And she said, "I know my own sin. I know that I deserve my punishment. I do not begrudge it." And I said, "It is out of your vanity that you would judge sin and salvation in the Lord's place. It is our mortal lot to suffer and to raise our voices in praise of Him who judges the sin and offers the salvation through our trials and tribulations time out of mind amen. Not even after Brother Whitfield, a godly man if ever one breathed God's breath, prayed for you and strove as never a man could except him," I said.

Because it is not us that can judge our sins or know what is sin in the Lord's eyes. She has had a hard life, but so does every woman. But you'd think from the way she talked that she knew more about sin and salvation than the Lord God Himself, than them who have strove and labored with the sin in this human world. When the only sin she ever committed was being partial to Jewel that never loved her and was its own punishment, in preference to Darl that was touched by God Himself and considered queer by us mortals and that did love her. I said, "There is your sin. And your punishment too. Jewel is your punishment. But where is your salvation? And life is short enough," I said, "to win eternal grace in. And God is a jealous God. It is His to judge and to mete; not yours."

"I know," she said. "I——" Then she stopped, and I said, "Know what?"

"Nothing," she said. "He is my cross and he will be my salvation. He will save me from the water and from the fire. Even though I have laid down my life, he will save me."

"How do you know, without you open your heart to Him and lift your voice in His praise?" I said. Then I realised that she did not mean God. I realised that out of the vanity of her heart she had spoken sacrilege. And I went down on my knees right there. I begged her to kneel and open her heart and cast from it the devil of vanity and cast herself upon the mercy of the Lord. But she wouldn't. She just sat there, lost in her vanity and her pride, that had closed her heart to God and set that selfish mortal boy in His place. Kneeling there I prayed for her. I prayed for that poor blind woman as I had never prayed for me and mine.

Addie

IN THE AFTERNOON when school was out and the last one had left with his little dirty snuffling nose, instead of going home I would go down the hill to the spring where I could be quiet and hate them. It would be quiet there then, with the water bubbling up and away and the sun slanting quiet in the trees and the quiet smelling of damp and rotting leaves and new earth; especially in the early spring, for it was worst then.

I could just remember how my father used to say that the reason for living was to get ready to stay dead a long time. And when I would have to look at them day after day, each with his and her secret and selfish thought, and blood strange to each other blood and strange to mine, and think that this seemed to be the only way I could get ready to stay dead, I would hate my father for having ever planted me. I would look forward to the times when they faulted, so I could whip them. When the switch fell I could feel it upon my flesh; when it welted and ridged it was my blood that ran, and I would think with each blow of the switch: Now you are aware of me! Now I am something in your secret and selfish life, who have marked your blood with my own for ever and ever.

And so I took Anse. I saw him pass the school house three or four times before I learned that he was driving four miles out of his way to do it. I noticed then how he was beginning to hump—a tall man and young—so that he looked already like a tall bird hunched in the cold weather, on the wagon seat. He would pass the school house, the wagon creaking slow, his head turning slow to watch the door of the school house as the wagon passed, until he went on around the curve and out of sight. One day I went to the door and stood there when he passed. When he saw me he looked quickly away and did not look back again.

In the early spring it was worst. Sometimes I thought that I could not bear it, lying in bed at night, with the wild geese going north and their honking coming faint and high and wild out of the wild darkness, and during the day it would seem as though I couldn't wait for the last one to go so I could go down to the spring. And so when I looked up that day and saw Anse standing there in his Sunday clothes, turning his hat round and round in his hands, I said:

"If you've got any womenfolks, why in the world dont they make you get your hair cut?"

"I aint got none," he said. Then he said suddenly, driving his eyes at me like two hounds in a strange yard: "That's what I come to see you about."

"And make you hold your shoulders up," I said. "You haven't got any? But you've got a house. They tell me you've got a house and a good farm. And you live there alone, doing for yourself, do you?" He just looked at me, turning the hat in his hands. "A new house," I said. "Are you going to get married?"

And he said again, holding his eyes to mine: "That's what I come to see you about."

Later he told me, "I aint got no people. So that wont be no worry to you. I dont reckon you can say the same."

"No. I have people. In Jefferson."

His face fell a little. "Well, I got a little property. I'm forehanded; I got a good honest name. I know how town folks are, but maybe when they talk to me. . . . . . ."

"They might listen," I said. "But they'll be hard to talk to." He was watching my face. "They're in the cemetery."

"But your living kin," he said. "They'll be different."

"Will they?" I said. "I dont know. I never had any other kind."

So I took Anse. And when I knew that I had Cash, I knew that living was terrible and that this was the answer to it. That was when I learned that words are no good; that words dont ever fit even what they are trying to say at. When he was born I knew that motherhood was invented by someone who had to have a word for it because the ones that had the children didn't care whether there was a word for it or not. I knew that fear was invented by someone that had never had the fear; pride, who never had the pride. I knew that it had been, not that they had dirty noses, but that we had had to use one another by words like spiders dangling by their mouths from a beam, swinging and twisting and never touching, and that only through the blows of the switch could my blood and their blood flow as one stream. I knew that it had been, not that my aloneness had to be violated over and over each day, but that it had never been violated until Cash came. Not even by Anse in the nights.

He had a word, too. Love, he called it. But I had been used to words for a long time. I knew that that word was like the others: just a shape to fill a lack; that when the right time came, you wouldn't need a word for that anymore than for pride or fear. Cash did not need to say it to me nor I to him, and I would say, Let Anse use it, if he wants to. So that it was Anse or love; love or Anse: it didn't matter.

I would think that even while I lay with him in the dark and Cash asleep in the cradle within the swing of my hand. I would think that if he were to wake and cry, I would suckle him, too. Anse or love: it didn't matter. My aloneness had been violated and then made whole again by the violation: time, Anse, love, what you will, outside the circle.

Then I found that I had Darl. At first I would not believe it. Then I believed that I would kill Anse. It was as though he had tricked me, hidden within a word like within a paper screen and struck me in the back through it. But then I realised that I had been tricked by words older than Anse or love, and that the same word had tricked Anse too, and that my revenge would be that he would never know I was taking revenge. And when Darl was born I asked Anse to promise to take me back to Jefferson when I died, because I knew that father had been right, even when he couldn't have known he was right anymore than I could have known I was wrong.

"Nonsense," Anse said; "you and me aint nigh done chapping yet, with just two."

He did not know that he was dead, then. Sometimes I would lie by him in the dark, hearing the land that was now of my blood and flesh, and I would think: Anse. Why Anse. Why are you Anse. I would think about his name until after a while I could see the word as a shape, a vessel, and I would watch him liquify and flow into it like cold molasses flowing out of the darkness into the vessel, until the jar stood full and motionless: a significant shape profoundly without life like an empty door frame; and then I would find that I had forgotten the name of the jar. I would think: The shape of my body where I used to be a virgin is in the shape of a   and I couldn't think *Anse*, couldn't remember *Anse*. It was not that I could think of myself as no longer unvirgin, because I was three now. And when I would think *Cash* and *Darl* that way until their names would die and solidify into a shape and then fade away, I would say, All right. It doesn't matter. It doesn't matter what they call them.

And so when Cora Tull would tell me I was not a true mother, I would think how words go straight up in a thin line, quick and harmless, and how terribly doing goes along the earth, clinging to it, so that after a while the two lines are too far apart for the same person to straddle from one to the other; and that sin and love and fear are just sounds that people who never sinned nor loved nor feared have for what they never had and cannot have until they forget the words. Like Cora, who could never even cook.

She would tell me what I owed to my children and to Anse and to God. I gave Anse the children. I did not ask for them. I did not even ask him for what he could have given me: not-Anse. That was my duty to him, to not ask that, and that duty I fulfilled. I would be I; I would let him be the shape and echo of his word. That was more than he asked, because he could not have asked for that and been Anse, using himself so with a word.

And then he died. He did not know he was dead. I would lie by him in the dark, hearing the dark land talking of God's love and His beauty and His sin; hearing the dark voicelessness in which the words are the deeds, and the other words that are not deeds, that are just the gaps in people's lacks, coming down like the cries of the geese out of the wild darkness in the old terrible nights, fumbling at the deeds like orphans to whom are pointed out in a crowd two faces and told, That is your father, your mother.

I believed that I had found it. I believed that the reason was the duty to the alive, to the terrible blood, the red bitter flood boiling through the land. I would think of sin as I would think of the clothes we both wore in the world's face, of the circumspection necessary because he was he and I was I; the sin the more utter and terrible since he was the instrument ordained by God who created the sin, to sanctify that sin He had created. While I waited for him in the woods, waiting for him before he saw me, I would think of him as dressed in sin. I would think of him as thinking of me as dressed also in sin, he the more beautiful since the garment which he had exchanged for sin was sanctified. I would think of the sin as garments which we would remove in order to shape and coerce the terrible blood to the forlorn echo of the dead word high in the air. Then I would lay with Anse again—I did not lie to him: I just refused, just as I refused my breast to Cash and Darl after their time was up—hearing the dark land talking the voiceless speech.

I hid nothing. I tried to deceive no one. I would not have cared. I merely took the precautions that he thought necessary for his sake, not for my safety, but just as I wore clothes in the world's face. And I would think then when Cora talked to me, of how the high dead words in time seemed to lose even the significance of their dead sound.

Then it was over. Over in the sense that he was gone and I knew that, see him again though I would, I would never again see him coming swift and secret to me in the woods dressed in sin like a gallant garment already blowing aside with the speed of his secret coming.

But for me it was not over. I mean, over in the sense of beginning and ending, because to me there was no beginning nor ending to anything then. I even held Anse refraining still, not that I was holding him recessional, but as though nothing else had ever been. My children were of me alone, of the wild blood boiling along the earth, of me and of all that lived; of none and of all. Then I found that I had Jewel. When I waked to remember to discover it, he was two months gone.

My father said that the reason for living is getting ready to stay dead. I knew at last what he meant and that he could not have known what he meant himself, because a man cannot know anything about cleaning up the house afterward. And so I have cleaned my house. With Jewel—I lay by the lamp, holding up my own head, watching him cap and suture it before he breathed—the wild blood boiled away and the sound of it ceased. Then there was only the milk, warm and calm, and I lying calm in the slow silence, getting ready to clean my house.

I gave Anse Dewey Dell to negative Jewel. Then I gave him Vardaman to replace the child I had robbed him of. And now he has three children that are his and not mine. And then I could get ready to die.

One day I was talking to Cora. She prayed for me because she believed I was blind to sin, wanting me to kneel and pray too, because people to whom sin is just a matter of words, to them salvation is just words too.

Whitfield

WHEN THEY told me she was dying, all that night I wrestled with Satan, and I emerged victorious. I woke to the enormity of my sin; I saw the true light at last, and I fell on my knees and confessed to God and asked His guidance and received it. "Rise," He said; "repair to that home in which you have put a living lie, among those people with whom you have outraged My Word; confess your sin aloud. It is for them, for that deceived husband, to forgive you: not I."

So I went. I heard that Tull's bridge was gone; I said "Thanks, O Lord, O Mighty Ruler of all;" for by those dangers and difficulties which I should have to surmount I saw that He had not abandoned me; that my reception again into His holy peace and love would be the sweeter for it. "Just let me not perish before I have begged the forgiveness of the man whom I betrayed," I prayed; "let me not be too late; let not the tale of mine and her transgression come from her lips instead of mine. She had sworn then that she would never tell it, but eternity is a fearsome thing to face: have I not wrestled thigh to thigh with Satan myself? let me not have also the sin of her broken vow upon my soul. Let not the waters of Thy Mighty Wrath encompass me until I have cleansed my soul in the presence of them whom I injured."

It was His hand that bore me safely above the flood, that fended from me the dangers of the waters. My horse was frightened, and my own heart failed me as the logs and the uprooted trees bore down upon my littleness. But not my soul: time after time I saw them averted at destruction's final instant, and I lifted my voice above the noise of the flood: "Praise to Thee, O Mighty Lord and King. By this token shall I cleanse my soul and gain again into the fold of Thy undying love."

I knew then that forgiveness was mine. The flood, the danger, behind, and as I rode on across the firm earth again and the scene of my Gethsemane drew closer and closer, I framed the words which I should use. I would enter the house; I would stop her before she had spoken; I would say to her husband: "Anse, I have sinned. Do with me as you will."

It was already as though it were done. My soul felt freer, quieter than it had in years; already I seemed to dwell in abiding peace again as I rode on. To either side I saw His hand; in my heart I could hear His voice: "Courage. I am with thee."

Then I reached Tull's house. His youngest girl came out and called to me as I was passing. She told me that she was already dead.

I have sinned, O Lord. Thou knowest the extent of my remorse and the will of my spirit. But He is merciful; He will accept the will for the deed, Who knew that when I framed the words of my confession it was to Anse I spoke them, even though he was not there. It was He in His infinite wisdom that restrained the tale from her dying lips as she lay surrounded by those who loved and trusted her; mine the travail by water which I sustained by the strength of His hand. Praise to Thee in Thy bounteous and omnipotent love; O praise.

I entered the house of bereavement, the lowly dwelling where another erring mortal lay while her soul faced the awful and irrevocable judgment, peace to her ashes.

"God's grace upon this house," I said.

Darl

O n the horse he rode up to Armstid's and *came back on the horse*, leading Armstid's team. We hitched up and laid Cash on top of Addie. When we laid him down he vomited again, but he got his head over the wagon bed in time.

"He taken a lick in the stomach, too," Vernon said.

"The horse may have kicked him in the stomach too," I said. "Did he kick you in the stomach, Cash?"

He tried to say something. Dewey Dell wiped his mouth again.

"What's he say?" Vernon said.

"What is it, Cash?" Dewey Dell said. She leaned down. "His tools," she said. Vernon got them and put them into the wagon. Dewey Dell lifted Cash's head so he could see. We drove on, Dewey Dell and I sitting beside Cash to steady him *and he riding on ahead on the horse*. Vernon stood watching us for a while. Then he turned and went back toward the bridge. He walked gingerly, beginning to flap the wet sleeves of his shirt as though he had just got wet.

He was sitting the horse before the gate. Armstid was waiting at the gate. We stopped *and he got down* and we lifted Cash down and carried him into the house, where Mrs Armstid had the bed ready. We left her and Dewey Dell undressing him.

We followed pa out to the wagon. He went back and got into the wagon and drove on, we following on foot, into the lot. The wetting had helped, because Armstid said, "You're welcome to the house. You can put it there." *He followed, leading the horse, and stood beside the wagon, the reins in his hand.*

"I thank you," pa said. "We'll use in the shed yonder. I know it's a imposition on you."

"You're welcome to the house," Armstid said. *He had that wooden look on his face again; that bold, surly, high-colored rigid look like his face and eyes were two colors of wood, the wrong one pale and the wrong one dark. His shirt was beginning to dry, but it still clung close upon him when he moved.*

"She would appreciate it," pa said.

We took the team out and rolled the wagon back under the shed. One side of the shed was open.

"It wont rain under," Armstid said. "But if you'd rather. . . . . . ."

Back of the barn was some rusted sheets of tin roofing. We took two of them and propped them against the open side.

"You're welcome to the house," Armstid said.

"I thank you," pa said. "I'd take it right kind if you'd give them a little snack."

"Sho," Armstid said. "Lula'll have supper ready soon as she gets Cash comfortable." *He had gone back to the horse and he was taking the saddle off, his damp shirt lapping flat to him when he moved.*

Pa wouldn't come in the house.

"Come in and eat," Armstid said. "It's nigh ready."

"I wouldn't crave nothing," pa said. "I thank you."

"You come in and dry and eat," Armstid said. "It'll be all right here."

"It's for her," pa said. "It's for her sake I am taking the food. I got no team, no nothing. But she will be grateful to ere a one of you."

"Sho," Armstid said. "You folks come in and dry."

But after Armstid gave pa a drink, he felt better, and when we went in to see about Cash *he hadn't come in with us. When I looked back he was leading the horse into the barn* he was already talking about getting another team, and by supper time he had good as bought it. *He is down there in the barn, sliding fluidly past the gaudy lunging swirl, into the stall with it. He climbs onto the manger and drags the hay down and leaves the stall and seeks and finds the curry-comb. Then he returns and slips quickly past the single crashing thump and up against the horse, where it cannot overreach. He applies the curry-comb, holding himself within the horse's striking radius with the agility of an acrobat, cursing the horse in a whisper of obscene caress. Its head flashes back, tooth-cropped; its eyes roll in the dusk like marbles on a gaudy velvet cloth as he strikes it upon the face with the back of the curry-comb.*

Armstid

B UT TIME I give him another sup of whisky and supper
was about ready, he had done already bought a team
from somebody, on a credit. Picking and choosing he were
by then, saying how he didn't like this span and wouldn't put
his money in nothing so-and-so owned, not even a hen coop.

"You might try Snopes," I said. "He's got three-four span.
Maybe one of them would suit you."

Then he begun to mumble his mouth, looking at me like it
was me that owned the only span of mules in the county and
wouldn't sell them to him, when I knew that like as not it
would be my team that would ever get them out of the lot at
all. Only I dont know what they would do with them, if they
had a team. Littlejohn had told me that the levee through
Haley bottom had done gone for two miles and that the only
way to get to Jefferson would be to go around by Mottson.
But that was Anse's business.

"He's a close man to trade with," he says, mumbling his
mouth. But when I give him another sup after supper, he
cheered up some. He was aiming to go back to the barn and
set up with her. Maybe he thought that if he just stayed down
there ready to take out, Santa Claus would maybe bring him
a span of mules. "But I reckon I can talk him around," he
says. "A man'll always help a fellow in a tight, if he's got ere
a drop of Christian blood in him."

"Of course you're welcome to the use of mine," I said, me
knowing how much he believed that was the reason.

"I thank you," he said. "She'll want to go in ourn," and
him knowing how much I believed that was the reason.

After supper Jewel rode over to the Bend to get Peabody.
I heard he was to be there today at Varner's. Jewel come back
about midnight. Peabody had gone down below Inverness
somewhere, but Uncle Billy come back with him, with his
satchel of horse-physic. Like he says, a man aint so different
from a horse or a mule, come long come short, except a mule
or a horse has got a little more sense. "What you been into
now, boy?" he says, looking at Cash. "Get me a mattress and
a chair and a glass of whisky," he says.

He made Cash drink the whisky, then he run Anse out of the room. "Lucky it was the same leg he broke last summer," Anse says, mournful, mumbling and blinking. "That's something."

We folded the mattress across Cash's legs and set the chair on the mattress and me and Jewel set on the chair and the gal held the lamp and Uncle Billy taken a chew of tobacco and went to work. Cash fought pretty hard for a while, until he fainted. Then he laid still, with big balls of sweat standing on his face like they had started to roll down and then stopped to wait for him.

When he waked up, Uncle Billy had done packed up and left. He kept on trying to say something until the gal leaned down and wiped his mouth. "It's his tools," she said.

"I brought them in," Darl said. "I got them."

He tried to talk again; she leaned down. "He wants to see them," she said. So Darl brought them in where he could see them. They shoved them under the side of the bed, where he could reach his hand and touch them when he felt better. Next morning Anse taken that horse and rode over to the Bend to see Snopes. Him and Jewel stood in the lot talking a while, then Anse got on the horse and rode off. I reckon that was the first time Jewel ever let anybody ride that horse, and until Anse come back he hung around in that swole-up way, watching the road like he was half a mind to take out after Anse and get the horse back.

Along toward nine oclock it begun to get hot. That was when I see the first buzzard. Because of the wetting, I reckon. Anyway it wasn't until well into the day that I see them. Lucky the breeze was setting away from the house, so it wasn't until well into the morning. But soon as I see them it was like I could smell it in the field a mile away from just watching them, and them circling and circling for everybody in the county to see what was in my barn.

I was still a good half a mile from the house when I heard that boy yelling. I thought maybe he might have fell into the well or something, so I whipped up and come into the lot on the lope.

There must have been a dozen of them setting along the ridge-pole of the barn, and that boy was chasing another one around the lot like it was a turkey and it just lifting enough to dodge him and go flopping back to the roof of the shed again where he had found it setting on the coffin. It had got hot then, right, and the breeze had dropped or changed or something, so I went and found Jewel, but Lula come out.

"You got to do something," she said. "It's a outrage."

"That's what I aim to do," I said.

"It's a outrage," she said. "He should be lawed for treating her so."

"He's getting her into the ground the best he can," I said. So I found Jewel and asked him if he didn't want to take one of the mules and go over to the Bend and see about Anse. He didn't say nothing. He just looked at me with his jaws going bone-white and them bone-white eyes of hisn, then he went and begun to call Darl.

"What you fixing to do?" I said.

He didn't answer. Darl come out. "Come on," Jewel said.

"What you aim to do?" Darl said.

"Going to move the wagon," Jewel said over his shoulder.

"Dont be a fool," I said. "I never meant nothing. You couldn't help it." And Darl hung back too, but nothing wouldn't suit Jewel.

"Shut your goddamn mouth," he says.

"It's got to be somewhere," Darl said. "We'll take out soon as pa gets back."

"You wont help me?" Jewel says, them white eyes of hisn kind of blaring and his face shaking like he had a aguer.

"No," Darl said. "I wont. Wait till pa gets back."

So I stood in the door and watched him push and haul at that wagon. It was on a downhill, and once I thought he was fixing to beat out the back end of the shed. Then the dinner bell rung. I called him, but he didn't look around. "Come on to dinner," I said. "Tell that boy." But he didn't answer, so I went on to dinner. The gal went down to get that boy, but she come back without him. About half through dinner we heard him yelling again, running that buzzard out.

"It's a outrage," Lula said; "a outrage."

"He's doing the best he can," I said. "A fellow dont trade with Snopes in thirty minutes. They'll set in the shade all afternoon to dicker."

"Do?" she says. "Do? He's done too much, already."

And I reckon he had. Trouble is, his quitting was just about to start our doing. He couldn't buy no team from nobody, let alone Snopes, withouten he had something to mortgage he didn't know would mortgage yet. And so when I went back to the field I looked at my mules and same as told them goodbye for a spell. And when I come back that evening and the sun shining all day on that shed, I wasn't so sho I would regret it.

He come riding up just as I went out to the porch, where they all was. He looked kind of funny: kind of more hangdog than common, and kind of proud too. Like he had done something he thought was cute but wasn't so sho now how other folks would take it.

"I got a team," he said.

"You bought a team from Snopes?" I said.

"I reckon Snopes aint the only man in this country that can drive a trade," he said.

"Sho," I said. He was looking at Jewel, with that funny look, but Jewel had done got down from the porch and was going toward the horse. To see what Anse had done to it, I reckon.

"Jewel," Anse says. Jewel looked back. "Come here," Anse says. Jewel come back a little and stopped again.

"What you want?" he said.

"So you got a team from Snopes," I said. "He'll send them over tonight, I reckon? You'll want a early start tomorrow, long as you'll have to go by Mottson."

Then he quit looking like he had been for a while. He got that badgered look like he used to have, mumbling his mouth.

"I do the best I can," he said. "Fore God, if there were ere a man in the living world suffered the trials and floutings I have suffered."

"A fellow that just beat Snopes in a trade ought to feel pretty good," I said. "What did you give him, Anse?"

He didn't look at me. "I give a chattel mortgage on my cultivator and seeder," he said.

"But they aint worth forty dollars. How far do you aim to get with a forty dollar team?"

They were all watching him now, quiet and steady. Jewel was stopped, halfway back, waiting to go on to the horse. "I give other things," Anse said. He begun to mumble his mouth again, standing there like he was waiting for somebody to hit him and him with his mind already made up not to do nothing about it.

"What other things?" Darl said.

"Hell," I said. "You take my team. You can bring them back. I'll get along someway."

"So that's what you were doing in Cash's clothes last night," Darl said. He said it just like he was reading it outen the paper. Like he never give a durn himself one way or the other. Jewel had come back now, standing there, looking at Anse with them marble eyes of hisn. "Cash aimed to buy that talking machine from Suratt with that money," Darl said.

Anse stood there, mumbling his mouth. Jewel watched him. He aint never blinked yet.

"But that's just eight dollars more," Darl said, in that voice like he was just listening and never give a durn himself. "That still wont buy a team."

Anse looked at Jewel, quick, kind of sliding his eyes that way, then he looked down again. "God knows, if there were ere a man," he says. Still they didn't say nothing. They just watched him, waiting, and him sliding his eyes toward their feet and up their legs but no higher. "And the horse," he says.

"What horse?" Jewel said. Anse just stood there. I be durn, if a man cant keep the upper hand of his sons, he ought to run them away from home, no matter how big they are. And if he cant do that, I be durn if he oughtn't to leave himself. I be durn if I wouldn't. "You mean, you tried to swap my horse?" Jewel says.

Anse stands there, dangle-armed. "For fifteen years I aint had a tooth in my head," he says. "God knows it. He knows in fifteen years I aint et the victuals He aimed for man to eat to keep his strength up, and me saving a nickel here and a nickel there so my family wouldn't suffer it, to buy them teeth so I could eat God's appointed food. I give that money. I thought that if I could do without eating, my sons could do without riding. God knows I did."

Jewel stands with his hands on his hips, looking at Anse.

Then he looks away. He looked out across the field, his face still as a rock, like it was somebody else talking about somebody else's horse and him not even listening. Then he spit, slow, and said "Hell" and he turned and went on to the gate and unhitched the horse and got on it. It was moving when he come into the saddle and by the time he was on it they was tearing down the road like the Law might have been behind them. They went out of sight that way, the two of them looking like some kind of a spotted cyclone.

"Well," I says. "You take my team," I said. But he wouldn't do it. And they wouldn't even stay, and that boy chasing them buzzards all day in the hot sun until he was nigh as crazy as the rest of them. "Leave Cash here, anyway," I said. But they wouldn't do that. They made a pallet for him with quilts on top of the coffin and laid him on it and set his tools by him, and we put my team in and hauled the wagon about a mile down the road.

"If we'll bother you here," Anse says, "just say so."

"Sho," I said. "It'll be fine here. Safe, too. Now let's go back and eat supper."

"I thank you," Anse said. "We got a little something in the basket. We can make out."

"Where'd you get it?" I said.

"We brought it from home."

"But it'll be stale now," I said. "Come and get some hot victuals."

But they wouldn't come. "I reckon we can make out," Anse said. So I went home and et and taken a basket back to them and tried again to make them come back to the house.

"I thank you," he said. "I reckon we can make out." So I left them there, squatting around a little fire, waiting; God knows what for.

I come on home. I kept thinking about them there, and about that fellow tearing away on that horse. And that would be the last they would see of him. And I be durn if I could blame him. Not for wanting to not give up his horse, but for getting shut of such a durn fool as Anse.

Or that's what I thought then. Because be durn if there aint something about a durn fellow like Anse that seems to make a man have to help him, even when he knows he'll be wanting to kick himself next minute. Because about a hour after breakfast next morning Eustace Grimm that works Snopes' place come up with a span of mules, hunting Anse.

"I thought him and Anse never traded," I said.

"Sho," Eustace said. "All they liked was the horse. Like I said to Mr Snopes, he was letting this team go for fifty dollars, because if his uncle Flem had a just kept them Texas horses when he owned them, Anse wouldn't a never——"

"The horse?" I said. "Anse's boy taken that horse and cleared out last night, probably half way to Texas by now, and Anse——"

"I didn't know who brung it," Eustace said. "I never see them. I just found the horse in the barn this morning when I went to feed, and I told Mr Snopes and he said to bring the team on over here."

Well, that'll be the last they'll ever see of him now, sho enough. Come Christmas time they'll maybe get a postal card from him in Texas, I reckon. And if it hadn't a been Jewel, I reckon it'd a been me; I owe him that much, myself. I be durn if Anse dont conjure a man, some way. I be durn if he aint a sight.

Vardaman

N OW THERE ARE seven of them, in little tall black circles.
"Look, Darl," I say; "see?"

He looks up. We watch them in little tall black circles of not-moving.

"Yesterday there were just four," I say.

There were more than four on the barn.

"Do you know what I would do if he tries to light on the wagon again?" I say.

"What would you do?" Darl says.

"I wouldn't let him light on her," I say. "I wouldn't let him light on Cash, either."

Cash is sick. He is sick on the box. But my mother is a fish.

"We got to get some medicine in Mottson," pa says. "I reckon we'll just have to."

"How do you feel, Cash?" Darl says.

"It dont bother none," Cash says.

"Do you want it propped a little higher?" Darl says.

Cash has a broken leg. He has had two broken legs. He lies on the box with a quilt rolled under his head and a piece of wood under his knee.

"I reckon we ought to left him at Armstid's," pa says.

I haven't got a broken leg and pa hasn't and Darl hasn't and   "It's just the bumps," Cash says. "It kind of grinds together a little on a bump. It dont bother none." *Jewel* has *gone away. He and his horse went away one supper time*

"It's because she wouldn't have us beholden," pa says. "Fore God, I do the best that ere a man" *Is it because Jewel's mother is a horse Darl? I said.*

"Maybe I can draw the ropes a little tighter," Darl says. *That's why Jewel and I were both in the shed and she was in the wagon because the horse lives in the barn and I had to keep on running the buzzard away from*

"If you just would," Cash says. And Dewey Dell hasn't got a broken leg and I haven't. Cash is my brother.

We stop. When Darl loosens the rope Cash begins to sweat again. His teeth look out.

"Hurt?" Darl says.

"I reckon you better put it back," Cash says.

Darl puts the rope back, pulling hard. Cash's teeth look out.

"Hurt?" Darl says.

"It dont bother none," Cash says.

"Do you want pa to drive slower?" Darl says.

"No," Cash says. "Aint no time to hang back. It dont bother none."

"We'll have to get some medicine at Mottson," pa says. "I reckon we'll have to."

"Tell him to go on," Cash says. We go on. Dewey Dell leans back and wipes Cash's face. Cash is my brother. *But Jewel's mother is a horse. My mother is a fish. Darl says that when we come to the water again I might see her and Dewey Dell said, She's in the box; how could she have got out? She got out through the holes I bored, into the water I said, and when we come to the water again I am going to see her. My mother is not in the box. My mother does not smell like that. My mother is a fish*

"Those cakes will be in fine shape by the time we get to Jefferson," Darl says.

Dewey Dell does not look around.

"You better try to sell them in Mottson," Darl says.

"When will we get to Mottson, Darl?" I say.

"Tomorrow," Darl says. "If this team dont rack to pieces. Snopes must have fed them on sawdust."

"Why did he feed them on sawdust, Darl?" I say.

"Look," Darl says. "See?"

Now there are nine of them, tall in little tall black circles.

When we come to the foot of the hill pa stops and Darl and Dewey Dell and I get out. Cash cant walk because he has a broken leg. "Come up, mules," pa says. The mules walk hard; the wagon creaks. Darl and Dewey Dell and I walk behind the wagon, up the hill. When we come to the top of the hill pa stops and we get back into the wagon.

Now there are ten of them, tall in little tall black circles on the sky.

Moseley

I HAPPENED to look up, and saw her outside the window, looking in. Not close to the glass, and not looking at anything in particular; just standing there with her head turned this way and her eyes full on me and kind of blank too, like she was waiting for a sign. When I looked up again she was moving toward the door.

She kind of bumbled at the screen door a minute, like they do, and came in. She had on a stiff-brimmed straw hat setting on the top of her head and she was carrying a package wrapped in newspaper: I thought that she had a quarter or a dollar at the most, and that after she stood around a while she would maybe buy a cheap comb or a bottle of nigger toilet water, so I never disturbed her for a minute or so except to notice that she was pretty in a kind of sullen, awkward way, and that she looked a sight better in her gingham dress and her own complexion than she would after she bought whatever she would finally decide on. Or tell that she wanted. I knew that she had already decided before she came in. But you have to let them take their time. So I went on with what I was doing, figuring to let Albert wait on her when he caught up at the fountain, when he came back to me.

"That woman," he said. "You better see what she wants."

"What does she want?" I said.

"I dont know. I cant get anything out of her. You better wait on her."

So I went around the counter. I saw that she was barefooted, standing with her feet flat and easy on the floor, like she was used to it. She was looking at me, hard, holding the package; I saw she had about as black a pair of eyes as ever I saw, and she was a stranger. I never remembered seeing her in Mottson before. "What can I do for you?" I said.

Still she didn't say anything. She stared at me without winking. Then she looked back at the folks at the fountain. Then she looked past me, toward the back of the store.

"Do you want to look at some toilet things?" I said. "Or is it medicine you want?"

"That's it," she said. She looked quick back at the fountain again. So I thought maybe her ma or somebody had sent her in for some of this female dope and she was ashamed to ask for it. I knew she couldn't have a complexion like hers and use it herself, let alone not being much more than old enough to barely know what it was for. It's a shame, the way they poison themselves with it. But a man's got to stock it or go out of business in this country.

"Oh," I said. "What do you use? We have——" She looked at me again, almost like she had said hush, and looked toward the back of the store again.

"I'd liefer go back there," she said.

"All right," I said. You have to humor them. You save time by it. I followed her to the back. She put her hand on the gate. "There's nothing back there but the prescription case," I said. "What do you want?" She stopped and looked at me. It was like she had taken some kind of a lid off her face, her eyes. It was her eyes: kind of dumb and hopeful and sullenly willing to be disappointed all at the same time. But she was in trouble of some sort; I could see that. "What's your trouble?" I said. "Tell me what it is you want. I'm pretty busy." I wasn't meaning to hurry her, but a man just hasn't got the time they have out there.

"It's the female trouble," she said.

"Oh," I said. "Is that all?" I thought maybe she was younger than she looked, and her first one had scared her, or maybe one had been a little abnormal as it will in young women. "Where's your ma?" I said. "Haven't you got one?"

"She's out yonder in the wagon," she said.

"Why not talk to her about it before you take any medicine," I said. "Any woman would have told you about it." She looked at me, and I looked at her again and said, "How old are you?"

"Seventeen," she said.

"Oh," I said. "I thought maybe you were. . . . . . ." She was watching me. But then, in the eyes all of them look like they had no age and knew everything in the world, anyhow. "Are you too regular, or not regular enough?"

She quit looking at me but she didn't move. "Yes," she said. "I reckon so. Yes."

"Well, which?" I said. "Dont you know?" It's a crime and

a shame; but after all, they'll buy it from somebody. She stood there, not looking at me. "You want something to stop it?" I said. "Is that it?"

"No," she said. "That's it. It's already stopped."

"Well, what——" Her face was lowered a little, still, like they do in all their dealings with a man so he dont ever know just where the lightning will strike next. "You are not married, are you?" I said.

"No."

"Oh," I said. "And how long has it been since it stopped? about five months maybe?"

"It aint been but two," she said.

"Well, I haven't got anything in my store you want to buy," I said, "unless it's a nipple. And I'd advise you to buy that and go back home and tell your pa, if you have one, and let him make somebody buy you a wedding license. Was that all you wanted?"

But she just stood there, not looking at me.

"I got the money to pay you," she said.

"Is it your own, or did he act enough of a man to give you the money?"

"He give it to me. Ten dollars. He said that would be enough."

"A thousand dollars wouldn't be enough in my store and ten cents wouldn't be enough," I said. "You take my advice and go home and tell your pa or your brothers if you have any or the first man you come to in the road."

But she didn't move. "Lafe said I could get it at the drugstore. He said to tell you me and him wouldn't never tell nobody you sold it to us."

"And I just wish your precious Lafe had come for it himself; that's what I wish. I dont know: I'd have had a little respect for him then. And you can go back and tell him I said so—if he aint halfway to Texas by now, which I dont doubt. Me, a respectable druggist, that's kept store and raised a family and been a church-member for fifty-six years in this town. I'm a good mind to tell your folks myself, if I can just find who they are."

She looked at me now, her eyes and face kind of blank again like when I first saw her through the window. "I didn't

know," she said. "He told me I could get something at the
drugstore. He said they might not want to sell it to me, but
if I had ten dollars and told them I wouldn't never tell nobody. . . ."

"He never said this drug-store," I said. "If he did or mentioned my name, I defy him to prove it. I defy him to repeat
it or I'll prosecute him to the full extent of the law, and you
can tell him so."

"But maybe another drugstore would," she said.

"Then I dont want to know it. Me, that's——" Then I
looked at her. But it's a hard life they have; sometimes a
man. . . . . .if there can ever be any excuse for sin, which
it cant be. And then, life wasn't made to be easy on folks:
they wouldn't ever have any reason to be good and die.
"Look here," I said. "You get that notion out of your head.
The Lord gave you what you have, even if He did use the
devil to do it; you let Him take it away from you if it's His
will to do so. You go on back to Lafe and you and him take
that ten dollars and get married with it."

"Lafe said I could get something at the drugstore," she
said.

"Then go and get it," I said. "You wont get it here."

She went out, carrying the package, her feet making a little
hissing on the floor. She bumbled again at the door and went
out. I could see her through the glass going on down the
street.

It was Albert told me about the rest of it. He said the
wagon was stopped in front of Grummet's hardware store,
with the ladies all scattering up and down the street with
handkerchiefs to their noses, and a crowd of hard-nosed men
and boys standing around the wagon, listening to the marshal
arguing with the man. He was a kind of tall, gaunted man
sitting on the wagon, saying it was a public street and he
reckoned he had as much right there as anybody, and the
marshal telling him he would have to move on; folks couldn't
stand it. It had been dead eight days, Albert said. They came
from some place out in Yoknapatawpha county, trying to get
to Jefferson with it. It must have been like a piece of rotten
cheese coming into an ant-hill, in that ramshackle wagon that
Albert said folks were scared would fall all to pieces before

they could get it out of town, with that home-made box and another fellow with a broken leg lying on a quilt on top of it, and the father and a little boy sitting on the seat and the marshal trying to make them get out of town.

"It's a public street," the man says. "I reckon we can stop to buy something same as airy other man. We got the money to pay for hit, and hit aint airy law that says a man cant spend his money where he wants."

They had stopped to buy some cement. The other son was in Grummet's, trying to make Grummet break a sack and let him have ten cents' worth, and finally Grummet broke the sack to get him out. They wanted the cement to fix the fellow's broken leg, someway.

"Why, you'll kill him," the marshal said. "You'll cause him to lose his leg. You take him on to a doctor, and you get this thing buried soon as you can. Dont you know you're liable to jail for endangering the public health?"

"We're doing the best we can," the father said. Then he told a long tale about how they had to wait for the wagon to come back and how the bridge was washed away and how they went eight miles to another bridge and it was gone too so they came back and swum the ford and the mules got drowned and how they got another team and found that the road was washed out and they had to come clean around by Mottson, and then the one with the cement came back and told him to shut up.

"We'll be gone in a minute," he told the marshal.

"We never aimed to bother nobody," the father said.

"You take that fellow to a doctor," the marshal told the one with the cement.

"I reckon he's all right," he said.

"It aint that we're hard-hearted," the marshal said. "But I reckon you can tell yourself how it is."

"Sho," the other said. "We'll take out soon as Dewey Dell comes back. She went to deliver a package."

So they stood there with the folks backed off with handkerchiefs to their faces, until in a minute the girl came up with that newspaper package.

"Come on," the one with the cement said, " we've lost too much time." So they got in the wagon and went on. And when I went to supper it still seemed like I could smell it. And the next day I met the marshal and I began to sniff and said,

"Smell anything?"

"I reckon they're in Jefferson by now," he said.

"Or in jail. Well, thank the Lord it's not our jail."

"That's a fact," he said.

Darl

"Here's a place," pa says. He pulls the team up and sits looking at the house. "We could get some water over yonder."

"All right," I say. "You'll have to borrow a bucket from them, Dewey Dell."

"God knows," pa says. "I wouldn't be beholden, God knows."

"If you see a good-sized can, you might bring it," I say. Dewey Dell gets down from the wagon, carrying the package. "You had more trouble than you expected, selling those cakes in Mottson," I say. How do our lives ravel out into the no-wind, no-sound, the weary gestures wearily recapitulant: echoes of old compulsions with no-hand on no-strings: in sunset we fall into furious attitudes, dead gestures of dolls. Cash broke his leg and now the sawdust is running out. He is bleeding to death is Cash.

"I wouldn't be beholden," pa says. "God knows."

"Then make some water yourself," I say. "We can use Cash's hat."

When Dewey Dell comes back the man comes with her. Then he stops and she comes on and he stands there and after a while he goes back to the house and stands on the porch, watching us.

"We better not try to lift him down," pa says. "We can fix it here."

"Do you want to be lifted down, Cash?" I say.

"Wont we get to Jefferson tomorrow?" he says. He is watching us, his eyes interrogatory, intent, and sad. "I can last it out."

"It'll be easier on you," pa says. "It'll keep it from rubbing together."

"I can last it," Cash says. "We'll lose time stopping."

"We done bought the cement, now," pa says.

"I could last it," Cash says. "It aint but one more day. It dont bother to speak of." He looks at us, his eyes wide in his thin gray face, questioning. "It sets up so," he says.

"We done bought it now," pa says.

I mix the cement in the can, stirring the slow water into the pale green thick coils. I bring the can to the wagon where Cash can see. He lies on his back, his thin profile in silhouette, ascetic and profound against the sky. "Does that look about right?" I say.

"You dont want too much water, or it wont work right," he says.

"Is this too much?"

"Maybe if you could get a little sand," he says. "It aint but one more day," he says. "It dont bother me none."

Vardaman goes back down the road to where we crossed the branch and returns with sand. He pours it slowly into the thick coiling in the can. I go to the wagon again.

"Does that look all right?"

"Yes," Cash says. "I could have lasted. It dont bother me none."

We loosen the splints and pour the cement over his leg, slow.

"Watch out for it," Cash says. "Dont get none on it if you can help."

"Yes," I say. Dewey Dell tears a piece of paper from the package and wipes the cement from the top of it as it drips from Cash's leg.

"How does that feel?"

"It feels fine," he says. "It's cold. It feels fine."

"If it'll just help you," pa says. "I asks your forgiveness. I never foreseen it no more than you."

"It feels fine," Cash says.

If you could just ravel out into time. That would be nice. It would be nice if you could just ravel out into time.

We replace the splints, the cords, drawing them tight, the cement in thick pale green slow surges among the cords, Cash watching us quietly with that profound questioning look.

"That'll steady it," I say.

"Ay," Cash says. "I'm obliged."

Then we all turn on the wagon and watch him. He is coming up the road behind us, wooden-backed, wooden-faced, moving only from his hips down. He comes up without a word, with his pale rigid eyes in his high sullen face, and gets into the wagon.

"Here's a hill," pa says. "I reckon you'll have to get out and walk."

Vardaman

DARL AND JEWEL and Dewey Dell and I are walking up the hill, behind the wagon. Jewel came back. He came up the road and got into the wagon. He was walking. Jewel hasn't got a horse anymore. Jewel is my brother. Cash is my brother. Cash has a broken leg. We fixed Cash's leg so it doesn't hurt. Cash is my brother. Jewel is my brother too, but he hasn't got a broken leg.

Now there are five of them, tall in little tall black circles.

"Where do they stay at night, Darl?" I say. "When we stop at night in the barn, where do they stay?"

The hill goes off into the sky. Then the sun comes up from behind the hill and the mules and the wagon and pa walk on the sun. You cannot watch them, walking slow on the sun. In Jefferson it is red on the track behind the glass. The track goes shining round and round. Dewey Dell says so.

Tonight I am going to see where they stay while we are in the barn.

Darl

"J EWEL," I say, "whose son are you?"

The breeze was setting up from the barn, so we put her under the apple tree, where the moonlight can dapple the apple tree upon the long slumbering flanks within which now and then she talks in little trickling bursts of secret and murmurous bubbling. I took Vardaman to listen. When we came up the cat leaped down from it and flicked away with silver claw and silver eye into the shadow.

"Your mother was a horse, but who was your father, Jewel?"

"You goddamn lying son of a bitch."

"Dont call me that," I say.

"You goddamn lying son of a bitch."

"Dont you call me that, Jewel." In the tall moonlight his eyes look like spots of white paper pasted on a high small football.

After supper Cash began to sweat a little. "It's getting a little hot," he said. "It was the sun shining on it all day, I reckon."

"You want some water poured on it?" we say. "Maybe that will ease it some."

"I'd be obliged," Cash said. "It was the sun shining on it, I reckon. I ought to thought and kept it covered."

"We ought to thought," we said. "You couldn't have suspicioned."

"I never noticed it getting hot," Cash said. "I ought to minded it."

So we poured the water over it. His leg and foot below the cement looked like they had been boiled. "Does that feel better?" we said.

"I'm obliged," Cash said. "It feels fine."

Dewey Dell wipes his face with the hem of her dress.

"See if you can get some sleep," we say.

"Sho," Cash says. "I'm right obliged. It feels fine now."

Jewel, I say, Who was your father, Jewel?

Goddamn you. Goddamn you.

143

Vardaman

S HE WAS under the apple tree and Darl and I go across the moon and the cat jumps down and runs and we can hear her inside the wood.

"Hear?" Darl says. "Put your ear close."

I put my ear close and I can hear her. Only I cant tell what she is saying.

"What is she saying, Darl?" I say. "Who is she talking to?"

"She's talking to God," Darl says. "She is calling on Him to help her."

"What does she want Him to do?" I say.

"She wants Him to hide her away from the sight of man," Darl says.

"Why does she want to hide her away from the sight of man, Darl?"

"So she can lay down her life," Darl says.

"Why does she want to lay down her life, Darl?"

"Listen," Darl says. We hear her. We hear her turn over on her side. "Listen," Darl says.

"She's turned over," I say. "She's looking at me through the wood."

"Yes," Darl says.

"How can she see through the wood, Darl?"

"Come," Darl says. "We must let her be quiet. Come."

"She cant see out there, because the holes are in the top," I say. "How can she see, Darl?"

"Let's go see about Cash," Darl says.

And I saw something Dewey Dell told me not to tell nobody

Cash is sick in his leg. We fixed his leg this afternoon, but he is sick in it again, lying on the bed. We pour water on his leg and then he feels fine.

"I feel fine," Cash says. "I'm obliged to you."

"Try to get some sleep," we say.

"I feel fine," Cash says. "I'm obliged to you."

And I saw something Dewey Dell told me not to tell nobody. It is not about pa and it is not about Cash and it is not about Jewel and it is not about Dewey Dell and it is not about me

Dewey Dell and I are going to sleep on the pallet. It is on

the back porch, where we can see the barn, and the moon shines on half of the pallet and we will lie half in the white and half in the black, with the moonlight on our legs. And then I am going to see where they stay at night while we are in the barn. We are not in the barn tonight but I can see the barn and so I am going to find where they stay at night.

We lie on the pallet, with our legs in the moon.

"Look," I say, "my legs look black. Your legs look black, too."

"Go to sleep," Dewey Dell says.

Jefferson is a far piece.

"Dewey Dell."

"What."

"If it's not Christmas now, how will it be there?"

It goes round and round on the shining track. Then the track goes shining round and round.

"Will what be there?"

"That train. In the window."

"You go to sleep. You can see tomorrow if it's there."

Maybe Santa Claus wont know they are town boys.

"Dewey Dell."

"You go to sleep. He aint going to let none of them town boys have it."

It was behind the window, red on the track, the track shining round and round. It made my heart hurt. And then it was pa and Jewel and Darl and Mr Gillespie's boy. Mr Gillespie's boy's legs come down under his nightshirt. When he goes into the moon, his legs fuzz. They go on around the house toward the apple tree.

"What are they going to do, Dewey Dell?"

They went around the house toward the apple tree.

"I can smell her," I say. "Can you smell her, too?"

"Hush," Dewey Dell says. "The wind's changed. Go to sleep."

And so I am going to know where they stay at night soon. They come around the house, going across the yard in the moon, carrying her on their shoulders. They carry her down to the barn, the moon shining flat and quiet on her. Then they come back and go into the house again. While they were in the moon, Mr Gillespie's boy's legs fuzzed. And then I waited and I said Dewey Dell? and then I waited and then I went to find where they stay at night and I saw something that Dewey Dell told me not to tell nobody.

Darl

AGAINST THE dark doorway he seems to materialise out of darkness, lean as a race horse in his underclothes in the beginning of the glare. He leaps to the ground with on his face an expression of furious unbelief. He has seen me without even turning his head or his eyes in which the glare swims like two small torches. "Come on," he says, leaping down the slope toward the barn.

For an instant longer he runs silver in the moonlight, then he springs out like a flat figure cut leanly from tin against an abrupt and soundless explosion as the whole loft of the barn takes fire at once, as though it had been stuffed with powder. The front, the conical façade with the square orifice of doorway broken only by the square squat shape of the coffin on the sawhorses like a cubistic bug, comes into relief. Behind me pa and Gillespie and Mack and Dewey Dell and Vardaman emerge from the house.

He pauses at the coffin, stooping, looking at me, his face furious. Overhead the flames sound like thunder; across us rushes a cool draft: there is no heat in it at all yet, and a handful of chaff lifts suddenly and sucks swiftly along the stalls where a horse is screaming. "Quick," I say; "the horses."

He glares a moment longer at me, then at the roof overhead, then he leaps toward the stall where the horse screams. It plunges and kicks, the sound of the crashing blows sucking up into the sound of the flames. They sound like an interminable train crossing an endless trestle. Gillespie and Mack pass me, in knee-length nightshirts, shouting, their voices thin and high and meaningless and at the same time profoundly wild and sad: ". . . . . .cow. . . . . .stall. . . . . ." Gillespie's nightshirt rushes ahead of him on the draft, ballooning about his hairy thighs.

The stall door has swung shut. Jewel thrusts it back with his buttocks and he appears, his back arched, the muscles ridged through his garment as he drags the horse out by its head. In the glare its eyes roll with soft, fleet, wild opaline fire; its muscles bunch and run as it flings its head about, lifting Jewel clear of the ground. He drags it on, slowly, terrifically; again he gives me across his shoulder a single glare furious and brief. Even when they are clear of the barn the horse continues to fight and lash backward toward the doorway until Gillespie passes me, stark-naked, his nightshirt wrapped about the mule's head, and beats the maddened horse on out of the door.

Jewel returns, running; again he looks down at the coffin. But he comes on. "Where's cow?" he cries, passing me. I follow him. In the stall Mack is struggling with the other mule. When its head turns into the glare I can see the wild rolling of its eye too, but it makes no sound. It just stands there, watching Mack over its shoulder, swinging its hind quarters toward him whenever he approaches. He looks back at us, his eyes and mouth three round holes in his face on which the freckles look like english peas on a plate. His voice is thin, high, faraway.

"I cant do nothing. . . . . . ." It is as though the sound had been swept from his lips and up and away, speaking back to us from an immense distance of exhaustion. Jewel slides past us; the mule whirls and lashes out, but he has already gained its head. I lean to Mack's ear:

"Nightshirt. Around his head."

Mack stares at me. Then he rips the nightshirt off and flings it over the mule's head, and it becomes docile at once. Jewel is yelling at him: "Cow? Cow?"

"Back," Mack cries. "Last stall."

The cow watches us as we enter. She is backed into the corner, head lowered, still chewing though rapidly. But she makes no move. Jewel has paused, looking up, and suddenly we watch the entire floor to the loft dissolve. It just turns to fire; a faint litter of sparks rains down. He glances about. Back under the trough is a three legged milking stool. He catches it up and swings it into the planking of the rear wall. He splinters a plank, then another, a third; we tear the fragments away. While we are stooping at the opening something charges into us from behind. It is the cow; with a single whistling breath she rushes between us and through the gap and into the outer glare, her tail erect and rigid as a broom nailed upright to the end of her spine.

Jewel turns back into the barn. "Here," I say; "Jewel!" I

grasp at him; he strikes my hand down. "You fool," I say, "dont you see you cant make it back yonder?" The hallway looks like a searchlight turned into rain. "Come on," I say, "around this way."

When we are through the gap he begins to run. "Jewel," I say, running. He darts around the corner. When I reach it he has almost reached the next one, running against the glare like that figure cut from tin. Pa and Gillespie and Mack are some distance away, watching the barn, pink against the darkness where for the time the moonlight has been vanquished. "Catch him!" I cry; "stop him!"

When I reach the front, he is struggling with Gillespie; the one lean in underclothes, the other stark naked. They are like two figures in a Greek frieze, isolated out of all reality by the red glare. Before I can reach them he has struck Gillespie to the ground and turned and run back into the barn.

The sound of it has become quite peaceful now, like the sound of the river did. We watch through the dissolving proscenium of the doorway as Jewel runs crouching to the far end of the coffin and stoops to it. For an instant he looks up and out at us through the rain of burning hay like a portière of flaming beads, and I can see his mouth shape as he calls my name.

"Jewel!" Dewey Dell cries; "Jewel!" It seems to me that I now hear the accumulation of her voice through the last five minutes, and I hear her scuffling and struggling as pa and Mack hold her, screaming "Jewel! Jewel!" But he is no longer looking at us. We see his sholders strain as he upends the coffin and slides it single-handed from the saw-horses. It looms unbelievably tall, hiding him: I would not have believed that Addie Bundren would have needed that much room to lie comfortable in; for another instant it stands upright while the sparks rain on it in scattering bursts as though they engendered other sparks from the contact. Then it topples forward, gaining momentum, revealing Jewel and the sparks raining on him too in engendering gusts, so that he appears to be enclosed in a thin nimbus of fire. Without stopping it overends and rears again, pauses, then crashes slowly forward and through the curtain. This time Jewel is riding upon it, clinging to it, until it crashes down and flings him forward and clear and Mack leaps forward into a thin smell of scorching meat and slaps at the widening crimson-edged holes that bloom like flowers in his undershirt.

Vardaman

When I went to find where they stay at night, I saw something. They said, "Where is Darl? Where did Darl go?"

They carried her back under the apple tree.

The barn was still red, but it wasn't a barn now. It was sunk down, and the red went swirling up. The barn went swirling up in little red pieces, against the sky and the stars so that the stars moved backward.

And then Cash was still awake. He turned his head from side to side, with sweat on his face.

"Do you want some more water on it, Cash?" Dewey Dell said.

Cash's leg and foot turned black. We held the lamp and looked at Cash's foot and leg where it was black.

"Your foot looks like a nigger's foot, Cash," I said.

"I reckon we'll have to bust it off," pa said.

"What in the tarnation you put it on there for," Mr Gillespie said.

"I thought it would steady it some," pa said. "I just aimed to help him."

They got the flat iron and the hammer. Dewey Dell held the lamp. They had to hit it hard. And then Cash went to sleep.

"He's asleep now," I said. "It cant hurt him while he's asleep."

It just cracked. It wouldn't come off.

"It'll take the hide, too," Mr Gillespie said. "Why in the tarnation you put it on there. Didn't none of you think to grease his leg first?"

"I just aimed to help him," pa said. "It was Darl put it on."

"Where is Darl?" they said.

"Didn't none of you have more sense than that?" Mr Gillespie said. "I'd a thought he would, anyway."

Jewel was lying on his face. His back was red. Dewey Dell put the medicine on it. The medicine was made out of butter and soot, to draw out the fire. Then his back was black.

"Does it hurt, Jewel?" I said. "Your back looks like a

nigger's, Jewel," I said. Cash's foot and leg looked like a nigger's. Then they broke it off. Cash's leg bled.

"You go on back and lay down," Dewey Dell said. "You
ought to be asleep."

"Where is Darl?" they said.

He is out there under the apple tree with her, lying on her.
He is there so the cat wont come back. I said, "Are you going
to keep the cat away, Darl?"

The moonlight dappled on him too. On her it was still, but
on Darl it dappled up and down.

"You needn't to cry," I said. "Jewel got her out. You
needn't to cry, Darl."

The barn is still red. It used to be redder than this. Then it
went swirling, making the stars run backward without falling.
It hurt my heart like the train did.

*When I went to find where they stay at night, I saw something
that Dewey Dell says I mustn't never tell nobody*

Darl

WE HAVE BEEN PASSING the signs for sometime now: the drug stores, the clothing stores, the patent medicine and the garages and cafés, and the mile-boards diminishing, becoming more starkly reaccruent: 3 mi. 2 mi. From the crest of a hill, as we get into the wagon again, we can see the smoke low and flat, seemingly unmoving in the unwinded afternoon.

"Is that it, Darl?" Vardaman says. "Is that Jefferson?" He too has lost flesh; like ours, his face has an expression strained, dreamy, and gaunt.

"Yes," I say. He lifts his head and looks at the sky. High against it they hang in narrowing circles, like the smoke, with an outward semblance of form and purpose, but with no inference of motion, progress or retrograde. We mount the wagon again where Cash lies on the box, the jagged shards of cement cracked about his leg. The shabby mules droop rattling and clanking down the hill.

"We'll have to take him to the doctor," pa says. "I reckon it aint no way around it." The back of Jewel's shirt, where it touches him, stains slow and black with grease. Life was created in the valleys. It blew up onto the hills on the old terrors, the old lusts, the old despairs. That's why you must walk up the hills so you can ride down.

Dewey Dell sits on the seat, the newspaper package on her lap. When we reach the foot of the hill where the road flattens between close walls of trees, she begins to look about quietly from one side of the road to the other. At last she says,

"I got to stop."

Pa looks at her, his shabby profile that of anticipant and disgruntled annoyance. He does not check the team. "What for?"

"I got to go to the bushes," Dewey Dell says.

Pa does not check the team. "Cant you wait till we get to town? It aint over a mile now."

"Stop," Dewey Dell says. "I got to go to the bushes."

Pa stops in the middle of the road and we watch Dewey Dell descend, carrying the package. She does not look back.

"Why not leave your cakes here?" I say. "We'll watch them."

She descends steadily, not looking at us.

"How would she know where to go to if she waited till we get to town?" Vardaman says. "Where would you go to do it in town, Dewey Dell?"

She lifts the package down and turns and disappears among the trees and undergrowth.

"Dont be no longer than you can help," pa says. "We aint got no time to waste." She does not answer. After a while we cannot hear her even. "We ought to done like Armstid and Gillespie said and sent word to town and had it dug and ready," he says.

"Why didn't you?" I say. "You could have telephoned."

"What for?" Jewel says. "Who the hell cant dig a hole in the ground?"

A car comes over the hill. It begins to sound the horn, slowing. It runs along the roadside in low gear, the outside wheels in the ditch, and passes us and goes on. Vardaman watches it until it is out of sight.

"How far is it now, Darl?" he says.

"Not far," I say.

"We ought to done it," pa says. "I just never wanted to be beholden to none except her flesh and blood."

"Who the hell cant dig a damn hole in the ground?" Jewel says.

"It aint respectful, talking that way about her grave," pa says. "You all dont know what it is. You never pure loved her, none of you." Jewel does not answer. He sits a little stiffly erect, his body arched away from his shirt. His high-colored jaw juts.

Dewey Dell returns. We watch her emerge from the bushes, carrying the package, and climb into the wagon. She now wears her Sunday dress, her beads, her shoes and stockings.

"I thought I told you to leave them clothes to home," pa says. She does not answer, does not look at us. She sets the package in the wagon and gets in. The wagon moves on.

"How many more hills now, Darl?" Vardaman says.

"Just one," I say. "The next one goes right up into town."

This hill is red sand, bordered on either hand by negro

cabins; against the sky ahead the massed telephone lines run, and the clock on the courthouse lifts among the trees. In the sand the wheels whisper, as though the very earth would hush our entry. We descend as the hill commences to rise.

We follow the wagon, the whispering wheels, passing the cabins where faces come suddenly to the doors, white-eyed. We hear sudden voices, ejaculant. Jewel has been looking from side to side; now his head turns forward and I can see his ears taking on a still deeper tone of furious red. Three negroes walk beside the road ahead of us; ten feet ahead of them a white man walks. When we pass the negroes their heads turn suddenly with that expression of shock and instinctive outrage. "Great God," one says; "what they got in that wagon?"

Jewel whirls. "Son of a bitches," he says. As he does so he is abreast of the white man, who has paused. It is as though Jewel had gone blind for the moment, for it is the white man toward whom he whirls.

"Darl!" Cash says from the wagon. I grasp at Jewel. The white man has fallen back a pace, his face still slack-jawed; then his jaw tightens, claps to. Jewel leans above him, his jaw muscles gone white.

"What did you say?" he says.

"Here," I say. "He dont mean anything, mister. Jewel," I say. When I touch him he swings at the man. I grasp his arm; we struggle. Jewel has never looked at me. He is trying to free his arm. When I see the man again he has an open knife in his hand.

"Hold up, mister," I say; "I've got him. Jewel," I say.

"Thinks because he's a goddamn town fellow," Jewel says, panting, wrenching at me. "Son of a bitch," he says.

The man moves. He begins to edge around me, watching Jewel, the knife low against his flank. "Cant no man call me that," he says. Pa has got down, and Dewey Dell is holding Jewel, pushing at him. I release him and face the man.

"Wait," I say. "He dont mean nothing. He's sick; got burned in a fire last night, and he aint himself."

"Fire or no fire," the man says, "cant no man call me that."

"He thought you said something to him," I say.

"I never said nothing to him. I never see him before."

"Fore God," pa says; "fore God."

"I know," I say. "He never meant anything. He'll take it back."

"Let him take it back, then."

"Put up your knife, and he will."

The man looks at me. He looks at Jewel. Jewel is quiet now.

"Put up your knife," I say.

The man shuts the knife.

"Fore God," pa says. "Fore God."

"Tell him you didn't mean anything, Jewel," I say.

"I thought he said something," Jewel says. "Just because he's——"

"Hush," I say. "Tell him you didn't mean it."

"I didn't mean it," Jewel says.

"He better not," the man says. "Calling me a——"

"Do you think he's afraid to call you that?" I say.

The man looks at me. "I never said that," he said.

"Dont think it, neither," Jewel says.

"Shut up," I say. "Come on. Drive on, pa."

The wagon moves. The man stands watching us. Jewel does not look back. "Jewel would a whipped him," Vardaman says.

We approach the crest, where the street runs, where cars go back and forth; the mules haul the wagon up and onto the crest and the street. Pa stops them. The street runs on ahead, where the square opens and the monument stands before the courthouse. We mount again while the heads turn with that expression which we know; save Jewel. He does not get on, even though the wagon has started again. "Get in, Jewel," I say. "Come on. Let's get away from here." But he does not get in. Instead he sets his foot on the turning hub of the rear wheel, one hand grasping the stanchion, and with the hub turning smoothly under his sole he lifts the other foot and squats there, staring straight ahead, motionless, lean, wooden-backed, as though carved squatting out of the lean wood.

Cash

IT WASN'T nothing else to do. It was either send him to Jackson, or have Gillespie sue us, because he knowed some way that Darl set fire to it. I dont know how he knowed, but he did. Vardaman seen him do it, but he swore he never told nobody but Dewey Dell and that she told him not to tell nobody. But Gillespie knowed it. But he would a suspicioned it sooner or later. He could have done it that night just watching the way Darl acted.

And so pa said, "I reckon there aint nothing else to do," and Jewel said,

"You want to fix him now?"

"Fix him?" pa said.

"Catch him and tie him up," Jewel said. "Goddamn it, do you want to wait until he sets fire to the goddamn team and wagon?"

But there wasn't no use in that. "There aint no use in that," I said. "We can wait till she is underground." A fellow that's going to spend the rest of his life locked up, he ought to be let to have what pleasure he can have before he goes.

"I reckon he ought to be there," pa says. "God knows, it's a trial on me. Seems like it aint no end to bad luck when once it starts."

Sometimes I aint so sho who's got ere a right to say when a man is crazy and when he aint. Sometimes I think it aint none of us pure crazy and aint none of us pure sane until the balance of us talks him that-a-way. It's like it aint so much what a fellow does, but it's the way the majority of folks is looking at him when he does it.

Because Jewel is too hard on him. Of course it was Jewel's horse was traded to get her that nigh to town, and in a sense it was the value of his horse Darl tried to burn up. But I thought more than once before we crossed the river and after, how it would be God's blessing if He did take her outen our hands and get shut of her in some clean way, and it seemed to me that when Jewel worked so to get her outen the river, he was going against God in a way, and then when Darl seen that it looked like one of us would have to do something, I can almost believe he done right in a way. But I dont reckon nothing excuses setting fire to a man's barn and endangering his stock and destroying his property. That's how I reckon a man is crazy. That's how he cant see eye to eye with other folks. And I reckon they aint nothing else to do with him but what the most folks says is right.

But it's a shame, in a way. Folks seems to get away from the olden right teaching that says to drive the nails down and trim the edges well always like it was for your own use and comfort you were making it. It's like some folks has the smooth, pretty boards to build a courthouse with and others dont have no more than rough lumber fitten to build a chicken coop. But it's better to build a tight chicken coop than a shoddy courthouse, and when they both build shoddy or build well, neither because it's one or tother is going to make a man feel the better nor the worse.

So we went up the street, toward the square, and he said, "We better take Cash to the doctor first. We can leave him there and come back for him." That's it. It's because me and him was born close together, and it nigh ten years before Jewel and Dewey Dell and Vardaman begun to come along. I feel kin to them, all right, but I dont know. And me being the oldest, and thinking already the very thing that he done: I dont know.

Pa was looking at me, then at him, mumbling his mouth.

"Go on," I said. "We'll get it done first."

"She would want us all there," pa says.

"Let's take Cash to the doctor first," Darl said. "She'll wait. She's already waited nine days."

"You all dont know," pa says. "The somebody you was young with and you growed old in her and she growed old in you, seeing the old coming on and it was the one somebody you could hear say it dont matter and know it was the truth outen the hard world and all a man's grief and trials. You all dont know."

"We got the digging to do, too," I said.

"Armstid and Gillespie both told you to send word ahead," Darl said. "Dont you want to go to Peabody's now, Cash?"

"Go on," I said. "It feels right easy now. It's best to get things done in the right place."

"If it was just dug," pa says. "We forgot our spade, too."

"Yes," Darl said. "I'll go to the hardware store. We'll have to buy one."

"It'll cost money," pa says.

"Do you begrudge her it?" Darl says.

"Go on and get a spade," Jewel said. "Here. Give me the money."

But pa didn't stop. "I reckon we can get a spade," he said. "I reckon there are Christians here." So Darl set still and we went on, with Jewel squatting on the tail-gate, watching the back of Darl's head. He looked like one of these bull dogs, one of these dogs that dont bark none, squatting against the rope, watching the thing he was waiting to jump at.

He set that way all the time we was in front of Mrs Bundren's house, hearing the music, watching the back of Darl's head with them hard white eyes of hisn.

The music was playing in the house. It was one of them graphophones. It was natural as a music-band.

"Do you want to go to Peabody's?" Darl said. "They can wait here and tell pa, and I'll drive you to Peabody's and come back for them."

"No," I said. It was better to get her underground, now we was this close, just waiting until pa borrowed the shovel. He drove along the street until we could hear the music.

"Maybe they got one here," he said. He pulled up at Mrs Bundren's. It was like he knowed. Sometimes I think that if a working man could see work as far ahead as a lazy man can see laziness. So he stopped there like he knowed, before that little new house, where the music was. We waited there, hearing it. I believe I could have dickered Suratt down to five dollars on that one of his. It's a comfortable thing, music is. "Maybe they got one here," pa says.

"You want Jewel to go," Darl says, "or do you reckon I better?"

"I reckon I better," pa says. He got down and went up the path and around the house to the back. The music stopped, then it started again.

"He'll get it, too," Darl said.

"Ay," I said. It was just like he knowed, like he could see through the walls and into the next ten minutes.

Only it was more than ten minutes. The music stopped and never commenced again for a good spell, where her and pa was talking at the back. We waited in the wagon.

"You let me take you back to Peabody's," Darl said.

"No," I said. "We'll get her underground."

"If he ever gets back," Jewel said. He begun to cuss. He started to get down from the wagon. "I'm going," he said.

Then we saw pa coming back. He had two spades, coming around the house. He laid them in the wagon and got in and we went on. The music never started again. Pa was looking back at the house. He kind of lifted his hand a little and I saw the shade pulled back a little at the window and her face in it.

But the curiousest thing was Dewey Dell. It surprised me. I see all the while how folks could say he was queer, but that was the very reason couldn't nobody hold it personal. It was like he was outside of it too, same as you, and getting mad at it would be kind of like getting mad at a mud-puddle that splashed you when you stepped in it. And then I always kind of had a idea that him and Dewey Dell kind of knowed things betwixt them. If I'd a said it was ere a one of us she liked better than ere a other, I'd a said it was Darl. But when we got it filled and covered and drove out the gate and turned into the lane where them fellows was waiting, when they come out and come on him and he jerked back, it was Dewey Dell that was on him before even Jewel could get at him. And then I believed I knowed how Gillespie knowed about how his barn taken fire.

She hadn't said a word, hadn't even looked at him, but when them fellows told him what they wanted and that they had come to get him and he throwed back, she jumped on him like a wild cat so that one of the fellows had to quit and hold her and her scratching and clawing at him like a wild cat, while the other one and pa and Jewel throwed Darl down and held him lying on his back, looking up at me.

"I thought you would have told me," he said. "I never thought you wouldn't have."

"Darl," I said. But he fought again, him and Jewel and the fellow, and the other one holding Dewey Dell and Vardaman yelling and Jewel saying,

"Kill him. Kill the son of a bitch."

It was bad so. It was bad. A fellow cant get away from a shoddy job. He cant do it. I tried to tell him, but he just said, "I thought you'd a told me. It's not that I," he said, then he begun to laugh. The other fellow pulled Jewel off of him and he sat there on the ground, laughing.

I tried to tell him. If I could have just moved, even set up. But I tried to tell him and he quit laughing, looking up at me.

"Do you want me to go?" he said.

"It'll be better for you," I said. "Down there it'll be quiet, with none of the bothering and such. It'll be better for you, Darl," I said.

"Better," he said. He begun to laugh again. "Better," he said. He couldn't hardly say it for laughing. He sat on the ground and us watching him, laughing and laughing. It was bad. It was bad so. I be durn if I could see anything to laugh at. Because there just aint nothing justifies the deliberate destruction of what a man has built with his own sweat and stored the fruit of his sweat into.

But I aint so sho that ere a man has the right to say what is crazy and what aint. It's like there was a fellow in every man that's done a-past the sanity or the insanity, that watches the sane and the insane doings of that man with the same horror and the same astonishment.

Peabody

I SAID, "I reckon a man in a tight might let Bill Varner patch him up like a damn mule, but I be damned if the man that'd let Anse Bundren treat him with raw cement aint got more spare legs than I have."

"They just aimed to ease hit some," he said.

"Aimed, hell," I said. "What in hell did Armstid mean by even letting them put you on that wagon again?"

"Hit was gittin right noticeable," he said. "We never had time to wait." I just looked at him. "Hit never bothered me none," he said.

"Dont you lie there and try to tell me you rode six days on a wagon without springs, with a broken leg and it never bothered you."

"It never bothered me much," he said.

"You mean, it never bothered Anse much," I said. "No more than it bothered him to throw that poor devil down in the public street and handcuff him like a damn murderer. Dont tell me. And dont tell me it aint going to bother you to lose sixty-odd square inches of skin to get that concrete off. And dont tell me it aint going to bother you to have to limp around on one short leg for the balance of your life—if you walk at all again. Concrete," I said. "God Amighty, why didn't Anse carry you to the nearest sawmill and stick your leg in the saw? That would have cured it. Then you all could have stuck his head into the saw and cured a whole family. . . . . . . Where is Anse, anyway? What's he up to now?"

"He's takin back them spades he borrowed," he said.

"That's right," I said. "Of course he'd have to borrow a spade to bury his wife with. Unless he could borrow a hole in the ground. Too bad you all didn't put him in it too. . . . . . . Does that hurt?"

"Not to speak of," he said, and the sweat big as marbles running down his face and his face about the color of blotting paper.

"Course not," I said. "About next summer you can hobble around fine on this leg. Then it wont bother you, not to

162

speak of. . . . . . . If you had anything you could call luck, you might say it was lucky this is the same leg you broke before," I said.

"Hit's what paw says," he said.

MacGowan

IT HAPPENED I am back of the prescription case, pouring up some chocolate sauce, when Jody comes back and says, "Say, Skeet, there's a woman up front that wants to see the doctor and when I said What doctor you want to see, she said she wants to see the doctor that works here and when I said There aint any doctor works here, she just stood there, looking back this way."

"What kind of a woman is it?" I says. "Tell her to go upstairs to Alford's office."

"Country woman," he says.

"Send her to the courthouse," I says. "Tell her all the doctors have gone to Memphis to a Barbers' Convention."

"All right," he says, going away. "She looks pretty good for a country girl," he says.

"Wait," I says. He waited and I went and peeped through the crack. But I couldn't tell nothing except she had a good leg against the light. "Is she young, you say?" I says.

"She looks like a pretty hot mamma, for a country girl," he says.

"Take this," I says, giving him the chocolate. I took off my apron and went up there. She looked pretty good. One of them black eyed ones that look like she'd as soon put a knife in you as not if you two-timed her. She looked pretty good. There wasn't nobody else in the store; it was dinner time.

"What can I do for you?" I says.

"Are you the doctor?" she says.

"Sure," I says. She quit looking at me and was kind of looking around.

"Can we go back yonder?" she says.

It was just a quarter past twelve, but I went and told Jody to kind of watch out and whistle if the old man come in sight, because he never got back before one.

"You better lay off of that," Jody says. "He'll fire your stern out of here so quick you cant wink."

"He dont never get back before one," I says. "You can see him go into the postoffice. You keep your eye peeled, now, and give me a whistle."

"What you going to do?" he says.

"You keep your eye out. I'll tell you later."

"Aint you going to give me no seconds on it?" he says.

"What the hell do you think this is?" I says; "a stud-farm? You watch out for him. I'm going into conference."

So I go on to the back. I stopped at the glass and smoothed my hair, then I went behind the prescription case, where she was waiting. She is looking at the medicine cabinet, then she looks at me.

"Now, madam," I says; " what is your trouble?"

"It's the female trouble," she says, watching me. "I got the money," she says.

"Ah," I says. "Have you got female troubles or do you want female troubles? If so, you come to the right doctor." Them country people. Half the time they dont know what they want, and the balance of the time they cant tell it to you. The clock said twenty past twelve.

"No," she says.

"No which?" I says.

"I aint had it," she says. "That's it." She looked at me. "I got the money," she says.

So I knew what she was talking about.

"Oh," I says. "You got something in your belly you wish you didn't have." She looks at me. "You wish you had a little more or a little less, huh?"

"I got the money," she says. "He said I could git something at the drugstore for hit."

"Who said so?" I says.

"He did," she says, looking at me.

"You dont want to call no names," I says. "The one that put the acorn in your belly? He the one that told you?" She dont say nothing. "You aint married, are you?" I says. I never saw no ring. But like as not, they aint heard yet out there that they use rings.

"I got the money," she says. She showed it to me, tied up in her handkerchief: a ten spot.

"I'll swear you have," I says. "He give it to you?"

"Yes," she says.

"Which one?" I says. She looks at me. "Which one of them give it to you?"

"It aint but one," she says. She looks at me.

"Go on," I says. She dont say nothing. The trouble about the cellar is, it aint but one way out and that's back up the inside stairs. The clock says twenty-five to one. "A pretty girl like you," I says.

She looks at me. She begins to tie the money back up in the handkerchief. "Excuse me a minute," I says. I go around the prescription case. "Did you hear about that fellow sprained his ear?" I says. "After that he couldn't even hear a belch."

"You better get her out from back there before the old man comes," Jody says.

"If you'll stay up there in front where he pays you to stay, he wont catch nobody but me," I says.

He goes on, slow, toward the front. "What you doing to her, Skeet?" he says.

"I cant tell you," I says. "It wouldn't be ethical. You go on up there and watch."

"Say, Skeet," he says.

"Ah, go on," I says. "I aint doing nothing but filling a pre-scription."

"He may not do nothing about that woman back there, but if he finds you monkeying with that prescription case, he'll kick your stern clean down them cellar stairs."

"My stern has been kicked by bigger bastards than him," I says. "Go back and watch out for him, now."

So I come back. The clock said fifteen to one. She is tying the money in the handkerchief. "You aint the doctor," she says.

"Sure I am," I says. She watches me. "Is it because I look too young, or am I too handsome?" I says. "We used to have a bunch of old water-jointed doctors here," I says; "Jefferson used to be a kind of Old Doctors' Home for them. But busi-ness started falling off and folks stayed so well until one day they found out that the women wouldn't never get sick at all. So they run all the old doctors out and got us young good-looking ones that the women would like and then the women begun to get sick again and so business picked up. They're doing that all over the country. Hadn't you heard about it? Maybe it's because you aint never needed a doctor."

"I need one now," she says.

"And you come to the right one," I says. "I already told you that."

"Have you got something for it?" she says. "I got the money."

"Well," I says, "of course a doctor has to learn all sorts of things while he's learning to roll calomel; he cant help himself. But I dont know about your trouble."

"He told me I could get something. He told me I could get it at the drugstore."

"Did he tell you the name of it?" I says. "You better go back and ask him."

She quit looking at me, kind of turning the handkerchief in her hands. "I got to do something," she says.

"How bad do you want to do something?" I says. She looks at me. "Of course, a doctor learns all sorts of things folks dont think he knows. But he aint supposed to tell all he knows. It's against the law."

Up front Jody says, "Skeet."

"Excuse me a minute," I says. I went up front. "Do you see him?" I says.

"Aint you done yet?" he says. "Maybe you better come up here and watch and let me do that consulting."

"Maybe you'll lay a egg," I says. I come back. She is looking at me. "Of course you realise that I could be put in the penitentiary for doing what you want," I says. "I would lose my license and then I'd have to go to work. You realise that?"

"I aint got but ten dollars," she says. "I could bring the rest next month, maybe."

"Pooh," I says, "ten dollars? You see, I cant put no price on my knowledge and skill. Certainly not for no little paltry sawbuck."

She looks at me. She dont even blink. "What you want, then?"

The clock said four to one. So I decided I better get her out. "You guess three times and then I'll show you," I says.

She dont even blink her eyes. "I got to do something," she says. She looks behind her and around, then she looks toward the front. "Gimme the medicine first," she says.

"You mean, you're ready to right now?" I says. "Here?"

"Gimme the medicine first," she says.

So I took a graduated glass and kind of turned my back to her and picked out a bottle that looked all right, because a man that would keep poison setting around in a unlabelled bottle ought to be in jail, anyway. It smelled like turpentine. I poured some into the glass and give it to her. She smelled it, looking at me across the glass.

"Hit smells like turpentine," she says.

"Sure," I says. "That's just the beginning of the treatment. You come back at ten oclock tonight and I'll give you the rest of it and perform the operation."

"Operation?" she says.

"It wont hurt you. You've had the same operation before. Ever hear about the hair of the dog?"

She looks at me. "Will it work?" she says.

"Sure it'll work. If you come back and get it."

So she drunk whatever it was without batting a eye, and went out. I went up front.

"Didn't you get it?" Jody says.

"Get what?" I says.

"Ah, come on," he says. "I aint going to try to beat your time."

"Oh, her," I says. "She just wanted a little medicine. She's got a bad case of dysentery and she's a little ashamed about mentioning it with a stranger there."

It was my night, anyway, so I helped the old bastard check up and I got his hat on him and got him out of the store by eight-thirty. I went as far as the corner with him and watched him until he passed under two street lamps and went on out of sight. Then I come back to the store and waited until nine-thirty and turned out the front lights and locked the door and left just one light burning at the back, and I went back and put some talcum powder into six capsules and kind of cleared up the cellar and then I was all ready.

She come in just at ten, before the clock had done striking. I let her in and she come in, walking fast. I looked out the door, but there wasn't nobody but a boy in overalls sitting on the curb. "You want something?" I says. He never said nothing, just looking at me. I locked the door and turned off the light and went on back. She was waiting. She didn't look at me now.

"Where is it?" she said.

I gave her the box of capsules. She held the box in her hand, looking at the capsules.

"Are you sure it'll work?" she says.

"Sure," I says. "When you take the rest of the treatment."

"Where do I take it?" she says.

"Down in the cellar," I says.

Vardaman

Now it is wider and lighter, but the stores are dark because they have all gone home. The stores are dark, but the lights pass on the windows when we pass. The lights are in the trees around the courthouse. They roost in the trees, but the courthouse is dark. The clock on it looks four ways, because it is not dark. The moon is not dark too. Not very dark. *Darl he went to Jackson is my brother Darl is my brother* Only it was over that way, shining on the track.

"Let's go that way, Dewey Dell," I say.

"What for?" Dewey Dell says. The track went shining around the window, it red on the track. But she said he would not sell it to the town boys. "But it will be there Christmas," Dewey Dell says. "You'll have to wait till then, when he brings it back."

Darl went to Jackson. Lots of people didn't go to Jackson. Darl is my brother. My brother is going to Jackson

While we walk the lights go around, roosting in the trees. On all sides it is the same. They go around the courthouse and then you cannot see them. But you can see them in the black windows beyond. They have all gone home to bed except me and Dewey Dell.

Going on the train to Jackson. My brother

There is a light in the store, far back. In the window are two big glasses of soda water, red and green. Two men could not drink them. Two mules could not. Two cows could not. *Darl*

A man comes to the door. He looks at Dewey Dell.

"You wait out here," Dewey Dell says.

"Why cant I come in?" I say. "I want to come in, too."

"You wait out here," she says.

"All right," I say.

Dewey Dell goes in.

Darl is my brother. Darl went crazy

The walk is harder than sitting on the ground. He is in the open door. He looks at me. "You want something?" he says. His head is slick. Jewel's head is slick sometimes. Cash's head is not slick. *Darl he went to Jackson my brother Darl* In the street he ate a banana. *Wouldn't you rather have bananas? Dewey Dell said. You wait till Christmas. It'll be there then. Then you can see it. So we are going to have some bananas. We are going to have a bag full, me and Dewey Dell.* He locks the door. Dewey Dell is inside. Then the light winks out.

He went to Jackson. He went crazy and went to Jackson both. Lots of people didn't go crazy. Pa and Cash and Jewel and Dewey Dell and me didn't go crazy. We never did go crazy. We didn't go to Jackson either. Darl

I hear the cow a long time, clopping   on the street. Then she comes into the square. She goes across the square, her head down   clopping   . She lows. There was nothing in the square before she lowed, but it wasn't empty. Now it is empty after she lowed. She goes on,   clopping   . She lows. *My brother is Darl. He went to Jackson on the train. He didn't go on the train to go crazy. He went crazy in our wagon. Darl* She has been in there a long time. And the cow is gone too. A long time. She has been in there longer than the cow was. But not as long as empty. *Darl is my brother. My brother Darl*

Dewey Dell comes out. She looks at me.

"Let's go around that way now," I say.

She looks at me. "It aint going to work," she says. "That son of a bitch."

"What aint going to work, Dewey Dell?"

"I just know it wont," she says. She is not looking at anything. "I just know it."

"Let's go that way," I say.

"We got to go back to the hotel. It's late. We got to slip back in."

"Cant we go by and see, anyway?"

"Hadn't you rather have bananas? Hadn't you rather?"

"All right." *My brother he went crazy and he went to Jackson too. Jackson is further away than crazy*

"It wont work," Dewey Dell says. "I just know it wont."

"What wont work?" I say. *He had to get on the train to go to Jackson. I have not been on the train, but Darl has been on the train. Darl. Darl is my brother. Darl. Darl*

Darl

DARL HAS GONE to Jackson. They put him on the train, laughing, down the long car laughing, the heads turning like the heads of owls when he passed. "What are you laughing at?" I said.

"Yes yes yes yes yes."

Two men put him on the train. They wore mismatched coats, bulging behind over their right hip pockets. Their necks were shaved to a hairline, as though the recent and simultaneous barbers had had a chalk-line like Cash's. "Is it the pistols you're laughing at?" I said. "Why do you laugh?" I said. "Is it because you hate the sound of laughing?"

They pulled two seats together so Darl could sit by the window to laugh. One of them sat beside him, the other sat on the seat facing him, riding backward. One of them had to ride backward because the state's money has a face to each backside and a backside to each face, and they are riding on the state's money which is incest. A nickel has a woman on one side and a buffalo on the other; two faces and no back. I dont know what that is. Darl had a little spy-glass he got in France at the war. In it it had a woman and a pig with two backs and no face. I know what that is. "Is that why you are laughing, Darl?"

"Yes yes yes yes yes yes."

The wagon stands on the square, hitched, the mules motionless, the reins wrapped about the seat-spring, the back of the wagon toward the courthouse. It looks no different from a hundred other wagons there; Jewel standing beside it and looking up the street like any other man in town that day, yet there is something different, distinctive. There is about it that unmistakable air of definite and imminent departure that trains have, perhaps due to the fact that Dewey Dell and Vardaman on the seat and Cash on a pallet in the wagon bed are eating bananas from a paper bag. "Is that why you are laughing, Darl?"

Darl is our brother, our brother Darl. Our brother Darl in

a cage in Jackson where, his grimed hands lying light in the quiet interstices, looking out he foams.

"Yes yes yes yes yes yes yes yes."

Dewey Dell

W HEN HE SAW the money I said, "It's not my money, it doesn't belong to me."

"Whose is it, then?"

"It's Cora Tull's money. It's Mrs Tull's. I sold the cakes for it."

"Ten dollars for two cakes?"

"Dont you touch it. It's not mine."

"You never had them cakes. It's a lie. It was them Sunday clothes you had in that package."

"Dont you touch it! If you take it you are a thief."

"My own daughter accuses me of being a thief. My own daughter."

"Pa. Pa."

"I have fed you and sheltered you. I give you love and care, yet my own daughter, the daughter of my dead wife, calls me a thief over her mother's grave."

"It's not mine, I tell you. If it was, God knows you could have it."

"Where did you get ten dollars?"

"Pa. Pa."

"You wont tell me. Did you come by it so shameful you dare not?"

"It's not mine, I tell you. Cant you understand it's not mine?"

"It's not like I wouldn't pay it back. But she calls her own father a thief."

"I cant, I tell you. I tell you it's not my money. God knows you could have it."

"I wouldn't take it. My own born daughter that has et my food for seventeen years, begrudges me the loan of ten dollars."

"It's not mine. I cant."

"Whose is it, then?"

"It was give to me. To buy something with."

"To buy what with?"

"Pa. Pa."

"It's just a loan. God knows, I hate for my blooden chil-

174

dren to reproach me. But I give them what was mine without stint. Cheerful I give them, without stint. And now they deny me. Addie. It was lucky for you you died, Addie."

"Pa. Pa."

"God knows it is."

He took the money and went out.

Cash

So when we stopped there to borrow the shovels we heard the graphophone playing in the house, and so when we got done with the shovels pa says, "I reckon I better take them back."

So we went back to the house. "We better take Cash on to Peabody's," Jewel said.

"It wont take but a minute," pa said. He got down from the wagon. The music was not playing now.

"Let Vardaman do it," Jewel said. "He can do it in half the time you can. Or here, you let me——"

"I reckon I better do it," pa says. "Long as it was me that borrowed them."

So we set in the wagon, but the music wasn't playing now. I reckon it's a good thing we aint got ere a one of them. I reckon I wouldn't never get no work done a-tall for listening to it. I dont know if a little music aint about the nicest thing a fellow can have. Seems like when he comes in tired of a night, it aint nothing could rest him like having a little music played and him resting. I have seen them that shuts up like a hand-grip, with a handle and all, so a fellow can carry it with him wherever he wants.

"What you reckon he's doing?" Jewel says. "I could a toted them shovels back and forth ten times by now."

"Let him take his time," I said. "He aint as spry as you, remember."

"Why didn't he let me take them back, then? We got to get your leg fixed up so we can start home tomorrow."

"We got plenty of time," I said. "I wonder what them machines costs on the installment."

"Installment of what?" Jewel said. "What you got to buy it with?"

"A fellow cant tell," I said. "I could a bought that one from Suratt for five dollars, I believe."

And so pa come back and we went to Peabody's. While we was there pa said he was going to the barbershop and get a shave. And so that night he said he had some business to tend to, kind of looking away from us while he said it, with his hair combed wet and slick and smelling sweet with perfume, but I said leave him be; I wouldn't mind hearing a little more of that music myself.

And so next morning he was gone again, then he come back and told us to get hitched up and ready to take out and he would meet us and when they was gone he said,

"I dont reckon you got no more money."

"Peabody just give me enough to pay the hotel with," I said. "We dont need nothing else, do we?"

"No," pa said; "no. We dont need nothing." He stood there, not looking at me.

"If it is something we got to have, I reckon maybe Peabody," I said.

"No," he said; "it aint nothing else. You all wait for me at the corner."

So Jewel got the team and come for me and they fixed me a pallet in the wagon and we drove across the square to the corner where pa said, and we was waiting there in the wagon, with Dewey Dell and Vardaman eating bananas, when we see them coming up the street. Pa was coming along with that kind of daresome and hangdog look all at once like when he has been up to something he knows ma aint going to like, carrying a grip in his hand, and Jewel says,

"Who's that?"

Then we see it wasn't the grip that made him look different; it was his face, and Jewel says, "He got them teeth."

It was a fact. It made him look a foot taller, kind of holding his head up, hangdog and proud too, and then we see her behind him, carrying the other grip—a kind of duck-shaped woman all dressed up, with them kind of hard-looking pop eyes like she was daring ere a man to say nothing. And there we set watching them, with Dewey Dell's and Vardaman's mouth half open and half-et bananas in their hands and her coming around from behind pa, looking at us like she dared ere a man. And then I see that the grip she was carrying was one of them little graphophones. It was for a fact, all shut up as pretty as a picture, and everytime a new record would come from the mail order and us setting in the house in the winter, listening to it, I would think what a shame Darl couldn't be to enjoy it too. But it is better so for him. This world is not his world; this life his life.

"It's Cash and Jewel and Vardaman and Dewey Dell," pa says, kind of hangdog and proud too, with his teeth and all, even if he wouldn't look at us. "Meet Mrs Bundren," he says.

SANCTUARY

I

FROM BEYOND the screen of bushes which surrounded the
spring, Popeye watched the man drinking. A faint path
led from the road to the spring. Popeye watched the man—a
tall, thin man, hatless, in worn gray flannel trousers and carrying a tweed coat over his arm—emerge from the path and
kneel to drink from the spring.

The spring welled up at the root of a beech tree and flowed
away upon a bottom of whorled and waved sand. It was surrounded by a thick growth of cane and brier, of cypress and
gum in which broken sunlight lay sourceless. Somewhere, hidden and secret yet nearby, a bird sang three notes and ceased.

In the spring the drinking man leaned his face to the broken and myriad reflection of his own drinking. When he rose
up he saw among them the shattered reflection of Popeye's
straw hat, though he had heard no sound.

He saw, facing him across the spring, a man of under size,
his hands in his coat pockets, a cigarette slanted from his chin.
His suit was black, with a tight, high-waisted coat. His trousers were rolled once and caked with mud above mud-caked
shoes. His face had a queer, bloodless color, as though seen
by electric light; against the sunny silence, in his slanted straw
hat and his slightly akimbo arms, he had that vicious depthless quality of stamped tin.

Behind him the bird sang again, three bars in monotonous
repetition: a sound meaningless and profound out of a suspirant and peaceful following silence which seemed to isolate
the spot, and out of which a moment later came the sound of
an automobile passing along a road and dying away.

The drinking man knelt beside the spring. "You've got a
pistol in that pocket, I suppose," he said.

Across the spring Popeye appeared to contemplate him
with two knobs of soft black rubber. "I'm asking you," Popeye said. "What's that in your pocket?"

The other man's coat was still across his arm. He lifted his
other hand toward the coat, out of one pocket of which protruded a crushed felt hat, from the other a book. "Which
pocket?" he said.

"Dont show me," Popeye said. "Tell me."

The other man stopped his hand. "It's a book."

"What book?" Popeye said.

"Just a book. The kind that people read. Some people do."

"Do you read books?" Popeye said.

The other man's hand was frozen above the coat. Across the spring they looked at one another. The cigarette wreathed its faint plume across Popeye's face, one side of his face squinted against the smoke like a mask carved into two simultaneous expressions.

From his hip pocket Popeye took a soiled handkerchief and spread it upon his heels. Then he squatted, facing the man across the spring. That was about four oclock on an afternoon in May. They squatted so, facing one another across the spring, for two hours. Now and then the bird sang back in the swamp, as though it were worked by a clock; twice more invisible automobiles passed along the highroad and died away. Again the bird sang.

"And of course you dont know the name of it," the man across the spring said. "I dont suppose you'd know a bird at all, without it was singing in a cage in a hotel lounge, or cost four dollars on a plate." Popeye said nothing. He squatted in his tight black suit, his right hand coat pocket sagging compactly against his flank, twisting and pinching cigarettes in his little, doll-like hands, spitting into the spring. His skin had a dead, dark pallor. His nose was faintly aquiline, and he had no chin at all. His face just went away, like the face of a wax doll set too near a hot fire and forgotten. Across his vest ran a platinum chain like a spider web. "Look here," the other man said. "My name is Horace Benbow. I'm a lawyer in Kinston. I used to live in Jefferson yonder; I'm on my way there now. Anybody in this county can tell you I am harmless. If it's whiskey, I dont care how much you all make or sell or buy. I just stopped here for a drink of water. All I want to do is get to town, to Jefferson."

Popeye's eyes looked like rubber knobs, like they'd give to the touch and then recover with the whorled smudge of the thumb on them.

"I want to reach Jefferson before dark," Benbow said. "You cant keep me here like this."

Without removing the cigarette Popeye spat past it into the spring.

"You cant stop me like this," Benbow said. "Suppose I break and run."

Popeye put his eyes on Benbow, like rubber. "Do you want to run?"

"No," Benbow said.

Popeye removed his eyes. "Well, dont, then."

Benbow heard the bird again, trying to recall the local name for it. On the invisible highroad another car passed, died away. Between them and the sound of it the sun was almost gone. From his trousers pocket Popeye took a dollar watch and looked at it and put it back in his pocket, loose like a coin.

Where the path from the spring joined the sandy byroad a tree had been recently felled, blocking the road. They climbed over the tree and went on, the highroad now behind them. In the sand were two shallow parallel depressions, but no mark of hoof. Where the branch from the spring seeped across it Benbow saw the prints of automobile tires. Ahead of him Popeye walked, his tight suit and stiff hat all angles, like a modernist lampstand.

The sand ceased. The road rose, curving, out of the jungle. It was almost dark. Popeye looked briefly over his shoulder. "Step out, Jack," he said.

"Why didn't we cut straight across up the hill?" Benbow said.

"Through all them trees?" Popeye said. His hat jerked in a dull, vicious gleam in the twilight as he looked down the hill where the jungle already lay like a lake of ink. "Jesus Christ."

It was almost dark. Popeye's gait had slowed. He walked now beside Benbow, and Benbow could see the continuous jerking of the hat from side to side as Popeye looked about with a sort of vicious cringing. The hat just reached Benbow's chin.

Then something, a shadow shaped with speed, stooped at them and on, leaving a rush of air upon their very faces, on a soundless feathering of taut wings, and Benbow felt Popeye's whole body spring against him and his hand clawing at his coat. "It's just an owl," Benbow said. "It's nothing but an owl." Then he said: "They call that Carolina wren a fishing-bird. That's what it is. What I couldn't think of back there," with Popeye crouching against him, clawing at his pocket and hissing through his teeth like a cat. He smells black, Benbow thought; he smells like that black stuff that ran out of Bovary's mouth and down upon her bridal veil when they raised her head.

A moment later, above a black, jagged mass of trees, the house lifted its stark square bulk against the failing sky.

The house was a gutted ruin rising gaunt and stark out of a grove of unpruned cedar trees. It was a landmark, known as the Old Frenchman place, built before the Civil War; a plantation house set in the middle of a tract of land; of cotton fields and gardens and lawns long since gone back to jungle, which the people of the neighborhood had been pulling down piecemeal for firewood for fifty years or digging with secret and sporadic optimism for the gold which the builder was reputed to have buried somewhere about the place when Grant came through the county on his Vicksburg campaign.

Three men were sitting in chairs on one end of the porch. In the depths of the open hall a faint light showed. The hall went straight back through the house. Popeye mounted the steps, the three men looking at him and his companion. "Here's the professor," he said, without stopping. He entered the house, the hall. He went on and crossed the back porch and turned and entered the room where the light was. It was the kitchen. A woman stood at the stove. She wore a faded calico dress. About her naked ankles a worn pair of man's brogans, unlaced, flapped when she moved. She looked back at Popeye, then to the stove again, where a pan of meat hissed.

Popeye stood in the door. His hat was slanted across his face. He took a cigarette from his pocket, without producing the pack, and pinched and fretted it and put it into his mouth and snapped a match on his thumbnail. "There's a bird out front," he said.

The woman did not look around. She turned the meat. "Why tell me?" she said. "I dont serve Lee's customers."

"It's a professor," Popeye said.

The woman turned, an iron fork suspended in her hand. Behind the stove, in shadow, was a wooden box. "A what?"

"Professor," Popeye said. "He's got a book with him."

"What's he doing here?"

"I dont know. I never thought to ask. Maybe to read the book."

"He came here?"

"I found him at the spring."

"Was he trying to find this house?"

"I dont know," Popeye said. "I never thought to ask." The woman was still looking at him. "I'll send him on to Jefferson on the truck," Popeye said. "He said he wants to go there."

"Why tell me about it?" the woman said.

"You cook. He'll want to eat."

"Yes," the woman said. She turned back to the stove. "I cook. I cook for crimps and spungs and feebs. Yes. I cook."

In the door Popeye watched her, the cigarette curling across his face. His hands were in his pockets. "You can quit. I'll take you back to Memphis Sunday. You can go to hustling again." He watched her back. "You're getting fat here. Laying off in the country. I wont tell them on Manuel street."

The woman turned, the fork in her hand. "You bastard," she said.

"Sure," Popeye said. "I wont tell them that Ruby Lamar is down in the country, wearing a pair of Lee Goodwin's throwed-away shoes, chopping her own firewood. No. I'll tell them Lee Goodwin is big rich."

"You bastard," the woman said. "You bastard."

"Sure," Popeye said. Then he turned his head. There was a shuffling sound across the porch, then a man entered. He was stooped, in overalls. He was barefoot; it was his bare feet which they had heard. He had a sunburned thatch of hair, matted and foul. He had pale furious eyes, a short soft beard like dirty gold in color.

"I be dawg if he aint a case, now," he said.

"What do you want?" the woman said. The man in overalls didn't answer. In passing, he looked at Popeye with a glance at once secret and alert, as though he were ready to laugh at a joke, waiting for the time to laugh. He crossed the kitchen with a shambling, bear-like gait, and still with that air of alert and gleeful secrecy, though in plain sight of them, he re-moved a loose board in the floor and took out a gallon jug. Popeye watched him, his forefingers in his vest, the cigarette (he had smoked it down without once touching it with his hand) curling across his face. His expression was savage, per-haps baleful; contemplative, watching the man in overalls re-cross the floor with a kind of alert diffidence, the jug clumsily concealed below his flank; he was watching Popeye, with that expression alert and ready for mirth, until he left the room. Again they heard his bare feet on the porch.

"Sure," Popeye said. "I wont tell them on Manuel street that Ruby Lamar is cooking for a dummy and a feeb too."

"You bastard," the woman said. "You bastard."

II

WHEN THE WOMAN entered the dining-room, carrying a platter of meat, Popeye and the man who had fetched the jug from the kitchen and the stranger were already at a table made by nailing three rough planks to two trestles. Coming into the light of the lamp which sat on the table, her face was sullen, not old; her eyes were cold. Watching her, Benbow did not see her look once at him as she set the platter on the table and stood for a moment with that veiled look with which women make a final survey of a table, and went and stooped above an open packing case in a corner of the room and took from it another plate and knife and fork, which she brought to the table and set before Benbow with a kind of abrupt yet unhurried finality, her sleeve brushing his shoulder.

As she was doing that, Goodwin entered. He wore muddy overalls. He had a lean, weathered face, the jaws covered by a black stubble; his hair was gray at the temples. He was leading by the arm an old man with a long white beard stained about the mouth. Benbow watched Goodwin seat the old man in a chair, where he sat obediently with that tentative and abject eagerness of a man who has but one pleasure left and whom the world can reach only through one sense, for he was both blind and deaf: a short man with a bald skull and a round, full-fleshed, rosy face in which his cataracted eyes looked like two clots of phlegm. Benbow watched him take a filthy rag from his pocket and regurgitate into the rag an almost colorless wad of what had once been chewing tobacco, and fold the rag up and put it into his pocket. The woman served his plate from the dish. The others were already eating, silently and steadily, but the old man sat there, his head bent over his plate, his beard working faintly. He fumbled at the plate with a diffident, shaking hand and found a small piece of meat and began to suck at it until the woman returned and rapped his knuckles. He put the meat back on the plate then and Benbow watched her cut up the food on the plate, meat, bread and all, and then pour sorghum over it. Then Benbow quit looking. When the meal was over, Goodwin led the old

man out again. Benbow watched the two of them pass out
the door and heard them go up the hall.

The men returned to the porch. The woman cleared the
table and carried the dishes to the kitchen. She set them on
the table and she went to the box behind the stove and she
stood over it for a time. Then she returned and put her own
supper on a plate and sat down to the table and ate and lit a
cigarette from the lamp and washed the dishes and put them
away. Then she went back up the hall. She did not go out
onto the porch. She stood just inside the door, listening to
them talking, listening to the stranger talking and to the thick,
soft sound of the jug as they passed it among themselves.
"That fool," the woman said. "What does he want. . . . . . ."
She listened to the stranger's voice; a quick, faintly outlandish
voice, the voice of a man given to much talk and not much
else. "Not to drinking, anyway," the woman said, quiet inside
the door. "He better get on to where he's going, where his
women folks can take care of him."

She listened to him. "From my window I could see the
grape arbor, and in the winter I could see the hammock too.
But in the winter it was just the hammock. That's why we
know nature is a she; because of that conspiracy between female flesh and female season. So each spring I could watch
the reaffirmation of the old ferment hiding the hammock; the
green-snared promise of unease. What blossoms grapes have,
that is. It's not much: a wild and waxlike bleeding less of
bloom than leaf, hiding and hiding the hammock, until along
in late May, in the twilight, her—Little Belle's—voice would
be like the murmur of the wild grape itself. She never would
say, 'Horace, this is Louis or Paul or Whoever' but 'It's just
Horace'. Just, you see; in a little white dress in the twilight,
the two of them all demure and quite alert and a little impatient. And I couldn't have felt any more foreign to her flesh
if I had begot it myself.

"So this morning—no; that was four days ago; it was
Thursday she got home from school and this is Tuesday—I
said, 'Honey, if you found him on the train, he probably belongs to the railroad company. You cant take him from the
railroad company; that's against the law, like the insulators
on the poles.'

" 'He's as good as you are. He goes to Tulane.'

" 'But on a train, honey,' I said.

" 'I've found them in worse places than on the train.'

" 'I know,' I said. 'So have I. But you dont bring them home, you know. You just step over them and go on. You dont soil your slippers, you know.'

"We were in the living room then; it was just before dinner; just the two of us in the house then. Belle had gone down town.

" 'What business is it of yours who comes to see me? You're not my father. You're just—just——'

" 'What?' I said. 'Just what?'

" 'Tell Mother, then! Tell her. That's what you're going to do. Tell her!'

" 'But on the train, honey,' I said. 'If he'd walked into your room in a hotel, I'd just kill him. But on the train, I'm disgusted. Let's send him along and start all over again.'

" 'You're a fine one to talk about finding things on the train! You're a fine one! Shrimp! Shrimp!' "

"He's crazy," the woman said, motionless inside the door. The stranger's voice went on, tumbling over itself, rapid and diffuse.

"Then she was saying 'No! No!' and me holding her and she clinging to me. 'I didn't mean that! Horace! Horace!' And I was smelling the slain flowers, the delicate dead flowers and tears, and then I saw her face in the mirror. There was a mirror behind her and another behind me, and she was watching herself in the one behind me, forgetting about the other one in which I could see her face, see her watching the back of my head with pure dissimulation. That's why nature is 'she' and Progress is 'he'; nature made the grape arbor, but Progress invented the mirror."

"He's crazy," the woman said inside the door, listening.

"But that wasn't quite it. I thought that maybe the spring, or maybe being forty-three years old, had upset me. I thought that maybe I would be all right if I just had a hill to lie on for a while——It was that country. Flat and rich and foul, so that the very winds seem to engender money out of it. Like you wouldn't be surprised to find that you could turn in the leaves off the trees, into the banks for cash. That Delta. Five thousand square miles, without any hill save the bumps of dirt the Indians made to stand on when the River overflowed.

"So I thought it was just a hill I wanted; it wasn't Little Belle that set me off. Do you know what it was?"

"He is," the woman said inside the door. "Lee ought not to let——"

Benbow had not waited for any answer. "It was a rag with rouge on it. I knew I would find it before I went into Belle's room. And there it was, stuffed behind the mirror: a handkerchief where she had wiped off the surplus paint when she dressed and stuck it behind the mantel. I put it into the clothes-bag and took my hat and walked out. I had got a lift on a truck before I found that I had no money with me. That was part of it too, you see; I couldn't cash a check. I couldn't get off the truck and go back to town and get some money. I couldn't do that. So I have been walking and bumming rides ever since. I slept one night in a sawdust pile at a mill, one night at a negro cabin, one night in a freight car on a siding. I just wanted a hill to lie on, you see. Then I would be all right. When you marry your own wife, you start off from scratch. . . . . . .maybe scratching. When you marry somebody else's wife, you start off maybe ten years behind, from somebody else's scratch and scratching. I just wanted a hill to lie on for a while."

"The fool," the woman said. "The poor fool." She stood inside the door. Popeye came through the hall from the back. He passed her without a word and went onto the porch.

"Come on," he said. "Let's get it loaded." She heard the three of them go away. She stood there. Then she heard the stranger get unsteadily out of his chair and cross the porch. Then she saw him, in faint silhouette against the sky, the lesser darkness: a thin man in shapeless clothes; a head of thinning and ill-kempt hair; and quite drunk. "They dont make him eat right," the woman said.

She was motionless, leaning lightly against the wall, he facing her. "Do you like living like this?" he said. "Why do you do it? You are young yet; you could go back to the cities and better yourself without lifting more than an eyelid." She didn't move, leaning lightly against the wall, her arms folded. "The poor, scared fool," she said.

"You see," he said, "I lack courage: that was left out of me. The machinery is all here, but it wont run." His hand fumbled across her cheek. "You are young yet." She didn't move, feeling his hand upon her face, touching her flesh as though he were trying to learn the shape and position of her bones and the texture of the flesh. "You have your whole life before you, practically. How old are you? You're not past thirty yet." His voice was not loud, almost a whisper.

When she spoke she did not lower her voice at all. She had not moved, her arms still folded across her breast. "Why did you leave your wife?" she said.

"Because she ate shrimp," he said. "I couldn't—You see, it was Friday, and I thought how at noon I'd go to the station and get the box of shrimp off the train and walk home with it, counting a hundred steps and changing hands with it, and it——"

"Did you do that every day?" the woman said.

"No. Just Friday. But I have done it for ten years, since we were married. And I still dont like to smell shrimp. But I wouldn't mind the carrying it home so much. I could stand that. It's because the package drips. All the way home it drips and drips, until after a while I follow myself to the station and stand aside and watch Horace Benbow take that box off the train and start home with it, changing hands every hundred steps, and I following him, thinking Here lies Horace Benbow in a fading series of small stinking spots on a Mississippi sidewalk."

"Oh," the woman said. She breathed quietly, her arms folded. She moved; he gave back and followed her down the hall. They entered the kitchen where a lamp burned. "You'll have to excuse the way I look," the woman said. She went to the box behind the stove and drew it out and stood above it, her hands hidden in the front of her garment. Benbow stood in the middle of the room. "I have to keep him in the box so the rats cant get to him," she said.

"What?" Benbow said. "What is it?" He approached, where he could see into the box. It contained a sleeping child, not a year old. He looked down at the pinched face quietly.

"Oh," he said. "You have a son." They looked down at the pinched, sleeping face of the child. There came a noise outside; feet came onto the back porch. The woman shoved the box back into the corner with her knee as Goodwin entered.

"All right," Goodwin said. "Tommy'll show you the way to the truck." He went away, on into the house.

Benbow looked at the woman. Her hands were still wrapped into her dress. "Thank you for the supper," he said. "Some day, maybe. . . ." He looked at her; she was watching him, her face not sullen so much, as cold, still. "Maybe I can do something for you in Jefferson. Send you something you need. . . . . . ."

She removed her hands from the fold of the dress in a turning, flicking motion; jerked them hidden again. "With all this dishwater and washing. . . . . . You might send me an orange stick," she said.

Walking in single file, Tommy and Benbow descended the hill from the house, following the abandoned road. Benbow looked back. The gaunt ruin of the house rose against the sky, above the massed and matted cedars, lightless, desolate, and profound. The road was an eroded scar too deep to be a road and too straight to be a ditch, gutted by winter freshets and choken with fern and rotted leaves and branches. Following Tommy, Benbow walked in a faint path where feet had worn the rotting vegetation down to the clay. Overhead an arching hedgerow of trees thinned against the sky.

The descent increased, curving. "It was about here that we saw the owl," Benbow said.

Ahead of him Tommy guffawed. "It skeered him too, I'll be bound," he said.

"Yes," Benbow said. He followed Tommy's vague shape, trying to walk carefully, to talk carefully, with that tedious concern of drunkenness.

"I be dog if he aint the skeeriest durn *white* man I ever see," Tommy said. "Here he was comin up the path to the porch and that ere dog come out from under the house and went up and sniffed his heels, like ere a dog will, and I be dog if he didn't flinch off like it was a moccasin and him barefoot, and whupped out that little artermatic pistol and shot it dead as a door-nail. I be durn if he didn't."

"Whose dog was it?" Horace said.

"Hit was mine," Tommy said. He chortled. "A old dog that wouldn't hurt a flea if hit could."

The road descended and flattened; Benbow's feet whispered into sand, walking carefully. Against the pale sand he could now see Tommy, moving at a shuffling shamble like a mule walks in sand, without seeming effort, his bare feet hissing, flicking the sand back in faint spouting gusts from each inward flick of his toes.

The bulky shadow of the felled tree blobbed across the road. Tommy climbed over it and Benbow followed, still carefully, gingerly, hauling himself through a mass of foliage not yet withered, smelling still green. "Some more of——" Tommy said. He turned. "Can you make it?"

"I'm all right," Horace said. He got his balance again. Tommy went on.

"Some more of Popeye's doins," Tommy said. " 'Twarn't no use, blockin this road like that. Just fixed it so we'd have to walk a mile to the trucks. I told him folks been comin out here to buy from Lee for four years now, and aint nobody bothered Lee yet. Besides gettin that car of hisn outen here again, big as it is. But 'twarn't no stoppin him. I be dog if he aint skeered of his own shadow."

"I'd be scared of it too," Benbow said. "If his shadow was mine."

Tommy guffawed, in undertone. The road was now a black tunnel floored with the impalpable defunctive glare of the sand. "It was about here that the path turned off to the spring," Benbow thought, trying to discern where the path notched into the jungle wall. They went on.

"Who drives the truck?" Benbow said. "Some more Memphis fellows?"

"Sho," Tommy said. "Hit's Popeye's truck."

"Why cant those Memphis folks stay in Memphis and let you all make your liquor in peace?"

"That's where the money is," Tommy said. "Aint no money in these here piddlin little quarts and half-a-gallons. Lee just does that for a-commodation, to pick up a extry dollar or two. It's in makin a run and gettin shut of it quick, where the money is."

"Oh," Benbow said. "Well, I think I'd rather starve than have that man around me."

Tommy guffawed. "Popeye's all right. He's just a little curious." He walked on, shapeless against the hushed glare of the road, the sandy road. "I be dog if he aint a case, now. Aint he?"

"Yes," Benbow said. "He's all of that."

The truck was waiting where the road, clay again, began to mount toward the gravel highway. Two men sat on the fender, smoking cigarettes; overhead the trees thinned against the stars of more than midnight.

"You took your time," one of the men said. "Didn't you? I aimed to be halfway to town by now. I got a woman waiting for me."

"Sure," the other man said. "Waiting on her back." The first man cursed him.

"We come as fast as we could," Tommy said. "Whyn't you fellows hang out a lantern? If me and him had a been the Law, we'd a had you, sho."

"Ah, go climb a tree, you mat-faced bastard," the first man said. They snapped their cigarettes away and got into the truck. Tommy guffawed, in undertone. Benbow turned and extended his hand.

"Goodbye," he said. "And much obliged, Mister——"

"My name's Tawmmy," the other said. His limp, calloused hand fumbled into Benbow's and pumped it solemnly once and fumbled away. He stood there, a squat, shapeless figure against the faint glare of the road, while Benbow lifted his foot for the step. He stumbled, catching himself.

"Watch yourself, Doc," a voice from the cab of the truck said. Benbow got in. The second man was laying a shotgun along the back of the seat. The truck got into motion and ground terrifically up the gutted slope and into the gravelled highroad and turned toward Jefferson and Memphis.

III

O N THE next afternoon Benbow was at his sister's home. It was in the country, four miles from Jefferson; the home of her husband's people. She was a widow, with a boy ten years old, living in a big house with her son and the great aunt of her husband: a woman of ninety, who lived in a wheel chair, who was known as Miss Jenny. She and Benbow were at the window, watching his sister and a young man walking in the garden. His sister had been a widow for ten years.

"Why hasn't she ever married again?" Benbow said.

"I ask you," Miss Jenny said. "A young woman needs a man."

"But not that one," Benbow said. He looked at the two people. The man wore flannels and a blue coat; a broad, plumpish young man with a swaggering air, vaguely collegiate. "She seems to like children. Maybe because she has one of her own now. Which one is that? Is that the same one she had last fall?"

"Gowan Stevens," Miss Jenny said. "You ought to remember Gowan."

"Yes," Benbow said. "I do now. I remember last October." At that time he had passed through Jefferson on his way home, and he had stopped overnight at his sister's. Through the same window he and Miss Jenny had watched the same two people walking in the same garden, where at that time the late, bright, dusty-odored flowers of October bloomed. At that time Stevens wore brown, and at that time he was new to Horace.

"He's only been coming out since he got home from Virginia last spring," Miss Jenny said. "The one then was that Jones boy; Herschell. Yes. Herschell."

"Ah," Benbow said. "An F.F.V., or just an unfortunate sojourner there?"

"At the school, the University. He went there. You dont remember him because he was still in diapers when you left Jefferson."

"Dont let Belle hear you say that," Benbow said. He

watched the two people. They approached the house and disappeared beyond it. A moment later they came up the stairs and into the room. Stevens came in, with his sleek head, his plump, assured face. Miss Jenny gave him her hand and he bent fatly and kissed it.

"Getting younger and prettier every day," he said. "I was just telling Narcissa that if you'd just get up out of that chair and be my girl, she wouldn't have a chance."

"I'm going to tomorrow," Miss Jenny said. "Narcissa——"

Narcissa was a big woman, with dark hair, a broad, stupid, serene face. She was in her customary white dress. "Horace, this is Gowan Stevens," she said. "My brother, Gowan."

"How do you do, sir," Stevens said. He gave Benbow's hand a quick, hard, high, close grip. At that moment the boy, Benbow Sartoris, Benbow's nephew, came in. "I've heard of you," Stevens said.

"Gowan went to Virginia," the boy said.

"Ah," Benbow said. "I've heard of it."

"Thanks," Stevens said. "But everybody cant go to Harvard."

"Thank you," Benbow said. "It was Oxford."

"Horace is always telling folks he went to Oxford so they'll think he means the state university, and he can tell them different," Miss Jenny said.

"Gowan goes to Oxford a lot," the boy said. "He's got a jelly there. He takes her to the dances. Dont you, Gowan?"

"Right, bud," Stevens said. "A red-headed one."

"Hush, Bory," Narcissa said. She looked at her brother. "How are Belle and Little Belle?" She almost said something else, then she ceased. Yet she looked at her brother, her gaze grave and intent.

"If you keep on expecting him to run off from Belle, he will do it," Miss Jenny said. "He'll do it someday. But Narcissa wouldn't be satisfied, even then," she said. "Some women wont want a man to marry a certain woman. But all the women will be mad if he ups and leaves her."

"You hush, now," Narcissa said.

"Yes, sir," Miss Jenny said. "Horace has been bucking at the halter for some time now. But you better not run against it too hard, Horace; it might not be fastened at the other end."

Across the hall a small bell rang. Stevens and Benbow both moved toward the handle of Miss Jenny's chair. "Will you forbear, sir?" Benbow said. "Since I seem to be the guest."

"Why, Horace," Miss Jenny said. "Narcissa, will you send up to the chest in the attic and get the duelling pistols?" She turned to the boy. "And you go on ahead and tell them to strike up the music, and to have two roses ready."

"Strike up what music?" the boy said.

"There are roses on the table," Narcissa said. "Gowan sent them. Come on to supper."

Through the window Benbow and Miss Jenny watched the two people, Narcissa still in white, Stevens in flannels and a blue coat, walking in the garden. "The Virginia gentleman one, who told us at supper that night about how they had taught him to drink like a gentleman. Put a beetle in alcohol, and you have a scarab; put a Mississippian in alcohol, and you have a gentleman——"

"Gowan Stevens," Miss Jenny said. They watched the two people disappear beyond the house. It was some time before he heard the two people come down the hall. When they entered, it was the boy instead of Stevens.

"He wouldn't stay," Narcissa said. "He's going to Oxford. There is to be a dance at the University Friday night. He has an engagement with a young lady."

"He should find ample field for gentlemanly drinking there," Horace said. "Gentlemanly anything else. I suppose that's why he is going down ahead of time."

"Taking an old girl to a dance," the boy said. "He's going to Starkville Saturday, to the base ball game. He said he'd take me, but you wont let me go."

IV

TOWNSPEOPLE TAKING after-supper drives through the college grounds or an oblivious and bemused faculty-member or a candidate for a master's degree on his way to the library would see Temple, a snatched coat under her arm and her long legs blonde with running, in speeding silhouette against the lighted windows of the Coop, as the women's dormitory was known, vanishing into the shadow beside the library wall, and perhaps a final squatting swirl of knickers or whatnot as she sprang into the car waiting there with engine running on that particular night. The cars belonged to town boys. Students in the University were not permitted to keep cars, and the men—hatless, in knickers and bright pull-overs—looked down upon the town boys who wore hats cupped rigidly upon pomaded heads, and coats a little too tight and trousers a little too full, with superiority and rage.

This was on week nights. On alternate Saturday evenings, at the Letter Club dances, or on the occasion of the three formal yearly balls, the town boys, lounging in attitudes of belligerent casualness, with their identical hats and upturned collars, watched her enter the gymnasium upon black collegiate arms and vanish in a swirling glitter upon a glittering swirl of music, with her high delicate head and her bold painted mouth and soft chin, her eyes blankly right and left looking, cool, predatory and discreet.

Later, the music wailing beyond the glass, they would watch her through the windows as she passed in swift rotation from one pair of black sleeves to the next, her waist shaped slender and urgent in the interval, her feet filling the rhythmic gap with music. Stooping they would drink from flasks and light cigarettes, then erect again, motionless against the light, the upturned collars, the hatted heads, would be like a row of hatted and muffled busts cut from black tin and nailed to the window-sills.

There would always be three or four of them there when the band played Home, Sweet Home, lounging near the exit, their faces cold, bellicose, a little drawn with sleeplessness, watching the couples emerge in a wan aftermath of motion and noise. Three of them watched Temple and Gowan Stevens come out, into the chill presage of spring dawn. Her face was quite pale, dusted over with recent powder, her hair in spent red curls. Her eyes, all pupil now, rested upon them for a blank moment. Then she lifted her hand in a wan gesture, whether at them or not, none could have said. They did not respond, no flicker in their cold eyes. They watched Gowan slip his arm into hers, and the fleet revelation of flank and thigh as she got into his car. It was a long, low roadster, with a jacklight.

"Who's that son bitch?" one said.

"My father's a judge," the second said in a bitter, lilting falsetto.

"Hell. Let's go to town."

They went on. Once they yelled at a car, but it did not stop. On the bridge across the railroad cutting they stopped and drank from a bottle. The last made to fling it over the railing. The second caught his arm.

"Let me have it," he said. He broke the bottle carefully and spread the fragments across the road. They watched him.

"You're not good enough to go to a college dance," the first said. "You poor bastard."

"My father's a judge," the other said, propping the jagged shards upright in the road.

"Here comes a car," the third said.

It had three headlights. They leaned against the railing, slanting their hats against the light, and watched Temple and Gowan pass. Temple's head was low and close. The car moved slowly.

"You poor bastard," the first said.

"Am I?" the second said. He took something from his pocket and flipped it out, whipping the sheer, faintly scented web across their faces. "Am I?"

"That's what you say."

"Doc got that step-in in Memphis," the third said. "Off a damn whore."

"You're a lying bastard," Doc said.

They watched the fan of light, the diminishing ruby tail-lamp, come to a stop at the Coop. The lights went off. After a while the car door slammed. The lights came on; the car moved away. It approached again. They leaned against the rail in a row, their hats slanted against the glare. The broken glass glinted in random sparks. The car drew up and stopped opposite them.

"You gentlemen going to town?" Gowan said, opening the door. They leaned against the rail, then the first said "Much obliged" gruffly and they got in, the two others in the rumble seat, the first beside Gowan.

"Pull over this way," he said. "Somebody broke a bottle there."

"Thanks," Gowan said. The car moved on. "You gentlemen going to Starkville tomorrow to the game?"

The ones in the rumble said nothing.

"I dont know," the first said. "I dont reckon so."

"I'm a stranger here," Gowan said. "I ran out of liquor tonight, and I've got a date early in the morning. Can you gentlemen tell me where I could get a quart?"

"It's mighty late," the first said. He turned to the others. "You know anybody he can find this time of night, Doc?"

"Luke might," the third said.

"Where does he live?" Gowan said.

"Go on," the first said. "I'll show you." They crossed the square and drove out of town about a half mile.

"This is the road to Taylor, isn't it?" Gowan said.

"Yes," the first said.

"I've got to drive down there early in the morning," Gowan said. "Got to get there before the special does. You gentlemen not going to the game, you say."

"I reckon not," the first said. "Stop here." A steep slope rose, crested by stunted blackjacks. "You wait here," the first said. Gowan switched off the lights. They could hear the other scrambling up the slope.

"Does Luke have good liquor?" Gowan said.

"Pretty good. Good as any, I reckon," the third said.

"If you dont like it, you dont have to drink it," Doc said. Gowan turned fatly and looked at him.

"It's as good as that you had tonight," the third said.

"You didn't have to drink that, neither," Doc said.

"They cant seem to make good liquor down here like they do up at school," Gowan said.

"Where you from?" the third said.

"Virgin——oh, Jefferson. I went to school at Virginia. Teach you how to drink, there."

The other two said nothing. The first returned, preceded by a minute shaling of earth down the slope. He had a fruit jar. Gowan lifted it against the sky. It was pale, innocent looking. He removed the cap and extended it.

"Drink."

The first took it and extended it to them in the rumble.

"Drink."

The third drank, but Doc refused. Gowan drank.

"Good God," he said, "how do you fellows drink this stuff?"

"We dont drink rotgut at Virginia," Doc said. Gowan turned in the seat and looked at him.

"Shut up, Doc," the third said. "Dont mind him," he said. "He's had a bellyache all night."

"Son bitch," Doc said.

"Did you call me that?" Gowan said.

" 'Course he didn't," the third said. "Doc's all right. Come on, Doc. Take a drink."

"I dont give a damn," Doc said. "Hand it here."

They returned to town. "The Shack'll be open," the first said. "At the depot."

It was a confectionery-lunchroom. It was empty save for a man in a soiled apron. They went to the rear and entered an alcove with a table and four chairs. The man brought four glasses and coca-colas. "Can I have some sugar and water and a lemon, Cap?" Gowan said. The man brought them. The others watched Gowan make a whiskey sour. "They taught me to drink it this way," he said. They watched him drink. "Hasn't got much kick, to me," he said, filling his glass from the jar. He drank that.

"You sure do drink it," the third said.

"I learned in a good school." There was a high window. Beyond it the sky was paler, fresher. "Have another, gentlemen," he said, filling his glass again. The others helped themselves moderately. "Up at school they consider it better to go down than to hedge," he said. They watched him drink that one. They saw his nostrils bead suddenly with sweat.

"That's all for him, too," Doc said.

"Who says so?" Gowan said. He poured an inch into the glass. "If we just had some decent liquor. I know a man in my county named Goodwin that makes——"

"That's what they call a drink up at school," Doc said.

Gowan looked at him. "Do you think so? Watch this." He poured into the glass. They watched the liquor rise.

"Look out, fellow," the third said. Gowan filled the glass level full and lifted it and emptied it steadily. He remembered setting the glass down carefully, then he became aware simultaneously of open air, of a chill gray freshness and an engine panting on a siding at the head of a dark string of cars, and that he was trying to tell someone that he had learned to drink like a gentleman. He was still trying to tell them, in a cramped dark place smelling of ammonia and creosote, vomiting into a receptacle, trying to tell them that he must be at Taylor at six-thirty, when the special arrived. The paroxysm passed; he felt extreme lassitude, weakness, a desire to lie down which was forcibly restrained, and in the flare of a match he leaned against the wall, his eyes focussing slowly upon a name written there in pencil. He shut one eye, propped against the wall, swaying and drooling, and read the name. Then he looked at them, wagging his head.

"Girl name. . . . . . Name girl I know. Good girl. Good sport. Got date take her to Stark. . . . . . Starkville. No chap'rone, see?" Leaning there, drooling, mumbling, he went to sleep.

At once he began to fight himself out of sleep. It seemed to him that it was immediately, yet he was aware of time passing all the while, and that time was a factor in his need to wake; that otherwise he would be sorry. For a long while he knew that his eyes were open, waiting for vision to return. Then he was seeing again, without knowing at once that he was awake.

He lay quite still. It seemed to him that, by breaking out of sleep, he had accomplished the purpose that he had waked himself for. He was lying in a cramped position under a low canopy, looking at the front of an unfamiliar building above which small clouds rosy with sunlight drove, quite empty of any sense. Then his abdominal muscles completed the retch upon which he had lost consciousness and he heaved himself up and sprawled into the foot of the car, banging his head on the door. The blow fetched him completely to and he opened the door and half fell to the ground and dragged himself up and turned toward the station at a stumbling run. He fell. On hands and knees he looked at the empty siding and up at the sunfilled sky with unbelief and despair. He rose and ran on, in his stained dinner jacket, his burst collar and broken hair. I passed out, he thought in a kind of rage, I passed out. *I passed out.*

The platform was deserted save for a negro with a broom. "Gret Gawd, white folks," he said.

"The train," Gowan said, "the special. The one that was on that track."

"Hit done lef. Bout five minutes ago." With the broom still in the arrested gesture of sweeping he watched Gowan turn and run back to the car and tumble into it.

The jar lay on the floor. He kicked it aside and started the engine. He knew that he needed something on his stomach, but there wasn't time. He looked down at the jar. His inside coiled coldly, but he raised the jar and drank, guzzling, choking the stuff down, clapping a cigarette into his mouth to restrain the paroxysm. Almost at once he felt better.

He crossed the square at forty miles an hour. It was six-fifteen. He took the Taylor road, increasing speed. He drank again from the jar without slowing down. When he reached Taylor the train was just pulling out of the station. He slammed in between two wagons as the last car passed. The vestibule opened; Temple sprang down and ran for a few steps beside the car while an official leaned down and shook his fist at her.

Gowan had got out. She turned and came toward him, walking swiftly. Then she paused, stopped, came on again, staring at his wild face and hair, at his ruined collar and shirt.

"You're drunk," she said. "You pig. You filthy pig."

"Had a big night. You dont know the half of it."

She looked about, at the bleak yellow station, the overalled men chewing slowly and watching her, down the track at the diminishing train, at the four puffs of vapor that had almost died away when the sound of the whistle came back. "You filthy pig," she said. "You cant go anywhere like this. You haven't even changed clothes." At the car she stopped again. "What's that behind you?"

"My canteen," Gowan said. "Get in."

She looked at him, her mouth boldly scarlet, her eyes watchful and cold beneath her brimless hat, a curled spill of red hair. She looked back at the station again, stark and ugly in the fresh morning. She sprang in, tucking her legs under her. "Let's get away from here." He started the car and turned it. "You'd better take me back to Oxford," she said. She looked back at the station. It now lay in shadow, in the shadow of a high scudding cloud. "You'd better," she said.

At two oclock that afternoon, running at good speed through a high murmurous desolation of pines, Gowan swung the car from the gravel into a narrow road between eroded banks, descending toward a bottom of cypress and gum. He wore a cheap blue workshirt beneath his dinner jacket. His eyes were bloodshot, puffed, his jowls covered by blue stubble, and looking at him, braced and clinging as the car leaped and bounced in the worn ruts, Temple thought His whiskers have grown since we left Dumfries. It was hair-oil he drank. He bought a bottle of hair-oil at Dumfries and drank it.

He looked at her, feeling her eyes. "Dont get your back up, now. It wont take a minute to run up to Goodwin's and get a bottle. It wont take ten minutes. I said I'd get you to Starkville before the train does, and I will. Dont you believe me?"

She said nothing, thinking of the pennant-draped train already in Starkville; of the colorful stands; the band, the yawning glitter of the bass horn; the green diamond dotted with players, crouching, uttering short, yelping cries like marsh-fowl disturbed by an alligator, not certain of where the danger is, motionless, poised, encouraging one another with short meaningless cries, plaintive, wary and forlorn.

"Trying to come over me with your innocent ways. Dont think I spent last night with a couple of your barber-shop jellies for nothing. Dont think I fed them my liquor just because I'm bighearted. You're pretty good, aren't you? Think you can play around all week with any badger-trimmed hick that owns a ford, and fool me on Saturday, dont you? Dont think I didn't see your name where it's written on that lavatory wall. Dont you believe me?"

She said nothing, bracing herself as the car lurched from one bank to the other of the cut, going too fast. He was still watching her, making no effort to steer it.

"By God, I want to see the woman that can——" The road flattened into sand, arched completely over, walled completely by a jungle of cane and brier. The car lurched from side to side in the loose ruts.

She saw the tree blocking the road, but she only braced herself anew. It seemed to her to be the logical and disastrous end to the train of circumstance in which she had become involved. She sat and watched rigidly and quietly as Gowan, apparently looking straight ahead, drove into the tree at twenty miles an hour. The car struck, bounded back, then drove into the tree again and turned onto its side.

She felt herself flying through the air, carrying a numbing shock upon her shoulder and a picture of two men peering from the fringe of cane at the roadside. She scrambled to her feet, her head reverted, and saw them step into the road, the one in a suit of tight black and a straw hat, smoking a cigarette, the other bareheaded, in overalls, carrying a shotgun, his bearded face gaped in slow astonishment. Still running her bones turned to water and she fell flat on her face, still running.

Without stopping she whirled and sat up, her mouth open upon a soundless wail behind her lost breath. The man in overalls was still looking at her, his mouth open in innocent astonishment within a short soft beard. The other man was leaning over the upturned car, his tight coat ridged across his shoulders. Then the engine ceased, though the lifted front wheel continued to spin idly, slowing.

V

THE MAN in overalls was barefoot also. He walked ahead of Temple and Gowan, the shotgun swinging in his hand, his splay feet apparently effortless in the sand into which Temple sank almost to the ankle at each step. From time to time he looked over his shoulder at them, at Gowan's bloody face and splotched clothes, at Temple struggling and lurching on her high heels.

"Putty hard walkin, aint it?" he said. "Ef she'll take off them high heel shoes, she'll git along better."

"Will I?" Temple said. She stopped and stood on alternate legs, holding to Gowan, and removed her slippers. The man watched her, looking at the slippers.

"Durn ef I could git ere two of my fingers into one of them things," he said. "Kin I look at em?" She gave him one. He turned it slowly in his hand. "Durn my hide," he said. He looked at Temple again with his pale, empty gaze. His hair grew innocent and straw-like, bleached on the crown, darkening about his ears and neck in untidy curls. "She's a right tall gal, too," he said. "With them skinny legs of hern. How much she weigh?" Temple extended her hand. He returned the slipper slowly, looking at her, at her belly and loins. "He aint laid no crop by yit, has he?"

"Come on," Gowan said, "let's get going. We've got to get a car and get back to Jefferson by night."

When the sand ceased Temple sat down and put her slippers on. She found the man watching her lifted thigh and she jerked her skirt down and sprang up. "Well," she said, "go on. Dont you know the way?"

The house came into sight, above the cedar grove beyond whose black interstices an apple orchard flaunted in the sunny afternoon. It was set in a ruined lawn, surrounded by abandoned grounds and fallen outbuildings. But nowhere was any sign of husbandry—plow or tool; in no direction was a planted field in sight—only a gaunt weather-stained ruin in a sombre grove through which the breeze drew with a sad, murmurous sound. Temple stopped.

"I dont want to go there," she said. "You go on and get the car," she told the man. "We'll wait here."

"He said fer y'all to come on to the house," the man said.

"Who did?" Temple said. "Does that black man think he can tell me what to do?"

"Ah, come on," Gowan said. "Let's see Goodwin and get a car. It's getting late. Mrs Goodwin's here, isn't she?"

"Hit's likely," the man said.

"Come on," Gowan said. They went on to the house. The man mounted to the porch and set the shotgun just inside the door.

"She's around somewher," he said. He looked at Temple again. "Hit aint no cause fer yo wife to fret," he said. "Lee'll git you to town, I reckon."

Temple looked at him. They looked at one another soberly, like two children or two dogs. "What's your name?"

"My name's Tawmmy," he said. "Hit aint no need to fret."

The hall was open through the house. She entered.

"Where you going?" Gowan said. "Why dont you wait out here?" She didn't answer. She went on down the hall. Behind her she could hear Gowan's and the man's voices. The back porch lay in sunlight, a segment of sunlight framed by the door. Beyond, she could see a weed-choked slope and a huge barn, broken-backed, tranquil in sunny desolation. To the right of the door she could see the corner either of a detached building or of a wing of the house. But she could hear no sound save the voices from the front.

She went on, slowly. Then she stopped. On the square of sunlight framed by the door lay the shadow of a man's head, and she half spun, poised with running. But the shadow wore no hat, so she turned and on tiptoe she went to the door and peered around it. A man sat in a splint-bottom chair, in the sunlight, the back of his bald, white-fringed head toward her, his hands crossed on the head of a rough stick. She emerged onto the back porch.

"Good afternoon," she said. The man did not move. She advanced again, then she glanced quickly over her shoulder. With the tail of her eye she thought she had seen a thread of smoke drift out the door in the detached room where the porch made an L, but it was gone. From a line between two posts in front of this door three square cloths hung damp and limp, as though recently washed, and a woman's undergarment of faded pink silk. It had been washed until the lace resembled a ragged, fibre-like fraying of the cloth itself. It bore a patch of pale calico, neatly sewn. Temple looked at the old man again.

For an instant she thought that his eyes were closed, then she believed that he had no eyes at all, for between the lids two objects like dirty yellowish clay marbles were fixed. "Gowan," she whispered, then she wailed "Gowan!" and turned running, her head reverted, just as a voice spoke beyond the door where she had thought to have seen smoke:

"He cant hear you. What do you want?"

She whirled again and without a break in her stride and still watching the old man, she ran right off the porch and fetched up on hands and knees in a litter of ashes and tin cans and bleached bones, and saw Popeye watching her from the corner of the house, his hands in his pockets and a slanted cigarette curling across his face. Still without stopping she scrambled onto the porch and sprang into the kitchen, where a woman sat at a table, a burning cigarette in her hand, watching the door.

VI

Popeye went on around the house. Gowan was leaning over the edge of the porch, dabbing gingerly at his bloody nose. The barefooted man squatted on his heels against the wall.

"For Christ's sake," Popeye said, "why cant you take him out back and wash him off? Do you want him sitting around here all day looking like a damn hog with its throat cut?" He snapped the cigarette into the weeds and sat on the top step and began to scrape his muddy shoes with a platinum penknife on the end of his watch chain.

The barefoot man rose.

"You said something about——" Gowan said.

"Pssst!" the other said. He began to wink and frown at Gowan, jerking his head at Popeye's back.

"And then you get on back down that road," Popeye said. "You hear?"

"I thought you was fixin to watch down ther," the man said.

"Dont think," Popeye said, scraping at his trouser-cuffs. "You've got along forty years without it. You do what I told you."

When they reached the back porch the barefoot man said: "He jest caint stand fer nobody——Aint he a cur'us feller, now? I be dawg ef he aint better'n a circus to——He wont stand fer nobody drinkin hyer cep Lee. Wont drink none hisself, and jest let me take one sup and I be dawg ef hit dont look like he'll have a catfit."

"He said you were forty years old," Gowan said.

" 'Taint that much," the other said.

"How old are you? Thirty?"

"I dont know. 'Taint as much as he said, though." The old man sat in the chair, in the sun. "Hit's jest Pap," the man said. The azure shadow of the cedars had reached the old man's feet. It was almost up to his knees. His hand came out and fumbled about his knees, dabbling into the shadow, and became still, wrist-deep in shadow. Then he rose and grasped the chair and, tapping ahead with the stick, he bore directly down upon them in a shuffling rush, so that they had to step quickly aside. He dragged the chair into the full sunlight and sat down again, his face lifted into the sun, his hands crossed on the head of the stick. "That's Pap," the man said. "Blind and deef both. I be dawg ef I wouldn't hate to be in a fix wher I couldn't tell and wouldn't even keer whut I was eatin."

On a plank fixed between two posts sat a galvanised pail, a tin basin, a cracked dish containing a lump of yellow soap. "To hell with water," Gowan said. "How about that drink?"

"Seems to me like you done already had too much. I be dawg ef you didn't drive that ere car straight into that tree."

"Come on. Haven't you got some hid out somewhere?"

"Mought be a little in the barn. But dont let him hyear us, er he'll find hit and po hit out." He went back to the door and peered up the hall. Then they left the porch and went toward the barn, crossing what had once been a kitchen garden choked now with cedar and blackjack saplings. Twice the man looked back over his shoulder. The second time he said:

"Yon's yo wife wantin somethin."

Temple stood in the kitchen door. "Gowan," she called.

"Wave yo hand er somethin," the man said. "Ef she dont hush, he's goin to hyear us." Gowan flapped his hand. They went on and entered the barn. Beside the entrance a crude ladder mounted. "Better wait twell I git up," the man said. "Hit's putty rotten; mought not hold us both."

"Why dont you fix it, then? Dont you use it everyday?"

"Hit's helt all right, so fur," the other said. He mounted. Then Gowan followed, through the trap, into yellow-barred gloom where the level sun fell through the broken walls and roof. "Walk wher I do," the man said. "You'll tromp on a loose boa'd and find yoself downstairs befo you know hit." He picked his way across the floor and dug an earthenware jug from a pile of rotting hay in the corner. "One place he wont look fer hit," he said. "Skeered of sp'ilin them gal's hands of hisn."

They drank. "I've seen you out hyer befo," the man said. "Caint call yo name, though."

"My name's Stevens. I've been buying liquor from Lee for three years. When'll he be back? We've got to get on to town."

"He'll be hyer soon. I've seen you befo. Nother feller fum Jefferson out hyer three-fo nights ago. I caint call his name neither. He sho was a talker, now. Kep on tellin how he up and quit his wife. Have some mo," he said; then he ceased and squatted slowly, the jug in his lifted hands, his head bent with listening. After a moment the voice spoke again, from the hallway beneath.

"Jack."

The man looked at Gowan. His jaw dropped into an expression of imbecile glee. What teeth he had were stained and ragged within his soft, tawny beard.

"You, Jack, up there," the voice said.

"Hyear him?" the man whispered, shaking with silent glee. "Callin me Jack. My name's Tawmmy."

"Come on," the voice said. "I know you're there."

"I reckon we better," Tommy said. "He jest lief take a shot up through the flo as not."

"For Christ's sake," Gowan said, "why didn't you—— Here," he shouted, "here we come!"

Popeye stood in the door, his forefingers in his vest. The sun had set. When they descended and appeared in the door Temple stepped from the back porch. She paused, watching them, then she came down the hill. She began to run.

"Didn't I tell you to get on down that road?" Popeye said.

"Me an him jest stepped down hyer a minute," Tommy said.

"Did I tell you to get on down that road, or didn't I?"

"Yeuh," Tommy said. "You told me." Popeye turned without so much as a glance at Gowan. Tommy followed. His back still shook with secret glee. Temple met Popeye halfway to the house. Without ceasing to run she appeared to pause. Even her flapping coat did not overtake her, yet for an appreciable instant she faced Popeye with a grimace of taut, toothed coquetry. He did not stop; the finicking swagger of his narrow back did not falter. Temple ran again. She passed Tommy and clutched Gowan's arm.

"Gowan, I'm scared. She said for me not to——You've been drinking again; you haven't even washed the blood—— She says for us to go away from here. . . . . . ." Her eyes were quite black, her face small and wan in the dusk. She looked toward the house. Popeye was just turning the corner. "She has to walk all the way to a spring for water; she—— They've got the cutest little baby in a box behind the stove. Gowan, she said for me not to be here after dark. She said to ask him. He's got a car. She said she didn't think he——"

"Ask who?" Gowan said. Tommy was looking back at them. Then he went on.

"That black man. She said she didn't think he would, but he might. Come on." They went toward the house. A path led around it to the front. The car was parked between the path and the house, in the tall weeds. Temple faced Gowan again, her hand lying upon the door of the car. "It wont take him any time, in this. I know a boy at home has one. It will run eighty. All he would have to do is just drive us to a town, because she said if we were married and I had to say we were. Just to a railroad. Maybe there's one closer than Jefferson," she whispered, staring at him, stroking her hand along the edge of the door.

"Oh," Gowan said, "I'm to do the asking. Is that it? You're all nuts. Do you think that ape will? I'd rather stay here a week than go anywhere with him."

"She said to. She said for me not to stay here."

"You're crazy as a loon. Come on here."

"You wont ask him? You wont do it?"

"No. Wait till Lee comes, I tell you. He'll get us a car."

They went on in the path. Popeye was leaning against a post, lighting a cigarette. Temple ran on up the broken steps. "Say," she said, "dont you want to drive us to town?"

He turned his head, the cigarette in his mouth, the match cupped between his hands. Temple's mouth was fixed in that cringing grimace. Popeye leaned the cigarette to the match. "No," he said.

"Come on," Temple said. "Be a sport. It wont take you any time in that Packard. How about it? We'll pay you."

Popeye inhaled. He snapped the match into the weeds. He said, in his soft, cold voice: "Make your whore lay off of me, Jack."

Gowan moved thickly, like a clumsy, good-tempered horse goaded suddenly. "Look here, now," he said. Popeye exhaled, the smoke jetting downward in two thin spurts. "I dont like that," Gowan said. "Do you know who you're talking to?" He continued that thick movement, like he could neither stop it nor complete it. "I dont like that." Popeye turned his head and looked at Gowan. Then he quit looking at him and Temple said suddenly:

"What river did you fall in with that suit on? Do you have to shave it off at night?" Then she was moving toward the door with Gowan's hand in the small of her back, her head reverted, her heels clattering. Popeye leaned motionless against the post, his head turned over his shoulder in profile.

"Do you want——" Gowan hissed.

"You mean old thing!" Temple cried. "You mean old thing!"

Gowan shoved her into the house. "Do you want him to slam your damn head off?" he said.

"You're scared of him!" Temple said. "You're scared!"

"Shut your mouth!" Gowan said. He began to shake her. Their feet scraped on the bare floor as though they were performing a clumsy dance, and clinging together they lurched into the wall. "Look out," he said, "you're getting all that stuff stirred up in me again." She broke free, running. He leaned against the wall and watched her in silhouette run out the back door.

She ran into the kitchen. It was dark save for a crack of light about the fire-door of the stove. She whirled and ran out the door and saw Gowan going down the hill toward the barn. He's going to drink some more, she thought; he's getting drunk again. That makes three times today. Still more dusk had grown in the hall. She stood on tiptoe, listening, thinking I'm hungry. I haven't eaten all day; thinking of the school, the lighted windows, the slow couples strolling toward the sound of the supper bell, and of her father sitting on the porch at home, his feet on the rail, watching a negro mow the lawn. She moved quietly on tiptoe. In the corner beside the door the shotgun leaned and she crowded into the corner beside it and began to cry.

Immediately she stopped and ceased breathing. Something was moving beyond the wall against which she leaned. It crossed the room with minute, blundering sounds, preceded by a dry tapping. It emerged into the hall and she screamed, feeling her lungs emptying long after all the air was expelled, and her diaphragm laboring long after her chest was empty, and watched the old man go down the hall at a wide-legged shuffling trot, the stick in one hand and the other elbow cocked at an acute angle from his middle. Running, she passed him—a dim, spraddled figure standing at the edge of the porch—and ran on into the kitchen and darted into the corner behind the stove. Crouching she drew the box out and drew it before her. Her hand touched the child's face, then she flung her arms around the box, clutching it, staring across it at the pale door and trying to pray. But she could not think of a single designation for the heavenly father, so she began to say "My father's a judge; my father's a judge" over and over until Goodwin ran lightly into the room. He struck a match and held it overhead and looked down at her until the flame reached his fingers.

"Hah," he said. She heard his light, swift feet twice, then his hand touched her cheek and he lifted her from behind the box by the scruff of the neck, like a kitten. "What are you doing in my house?" he said.

VII

F ROM SOMEWHERE beyond the lamplit hall she could hear the voices—a word; now and then a laugh: the harsh, derisive laugh of a man easily brought to mirth by youth or by age, cutting across the spluttering of frying meat on the stove where the woman stood. Once she heard two of them come down the hall in their heavy shoes, and a moment later the clatter of the dipper in the galvanised pail and the voice that had laughed, cursing. Holding her coat close she peered around the door with the wide, abashed curiosity of a child, and saw Gowan and a second man in khaki breeches. He's getting drunk again, she thought. He's got drunk four times since we left Taylor.

"Is he your brother?" she said.

"Who?" the woman said. "My what?" she turned the meat on the hissing skillet.

"I thought maybe your young brother was here."

"God," the woman said. She turned the meat with a wire fork. "I hope not."

"Where is your brother?" Temple said, peering around the door. "I've got four brothers. Two are lawyers and one's a newspaper man. The other's still in school. At Yale. My father's a judge. Judge Drake of Jackson." She thought of her father sitting on the veranda, in a linen suit, a palm leaf fan in his hand, watching the negro mow the lawn.

The woman opened the oven and looked in. "Nobody asked you to come out here. I didn't ask you to stay. I told you to go while it was daylight."

"How could I? I asked him. Gowan wouldn't, so I had to ask him."

The woman closed the oven and turned and looked at Temple, her back to the light. "How could you? Do you know how I get my water? I walk after it. A mile. Six times a day. Add that up. Not because I am somewhere I am afraid to stay." She went to the table and took up a pack of cigarettes and shook one out.

"May I have one?" Temple said. The woman flipped the pack along the table. She removed the chimney from the lamp

and lit hers at the wick. Temple took up the pack and stood
listening to Gowan and the other man go back into the
house. "There are so many of them," she said in a wailing
tone, watching the cigarette crush slowly in her fingers. "But
maybe, with so many of them. . . . . . ." The woman had
gone back to the stove. She turned the meat. "Gowan kept
on getting drunk again. He got drunk three times today. He
was drunk when I got off the train at Taylor and I am on
probation and I told him what would happen and I tried to
get him to throw the jar away and when we stopped at that
little country store to buy a shirt he got drunk again. And so
we hadn't eaten and we stopped at Dumfries and he went
into the restaurant but I was too worried to eat and I couldn't
find him and then he came up another street and I felt the
bottle in his pocket before he knocked my hand away. He
kept on saying I had his lighter and then when he lost it and
I told him he had, he swore he never owned one in his life."

The meat hissed and spluttered in the skillet. "He got
drunk three separate times," Temple said. "Three separate
times in one day. Buddy—that's Hubert, my youngest
brother—said that if he ever caught me with a drunk man,
he'd beat hell out of me. And now I'm with one that gets
drunk three times in one day." Leaning her hip against the
table, her hand crushing the cigarette, she began to laugh.
"Dont you think that's funny?" she said. Then she quit laughing by holding her breath, and she could hear the faint gut-
tering the lamp made, and the meat in the skillet and the
hissing of the kettle on the stove, and the voices, the harsh,
abrupt, meaningless masculine sounds from the house. "And
you have to cook for all of them every night. All those men
eating here, the house full of them at night, in the
dark. . . . . . ." She dropped the crushed cigarette. "May I
hold the baby? I know how; I'll hold him good." She ran to
the box, stooping, and lifted the sleeping child. It opened its
eyes, whimpering. "Now, now; Temple's got it." She rocked
it, held high and awkward in her thin arms. "Listen," she
said, looking at the woman's back, " will you ask him? your
husband, I mean. He can get a car and take me somewhere.
Will you? Will you ask him?" The child had stopped whimpering. Its lead-colored eyelids showed a thin line of eyeball.

"I'm not afraid," Temple said. "Things like that dont happen. Do they? They're just like other people. You're just like other people. With a little baby. And besides, my father's a ju-judge. The gu-governor comes to our house to e-eat—— What a cute little bu-ba-a-by," she wailed, lifting the child to her face; "if bad mans hurts Temple, us'll tell the governor's soldiers, wont us?"

"Like what people?" the woman said, turning the meat. "Do you think Lee hasn't anything better to do than chase after every one of you cheap little——" She opened the fire door and threw her cigarette in and slammed the door. In nuzzling at the child Temple had pushed her hat onto the back of her head at a precarious dissolute angle above her clotted curls. "Why did you come here?"

"It was Gowan. I begged him. We had already missed the ball game, but I begged him if he'd just get me to Starkville before the special started back, they wouldn't know I wasn't on it, because the ones that saw me get off wouldn't tell. But he wouldn't. He said we'd stop here just a minute and get some more whiskey and he was already drunk then. He had gotten drunk again since we left Taylor and I'm on probation and Daddy would just die. But he wouldn't do it. He got drunk again while I was begging him to take me to a town anywhere and let me out."

"On probation?" the woman said.

"For slipping out at night. Because only town boys can have cars, and when you had a date with a town boy on Friday or Saturday or Sunday, the boys in school wouldn't have a date with you, because they cant have cars. So I had to slip out. And a girl that didn't like me told the Dean, because I had a date with a boy she liked and he never asked her for another date. So I had to."

"If you didn't slip out, you wouldn't get to go riding," the woman said. "Is that it? And now when you slipped out once too often, you're squealing."

"Gowan's not a town boy. He's from Jefferson. He went to Virginia. He kept on saying how they had taught him to drink like a gentleman, and I begged him just to let me out anywhere and lend me enough money for a ticket because I only had two dollars, but he——"

"Oh, I know your sort," the woman said. "Honest women. Too good to have anything to do with common people. You'll slip out at night with the kids, but just let a man come along." She turned the meat. "Take all you can get, and give nothing. 'I'm a pure girl; I dont do that'. You'll slip out with the kids and burn their gasoline and eat their food, but just let a man so much as look at you and you faint away because your father the judge and your four brothers might not like it. But just let you get into a jam, then who do you come crying to? to us, the ones that are not good enough to lace the judge's almighty shoes." Across the child Temple gazed at the woman's back, her face like a small pale mask beneath the precarious hat.

"My brother said he would kill Frank. He didn't say he would give me a whipping if he caught me with him; he said he would kill the goddam son of a bitch in his yellow buggy and my father cursed my brother and said he could run his family a while longer and he drove me into the house and locked me in and went down to the bridge to wait for Frank. But I wasn't a coward. I climbed down the gutter and headed Frank off and told him. I begged him to go away, but he said we'd both go. When we got back in the buggy I knew it had been the last time. I knew it, and I begged him again to go away, but he said he'd drive me home to get my suit case and we'd tell father. He wasn't a coward either. My father was sitting on the porch. He said 'Get out of that buggy' and I got out and I begged Frank to go on, but he got out too and we came up the path and father reached around inside the door and got the shotgun. I got in front of Frank and father said 'Do you want it too?' and I tried to stay in front but Frank shoved me behind him and held me and father shot him and said 'Get down there and sup your dirt, you whore'."

"I have been called that," Temple whispered, holding the sleeping child in her high thin arms, gazing at the woman's back.

"But you good women. Cheap sports. Giving nothing, then when you're caught. . . . . . . Do you know what you've got into now?" she looked across her shoulder, the fork in her hand. "Do you think you're meeting kids now? kids that give a damn whether you like it or not? Let me tell you whose house you've come into without being asked or wanted; who you're expecting to drop everything and carry you back where you had no business ever leaving. When he was a soldier in the Philippines he killed another soldier over one of those nigger women and they sent him to Leavenworth. Then the war came and they let him out to go to it. He got two medals, and when it was over they put him back in Leavenworth until the lawyer got a congressman to get him out. Then I could quit jazzing again——"

"Jazzing?" Temple whispered, holding the child, looking herself no more than an elongated and leggy infant in her scant dress and uptilted hat.

"Yes, putty-face!" the woman said. "How do you suppose I paid that lawyer? And that's the sort of man you think will care that much——" with the fork in her hand she came and snapped her fingers softly and viciously in Temple's face "——what happens to you. And you, you little doll-faced slut, that think you cant come into a room where a man is without him. . . . . . ." Beneath the faded garment her breast moved deep and full. With her hands on her hips she looked at Temple with cold, blazing eyes. "Man? You've never seen a real man. You dont know what it is to be wanted by a real man. And thank your stars you haven't and never will, for then you'd find just what that little putty face is worth, and all the rest of it you think you are jealous of when you're just scared of it. And if he is just man enough to call you whore, you'll say Yes Yes and you'll crawl naked in the dirt and the mire for him to call you that. . . . . . Give me that baby." Temple held the child, gazing at the woman, her mouth moving as if she were saying Yes Yes Yes. The woman threw the fork onto the table. "Turn loose," she said, lifting the child. It opened its eyes and wailed. The woman drew a chair out and sat down, the child upon her lap. "Will you hand me one of those diapers on the line yonder?" she said. Temple stood in the floor, her lips still moving. "You're scared to go out there, aren't you?" the woman said. She rose.

"No," Temple said; "I'll get——"

"I'll get it." The unlaced brogans scuffed across the kitchen. She returned and drew another chair up to the stove and spread the two remaining cloths and the undergarment on it, and sat again and laid the child across her lap. It wailed. "Hush," she said, "hush, now," her face in the lamplight taking a serene, brooding quality. She changed the child and laid it in the box. Then she took a platter down from a cupboard curtained by a split towsack and took up the fork and came and looked into Temple's face again.

"Listen. If I get a car for you, will you get out of here?" she said. Staring at her Temple moved her mouth as though she were experimenting with words, tasting them. "Will you go out the back and get into it and go away and never come back here?"

"Yes," Temple whispered, "anywhere. Anything."

Without seeming to move her cold eyes at all the woman looked Temple up and down. Temple could feel all her muscles shrinking like severed vines in the noon sun. "You poor little gutless fool," the woman said in her cold undertone. "Playing at it."

"I didn't. I didn't."

"You'll have something to tell them now, when you get back. Wont you?" Face to face, their voices were like shadows upon two close blank walls. "Playing at it."

"Anything. Just so I get away. Anywhere."

"It's not Lee I'm afraid of. Do you think he plays the dog after every hot little bitch that comes along? It's you."

"Yes. I'll go anywhere."

"I know your sort. I've seen them. All running, but not too fast. Not so fast you cant tell a real man when you see him. Do you think you've got the only one in the world?"

"Gowan," Temple whispered, "Gowan."

"I have slaved for that man," the woman whispered, her lips scarce moving, in her still, dispassionate voice. It was as though she were reciting a formula for bread. "I worked night shift as a waitress so I could see him Sundays at the prison. I lived two years in a single room, cooking over a gas-jet, because I promised him. I lied to him and made money to get him out of prison, and when I told him how I made it, he beat me. And now you must come here where you're not wanted. Nobody asked you to come here. Nobody cares whether you are afraid or not. Afraid? You haven't the guts to be really afraid, anymore than you have to be in love."

"I'll pay you," Temple whispered. "Anything you say. My father will give it to me." The woman watched her, her face motionless, as rigid as when she had been speaking. "I'll send you clothes. I have a new fur coat. I just wore it since Christmas. It's as good as new."

The woman laughed. Her mouth laughed, with no sound, no movement of her face. "Clothes? I had three fur coats once. I gave one of them to a woman in an alley by a saloon. Clothes? God." She turned suddenly. "I'll get a car. You get away from here and dont you ever come back. Do you hear?"

"Yes," Temple whispered. Motionless, pale, like a sleepwalker she watched the woman transfer the meat to the platter and pour the gravy over it. From the oven she took a pan of biscuits and put them on a plate. "Can I help you?" Temple whispered. The woman said nothing. She took up the two plates and went out. Temple went to the table and took a cigarette from the pack and stood staring stupidly at the lamp. One side of the chimney was blackened. Across it a crack ran in a thin silver curve. The lamp was of tin, coated about the neck with dirty grease. She lit hers at the lamp, someway, Temple thought, holding the cigarette in her hand, staring at the uneven flame. The woman returned. She caught up the corner of her skirt and lifted the smutty coffee-pot from the stove.

"Can I take that?" Temple said.

"No. Come on and get your supper." She went out.

Temple stood at the table, the cigarette in her hand. The shadow of the stove fell upon the box where the child lay. Upon the lumpy wad of bedding it could be distinguished only by a series of pale shadows in soft small curves, and she went and stood over the box and looked down at its putty-colored face and bluish eyelids. A thin whisper of shadow cupped its head and lay moist upon its brow; one thin arm, upflung, lay curl-palmed beside its cheek. Temple stooped above the box.

"He's going to die," Temple whispered. Bending, her shadow loomed high upon the wall, her coat shapeless, her hat tilted monstrously above a monstrous escaping of hair. "Poor little baby," she whispered, "poor little baby." The men's voices grew louder. She heard a trampling of feet in the hall, a rasping of chairs, the voice of the man who had laughed above them, laughing again. She turned, motionless again, watching the door. The woman entered.

"Go and eat your supper," she said.

"The car," Temple said. "I could go now, while they're eating."

"What car?" the woman said. "Go on and eat. Nobody's going to hurt you."

"I'm not hungry. I haven't eaten today. I'm not hungry at all."

"Go and eat your supper," she said.

"I'll wait and eat when you do."

"Go on and eat your supper. I've got to get done here some time tonight."

VIII

T<small>EMPLE ENTERED</small> the dining-room from the kitchen, her face fixed in a cringing, placative expression; she was quite blind when she entered, holding her coat about her, her hat thrust upward and back at that dissolute angle. After a moment she saw Tommy. She went straight toward him, as if she had been looking for him all the while. Something intervened: a hard forearm; she attempted to evade it, looking at Tommy.

"Here," Gowan said across the table, his chair rasping back, "you come around here."

"Outside, brother," the one who had stopped her said, whom she recognised then as the one who had laughed so often; "you're drunk. Come here, kid." His hard forearm came across her middle. She thrust against it, grinning rigidly at Tommy. "Move down, Tommy," the man said. "Aint you got no manners, you mat-faced bastard?" Tommy guffawed, scraping his chair along the floor. The man drew her toward him by the wrist. Across the table Gowan stood up, propping himself on the table. She began to resist, grinning at Tommy, picking at the man's fingers.

"Quit that, Van," Goodwin said.

"Right on my lap here," Van said.

"Let her go," Goodwin said.

"Who'll make me?" Van said. "Who's big enough?"

"Let her go," Goodwin said. Then she was free. She began to back slowly away. Behind her the woman, entering with a dish, stepped aside. Still smiling her aching, rigid grimace Temple backed from the room. In the hall she whirled and ran. She ran right off the porch, into the weeds, and sped on. She ran to the road and down it for fifty yards in the darkness, then without a break she whirled and ran back to the house and sprang onto the porch and crouched against the door just as someone came up the hall. It was Tommy.

"Oh, hyer you are," he said. He thrust something awkwardly at her. "Hyer," he said.

"What is it?" she whispered.

"Little bite of victuals. I bet you aint et since mawnin."

"No. Not then, even," she whispered.

"You eat a little mite and you'll feel better," he said, poking the plate at her. "You set down hyer and eat a little bite wher wont nobody bother you. Durn them fellers."

Temple leaned around the door, past his dim shape, her face wan as a small ghost in the refracted light from the dining-room. "Mrs——Mrs. . . . . . ." she whispered.

"She's in the kitchen. Want me to go back there with you?" In the dining-room a chair scraped. Between blinks Tommy saw Temple in the path, her body slender and motionless for a moment as though waiting for some laggard part to catch up. Then she was gone like a shadow around the corner of the house. He stood in the door, the plate of food in his hand. Then he turned his head and looked down the hall just in time to see her flit across the darkness toward the kitchen. "Durn them fellers."

He was standing there when the others returned to the porch.

"He's got a plate of grub," Van said. "He's trying to get his with a plate full of ham."

"Git my whut?" Tommy said.

"Look here," Gowan said.

Van struck the plate from Tommy's hand. He turned to Gowan. "Dont you like it?"

"No," Gowan said, "I dont."

"What are you going to do about it?" Van said.

"Van," Goodwin said.

"Do you think you're big enough to not like it?" Van said.

"I am," Goodwin said.

When Van went back to the kitchen Tommy followed him. He stopped at the door and heard Van in the kitchen.

"Come for a walk, little bit," Van said.

"Get out of here, Van," the woman said.

"Come for a little walk," Van said. "I'm a good guy. Ruby'll tell you."

"Get out of here, now," the woman said. "Do you want me to call Lee?" Van stood against the light, in a khaki shirt and breeches, a cigarette behind his ear against the smooth sweep of his blond hair. Beyond him Temple stood behind the chair in which the woman sat at the table, her mouth open a little, her eyes quite black.

When Tommy went back to the porch with the jug he said to Goodwin: "Why dont them fellers quit pesterin that gal?"

"Who's pestering her?"

"Van is. She's skeered. Whyn't they leave her be?"

"It's none of your business. You keep out of it. You hear?"

"Them fellers ought to quit pesterin her," Tommy said. He squatted against the wall. They were drinking, passing the jug back and forth, talking. With the top of his mind he listened to them, to Van's gross and stupid tales of city life, with rapt interest, guffawing now and then, drinking in his turn. Van and Gowan were doing the talking, and Tommy listened to them. "Them two's fixin to have hit out with one another," he whispered to Goodwin in a chair beside him. "Hyear em?" They were talking quite loud; Goodwin moved swiftly and lightly from his chair, his feet striking the floor with light thuds; Tommy saw Van standing and Gowan holding himself erect by the back of his chair.

"I never meant——" Van said.

"Dont say it, then," Goodwin said.

Gowan said something. That durn feller, Tommy thought. Cant even talk no more.

"Shut up, you," Goodwin said.

"Think talk bout my——" Gowan said. He moved, swayed against the chair. It fell over. Gowan blundered into the wall.

"By God, I'll——" Van said.

"——ginia gentleman; I dont give a——" Gowan said. Goodwin flung him aside with a backhanded blow of his arm, and grasped Van. Gowan fell against the wall.

"When I say sit down, I mean it," Goodwin said.

After that they were quiet for a while. Goodwin returned to his chair. They began to talk again, passing the jug, and Tommy listened. But soon he began to think about Temple again. He would feel his feet scouring on the floor and his whole body writhing in an acute discomfort. "They ought to let that gal alone," he whispered to Goodwin. "They ought to quit pesterin her."

"It's none of your business," Goodwin said. "Let every damned one of them. . . . . . ."

"They ought to quit pesterin her."

Popeye came out the door. He lit a cigarette. Tommy watched his face flare out between his hands, his cheeks sucking; he followed with his eyes the small comet of the match into the weeds. Him too, he said. Two of em; his body writhing slowly. Pore little crittur. I be dawg ef I aint a mind to go down to the barn and stay there, I be dawg ef I aint. He rose, his feet making no sound on the porch. He stepped down into the path and went around the house. There was a light in the window there. Dont nobody never use in there, he said, stopping, then he said, That's where she'll be stayin, and he went to the window and looked in. The sash was down. Across a missing pane a sheet of rusted tin was nailed.

Temple was sitting on the bed, her legs tucked under her, erect, her hands lying in her lap, her hat tilted on the back of her head. She looked quite small, her very attitude an outrage to muscle and tissue of more than seventeen and more compatible with eight or ten, her elbows close to her sides, her face turned toward the door against which a chair was wedged. There was nothing in the room save the bed, with its faded patchwork quilt, and the chair. The walls had been plastered once, but the plaster had cracked and fallen in places, exposing the lathing and molded shreds of cloth. On the wall hung a raincoat and a khaki-covered canteen.

Temple's head began to move. It turned slowly, as if she were following the passage of someone beyond the wall. It turned on to an excruciating degree, though no other muscle moved, like one of those papier-mâché Easter toys filled with candy, and became motionless in that reverted position. Then it turned back, slowly, as though pacing invisible feet beyond the wall, back to the chair against the door and became motionless there for a moment. Then she faced forward and Tommy watched her take a tiny watch from the top of her stocking and look at it. With the watch in her hand she lifted her head and looked directly at him, her eyes calm and empty as two holes. After a while she looked down at the watch again and returned it to her stocking.

She rose from the bed and removed her coat and stood motionless, arrowlike in her scant dress, her head bent, her hands clasped before her. She sat on the bed again. She sat with her legs close together, her head bent. She raised her head and looked about the room. Tommy could hear the voices from the dark porch. They rose again, then sank to the steady murmur.

Temple sprang to her feet. She unfastened her dress, her arms arched thin and high, her shadow anticking her movements. In a single motion she was out of it, crouching a little, match-thin in her scant undergarments. Her head emerged facing the chair against the door. She hurled the dress away, her hand reaching for the coat. She scrabbled it up and swept it about her, pawing at the sleeves. Then, the coat clutched to her breast, she whirled and looked straight into Tommy's eyes and whirled and ran and flung herself upon the chair. "Durn them fellers," Tommy whispered, "durn them fellers." He could hear them on the front porch and his body began again to writhe slowly in an acute unhappiness. "Durn them fellers."

When he looked into the room again Temple was moving toward him, holding the coat about her. She took the raincoat from the nail and put it on over her own coat and fastened it. She lifted the canteen down and returned to the bed. She laid the canteen on the bed and picked her dress up from the floor and brushed it with her hand and folded it carefully and laid it on the bed. Then she turned back the quilt, exposing the mattress. There was no linen, no pillow, and when she touched the mattress it gave forth a faint dry whisper of shucks.

She removed her slippers and set them on the bed and got in beneath the quilt. Tommy could hear the mattress crackle. She didn't lie down at once. She sat upright, quite still, the hat tilted rakishly upon the back of her head. Then she moved the canteen, the dress and the slippers beside her head and drew the raincoat about her legs and lay down, drawing the quilt up, then she sat up and removed the hat and shook her hair out and laid the hat with the other garments and prepared to lie down again. Again she paused. She opened the raincoat and produced a compact from somewhere and, watching her motions in the tiny mirror, she spread and fluffed her hair with her fingers and powdered her face and replaced the compact and looked at the watch again and fastened the raincoat. She moved the garments one by one under the quilt and lay down and drew the quilt to her chin. The voices had got quiet for a moment and in the silence Tommy could hear a faint, steady chatter of the shucks inside the mattress where Temple lay, her hands crossed on her breast and her legs straight and close and decorous, like an effigy on an ancient tomb.

The voices were still; he had completely forgot them until he heard Goodwin say "Stop it. Stop that!" A chair crashed over; he heard Goodwin's light thudding feet; the chair clattered along the porch as though it had been kicked aside, and crouching, his elbows out a little in squat, bear-like alertness, Tommy heard dry, light sounds like billiard balls. "Tommy," Goodwin said.

When necessary he could move with that thick, lightning-like celerity of badgers or coons. He was around the house and on the porch in time to see Gowan slam into the wall and slump along it and plunge full length off the porch into the weeds, and Popeye in the door, his head thrust forward. "Grab him there!" Goodwin said. Tommy sprang upon Popeye in a sidling rush.

"I got—hah!" he said as Popeye slashed savagely at his face; "you would, would you? Hole up hyer."

Popeye ceased. "Jesus Christ. You let them sit around here all night, swilling that goddam stuff; I told you. Jesus Christ."

Goodwin and Van were a single shadow, locked and hushed and furious. "Let go!" Van shouted. "I'll kill——" Tommy sprang to them. They jammed Van against the wall and held him motionless.

"Got him?" Goodwin said.

"Yeuh. I got him. Hole up hyer. You done whupped him."

"By God, I'll——"

"Now, now; whut you want to kill him fer? You caint eat him, kin you? You want Mr Popeye to start guttin us all with that ere artermatic?"

Then it was over, gone like a furious gust of black wind, leaving a peaceful vacuum in which they moved quietly about, lifting Gowan out of the weeds with low-spoken, amicable directions to one another. They carried him into the hall, where the woman stood, and to the door of the room where Temple was.

"She's locked it," Van said. He struck the door, high. "Open the door," he shouted. "We're bringing you a customer."

"Hush," Goodwin said. "There's no lock on it. Push it."

"Sure," Van said; "I'll push it." He kicked it. The chair buckled and sprang into the room. Van banged the door open and they entered, carrying Gowan's legs. Van kicked the chair across the room. Then he saw Temple standing in the corner behind the bed. His hair was broken about his face, long as a girl's. He flung it back with a toss of his head. His chin was bloody and he deliberately spat blood onto the floor.

"Go on," Goodwin said, carrying Gowan's shoulders, "put him on the bed." They swung Gowan onto the bed. His bloody head lolled over the edge. Van jerked him over and slammed him into the mattress. He groaned, lifting his hand. Van struck him across the face with his palm.

"Lie still, you——"

"Let be," Goodwin said. He caught Van's hand. For an instant they glared at one another.

"I said, Let be," Goodwin said. "Get out of here."

"Got proteck. . . . . . ." Gowan muttered ". . . .girl. 'Ginia gem. . . . . . gemman got proteck. . . . . ."

"Get out of here, now," Goodwin said.

The woman stood in the door beside Tommy, her back against the door frame. Beneath a cheap coat her nightdress dropped to her feet.

Van lifted Temple's dress from the bed. "Van," Goodwin said. "I said get out."

"I heard you," Van said. He shook the dress out. Then he looked at Temple in the corner, her arms crossed, her hands clutching her shoulders. Goodwin moved toward Van. He dropped the dress and went around the bed. Popeye came in the door, a cigarette in his fingers. Beside the woman Tommy drew his breath hissing through his ragged teeth.

He saw Van take hold of the raincoat upon Temple's breast and rip it open. Then Goodwin sprang between them; he saw Van duck, whirling, and Temple fumbling at the torn raincoat. Van and Goodwin were now in the middle of the floor, swinging at one another, then he was watching Popeye walking toward Temple. With the corner of his eye he saw Van lying on the floor and Goodwin standing over him, stooped a little, watching Popeye's back.

"Popeye," Goodwin said. Popeye went on, the cigarette trailing back over his shoulder, his head turned a little as though he were not looking where he was going, the cigarette slanted as though his mouth were somewhere under the turn of his jaw. "Dont touch her," Goodwin said.

Popeye stopped before Temple, his face turned a little aside. His right hand lay in his coat pocket. Beneath the raincoat on Temple's breast Tommy could see the movement of the other hand, communicating a shadow of movement to the coat.

"Take your hand away," Goodwin said. "Move it."

Popeye moved his hand. He turned, his hands in his coat pockets, looking at Goodwin. He crossed the room, watching Goodwin. Then he turned his back on him and went out the door.

"Here, Tommy," Goodwin said quietly, "grab hold of this." They lifted Van and carried him out. The woman stepped aside. She leaned against the wall, holding her coat together. Across the room Temple stood crouched into the corner, fumbling at the torn raincoat. Gowan began to snore.

Goodwin returned. "You'd better go back to bed," he said. The woman didn't move. He put his hand on her shoulder. "Ruby."

"While you finish the trick Van started and you wouldn't let him finish? You poor fool. You poor fool."

"Come on, now," he said, his hand on her shoulder. "Go back to bed."

"But dont come back. Dont bother to come back. I wont be there. You owe me nothing. Dont think you do."

Goodwin took her wrists and drew them steadily apart. Slowly and steadily he carried her hands around behind her and held them in one of his. With the other hand he opened the coat. The nightdress was of faded pink crepe, lace-trimmed, laundered and laundered until, like the garment on the wire, the lace was a fibrous mass.

"Hah," he said. "Dressed for company."

"Whose fault is it if this is the only one I have? Whose fault is it? Not mine. I've given them away to nigger maids after one night. But do you think any nigger would take this and not laugh in my face?"

He let the coat fall to. He released her hands and she drew the coat together. With his hand on her shoulder he began to push her toward the door. "Go on," he said. Her shoulder gave. It alone moved, her body turning on her hips, her face reverted, watching him. "Go on," he said. But her torso alone turned, her hips and head still touching the wall. He turned and crossed the room and went swiftly around the bed and caught Temple by the front of the raincoat with one hand. He began to shake her. Holding her up by the gathered wad of coat he shook her, her small body clattering soundlessly inside the loose garment, her shoulders and thighs thumping against the wall. "You little fool!" he said. "You little fool!" Her eyes were quite wide, almost black, the lamplight on her face and two tiny reflections of his face in her pupils like peas in two inkwells.

He released her. She began to sink to the floor, the raincoat rustling about her. He caught her up and began to shake her again, looking over his shoulder at the woman. "Get the lamp," he said. The woman did not move. Her head was bent a little; she appeared to muse upon them. Goodwin swept his other arm under Temple's knees. She felt herself swooping, then she was lying on the bed beside Gowan, on her back, jouncing to the dying chatter of the shucks. She watched him cross the room and lift the lamp from the mantel. The woman had turned her head, following him also, her face sharpening out of the approaching lamp in profile. "Go on," he said. She turned, her face turning into shadow, the lamp now on her back and on his hand on her shoulder. His shadow blotted the room completely; his arm in silhouette backreaching, drew to the door. Gowan snored, each respiration choking to a huddle fall, as though he would never breathe again.

Tommy was outside the door, in the hall.

"They gone down to the truck yet?" Goodwin said.

"Not yit," Tommy said.

"Better go and see about it," Goodwin said. They went on. Tommy watched them enter another door. Then he went to the kitchen, silent on his bare feet, his neck craned a little with listening. In the kitchen Popeye sat, straddling a chair, smoking. Van stood at the table, before a fragment of mirror, combing his hair with a pocket comb. Upon the table lay a damp, bloodstained cloth and a burning cigarette. Tommy squatted outside the door, in the darkness.

He was there when Goodwin came out with the raincoat. Goodwin entered the kitchen without seeing him. "Where's Tommy?" he said. Tommy heard Popeye say something, then Goodwin emerged with Van following him, the raincoat on his arm now. "Come on, now," Goodwin said. "Let's get that stuff out of here."

Tommy's pale eyes began to glow faintly, like those of a cat. The woman could see them in the darkness when he crept into the room after Popeye, and while Popeye stood over the bed where Temple lay. They glowed suddenly out of the darkness at her, then they went away and she could hear him breathing beside her; again they glowed up at her with a quality furious and questioning and sad and went away again and he crept behind Popeye from the room.

He saw Popeye return to the kitchen, but he did not follow at once. He stopped at the hall door and squatted there. His body began to writhe again in shocked indecision, his bare feet whispering on the floor with a faint, rocking movement as he swayed from side to side, his hands wringing slowly against his flanks. And Lee too, he said, And Lee too. Durn them fellers. Durn them fellers. Twice he stole along the porch until he could see the shadow of Popeye's hat on the kitchen floor, then returned to the hall and the door beyond which Temple lay and where Gowan snored. The third time he smelled Popeye's cigarette. Ef he'll jest keep that up, he said. And Lee too, he said, rocking from side to side in a dull, excruciating agony, And Lee too.

When Goodwin came up the slope and onto the back porch Tommy was squatting just outside the door again. "What in hell——" Goodwin said. "Why didn't you come on? I've been looking for you for ten minutes." He glared at Tommy, then he looked into the kitchen. "You ready?" he said. Popeye came to the door. Goodwin looked at Tommy again. "What have you been doing?"

Popeye looked at Tommy. Tommy stood now, rubbing his instep with the other foot, looking at Popeye.

"What're you doing here?" Popeye said.

"Aint doin nothin," Tommy said.

"Are you following me around?"

"I aint trailin nobody," Tommy said sullenly.

"Well, dont, then," Popeye said.

"Come on," Goodwin said. "Van's waiting." They went on. Tommy followed them. Once he looked back at the house, then he shambled on behind them. From time to time he would feel that acute surge go over him, like his blood was too hot all of a sudden, dying away into that warm unhappy feeling that fiddle music gave him. Durn them fellers, he whispered, Durn them fellers.

IX

THE ROOM was dark. The woman stood inside the door, against the wall, in the cheap coat, the lace-trimmed crepe nightgown, just inside the lockless door. She could hear Gowan snoring in the bed, and the other men moving about, on the porch and in the hall and in the kitchen, talking, their voices indistinguishable through the door. After a while they got quiet. Then she could hear nothing at all save Gowan as he choked and snored and moaned through his battered nose and face.

She heard the door open. The man came in, without trying to be silent. He entered, passing within a foot of her. She knew it was Goodwin before he spoke. He went to the bed. "I want the raincoat," he said. "Sit up and take it off." The woman could hear the shucks in the mattress as Temple sat up and Goodwin took the raincoat off of her. He returned across the floor and went out.

She stood just inside the door. She could tell all of them by the way they breathed. Then, without having heard, felt, the door open, she began to smell something: the brilliantine which Popeye used on his hair. She did not see Popeye at all when he entered and passed her; she did not know he had entered yet; she was waiting for him; until Tommy entered, following Popeye. Tommy crept into the room, also sound-less; she would have been no more aware of his entrance than of Popeye's, if it hadn't been for his eyes. They glowed, breast-high, with a profound interrogation, then they disap-peared and the woman could then feel him, squatting beside her; she knew that he too was looking toward the bed over which Popeye stood in the darkness, upon which Temple and Gowan lay, with Gowan snoring and choking and snoring. The woman stood just inside the door.

She could hear no sound from the shucks, so she remained motionless beside the door, with Tommy squatting beside her, his face toward the invisible bed. Then she smelled the brilliantine again. Or rather, she felt Tommy move from be-side her, without a sound, as though the stealthy evacuation of his position blew soft and cold upon her in the black

234

silence; without seeing or hearing him, she knew that he had crept again from the room, following Popeye. She heard them go down the hall; the last sound died out of the house.

She went to the bed. Temple did not move until the woman touched her. Then she began to struggle. The woman found Temple's mouth and put her hand over it, though Temple had not attempted to scream. She lay on the shuck mattress, turning and thrashing her body from side to side, rolling her head, holding the coat together across her breast but making no sound.

"You fool!" the woman said in a thin, fierce whisper. "It's me. It's just me."

Temple ceased to roll her head, but she still thrashed from side to side beneath the woman's hand. "I'll tell my father!" she said. "I'll tell my father!"

The woman held her. "Get up," she said. Temple ceased to struggle. She lay still, rigid. The woman could hear her wild breathing. "Will you get up and walk quiet?" the woman said.

"Yes!" Temple said. "Will you get me out of here? Will you? Will you?"

"Yes," the woman said. "Get up." Temple got up, the shucks whispering. In the further darkness Gowan snored, savage and profound. At first Temple couldn't stand alone. The woman held her up. "Stop it," the woman said. "You've got to stop it. You've got to be quiet."

"I want my clothes," Temple whispered. "I haven't got anything on but. . . . . . ."

"Do you want your clothes," the woman said, "or do you want to get out of here?"

"Yes," Temple said. "Anything. If you'll just get me out of here."

On their bare feet they moved like ghosts. They left the house and crossed the porch and went on toward the barn. When they were about fifty yards from the house the woman stopped and turned and jerked Temple up to her, and gripping her by the shoulders, their faces close together, she cursed Temple in a whisper, a sound no louder than a sigh and filled with fury. Then she flung her away and they went on. They entered the hallway. It was pitch dark. Temple heard the woman fumbling at the wall. A door creaked open; the

woman took her arm and guided her up a single step into a
floored room where she could feel walls and smell a faint,
dusty odor of grain, and closed the door behind them. As she
did so something rushed invisibly nearby in a scurrying scrabble, a dying whisper of fairy feet. Temple whirled, treading
on something that rolled under her foot, and sprang toward
the woman.

"It's just a rat," the woman said, but Temple hurled herself
upon the other, flinging her arms about her, trying to snatch
both feet from the floor.

"A rat?" she wailed, "a rat? Open the door! Quick!"

"Stop it! Stop it!" the woman hissed. She held Temple until
she ceased. Then they knelt side by side against the wall. After
a while the woman whispered: "There's some cottonseed-
hulls over there. You can lie down." Temple didn't answer.
She crouched against the woman, shaking slowly, and they
squatted there in the black darkness, against the wall.

X

WHILE THE WOMAN was cooking breakfast, the child still—or already—asleep in the box behind the stove, she heard a blundering sound approaching across the porch and stop at the door. When she looked around she saw the wild and battered and bloody apparition which she recognised as Gowan. His face, beneath a two-days' stubble, was marked, his lip was cut. One eye was closed and the front of his shirt and coat were blood-stained to the waist. Through his swollen and stiffened lips he was trying to say something. At first the woman could not understand a word. "Go and bathe your face," she said. "Wait. Come in here and sit down. I'll get the basin."

He looked at her, trying to talk. "Oh," the woman said. "She's all right. She's down there in the crib, asleep." She had to repeat it three or four times, patiently. "In the crib. Asleep. I stayed with her until daylight. Go wash your face, now."

Gowan got a little calmer then. He began to talk about getting a car.

"The nearest one is at Tull's, two miles away," the woman said. "Wash your face and eat some breakfast."

Gowan entered the kitchen, talking about getting the car. "I'll get it and take her on back to school. One of the other girls will slip her in. It'll be all right then. Dont you think it'll be all right then?" He came to the table and took a cigarette from the pack and tried to light it with his shaking hands. He had trouble putting it into his mouth, and he could not light it at all until the woman came and held the match. But he took but one draw, then he stood, holding the cigarette in his hand, looking at it with his one good eye in a kind of dull amazement. He threw the cigarette away and turned toward the door, staggering and catching himself. "Go get car," he said.

"Get something to eat first," the woman said. "Maybe a cup of coffee will help you."

"Go get car," Gowan said. When he crossed the porch he paused long enough to splash some water upon his face, without helping his appearance much.

When he left the house he was still groggy and he thought that he was still drunk. He could remember only vaguely what had happened. He had got Van and the wreck confused and he did not know that he had been knocked out twice. He only remembered that he had passed out some time early in the night, and he thought that he was still drunk. But when he reached the wrecked car and saw the path and followed it to the spring and drank of the cold water, he found that it was a drink he wanted, and he knelt there, bathing his face in the cold water and trying to examine his reflection in the broken surface, whispering Jesus Christ to himself in a kind of despair. He thought about returning to the house for a drink, then he thought of having to face Temple, the men; of Temple there among them.

When he reached the highroad the sun was well up, warm. I'll get cleaned up some, he said. And coming back with a car. I'll decide what to say to her on the way to town; thinking of Temple returning among people who knew him, who might know him. I passed out twice, he said. *I passed out twice*. Jesus Christ, Jesus Christ he whispered, his body writhing inside his disreputable and bloody clothes in an agony of rage and shame.

His head began to clear with air and motion, but as he began to feel better physically the blackness of the future increased. Town, the world, began to appear as a black cul-de-sac; a place in which he must walk forever more, his whole body cringing and flinching from whispering eyes when he had passed, and when in midmorning he reached the house he sought, the prospect of facing Temple again was more than he could bear. So he engaged the car and directed the man and paid him and went on. A little later a car going in the opposite direction stopped and picked him up.

XI

T EMPLE WAKED lying in a tight ball, with narrow bars of
sunlight falling across her face like the tines of a golden
fork, and while the stiffened blood trickled and tingled
through her cramped muscles she lay gazing quietly up at the
ceiling. Like the walls, it was of rough planks crudely laid,
each plank separated from the next by a thin line of blackness;
in the corner a square opening above a ladder gave into a
gloomy loft shot with thin pencils of sun also. From nails in
the walls broken bits of desiccated harness hung, and she lay
plucking tentatively at the substance in which she lay. She
gathered a handful of it and lifted her head, and saw within
her fallen coat naked flesh between brassiere and knickers and
knickers and stockings. Then she remembered the rat and
scrambled up and sprang to the door, clawing at it, still
clutching the fist full of cottonseed-hulls, her face puffed with
the hard slumber of seventeen.

She had expected the door to be locked and for a time she
could not pull it open, her numb hands scoring at the undressed planks until she could hear her finger nails. It swung
back and she sprang out. At once she sprang back into the
crib and banged the door to. The blind man was coming
down the slope at a scuffling trot, tapping ahead with the
stick, the other hand at his waist, clutching a wad of his trousers. He passed the crib with his braces dangling about his
hips, his gymnasium shoes scuffing in the dry chaff of the
hallway, and passed from view, the stick rattling lightly along
the rank of empty stalls.

Temple crouched against the door, clutching her coat about
her. She could hear him back there in one of the stalls. She
opened the door and peered out, at the house in the bright
May sunshine, the sabbath peace, and she thought about the
girls and men leaving the dormitories in their new Spring
clothes, strolling along the shaded streets toward the cool,
unhurried sound of bells. She lifted her foot and examined
the soiled sole of her stocking, brushing at it with her palm,
then at the other one.

The blind man's stick clattered again. She jerked her head

back and closed the door to a crack and watched him pass, slower now, hunching his braces onto his shoulders. He mounted the slope and entered the house. Then she opened the door and stepped gingerly down.

She walked swiftly to the house, her stockinged feet flinching and cringing from the rough earth, watching the house. She mounted to the porch and entered the kitchen and stopped, listening into the silence. The stove was cold. Upon it the blackened coffee-pot sat, and a soiled skillet; upon the table soiled dishes were piled at random. I haven't eaten since . . . . . . .since. . . . . . Yesterday was one day, she thought, but I didn't eat then. I haven't eaten since . . . . . . .and that night was the dance, and I didn't eat any supper. I haven't eaten since dinner Friday, she thought. And now it's Sunday, thinking about the bells in cool steeples against the blue, and pigeons crooning about the belfries like echoes of the organ's bass. She returned to the door and peered out. Then she emerged, clutching the coat about her.

She entered the house and sped up the hall. The sun lay now on the front porch and she ran with a craning motion of her head, watching the patch of sun framed in the door. It was empty. She reached the door to the right of the entrance and opened it and sprang into the room and shut the door and leaned her back against it. The bed was empty. A faded patchwork quilt was wadded across it. A khaki-covered canteen and one slipper lay on the bed. On the floor her dress and hat lay.

She picked up the dress and hat and tried to brush them with her hand and with the corner of her coat. Then she sought the other slipper, moving the quilt, stooping to look under the bed. At last she found it in the fireplace, in a litter of wood ashes between an iron fire-dog and an overturned stack of bricks, lying on its side, half full of ashes, as though it had been flung or kicked there. She emptied it and wiped it on her coat and laid it on the bed and took the canteen and hung it on a nail in the wall. It bore the letters U S and a blurred number in black stencil. Then she removed the coat and dressed.

Long legged, thin armed, with high small buttocks—a small childish figure no longer quite a child, not yet quite a woman—she moved swiftly, smoothing her stockings and writhing into her scant, narrow dress. Now I can stand anything, she thought quietly, with a kind of dull, spent astonishment; I can stand just anything. From the top of one stocking she removed a watch on a broken black ribbon. Nine oclock. With her fingers she combed her matted curls, combing out three or four cottonseed-hulls. She took up the coat and hat and listened again at the door.

She returned to the back porch. In the basin was a residue of dirty water. She rinsed it and filled it and bathed her face. A soiled towel hung from a nail. She used it gingerly, then she took a compact from her coat and was using it when she found the woman watching her in the kitchen door.

"Good morning," Temple said. The woman held the child on her hip. It was asleep. "Hello, baby," Temple said, stooping; "you wan s'eep all day? Look at Temple." They entered the kitchen. The woman poured coffee into a cup.

"It's cold, I expect," she said. "Unless you want to make up the fire." From the oven she took a pan of bread.

"No," Temple said, sipping the lukewarm coffee, feeling her insides move in small, trickling clots, like loose shot. "I'm not hungry. I haven't eaten in two days, but I'm not hungry. Isn't that funny? I haven't eaten in. . . . . . ." She looked at the woman's back with a fixed placative grimace. "You haven't got a bathroom, have you?"

"What?" the woman said. She looked at Temple across her shoulder while Temple stared at her with that grimace of cringing and placative assurance. From a shelf the woman took a mail-order catalogue and tore out a few leaves and handed them to Temple. "You'll have to go to the barn, like we do."

"Will I?" Temple said, holding the paper. "The barn."

"They're all gone," the woman said. "They wont be back this morning."

"Yes," Temple said. "The barn."

"Yes; the barn," the woman said. "Unless you're too pure to have to."

"Yes," Temple said. She looked out the door, across the weed-choked clearing. Between the sombre spacing of the cedars the orchard lay bright in the sunlight. She donned

the coat and hat and went toward the barn, the torn leaves in
her hand, splotched over with small cuts of clothes-pins and
patent wringers and washing-powder, and entered the hallway. She stopped, folding and folding the sheets, then she
went on, with swift, cringing glances at the empty stalls. She
walked right through the barn. It was open at the back, upon
a mass of jimson weed in savage white-and-lavender bloom.
She walked on into the sunlight again, into the weeds. Then
she began to run, snatching her feet up almost before they
touched the earth, the weeds slashing at her with huge, moist,
malodorous blossoms. She stooped and twisted through a
fence of sagging rusty wire and ran downhill among trees.

At the bottom of the hill a narrow scar of sand divided the
two slopes of a small valley, winding in a series of dazzling
splotches where the sun found it. Temple stood in the sand,
listening to the birds among the sunshot leaves, listening,
looking about. She followed the dry runlet to where a jutting
shoulder formed a nook matted with briers. Among the new
green last year's dead leaves from the branches overhead
clung, not yet fallen to earth. She stood here for a while,
folding and folding the sheets in her fingers, in a kind of despair. When she rose she saw, upon the glittering mass of
leaves along the crest of the ditch, the squatting outline of a
man.

For an instant she stood and watched herself run out of her
body, out of one slipper. She watched her legs twinkle against
the sand, through the flecks of sunlight, for several yards,
then whirl and run back and snatch up the slipper and whirl
and run again.

When she caught a glimpse of the house she was opposite
the front porch. The blind man sat in a chair, his face lifted
into the sun. At the edge of the woods she stopped and put
on the slipper. She crossed the ruined lawn and sprang onto
the porch and ran down the hall. When she reached the back
porch she saw a man in the door of the barn, looking toward
the house. She crossed the porch in two strides and entered
the kitchen, where the woman sat at the table, smoking, the
child on her lap.

"He was watching me!" Temple said. "He was watching me
all the time!" She leaned beside the door, peering out, then

she came to the woman, her face small and pale, her eyes like holes burned with a cigar, and laid her hand on the cold stove.

"Who was?" the woman said.

"Yes," Temple said. "He was there in the bushes, watching me all the time." She looked toward the door, then back at the woman, and saw her hand lying on the stove. She snatched it up with a wailing shriek, clapping it against her mouth, and turned and ran toward the door. The woman caught her arm, still carrying the child on the other, and Temple sprang back into the kitchen. Goodwin was coming toward the house. He looked once at them and went on into the hall.

Temple began to struggle. "Let go," she whispered, "let go! Let go!" She surged and plunged, grinding the woman's hand against the door jamb until she was free. She sprang from the porch and ran toward the barn and into the hallway and climbed the ladder and scrambled through the trap and to her feet again, running toward the pile of rotting hay.

Then suddenly she ran upside down in a rushing interval; she could see her legs still running in space, and she struck lightly and solidly on her back and lay still, staring up at an oblong yawn that closed with a clattering vibration of loose planks. Faint dust sifted down across the bars of sunlight.

Her hand moved in the substance in which she lay, then she remembered the rat a second time. Her whole body surged in an involuted spurning movement that brought her to her feet in the loose hulls, so that she flung her hands out and caught herself upright, a hand on either angle of the corner, her face not twelve inches from the cross beam on which the rat crouched. For an instant they stared eye to eye, then its eyes glowed suddenly like two tiny electric bulbs and it leaped at her head just as she sprang backward, treading again on something that rolled under her foot.

She fell toward the opposite corner, on her face in the hulls and a few scattered corn-cobs gnawed bone-clean. Something thudded against the wall and struck her head in ricochet. The rat was in that corner now, on the floor. Again their faces were not twelve inches apart, the rat's eyes glowing and fading as though worked by lungs. Then it stood erect, its back to the corner, its forepaws curled against its chest, and began to squeak at her in tiny plaintive gasps. She backed away on hands and knees, watching it. Then she got to her feet and sprang at the door, hammering at it, watching the rat over her shoulder, her body arched against the door, rasping at the planks with her bare hands.

XII

THE WOMAN stood in the kitchen door, holding the child, until Goodwin emerged from the house. The lobes of his nostrils were quite white against his brown face, and she said: "God, are you drunk too?" He came along the porch. "She's not here," the woman said. "You cant find her." He brushed past her, trailing a reek of whiskey. She turned, watching him. He looked swiftly about the kitchen, then he turned and looked at her standing in the door, blocking it. "You wont find her," she said. "She's gone." He came toward her, lifting his hand. "Dont put your hand on me," she said. He gripped her arm, slowly. His eyes were a little bloodshot. The lobes of his nostrils looked like wax.

"Take your hand off me," she said. "Take it off." Slowly he drew her out of the door. She began to curse him. "Do you think you can? Do you think I'll let you? Or any other little slut?" Motionless, facing one another like the first position of a dance, they stood in a mounting terrific muscular hiatus.

With scarce any movement at all he flung her aside in a complete revolution that fetched her up against the table, her arm flung back for balance, her body bent and her hand fumbling behind her among the soiled dishes, watching him across the inert body of the child. He walked toward her. "Stand back," she said, lifting her hand slightly, bringing the butcher knife into view. "Stand back." He came steadily toward her, then she struck at him with the knife.

He caught her wrist. She began to struggle. He plucked the child from her and laid it on the table and caught her other hand as it flicked at his face, and holding both wrists in one hand, he slapped her. It made a dry, flat sound. He slapped her again, first on one cheek, then the other, rocking her head from side to side. "That's what I do to them," he said, slapping her. "See?" He released her. She stumbled backward against the table and caught up the child and half crouched between the table and the wall, watching him as he turned and left the room.

She knelt in the corner, holding the child. It had not stirred. She laid her palm first on one cheek, then on the

other. She rose and laid the child in the box and took a sunbonnet from a nail and put it on. From another nail she took
a coat trimmed with what had once been white fur, and took
up the child and left the room.

Tommy was standing in the barn, beside the crib, looking
toward the house. The old man sat on the front porch, in the
sun. She went down the steps and followed the path to the
road and went on without looking back. When she came to
the tree and the wrecked car she turned from the road, into a
path. After a hundred yards or so she reached the spring and
sat down beside it, the child on her lap and the hem of her
skirt turned back over its sleeping face.

Popeye came out of the bushes, walking gingerly in his
muddy shoes, and stood looking down at her across the
spring. His hand flicked to his coat and he fretted and twisted
a cigarette and put it into his mouth and snapped a match
with his thumb. "Jesus Christ," he said, "I told him about
letting them sit around all night, swilling that goddam stuff.
There ought to be a law." He looked away in the direction in
which the house lay. Then he looked at the woman, at the
top of her sunbonnet. "Goofy house," he said. "That's what
it is. It's not four days ago I find a bastard squatting here,
asking me if I read books. Like he would jump me with a
book or something. Take me for a ride with the telephone
directory." Again he looked off toward the house, jerking his
neck forth as if his collar were too tight. He looked down at
the top of the sunbonnet. "I'm going to town, see?" he said.
"I'm clearing out. I've got enough of this." She did not look
up. She adjusted the hem of the skirt above the child's face.
Popeye went on, with light, finicking sounds in the underbrush. Then they ceased. Somewhere in the swamp a bird
sang.

Before he reached the house Popeye left the road and followed a wooded slope. When he emerged he saw Goodwin
standing behind a tree in the orchard, looking toward the
barn. Popeye stopped at the edge of the wood and looked at
Goodwin's back. He put another cigarette into his mouth and
thrust his fingers into his vest. He went on across the orchard,
walking gingerly. Goodwin heard him and looked over his

shoulder. Popeye took a match from his vest, flicked it into flame and lit the cigarette. Goodwin looked toward the barn again and Popeye stood at his shoulder, looking toward the barn.

"Who's down there?" he said. Goodwin said nothing. Popeye jetted smoke from his nostrils. "I'm clearing out," he said. Goodwin said nothing, watching the barn. "I said, I'm getting out of here," Popeye said. Without turning his head Goodwin cursed him. Popeye smoked quietly, the cigarette wreathing across his still, soft, black gaze. Then he turned and went toward the house. The old man sat in the sun. Popeye did not enter the house. Instead he went on across the lawn and into the cedars until he was hidden from the house. Then he turned and crossed the garden and the weed-choked lot and entered the barn from the rear.

Tommy squatted on his heels beside the crib door, looking toward the house. Popeye looked at him a while, smoking. Then he snapped the cigarette away and entered a stall quietly. Above the manger was a wooden rack for hay, just under an opening in the loft floor. Popeye climbed into the rack and drew himself silently into the loft, his tight coat strained into thin ridges across his narrow shoulders and back.

XIII

TOMMY WAS STANDING in the hallway of the barn when Temple at last got the door of the crib open. When she recognised him she was half spun, leaping back, then she whirled and ran toward him and sprang down, clutching his arm. Then she saw Goodwin standing in the back door of the house and she whirled and leaped back into the crib and turned and leaned her head around the door, her voice making a thin eeeeeeeeeeeeee sound like bubbles in a bottle. She leaned there, scrabbling her hands on the door, trying to pull it to, hearing Tommy's voice.

". . . . . . Lee says hit wont hurt you none. All you got to do is lay down. . . . . ." It was a dry sort of sound, not in her consciousness at all, nor his pale eyes beneath the shaggy thatch. She leaned in the door, wailing, trying to shut it. Then she felt his hand clumsily on her thigh. ". . . . . .says hit wont hurt you none. All you got to do is. . . . . ."

She looked at him, his diffident, hard hand on her hip. "Yes," she said, "all right. Dont you let him in here."

"You mean fer me not to let none of them in hyer?"

"All right. I'm not scared of rats. You stay there and dont let him in."

"All right. I'll fix hit so caint nobody git to you. I'll be right hyer."

"All right. Shut the door. Dont let him in here."

"All right." He shut the door. She leaned in it, looking toward the house. He pushed her back so he could close the door. "Hit aint goin to hurt you none, Lee says. All you got to do is lay down."

"All right. I will. Dont you let him in here." The door closed. She heard him drive the hasp to. Then he shook the door.

"Hit's fastened," he said. "Caint nobody git to you now. I'll be right hyer."

He squatted on his heels in the chaff, looking at the house. After a while he saw Goodwin come to the back door and look toward him, and squatting, clasping his knees, Tommy's eyes glowed again, the pale irises appearing for an instant to spin on the pupils like tiny wheels. He squatted there, his lip lifted a little, until Goodwin went back into the house. Then he sighed, expelling his breath, and he looked at the blank door of the crib and again his eyes glowed with a diffident, groping, hungry fire and he began to rub his hands slowly on his shanks, rocking a little from side to side. Then he ceased, became rigid, and watched Goodwin move swiftly across the corner of the house and into the cedars. He squatted rigid, his lip lifted a little upon his ragged teeth.

Sitting in the cottonseed-hulls, in the litter of gnawed corncobs, Temple lifted her head suddenly toward the trap at the top of the ladder. She heard Popeye cross the floor of the loft, then his foot appeared, groping gingerly for the step. He descended, watching her over his shoulder.

She sat quite motionless, her mouth open a little. He stood looking at her. He began to thrust his chin out in a series of jerks, as though his collar were too tight. He lifted his elbows and brushed them with his palm, and the skirt of his coat, then he crossed her field of vision, moving without a sound, his hand in his coat pocket. He tried the door. Then he shook it.

"Open the door," he said.

There was no sound. Then Tommy whispered: "Who's that?"

"Open the door," Popeye said. The door opened. Tommy looked at Popeye. He blinked.

"I didn't know you was in hyer," he said. He made to look past Popeye, into the crib. Popeye laid his hand flat on Tommy's face and thrust him back and leaned past him and looked up at the house. Then he looked at Tommy.

"Didn't I tell you about following me?"

"I wasn't following you," Tommy said. "I was watching him," jerking his head toward the house.

"Watch him, then," Popeye said. Tommy turned his head and looked toward the house and Popeye drew his hand from his coat pocket.

To Temple, sitting in the cottonseed-hulls and the corn-cobs, the sound was no louder than the striking of a match: a short, minor sound shutting down upon the scene, the instant, with a profound finality, completely isolating it, and she sat there, her legs straight before her, her hands limp and palm-up on her lap, looking at Popeye's tight back and the ridges of his coat across the shoulders as he leaned out the door, the pistol behind him, against his flank, wisping thinly along his leg.

He turned and looked at her. He waggled the pistol slightly and put it back in his coat, then he walked toward her. Moving, he made no sound at all; the released door yawned and clapped against the jamb, but it made no sound either; it was as though sound and silence had become inverted. She could hear silence in a thick rustling as he moved toward her through it, thrusting it aside, and she began to say Something is going to happen to me. She was saying it to the old man with the yellow clots for eyes. "Something is happening to me!" she screamed at him, sitting in his chair in the sunlight, his hands crossed on the top of the stick. "I told you it was!" she screamed, voiding the words like hot silent bubbles into the bright silence about them until he turned his head and the two phlegm-clots above her where she lay tossing and thrashing on the rough, sunny boards. "I told you! I told you all the time!"

XIV

WHILE SHE was sitting beside the spring, with the sleeping child upon her knees, the woman discovered that she had forgot its bottle. She sat there for about an hour after Popeye left her. Then she returned to the road and turned back toward the house. When she was about halfway back to the house, carrying the child in her arms, Popeye's car passed her. She heard it coming and she got out of the road and stood there and watched it come dropping down the hill. Temple and Popeye were in it. Popeye did not make any sign, though Temple looked full at the woman. From beneath her hat Temple looked the woman full in the face, without any sign of recognition whatever. The face did not turn, the eyes did not wake; to the woman beside the road it was like a small, dead-colored mask drawn past her on a string and then away. The car went on, lurching and jolting in the ruts. The woman went on to the house.

The blind man was sitting on the front porch, in the sun. When she entered the hall, she was walking fast. She was not aware of the child's thin weight. She found Goodwin in their bedroom. He was in the act of putting on a frayed tie; looking at him, she saw that he had just shaved.

"Yes," she said. "What is it? What is it?"

"I've got to walk up to Tull's and telephone for the sheriff," he said.

"The sheriff," she said. "Yes. All right." She came to the bed and laid the child carefully down. "To Tull's," she said. "Yes. He's got a phone."

"You'll have to cook," Goodwin said. "There's Pap."

"You can give him some cold bread. He wont mind. There's some left in the stove. He wont mind."

"I'll go," Goodwin said. "You stay here."

"To Tull's," she said. "All right." Tull was the man at whose house Gowan had found a car. It was two miles away. Tull's family was at dinner. They asked her to stop. "I just want to use the telephone," she said. The telephone was in the dining-room, where they were eating. She called, with them sitting about the table. She didn't know the number. "The Sheriff,"

she said patiently into the mouthpiece. Then she got the sheriff, with Tull's family sitting about the table, about the Sunday dinner. "A dead man. You pass Mr Tull's about a mile
and turn off to the right. . . . . . . Yes, the Old Frenchman
place. Yes. This is Mrs Goodwin talking. . . . Goodwin.
Yes."

XV

BENBOW REACHED his sister's home in the middle of the afternoon. It was four miles from town, Jefferson. He and his sister were born in Jefferson, seven years apart, in a house which they still owned, though his sister had wanted to sell the house when Benbow married the divorced wife of a man named Mitchell and moved to Kinston. Benbow would not agree to sell, though he had built a new bungalow in Kinston on borrowed money upon which he was still paying interest.

When he arrived, there was no one about. He entered the house and he was sitting in the dim parlor behind the closed blinds, when he heard his sister come down the stairs, still unaware of his arrival. He made no sound. She had almost crossed the parlor door and vanished when she paused and looked full at him, without outward surprise, with that serene and stupid impregnability of heroic statuary; she was in white. "Oh, Horace," she said.

He did not rise. He sat with something of the air of a guilty small boy. "How did you——" he said. "Did Belle——"

"Of course. She wired me Saturday. That you had left, and if you came here, to tell you that she had gone back home to Kentucky and had sent for Little Belle."

"Ah, damnation," Benbow said.

"Why?" his sister said. "You want to leave home yourself, but you dont want her to leave."

He stayed at his sister's two days. She had never been given to talking, living a life of serene vegetation like perpetual corn or wheat in a sheltered garden instead of a field, and during those two days she came and went about the house with an air of tranquil and faintly ludicrous tragic disapproval.

After supper they sat in Miss Jenny's room, where Narcissa would read the Memphis paper before taking the boy off to bed. When she went out of the room, Miss Jenny looked at Benbow.

"Go back home, Horace," she said.

"Not to Kinston," Benbow said. "I hadn't intended to stay

here, anyway. It wasn't Narcissa I was running to. I haven't quit one woman to run to the skirts of another."

"If you keep on telling yourself that you may believe it, someday," Miss Jenny said. "Then what'll you do?"

"You're right," Benbow said. "Then I'd have to stay at home."

His sister returned. She entered the room with a definite air. "Now for it," Benbow said. His sister had not spoken directly to him all day.

"What are you going to do, Horace?" she said. "You must have business of some sort there in Kinston that should be attended to."

"Even Horace must have," Miss Jenny said. "What I want to know is, why he left. Did you find a man under the bed, Horace?"

"No such luck," Benbow said. "It was Friday, and all of a sudden I knew that I could not go to the station and get that box of shrimp and——"

"But you have been doing that for ten years," his sister said.

"I know. That's how I know that I will never learn to like smelling shrimp."

"Was that why you left Belle?" Miss Jenny said. She looked at him. "It took you a long time to learn that, if a woman dont make a very good wife for one man, she aint likely to for another, didn't it?"

"But to walk out just like a nigger," Narcissa said. "And to mix yourself up with moonshiners and street-walkers."

"Well, he's gone and left the street-walker too," Miss Jenny said. "Unless you're going to walk the streets with that orange-stick in your pocket until she comes to town."

"Yes," Benbow said. He told again about the three of them, himself and Goodwin and Tommy sitting on the porch, drinking from the jug and talking, and Popeye lurking about the house, coming out from time to time to ask Tommy to light a lantern and go down to the barn with him and Tommy wouldn't do it and Popeye would curse him, and Tommy sitting on the floor, scouring his bare feet on the boards with a faint, hissing noise, chortling: "Aint he a sight, now?"

"You could feel the pistol on him just like you knew he had

a navel," Benbow said. "He wouldn't drink, because he said it made him sick to his stomach like a dog; he wouldn't stay and talk with us; he wouldn't do anything: just lurking about, smoking his cigarettes, like a sullen and sick child.

"Goodwin and I were both talking. He had been a cavalry sergeant in the Philippines and on the Border, and in an infantry regiment in France; he never told me why he changed, transferred to infantry and lost his rank. He might have killed someone, might have deserted. He was talking about Manila and Mexican girls, and that halfwit chortling and glugging at the jug and shoving it at me: 'Take some mo'; and then I knew that the woman was just behind the door, listening to us. They are not married. I know that just like I know that that little black man had that flat little pistol in his coat pocket. But she's out there, doing a nigger's work, that's owned diamonds and automobiles too in her day, and bought them with a harder currency than cash. And that blind man, that old man sitting there at the table, waiting for somebody to feed him, with that immobility of blind people, like it was the backs of their eyeballs you looked at while they were hearing music you couldn't hear; that Goodwin led out of the room and completely off the earth, as far as I know. I never saw him again. I never knew who he was, who he was kin to. Maybe not to anybody. Maybe that old Frenchman that built the house a hundred years ago didn't want him either and just left him there when he died or moved away."

The next morning Benbow got the key to the house from his sister, and went into town. The house was on a side street, unoccupied now for ten years. He opened the house, drawing the nails from the windows. The furniture had not been moved. In a pair of new overalls, with mops and pails, he scoured the floors. At noon he went down town and bought bedding and some tinned food. He was still at work at six oclock when his sister drove up in her car.

"Come on home, Horace," she said. "Dont you see you cant do this?"

"I found that out right after I started," Benbow said. "Until this morning I thought that anybody with one arm and a pail of water could wash a floor."

"Horace," she said.

"I'm the oldest, remember," he said. "I'm going to stay here. I have some cover." He went to the hotel for supper. When he returned, his sister's car was again in the drive. The negro driver had brought a bundle of bedclothing.

"Miss Narcissa say for you to use them," the negro said. Benbow put the bundle into a closet and made a bed with the ones which he had bought.

Next day at noon, eating his cold food at the kitchen table, he saw through the window a wagon stop in the street. Three women got down and standing on the curb they made unabashed toilets, smoothing skirts and stockings, brushing one another's back, opening parcels and donning various finery. The wagon had gone on. They followed, on foot, and he remembered that it was Saturday. He removed the overalls and dressed and left the house.

The street opened into a broader one. To the left it went on to the square, the opening between two buildings black with a slow, continuous throng, like two streams of ants, above which the cupola of the courthouse rose from a clump of oaks and locusts covered with ragged snow. He went on toward the square. Empty wagons still passed him and he passed still more women on foot, black and white, unmistakable by the unease of their garments as well as by their method of walking, believing that town dwellers would take them for town dwellers too, not even fooling one another.

The adjacent alleys were choked with tethered wagons, the teams reversed and nuzzling gnawed corn-ears over the tailboards. The square was lined two-deep with ranked cars, while the owners of them and of the wagons thronged in slow overalls and khaki, in mail-order scarves and parasols, in and out of the stores, soiling the pavement with fruit- and peanut-hulls. Slow as sheep they moved, tranquil, impassable, filling the passages, contemplating the fretful hurrying of those in urban shirts and collars with the large, mild inscrutability of cattle or of gods, functioning outside of time, having left time lying upon the slow and imponderable land green with corn and cotton in the yellow afternoon.

Horace moved among them, swept here and there by the deliberate current, without impatience. Some of them he knew; most of the merchants and professional men remembered him as a boy, a youth, a brother lawyer—beyond a foamy screen of locust branches he could see the dingy second-story windows where he and his father had practised, the glass still innocent of water and soap as then—and he stopped now and then and talked with them in unhurried backwaters.

The sunny air was filled with competitive radios and phonographs in the doors of drug- and music-stores. Before these doors a throng stood all day, listening. The pieces which moved them were ballads simple in melody and theme, of bereavement and retribution and repentance metallically sung, blurred, emphasised by static or needle—disembodied voices blaring from imitation wood cabinets or pebble-grain hornmouths above the rapt faces, the gnarled slow hands long shaped to the imperious earth, lugubrious, harsh, and sad.

That was Saturday, in May: no time to leave the land. Yet on Monday they were back again, most of them, in clumps about the courthouse and the square, and trading a little in the stores since they were here, in their khaki and overalls and collarless shirts. All day long a knot of them stood about the door to the undertaker's parlor, and boys and youths with and without schoolbooks leaned with flattened noses against the glass, and the bolder ones and the younger men of the town entered in twos and threes to look at the man called Tommy. He lay on a wooden table, barefoot, in overalls, the sun-bleached curls on the back of his head matted with dried blood and singed with powder, while the coroner sat over him, trying to ascertain his last name. But none knew it, not even those who had known him for fifteen years about the countryside, nor the merchants who on infrequent Saturdays had seen him in town, barefoot, hatless, with his rapt, empty gaze and his cheek bulged innocently by a peppermint jawbreaker. For all general knowledge, he had none.

XVI

O N THE DAY when the sheriff brought Goodwin to town,
there was a negro murderer in the jail, who had killed
his wife; slashed her throat with a razor so that, her whole
head tossing further and further backward from the bloody
regurgitation of her bubbling throat, she ran out the cabin
door and for six or seven steps up the quiet moonlit lane.
He would lean in the window in the evening and sing. After
supper a few negroes gathered along the fence below—
natty, shoddy suits and sweat-stained overalls shoulder to
shoulder—and in chorus with the murderer, they sang
spirituals while white people slowed and stopped in the leafed
darkness that was almost summer, to listen to those who were
sure to die and him who was already dead singing about
heaven and being tired; or perhaps in the interval between
songs a rich, sourceless voice coming out of the high darkness where the ragged shadow of the heaven-tree which
snooded the street lamp at the corner fretted and mourned:
"Fo days mo! Den dey ghy stroy de bes ba'ytone singer in
nawth Mississippi!"

Sometimes during the day he would lean there, singing
alone then, though after a while one or two ragamuffin boys
or negroes with delivery baskets like as not, would halt at the
fence, and the white men sitting in tilted chairs along the oil-
foul wall of the garage across the street would listen above
their steady jaws. "One day mo! Den Ise a gawn po sonnen
bitch. Say, Aint no place fer you in heavum! Say, Aint no
place fer you in hell! Say, Aint no place fer you in jail!"

"Damn that fellow," Goodwin said, jerking up his black
head, his gaunt, brown, faintly harried face. "I aint in any
position to wish any man that sort of luck, but I'll be
damned. . . . . . ." He wouldn't talk. "I didn't do it. You
know that, yourself. You know I wouldn't have. I aint going
to say what I think. I didn't do it. They've got to hang it on
me first. Let them do that. I'm clear. But if I talk, if I say
what I think or believe, I wont be clear." He was sitting on
the cot in his cell. He looked up at the windows: two orifices
not much larger than sabre slashes.

"Is he that good a shot?" Benbow said. "To hit a man through one of those windows?"

Goodwin looked at him. "Who?"

"Popeye," Benbow said.

"Did Popeye do it?" Goodwin said.

"Didn't he?" Benbow said.

"I've told all I'm going to tell. I dont have to clear myself; it's up to them to hang it on me."

"Then what do you want with a lawyer?" Benbow said. "What do you want me to do?"

Goodwin was not looking at him. "If you'll just promise to get the kid a good newspaper grift when he's big enough to make change," he said. "Ruby'll be all right. Wont you, old gal?" He put his hand on the woman's head, scouring her hair with his hand. She sat on the cot beside him, holding the child on her lap. It lay in a sort of drugged immobility, like the children which beggars on Paris streets carry, its pinched face slick with faint moisture, its hair a damp whisper of shadow across its gaunt, veined skull, a thin crescent of white showing beneath its lead-colored eyelids.

The woman wore a dress of gray crepe, neatly brushed and skilfully darned by hand. Parallel with each seam was that faint, narrow, glazed imprint which another woman would recognise at a hundred yards with one glance. On the shoulder was a purple ornament of the sort that may be bought in ten cent stores or by mail order; on the cot beside her lay a gray hat with a neatly darned veil; looking at it, Benbow could not remember when he had seen one before, when women ceased to wear veils.

He took the woman to his house. They walked, she carrying the child while Benbow carried a bottle of milk and a few groceries, food in tin cans. The child still slept. "Maybe you hold it too much," he said. "Suppose we get a nurse for it."

He left her at the house and returned to town, to a telephone, and he telephoned out to his sister's, for the car. The car came for him. He told his sister and Miss Jenny about the case over the supper table.

"You're just meddling!" his sister said, her serene face, her voice, furious. "When you took another man's wife and child away from him I thought it was dreadful, but I said At least he will not have the face to ever come back here again. And when you just walked out of the house like a nigger and left her I thought that was dreadful too, but I would not let myself believe you meant to leave her for good. And then when you insisted without any reason at all on leaving here and opening the house, scrubbing it yourself and all the town looking on and living there like a tramp, refusing to stay here where everybody would expect you to stay and think it funny when you wouldn't; and now to deliberately mix yourself up with a woman you said yourself was a street-walker, a murderer's woman."

"I cant help it. She has nothing, no one. In a madeover dress all neatly about five years out of mode, and that child that never has been more than half alive, wrapped in a piece of blanket scrubbed almost cotton-white. Asking nothing of anyone except to be let alone, trying to make something out of her life when all you sheltered chaste women——"

"Do you mean to say a moonshiner hasn't got the money to hire the best lawyer in the country?" Miss Jenny said.

"It's not that," Horace said. "I'm sure he could get a better lawyer. It's that——"

"Horace," his sister said. She had been watching him. "Where is that woman?" Miss Jenny was watching him too, sitting a little forward in the wheel chair. "Did you take that woman into my house?"

"It's my house too, honey." She did not know that for ten years he had been lying to his wife in order to pay interest on a mortgage on the stucco house he had built for her in Kinston, so that his sister might not rent to strangers that other house in Jefferson which his wife did not know he still owned any share in. "As long as it's vacant, and with that child——"

"The house where my father and mother and your father and mother, the house where I——I wont have it. I wont have it."

"Just for one night, then. I'll take her to the hotel in the morning. Think of her, alone, with that baby. . . . . . . Suppose it were you and Bory, and your husband accused of a murder you knew he didn't——"

"I dont want to think about her. I wish I had never heard of the whole thing. To think that my brother——Dont you see that you are always having to clean up after yourself? It's not that there's litter left; it's that you——that——But to bring a street-walker, a murderess, into the house where I was born."

"Fiddlesticks," Miss Jenny said. "But, Horace, aint that what the lawyers call collusion? connivance?" Horace looked at her. "It seems to me you've already had a little more to do with these folks than the lawyer in the case should have. You were out there where it happened yourself not long ago. Folks might begin to think you know more than you've told."

"That's so," Horace said, "Mrs Blackstone. And sometimes I have wondered why I haven't got rich at the law. Maybe I will, when I get old enough to attend the same law school you did."

"If I were you," Miss Jenny said, "I'd drive back to town now and take her to the hotel and get her settled. It's not late."

"And go on back to Kinston until the whole thing is over," Narcissa said. "These people are not your people. Why must you do such things?"

"I cannot stand idly by and see injustice——"

"You wont ever catch up with injustice, Horace," Miss Jenny said.

"Well, that irony which lurks in events, then."

"Hmmph," Miss Jenny said. "It must be because she is one woman you know that dont know anything about that shrimp."

"Anyway, I've talked too much, as usual," Horace said. "So I'll have to trust you all——"

"Fiddlesticks," Miss Jenny said. "Do you think Narcissa'd want anybody to know that any of her folks could know people that would do anything as natural as make love or rob or steal?" There was that quality about his sister. During all the four days between Kinston and Jefferson he had counted on that imperviousness. He hadn't expected her—any woman— to bother very much over a man she had neither married nor borne when she had one she did bear to cherish and fret over. But he had expected that imperviousness, since she had had it thirty-six years.

When he reached the house in town a light burned in one

room. He entered, crossing floors which he had scrubbed
himself, revealing at the time no more skill with a mop than
he had expected, than he had with the lost hammer with
which he nailed the windows down and the shutters to ten
years ago, who could not even learn to drive a motor car. But
that was ten years ago, the hammer replaced by the new one
with which he had drawn the clumsy nails, the windows open
upon scrubbed floor spaces still as dead pools within the
ghostly embrace of hooded furniture.

The woman was still up, dressed save for the hat. It lay on
the bed where the child slept. Lying together there, they lent
to the room a quality of transience more unmistakable than
the makeshift light, the smug paradox of the made bed in a
room otherwise redolent of long unoccupation. It was as
though femininity were a current running through a wire
along which a certain number of identical bulbs were hung.

"I've got some things in the kitchen," she said. "I wont be
but a minute."

The child lay on the bed, beneath the unshaded light, and
he wondered why women, in quitting a house, will remove
all the lamp shades even though they touch nothing else;
looking down at the child, at its bluish eyelids showing a faint
crescent of bluish white against its lead-colored cheeks, the
moist shadow of hair capping its skull, its hands uplifted,
curl-palmed, sweating too, thinking Good God. Good
God.

He was thinking of the first time he had seen it, lying in a
wooden box behind the stove in that ruined house twelve
miles from town; of Popeye's black presence lying upon the
house like the shadow of something no larger than a match
falling monstrous and portentous upon something else otherwise familiar and everyday and twenty times its size; of the
two of them—himself and the woman—in the kitchen
lighted by a cracked and smutty lamp on a table of clean,
spartan dishes and Goodwin and Popeye somewhere in the
outer darkness peaceful with insects and frogs yet filled too
with Popeye's presence in black and nameless threat. The
woman drew the box out from behind the stove and stood
above it, her hands still hidden in her shapeless garment. "I
have to keep him in this so the rats cant get to him," she said.

"Oh," Horace said, "you have a son." Then she showed him her hands, flung them out in a gesture at once spontaneous and diffident and self-conscious and proud, and told him he might bring her an orange-stick.

She returned, with something wrapped discreetly in a piece of newspaper. He knew that it was a diaper, freshly washed, even before she said: "I made a fire in the stove. I guess I overstepped."

"Of course not," he said. "It's merely a matter of legal precaution, you see," he said. "Better to put everybody to a little temporary discomfort than to jeopardise our case." She did not appear to be listening. She spread the blanket on the bed and lifted the child onto it. "You understand how it is," Horace said. "If the judge suspected that I knew more about it than the facts would warrant——I mean, we must try to give everybody the idea that holding Lee for that killing is just——"

"Do you live in Jefferson?" she said, wrapping the blanket about the child.

"No. I live in Kinston. I used to——I have practised here, though."

"You have kinfolks here, though. Women. That used to live in this house." She lifted the child, tucking the blanket about it. Then she looked at him. "It's all right. I know how it is. You've been kind."

"Damn it," he said, "do you think——Come on. Let's go on to the hotel. You get a good night's rest, and I'll be in early in the morning. Let me take it."

"I've got him," she said. She started to say something else, looking at him quietly for a moment, but she went on. He turned out the light and followed and locked the door. She was already in the car. He got in.

"Hotel, Isom," he said. "I never did learn to drive one," he said. "Sometimes, when I think of all the time I have spent not learning to do things. . . . . . ."

The street was narrow, quiet. It was paved now, though he could remember when, after a rain, it had been a canal of blackish substance half earth, half water, with murmuring gutters in which he and Narcissa paddled and splashed with tucked-up garments and muddy bottoms, after the crudest of whittled boats, or made loblollies by treading and treading in one spot with the intense oblivion of alchemists. He could remember when, innocent of concrete, the street was bordered on either side by paths of red brick tediously and unevenly laid and worn in rich, random maroon mosaic into the black earth which the noon sun never reached; at that moment, pressed into the concrete near the entrance of the drive, were the prints of his and his sister's naked feet in the artificial stone.

The infrequent lamps mounted to crescendo beneath the arcade of a fillingstation at the corner. The woman leaned suddenly forward. "Stop here, please, boy," she said. Isom put on the brakes. "I'll get out here and walk," she said.

"You'll do nothing of the kind," Horace said. "Go on, Isom."

"No; wait," the woman said. "We'll be passing people that know you. And then the square."

"Nonsense," Horace said. "Go on, Isom."

"You get out and wait, then," she said. "He can come straight back."

"You'll do no such thing," Horace said. "By heaven, I—— Drive on, Isom!"

"You'd better," the woman said. She sat back in the seat. Then she leaned forward again. "Listen. You've been kind. You mean all right, but——"

"You dont think I am lawyer enough, you mean?"

"I guess I've got just what was coming to me. There's no use fighting it."

"Certainly not, if you feel that way about it. But you dont. Or you'd have told Isom to drive you to the railroad station. Wouldn't you?" She was looking down at the child, fretting the blanket about its face. "You get a good night's rest and I'll be in early tomorrow." They passed the jail—a square building slashed harshly by pale slits of light. Only the central window was wide enough to be called a window, crisscrossed by slender bars. In it the negro murderer leaned; below along the fence a row of heads hatted and bare above work-thickened shoulders, and the blended voices swelled rich and sad into the soft, depthless evening, singing of heaven and being tired. "Dont you worry at all, now. Everybody knows Lee didn't do it."

They drew up to the hotel, where the drummers sat in chairs along the curb, listening to the singing. "I must——" the woman said. Horace got down and held the door open. She didn't move. "Listen. I've got to tell——"

"Yes," Horace said, extending his hand. "I know. I'll be in early tomorrow." He helped her down. They entered the hotel, the drummers turning to watch her legs, and went to the desk. The singing followed them, dimmed by the walls, the lights.

The woman stood quietly nearby, holding the child, until Horace had done.

"Listen," she said. The porter went on with the key, toward the stairs. Horace touched her arm, turning her that way. "I've got to tell you," she said.

"In the morning," he said. "I'll be in early," he said, guiding her toward the stairs. Still she hung back, looking at him; then she freed her arm by turning to face him.

"All right, then," she said. She said, in a low, level tone, her face bent a little toward the child: "We haven't got any money. I'll tell you now. That last batch Popeye didn't——"

"Yes, yes," Horace said; "first thing in the morning. I'll be in by the time you finish breakfast. Goodnight." He returned to the car, into the sound of the singing. "Home, Isom," he said. They turned and passed the jail again and the leaning shape beyond the bars and the heads along the fence. Upon the barred and slitted wall the splotched shadow of the heaven tree shuddered and pulsed monstrously in scarce any wind; rich and sad, the singing fell behind. The car went on, smooth and swift, passing the narrow street. "Here," Horace said, " where are you——" Isom clapped on the brakes.

"Miss Narcissa say to bring you back out home," he said.

"Oh, she did?" Horace said. "That was kind of her. You can tell her I changed her mind."

Isom backed and turned into the narrow street and then into the cedar drive, the lights lifting and boring ahead into the unpruned tunnel as though into the most profound blackness of the sea, as though among straying rigid shapes to which not even light could give color. The car stopped at the door and Horace got out. "You might tell her it was not to her I ran," he said. "Can you remember that?"

XVII

THE LAST trumpet-shaped bloom had fallen from the heaven tree at the corner of the jail yard. They lay thick, viscid underfoot, sweet and oversweet in the nostrils with a sweetness surfeitive and moribund, and at night now the ragged shadow of full-fledged leaves pulsed upon the barred window in shabby rise and fall. The window was in the general room, the white-washed walls of which were stained with dirty hands, scribbled and scratched over with names and dates and blasphemous and obscene doggerel in pencil or nail or knifeblade. Nightlily the negro murderer leaned there, his face checkered by the shadow of the grating in the restless interstices of leaves, singing in chorus with those along the fence below.

Sometimes during the day he sang also, alone then save for the slowing passerby and ragamuffin boys and the garage men across the way. "One day mo! Aint no place fer you in heavum! Aint no place fer you in hell! Aint no place fer you in whitefolks' jail! Nigger, whar you gwine to? Whar you gwine to, nigger?"

Each morning Isom fetched in a bottle of milk, which Horace delivered to the woman at the hotel, for the child. On Sunday afternoon he went out to his sister's. He left the woman sitting on the cot in Goodwin's cell, the child on her lap. Heretofore it had lain in that drugged apathy, its eyelids closed to thin crescents, but today it moved now and then in frail, galvanic jerks, whimpering.

Horace went up to Miss Jenny's room. His sister had not appeared. "He wont talk," Horace said. "He just says they will have to prove he did it. He said they had nothing on him, no more than on the child. He wouldn't even consider bond, if he could have got it. He says he is better off in the jail. And I suppose he is. His business out there is finished now, even if the sheriff hadn't found his kettles and destroyed——"

"Kettles?"

"His still. After he surrendered, they hunted around until they found the still. They knew what he was doing, but they

266

waited until he was down. Then they all jumped on him. The good customers, that had been buying whiskey from him and drinking all that he would give them free and maybe trying to make love to his wife behind his back. You should hear them down town. This morning the Baptist minister took him for a text. Not only as a murderer, but as an adulterer; a polluter of the free Democratico-Protestant atmosphere of Yoknapatawpha county. I gathered that his idea was that Goodwin and the woman should both be burned as a sole example to that child; the child to be reared and taught the English language for the sole end of being taught that it was begot in sin by two people who suffered by fire for having begot it. Good God, can a man, a civilised man, seriously. . . . . . ."

"They're just Baptists," Miss Jenny said. "What about the money?"

"He had a little, almost a hundred and sixty dollars. It was buried in a can in the barn. They let him dig that up. 'That'll keep her' he says 'until it's over. Then we'll clear out. We've been intending to for a good while. If I'd listened to her, we'd have been gone already. You've been a good girl' he says. She was sitting on the cot beside him, holding the baby, and he took her chin in his hand and shook her head a little."

"It's a good thing Narcissa aint going to be on that jury," Miss Jenny said.

"Yes. But the fool wont even let me mention that that gorilla was ever on the place. He said 'They cant prove anything on me. I've been in a jam before. Everybody that knows anything about me knows that I wouldn't hurt a feeb.' But that wasn't the reason he doesn't want it told about that thug. And he knew I knew it wasn't, because he kept on talking, sitting there in his overalls, rolling his cigarettes with the sack hanging in his teeth. 'I'll just stay here until it blows over. I'll be better off here; cant do anything outside, anyway. And this will keep her, with maybe something over for you until you're better paid.'

"But I knew what he was thinking. 'I didn't know you were a coward' I said.

" 'You do like I say' he said. 'I'll be all right here'. But he doesn't. . . . . . ." He sat forward, rubbing his hands slowly. "He doesn't realise. . . . . . . Dammit, say what you want to, but there's a corruption about even looking upon evil, even by accident; you cannot haggle, traffic, with putrefaction——You've seen how Narcissa, just hearing about it, how it's made her restless and suspicious. I thought I had come back here of my own accord, but now I see that——Do you suppose she thought I was bringing that woman into the house at night, or something like that?"

"I did too, at first," Miss Jenny said. "But I reckon now she's learned that you'll work harder for whatever reason you think you have, than for anything anybody could offer you or give you."

"You mean, she'd let me think they never had any money, when she——"

"Why not? Aint you doing all right without it?"

Narcissa entered.

"We were just talking about murder and crime," Miss Jenny said.

"I hope you're through, then," Narcissa said. She did not sit down.

"Narcissa has her sorrows too," Miss Jenny said. "Dont you, Narcissa?"

"What now?" Horace said. "She hasn't caught Bory with alcohol on his breath, has she?"

"She's been jilted. Her beau's gone and left her."

"You're such a fool," Narcissa said.

"Yes, sir," Miss Jenny said, "Gowan Stevens has thrown her down. He didn't even come back from that Oxford dance to say goodbye. He just wrote her a letter." She began to search about her in the chair. "And now I flinch everytime the doorbell rings, thinking that his mother——"

"Miss Jenny," Narcissa said, "you give me my letter."

"Wait," Miss Jenny said, "here it is. Now, what do you think of that for a delicate operation on the human heart without anaesthetic? I'm beginning to believe all this I hear, about how young folks learn all the things in order to get married, that we had to get married in order to learn."

Horace took the single sheet.

Narcissa my dear

This has no heading. I wish it could have no date. But if my heart were as blank as this page, this would not be necessary at all. I will not see you again. I cannot write it, for I have gone through with an experience which I cannot face. I have but one rift in the darkness, that is that I have injured no one save myself by my folly, and that the extent of that folly you will never learn. I need not say that the hope that you never learn it is the sole reason why I will not see you again. Think as well of me as you can. I wish I had the right to say, if you learn of my folly think not the less of me.

G.

Horace read the note, the single sheet. He held it between his hands. He did not say anything for a while.

"Good Lord," Horace said. "Someone mistook him for a Mississippi man on the dance floor."

"I think, if I were you——" Narcissa said. After a moment she said: "How much longer is this going to last, Horace?"

"Not any longer than I can help. If you know of any way in which I can get him out of that jail by tomorrow. . . ."

"There's only one way," she said. She looked at him a moment. Then she turned toward the door. "Which way did Bory go? Dinner'll be ready soon." She went out.

"And you know what that way is," Miss Jenny said. "If you aint got any backbone."

"I'll know whether or not I have any backbone when you tell me what the other way is."

"Go back to Belle," Miss Jenny said. "Go back home."

The negro murderer was to be hung on a Saturday without pomp, buried without circumstance: one night he would be singing at the barred window and yelling down out of the soft myriad darkness of a May night; the next night he would be gone, leaving the window for Goodwin. Goodwin had been bound over for the June term of court, without bail. But still he would not agree to let Horace divulge Popeye's presence at the scene of the murder.

"I tell you, they've got nothing on me," Goodwin said.

"How do you know they haven't?" Horace said.

"Well, no matter what they think they have on me, I stand a chance in court. But just let it get to Memphis that I said he was anywhere around there, what chance do you think I'd have to get back to this cell after I testified?"

"You've got the law, justice, civilization."

"Sure, if I spend the rest of my life squatting in that corner yonder. Come here." He led Horace to the window. "There are five windows in that hotel yonder that look into this one. And I've seen him light matches with a pistol at twenty feet. Why, damn it all, I'd never get back here from the courtroom the day I testified that."

"But there's such a thing as obstruct——"

"Obstructing damnation. Let them prove I did it. Tommy was found in the barn, shot from behind. Let them find the pistol. I was there, waiting. I didn't try to run. I could have, but I didn't. It was me notified the sheriff. Of course my being there alone except for her and Pap looked bad. If it was a stall, dont common sense tell you I'd have invented a better one?"

"You're not being tried by common sense," Horace said. "You're being tried by a jury."

"Then let them make the best of it. That's all they'll get. The dead man is in the barn, hadn't been touched; me and my wife and child and Pap in the house; nothing in the house touched; me the one that sent for the sheriff. No, no; I know I run a chance this way, but let me just open my head about that fellow, and there's no chance to it. I know what I'll get."

"But you heard the shot," Horace said. "You have already told that."

"No," he said, "I didn't. I didn't hear anything. I dont know anything about it. . . . . . . Do you mind waiting outside a minute while I talk to Ruby?"

It was five minutes before she joined him. He said:

"There's something about this that I dont know yet; that you and Lee haven't told me. Something he just warned you not to tell me. Isn't there?" She walked beside him, carrying the child. It was still whimpering now and then, tossing its thin body in sudden jerks. She tried to soothe it, crooning to it, rocking it in her arms. "Maybe you carry it too much,"

Horace said; "maybe if you could leave it at the hotel. . . ."

"I guess Lee knows what to do," she said.

"But the lawyer should know all the facts, everything. He is the one to decide what to tell and what not to tell. Else, why have one? That's like paying a dentist to fix your teeth and then refusing to let him look into your mouth, dont you see? You wouldn't treat a dentist or a doctor this way." She said nothing, her head bent over the child. It wailed.

"Hush," she said, "hush, now."

"And worse than that, there's such a thing called obstructing justice. Suppose he swears there was nobody else there, suppose he is about to be cleared—which is not likely—and somebody turns up who saw Popeye about the place, or saw his car leaving. Then they'll say, if Lee didn't tell the truth about an unimportant thing, why should we believe him when his neck's in danger?"

They reached the hotel. He opened the door for her. She did not look at him. "I guess Lee knows best," she said, going in. The child wailed, a thin, whimpering, distressful cry. "Hush," she said. "Shhhhhhhhhhhh."

Isom had been to fetch Narcissa from a party; it was late when the car stopped at the corner and picked him up. A few of the lights were beginning to come on, and men were already drifting back toward the square after supper, but it was still too early for the negro murderer to begin to sing. "And he'd better sing fast, too," Horace said. "He's only got two days more." But he was not there yet. The jail faced west; a last faint copper-colored light lay upon the dingy grating and upon the small, pale blob of a hand, and in scarce any wind a blue wisp of tobacco floated out and dissolved raggedly away. "If it wasn't bad enough to have her husband there, without that poor brute counting his remaining breaths at the top of his voice. . . . . ."

"Maybe they'll wait and hang them both together," Narcissa said. "They do that sometimes, dont they?"

That night Horace built a small fire in the grate. It was not cool. He was using only one room now, taking his meals at the hotel; the rest of the house was locked again. He tried to read, then he gave up and undressed and went to bed, watching the fire die in the grate. He heard the town clock strike twelve. "When this is over, I think I'll go to Europe," he said. "I need a change. Either I, or Mississippi, one."

Maybe a few of them would still be gathered along the fence, since this would be his last night; the thick, small-headed shape of him would be clinging to the bars, gorilla-like, singing, while upon his shadow, upon the checkered orifice of the window, the ragged grief of the heaven tree would pulse and change, the last bloom fallen now in viscid smears upon the sidewalk. Horace turned again in the bed. "They ought to clean that damn mess off the sidewalk," he said. "Damn. Damn. Damn."

He was sleeping late the next morning; he had seen daylight. He was wakened by someone knocking at the door. It was half-past six. He went to the door. The negro porter of the hotel stood there.

"What?" Horace said. "Is it Mrs Goodwin?"

"She say for you to come when you up," the negro said.

"Tell her I'll be there in ten minutes."

As he entered the hotel he passed a young man with a small black bag, such as doctors carry. Horace went on up. The woman was standing in the half-open door, looking down the hall.

"I finally got the doctor," she said. "But I wanted any-way. . . . . . ." The child lay on the bed, its eyes shut, flushed and sweating, its curled hands above its head in the attitude of one crucified, breathing in short, whistling gasps. "He was sick all last night. I went and got some medicine and I tried to keep him quiet until daylight. At last I got the doctor." She stood beside the bed, looking down at the child. "There was a woman there," she said. "A young girl."

"A——" Horace said. "Oh," he said. "Yes. You'd better tell me about it."

XVIII

POPEYE DROVE swiftly but without any quality of haste or
of flight, down the clay road and into the sand. Temple
was beside him. Her hat was jammed onto the back of her
head, her hair escaping beneath the crumpled brim in matted
clots. Her face looked like a sleep-walker's as she swayed
limply to the lurching of the car. She lurched against Popeye,
lifting her hand in limp reflex. Without releasing the wheel
he thrust her back with his elbow. "Brace yourself," he said.
"Come on, now."

Before they came to the tree they passed the woman. She
stood beside the road, carrying the child, the hem of her dress
folded back over its face, and she looked at them quietly from
beneath the faded sunbonnet, flicking swiftly in and out of
Temple's vision without any motion, any sign.

When they reached the tree Popeye swung the car out of
the road and drove it crashing into the undergrowth and
through the prone tree-top and back into the road again in a
running popping of cane-stalks like musketry along a trench,
without any diminution of speed. Beside the tree Gowan's car
lay on its side. Temple looked vaguely and stupidly at it as it
too shot behind.

Popeye swung back into the sandy ruts. Yet there was no
flight in the action: he performed it with a certain vicious
petulance, that was all. It was a powerful car. Even in the
sand it held forty miles an hour, and up the narrow gulch to
the highroad, where he turned north. Sitting beside him,
braced against jolts that had already given way to a smooth
increasing hiss of gravel, Temple gazed dully forward as the
road she had traversed yesterday began to flee backward
under the wheels as onto a spool, feeling her blood seeping
slowly inside her loins. She sat limp in the corner of the seat,
watching the steady backward rush of the land—pines in
opening vistas splashed with fading dogwood; sedge; fields
green with new cotton and empty of any movement, peaceful,
as though Sunday were a quality of atmosphere, of light and
shade—sitting with her legs close together, listening to the

hot minute seeping of her blood, saying dully to herself, I'm still bleeding. I'm still bleeding.

It was a bright, soft day, a wanton morning filled with that unbelievable soft radiance of May, rife with a promise of noon and of heat, with high fat clouds like gobs of whipped cream floating lightly as reflections in a mirror, their shadows scudding sedately across the road. It had been a lavender spring. The fruit trees, the white ones, had been in small leaf when the blooms matured; they had never attained that brilliant whiteness of last spring, and the dogwood had come into full bloom after the leaf also, in green retrograde before crescendo. But lilac and wistaria and redbud, even the shabby heaven trees, had never been finer, fulgent, with a burning scent blowing for a hundred yards along the vagrant air of April and May. The bougainvillia against the veranda would be large as basketballs and lightly poised as balloons, and looking vacantly and stupidly at the rushing roadside Temple began to scream.

It started as a wail, rising, cut suddenly off by Popeye's hand. With her hands lying on her lap, sitting erect, she screamed, tasting the gritty acridity of his fingers while the car slewed squealing in the gravel, feeling her secret blood. Then he gripped her by the back of the neck and she sat motionless, her mouth round and open like a small empty cave. He shook her head.

"Shut it," he said, "shut it;" gripping her silent. "Look at yourself. Here." With the other hand he swung the mirror on the windshield around and she looked at her image, at the uptilted hat and her matted hair and her round mouth. She began to fumble at her coat pockets, looking at her reflection. He released her and she produced the compact and opened it and peered into the mirror, whimpering a little. She powdered her face and rouged her mouth and straightened her hat, whimpering into the tiny mirror on her lap while Popeye watched her. He lit a cigarette. "Aint you ashamed of yourself?" he said.

"It's still running," she whimpered. "I can feel it." With the lipstick poised she looked at him and opened her mouth again. He gripped her by the back of the neck.

"Stop it, now. You going to shut it?"

"Yes," she whimpered.

"See you do, then. Come on. Get yourself fixed."

She put the compact away. He started the car again.

The road began to thicken with pleasure cars Sunday-bent—small, clay-crusted Fords and Chevrolets; an occasional larger car moving swiftly, with swathed women, and dust-covered hampers; trucks filled with wooden-faced country people in garments like a colored wood meticulously carved; now and then a wagon or a buggy. Before a weathered frame church on a hill the grove was full of tethered teams and battered cars and trucks. The woods gave away to fields; houses became more frequent. Low above the skyline, above roofs and a spire or two, smoke hung. The gravel became asphalt and they entered Dumfries.

Temple began to look about, like one waking from sleep. "Not here!" she said. "I cant——"

"Hush it, now," Popeye said.

"I cant——I might——" she whimpered. "I'm hungry," she said. "I haven't eaten since. . . . . ."

"Ah, you aint hungry. Wait till we get to town."

She looked about with dazed, glassy eyes. "There might be people here. . . . . ." He swung in toward a fillingstation. "I cant get out," she whimpered. "It's still running, I tell you!"

"Who told you to get out?" He descended and looked at her across the wheel. "Dont you move." She watched him go up the street and enter a door. It was a dingy confectionery. He bought a pack of cigarettes and put one in his mouth. "Gimme a couple of bars of candy," he said.

"What kind?"

"Candy," he said. Under a glass bell on the counter a plate of sandwiches sat. He took one and flipped a dollar on the counter and turned toward the door.

"Here's your change," the clerk said.

"Keep it," he said. "You'll get rich faster."

When he saw the car it was empty. He stopped ten feet away and changed the sandwich to his left hand, the unlighted cigarette slanted beneath his chin. The mechanic, hanging the hose up, saw him and jerked his thumb toward the corner of the building.

Beyond the corner the wall made an offset. In the niche was a greasy barrel half full of scraps of metal and rubber. Between the barrel and the wall Temple crouched. "He nearly saw me!" she whispered. "He was almost looking right at me!"

"Who?" Popeye said. He looked back up the street. "Who saw you?"

"He was coming right toward me! A boy. At school. He was looking right toward——"

"Come on. Come out of it."

"He was look——" Popeye took her by the arm. She crouched in the corner, jerking at the arm he held, her wan face craned around the corner.

"Come on, now." Then his hand was at the back of her neck, gripping it.

"Oh," she wailed in a choked voice. It was as though he were lifting her slowly erect by that one hand. Excepting that, there was no movement between them. Side by side, almost of a height, they appeared as decorous as two acquaintances stopped to pass the time of day before entering church.

"Are you coming?" he said. "Are you?"

"I cant. It's down to my stocking now. Look." She lifted her skirt away in a shrinking gesture, then she dropped the skirt and rose again, her torso arching backward, her soundless mouth open as he gripped her. He released her.

"Will you come now?"

She came out from behind the barrel. He took her arm.

"It's all over the back of my coat," she whimpered. "Look and see."

"You're all right. I'll get you another coat tomorrow. Come on."

They returned to the car. At the corner she hung back again. "You want some more of it, do you?" he whispered, not touching her. "Do you?" She went on and got into the car quietly. He took the wheel. "Here, I got you a sandwich." He took it from his pocket and put it in her hand. "Come on, now. Eat it." She took a bite obediently. He started the car and took the Memphis road. Again, the bitten sandwich in her hand, she ceased chewing and opened her mouth in that round, hopeless expression of a child; again his hand left the wheel and gripped the back of her neck and she sat motionless, gazing straight at him, her mouth open and the half chewed mass of bread and meat lying upon her tongue.

They reached Memphis in midafternoon. At the foot of the bluff below Main Street Popeye turned into a narrow street of smoke-grimed frame houses with tiers of wooden galleries, set a little back in grassless plots, with now and then a forlorn and hardy tree of some shabby species—gaunt, lop-branched magnolias, a stunted elm or a locust in grayish, cadaverous bloom—interspersed by rear ends of garages; a scrap-heap in a vacant lot; a low-doored cavern of an equivocal appearance where an oilcloth-covered counter and a row of backless stools, a metal coffee-urn and a fat man in a dirty apron with a toothpick in his mouth, stood for an instant out of the gloom with an effect as of a sinister and meaningless photograph poorly made. From the bluff, beyond a line of office buildings terraced sharply against the sunfilled sky, came a sound of traffic—motor horns, trolleys—passing high overhead on the river breeze; at the end of the street a trolley materialised in the narrow gap with an effect as of magic and vanished with a stupendous clatter. On a second storey gallery a young negress in her underclothes smoked a cigarette sullenly, her arms on the balustrade.

Popeye drew up before one of the dingy three-storey houses, the entrance of which was hidden by a dingy lattice cubicle leaning a little awry. In the grimy grassplot before it two of those small, woolly, white, worm-like dogs, one with a pink, the other a blue, ribbon about its neck, moved about with an air of sluggish and obscene paradox. In the sunlight their coats looked as though they had been cleaned with gasoline.

Later Temple could hear them outside her door, whimpering and scuffing, or, rushing thickly in when the negro maid opened the door, climbing and sprawling onto the bed and into Miss Reba's lap with wheezy, flatulent sounds, billowing into the rich pneumasis of her breast and tonguing along the metal tankard which she waved in one ringed hand as she talked.

"Anybody in Memphis can tell you who Reba Rivers is. Ask any man on the street, cop or not. I've had some of the biggest men in Memphis right here in this house, bankers, lawyers, doctors—all of them. I've had two police captains drinking beer in my dining-room and the commissioner himself upstairs with one of my girls. They got drunk and crashed the door in on him and found him buck-nekkid, dancing the highland fling. A man fifty years old, seven foot tall, with a head like a peanut. He was a fine fellow. He knew me. They all know Reba Rivers. Spend their money here like water, they have. They know me. I aint never double-crossed nobody, honey." She drank beer, breathing thickly into the tankard, the other hand, ringed with yellow diamonds as large as gravel, lost among the lush billows of her breast.

Her slightest movement appeared to be accomplished by an expenditure of breath out of all proportion to any pleasure the movement could afford her. Almost as soon as they entered the house she began to tell Temple about her asthma, toiling up the stairs in front of them, planting her feet heavily in worsted bedroom slippers, a wooden rosary in one hand and the tankard in the other. She had just returned from church, in a black silk gown and a hat savagely flowered; the lower half of the tankard was still frosted with inner chill. She moved heavily from big thigh to thigh, the two dogs moiling underfoot, talking steadily back across her shoulder in a harsh, expiring, maternal voice.

"Popeye knew better than to bring you anywhere else but to my house. I been after him for, how many years I been after you to get you a girl, honey? What I say, a young fellow cant no more live without a girl than. . . . . . ." Panting, she fell to cursing the dogs under her feet, stopping to shove them aside. "Get back down there," she said, shaking the rosary at them. They snarled at her in vicious falsetto, baring their teeth, and she leaned against the wall in a thin aroma of beer, her hand to her breast, her mouth open, her eyes fixed in a glare of sad terror of all breathing as she besought breath, the tankard a squat soft gleam like dull silver lifted in the gloom.

The narrow stairwell turned back upon itself in a succession of niggard reaches. The light, falling through a thickly-curtained door at the front and through a shuttered window at the rear of each stage, had a weary quality. A spent quality;

defunctive, exhausted—a protracted weariness like a vitiated backwater beyond sunlight and the vivid noises of sunlight and day. There was a defunctive odor of irregular food, vaguely alcoholic, and Temple even in her ignorance seemed to be surrounded by a ghostly promiscuity of intimate garments, of discreet whispers of flesh stale and oft-assailed and impregnable beyond each silent door which they passed. Behind her, about hers and Miss Reba's feet the two dogs scrabbled in nappy gleams, their claws clicking on the metal strips which bound the carpet to the stairs.

Later, lying in bed, a towel wrapped about her naked loins, she could hear them sniffing and whining outside the door. Her coat and hat hung on nails in the door, her dress and stockings lay upon a chair, and it seemed to her that she could hear the rhythmic splash-splash of the washing-board somewhere and she flung herself again in an agony for concealment as she had when they took her knickers off.

"Now, now," Miss Reba said. "I bled for four days, myself. It aint nothing. Doctor Quinn'll stop it in two minutes, and Minnie'll have them all washed and pressed and you wont never know it. That blood'll be worth a thousand dollars to you, honey." She lifted the tankard, the flowers on her hat rigidly moribund, nodding in macabre was hael. "Us poor girls," she said. The drawn shades, cracked into a myriad pattern like old skin, blew faintly on the bright air, breathing into the room on waning surges the sound of Sabbath traffic, festive, steady, evanescent. Temple lay motionless in the bed, her legs straight and close, the covers to her chin and her face small and wan, framed in the rich sprawl of her hair. Miss Reba lowered the tankard, gasping for breath. In her hoarse, fainting voice she began to tell Temple how lucky she was.

"Every girl in the district has been trying to get him, honey. There's one, a little married woman slips down here sometimes, she offered Minnie twenty-five dollars just to get him into the room, that's all. But do you think he'd so much as look at one of them? Girls that have took in a hundred dollars a night. No, sir. Spend his money like water, but do you think he'd look at one of them except to dance with her? I always knowed it wasn't going to be none of these here common whores he'd take. I'd tell them, I'd say, the one of yez that gets him'll wear diamonds, I says, but it aint going to be none of you common whores, and now Minnie'll have them washed and pressed until you wont know it."

"I cant wear it again," Temple whispered. "I cant."

"No more you'll have to, if you dont want. You can give them to Minnie, though I dont know what she'll do with them except maybe——" At the door the dogs began to whimper louder. Feet approached. The door opened. A negro maid entered, carrying a tray bearing a quart bottle of beer and a glass of gin, the dogs surging in around her feet. "And tomorrow the stores'll be open and me and you'll go shopping, like he said for us to. Like I said, the girl that gets him'll wear diamonds: you just see if I wasn't——" she turned, mountainous, the tankard lifted, as the two dogs scrambled onto the bed and then onto her lap, snapping viciously at one another. From their curled shapeless faces bead-like eyes glared with choleric ferocity, their mouths gaped pinkly upon needle-like teeth. "Reba!" Miss Reba said, "get down! You, Mr Binford!" flinging them down, their teeth clicking about her hands. "You just bite me, you—— Did you get Miss——What's your name, honey? I didn't quite catch it."

"Temple," Temple whispered.

"I mean, your first name, honey. We dont stand on no ceremony here."

"That's it. Temple. Temple Drake."

"You got a boy's name, aint you?——Miss Temple's things washed, Minnie?"

"Yessum," the maid said. "Hit's dryin now hind the stove." She came with the tray, shoving the dogs gingerly aside while they clicked their teeth at her ankles.

"You wash it out good?"

"I had a time with it," Minnie said. "Seem like that the most hardest blood of all to get——" With a convulsive movement Temple flopped over, ducking her head beneath the covers. She felt Miss Reba's hand.

"Now, now. Now, now. Here, take your drink. This one's on me. I aint going to let no girl of Popeye's——"

"I dont want anymore," Temple said.

"Now, now," Miss Reba said. "Drink it and you'll feel

better." She lifted Temple's head. Temple clutched the covers to her throat. Miss Reba held the glass to her lips. She gulped it, writhed down again, clutching the covers about her, her eyes wide and black above the covers. "I bet you got that towel disarranged," Miss Reba said, putting her hand on the covers.

"No," Temple whispered. "It's all right. It's still there." She shrank, cringing; they could see the cringing of her legs beneath the covers.

"Did you get Dr Quinn, Minnie?" Miss Reba said.

"Yessum." Minnie was filling the tankard from the bottle, a dull frosting pacing the rise of liquor within the metal. "He say he dont make no Sunday afternoon calls."

"Did you tell him who wanted him? Did you tell him Miss Reba wanted him?"

"Yessum. He say he dont——"

"You go back and tell that suh——You tell him I'll—— No; wait." She rose heavily. "Sending a message like that back to me, that can put him in jail three times over." She waddled toward the door, the dogs crowding about the felt slippers. The maid followed and closed the door. Temple could hear Miss Reba cursing the dogs as she descended the stairs with terrific slowness. The sounds died away.

The shades blew steadily in the windows, with faint rasping sounds. Temple began to hear a clock. It sat on the mantel above a grate filled with fluted green paper. The clock was of flowered china, supported by four china nymphs. It had only one hand, scrolled and gilded, halfway between ten and eleven, lending to the otherwise blank face a quality of unequivocal assertion, as though it had nothing whatever to do with time.

Temple rose from the bed. Holding the towel about her she stole toward the door, her ears acute, her eyes a little blind with the strain of listening. It was twilight; in a dim mirror, a pellucid oblong of dusk set on end, she had a glimpse of herself like a thin ghost, a pale shadow moving in the uttermost profundity of shadow. She reached the door. At once she began to hear a hundred conflicting sounds in a single converging threat and she clawed furiously at the door until she found the bolt, dropping the towel to drive it home. Then she caught up the towel, her face averted, and ran back and sprang into the bed and clawed the covers to her chin and lay there, listening to the secret whisper of her blood.

They knocked at the door for some time before she made any sound. "It's the doctor, honey," Miss Reba panted harshly. "Come on, now. Be a good girl."

"I cant," Temple said, her voice faint and small. "I'm in bed."

"Come on, now. He wants to fix you up." She panted harshly. "My God, if I could just get one full breath again. I aint had a full breath since. . . . . . ." Low down beyond the door Temple could hear the dogs. "Honey."

She rose from the bed, holding the towel about her. She went to the door, silently.

"Honey," Miss Reba said.

"Wait," Temple said. "Let me get back to the bed before Let me get"

"There's a good girl," Miss Reba said. "I knowed she was going to be good."

"Count ten, now," Temple said. "Will you count ten, now?" she said against the wood. She slipped the bolt soundlessly, then she turned and sped back to the bed, her naked feet in pattering diminuendo.

The doctor was a fattish man with thin, curly hair. He wore horn-rimmed glasses which lent to his eyes no distortion at all, as though they were of clear glass and worn for decorum's sake. Temple watched him across the covers, holding them to her throat. "Make them go out," she whispered; "if they'll just go out."

"Now, now," Miss Reba said, "he's going to fix you up."

Temple clung to the covers.

"If the little lady will just let . . ." the doctor said. His hair evaporated finely from his brow. His mouth nipped in at the corners, his lips full and wet and red. Behind the glasses his eyes looked like little bicycle wheels at dizzy speed; a metallic hazel. He put out a thick, white hand bearing a masonic ring, haired over with fine reddish fuzz to the second knuckle-joints. Cold air slipped down her body, below her thighs; her eyes were closed. Lying on her back, her legs close together,

she began to cry, hopelessly and passively, like a child in a
dentist's waiting-room.

"Now, now," Miss Reba said, "take another sup of gin,
honey. It'll make you feel better."

In the window the cracked shade, yawning now and then
with a faint rasp against the frame, let twilight into the room
in fainting surges. From beneath the shade the smoke-colored
twilight emerged in slow puffs like signal smoke from a blanket, thickening in the room. The china figures which supported the clock gleamed in hushed smooth flexions: knee,
elbow, flank, arm and breast in attitudes of voluptuous lassitude. The glass face, become mirror-like, appeared to hold all
reluctant light, holding in its tranquil depths a quiet gesture
of moribund time, one-armed like a veteran from the wars.
Half past ten oclock. Temple lay in the bed, looking at the
clock, thinking about half-past-ten-oclock.

She wore a too-large gown of cerise crepe, black against
the linen. Her hair was a black sprawl, combed out now; her
face, throat and arms outside the covers were gray. After the
others left the room she lay for a time, head and all beneath
the covers. She lay so until she heard the door shut and the
descending feet, the doctor's light, unceasing voice and Miss
Reba's labored breath grow twilight-colored in the dingy hall
and die away. Then she sprang from the bed and ran to the
door and shot the bolt and ran back and hurled the covers
over her head again, lying in a tight knot until the air was
exhausted.

A final saffron-colored light lay upon the ceiling and the
upper walls, tinged already with purple by the serrated pali-
sade of Main Street high against the western sky. She watched
it fade as the successive yawns of the shade consumed it. She
watched the final light condense into the clock face, and the
dial change from a round orifice in the darkness to a disc
suspended in nothingness, the original chaos, and change in
turn to a crystal ball holding in its still and cryptic depths the
ordered chaos of the intricate and shadowy world upon
whose scarred flanks the old wounds whirl onward at dizzy
speed into darkness lurking with new disasters.

She was thinking about half-past-ten-oclock. The hour for

dressing for a dance, if you were popular enough not to have to be on time. The air would be steamy with recent baths, and perhaps powder in the light like chaff in barn-lofts, and they looking at one another, comparing, talking whether you could do more damage if you could just walk out on the floor like you were now. Some wouldn't, mostly ones with short legs. Some of them were all right, but they just wouldn't. They wouldn't say why. The worst one of all said boys thought all girls were ugly except when they were dressed. She said the Snake had been seeing Eve for several days and never noticed her until Adam made her put on a fig leaf. How do you know? they said, and she said because the Snake was there before Adam, because he was the first one thrown out of heaven; he was there all the time. But that wasn't what they meant and they said, How do you know, and Temple thought of her kind of backed up against the dressing table and the rest of them in a circle around her with their combed hair and their shoulders smelling of scented soap and the light powder in the air and their eyes like knives until you could almost watch her flesh where the eyes were touching it, and her eyes in her ugly face courageous and frightened and daring, and they all saying, How do you know? until she told them and held up her hand and swore she had. That was when the youngest one turned and ran out of the room. She locked herself in the bath and they could hear her being sick.

She thought about half-past-ten-oclock in the morning. Sunday morning, and the couples strolling toward church. She remembered it was still Sunday, the same Sunday, looking at the fading peaceful gesture of the clock. Maybe it was half-past-ten this morning, that half-past-ten-oclock. Then I'm not here, she thought. This is not me. Then I'm at school. I have a date tonight with. . . . . . .thinking of the student with whom she had the date. But she couldn't remember who it would be. She kept the dates written down in her Latin 'pony', so she didn't have to bother about who it was. She'd just dress, and after a while somebody would call for her. So I better get up and dress, she said, looking at the clock.

She rose and crossed the room quietly. She watched the

clock face, but although she could see a warped turmoil of faint light and shadow in geometric miniature swinging across it, she could not see herself. It's this nightie, she thought, looking at her arms, her breast rising out of a dissolving pall beneath which her toes peeped in pale, fleet intervals as she walked. She drew the bolt quietly and returned to the bed and lay with her head cradled in her arms.

There was still a little light in the room. She found that she was hearing her watch; had been hearing it for some time. She discovered that the house was full of noises, seeping into the room muffled and indistinguishable, as though from a distance. A bell rang faintly and shrilly somewhere; someone mounted the stairs in a swishing garment. The feet went on past the door and mounted another stair and ceased. She listened to the watch. A car started beneath the window with a grind of gears; again the faint bell rang, shrill and prolonged. She found that the faint light yet in the room was from a street lamp. Then she realised that it was night and that the darkness beyond was full of the sound of the city.

She heard the two dogs come up the stairs in a furious scrabble. The noise passed the door and stopped, became utterly still; so still that she could almost see them crouching there in the dark against the wall, watching the stairs. One of them was named Mister something, Temple thought, waiting to hear Miss Reba's feet on the stairs. But it was not Miss Reba; they came too steadily and too lightly. The door opened; the dogs surged in in two shapeless blurs and scuttled under the bed and crouched, whimpering. "You, dawgs!" Minnie's voice said. "You make me spill this." The light came on. Minnie carried a tray. "I got you some supper," she said. "Where them dawgs gone to?"

"Under the bed," Temple said. "I dont want any."

Minnie came and set the tray on the bed and looked down at Temple, her pleasant face knowing and placid. "You want me to——" she said, extending her hand. Temple turned her face quickly away. She heard Minnie kneel, cajoling the dogs, the dogs snarling back at her with whimpering, asthmatic snarls and clicking teeth. "Come outen there, now," Minnie said. "They know fo Miss Reba do when she fixing to get drunk. You, Mr Binford!"

Temple raised her head. "Mr Binford?"

"He the one with the blue ribbon," Minnie said. Stooping, she flapped her arm at the dogs. They were backed against the wall at the head of the bed, snapping and snarling at her in mad terror. "Mr Binford was Miss Reba's man. Was landlord here eleven years until he die bout two years ago. Next day Miss Reba get these dawgs, name one Mr Binford and other Miss Reba. Whenever she go to the cemetery she start drinking like this evening, then they both got to run. But Mr Binford ketch it sho nough. Last time she throw him outen upstair window and go down and empty Mr Binford's clothes closet and throw everything out in the street except what he buried in."

"Oh," Temple said. "No wonder they're scared. Let them stay under there. They wont bother me."

"Reckon I have to. Mr Binford aint going to leave this room, not if he know it." She stood again, looking down at Temple. "Eat that supper," she said. "You feel better. I done slip you a drink of gin, too."

"I dont want any," Temple said, turning her face away. She heard Minnie leave the room. The door closed quietly. Under the bed the dogs crouched against the wall in that rigid and furious terror.

The light hung from the center of the ceiling, beneath a fluted shade of rose-colored paper browned where the bulb bulged it. The floor was covered by a figured maroon-tinted carpet tacked down in strips; the olive-tinted walls bore two framed lithographs. From the two windows curtains of machine lace hung, dust-colored, like strips of lightly congealed dust set on end. The whole room had an air of musty stodginess, decorum; in the wavy mirror of a cheap varnished dresser, as in a stagnant pool, there seemed to linger spent ghosts of voluptuous gestures and dead lusts. In the corner, upon a faded scarred strip of oilcloth tacked over the carpet, sat a washstand bearing a flowered bowl and pitcher and a row of towels; in the corner behind it sat a slop jar dressed also in fluted rose-colored paper.

Beneath the bed the dogs made no sound. Temple moved slightly; the dry complaint of mattress and springs died into the terrific silence in which they crouched. She thought of them, woolly, shapeless; savage, petulant, spoiled, the flatulent monotony of their sheltered lives snatched up without warning by an incomprehensible moment of terror and fear of bodily annihilation at the very hands which symbolised by ordinary the licensed tranquillity of their lives.

The house was full of sounds. Indistinguishable, remote, they came in to her with a quality of awakening, resurgence, as though the house itself had been asleep, rousing itself with dark; she heard something which might have been a burst of laughter in a shrill woman voice. Steamy odors from the tray drifted across her face. She turned her head and looked at it, at the covered and uncovered dishes of thick china. In the midst of them sat the glass of pale gin, a pack of cigarettes and a box of matches. She rose on her elbow, catching up the slipping gown. She lifted the covers upon a thick steak, potatoes, green peas; rolls; an anonymous pinkish mass which some sense—elimination, perhaps—identified as a sweet. She drew the slipping gown up again, thinking about them eating down at school in a bright uproar of voices and clattering forks; of her father and brothers at the supper table at home; thinking about the borrowed gown and Miss Reba saying that they would go shopping tomorrow. And I've just got two dollars, she thought.

When she looked at the food she found that she was not hungry at all, didn't even want to look at it. She lifted the glass and gulped it empty, her face wry, and set it down and turned her face hurriedly from the tray, fumbling for the cigarettes. When she went to strike the match she looked at the tray again and took up a strip of potato gingerly in her fingers and ate it. She ate another, the unlighted cigarette in her other hand. Then she put the cigarette down and took up the knife and fork and began to eat, pausing from time to time to draw the gown up onto her shoulder.

When she finished eating she lit the cigarette. She heard the bell again, then another in a slightly different key. Across a shrill rush of a woman's voice a door banged. Two people mounted the stairs and passed the door; she heard Miss Reba's voice booming from somewhere and listened to her toiling slowly up the stairs. Temple watched the door until it opened and Miss Reba stood in it, the tankard in her hand.

She now wore a bulging house dress and a widow's bonnet
with a veil. She entered on the flowered felt slippers. Beneath
the bed the two dogs made a stifled concerted sound of utter
despair.

The dress, unfastened in the back, hung lumpily about Miss
Reba's shoulders. One ringed hand lay on her breast, the
other held the tankard high. Her open mouth, studded with
gold-fillings, gaped upon the harsh labor of her breathing.

"Oh God oh God," she said. The dogs surged out from
beneath the bed and hurled themselves toward the door in a
mad scrabble. As they rushed past her she turned and flung
the tankard at them. It struck the door jamb, splashing up the
wall, and rebounded with a forlorn clatter. She drew her
breath whistling, clutching her breast. She came to the bed
and looked down at Temple through the veil. "We was happy
as two doves," she wailed, choking, her rings smoldering in
hot glints within her billowing breast. "Then he had to go
and die on me." She drew her breath whistling, her mouth
gaped, shaping the hidden agony of her thwarted lungs, her
eyes pale and round with stricken bafflement, protuberant.
"As two doves," she roared in a harsh, choking voice.

Again time had overtaken the dead gesture behind the
clock crystal: Temple's watch on the table beside the bed said
half-past-ten. For two hours she had lain undisturbed, listening. She could distinguish voices now from below stairs. She
had been hearing them for some time, lying in the room's
musty isolation. Later a mechanical piano began to play. Now
and then she heard automobile brakes in the street beneath
the window; once two voices quarrelling bitterly came up and
beneath the shade.

She heard two people—a man and a woman—mount the
stairs and enter the room next hers. Then she heard Miss
Reba toil up the stairs and pass her door, and lying in the
bed, her eyes wide and still, she heard Miss Reba hammering
at the next door with the metal tankard and shouting into the
wood. Beyond the door the man and woman were utterly
quiet, so quiet that Temple thought of the dogs again,
thought of them crouching against the wall under the bed in
that rigid fury of terror and despair. She listened to Miss

Reba's voice shouting hoarsely into the blank wood. It died away into terrific gasping, then it rose again in the gross and virile cursing of a man. Beyond the wall the man and woman made no sound. Temple lay staring at the wall beyond which Miss Reba's voice rose again as she hammered at the door with the tankard.

Temple neither saw nor heard her door when it opened. She just happened to look toward it after how long she did not know, and saw Popeye standing there, his hat slanted across his face. Still without making any sound he entered and shut the door and shot the bolt and came toward the bed. As slowly she began to shrink into the bed, drawing the covers up to her chin, watching him across the covers. He came and looked down at her. She writhed slowly in a cringing movement, cringing upon herself in as complete an isolation as though she were bound to a church steeple. She grinned at him, her mouth warped over the rigid, placative porcelain of her grimace.

When he put his hand on her she began to whimper. "No, no," she whispered, "he said I cant now he said. . . . . . ."
He jerked the covers back and flung them aside. She lay motionless, her palms lifted, her flesh beneath the envelope of her loins cringing rearward in furious disintegration like frightened people in a crowd. When he advanced his hand again she thought he was going to strike her. Watching his face, she saw it beginning to twitch and jerk like that of a child about to cry, and she heard him begin to make a whimpering sound. He gripped the top of the gown. She caught his wrists and began to toss from side to side, opening her mouth to scream. His hand clapped over her mouth, and gripping his wrist, the saliva drooling between his fingers, her body thrashing furiously from thigh to thigh, she saw him crouching beside the bed, his face wrung above his absent chin, his bluish lips protruding as though he were blowing upon hot soup, making a high whinnying sound like a horse. Beyond the wall Miss Reba filled the hall, the house, with a harsh choking uproar of obscene cursing.

XIX

"**B**ut that girl," Horace said. "She was all right. You know she was all right when you left the house. When you saw her in the car with him. He was just giving her a lift to town. She was all right. You know she was all right."

The woman sat on the edge of the bed, looking down at the child. It lay beneath the faded, clean blanket, its hands upflung beside its head, as though it had died in the presence of an unbearable agony which had not had time to touch it. Its eyes were half open, the balls rolled back into the skull so that only the white showed, in color like weak milk. Its face was still damp with perspiration, but its breathing was easier. It no longer breathed in those weak, whistling gasps as it had when Horace entered the room. On a chair beside the bed sat a tumbler half full of faintly discolored water, with a spoon in it. Through the open window came the myriad noises of the square—cars, wagons, footsteps on the pavement beneath—and through it Horace could see the courthouse, with men pitching dollars back and forth between holes in the bare earth beneath the locusts and water oaks.

The woman brooded above the child. "Nobody wanted her out there. Lee has told them and told them they must not bring women out there, and I told her before it got dark they were not her kind of people and to get away from there. It was that fellow that brought her. He was out there on the porch with them, still drinking, because when he came in to supper he couldn't hardly walk, even. He hadn't even tried to wash the blood off of his face. Little shirt-tail boys that think because Lee breaks the law, they can come out there and treat our house like a. . . . . . . Grown people are bad, but at least they take buying whiskey like buying anything else; it's the ones like him, the ones that are too young to realise that people dont break the law just for a holiday." Horace could see her clenched hands writhing in her lap. "God, if I had my way, I'd hang every man that makes it or buys it or drinks it, every one of them.

"But why must it have been me, us? What had I ever done to her, to her kind? I told her to get away from there. I told her not to stay there until dark. But that fellow that brought her was getting drunk again, and him and Van picking at each other. If she'd just stopped running around where they had to look at her. She wouldn't stay anywhere. She'd just dash out one door, and in a minute she'd come running in from the other direction. And if he'd just let Van alone, because Van had to go back on the truck at midnight, and so Popeye would have made him behave. And Saturday night too, and them sitting up all night drinking anyway, and I had gone through it and gone through it and I'd tell Lee to let's get away, that he was getting nowhere, and he would have these spells like last night, and no doctor, no telephone. And then she had to come out there, after I had slaved for him, slaved for him." Motionless, her head bent and her hands still in her lap, she had that spent immobility of a chimney rising above the ruin of a house in the aftermath of a cyclone.

"Standing there in the corner behind the bed, with that raincoat on. She was that scared, when they brought the fellow in, all bloody again. They laid him on the bed and Van hit him again and Lee caught Van's arm, and her standing there with her eyes like the holes in one of these masks. The raincoat was hanging on the wall, and she had it on, over her coat. Her dress was all folded up on the bed. They threw the fellow right on top of it, blood and all, and I said 'God, are you drunk too?' but Lee just looked at me and I saw that his nose was white already, like it gets when he's drunk.

"There wasn't any lock on the door, but I thought that pretty soon they'd have to go and see about the truck and then I could do something. Then Lee made me go out too, and he took the lamp out, so I had to wait until they went back to the porch before I could go back. I stood just inside the door. The fellow was snoring, in the bed there, breathing hard, with his nose and mouth all battered up again, and I could hear them on the porch. Then they would be outdoors, around the house and at the back too I could hear them. Then they got quiet.

"I stood there, against the wall. He would snore and choke and catch his breath and moan, sort of, and I would think about that girl lying there in the dark, with her eyes open, listening to them, and me having to stand there, waiting for them to go away so I could do something. I told her to go away. I said 'What fault is it of mine if you're not married? I dont want you here a bit more than you want to be here.' I said 'I've lived my life without any help from people of your sort; what right have you got to look to me for help?' Because I've done everything for him. I've been in the dirt for him. I've put everything behind me and all I ask was to be let alone.

"Then I heard the door open. I could tell Lee by the way he breathes. He went to the bed and said 'I want the raincoat. Sit up and take it off' and I could hear the shucks rattling while he took it off of her, then he went out. He just got the raincoat and went out. It was Van's coat.

"And I have walked around that house so much at night, with those men there, men living off of Lee's risk, men that wouldn't lift a finger for him if he got caught, until I could tell any of them by the way they breathed, and I could tell Popeye by the smell of that stuff on his hair. Tommy was following him. He came in the door behind Popeye and looked at me and I could see his eyes, like a cat. Then his eyes went away and I could feel him sort of squatting against me, and we could hear Popeye over where the bed was and that fellow snoring and snoring.

"I could just hear little faint sounds, from the shucks, so I knew it was all right yet, and in a minute Popeye came on back, and Tommy followed him out, creeping along behind him, and I stood there until I heard them go down to the truck. Then I went to the bed. When I touched her she began to fight. I was trying to put my hand over her mouth so she couldn't make a noise, but she didn't anyway. She just lay there, thrashing about, rolling her head from one side to the other, holding to the coat.

" 'You fool!' I says 'It's me—the woman.' "

"But that girl," Horace said. "She was all right. When you were coming back to the house the next morning after the baby's bottle, you saw her and knew she was all right." The room gave onto the square. Through the window he could see the young men pitching dollars in the courthouse yard, and the wagons passing or tethered about the hitching chains, and he could hear the footsteps and voices of people on the slow and unhurried pavement below the window; the people buying comfortable things to take home and eat at quiet tables. "You know she was all right."

That night Horace went out to his sister's, in a hired car; he did not telephone. He found Miss Jenny in her room. "Well," she said. "Narcissa will——"

"I dont want to see her." Horace said. "Her nice, well-bred young man. Her Virginia gentleman. I know why he didn't come back."

"Who? Gowan?"

"Yes; Gowan. And, by the Lord, he'd better not come back. By God, when I think that I had the opportunity——"

"What? What did he do?"

"He carried a little fool girl out there with him that day and got drunk and ran off and left her. That's what he did. If it hadn't been for that woman——And when I think of people like that walking the earth with impunity just because he has a balloon-tailed suit and went through the astonishing experience of having attended Virginia. . . . . . . On any train or in any hotel, on the street; anywhere, mind you——"

"Oh," Miss Jenny said. "I didn't understand at first who you meant. Well," she said. "You remember that last time he was here, just after you came? the day he wouldn't stay for supper and went to Oxford?"

"Yes. And when I think how I could have——"

"He asked Narcissa to marry him. She told him that one child was enough for her."

"I said she has no heart. She cannot be satisfied with less than insult."

"So he got mad and said he would go to Oxford, where there was a woman he was reasonably confident he would not appear ridiculous to: something like that. Well." She looked at him, her neck bowed to see across her spectacles. "I'll declare, a male parent is a funny thing, but just let a man have a hand in the affairs of a female that's no kin to him. . . . . . . What is it that makes a man think that the female flesh he marries or begets might misbehave, but all he didn't marry or get is bound to?"

"Yes," Horace said, "and thank God she isn't my flesh and

blood. I can reconcile myself to her having to be exposed to a scoundrel now and then, but to think that at any moment she may become involved with a fool."

"Well, what are you going to do about it? Start some kind of roach campaign?"

"I'm going to do what she said; I'm going to have a law passed making it obligatory upon everyone to shoot any man less than fifty years old that makes, buys, sells or thinks whiskey. . . . . . .scoundrel I can face, but to think of her being exposed to any fool. . . . . . ."

He returned to town. The night was warm, the darkness filled with the sound of new-fledged cicadas. He was using a bed, one chair, a bureau on which he had spread a towel and upon which lay his brushes, his watch, his pipe and tobacco pouch, and, propped against a book, a photograph of his step-daughter, Little Belle. Upon the glazed surface a high-light lay. He shifted the photograph until the face came clear. He stood before it, looking at the sweet, inscrutable face which looked in turn at something just beyond his shoulder, out of the dead cardboard. He was thinking of the grape ar-bor in Kinston, of summer twilight and the murmur of voices darkening into silence as he approached, who meant them, her, no harm; who meant her less than harm, good God; darkening into the pale whisper of her white dress, of the delicate and urgent mammalian whisper of that curious small flesh which he had not begot and in which appeared to be vatted delicately some seething sympathy with the blossoming grape.

He moved, suddenly. As of its own accord the photograph had shifted, slipping a little from its precarious balancing against the book. The image blurred into the highlight, like something familiar seen beneath disturbed though clear wa-ter; he looked at the familiar image with a kind of quiet hor-ror and despair, at a face suddenly older in sin than he would ever be, a face more blurred than sweet, at eyes more secret than soft. In reaching for it, he knocked it flat; whereupon once more the face mused tenderly behind the rigid travesty of the painted mouth, contemplating something beyond his shoulder. He lay in bed, dressed, with the light burning, until he heard the court-house clock strike three. Then he left the house, putting his watch and his tobacco pouch into his pocket.

The railroad station was three quarters of a mile away. The waiting room was lit by a single weak bulb. It was empty save for a man in overalls asleep on a bench, his head on his folded coat, snoring, and a woman in a calico dress, in a dingy shawl and a new hat trimmed with rigid and moribund flowers set square and awkward on her head. Her head was bent; she may have been asleep; her hands crossed on a paper-wrapped parcel upon her lap, a straw suit case at her feet. It was then that Horace found that he had forgot his pipe.

The train came, finding him tramping back and forth along the cinder-packed right-of-way. The man and woman got on, the man carrying his rumpled coat, the woman the parcel and the suit case. He followed them into the day coach filled with snoring, with bodies sprawled half into the aisle as though in the aftermath of a sudden and violent destruction, with dropped heads, open-mouthed, their throats turned profoundly upward as though waiting the stroke of knives.

He dozed. The train clicked on, stopped, jolted. He waked and dozed again. Someone shook him out of sleep into a primrose dawn, among unshaven puffy faces washed lightly over as though with the paling ultimate stain of a holocaust, blinking at one another with dead eyes into which personality returned in secret opaque waves. He got off, had breakfast, and took another accommodation, entering a car where a child wailed hopelessly, crunching peanut-shells under his feet as he moved up the car in a stale ammoniac odor until he found a seat beside a man. A moment later the man leaned forward and spat tobacco juice between his knees. Horace rose quickly and went forward into the smoking car. It was full too, the door between it and the jim crow car swinging open. Standing in the aisle he could look forward into a diminishing corridor of green plush seat-backs topped by hatted cannonballs swaying in unison, while gusts of talk and laughter blew back and kept in steady motion the blue acrid air in which white men sat, spitting into the aisle.

He changed again. The waiting crowd was composed half of young men in collegiate clothes with small cryptic badges on their shirts and vests, and two girls with painted small faces and scant bright dresses like identical artificial flowers surrounded each by bright and restless bees. When the train came they pushed gaily forward, talking and laughing, shouldering aside older people with gay rudeness, clashing and slamming seats back and settling themselves, turning their faces up out of laughter, their cold faces still toothed with it, as three middle-aged women moved down the car, looking tentatively left and right at the filled seats.

The two girls sat together, removing a fawn and a blue hat, lifting slender hands and preening not-quite-formless fingers about their close heads seen between the sprawled elbows and the leaning heads of two youths hanging over the back of the seat and surrounded by colored hat bands at various heights where the owners sat on the seat arms or stood in the aisle; and presently the conductor's cap as he thrust among them with plaintive, fretful cries, like a bird.

"Tickets. Tickets, please," he chanted. For an instant they held him there, invisible save for his cap. Then two young men slipped swiftly back and into the seat behind Horace. He could hear them breathing. Forward the conductor's punch clicked twice. He came on back. "Tickets," he chanted. "Tickets." He took Horace's and stopped where the youths sat.

"You already got mine," one said. "Up there."

"Where's your check?" the conductor said.

"You never gave us any. You got our tickets, though. Mine was number——" he repeated a number glibly, in a frank, pleasant tone. "Did you notice the number of yours, Shack?"

The second one repeated a number in a frank, pleasant tone. "Sure you got ours. Look and see." He began to whistle between his teeth, a broken dance rhythm, unmusical.

"Do you eat at Gordon hall?" the other said.

"No. I have natural halitosis." The conductor went on. The whistle reached crescendo, clapped off by his hands on his knees, ejaculating duh-duh-duh. Then he just squalled, meaningless, vertiginous; to Horace it was like sitting before a series of printed pages turned in furious snatches, leaving a series of cryptic, headless and tailless evocations on the mind.

"She's travelled a thousand miles without a ticket."

"Marge too."

"Beth too."

"Duh-duh-duh."

"Marge too."

"I'm going to punch mine Friday night."

"Eeeeyow."

"Do you like liver?"

"I cant reach that far."

"Eeeeeyow."

They whistled, clapping their heels on the floor to furious crescendo, saying duh-duh-duh. The first jolted the seat back against Horace's head. He rose. "Come on," he said. "He's done gone." Again the seat jarred into Horace and he watched them return and join the group that blocked the aisle, saw one of them lay his bold, rough hand flat upon one of the bright, soft faces uptilted to them. Beyond the group a countrywoman with an infant in her arms stood braced against a seat. From time to time she looked back at the blocked aisle and the empty seats beyond.

At Oxford he descended into a throng of them at the station, hatless, in bright dresses, now and then with books in their hands and surrounded still by swarms of colored shirts. Impassable, swinging hands with their escorts, objects of casual and puppyish pawings, they dawdled up the hill toward the college, swinging their little hips, looking at Horace with cold, blank eyes as he stepped off the walk in order to pass them.

At the top of the hill three paths diverged through a broad grove beyond which, in green vistas, buildings in red brick or gray stone gleamed, and where a clear soprano bell began to ring. The procession became three streams, thinning rapidly upon the dawdling couples swinging hands, strolling in erratic surges, lurching into one another with puppyish squeals, with the random intense purposelessness of children.

The broader path led to the postoffice. He entered and waited until the window was clear.

"I'm trying to find a young lady, Miss Temple Drake. I probably just missed her, didn't I?"

"She's not here any longer," the clerk said. "She quit school about two weeks ago." He was young: a dull, smooth face behind horn glasses, the hair meticulous. After a time Horace heard himself asking quietly:

"You dont know where she went?"

The clerk looked at him. He leaned, lowering his voice: "Are you another detective?"

"Yes," Horace said, "yes. No matter. It doesn't matter." Then he was walking quietly down the steps, into the sunlight again. He stood there while on both sides of him they passed in a steady stream of little colored dresses, bare-armed, with close bright heads, with that identical cool, innocent, unabashed expression which he knew well in their eyes, above the savage identical paint upon their mouths; like music moving, like honey poured in sunlight, pagan and evanescent and serene, thinly evocative of all lost days and outpaced delights, in the sun. Bright, trembling with heat, it lay in open glades of miragelike glimpses of stone or brick: columns without tops, towers apparently floating above a green cloud in slow ruin against the southwest wind, sinister, imponderable, bland; and he standing there listening to the sweet cloistral bell, thinking Now what? What now? and answering himself: Why, nothing. Nothing. It's finished.

He returned to the station an hour before the train was due, a filled but unlighted cob pipe in his hand. In the lavatory he saw, scrawled on the foul, stained wall, her pencilled name. Temple Drake. He read it quietly, his head bent, slowly fingering the unlighted pipe.

A half hour before the train came they began to gather, strolling down the hill and gathering along the platform with thin, bright, raucous laughter, their blonde legs monotonous, their bodies moving continually inside their scant garments with that awkward and voluptuous purposelessness of the young.

The return train carried a pullman. He went on through the day coach and entered it. There was only one other occupant: a man in the center of the car, next the window, bareheaded, leaning back, his elbow on the window sill and an unlighted cigar in his ringed hand. When the train drew away, passing the sleek crowns in increasing reverse, the other passenger rose and went forward toward the day coach. He carried an overcoat on his arm, and a soiled, light-colored felt hat. With the corner of his eye Horace saw his hand fumbling at his breast pocket, and he remarked the severe trim of hair across the man's vast, soft, white neck. Like with a guillotine, Horace thought, watching the man sidle past the porter in the aisle and vanish, passing out of his sight and his mind in the act of flinging the hat onto his head. The train sped on, swaying on the curves, flashing past an occasional house, through cuts and across valleys where young cotton wheeled slowly in fanlike rows.

The train checked speed; a jerk came back, and four whistle-blasts. The man in the soiled hat entered, taking a cigar from his breast pocket. He came down the aisle swiftly, looking at Horace. He slowed, the cigar in his fingers. The train jolted again. The man flung his hand out and caught the back of the seat facing Horace.

"Aint this Judge Benbow?" he said. Horace looked up into a vast, puffy face without any mark of age or thought whatever—a majestic sweep of flesh on either side of a small blunt nose, like looking out over a mesa, yet withal some indefinable quality of delicate paradox, as though the Creator had completed his joke by lighting the munificent expenditure of putty with something originally intended for some weak, acquisitive creature like a squirrel or a rat. "Dont I address Judge Benbow?" he said, offering his hand. "I'm Senator Snopes, Cla'ence Snopes."

"Oh," Horace said, "yes. Thanks," he said, "but I'm afraid you anticipate a little. Hope, rather."

The other waved the cigar, the other hand, palm-up, the third finger discolored faintly at the base of a huge ring, in Horace's face. Horace shook it and freed his hand. "I thought I recognised you when you got on at Oxford," Snopes said, "but I——May I set down?" he said, already shoving at Horace's knee with his leg. He flung the overcoat—a shoddy blue garment with a greasy velvet collar—on the seat and sat down as the train stopped. "Yes, sir, I'm always glad to see any of the boys, any time. . . . . . ." He leaned across Horace and peered out the window at a small dingy station with its cryptic bulletin board chalked over, an express truck bearing a wire chicken coop containing two forlorn fowls, at three or four men in overalls gone restfully against the wall, chewing. " 'Course you aint in my county no longer, but what I say a man's friends is his friends, whichever way they vote.

Because a friend is a friend, and whether he can do anything for me or not. . . . . . ." He leaned back, the unlighted cigar in his fingers. "You aint come all the way up from the big town, then."

"No," Horace said.

"Anytime you're in Jackson, I'll be glad to accommodate you as if you was still in my county. Dont no man stay so busy he aint got time for his old friends, what I say. Let's see, you're in Kinston, now, aint you? I know your senators. Fine men, both of them, but I just caint call their names."

"I really couldn't say, myself," Horace said. The train started. Snopes leaned into the aisle, looking back. His light gray suit had been pressed but not cleaned. "Well," he said. He rose and took up the overcoat. "Any time you're in the city. . . . . . . You going to Jefferson, I reckon?"

"Yes," Horace said.

"I'll see you again, then."

"Why not ride back here?" Horace said. "You'll find it more comfortable."

"I'm going up and have a smoke," Snopes said, waving the cigar. "I'll see you again."

"You can smoke here. There aren't any ladies."

"Sure," Snopes said. "I'll see you at Holly Springs." He went on back toward the day coach and passed out of sight with the cigar in his mouth. Horace remembered him ten years ago as a hulking, dull youth, son of a restaurant-owner, member of a family which had been moving from the Frenchman's Bend neighborhood into Jefferson for the past twenty years, in sections; a family of enough ramifications to have elected him to the legislature without recourse to a public polling.

He sat quite still, the cold pipe in his hand. He rose and went forward through the day coach, then into the smoker. Snopes was in the aisle, his thigh draped over the arm of a seat where four men sat, using the unlighted cigar to gesture with. Horace caught his eye and beckoned from the vestibule. A moment later Snopes joined him, the overcoat on his arm.

"How are things going at the capital?" Horace said.

Snopes began to speak in his harsh, assertive voice. There emerged gradually a picture of stupid chicanery and petty corruption for stupid and petty ends, conducted principally in hotel rooms into which bellboys whisked with bulging jackets upon discreet flicks of skirts in swift closet doors. "Anytime you're in town," he said. "I always like to show the boys around. Ask anybody in town; they'll tell you if it's there, Cla'ence Snopes'll know where it is. You got a pretty tough case up home there, what I hear."

"Cant tell yet," Horace said. He said: "I stopped off at Oxford today, at the university, speaking to some of my step-daughter's friends. One of her best friends is no longer in school there. A young lady from Jackson named Temple Drake."

Snopes was watching him with thick, small, opaque eyes. "Oh, yes; Judge Drake's gal," he said. "The one that ran away."

"Ran away?" Horace said. "Ran back home, did she? What was the trouble? Fail in her work?"

"I dont know. When it come out in the paper folks thought she'd run off with some fellow. One of them companionate marriages."

"But when she turned up at home, they knew it wasn't that, I reckon. Well, well, Belle'll be surprised. What's she doing now? Running around Jackson, I suppose?"

"She aint there."

"Not?" Horace said. He could feel the other watching him. "Where is she?"

"Her paw sent her up north somewhere, with an aunt. Michigan. It was in the papers couple days later."

"Oh," Horace said. He still held the cold pipe, and he discovered his hand searching his pocket for a match. He drew a deep breath. "That Jackson paper's a pretty good paper. It's considered the most reliable paper in the state, isn't it?"

"Sure," Snopes said. "You was at Oxford trying to locate her?"

"No, no. I just happened to meet a friend of my daughter who told me she had left school. Well, I'll see you at Holly Springs."

"Sure," Snopes said. Horace returned to the pullman and sat down and lit the pipe.

When the train slowed for Holly Springs he went to the

vestibule, then he stepped quickly back into the car. Snopes emerged from the day coach as the porter opened the door and swung down the step, stool in hand. Snopes descended. He took something from his breast pocket and gave it to the porter. "Here, George," he said, "have a cigar."

Horace descended. Snopes went on, the soiled hat towering half a head above any other. Horace looked at the porter.

"He gave it to you, did he?"

The porter chucked the cigar on his palm. He put it in his pocket.

"What're you going to do with it?" Horace said.

"I wouldn't give it to nobody I know," the porter said.

"Does he do this very often?"

"Three-four times a year. Seems like I always git him, too. . . . . . . Thank' suh."

Horace saw Snopes enter the waiting-room; the soiled hat, the vast neck, passed again out of his mind. He filled the pipe again.

From a block away he heard the Memphis-bound train come in. It was at the platform when he reached the station. Beside the open vestibule Snopes stood, talking with two youths in new straw hats, with something vaguely mentorial about his thick shoulders and his gestures. The train whistled. The two youths got on. Horace stepped back around the corner of the station.

When his train came he saw Snopes get on ahead of him and enter the smoker. Horace knocked out his pipe and entered the day coach and found a seat at the rear, facing backward.

XX

As HORACE was leaving the station at Jefferson a townward-bound car slowed beside him. It was the taxi which he used to go out to his sister's. "I'll give you a ride, this time," the driver said.

"Much obliged," Horace said. He got in. When the car entered the square, the court-house clock said only twenty minutes past eight, yet there was no light in the hotel room window. "Maybe the child's asleep," Horace said. He said, "If you'll just drop me at the hotel——" Then he found that the driver was watching him, with a kind of discreet curiosity.

"You been out of town today," the driver said.

"Yes," Horace said. "What is it? What happened here today?"

"She aint staying at the hotel anymore. I heard Mrs Walker taken her in at the jail."

"Oh," Horace said. "I'll get out at the hotel."

The lobby was empty. After a moment the proprietor appeared: a tight, iron-gray man with a toothpick, his vest open upon a neat paunch. The woman was not there. "It's these church ladies," he said. He lowered his voice, the toothpick in his fingers. "They come in this morning. A committee of them. You know how it is, I reckon."

"You mean to say you let the Baptist church dictate who your guests shall be?"

"It's them ladies. You know how it is, once they get set on a thing. A man might just as well give up and do like they say. Of course, with me——"

"By God, if there was a man——"

"Shhhhhh," the proprietor said. "You know how it is when them——"

"But of course there wasn't a man who would——And you call yourself one, that'll let——"

"I got a certain position to keep up myself," the proprietor said in a placative tone. "If you come right down to it." He stepped back a little, against the desk. "I reckon I can say who'll stay in my house and who wont," he said. "And I know some more folks around here that better do the same thing. Not no mile off, neither. I aint beholden to no man. Not to you, noways."

"Where is she now? or did they drive her out of town?"

"That aint my affair, where folks go after they check out," the proprietor said, turning his back. He said: "I reckon somebody took her in, though."

"Yes," Horace said. "Christians. Christians." He turned toward the door. The proprietor called him. He turned. The other was taking a paper down from a pigeon-hole. Horace returned to the desk. The paper lay on the desk. The proprietor leaned with his hands on the desk, the toothpick tilted in his mouth.

"She said you'd pay it," he said.

He paid the bill, counting the money down with shaking hands. He entered the jail yard and went to the door and knocked. After a while a lank, slattern woman came with a lamp, holding a man's coat across her breast. She peered at him and said before he could speak:

"You're lookin fer Miz Goodwin, I reckon."

"Yes. How did——Did——"

"You're the lawyer. I've seed you befo. She's hyer. Sleepin now."

"Thanks," Horace said, "thanks. I knew that someone—— I didn't believe that——"

"I reckon I kin always find a bed fer a woman and child," the woman said. "I dont keer whut Ed says. Was you wantin her special? She's sleepin now."

"No, no; I just wanted to——"

The woman watched him across the lamp. " 'Taint no need botherin her, then. You kin come around in the mawnin and git her a boa'din-place. 'Taint no hurry."

On the next afternoon Horace went out to his sister's, again in a hired car. He told her what had happened. "I'll have to take her home now."

"Not into my house," Narcissa said.

He looked at her. Then he began to fill his pipe slowly and carefully. "It's not a matter of choice, my dear. You must see that."

"Not in my house," Narcissa said. "I thought we settled that."

He struck the match and lit the pipe and put the match carefully into the fireplace. "Do you realise that she has been practically turned into the streets? That——"

"That shouldn't be a hardship. She ought to be used to that."

He looked at her. He put the pipe in his mouth and smoked it to a careful coal, watching his hand tremble upon the stem. "Listen. By tomorrow they will probably ask her to leave town. Just because she happens not to be married to the man whose child she carries about these sanctified streets. But who told them? That's what I want to know. I know that nobody in Jefferson knew it except——"

"You were the first I heard tell it," Miss Jenny said. "But, Narcissa, why——"

"Not in my house," Narcissa said.

"Well," Horace said. He drew the pipe to an even coal. "That settles it, of course," he said, in a dry, light voice.

She rose. "Will you stay here tonight?"

"What? No. No. I'll——I told her I'd come for her at the jail and. . . . . . ." He sucked at his pipe. "Well, I dont suppose it matters. I hope it doesn't."

She was still paused, turning. "Will you stay or not?"

"I could even tell her I had a puncture," Horace said. "Time's not such a bad thing after all. Use it right, and you can stretch anything out, like a rubber band, until it busts somewhere, and there you are, with all tragedy and despair in two little knots between thumb and finger of each hand."

"Will you stay, or wont you stay, Horace?" Narcissa said.

"I think I'll stay," Horace said.

He was in bed. He had been lying in the dark for about an hour, when the door of the room opened, felt rather than seen or heard. It was his sister. He rose to his elbow. She took shape vaguely, approaching the bed. She came and looked down at him. "How much longer are you going to keep this up?" she said.

"Just until morning," he said. "I'm going back to town. You need not see me again."

She stood beside the bed, motionless. After a moment her cold unbending voice came down to him: "You know what I mean."

"I promise not to bring her into your house again. You can send Isom in to hide in the canna bed." She said nothing. "Surely you dont object to my living there, do you?"

"I dont care where you live. The question is, where I live. I live here, in this town. I'll have to stay here. But you're a man. It doesn't matter to you. You can go away."

"Oh," he said. He lay quite still. She stood above him, motionless. They spoke quietly, as though they were discussing wall-paper, food.

"Dont you see, this is my home, where I must spend the rest of my life. Where I was born. I dont care where else you go nor what you do. I dont care how many women you have nor who they are. But I cannot have my brother mixed up with a woman people are talking about. I dont expect you to have consideration for me; I ask you to have consideration for our father and mother. Take her to Memphis. They say you refused to let the man have bond to get out of jail; take her on to Memphis. You can think of a lie to tell him about that, too."

"Oh. So you think that, do you?"

"I dont think anything about it. I dont care. That's what people in town think. So it doesn't matter whether it's true or not. What I do mind is, everyday you force me to have to tell lies for you. Go away from here, Horace. Anybody but you would realise it's a case of cold-blooded murder."

"And over her, of course. I suppose they say that too, out of their odorous and omnipotent sanctity. Do they say yet that it was I killed him?"

"I dont see that it makes any difference who did it. The question is, are you going to stay mixed up with it? When people already believe you and she are slipping into my house at night." Her cold, unbending voice shaped the words in the darkness above him. Through the window, upon the blowing darkness, came the drowsy dissonance of cicada and cricket.

"Do you believe that?" he said.

"It doesn't matter what I believe. Go on away, Horace. I ask it."

"And leave her—them, flat?"

"Hire a lawyer, if he still insists he's innocent. I'll pay for it. You can get a better criminal lawyer than you are. She wont know it. She wont even care. Cant you see that she is just leading you on to get him out of jail for nothing? Dont you know that woman has got money hidden away somewhere? You're going back into town tomorrow, are you?" She turned, began to dissolve into the blackness. "You wont leave before breakfast."

The next morning at breakfast, his sister said: "Who will be the lawyer on the other side of the case?"

"District Attorney. Why?"

She rang the bell and sent for fresh bread. Horace watched her. "Why do you ask that?" Then he said: "Damn little squirt." He was talking about the district attorney, who had also been raised in Jefferson and who had gone to the town school with them. "I believe he was at the bottom of that business night before last. The hotel. Getting her turned out of the hotel for public effect, political capital. By God, if I knew that, believed that he had done that just to get elected to Congress. . . . . ."

After Horace left, Narcissa went up to Miss Jenny's room. "Who is the District Attorney?" she said.

"You've known him all your life," Miss Jenny said. "You even elected him. Eustace Graham. What do you want to know for? Are you looking around for a substitute for Gowan Stevens?"

"I just wondered," Narcissa said.

"Fiddlesticks," Miss Jenny said. "You dont wonder. You just do things and then stop until the next time to do something comes around."

Horace met Snopes emerging from the barbershop, his jowls gray with powder, moving in an effluvium of pomade. In the bosom of his shirt, beneath his bow tie, he wore an imitation ruby stud which matched his ring. The tie was of blue polka-dots; the very white spots on it appeared dirty when seen close; the whole man with his shaved neck and pressed clothes and gleaming shoes emanated somehow the idea that he had been dry-cleaned rather than washed.

"Well, Judge," he said, "I hear you're having some trouble gittin a boarding-place for that client of yourn. Like I always say——" he leaned, his voice lowered, his mud-colored eyes roving aside "——the church aint got no place in politics, and women aint got no place in neither one, let alone the law. Let them stay at home and they'll find plenty to do without upsetting a man's law-suit. And besides, a man aint no more than human, and what he does aint nobody's business but his. What you done with her?"

"She's at the jail," Horace said. He spoke shortly, making to pass on. The other blocked his way with an effect of clumsy accident.

"You got them all stirred up, anyhow. Folks is saying you wouldn't git Goodwin no bond, so he'd have to stay——" again Horace made to pass on. "Half the trouble in this world is caused by women, I always say. Like that girl gittin her paw all stirred up, running off like she done. I reckon he done the right thing sending her clean outen the state."

"Yes," Horace said in a dry, furious voice.

"I'm mighty glad to hear your case is going all right. Between you and me, I'd like to see a good lawyer make a monkey outen that District Attorney. Give a fellow like that a little county office and he gits too big for his pants right away. Well, glad to've saw you. I got some business up town for a day or two. I dont reckon you'll be going up that-a-way?"

"What?" Horace said. "Up where?"

"Memphis. Anything I can do for you?"

"No," Horace said. He went on. For a short distance he could not see at all. He tramped steadily, the muscles beside his jaws beginning to ache, passing people who spoke to him, unawares.

XXI

As the train neared Memphis Virgil Snopes ceased talking and began to grow quieter and quieter, while on the contrary his companion, eating from a paraffin-paper package of popcorn and molasses, grew livelier and livelier with a quality something like intoxication, seeming not to notice the inverse state of his friend. He was still talking away when, carrying their new, imitation leather suit cases, their new hats slanted above their shaven necks, they descended at the station. In the waiting room Fonzo said:

"Well, what're we going to do first?" Virgil said nothing. Someone jostled them; Fonzo caught at his hat. "What we going to do?" he said. Then he looked at Virgil, at his face. "What's the matter?"

"Aint nothing the matter," Virgil said.

"Well, what're we going to do? You been here before. I aint."

"I reckon we better kind of look around," Virgil said.

Fonzo was watching him, his blue eyes like china. "What's the matter with you? All the time on the train you was talking about how many times you been to Memphis. I bet you aint never bu——" Someone jostled them, thrust them apart; a stream of people began to flow between them. Clutching his suit case and hat Fonzo fought his way back to his friend.

"I have, too," Virgil said, looking glassily about.

"Well, what we going to do, then? It wont be open till eight oclock in the morning."

"What you in such a rush for, then?"

"Well, I dont aim to stay here all night. . . . What did you do when you was here before?"

"Went to the hotel," Virgil said.

"Which one? They got more than one here. You reckon all these folks could stay in one hotel? Which one was it?"

Virgil's eyes were also a pale, false blue. He looked glassily about. "The Gayoso hotel," he said.

"Well, let's go to it," Fonzo said. They moved toward the exit. A man shouted "taxi" at them; a redcap tried to take

Fonzo's bag. "Look out," he said, drawing it back. On the street more cabmen barked at them.

"So this is Memphis," Fonzo said. "Which way is it, now?" He had no answer. He looked around and saw Virgil in the act of turning away from a cabman. "What you——"

"Up this way," Virgil said. "It aint far."

It was a mile and a half. From time to time they swapped hands with the bags. "So this is Memphis," Fonzo said. "Where have I been all my life?" When they entered the Gayoso a porter offered to take the bags. They brushed past him and entered, walking gingerly on the tile floor. Virgil stopped.

"Come on," Fonzo said.

"Wait," Virgil said.

"Thought you was here before," Fonzo said.

"I was. This hyer place is too high. They'll want a dollar a day here."

"What we going to do, then?"

"Let's kind of look around."

They returned to the street. It was five oclock. They went on, looking about, carrying the suit cases. They came to another hotel. Looking in they saw marble, brass cuspidors, hurrying bellboys, people sitting among potted plants.

"That un'll be just as bad," Virgil said.

"What we going to do then? We caint walk around all night."

"Let's git off this hyer street," Virgil said. They left Main Street. At the next corner Virgil turned again. "Let's look down this-a-way. Git away from all that ere plate glass and monkey niggers. That's what you have to pay for in them places."

"Why? It's already bought when we got there. How come we have to pay for it?"

"Suppose somebody broke it while we was there. Suppose they couldn't ketch who done it. Do you reckon they'd let us out withouten we paid our share?"

At five-thirty they entered a narrow dingy street of frame houses and junk yards. Presently they came to a three storey house in a small grassless yard. Before the entrance a lattice-work false entry leaned. On the steps sat a big woman in a mother hubbard, watching two fluffy white dogs which moved about the yard.

"Let's try that un," Fonzo said.

"That aint no hotel. Where's ere sign?"

"Why aint it?" Fonzo said. " 'Course it is. Who ever heard of anybody just living in a three storey house?"

"We cant go in this-a-way," Virgil said. "This hyer's the back. Dont you see that privy?" jerking his head toward the lattice.

"Well, let's go around to the front, then," Fonzo said. "Come on."

They went around the block. The opposite side was filled by a row of automobile sales-rooms. They stood in the middle of the block, their suit cases in their right hands.

"I dont believe you ever was here before, noways," Fonzo said.

"Let's go back. That must a been the front."

"With the privy built onto the front door?" Fonzo said.

"We can ask that lady."

"Who can? I aint."

"Let's go back and see, anyway."

They returned. The woman and the dogs were gone.

"Now you done it," Fonzo said. "Aint you?"

"Let's wait a while. Maybe she'll come back."

"It's almost seven oclock," Fonzo said.

They set the bags down beside the fence. The lights had come on, quivering high in the serried windows against the tall serene western sky.

"I can smell ham, too," Fonzo said.

A cab drew up. A plump blonde woman got out, followed by a man. They watched them go up the walk and enter the lattice. Fonzo sucked his breath across his teeth. "Durned if they didn't," he whispered.

"Maybe it's her husband," Virgil said.

Fonzo picked up his bag. "Come on."

"Wait," Virgil said. "Give them a little time."

They waited. The man came out and got in the cab and went away.

"Caint be her husband," Fonzo said. "I wouldn't a never left. Come on." He entered the gate.

"Wait," Virgil said.

"You can," Fonzo said. Virgil took his bag and followed. He stopped while Fonzo opened the lattice gingerly and peered in. "Aw, hell," he said. He entered. There was another door, with curtained glass. Fonzo knocked.

"Why didn't you push that ere button?" Virgil said. "Dont you know city folks dont answer no knock?"

"All right," Fonzo said. He rang the bell. The door opened. It was the woman in the mother hubbard; they could hear the dogs behind her.

"Got ere extra room?" Fonzo said.

Miss Reba looked at them, at their new hats and the suit cases.

"Who sent you here?" she said.

"Didn't nobody. We just picked it out." Miss Reba looked at him. "Them hotels is too high."

Miss Reba breathed harshly. "What you boys doing?"

"We come hyer on business," Fonzo said. "We aim to stay a good spell."

"If it aint too high," Virgil said.

Miss Reba looked at him. "Where you from, honey?"

They told her, and their names. "We aim to be hyer a month or more, if it suits us."

"Why, I reckon so," she said after a while. She looked at them. "I can let you have a room, but I'll have to charge you extra whenever you do business in it. I got my living to make like everybody else."

"We aint," Fonzo said. "We'll do our business at the college."

"What college?" Miss Reba said.

"The barber's college," Fonzo said.

"Look here," Miss Reba said, "you little whipper-snapper." Then she began to laugh, her hand at her breast. They watched her soberly while she laughed in harsh gasps. "Lord, Lord," she said. "Come in here."

The room was at the top of the house, at the back. Miss Reba showed them the bath. When she put her hand on the door a woman's voice said: "Just a minute, dearie" and the door opened and she passed them, in a kimono. They watched her go up the hall, rocked a little to their young foundations by a trail of scent which she left. Fonzo nudged Virgil surreptitiously. In their room again he said:

"That was another one. She's got two daughters. Hold me, big boy; I'm heading for the hen-house."

They didn't go to sleep for some time that first night, what with the strange bed and room and the voices. They could hear the city, evocative and strange, imminent and remote; threat and promise both—a deep, steady sound upon which invisible lights glittered and wavered: colored coiling shapes of splendor in which already women were beginning to move in suave attitudes of new delights and strange nostalgic promises. Fonzo thought of himself surrounded by tier upon tier of drawn shades, rose-colored, beyond which, in a murmur of silk, in panting whispers, the apotheosis of his youth assumed a thousand avatars. Maybe it'll begin tomorrow, he thought; maybe by tomorrow night. . . . . . A crack of light came over the top of the shade and sprawled in a spreading fan upon the ceiling. Beneath the window he could hear a voice, a woman's, then a man's: they blended, murmured; a door closed. Someone came up the stairs in swishing garments, on the swift hard heels of a woman.

He began to hear sounds in the house: voices, laughter; a mechanical piano began to play. "Hear them?" he whispered.

"She's got a big family, I reckon," Virgil said, his voice already dull with sleep.

"Family, hell," Fonzo said. "It's a party. Wish I was to it."

On the third day as they were leaving the house in the morning, Miss Reba met them at the door. She wanted to use their room in the afternoons while they were absent. There was to be a detective's convention in town and business would look up some, she said. "Your things'll be all right. I'll have Minnie lock everything up before hand. Aint nobody going to steal nothing from you in my house."

"What business you reckon she's in?" Fonzo said when they reached the street.

"Dont know," Virgil said.

"Wish I worked for her, anyway," Fonzo said. "With all them women in kimonos and such running around."

"Wouldn't do you no good," Virgil said. "They're all married. Aint you heard them?"

The next afternoon when they returned from the school they found a woman's undergarment under the washstand. Fonzo picked it up. "She's a dress-maker," he said.

"Reckon so," Virgil said. "Look and see if they taken anything of yourn."

The house appeared to be filled with people who did not sleep at night at all. They could hear them at all hours, running up and down the stairs, and always Fonzo would be conscious of women, of female flesh. It got to where he seemed to lie in his celibate bed surrounded by women, and he would lie beside the steadily snoring Virgil, his ears strained for the murmurs, the whispers of silk that came through the walls and the floor, that seemed to be as much a part of both as the planks and the plaster, thinking that he had been in Memphis ten days, yet the extent of his acquaintance was a few of his fellow pupils at the school. After Virgil was asleep he would rise and unlock the door and leave it ajar, but nothing happened.

On the twelfth day he told Virgil they were going visiting, with one of the barber-students.

"Where?" Virgil said.

"That's all right. You come on. I done found out something. And when I think I been here two weeks without knowing about it. . . . . . ."

"What's it going to cost?" Virgil said.

"When'd you ever have any fun for nothing?" Fonzo said. "Come on."

"I'll go," Virgil said. "But I aint going to promise to spend nothing."

"You wait and say that when we get there," Fonzo said.

The barber took them to a brothel. When they came out Fonzo said: "And to think I been here two weeks without never knowing about that house."

"I wisht you hadn't never learned," Virgil said. "It cost three dollars."

"Wasn't it worth it?" Fonzo said.

"Aint nothing worth three dollars you caint tote off with you," Virgil said.

When they reached home Fonzo stopped. "We got to sneak in, now," he said. "If she was to find out where we been and what we been doing, she might not let us stay in the house with them ladies no more."

"That's so," Virgil said. "Durn you. Hyer you done made me spend three dollars, and now you fixing to git us both throwed out."

"You do like I do," Fonzo said. "That's all you got to do. Dont say nothing."

Minnie let them in. The piano was going full blast. Miss Reba appeared in a door, with a tin cup in her hand. "Well, well," she said, "you boys been out mighty late tonight."

"Yessum," Fonzo said, prodding Virgil toward the stairs. "We been to prayer-meeting."

In bed, in the dark, they could still hear the piano.

"You made me spend three dollars," Virgil said.

"Aw, shut up," Fonzo said. "When I think I been here for two whole weeks almost. . . . . . ."

The next afternoon they came home through the dusk, with the lights winking on, beginning to flare and gleam, and the women on their twinkling blonde legs meeting men and getting into automobiles and such.

"How about that three dollars now?" Fonzo said.

"I reckon we better not go ever night," Virgil said. "It'll cost too much."

"That's right," Fonzo said. "Somebody might see us and tell her."

They waited two nights. "Now it'll be six dollars," Virgil said.

"Dont come, then," Fonzo said.

When they returned home Fonzo said: "Try to act like something, this time. She near about caught us before on account of the way you acted."

"What if she does?" Virgil said in a sullen voice. "She caint eat us."

They stood outside the lattice, whispering.

"How you know she caint?" Fonzo said.

"She dont want to, then."

"How you know she dont want to?"

"Maybe she dont," Virgil said. Fonzo opened the lattice door. "I caint eat that six dollars, noways," Virgil said. "Wisht I could."

Minnie let them in. She said: "Somebody huntin you all."
They waited in the hall.

"We done caught now," Virgil said. "I told you about
throwing that money away."

"Aw, shut up," Fonzo said.

A man emerged from a door, a big man with his hat cocked
over one ear, his arm about a blonde woman in a red dress.
"There's Cla'ence," Virgil said.

In their room Clarence said: "How'd you get into this
place?"

"Just found it," Virgil said. They told him about it. He sat
on the bed, in his soiled hat, a cigar in his fingers.

"Where you been tonight?" he said. They didn't answer.
They looked at him with blank, watchful faces. "Come on. I
know. Where was it?" They told him.

"Cost me three dollars, too," Virgil said.

"I'll be durned if you aint the biggest fool this side of Jackson," Clarence said. "Come on here." They followed sheep-
ishly. He led them from the house and for three or four
blocks. They crossed a street of negro stores and theatres and
turned into a narrow, dark street and stopped at a house with
red shades in the lighted windows. Clarence rang the bell.
They could hear music inside, and shrill voices, and feet. They
were admitted into a bare hallway where two shabby negro
men argued with a drunk white man in greasy overalls.
Through an open door they saw a room filled with coffee-
colored women in bright dresses, with ornate hair and golden
smiles.

"Them's niggers," Virgil said.

" 'Course they're niggers," Clarence said. "But see this?" he
waved a banknote in his cousin's face. "This stuff is color-
blind."

XXII

O**N THE THIRD DAY** of his search, Horace found a domicile for the woman and child. It was in the ramshackle house of an old half-crazed white woman who was believed to manufacture spells for negroes. It was on the edge of town, set in a tiny plot of ground choked and massed with waist-high herbage in an unbroken jungle across the front. At the back a path had been trodden from the broken gate to the door. All night a dim light burned in the crazy depths of the house and at almost any hour of the twenty-four a wagon or a buggy might be seen tethered in the lane behind it and a negro entering or leaving the back door.

The house had been entered once by officers searching for whiskey. They found nothing save a few dried bunches of weeds, and a collection of dirty bottles containing liquid of which they could say nothing surely save that it was not alcoholic, while the old woman, held by two men, her lank grayish hair shaken before the glittering collapse of her face, screamed invective at them in her cracked voice. In a lean-to shed room containing a bed and a barrel of anonymous refuse and trash in which mice rattled all night long, the woman found a home.

"You'll be all right here," Horace said. "You can always get me by telephone, at——" giving her the name of a neighbor. "No: wait; tomorrow I'll have the telephone put back in. Then you can——"

"Yes," the woman said. "I reckon you better not be coming out here."

"Why? Do you think that would——that I'd care a damn what——"

"You have to live here."

"I'm damned if I do. I've already let too many women run my affairs for me as it is, and if these uxorious. . . . . . ." But he knew he was just talking. He knew that she knew it too, out of that feminine reserve of unflagging suspicion of all peoples' actions which seems at first to be mere affinity for evil but which is in reality practical wisdom.

317

"I guess I'll find you if there's any need," she said. "There's not anything else I could do."

"By God," Horace said, "dont you let them. . . . Bitches," he said; "bitches."

The next day he had the telephone installed. He did not see his sister for a week; she had no way of learning that he had a phone, yet when, a week before the opening of Court, the telephone shrilled into the quiet where he sat reading one evening, he thought it was Narcissa until, across a remote blaring of victrola or radio music, a man's voice spoke in a guarded, tomblike tone.

"This is Snopes," it said. "How're you, Judge?"

"What?" Horace said. "Who is it?"

"Senator Snopes. Cla'ence Snopes." The victrola blared, faint, far away; he could see the man, the soiled hat, the thick shoulders, leaning above the instrument—in a drugstore or a restaurant—whispering into it behind a soft, huge, ringed hand, the telephone toylike in the other.

"Oh," Horace said. "Yes? What is it?"

"I got a little piece of information that might interest you."

"Information that would interest me?"

"I reckon so. That would interest a couple of parties." Against Horace's ear the radio or the victrola performed a reedy arpeggio of saxophones. Obscene, facile, they seemed to be quarreling with one another like two dexterous monkeys in a cage. He could hear the gross breathing of the man at the other end of the wire.

"All right," he said. "What do you know that would interest me?"

"I'll let you judge that."

"All right. I'll be down town in the morning. You can find me somewhere." Then he said immediately: "Hello!" The man sounded as though he were breathing in Horace's ear: a placid, gross sound, suddenly portentous somehow. "Hello!" Horace said.

"It evidently dont interest you, then. I reckon I'll dicker with the other party and not trouble you no more. Goodbye."

"No; wait," Horace said. "Hello! Hello!"

"Yeuh?"

"I'll come down tonight. I'll be there in about fifteen——"

" 'Taint no need of that," Snopes said. "I got my car. I'll drive up there."

He walked down to the gate. There was a moon tonight. Within the black-and-silver tunnel of cedars fireflies drifted in fatuous pinpricks. The cedars were black and pointed on the sky like a paper silhouette; the sloping lawn had a faint sheen, a patina like silver. Somewhere a whippoorwill called, reiterant, tremulous, plaintful above the insects. Three cars passed. The fourth slowed and swung toward the gate. Horace stepped into the light. Behind the wheel Snopes loomed bulkily, giving the impression of having been inserted into the car before the top was put on. He extended his hand.

"How're you tonight, Judge? Didn't know you was living in town again until I tried to call you out to Mrs Sartorises."

"Well, thanks," Horace said. He freed his hand. "What's this you've got hold of?"

Snopes creased himself across the wheel and peered out beneath the top, toward the house.

"We'll talk here," Horace said. "Save you having to turn around."

"It aint very private here," Snopes said. "But that's for you to say." Huge and thick he loomed, hunched, his featureless face moonlike itself in the refraction of the moon. Horace could feel Snopes watching him, with that sense of portent which had come over the wire; a quality calculating and cunning and pregnant. It seemed to him that he watched his mind flicking this way and that, striking always that vast, soft, inert bulk, as though it were caught in an avalanche of cottonseed-hulls.

"Let's go to the house," Horace said. Snopes opened the door. "Go on," Horace said. "I'll walk up." Snopes drove on. He was getting out of the car when Horace overtook him. "Well, what is it?" Horace said.

Again Snopes looked at the house. "Keeping batch, are you?" he said. Horace said nothing. "Like I always say, ever married man ought to have a little place of his own, where he can git off to himself without it being nobody's business what he does. 'Course a man owes something to his wife, but what they dont know caint hurt them, does it? Long's he does that,

I caint see where she's got ere kick coming. Aint that what you say?"

"She's not here," Horace said, "if that's what you're hinting at. What did you want to see me about?"

Again he felt Snopes watching him, the unabashed stare calculating and completely unbelieving. "Well, I always say, caint nobody tend to a man's private business but himself. I aint blaming you. But when you know me better, you'll know I aint loose-mouthed. I been around. I been there. . . . Have a cigar?" His big hand flicked to his breast and offered two cigars.

"No, thanks."

Snopes lit a cigar, his face coming out of the match like a pie set on edge.

"What did you want to see me about?" Horace said.

Snopes puffed the cigar. "Couple days ago I come onto a piece of information which will be of value to you, if I aint mistook."

"Oh. Of value. What value?"

"I'll leave that to you. I got another party I could dicker with, but being as me and you was fellow-townsmen and all that."

Here and there Horace's mind flicked and darted. Snopes' family originated somewhere near Frenchman's Bend and still lived there. He knew of the devious means by which information passed from man to man of that illiterate race which populated that section of the county. But surely it cant be something he'd try to sell to the State, he thought. Even he is not that big a fool.

"You'd better tell me what it is, then," he said.

He could feel Snopes watching him. "You remember one day you got on the train at Oxford, where you'd been on some bus—"

"Yes," Horace said.

Snopes puffed the cigar to an even coal, carefully, at some length. He raised his hand and drew it across the back of his neck. "You recall speaking to me about a girl."

"Yes. Then what?"

"That's for you to say."

He could smell the honeysuckle as it bore up the silver

slope, and he heard the whippoorwill, liquid, plaintful, reiterant. "You mean, you know where she is?" Snopes said nothing. "And that for a price you'll tell?" Snopes said nothing. Horace shut his hands and put them in his pockets, shut against his flanks. "What makes you think that information will interest me?"

"That's for you to judge. I aint conducting no murder case. I wasn't down there at Oxford looking for her. Of course, if it dont, I'll dicker with the other party. I just give you the chance."

Horace turned toward the steps. He moved gingerly, like an old man. "Let's sit down," he said. Snopes followed and sat on the step. They sat in the moonlight. "You know where she is?"

"I seen her." Again he drew his hand across the back of his neck. "Yes, sir. If she aint—hasn't been there, you can git your money back. I caint say no fairer, can I?"

"And what's your price?" Horace said. Snopes puffed the cigar to a careful coal. "Go on," Horace said. "I'm not going to haggle." Snopes told him. "All right," Horace said. "I'll pay it." He drew his knees up and set his elbows on them and laid his hands to his face. "Where is——Wait. Are you a Baptist, by any chance?"

"My folks is. I'm putty liberal, myself. I aint hidebound in no sense, as you'll find when you know me better."

"All right," Horace said from behind his hands. "Where is she?"

"I'll trust you," Snopes said. "She's in a Memphis 'ho'-house."

XXIII

As HORACE ENTERED Miss Reba's gate and approached the lattice door, someone called his name from behind him. It was evening; the windows in the weathered, scaling wall were close pale squares. He paused and looked back. Around an adjacent corner Snopes' head peered, turkey-like. He stepped into view. He looked up at the house, then both ways along the street. He came along the fence and entered the gate with a wary air.

"Well, Judge," he said. "Boys will be boys, wont they?" He didn't offer to shake hands. Instead he bulked above Horace with that air somehow assured and alert at the same time, glancing over his shoulder at the street. "Like I say, it never done no man no harm to git out now and then and——"

"What is it now?" Horace said. "What do you want with me?"

"Now, now, Judge. I aint going to tell this at home. Git that idea clean out of your mind. If us boys started telling what we know, caint none of us git off a train at Jefferson again, hey?"

"You know as well as I do what I'm doing here. What do you want with me?"

"Sure; sure," Snopes said. "I know how a feller feels, married and all and not being sho where his wife is at." Between jerky glances over his shoulder he winked at Horace. "Make your mind easy. It's the same with me as if the grave knowed it. Only I hate to see a good——" Horace had gone on toward the door. "Judge," Snopes said in a penetrant undertone. Horace turned. "Dont stay."

"Dont stay?"

"See her and then leave. It's a sucker place. Place for farm-boys. Higher'n Monte Carlo. I'll wait out hyer and I'll show you a place where——" Horace went on and entered the lattice. Two hours later, as he sat talking to Miss Reba in her room while beyond the door feet and now and then voices came and went in the hall and on the stairs, Minnie entered with a torn scrap of paper and brought it to Horace.

"What's that?" Miss Reba said.

"That big pie-face-ted man left it fer him," Minnie said. "He say fer you to come on down there."

"Did you let him in?" Miss Reba said.

"Nome. He never tried to git in."

"I guess not," Miss Reba said. She grunted. "Do you know him?" she said to Horace.

"Yes. I cant seem to help myself," Horace said. He opened the paper. Torn from a handbill, it bore an address in pencil in a neat, flowing hand.

"He turned up here about two weeks ago," Miss Reba said. "Come in looking for two boys and sat around the dining-room blowing his head off and feeling the girls' behinds, but if he ever spent a cent I dont know it. Did he ever give you an order, Minnie?"

"Nome," Minnie said.

"And couple of nights later he was here again. Didn't spend nuttin, didn't do nuttin but talk, and I says to him 'Look here, mister, folks what uses this waiting-room has got to get on the train now and then.' So next time he brought a half-pint of whiskey with him. I dont mind that, from a good customer. But when a fellow like him comes here three times, pinching my girls and bringing one half-pint of whiskey and ordering four coca-colas. . . . . . Just a cheap, vulgar man, honey. So I told Minnie not to let him in anymore, and here one afternoon I aint no more than laid down for a nap when——I never did find out what he done to Minnie to get in. I know he never give her nuttin. How did he do it, Minnie? He must a showed you something you never seen before. Didn't he?"

Minnie tossed her head. "He aint got nothing I wantin to see. I done seed too many now fer my own good." Minnie's husband had quit her. He didn't approve of Minnie's business. He was a cook in a restaurant and he took all the clothes and jewelry the white ladies had given Minnie and went off with a waitress in the restaurant.

"He kept on asking and hinting around about that girl," Miss Reba said, "and me telling him to go ask Popeye if he wanted to know right bad. Not telling him nuttin except to get out and stay out, see; so this day it's about two in the afternoon and I'm asleep and Minnie lets him in and he asks her who's here and she tells him aint nobody, and he goes on up stairs. And Minnie says about that time Popeye comes in. She says she dont know what to do. She's scared not to let him in, and she says she knows if she does and he spatters that big bastard all over the upstairs floor, she knows I'll fire her and her husband just quit her and all.

"So Popeye goes on upstairs on them cat feet of his and comes on your friend on his knees, peeping through the keyhole. Minnie says Popeye stood behind him for about a minute, with his hat cocked over one eye. She says he took out a cigarette and struck a match on his thumbnail without no noise and lit it and then she says he reached over and held the match to the back of your friend's neck, and Minnie says she stood there halfway up the stairs and watched them: that fellow kneeling there with his face like a pie took out of the oven too soon and Popeye squirting smoke through his nose and kind of jerking his head at him. Then she come on down and in about ten seconds here he comes down the stairs with both hands on top of his head, going wump-wump-wump inside like one of these here big dray-horses, and he pawed at the door for about a minute, moaning to himself like the wind in a chimney Minnie says, until she opened the door and left him out. And that's the last time he's even rung this bell until tonight. . . . Let me see that." Horace gave her the paper. "That's a nigger whore-house," she said. "The lous——Minnie, tell him his friend aint here. Tell him I dont know where he went."

Minnie went out. Miss Reba said:

"I've had all sorts of men in my house, but I got to draw the line somewhere. I had lawyers, too. I had the biggest lawyer in Memphis back there in my dining-room, treating my girls. A millionaire. He weighed two hundred and eighty pounds and he had his own special bed made and sent down here. It's upstairs right this minute. But all in the way of my business, not theirs. I aint going to have none of my girls pestered by lawyers without good reason."

"And you dont consider this good reason? that a man is being tried for his life for something he didn't do? You may be guilty right now of harboring a fugitive from justice."

"Then let them come take him. I got nuttin to do with it.

I had too many police in this house to be scared of them."
She raised the tankard and drank and drew the back of her
hand across her mouth. "I aint going to have nuttin to do
with nuttin I dont know about. What Popeye done outside is
his business. When he starts killing folks in my house, then
I'll take a hand."

"Have you any children?" She looked at him. "I dont mean
to pry into your affairs," he said. "I was just thinking about
that woman. She'll be on the streets again, and God only
knows what will become of that baby."

"Yes," Miss Reba said. "I'm supporting four, in a Arkansaw
home now. Not mine, though." She lifted the tankard and
looked into it, oscillating it gently. She set it down again. "It
better not been born at all," she said. "None of them had."
She rose and came toward him, moving heavily, and stood
above him with her harsh breath. She put her hand on his
head and tilted his face up. "You aint lying to me, are you?"
she said, her eyes piercing and intent and sad. "No, you aint."
She released him. "Wait here a minute. I'll see." She went out.
He heard her speak to Minnie in the hall, then he heard her
toil up the stairs.

He sat quietly as she had left him. The room contained a
wooden bed, a painted screen, three over-stuffed chairs, a wall
safe. The dressing-table was littered with toilet articles tied in
pink satin bows. The mantel supported a wax lily beneath a
glass bell; above it, draped in black, the photograph of a
meek-looking man with an enormous moustache. On the
walls hung a few lithographs of spurious Greek scenes, and
one picture done in tatting. Horace rose and went to the
door. Minnie sat in a chair in the dim hall.

"Minnie," he said, "I've got to have a drink. A big one."

He had just finished it when Minnie entered again. "She
say fer you to come on up," she said.

He mounted the stairs. Miss Reba waited at the top. She
led the way up the hall and opened a door into a dark room.
"You'll have to talk to her in the dark," she said. "She wont
have no light." Light from the hall fell through the door and
across the bed. "This aint hers," Miss Reba said. "Wouldn't
even see you in her room at all. I reckon you better humor
her until you find out what you want." They entered. The

light fell across the bed, upon a motionless curving ridge of
bedclothing, the general tone of the bed unbroken. She'll
smother, Horace thought. "Honey," Miss Reba said. The
ridge did not move. "Here he is, honey. Long as you're all
covered up, let's have some light. Then we can close the
door." She turned the light on.

"She'll smother," Horace said.

"She'll come out in a minute," Miss Reba said. "Go on.
Tell her what you want. I better stay. But dont mind me. I
couldn't a stayed in my business without learning to be deaf
and dumb a long time before this. And if I'd ever a had any
curiosity, I'd have worn it out long ago in this house. Here's
a chair." She turned, but Horace anticipated her and drew up
two chairs. He sat down beside the bed and, talking at the
top of the unstirring ridge, he told her what he wanted.

"I just want to know what really happened. You wont commit yourself. I know that you didn't do it. I'll promise before
you tell me a thing that you wont have to testify in Court
unless they are going to hang him without it. I know how
you feel. I wouldn't bother you if the man's life were not at
stake."

The ridge did not move.

"They're going to hang him for something he never done,"
Miss Reba said. "And she wont have nuttin, nobody. And
you with diamonds, and her with that poor little kid. You
seen it, didn't you?"

The ridge did not move.

"I know how you feel," Horace said. "You can use a different name, wear clothes nobody will recognise you in, glasses."

"They aint going to catch Popeye, honey," Miss Reba said.
"Smart as he is. You dont know his name, noway, and if you
have to go and tell them in the court, I'll send him word after
you leave and he'll go somewheres and send for you. You and
him dont want to stay here in Memphis. The lawyer'll take
care of you and you wont have to tell nuttin you——" The
ridge moved. Temple flung the covers back and sat up. Her
head was tousled, her face puffed, two spots of rouge on her
cheekbones and her mouth painted into a savage cupid's bow.
She stared for an instant at Horace with black antagonism,
then she looked away.

"I want a drink," she said, pulling up the shoulder of her gown.

"Lie down," Miss Reba said. "You'll catch cold."

"I want another drink," Temple said.

"Lie down and cover up your nekkidness, anyway," Miss Reba said, rising. "You already had three since supper."

Temple dragged the gown up again. She looked at Horace. "You give me a drink, then."

"Come on, honey," Miss Reba said, trying to push her down. "Lie down and get covered up and tell him about that business. I'll get you a drink in a minute."

"Let me alone," Temple said, writhing free. Miss Reba drew the covers about her shoulders. "Give me a cigarette, then. Have you got one?" she asked Horace.

"I'll get you one in a minute," Miss Reba said. "Will you do what he wants you to?"

"What?" Temple said. She looked at Horace with her black, belligerent stare.

"You needn't tell me where your—he——" Horace said.

"Dont think I'm afraid to tell," Temple said. "I'll tell it anywhere. Dont think I'm afraid. I want a drink."

"You tell him, and I'll get you one," Miss Reba said.

Sitting up in the bed, the covers about her shoulders, Temple told him of the night she had spent in the ruined house, from the time she entered the room and tried to wedge the door with the chair, until the woman came to the bed and led her out. That was the only part of the whole experience which appeared to have left any impression on her at all: the night which she had spent in comparative inviolation. Now and then Horace would attempt to get her on ahead to the crime itself, but she would elude him and return to herself sitting on the bed, listening to the men on the porch, or lying in the dark while they entered the room and came to the bed and stood there above her.

"Yes; that," she would say. "It just happened. I dont know. I had been scared so long that I guess I had just gotten used to being. So I just sat there in those cottonseeds and watched him. I thought it was the rat at first. There were two of them there. One was in one corner looking at me and the other was in the other corner. I dont know what they lived on, because there wasn't anything there but corn-cobs and cotton-seeds. Maybe they went to the house to eat. But there wasn't any in the house. I never did hear one in the house. I thought it might have been a rat when I first heard them, but you can feel people in a dark room: did you know that? You dont have to see them. You can feel them like you can in a car when they begin to look for a good place to stop—you know: park for a while." She went on like that, in one of those bright, chatty monologues which women can carry on when they realise that they have the center of the stage; suddenly Horace realised that she was recounting the experience with actual pride, a sort of naive and impersonal vanity, as though she were making it up, looking from him to Miss Reba with quick, darting glances like a dog driving two cattle along a lane.

"And so whenever I breathed I'd hear those shucks. I dont see how anybody ever sleeps on a bed like that. But maybe you get used to it. Or maybe they're tired at night. Because when I breathed I could hear them, even when I was just sitting on the bed. I didn't see how it could be just breathing, so I'd sit as still as I could, but I could still hear them. That's because breathing goes down. You think it goes up, but it doesn't. It goes down you, and I'd hear them getting drunk on the porch. I got to thinking I could see where their heads were leaning back against the wall and I'd say Now this one's drinking out of the jug. Now that one's drinking. Like the mashed-in place on the pillow after you got up, you know.

"That was when I got to thinking a funny thing. You know how you do when you're scared. I was looking at my legs and I'd try to make like I was a boy. I was thinking about if I just was a boy and then I tried to make myself into one by thinking. You know how you do things like that. Like when you know one problem in class and when they come to that you look at him and think right hard, Call on me. Call on me. Call on me. I'd think about what they tell children, about kissing your elbow, and I tried to. I actually did. I was that scared, and I'd wonder if I could tell when it happened. I mean, before I looked, and I'd think I had and how I'd go out and show them—you know. I'd strike a match and say Look. See? Let me alone, now. And then I could go back to bed. I'd think how I could go to bed and go to sleep then, because I was sleepy. I was so sleepy I simply couldn't hardly hold my eyes open.

"So I'd hold my eyes tight shut and say Now I am. I am now. I'd look at my legs and I'd think about how much I had done for them. I'd think about how many dances I had taken them to—crazy, like that. Because I thought how much I'd done for them, and now they'd gotten me into this. So I'd think about praying to be changed into a boy and I would pray and then I'd sit right still and wait. Then I'd think maybe I couldn't tell it and I'd get ready to look. Then I'd think maybe it was too soon to look; that if I looked too soon I'd spoil it and then it wouldn't, sure enough. So I'd count. I said to count fifty at first, then I thought it was still too soon, and I'd say to count fifty more. Then I'd think if I didn't look at the right time, it would be too late.

"Then I thought about fastening myself up some way. There was a girl went abroad one summer that told me about a kind of iron belt in a museum a king or something used to lock the queen up in when he had to go away, and I thought if I just had that. That was why I got the raincoat and put it on. The canteen was hanging by it and I got it too and put it in the——"

"Canteen?" Horace said. "Why did you do that?"

"I dont know why I took it. I was just scared to leave it there, I guess. But I was thinking if I just had that French thing. I was thinking maybe it would have long sharp spikes on it and he wouldn't know it until too late and I'd jab it into him. I'd jab it all the way through him and I'd think about the blood running on me and how I'd say I guess that'll teach you! I guess you'll let me alone now! I'd say. I didn't know it was going to be just the other way. . . . . . I want a drink."

"I'll get you one in a minute," Miss Reba said. "Go on and tell him."

"Oh, yes; this was something else funny I did." She told about lying in the darkness with Gowan snoring beside her, listening to the shucks and hearing the darkness full of movement, feeling Popeye approaching. She could hear the blood in her veins, and the little muscles at the corners of her eyes cracking faintly wider and wider, and she could feel her nostrils going alternately cool and warm. Then he was standing over and she was saying Come on. Touch me. Touch me! You're a coward if you dont. Coward! Coward!

"I wanted to go to sleep, you see. And he just kept on standing there. I thought if he'd just go on and get it over with, I could go to sleep. So I'd say You're a coward if you dont! You're a coward if you dont! and I could feel my mouth getting fixed to scream, and that little hot ball inside you that screams. Then it touched me, that nasty little cold hand, fiddling around inside the coat where I was naked. It was like alive ice and my skin started jumping away from it like those little flying fish in front of a boat. It was like my skin knew which way it was going to go before it started moving, and my skin would keep on jerking just ahead of it like there wouldn't be anything there when the hand got there.

"Then it got down to where my insides begin, and I hadn't eaten since yesterday at dinner and my insides started bubbling and going on and the shucks began to make so much noise it was like laughing. I'd think they were laughing at me because all the time his hand was going inside the top of my knickers and I hadn't changed into a boy yet.

"That was the funny thing, because I wasn't breathing then. I hadn't breathed in a long time. So I thought I was dead. Then I did a funny thing. I could see myself in the coffin. I looked sweet—you know: all in white. I had on a veil like a bride, and I was crying because I was dead or looked sweet or something. No: it was because they had put shucks in the coffin. I was crying because they had put shucks in the coffin where I was dead, but all the time I could feel my nose going cold and hot and cold and hot, and I could see all the people sitting around the coffin, saying Dont she look sweet. Dont she look sweet.

"But I kept on saying Coward! Coward! Touch me, coward! I got mad, because he was so long doing it. I'd talk to him. I'd say Do you think I'm going to lie here all night, just waiting on you? I'd say. Let me tell you what I'll do, I'd say. And I'd lie there with the shucks laughing at me and me jerking away in front of his hand and I'd think what I'd say to him. I'd talk to him like the teacher does in school, and then

I was a teacher in school and it was a little black thing like a
nigger boy, kind of, and I was the teacher. Because I'd say
How old am I? and I'd say I'm forty-five years old. I had iron-
gray hair and spectacles and I was all big up here like women
get. I had on a gray tailored suit, and I never could wear gray.
And I was telling it what I'd do, and it kind of drawing up
and drawing up like it could already see the switch.

"Then I said That wont do. I ought to be a man. So I was
an old man, with a long white beard, and then the little black
man got littler and littler and I was saying Now. You see now.
I'm a man now. Then I thought about being a man, and as
soon as I thought it, it happened. It made a kind of plopping
sound, like blowing a little rubber tube wrong-side outward.
It felt cold, like the inside of your mouth when you hold it
open. I could feel it, and I lay right still to keep from laughing about how surprised he was going to be. I could feel the
jerking going on inside my knickers ahead of his hand and me
lying there trying not to laugh about how surprised and mad
he was going to be in about a minute. Then all of a sudden I
went to sleep. I couldn't even stay awake until his hand got
there. I just went to sleep. I couldn't even feel myself jerking
in front of his hand, but I could hear the shucks. I didn't
wake up until that woman came and took me down to the
crib."

As he was leaving the house Miss Reba said: "I wish you'd
get her down there and not let her come back. I'd find her
folks myself, if I knowed how to go about it. But you know
how. . . . . . . She'll be dead, or in the asylum in a year,
way him and her go on up there in that room. There's something funny about it that I aint found out about yet. Maybe
it's her. She wasn't born for this kind of life. You have to be
born for this like you have to be born a butcher or a barber,
I guess. Wouldn't anybody be either of them just for money
or fun."

Better for her if she were dead tonight, Horace thought,
walking on. For me, too. He thought of her, Popeye, the
woman, the child, Goodwin, all put into a single chamber,
bare, lethal, immediate and profound: a single blotting instant between the indignation and the surprise. And I too;
thinking how that were the only solution. Removed, cauter-

ised out of the old and tragic flank of the world. And I, too, now that we're all isolated; thinking of a gentle dark wind blowing in the long corridors of sleep; of lying beneath a low cozy roof under the long sound of the rain: the evil, the injustice, the tears. In an alley-mouth two figures stood, face to face, not touching; the man speaking in a low tone unprintable epithet after epithet in a caressing whisper, the woman motionless before him as though in a musing swoon of voluptuous ecstasy. Perhaps it is upon the instant that we realise, admit, that there is a logical pattern to evil, that we die, he thought, thinking of the expression he had once seen in the eyes of a dead child, and of other dead: the cooling indignation, the shocked despair fading, leaving two empty globes in which the motionless world lurked profoundly in miniature.

He did not even return to his hotel. He went to the station. He could get a train at midnight. He had a cup of coffee and wished immediately that he had not, for it lay in a hot ball on his stomach. Three hours later, when he got off at Jefferson, it was still there, unassimilated. He walked to town and crossed the deserted square. He thought of the other morning when he had crossed it. It was as though there had not been any elapsed time between: the same gesture of the lighted clock-face, the same vulture-like shadows in the doorways; it might be the same morning and he had merely crossed the square, about-faced and was returning; all between a dream filled with all the nightmare shapes it had taken him forty-three years to invent, concentrated in a hot, hard lump in his stomach. Suddenly he was walking fast, the coffee jolting like a hot, heavy rock inside him.

He walked quietly up the drive, beginning to smell the honeysuckle from the fence. The house was dark, still, as though it were marooned in space by the ebb of all time. The insects had fallen to a low monotonous pitch, everywhere, nowhere, spent, as though the sound were the chemical agony of a world left stark and dying above the tide-edge of the fluid in which it lived and breathed. The moon stood overhead, but without light; the earth lay beneath, without darkness. He opened the door and felt his way into the room and to the light. The voice of the night—insects, whatever it was—had followed him into the house; he knew suddenly that it was the friction of the earth on its axis, approaching that moment when it must decide to turn on or to remain forever still: a motionless ball in cooling space, across which a thick smell of honeysuckle writhed like cold smoke.

He found the light and turned it on. The photograph sat on the dresser. He took it up, holding it in his hands. Enclosed by the narrow imprint of the missing frame Little Belle's face dreamed with that quality of sweet chiaroscuro. Communicated to the cardboard by some quality of the light or perhaps by some infinitesimal movement of his hands, his own breathing, the face appeared to breathe in his palms in a shallow bath of highlight, beneath the slow, smoke-like tongues of invisible honeysuckle. Almost palpable enough to be seen, the scent filled the room and the small face seemed to swoon in a voluptuous languor, blurring still more, fading, leaving upon his eye a soft and fading aftermath of invitation and voluptuous promise and secret affirmation like a scent itself.

Then he knew what that sensation in his stomach meant. He put the photograph down hurriedly and went to the bathroom. He opened the door running and fumbled at the light. But he had not time to find it and he gave over and plunged forward and struck the lavatory and leaned upon his braced arms while the shucks set up a terrific uproar beneath her thighs. Lying with her head lifted slightly, her chin depressed like a figure lifted down from a crucifix, she watched something black and furious go roaring out of her pale body. She was bound naked on her back on a flat car moving at speed through a black tunnel, the blackness streaming in rigid threads overhead, a roar of iron wheels in her ears. The car shot bodily from the tunnel in a long upward slant, the darkness overhead now shredded with parallel attenuations of living fire, toward a crescendo like a held breath, an interval in which she would swing faintly and lazily in nothingness filled with pale, myriad points of light. Far beneath her she could hear the faint, furious uproar of the shucks.

XXIV

THE FIRST TIME Temple went to the head of the stairs
Minnie's eyeballs rolled out of the dusky light beside
Miss Reba's door. Leaning once more within her bolted door
Temple heard Miss Reba toil up the stairs and knock. Temple
leaned silently against the door while Miss Reba panted and
wheezed beyond it with a mixture of blandishment and
threat. She made no sound. After a while Miss Reba went
back down the stairs.

Temple turned from the door and stood in the center of the
room, beating her hands silently together, her eyes black in
her livid face. She wore a street dress, a hat. She removed the
hat and hurled it into a corner and went and flung herself face
down upon the bed. The bed had not been made. The table
beside it was littered with cigarette stubs, the adjacent floor
strewn with ashes. The pillow slip on that side was spotted
with brown holes. Often in the night she would wake to
smell tobacco and to see the single ruby eye where Popeye's
mouth would be.

It was midmorning. A thin bar of sunlight fell beneath the
drawn shade of the south window, lying upon the sill and
then upon the floor in a narrow band. The house was utterly
quiet, with that quality as of spent breathing which it had
in midmorning. Now and then a car passed in the street
beneath.

Temple turned over on the bed. When she did so she saw
one of Popeye's innumerable black suits lying across a chair.
She lay looking at it for a while, then she rose and snatched
the garments up and hurled them into the corner where the
hat was. In another corner was a closet improvised by a print
curtain. It contained dresses of all sorts and all new. She
ripped them down in furious wads and flung them after the
suit, and a row of hats from a shelf. Another of Popeye's suits
hung there also. She flung it down. Behind it, hanging from
a nail, was an automatic pistol in a holster of oiled silk. She
took it down gingerly and removed the pistol and stood with
it in her hand. After a moment she went to the bed and hid
it beneath the pillow.

The dressing-table was cluttered with toilet-things—brushes and mirrors, also new; with flasks and jars of delicate and bizarre shapes, bearing French labels. One by one she gathered them up and hurled them into the corner in thuds and splintering crashes. Among them lay a platinum bag: a delicate webbing of metal upon the smug orange gleam of banknotes. This followed the other things into the corner and she returned to the bed and lay again on her face in a slow thickening of expensive scent.

At noon Minnie tapped at the door. "Here yo dinner." Temple didn't move. "I ghy leave it here by the door. You can git it when you wants it." Her feet went away. Temple did not move.

Slowly the bar of sunlight shifted across the floor; the western side of the window-frame was now in shadow. Temple sat up, her head turned aside as though she were listening, fingering with deft habitude at her hair. She rose quietly and went to the door and listened again. Then she opened it. The tray sat on the floor. She stepped over it and went to the stairs and peered over the rail. After a while she made Minnie out, sitting in a chair in the hall.

"Minnie," she said. Minnie's head jerked up; again her eyes rolled whitely. "Bring me a drink," Temple said. She returned to her room. She waited fifteen minutes. She banged the door and was tramping furiously down the stairs when Minnie appeared in the hall.

"Yessum," Minnie said, "Miss Reba say——We aint got no——" Miss Reba's door opened. Without looking up at Temple she spoke to Minnie. Minnie lifted her voice again. "Yessum; all right. I bring it up in just a minute."

"You'd better," Temple said. She returned and stood just inside the door until she heard Minnie mount the stairs. Temple opened the door, holding it just ajar.

"Aint you going to eat no dinner?" Minnie said, thrusting at the door with her knee. Temple held it to.

"Where is it?" she said.

"I aint straightened your room up this mawnin," Minnie said.

"Give it here," Temple said, reaching her hand through the crack. She took the glass from the tray.

"You better make that un last," Minnie said. "Miss Reba say you aint ghy git no more. . . . . . . What you want to treat him this-a-way, fer? Way he spend his money on you, you ought to be ashamed. He a right pretty little man, even if he aint no John Gilbert, and way he spendin his money——" Temple shut the door and shot the bolt. She drank the gin and drew a chair up to the bed and lit a cigarette and sat down with her feet on the bed. After a while she moved the chair to the window and lifted the shade a little so she could see the street beneath. She lit another cigarette.

At five oclock she saw Miss Reba emerge, in the black silk and flowered hat, and go down the street. She sprang up and dug the hat from the mass of clothes in the corner and put it on. At the door she turned and went back to the corner and exhumed the platinum purse and descended the stairs. Minnie was in the hall.

"I'll give you ten dollars," Temple said. "I wont be gone ten minutes."

"I caint do it, Miss Temple. Hit be worth my job if Miss Reba find it out, and my th'oat too, if Mist Popeye do."

"I swear I'll be back in ten minutes. I swear I will. Twenty dollars." She put the bill in Minnie's hand.

"You better come back," Minnie said, opening the door. "If you aint back here in ten minutes, I aint going to be, neither."

Temple opened the lattice and peered out. The street was empty save for a taxi at the curb across the way, and a man in a cap standing in a door beyond it. She went down the street, walking swiftly. At the corner a cab overtook her, slowing, the driver looking at her interrogatively. She turned into the drug store at the corner and went back to the telephone booth. Then she returned to the house. As she turned the corner she met the man in the cap who had been leaning in the door. She entered the lattice. Minnie opened the door.

"Thank goodness," Minnie said. "When that cab over there started up, I got ready to pack up too. If you aint ghy say nothing about it, I git you a drink."

When Minnie fetched the gin Temple started to drink it. Her hand was trembling and there was a sort of elation in her face as she stood again just inside the door, listening, the glass

in her hand. I'll need it later, she said. I'll need more than
that. She covered the glass with a saucer and hid it carefully.
Then she dug into the mass of garments in the corner and
found a dancing-frock and shook it out and hung it back in
the closet. She looked at the other things a moment, but she
returned to the bed and lay down again. At once she rose and
drew the chair up and sat down, her feet on the unmade bed.
While daylight died slowly in the room she sat smoking cigarette after cigarette, listening to every sound on the stairs.

At half-past six Minnie brought her supper up. On the tray
was another glass of gin. "Miss Reba sont this un," she said.
"She say, how you feelin?"

"Tell her, all right," Temple said. "I'm going to have a bath
and then go to bed, tell her."

When Minnie was gone Temple poured the two drinks into
a tumbler and gloated over it, the glass shaking in her hands.
She set it carefully away and covered it and ate her supper
from the bed. When she finished she lit a cigarette. Her
movements were jerky; she smoked swiftly, moving about the
room. She stood for a moment at the window, the shade
lifted aside, then she dropped it and turned into the room
again, spying herself in the mirror. She turned before it,
studying herself, puffing at the cigarette.

She snapped it behind her, toward the fireplace, and went
to the mirror and combed her hair. She ripped the curtain
aside and took the dress down and laid it on the bed and
returned and drew out a drawer in the dresser and took a
garment out. She paused with the garment in her hand, then
she replaced it and closed the drawer and caught up the frock
swiftly and hung it back in the closet. A moment later she
found herself walking up and down the room, another cigarette burning in her hand, without any recollection of having
lit it. She flung it away and went to the table and looked at
her watch and propped it against the pack of cigarettes so she
could see it from the bed, and lay down. When she did so she
felt the pistol through the pillow. She slipped it out and
looked at it, then she slid it under her flank and lay motionless, her legs straight, her hands behind her head, her eyes
focussing into black pinheads at every sound on the stairs.

At nine she rose. She picked up the pistol again; after a

moment she thrust it beneath the mattress and undressed and in a spurious Chinese robe splotched with gold dragons and jade and scarlet flowers she left the room. When she returned her hair curled damply about her face. She went to the washstand and took up the tumbler, holding it in her hands, but she set it down again.

She dressed, retrieving the bottles and jars from the corner. Her motions before the glass were furious yet painstaking. She went to the washstand and took up the glass, but again she paused and went to the corner and got her coat and put it on and put the platinum bag in the pocket and leaned once more to the mirror. Then she went and took up the glass and gulped the gin and left the room, walking swiftly.

A single light burned in the hall. It was empty. She could hear voices in Miss Reba's room, but the lower hall was deserted. She descended swiftly and silently and gained the door. She believed that it would be at the door that they would stop her and she thought of the pistol with acute regret, almost pausing, knowing that she would use it without any compunction whatever, with a kind of pleasure. She sprang to the door and pawed at the bolt, her head turned over her shoulder.

It opened. She sprang out and out the lattice door and ran down the walk and out the gate. As she did so a car, moving slowly along the curb, stopped opposite her. Popeye sat at the wheel. Without any apparent movement from him the door swung open. He made no movement, spoke no word. He just sat there, the straw hat slanted a little aside.

"I wont!" Temple said. "I wont!"

He made no movement, no sound. She came to the car.

"I wont, I tell you!" Then she cried wildly: "You're scared of him! You're scared to!"

"I'm giving him his chance," he said. "Will you go back in that house, or will you get in this car?"

"You're scared to!"

"I'm giving him his chance," he said, in his cold soft voice. "Come on. Make up your mind."

She leaned forward, putting her hand on his arm. "Popeye," she said; "daddy." His arm felt frail, no larger than a child's, dead and hard and light as a stick.

"I dont care which you do," he said. "But do it. Come on."

She leaned toward him, her hand on his arm. Then she got into the car. "You wont do it. You're afraid to. He's a better man than you are."

He reached across and shut the door. "Where?" he said. "Grotto?"

"He's a better man than you are!" Temple said shrilly. "You're not even a man! He knows it. Who does know it if he dont?" The car was in motion. She began to shriek at him. "You, a man, a bold bad man, when you cant even——When you had to bring a real man in to——And you hanging over the bed, moaning and slobbering like a——You couldn't fool me but once, could you? No wonder I bled and bluh——" his hand came over her mouth, hard, his nails going into her flesh. With the other hand he drove the car at reckless speed. When they passed beneath lights she could see him watching her as she struggled, tugging at his hand, whipping her head this way and that.

She ceased struggling, but she continued to twist her head from side to side, tugging at his hand. One finger, ringed with a thick ring, held her lips apart, his finger-tips digging into her cheek. With the other hand he whipped the car in and out of traffic, bearing down upon other cars until they slewed aside with brakes squealing, shooting recklessly across intersections. Once a policeman shouted at them, but he did not even look around.

Temple began to whimper, moaning behind his hand, drooling upon his fingers. The ring was like a dentist's instrument; she could not close her lips to regurgitate. When he removed it she could feel the imprint of his fingers cold on her jaw. She lifted her hand to it.

"You hurt my mouth," she whimpered. They were approaching the outskirts of the city, the speedometer at fifty miles. His hat slanted above his delicate hooked profile. She nursed her jaw. The houses gave way to broad, dark subdivisions out of which realtors' signs loomed abrupt and ghostly, with a quality of forlorn assurance. Between them low, far lights hung in the cool empty darkness blowing with fireflies. She began to cry quietly, feeling the cooling double drink of gin inside her. "You hurt my mouth," she said in a voice small and faint with self-pity. She nursed her jaw with experimental fingers, pressing harder and harder until she found a twinge. "You'll be sorry for this," she said in a muffled voice. "When I tell Red. Dont you wish you were Red? Dont you? Dont you wish you could do what he can do? Dont you wish he was the one watching us instead of you?"

They turned into the Grotto, passing along a closely curtained wall from which a sultry burst of music came. She sprang out while he was locking the car and ran on up the steps. "I gave you your chance," she said. "You brought me here. I didn't ask you to come."

She went to the washroom. In the mirror she examined her face. "Shucks," she said, "it didn't leave a mark, even;" drawing the flesh this way and that. "Little runt," she said, peering at her reflection. She added a phrase, glibly obscene, with a detached parrotlike effect. She painted her mouth again. Another woman entered. They examined one another's clothes with brief, covert, cold, embracing glances.

Popeye was standing at the door to the dance-hall, a cigarette in his fingers.

"I gave you your chance," Temple said. "You didn't have to come."

"I dont take chances," he said.

"You took one," Temple said. "Are you sorry? Huh?"

"Go on," he said, his hand on her back. She was in the act of stepping over the sill when she turned and looked at him, their eyes almost on a level; then her hand flicked toward his armpit. He caught her wrist; the other hand flicked toward him. He caught that one too in his soft, cold hand. They looked eye to eye, her mouth open and the rouge spots darkening slowly on her face.

"I gave you your chance back there in town," he said. "You took it."

Behind her the music beat, sultry, evocative; filled with movement of feet, the voluptuous hysteria of muscles warming the scent of flesh, of the blood. "Oh, God; oh, God," she said, her lips scarce moving. "I'll go. I'll go back."

"You took it," he said. "Go on."

In his grasp her hands made tentative plucking motions at his coat just out of reach of her finger-tips. Slowly he was turning her toward the door, her head reverted. "You just dare!" she cried. "You just——" His hand closed upon the back of her neck, his fingers like steel, yet cold and light as aluminum. She could hear the vertebrae grating faintly together, and his voice, cold and still.

"Will you?"

She nodded her head. Then they were dancing. She could still feel his hand at her neck. Across his shoulder she looked swiftly about the room, her gaze flicking from face to face among the dancers. Beyond a low arch, in another room, a group stood about the crap-table. She leaned this way and that, trying to see the faces of the group.

Then she saw the four men. They were sitting at a table near the door. One of them was chewing gum; the whole lower part of his face seemed to be cropped with teeth of an unbelievable whiteness and size. When she saw them she swung Popeye around with his back to them, working the two of them toward the door again. Once more her harried gaze flew from face to face in the crowd.

When she looked again two of the men had risen. They approached. She dragged Popeye into their path, still keeping his back turned to them. The men paused and essayed to go around her; again she backed Popeye into their path. She was trying to say something to him, but her mouth felt cold. It was like trying to pick up a pin with the fingers numb. Suddenly she felt herself lifted bodily aside, Popeye's small arms light and rigid as aluminum. She stumbled back against the wall and watched the two men leave the room. "I'll go back," she said. "I'll go back." She began to laugh shrilly.

"Shut it," Popeye said. "Are you going to shut it?"

"Get me a drink," she said. She felt his hand; her legs felt cold too, like they were not hers. They were sitting at a table. Two tables away the man was still chewing, his elbows on the table. The fourth man sat on his spine, smoking, his coat buttoned across his chest.

She watched hands: a brown one in a white sleeve, a soiled white one beneath a dirty cuff, setting bottles on the table. She had a glass in her hand. She drank, gulping; with the glass in her hand she saw Red standing in the door, in a gray suit and a spotted bow tie. He looked like a college boy, and he looked about the room until he saw her. He looked at the back of Popeye's head, then at her as she sat with the glass in her hand. The two men at the other table had not moved. She could see the faint, steady movement of the one's ears as he chewed. The music started.

She held Popeye's back toward Red. He was still watching her, almost a head taller than anybody else. "Come on," she said in Popeye's ear. "If you're going to dance, dance."

She had another drink. They danced again. Red had disappeared. When the music ceased she had another drink. It did no good. It merely lay hot and hard inside her. "Come on," she said, "dont quit." But he wouldn't get up, and she stood over him, her muscles flinching and jerking with exhaustion and terror. She began to jeer at him. "Call yourself a man, a bold, bad man, and let a girl dance you off your feet." Then her face drained, became small and haggard and sincere; she spoke like a child, with sober despair. "Popeye." He sat with his hands on the table, finicking with a cigarette, the second glass with its melting ice before him. She put her hand on his shoulder. "Daddy," she said. Moving to shield them from the room, her hand stole toward his arm pit, touching the butt of the flat pistol. It lay rigid in the light, dead vise of his arm and side. "Give it to me," she whispered. "Daddy. Daddy." She leaned her thigh against his shoulder, caressing his arm with her flank. "Give it to me, daddy," she whispered. Suddenly her hand began to steal down his body in a swift, covert movement; then it snapped away in a movement of revulsion. "I forgot," she whispered; "I didn't mean . . . . I didn't. . . . . . ."

One of the men at the other table hissed once through his teeth. "Sit down," Popeye said. She sat down. She filled her glass, watching her hands perform the action. Then she was watching the corner of the gray coat. He's got a broken button, she thought stupidly. Popeye had not moved.

"Dance this?" Red said.

His head was bent but he was not looking at her. He was turned a little, facing the two men at the other table. Still Popeye did not move. He shredded delicately the end of the cigarette, pinching the tobacco off. Then he put it into his mouth.

"I'm not dancing," Temple said through her cold lips.

"Not?" Red said. He said, in a level tone, without moving: "How's the boy?"

"Fine," Popeye said. Temple watched him scrape a match, saw the flame distorted through glass. "You've had enough," Popeye said. His hand took the glass from her lips. She watched him empty it into the ice bowl. The music started again. She sat looking quietly about the room. A voice began to buzz faintly at her hearing, then Popeye was gripping her wrist, shaking it, and she found that her mouth was open and that she must have been making a noise of some sort with it. "Shut it, now," he said. "You can have one more." He poured the drink into the glass.

"I haven't felt it at all," she said. He gave her the glass. She drank. When she set the glass down she realised that she was drunk. She believed that she had been drunk for some time. She thought that perhaps she had passed out and that it had already happened. She could hear herself saying I hope it has. I hope it has. Then she believed it had and she was overcome by a sense of bereavement and of physical desire. She thought, It will never be again, and she sat in a floating swoon of agonised sorrow and erotic longing, thinking of Red's body, watching her hand holding the empty bottle over the glass.

"You've drunk it all," Popeye said. "Get up, now. Dance it off." They danced again. She moved stiffly and languidly, her eyes open but unseeing; her body following the music without hearing the tune for a time. Then she became aware that the orchestra was playing the same tune as when Red was asking her to dance. If that were so, then it couldn't have happened yet. She felt a wild surge of relief. It was not too late: Red was still alive; she felt long shuddering waves of physical desire going over her, draining the color from her mouth, drawing her eyeballs back into her skull in a shuddering swoon.

They were at the crap table. She could hear herself shouting to the dice. She was rolling them, winning; the counters were piling up in front of her as Popeye drew them in, coaching her, correcting her in his soft, querulous voice. He stood beside her, shorter than she.

He had the cup himself. She stood beside him cunningly, feeling the desire going over her in wave after wave, involved with the music and with the smell of her own flesh. She became quiet. By infinitesimal inches she moved aside until someone slipped into her place. Then she was walking swiftly and carefully across the floor toward the door, the dancers, the music swirling slowly about her in a bright myriad wave. The table where the two men had sat was empty, but she did not even glance at it. She entered the corridor. A waiter met her.

"Room," she said. "Hurry."

The room contained a table and four chairs. The waiter turned on the light and stood in the door. She jerked her hand at him; he went out. She leaned against the table on her braced arms, watching the door, until Red entered.

He came toward her. She did not move. Her eyes began to grow darker and darker, lifting into her skull above a half moon of white, without focus, with the blank rigidity of a statue's eyes. She began to say Ah-ah-ah-ah in an expiring voice, her body arching slowly backward as though faced by an exquisite torture. When he touched her she sprang like a bow, hurling herself upon him, her mouth gaped and ugly like that of a dying fish as she writhed her loins against him.

He dragged his face free by main strength. With her hips grinding against him, her mouth gaping in straining protrusion, bloodless, she began to speak. "Let's hurry. Anywhere. I've quit him. I told him so. It's not my fault. Is it my fault? You dont need your hat and I dont either. He came here to kill you but I said I gave him his chance. It wasn't my fault. And now it'll just be us. Without him there watching. Come on. What're you waiting for?" She strained her mouth toward him, dragging his head down, making a whimpering moan. He held his face free. "I told him I was. I said if you bring me here. I gave you your chance I said. And now he's got them there to bump you off. But you're not afraid. Are you?"

"Did you know that when you telephoned me?" he said.

"What? He said I wasn't to see you again. He said he'd kill you. But he had me followed when I telephoned. I saw him. But you're not afraid. He's not even a man, but you are. You're a man. You're a man." She began to grind against him, dragging at his head, murmuring to him in parrotlike under-world epithet, the saliva running pale over her bloodless lips. "Are you afraid?"

"Of that dopey bastard?" Lifting her bodily he turned so that he faced the door, and slipped his right hand free. She did not seem to be aware that he had moved.

"Please. Please. Please. Please. Dont make me wait. I'm burning up."

"All right. You go on back. You wait till I give you the sign. Will you go on back?"

"I cant wait. You've got to. I'm on fire, I tell you." She clung to him. Together they blundered across the room to-ward the door, he holding her clear of his right side; she in a voluptuous swoon, unaware that they were moving, straining at him as though she were trying to touch him with all of her body-surface at once. He freed himself and thrust her into the passage.

"Go on," he said. "I'll be there in a minute."

"You wont be long? I'm on fire. I'm dying, I tell you."

"No. Not long. Go on, now."

The music was playing. She moved up the corridor, stag-gering a little. She thought that she was leaning against the wall, when she found that she was dancing again; then that she was dancing with two men at once; then she found that she was not dancing but that she was moving toward the door between the man with the chewing gum and the one with the buttoned coat. She tried to stop, but they had her under the arms; she opened her mouth to scream, taking one last despairing look about the swirling room.

"Yell," the man with the buttoned coat said. "Just try it once."

Red was at the crap table. She saw his head turned, the cup in his lifted hand. With it he made her a short, cheery salute. He watched her disappear through the door, between the two men. Then he looked briefly about the room. His face was bold and calm, but there were two white lines at the base of his nostrils and his forehead was damp. He rattled the cup and threw the dice steadily.

"Eleven," the dealer said.

"Let it lay," Red said. "I'll pass a million times tonight."

They helped Temple into the car. The man in the buttoned coat took the wheel. Where the drive joined the lane that led to the highroad a long touring car was parked. When they passed it Temple saw, leaning to a cupped match, Popeye's delicate hooked profile beneath the slanted hat as he lit the cigarette. The match flipped outward like a dying star in miniature, sucked with the profile into darkness by the rush of their passing.

XXV

THE TABLES had been moved to one end of the dance floor. On each one was a black table-cloth. The curtains were still drawn; a thick, salmon-colored light fell through them. Just beneath the orchestra platform the coffin sat. It was an expensive one: black, with silver fittings, the trestles hidden by a mass of flowers. In wreaths and crosses and other shapes of ceremonial mortality, the mass appeared to break in a symbolical wave over the bier and on upon the platform and the piano, the scent of them thickly oppressive.

The proprietor of the place moved about among the tables, speaking to the arrivals as they entered and found seats. The negro waiters, in black shirts beneath their starched jackets, were already moving in and out with glasses and bottles of ginger ale. They moved with swaggering and decorous repression; already the scene was vivid, with a hushed, macabre air a little febrile.

The archway to the dice-room was draped in black. A black pall lay upon the crap table, upon which the overflow of floral shapes was beginning to accumulate. People entered steadily, the men in dark suits of decorous restraint, others in the light, bright shades of spring, increasing the atmosphere of macabre paradox. The women—the younger ones—wore bright colors also, in hats and scarves; the older ones in sober gray and black and navy blue, and glittering with diamonds: matronly figures resembling housewives on a Sunday afternoon excursion.

The room began to hum with shrill, hushed talk. The waiters moved here and there with high, precarious trays, their white jackets and black shirts resembling photograph negatives. The proprietor went from table to table with his bald head, a huge diamond in his black cravat, followed by the bouncer, a thick, muscle-bound, bullet-headed man who appeared to be on the point of bursting out of his dinner-jacket through the rear, like a cocoon.

In a private dining-room, on a table draped in black, sat a huge bowl of punch floating with ice and sliced fruit. Beside it leaned a fat man in a shapeless greenish suit, from the sleeves of which dirty cuffs fell upon hands rimmed with black nails. The soiled collar was wilted about his neck in limp folds, knotted by a greasy black tie with an imitation ruby stud. His face gleamed with moisture and he adjured the throng about the bowl in a harsh voice:

"Come on, folks. It's on Gene. It dont cost you nothing. Step up and drink. There wasn't never a better boy walked than him." They drank and fell back, replaced by others with extended cups. From time to time a waiter entered with ice and fruit and dumped them into the bowl; from a suit case under the table Gene drew fresh bottles and decanted them into the bowl; then, proprietorial, adjurant, sweating, he resumed his harsh monologue, mopping his face on his sleeve. "Come on, folks. It's all on Gene. I aint nothing but a bootlegger, but he never had a better friend than me. Step up and drink, folks. There's more where that come from."

From the dance hall came a strain of music. The people entered and found seats. On the platform was the orchestra from a downtown hotel, in dinner coats. The proprietor and a second man were conferring with the leader.

"Let them play jazz," the second man said. "Never nobody liked dancing no better than Red."

"No, no," the proprietor said. "Time Gene gets them all ginned up on free whiskey, they'll start dancing. It'll look bad."

"How about the Blue Danube?" the leader said.

"No, no; dont play no blues, I tell you," the proprietor said. "There's a dead man in that bier."

"That's not blues," the leader said.

"What is it?" the second man said.

"A waltz. Strauss."

"A wop?" the second man said. "Like hell. Red was an American. You may not be, but he was. Dont you know anything American? Play I Cant Give You Anything but Love. He always liked that."

"And get them all to dancing?" the proprietor said. He glanced back at the tables, where the women were beginning to talk a little shrilly. "You better start off with Nearer, My God, To Thee," he said, "and sober them up some. I told Gene it was risky about that punch, starting it so soon. My suggestion was to wait until we started back to town. But I might have knowed somebody'd have to turn it into a carnival. Better start off solemn and keep it up until I give you the sign."

"Red wouldn't like it solemn," the second man said. "And you know it."

"Let him go somewheres else, then," the proprietor said. "I just done this as an accommodation. I aint running no funeral parlor."

The orchestra played Nearer, My God, To Thee. The audience grew quiet. A woman in a red dress came in the door unsteadily. "Whoopee," she said, "so long, Red. He'll be in hell before I could even reach Little Rock."

"Shhhhhhhh!" voices said. She fell into a seat. Gene came to the door and stood there until the music stopped.

"Come on, folks," he shouted, jerking his arms in a fat, sweeping gesture, "come and get it. It's on Gene. I dont want a dry throat or eye in this place in ten minutes." Those at the rear moved toward the door. The proprietor sprang to his feet and jerked his hand at the orchestra. The cornetist rose and played In That Haven of Rest in solo, but the crowd at the back of the room continued to dwindle through the door where Gene stood waving his arm. Two middle-aged women were weeping quietly beneath flowered hats.

They surged and clamored about the diminishing bowl. From the dance hall came the rich blare of the cornet. Two soiled young men worked their way toward the table, shouting "Gangway. Gangway" monotonously, carrying suit cases. They opened them and set bottles on the table, while Gene, frankly weeping now, opened them and decanted them into the bowl. "Come up, folks. I couldn't a loved him no better if he'd a been my own son," he shouted hoarsely, dragging his sleeve across his face.

A waiter edged up to the table with a bowl of ice and fruit and went to put them into the punch bowl. "What the hell you doing?" Gene said, "putting that slop in there? Get to hell away from here."

"Ra-a-a-a-y-y-y-y!" they shouted, clashing their cups, drowning all save the pantomime as Gene knocked the bowl of fruit from the waiter's hand and fell again to dumping raw liquor into the bowl, sploshing it into and upon the extended hands and cups. The two youths opened bottles furiously.

As though swept there upon a brassy blare of music the proprietor appeared in the door, his face harried, waving his arms. "Come on, folks," he shouted, "let's finish the musical program. It's costing us money."

"Hell with it," they shouted.

"Costing who money?"

"Who cares?"

"Costing who money?"

"Who begrudges it? I'll pay it. By God, I'll buy him two funerals."

"Folks! Folks!" the proprietor shouted. "Dont you realise there's a bier in that room?"

"Costing who money?"

"Beer?" Gene said. "Beer?" he said in a broken voice. "Is anybody here trying to insult me by——"

"He begrudges Red the money."

"Who does?"

"Joe does, the cheap son of a bitch."

"Is somebody here trying to insult me——"

"Let's move the funeral, then. This is not the only place in town."

"Let's move Joe."

"Put the son of a bitch in a coffin. Let's have two funerals."

"Beer? Beer? Is somebody——"

"Put the son of a bitch in a coffin. See how he likes it."

"Put the son of a bitch in a coffin," the woman in red shrieked. They rushed toward the door, where the proprietor stood waving his hands above his head, his voice shrieking out of the uproar before he turned and fled.

In the main room a male quartet engaged from a vaudeville house was singing. They were singing mother songs in close harmony; they sang Sonny Boy. The weeping was general among the older women. Waiters were now carrying cups of punch in to them and they sat holding the cups in their fat, ringed hands, crying.

The orchestra played again. The woman in red staggered into the room. "Come on, Joe," she shouted, "open the game. Get that damn stiff out of here and open the game." A man tried to hold her; she turned upon him with a burst of filthy language and went on to the shrouded crap table and hurled a wreath to the floor. The proprietor rushed toward her, followed by the bouncer. The proprietor grasped the woman as she lifted another floral piece. The man who had tried to hold her intervened, the woman cursing shrilly and striking at both of them impartially with the wreath. The bouncer caught the man's arm; he whirled and struck at the bouncer, who knocked him halfway across the room. Three more men entered. The fourth rose from the floor and all four of them rushed at the bouncer.

He felled the first and whirled and sprang with unbelievable celerity, into the main room. The orchestra was playing. It was immediately drowned in a sudden pandemonium of chairs and screams. The bouncer whirled again and met the rush of the four men. They mingled; a second man flew out and skittered along the floor on his back; the bouncer sprang free. Then he whirled and rushed them and in a whirling plunge they bore down upon the bier and crashed into it. The orchestra had ceased and were now climbing onto their chairs, with their instruments. The floral offerings flew; the coffin teetered. "Catch it!" a voice shouted. They sprang forward, but the coffin crashed heavily to the floor, coming open. The corpse tumbled slowly and sedately out and came to rest with its face in the center of a wreath.

"Play something!" the proprietor bawled, waving his arms; "play! Play!"

When they raised the corpse the wreath came too, attached to him by a hidden end of wire driven into his cheek. He had worn a cap which, tumbling off, exposed a small blue hole in the center of his forehead. It had been neatly plugged with wax and was painted, but the wax had been jarred out and lost. They couldn't find it, but by unfastening the snap in the peak, they could draw the cap down to his eyes.

As the cortège neared the downtown section more cars joined it. The hearse was followed by six Packard touring cars with the tops back, driven by liveried chauffeurs and filled with flowers. They looked exactly alike and were of the type rented by the hour by the better class agencies. Next came a nondescript line of taxis, roadsters, sedans, which increased as the procession moved slowly through the restricted district where faces peered from beneath lowered shades, toward the main artery that led back out of town, toward the cemetery.

On the avenue the hearse increased its speed, the procession stretching out at swift intervals. Presently the private cars and the cabs began to drop out. At each intersection they would turn this way or that, until at last only the hearse and the six Packards were left, each carrying no occupant save the liveried driver. The street was broad and now infrequent, with a white line down the center that diminished on ahead into the smooth asphalt emptiness. Soon the hearse was making forty miles an hour and then forty-five and then fifty.

One of the cabs drew up at Miss Reba's door. She got out, followed by a thin woman in sober, severe clothes and gold nose-glasses, and a short plump woman in a plumed hat, her face hidden by a handkerchief, and a small bullet-headed boy of five or six. The woman with the handkerchief continued to sob in snuffy gasps as they went up the walk and entered the lattice. Beyond the house door the dogs set up a falsetto uproar. When Minnie opened the door they surged about Miss Reba's feet. She kicked them aside. Again they assailed her with snapping eagerness; again she flung them back against the wall in muted thuds.

"Come in, come in," she said, her hand to her breast. Once inside the house the woman with the handkerchief began to weep aloud.

"Didn't he look sweet?" she wailed. "Didn't he look sweet!"

"Now, now," Miss Reba said, leading the way to her room, "come in and have some beer. You'll feel better. Minnie!" They entered the room with the decorated dresser, the safe, the screen, the draped portrait. "Sit down, sit down," she panted, shoving the chairs forward. She lowered herself into one and stooped terrifically toward her feet.

"Uncle Bud, honey," the weeping woman said, dabbing at her eyes, "come and unlace Miss Reba's shoes."

The boy knelt and removed Miss Reba's shoes. "And if you'll just reach me them house slippers under the bed there, honey," Miss Reba said. The boy fetched the slippers. Minnie entered, followed by the dogs. They rushed at Miss Reba and began to worry the shoes she had just removed.

"Scat!" the boy said, striking at one of them with his hand. The dog's head snapped around, its teeth clicking, its half-hidden eyes bright and malevolent. The boy recoiled. "You bite me, you thon bitch," he said.

"Uncle Bud!" the fat woman said, her round face, ridged in fatty folds and streaked with tears, turned upon the boy in shocked surprise, the plumes nodding precariously above it. Uncle Bud's head was quite round, his nose bridged with freckles like splotches of huge summer rain on a sidewalk. The other woman sat primly erect, in gold nose-glasses on a gold chain and neat iron-gray hair. She looked like a school-teacher. "The very idea!" the fat woman said. "How in the world he can learn such words on a Arkansaw farm, I dont know."

"They'll learn meanness anywhere," Miss Reba said. Minnie leaned down a tray bearing three frosted tankards. Uncle Bud watched with round cornflower eyes as they took one each. The fat woman began to cry again.

"He looked so sweet!" she wailed.

"We all got to suffer it," Miss Reba said. "Well, may it be a long day," lifting her tankard. They drank, bowing formally to one another. The fat woman dried her eyes; the two guests wiped their lips with prim decorum. The thin one coughed delicately aside, behind her hand.

"Such good beer," she said.

"Aint it?" the fat one said. "I always say it's the greatest pleasure I have to call on Miss Reba."

They began to talk politely, in decorous half-completed sentences, with little gasps of agreement. The boy had moved aimlessly to the window, peering beneath the lifted shade.

"How long's he going to be with you, Miss Myrtle?" Miss Reba said.

"Just till Sat'dy," the fat woman said. "Then he'll go back home. It makes a right nice little change for him, with me for a week or two. And I enjoy having him."

"Children are such a comfort to a body," the thin one said.

"Yes," Miss Myrtle said. "Is them two nice young fellows still with you, Miss Reba?"

"Yes," Miss Reba said. "I think I got to get shut of them, though. I aint specially tender-hearted, but after all it aint no use in helping young folks to learn this world's meanness until they have to. I already had to stop the girls running around the house without no clothes on, and they dont like it."

They drank again, decorously, handling the tankards delicately, save Miss Reba who grasped hers as though it were a weapon, her other hand lost in her breast. She set her tankard down empty. "I get so dry, seems like," she said. "Wont you ladies have another?" They murmured, ceremoniously. "Minnie!" Miss Reba shouted.

Minnie came and filled the tankards again. "Reely, I'm right ashamed," Miss Myrtle said. "But Miss Reba has such good beer. And then we've all had a kind of upsetting afternoon."

"I'm just surprised it wasn't upset no more," Miss Reba said. "Giving away all that free liquor like Gene done."

"It must have cost a good piece of jack," the thin woman said.

"I believe you," Miss Reba said. "And who got anything out of it? Tell me that. Except the privilege of having his place hell-full of folks not spending a cent." She had set her tankard on the table beside her chair. Suddenly she turned her head sharply and looked at it. Uncle Bud was now behind her chair, leaning against the table. "You aint been into my beer, have you, boy?" she said.

"You, Uncle Bud," Miss Myrtle said. "Aint you ashamed? I declare, it's getting so I dont dare take him nowhere. I never see such a boy for snitching beer in my life. You come out here and play, now. Come on."

"Yessum," Uncle Bud said. He moved, in no particular direction. Miss Reba drank and set the tankard back on the table and rose.

"Since we all been kind of tore up," she said, "maybe I can prevail on you ladies to have a little sup of gin?"

"No; reely," Miss Myrtle said.

"Miss Reba's the perfect hostess," the thin one said. "How many times you heard me say that, Miss Myrtle?"

"I wouldn't undertake to say, dearie," Miss Myrtle said.

Miss Reba vanished behind the screen.

"Did you ever see it so warm for June, Miss Lorraine?" Miss Myrtle said.

"I never did," the thin woman said. Miss Myrtle's face began to crinkle again. Setting her tankard down she began to fumble for her handkerchief.

"It just comes over me like this," she said, "and them singing that Sonny Boy and all. He looked so sweet," she wailed.

"Now, now," Miss Lorraine said. "Drink a little beer. You'll feel better. Miss Myrtle's took again," she said, raising her voice.

"I got too tender a heart," Miss Myrtle said. She snuffled behind the handkerchief, groping for her tankard. She groped for a moment, then it touched her hand. She looked quickly up. "You, Uncle Bud!" she said. "Didn't I tell you to come out from behind there and play? Would you believe it? The other afternoon when we left here I was so mortified I didn't know what to do. I was ashamed to be seen on the street with a drunk boy like you."

Miss Reba emerged from behind the screen with three glasses of gin. "This'll put some heart into us," she said. "We're setting here like three old sick cats." They bowed formally and drank, patting their lips. Then they began to talk. They were all talking at once, again in half-completed sentences, but without pauses for agreement or affirmation.

"It's us girls," Miss Myrtle said. "Men just cant seem to take us and leave us for what we are. They make us what we are, then they expect us to be different. Expect us not to never look at another man, while they come and go as they please."

"A woman that wants to fool with more than one man at a time is a fool," Miss Reba said. "They're all trouble, and why do you want to double your trouble? And the woman that cant stay true to a good man when she gets him, a free-hearted spender that never give her a hour's uneasiness or a hard word. . . . . ." looking at them, her eyes began to fill with a sad, unutterable expression, of baffled and patient despair.

"Now, now," Miss Myrtle said. She leaned forward and patted Miss Reba's huge hand. Miss Lorraine made a faint clucking sound with her tongue. "You'll get yourself started."

"He was such a good man," Miss Reba said. "We was like two doves. For eleven years we was like two doves."

"Now, dearie; now, dearie," Miss Myrtle said.

"It's when it comes over me like this," Miss Reba said. "Seeing that boy laying there under them flowers."

"He never had no more than Mr Binford had," Miss Myrtle said. "Now, now. Drink a little beer."

Miss Reba brushed her sleeve across her eyes. She drank some beer.

"He ought to known better than to take a chance with Popeye's girl," Miss Lorraine said.

"Men dont never learn better than that, dearie," Miss Myrtle said. "Where you reckon they went, Miss Reba?"

"I dont know and I dont care," Miss Reba said. "And how soon they catch him and burn him for killing that boy, I dont care neither. I dont care none."

"He goes all the way to Pensacola every summer to see his mother," Miss Myrtle said. "A man that'll do that cant be all bad."

"I dont know how bad you like them, then," Miss Reba said. "Me trying to run a respectable house, that's been running a shooting-gallery for twenty years, and him trying to turn it into a peep-show."

"It's us poor girls," Miss Myrtle said, "causes all the trouble and gets all the suffering."

"I heard two years ago he wasn't no good that way," Miss Lorraine said.

"I knew it all the time," Miss Reba said. "A young man spending his money like water on girls and not never going to bed with one. It's against nature. All the girls thought it was because he had a little woman out in town somewhere, but I says mark my words, there's something funny about him. There's a funny business somewhere."

"He was a free spender, all right," Miss Lorraine said.

"The clothes and jewelry that girl bought, it was a shame," Miss Reba said. "There was a Chinee robe she paid a hundred dollars for—imported, it was—and perfume at ten dollars an ounce; and next morning when I went up there, they was all wadded in the corner and the perfume and rouge busted all over them like a cyclone. That's what she'd do when she got mad at him, when he'd beat her. After he shut her up and wouldn't let her leave the house. Having the front of my house watched like it was a. . . . . . ." She raised the tankard from the table to her lips. Then she halted it, blinking. "Where's my——"

"Uncle Bud!" Miss Myrtle said. She grasped the boy by the arm and snatched him out from behind Miss Reba's chair and shook him, his round head bobbing on his shoulders with an expression of equable idiocy. "Aint you ashamed? Aint you *ashamed*? Why cant you stay out of these ladies' beer? I'm a good mind to take that dollar back and make you buy Miss Reba a can of beer, I am for a fact. Now, you go over there by that window and stay there, you hear?"

"Nonsense," Miss Reba said. "There wasn't much left. You ladies are about ready too, aint you? Minnie!"

Miss Lorraine touched her mouth with her handkerchief. Behind her glasses her eyes rolled aside in a veiled, secret look. She laid the other hand to her flat spinster's breast.

"We forgot about your heart, honey," Miss Myrtle said. "Dont you reckon you better take gin this time?"

"Reely, I——" Miss Lorraine said.

"Yes; do," Miss Reba said. She rose heavily and fetched three more glasses of gin from behind the screen. Minnie entered and refilled the tankards. They drank, patting their lips.

"That's what was going on, was it?" Miss Lorraine said.

"First I knowed was when Minnie told me there was something funny going on," Miss Reba said. "How he wasn't here hardly at all, gone about every other night, and that when he was here, there wasn't no signs at all the next morning when she cleaned up. She'd hear them quarrelling, and she said it was her wanting to get out and he wouldn't let her. With all them clothes he was buying her, mind, he didn't want her to leave the house, and she'd get mad and lock the door and wouldn't even let him in."

"Maybe he went off and got fixed up with one of these glands, these monkey glands, and it quit on him," Miss Myrtle said.

"Then one morning he come in with Red and took him up there. They stayed about an hour and left, and Popeye didn't show up again until next morning. Then him and Red come back and stayed up there about an hour. When they left, Minnie come and told me what was going on, so next day I waited for them. I called him in here and I says 'Look here, you son of a buh—' " She ceased. For an instant the three of them sat motionless, a little forward. Then slowly their heads turned and they looked at the boy leaning against the table.

"Uncle Bud, honey," Miss Myrtle said, "dont you want to go and play in the yard with Reba and Mr Binford?"

"Yessum," the boy said. He went toward the door. They watched him until the door closed upon him. Miss Lorraine drew her chair up; they leaned together.

"And that's what they was doing?" Miss Myrtle said.

"I says 'I been running a house for twenty years, but this is the first time I ever had anything like this going on in it. If you want to turn a stud in to your girl' I says 'go somewhere else to do it. I aint going to have my house turned into no French joint.' "

"The son of a bitch," Miss Lorraine said.

"He'd ought to've had sense enough to got a old ugly man," Miss Myrtle said. "Tempting us poor girls like that."

"Men always expects us to resist temptation," Miss Lorraine said. She was sitting upright like a school-teacher. "The lousy son of a bitch."

"Except what they offers themselves," Miss Reba said. "Then watch them. . . . Every morning for four days that was going on, then they didn't come back. For a week Popeye didn't show up at all, and that girl wild as a young mare. I thought he was out of town on business maybe, until Minnie told me he wasn't and that he give her five dollars a day not to let that girl out of the house nor use the telephone. And me trying to get word to him to come and take her out of my house because I didn't want nuttin like that going on in it. Yes, sir, Minnie said the two of them would be nekkid as two snakes, and Popeye hanging over the foot of the bed without even his hat took off, making a kind of whinnying sound."

"Maybe he was cheering for them," Miss Lorraine said. "The lousy son of a bitch."

Feet came up the hall; they could hear Minnie's voice lifted in adjuration. The door opened. She entered, holding Uncle Bud erect by one hand. Limp-kneed he dangled, his face fixed in an expression of glassy idiocy. "Miss Reba," Minnie said, "this boy done broke in the icebox and drunk a whole bottle of beer. You, boy!" she said, shaking him, "stan up!" Limply he dangled, his face rigid in a slobbering grin. Then upon it came an expression of concern, consternation; Minnie swung him sharply away from her as he began to vomit.

XXVI

WHEN THE SUN ROSE, Horace had not been to bed nor even undressed. He was just finishing a letter to his wife, addressed to her at her father's in Kentucky, asking for a divorce. He sat at the table, looking down at the single page written neatly and illegibly over, feeling quiet and empty for the first time since he had found Popeye watching him across the spring four weeks ago. While he was sitting there he began to smell coffee from somewhere. "I'll finish this business and then I'll go to Europe. I am sick. I am too old for this. I was born too old for it, and so I am sick to death for quiet."

He shaved and made coffee and drank a cup and ate some bread. When he passed the hotel, the bus which met the morning train was at the curb, with the drummers getting into it. Clarence Snopes was one of them, carrying a tan suit case.

"Going down to Jackson for a couple of days on a little business," he said. "Too bad I missed you last night. I come on back in a car. I reckon you was settled for the night, maybe?" He looked down at Horace, vast, pasty, his intention unmistakable. "I could have took you to a place most folks dont know about. Where a man can do just whatever he is big enough to do. But there'll be another time, since I done got to know you better." He lowered his voice a little, moving a little aside. "Dont you be uneasy. I aint a talker. When I'm here, in Jefferson, I'm one fellow; what I am up town with a bunch of good sports aint nobody's business but mine and theirn. Aint that right?"

Later in the morning, from a distance he saw his sister on the street ahead of him turn and disappear into a door. He tried to find her by looking into all the stores within the radius of where she must have turned, and asking the clerks. She was in none of them. The only place he did not investigate was a stairway that mounted between two stores, to a corridor of offices on the first floor, one of which was that of the District Attorney, Eustace Graham.

Graham had a club foot, which had elected him to the

office he now held. He worked his way into and through the State University; as a youth the town remembered him as driving wagons and trucks for grocery stores. During his first year at the University he made a name for himself by his industry. He waited on table in the commons and he had the government contract for carrying the mail to and from the local postoffice at the arrival of each train, hobbling along with the sack over his shoulder: a pleasant, open-faced young man with a word for everyone and a certain alert rapacity about the eyes. During his second year he let his mail contract lapse and he resigned from his job in the commons; he also had a new suit. People were glad that he had saved through his industry to where he could give all his time to his studies. He was in the law school then, and the law professors groomed him like a race-horse. He graduated well, though without distinction. "Because he was handicapped at the start," the professors said. "If he had had the same start that the others had. . . . He will go far," they said.

It was not until he had left school that they learned that he had been playing poker for three years in the office of a livery stable, behind drawn shades. When, two years out of school, he got elected to the State legislature, they began to tell an anecdote of his school days.

It was in the poker game in the livery stable office. The bet came to Graham. He looked across the table at the owner of the stable, who was his only remaining opponent.

"How much have you got there, Mr Harris?" he said.

"Forty-two dollars, Eustace," the proprietor said. Eustace shoved some chips into the pot. "How much is that?" the proprietor said.

"Forty-two dollars, Mr Harris."

"Hmmm," the proprietor said. He examined his hand. "How many cards did you draw, Eustace?"

"Three, Mr Harris."

"Hmmm. Who dealt the cards, Eustace?"

"I did, Mr Harris."

"I pass, Eustace."

He had been District Attorney but a short time, yet already he had let it be known that he would announce for Congress on his record of convictions, so when he found himself facing

Narcissa across the desk in his dingy office, his expression was like that when he had put the forty-two dollars into the pot.

"I only wish it weren't your brother," he said. "I hate to see a brother-in-arms, you might say, with a bad case." She was watching him with a blank, enveloping look. "After all, we've got to protect society, even when it does seem. . . . . . ."

"Are you sure he cant win?" she said.

"Well, the first principle of law is, God alone knows what the jury will do. Of course, you cant expect——"

"But you dont think he will."

"Naturally, I——"

"You have good reason to think he cant. I suppose you know things about it that he doesn't."

He looked at her briefly. Then he picked up a pen from his desk and began to scrape at the point with a paper cutter. "This is purely confidential. I am violating my oath of office; I wont have to tell you that. But it may save you worry to know that he hasn't a chance in the world. I know what the disappointment will be to him, but that cant be helped. We happen to know that the man is guilty. So if there's any way you know of to get your brother out of the case, I'd advise you to do it. A losing lawyer is like a losing anything else, ballplayer or merchant or doctor: his business is to——"

"So the quicker he loses, the better it would be, wouldn't it?" she said. "If they hung the man and got it over with." His hands became perfectly still. He did not look up. She said, her tone cold and level: "I have reasons for wanting Horace out of this case. The sooner the better. Three nights ago that Snopes, the one in the legislature, telephoned out home, trying to find him. The next day he went to Memphis. I dont know what for. You'll have to find that out yourself. I just want Horace out of this business as soon as possible."

She rose and moved toward the door. He hobbled over to open it; again she put that cold, still, unfathomable gaze upon him as though he were a dog or a cow and she waited for it to get out of her path. Then she was gone. He closed the door and struck a clumsy clog-step, snapping his fingers just as the door opened again; he snapped his hands toward his tie and looked at her in the door, holding it open.

"What day do you think it will be over with?" she said.

"Why, I cuh—Court opens the twentieth," he said. "It will be the first case. Say. . . . Two days. Or three at the most, with your kind assistance. And I need not assure you that this will be held in strictest confidence between us. . . . . . ."
He moved toward her, but her blank calculating gaze was like a wall, surrounding him.

"That will be the twenty-fourth." Then she was looking at him again. "Thank you," she said, and closed the door.

That night she wrote Belle that Horace would be home on the twenty-fourth. She telephoned Horace and asked for Belle's address.

"Why?" Horace said.

"I'm going to write her a letter," she said, her voice tranquil, without threat. Dammit, Horace thought, holding the dead wire in his hand, How can I be expected to combat people who will not even employ subterfuge. But soon he forgot it, forgot that she had called. He did not see her again before the trial opened.

Two days before it opened Snopes emerged from a dentist's office and stood at the curb, spitting. He took a gold-wrapped cigar from his pocket and removed the foil and put the cigar gingerly between his teeth. He had a black eye, and the bridge of his nose was bound in soiled adhesive tape. "Got hit by a car in Jackson," he told them in the barber-shop. "But dont think I never made the bastard pay," he said, showing a sheaf of yellow bills. He put them into a notecase and stowed it away. "I'm an American," he said. "I dont brag about it, because I was born one. And I been a decent Baptist all my life, too. Oh, I aint no preacher and I aint no old maid; I been around with the boys now and then, but I reckon I aint no worse than lots of folks that pretends to sing loud in church. But the lowest, cheapest thing on this earth aint a nigger: it's a jew. We need laws against them. Drastic laws. When a durn lowlife jew can come to a free country like this and just because he's got a law degree, it's time to put a stop to things. A jew is the lowest thing on this creation. And the lowest kind of jew is a jew lawyer. And the lowest kind of jew lawyer is a Memphis jew lawyer. When a jew lawyer can hold up an American, a white man, and not give him but ten dollars for something that two Americans, Americans, south-ron gentlemen; a judge living in the capital of the State of Mississippi and a lawyer that's going to be as big a man as his pa some day, and a judge too; when they give him ten times as much for the same thing than the lowlife jew, we need a law. I been a liberal spender all my life; whatever I had has always been my friends' too. But when a durn, stinking, lowlife jew will refuse to pay an American one tenth of what another American, and a judge at that——"

"Why did you sell it to him, then?" the barber said.

"What?" Snopes said. The barber was looking at him.

"What was you trying to sell to that car when it run over you?" the barber said.

"Have a cigar," Snopes said.

XXVII

Tᴴᴱ ᴛʀɪᴀʟ was set for the twentieth of June. A week after his Memphis visit, Horace telephoned Miss Reba. "Just to know if she's still there," he said. "So I can reach her if I need to."

"She's here," Miss Reba said. "But this reaching. I dont like it. I dont want no cops around here unless they are on my business."

"It'll be only a bailiff," Horace said. "Someone to hand a paper into her own hand."

"Let the postman do it, then," Miss Reba said. "He comes here anyway. In a uniform too. He dont look no worse in it than a full-blowed cop, neither. Let him do it."

"I wont bother you," Horace said. "I wont make you any trouble."

"I know you aint," Miss Reba said. Her voice was thin, harsh, over the wire. "I aint going to let you. Minnie's done took a crying spell tonight, over that bastard that left her, and me and Miss Myrtle was sitting here, and we got started crying too. Me and Minnie and Miss Myrtle. We drunk up a whole new bottle of gin. I cant afford that. So dont you be sending no jay cops up here with no letters for nobody. You telephone me and I'll turn them both out on the street and you can have them arrested there."

On the night of the nineteenth he telephoned her again. He had some trouble in getting in touch with her.

"They're gone," she said. "Both of them. Dont you read no papers?"

"What papers?" Horace said. "Hello. Hello!"

"They aint here no more, I said," Miss Reba said. "I dont know nuttin about them and I dont want to know nuttin except who's going to pay me a week's room rent on——"

"But cant you find where she went to? I may need her."

"I dont know nuttin and I dont want to know nuttin," Miss Reba said. He heard the receiver click. Yet the disconnection was not made at once. He heard the receiver thud onto the table where the telephone sat, and he could hear Miss Reba shouting for Minnie: "Minnie.   Minnie!"

Then some hand lifted the receiver and set it onto the hook; the wire clicked in his ear. After a while a detached Delsarteish voice said: "Pine Bluff dizzent. . . . Enkyew!"

The trial opened the next day. On the table lay the sparse objects which the District Attorney was offering: the bullet from Tommy's skull, a stoneware jug containing corn whiskey.

"I will call Mrs Goodwin to the stand," Horace said. He did not look back. He could feel Goodwin's eyes on his back as he helped the woman into the chair. She was sworn, the child lying on her lap. She repeated the story as she had told it to him on the day after the child was ill. Twice Goodwin tried to interrupt and was silenced by the Court. Horace would not look at him.

The woman finished her story. She sat erect in the chair, in her neat, worn gray dress and hat with the darned veil, the purple ornament on her shoulder. The child lay on her lap, its eyes closed in that drugged immobility. For a while her hand hovered about its face, performing those needless maternal actions as though unawares.

Horace went and sat down. Then only did he look at Goodwin. But the other sat quietly now, his arms folded and his head bent a little, but Horace could see that his nostrils were waxy white with rage against his dark face. He leaned toward him and whispered, but Goodwin did not move.

The District Attorney now faced the woman.

"Mrs Goodwin," he said, " what was the date of your marriage to Mr Goodwin?"

"I object!" Horace said, on his feet.

"Can the prosecution show how this question is relevant?" the Court said.

"I waive, your Honor," the District Attorney said, glancing at the jury.

When court adjourned for the day Goodwin said bitterly: "Well, you've said you would kill me someday, but I didn't think you meant it. I didn't think that you——"

"Dont be a fool," Horace said. "Dont you see your case is won? That they are reduced to trying to impugn the character of your witness?" But when they left the jail he found the woman still watching him from some deep reserve of foreboding. "You mustn't worry at all, I tell you. You may know more about making whiskey or love than I do, but I know more about criminal procedure than you, remember."

"You dont think I made a mistake?"

"I know you didn't. Dont you see how that explodes their case? The best they can hope for now is a hung jury. And the chances of that are not one in fifty. I tell you, he'll walk out of that jail tomorrow a free man."

"Then I guess it's time to think about paying you."

"Yes," Horace said, "all right. I'll come out tonight."

"Tonight?"

"Yes. He may call you back to the stand tomorrow. We'd better prepare for it, anyway."

At eight oclock he entered the mad woman's yard. A single light burned in the crazy depths of the house, like a firefly caught in a brier patch, but the woman did not appear when he called. He went to the door and knocked. A shrill voice shouted something; he waited a moment. He was about to knock again when he heard the voice again, shrill and wild and faint, as though from a distance, like a reedy pipe buried by an avalanche. He circled the house in the rank, waist-high weeds. The kitchen door was open. The lamp was there, dim in a smutty chimney, filling the room—a jumble of looming shapes rank with old foul female flesh—not with light but with shadow. White eyeballs rolled in a high, tight bullet head in brown gleams above a torn singlet strapped into overalls. Beyond the negro the mad woman turned in an open cupboard, brushing her lank hair back with her forearm.

"Your bitch has gone to jail," she said. "Go on with her."

"Jail?" Horace said.

"That's what I said. Where the good folks live. When you get a husband, keep him in jail where he cant bother you." She turned to the negro, a small flask in her hand. "Come on, dearie. Give me a dollar for it. You got plenty money."

Horace returned to town, to the jail. They admitted him. He mounted the stairs; the jailer locked a door behind him.

The woman admitted him to the cell. The child lay on the cot. Goodwin sat beside it, his arms crossed, his legs extended in the attitude of a man in the last stage of physical exhaustion.

"Why are you sitting there, in front of that slit?" Horace said. "Why not get into the corner, and we'll put the mattress over you."

"You come to see it done, did you?" Goodwin said. "Well, that's no more than right. It's your job. You promised I wouldn't hang, didn't you?"

"You've got an hour yet," Horace said. "The Memphis train doesn't get here until eight-thirty. He's surely got better sense than to come here in that canary-colored car." He turned to the woman. "But you. I thought better of you. I know that he and I are fools, but I expected better of you."

"You're doing her a favor," Goodwin said. "She might have hung on with me until she was too old to hustle a good man. If you'll just promise to get the kid a newspaper grift when he's old enough to make change, I'll be easy in my mind."

The woman had returned to the cot. She lifted the child onto her lap. Horace went to her. He said: "You come on, now. Nothing's going to happen. He'll be all right here. He knows it. You've got to go home and get some sleep, because you'll both be leaving here tomorrow. Come, now."

"I reckon I better stay," she said.

"Damn it, dont you know that putting yourself in the position for disaster is the surest way in the world to bring it about? Hasn't your own experience shown you that? Lee knows it. Lee, make her stop this."

"Go on, Ruby," Goodwin said. "Go home and go to bed."

"I reckon I better stay," she said.

Horace stood over them. The woman mused above the child, her face bent and her whole body motionless. Goodwin leaned back against the wall, his brown wrists folded into the faded sleeves of his shirt. "You're a man now," Horace said. "Aren't you? I wish that jury could see you now, locked up in a concrete cell, scaring women and children with fifth grade ghost stories. They'd know you never had the guts to kill anybody."

"You better go on and go to bed yourself," Goodwin said. "We could sleep here, if there wasn't so much noise going on."

"No; that's too sensible for us to do," Horace said. He left the cell. The jailer unlocked the door for him and he quitted the building. In ten minutes he returned, with a parcel. Goodwin had not moved. The woman watched him open the package. It contained a bottle of milk, a box of candy, a box of cigars. He gave Goodwin one of the cigars and took one himself. "You brought his bottle, didn't you?"

The woman produced the bottle from a bundle beneath the cot. "It's got some in it," she said. She filled it from the bottle. Horace lit his and Goodwin's cigars. When he looked again the bottle was gone.

"Not time to feed him yet?" he said.

"I'm warming it," the woman said.

"Oh," Horace said. He tilted the chair against the wall, across the cell from the cot.

"Here's room on the bed," the woman said. "It's softer. Some."

"Not enough to change, though," Horace said.

"Look here," Goodwin said, "you go on home. No use in you doing this."

"We've got a little work to do," Horace said. "That lawyer'll call her again in the morning. That's his only chance: to invalidate her testimony someway. You might try to get some sleep while we go over it."

"All right," Goodwin said.

Horace began to drill the woman, tramping back and forth upon the narrow floor. Goodwin finished his cigar and sat motionless again, his arms folded and his head bent. The clock above the square struck nine and then ten. The child whimpered, stirred. The woman stopped and changed it and took the bottle from beneath her flank and fed it. Then she leaned forward carefully and looked into Goodwin's face. "He's asleep," she whispered.

"Shall we lay him down?" Horace whispered.

"No. Let him stay there." Moving quietly she laid the child on the cot and moved herself to the other end of it. Horace carried the chair over beside her. They spoke in whispers.

The clock struck eleven. Still Horace drilled her, going over and over the imaginary scene. At last he said: "I think that's all. Can you remember it, now? If he should ask you anything you cant answer in the exact words you've learned tonight, just say nothing for a moment. I'll attend to the rest. Can you remember, now?"

"Yes," she whispered. He reached across and took the box of candy from the cot and opened it, the glazed paper crackling faintly. She took a piece. Goodwin had not moved. She looked at him, then at the narrow slit of window.

"Stop that," Horace whispered. "He couldn't reach him through that window with a hat-pin, let alone a bullet. Dont you know that?"

"Yes," she said. She held the bon-bon in her hand. She was not looking at him. "I know what you're thinking," she whispered.

"What?"

"When you got to the house and I wasn't there. I know what you're thinking." Horace watched her, her averted face. "You said tonight was the time to start paying you."

For a while longer he looked at her. "Ah," he said. "O tempora! O mores! O hell! Can you stupid mammals never believe that any man, every man——You thought that was what I was coming for? You thought that if I had intended to, I'd have waited this long?"

She looked at him briefly. "It wouldn't have done you any good if you hadn't waited."

"What? Oh. Well. But you would have tonight?"

"I thought that was what——"

"You would now, then?" She looked around at Goodwin. He was snoring a little. "Oh, I dont mean right this minute," he whispered. "But you'll pay on demand."

"I thought that was what you meant. I told you we didn't have——If that aint enough pay, I dont know that I blame you."

"It's not that. You know it's not that. But cant you see that perhaps a man might do something just because he knew it was right, necessary to the harmony of things that it be done?"

The woman turned the bon-bon slowly in her hand. "I thought you were mad about him."

"Lee?"

"No. Him." She touched the child. "Because I'd have to bring him with us."

"You mean, with him at the foot of the bed, maybe? perhaps you holding him by the leg all the time, so he wouldn't fall off?"

She looked at him, her eyes grave and blank and contemplative. Outside the clock struck twelve.

"Good God," he whispered. "What kind of men have you known?"

"I got him out of jail once that way. Out of Leavenworth, too. When they knew he was guilty."

"You did?" Horace said. "Here. Take another piece. That one's about worn out." She looked down at her chocolate-stained fingers and the shapeless bon-bon. She dropped it behind the cot. Horace extended his handkerchief.

"It'll soil it," she said. "Wait." She wiped her fingers on the child's discarded garment and sat again, her hands clasped in her lap. Goodwin was snoring regularly. "When he went to the Philippines he left me in San Francisco. I got a job and I lived in a hall room, cooking over a gas-jet, because I told him I would. I didn't know how long he'd be gone, but I promised him I would and he knew I would. When he killed that other soldier over that nigger woman, I didn't even know it. I didn't get a letter from him for five months. It was just when I happened to see an old newspaper I was spreading on a closet shelf in the place where I worked that I saw the regiment was coming home, and when I looked at the calendar it was that day. I'd been good all that time. I'd had good chances; everyday I had them with the men coming in the restaurant.

"They wouldn't let me off to go and meet the ship, so I had to quit. Then they wouldn't let me see him, wouldn't even let me on the ship. I stood there while they came marching off of it, watching for him and asking the ones that passed if they knew where he was and them kidding me if I had a date that night, telling me they never heard of him or that he was dead or he had run off to Japan with the colonel's wife. I tried to get on the ship again, but they wouldn't let me. So that night I dressed up and went to the cabarets until I found one of them and let him pick me up, and he told me. It was like I had died. I sat there with the music playing and all, and that drunk soldier pawing at me, and me wondering why I

didn't let go, go on with him, get drunk and never sober up
again and me thinking And this is the sort of animal I wasted
a year over. I guess that was why I didn't.

"Anyway, I didn't. I went back to my room and the next
day I started looking for him. I kept on, with them telling me
lies and trying to make me, until I found he was in Leavenworth. I didn't have enough money for a ticket, so I had to
get another job. It took two months to get enough money.
Then I went to Leavenworth. I got another job as waitress,
in Childs', nightshifts, so I could see Lee every other Sunday
afternoon. We decided to get a lawyer. We didn't know that
a lawyer couldn't do anything for a federal prisoner. The lawyer didn't tell me, and I hadn't told Lee how I was getting
the lawyer. He thought I had saved some money. I lived with
the lawyer two months before I found it out.

"Then the war came and they let Lee out and sent him to
France. I went to New York and got a job in a munitions
plant. I stayed straight too, with the cities full of soldiers with
money to spend, and even the little ratty girls wearing silk.
But I stayed straight. Then he came home. I was at the ship
to meet him. He got off under arrest and they sent him back
to Leavenworth for killing that soldier three years ago. Then
I got a lawyer to get a Congressman to get him out. I gave
him all the money I had saved too. So when Lee got out, we
had nothing. He said we'd get married, but we couldn't
afford to. And when I told him about the lawyer, he beat
me."

Again she dropped a shapeless piece of candy behind the
cot and wiped her hands on the garment. She chose another
piece from the box and ate it. Chewing, she looked at Horace, turning upon him a blank, musing gaze for an unhurried
moment. Through the slotted window the darkness came chill
and dead.

Goodwin ceased snoring. He stirred and sat up.

"What time is it?" he said.

"What?" Horace said. He looked at his watch. "Half-past
two."

"He must have had a puncture," Goodwin said.

Toward dawn Horace himself slept, sitting in the chair.
When he waked a narrow rosy pencil of sunlight fell level

through the window. Goodwin and the woman were talking quietly on the cot. Goodwin looked at him bleakly.

"Morning," he said.

"I hope you slept off that nightmare of yours," Horace said.

"If I did, it's the last one I'll have. They say you dont dream there."

"You've certainly done enough not to miss it," Horace said. "I suppose you'll believe us, after this."

"Believe, hell," Goodwin said, who had sat so quiet, so contained, with his saturnine face, negligent in his overalls and blue shirt; "do you think for one minute that man is going to let me walk out of that door and up the street and into that courthouse, after yesterday? What sort of men have you lived with all your life? In a nursery? I wouldn't do that, myself."

"If he does, he has sprung his own trap," Horace said.

"What good will that do me? Let me tell——"

"Lee," the woman said.

"——you something: the next time you want to play dice with a man's neck——"

"Lee," she said. She was stroking her hand slowly on his head, back and forth. She began to smooth his hair into a part, patting his collarless shirt smooth. Horace watched them.

"Would you like to stay here today?" he said quietly. "I can fix it."

"No," Goodwin said. "I'm sick of it. I'm going to get it over with. Just tell that goddamned deputy not to walk too close to me. You and her better go and eat breakfast."

"I'm not hungry," the woman said.

"You go on like I told you," Goodwin said.

"Lee."

"Come," Horace said. "You can come back afterward."

Outside, in the fresh morning, he began to breathe deeply. "Fill your lungs," he said. "A night in that place would give anyone the jim-jams. The idea of three grown people. . . . My Lord, sometimes I believe that we are all children, except children themselves. But today will be the last. By noon he'll walk out of there a free man: do you realise that?"

They walked on in the fresh sunlight, beneath the high, soft sky. High against the blue fat little clouds blew up from the south-west, and the cool steady breeze shivered and twinkled in the locusts where the blooms had long since fallen.

"I dont know how you'll get paid," she said.

"Forget it. I've been paid. You wont understand it, but my soul has served an apprenticeship that has lasted for forty-three years. Forty-three years. Half again as long as you have lived. So you see that folly, as well as poverty, cares for its own."

"And you know that he——that——"

"Stop it, now. We dreamed that away, too. God is foolish at times, but at least He's a gentleman. Dont you know that?"

"I always thought of Him as a man," the woman said.

The bell was already ringing when Horace crossed the square toward the courthouse. Already the square was filled with wagons and cars, and the overalls and khaki thronged slowly beneath the gothic entrance of the building. Overhead the clock was striking nine as he mounted the stairs.

The broad double doors at the head of the cramped stair were open. From beyond them came a steady preliminary stir of people settling themselves. Above the seat-backs Horace could see their heads—bald heads, gray heads, shaggy heads and heads trimmed to recent feather-edge above sun-baked necks, oiled heads above urban collars and here and there a sunbonnet or a flowered hat.

The hum of their voices and movements came back upon the steady draft which blew through the door. The air entered the open windows and blew over the heads and back to Horace in the door, laden with smells of tobacco and stale sweat and the earth and with that unmistakable odor of courtrooms; that musty odor of spent lusts and greeds and bickerings and bitterness, and withal a certain clumsy stability in lieu of anything better. The windows gave upon balconies close under the arched porticoes. The breeze drew through them, bearing the chirp and coo of sparrows and pigeons that nested in the eaves, and now and then the sound of a motor horn from the square below, rising out of and sinking back into a hollow rumble of feet in the corridor below and on the stairs.

The Bench was empty. At one side, at the long table, he could see Goodwin's black head and gaunt brown face, and the woman's gray hat. At the other end of the table sat a man picking his teeth. His skull was capped closely by tightly-curled black hair thinning upon a bald spot. He had a long, pale nose. He wore a tan palm beach suit; upon the table near him lay a smart leather brief-case and a straw hat with a red-and-tan band, and he gazed lazily out a window above the ranked heads, picking his teeth. Horace stopped just within the door. "It's a lawyer," he said. "A Jew lawyer from Memphis." Then he was looking at the backs of the heads about the table, where the witnesses and such would be. "I know what I'll find before I find it," he said. "She will have on a black hat."

He walked up the aisle. From beyond the balcony window where the sound of the bell seemed to be and where beneath the eaves the guttural pigeons crooned, the voice of the bailiff came:

"The honorable Circuit Court of Yoknapatawpha county is now open according to law. . . . . . ."

Temple had on a black hat. The clerk called her name twice before she moved and took the stand. After a while Horace realised that he was being spoken to, a little testily, by the Court.

"Is this your witness, Mr Benbow?"

"It is, your Honor."

"You wish her sworn and recorded?"

"I do, your Honor."

Beyond the window, beneath the unhurried pigeons, the bailiff's voice still droned, reiterant, importunate, and detached, though the sound of the bell had ceased.

XXVIII

THE DISTRICT ATTORNEY faced the jury. "I offer as evidence this object which was found at the scene of the crime." He held in his hand a corn-cob. It appeared to have been dipped in dark brownish paint. "The reason this was not offered sooner is that its bearing on the case was not made clear until the testimony of the defendant's wife which I have just caused to be read aloud to you gentlemen from the record.

"You have just heard the testimony of the chemist and the gynecologist—who is, as you gentlemen know, an authority on the most sacred affairs of that most sacred thing in life: womanhood—who says that this is no longer a matter for the hangman, but for a bonfire of gasoline——"

"I object!" Horace said: "The prosecution is attempting to sway——"

"Sustained," the Court said. "Strike out the phrase beginning 'who says that', mister clerk. You may instruct the jury to disregard it, Mr Benbow. Keep to the matter in hand, Mr District Attorney."

The District Attorney bowed. He turned to the witness stand, where Temple sat. From beneath her black hat her hair escaped in tight red curls like clots of resin. The hat bore a rhinestone ornament. Upon her black satin lap lay a platinum bag. Her pale tan coat was open upon a shoulder knot of purple. Her hands lay motionless, palm-up on her lap. Her long blonde legs slanted, lax-ankled, her two motionless slippers with their glittering buckles lay on their sides as though empty. Above the ranked intent faces white and pallid as the floating bellies of dead fish, she sat in an attitude at once detached and cringing, her gaze fixed on something at the back of the room. Her face was quite pale, the two spots of rouge like paper discs pasted on her cheek bones, her mouth painted into a savage and perfect bow, also like something both symbolical and cryptic cut carefully from purple paper and pasted there.

The District Attorney stood before her.

"What is your name?" She did not answer. She moved her head slightly, as though he had obstructed her view, gazing at something in the back of the room. "What is your name?" he repeated, moving also, into the line of her vision again. Her mouth moved. "Louder," he said. "Speak out. No one will hurt you. Let these good men, these fathers and husbands, hear what you have to say and right your wrong for you."

The Court glanced at Horace, his eyebrows raised. But Horace made no move. He sat with his head bent a little, his hands clutched in his lap.

"Temple Drake," Temple said.

"Your age?"

"Eighteen."

"Where is your home?"

"Memphis," she said in a scarce distinguishable voice.

"Speak a little louder. These men will not hurt you. They are here to right the wrong you have suffered. Where did you live before you went to Memphis?"

"In Jackson."

"Have you relations there?"

"Yes."

"Come. Tell these good men——"

"My father."

"Your mother is dead?"

"Yes."

"Have you any sisters?"

"No."

"You are your father's only daughter?"

Again the Court looked at Horace; again he made no move.

"Yes."

"Where have you been living since May twelfth of this year?" Her head moved faintly, as though she would see beyond him. He moved into her line of vision, holding her eyes. She stared at him again, giving her parrotlike answers.

"Did your father know you were there?"

"No."

"Where did he think you were?"

"He thought I was in school."

"You were in hiding, then, because something had happened to you and you dared not——"

"I object!" Horace said. "The question is lead——"

"Sustained," the Court said. "I have been on the point of warning you for some time, Mr Attorney, but defendant would not take exception, for some reason."

The District Attorney bowed toward the Bench. He turned to the witness and held her eyes again.

"Where were you on Sunday morning, May twelfth?"

"I was in the crib."

The room sighed, its collective breath hissing in the musty silence. Some newcomers entered, but they stopped at the rear of the room in a clump and stood there. Temple's head had moved again. The District Attorney caught her gaze and held it. He half turned and pointed at Goodwin.

"Did you ever see that man before?" She gazed at the District Attorney, her face quite rigid, empty. From a short distance her eyes, the two spots of rouge and her mouth, were like five meaningless objects in a small heart-shaped dish. "Look where I am pointing."

"Yes."

"Where did you see him?"

"In the crib."

"What were you doing in the crib?"

"I was hiding."

"Who were you hiding from?"

"From him."

"That man there? Look where I am pointing."

"Yes."

"But he found you."

"Yes."

"Was anyone else there?"

"Tommy was. He said——"

"Was he inside the crib or outside?"

"He was outside by the door. He was watching. He said he wouldn't let——"

"Just a minute. Did you ask him not to let anyone in?"

"Yes."

"And he locked the door on the outside?"

"Yes."

"But Goodwin came in."

"Yes."

"Did he have anything in his hand?"

"He had the pistol."

"Did Tommy try to stop him?"

"Yes. He said he——"

"Wait. What did he do to Tommy?"

She gazed at him.

"He had the pistol in his hand. What did he do then?"

"He shot him." The District Attorney stepped aside. At once the girl's gaze went to the back of the room and became fixed there. The District Attorney returned, stepped into her line of vision. She moved her head; he caught her gaze and held it and lifted the stained corn-cob before her eyes. The room sighed, a long hissing breath.

"Did you ever see this before?"

"Yes."

The District Attorney turned away. "Your Honor and gentlemen, you have listened to this horrible, this unbelievable, story which this young girl has told; you have seen the evidence and heard the doctor's testimony: I shall no longer subject this ruined, defenseless child to the agony of——" he ceased; the heads turned as one and watched a man come stalking up the aisle toward the Bench. He walked steadily, paced and followed by a slow gaping of the small white faces, a slow hissing of collars. He had neat white hair and a clipped moustache like a bar of hammered silver against his dark skin. His eyes were pouched a little. A small paunch was buttoned snugly into his immaculate linen suit. He carried a panama hat in one hand and a slender black stick in the other. He walked steadily up the aisle in a slow expulsion of silence like a prolonged sigh, looking to neither side. He passed the witness stand without a glance at the witness, who still gazed at something in the back of the room, walking right through her line of vision like a runner crossing a tape, and stopped before the bar above which the Court had half-risen, his arms on the desk.

"Your Honor," the old man said, "is the Court done with this witness?"

"Yes, sir, Judge," the Court said; "yes, sir. Defendant, do you waive——"

The old man turned slowly, erect above the held breaths, the little white faces, and looked down at the six people at the counsel table. Behind him the witness had not moved. She sat in her attitude of childish immobility, gazing like a drugged person above the faces, toward the rear of the room. The old man turned to her and extended his hand. She did not move. The room expelled its breath, sucked it quickly in and held it again. The old man touched her arm. She turned her head toward him, her eyes blank and all pupil above the three savage spots of rouge. She put her hand in his and rose, the platinum bag slipping from her lap to the floor with a thin clash, gazing again at the back of the room. With the toe of his small gleaming shoe the old man flipped the bag into the corner where the jury-box joined the Bench, where a spittoon sat, and steadied the girl down from the dais. The room breathed again as they moved on down the aisle.

Half way down the aisle the girl stopped again, slender in her smart open coat, her blank face rigid, then she moved on, her hand in the old man's. They returned down the aisle, the old man erect beside her, looking to neither side, paced by that slow whisper of collars. Again the girl stopped. She began to cringe back, her body arching slowly, her arm tautening in the old man's grasp. He bent toward her, speaking; she moved again, in that shrinking and rapt abasement. Four younger men were standing stiffly erect near the exit. They stood like soldiers, staring straight ahead until the old man and the girl reached them. Then they moved and surrounded the other two, and in a close body, the girl hidden among them, they moved toward the door. Here they stopped again; the girl could be seen shrunk against the wall just inside the door, her body arched again. She appeared to be clinging there, then the five bodies hid her again and again in a close body the group passed through the door and disappeared. The room breathed: a buzzing sound like a wind getting up. It moved forward with a slow increasing rush, on above the long table where the prisoner and the woman with the child and Horace and the District Attorney and the Memphis lawyer sat, and across the jury and against the Bench in a long sigh. The Memphis lawyer was sitting on his spine, gazing dreamily out the window. The child made a fretful sound, whimpering.

"Hush," the woman said. "Shhhhhhhh."

XXIX

T HE JURY was out eight minutes. When Horace left the
courthouse it was getting toward dusk. The tethered
wagons were taking out, some of them to face twelve and
sixteen miles of country road. Narcissa was waiting for him
in the car. He emerged among the overalls, slowly; he got
into the car stiffly, like an old man, with a drawn face. "Do
you want to go home?" Narcissa said.

"Yes," Horace said.

"I mean, to the house, or out home?"

"Yes," Horace said.

She was driving the car. The engine was running. She
looked at him, in a new dark dress with a severe white collar,
a dark hat.

"Which one?"

"Home," he said. "I dont care. Just home."

They passed the jail. Standing along the fence were the
loafers, the countrymen, the blackguard boys and youths who
had followed Goodwin and the deputy from the courthouse.
Beside the gate the woman stood, in the gray hat with the
veil, carrying the child in her arms. "Standing where he can
see it through the window," Horace said. "I smell ham, too.
Maybe he'll be eating ham before we get home." Then he began
to cry, sitting in the car beside his sister. She drove steadily, not fast. Soon they had left the town and the stout rows of
young cotton swung at either hand in parallel and diminishing retrograde. There was still a little snow of locust blooms
on the mounting drive. "It does last," Horace said. "Spring
does. You'd almost think there was some purpose to it."

He stayed to supper. He ate a lot. "I'll go and see about
your room," his sister said, quite gently.

"All right," Horace said. "It's nice of you." She went out.
Miss Jenny's wheel chair sat on a platform slotted for the
wheels. "It's nice of her," Horace said. "I think I'll go outside
and smoke my pipe."

"Since when have you quit smoking it in here?" Miss Jenny
said.

"Yes," Horace said. "It was nice of her." He walked across

the porch. "I intended to stop here," Horace said. He watched himself cross the porch and then tread the diffident snow of the last locusts; he turned out of the iron gates, onto the gravel. After about a mile a car slowed and offered him a ride. "I'm just walking before supper," he said; "I'll turn back soon." After another mile he could see the lights of town. It was a faint glare, low and close. It got stronger as he approached. Before he reached town he began to hear the sound, the voices. Then he saw the people, a shifting mass filling the street, and the bleak, shallow yard above which the square and slotted bulk of the jail loomed. In the yard, beneath the barred window, a man in his shirt sleeves faced the crowd, hoarse, gesticulant. The barred window was empty.

Horace went on toward the square. The sheriff was among the drummers before the hotel, standing along the curb. He was a fat man, with a broad, dull face which belied the expression of concern about his eyes. "They wont do anything," he said. "There is too much talk. Noise. And too early. When a mob means business, it dont take that much time and talk. And it dont go about its business where every man can see it."

The crowd stayed in the street until late. It was quite orderly, though. It was as though most of them had come to see, to look at the jail and the barred window, or to listen to the man in shirt sleeves. After a while he talked himself out. Then they began to move away, back to the square and some of them homeward, until there was left only a small group beneath the arc light at the entrance to the square, among whom were two temporary deputies, and the night marshal in a broad pale hat, a flash light, a time clock and a pistol. "Git on home now," he said. "Show's over. You boys done had your fun. Git on home to bed, now."

The drummers sat a little while longer along the curb before the hotel, Horace among them; the south-bound train ran at one oclock. "They're going to let him get away with it, are they?" a drummer said. "With that corn cob? What kind of folks have you got here? What does it take to make you folks mad?"

"He wouldn't a never got to trial, in my town," a second said.

"To jail, even," a third said. "Who was she?"

"College girl. Good looker. Didn't you see her?"

"I saw her. She was some baby. Jeez. I wouldn't have used no cob."

Then the square was quiet. The clock struck eleven; the drummers went in and the negro porter came and turned the chairs back into the wall. "You waiting for the train?" he said to Horace.

"Yes. Have you got a report on it yet?"

"It's on time. But that's two hours yet. You could lay down in the Sample Room, if you want."

"Can I?" Horace said.

"I'll show you," the negro said. The Sample Room was where the drummers showed their wares. It contained a sofa. Horace turned off the light and lay down on the sofa. He could see the trees about the courthouse, and one wing of the building rising above the quiet and empty square. But people were not asleep. He could feel the wakefulness, the people awake about the town. "I could not have gone to sleep, anyway," he said to himself.

He heard the clock strike twelve. Then—it might have been thirty minutes or maybe longer than that—he heard someone pass under the window, running. The runner's feet sounded louder than a horse, echoing across the empty square, the peaceful hours given to sleeping. It was not a sound Horace heard now; it was something in the air which the sound of the running feet died into.

When he went down the corridor toward the stairs he did not know he was running until he heard beyond a door a voice say, "Fire! It's a. . . . . . ." Then he had passed it. "I scared him," Horace said. "He's just from Saint Louis, maybe, and he's not used to this." He ran out of the hotel, onto the street. Ahead of him the proprietor had just run, ludicrous; a broad man with his trousers clutched before him and his braces dangling beneath his nightshirt, a tousled fringe of hair standing wildly about his bald head; three other men passed the hotel running. They appeared to come from nowhere, to emerge in midstride out of nothingness, fully dressed in the middle of the street, running.

"It is a fire," Horace said. He could see the glare; against it the jail loomed in stark and savage silhouette.

"It's in that vacant lot," the proprietor said, clutching his trousers. "I cant go because there aint anybody on the desk. . . . . . ."

Horace ran. Ahead of him he saw other figures running, turning into the alley beside the jail; then he heard the sound, of the fire; the furious sound of gasoline. He turned into the alley. He could see the blaze, in the center of a vacant lot where on market days wagons were tethered. Against the flames black figures showed, antic; he could hear panting shouts; through a fleeting gap he saw a man turn and run, a mass of flames, still carrying a five-gallon coal oil can which exploded with a rocket-like glare while he carried it, running.

He ran into the throng, into the circle which had formed about a blazing mass in the middle of the lot. From one side of the circle came the screams of the man about whom the coal oil can had exploded, but from the central mass of fire there came no sound at all. It was now indistinguishable, the flames whirling in long and thunderous plumes from a white-hot mass out of which there defined themselves faintly the ends of a few posts and planks. Horace ran among them; they were holding him, but he did not know it; they were talking, but he could not hear the voices.

"It's his lawyer."

"Here's the man that defended him. That tried to get him clear."

"Put him in, too. There's enough left to burn a lawyer."

"Do to the lawyer what we did to him. What he did to her. Only we never used a cob. We made him wish we had used a cob."

Horace couldn't hear them. He couldn't hear the man who had got burned screaming. He couldn't hear the fire, though it still swirled upward unabated, as though it were living upon itself, and soundless: a voice of fury like in a dream, roaring silently out of a peaceful void.

XXX

THE TRAINS at Kinston were met by an old man who drove a seven passenger car. He was thin, with gray eyes and a gray moustache with waxed ends. In the old days, before the town boomed suddenly into a lumber town, he was a planter, a landholder, son of one of the first settlers. He lost his property through greed and gullibility, and he began to drive a hack back and forth between town and the trains, with his waxed moustache, in a top hat and a worn Prince Albert coat, telling the drummers how he used to lead Kinston society; now he drove it.

After the horse era passed, he bought a car, still meeting the trains. He still wore his waxed moustache, though the top hat was replaced by a cap, the frock coat by a suit of gray striped with red made by Jews in the New York tenement district. "Here you are," he said, when Horace descended from the train. "Put your bag into the car," he said. He got in himself. Horace got into the front seat beside him. "You are one train late," he said.

"Late?" Horace said.

"She got in this morning. I took her home. Your wife."

"Oh," Horace said. "She's home?"

The other started the car and backed and turned. It was a good, powerful car, moving easily. "When did you expect her? . . . ." They went on. "I see where they burned that fellow over at Jefferson. I guess you saw it."

"Yes," Horace said. "Yes. I heard about it."

"Served him right," the driver said. "We got to protect our girls. Might need them ourselves."

They turned, following a street. There was a corner, beneath an arc light. "I'll get out here," Horace said.

"I'll take you on to the door," the driver said.

"I'll get out here," Horace said. "Save you having to turn."

"Suit yourself," the driver said. "You're paying for it, anyway."

Horace got out and lifted out his suit case; the driver did not offer to touch it. The car went on. Horace picked up the suit case, the one which had stayed in the closet at his sister's

385

home for ten years and which he had brought into town with him on the morning when she had asked him the name of the District Attorney.

His house was new, on a fairish piece of lawn, the trees, the poplars and maples which he had set out, still new. Before he reached the house, he saw the rose colored shade at his wife's windows. He entered the house from the back and came to her door and looked into the room. She was reading in bed, a broad magazine with a colored back. The lamp had a rose colored shade. On the table sat an open box of chocolates.

"I came back," Horace said.

She looked at him across the magazine.

"Did you lock the back door?" she said.

"Yes, I knew she would be," Horace said. "Have you to-night. . . . . . ."

"Have I what?"

"Little Belle. Did you telephone. . . . . . ."

"What for? She's at that house party. Why shouldn't she be? Why should she have to disrupt her plans, refuse an invitation?"

"Yes," Horace said. "I knew she would be. Did you. . . . . . ."

"I talked to her night before last. Go lock the back door."

"Yes," Horace said. "She's all right. Of course she is. I'll just. . . . . . ." The telephone sat on a table in the dark hall. The number was on a rural line; it took some time. Horace sat beside the telephone. He had left the door at the end of the hall open. Through it the light airs of the summer night drew, vague, disturbing. "Night is hard on old people," he said quietly, holding the receiver. "Summer nights are hard on them. Something should be done about it. A law."

From her room Belle called his name, in the voice of a reclining person. "I called her night before last. Why must you bother her?"

"I know," Horace said. "I wont be long at it."

He held the receiver, looking at the door through which the vague, troubling wind came. He began to say something out of a book he had read: "Less oft is peace. Less oft is peace," he said.

The wire answered. "Hello! Hello! Belle?" Horace said.

"Yes?" her voice came back thin and faint. "What is it? Is anything wrong?"

"No, no," Horace said. "I just wanted to tell you hello and good-night."

"Tell what? What is it? Who is speaking?" Horace held the receiver, sitting in the dark hall.

"It's me, Horace. Horace. I just wanted to——"

Over the thin wire there came a scuffling sound; he could hear Little Belle breathe. Then a voice said, a masculine voice: "Hello, Horace; I want you to meet a——"

"Hush!" Little Belle's voice said, thin and faint; again Horace heard them scuffling; a breathless interval. "Stop it!" Little Belle's voice said. "It's Horace! I live with him!" Horace held the receiver to his ear. Little Belle's voice was breathless, controlled, cool, discreet, detached. "Hello. Horace. Is Mamma all right?"

"Yes. We're all right. I just wanted to tell you. . . . . ."

"Oh. Good-night."

"Good-night. Are you having a good time?"

"Yes. Yes. I'll write tomorrow. Didn't Mamma get my letter today?"

"I dont know. I just——"

"Maybe I forgot to mail it. I wont forget tomorrow, though. I'll write tomorrow. Was that all you wanted?"

"Yes. Just wanted to tell you. . . . . ."

He put the receiver back; he heard the wire die. The light from his wife's room fell across the hall. "Lock the back door," she said.

XXXI

WHILE ON HIS WAY to Pensacola to visit his mother, Popeye was arrested in Birmingham for the murder of a policeman in a small Alabama town on June 17 of that year. He was arrested in August. It was on the night of June 17 that Temple had passed him sitting in the parked car beside the road house on the night when Red had been killed.

Each summer Popeye went to see his mother. She thought he was a night clerk in a Memphis hotel.

His mother was the daughter of a boarding house keeper. His father had been a professional strike breaker hired by the street railway company to break a strike in 1900. His mother at that time was working in a department store downtown. For three nights she rode home on the car beside the motorman's seat on which Popeye's father rode. One night the strike breaker got off at her corner with her and walked to her home.

"Wont you get fired?" she said.

"By who?" the strike breaker said. They walked along together. He was well-dressed. "Them others would take me that quick. They know it, too."

"Who would take you?"

"The strikers. I dont care a damn who is running the car, see. I'll ride with one as soon as another. Sooner, if I could make this route every night at this time."

She walked beside him. "You dont mean that," she said.

"Sure I do." He took her arm.

"I guess you'd just as soon be married to one as another, the same way."

"Who told you that?" he said. "Have them bastards been talking about me?"

A month later she told him that they would have to be married.

"How do you mean, have to?" he said.

"I dont dare to tell them. I would have to go away. I dont dare."

"Well, dont get upset. I'd just as lief. I have to pass here every night anyway."

They were married. He would pass the corner at night. He would ring the foot-bell. Sometimes he would come home. He would give her money. Her mother liked him; he would come roaring into the house at dinner time on Sunday, calling the other clients, even the old ones, by their first names. Then one day he didn't come back; he didn't ring the foot-bell when the trolley passed. The strike was over by then. She had a Christmas card from him; a picture, with a bell and an embossed wreath in gilt, from a Georgia town. It said: "The boys trying to fix it up here. But these folks awful slow. Will maybe move on until we strike a good town ha ha." The word, strike, was underscored.

Three weeks after her marriage, she had begun to ail. She was pregnant then. She did not go to a doctor, because an old negro woman told her what was wrong. Popeye was born on the Christmas day on which the card was received. At first they thought he was blind. Then they found that he was not blind, though he did not learn to walk and talk until he was about four years old. In the mean time, the second husband of her mother, an undersized, snuffy man with a mild, rich moustache, who pottered about the house; he fixed all the broken steps and leaky drains and such; left home one afternoon with a check signed in blank to pay a twelve dollar butcher's bill. He never came back. He drew from the bank his wife's fourteen hundred dollar savings account, and disappeared.

The daughter was still working downtown, while her mother tended the child. One afternoon one of the clients returned and found his room on fire. He put it out; a week later he found a smudge in his waste-basket. The grandmother was tending the child. She carried it about with her. One evening she was not in sight. The whole household turned out. A neighbor turned in a fire alarm and the firemen found the grandmother in the attic, stamping out a fire in a handful of excelsior in the center of the floor, the child asleep in a discarded mattress nearby.

"Them bastards are trying to get him," the old woman said. "They set the house on fire." The next day, all the clients left.

The young woman quit her job. She stayed at home all the

time. "You ought to get out and get some air," the grand-mother said.

"I get enough air," the daughter said.

"You could go out and buy the groceries," the mother said. "You could buy them cheaper."

"We get them cheap enough."

She would watch all the fires; she would not have a match in the house. She kept a few hidden behind a brick in the outside wall. Popeye was three years old then. He looked about one, though he could eat pretty well. A doctor had told his mother to feed him eggs cooked in olive oil. One after-noon the grocer's boy, entering the area-way on a bicycle, skidded and fell. Something leaked from the package. "It aint eggs," the boy said. "See?" It was a bottle of olive oil. "You ought to buy that oil in cans, anyway," the boy said. "He cant tell no difference in it. I'll bring you another one. And you want to have that gate fixed. Do you want I should break my neck on it?"

He had not returned by six oclock. It was summer. There was no fire, not a match in the house. "I'll be back in five minutes," the daughter said.

She left the house. The grandmother watched her disap-pear. Then she wrapped the child up in a light blanket and left the house. The street was a side street, just off a main street where there were markets, where the rich people in lim-ousines stopped on the way home to shop. When she reached the corner, a car was just drawing in to the curb. A woman got out and entered a store, leaving a negro driver behind the wheel. She went to the car.

"I want a half a dollar," she said.

The negro looked at her. "A which?"

"A half a dollar. The boy busted the bottle."

"Oh," the negro said. He reached in his pocket. "How am I going to keep it straight, with you collecting out here? Did she send you for the money out here?"

"I want a half a dollar. He busted the bottle."

"I reckon I better go in, then," the negro said. "Seem like to me you folks would see that folks got what they buy, folks that been trading here long as we is."

"It's a half a dollar," the woman said. He gave her a half

dollar and entered the store. The woman watched him. Then she laid the child on the seat of the car, and followed the negro. It was a self-serve place, where the customers moved slowly along a railing in single file. The negro was next to the white woman who had left the car. The grandmother watched the woman pass back to the negro a loose handful of bottles of sauce and catsup. "That'll be a dollar and a quarter," she said. The negro gave her the money. She took it and passed them and crossed the room. There was a bottle of imported Italian olive oil, with a price tag. "I got twenty-eight cents more," she said. She moved on, watching the price tags, until she found one that said twenty-eight cents. It was seven bars of bath soap. With the two parcels she left the store. There was a policeman at the corner. "I'm out of matches," she said.

The policeman dug into his pocket. "Why didn't you buy some while you were there?" he said.

"I just forgot it. You know how it is, shopping with a child."

"Where is the child?" the policeman said.

"I traded it in," the woman said.

"You ought to be in vaudeville," the policeman said. "How many matches do you want? I aint got but one or two."

"Just one," the woman said. "I never do light a fire with but one."

"You ought to be in vaudeville," the policeman said. "You'd bring down the house."

"I am," the woman said. "I bring down the house."

"What house?" He looked at her. "The poor house?"

"I'll bring it down," the woman said. "You watch the papers tomorrow. I hope they get my name right."

"What's your name? Calvin Coolidge?"

"No, sir. That's my boy."

"Oh. That's why you had so much trouble shopping, is it? You ought to be in vaudeville. . . . Will two matches be enough?"

They had had three alarms from that address, so they didn't hurry. The first to arrive was the daughter. The door was locked, and when the firemen came and chopped it down, the house was already gutted. The grandmother was leaning out an upstairs window through which the smoke already curled. "Them bastards," she said. "They thought they would get him. But I told them I would show them. I told them so."

The mother thought that Popeye had perished also. They held her, shrieking, while the shouting face of the grandmother vanished into the smoke, and the shell of the house caved in; that was where the woman and the policeman carrying the child, found her: a young woman with a wild face, her mouth open, looking at the child with a vague air, scouring her loose hair slowly upward from her temples with both hands. She never wholly recovered. What with the hard work and the lack of fresh air, diversion, and the disease, the legacy which her brief husband had left her, she was not in any condition to stand shock, and there were times when she still believed that the child had perished, even though she held it in her arms crooning above it.

Popeye might well have been dead. He had no hair at all until he was five years old, by which time he was already a kind of day pupil at an institution: an undersized, weak child with a stomach so delicate that the slightest deviation from a strict regimen fixed for him by the doctor would throw him into convulsions. "Alcohol would kill him like strychnine," the doctor said. "And he will never be a man, properly speaking. With care, he will live some time longer. But he will never be any older than he is now." He was talking to the woman who had found Popeye in her car that day when his grandmother burned the house down and at whose instigation Popeye was under the doctor's care. She would fetch him to her home in afternoons and for holidays, where he would play by himself. She decided to have a children's party for him. She told him about it, bought him a new suit. When the afternoon of the party came and the guests began to arrive, Popeye could not be found. Finally a servant found a bathroom door locked. They called the child, but got no answer. They sent for a locksmith, but in the meantime the woman, frightened, had the door broken in with an axe. The bathroom was empty. The window was open. It gave onto a lower roof, from which a drain-pipe descended to the ground. But Popeye was gone. On the floor lay a wicker cage

in which two lovebirds lived; beside it lay the birds themselves, and the bloody scissors with which he had cut them
up alive.

Three months later, at the instigation of a neighbor of his
mother, Popeye was arrested and sent to a home for incorrigible children. He had cut up a half-grown kitten the same
way.

His mother was an invalid. The woman who had tried to
befriend the child supported her, letting her do needlework
and such. After Popeye was out—he was let out after five
years, his behavior having been impeccable, as being cured—
he would write to her two or three times a year, from Mobile
and then New Orleans and then Memphis. Each summer he
would return home to see her, prosperous, quiet, thin, black,
and uncommunicative in his narrow black suits. He told her
that his business was being night clerk in hotels; that, following his profession, he would move from town to town, as a
doctor or a lawyer might.

While he was on his way home that summer they arrested
him for killing a man in one town and at an hour when he
was in another town killing somebody else—that man who
made money and had nothing he could do with it, spend it
for, since he knew that alcohol would kill him like poison,
who had no friends and had never known a woman and knew
he could never—and he said, "For Christ's sake," looking
about the cell in the jail of the town where the policeman had
been killed, his free hand (the other was handcuffed to the
officer who had brought him from Birmingham) finicking a
cigarette from his coat.

"Let him send for his lawyer," they said, "and get that off
his chest. You want to wire?"

"Nah," he said, his cold, soft eyes touching briefly the cot,
the high small window, the grated door through which the
light fell. They removed the handcuff; Popeye's hand appeared to flick a small flame out of thin air. He lit the cigarette and snapped the match toward the door. "What do I
want with a lawyer? I never was in——What's the name of
this dump?"

They told him. "You forgot, have you?"

"He wont forget it no more," another said.

"Except he'll remember his lawyer's name by morning," the first said.

They left him smoking on the cot. He heard doors clash. Now and then he heard voices from the other cells; somewhere down the corridor a negro was singing. Popeye lay on the cot, his feet crossed in small, gleaming black shoes. "For Christ's sake," he said.

The next morning the judge asked him if he wanted a lawyer.

"What for?" he said. "I told them last night I never was here before in my life. I dont like your town well enough to bring a stranger here for nothing."

The judge and the bailiff conferred aside.

"You'd better get your lawyer," the judge said.

"All right," Popeye said. He turned and spoke generally into the room: "Any of you ginneys want a one-day job?"

The judge rapped on the table. Popeye turned back, his tight shoulders lifted in a faint shrug, his hand moving toward the pocket where he carried his cigarettes. The judge appointed him counsel, a young man just out of law school.

"And I wont bother about being sprung," Popeye said. "Get it over with all at once."

"You wouldn't get any bail from me, anyway," the judge told him.

"Yeuh?" Popeye said. "All right, Jack," he told his lawyer, "get going. I'm due in Pensacola right now."

"Take the prisoner back to jail," the judge said.

His lawyer had an ugly, eager, earnest face. He rattled on with a kind of gaunt enthusiasm while Popeye lay on the cot, smoking, his hat over his eyes, motionless as a basking snake save for the periodical movement of the hand that held the cigarette. At last he said: "Here. I aint the judge. Tell him all this."

"But I've got——"

"Sure. Tell it to them. I dont know nothing about it. I wasn't even there. Get out and walk it off."

The trial lasted one day. While a fellow policeman, a cigar-clerk, a telephone girl testified, while his own lawyer rebutted in a gaunt mixture of uncouth enthusiasm and earnest ill-judgment, Popeye lounged in his chair, looking out the window above the jury's heads. Now and then he yawned; his hand moved to the pocket where his cigarettes lay, then refrained and rested idle against the black cloth of his suit, in the waxy lifelessness of shape and size like the hand of a doll.

The jury was out eight minutes. They stood and looked at him and said he was guilty. Motionless, his position unchanged, he looked back at them in a slow silence for several moments. "Well, for Christ's sake," he said.

The judge rapped sharply with his gavel; the officer touched his arm.

"I'll appeal," the lawyer babbled, plunging along beside him. "I'll fight them through every court——"

"Sure," Popeye said, lying on the cot and lighting a cigarette; "but not in here. Beat it, now. Go take a pill."

The District Attorney was already making his plans for the appeal. "It was too easy," he said. "He took it——Did you see how he took it? like he might be listening to a song he was too lazy to either like or dislike, and the Court telling him on what day they were going to break his neck. Probably got a Memphis lawyer already there outside the supreme court door now, waiting for a wire. I know them. It's them thugs like that that have made justice a laughing-stock, until even when we get a conviction, everybody knows it wont hold."

Popeye sent for the turnkey and gave him a hundred dollar bill. He wanted a shaving-kit and cigarettes. "Keep the change and let me know when it's smoked up," he said.

"I reckon you wont be smoking with me much longer," the turnkey said. "You'll get a good lawyer, this time."

"Dont forget that lotion," Popeye said. "Ed Pinaud." He called it "Py-nawd."

It had been a gray summer, a little cool. Little daylight ever reached the cell, and a light burned in the corridor all the time, falling into the cell in a broad pale mosaic, reaching the cot where his feet lay. The turnkey gave him a chair. He used it for a table; upon it the dollar watch lay, and a carton of cigarettes and a cracked soup bowl of stubs, and he lay on the cot, smoking and contemplating his feet while day after day passed. The gleam of his shoes grew duller, and his clothes needed pressing, because he lay in them all the time, since it was cool in the stone cell.

One day the turnkey said: "There's folks here says that deppity invited killing. He done two-three mean things folks knows about." Popeye smoked, his hat over his face. The turnkey said: "They might not a sent your telegram. You want me to send another one for you?" Leaning against the grating he could see Popeye's feet, his thin, black legs motionless, merging into the delicate bulk of his prone body and the hat slanted across his averted face, the cigarette in one small hand. His feet were in shadow, in the shadow of the turnkey's body where it blotted out the grating. After a while the turnkey went away quietly.

When he had six days left the turnkey offered to bring him magazines, a deck of cards.

"What for?" Popeye said. For the first time he looked at the turnkey, his head lifted, in his smooth, pallid face his eyes round and soft as those prehensile tips on a child's toy arrows. Then he lay back again. After that each morning the turnkey thrust a rolled newspaper through the door. They fell to the floor and lay there, accumulating, unrolling and flattening slowly of their own weight in diurnal progression.

When he had three days left a Memphis lawyer arrived. Unbidden, he rushed up to the cell. All that morning the turnkey heard his voice raised in pleading and anger and expostulation; by noon he was hoarse, his voice not much louder than a whisper.

"Are you just going to lie here and let——"

"I'm all right," Popeye said. "I didn't send for you. Keep your nose out."

"Do you want to hang? Is that it? Are you trying to commit suicide? Are you so tired of dragging down jack that. . . . You, the smartest——"

"I told you once. I've got enough on you."

"You, to have it hung on you by a small-time j.p.! When I go back to Memphis and tell them, they wont believe it."

"Dont tell them, then." He lay for a time while the lawyer looked at him in baffled and raging unbelief. "Them durn

hicks," Popeye said. "Jesus Christ. . . . . . . Beat it, now,"
he said. "I told you. I'm all right."

On the night before, a minister came in.

"Will you let me pray with you?" he said.

"Sure," Popeye said; "go ahead. Dont mind me."

The minister knelt beside the cot where Popeye lay smoking. After a while the minister heard him rise and cross the
floor, then return to the cot. When he rose Popeye was lying
on the cot, smoking. The minister looked behind him, where
he had heard Popeye moving and saw twelve marks at spaced
intervals along the base of the wall, as though marked there
with burned matches. Two of the spaces were filled with cigarette stubs laid in neat rows. In the third space were two
stubs. Before he departed he watched Popeye rise and go
there and crush out two more stubs and lay them carefully
beside the others.

Just after five oclock the minister returned. All the spaces
were filled save the twelfth one. It was three quarters complete. Popeye was lying on the cot. "Ready to go?" he said.

"Not yet," the minister said. "Try to pray," he said. "Try."

"Sure," Popeye said; "go ahead." The minister knelt again.
He heard Popeye rise once and cross the floor and then
return.

At five-thirty the turnkey came. "I brought——" he
said. He held his closed fist dumbly through the grating.
"Here's your change from that hundred you never——I
brought. . . . . . . It's forty-eight dollars," he said. "Wait;
I'll count it again; I dont know exactly, but I can give you a
list——them tickets. . . . . . ."

"Keep it," Popeye said, without moving. "Buy yourself a
hoop."

They came for him at six. The minister went with him, his
hand under Popeye's elbow, and he stood beneath the scaf-
fold praying, while they adjusted the rope, dragging it over
Popeye's sleek, oiled head, breaking his hair loose. His hands
were tied, so he began to jerk his head, flipping his hair back
each time it fell forward again, while the minister prayed, the
others motionless at their posts with bowed heads.

Popeye began to jerk his neck forward in little jerks.
"Psssst!" he said, the sound cutting sharp into the drone of

the minister's voice; "pssssst!" The sheriff looked at him; he quit jerking his neck and stood rigid, as though he had an egg balanced on his head. "Fix my hair, Jack," he said.

"Sure," the sheriff said. "I'll fix it for you;" springing the trap.

It had been a gray day, a gray summer, a gray year. On the street old men wore overcoats, and in the Luxembourg Gardens as Temple and her father passed the women sat knitting in shawls and even the men playing croquet played in coats and capes, and in the sad gloom of the chestnut trees the dry click of balls, the random shouts of children, had that quality of autumn, gallant and evanescent and forlorn. From beyond the circle with its spurious Greek balustrade, clotted with movement, filled with a gray light of the same color and texture as the water which the fountain played into the pool, came a steady crash of music. They went on, passed the pool where the children and an old man in a shabby brown overcoat sailed toy boats, and entered the trees again and found seats. Immediately an old woman came with decrepit promptitude and collected four sous.

In the pavilion a band in the horizon blue of the army played Massenet and Scriabin, and Berlioz like a thin coating of tortured Tschaikovsky on a slice of stale bread, while the twilight dissolved in wet gleams from the branches, onto the pavilion and the sombre toadstools of umbrellas. Rich and resonant the brasses crashed and died in the thick green twilight, rolling over them in rich sad waves. Temple yawned behind her hand, then she took out a compact and opened it upon a face in miniature sullen and discontented and sad. Beside her her father sat, his hands crossed on the head of his stick, the rigid bar of his moustache beaded with moisture like frosted silver. She closed the compact and from beneath her smart new hat she seemed to follow with her eyes the waves of music, to dissolve into the dying brasses, across the pool and the opposite semicircle of trees where at sombre intervals the dead tranquil queens in stained marble mused, and on into the sky lying prone and vanquished in the embrace of the season of rain and death.

LIGHT IN AUGUST

I

Sitting beside the road, watching the wagon mount the hill toward her, Lena thinks, 'I have come from Alabama: a fur piece. All the way from Alabama a-walking. A fur piece.' Thinking *although I have not been quite a month on the road I am already in Mississippi, further from home than I have ever been before. I am now further from Doane's Mill than I have been since I was twelve years old*

She had never even been to Doane's Mill until after her father and mother died, though six or eight times a year she went to town on Saturday, in the wagon, in a mailorder dress and her bare feet flat in the wagon bed and her shoes wrapped in a piece of paper beside her on the seat. She would put on the shoes just before the wagon reached town. After she got to be a big girl she would ask her father to stop the wagon at the edge of town and she would get down and walk. She would not tell her father why she wanted to walk in instead of riding. He thought that it was because of the smooth streets, the sidewalks. But it was because she believed that the people who saw her and whom she passed on foot would believe that she lived in the town too.

When she was twelve years old her father and mother died in the same summer, in a log house of three rooms and a hall, without screens, in a room lighted by a bugswirled kerosene lamp, the naked floor worn smooth as old silver by naked feet. She was the youngest living child. Her mother died first. She said, "Take care of paw." Lena did so. Then one day her father said, "You go to Doane's Mill with McKinley. You get ready to go, be ready when he comes." Then he died. Mc-Kinley, the brother, arrived in a wagon. They buried the father in a grove behind a country church one afternoon, with a pine headstone. The next morning she departed forever, though it is possible that she did not know this at the time, in the wagon with McKinley, for Doane's Mill. The wagon was borrowed and the brother had promised to return it by nightfall.

The brother worked in the mill. All the men in the village

worked in the mill or for it. It was cutting pine. It had been
there seven years and in seven years more it would destroy all
the timber within its reach. Then some of the machinery and
most of the men who ran it and existed because of and for it
would be loaded onto freight cars and moved away. But some
of the machinery would be left, since new pieces could always
be bought on the installment plan—gaunt, staring, motionless wheels rising from mounds of brick rubble and ragged
weeds with a quality profoundly astonishing, and gutted boil-
ers lifting their rusting and unsmoking stacks with an air
stubborn, baffled and bemused upon a stumppocked scene of
profound and peaceful desolation, unplowed, untilled, gut-
ting slowly into red and choked ravines beneath the long
quiet rains of autumn and the galloping fury of vernal equi-
noxes. Then the hamlet which at its best day had borne no
name listed on Postoffice Department annals would not now
even be remembered by the hookwormridden heirs at large
who pulled the buildings down and burned them in cook-
stoves and winter grates.

There were perhaps five families there when Lena arrived.
There was a track and a station, and once a day a mixed train
fled shrieking through it. The train could be stopped with a
red flag, but by ordinary it appeared out of the devastated
hills with apparitionlike suddenness and wailing like a ban-
shee, athwart and past that little less-than-village like a forgotten bead from a broken string. The brother was twenty
years her senior. She hardly remembered him at all when she
came to live with him. He lived in a four room and unpainted
house with his labor- and childridden wife. For almost half of
every year the sister-in-law was either lying in or recovering.
During this time Lena did all the housework and took care of
the other children. Later she told herself, 'I reckon that's why
I got one so quick myself.'

She slept in a leanto room at the back of the house. It had
a window which she learned to open and close again in the
dark without making a sound, even though there also slept in
the leanto room at first her oldest nephew and then the two
oldest and then the three. She had lived there eight years before she opened the window for the first time. She had not
opened it a dozen times hardly before she discovered that she

should not have opened it at all. She said to herself, 'That's just my luck.'

The sister-in-law told the brother. Then he remarked her changing shape, which he should have noticed some time before. He was a hard man. Softness and gentleness and youth (he was just forty) and almost everything else except a kind of stubborn and despairing fortitude and the bleak heritage of his bloodpride had been sweated out of him. He called her whore. He accused the right man (young bachelors, or sawdust Casanovas anyway, were even fewer in number than families) but she would not admit it, though the man had departed six months ago. She just repeated stubbornly, "He's going to send for me. He said he would send for me"; unshakable, sheeplike, having drawn upon that reserve of patient and steadfast fidelity upon which the Lucas Burches depend and trust, even though they do not intend to be present when the need for it arises. Two weeks later she climbed again through the window. It was a little difficult, this time. 'If it had been this hard to do before, I reckon I would not be doing it now,' she thought. She could have departed by the door, by daylight. Nobody would have stopped her. Perhaps she knew that. But she chose to go by night, and through the window. She carried a palm leaf fan and a small bundle tied neatly in a bandanna handkerchief. It contained among other things thirtyfive cents in nickels and dimes. Her shoes were a pair of his own which her brother had given to her. They were but slightly worn, since in the summer neither of them wore shoes at all. When she felt the dust of the road beneath her feet she removed the shoes and carried them in her hand.

She has been doing that now for almost four weeks. Behind her the four weeks, the evocation of *far* is a peaceful corridor paved with unflagging and tranquil faith and peopled with kind and nameless faces and voices: *Lucas Burch? I dont know. I dont know of anybody by that name around here. This road? It goes to Pocahontas. He might be there. It's possible. Here's a wagon that's going a piece of the way. It will take you that far;* backrolling now behind her a long monotonous succession of peaceful and undeviating changes from day to dark and dark to day again, through which she advanced in identical and anonymous and deliberate wagons as though through a succession of creakwheeled and limpeared avatars, like something moving forever and without progress across an urn.

The wagon mounts the hill toward her. She passed it about a mile back down the road. It was standing beside the road, the mules asleep in the traces and their heads pointed in the direction in which she walked. She saw it and she saw the two men squatting beside a barn beyond the fence. She looked at the wagon and the men once: a single glance allembracing, swift, innocent and profound. She did not stop; very likely the men beyond the fence had not seen her even look at the wagon nor at them. Neither did she look back. She went on out of sight, walking slowly, the shoes unlaced about her ankles, until she reached the top of the hill a mile beyond. Then she sat down on the ditchbank, with her feet in the shallow ditch, and removed the shoes. After a while she began to hear the wagon. She heard it for some time. Then it came into sight, mounting the hill.

The sharp and brittle crack and clatter of its weathered and ungreased wood and metal is slow and terrific: a series of dry sluggish reports carrying for a half mile across the hot still pinewiney silence of the August afternoon. Though the mules plod in a steady and unflagging hypnosis, the vehicle does not seem to progress. It seems to hang suspended in the middle distance forever and forever, so infinitesimal is its progress, like a shabby bead upon the mild red string of road. So much so is this that in the watching of it the eye loses it as sight and sense drowsily merge and blend, like the road itself, with all the peaceful and monotonous changes between darkness and day, like already measured thread being rewound onto a spool. So that at last, as though out of some trivial and unimportant region beyond even distance, the sound of it seems to come slow and terrific and without meaning, as though it were a ghost travelling a half mile ahead of its own shape. 'That far within my hearing before my seeing,' Lena thinks. She thinks of herself as already moving, riding again, thinking *Then it will be as if I were riding for a half mile before I even got into the wagon, before the wagon even got to where I was waiting, and that when the wagon is empty of me again it will go on for a half mile with me still in it* She waits, not even watching the wagon now, while thinking goes idle and swift and smooth, filled with nameless kind faces and voices: *Lucas Burch? You say you tried in Pocahontas? This road? It goes to Springvale. You wait here. There will be a wagon passing soon that will take you as far as it goes* Thinking, 'And if he is going all the way to Jefferson, I will be riding within the hearing of Lucas Burch before his seeing. He will hear the wagon, but he wont know. So there will be one within his hearing before his seeing. And then he will see me and he will be excited. And so there will be two within his seeing before his remembering.'

While Armstid and Winterbottom were squatting against the shady wall of Winterbottom's stable, they saw her pass in the road. They saw at once that she was young, pregnant, and a stranger. "I wonder where she got that belly," Winterbottom said.

"I wonder how far she has brought it afoot," Armstid said.

"Visiting somebody back down the road, I reckon," Winterbottom said.

"I reckon not. Or I would have heard. And it aint nobody up my way, neither. I would have heard that, too."

"I reckon she knows where she is going," Winterbottom said. "She walks like it."

"She'll have company, before she goes much further," Armstid said. The woman had now gone on, slowly, with her swelling and unmistakable burden. Neither of them had seen her so much as glance at them when she passed in a shapeless garment of faded blue, carrying a palm leaf fan and a small cloth bundle. "She aint come from nowhere close," Armstid said. "She's hitting that lick like she's been at it for a right smart while and had a right smart piece to go yet."

"She must be visiting around here somewhere," Winterbottom said.

"I reckon I would have heard about it," Armstid said. The woman went on. She had not looked back. She went out of sight up the road: swollen, slow, deliberate, unhurried and tireless as augmenting afternoon itself. She walked out of their talking too; perhaps out of their minds too. Because after a while Armstid said what he had come to say. He had

already made two previous trips, coming in his wagon five
miles and squatting and spitting for three hours beneath the
shady wall of Winterbottom's barn with the timeless unhaste
and indirection of his kind, in order to say it. It was to make
Winterbottom an offer for a cultivator which Winterbottom
wanted to sell. At last Armstid looked at the sun and offered
the price which he had decided to offer while lying in bed
three nights ago. "I know of one in Jefferson I can buy at that
figure," he said.

"I reckon you better buy it," Winterbottom said. "It sounds
like a bargain."

"Sho," Armstid said. He spat. He looked again at the sun,
and rose. "Well, I reckon I better get on toward home."

He got into his wagon and waked the mules. That is, he
put them into motion, since only a negro can tell when a
mule is asleep or awake. Winterbottom followed him to the
fence, leaning his arms on the top rail. "Yes, sir," he said. "I'd
sho buy that cultivator at that figure. If you dont take it, I be
dog if I aint a good mind to buy it, myself, at that price. I
reckon the fellow that owns it aint got a span of mules to sell
for about five dollars, has he?"

"Sho," Armstid said. He drove on, the wagon beginning to
fall into its slow and mileconsuming clatter. Neither does he
look back. Apparently he is not looking ahead either, because
he does not see the woman sitting in the ditch beside the road
until the wagon has almost reached the top of the hill. In the
instant in which he recognises the blue dress he cannot tell if
she has ever seen the wagon at all. And no one could have
known that he had ever looked at her either as, without any
semblance of progress in either of them, they draw slowly
together as the wagon crawls terrifically toward her in its slow
palpable aura of somnolence and red dust in which the steady
feet of the mules move dreamlike and punctuate by the sparse
jingle of harness and the limber bobbing of jackrabbit ears,
the mules still neither asleep nor awake as he halts them.

From beneath a sunbonnet of faded blue, weathered now
by other than formal soap and water, she looks up at him
quietly and pleasantly: young, pleasantfaced, candid, friendly,
and alert. She does not move yet. Beneath the faded garment

of that same weathered blue her body is shapeless and immobile. The fan and the bundle lie on her lap. She wears no stockings. Her bare feet rest side by side in the shallow ditch. The pair of dusty, heavy, manlooking shoes beside them are not more inert. In the halted wagon Armstid sits, humped, bleacheyed. He sees that the rim of the fan is bound neatly in the same faded blue as the sunbonnet and the dress.

"How far you going?" he says.

"I was trying to get up the road a pieceways before dark," she says. She rises and takes up the shoes. She climbs slowly and deliberately into the road, approaching the wagon. Armstid does not descend to help her. He merely holds the team still while she climbs heavily over the wheel and sets the shoes beneath the seat. Then the wagon moves on. "I thank you," she says. "It was right tiring afoot."

Apparently Armstid has never once looked full at her. Yet he has already seen that she wears no wedding ring. He does not look at her now. Again the wagon settles into its slow clatter. "How far you come from?" he says.

She expels her breath. It is not a sigh so much as a peaceful expiration, as though of peaceful astonishment. "A right good piece, it seems now. I come from Alabama."

"Alabama? In your shape? Where's your folks?"

She does not look at him, either. "I'm looking to meet him up this way. You might know him. His name is Lucas Burch. They told me back yonder a ways that he is in Jefferson, working for the planing mill."

"Lucas Burch." Armstid's tone is almost identical with hers. They sit side by side on the sagging and brokenspringed seat. He can see her hands upon her lap and her profile beneath the sunbonnet; from the corner of his eye he sees it. She seems to be watching the road as it unrolls between the limber ears of the mules. "And you come all the way here, afoot, by yourself, hunting for him?"

She does not answer for a moment. Then she says: "Folks have been kind. They have been right kind."

"Womenfolks too?" From the corner of his eye he watches her profile, thinking *I dont know what Martha's going to say* thinking, 'I reckon I do know what Martha's going to say. I reckon womenfolks are likely to be good without being very kind. Men, now, might. But it's only a bad woman herself that is likely to be very kind to another woman that needs the kindness' thinking *Yes I do. I know exactly what Martha is going to say*

She sits a little forward, quite still, her profile quite still, her cheek. "It's a strange thing," she says.

"How folks can look at a strange young gal walking the road in your shape and know that her husband has left her?" She does not move. The wagon now has a kind of rhythm, its ungreased and outraged wood one with the slow afternoon, the road, the heat. "And you aim to find him up here."

She does not move, apparently watching the slow road between the ears of the mules, the distance perhaps roadcarved and definite. "I reckon I'll find him. It wont be hard. He'll be where the most folks are gathered together, and the laughing and joking is. He always was a hand for that."

Armstid grunts, a sound savage, brusque. "Get up, mules," he says; he says to himself, between thinking and saying aloud: 'I reckon she will. I reckon that fellow is fixing to find that he made a bad mistake when he stopped this side of Arkansas, or even Texas.'

The sun is slanting, an hour above the horizon now, above the swift coming of the summer night. The lane turns from the road, quieter even than the road. "Here we are," Armstid says.

The woman moves at once. She reaches down and finds the shoes; apparently she is not even going to delay the wagon long enough to put them on. "I thank you kindly," she says. "It was a help."

The wagon is halted again. The woman is preparing to descend. "Even if you get to Varner's store before sundown, you'll still be twelve miles from Jefferson," Armstid says.

She holds the shoes, the bundle, the fan awkwardly in one hand, the other free to help her down. "I reckon I better get on," she says.

Armstid does not touch her. "You come on and stay the night at my house," he says; " where womenfolks——where a woman can . . . if you——You come on, now. I'll take you on to Varner's first thing in the morning, and you can get a ride in to town. There will be somebody going, on a Saturday. He aint going to get away on you overnight. If he is in Jefferson at all, he will still be there tomorrow."

She sits quite still, her possessions gathered into her hand for dismounting. She is looking ahead, to where the road curves on and away, crossslanted with shadows. "I reckon I got a few days left."

"Sho. You got plenty of time yet. Only you are liable to have some company at any time now that cant walk. You come on home with me." He puts the mules into motion without waiting for a reply. The wagon enters the lane, the dim road. The woman sits back, though she still holds the fan, the bundle, the shoes.

"I wouldn't be beholden," she says. "I wouldn't trouble."

"Sho," Armstid says. "You come on with me." For the first time the mules move swiftly of their own accord. "Smelling corn," Armstid says, thinking 'But that's the woman of it. Her own self one of the first ones to cut the ground from under a sister woman, she'll walk the public country herself without shame because she knows that folks, menfolks, will take care of her. She dont care nothing about womenfolks. It wasn't any woman that got her into what she dont even call trouble. Yes, sir. You just let one of them get married or get into trouble without being married, and right then and there is where she secedes from the woman race and species and spends the balance of her life trying to get joined up with the man race. That's why they dip snuff and smoke and want to vote.'

When the wagon passes the house and goes on toward the barnlot, his wife is watching it from the front door. He does not look in that direction; he does not need to look to know that she will be there, is there. 'Yes,' he thinks, with sardonic ruefulness, turning the mules into the open gate, 'I know exactly what she is going to say. I reckon I know exactly.' He halts the wagon. He does not need to look to know that his wife is now in the kitchen, not watching now; just waiting. He halts the wagon. "You go on to the house," he says; he has already descended and the woman is now climbing slowly down, with that inwardlistening deliberation. "When you meet somebody, it will be Martha. I'll be in when I feed the stock." He does not watch her cross the lot and go on toward the kitchen. He does not need to. Step by step with her he enters the kitchen door also and comes upon the woman who now watches the kitchen door exactly as she had watched the wagon pass from the front one. 'I reckon I know exactly what she will say,' he thinks.

He takes the team out and waters and stalls and feeds them, and lets the cows in from the pasture. Then he goes to the kitchen. She is still there, the gray woman with a cold, harsh, irascible face, who bore five children in six years and raised them to man- and womanhood. She is not idle. He does not look at her. He goes to the sink and fills a pan from the pail and turns his sleeves back. "Her name is Burch," he says. "At least that's what she says the fellow's name is that she is hunting for. Lucas Burch. Somebody told her back down the road a ways that he is in Jefferson now." He begins to wash, his back to her. "She come all the way from Alabama, alone and afoot, she says."

Mrs Armstid does not look around. She is busy at the table. "She's going to quit being alone a good while before she sees Alabama again," she says.

"Or that fellow Burch either, I reckon." He is quite busy at the sink, with the soap and water. And he can feel her looking at him, at the back of his head, his shoulders in the shirt of sweatfaded blue. "She says that somebody down at Samson's told her there is a fellow named Burch or something working at the planing mill in Jefferson."

"And she expects to find him there. Waiting. With the house all furnished and all."

He cannot tell from her voice if she is watching him or not now. He towels himself with a split floursack. "Maybe she will. If it's running away from her he's after, I reckon he's going to find out he made a bad mistake when he stopped before he put the Mississippi river between them." And now he knows that she is watching him: the gray woman not plump and not thin, manhard, workhard, in a serviceable gray garment worn savage and brusque, her hands on her hips, her face like those of generals who have been defeated in battle.

"You men," she says.

"What do you want to do about it? Turn her out? let her sleep in the barn maybe?"

"You men," she says. "You durn men."

They enter the kitchen together, though Mrs Armstid is in front. She goes straight to the stove. Lena stands just within the door. Her head is uncovered now, her hair combed smooth. Even the blue garment looks freshened and rested. She looks on while Mrs Armstid at the stove clashes the metal eyes and handles the sticks of wood with the abrupt savageness of a man. "I would like to help," Lena says.

Mrs Armstid does not look around. She clashes the stove savagely. "You stay where you are. You keep off your feet now, and you'll keep off your back a while longer maybe."

"It would be a beholden kindness to let me help."

"You stay where you are. I been doing this three times a day for thirty years now. The time when I needed help with it is done passed." She is busy at the stove, not backlooking. "Armstid says your name is Burch."

"Yes," the other says. Her voice is quite grave now, quite quiet. She sits quite still, her hands motionless upon her lap. And Mrs Armstid does not look around either. She is still busy at the stove. It appears to require an amount of attention out of all proportion to the savage finality with which she built the fire. It appears to engage as much of her attention as if it were an expensive watch.

"Is your name Burch yet?" Mrs Armstid says.

The young woman does not answer at once. Mrs Armstid does not rattle the stove now, though her back is still toward the younger woman. Then she turns. They look at one another, suddenly naked, watching one another: the young woman in the chair, with her neat hair and her inert hands upon her lap, and the older one beside the stove, turning, motionless too, with a savage screw of gray hair at the base of her skull and a face that might have been carved in sandstone. Then the younger one speaks.

"I told you false. My name is not Burch yet. It's Lena Grove."

They look at one another. Mrs Armstid's voice is neither cold nor warm. It is not anything at all. "And so you want to catch up with him so your name will be Burch in time. Is that it?"

Lena is looking down now, as though watching her hands upon her lap. Her voice is quiet, dogged. Yet it is serene. "I dont reckon I need any promise from Lucas. It just happened unfortunate so, that he had to go away. His plans just never worked out right for him to come back for me like he aimed to. I reckon me and him didn't need to make word promises. When he found out that night that he would have to go, he——"

"Found out what night? The night you told him about that chap?"

The other does not answer for a moment. Her face is calm as stone, but not hard. Its doggedness has a soft quality, an inwardlighted quality of tranquil and calm unreason and detachment. Mrs Armstid watches her. Lena is not looking at the other woman while she speaks. "He had done got the word about how he might have to leave a long time before that. He just never told me sooner because he didn't want to worry me with it. When he first heard about how he might have to leave, he knowed then it would be best to go, that he could get along faster somewhere where the foreman wouldn't be down on him. But he kept on putting it off. But when this here happened, we couldn't put it off no longer then. The foreman was down on Lucas because he didn't like him because Lucas was young and full of life all the time and the foreman wanted Lucas' job to give it to a cousin of his. But he hadn't aimed to tell me because it would just worry me. But when this here happened, we couldn't wait any longer. I was the one that said for him to go. He said he would stay if I said so, whether the foreman treated him right or not. But I said for him to go. He never wanted to go, even then. But I said for him to. To just send me word when he was ready for me to come. And then his plans just never worked out for him to send for me in time, like he aimed. Going away among strangers like that, a young fellow needs time to get settled down. He never knowed that when he left, that he would need more time to get settled down in than he figured on. Especially a young fellow full of life like Lucas, that likes folks and jollifying, and liked by folks in turn. He didn't know it would take longer than he planned, being young, and folks always after him because he is a hand for laughing and joking, interfering with his work unbeknownst to him because he never wanted to hurt folks' feelings. And I wanted him to have his last enjoyment, because marriage is different with a young fellow, a lively young fellow, and a woman. It lasts so long with a lively young fellow. Dont you think so?"

Mrs Armstid does not answer. She looks at the other sitting in the chair with her smooth hair and her still hands lying upon her lap and her soft and musing face. "Like as not, he already sent me the word and it got lost on the way. It's a right far piece from here to Alabama even, and I aint to Jefferson yet. I told him I would not expect him to write, being as he aint any hand for letters. 'You just send me your mouthword when you are ready for me,' I told him. 'I'll be waiting.' It worried me a little at first, after he left, because my name wasn't Burch yet and my brother and his folks not knowing Lucas as well as I knew him. How could they?" Into her face there comes slowly an expression of soft and bright surprise, as if she had just thought of something which she had not even been aware that she did not know. "How could they be expected to, you see. But he had to get settled down first; it was him would have all the trouble of being among strangers, and me with nothing to bother about except to just wait while he had all the bother and trouble. But after a while I reckon I just got too busy getting this chap up to his time to worry about what my name was or what folks thought. But me and Lucas dont need no word promises between us. It was something unexpected come up, or he even sent the word and it got lost. So one day I just decided to up and not wait any longer."

"How did you know which way to go when you started?"

Lena is watching her hands. They are moving now, plaiting with rapt bemusement a fold of her skirt. It is not diffidence, shyness. It is apparently some musing reflex of the hand alone. "I just kept asking. With Lucas a lively young fellow that got to know folks easy and quick, I knew that wherever he had been, folks would remember him. So I kept asking. And folks was right kind. And sure enough, I heard two days back on the road that he is in Jefferson, working for the planing mill."

Mrs Armstid watches the lowered face. Her hands are on her hips and she watches the younger woman with an expression of cold and impersonal contempt. "And you believe that he will be there when you get there. Granted that he ever was there at all. That he will hear you are in the same town with him, and still be there when the sun sets."

Lena's lowered face is grave, quiet. Her hand has ceased now. It lies quite still on her lap, as if it had died there. Her voice is quiet, tranquil, stubborn. "I reckon a family ought to all be together when a chap comes. Specially the first one. I reckon the Lord will see to that."

"And I reckon He will have to," Mrs Armstid says, savagely, harshly. Armstid is in bed, his head propped up a little, watching her across the footboard as, still dressed, she stoops into the light of the lamp upon the dresser, hunting violently in a drawer. She produces a metal box and unlocks it with a key suspended about her neck and takes out a cloth sack which she opens and produces a small china effigy of a rooster with a slot in its back. It jingles with coins as she moves it and upends it and shakes it violently above the top of the dresser, shaking from the slot coins in a meagre dribbling. Armstid in the bed watches her.

"What are you fixing to do with your eggmoney this time of night?" he says.

"I reckon it's mine to do with what I like." She stoops into the lamp, her face harsh, bitter. "God knows it was me sweated over them and nursed them. You never lifted no hand."

"Sho," he says. "I reckon it aint any human in this country is going to dispute them hens with you, lessen it's the possums and the snakes. That rooster bank, neither," he says. Because, stooping suddenly, she jerks off one shoe and strikes the china bank a single shattering blow. From the bed, reclining, Armstid watches her gather the remaining coins from among the china fragments and drop them with the others into the sack and knot it and reknot it three or four times with savage finality.

"You give that to her," she says. "And come sunup you hitch up the team and take her away from here. Take her all the way to Jefferson, if you want."

"I reckon she can get a ride in from Varner's store," he says.

Mrs Armstid rose before day and cooked breakfast. It was on the table when Armstid came in from milking. "Go tell her to come and eat," Mrs Armstid said. When he and Lena returned to the kitchen, Mrs Armstid was not there. Lena looked about the room once, pausing at the door with less than a pause, her face already fixed in an expression immanent with smiling, with speech, prepared speech, Armstid knew. But she said nothing; the pause was less than a pause.

"Let's eat and get on," Armstid said. "You still got a right good piece to go." He watched her eat, again with the tranquil and hearty decorum of last night's supper, though there was now corrupting it a quality of polite and almost finicking restraint. Then he gave her the knotted cloth sack. She took it, her face pleased, warm, though not very much surprised.

"Why, it's right kind of her," she said. "But I wont need it. I'm so nigh there now."

"I reckon you better keep it. I reckon you done noticed how Martha aint much on being crossed in what she aims to do."

"It's right kind," Lena said. She tied the money up in the bandanna bundle and put on the sunbonnet. The wagon was waiting. When they drove down the lane, past the house, she looked back at it. "It was right kind of you all," she said.

"She done it," Armstid said. "I reckon I cant claim no credit."

"It was right kind, anyway. You'll have to say goodbye to her for me. I had hopened to see her myself, but . . . . . ."

"Sho," Armstid said. "I reckon she was busy or something. I'll tell her."

They drove up to the store in the early sunlight, with the squatting men already spitting across the heelgnawed porch, watching her descend slowly and carefully from the wagon seat, carrying the bundle and the fan. Again Armstid did not move to assist her. He said from the seat: "This here is Miz Burch. She wants to go to Jefferson. If anybody is going in today, she will take it kind to ride with them."

She reached the earth, in the heavy, dusty shoes. She looked up at him, serene, peaceful. "It's been right kind," she said.

"Sho," Armstid said. "I reckon you can get to town now." He looked down at her. Then it seemed an interminable while that he watched his tongue seek words, thinking quiet and swift, thought fleeing *A man. All men. He will pass up a hundred chances to do good for one chance to meddle where meddling is not wanted. He will overlook and fail to see chances, opportunities, for riches and fame and welldoing, and even sometimes for evil. But he wont fail to see a chance to meddle* Then his tongue found words, he listening, perhaps with the same astonishment that she did: "Only I wouldn't set too much store by. . . . . .store in . . ." thinking *She is not listening. If she could hear words like that she would not be getting down from this wagon, with that belly and that fan and that little bundle, alone, bound for a place she never saw before and hunting for a man she aint going to ever see again and that she has already seen one time too many as it is* "—any time you are passing back this way, tomorrow or even tonight. . . . . ."

"I reckon I'll be all right now," she said. "They told me he is there."

He turned the wagon and drove back home, sitting hunched, bleacheyed, on the sagging seat, thinking, 'It wouldn't have done any good. She would not have believed the telling and hearing it any more than she will believe the thinking that's been going on all around her for. . . . . . It's four weeks now, she said. No more than she will feel it and believe it now. Setting there on that top step, with her hands in her lap and them fellows squatting there and spitting past her into the road. And not even waiting for them to ask her about it before she begins to tell. Telling them of her own accord about that durn fellow like she never had nothing particular to either hide or tell, even when Jody Varner or some of them will tell her that that fellow in Jefferson at the planing mill is named Bunch and not Burch; and that not worrying her either. I reckon she knows more than even Martha does, like when she told Martha last night about how the Lord will see that what is right will get done.'

It required only one or two questions. Then, sitting on the top step, the fan and the bundle upon her lap, Lena tells her story again, with that patient and transparent recapitulation of a lying child, the squatting overalled men listening quietly.

"That fellow's name is Bunch," Varner says. "He's been working there at the mill about seven years. How do you know that Burch is there too?"

She is looking away up the road, in the direction of Jefferson. Her face is calm, waiting, a little detached without being bemused. "I reckon he'll be there. At that planing mill and all. Lucas always did like excitement. He never did like to live quiet. That's why it never suited him back at Doane's Mill. Why he—we decided to make a change: for money and excitement."

"For money and excitement," Varner says. "Lucas aint the first young buck that's throwed over what he was bred to do and them that depended on him doing it, for money and excitement."

But she is not listening apparently. She sits quietly on the top step, watching the road where it curves away, empty and mounting, toward Jefferson. The squatting men along the wall look at her still and placid face and they think as Armstid thought and as Varner thinks: that she is thinking of a scoundrel who deserted her in trouble and whom they believe that she will never see again, save his coattails perhaps already boardflat with running. 'Or maybe it's about that Sloane's or Bone's Mill she is thinking,' Varner thinks. 'I reckon that even a fool gal dont have to come as far as Mississippi to find out that whatever place she run from aint going to be a whole lot different or worse than the place she is at. Even if it has got a brother in it that objects to his sister's nightprowling' thinking *I would have done the same as the brother; the father would have done the same. She has no mother because fatherblood hates with love and pride, but motherblood with hate loves and cohabits*

She is not thinking about this at all. She is thinking about the coins knotted in the bundle beneath her hands. She is remembering breakfast, thinking how she can enter the store this moment and buy cheese and crackers and even sardines if she likes. At Armstid's she had had but a cup of coffee and a piece of cornbread: nothing more, though Armstid pressed her. 'I et polite,' she thinks, her hands lying upon the bundle, knowing the hidden coins, remembering the single cup of coffee, the decorous morsel of strange bread; thinking with a sort of serene pride: 'Like a lady I et. Like a lady travelling. But now I can buy sardines too if I should so wish.'

So she seems to muse upon the mounting road while the slowspitting and squatting men watch her covertly, believing that she is thinking about the man and the approaching crisis, when in reality she is waging a mild battle with that providential caution of the old earth of and with and by which she lives. This time she conquers. She rises and walking a little awkwardly, a little carefully, she traverses the ranked battery of maneyes and enters the store, the clerk following. 'I'm a-going to do it,' she thinks, even while ordering the cheese and crackers; 'I'm a-going to do it', saying aloud: "And a box of sardines." She calls them *sour-deens*. "A nickel box."

"We aint got no nickel sardines," the clerk says. "Sardines is fifteen cents." He also calls them *sour-deens*.

She muses. "What have you got in a can for a nickel?"

"Aint got nothing except shoeblacking. I dont reckon you want that. Not to eat, noway."

"I reckon I'll take the fifteen cent ones, then." She unties the bundle and the knotted sack. It requires some time to solve the knots. But she unties them patiently, one by one, and pays and knots the sack and the bundle again and takes up her purchase. When she emerges onto the porch there is a wagon standing at the steps. A man is on the seat.

"Here's a wagon going to town," they tell her. "He will take you in."

Her face wakes, serene, slow, warm. "Why, you're right kind," she says.

The wagon moves slowly, steadily, as if here within the sunny loneliness of the enormous land it were outside of, beyond all time and all haste. From Varner's store to Jefferson it is twelve miles. "Will we get there before dinner time?" she says.

The driver spits. "We mought," he says.

Apparently he has never looked at her, not even when she got into the wagon. Apparently she has never looked at him, either. She does not do so now. "I reckon you go to Jefferson a right smart."

He says, "Some." The wagon creaks on. Fields and woods seem to hang in some inescapable middle distance, at once static and fluid, quick, like mirages. Yet the wagon passes them.

"I reckon you dont know anybody in Jefferson named Lucas Burch."

"Burch?"

"I'm looking to meet him there. He works at the planing mill."

"No," the driver says. "I dont know that I know him. But likely there is a right smart of folks in Jefferson I dont know. Likely he is there."

"I'll declare, I hope so. Travelling is getting right bothersome."

The driver does not look at her. "How far have you come, looking for him?"

"From Alabama. It's a right fur piece."

He does not look at her. His voice is quite casual. "How did your folks come to let you start out, in your shape?"

"My folks are dead. I live with my brother. I just decided to come on."

"I see. He sent you word to come to Jefferson."

She does not answer. He can see beneath the sunbonnet her calm profile. The wagon goes on, slow, timeless. The red and unhurried miles unroll beneath the steady feet of the mules, beneath the creaking and clanking wheels. The sun stands now high overhead; the shadow of the sunbonnet now falls across her lap. She looks up at the sun. "I reckon it's time to eat," she says. He watches from the corner of his eye as she opens the cheese and crackers and the sardines, and offers them.

"I wouldn't care for none," he says.

"I'd take it kind for you to share."

"I wouldn't care to. You go ahead and eat."

She begins to eat. She eats slowly, steadily, sucking the rich sardine oil from her fingers with slow and complete relish. Then she stops, not abruptly, yet with utter completeness, her jaw stilled in midchewing, a bitten cracker in her hand and her face lowered a little and her eyes blank, as if she were listening to something very far away or so near as to be inside her. Her face has drained of color, of its full, hearty blood, and she sits quite still, hearing and feeling the implacable and immemorial earth, but without fear or alarm. 'It's twins at least,' she says to herself, without lip movement, without sound. Then the spasm passes. She eats again. The wagon has not stopped; time has not stopped. The wagon crests the final hill and they see smoke.

"Jefferson," the driver says.

"Well, I'll declare," she says. "We are almost there, aint we?"

It is the man now who does not hear. He is looking ahead, across the valley toward the town on the opposite ridge. Following his pointing whip, she sees two columns of smoke: the one the heavy density of burning coal above a tall stack, the other a tall yellow column standing apparently from among a clump of trees some distance beyond the town. "That's a house burning," the driver says. "See?"

But she in turn again does not seem to be listening, to hear. "My, my," she says; "here I aint been on the road but four weeks, and now I am in Jefferson already. My, my. A body does get around."

II

BYRON BUNCH knows this: It was one Friday morning three years ago. And the group of men at work in the planer shed looked up, and saw the stranger standing there, watching them. They did not know how long he had been there. He looked like a tramp, yet not like a tramp either. His shoes were dusty and his trousers were soiled too. But they were of decent serge, sharply creased, and his shirt was soiled but it was a white shirt, and he wore a tie and a stiffbrim straw hat that was quite new, cocked at an angle arrogant and baleful above his still face. He did not look like a professional hobo in his professional rags, but there was something definitely rootless about him, as though no town nor city was his, no street, no walls, no square of earth his home. And that he carried this knowledge with him always as though it were a banner, with a quality ruthless, lonely, and almost proud. "As if," as the men said later, "he was just down on his luck for a time, and that he didn't intend to stay down on it and didn't give a damn much how he rose up." He was young. And Byron watched him standing there and looking at the men in sweatstained overalls, with a cigarette in one side of his mouth and his face darkly and contemptuously still, drawn down a little on one side because of the smoke. After a while he spat the cigarette without touching his hand to it and turned and went on to the mill office while the men in faded and worksoiled overalls looked at his back with a sort of baffled outrage. "We ought to run him through the planer," the foreman said. "Maybe that will take that look off his face."

They did not know who he was. None of them had ever seen him before. "Except that's a pretty risky look for a man to wear on his face in public," one said. "He might forget and use it somewhere where somebody wont like it." Then they dismissed him, from the talk, anyway. They went back to their work among the whirring and grating belts and shafts. But it was not ten minutes before the mill superintendent entered, with the stranger behind him.

"Put this man on," the superintendent said to the foreman.

"He says he can handle a scoop, anyhow. You can put him on the sawdust pile."

The others had not stopped work, yet there was not a man in the shed who was not again watching the stranger in his soiled city clothes, with his dark, insufferable face and his whole air of cold and quiet contempt. The foreman looked at him, briefly, his gaze as cold as the other's. "Is he going to do it in them clothes?"

"That's his business," the superintendent said. "I'm not hiring his clothes."

"Well, whatever he wears suits me if it suits you and him," the foreman said. "All right, mister," he said. "Go down yonder and get a scoop and help them fellows move that sawdust."

The newcomer turned without a word. The others watched him go down to the sawdust pile and vanish and reappear with a shovel and go to work. The foreman and the superintendent were talking at the door. They parted and the foreman returned. "His name is Christmas," he said.

"His name is what?" one said.

"Christmas."

"Is he a foreigner?"

"Did you ever hear of a white man named Christmas?" the foreman said.

"I never heard of nobody a-tall named it," the other said.

And that was the first time Byron remembered that he had ever thought how a man's name, which is supposed to be just the sound for who he is, can be somehow an augur of what he will do, if other men can only read the meaning in time. It seemed to him that none of them had looked especially at the stranger until they heard his name. But as soon as they heard it, it was as though there was something in the sound of it that was trying to tell them what to expect; that he carried with him his own inescapable warning, like a flower its scent or a rattlesnake its rattle. Only none of them had sense enough to recognise it. They just thought that he was a foreigner, and as they watched him for the rest of that Friday, working in that tie and the straw hat and the creased trousers, they said among themselves that that was the way men in his country worked; though there were others who said, "He'll change clothes tonight. He wont have on them Sunday clothes when he comes to work in the morning."

Saturday morning came. As the late arrivals came up just before the whistle blew, they were already saying "Did he—— Where——" The others pointed. The new man was standing alone down at the sawdust pile. His shovel was beside him, and he stood in the same garments of yesterday, with the arrogant hat, smoking a cigarette. "He was there when we come," the first ones said. "Just standing there, like that. Like he hadn't never been to bed, even."

He did not talk to any of them at all. And none of them tried to talk to him. But they were all conscious of him, of the steady back   (he worked well enough, with a kind of baleful and restrained steadiness)   and arms. Noon came. With the exception of Byron, they had brought no lunch with them today, and they began to gather up their belongings preparatory to quitting until Monday. Byron went alone with his lunch pail to the pump house where they usually ate, and sat down. Then something caused him to look up. A short distance away the stranger was leaning against a post, smoking. Byron knew that he had been there when he entered, and would not even bother to go away. Or worse: that he had come there deliberately, ignoring Byron as if he were another post. "Aint you going to knock off?" Byron said.

The other expelled smoke. Then he looked at Byron. His face was gaunt, the flesh a level dead parchment color. Not the skin: the flesh itself, as though the skull had been molded in a still and deadly regularity and then baked in a fierce oven. "How much do they pay for overtime?" he said. And then Byron knew. He knew then why the other worked in the Sunday clothes, and why he had had no lunch with him either yesterday or today, and why he had not quit with the others at noon. He knew as well as if the man had told him that he did not have a nickel in his pockets and that in all likelihood he had lived on cigarettes for two or three days now. Almost with the thought Byron was offering his own pail, the action as reflex as the thought. Because before the act was completed the man, without changing his indolent and contemptuous attitude, turned his face and looked once at the proffered pail through the drooping smoke of the cigarette. "I aint hungry. Keep your muck."

Monday morning came and Byron proved himself right. The man came to work in new overalls, and with a paper bag of food. But he did not squat with them in the pump house to eat at noon, and the look was still on his face. "Let it stay there," the foreman said. "Simms aint hiring his face anymore than his clothes."

Simms hadn't hired the stranger's tongue, either, Byron thought. At least, Christmas didn't seem to think so, to act so. He still had nothing to say to anyone, even after six months. No one knew what he did between mill hours. Now and then one of his fellow workers would pass him on the square down town after supper, and it would be as though Christmas had never seen the other before. He would be wearing then the new hat and the ironed trousers and the cigarette in one side of his mouth and the smoke sneering across his face. No one knew where he lived, slept at night, save that now and then someone would see him following a path that came up through the woods on the edge of town, as if he might live out that way somewhere.

This is not what Byron knows now. This is just what he knew then, what he heard and watched as it came to his knowledge. None of them knew then where Christmas lived and what he was actually doing behind the veil, the screen, of his negro's job at the mill. Possibly no one would ever have known it if it had not been for the other stranger, Brown. But as soon as Brown told, there were a dozen men who admitted having bought whiskey from Christmas for over two years, meeting him at night and alone in the woods behind an old colonial plantation house two miles from town, in which a middleaged spinster named Burden lived alone. But even the ones who bought the whiskey did not know that Christmas was actually living in a tumble down negro cabin on Miss Burden's place, and that he had been living in it for more than two years.

Then one day about six months ago another stranger appeared at the mill as Christmas had done, seeking work. He was young too, tall, already in overalls which looked as though he had been in them constantly for some time, and he looked as though he had been travelling light also. He had an alert, weakly handsome face with a small white scar beside the mouth that looked as if it had been contemplated a great deal in the mirror, and a way of jerking his head quickly and glancing over his shoulder like a mule does in front of an automobile in the road, Byron thought. But it was not alone backwatching, alarm; it seemed also to Byron to possess a quality of assurance, brass, as though the man were reiterating and insisting all the while that he was afraid of nothing that might or could approach him from behind. And when Mooney, the foreman, saw the new hand, Byron believed that he and Mooney had the same thought. Mooney said: "Well, Simms is safe from hiring anything at all when he put that fellow on. He never even hired a whole pair of pants."

"That's so," Byron said. "He puts me in mind of one of these cars running along the street with a radio in it. You cant make out what it is saying and the car aint going anywhere in particular and when you look at it close you see that there aint even anybody in it."

"Yes," Mooney said. "He puts me in mind of a horse. Not a mean horse. Just a worthless horse. Looks fine in the pasture, but it's always down in the spring bottom when anybody comes to the gate with a bridle. Runs fast, all right, but it's always got a sore hoof when hitching-up time comes."

"But I reckon maybe the mares like him," Byron said.

"Sho," Mooney said. "I dont reckon he'd do even a mare any permanent harm."

The new hand went to work down in the sawdust pile with Christmas. With a lot of motion to it, telling everybody who he was and where he had been, in a tone and manner that was the essence of the man himself, that carried within itself its own confounding and mendacity. So that a man put no more belief in what he said that he had done than in what he said his name was, Byron thought. There was no reason why his name should not have been Brown. It was that, looking at him, a man would know that at some time in his life he would reach some crisis in his own foolishness when he would change his name, and that he would think of Brown to change it to with a kind of gleeful exultation, as though the name had never been invented. The thing was, there was no reason why he should have had or have needed any name at all. Nobody cared, just as Byron believed that no one (wearing pants, anyway) cared where he came from nor where he went nor how long he stayed. Because wherever he came from and wherever he had been, a man knew that he was just living on the country, like a locust. It was as though he had been doing it for so long now that all of him had become scattered and diffused and now there was nothing left but the transparent and weightless shell blown oblivious and without destination upon whatever wind.

He worked some, though, after a fashion. Byron believed that there was not even enough left of him to do a good, shrewd job of shirking. To desire to shirk, even, since a man must be better than common to do a good job of malingering, the same as a good job at anything else: of stealing and murdering even. He must be aiming at some specific and definite goal, working toward it. And he believed that Brown was not. They heard how he went and lost his entire first week's pay in a crap game on the first Saturday night. Byron said to Mooney: "I am surprised at that. I would have thought that maybe shooting dice would be the one thing he could do."

"Him?" Mooney said. "What makes you think that he could be good at any kind of devilment when he aint any good at anything as easy as shovelling sawdust? that he could fool anybody with anything as hard to handle as a pair of dice, when he cant with anything as easy to handle as a scoop?" Then he said, "Well, I reckon there aint any man so sorry he cant beat somebody doing something. Because he can at least beat that Christmas doing nothing at all."

"Sho," Byron said. "I reckon that being good is about the easiest thing in the world for a lazy man."

"I reckon he'd be bad fast enough," Mooney said, "if he just had somebody to show him how."

"Well, he'll find that fellow somewhere, sooner or later," Byron said. They both turned and looked down at the sawdust pile, where Brown and Christmas labored, the one with that brooding and savage steadiness, the other with a high-armed and erratic motion which could not have been fooling even itself.

"I reckon so," Mooney said. "But if I aimed to be bad, I'd sho hate to have him for my partner."

Like Christmas, Brown came to work in the same clothes which he wore on the street. But unlike Christmas, he made no change in his costume for some time. "He'll win just enough in that crap game some Saturday night to buy a new suit and still have fifty cents in nickels to rattle in his pocket," Mooney said. "And on the next Monday morning we aint going to see him again." Meanwhile Brown continued to come to work in the same overalls and shirt in which he had arrived in Jefferson, losing his week's pay in the Saturday night dice game or perhaps winning a little, greeting either the one or the other with the same shouts of imbecile laughter, joking and chaffing with the very men who in all likelihood were periodically robbing him. Then one day they heard that he had won sixty dollars. "Well, that's the last we'll see of him," one said.

"I dont know," Mooney said. "Sixty dollars is the wrong figure. If it had been either ten dollars or five hundred, I reckon you'd be right. But not just sixty. He'll just feel now that he is settled down good here, drawing at last somewhere about what he is worth a week." And on Monday he did return to work, in the overalls; they saw them, Brown and Christmas, down at the sawdust pile. They had been watching the two of them down there from the day when Brown went to work: Christmas jabbing his shovel into the sawdust slowly and steadily and hard, as though he were chopping up a buried snake ("or a man," Mooney said) and Brown leaning on his shovel while he apparently told Christmas a story, an anecdote. Because presently he would laugh, shout with laughter, his head backflung, while beside him the other man worked with silent and unflagging savageness. Then Brown would fall to again, working for a time once again as fast as Christmas, but picking up less and less in the scoop until at last the shovel would not even touch the sawdust in its flagging arc. Then he would lean upon it again and apparently finish whatever it was that he was telling Christmas, telling to

the man who did not even seem to hear his voice. As if the
other were a mile away, or spoke a different language from
the one he knew, Byron thought. And they would be seen
together down town on Saturday evening sometimes: Christmas in his neat, soberly austere serge-and-white and the straw
hat, and Brown in his new suit (it was tan, with a red criss-
cross, and he had a colored shirt and a hat like Christmas' but
with a colored band) talking and laughing, his voice heard
clear across the square and back again in echo, somewhat as a
meaningless sound in a church seems to come from everywhere at once. Like he aimed for everybody to see how he
and Christmas were buddies, Byron thought. And then
Christmas would turn and with that still, sullen face of his
walk out of whatever small gathering the sheer empty sound
of Brown's voice had surrounded them with, with Brown following, still laughing and talking. And each time the other
workmen would say, "Well, he wont be back on the job Monday morning." But each Monday he was back. It was Christmas who quit first.

He quit one Saturday night, without warning, after almost
three years. It was Brown who informed them that Christmas
had quit. Some of the other workers were family men and
some were bachelors and they were of different ages and they
led a catholic variety of lives, yet on Monday morning they
all came to work with a kind of gravity, almost decorum.
Some of them were young, and they drank and gambled on
Saturday night, and even went to Memphis now and then.
Yet on Monday morning they came quietly and soberly to
work, in clean overalls and clean shirts, waiting quietly until
the whistle blew and then going quietly to work, as though
there were still something of sabbath in the overlingering air
which established a tenet that, no matter what a man had
done with his sabbath, to come quiet and clean to work on
Monday morning was no more than seemly and right to do.

That is what they had always remarked about Brown. On
Monday morning as likely as not he would appear in the same
soiled clothes of last week, and with a black stubble that had
known no razor. And he would be more noisy than ever,
shouting and playing the pranks of a child of ten. To the
sober others it did not look right. To them it was as though

he had arrived naked, or drunk. Hence it was Brown who on this Monday morning notified them that Christmas had quit. He arrived late, but that was not it. He hadn't shaved, either; but that was not it. He was quiet. For a time they did not know that he was even present, who by that time should have had half the men there cursing him, and some in good earnest. He appeared just as the whistle blew and went straight to the sawdust pile and went to work without a word to anyone, even when one man spoke to him. And then they saw that he was down there alone, that Christmas, his partner, was not there. When the foreman came in, one said: "Well, I see you have lost one of your apprentice firemen."

Mooney looked down to where Brown was spading into the sawdust pile as though it were eggs. He spat briefly. "Yes. He got rich too fast. This little old job couldn't hold him."

"Got rich?" another said.

"One of them did," Mooney said, still watching Brown. "I saw them yesterday riding in a new car. He——" he jerked his head toward Brown "——was driving it. I wasn't surprised at that. I am just surprised that even one of them come to work today."

"Well, I dont reckon Simms will have any trouble finding a man to fill his shoes in these times," the other said.

"He wouldn't have any trouble doing that at any time," Mooney said.

"It looked to me like he was doing pretty well."

"Oh," Mooney said. "I see. You are talking about Christmas."

"Who were you talking about? Has Brown said he is quitting too?"

"You reckon he's going to stay down there, working, with the other one riding around town all day in that new car?"

"Oh." The other looked at Brown too. "I wonder where they got that car."

"I dont," Mooney said. "What I wonder is, if Brown is going to quit at noon or work on until six oclock."

"Well," Byron said, "if I could get rich enough out here to buy a new automobile, I'd quit too."

One or two of the others looked at Byron. They smiled a little. "They never got that rich out here," one said. Byron looked at him. "I reckon Byron stays out of meanness too much himself to keep up with other folks'," the other said. They looked at Byron. "Brown is what you might call a public servant. Christmas used to make them come way out to them woods back of Miss Burden's place, at night; now Brown brings it right into town for them. I hear tell how if you just know the pass word, you can buy a pint of whiskey out of his shirt front in any alley on a Saturday night."

"What's the pass word?" another said. "Six bits?"

Byron looked from face to face. "Is that a fact? Is that what they are doing?"

"That's what Brown is doing. I dont know about Christmas. I wouldn't swear to it. But Brown aint going to be far away from where Christmas is at. Like to like, as the old folks say."

"That's a fact," another said. "Whether Christmas is in it or not, I reckon we aint going to know. He aint going to walk around in public with his pants down, like Brown does."

"He aint going to need to," Mooney said, looking at Brown.

And Mooney was right. They watched Brown until noon, down there at the sawdust pile by himself. Then the whistle blew and they got their lunch pails and squatted in the pump shed and began to eat. Brown came in, glum, his face at once sullen and injured looking, like a child's, and squatted among them, his hands dangling between his knees. He had no lunch with him today.

"Aint you going to eat any dinner?" one said.

"Cold muck out of a dirty lard bucket?" Brown said. "Starting in at daylight and slaving all day like a durn nigger, with a hour off at noon to eat cold muck out of a tin bucket."

"Well, maybe some folks work like the niggers work where they come from," Mooney said. "But a nigger wouldn't last till the noon whistle, working on this job like some white folks work on it."

But Brown did not seem to hear, to be listening, squatting with his sullen face and his dangling hands. It was as though he were not listening to any save himself, listening to himself: "A fool. A man is a fool that will do it."

"You are not chained to that scoop," Mooney said.

"You durn right I aint," Brown said.

Then the whistle blew. They went back to work. They watched Brown down at the sawdust pile. He would dig for a while, then he would begin to slow, moving slower and slower until at last he would be clutching the shovel as though it were a riding whip, and they could see that he was talking to himself. "Because there aint nobody else down there for him to tell it to," one said.

"It's not that," Mooney said. "He hasn't quite convinced himself yet. He aint quite sold yet."

"Sold on what?"

"On the idea that he's a bigger fool than even I think he is," Mooney said.

The next morning he did not appear. "His address from now on will be the barbershop," one said.

"Or that alley just behind it," another said.

"I reckon we'll see him once more," Mooney said. "He'll be out here once more to draw his time for yesterday."

Which he did. About eleven oclock he came up. He wore now the new suit and the straw hat, and he stopped at the shed and stood there looking at the working men as Christmas had done on that day three years ago, as if somehow the very attitudes of the master's dead life motivated, unawares to him, the willing muscles of the disciple who had learned too quick and too well. But Brown merely contrived to look scattered and emptily swaggering where the master had looked sullen and quiet and fatal as a snake. "Lay into it, you slaving bastards!" Brown said, in a merry, loud voice cropped with teeth.

Mooney looked at Brown. Then Brown's teeth didn't show. "You aint calling me that," Mooney said. "Are you?"

Brown's mobile face performed one of those instantaneous changes which they knew. Like it was so scattered and so lightly built that it wasn't any trouble for even him to change it, Byron thought. "I wasn't talking to you," Brown said.

"Oh, I see." Mooney's tone was quite pleasant, easy. "It was these other fellows you were calling a bastard."

Immediately a second one said: "Were you calling that at me?"

"I was just talking to myself," Brown said.

"Well, you have told God's truth for once in your life,"

Mooney said. "The half of it, that is. Do you want me to come up there and whisper the other half in your ear?"

And that was the last they saw of him at the mill, though Byron knows and remembers now the new car (with presently a crumpled fender or two) about the town, idle, destinationless, and constant, with Brown lolling behind the wheel and not making a very good job of being dissolute and enviable and idle. Now and then Christmas would be with him, but not often. And it is now no secret what they were doing. It is a byword among young men and even boys that whiskey can be bought from Brown almost on sight, and the town is just waiting for him to get caught, to produce from his raincoat and offer to sell it to an undercover man. They still do not know for certain if Christmas is connected with it, save that no one believes that Brown alone has sense enough to make a profit even from bootlegging, and some of them know that Christmas and Brown both live in a cabin on the Burden place. But even these do not know if Miss Burden knows it or not, and if they did, they would not tell her. She lives in the big house alone, a woman of middleage. She has lived in the house since she was born, yet she is still a stranger, a foreigner whose people moved in from the North during Reconstruction. A Yankee, a lover of negroes, about whom in the town there is still talk of queer relations with negroes in the town and out of it, despite the fact that it is now sixty years since her grandfather and her brother were killed on the square by an ex slaveowner over a question of negro votes in a state election. But it still lingers about her and about the place: something dark and outlandish and threatful, even though she is but a woman and but the descendant of them whom the ancestors of the town had reason (or thought that they had) to hate and dread. But it is there: the descendants of both in their relationship to one another's ghosts, with between them the phantom of the old spilled blood and the old horror and anger and fear.

If there had been love once, man or woman would have said that Byron Bunch had forgotten her. Or she (meaning

love) him, more like—that small man who will not see thirty
again, who has spent six days of every week for seven years at
the planing mill, feeding boards into the machinery. Saturday
afternoons too he spends there, alone now, with the other
workmen all down town in their Sunday clothes and neckties,
in that terrific and aimless and restive idleness of men who
labor.

On these Saturday afternoons he loads the finished boards
into freight cars, since he cannot operate the planer alone,
keeping his own time to the final second of an imaginary
whistle. The other workmen, the town itself or that part of it
which remembers or thinks about him, believe that he does it
for the overtime which he receives. Perhaps this is the reason.
Man knows so little about his fellows. In his eyes all men or
women act upon what he believes would motivate him if he
were mad enough to do what that other man or woman is
doing. In fact, there is but one man in the town who could
speak with any certainty about Bunch, and with this man the
town does not know that Bunch has any intercourse, since
they meet and talk only at night. This man's name is Hightower. Twenty-five years ago he was minister of one of the
principal churches, perhaps the principal church. This man
alone knows where Bunch goes each Saturday evening when
the imaginary whistle blows (or when Bunch's huge silver
watch says that it has blown). Mrs Beard, at whose boarding
house Bunch lives, knows only that shortly after six oclock
each Saturday Bunch enters, bathes and changes to a suit of
cheap serge which is not new, eats his supper and saddles the
mule which he stables in a shed behind the house which
Bunch himself patched up and roofed, and departs on the
mule. She does not know where he goes. It is the minister
Hightower alone who knows that Bunch rides thirty miles
into the country and spends Sunday leading the choir in a
country church—a service which lasts all day long. Then
some time around midnight he saddles the mule again and
rides back to Jefferson at a steady, allnight jog. And on Monday morning, in his clean overalls and shirt he will be on hand
at the mill when the whistle blows. Mrs Beard knows only
that from Saturday's supper to Monday's breakfast each week
his room and the mule's homemade stable will be vacant.

Hightower alone knows where he goes and what he does there, because two or three nights a week Bunch visits Hightower in the small house where the exminister lives alone, in what the town calls his disgrace—the house unpainted, small, obscure, poorly lighted, mansmelling, manstale. Here the two of them sit in the minister's study, talking quietly: the slight, nondescript man who is utterly unaware that he is a man of mystery among his fellow workers, and the fifty-year-old outcast who has been denied by his church.

Then Byron fell in love. He fell in love contrary to all the tradition of his austere and jealous country raising which demands in the object physical inviolability. It happens on a Saturday afternoon while he is alone at the mill. Two miles away the house is still burning, the yellow smoke standing straight as a monument on the horizon. They saw it before noon, when the smoke first rose above the trees, before the whistle blew and the others departed. "I reckon Byron'll quit too, today," they said. "With a free fire to watch."

"It's a big fire," another said. "What can it be? I dont remember anything out that way big enough to make all that smoke except that Burden house."

"Maybe that's what it is," another said. "My pappy says he can remember how fifty years ago folks said it ought to be burned, and with a little human fat meat to start it good."

"Maybe your pappy slipped out there and set it afire," a third said. They laughed. Then they went back to work, waiting for the whistle, pausing now and then to look at the smoke. After a while a truck loaded with logs drove in. They asked the truck driver, who had come through town.

"Burden," the driver said. "Yes. That's the name. Somebody in town said that the sheriff had gone out there too."

"Well, I reckon Watt Kennedy likes to watch a fire, even if he does have to take that badge with him," one said.

"From the way the square looks," the driver said, "he wont have much trouble finding anybody he wants out there to arrest."

The noon whistle blew. The others departed. Byron ate his lunch, the silver watch open beside him. When it said one oclock, he went back to work. He was alone in the loading shed, making his steady and interminable journeys between the shed and the car, with a piece of folded tow sack upon his shoulder for a pad and bearing upon the pad stacked burdens of staves which another would have said he could not raise nor carry, when Lena Grove walked into the door behind him, her face already shaped with serene anticipatory smiling, her mouth already shaped upon a name. He hears her and turns and sees her face fade like the dying agitation of a dropped pebble in a spring.

"You aint him," she says behind her fading smile, with the grave astonishment of a child.

"No ma'am," Byron says. He pauses, half turning with the balanced staves. "I dont reckon I am. Who is it I aint?"

"Lucas Burch. They told me——"

"Lucas Burch?"

"They told me I would find him out here." She speaks with a kind of serene suspicion, watching him without blinking, as if she believes that he is trying to trick her. "When I got close to town they kept a-calling it Bunch instead of Burch. But I just thought they was saying it wrong. Or maybe I just heard it wrong."

"Yes, ma'am," he says. "That's what it is: Bunch. Byron Bunch." With the staves still balanced on his shoulder he looks at her, at her swollen body, her heavy loins, at the red dust upon the man's heavy shoes upon her feet. "Are you Miz Burch?"

She does not answer at once. She stands there just inside the door, watching him intently but without alarm, with that untroubled, faintly baffled, faintly suspicious gaze. Her eyes are quite blue. But in them is that shadow of the belief that he is trying to deceive her. "They told me away back on the road that Lucas is working at the planing mill in Jefferson. Lots of them told me. And I got to Jefferson and they told me where the planing mill was, and I asked in town about Lucas Burch and they said 'Maybe you mean Bunch' and so I thought they had just got the name wrong and so it wouldn't make any difference. Even when they told me the man they meant wasn't dark complected. You aint telling me you dont know Lucas Burch out here."

Byron puts down the load of staves, in a neat stack, ready to be taken up again. "No, ma'am. Not out here. Not no Lucas Burch out here. And I know all the folks that work here. He may work somewhere in town. Or at another mill."

"Is there another planing mill?"

"No, ma'am. There's some saw mills, a right smart of them, though."

She watches him. "They told me back down the road that he worked for the planing mill."

"I dont know of any here by that name," Byron says. "I dont recall none named Burch except me, and my name is Bunch."

She continues to watch him with that expression not so much concerned for the future as suspicious of the now. Then she breathes. It is not a sigh: she just breathes deeply and quietly once. "Well," she says. She half turns and glances about, at the sawn boards, the stacked staves. "I reckon I'll set down a while. It's right tiring, walking over them hard streets from town. It seems like walking out here from town tired me more than all that way from Alabama did." She is moving toward a low stack of planks.

"Wait," Byron says. He almost springs forward, slipping the sack pad from his shoulder. The woman arrests herself in the act of sitting and Byron spreads the sack on the planks. "You'll set easier."

"Why, you're right kind." She sits down.

"I reckon it'll set a little easier," Byron says. He takes from his pocket the silver watch and looks at it; then he too sits, at the other end of the stack of lumber. "I reckon five minutes will be about right."

"Five minutes to rest?" she says.

"Five minutes from when you come in. It looks like I done already started resting. I keep my own time on Saturday evenings," he says.

"And every time you stop for a minute, you keep a count of it? How will they know you stopped? A few minutes wouldn't make no difference, would it?"

"I reckon I aint paid for setting down," he says. "So you come from Alabama."

She tells him, in his turn, sitting on the towsack pad,

heavybodied, her face quiet and tranquil, and he watching her as quietly; telling him more than she knows that she is telling, as she has been doing now to the strange faces among whom she has travelled for four weeks with the untroubled unhaste of a change of season. And Byron in his turn gets the picture of a young woman betrayed and deserted and not even aware that she has been deserted, and whose name is not yet Burch.

"No, I dont reckon I know him," he says at last. "There aint anybody but me out here this evening, anyway. The rest of them are all out yonder at that fire, more than like." He shows her the yellow pillar of smoke standing tall and windless above the trees.

"We could see it from the wagon before we got to town," she says. "It's a right big fire."

"It's a right big old house. It's been there a long time. Dont nobody live in it but one lady, by herself. I reckon there are folks in this town will call it a judgment on her, even now. She is a Yankee. Her folks come down here in the Reconstruction, to stir up the niggers. Two of them got killed doing it. They say she is still mixed up with niggers. Visits them when they are sick, like they was white. Wont have a cook because it would have to be a nigger cook. Folks say she claims that niggers are the same as white folks. That's why folks dont never go out there. Except one." She is watching him, listening. Now he does not look at her, looking a little aside. "Or maybe two, from what I hear. I hope they was out there in time to help her move her furniture out. Maybe they was."

"Maybe who was?"

"Two fellows named Joe that live out that way somewhere. Joe Christmas and Joe Brown."

"Joe Christmas? That's a funny name."

"He's a funny fellow." Again he looks a little aside from her interested face. "His partner's a sight, too. Brown. He used to work here too. But they done quit now, both of them. Which aint nobody's loss, I reckon."

The woman sits on the towsack pad, interested, tranquil. The two of them might be sitting in their Sunday clothes, in splint chairs on the patinasmooth earth before a country cabin on a sabbath afternoon. "Is his partner named Joe too?"

"Yes, ma'am. Joe Brown. But I reckon that may be his right name. Because when you think of a fellow named Joe Brown, you think of a bigmouthed fellow that's always laughing and talking loud. And so I reckon that is his right name, even if Joe Brown does seem a little kind of too quick and too easy for a natural name, somehow. But I reckon it is his, all right. Because if he drew time on his mouth, he would be owning this here mill right this minute. Folks seem to like him, though. Him and Christmas get along, anyway."

She is watching him. Her face is still serene, but now it is quite grave, her eyes quite grave and quite intent. "What do him and the other one do?"

"Nothing they hadn't ought to, I reckon. At least, they aint been caught at it yet. Brown used to work here, some; what time he had off from laughing and playing jokes on folks. But Christmas has retired. They live out yonder together, out there somewhere where that house is burning. And I have heard what they do to make a living. But that aint none of my business in the first place. And in the second place, most of what folks tells on other folks aint true to begin with. And so I reckon I aint no better than nobody else."

She is watching him. She is not even blinking. "And he says his name is Brown." It might have been a question, but she does not wait for an answer. "What kind of tales have you heard about what they do?"

"I would injure no man," Byron says. "I reckon I ought not to talked so much. For a fact, it looks like a fellow is bound to get into mischief soon as he quits working."

"What kind of tales?" she says. She has not moved. Her tone is quiet, but Byron is already in love, though he does not yet know it. He does not look at her, feeling her grave, intent gaze upon his face, his mouth.

"Some claim they are selling whiskey. Keeping it hid out there where that house is burning. And there is some tale about Brown was drunk down town one Saturday night and he pretty near told something that ought not to been told, about him and Christmas in Memphis one night, or on a dark road close to Memphis, that had a pistol in it. Maybe two pistols. Because Christmas come in quick and shut Brown up and took him away. Something that Christmas didn't want told, anyway, and that even Brown would have had better sense than to told if he hadn't been drunk. That's what I heard. I wasn't there, myself." When he raises his face now he finds that he has looked down again before he even met her eyes. He seems to have already a foreknowledge of something now irrevocable, not to be recalled, who had believed that out here at the mill alone on Saturday afternoon he would be where the chance to do hurt or harm could not have found him.

"What does he look like?" she says.

"Christmas? Why——"

"I dont mean Christmas."

"Oh. Brown. Yes. Tall, young. Dark complected; women-folks calls him handsome, a right smart do, I hear tell. A big hand for laughing and frolicking and playing jokes on folks. But I. . . . . ." His voice ceases. He cannot look at her, feeling her steady, sober gaze upon his face.

"Joe Brown," she says. "Has he got a little white scar right here by his mouth?"

And he cannot look at her, and he sits there on the stacked lumber when it is too late, and he could have bitten his tongue in two.

III

From his study window he can see the street. It is not far away, since the lawn is not deep. It is a small lawn, containing a half dozen lowgrowing maples. The house, the brown, unpainted and unobtrusive bungalow is small too and by bushing crepe myrtle and syringa and althea almost hidden save for that gap through which from the study window he watches the street. So hidden it is that the light from the corner street lamp scarcely touches it.

From the window he can also see the sign, which he calls his monument. It is planted in the corner of the yard, low, facing the street. It is three feet long and eighteen inches high—a neat oblong presenting its face to who passes and its back to him. But he does not need to read it because he made the sign with hammer and saw, neatly, and he painted the legend which it bears, neatly too, tediously, when he realised that he would have to begin to have to have money for bread and fire and clothing. When he quitted the seminary he had a small income inherited from his father, which, as soon as he got his church, he forwarded promptly on receipt of the quarterly checks to an institution for delinquent girls in Memphis. Then he lost his church, he lost the Church, and the bitterest thing which he believed that he had ever faced—more bitter even than the bereavement and the shame—was the letter which he wrote them to say that from now on he could send them but half the sum which he had previously sent.

So he continued to send them half of a revenue which in its entirety would little more than have kept him. "Luckily there are things which I can do," he said at the time. Hence the sign, carpentered neatly by himself and by himself lettered, with bits of broken glass contrived cunningly into the paint, so that at night, when the corner street lamp shone upon it, the letters glittered with an effect as of Christmas:

REV. GAIL HIGHTOWER, D.D.
Art Lessons
Handpainted Xmas & Anniversary Cards
Photographs Developed

But that was years ago, and he had had no art pupils and few enough Christmas cards and photograph plates, and the paint and the shattered glass had weathered out of the fading letters. They were still readable, however; though, like Hightower himself, few of the townspeople needed to read them anymore. But now and then a negro nursemaid with her white charges would loiter there and spell them aloud with that vacuous idiocy of her idle and illiterate kind, or a stranger happening along the quiet and remote and unpaved and littleused street would pause and read the sign and then look up at the small, brown, almost concealed house, and pass on; now and then the stranger would mention the sign to some acquaintance in the town. "Oh yes," the friend would say. "Hightower. He lives there by himself. He come here as minister of the Presbyterian church, but his wife went bad on him. She would slip off to Memphis now and then and have a good time. About twenty-five years ago, that was, right after he come here. Some folks claimed he knew about it. That he couldn't or wouldn't satisfy her himself and that he knew what she was doing. Then one Saturday night she got killed, in a house or something in Memphis. Papers full of it. He had to resign from the church, but he wouldn't leave Jefferson, for some reason. They tried to get him to, for his own sake as well as the town's, the church's. That was pretty bad on the church, you see. Having strangers come here and hear about it, and him refusing to leave the town. But he wouldn't go away. He has lived out there on what used to be the main street ever since, by himself. At least it aint a principal street anymore. That's something. But then he dont worry anybody anymore, and I reckon most folks have forgot about him. Does his own housework. I dont reckon anybody's even been inside that house in twenty-five years. We dont know why he stays here. But any day you pass along there about dusk or nightfall, you can see him sitting in the window. Just sitting there. The rest of the time folks wont hardly see him around the place at all, except now and then working in his garden."

So the sign which he carpentered and lettered is even less to him than it is to the town; he is no longer conscious of it as a sign, a message. He does not remember it at all until he takes his place in the study window just before dusk. Then it

is just a familiar low oblong shape without any significance at
all, low at the street end of the shallow lawn; it too might
have grown up out of the tragic and inescapable earth along
with the low spreading maples and the shrubs, without help
or hindrance from him. He no longer even looks at it, as he
does not actually see the trees beneath and through which he
watches the street, waiting for nightfall, the moment of night.
The house, the study, is dark behind him, and he is waiting
for that instant when all light has failed out of the sky and it
would be night save for that faint light which daygranaried
leaf and grass blade reluctant suspire, making still a little light
on earth though night itself has come. *Now, soon,* he thinks;
soon, now He does not say even to himself: "There remains
yet something of honor and pride, of life."

When Byron Bunch first came to Jefferson seven years ago
and saw that little sign   *Gail Hightower D.D. Art Lessons
Christmas Cards Photographs Developed*   he thought 'D.D.
What is D.D.' and he asked and they told him it meant Done
Damned. Gail Hightower Done Damned in Jefferson anyway, they told him. And how Hightower had come straight
to Jefferson from the seminary, refusing to accept any other
call; how he had pulled every string he could in order to be
sent to Jefferson. And how he arrived with his young wife,
descending from the train in a state of excitement already,
talking, telling the old men and women who were the pillars
of the church how he had set his mind on Jefferson from the
first, since he had first decided to become a minister; telling
them with a kind of glee of the letters he had written and the
worrying he had done and the influence he had used in order
to be called here. To the people of the town it sounded like a
horsetrader's glee over an advantageous trade. Perhaps that is
how it sounded to the elders. Because they listened to him
with something cold and astonished and dubious, since he
sounded like it was the town he desired to live in and not the
church and the people who composed the church, that he
wanted to serve. As if he did not care about the people, the
living people, about whether they wanted him here or not.

And he being young too, and the old men and the old women trying to talk down his gleeful excitement with serious matters of the church and its responsibilities and his own. And they told Byron how the young minister was still excited even after six months, still talking about the Civil War and his grandfather, a cavalryman, who was killed, and about General Grant's stores burning in Jefferson until it did not make sense at all. They told Byron how he seemed to talk that way in the pulpit too, wild too in the pulpit, using religion as though it were a dream. Not a nightmare, but something which went faster than the words in the Book; a sort of cyclone that did not even need to touch the actual earth. And the old men and women did not like that, either.

It was as if he couldn't get religion and that galloping cavalry and his dead grandfather shot from the galloping horse untangled from each other, even in the pulpit. And that he could not untangle them in his private life, at home either, perhaps. Perhaps he did not even try to at home, Byron thought, thinking how that is the sort of thing that men do to the women who belong to them; thinking that that is why women have to be strong and should not be held blameable for what they do with or for or because of men, since God knew that being anybody's wife was a tricky enough business. They told him how the wife was a small, quietlooking girl who at first the town thought just had nothing to say for herself. But the town said that if Hightower had just been a more dependable kind of man, the kind of man a minister should be instead of being born about thirty years after the only day he seemed to have ever lived in—that day when his grandfather was shot from the galloping horse—she would have been all right too. But he was not, and the neighbors would hear her weeping in the parsonage in the afternoons or late at night, and the neighbors knowing that the husband would not know what to do about it because he did not know what was wrong. And how sometimes she would not even come to the church, where her own husband was preaching, even on Sunday, and they would look at him and wonder if he even knew that she was not there, if he had not even forgot that he ever had a wife, up there in the pulpit with his hands flying around him and the dogma he was

posed to preach all full of galloping cavalry and defeat and
glory just as when he tried to tell them on the street about
the galloping horses, it in turn would get all mixed up with
absolution and choirs of martial seraphim, until it was natural
that the old men and women should believe that what he
preached in God's own house on God's own day verged on
actual sacrilege.

And they told Byron how after about a year in Jefferson,
the wife began to wear that frozen look on her face, and when
the church ladies would go to call Hightower would meet
them alone, in his shirt sleeves and without any collar, in a
flurry, and for a time it would seem as though he could not
even think what they had come for and what he ought to do.
Then he would invite them in and excuse himself and go out.
And they would not hear a sound anywhere in the house,
sitting there in their Sunday dresses, looking at one another
and about the room, listening and not hearing a sound. And
then he would come back with his coat and collar on and sit
and talk with them about the church and the sick, and they
talking back, bright and quiet, still listening and maybe
watching the door, maybe wondering if he knew what they
believed that they already knew.

The ladies quit going there. Soon they did not even see the
minister's wife on the street anymore. And he still acting like
there was nothing wrong. And then she would be gone for a
day or two; they would see her get on the early train, with her
face beginning to get thin and gaunted as though she never ate
enough and that frozen look on it as if she were not seeing
what she was looking at. And he would tell that she had gone
to visit her people downstate somewhere, until one day, during one of her absences, a Jefferson woman shopping in
Memphis saw her walking fast into a hotel there. It was one
Saturday that the woman returned home and told it. But the
next day Hightower was in the pulpit, with religion and the
galloping cavalry all mixed up again, and the wife returned
Monday and the following Sunday she came to church again,
for the first time in six or seven months, sitting by herself at
the rear of the church. She came every Sunday after that for
a while. Then she was gone again, in the middle of the week
this time   (it was in July and hot)   and Hightower said that

she had gone to see her folks again, in the country where it would be cool; and the old men, the elders, and the old women watching him, not knowing if he believed what he was telling or not, and the young people talking behind his back.

But they could not tell whether he himself believed or not what he told them, if he cared or not, with his religion and his grandfather being shot from the galloping horse all mixed up, as though the seed which his grandfather had transmitted to him had been on the horse too that night and had been killed too and time had stopped there and then for the seed and nothing had happened in time since, not even him.

The wife returned before Sunday. It was hot; the old people said that it was the hottest spell which the town had ever known. She came to church that Sunday and took her seat on a bench at the back, alone. In the middle of the sermon she sprang from the bench and began to scream, to shriek something toward the pulpit, shaking her hands toward the pulpit where her husband had ceased talking, leaning forward with his hands raised and stopped. Some people nearby tried to hold her but she fought them, and they told Byron how she stood there, in the aisle now, shrieking and shaking her hands at the pulpit where her husband leaned with his hand still raised and his wild face frozen in the shape of the thundering and allegorical period which he had not completed. They did not know whether she was shaking her hands at him or at God. Then he came down and approached and she stopped fighting then and he led her out, with the heads turning as they passed, until the superintendent told the organist to play. That afternoon the elders held a meeting behind locked doors. The people did not know what went on behind them, save that Hightower returned and entered the vestry room and closed the door behind him too.

But the people did not know what had happened. They only knew that the church made up a sum to send the wife to an institution, a sanatorium, and that Hightower took her there and came back and preached the next Sunday, as usual. The women, the neighbors, some of whom had not entered the parsonage in months, were kind to him, taking him dishes now and then, telling one another and their husbands what a mess the parsonage was in, and how the minister seemed to eat like an animal—just when he got hungry and just whatever he could find. Every two weeks he would go and visit his wife in the sanatorium, but he always returned after a day or so; and on Sunday, in the pulpit again, it was as though the whole thing had never happened. The people would ask about her health, curious and kind, and he would thank them. Then Sunday he would be again in the pulpit, with his wild hands and his wild rapt eager voice in which like phantoms God and salvation and the galloping horses and his dead grandfather thundered, while below him the elders sat, and the congregation, puzzled and outraged. In the fall the wife came home. She looked better. She had put on a little flesh. She had changed more than that, even. Perhaps it was that she seemed chastened now; awake, anyway. Anyhow she was now like the ladies had wanted her to be all the time, as they believed that the minister's wife should be. She attended church and prayer meeting regularly, and the ladies called upon her and she called upon them, sitting quiet and humble, even in her own house, while they told her how to run it and what to wear and what to make her husband eat.

It might even be said that they forgave her. No crime or transgression had been actually named and no penance had been actually set. But the town did not believe that the ladies had forgot those previous mysterious trips, with Memphis as their destination and for that purpose regarding which all had the same conviction, though none ever put it into words, spoke it aloud, since the town believed that good women dont forget things easily, good or bad, lest the taste and savor of forgiveness die from the palate of conscience. Because the town believed that the ladies knew the truth, since it believed that bad women can be fooled by badness, since they have to spend some of their time not being suspicious. But that no good woman can be fooled by it because, by being good herself, she does not need to worry anymore about hers or anybody else's goodness; hence she has plenty of time to smell out sin. That was why, they believed, that good can fool her almost any time into believing that it is evil, but that evil itself can never fool her. So when after four or five months the wife went away again on a visit and the husband said again that she had gone to visit her people, the town believed that this time even he was not fooled. Anyway, she came back and he went on preaching every Sunday like nothing had happened, making his calls on the people and the sick and talking about the church. But the wife did not come to church anymore, and soon the ladies stopped calling on her, going to the parsonage at all. And even the neighbors on either side would no longer see her about the house. And soon it was as though she were not there; as though everyone had agreed that she was not there, that the minister did not even have a wife. And he preaching to them every Sunday, not even telling them now that she had gone to visit her people. Maybe he was glad of that, the town thought. Maybe he was glad to not have to lie anymore.

So nobody saw her when she got on the train that Friday, or maybe it was Saturday, the day itself. It was Sunday morning's paper which they saw, telling how she had jumped or fallen from a hotel window in Memphis Saturday night, and was dead. There had been a man in the room with her. He was arrested. He was drunk. They were registered as man and wife, under a fictitious name. The police found her rightful name where she had written it herself on a piece of paper and then torn it up and thrown it into the waste basket. The papers printed it, with the story: wife of the Reverend Gail Hightower, of Jefferson, Mississippi. And the story told how the paper telephoned to the husband at two a.m. and how the husband said that he had nothing to say. And when they reached the church that Sunday morning the yard was full of Memphis reporters taking pictures of the church and the parsonage. Then Hightower came. The reporters tried to stop him but he walked right through them and into the church and up into the pulpit. The old ladies and some of the old men were already in the church, horrified and outraged, not so much about the Memphis business as about the presence of the reporters. But when Hightower came in and actually went up into the pulpit, they forgot about the reporters even. The ladies got up first and began to leave. Then the men got up too, and then the church was empty save for the minister in the pulpit, leaning a little forward, with the Book open and his hands propped on either side of it and his head not bowed either, and the Memphis reporters (they had followed him

into the church)   sitting in a line in the rear pew. They said
he was not watching his congregation leaving; he was not
looking at anything.

They told Byron about it; about how at last the minister
closed the Book, carefully, and came down into the empty
church and walked up the aisle without once looking at the
row of reporters, like the congregation had done, and went
out the door. There were some photographers waiting out in
front, with the cameras all set up and their heads under the
black cloths. The minister had evidently expected this. Because he emerged from the church with an open hymn book
held before his face. But the cameramen had evidently expected that too. Because they fooled him. Very likely he was
not used to it and so was easily fooled, they told Byron. One
of the cameramen had his machine set up to one side, and the
minister did not see that one at all, or until too late. He was
keeping his face concealed from the one in front, and next
day when the picture came out in the paper it had been taken
from the side, with the minister in the middle of a step, holding the hymn book before his face. And behind the book his
lips were drawn back as though he were smiling. But his teeth
were tight together and his face looked like the face of Satan
in the old prints. The next day he brought his wife home and
buried her. The town came to the ceremony. It was not a
funeral. He did not take the body to the church at all. He
took it straight to the cemetery and he was preparing to read
from the Book himself when another minister came forward
and took it from his hand. A lot of the people, the younger
ones, remained after he and the others had gone, looking at
the grave.

Then even the members of the other churches knew that
his own had asked him to resign, and that he refused. The
next Sunday a lot of them from the other churches came to
his church to see what would happen. He came and entered
the church. The congregation as one rose and walked out,
leaving the minister and those from the other churches who
had come as though to a show. So he preached to them, as
he had always preached: with that rapt fury which they had
considered sacrilege and which those from the other churches
believed to be out and out insanity.

He would not resign. The elders asked the church board to recall him. But after the story, the pictures in the papers and all, no other town would have him either. There was nothing against him personally, they all insisted. He was just unlucky. He was just born unlucky. So the people quit coming to the church at all, even the ones from the other churches who had come out of curiosity for a time: he was no longer even a show now; he was now only an outrage. But he would reach the church at the old hour each Sunday morning and go to the pulpit, and the congregation would rise and leave, and the loafers and such would gather along the street outside and listen to him preaching and praying in the empty church. And the Sunday after that when he arrived the door was locked, and the loafers watched him try the door and then desist and stand there with his face still not bowed, with the street lined with men who never went to church anyway, and little boys who did not know exactly what it was but that it was something, stopping and looking with still round eyes at the man standing quite motionless before the locked door. The next day the town heard how he had gone to the elders and resigned his pulpit for the good of the church.

Then the town was sorry with being glad, as people sometimes are sorry for those whom they have at last forced to do as they wanted them to. They thought of course that he would go away now, and the church made up a collection for him to go away on and settle somewhere else. Then he refused to leave the town. They told Byron of the consternation, the more than outrage, when they learned that he had bought the little house on the back street where he now lives and has lived ever since; and the elders held another meeting because they said that they had given him the money to go away on, and when he spent it for something else he had accepted the money under false pretences. They went to him and told him so. He asked them to excuse him; he returned to the room with the sum which had been given him, to the exact penny and in the exact denominations, and insisted that they take it back. But they refused, and he would not tell where he had got the money to buy the house with. So by the next day, they told Byron, there were some who said that he had insured his wife's life and then paid someone to murder her. But everyone knew that this was not so, including the ones who told and repeated it and the ones who listened when it was told.

But he would not leave the town. Then one day they saw the little sign which he had made and painted himself and set in his front yard, and they knew that he meant to stay. He still kept the cook, a negro woman. He had had her all the time. But they told Byron how as soon as his wife was dead, the people seemed to realise all at once that the negro was a woman, that he had that negro woman in the house alone with him all day. And how the wife was hardly cold in the shameful grave before the whispering began. About how he had made his wife go bad and commit suicide because he was not a natural husband, a natural man, and that the negro woman was the reason. And that's all it took; all that was lacking. Byron listened quietly, thinking to himself how people everywhere are about the same, but that it did seem that in a small town, where evil is harder to accomplish, where opportunities for privacy are scarcer, that people can invent more of it in other people's names. Because that was all it required: that idea, that single idle word blown from mind to mind. One day the cook quit. They heard how one night a party of carelessly masked men went to the minister's house and ordered him to fire her. Then they heard how the next day the woman told that she quit herself because her employer asked her to do something which she said was against God and nature. And it was said that some masked men had scared her into quitting because she was what is known as a high brown and it was known that there were two or three men in the town who would object to her doing whatever it was which she considered contrary to God and nature, since, as some of the younger men said, if a nigger woman considered it against God and nature, it must be pretty bad. Anyway, the minister couldn't—or didn't—get another woman cook. Possibly the men scared all the other negro women in town that same night. So he did his own cooking for a while, until they heard one day that he had a negro man to cook for him. And that finished him, sure enough. Because that evening some men, not masked either, took the negro man out and whipped him. And when Hightower waked the next morning his study window was broken and on the floor lay a brick with a note tied to it, commanding him to get out of town by sunset and signed K.K.K. And he did not go, and on the second morning a man found him in the woods about a mile from town. He had been tied to a tree and beaten unconscious.

He refused to tell who had done it. The town knew that that was wrong, and some of the men came to him and tried again to persuade him to leave Jefferson, for his own good, telling him that next time they might kill him. But he refused to leave. He would not even talk about the beating, even when they offered to prosecute the men who had done it. But he would do neither. He would neither tell, nor depart. Then all of a sudden the whole thing seemed to blow away, like an evil wind. It was as though the town realised at last that he would be a part of its life until he died, and that they might as well become reconciled. As though, Byron thought, the entire affair had been a lot of people performing a play and that now and at last they had all played out the parts which had been allotted them and now they could live quietly with one another. They let the minister alone. They would see him working in the yard or the garden, and on the street and in the stores with a small basket on his arm, and they would speak to him. They knew that he did his own cooking and housework, and after a while the neighbors began to send him dishes again, though they were the sort of dishes which they would have sent to a poor mill family. But it was food, and wellmeant. Because, as Byron thought, people forget a lot in twenty years. 'Why,' he thinks, 'I dont reckon there is anybody in Jefferson that knows that he sits in that window from sundown to full dark every day that comes, except me. Or what the inside of that house looks like. And they dont even know that I know, or likely they'd take us both out and whip us again, since folks dont seem to forget much longer than they remember.' Because there is one other thing, which came into Byron's own knowledge and observation, in his own time since he came to Jefferson to live.

Hightower read a great deal. That is, Byron had examined with a kind of musing and respectful consternation the books which lined the study walls: books of religion and history and science of whose very existence Byron had never heard. One day about four years ago a negro man came running up to the minister's house from his cabin on the edge of town immediately behind it, and said that his wife was at childbed. Hightower had no telephone and he told the negro to run next door and call a doctor. He watched the negro go to the gate of the next house. But instead of entering, the negro stood there for a time and then went on up the street toward town, walking; Hightower knew that the man would walk all the way to town and then spend probably thirty minutes more getting in touch with a doctor, in his fumbling and timeless negro fashion, instead of asking some white woman to telephone for him. Then he went to his kitchen door and he could hear the woman in the not so distant cabin, wailing. He waited no longer. He ran down to the cabin and found that the woman had got out of bed, for what reason he never learned, and she was now on her hands and knees on the floor, trying to get back into the bed, screaming and wailing. He got her back into the bed and told her to lie still, frightened her into obeying him, and ran back to his house and took one of the books from the study shelf and got his razor and some cord and ran back to the cabin and delivered the child. But it was already dead; the doctor when arrived said that she had doubtless injured it when she left the bed where Hightower found her. He also approved of Hightower's work, and the husband was satisfied too.

'But it was just too close to that other business,' Byron thought, 'even despite the fifteen years between them.' Because within two days there were those who said that the child was Hightower's and that he had let it die deliberately. But Byron believed that even the ones who said this did not believe it. He believed that the town had had the habit of saying things about the disgraced minister which they did not believe themselves, for too long a time to break themselves of it. 'Because always,' he thinks, 'when anything gets to be a habit, it also manages to get a right good distance away from truth and fact.' And he remembers one evening when he and Hightower were talking together and Hightower said: "They are good people. They must believe what they must believe, especially as it was I who was at one time both master and

servant of their believing. And so it is not for me to outrage
their believing nor for Byron Bunch to say that they are
wrong. Because all that any man can hope for is to be permitted to live quietly among his fellows." That was soon after
Byron had heard the story, shortly after the evening visits to
Hightower's study began and Byron still wondered why the
other remained in Jefferson, almost within sight of, and
within hearing of, the church which had disowned and expelled him. One evening Byron asked him.

"Why do you spend your Saturday afternoons working at
the mill while other men are taking pleasure down town?"
Hightower said.

"I dont know," Byron said. "I reckon that's just my life."

"And I reckon this is just my life, too," the other said. 'But
I know now why it is,' Byron thinks. 'It is because a fellow is
more afraid of the trouble he might have than he ever is of
the trouble he's already got. He'll cling to trouble he's used
to before he'll risk a change. Yes. A man will talk about how
he'd like to escape from living folks. But it's the dead folks
that do him the damage. It's the dead ones that lay quiet in
one place and dont try to hold him, that he cant escape from.'

They have thundered past now and crashed silently on into
the dusk; night has fully come. Yet he still sits at the study
window, the room still dark behind him. The street lamp at
the corner flickers and glares, so that the bitten shadows of
the unwinded maples seem to toss faintly upon the August
darkness. From a distance, quite faint though quite clear, he
can hear the sonorous waves of massed voices from the
church: a sound at once austere and rich, abject and proud,
swelling and falling in the quiet summer darkness like a har-
monic tide.

Then he sees a man approaching along the street. On a
week night he would have recognised the figure, the shape,
the carriage and gait. But on Sunday evening, and with the
echo of the phantom hooves still crashing soundlessly in the
duskfilled study, he watches quietly the puny, unhorsed figure
moving with that precarious and meretricious cleverness of

animals balanced on their hinder legs; that cleverness of which the man animal is so fatuously proud and which constantly betrays him by means of natural laws like gravity and ice, and by the very extraneous objects which he has himself invented, like motor cars and furniture in the dark, and the very refuse of his own eating left upon floor or pavement; and he thinks quietly how right the ancients were in making the horse an attribute and symbol of warriors and kings, when he sees the man in the street pass the low sign and turn into his gate and approach the house. He sits forward then, watching the man come up the dark walk toward the dark door; he hears the man stumble heavily at the dark bottom step. "Byron Bunch," he says. "In town on Sunday night. Byron Bunch in town on Sunday."

IV

T HEY SIT facing one another across the desk. The study is
lighted now, by a greenshaded reading lamp sitting upon
the desk. Hightower sits behind it, in an ancient swivel chair,
Byron in a straight chair opposite. Both their faces are just
without the direct downward pool of light from the shaded
lamp. Through the open window the sound of singing from
the distant church comes. Byron talks in a flat, level voice.

"It was a strange thing. I thought that if there ever was a
place where a man would be where the chance to do harm
could not have found him, it would have been out there at
the mill on a Saturday evening. And with the house burning
too, right in my face, you might say. It was like all the time I
was eating dinner and I would look up now and then and see
that smoke and I would think 'Well, I wont see a soul out
here this evening, anyway. I aint going to be interrupted this
evening, at least.' And then I looked up and there she was,
with her face all fixed for smiling and with her mouth all fixed
to say his name, when she saw that I wasn't him. And I never
knowed any better than to blab the whole thing." He gri-
maces faintly. It is not a smile. His upper lip just lifts momentarily, the movement, even the surface wrinkling, travelling no
further and vanishing almost at once. "I never even suspicioned then that what I didn't know was not the worst of it."

"It must have been a strange thing that could keep Byron
Bunch in Jefferson over Sunday," Hightower says. "But she
was looking for him. And you helped her to find him. Wasn't
what you did what she wanted, what she had come all the
way from Alabama to find?"

"I reckon I told her, all right. I reckon it aint any question
about that. With her watching me, sitting there, swolebellied,
watching me with them eyes that a man could not have lied
to if he had wanted. And me blabbing on, with that smoke
right yonder in plain sight like it was put there to warn me,
to make me watch my mouth only I never had the sense to
see it."

"Oh," Hightower says. "The house that burned yesterday.
But I dont see any connection between——Whose house was

it? I saw the smoke, myself, and I asked a passing negro, but
he didn't know."

"That old Burden house," Byron says. He looks at the
other. They look at one another. Hightower is a tall man, and
he was thin once. But he is not thin now. His skin is the color
of flour sacking and his upper body in shape is like a loosely
filled sack falling from his gaunt shoulders of its own weight,
upon his lap. Then Byron says, "You aint heard yet." The
other watches him. He says, in a musing tone: "That would
be for me to do too. To tell on two days to two folks something they aint going to want to hear and that they hadn't
ought to have to hear at all."

"What is this that you think I will not want to hear? What
is it that I have not heard?"

"Not the fire," Byron says. "They got out of the fire all
right."

"They? I understood that Miss Burden lived there alone."

Again Byron looks at the other for a moment. But Hightower's face is merely grave and interested. "Brown and
Christmas," Byron says. Still Hightower's face does not
change in expression. "You aint heard that, even," Byron says.
"They lived out there."

"Lived out there? They boarded in the house?"

"No. In a old nigger cabin in the back. Christmas fixed it
up three years ago. He's been living in it ever since, with folks
wondering where he slept at night. Then when him and
Brown set up together, he took Brown in with him."

"Oh," Hightower said. "But I dont see. . . . . . If they
were comfortable, and Miss Burden didn't——"

"I reckon they got along. They were selling whiskey, using
that old place for a headquarters, a blind. I dont reckon she
knew that, about the whiskey. Leastways, folks dont know if
she ever knew or not. They say that Christmas started it by
himself three years ago, just selling to a few regular customers
that didn't even know one another. But when he took Brown
in with him, I reckon Brown wanted to spread out. Selling it
by the half a pint out of his shirt bosom in any alley and to
anybody. Selling what he never drunk, that is. And I reckon
the way they got the whiskey they sold would not have stood
much looking into. Because about two weeks after Brown

quit out at the mill and taken to riding around in that new car for his steady work, he was down town drunk one Saturday night and bragging to a crowd in the barbershop something about him and Christmas in Memphis one night, or on a road close to Memphis. Something about them and that new car hid in the bushes and Christmas with a pistol, and a lot more about a truck and a hundred gallons of something, until Christmas come in quick and walked up to him and jerked him out of the chair. And Christmas saying in that quiet voice of his, that aint pleasant and aint mad either: 'You ought to be careful about drinking so much of this Jefferson hair tonic. It's gone to your head. First thing you know you'll have a hairlip.' Holding Brown up he was with one hand and slapping his face with the other. They didn't look like hard licks. But the folks could see the red even through Brown's whiskers when Christmas' hand would come away between licks. 'You come out and get some fresh air,' Christmas says. 'You're keeping these folks from working.'" He muses. He speaks again: "And there she was, sitting there on them staves, watching me and me blabbing the whole thing to her, and her watching me. And then she says 'Did he have a little white scar right here by his mouth?'"

"And Brown is the man," Hightower says. He sits motionless, watching Byron with a sort of quiet astonishment. There is nothing militant in it, nothing of outraged morality. It is as though he were listening to the doings of people of a different race. "Her husband a bootlegger. Well, well, well." Yet Byron can see in the other's face something latent, about to wake, of which Hightower himself is unaware, as if something inside the man were trying to warn or prepare him. But Byron thinks that this is just the reflection of what he himself already knows and is about to tell.

"And so I had already told her before I knew it. And I could have bit my tongue in two, even then, even when I thought that that was all." He is not looking at the other now. Through the window, faint yet clear, the blended organ and voices come from the distant church, across the still evening. *I wonder if he hears it too* Byron thinks *Or maybe he has listened to it so much and so long that he dont even hear it anymore. Dont even need to not listen* "And she set there all the evening while I worked, and the smoke dying away at last, and me trying to think what to tell her and what to do. She wanted to go right on out there, for me to tell her the way. When I told her it was two miles she just kind of smiled, like I was a child or something. 'I done come all the way from Alabama,' she said. 'I reckon I aint going to worry about two miles more.' And then I told her. . . . . . ." His voice ceases. He appears to contemplate the floor at his feet. He looks up. "I lied, I reckon. Only in a way it was not a lie. It was because I knowed there would be folks out there watching the fire, and her coming up, trying to find him. I didn't know myself, then, the other. The rest of it. The worst of it. So I told her that he was busy at a job he had, and that the best time to find him would be down town after six oclock. And that was the truth. Because I reckon he does call it work, carrying all them cold little bottles nekkid against his chest, and if he ever was away from the square it was just because he was a little behind in getting back or had just stepped into a alley for a minute. So I persuaded her to wait and she set there and I went on working, trying to decide what to do. When I think now how worried I was on what little I knowed, now when I know the rest of it, it dont seem like I had anything then to worry me at all. All day I have been thinking how easy it would be if I could just turn back to yesterday and not have any more to worry me than I had then."

"I still cannot see what you have to worry about," Hightower says. "It is not your fault that the man is what he is or she what she is. You did what you could. All that any stranger could be expected to do. Unless. . . . . . ." His voice ceases also. Then it dies away on that inflection, as if idle thinking had become speculation and then something like concern. Opposite him Byron sits without moving, his face lowered and grave. And opposite Byron, Hightower does not yet think *love*. He remembers only that Byron is still young and has led a life of celibacy and hard labor, and that by Byron's telling the woman whom he has never seen possesses some disturbing quality at least, even though Byron still believes that it is only pity. So he watches Byron now with a certain narrowness neither cold nor warm, while Byron continues in that flat voice: about how at six oclock he had still decided on nothing; that when he and Lena reached the square he was still undecided. And now there begins to come into Hightower's puzzled expression a quality of shrinking and foreboding as Byron talks quietly, telling about how he decided after they reached the square to take Lena on to Mrs Beard's. And Byron talking quietly, thinking, remembering: It was like something gone through the air, the evening, making the familiar faces of men appear strange, and he, who had not yet heard, without having to know that something had happened which made of the former dilemma of his innocence a matter for children, so that he knew before he knew what had happened, that Lena must not hear about it. He did not even have to be told in words that he had surely found the lost Lucas Burch; it seemed to him now that only the crassest fatuousness and imbecility should have kept him unaware. It seemed to him that fate, circumstance, had set a warning in the sky all day long in that pillar of yellow smoke, and he too stupid to read it. And so he would not let them tell—the men whom they passed, the air that blew upon them full of it—lest she hear too. Perhaps he knew at the time that she would have to know, hear, it sooner or later; that in a way it was her right to know. It just seemed to him that if he could only get her across the square and into a house his responsibility would be discharged. Not responsibility for the evil to which he held himself for no other reason than that of having spent the afternoon with her while it was happening, having been chosen by circumstance to represent Jefferson to her who had come afoot and without money for thirty days in order to reach there. He did not hope nor intend to avoid that responsibility. It was just to give himself and her time to be shocked and surprised. He tells it quietly, fumbling, his face lowered, in his flat, inflectionless voice, while across the desk Hightower watches him with that expression of shrinking and denial.

They reached the boarding house at last and entered it. It was as though she felt foreboding too, watching him as they stood in the hall, speaking for the first time: "What is it them men were trying to tell you? What is it about that burned house?"

"It wasn't anything," he said, his voice sounding dry and light to him. "Just something about Miss Burden got hurt in the fire."

"How got hurt? How bad hurt?"

"I reckon not bad. Maybe not hurt at all. Just folks talking, like as not. Like they will." He could not look at her, meet her eyes at all. But he could feel her watching him, and he seemed to hear a myriad sounds: voices, the hushed tense voices about the town, about the square through which he had hurried her, where men met among the safe and familiar lights, telling it. The house too seemed filled with familiar sounds, but mostly with inertia, a terrible procrastination as he gazed down the dim hall, thinking *Why dont she come on. Why dont she come on* Then Mrs Beard did come: a comfortable woman, with red arms and untidy grayish hair. "This here is Miz Burch," he said. His expression was almost a glare: importunate, urgent. "She just got to town from Alabama. She is looking to meet her husband here. He aint come yet. So I brought her here, where she can rest some before she gets mixed up in the excitement of town. She aint been in town or talked to anybody yet, and so I thought maybe you could fix her up a place to get rested some before she has to hear talking and. . . . . . ." His voice ceased, died, recapitulant, urgent, importunate. Then he believed that she had got his meaning. Later he knew that it was not because of his asking that she refrained from telling what he knew that she had also heard, but because she had already noticed the pregnancy and that she would have kept the matter hidden anyway. She looked at Lena, once, completely, as strange women had been doing for four weeks now.

"How long does she aim to stay?" Mrs Beard said.

"Just a night or two," Byron said. "Maybe just tonight. She's looking to meet her husband here. She just got in, and she aint had time to ask or inquire——" His voice was still recapitulant, meaningful. Mrs Beard watched him now. He thought that she was still trying to get his meaning. But what she was doing was watching him grope, believing (or about to believe) that his fumbling had a different reason and meaning. Then she looked at Lena again. Her eyes were not exactly cold. But they were not warm.

"I reckon she aint got any business trying to go anywhere right now," she said.

"That's what I thought," Byron said, quickly, eagerly. "With all the talk and excitement she might have to listen to, after not hearing no talk and excitement. . . . . . . If you are crowded tonight, I thought she might have my room."

"Yes," Mrs Beard said immediately. "You'll be taking out in a few minutes, anyway. You want her to have your room until you get back Monday morning?"

"I aint going tonight," Byron said. He did not look away. "I wont be able to go this time." He looked straight into cold, already disbelieving eyes, watching her in turn trying to read his own, believing that she read what was there instead of what she believed was there. They say that it is the practiced liar who can deceive. But so often the practiced and chronic liar deceives only himself; it is the man who all his life has been selfconvicted of veracity whose lies find quickest credence.

"Oh," Mrs Beard said. She looked at Lena again. "Aint she got any acquaintances in Jefferson?"

"She dont know nobody here," Byron said. "Not this side of Alabama. Likely Mr Burch will show up in the morning."

"Oh," Mrs Beard said. "Where are you going to sleep?" But she did not wait for an answer. "I reckon I can fix her up a cot in my room for tonight. If she wont object to that."

"That'll be fine," Byron said. "It'll be fine."

When the supper bell rang, he was all prepared. He had found a chance to speak to Mrs Beard. He had spent more time in inventing that lie than any yet. And then it was not necessary; that which he was trying to shield was its own protection. "Them men will be talking about it at the table," Mrs Beard said. "I reckon a woman in her shape (*and having to find a husband named Burch at the same time* she thought with dry irony) aint got no business listening to any more of man's devilment. You bring her in later, after they have all et." Which Byron did. Lena ate heartily again, with that grave and hearty decorum, almost going to sleep in her plate before she had finished.

"It's right tiring, travelling is," she explained.

"You go set in the parlor and I'll fix your cot," Mrs Beard said.

"I'd like to help," Lena said. But even Byron could see that she would not; that she was dead for sleep.

"You go set in the parlor," Mrs Beard said. "I reckon Mr Bunch wont mind keeping you company for a minute or two."

"I didn't dare leave her alone," Byron says. Beyond the desk Hightower has not moved. "And there we was setting, at the very time when it was all coming out down town at the sheriff's office, at the very time when Brown was telling it all; about him and Christmas and the whiskey and all. Only the whiskey wasn't much news to folks, not since he had took Brown for a partner. I reckon the only thing folks wondered about was why Christmas ever took up with Brown. Maybe it was because like not only finds like; it cant even escape from being found by its like. Even when it's just like in one thing, because even them two with the same like was different. Christmas dared the law to make money, and Brown dared the law because he never even had sense enough to know he was doing it. Like that night in the barbershop and him drunk and talking loud until Christmas kind of run in and dragged him out. And Mr Maxey said 'What do you reckon that was he pretty near told on himself and that other one?' and Captain McLendon said 'I dont reckon about it at all.' and Mr Maxey said 'Do you reckon they was actually holding up somebody else's liquor truck?' and McLendon said 'Would it surprise you to hear that that fellow Christmas hadn't done no worse than that in his life?'

"That's what Brown was telling last night. But everybody knew about that. They had been saying for a good while that somebody ought to tell Miss Burden. But I reckon there wasn't anybody that wanted to go out there and tell her, because nobody knowed what was going to happen then. I reckon there are folks born here that never even saw her. I dont reckon I'd wanted to go out there to that old house where nobody ever saw her unless maybe it was folks in a passing wagon that would see her now and then standing in the yard in a dress and sunbonnet that some nigger women I know wouldn't have wore for its shape and how it made her look. Or maybe she already knew it. Being a Yankee and all, maybe she didn't mind. And then couldn't nobody have known what was going to happen.

"And so I didn't dare leave her alone until she was in bed. I aimed to come out and see you last night, right away. But I never dared to leave her. Them other boarders was passing up and down the hall and I didn't know when one of them would take a notion to come in and start talking about it and tell the whole thing; I could already hear them talking about it on the porch, and her still watching me with her face all fixed to ask me again about that fire. And so I didn't dare leave her. And we was setting there in the parlor and she couldn't hardly keep her eyes open then, and me telling her how I would find him for her all right, only I wanted to come and talk to a preacher I knowed that could help her to get in touch with him. And her setting there with her eyes closed while I was telling her, not knowing that I knew that her and that fellow wasn't married yet. She thought she had fooled everybody. And she asked me what kind of a man it was that I aimed to tell about her to and I told her and her setting there with her eyes closed so that at last I said 'You aint heard a word I been saying' and she kind of roused up, but without opening her eyes, and said 'Can he still marry folks?' and I said 'What? Can he what?' and she said 'Is he still enough of a preacher to marry folks?' "

Hightower has not moved. He sits erect behind the desk, his forearms parallel upon the armrests of the chair. He wears neither collar nor coat. His face is at once gaunt and flabby; it is as though there were two faces, one imposed upon the other, looking out from beneath the pale, bald skull surrounded by a fringe of gray hair, from behind the twin motionless glares of his spectacles. That part of his torso visible above the desk is shapeless, almost monstrous, with a soft and sedentary obesity. He sits rigid; on his face now that expression of denial and flight has become definite. "Byron," he says; "Byron. What is this you are telling me?"

Byron ceases. He looks quietly at the other, with an expression of commiseration and pity. "I knowed you had not heard yet. I knowed it would be for me to tell you."

They look at one another. "What is it I haven't heard yet?"

"About Christmas. About yesterday and Christmas. Christmas is part nigger. About him and Brown and yesterday."

"Part negro," Hightower says. His voice sounds light, trivial, like a thistle bloom falling into silence without a sound, without any weight. He does not move. For a moment longer he does not move. Then there seems to come over his whole body, as if its parts were mobile like face features, that shrinking and denial, and Byron sees that the still, flaccid, big face is suddenly slick with sweat. But his voice is light and calm. "What about Christmas and Brown and yesterday?" he says.

The sound of music from the distant church has long since ceased. Now there is no sound in the room save the steady shrilling of insects and the monotonous sound of Byron's voice. Beyond the desk Hightower sits erect. Between his parallel and downturned palms and with his lower body concealed by the desk, his attitude is that of an eastern idol.

"It was yesterday morning. There was a countryman coming to town in a wagon with his family. He was the one that found the fire. No: he was the second one to get there, because he told how there was already one fellow there when he broke down the door. He told about how he come into sight of the house and he said to his wife how it was a right smart of smoke coming out of that kitchen, and about how the wagon come on and then his wife said 'That house is afire.' And I reckon maybe he stopped the wagon and they set there in the wagon for a while, looking at the smoke, and I reckon that after a while he said 'It looks like it is.' And I reckon it was his wife that made him get down and go and see. 'They dont know it's afire' she said, I reckon. 'You go up there and tell them'. And he got out of the wagon and went up onto the porch and stood there, hollering 'Hello. Hello' for a while. He told how he could hear the fire then, inside the house, and then he hit the door a lick with his shoulder and went in and then he found the one that had found that fire first. It was Brown. But the countryman didn't know that. He just said it was a drunk man in the hall that looked like he had just finished falling down the stairs, and the countryman said 'Your house is afire, mister' before he realised how drunk the man was. And he told how the drunk man kept on saying how there wasn't nobody upstairs and that the upstairs was all afire anyway and there wasn't any use trying to save anything from up there.

"But the countryman knew there couldn't be that much fire upstairs because the fire was all back toward the kitchen. And besides, the man was too drunk to know, anyway. And he told how he suspected there was something wrong from the way the drunk man was trying to keep him from going upstairs. So he started upstairs, and the drunk fellow trying to hold him back, and he shoved the drunk man away and went on up the stairs. He told how the drunk man tried to follow him, still telling him how it wasn't anything upstairs, and he said that when he come back down again and thought about the drunk fellow, he was gone. But I reckon it was some time before he remembered to think about Brown again. Because he went on up the stairs and begun hollering again, opening the doors, and then he opened the right door and he found her."

He ceases. Then there is no sound in the room save the insects. Beyond the open window the steady insects pulse and beat, drowsy and myriad. "Found her," Hightower says. "It was Miss Burden he found." He does not move. Byron does not look at him. He might be contemplating his hands upon his lap while he talks.

"She was lying on the floor. Her head had been cut pretty near off; a lady with the beginning of gray hair. The man said how he stood there and he could hear the fire and there was smoke in the room itself now, like it had done followed him in. And how he was afraid to try to pick her up and carry her out because her head might come clean off. And then he said how he run back down the stairs again and out the front without even noticing that the drunk fellow was gone, and down to the road and told his wife to whip the team on to the nearest telephone and call for the sheriff too. And how he run back around the house to the cistern and he said he was already drawing up a bucket of water before he realised how foolish that was, with the whole back end of the house afire good now. So he run back into the house and up the stairs again and into the room and jerked a cover off the bed and rolled her onto it and caught up the corners and swung it onto his back like a sack of meal and carried it out of the house and laid it down under a tree. And he said that what he was scared of happened. Because the cover fell open and she was laying on her side, facing one way, and her head was turned clean around like she was looking behind her. And he said how if she could just have done that when she was alive, she might not have been doing it now."

Byron ceases and looks, glances once, at the man beyond the desk. Hightower has not moved. His face about the twin blank glares of the spectacles is sweating quietly and steadily. "And the sheriff come out, and the fire department come too. But there wasn't nothing it could do because there wasn't any water for the hose. And that old house burned all evening and I could see the smoke from the mill and I showed it to her when she come up, because I didn't know then. And they brought Miss Burden to town, and there was a paper at the bank that she had told them would tell what to do with her when she died. It said how she had a nephew in the North where she come from, her folks come from. And they telegraphed the nephew and in two hours they got the answer that the nephew would pay a thousand dollars' reward for who done it.

"And Christmas and Brown were both gone. The sheriff found out how somebody had been living in that cabin, and then right off everybody begun to tell about Christmas and Brown, that had kept it a secret long enough for one of them or maybe both of them to murder that lady. But nobody could find either one of them until last night. The country-man didn't know it was Brown that he found drunk in the house. Folks thought that him and Christmas had both run, maybe. And then last night Brown showed up. He was sober then, and he come onto the square about eight oclock, wild, yelling about how it was Christmas that killed her and making his claim on that thousand dollars. They got the officers and took him to the sheriff's office and they told him the

reward would be his all right soon as he caught Christmas
and proved he done it. And so Brown told. He told about
how Christmas had been living with Miss Burden like man
and wife for three years, until Brown and him teamed up. At
first, when he moved out to live in the cabin with Christmas,
Brown said that Christmas told him he had been sleeping in
the cabin all the time. Then he said how one night he hadn't
gone to sleep and he told how he heard Christmas get up out
of bed and come and stand over Brown's cot for a while, like
he was listening, and then he tiptoed to the door and opened
it quiet and went out. And Brown said how he got up and
followed Christmas and saw him go up to the big house and
go in the back door, like either it was left open for him or he
had a key to it. Then Brown come on back to the cabin and
got into bed. But he said how he couldn't go to sleep for
laughing, thinking about how smart Christmas thought he
was. And he was laying there when Christmas come back in
about a hour. Then he said how he couldn't keep from laughing no longer, and he says to Christmas 'You old son of a
gun'. Then he said how Christmas got right still in the dark,
and how he laid there laughing, telling Christmas how he
wasn't such a slick one after all and joking Christmas about
gray hair and about how if Christmas wanted him to, he
would take it week about with him paying the house rent.

"Then he told how he found out that night that sooner or
later Christmas was going to kill her or somebody. He said
he was laying there, laughing, thinking that Christmas would
just maybe get back in bed again, when Christmas struck a
match. Then Brown said he quit laughing and he laid there
and watched Christmas light the lantern and set it on the box
by Brown's cot. Then Brown said how he wasn't laughing
and he laid there and Christmas standing there by the cot,
looking down at him. 'Now you got a good joke' Christmas
says. 'You can get a good laugh, telling them in the barbershop tomorrow night'. And Brown said he didn't know that
Christmas was mad and that he kind of said something back
to Christmas, not meaning to make him mad, and Christmas
said, in that still way of his: 'You dont get enough sleep. You
stay awake too much. Maybe you ought to sleep more' and
Brown said 'How much more?' and Christmas said 'Maybe

from now on'. And Brown said how he realised then that Christmas was mad and that it wasn't no time to joke him, and he said 'Aint we buddies? What would I want to tell something that aint none of my business? Cant you trust me?' and Christmas said 'I dont know. I dont care, neither. But you can trust me.' And he looked at Brown. 'Cant you trust me?' and Brown said he said 'Yes'.

"And he told then about how he was afraid that Christmas would kill Miss Burden some night, and the sheriff asked him how come he never reported his fear and Brown said he thought how maybe by not saying nothing he could stay out there and prevent it, without having to bother the officers with it; and the sheriff kind of grunted and said that was thoughtful of Brown and that Miss Burden would sholy appreciate it if she knowed. And then I reckon it begun to dawn on Brown that he had a kind of rat smell too. Because he started in telling about how it was Miss Burden that bought Christmas that auto and how he would try to persuade Christmas to quit selling whiskey before he got them both into trouble; and the officers watching him and him talking faster and faster and more and more; about how he had been awake early Saturday morning and saw Christmas get up about dawn and go out. And Brown knew where Christmas was going, and about seven oclock Christmas come back into the cabin and stood there, looking at Brown. 'I've done it,' Christmas says. 'Done what?' Brown says. 'Go up to the house and see,' Christmas says. And Brown said how he was afraid then, but that he never suspected the truth. He just said that at the outside all he expected was that maybe Christmas just beat her some. And he said how Christmas went out again and then he got up and dressed and he was making a fire to cook his breakfast when he happened to look out the door and he said how all the kitchen was afire up at the big house.

" 'What time was this?' the sheriff says.

" 'About eight oclock, I reckon,' Brown says. 'When a man would naturally be getting up. Unless he is rich. And God knows I aint that.'

" 'And that fire wasn't reported until nigh eleven oclock,'

the sheriff says. 'And that house was still burning at three p.m. You mean to say a old wooden house, even a big one, would need six hours to burn down in?'

"And Brown was setting there, looking this way and that, with them fellows watching him in a circle, hemming him in. 'I'm just telling you the truth,' Brown says. 'That's what you asked for.' He was looking this way and that, jerking his head. Then he kind of hollered: 'How do I know what time it was. Do you expect a man doing the work of a nigger slave at a sawmill to be rich enough to own a watch?'

" 'You aint worked at no sawmill nor at anything else in six weeks,' the marshal says. 'And a man that can afford to ride around all day long in a new car can afford to pass the court-house often enough to see the clock and keep up with the time.'

" 'It wasn't none of my car, I tell you!' Brown says. 'It was his. She bought it and give it to him; the woman he murdered give it to him.'

" 'That's neither here nor there,' the sheriff says. 'Let him tell the rest of it.'

"And so Brown went on then, talking louder and louder and faster and faster, like he was trying to hide Joe Brown behind what he was telling on Christmas until Brown could get his chance to make a grab at that thousand dollars. It beats all how some folks think that making or getting money is a kind of game where there are not any rules at all. He told about how even when he saw the fire, he never dreamed that she would still be in the house, let alone dead. He said how he never even thought to look into the house at all; that he was just figuring on how to put out the fire.

" 'And that was round eight a.m.,' the sheriff says. 'Or so you claim. And Hamp Waller's wife never reported that fire until nigh eleven. It took you a right smart while to find out you couldn't put out that fire with your bare hands.' And Brown sitting there in the middle of them (they had locked the door, but the windows was lined with folks' faces against the glass) with his eyes going this way and that and his lip lifted away from his teeth. 'Hamp says that after he broke in the door, there was already a man inside that house,' the sheriff says. 'And that that man tried to keep him from going up the stairs.' And him setting there in the center of them, with his eyes going and going.

"I reckon he was desperate by then. I reckon he could not only see that thousand dollars getting further and further away from him, but that he could begin to see somebody else getting it. I reckon it was like he could see himself with that thousand dollars right in his hand for somebody else to have the spending of it. Because they said it was like he had been saving what he told them next for just such a time as this. Like he had knowed that if it come to a pinch, this would save him, even if it was almost worse for a white man to admit what he would have to admit than to be accused of the murder itself. 'That's right,' he says. 'Go on. Accuse me. Accuse the white man that's trying to help you with what he knows. Accuse the white man and let the nigger go free. Accuse the white and let the nigger run.'

" 'Nigger?' the sheriff said. 'Nigger?'

"It's like he knew he had them then. Like nothing they could believe he had done would be as bad as what he could tell that somebody else had done. 'You're so smart,' he says. 'The folks in this town is so smart. Fooled for three years. Calling him a foreigner for three years, when soon as I watched him three days I knew he wasn't no more a foreigner than I am. I knew before he even told me himself.' And them watching him now, and looking now and then at one another.

" 'You better be careful what you are saying, if it is a white man you are talking about,' the marshal says. 'I dont care if he is a murderer or not.'

" 'I'm talking about Christmas,' Brown says. 'The man that killed that white woman after he had done lived with her in plain sight of this whole town, and you all letting him get further and further away while you are accusing the one fellow that can find him for you, that knows what he done. He's got nigger blood in him. I knowed it when I first saw him. But you folks, you smart sheriffs and such. One time he even admitted it, told me he was part nigger. Maybe he was drunk when he done it: I dont know. Anyway, the next morning after he told me he come to me and he says   (Brown was talking fast now, kind of glaring his eyes and his teeth both around at them, from one to another) he said to me "I made a mistake last night. Dont you make the same one" and I said "How do you mean a mistake?" and he said "You think a minute" and I thought about something he done one night when me and him was in Memphis and I knowed my life wouldn't be worth nothing if I ever crossed him and so I said "I reckon I know what you mean. I aint going to meddle in what aint none of my business. I aint never done that yet, that I know of". And you'd have said that, too,' Brown says, ' way out there, alone in that cabin with him and nobody to hear you if you was to holler. You'd have been scared too, until the folks you was trying to help turned in and accused you of the killing you never done.' And there he sat, with his eyes going and going, and them in the room watching him and the faces pressed against the window from outside.

" 'A nigger,' the marshal said. 'I always thought there was something funny about that fellow.'

"Then the sheriff talked to Brown again. 'And that's why you didn't tell what was going on out there until tonight?'

"And Brown setting there in the midst of them, with his lips snarled back and that little scar by his mouth white as a popcorn. 'You just show me the man that would a done different,' he says. 'That's all I ask. Just show me the man that would a lived with him enough to know him like I done, and done different.'

" 'Well,' the sheriff says, 'I believe you are telling the truth at last. You go on with Buck, now, and get a good sleep. I'll attend to Christmas.'

" 'I reckon that means the jail,' Brown says. 'I reckon you'll lock me up in jail while you get the reward.'

" 'You shut your mouth,' the sheriff says, not mad. 'If that reward is yours, I'll see that you get it. Take him on, Buck.'

"The marshal come over and touched Brown's shoulder and he got up. When they went out the door the ones that had been watching through the window crowded up: 'Have you got him, Buck? Is he the one that done it?'

" 'No,' Buck says. 'You boys get on home. Get on to bed, now.' "

Byron's voice ceases. Its flat, inflectionless, countrybred

singsong dies into silence. He is now looking at Hightower with that look compassionate and troubled and still, watching across the desk the man who sits there with his eyes closed and the sweat running down his face like tears. Hightower speaks: "Is it certain, proved, that he has negro blood? Think, Byron; what it will mean when the people——if they catch. . . . . . . Poor man. Poor mankind."

"That's what Brown says," Byron says, his tone quiet, stubborn, convinced. "And even a liar can be scared into telling the truth, same as a honest man can be tortured into telling a lie."

"Yes," Hightower says. He sits with his eyes closed, erect. "But they have not caught him yet. They have not caught him yet, Byron."

Neither is Byron looking at the other. "Not yet. Not the last I heard. They took some blood hounds out there today. But they hadn't caught him when I heard last."

"And Brown?"

"Brown," Byron says. "Him. He went with them. He may have helped Christmas do it. But I dont reckon so. I reckon that setting fire to the house was about his limit. And why he done that, if he did, I reckon even he dont know. Unless maybe he thought that if the whole thing was just burned up, it would kind of not ever been at all, and then him and Christmas could go on riding around in that new car. I reckon he figured that what Christmas committed was not so much a sin as a mistake." His face is musing, downlooking; again it cracks faintly, with a kind of sardonic weariness. "I reckon he's safe enough. I reckon she can find him now any time she wants, provided him and the sheriff aint out with the dogs. He aint trying to run—not with that thousand dollars hanging over his head, you might say. I reckon he wants to catch Christmas worse than any man of them. He goes with them. They take him out of the jail and he goes along with them, and then they all come back to town and lock Brown up again. It's right queer. Kind of a murderer trying to catch himself to get his own reward. He dont seem to mind though, except to begrudge the time while they aint out on the trail, the time wasted setting down. Yes. I'll tell her tomorrow. I'll just tell her that he is in hock for the time being, him and them two dogs. Maybe I'll take her to town where she can see them, all three of them hitched to the other men, a-straining and yapping."

"You haven't told her yet."

"I aint told her. Nor him. Because he might run again, reward or no reward. And maybe if he can catch Christmas and get that reward, he will marry her in time. But she dont know yet, no more than she knowed yesterday when she got down from that wagon on the square. Swolebellied, getting down slow from that strange wagon, among them strange faces, telling herself with a kind of quiet astonishment, only I dont reckon it was any astonishment in it, because she had come slow and afoot and telling never bothered her: 'My, my. Here I have come clean from Alabama, and now I am in Jefferson at last, sure enough.' "

V

IT WAS after midnight. Though Christmas had been in bed for two hours, he was not yet asleep. He heard Brown before he saw him. He heard Brown approach the door and then blunder into it, in silhouette propping himself erect in the door. Brown was breathing heavily. Standing there between his propped arms, Brown began to sing in a saccharine and nasal tenor. The very longdrawn pitch of his voice seemed to smell of whiskey. "Shut it," Christmas said. He did not move and his voice was not raised. Yet Brown ceased at once. He stood for a moment longer in the door, propping himself upright. Then he let go of the door and Christmas heard him stumble into the room; a moment later he blundered into something. There was an interval filled with hard, labored breathing. Then Brown fell to the floor with a tremendous clatter, striking the cot on which Christmas lay and filling the room with loud and idiot laughter.

Christmas rose from his cot. Invisible beneath him Brown lay on the floor, laughing, making no effort to rise. "Shut it!" Christmas said. Brown still laughed. Christmas stepped across Brown and put his hand out toward where a wooden box that served for table sat, on which the lantern and matches were kept. But he could not find the box, and then he remembered the sound of the breaking lantern when Brown fell. He stooped, astride Brown, and found his collar and hauled him out from beneath the cot and raised Brown's head and began to strike him with his flat hand, short, vicious, and hard, until Brown ceased laughing.

Brown was limp. Christmas held his head up, cursing him in a voice level as whispering. He dragged Brown over to the other cot and flung him onto it, face up. Brown began to laugh again. Christmas put his hand flat upon Brown's mouth and nose, shutting his jaw with his left hand while with the right he struck Brown again with those hard, slow, measured blows, as if he were meting them out by count. Brown had stopped laughing. He struggled. Beneath Christmas' hand he began to make a choked, gurgling noise, struggling. Christmas held him until he ceased and became still. Then Christmas slacked his hand a little. "Will you be quiet now?" he said. "Will you?"

Brown struggled again. "Take your black hand off of me, you damn niggerblooded——" The hand shut down again. Again Christmas struck him with the other hand upon the face. Brown ceased and lay still again. Christmas slacked his hand. After a moment Brown spoke, in a tone cunning, not loud: "You're a nigger, see? You said so yourself. You told me. But I'm white. I'm a wh——" The hand shut down. Again Brown struggled, making a choked whimpering sound beneath the hand, drooling upon the fingers. When he stopped struggling, the hand slacked. Then he lay still, breathing hard.

"Will you now?" Christmas said.

"Yes," Brown said. He breathed noisily. "Let me breathe. I'll be quiet. Let me breathe."

Christmas slacked his hand but he did not remove it. Beneath it Brown breathed easier, his breath came and went easier, with less noise. But Christmas did not remove the hand. He stood in the darkness above the prone body, with Brown's breath alternately hot and cold on his fingers, thinking quietly *Something is going to happen to me. I am going to do something* Without removing his left hand from Brown's face he could reach with his right across to his cot, to his pillow beneath which lay his razor with its five inch blade. But he did not do it. Perhaps thinking had already gone far enough and dark enough to tell him *This is not the right one* Anyway he did not reach for the razor. After a time he removed his hand from Brown's face. But he did not go away. He still stood above the cot, his own breathing so quiet, so calm, as to make no sound even to himself. Invisible too, Brown breathed quieter now, and after a while Christmas returned and sat upon his cot and fumbled a cigarette and a match from his trousers hanging on the wall. In the flare of the match Brown was visible. Before taking the light, Christmas lifted the match and looked at Brown. Brown lay on his back, sprawled, one arm dangling to the floor. His mouth was open. While Christmas watched, he began to snore.

Christmas lit the cigarette and snapped the match toward the open door, watching the flame vanish in midair. Then he was listening for the light, trivial sound which the dead match would make when it struck the floor; and then it seemed to him that he heard it. Then it seemed to him, sitting on the cot in the dark room, that he was hearing a myriad sounds of no greater volume—voices, murmurs, whispers: of trees, darkness, earth; people: his own voice; other voices evocative of names and times and places—which he had been conscious of all his life without knowing it, which were his life, thinking *God perhaps and me not knowing that too* He could see it like a printed sentence, fullborn and already dead *God loves me too* like the faded and weathered letters on a last year's billboard *God loves me too*

He smoked the cigarette down without once touching it with his hand. He snapped it too toward the door. Unlike the match, it did not vanish in midflight. He watched it twinkle end over end through the door. He lay back on the cot, his hands behind his head, as a man lies who does not expect to sleep, thinking *I have been in bed now since ten oclock and I have not gone to sleep. I do not know what time it is but it is later than midnight and I have not yet been asleep* "It's because she started praying over me," he said. He spoke aloud, his voice sudden and loud in the dark room, above Brown's drunken snoring. "That's it. Because she started praying over me."

He rose from the cot. His bare feet made no sound. He stood in the darkness, in his underclothes. On the other cot Brown snored. For a moment Christmas stood, his head turned toward the sound. Then he went on toward the door. In his underclothes and barefoot he left the cabin. It was a little lighter outdoors. Overhead the slow constellations wheeled, the stars of which he had been aware for thirty years and not one of which had any name to him or meant anything at all by shape or brightness or position. Ahead, rising from out a close mass of trees, he could see one chimney and one gable of the house. The house itself was invisible and dark. No light shown and no sound came from it when he approached and stood beneath the window of the room where she slept, thinking *If she is asleep too. If she is asleep* The doors were never locked, and it used to be that at whatever hour between dark and dawn that the desire took him, he would enter the house and go to her bedroom and take his sure way through the darkness to her bed. Sometimes she would be awake and waiting and she would speak his name. At others he would waken her with his hard brutal hand and sometimes take her as hard and as brutally before she was good awake.

That was two years ago, two years behind them now, thinking *Perhaps that is where outrage lies. Perhaps I believe that I have been tricked, fooled. That she lied to me about her age, about what happens to women at a certain age* He said, aloud, solitary, in the darkness beneath the dark window: "She ought not to started praying over me. She would have been all right if she hadn't started praying over me. It was not her fault that she got too old to be any good any more. But she ought to have had better sense than to pray over me." He began to curse her. He stood beneath the dark window, cursing her with slow and calculated obscenity. He was not looking at the window. In the less than halflight he appeared to be watching his body, seeming to watch it turning slow and lascivious in a whispering of gutter filth like a drowned corpse in a thick still black pool of more than water. He touched himself with his flat hands, hard, drawing his hands hard up his abdomen and chest inside his undergarment. It was held together by a single button at the top. Once he had owned garments with intact buttons. A woman had sewed them on. That was for a time, during a time. Then the time passed. After that he would purloin his own garments from the family wash before she could get to them and replace the missing buttons. When she foiled him he set himself deliberately to learn and remember which buttons were missing and had been restored. With his pocket knife and with the cold and bloodless deliberation of a surgeon he would cut off the buttons which she had just replaced.

His right hand slid fast and smooth as the knife blade had ever done, up the opening in the garment. Edgewise it struck the remaining button a light, swift blow. The dark air breathed upon him, breathed smoothly as the garment slipped down his legs, the cool mouth of darkness, the soft cool tongue. Moving again, he could feel the dark air like water; he could feel the dew under his feet as he had never felt dew before. He passed through the broken gate and

stopped beside the road. The August weeds were thightall.
Upon the leaves and stalks dust of a month of passing wagons
lay. The road ran before him. It was a little paler than the
darkness of trees and earth. In one direction town lay. In the
other the road rose to a hill. After a time a light began to
grow beyond the hill, defining it. Then he could hear the car.
He did not move. He stood with his hands on his hips, naked, thighdeep in the dusty weeds, while the car came over
the hill and approached, the lights full upon him. He watched
his body grow white out of the darkness like a kodak print
emerging from the liquid. He looked straight into the headlights as it shot past. From it a woman's shrill voice flew back,
shrieking. "White bastards!" he shouted. "That's not the first
of your bitches that ever saw. . . . . . ." But the car was
gone. There was no one to hear, to listen. It was gone, sucking its dust and its light with it and behind it, sucking with
it the white woman's fading cry. He was cold now. It was as
though he had merely come there to be present at a finality,
and the finality had now occurred and he was free again. He
returned to the house. Beneath the dark window he paused
and hunted and found his undergarment and put it on. There
was no remaining button at all now and he had to hold it
together as he returned to the cabin. Already he could hear
Brown snoring. He stood for a while at the door, motionless
and silent, listening to the long, harsh, uneven suspirations
ending each in a choked gurgle. 'I must have hurt his nose
more than I knew,' he thought. 'Damn son of a bitch.' He
entered and went to his cot, preparing to lie down. He was
in the act of reclining when he stopped, halted, halfreclining.
Perhaps the thought of himself lying there until daylight, with
the drunken man snoring in the darkness and the intervals
filled with the myriad voices, was more than he could bear.
Because he sat up and fumbled quietly beneath his cot and
found his shoes and slipped them on and took from the cot
the single half cotton blanket which composed his bedding,
and left the cabin. About three hundred yards away the stable
stood. It was falling down and there had not been a horse in
it in thirty years, yet it was toward the stable that he went.
He was walking quite fast. He was thinking now, aloud now,
"Why in hell do I want to smell horses?" Then he said,

fumbling: "It's because they are not women. Even a mare horse is a kind of man."

He slept less than two hours. When he waked dawn was just beginning. Lying in the single blanket upon the loosely planked floor of the sagging and gloomy cavern acrid with the thin dust of departed hay and faintly ammoniac with that breathless desertion of old stables, he could see through the shutterless window in the eastern wall the primrose sky and the high, pale morning star of full summer.

He felt quite rested, as if he had slept an unbroken eight hours. It was the unexpected sleep, since he had not expected to sleep at all. With his feet again in the unlaced shoes and the folded blanket beneath his arm he descended the perpendicular ladder, feeling for the rotting and invisible rungs with his feet, lowering himself from rung to rung in onehanded swoops. He emerged into the gray and yellow of dawn, the clean chill, breathing it deep.

The cabin now stood sharp against the increasing east, and the clump of trees also within which the house was hidden save for the single chimney. The dew was heavy in the tall grass. His shoes were wet at once. The leather was cold to his feet; against his bare legs the wet grass blades were like strokes of limber icicles. Brown had stopped snoring. When Christmas entered he could see Brown by the light from the eastern window. He breathed quietly now. 'Sober now,' Christmas thought. 'Sober and dont know it. Poor bastard.' He looked at Brown. 'Poor bastard. He'll be mad when he wakes up and finds out that he is sober again. Take him maybe a whole hour to get back drunk again.' He put down the blanket and dressed, in the serge trousers, the white shirt a little soiled now, the bow tie. He was smoking. Nailed to the wall was a shard of mirror. In the fragment he watched his dim face as he knotted the tie. The stiff hat hung on a nail. He did not take it down. He took instead a cloth cap from another nail, and from the floor beneath his cot a magazine of that type whose covers bear either pictures of young women in underclothes or pictures of men in the

act of shooting one another with pistols. From beneath the
pillow on his cot he took his razor and a brush and a stick
of shaving soap and put them into his pocket.

When he left the cabin it was quite light. The birds were
in full chorus. This time he turned his back on the house. He
went on past the stable and entered the pasture beyond it.
His shoes and his trouser legs were soon sopping with gray
dew. He paused and rolled his trousers gingerly to his knees
and went on. At the end of the pasture woods began. The
dew was not so heavy here, and he rolled his trousers down
again. After a while he came to a small valley in which a
spring rose. He put down the magazine and gathered twigs
and dried brush and made a fire and sat, his back against a
tree and his feet to the blaze. Presently his wet shoes began
to steam. Then he could feel the heat moving up his legs, and
then all of a sudden he opened his eyes and saw the high sun
and that the fire had burned completely out, and he knew that
he had been asleep. 'Damned if I haven't,' he thought.
'Damned if I haven't slept again.'

He had slept more than two hours this time, because the
sun was shining down upon the spring itself, glinting and
glancing upon the ceaseless water. He rose, stretching his
cramped and stiffened back, waking his tingling muscles.
From his pocket he took the razor, the brush, the soap.
Kneeling beside the spring he shaved, using the water's surface for glass, stropping the long bright razor on his
shoe.

He concealed the shaving things and the magazine in a
clump of bushes and put on the tie again. When he left the
spring he bore now well away from the house. When he
reached the road he was a half mile beyond the house. A short
distance further on stood a small store with a gasoline pump
before it. He entered the store and a woman sold him crackers and a tin of potted meat. He returned to the spring, the
dead fire.

He ate his breakfast with his back against the tree, reading
the magazine while he ate. He had previously read but one
story; he began now upon the second one, reading the magazine straight through as though it were a novel. Now and
then he would look up from the page, chewing, into the

sunshot leaves which arched the ditch. 'Maybe I have already done it,' he thought. 'Maybe it is no longer now waiting to be done'. It seemed to him that he could see the yellow day opening peacefully on before him, like a corridor, an arras, into a still chiaroscuro without urgency. It seemed to him that as he sat there the yellow day contemplated him drowsily, like a prone and somnolent yellow cat. Then he read again. He turned the pages in steady progression, though now and then he would seem to linger upon one page, one line, perhaps one word. He would not look up then. He would not move, apparently arrested and held immobile by a single word which had perhaps not yet impacted, his whole being suspended by the single trivial combination of letters in quiet and sunny space, so that hanging motionless and without physical weight he seemed to watch the slow flowing of time beneath him, thinking   *All I wanted was peace* thinking, 'She ought not to started praying over me.'

When he reached the last story he stopped reading and counted the remaining pages. Then he looked at the sun and read again. He read now like a man walking along a street might count the cracks in the pavement, to the last and final page, the last and final word. Then he rose and struck a match to the magazine and prodded it patiently until it was consumed. With the shaving things in his pocket he went on down the ditch.

After a while it broadened: a smooth, sandblanched floor between steep shelving walls choked, flank and crest, with brier and brush. Over it trees still arched, and in a small cove in one flank a mass of dead brush lay, filling the cove. He began to drag the brush to one side, clearing the cove and exposing a short handled shovel. With the shovel he began to dig in the sand which the brush had concealed, exhuming one by one six metal tins with screw tops. He did not unscrew the caps. He laid the tins on their sides and with the sharp edge of the shovel he pierced them, the sand beneath them darkening as the whiskey spurted and poured, the sunny solitude, the air, becoming redolent with alcohol. He emptied them thoroughly, unhurried, his face completely cold, masklike almost. When they were all empty he tumbled them back into the hole and buried them roughly and dragged the brush back and hid the shovel again. The brush hid the stain but it could not hide the scent, the smell. He looked at the sun again. It was now afternoon.

At seven oclock that evening he was in town, in a restaurant on a side street, eating his supper, sitting on a backless stool at a frictionsmooth wooden counter, eating.

At nine oclock he was standing outside the barbershop, looking through the window at the man whom he had taken for a partner. He stood quite still, with his hands in his trousers and cigarette smoke drifting across his still face and the cloth cap worn, like the stiff hat, at that angle at once swaggering and baleful. So cold, so baleful he stood there that Brown inside the shop, among the lights, the air heavy with lotion and hot soap, gesticulant, thickvoiced, in the soiled redbarred trousers and the soiled colored shirt, looked up in midvoice and with his drunken eyes looked into the eyes of the man beyond the glass. So still and baleful that a negro youth shuffling up the street whistling saw Christmas' profile and ceased whistling and edged away and slid past behind him, turning, looking back over his shoulder. But Christmas was moving himself now. It was as if he had just paused there for Brown to look at him.

He went on, not fast, away from the square. The street, a quiet one at all times, was deserted at this hour. It led down through the negro section, Freedman Town, to the station. At seven oclock he would have passed people, white and black, going toward the square and the picture show; at half past nine they would have been going back home. But the picture show had not turned out yet, and he now had the street to himself. He went on, passing still between the homes of white people, from street lamp to street lamp, the heavy shadows of oak and maple leaves sliding like scraps of black velvet across his white shirt. Nothing can look quite as lonely as a big man going along an empty street. Yet though he was not large, not tall, he contrived somehow to look more lonely than a lone telephone pole in the middle of a desert. In the wide, empty, shadowbrooded street he looked like a phantom, a spirit, strayed out of its own world, and lost.

Then he found himself. Without his being aware the street had begun to slope and before he knew it he was in Freedman Town, surrounded by the summer smell and the summer voices of invisible negroes. They seemed to enclose him like bodiless voices murmuring talking laughing in a language not his. As from the bottom of a thick black pit he saw himself enclosed by cabinshapes, vague, kerosenelit, so that the street lamps themselves seemed to be further spaced, as if the black life, the black breathing had compounded the substance of breath so that not only voices but moving bodies and light itself must become fluid and accrete slowly from particle to particle, of and with the now ponderable night inseparable and one.

He was standing still now, breathing quite hard, glaring this way and that. About him the cabins were shaped blackly out of blackness by the faint, sultry glow of kerosene lamps. On all sides, even within him, the bodiless fecundmellow voices of negro women murmured. It was as though he and all other manshaped life about him had been returned to the lightless hot wet primogenitive Female. He began to run, glaring, his teeth glaring, his inbreath cold on his dry teeth and lips, toward the next street lamp. Beneath it a narrow and rutted lane turned and mounted to the parallel street, out of the black hollow. He turned into it running and plunged up the sharp ascent, his heart hammering, and into the higher street. He stopped here, panting, glaring, his heart thudding as if it could not or would not yet believe that the air now was the cold hard air of white people.

Then he became cool. The negro smell, the negro voices, were behind and below him now. To his left lay the square, the clustered lights: low bright birds in stillwinged and tremulous suspension. To the right the street lamps marched on, spaced, intermittent with bitten and unstirring branches. He went on, slowly again, his back toward the square, passing again between the houses of white people. There were people on these porches too, and in chairs upon the lawns; but he could walk quiet here. Now and then he could see them: heads in silhouette, a white blurred garmented shape; on a lighted veranda four people sat about a card table, the white faces intent and sharp in the low light, the bare arms of the women glaring smooth and white above the trivial cards. 'That's all I wanted,' he thought. 'That dont seem like a whole lot to ask.'

This street in turn began to slope. But it sloped safely. His steady white shirt and pacing dark legs died among long shadows bulging square and huge against the August stars: a cotton warehouse, a horizontal and cylindrical tank like the torso of a beheaded mastodon, a line of freight cars. He crossed the tracks, the rails coming momentarily into twin green glints from a switch lamp, glinting away again. Beyond the tracks woods began. But he found the path unerringly. It mounted, among the trees, the lights of the town now beginning to come into view again across the valley where the railroad ran. But he did not look back until he reached the crest of the hill. Then he could see the town, the glare, the individual lights where streets radiated from the square. He could see the street down which he had come, and the other street, the one which had almost betrayed him; and further away and at right angles, the far bright rampart of the town itself, and in the angle between the black pit from which he had fled with drumming heart and glaring lips. No light came from it, from here no breath, no odor. It just lay there, black, impenetrable, in its garland of Augusttremulous lights. It might have been the original quarry, abyss itself.

His way was sure, despite the trees, the darkness. He never once lost the path which he could not even see. The woods continued for a mile. He emerged into a road, with dust under his feet. He could see now, the vague spreading world, the horizon. Here and there faint windows glowed. But most of the cabins were dark. Nevertheless his blood began again, talking and talking. He walked fast, in time to it; he seemed to be aware that the group were negroes before he could have seen or heard them at all, before they even came in sight vaguely against the defunctive dust. There were five or six of them, in a straggling body yet vaguely paired; again there reached him, above the noise of his own blood, the rich murmur of womenvoices. He was walking directly toward them, walking fast. They had seen him and they gave to one side of the road, the voices ceasing. He too changed direction, crossing toward them as if he intended to walk them down. In a single movement and as though at a spoken command the women faded back and were going around him, giving him a wide berth. One of the men followed them as if he were driving them before him, looking over his shoulder as he passed. The other two men had halted in the road, facing Christmas. Christmas had stopped also. Neither seemed to be moving, yet they approached, looming, like two shadows drifting up. He could smell negro; he could smell cheap cloth and sweat. The head of the negro, higher than his own, seemed to stoop, out of the sky, against the sky. "It's a white man," he said, without turning his head, quietly. "What you want, whitefolks? You looking for somebody?" The voice was not threatful. Neither was it servile.

"Come on away from there, Jupe," the one who had followed the women said.

"Who you looking for, cap'm?" the negro said.

"Jupe," one of the women said, her voice a little high. "You come on, now."

For a moment longer the two heads, the light and the dark, seemed to hang suspended in the darkness, breathing upon one another. Then the negro's head seemed to float away; a cool wind blew from somewhere. Christmas, turning slowly, watching them dissolve and fade again into the pale road, found that he had the razor in his hand. It was not open. It was not from fear. "Bitches!" he said, quite loud. "Sons of bitches!"

The wind blew dark and cool; the dust even through his shoes was cool. 'What in hell is the matter with me?' he thought. He put the razor back into his pocket and stopped and lit a cigarette. He had to moisten his lips several times to hold the cigarette. In the light of the match he could watch his own hands shake. 'All this trouble,' he thought. "All this damn trouble," he said aloud, walking again. He looked up at the stars, the sky. 'It must be near ten now,' he thought; and then almost with the thought he heard the clock on the courthouse two miles away. Slow, measured, clear the ten strokes came. He counted them, stopped again in the lonely and empty road. 'Ten oclock,' he thought. 'I heard ten strike last night too. And eleven. And twelve. But I didn't hear one. Maybe the wind had changed.'

When he heard eleven strike tonight he was sitting with his back against a tree inside the broken gate, while behind him again the house was dark and hidden in its shaggy grove. He was not thinking *Maybe she is not asleep either* tonight. He was not thinking at all now; thinking had not begun now; the voices had not begun now either. He just sat there, not moving, until after a while he heard the clock two miles away strike twelve. Then he rose and moved toward the house. He didn't go fast. He didn't think even then *Something is going to happen. Something is going to happen to me*

VI

MEMORY BELIEVES before knowing remembers. Believes longer than recollects, longer than knowing even wonders. Knows remembers believes a corridor in a big long garbled cold echoing building of dark red brick sootbleakened by more chimneys than its own, set in a grassless cinder-strewnpacked compound surrounded by smoking factory purlieus and enclosed by a ten foot steel-and-wire fence like a penitentiary or a zoo, where in random erratic surges, with sparrowlike childtrebling, orphans in identical and uniform blue denim in and out of remembering but in knowing constant as the bleak walls, the bleak windows where in rain soot from the yearly adjacenting chimneys streaked like black tears.

In the quiet and empty corridor, during the quiet hour of early afternoon, he was like a shadow, small even for five years, sober and quiet as a shadow. Another in the corridor could not have said just when and where he vanished, into what door, what room. But there was no one else in the corridor at this hour. He knew that. He had been doing this for almost a year, ever since the day when he discovered by accident the toothpaste which the dietitian used.

Once in the room, he went directly on his bare and silent feet to the washstand and found the tube. He was watching the pink worm coil smooth and cool and slow onto his parchmentcolored finger when he heard footsteps in the corridor and then voices just beyond the door. Perhaps he recognised the dietitian's voice. Anyway, he did not wait to see if they were going to pass the door or not. With the tube in his hand and still silent as a shadow on his bare feet he crossed the room and slipped beneath a cloth curtain which screened off one corner of the room. Here he squatted, among delicate shoes and suspended soft womangarments. Crouching, he heard the dietitian and her companion enter the room.

The dietitian was nothing to him yet, save a mechanical adjunct to eating, food, the diningroom, the ceremony of eating at the wooden forms, coming now and then into his vision without impacting at all except as something of pleasing association and pleasing in herself to look at—young, a little fullbodied, smooth, pink-and-white, making his mind think of the diningroom, making his mouth think of something sweet and sticky to eat, and also pinkcolored and surreptitious. On that first day when he discovered the toothpaste in her room he had gone directly there, who had never heard of toothpaste either, as if he already knew that she would possess something of that nature and he would find it. He knew the voice of her companion also. It was that of a young interne from the county hospital who was assistant to the parochial doctor, he too a familiar figure about the house and also not yet an enemy.

He was safe now, behind the curtain. When they went away, he would replace the toothpaste and also leave. So he squatted behind the curtain, hearing without listening to it the woman's tense whispering voice: "No! No! Not here. Not now. They'll catch us. Somebody will——No, Charley! Please!" The man's words he could not understand at all. The voice was lowered too. It had a ruthless sound, as the voices of all men did to him yet, since he was too young yet to escape from the world of women for that brief respite before he escaped back into it to remain until the hour of his death. He heard other sounds which he did know: a scuffing as of feet, the turn of the key in the door. "No, Charley! Charley, please! Please, Charley!" the woman's whisper said. He heard other sounds, rustlings, whisperings, not voices. He was not listening; he was just waiting, thinking without particular interest or attention that it was a strange hour to be going to bed. Again the woman's fainting whisper came through the thin curtain: "I'm scared! Hurry! Hurry!"

He squatted among the soft womansmelling garments and the shoes. He saw by feel alone now the ruined, oncecylindrical tube. By taste and not seeing he contemplated the cool invisible worm as it coiled onto his finger and smeared sharp, automatonlike and sweet, into his mouth. By ordinary he would have taken a single mouthful and then replaced the tube and left the room. Even at five, he knew that he must not take more than that. Perhaps it was the animal warning him that more would make him sick; perhaps the human being warning him that if he took more than that, she would miss it. This was the first time he had taken more. By now, hiding and waiting, he had taken a good deal more. By feel he could see the diminishing tube. He began to sweat. Then he found that he had been sweating for some time, that for some time now he had been doing nothing else but sweating. He was not hearing anything at all now. Very likely he would not have heard a gunshot beyond the curtain. He seemed to be turned in upon himself, watching himself sweating, watching himself smear another worm of paste into his mouth which his stomach did not want. Sure enough, it refused to go down. Motionless now, utterly contemplative, he seemed to stoop above himself like a chemist in his laboratory, waiting. He didn't have to wait long. At once the paste which he had already swallowed lifted inside him, trying to get back out, into the air where it was cool. It was no longer sweet. In the rife, pinkwomansmelling obscurity behind the curtain he squatted, pinkfoamed, listening to his insides, waiting with astonished fatalism for what was about to happen to him. Then it happened. He said to himself with complete and passive surrender: 'Well, here I am.'

When the curtain fled back he did not look up. When hands dragged him violently out of his vomit he did not resist. He hung from the hands, limp, looking with slackjawed and glassy idiocy into a face no longer smooth pink-and-white, surrounded now by wild and dishevelled hair whose smooth bands once made him think of candy. "You little rat!" the thin, furious voice hissed; "you little rat! Spying on me! You little nigger bastard!"

The dietitian was twentyseven—old enough to have to take a few amorous risks but still young enough to attach a great deal of importance not so much to love, but to being caught at it. She was also stupid enough to believe that a child of five not only could deduce the truth from what he had heard, but that he would want to tell it as an adult would. So when during the following two days she could seem to look nowhere and be nowhere without finding the child watching her with the profound and intent interrogation of an animal, she foisted upon him more of the attributes of an adult: she believed that he not only intended to tell, but that he deferred doing it deliberately in order to make her suffer more. It never occurred to her that he believed that he was the one who had been taken in sin and was being tortured with punishment deferred and that he was putting himself in her way in order to get it over with, get his whipping and strike the balance and write it off.

By the second day she was well nigh desperate. She did not sleep at night. She lay most of the night now tense, teeth and hands clenched, panting with fury and terror and worst of all, regret: that blind fury to turn back time just for an hour, a second. This was to the exclusion of even love during the time. The young doctor was now, even less than the child, merely an instrument of her disaster and not even that of her salvation. She could not have said which she hated most. She could not even say when she was asleep and when she was awake. Because always against her eyelids or upon her retinae was that still, grave, inescapable, parchmentcolored face watching her.

On the third day she came out of the coma state, the waking sleep through which during the hours of light and faces she carried her own face like an aching mask in a fixed grimace of dissimulation that dared not flag. On the third day she acted. She had no trouble finding him. It was in the corridor, the empty corridor during the quiet hour after dinner. He was there, doing nothing at all. Perhaps he had followed her. No one else could have said if he were waiting there or not. But she found him without surprise and he heard and turned and saw her without surprise: the two faces, the one no longer smooth pink-and-white, the other grave, sobereyed, perfectly empty of everything except waiting. 'Now I'll get it over with,' he thought.

"Listen," she said. Then she stopped, looking at him. It was as though she could not think what to say next. The child waited, still, motionless. Slowly and gradually the muscles of his backside were becoming flat and rigid and tense as boards. "Are you going to tell?" she said.

He didn't answer. He believed that anyone should have known that the last thing in the world he would do would be to tell about the toothpaste, the vomit. He was not looking at her face. He was watching her hands, waiting. One of them was clenched inside her skirt pocket. Through the cloth he could see that it was clenched hard. He had never been struck with a fist. Yet neither had he ever waited three days to be punished. When he saw the hand emerge from the pocket he believed that she was about to strike him. But she did not; the hand just opened beneath his eyes. Upon it lay a silver dollar. Her voice was thin, urgent, whispering, though the corridor was empty about them. "You can buy a lot with this. A whole dollar." He had never seen a dollar before, though he knew what it was. He looked at it. He wanted it as he would have wanted the bright cap from a beer bottle. But he did not believe that she would give it to him, because he would not give it to her if it were his. He didn't know what she wanted him to do. He was waiting to get whipped and then be released. Her voice went on, urgent, tense, fast: "A whole dollar. See? How much you could buy. Some to eat every day for a week. And next month maybe I'll give you another one."

He did not move nor speak. He might have been carven, a large toy: small, still, round headed and round eyed, in overalls. He was still with astonishment, shock, outrage. Looking at the dollar, he seemed to see ranked tubes of toothpaste like corded wood, endless and terrifying; his whole being coiled in a rich and passionate revulsion. "I dont want no more," he said. 'I dont never want no more,' he thought.

Then he didn't dare even look at her face. He could feel her, hear her, her long shuddering breath. *Now it's coming* he thought in a flashing instant. But she didn't even shake him. She just held him, hard, not shaking him, as if her hand too didn't know what it wanted to do next. Her face was so near that he could feel her breath on his cheek. He didn't need to look up to know what her face looked like now. "Tell!" she said. "Tell, then! You little nigger bastard! You nigger bastard!"

That was the third day. On the fourth day she became quite calmly and completely mad. She no longer planned at all. Her subsequent actions followed a kind of divination, as if the days and the unsleeping nights during which she had nursed behind that calm mask her fear and fury had turned her psychic along with her natural female infallibility for the spontaneous comprehension of evil.

She was quite calm now. She had escaped for the moment from even urgency. It was as though now she had time to look about and plan. Looking about the scene her glance, her mind, her thought, went full and straight and instantaneous to the janitor sitting in the door of the furnace room. There was no ratiocination in it, no design. She just seemed to look outside herself for one moment like a passenger in a car, and saw without any surprise at all that small, dirty man sitting in a splint chair in a sootgrimed doorway, reading through steel-rimmed spectacles from a book upon his knees—a figure, almost a fixture, of which she had been aware for five years now without once having actually looked at him. She would not have recognised his face on the street. She would have passed him without knowing him, even though he was a man. Her life now seemed straight and simple as a corridor with him sitting at the end of it. She went to him at once, already in motion upon the dingy path before she was aware that she had started.

He was sitting in his splint chair in the doorway, the open book upon his knees. When she approached she saw that it was the Bible. But she just noticed this, as she might have noticed a fly upon his leg. "You hate him too," she said. "You've been watching him too. I've seen you. Dont say you dont." He looked up at her face, the spectacles propped now above his brows. He was not an old man. In his present occupation he was an incongruity. He was a hard man, in his prime; a man who should have been living a hard and active life, and whom time, circumstance, something, had betrayed, sweeping the hale body and thinking of a man of fortyfive into a backwater suitable for a man of sixty or sixtyfive. "You know," she said. "You knew before the other children started calling him Nigger. You came out here at the same time. You weren't working here a month before that Christmas night when Charley found him on the doorstep yonder. Tell me." The janitor's face was round, a little flabby, quite dirty, with a dirty stubble. His eyes were quite clear, quite gray, quite cold. They were quite mad too. But the woman did not notice that. Or perhaps they did not look mad to her. So they

faced one another in the coalgrimed doorway, mad eyes looking into mad eyes, mad voice talking to mad voice as calm
and quiet and terse as two conspirators. "I've watched you for
five years." She believed that she was telling the truth. "Sitting here in this very chair, watching him. You never sit here
except when the children are outdoors. But as soon as they
come out, you bring this chair here to the door and sit in it
where you can watch them. Watching him and hearing the
other children calling him Nigger. That's what you are doing.
I know. You came here just to do that, to watch him and hate
him. You were here ready when he came. Maybe you brought
him and left him on the step yonder yourself. But anyway you
know. And I've got to know. When he tells I will be fired.
And Charley may——will——Tell me. Tell me, now."

"Ah," the janitor said. "I knowed he would be there to
catch you when God's time came. I knowed. I know who set
him there, a sign and a damnation for bitchery."

"Yes. He was right behind the curtain. As close as you are.
You tell me, now. I've seen your eyes when you look at him.
Watched you. For five years."

"I know," he said. "I know evil. Aint I made evil to get up
and walk God's world? A walking pollution in God's own
face I made it. Out of the mouths of little children He never
concealed it. You have heard them. I never told them to say
it, to call him in his rightful nature, by the name of his damnation. I never told them. They knowed. They was told, but
it wasn't by me. I just waited, on His own good time, when
He would see fitten to reveal it to His living world. And it's
come now. This is the sign, wrote again in womansinning
and bitchery."

"Yes. But what must I do? Tell me."

"Wait. Like I waited. Five years I waited for the Lord to
move and show His will. And He done it. You wait too.
When He is ready for it He will show His will to them that
have the sayso."

"Yes. The sayso." They glared at one another, still, breathing quietly.

"The madam. When He is ready, He will reveal it to her."

"You mean, if the madam knows, she will send him away?
Yes. But I cant wait."

"No more can you hurry the Lord God. Aint I waited five years?"

She began to beat her hands lightly together. "But dont you see? This may be the Lord's way. For you to tell me. Because you know. Maybe it's His way for you to tell me and me to tell the madam." Her mad eyes were quite calm, her mad voice patient and calm: it was only her light unceasing hands.

"You'll wait, the same as I waited," he said. "You have felt the weight of the Lord's remorseful hand for maybe three days. I have lived under it for five years, watching and waiting for His own good time, because my sin is greater than your sin." Though he was looking directly at her face he did not seem to see her at all, his eyes did not. They looked like they were blind, wide open, icecold, fanatical. "To what I done and what I suffered to expiate it, what you done and are womansuffering aint no more than a handful of rotten dirt. I done bore mine five years; who are you to hurry Almighty God with your little womanfilth?"

She turned, at once. "Well. You dont have to tell me. I know, anyway. I've known it all the time that he's part nigger." She returned to the house. She did not walk fast now and she yawned, terrifically. 'All I have to do is to think of some way to make the madam believe it. He wont tell her, back me up.' She yawned again, tremendously, her face emptied now of everything save yawning and then emptied even of yawning. She had just thought of something else. She had not thought of it before, but she believed that she had, had known it all the while, because it seemed so right: he would not only be removed; he would be punished for having given her terror and worry. 'They'll send him to the nigger orphanage,' she thought. 'Of course. They will have to.'

She did not even go to the matron at once. She had started there, but instead of turning toward the office door she saw herself passing it, going on toward the stairs and mounting. It was as though she followed herself to see where she was going. In the corridor, quiet and empty now, she yawned again, with utter relaxation. She entered her room and locked the door and took off her clothes and got into bed. The shades were drawn and she lay still in the more than halfdark, on her back. Her eyes were closed and her face was empty and smooth. After a while she began to open her legs and close them slowly, feeling the sheets flow cool and smooth over them and then flow warm and smooth again. Thinking seemed to hang suspended between the sleep which she had not had now in three nights and the sleep which she was about to receive, her body open to accept sleep as though sleep were a man. 'All I need do is to make the madam believe,' she thought. And then she thought *He will look just like a pea in a pan full of coffee beans*

That was in the afternoon. At nine that evening she was undressing again when she heard the janitor come up the corridor, toward her door. She did not, could not, know who it was, then somehow she did know, hearing the steady feet and then a knock at the door which already began to open before she could spring to it. She didn't call; she sprang to the door, putting her weight against it, holding it to. "I'm undressing!" she said, in a thin, agonised voice, knowing who it was. He didn't answer, his weight firm and steady against the crawling door, beyond the crawling gap. "You cant come in here!" she cried, hardly louder than a whisper. "Dont you know that they. . . . . ." Her voice was panting, fainting, and desperate. He did not answer. She tried to halt and hold the slow inward crawling of the door. "Let me get some clothes on, and I'll come out there. Will you do that?" She spoke in that fainting whisper, her tone light, inconsequential, like that of one speaking to an unpredictable child or a maniac: soothing, cajoling: "You wait, now. Do you hear? Will you wait, now?" He did not answer. The slow and irresistible crawling of the door did not cease. Leaning against it, wearing nothing save her undergarment, she was like a puppet in some burlesque of rapine and despair. Leaning, downlooking, immobile, she appeared to be in deepest thought, as if the puppet in the midst of the scene had gone astray within itself. Then she turned, releasing the door, and sprang back to the bed, whipping up without looking at it a garment and whirling to face the door, clutching the garment at her breast, huddling. He had already entered; apparently he had been watching her and waiting during the whole blind interval of fumbling and interminable haste.

He still wore the overalls and he now wore his hat. He did not remove it. Again his cold mad gray eyes did not seem to see her, to look at her at all. "If the Lord Himself come into the room of one of you," he said, "you would believe He come in bitchery." He said, "Have you told her?"

The woman sat on the bed. She seemed to sink slowly back upon it, clutching the garment, watching him, her face blanched. "Told her?"

"What will she do with him?"

"Do?" She watched him: those bright, still eyes that seemed not to look at her so much as to envelop her. Her mouth hung open like the mouth of an idiot.

"Where will they send him to?" She didn't answer. "Dont lie to me, to the Lord God. They'll send him to the one for niggers." Her mouth closed; it was as if she had discovered at last what he was talking about. "Ay, I've thought it out. They'll send him to the one for nigger children." She didn't answer, but she was watching him now, her eyes still a little fearful but secret too, calculating. Now he was looking at her; his eyes seemed to contract upon her shape and being. "Answer me, Jezebel!" he shouted.

"Shhhhhhhhh!" she said. "Yes. They'll have to. When they find. . . . . . ."

"Ah," he said. His gaze faded; the eyes released her and enveloped her again. Looking at them, she seemed to see herself as less than nothing in them, trivial as a twig floating upon a pool. Then his eyes became almost human. He began to look about the womanroom as if he had never seen one before: the close room, warm, littered, womanpinksmelling. "Womanfilth," he said. "Before the face of God." He turned and went out. After a while the woman rose. She stood for a time, clutching the garment, motionless, idiotic, staring at the empty door as if she could not think what to tell herself to do. Then she ran. She sprang to the door, flinging herself upon it, crashing it to and locking it, leaning against it, panting, clutching the turned key in both hands.

At breakfast time the next morning the janitor and the child were missing. No trace of them could be found. The police were notified at once. A side door was found to be unlocked, to which the janitor had a key.

"It's because he knows," the dietitian told the matron.

"Knows what?"

"That that child, that Christmas boy, is a nigger."

"A what?" the matron said. Backthrust in her chair, she glared at the younger woman. "A ne——I dont believe it!" she cried. "I dont believe it!"

"You dont have to believe it," the other said. "But he knows it. He stole him away because of it."

The matron was past fifty, flabby faced, with weak, kind, frustrated eyes. "I dont believe it!" she said. But on the third day she sent for the dietitian. She looked as if she had not slept in some time. The dietitian, on the contrary, was quite fresh, quite serene. She was still unshaken when the matron told her the news, that the man and the child had been found. "At Little Rock," the matron said. "He tried to put the child into an orphanage there. They thought he was crazy and held him until the police came." She looked at the younger woman. "You told me. . . . . . The other day you said. . . . . . How did you know about this?"

The dietitian did not look away. "I didn't. I had no idea at all. Of course I knew it didn't mean anything when the other children called him Nigger——"

"Nigger?" the matron said. "The other children?"

"They have been calling him Nigger for years. Sometimes I think that children have a way of knowing things that grown people of your and my age dont see. Children, and old people like him, like that old man. That's why he always sat in the door yonder while they were playing in the yard: watching that child. Maybe he found it out from hearing the other children call him Nigger. But he might have known before hand. If you remember, they came here about the same time. He hadn't been working here hardly a month before the night—that Christmas, dont you remember—when Ch— they found the baby on the doorstep." She spoke smoothly, watching the baffled, shrinking eyes of the older woman full upon her own as though she could not remove them. The dietitian's eyes were bland and innocent. "And so the other day we were talking and he was trying to tell me something about the child. It was something he wanted to tell me, tell somebody, and finally he lost his nerve maybe and wouldn't tell it, and so I left him. I wasn't thinking about it at all. It had gone completely out of my mind when——" Her voice ceased. She gazed at the matron while into her face there came an expression of enlightenment, sudden comprehension; none could have said if it were simulated or not. "Why, that's why it. . . . . . . Why, I see it all, now. What happened just the day before they were gone, missing. I was in the corridor, going to my room; it was the same day I happened to be talking to him and he refused to tell me whatever it was he started to tell, when all of a sudden he came up and stopped me; I thought then it was funny because I had never before seen him inside the house. And he said—he sounded crazy, he looked crazy. I was scared, too scared to move, with him blocking the corridor—he said 'Have you told her yet?' and I said 'Told who? Told who what?' and then I realised he meant you; if I had told you that he had tried to tell me something about the child. But I didn't know what he meant for me to tell you and I wanted to scream and then he said 'What will she do if she finds it out?' and I didn't know what to say or how to get away from him and then he said 'You dont have to tell me. I know what she will do. She will send him to the one for niggers.' "

"For negroes?"

"I dont see how we failed to see it as long as we did. You can look at his face now, his eyes and hair. Of course it's terrible. But that's where he will have to go, I suppose."

Behind her glasses the weak, troubled eyes of the matron had a harried, jellied look, as if she were trying to force them to something beyond their physical cohesiveness. "But why did he want to take the child away?"

"Well, if you want to know what I think, I think he is crazy. If you could have seen him in the corridor that ni— day like I did. Of course it's bad for the child to have to go to the nigger home, after this, after growing up with white people. It's not his fault what he is. But it's not our fault, either—" She ceased, watching the matron. Behind the glasses the older woman's eyes were still harried, weak, hopeless; her mouth was trembling as she shaped speech with it. Her words were hopeless too, but they were decisive enough, determined enough.

"We must place him. We must place him at once. What applications have we? If you will hand me the file. . . . . . ."

When the child wakened, he was being carried. It was pitchdark and cold; he was being carried down stairs by someone who moved with silent and infinite care. Pressed between him and one of the arms which supported him was a wad which he knew to be his clothes. He made no outcry, no sound. He knew where he was by the smell, the air, of the back stairway which led down to the side door from the room in which his bed had been one among forty others since he could remember. He knew also by smell that the person who carried him was a man. But he made no sound, lying as still and as lax as while he had been asleep, riding high in the invisible arms, moving, descending slowly toward the side door which gave onto the playground.

He didn't know who was carrying him. He didn't bother about it because he believed that he knew where he was going. Or why, that is. He didn't bother about where either, yet. It went back two years, to when he was three years old. One day there was missing from among them a girl of twelve named Alice. He had liked her, enough to let her mother him a little; perhaps because of it. And so to him she was as mature, almost as large in size, as the adult women who ordered his eating and washing and sleeping, with the difference that she was not and never would be his enemy. One night she waked him. She was telling him goodbye but he did not know it. He was sleepy and a little annoyed, never full awake, suffering her because she had always tried to be good to him. He didn't know that she was crying because he did not know that grown people cried, and by the time he learned that, memory had forgotten her. He went back into sleep while still suffering her, and the next morning she was gone. Vanished, no trace of her left, not even a garment, the very bed in which she had slept already occupied by a new boy. He never did know where she went to. That day he listened while a few of the older girls who had helped her prepare to leave in that same hushed, secret sibilance in which a half dozen young girls help prepare the seventh one for marriage told, still batebreathed, about the new dress, the new shoes, the carriage which had fetched her away. He knew then that she had gone for good, had passed beyond the iron gates in the steel fence. He seemed to see her then, grown heroic at the instant of vanishment beyond the clashedto gates, fading without diminution of size into something nameless and splendid, like a sunset. It was more than a year before he knew that she had not been the first and would not be the last. That there had been more than Alice to vanish beyond the clashedto gates, in a new dress or new overalls, with a small neat bundle less large sometimes than a shoebox. He believed that that was what was happening to him now. He believed that he knew now how they had all managed to depart without leaving any trace behind them. He believed that they had been carried out, as he was being, in the dead of night.

Now he could feel the door. It was quite near now; he knew to the exact number how many more invisible steps remained to which in turn the man who carried him would lower himself with that infinite and silent care. Against his cheek he could feel the man's quiet, fast, warm breathing; beneath him he could feel the tense and rigid arms, the wadded lump which he knew was his clothing caught up by feel in the dark. The man stopped. As he stooped the child's feet swung down and touched the floor, his toes curling away from the ironcold planks. The man spoke, for the first time. "Stand up," he said. Then the child knew who he was.

He recognised the man at once, without surprise. The surprise would have been the matron's if she had known how well he did know the man. He did not know the man's name and in the three years since he had been a sentient creature they had not spoken a hundred words. But the man was a more definite person than anyone else in his life, not excepting the girl Alice. Even at three years of age the child knew that there was something between them that did not need to be spoken. He knew that he was never on the playground for an instant that the man was not watching him from the chair in the furnace room door, and that the man was watching him with a profound and unflagging attention. If the child had been older he would perhaps have thought *He hates me and fears me. So much so that he cannot let me out of his sight* With more vocabulary but no more age he might have thought *That is why I am different from the others: because he is watching me all the time* He accepted it. So he was not surprised when he found who it was who had taken him, sleeping, from his bed and carried him downstairs; as, standing beside the door in the cold pitch dark while the man helped him put on his clothes, he might have thought *He hates me enough even to try to prevent something that is about to happen to me coming to pass*

He dressed obediently, shivering, as swiftly as he could, the two of them fumbling at the small garments, getting them on him somehow. "Your shoes," the man said, in that dying whisper. "Here." The child sat on the cold floor, putting on the shoes. The man was not touching him now, but the child could hear, feel, that the man was stooped too, engaged in something. 'He's putting on his shoes too,' he thought. The man touched him again, groping, lifting him to his feet. His shoes were not laced. He had not learned to do that by himself yet. He did not tell the man that he had not laced them. He made no sound at all. He just stood there and then a bigger garment enveloped him completely—by its smell he knew that it belonged to the man—and then he was lifted again. The door opened, inyawned. The fresh cold air rushed in, and light from the lamps along the street; he could see the lights the blank factory walls and the tall unsmoking chimneys against the stars. Against the street light the steel fence was like a parade of starved soldiers. As they crossed the empty playground his dangling feet swung rhythmically to the man's striding, the unlaced shoes flapping about his ankles. They reached the iron gates and passed through.

They did not have to wait long for the street car. If he had been older he would have remarked how well the man had timed himself. But he didn't wonder or notice. He just stood on the corner beside the man, in the unlaced shoes, enveloped to the heels in the man's coat, his eyes round and wide, his small face still, awake. The car came up, the row of windows, jarring to a stop and humming while they entered. It was almost empty, since the hour was past two oclock. Now the man noticed the unlaced shoes and laced them, the child watching, quite still on the seat, his legs thrust straight out before him. The station was a long distance away, and he had ridden on a streetcar before, so when they reached the station he was asleep. When he waked it was daylight and they had been on the train for some time. He had never ridden on a train before, but no one could have told it. He sat quite still, as in the streetcar, completely enveloped in the man's coat save for his outthrust legs and his head, watching the country—hills and trees and cows and such—that he had never seen before flowing past. When the man saw that he was awake he produced food from a piece of newspaper. It was bread, with ham between. "Here," the man said. He took the food and ate, looking out the window.

He said no word, he had shown no surprise, not even when on the third day the policemen came and got him and the man. The place where they now were was no different from the one which they had left in the night—the same children, with different names; the same grown people, with different smells: he could see no more reason why he should not have stayed there than why he should ever have left the first one. But he was not surprised when they came and told him again to get up and dress, neglecting to tell him why or where he was going now. Perhaps he knew that he was going back; perhaps with his child's clairvoyance he had known all the while what the man had not: that it would not, could not, last. On the train again he saw the same hills, the same trees, the same cows, but from another side, another direction. The policeman gave him food. It was bread, with ham between, though it did not come out of a scrap of newspaper. He noticed that, but he said nothing, perhaps thought nothing.

Then he was home again. Perhaps he expected to be punished upon his return, for what, what crime exactly, he did not expect to know, since he had already learned that, though children can accept adults as adults, adults can never accept children as anything but adults too. He had already forgot the toothpaste affair. He was now avoiding the dietitian just as, a month ago, he had been putting himself in her way. He was so busy avoiding her that he had long since forgot the reason for it; soon he had forgotten the trip too, since he was never to know that there was any connection between them. Now and then he thought of it, hazily and vaguely. But that was only when he would look toward the door to the furnace room and remember the man who used to sit there and watch him and who was now gone, completely, without leaving any trace, not even the splint chair in the doorway, after the fashion of all who departed from there. Where he may have gone to also the child did not even think or even wonder.

One evening they came to the schoolroom and got him. It was two weeks before Christmas. Two of the young women —the dietitian was not one—took him to the bathroom and washed him and combed his damp hair and dressed him in clean overalls and fetched him to the matron's office. In the office sat a man, a stranger. And he looked at the man and he knew before the matron even spoke. Perhaps memory knowing, knowing beginning to remember; perhaps even desire, since five is still too young to have learned enough despair to hope. Perhaps he remembered suddenly the train ride and the food, since even memory did not go much further back than that. "Joseph," the matron said; "how would you like to go and live with some nice people in the country?"

He stood there, his ears and face red and burning with harsh soap and harsh towelling, in the stiff new overalls, listening to the stranger. He had looked once and saw a thickish man with a close brown beard and hair cut close though not recently. Hair and beard both had a hard, vigorous quality, unsilvered, as though the pigmentation were impervious to the forty and more years which the face revealed. The eyes were lightcolored, cold. He wore a suit of hard, decent black. On his knee rested a black hat held in a blunt clean hand shut, even on the soft felt of the hat, into a fist. Across his vest ran a heavy silver watch chain. His thick black shoes were planted side by side; they had been polished by hand. Even the child of five years, looking at him, knew that he did not use tobacco himself and would not tolerate it in others. But he did not look at the man because of his eyes.

He could feel the man looking at him though, with a stare cold and intent and yet not deliberately harsh. It was the same stare with which he might have examined a horse or a second hand plow, convinced before hand that he would see flaws, convinced before hand that he would buy. His voice was deliberate, infrequent, ponderous; the voice of a man who demanded that he be listened to not so much with attention but in silence. "And you either cannot or will not tell me anything more about his parentage."

The matron did not look at him. Behind her glasses her eyes apparently had jellied, for the time at least. She said immediately, almost a little too immediately: "We make no effort to ascertain their parentage. As I told you before, he was left on the doorstep here on Christmas eve will be five years this two weeks. If the child's parentage is important to you, you had better not adopt one at all."

"I would not mean just that," the stranger said. His tone now was a little placative. He contrived at once to apologise without surrendering one jot of his conviction. "I would have thought to talk with Miss Atkins (this was the dietitian's name) since it was with her I have been in correspondence."

Again the matron's voice was cold and immediate, speaking almost before his had ceased: "I can perhaps give you as much information about this or any other of our children as Miss Atkins can, since her official connection here is only with the diningroom and kitchen. It just happened that in this case she was kind enough to act as secretary in our correspondence with you."

"It's no matter," the stranger said. "It's no matter. I had just thought. . . . . . ."

"Just thought what? We force no one to take our children, nor do we force the children to go against their wishes, if their reasons are sound ones. That is a matter for the two parties to settle between themselves. We only advise."

"Ay," the stranger said. "It's no matter, as I just said to you. I've no doubt the tyke will do. He will find a good home with Mrs McEachern and me. We are not young now, and we like quiet ways. And he'll find no fancy food and no idleness. Nor neither more work than will be good for him. I make no doubt that with us he will grow up to fear God and abhor idleness and vanity despite his origin."

Thus the promissory note which he had signed with a tube

of toothpaste on that afternoon two months ago was recalled, the yet oblivious executor of it sitting wrapped in a clean horse blanket, small, shapeless, immobile, on the seat of a light buggy jolting through the December twilight up a frozen and rutted lane. They had driven all that day. At noon the man had fed him, taking from beneath the seat a cardboard box containing country food cooked three days ago. But only now did the man speak to him. He spoke a single word, pointing up the lane with a mittened fist which clutched the whip, toward a single light which shown in the dusk. "Home," he said. The child said nothing. The man looked down at him. The man was bundled too against the cold, squat, big, shapeless, somehow rocklike, indomitable, not so much ungentle as ruthless. "I said, there is your home." Still the child didn't answer. He had never seen a home, so there was nothing for him to say about it. And he was not old enough to talk and say nothing at the same time. "You will find food and shelter and the care of Christian people," the man said. "And the work within your strength that will keep you out of mischief. For I will have you learn soon that the two abominations are sloth and idle thinking, the two virtues are work and the fear of God." Still the child said nothing. He had neither ever worked nor feared God. He knew less about God than about work. He had seen work going on in the person of men with rakes and shovels about the playground six days each week, but God had only occurred on Sunday. And then—save for the concomitant ordeal of cleanliness—it was music that pleased the ear and words that did not trouble the ear at all——on the whole, pleasant, even if a little tiresome. He said nothing at all. The buggy jolted on, the stout, wellkept team eagering, homing, barning.

There was one other thing which he was not to remember until later, when memory no longer accepted his face, accepted the surface of remembering. They were in the matron's office; he standing motionless, not looking at the stranger's eyes which he could feel upon him, waiting for the stranger to say what his eyes were thinking. Then it came: "Christmas. A heathenish name. Sacrilege. I will change that."

"That will be your legal right," the matron said. "We are not interested in what they are called, but in how they are treated."

But the stranger was not listening to anyone anymore than he was talking to anyone. "From now on his name will be McEachern."

"That will be suitable," the matron said. "To give him your name."

"He will eat my bread and he will observe my religion," the stranger said. "Why should he not bear my name?"

The child was not listening. He was not bothered. He did not especially care, anymore than if the man had said the day was hot when it was not hot. He didn't even bother to say to himself *My name aint McEachern. My name is Christmas* There was no need to bother about that yet. There was plenty of time.

"Why not, indeed?" the matron said.

VII

A ND MEMORY KNOWS this; twenty years later memory is still to believe *On this day I became a man*

The clean, spartan room was redolent of Sunday. In the windows the clean, darned curtains stirred faintly in a breeze smelling of turned earth and crabapple. Upon the yellow imitation oak melodeon with its pedals padded with pieces of frayed and outworn carpet sat a fruit jar filled with larkspur. The boy sat in a straight chair beside the table on which was a nickel lamp and an enormous Bible with brass clasps and hinges and a brass lock. He wore a clean white shirt without a collar. His trousers were dark, harsh, and new. His shoes had been polished recently and clumsily, as a boy of eight would polish them, with small dull patches here and there, particularly about the heels, where the polish had failed to overlap. Upon the table, facing him and open, lay a Presbyterian catechism.

McEachern stood beside the table. He wore a clean, glazed shirt, and the same black trousers in which the boy had first seen him. His hair, damp, still unsilvered, was combed clean and stiff upon his round skull. His beard was also combed, also still damp. "You have not tried to learn it," he said.

The boy did not look up. He did not move. But the face of the man was not more rocklike. "I did try."

"Then try again. I'll give you another hour." From his pocket McEachern took a thick silver watch and laid it faceup on the table and drew up a second straight, hard chair to the table and sat down, his clean, scrubbed hands on his knees, his heavy polished shoes set squarely. On them were no patches where the polish had failed to overlap. There had been last night at suppertime, though. And later the boy, undressed for bed and in his shirt, had received a whipping and then polished them again. The boy sat at the table. His face was bent, still, expressionless. Into the bleak, clean room the springfilled air blew in fainting gusts.

That was at nine oclock. They had been there since eight. There were churches nearby, but the Presbyterian church was five miles away; it would take an hour to drive it. At half past nine Mrs McEachern came in. She was dressed, in black, with a bonnet—a small woman, entering timidly, a little hunched, with a beaten face. She looked fifteen years older than the rugged and vigorous husband. She did not quite enter the room. She just came within the door and stood there for a moment, in her bonnet and her dress of rusty yet often-brushed black, carrying an umbrella and a palm leaf fan, with something queer about her eyes, as if whatever she saw or heard, she saw or heard through a more immediate man-shape or manvoice, as if she were the medium and the vigorous and ruthless husband the control. He may have heard her. But he neither looked up nor spoke. She turned and went away.

Exactly on the dot of the hour McEachern raised his head. "Do you know it now?" he said.

The boy did not move. "No," he said.

McEachern rose, deliberately, without haste. He took up the watch and closed it and returned it to his pocket, looping the chain again through his suspender. "Come," he said. He did not look back. The boy followed, down the hall, toward the rear; he too walked erect and in silence, his head up. There was a very kinship of stubbornness like a transmitted resemblance in their backs. Mrs McEachern was in the kitchen. She still wore the hat, still carried the umbrella and the fan. She was watching the door when they passed it. "Pa," she said. Neither of them so much as looked at her. They might not have heard, she might not have spoken, at all. They went on, in steady single file, the two backs in their rigid abnegation of all compromise more alike than actual blood could have made them. They crossed the back yard and went on toward the stable and entered. McEachern opened the crib door and stood aside. The boy entered the crib. McEachern took from the wall a harness strap. It was neither new nor old, like his shoes. It was clean, like the shoes, and it smelled like the man smelled: an odor of clean hard virile living leather. He looked down at the boy.

"Where is the book?" he said. The boy stood before him, still, his face calm and a little pale beneath the smooth parchment skin. "You did not bring it," McEachern said. "Go back and get it." His voice was not unkind. It was not human, personal, at all. It was just cold, implacable, like written or printed words. The boy turned and went out.

When he reached the house Mrs McEachern was in the hall. "Joe," she said. He did not answer. He didn't even look at her, at her face, at the stiff movement of one half lifted hand in stiff caricature of the softest movement which human hand can make. He walked stiffly past her, rigidfaced, his face rigid with pride perhaps and despair. Or maybe it was vanity, the stupid vanity of a man. He got the catechism from the table and returned to the stable.

McEachern was waiting, holding the strap. "Put it down," he said. The boy laid the book on the floor. "Not there," McEachern said, without heat. "You would believe that a stable floor, the stamping place of beasts, is the proper place for the word of God. But I'll learn you that, too." He took up the book himself and laid it on a ledge. "Take down your pants," he said. "We'll not soil them."

Then the boy stood, his trousers collapsed about his feet, his legs revealed beneath his brief shirt. He stood, slight and erect. When the strap fell he did not flinch, no quiver passed over his face. He was looking straight ahead, with a rapt, calm expression like a monk in a picture. McEachern began to strike methodically, with slow and deliberate force, still without heat or anger. It would have been hard to say which face was the more rapt, more calm, more convinced.

He struck ten times, then he stopped. "Take the book," he said. "Leave your pants be." He handed the boy the catechism. The boy took it. He stood so, erect, his face and the pamphlet lifted, his attitude one of exaltation. Save for surplice he might have been a Catholic choir boy, with for nave the looming and shadowy crib, the rough planked wall beyond which in the ammoniac and dryscented obscurity beasts stirred now and then with snorts and indolent thuds. McEachern lowered himself stiffly to the top of a feed box, spreadkneed, one hand on his knee and the silver watch in the other palm, his clean, bearded face as firm as carved stone, his eyes ruthless, cold, but not unkind.

They remained so for another hour. Before it was up Mrs McEachern came to the back door of the house. But she did not speak. She just stood there, looking at the stable, in the hat, with the umbrella and the fan. Then she went back into the house.

Again on the exact second of the hour McEachern returned the watch to his pocket. "Do you know it now?" he said. The boy didn't answer, rigid, erect, holding the open pamphlet before his face. McEachern took the book from between his hands. Otherwise, the boy did not move at all. "Repeat your catechism," McEachern said. The boy stared straight at the wall before him. His face was now quite white despite the smooth rich pallor of his skin. Carefully and deliberately McEachern laid the book upon the ledge and took up the strap. He struck ten times. When he finished, the boy stood for a moment longer motionless. He had had no breakfast yet; neither of them had eaten breakfast yet. Then the boy staggered and would have fallen if the man had not caught his arm, holding him up. "Come," McEachern said, trying to lead him to the feed box. "Sit down here."

"No," the boy said. His arm began to jerk in the man's grasp. McEachern released him.

"Are you all right? Are you sick?"

"No," the boy said. His voice was faint, his face was quite white.

"Take the book," McEachern said, putting it into the boy's hand. Through the crib window Mrs McEachern came into view, emerging from the house. She now wore a faded mother hubbard and a sunbonnet, and she carried a cedar bucket. She crossed the window without looking toward the crib, and vanished. After a time the slow creak of a well pulley reached them, coming with a peaceful, startling quality upon the sabbath air. Then she appeared again in the window, her body balanced now to the bucket's weight in her hand, and reentered the house without looking toward the stable.

Again on the dot of the hour McEachern looked up from the watch. "Have you learned it?" he said. The boy did not answer, did not move. When McEachern approached he saw that the boy was not looking at the page at all, that his eyes were quite fixed and quite blank. When he put his hand on the book he found that the boy was clinging to it as if it were a rope or a post. When McEachern took the book forcibly from his hands, the boy fell at full length to the floor and did not move again.

When he came to it was late afternoon. He was in his own bed in the attic room with its lowpitched roof. The room was quiet, already filling with twilight. He felt quite well, and he lay for some time, looking peacefully up at the slanted ceiling overhead, before he became aware that there was someone sitting beside the bed. It was McEachern. He now wore his everyday clothes also—not the overalls in which he went to the field, but a faded clean shirt without a collar, and faded, clean khaki trousers. "You are awake," he said. His hand came forth and turned back the cover. "Come," he said.

The boy did not move. "Are you going to whip me again?"

"Come," McEachern said. "Get up." The boy rose from the bed and stood, thin, in clumsy cotton underclothes. McEachern was moving also, thickly, with clumsy, musclebound movements, as if at the expenditure of tremendous effort; the boy, watching with the amazeless interest of a child, saw the man kneel slowly and heavily beside the bed. "Kneel down," McEachern said. The boy knelt; the two of them knelt in the close, twilit room: the small figure in cutdown underwear, the ruthless man who had never known either pity or doubt. McEachern began to pray. He prayed for a long time, his voice droning, soporific, monotonous. He asked that he be forgiven for trespass against the Sabbath and for lifting his hand against a child, an orphan, who was dear to God. He asked that the child's stubborn heart be softened and that the sin of disobedience be forgiven him also, through the advocacy of the man whom he had flouted and disobeyed, requesting that Almighty be as magnanimous as himself, and by and through and because of conscious grace.

He finished and rose, heaving to his feet. The boy still knelt. He did not move at all. But his eyes were open (his face had never been hidden or even lowered) and his face was quite calm; calm, peaceful, quite inscrutable. He heard the man fumble at the table on which the lamp sat. A match scraped, spurted; the flame steadied upon the wick, beneath the globe upon which the man's hand appeared now as if it had been dipped in blood. The shadows whirled and steadied. McEachern lifted something from the table beside the lamp:

the catechism. He looked down at the boy: a nose, a cheek jutting, granitelike, bearded to the caverned and spectacled eyesocket. "Take the book," he said.

It had begun that Sunday morning before breakfast. He had had no breakfast; likely neither he nor the man had once thought of that. The man himself had eaten no breakfast, though he had gone to the table and demanded absolution for the food and for the necessity of eating it. At the noon meal he had been asleep, from nervous exhaustion. And at supper time neither of them had thought of food. The boy did not even know what was wrong with him, why he felt weak and peaceful.

That was how he felt as he lay in bed. The lamp was still burning; it was now full dark outside. Some time had elapsed, but it seemed to him that if he turned his head he would still see the two of them, himself and the man, kneeling beside the bed, or anyway, in the rug the indentations of the twin pairs of knees without tangible substance. Even the air seemed still to excrete that monotonous voice as of someone talking in a dream, talking, adjuring, arguing with a Presence who could not even make a phantom indentation in an actual rug.

He was lying so, on his back, his hands crossed on his breast like a tomb effigy, when he heard again feet on the cramped stairs. They were not the man's; he had heard McEachern drive away in the buggy, departing in the twilight to drive three miles and to a church which was not Presbyterian, to serve the expiation which he had set himself for the morning.

Without turning his head the boy heard Mrs McEachern toil slowly up the stairs. He heard her approach across the floor. He did not look, though after a time her shadow came and fell upon the wall where he could see it, and he saw that she was carrying something. It was a tray of food. She set the tray on the bed. He had not once looked at her. He had not moved. "Joe," she said. He didn't move. "Joe," she said. She could see that his eyes were open. She did not touch him.

"I aint hungry," he said.

She didn't move. She stood, her hands folded into her apron. She didn't seem to be looking at him, either. She seemed to be speaking to the wall beyond the bed. "I know what you think. It aint that. He never told me to bring it to you. It was me that thought to do it. He dont know. It aint any food he sent you." He didn't move. His face was calm as a graven face, looking up at the steep pitch of the plank ceiling. "You haven't eaten today. Sit up and eat. It wasn't him that told me to bring it to you. He dont know it. I waited until he was gone and then I fixed it myself."

He sat up then. While she watched him he rose from the bed and took the tray and carried it to the corner and turned it upside down, dumping the dishes and food and all onto the floor. Then he returned to the bed, carrying the empty tray like it was a monstrance and he the bearer, his surplice the cutdown undergarment which had been bought for a man to wear. She was not watching him now, though she had not moved. Her hands were still rolled into her apron. He got back into bed and lay again on his back, his eyes wide and still upon the ceiling. He could see her motionless shadow, shapeless, a little hunched. Then it went away. He did not look, but he could hear her kneel in the corner, gathering the broken dishes back into the tray. Then she left the room. It was quite still then. The lamp burned steadily above the steady wick; on the wall the flitting shadows of whirling moths were as large as birds. From beyond the window he could smell, feel, darkness, spring, the earth.

He was just eight then. It was years later that memory knew what he was remembering; years after that night when, an hour later, he rose from the bed and went and knelt in the corner as he had not knelt on the rug, and above the outraged food kneeling, with his hands ate, like a savage, like a dog.

It was dusk; already he should have been miles toward home. Although his Saturday afternoons were free, he had never before been this far from home this late. When he reached home he would be whipped. But not for what he might have or might not have done during his absence. When

he reached home he would receive the same whipping though
he had committed no sin as he would receive if McEachern
had seen him commit it.

But perhaps he did not yet know himself that he was not
going to commit the sin. The five of them were gathered quietly in the dusk about the sagging doorway of a deserted sawmill shed where, waiting hidden a hundred yards away, they
had watched the negro girl enter and look back once and then
vanish. One of the older boys had arranged it and he went in
first. The others, boys in identical overalls, who lived within
a three mile radius, who, like the one whom they knew as Joe
McEachern, could at fourteen and fifteen plow and milk and
chop wood like grown men, drew straws for turns. Perhaps
he did not even think of it as a sin until he thought of the
man who would be waiting for him at home, since to fourteen the paramount sin would be to be publicly convicted of
virginity.

His turn came. He entered the shed. It was dark. At once
he was overcome by a terrible haste. There was something in
him trying to get out, like when he had used to think of
toothpaste. But he could not move at once, standing there,
smelling the woman smelling the negro all at once; enclosed
by the womanshenegro and the haste, driven, having to wait
until she spoke: a guiding sound that was no particular word
and completely unaware. Then it seemed to him that he could
see her—something, prone, abject; her eyes perhaps. Leaning, he seemed to look down into a black well and at the
bottom saw two glints like reflections of dead stars. He was
moving, because his foot touched her. Then it touched her
again because he kicked her. He kicked her hard, kicking into
and through a choked wail of surprise and fear. She began to
scream, he jerking her up, clutching her by the arm, hitting
at her with wide, wild blows, striking at the voice perhaps,
feeling her flesh anyway, enclosed by the womanshenegro and
the haste.

Then she fled beneath his fist, and he too fled backward as
the others fell upon him, swarming, grappling, fumbling, he
striking back, his breath hissing with rage and despair. Then
it was male he smelled, they smelled; somewhere beneath it
the She scuttling, screaming. They trampled and swayed,

striking at whatever hand or body touched, until they all went down in a mass, he underneath. Yet he still struggled, fighting, weeping. There was no She at all now. They just fought; it was as if a wind had blown among them, hard and clean. They held him down now, holding him helpless. "Will you quit now? We got you. Promise to quit now."

"No," he said. He heaved, twisting.

"Quit, Joe! You cant fight all of us. Dont nobody want to fight you, anyway."

"No," he said, panting, struggling. None of them could see, tell who was who. They had completely forgot about the girl, why they had fought, if they had ever known. On the part of the other four it had been purely automatic and reflex: that spontaneous compulsion of the male to fight with or because of or over the partner with which he has recently or is about to copulate. But none of them knew why he had fought. And he could not have told them. They held him to the earth, talking to one another in quiet, strained voices.

"Some of you all back there get away. Then the rest of us will turn him loose at the same time."

"Who's got him? Who is this I've got?"

"Here; turn loose. Now wait: here he is. Me and——" Again the mass of them surged, struggled. They held him again. "We got him here. You all turn loose and get out. Give us room."

Two of them rose and backed away, into the door. Then the other two seemed to explode upward out of the earth, the duskfilled shed, already running. Joe struck at them as soon as he was free, but they were already clear. Lying on his back he watched the four of them run on in the dusk, slowing, turning to look back. He rose and emerged from the shed. He stood in the door, brushing himself off, this too purely automatic, while a short distance away they huddled quietly and looked back at him. He did not look at them. He went on, his overalls duskcolored in the dusk. It was late now. The evening star was rich and heavy as a jasmine bloom. He did not look back once. He went on, fading, phantomlike; the four boys who watched him huddled quietly, their faces small and pale with dusk. From the group a voice spoke suddenly, loud: "Yaaah!" He did not look back. A second voice said quietly, carrying quietly, clear: "See you tomorrow at church, Joe." He didn't answer. He went on. Now and then he brushed at his overalls, mechanically, with his hands.

When he came in sight of home all light had departed from the west. In the pasture behind the barn there was a spring: a clump of willows in the darkness smelt and heard but not seen. When he approached the fluting of young frogs ceased like so many strings cut with simultaneous scissors. He knelt; it was too dark to discern even his silhouetted head. He bathed his face, his swollen eye. He went on, crossing the pasture toward the kitchen light. It seemed to watch him, biding and threatful, like an eye.

When he reached the lot fence he stopped, looking at the light in the kitchen window. He stood there for a while, leaning on the fence. The grass was aloud, alive with crickets. Against the dewgray earth and the dark bands of trees fireflies drifted and faded, erratic and random. A mockingbird sang in a tree beside the house. Behind him, in the woods beyond the spring, two whippoorwills whistled. Beyond them, as though beyond some ultimate horizon of summer, a hound howled. Then he crossed the fence and saw someone sitting quite motionless in the door to the stable in which waited the two cows which he had not yet milked.

He seemed to recognise McEachern without surprise, as if the whole situation were perfectly logical and reasonable and inescapable. Perhaps he was thinking then how he and the man could always count upon one another, depend upon one another; that it was the woman alone who was unpredictable. Perhaps he saw no incongruity at all in the fact that he was about to be punished, who had refrained from what McEachern would consider the cardinal sin which he could commit, exactly the same as if he had committed it. McEachern did not rise. He still sat, stolid and rocklike, his shirt a white blur in the door's black yawn. "I have milked and fed," he said. Then he rose, deliberately. Perhaps the boy knew that he already held the strap in his hand. It rose and fell, deliberate, numbered, with deliberate, flat reports. The boy's body might have been wood or stone; a post or a tower upon which the sentient part of him mused like a hermit, contemplative and remote with ecstasy and selfcrucifixion.

As they approached the kitchen they walked side by side. When the light from the window fell upon them the man stopped and turned, leaning, peering. "Fighting," he said. "What was it about?"

The boy did not answer. His face was quite still, composed. After a while he answered. His voice was quiet, cold. "Nothing."

They stood there. "You mean, you cant tell or you wont tell?" The boy did not answer. He was not looking down. He was not looking at anything. "Then, if you dont know you are a fool. And if you wont tell you have been a knave. Have you been to a woman?"

"No," the boy said. The man looked at him. When he spoke his tone was musing.

"You have never lied to me. That I know of, that is." He looked at the boy, at the still profile. "Who were you fighting with?"

"There was more than one."

"Ah," the man said. "You left marks on them, I trust?"

"I dont know. I reckon so."

"Ah," the man said. "Go and wash. Supper is ready."

When he went to bed that night his mind was made up to run away. He felt like an eagle: hard, sufficient, potent, remorseless, strong. But that passed, though he did not then know that, like the eagle, his own flesh as well as all space was still a cage.

McEachern did not actually miss the heifer for two days. Then he found the new suit where it was hidden in the barn; on examining it he knew that it had never been worn. He found the suit in the forenoon. But he said nothing about it. That evening he entered the barn where Joe was milking. Sitting on the low stool, his head bent against the cow's flank, the boy's body was now by height at least the body of a man. But McEachern did not see that. If he saw anything at all, it was the child, the orphan of five years who had sat with the still and alert and unrecking passiveness of an animal on the seat of his buggy on that December evening twelve years ago. "I dont see your heifer," McEachern said. Joe didn't answer. He bent above the bucket, above the steady hissing of milk. McEachern stood behind and above him, looking down at him. "I said, your heifer has not come up."

"I know it," Joe said. "I reckon she is down at the creek. I'll look after her, being as she belongs to me."

"Ah," McEachern said. His voice was not raised. "The creek at night is no place for a fifty dollar cow."

"It'll be my loss, then," Joe said. "It was my cow."

"Was?" McEachern said. "Did you say *was* my cow?"

Joe did not look up. Between his fingers the milk hissed steadily into the pail. Behind him he heard McEachern move. But Joe did not look around until the milk no longer responded. Then he turned. McEachern was sitting on a wooden block in the door. "You had better take the milk on to the house first," he said.

Joe stood, the pail swinging from his hand. His voice was dogged though quiet. "I'll find her in the morning."

"Take the milk on to the house," McEachern said. "I will wait for you here."

For a moment longer Joe stood there. Then he moved. He emerged and went on to the kitchen. Mrs McEachern came in as he was setting the pail onto the table. "Supper is ready," she said. "Has Mr McEachern come to the house yet?"

Joe was turning away, back toward the door. "He'll be in soon," he said. He could feel the woman watching him. She said, in a tone tentative, anxious:

"You'll have just time to wash."

"We'll be in soon." He returned to the barn. Mrs McEachern came to the door and looked after him. It was not yet full dark and she could see her husband standing in the barn door. She did not call. She just stood there and watched the two men meet. She could not hear what they said.

"She will be down at the creek, you say," McEachern said.

"I said she may be. This is a good sized pasture."

"Ah," McEachern said. Both their voices were quiet. "Where do you think she will be?"

"I dont know. I aint no cow. I dont know where she might be."

McEachern moved. "We'll go see," he said. They entered the pasture in single file. The creek was a quarter of a mile distant. Against the dark band of trees where it flowed fireflies winked and faded. They reached these trees. The trunks of them were choked with marshy undergrowth, hard to penetrate even by day. "Call her," McEachern said. Joe did not answer. He did not move. They faced one another.

"She's my cow," Joe said. "You gave her to me. I raised her from a calf because you gave her to me to be my own."

"Yes," McEachern said. "I gave her to you. To teach you the responsibility of possessing, owning, ownership. The responsibility of the owner to that which he owns under God's sufferance. To teach you foresight and aggrandisement. Call her."

For a while longer they faced one another. Perhaps they were looking at one another. Then Joe turned and went on along the marsh, McEachern following. "Why dont you call her?" he said. Joe did not answer. He did not seem to be watching the marsh, the creek, at all. On the contrary he was watching the single light which marked the house, looking back now and then as if he were gauging his distance from it. They did not go fast, yet in time they came to the boundary fence which marked the end of the pasture. It was now full dark. When he reached the fence Joe turned and stopped. Now he looked at the other. Again they stood face to face. Then McEachern said: "What have you done with that heifer?"

"I sold her," Joe said.

"Ah. You sold her. And what did you get for her, might I ask?"

They could not distinguish one another's face now. They were just shapes, almost of a height, though McEachern was the thicker. Above the white blur of his shirt McEachern's head resembled one of the marble cannonballs on Civil War monuments. "It was my cow," Joe said. "If she wasn't mine, why did you tell me she was? Why did you give her to me?"

"You are quite right. She was your own. I have not yet chidden you for selling her, provided you got a good price. And even if you were beat in the trade, which with a boy of eighteen is more than like to be so, I will not chide you for that. Though you would better have asked the advice of some one older in the ways of the world. But you must learn, as I did. What I ask is, Where have you put the money for safekeeping?" Joe didn't answer. They faced one another. "You gave it to your fostermother to keep for you, belike?"

"Yes," Joe said. His mouth said it, told the lie. He had not intended to answer at all. He heard his mouth say the word with a kind of shocked astonishment. Then it was too late. "I gave it to her to put away," he said.

"Ah," McEachern said. He sighed; it was a sound almost luxurious, of satisfaction and victory. "And you will doubtless say also that it was your fostermother who bought the new suit which I found hid in the loft. You have revealed every other sin of which you are capable: sloth, and ingratitude, and irreverence and blasphemy. And now I have taken you in the remaining two: lying and lechery. What else would you want with a new suit if you were not whoring?" And then he acknowledged that the child whom he had adopted twelve years ago was a man. Facing him, the two of them almost toe to toe, he struck at Joe with his fist.

Joe took the first two blows; perhaps from habit, perhaps from surprise. But he took them, feeling twice the man's hard fist crash into his face. Then he sprang back, crouched, licking blood, panting. They faced one another. "Dont you hit me again," he said.

Later, lying cold and rigid in his bed in the attic, he heard their voices coming up the cramped stairs from the room beneath.

"I bought it for him!" Mrs McEachern said. "I did! I bought it with my butter money. You said that I could have . . . . could spend——Simon! Simon!"

"You are a clumsier liar than even he," the man said. His

voice came, measured, harsh, without heat, up the cramped stair to where Joe lay in bed. He was not listening to it. "Kneel down. Kneel down. KNEEL DOWN, WOMAN. Ask grace and pardon of God; not of me."

She had always tried to be kind to him, from that first December evening twelve years ago. She was waiting on the porch—a patient, beaten creature without sex demarcation at all save the neat screw of graying hair and the skirt— when the buggy drove up. It was as though instead of having been subtly slain and corrupted by the ruthless and bigoted man into something beyond his intending and her knowing, she had been hammered stubbornly thinner and thinner like some passive and dully malleable metal, into an attenuation of dumb hopes and frustrated desires now faint and pale as dead ashes.

When the buggy stopped she came forward as though she had already planned it, practiced it: how she would lift him down from the seat and carry him into the house. He had never been carried by a woman since he was big enough to walk. He squirmed down and entered the house on his own feet, marched in, small, shapeless in his wrappings. She followed, hovering about him. She made him sit down; it was as though she hovered about with a kind of strained alertness, an air baffled and alert, waiting to spring in again and try to make himself and her act as she had planned for them to act. Kneeling before him she was trying to take off his shoes, until he realised what she wanted. He put her hands away and removed the shoes himself, not setting them onto the floor though. He held to them. She stripped off his stockings and then she fetched a basin of hot water, fetched it so immediately that anyone but a child would have known that she must have had it ready and waiting all day probably. He spoke for the first time, then. "I done washed just yesterday," he said.

She didn't answer. She knelt before him while he watched the crown of her head and her hands fumbling a little clumsily about his feet. He didn't try to help her now. He didn't know what she was trying to do, not even when he was sitting with his cold feet in the warm water. He didn't know that that was all, because it felt too good. He was waiting for the rest of it to begin; the part that would not be pleasant, whatever it would be. This had never happened to him before either.

Later she put him to bed. For two years almost he had been dressing and undressing himself, unnoticed and unassisted save by occasional Alices. He was already too tired to go to sleep at once, and now he was puzzled and hence nervous, waiting until she went out so he could sleep. Then she did not go out. Instead she drew a chair up to the bed and sat down. There was no fire in the room; it was cold. She had a shawl now about her shoulders, huddled into the shawl, her breath vaporising as though she were smoking. And he became wide awake now. He was waiting for the part to begin which he would not like, whatever it was, whatever it was that he had done. He didn't know that this was all. This had never happened to him before either.

It began on that night. He believed that it was to go on for the rest of his life. At seventeen, looking back he could see now the long series of trivial, clumsy, vain efforts born of frustration and fumbling and dumb instinct: the dishes she would prepare for him in secret and then insist on his accepting and eating them in secret, when he did not want them and he knew that McEachern would not care anyway; the times when, like tonight, she would try to get herself between him and the punishment which, deserved or not, just or unjust, was impersonal, both the man and the boy accepting it as a natural and inescapable fact until she, getting in the way, must give it an odor, an attenuation, an aftertaste.

Sometimes he thought that he would tell her alone. Have her who in her helplessness could neither alter it nor ignore it, know it and need to hide it from the man whose immediate and predictable reaction to the knowledge would so obliterate it as a factor in their relations that it would never appear again. To say to her in secret, in secret payment for the secret dishes which he had not wanted: "Listen. He says he has nursed a blasphemer and an ingrate. I dare you to tell him what he has nursed. That he has nursed a nigger beneath his own roof, with his own food at his own table."

Because she had always been kind to him. The man, the hard, just, ruthless man, merely depended on him to act in a certain way and to receive the as certain reward or punishment, just as he could depend on the man to react in a certain way to his own certain doings and misdoings. It was the woman who, with a woman's affinity and instinct for secrecy, for casting a faint taint of evil about the most trivial and innocent actions. Behind a loose board in the wall of his attic room she had hidden a small hoard of money in a tin can. The amount was trivial and it was apparently a secret to no one but her husband, and the boy believed that he would not have cared. But it had never been a secret from him. Even while he was still a child she would take him with her when with all the intense and mysterious caution of a playing child she would creep to the attic and add to the hoard meagre and infrequent and terrific nickels and dimes (fruit of what small chicanery and deceptions with none anywhere under the sun to say her nay he did not know), putting into the can beneath his round grave eyes coins whose value he did not even recognise. It was she who trusted him, who insisted on trusting him as she insisted on his eating: by conspiracy, in secret, making a secret of the very fact which the act of trusting was supposed to exemplify.

It was not the hard work which he hated, nor the punishment and injustice. He was used to that before he ever saw either of them. He expected no less, and so he was neither outraged nor surprised. It was the woman: that soft kindness which he believed himself doomed to be forever victim of and which he hated worse than he did the hard and ruthless justice of men. 'She is trying to make me cry,' he thought, lying cold and rigid in his bed, his hands beneath his head and the moonlight falling across his body, hearing the steady murmur of the man's voice as it mounted the stairway on its first heavenward stage; 'She was trying to make me cry. Then she thinks that they would have had me.'

VIII

MOVING QUIETLY, he took the rope from its hiding place. One end of it was already prepared for making fast inside the window. Now it took him no time at all to reach the ground and to return; now, with more than a year of practice, he could mount the rope hand over hand, without once touching the wall of the house, with the shadowlike agility of a cat. Leaning from the window he let the free end whisper down. In the moonlight it looked not less frail than a spider skein. Then, with his shoes tied together and strung through his belt behind him, he slid down the rope, passing swift as a shadow across the window where the old people slept. The rope hung directly before the window. He drew it tautly aside, flat against the house, and tied it. Then he went on through the moonlight to the stable and mounted to the loft and took the new suit from its hiding place. It was wrapped in paper, carefully. Before unwrapping it he felt with his hands about the folds of the paper. 'He found it,' he thought. 'He knows.' He said aloud, whispering: "The bastard. The son of a bitch."

He dressed in the dark, swiftly. He was already late, because he had had to give them time to get to sleep after all the uproar about the heifer, the uproar which the woman had caused by meddling after it was all over, settled for the night, anyway. The bundle included a white shirt and a tie. He put the tie into his pocket, but he put on the coat so that the white shirt would not be so visible in the moonlight. He descended and emerged from the stable. The new cloth, after his soft, oftenwashed overalls, felt rich and harsh. The house squatted in the moonlight, dark, profound, a little treacherous. It was as though in the moonlight the house had acquired personality: threatful, deceptive. He passed it and entered the lane. He took from his pocket a dollar watch. He had bought it three days ago, with some of the money. But he had never owned a watch before and so he had forgot to wind it. But he did not need the watch to tell him that he was already late.

The lane went straight beneath the moon, bordered on

each side by trees whose shadowed branches lay thick and sharp as black paint upon the mild dust. He walked fast, the house now behind him, himself now not visible from the house. The highroad passed the lane a short distance ahead. He expected at any moment to see the car rush past, since he had told her that if he were not waiting at the mouth of the lane, he would meet her at the schoolhouse where the dance was being held. But no car passed, and when he reached the highroad he could hear nothing. The road, the night, were empty. 'Maybe she has already passed,' he thought. He took out the dead watch again and looked at it. The watch was dead because he had had no chance to wind it. He had been made late by them who had given him no opportunity to wind the watch and so know if he were late or not. Up the dark lane, in the now invisible house, the woman now lay asleep, since she had done all she could to make him late. He looked that way, up the lane; he stopped in the act of looking and thinking; mind and body as if on the same switch, believing that he had seen movement among the shadows in the lane. Then he thought that he had not, that it might perhaps have been something in his mind projected like a shadow on a wall. 'But I hope it is him,' he thought. 'I wish it was him. I wish he would follow me and see me get into the car. I wish he would try to follow us. I wish he would try to stop me.' But he could see nothing in the lane. It was empty, intermittent with treacherous shadows. Then he heard, from far down the road toward town, the sound of the car. Looking, he saw presently the glare of the lights.

She was a waitress in a small, dingy, back street restaurant in town. Even a casual adult glance could tell that she would never see thirty again. But to Joe she probably did not look more than seventeen too, because of her smallness. She was not only not tall, she was slight, almost childlike. But the adult look saw that the smallness was not due to any natural slenderness but to some inner corruption of the spirit itself: a slenderness which had never been young, in not one of whose curves anything youthful had ever lived or lingered. Her hair was dark. Her face was prominently boned, always down-looking, as if her head were set so on her neck, a little out of line. Her eyes were like the button eyes of a toy animal: a quality beyond even hardness, without being hard.

It was because of her smallness that he ever attempted her, as if her smallness should have or might have protected her from the roving and predatory eyes of most men, leaving his chances better. If she had been a big woman he would not have dared. He would have thought, 'It wont be any use. She will already have a fellow, a man.'

It began in the fall when he was seventeen. It was a day in the middle of the week. Usually when they came to town it would be Saturday and they would bring food with them— cold dinner in a basket purchased and kept for that purpose— with the intention of spending the day. This time McEachern came to see a lawyer, with the intention of finishing his business and being home again by dinnertime. But it was almost twelve oclock when he emerged onto the street where Joe waited for him. He came into sight looking at his watch. Then he looked at a municipal clock in the courthouse tower and then at the sun, with an expression of exasperation and outrage. He looked at Joe also with that expression, the open watch in his hand, his eyes cold, fretted. He seemed to be examining and weighing for the first time the boy whom he had raised from childhood. Then he turned. "Come," he said. "It cant be helped now."

The town was a railroad division point. Even in midweek there were many men about the streets. The whole air of the place was masculine, transient: a population even whose husbands were at home only at intervals and on holiday—a population of men who led esoteric lives whose actual scenes were removed and whose intermittent presence was pandered to like that of patrons in a theatre.

Joe had never before seen the place to which McEachern took him. It was a restaurant on a back street—a narrow dingy doorway between two dingy windows. He did not know that it was a restaurant at first. There was no sign outside and he could neither smell nor hear food cooking. What he saw was a long wooden counter lined with backless stools,

and a big, blonde woman behind a cigar case near the front
and a clump of men at the far end of the counter, not eating,
who all turned as one and looked at him and McEachern
when they entered, through the smoke of cigarettes. Nobody
said anything at all. They just looked at McEachern and Joe
as if breathing had stopped with talking, as if even the cigarette smoke had stopped and now drifted aimlessly of its own
weight. The men were not in overalls and they all wore hats,
and their faces were all alike: not young and not old; not
farmers and not townsmen either. They looked like people
who had just got off a train and who would be gone tomorrow and who did not have any address.

Sitting on two of the backless stools at the counter, Mc-
Eachern and Joe ate. Joe ate fast because McEachern was eating fast. Beside him the man, even in the act of eating,
seemed to sit in a kind of stiffbacked outrage. The food which
McEachern ordered was simple: quickly prepared and quickly
eaten. But Joe knew that parsimony had no part in this. Parsimony might have brought them here in preference to another place, but he knew that it was a desire to depart quickly
that had chosen the food. As soon as he laid down his knife
and fork, McEachern said, "Come", already getting down
from his stool. At the cigar counter McEachern paid the
brasshaired woman. There was about her a quality impervious
to time: a belligerent and diamondsurfaced respectability. She
had not so much as looked at them, even when they entered
and even when McEachern gave her money. Still without
looking at them she made the change, correctly and swiftly,
sliding the coins onto the glass counter almost before Mc-
Eachern had offered the bill; herself somehow definite behind
the false glitter of the careful hair, the careful face, like a
carved lioness guarding a portal, presenting respectability like
a shield behind which the clotted and idle and equivocal men
could slant their hats and their thwartfacecurled cigarettes.
McEachern counted his change and they went out, into the
street. He was looking at Joe again. He said: "I'll have you
remember that place. There are places in this world where a
man may go but a boy, a youth of your age, may not. That
is one of them. Maybe you should never have gone there. But

you must see such so you will know what to avoid and shun. Perhaps it was as well that you saw it with me present to explain and warn you. And the dinner there is cheap."

"What is the matter with it?" Joe said.

"That is the business of the town and not of yours. You will only mark my words: I'll not have you go there again unless I am with you. Which will not be again. We'll bring dinner next time, early or no early."

That was what he saw that day while he was eating swiftly beside the unbending and quietly outraged man, the two of them completely isolated at the center of the long counter with at one end of it the brasshaired woman and at the other the group of men, and the waitress with her demure and downlooking face and her big, too big, hands setting the plates and cups, her head rising from beyond the counter at about the height of a tall child. Then he and McEachern departed. He did not expect ever to return. It was not that McEachern had forbidden him. He just did not believe that his life would ever again chance there. It was as if he said to himself, 'They are not my people. I can see them but I dont know what they are doing nor why. I can hear them but I dont know what they are saying nor why nor to whom. I know that there is something about it beside food, eating. But I dont know what. And I never will know.'

So it passed from the surface of thinking. Now and then during the next six months he returned to town, but he did not again even see or pass the restaurant. He could have. But he didn't think to. Perhaps he did not need to. More often that he knew perhaps thinking would have suddenly flowed into a picture, shaping, shaped: the long, barren, somehow equivocal counter with the still, coldfaced, violenthaired woman at one end as though guarding it, and at the other men with inwardleaning heads, smoking steadily, lighting and throwing away their constant cigarettes, and the waitress, the woman not much larger than a child going back and forth to the kitchen with her arms overladen with dishes, having to pass on each journey within touching distance of the men who leaned with their slanted hats and spoke to her through the cigarette smoke, murmured to her somewhere near mirth or exultation, and her face musing, demure, downcast, as if she had not heard. 'I dont even know what they are saying to her,' he thought, thinking *I dont even know that what they are saying to her is something that men do not say to a passing child* believing *I do not know yet that in the instant of sleep the eyelid closing prisons within the eye's self her face demure, pensive; tragic, sad, and young; waiting, colored with all the vague and formless magic of young desire. That already there is something for love to feed upon: that sleeping I know now why I struck refraining that negro girl three years ago and that she must know it too and be proud too, with waiting and pride*

So he did not expect to see her again, since love in the young requires as little of hope as of desire to feed upon. Very likely he was as much surprised by his action and what it inferred and revealed as McEachern would have been. It was on Saturday this time, in the spring now. He had turned eighteen. Again McEachern had to see the lawyer. But he was prepared now. "I'll be there an hour," he said. "You can walk about and see the town." Again he looked at Joe, hard, calculating, again a little fretted, like a just man forced to compromise between justice and judgment. "Here," he said. He opened his purse and took a coin from it. It was a dime. "You might try not to throw it away as soon as you can find someone who will take it. It's a strange thing," he said fretfully, looking at Joe, "but it seems impossible for a man to learn the value of money without first having to learn to waste it. You will be here in one hour."

He took that coin and went straight to the restaurant. He did not even put the coin into his pocket. He did it without plan or design, almost without volition, as if his feet ordered his action and not his head. He carried the dime clutched hot and small in his palm as a child might. He entered the screen door, clumsily, stumbling a little. The blonde woman behind the cigar case (it was as if she had not moved in the six months, not altered one strand of her hard bright brassridged hair or even her dress) watched him. At the far end of the counter the group of men with their tilted hats and their cigarettes and their odor of barbershops, watched him. The proprietor was among them. He noticed, saw, the proprietor for the first time. Like the other men, the proprietor wore a hat and was smoking. He was not a big man, not much bigger

than Joe himself, with a cigarette burning in one corner of his
mouth as though to be out of the way of talking. From that
face squinted and still behind the curling smoke from the cigarette which was not touched once with hand until it burned
down and was spat out and ground beneath a heel, Joe was
to acquire one of his own mannerisms. But not yet. That was
to come later, when life had begun to go so fast that accepting would take the place of knowing and believing. Now he
just looked at the man who leaned upon the counter from the
inward side, in a dirty apron which he wore as a footpad
might assume for the moment a false beard. The accepting
was to come later, along with the whole sum of entire outrage
to credulity: these two people as husband and wife, the establishment as a business for eating, with the successive imported
waitresses clumsy with the cheap dishes of simple food as
business justified; and himself accepting, taking, during his
brief and violent holiday like a young stallion in a state of
unbelieving and ecstatic astonishment in a hidden pasture of
tired and professional mares, himself in turn victim of nameless and unnumbered men.

But that was not yet. He went to the counter, clutching the
dime. He believed that the men had all stopped talking to
watch him, because he could hear nothing now save a vicious
frying sound from beyond the kitchen door, thinking *She's
back there. That's why I dont see her* He slid onto a stool. He
believed that they were all watching him. He believed that
the blonde woman behind the cigar case was looking at him,
and the proprietor too, across whose face now the smoke of
the cigarette would have become quite still in its lazy vapor-
ing. Then the proprietor spoke a single word. Joe knew that he
had not moved nor touched the cigarette. "Bobbie," he said.

A man's name. It was not thinking. It was too fast, too
complete: *She's gone. They have got a man in her place. I have
wasted the dime, like he said* He believed that he could not
leave now; that if he tried to go out, the blonde woman
would stop him. He believed that the men at the back knew
this and were laughing at him. So he sat quite still on the
stool, looking down, the dime clutched in his palm. He did
not see the waitress until the two overlarge hands appeared
upon the counter opposite him and into sight. He could see

the figured pattern of her dress and the bib of an apron and the two bigknuckled hands lying on the edge of the counter as completely immobile as if they were something she had fetched in from the kitchen. "Coffee and pie," he said.

Her voice sounded downcast, quite empty. "Lemon cocoanut chocolate."

In proportion to the height from which her voice came, the hands could not be her hands at all. "Yes," Joe said.

The hands did not move. The voice did not move. "Lemon cocoanut chocolate. Which kind." To the others they must have looked quite strange. Facing one another across the dark, stained, greasecrusted and frictionsmooth counter, they must have looked a little like they were praying: the youth countryfaced, in clean and spartan clothing, with an awkwardness which invested him with a quality unworldly and innocent; and the woman opposite him, downcast, still, waiting, who because of her smallness partook likewise of that quality of his, of something beyond flesh. Her face was highboned, gaunt. The flesh was taut across her cheekbones, circled darkly about the eyes; beneath the lowered lids her eyes seemed to be without depth, as if they could not even reflect. Her lower jaw seemed too narrow to contain two rows of teeth.

"Cocoanut," Joe said. His mouth said it, because immediately he wanted to unsay it. He had only the dime. He had been holding it too hard to have realised yet that it was only a dime. His hand sweated about it, upon it. He believed that the men were watching him and laughing again. He could not hear them and he did not look at them. But he believed that they were. The hands had gone away. Then they returned, setting a plate and a cup before him. He looked at her now, at her face. "How much is pie?" he said.

"Pie is ten cents." She was just standing there before him, beyond the counter, with her big hands again lying on the dark wood, with that quality spent and waiting. She had never looked at him. He said, in a faint, desperate voice:

"I reckon I dont want no coffee."

For a while she did not move. Then one of the big hands moved and took up the coffee cup; hand and cup vanished. He sat still, downlooking too, waiting. Then it came. It was not the proprietor. It was the woman behind the cigar case. "What's that?" she said.

"He dont want the coffee," the waitress said. Her voice, speaking, moved on, as if she had not paused at the question. Her voice was flat, quiet. The other woman's voice was quiet too.

"Didn't he order coffee too?" she said.

"No," the waitress said, in that level voice that was still in motion, going away. "I misunderstood."

When he got out, when his spirit wrung with abasement and regret and passionate for hiding scuttled past the cold face of the woman behind the cigar case, he believed that he knew he would and could never see her again. He did not believe that he could bear to see her again, even look at the street, the dingy doorway, even from a distance, again, not thinking yet *It's terrible to be young. It's terrible. Terrible* When Saturdays came he found, invented, reasons to decline to go to town, with McEachern watching him, though not with actual suspicion yet. He passed the days by working hard, too hard; McEachern contemplated the work with suspicion. But there was nothing which the man could know, deduce. Working was permitted him. Then he could get the nights passed, since he would be too tired to lie awake. And in time even the despair and the regret and the shame grew less. He did not cease to remember it, to react to it. But now it had become wornout, like a gramophone record: familiar only because of the worn threading which blurred the voices. After a while even McEachern accepted a fact. He said:

"I have been watching you lately. And now there is nothing for it but I must misdoubt my own eyes or else believe that at last you are beginning to accept what the Lord has seen fit to allot you. But I will not have you grow vain because I have spoken well of it. You'll have time and opportunity (and inclination too, I dont doubt) to make me regret that I have spoken. To fall into sloth and idleness again. However, reward was created for man the same as chastisement. Do you see that heifer yonder? From today that calf is your own. See that I do not later regret it."

Joe thanked him. Then he could look at the calf and say, aloud: "That belongs to me." Then he looked at it, and it was again too fast and too complete to be thinking: *That is not a gift. It is not even a promise: it is a threat* thinking, 'I didn't ask for it. He gave it to me. I didn't ask for it' believing *God knows, I have earned it*

It was a month later. It was Saturday morning. "I thought you did not like town anymore," McEachern said.

"I reckon one more trip wont hurt me," Joe said. He had a half dollar in his pocket. Mrs McEachern had given it to him. He had asked for a nickel. She insisted that he take the half dollar. He took it, holding it on his palm, cold, contemptuously.

"I suppose not," McEachern said. "You have worked hard, too. But town is no good habit for a man who has yet to make his way."

He did not need to escape, though he would have, even by violence perhaps. But McEachern made it easy. He went to the restaurant, fast. He entered without stumbling now. The waitress was not there. Perhaps he saw, noticed that she wasn't. He stopped at the cigar counter, behind which the woman sat, laying the half dollar on the counter. "I owe a nickel. For a cup of coffee. I said pie and coffee, before I knew that pie was a dime. I owe you a nickel." He did not look toward the rear. The men were there, in their slanted hats and with their cigarettes. The proprietor was there; waiting, Joe heard him at last, in the dirty apron, speaking past the cigarette:

"What is it? What does he want?"

"He says he owes Bobbie a nickel," the woman said. "He wants to give Bobbie a nickel." Her voice was quiet. The proprietor's voice was quiet.

"Well for Christ's sake," he said. To Joe the room was full of listening. He heard, not hearing; he saw, not looking. He was now moving toward the door. The half dollar lay on the glass counter. Even from the rear of the room the proprietor could see it, since he said, "What's that for?"

"He says he owes for a cup of coffee," the woman said.

Joe had almost reached the door. "Here, Jack," the man said. Joe did not stop. "Give him his money," the man said, flatvoiced, not yet moving. The cigarette smoke would curl still across his face, unwinded by any movement. "Give it back to him," the man said. "I dont know what his racket is. But he cant work it here. Give it back to him. You better go back to the farm, Hiram. Maybe you can make a girl there with a nickel."

Now he was in the street, sweating the half dollar, the coin sweating his hand, larger than a cartwheel, feeling. He walked in laughter. He had passed through the door upon it, upon the laughing of the men. It swept and carried him along the street; then it began to flow past him, dying away, letting him to earth, pavement. He and the waitress were facing one another. She did not see him at once, walking swiftly, down-looking, in a dark dress and a hat. Again, stopped, she did not even look at him, having already looked at him, allseeing, like when she had set the coffee and the pie on the counter. She said, "Oh. And you come back to give it to me. Before them. And they kidded you. Well, say."

"I thought you might have had to pay for it, yourself. I thought——"

"Well, say. Can you tie that. Can you, now."

They were not looking at one another, standing face to face. To another they must have looked like two monks met during the hour of contemplation in a garden path. "I just thought that I. . . . . . ."

"Where do you live?" she said. "In the country? Well, say. What's your name?"

"It's not McEachern," he said. "It's Christmas."

"Christmas? Is that your name? Christmas? Well, say."

On the Saturday afternoons during and after adolescence he and the other four or five boys hunted and fished. He saw girls only at church, on Sunday. They were associated with Sunday and with church. So he could not notice them. To do so would be, even to him, a retraction of his religious hatred. But he and the other boys talked about girls. Perhaps some of them—the one who arranged with the negro girl that afternoon, for instance—knew. "They all want to," he told the others. "But sometimes they cant." The others did not know that. They did not know that all girls wanted to, let alone that there were times when they could not. They thought differently. But to admit that they did not know the latter would be to admit that they had not discovered the former. So they listened while the boy told them. "It's something that happens to them once a month." He described his idea of the physical ceremony. Perhaps he knew. Anyway he was graphic enough, convincing enough. If he had tried to describe it as a mental state, something which he only believed, they would not have listened. But he drew a picture, physical, actual, to be discerned by the sense of smell and even of sight. It moved them: the temporary and abject helplessness of that which tantalised and frustrated desire; the smooth and superior shape in which volition dwelled doomed to be at stated and inescapable intervals victims of periodical filth. That was how the boy told it, with the other five listening quietly, looking at one another, questioning and secret. On the next Saturday Joe did not go hunting with them. McEachern thought that he had already gone, since the gun was missing. But Joe was hidden in the barn. He stayed there all that day. On the Saturday following he did go, but alone, early, before the boys called for him. But he did not hunt. He was not three miles from home when in the late afternoon he shot a sheep. He found the flock in a hidden valley and stalked and killed one with the gun. Then he knelt, his hands in the yet warm blood of the dying beast, trembling, drymouthed, backglaring. Then he got over it, recovered. He did not forget what the boy had told him. He just accepted it. He found that he could live with it, side by side with it. It was as if he said, illogical and desperately calm   *All right. It is so, then. But not to me. Not in my life and my love*   Then it was three or four years ago and he had forgotten it, in the sense that a fact is forgotten when it once succumbs to the mind's insistence that it be neither true nor false.

He met the waitress on the Monday night following the Saturday on which he had tried to pay for the cup of coffee. He did not have the rope then. He climbed from his window and dropped the ten feet to the earth and walked the five miles in to town. He did not think at all about how he would get back into his room.

He reached town and went to the corner where she had

told him to wait. It was a quiet corner and he was quite early, thinking *I will have to remember. To let her show me what to do and how to do it and when. To not let her find out that I dont know, that I will have to find out from her*

He had been waiting for over an hour when she appeared. He had been that early. She came up on foot. She came and stood before him, small, with that air steadfast, waiting, downlooking, coming up out of the darkness. "Here you are," she said.

"I got here soon as I could. I had to wait for them to go to sleep. I was afraid I would be late."

"Have you been here long? How long?"

"I dont know. I ran, most of the way. I was afraid I would be late."

"You ran? All them three miles?"

"It's five miles. It's not three."

"Well, say." Then they did not talk. They stood there, two shadows facing one another. More than a year later, remembering that night, he said, suddenly knowing *It was like she was waiting for me to hit her* "Well," she said.

He had begun now to tremble a little. He could smell her, smell the waiting: still, wise, a little weary; thinking *She's waiting for me to start and I dont know how* Even to himself his voice sounded idiotic. "I reckon it's late."

"Late?"

"I thought maybe they would be waiting for you. Waiting up until you. . . . . . ."

"Waiting for. . . . . . Waiting for. . . . . . ." Her voice died, ceased. She said, not moving; they stood like two shadows: "I live with Mame and Max. You know. The restaurant. You ought to remember them, trying to pay that nickel. . . . . . ." She began to laugh. There was no mirth in it, nothing in it. "When I think of that. When I think of you coming in there, with that nickel." Then she stopped laughing. There was no cessation of mirth in that, either. The still, abject, downlooking voice reached him. "I made a mistake tonight. I forgot something." Perhaps she was waiting for him to ask her what it was. But he did not. He just stood there, with the still, downspeaking voice dying somewhere about his ears. He had forgot about the shot sheep. He had lived with the fact which the older boy had told him too long now. With the slain sheep he had bought immunity from it for too long now for it to be alive. So he could not understand at first what she was trying to tell him. They stood at the corner. It was at the edge of town, where the street became a road that ran on beyond the ordered and measured lawns, between small, random houses and barren fields—the small, cheap houses which compose the purlieus of such towns. She said, "Listen. I'm sick tonight." He did not understand. He said nothing. Perhaps he did not need to understand. Perhaps he had already expected some fateful mischance, thinking, 'It was too good to be true, anyway'; thinking too fast for even thought: *In a moment she will vanish. She will not be. And then I will be back home, in bed, not having left it at all* Her voice went on: "I forgot about the day of the month when I told you Monday night. You surprised me, I guess. There on the street Saturday. I forgot what day it was, anyhow. Until after you had gone."

His voice was as quiet as hers. "How sick? Haven't you got some medicine at home that you can take?"

"Haven't I got. . . . . . ." Her voice died. She said, "Well, say." She said suddenly: "It's late. And you with four miles to walk."

"I've already walked it now. I'm here now." His voice was quiet, hopeless, calm. "I reckon it's getting late," he said. Then something changed. Not looking at him, she sensed something before she heard it in his hard voice: "What kind of sickness have you got?"

She didn't answer at once. Then she said, still, downlooking: "You haven't ever had a sweetheart, yet. I'll bet you haven't." He didn't answer. "Have you?" He didn't answer. She moved. She touched him for the first time. She came and took his arm, lightly, in both hands. Looking down, he could see the dark shape of the lowered head which appeared to have been set out of line a little on the neck when she was born. She told him, halting, clumsily, using the only words which she knew perhaps. But he had heard it before. He had already fled backward, past the slain sheep, the price paid for immunity, to the afternoon when, sitting on a creek bank, he had been not hurt or astonished so much as outraged. The arm which she held jerked free. She did not believe that he had intended to strike her; she believed otherwise, in fact. But the result was the same. As he faded on down the road, the shape, the shadow, she believed that he was running. She could hear his feet for some time after she could no longer see him. She did not move at once. She stood as he had left her, motionless, downlooking, as though waiting for the blow which she had already received.

He was not running. But he was walking fast, and in a direction that was taking him further yet from home, from the house five miles away which he had left by climbing from a window and which he had not yet planned any way of re-entering. He went on down the road fast and turned from it and sprang over a fence, into plowed earth. Something was growing in the furrows. Beyond were woods, trees. He reached the woods and entered, among the hard trunks, the branchshadowed quiet, hardfeeling, hardsmelling, invisible. In the notseeing and the hardknowing as though in a cave he seemed to see a diminishing row of suavely shaped urns in moonlight, blanched. And not one was perfect. Each one was cracked and from each crack there issued something liquid, deathcolored, and foul. He touched a tree, leaning his propped arms against it, seeing the ranked and moonlit urns. He vomited.

On the next Monday night he had the rope. He was waiting at the same corner; he was quite early again. Then he saw her. She came up to where he stood. "I thought maybe you wouldn't be here," she said.

"Did you?" He took her arm, drawing her on down the road.

"Where are we going?" she said. He didn't answer, drawing her on. She had to trot to keep up. She trotted clumsily: an animal impeded by that which distinguished her from animals: her heels, her clothes, her smallness. He drew her from the road, toward the fence which he had crossed a week ago. "Wait," she said, the words jolting from her mouth. "The fence——I cant——" As she stooped to go through, between the strands of wire which he had stepped over, her dress caught. He leaned and jerked it free with a ripping sound.

"I'll buy you another one," he said. She said nothing. She let herself be half carried and half dragged among the growing plants, the furrows, and into the woods, the trees.

He kept the rope, neatly coiled, behind the same loose board in his attic room where Mrs McEachern kept her hoard of nickels and dimes, with the difference that the rope was thrust further back into the hole than Mrs McEachern could reach. He had got the idea from her. Sometimes, with the old couple snoring in the room beneath, when he lifted out the silent rope he would think of the paradox. Sometimes he thought about telling her; of showing her where he kept hidden the implement of his sin, having got the idea, learned how and where to hide it, from her. But he knew that she would merely want to help him conceal it; that she would want him to sin in order that she could help him hide it; that she would at last make such a todo of meaningful whispers and signals that McEachern would have to suspect something despite himself.

Thus he began to steal, to take money from the hoard. It is very possible that the woman did not suggest it to him, never mentioned money to him. It is possible that he did not even know that he was paying with money for pleasure. It was that he had watched for years Mrs McEachern hide money in a certain place. Then he himself had something which it was necessary to hide. He put it in the safest place which he knew. Each time he hid or retrieved the rope, he saw the tin can containing money.

The first time he took fifty cents. He debated for some time between fifty cents and a quarter. Then he took the fifty cents because that was the exact sum he needed. With it he bought a stale and flyspecked box of candy from a man who had won it for ten cents on a punching board in a store. He gave it to the waitress. It was the first thing which he had ever given her. He gave it to her as if no one had ever thought of giving her anything before. Her expression was a little strange when she took the tawdry, shabby box into her big hands. She was sitting at the time on her bed in her bedroom in the small house where she lived with the man and woman called Max and Mame. One night about a week before the man came into the room. She was undressing, sitting on the bed while she removed her stockings. He came in and leaned against the bureau, smoking.

"A rich farmer," he said. "John Jacob Astor from the cowshed."

She had covered herself, sitting on the bed, still, down-looking. "He pays me."

"With what? Hasn't he used up that nickel yet?" He looked at her. "A setup for hayseeds. That's what I brought you down here from Memphis for. Maybe I'd better start giving away grub too."

"I'm not doing it on your time."

"Sure. I cant stop you. I just hate to see you. A kid, that never saw a whole dollar at one time in his life. With this town full of guys making good jack, that would treat you right."

"Maybe I like him. Maybe you hadn't thought of that."

He looked at her, at the still and lowered crown of her head as she sat on the bed, her hands on her lap. He leaned against the bureau, smoking. He said, "Mame!" After a while he said again, "Mame! Come in here." The walls were thin. After a while the big blonde woman came up the hall, without haste. They could both hear her. She entered. "Get this," the man said. "She says maybe she likes him best. It's Romeo and Juliet. For sweet Jesus."

The blonde woman looked at the dark crown of the waitress' head. "What about that?"

"Nothing. It's fine. Max Confrey presenting Miss Bobbie Allen, the youth's companion."

"Go out," the woman said.

"Sure. I just brought her change for a nickel." He went out. The waitress had not moved. The blonde woman went to the bureau and leaned against it, looking at the other's lowered head.

"Does he ever pay you?" she said.

The waitress did not move. "Yes. He pays me."

The blonde woman looked at her, leaning against the bureau as Max had done. "Coming all the way down here from Memphis. Bringing it all the way down here to give it away."

The waitress did not move. "I'm not hurting Max."

The blonde woman looked at the other's lowered head. Then she turned and went toward the door. "See that you dont," she said. "This wont last forever. These little towns wont stand for this long. I know. I came from one of them."

Sitting on the bed, holding the cheap, florid candy box in her hands, she sat as she had sat while the blonde woman talked to her. But it was now Joe who leaned against the bureau and looked at her. She began to laugh. She laughed, holding the gaudy box in her bigknuckled hands. Joe watched her. He watched her rise and pass him, her face lowered. She passed through the door and called Max by name. Joe had never seen Max save in the restaurant, in the hat and the dirty apron. When Max entered he was not even smoking. He thrust out his hand. "How are you, Romeo?" he said.

Joe was shaking hands almost before he had recognised the man. "My name's Joe McEachern," he said. The blonde woman had also entered. It was also the first time he had ever seen her save in the restaurant. He saw her enter, watching her, watching the waitress open the box. She extended it.

"Joe brought it to me," she said.

The blonde woman looked at the box, once. She did not even move her hand. "Thanks," she said. The man also looked at the box, without moving his hand.

"Well, well, well," he said. "Sometimes Christmas lasts a good while. Hey, Romeo?" Joe had moved a little away from the bureau. He had never been in the house before. He was looking at the man, with on his face an expression a little placative and baffled though not alarmed, watching the man's inscrutable and monklike face. But he said nothing. It was the waitress who said,

"If you dont like it, you dont have to eat it." He watched Max, watching his face, hearing the waitress' voice; the voice downlooking: "Not doing you nor nobody else any harm . . . . Not on his time. . . . . . ." He was not watching her nor the blonde woman either. He was watching Max, with that expression puzzled, placative, not afraid. The blonde woman now spoke; it was as though they were speaking of him and in his presence and in a tongue which they knew that he did not know.

"Come on out," the blonde woman said.

"For sweet Jesus," Max said. "I was just going to give Romeo a drink on the house."

"Does he want one?" the blonde woman said. Even when she addressed Joe directly it was as if she still spoke to Max. "Do you want a drink?"

"Dont hold him in suspense because of his past behavior. Tell him it's on the house."

"I dont know," Joe said. "I never tried it."

"Never tried anything on the house," Max said. "For sweet Jesus." He had not looked at Joe once again after he entered the room. Again it was as if they talked at and because of him, in a language which he did not understand.

"Come on," the blonde woman said. "Come on, now."

They went out. The blonde woman had never looked at him at all, and the man, without looking at him, had never ceased. Then they were gone. Joe stood beside the bureau. In the middle of the floor the waitress stood, downlooking, with the open box of candy in her hand. The room was close, smelling of stale scent. Joe had never seen it before. He had not believed that he ever would. The shades were drawn. The single bulb burned at the end of a cord, shaded by a magazine page pinned about it and already turned brown from the heat. "It's all right," he said. "It's all right." She didn't answer nor move. He thought of the darkness outside, the night in which they had been alone before. "Let's go," he said.

"Go?" she said. Then he looked at her. "Go where?" she said. "What for?" Still he did not understand her. He watched her come to the bureau and set the box of candy upon it. While he watched, she began to take her clothes off, ripping them off and flinging them down.

He said, "Here? In here?" It was the first time he had ever seen a naked woman, though he had been her lover for a month. But even then he did not even know that he had not known what to expect to see.

That night they talked. They lay in the bed, in the dark, talking. Or he talked, that is. All the time he was thinking 'Jesus. Jesus. So this is it.' He lay naked too, beside her, touching her with his hand and talking about her. Not about where she had come from and what she had even done, but about her body as if no one had ever done this before, with her or with anyone else. It was as if with speech he were learning about women's bodies, with the curiosity of a child. She told him about the sickness of the first night. It did not shock him now. Like the nakedness and the physical shape, it was like something which had never happened or existed before. So he told her in turn what he knew to tell. He told about the negro girl in the mill shed on that afternoon three years ago. He told her quietly and peacefully, lying beside her, touching her. Perhaps he could not even have said if she listened or not. Then he said, "You noticed my skin, my hair," waiting for her to answer, his hand slow on her body.

She whispered also. "Yes. I thought maybe you were a foreigner. That you never come from around here."

"It's different from that, even. More than just a foreigner. You cant guess."

"What? How more different?"

"Guess."

Their voices were quiet. It was still, quiet; night now known, not to be desired, pined for. "I cant. What are you?"

His hand was slow and quiet on her invisible flank. He did not answer at once. It was not as if he were tantalising her. It was as if he just had not thought to speak on. She asked him again. Then he told her. "I got some nigger blood in me."

Then she lay perfectly still, with a different stillness. But he did not seem to notice it. He lay peacefully too, his hand slow up and down her flank. "You're what?" she said.

"I think I got some nigger blood in me." His eyes were closed, his hand slow and unceasing. "I dont know. I believe I have."

She did not move. She said at once: "You're lying."

"All right," he said, not moving, his hand not ceasing.

"I dont believe it," her voice said in the darkness.

"All right," he said, his hand not ceasing.

The next Saturday he took another half dollar from Mrs McEachern's hiding place and gave it to the waitress. A day or two later he had reason to believe that Mrs McEachern had missed the money and that she suspected him of having taken it. Because she lay in wait for him until he knew that she knew that McEachern would not interrupt them. Then she said, "Joe." He paused and looked at her, knowing that she would not be looking at him. She said, not looking at him, her voice flat, level: "I know how a young man growing up needs money. More than p—Mr McEachern gives you. . . . . . ." He looked at her, until her voice ceased and died away. Apparently he was waiting for it to cease. Then he said,

"Money? What do I want with money?"

On the next Saturday he earned two dollars chopping wood for a neighbor. He lied to McEachern about where he was going and where he had been and what he had done there. He gave the money to the waitress. McEachern found out about the work. Perhaps he believed that Joe had hidden the money. Mrs McEachern may have told him so.

Perhaps two nights a week Joe and the waitress went to her room. He did not know at first that anyone else had ever done that. Perhaps he believed that some peculiar dispensation had been made in his favor, for his sake. Very likely until the last he still believed that Max and Mame had to be placated, not for the actual fact, but because of his presence there. But he did not see them again in the house, though he knew that they were there. But he did not know for certain if they knew that he was there or had ever returned after the night of the candy.

Usually they met outside, went somewhere else or just loitered on the way to where she lived. Perhaps he believed up to the last that he had suggested it. Then one night she did not meet him where he waited. He waited until the clock in the courthouse struck twelve. Then he went on to where she lived. He had never done that before, though even then he could not have said that she had ever forbidden him to come there unless she was with him. But he went there that night, expecting to find the house dark and asleep. The house was dark, but it was not asleep. He knew that, that beyond the dark shades of her room people were not asleep and that she was not there alone. How he knew it he could not have said. Neither would he admit what he knew. 'It's just Max,' he thought. 'It's just Max.' But he knew better. He knew that there was a man in the room with her. He did not see her for two weeks, though he knew that she was waiting for him. Then one night he was at the corner when she appeared. He struck her, without warning, feeling her flesh. He knew then what even yet he had not believed. "Oh," she cried. He struck her again. "Not here!" she whispered. "Not here!" Then he found that he was crying. He had not cried since he could remember. He cried, cursing her, striking her. Then she was holding him. Even the reason for striking her was gone then. "Now, now," she said. "Now, now."

They did not leave the corner even that night. They did not walk on loitering nor leave the road. They sat on a sloping grassbank and talked. She talked this time, telling him. It did not take much telling. He could see now what he discovered that he had known all the time: the idle men in the restaurant, with their cigarettes bobbing as they spoke to her in passing, and she going back and forth, constant, downlooking, and abject. Listening to her voice, he seemed to smell the odorreek of all anonymous men above dirt. Her head was a little lowered as she talked, the big hands still on her lap. He could not see, of course. He did not have to see. "I thought you knew," she said.

"No," he said. "I reckon I didn't."

"I thought you did."

"No," he said. "I dont reckon I did."

Two weeks later he had begun to smoke, squinting his face against the smoke, and he drank too. He would drink at night with Max and Mame and sometimes three or four other men and usually another woman or two, sometimes from the town, but usually strangers who would come in from Memphis and stay a week or a month, as waitresses behind the restaurant counter where the idle men gathered all day. He did not always know their names, but he could cock his hat as they did; during the evenings behind the drawn shades of the diningroom at Max's he cocked it so and spoke of the waitress to the others, even in her presence, in his loud, drunken, despairing young voice, calling her his whore. Now and then in Max's car he took her to dances in the country, always careful that McEachern should not hear about it. "I dont know which he would be madder at," he told her; "at you or at the dancing." Once they had to put him to bed, helpless, in the house where he had not even ever dreamed at one time that he could enter. The next morning the waitress drove him out home before daylight so he could get into the house before he was caught. And during the day McEachern watched him with dour and grudging approval.

"But you have still plenty of time to make me regret that heifer," McEachern said.

IX

MCEACHERN LAY in bed. The room was dark, but he was not asleep. He lay beside Mrs McEachern, whom he did believe to be sleeping, thinking fast and hard, thinking 'The suit has been worn. But when. It could not have been during the day, because he is beneath my eyes, except on Saturday afternoons. But on any Saturday afternoon he could go to the barn, remove and hide the fit clothing which I require him to wear, and then don apparel which he would and could need only as some adjunct to sinning.' It was as if he knew then, had been told. That would infer then that the garments were worn in secret, and therefore in all likelihood, at night. And if that were so, he refused to believe that the boy had other than one purpose: lechery. He had never committed lechery himself and he had not once failed to refuse to listen to anyone who talked about it. Yet within about thirty minutes of intensive thinking he knew almost as much of Joe's doings as Joe himself could have told him, with the exception of names and places. Very likely he would not have believed those even from Joe's mouth, since men of his kind usually have just as firmly fixed convictions about the mechanics, the theatring of evil as about those of good. Thus bigotry and clairvoyance were practically one, only the bigotry was a little slow, for as Joe, descending on his rope, slid like a fast shadow across the open and moonfilled window behind which McEachern lay, McEachern did not at once recognise him or perhaps believe what he saw, even though he could see the very rope itself. And when he got to the window Joe had already drawn the rope back and made it fast and was now on his way toward the barn. As McEachern watched him from the window, he felt something of that pure and impersonal outrage which a judge must feel were he to see a man on trial for his life lean and spit on the bailiff's sleeve.

Hidden in the shadows of the lane halfway between the house and the road, he could see Joe at the mouth of the lane. He too heard the car and saw it come up and stop and Joe get into it. Possibly he did not even care who else was in it. Perhaps he already knew, and his purpose had been merely to see in which direction it went. Perhaps he believed that he knew that too, since the car could have gone almost anywhere in a country full of possible destinations with roads that led to them. Because he turned now back toward the house, walking fast, in that same pure and impersonal outrage, as if he believed so that he would be guided by some greater and purer outrage that he would not even need to doubt personal faculties. In carpet slippers, without a hat, his nightshirt thrust into his trousers and his braces dangling, he went straight as an arrow to the stable and saddled his big, old, strong white horse and returned back down the lane and to the road at a heavy gallop, though Mrs McEachern from the kitchen door called his name when he rode out of the lot. He turned into the road at that slow and ponderous gallop, the two of them, man and beast, leaning a little stiffly forward as though in some juggernaut-ish simulation of terrific speed though the actual speed itself was absent, as if in that cold and implacable and un-deviating conviction of both omnipotence and clairvoyance of which they both partook known destination and speed were not necessary.

He rode at that same speed straight to the place which he sought and which he had found out of a whole night and almost a whole half of a county, though it was not that far distant. He had gone hardly four miles when he heard music ahead and then he saw beside the road lights in a school-house, a oneroom building. He had known where the build-ing was, but he had had neither reason nor manner of knowing that there would be a dance held in it. But he rode straight to it and into the random shadows of parked cars and buggies and saddled horses and mules which filled the grove which surrounded the school, and dismounted almost before the horse had stopped. He did not even tether it. He got down, and in the carpet slippers and the dangling braces and his round head and his short, blunt, outraged beard ran to-ward the open door and the open windows where the music came and where kerosenelit shadows passed in a certain or-derly uproar.

Perhaps, if he were thinking at all, he believed that he had been guided and were now being propelled by some militant Michael Himself as he entered the room. Apparently his eyes were not even momentarily at fault with the sudden light and the motion as he thrust among bodies with turned heads as, followed by a wake of astonishment and incipient pandemonium, he ran toward the youth whom he had adopted of his own free will and whom he had tried to raise as he was convinced was right. Joe and the waitress were dancing and Joe had not seen him yet. The woman had never seen him but once, but perhaps she remembered him, or perhaps his appearance now was enough. Because she stopped dancing and upon her face came an expression very like horror, which Joe saw and turned. As he turned, McEachern was upon them. Neither had McEachern ever seen the woman but once, and very likely then he had not looked at her, just as he had refused to listen when men spoke of fornication. Yet he went straight to her, ignoring Joe for the moment. "Away, Jezebel!" he said. His voice thundered, into the shocked silence, the shocked surrounding faces beneath the kerosene lamps, into the ceased music, into the peaceful moonlit night of young summer. "Away, harlot!"

Perhaps it did not seem to him that he had been moving fast nor that his voice was loud. Very likely he seemed to himself to be standing just and rocklike and with neither haste nor anger while on all sides the sluttishness of weak human man seethed in a long sigh of terror about the actual representative of the wrathful and retributive Throne. Perhaps they were not even his hands which struck at the face of the youth whom he had nurtured and sheltered and clothed from a child, and perhaps when the face ducked the blow and came up again it was not the face of that child. But he could not have been surprised at that, since it was not that child's face which he was concerned with: it was the face of Satan, which he knew as well. And when, staring at the face, he walked steadily toward it with his hand still raised, very likely he walked toward it in the furious and dreamlike exaltation of a martyr who has already been absolved, into the descending chair which Joe swung at his head, and into nothingness. Perhaps the nothingness astonished him a little, but not much, and not for long.

Then to Joe it all rushed away, roaring, dying, leaving him in the center of the floor, the shattered chair clutched in his hand, looking down at his adopted father. McEachern lay on his back. He looked quite peaceful now. He appeared to sleep: bluntheaded, indomitable even in repose, even the blood on his forehead peaceful and quiet.

Joe was breathing hard. He could hear it, and also something else, thin and shrill and far away. He seemed to listen to it for a long time before he recognised it for a voice, a woman's voice. He looked and saw two men holding her and she writhing and struggling, her hair shaken forward, her white face wrung and ugly beneath the splotches of savage paint, her mouth a small jagged hole filled with shrieking. "Calling me a harlot!" she screamed, wrenching at the men who held her. "That old son of a bitch! Let go! Let go!" Then her voice stopped making words again and just screamed; she writhed and threshed, trying to bite the hands of the men who struggled with her.

Still carrying the shattered chair Joe walked toward her. About the walls, huddling, clotted, the others watched him: the girls in stiff offcolors and mailorder stockings and heels; the men, young men in illcut and boardlike garments also from the mailorder, with hard, ruined hands and eyes already revealing a heritage of patient brooding upon endless furrows and the slow buttocks of mules. Joe began to run, brandishing the chair. "Let her go!" he said. At once she ceased struggling and turned on him the fury, the shrieking, as if she had just seen him, realised that he was also there.

"And you! You brought me here. Goddamn bastard clodhopper. Bastard you! Son of a bitch you and him too. Putting him at me that never ever saw——" Joe did not appear to be running at anyone in particular, and his face was quite calm beneath the uplifted chair. The others fell back from about the woman, freeing her, though she continued to wrench her arms as if she did not yet realise it.

"Get out of here!" Joe shouted. He whirled, swinging the chair; yet his face was still quite calm. "Back!" he said, though no one had moved toward him at all. They were all as still and as silent as the man on the floor. He swung the chair, backing now toward the door. "Stand back! I said I would kill him some day! I told him so!" He swung the chair about him, calmfaced, backing toward the door. "Dont a one of you move, now," he said, looking steadily and ceaselessly at faces that might have been masks. Then he flung the chair down and whirled and sprang out the door, into soft, dappled moonlight. He overtook the waitress as she was getting into the car in which they had come. He was panting, yet his voice was calm too: a sleeping face merely breathing hard enough to make sounds. "Get on back to town," he said. "I'll be there soon as I. . . . . ." Apparently he was not aware of what he was saying nor of what was happening; when the woman turned suddenly in the door of the car and began to beat him in the face he did not move, his voice did not change: "Yes. That's right. I'll be there soon as I——" Then he turned and ran, while she was still striking at him.

He could not have known where McEachern had left the horse, nor for certain if it was even there. Yet he ran straight to it, with something of his adopted father's complete faith in an infallibility in events. He got onto it and swung it back toward the road. The car had already turned into the road. He saw the taillight diminish and disappear.

The old, strong, farmbred horse returned home at its slow and steady canter. The youth upon its back rode lightly, balanced lightly, leaning well forward, exulting perhaps at that moment as Faustus had, of having put behind now at once and for all the Shalt Not, of being free at last of honor and law. In the motion the sweet sharp sweat of the horse blew, sulphuric; the invisible wind flew past. He cried aloud, "I have done it! I have done it! I told them I would!"

He entered the lane and rode through the moonlight up to the house without slowing. He had thought it would be dark, but it was not. He did not pause; the careful and hidden rope were as much a part of his dead life now as honor and hope, and the old wearying woman who had been one of his enemies for thirteen years and who was now awake, waiting for him. The light was in hers and McEachern's bedroom and she was standing in the door, with a shawl over her nightdress. "Joe?" she said. He came down the hall fast. His face looked as McEachern had seen it as the chair fell. Perhaps she could not yet see it good. "What is it?" she said. "Paw rode away on the horse. I heard. . . . . . ." She saw his face then. But she did not even have time to step back. He did not strike her; his hand on her arm was quite gentle. It was just hurried, getting her out of the path, out of the door. He swept her aside as he might have a curtain across the door.

"He's at a dance," he said. "Get away, old woman." She turned, clutching the shawl with one hand, her other against the door face as she fell back, watching him as he crossed the room and began to run up the stairs which mounted to his attic. Without stopping he looked back. Then she could see his teeth shining in the lamp. "At a dance, you hear? He's not dancing, though." He laughed back, into the lamp; he turned his head and his laughing, running on up the stairs, vanishing as he ran, vanishing upward from the head down as if he were running headfirst and laughing into something that was obliterating him like a picture in chalk being erased from a blackboard.

She followed, toiling up the stairs. She began to follow almost as soon as he passed her, as if that implacable urgency which had carried her husband away had returned like a cloak on the shoulders of the boy and had been passed from him in turn to her. She dragged herself up the cramped stair, clutching the rail with one hand and the shawl with the other. She was not speaking, not calling to him. It was as though she were a phantom obeying the command sent back by the absent master. Joe had not lighted his lamp. But the room was filled with refracted moonglow, and even without that very likely she could have told what he was doing. She held herself upright by the wall, fumbling her hand along the wall until she reached the bed and sank onto it, sitting. It had taken her some time, because when she looked toward where the loose plank was, he was already approaching toward the bed, where the moonlight fell directly, and she watched him empty the tin can onto the bed and sweep the small mass of coins and bills into his hand and ram the hand into his pocket. Only then did he look at her as she sat, backfallen a little now, propped on one arm and holding the shawl with the other hand. "I didn't ask you for it," he said. "Remember that. I didn't ask, because I was afraid you would give it to me. I just took it. Dont forget that." He was turning almost before his voice ceased. She watched him turn into the lamplight which fell up the stair, descending. He passed out of sight, but she could still hear him. She heard him in the hall again, fast, and after a while she heard the horse again, galloping; and after a while the sound of the horse ceased.

A clock was striking one somewhere when Joe urged the now spent old horse through the main street of town. The horse had been breathing hard for some time now, but Joe still held it at a stumbling trot with a heavy stick that fell rhythmically across its rump. It was not a switch: it was a section of broom handle which had been driven into Mrs McEachern's flower bed in front of the house for something to grow on. Though the horse was still going through the motion of galloping, it was not moving much faster than a man could walk. The stick too rose and fell with the same spent and terrific slowness, the youth on the horse's back leaning forward as if he did not know that the horse had flagged, or as though to lift forward and onward the failing beast whose slow hooves rang with a measured hollow sound through the empty and moondappled street. It—the horse and the rider—had a strange, dreamy effect, like a moving picture in slow motion as it galloped steady and flagging up the street and toward the old corner where he used to wait, less urgent perhaps but not less eager, and more young.

The horse was not even trotting now, on stiff legs, its breathing deep and labored and rasping, each breath a groan. The stick still fell; as the progress of the horse slowed, the speed of the stick increased in exact ratio. But the horse slowed, sheering in to the curb. Joe pulled at its head, beating it, but it slowed into the curb and stopped, shadowdappled, its head down, trembling, its breathing almost like a human voice. Yet still the rider leaned forward in the arrested saddle, in the attitude of terrific speed, beating the horse across the rump with the stick. Save for the rise and fall of the stick and the groaning respirations of the animal, they might have been an equestrian statue strayed from its pedestal and come to rest in an attitude of ultimate exhaustion in a quiet and empty street splotched and dappled by moonshadows.

Joe descended. He went to the horse's head and began to tug it, as if he would drag it into motion by main strength and then spring onto its back. The horse did not move. He desisted; he seemed to be leaning a little toward the horse. Again they were motionless: the spent beast and the youth, facing one another, their heads quite near, as if carved in an attitude of listening or of prayer or of consultation. Then Joe raised the stick and fell to beating the horse about its motionless head. He beat it steadily until the stick broke. He continued to strike it with a fragment not much longer than his hand. But perhaps he realised that he was inflicting no pain, or perhaps his arm grew tired at last, because he threw the stick away and turned, whirled, already in full stride. He did not look back. Diminishing, his white shirt pulsing and fading in the moonshadows, he ran as completely out of the life of the horse as if it had never existed.

He passed the corner where he used to wait. If he noticed, thought, at all, he must have said *My God how long. How long ago that was* The street curved into the gravel road. He had almost a mile yet to go, so he ran not fast but carefully, steadily, his face lowered a little as if he contemplated the spurned road beneath his feet, his elbows at his sides like a trained runner. The road curved on, moonblanched, bordered at wide intervals by the small, random, new, terrible little houses in which people who came yesterday from nowhere and tomorrow will be gone wherenot, dwell on the edges of towns. They were all dark save the one toward which he ran.

He reached the house and turned from the road, running, his feet measured and loud in the late silence. Perhaps he could see already the waitress, in a dark dress for travelling, with her hat on and her bag packed, waiting (how they were to go anywhere, by what means depart, likely he had never thought). And perhaps Max and Mame too, likely undressed—Max coatless or maybe even in his undershirt, and Mame in the light blue kimono—the two of them bustling about in that loud, cheerful, seeing-someone-off way. But actually he was not thinking at all, since he had never told the waitress to get ready to leave at all. Perhaps he believed that he had told her, or that she should know, since his recent doings and his future plans must have seemed to him simple enough for anyone to understand. Perhaps he even believed that he had told her he was going home in order to get money when she got into the car.

He ran onto the porch. Heretofore, even during his heydey in the house, his impulse had been always to glide from the road and into the shadow of the porch and into the house itself where he was expected, as swiftly and inconspicuously as possible. He knocked. There was a light in her room, and another at the end of the hall, as he had expected; and voices from beyond the curtained windows too, several voices which he could discern to be intent rather than cheerful: that he expected too, thinking *Perhaps they think I am not coming. That damn horse. That damn horse* He knocked again, louder, putting his hand on the knob, shaking it, pressing his face against the curtained glass in the front door. The voices ceased. Then there was no sound whatever from within the house. The two lights, the lighted shade to her room and the opaque curtain in the door, burned with a steady and unwavering glare, as if all the people in the house had suddenly died when he touched the knob. He knocked again, with scarce interval between; he was still knocking when the door (no shadow had fallen upon the curtain and no step had approached beyond it) fled suddenly and silently from under his rapping hand. He was already stepping across the threshold as if he were attached to the door, when Max emerged from behind it, blocking it. He was completely dressed, even to the hat. "Well, well, well," he said. His voice was not loud, and it was almost as if he had drawn Joe swiftly into the hall and shut the door and locked it before Joe knew that he was inside. Yet his voice held again that ambiguous quality, that quality hearty and completely empty and completely without pleasure or mirth, like a shell, like something he carried before his face and watched Joe through it, which in the past had caused Joe to look at Max with something between puzzlement and anger. "Here's Romeo at last," he said. "The Beale Street Playboy." Then he spoke a little louder, saying Romeo quite loud. "Come in and meet the folks."

Joe was already moving toward the door which he knew, very nearly running again, if he had ever actually stopped. He was not listening to Max. He had never heard of Beale Street, that three or four Memphis city blocks in comparison with which Harlem is a movie set. Joe had not looked at anything. Because suddenly he saw the blonde woman standing in the hall at the rear. He had not seen her emerge into the hall at all, yet it was empty when he entered. And then suddenly she was standing there. She was dressed, in a dark skirt, and she held a hat in her hand. And just beyond an open dark door beside him was a pile of luggage, several bags. Perhaps he did not see them. Or perhaps looking saw once, faster than thought *I didn't think she would have that many* Perhaps he thought then for the first time that they had nothing to travel in, thinking *How can I carry all those* But he did not pause, already turning toward the door which he knew. It was only as he put his hand on the door that he became aware of complete silence beyond it, a silence which he at eighteen knew that it would take more than one person to make. But he did not pause; perhaps he was not even aware that the hall was empty again, that the blonde woman had vanished again without his having seen or heard her move.

He opened the door. He was running now; that is, as a man might run far ahead of himself and his knowing in the act of stopping stock still. The waitress sat on the bed as he had seen her sitting so many times. She wore the dark dress and the hat, as he had expected, known. She sat with her face lowered, not even looking at the door when it opened, a cigarette burning in one still hand that looked almost monstrous in its immobility against the dark dress. And in the same instant he saw the second man. He had never seen the man before. But he did not realise this now. It was only later that he remembered that, and remembered the piled luggage in the dark room which he had looked at for an instant while thought went faster than seeing.

The stranger sat on the bed too, also smoking. His hat was

tipped forward so that the shadow of the brim fell across his mouth. He was not old, yet he did not look young either. He and Max might have been brothers in the sense that any two white men strayed suddenly into an African village might look like brothers to them who live there. His face, his chin where the light fell upon it, was still. Whether or not the stranger was looking at him, Joe did not know. And that Max was standing just behind him Joe did not know either. And he heard their actual voices without knowing what they said, without even listening: *Ask him*

How would he know Perhaps he heard the words. But likely not. Likely they were as yet no more significant than the rasping of insects beyond the closedrawn window, or the packed bags which he had looked at and had not yet seen. *He cleared out right afterward, Bobbie said*

He might know. Let's find out if we can just what we are running from, at least

Though Joe had not moved since he entered, he was still running. When Max touched his shoulder he turned as if he had been halted in midstride. He had not been aware that Max was even in the room. He looked at Max over his shoulder with a kind of furious annoyance. "Let's have it, kid," Max said. "What about it?"

"What about what?" Joe said.

"The old guy. Do you think you croaked him? Let's have it straight. You dont want to get Bobbie in a jam."

"Bobbie," Joe said, thinking *Bobbie. Bobbie* He turned, running again; this time Max caught his shoulder, though not hard.

"Come on," Max said. "Aint we all friends here? Did you croak him?"

"Croak him?" Joe said, in that fretted tone of impatience and restraint, as if he were being detained and questioned by a child.

The stranger spoke. "The one you crowned with the chair. Is he dead?"

"Dead?" Joe said. He looked at the stranger. When he did so, he saw the waitress again and he ran again. He actually moved now. He had completely dismissed the two men from his mind. He went to the bed, dragging at his pocket, on his face an expression both exalted and victorious. The waitress did not look at him. She had not looked at him once since he entered, though very likely he had completely forgot that. She had not moved; the cigarette still burned in her hand. Her motionless hand looked as big and dead and pale as a piece of cooking meat. Again someone grasped him by the shoulder. It was the stranger now. The stranger and Max stood shoulder to shoulder, looking at Joe.

"Quit stalling," the stranger said. "If you croaked the guy, say so. It cant be any secret long. They are bound to hear about it by next month at the outside."

"I dont know, I tell you!" Joe said. He looked from one to the other, fretted but not yet glaring. "I hit him. He fell down. I told him I was going to do it someday." He looked from one to the other of the still, almost identical faces. He began to jerk his shoulder under the stranger's hand.

Max spoke. "What did you come here for, then?"

"What did——" Joe said. "What did I. . . . . . ." he said, in a tone of fainting amazement, glaring from face to face with a sort of outraged yet still patient exasperation. "What did I come for? I came to get Bobbie. Do you think that I——when I went all the way home to get the money to get married——" Again he completely forgot, dismissed them. He jerked free and turned to the woman with once more that expression oblivious, exalted, and proud. Very likely at that moment the two men were blown as completely out of his life as two scraps of paper. Very likely he was not even aware when Max went to the door and called and a moment later the blonde woman entered. He was bending above the bed upon which sat the immobile and downlooking waitress, stooping above her, dragging the wadded mass of coins and bills from his pocket, onto her lap and onto the bed beside her. "Here! Look at it. Look. I've got. See?"

Then the wind blew upon him again, like in the school house three hours ago among the gaped faces there of which he had for the time been oblivious. He stood in a quiet, dreamlike state, erect now where the upward spring of the sitting waitress had knocked him, and saw her, on her feet, gather up the wadded and scattered money and fling it; he saw quietly her face strained, the mouth screaming, the eyes screaming too. He alone of them all seemed to himself quiet, calm; his voice alone quiet enough to register upon the ear: "You mean you wont?" he said. "You mean, you wont?"

It was very much like it had been in the school house: someone holding her as she struggled and shrieked, her hair wild with the jerking and tossing of her head; her face, even her mouth, in contrast to the hair as still as a dead mouth in a dead face. "Bastard! Son of a bitch! Getting me into a jam, that always treated you like you were a white man. A white man!"

But very likely to him even yet it was just noise, not registering at all: just a part of the long wind. He just stared at her, at the face which he had never seen before, saying quietly (whether aloud or not, he could not have said) in a slow amazement: *Why, I committed murder for her. I even stole for her* as if he had just heard of it, thought of it, been told that he had done it.

Then she too seemed to blow out of his life on the long wind like a third scrap of paper. He began to swing his arm as if the hand still clutched the shattered chair. The blonde woman had been in the room some time. He saw her for the first time, without surprise, having apparently materialised out of thin air, motionless, with that diamondsurfaced tranquillity which invested her with a respectability as implacable and calm as the white lifted glove of a policeman, not a hair out of place. She now wore the pale blue kimono over the dark garment for travelling. She said quietly: "Take him. Let's get out of here. There'll be a cop out here soon. They'll know where to look for him."

Perhaps Joe did not hear her at all, nor the screaming waitress: "He told me himself he was a nigger! The son of a bitch! Me f . ing for nothing a nigger son of a bitch that would get me in a jam with clodhopper police. At a clodhopper dance!" Perhaps he heard only the long wind, as, swinging his hand as though it still clutched the chair, he sprang forward upon the two men. Very likely he did not even know that they were already moving toward him. Because with something of the exaltation of his adopted father he sprang full and of his own accord into the stranger's fist. Perhaps he did not feel either blow, though the stranger struck him twice in the face before he reached the floor, where like the man whom he had struck down, he lay upon his back, quite still. But he was not out because his eyes were still open, looking quietly up at them. There was nothing in his eyes at all, no pain, no surprise. But apparently he could not move; he just lay there with a profoundly contemplative expression, looking quietly up at the two men, and the blonde woman still as immobile and completely finished and surfaced as a cast statue. Perhaps he could not hear the voices either, or perhaps he did and they once more had no more significance than the dry buzzing of the steady insects beyond the window:

Bitching up as sweet a little setup as I could have wanted

He ought to stay away from bitches

He cant help himself. He was born too close to one

Is he really a nigger? He dont look like one

That's what he told Bobbie one night. But I guess she still dont know any more about what he is than he does. These country bastards are liable to be anything

We'll find out. We'll see if his blood is black Lying peaceful and still Joe watched the stranger lean down and lift his head from the floor and strike him again in the face, this time with a short slashing blow. After a moment he licked his lip a little, somewhat as a child might lick a cooking spoon. He watched the stranger's hand go back. But it did not fall.

That's enough. Let's get on to Memphis

Just one more Joe lay quietly and watched the hand. Then Max was beside the stranger, stooping too. *We'll need a little more blood to tell for sure*

Sure. He dont need to worry. This one is on the house too

The hand did not fall. Then the blonde woman was there too. She was holding the stranger's lifted arm by the wrist. *I said that will do*

X

KNOWING NOT GRIEVING remembers a thousand savage and lonely streets. They run from that night when he lay and heard the final footfall and then the final door (they did not even turn the light out) and then lay quietly, on his back, with open eyes while above the suspended globe burned with aching and unwavering glare as though in the house where all the people had died. He did not know how long he lay there. He was not thinking at all, not suffering. Perhaps he was conscious of somewhere within him the two severed wireends of volition and sentience lying, not touching now, waiting to touch, to knit anew so that he could move. While they finished their preparations to depart they stepped now and then across him, like people about to vacate a house forever will across some object which they intend to leave. *here bobbie here kid heres your comb you forgot it heres romeos chicken feed too jesus he must have tapped the sunday school till on the way out its bobbies now didnt you see him give it to her didnt you see old bighearted thats right pick it up kid you can keep it as an installment or a souvenir or something what dont she want it well say thats too bad now thats tough but we cant leave it lay here on the floor itll rot a hole in the floor its already helped to rot one hole pretty big for its size pretty big for any size hey bobbie hey kid sure ill just keep it for bobbie like hell you will well i mean ill keep half of it for bobbie leave it there you bastards what do you want with it it belongs to him well for sweet jesus what does he want with it he doesnt use money he doesnt need it ask bobbie if he needs money they give it to him that the rest of us have to pay for it leave it there i said like hell this aint mine to leave its bobbies it aint yours neither unless sweet jesus youre going to tell me he owes you jack too that he has been f.ing you too behind my back on credit i said leave it go chase yourself it aint but five or six bucks apiece* Then the blonde woman stood above him and stooping, he watching quietly, she lifted her skirt and took from the top of her stocking a flat folded sheaf of banknotes and removed one and stopped and thrust it into the fob pocket of his trousers. Then she was gone. *get on get out of here you aint ready yet yourself you got to put that kimono in and close your bag and*

*powder your face again bring my bag and hat in here go on now
and you take bobbie and them other bags and get in the car and
wait for me and max you think im going to leave either one of you
here alone to steal that one off of him too go on now get out of here*

Then they were gone: the final feet, the final door. Then he
heard the car drown the noise of the insects, riding above,
sinking to the level, sinking below the level so that he heard
only the insects. He lay there beneath the light. He could not
move yet, as he could look without actually seeing, hear without actually knowing; the two wireends not yet knit as he lay
peacefully, licking his lips now and then as a child does.

Then the wireends knit and made connection. He did not
know the exact instant, save that suddenly he was aware of
his ringing head, and he sat up slowly, discovering himself
again, getting to his feet. He was dizzy; the room went round
him, slowly and smoothly as thinking, so that thinking said
Not yet But he still felt no pain, not even when, propped
before the bureau, he examined in the glass his swollen and
bloody face and touched his face. "Sweet Jesus," he said.
"They sure beat me up." He was not thinking yet; it had not
yet risen that far *I reckon I better get out of here I reckon I
better get out of here* He went toward the door, his hands out
before him like a blind man or a sleepwalker. He was in the
hall without having remembered passing through the door,
and he found himself in another bedroom while he still hoped
perhaps not believed that he was moving toward the front
door. It was small too. Yet it still seemed to be filled with the
presence of the blonde woman, its very cramped harsh walls
bulged outward with that militant and diamondsurfaced respectability. On the bare bureau sat a pint bottle almost full
of whiskey. He drank it, slowly, not feeling the fire at all,
holding himself upright by holding to the bureau. The whiskey went down his throat cold as molasses, without taste. He
set the empty bottle down and leaned on the bureau, his head
lowered, not thinking, waiting perhaps without knowing it,
perhaps not even waiting. Then the whiskey began to burn in
him and he began to shake his head slowly from side to side,
while thinking became one with the slow, hot coiling and
recoiling of his entrails: 'I got to get out of here.' He reentered the hall. Now it was his head that was clear and his

body that would not behave. He had to coax it along the hall,
sliding it along one wall toward the front, thinking, 'Come
on, now; pull yourself together. I got to get out.' thinking
If I can just get it outside, into the air, the cool air, the cool dark
He watched his hands fumbling at the door, trying to help
them, to coax and control them. 'Anyway, they didn't lock it
on me,' he thought. 'Sweet Jesus, I could not have got out
until morning then. It never would have opened a window
and climbed through it.' He opened the door at last and
passed out and closed the door behind him, arguing again
with his body which did not want to bother to close the
door, having to be forced to close it upon the empty house
where the two lights burned with their dead and unwavering
glare, not knowing that the house was empty and not caring,
not caring anymore for silence and desolation than they had
cared for the cheap and brutal nights of stale oftused glasses
and stale oftused beds. His body was acquiescing better, becoming docile. He stepped from the dark porch, into the
moonlight, and with his bloody head and his empty stomach
hot, savage, and courageous with whiskey, he entered the
street which was to run for fifteen years.

The whiskey died away in time and was renewed and died
again, but the street ran on. From that night the thousand
streets ran as one street, with imperceptible corners and
changes of scene, broken by intervals of begged and stolen
rides, on trains and trucks, and on country wagons with he at
twenty and twentyfive and thirty sitting on the seat with his
still, hard face and the clothes (even when soiled and worn)
of a city man and the driver of the wagon not knowing who
or what the passenger was and not daring to ask. The street
ran into Oklahoma and Missouri and as far south as Mexico
and then back north to Chicago and Detroit and then back
south again and at last to Mississippi. It was fifteen years
long: it ran between the savage and spurious board fronts of
oil towns where, his inevitable serge clothing and light shoes
black with bottomless mud, he ate crude food from tin dishes
that cost him ten and fifteen dollars a meal and payed for
them with a roll of banknotes the size of a bullfrog and
stained too with the rich mud that seemed as bottomless as
the gold which it excreted. It ran through yellow wheat fields

waving beneath the fierce yellow days of labor and hard sleep in haystacks beneath the cold mad moon of September, and the brittle stars: he was in turn laborer, miner, prospector, gambling tout; he enlisted in the army, served four months and deserted and was never caught. And always, sooner or later, the street ran through cities, through an identical and wellnigh interchangeable section of cities without remembered names, where beneath the dark and equivocal and symbolical archways of midnight he bedded with the women and paid them when he had the money, and when he did not have it he bedded anyway and then told them that he was a negro. For a while it worked; that was while he was still in the south. It was quite simple, quite easy. Usually all he risked was a cursing from the woman and the matron of the house, though now and then he was beaten unconscious by other patrons, to waken later in the street or in the jail.

That was while he was still in the (comparatively speaking) south. Because one night it did not work. He rose from the bed and told the woman that he was a negro. "You are?" she said. "I thought maybe you were just another wop or something." She looked at him, without particular interest; then she evidently saw something in his face: she said, "What about it? You look all right. You ought to seen the shine I turned out just before your turn came." She was looking at him. She was quite still now. "Say, what do you think this dump is, anyhow? The Ritz hotel?" Then she quit talking. She was watching his face and she began to move backward slowly before him, staring at him, her face draining, her mouth open to scream. Then she did scream. It took two policemen to subdue him. At first they thought that the woman was dead.

He was sick after that. He did not know until then that there were white women who would take a man with a black skin. He stayed sick for two years. Sometimes he would remember how he had once tricked or teased white men into calling him a negro in order to fight them, to beat them or be beaten; now he fought the negro who called him white. He was in the north now, in Chicago and then Detroit. He lived with negroes, shunning white people. He ate with them, slept with them, belligerent, unpredictable, uncommunicative.

He now lived as man and wife with a woman who resembled an ebony carving. At night he would lie in bed beside her, sleepless, beginning to breathe deep and hard. He would do it deliberately, feeling, even watching, his white chest arch deeper and deeper within his ribcage, trying to breathe into himself the dark odor, the dark and inscrutable thinking and being of negroes, with each suspiration trying to expel from himself the white blood and the white thinking and being. And all the while his nostrils at the odor which he was trying to make his own would whiten and tauten, his whole being writhe and strain with physical outrage and spiritual denial.

He thought that it was loneliness which he was trying to escape and not himself. But the street ran on: catlike, one place was the same as another to him. But in none of them could he be quiet. But the street ran on in its moods and phases, always empty: he might have seen himself as in numberless avatars, in silence, doomed with motion, driven by the courage of flagged and spurred despair; by the despair of courage whose opportunities had to be flagged and spurred. He was thirtythree years old.

One afternoon the street had become a Mississippi country road. He had been put off a southbound freight train near a small town. He did not know the name of the town; he didn't care what word it used for name. He didn't even see it, anyway. He skirted it, following the woods, and came to the road and looked in both directions. It was not a gravelled road, though it looked to be fairly well used. He saw several negro cabins scattered here and there along it; then he saw, about a half mile away, a larger house. It was a big house set in a grove of trees; obviously a place of some pretensions at one time. But now the trees needed pruning and the house had not been painted in years. But he could tell that it was inhabited, and he had not eaten in twentyfour hours. 'That one might do,' he thought.

But he did not approach it at once, though the afternoon was drawing on. Instead he turned his back upon it and went on in the other direction, in his soiled white shirt and worn serge trousers and his cracked, dusty, townshaped shoes, his cloth cap set at an arrogant angle above a threeday's stubble. Yet even then he did not look like a tramp; at least apparently not to the negro boy whom he met presently coming up the road and swinging a tin bucket. He stopped the boy. "Who lives in the big house back there?" he said.

"That where Miz Burden stay at."

"Mr and Mrs Burden?"

"No, sir. Aint no Mr Burden. Aint nobody live there but her."

"Oh. An old woman, I guess."

"No, sir. Miz Burden aint old. Aint young neither."

"And she lives there by herself. Dont she get scared?"

"Who going to harm her, right here at town? Colored folks around here looks after her."

"Colored folks look after her?"

At once it was as if the boy had closed a door between himself and the man who questioned him. "I reckon aint nobody round here going to do her no harm. She aint harmed nobody."

"I guess not," Christmas said. "How far is it to the next town over this way?"

"Bout thirty miles, they say. You aint fixing to walk it, is you?"

"No," Christmas said. He turned then, going on. The boy looked after him. Then he too turned, walking again, the tin bucket swinging against his faded flank. A few steps later he looked back. The man who had questioned him was walking on, steadily though not fast. The boy went on again, in his faded, patched, scant overalls. He was barefoot. Presently he began to shuffle, still moving forward, the red dust rising about his lean, chocolatecolored shanks and the frayed legs of the tooshort overalls; he began to chant, tuneless, rhythmic, musical, though on a single note:

> *Say dont didn't.*
> *Didn't dont who.*
> *Want dat yaller gal's*
> *Pudden dont hide.*

Lying in a tangle of shrubbery a hundred yards from the house, Christmas heard a far clock strike nine and then ten.

Before him the house bulked square and huge from its mass of trees. There was a light in one window upstairs. The shades were not drawn and he could see that the light was a kerosene lamp, and now and then he saw through the window the shadow of a moving person cross the further wall. But he never saw the person at all. After a while the light went out.

The house was now dark; he quit watching it then. He lay in the copse, on his belly on the dark earth. In the copse the darkness was impenetrable; through his shirt and trousers it felt a little chill, close, faintly dank, as if the sun never reached the atmosphere which the copse held. He could feel the neversunned earth strike, slow and receptive, against him through his clothes: groin, hip, belly, breast, forearms. His arms were crossed, his forehead rested upon them, in his nostrils the damp rich odor of the dark and fecund earth.

He did not look once again toward the dark house. He lay perfectly still in the copse for more than an hour before he rose up and emerged. He did not creep. There was nothing skulking nor even especially careful about his approach to the house. He simply went quietly as if that were his natural manner of moving and passed around the now dimensionless bulk of the house, toward the rear, where the kitchen would be. He made no more noise than a cat as he paused and stood for a while beneath the window where the light had shown. In the grass about his feet the crickets, which had ceased as he moved, keeping a little island of silence about him like thin yellow shadow of their small voices, began again, ceasing again when he moved with that tiny and alert suddenness. From the rear of the house a single storey wing projected. 'That will be the kitchen,' he thought. 'Yes. That will be it.' He walked without sound, moving in his tiny island of abruptly ceased insects. He could discern a door in the kitchen wall. He would have found it unlocked if he had tried it. But he did not. He passed it and paused beneath a window. Before he tried it he remembered that he had seen no screen in the lighted window upstairs.

The window was even open, propped open with a stick. 'What do you think about that,' he thought. He stood beside the window, his hands on the sill, breathing quietly, not lis-

tening, not hurrying, as if there were no need for haste anywhere under the sun. 'Well. Well. Well. What do you know
about that. Well. Well. Well.' Then he climbed into the window; he seemed to flow into the dark kitchen: a shadow returning without a sound and without locomotion to the
allmother of obscurity and darkness. Perhaps he thought of
that other window which he had used to use and of the rope
upon which he had had to rely; perhaps not.

Very likely not, no more than a cat would recall another
window; like the cat, he also seemed to see in the darkness as
he moved as unerringly toward the food which he wanted as
if he knew where it would be; that, or were being manipu-
lated by an agent which did know. He ate something from an
invisible dish, with invisible fingers: invisible food. He did
not care what it would be. He did not know that he had even
wondered or tasted until his jaw stopped suddenly in midchewing and thinking fled for twentyfive years back down the
street, past all the imperceptible corners of bitter defeats and
more bitter victories, and five miles even beyond a corner
where he used to wait in the terrible early time of love, for
someone whose name he had forgot; five miles even beyond
that it went *I'll know it in a minute. I have eaten it before,*
somewhere. In a minute I will memory clicking knowing *I*
see I see I more than see hear I hear I see my head bent I hear the
monotonous dogmatic voice which I believe will never cease going
on and on forever and peeping I see the indomitable bullet head
the clean blunt beard they too bent and I thinking How can he be
so nothungry and I smelling my mouth and tongue weeping the
hot salt of waiting my eyes tasting the hot steam from the dish
"It's peas," he said, aloud. "For sweet Jesus. Field peas
cooked with molasses."

More of him than thinking may have been absent; he
should have heard the sound before he did, since whoever
was creating it was trying no more for silence and caution
than he had. Perhaps he did hear it. But he did not move at
all as the soft sound of slippered feet approached the kitchen
from the house side of it, and when he did at last turn suddenly, his eyes glowing suddenly, he saw already beneath the
door which entered the house itself, the faint approaching
light. The open window was at his hand: he could have been

through it in a single step almost. But he did not move. He didn't even set down the dish. He did not even cease to chew. Thus he was standing in the center of the room, holding the dish and chewing, when the door opened and the woman entered. She wore a faded dressing gown and she carried a candle, holding it high, so that its light fell upon her face: a face quiet, grave, utterly unalarmed. In the soft light of the candle she looked to be not much past thirty. She stood in the door. They looked at one another for more than a minute, almost in the same attitude: he with the dish, she with the candle. He had stopped chewing now.

"If it is just food you want, you will find that," she said in a voice calm, a little deep, quite cold.

XI

B Y THE LIGHT of the candle she did not look much more
than thirty, in the soft light downfalling upon the soft-
ungirdled presence of a woman prepared for sleep. When he
saw her by daylight he knew that she was better than thirtyfive. Later she told him that she was forty. 'Which means
either fortyone or fortynine, from the way she said it,' he
thought. But it was not that first night, nor for many succeeding ones, that she told him that much even.

She told him very little, anyway. They talked very little, and
that casually, even after he was the lover of her spinster's bed.
Sometimes he could almost believe that they did not talk at
all, that he didn't know her at all. It was as though there were
two people: the one whom he saw now and then by day and
looked at while they spoke to one another with speech that
told nothing at all since it didn't try to and didn't intend to;
the other with whom he lay at night and didn't even see,
speak to, at all.

Even after a year (he was working at the planing mill now)
when he saw her by day at all, it would be on Saturday afternoon or Sunday or when he would come to the house for the
food which she would prepare for him and leave upon the
kitchen table. Now and then she would come to the kitchen,
though she would never stay while he ate, and at times she
met him at the back porch, where during the first four or five
months of his residence in the cabin below the house, they
would stand for a while and talk almost like strangers. They
always stood: she in one of her apparently endless succession
of clean calico house dresses and sometimes a cloth sunbonnet
like a countrywoman, and he in a clean white shirt now and
the serge trousers creased now every week. They never sat
down to talk. He had never seen her sitting save one time
when he looked through a downstairs window and saw her
writing at a desk in the room. And it was a year after he had
remarked without curiosity the volume of mail which she received and sent, and that for a certain period of each forenoon
she would sit at the worn, scarred, rolltop desk in one of the
scarceused and sparsely furnished downstairs rooms, writing

steadily, before he learned that what she received were business and private documents with fifty different postmarks and that what she sent were replies—advice, business, financial and religious, to the presidents and faculties and trustees, and advice personal and practical to young girl students and even alumnae, of a dozen negro schools and colleges through the south. Now and then she would be absent from home three and four days at a time, and though he could now see her at his will on any night, it was a year before he learned that in these absences she visited the schools in person and talked to the teachers and the students. Her business affairs were conducted by a negro lawyer in Memphis, who was a trustee of one of the schools, and in whose safe, along with her will, reposed the written instructions (in her own hand) for the disposal of her body after death. When he learned that, he understood the town's attitude toward her, though he knew that the town did not know as much as he did. He said to himself: 'Then I wont be bothered here.'

One day he realised that she had never invited him inside the house proper. He had never been further than the kitchen, which he had already entered of his own accord, thinking, liplifted, 'She couldn't keep me out of here. I guess she knows that.' And he had never entered the kitchen by day save when he came to get the food which she prepared for him and set out upon the table. And when he entered the house at night it was as he had entered it that first night; he felt like a thief, a robber, even while he mounted to the bedroom where she waited. Even after a year it was as though he entered by stealth to despoil her virginity each time anew. It was as though each turn of dark saw him faced again with the necessity to despoil again that which he had already despoiled—or never had and never would.

Sometimes he thought of it in that way, remembering the hard, untearful and unselfpitying and almost manlike yielding of that surrender. A spiritual privacy so long intact that its own instinct for preservation had immolated it, its physical phase the strength and fortitude of a man. A dual personality: the one the woman at first sight of whom in the lifted candle (or perhaps the very sound of the slippered approaching feet) there had opened before him, instantaneous as a landscape in a lightningflash, a horizon of physical security and adultery if not pleasure; the other the mantrained muscles and the mantrained habit of thinking born of heritage and environment with which he had to fight up to the final instant. There was no feminine vacillation, no coyness of obvious desire and intention to succumb at last. It was as if he struggled physically with another man for an object of no actual value to either, and for which they struggled on principle alone.

When he saw her next, he thought, 'My God. How little I know about women, when I thought I knew so much.' It was on the very next day; looking at her, being spoken to by her, it was as though what memory of less than twelve hours knew to be true could never have happened, thinking *Under her clothes she cant even be made so that it could have happened* He had not started to work at the mill then. Most of that day he spent lying on his back on the cot which she had loaned him, in the cabin which she had given him to live in, smoking, his hands beneath his head. 'My God,' he thought, 'it was like I was the woman and she was the man.' But that was not right, either. Because she had resisted to the very last. But it was not woman resistance, that resistance which, if really meant, cannot be overcome by any man for the reason that the woman observes no rules of physical combat. But she had resisted fair, by the rules that decreed that upon a certain crisis one was defeated, whether the end of resistance had come or not. That night he waited until he saw the light go out in the kitchen and then come on in her room. He went to the house. He did not go in eagerness, but in a quiet rage. "I'll show her," he said aloud. He did not try to be quiet. He entered the house boldly and mounted the stairs; she heard him at once. "Who is it?" she said. But there was no alarm in her tone. He didn't answer. He mounted the stairs and entered the room. She was still dressed, turning, watching the door as he entered. But she did not speak to him. She just watched him as he went to the table and blew out the lamp, thinking, 'Now she'll run.' And so he sprang forward, toward the door to intercept her. But she did not flee. He found her in the dark exactly where the light had lost her, in the same attitude. He began to tear at her clothes. He was talking to

her, in a tense, hard, low voice: "I'll show you! I'll show the
bitch!" She did not resist at all. It was almost as though she
were helping him, with small changes of position of limbs
when the ultimate need for help arose. But beneath his hands
the body might have been the body of a dead woman not yet
stiffened. But he did not desist; though his hands were hard
and urgent it was with rage alone. 'At least I have made a
woman of her at last,' he thought. 'Now she hates me. I have
taught her that, at least.'

The next day he lay again all day long on his cot in the
cabin. He ate nothing; he did not even go to the kitchen to
see if she had left food for him. He was waiting for sunset,
dusk. 'Then I'll blow,' he thought. He did not expect ever to
see her again. 'Better blow,' he thought. 'Not give her the
chance to turn me out of the cabin too. That much, anyway.
No white woman ever did that. Only a nigger woman ever
give me the air, turned me out.' So he lay on the cot, smoking, waiting for sunset. Through the open door he watched
the sun slant and lengthen and turn copper. Then the copper
faded into lilac, into the fading lilac of full dusk. He could
hear the frogs then, and fireflies began to drift across the open
frame of the door, growing brighter as the dusk faded. Then
he rose. He owned nothing but the razor; when he had put
that into his pocket, he was ready to travel one mile or a
thousand, wherever the street of the imperceptible corners
should choose to run again. Yet when he moved, it was toward the house. It was as though, as soon as he found that
his feet intended to go there, that he let go, seemed to float,
surrendered, thinking *All right All right* floating, riding
across the dusk, up to the house and onto the back porch and
to the door by which he would enter, that was never locked.
But when he put his hand upon it, it would not open. Perhaps for the moment neither hand nor believing would believe; he seemed to stand there, quiet, not yet thinking,
watching his hand shaking the door, hearing the sound of the
bolt on the inside. He turned away quietly. He was not yet
raging. He went to the kitchen door. He expected that to be
locked also. But he did not realise until he found that it was
open, that he had wanted it to be. When he found that it was
not locked it was like an insult. It was as though some enemy

upon whom he had wreaked his utmost of violence and contumely stood, unscathed and unscarred, and contemplated him with a musing and insufferable contempt. When he entered the kitchen, he did not approach the door into the house proper, the door in which she had appeared with the candle on the night when he first saw her. He went directly to the table where she set out his food. He did not need to see. His hands saw; the dishes were still a little warm, thinking *Set out for the nigger. For the nigger.*

He seemed to watch his hand as if from a distance. He watched it pick up a dish and swing it up and back and hold it there while he breathed deep and slow, intensely cogitant. He heard his voice say aloud, as if he were playing a game: "Ham," and watched his hand swing and hurl the dish crashing into the wall, the invisible wall, waiting for the crash to subside and silence to flow completely back before taking up another one. He held this dish poised, sniffing. This one required some time. "Beans or greens?" he said. "Beans or spinach? . . . . All right. Call it beans." He hurled it, hard, waiting until the crash ceased. He raised the third dish. "Something with onions," he said, thinking *This is fun. Why didn't I think of this before?* "Woman's muck." He hurled it, hard and slow, hearing the crash, waiting. Now he heard something else: feet within the house, approaching the door. 'She'll have the lamp this time,' he thought, thinking *If I were to look now, I could see the light under the door* as his hand swung up and back *now she has almost reached the door* "Potatoes," he said at last, with judicial finality. He did not look around, even when he heard the bolt in the door and heard the door inyawn and light fell upon him where he stood with the dish poised. "Yes, it's potatoes," he said, in the preoccupied and oblivious tone of a child playing alone. He could both see and hear this crash. Then the light went away; again he heard the door yawn, again he heard the bolt. He had not yet looked around. He took up the next dish. "Beets," he said. "I dont like beets, anyhow."

The next day he went to work at the planing mill. He went to work on Friday. He had eaten nothing now since Wednesday night. He drew no pay until Saturday evening, working overtime Saturday afternoon. He ate Saturday night, in a restaurant downtown, for the first time in three days. He did not return to the house. For a time he would not even look toward it when he left or entered the cabin. At the end of six months he had worn a private path between the cabin and the mill. It ran almost stringstraight, avoiding all houses, entering the woods soon and running straight and with daily increasing definition and precision, to the sawdust pile where he worked. And always, when the whistle blew at five thirty, he returned by it to the cabin, to change into the white shirt and the dark creased trousers before walking the two miles back to town to eat, as if he were ashamed of the overalls. Or perhaps it was not shame, though very likely he could no more have said what it was than he could have said that it was not shame.

He no longer deliberately avoided looking at the house; neither did he deliberately look at it. For a while he believed that she would send for him. 'She'll make the first sign,' he thought. But she did not; after a while he believed that he no longer expected it. Yet on the first time that he deliberately looked again toward the house, he felt a shocking surge and fall of blood; then he knew that he had been afraid all the time that she would be in sight, that she had been watching him all the while with that perspicuous and still contempt; he felt a sensation of sweating, of having surmounted an ordeal. 'That's over,' he thought. 'I have done that now.' So that when one day he did see her, there was no shock. Perhaps he was prepared. Anyway, there was no shocking surge and drop of blood when he looked up, completely by chance, and saw her in the back yard, in a gray dress and the sunbonnet. He could not tell if she had been watching him or had seen him or were watching him now or not. 'You dont bother me and I dont bother you,' he thought, thinking *I dreamed it. It didn't happen. She has nothing under her clothes so that it could have happened*

He went to work in the spring. One evening in September he returned home and entered the cabin and stopped in midstride, in complete astonishment. She was sitting on the cot, looking at him. Her head was bare. He had never seen it bare before, though he had felt in the dark the loose abandon of her hair, not yet wild, on a dark pillow. But he had never seen her hair before and he stood staring at it alone while she watched him; he said suddenly to himself, in the instant of moving again: 'She's trying to. *I had expected it to have gray in it* She's trying to be a woman and she dont know how.' Thinking, knowing *She has come to talk to me* Two hours later she was still talking, they sitting side by side on the cot in the now dark cabin. She told him that she was fortyone years old and that she had been born in the house yonder and had lived there ever since. That she had never been away from Jefferson for a longer period than six months at any time and these only at wide intervals filled with homesickness for the sheer boards and nails, the earth and trees and shrubs, which composed the place which was a foreign land to her and her people; when she spoke even now, after forty years, among the slurred consonants and the flat vowels of the land where her life had been cast, New England talked as plainly as it did in the speech of her kin who had never left New Hampshire and whom she had seen perhaps three times in her life, her forty years. Sitting beside her on the dark cot while the light failed and at last her voice was without source, steady, interminable, pitched almost like the voice of a man, Christmas thought, 'She is like all the rest of them. Whether they are seventeen or fortyseven, when they finally come to surrender completely, it's going to be in words.'

Calvin Burden was the son of a minister named Nathaniel Burrington. The youngest of ten children, he ran away from home at the age of twelve, before he could write his name (or would write it, his father believed) on a ship. He made the voyage around the Horn to California and turned Catholic; he lived for a year in a monastery. Ten years later he reached Missouri from the west. Three weeks after he arrived he was married, to the daughter of a family of Huguenot stock which had emigrated from Carolina by way of Kentucky. On the day after the wedding he said, "I guess I had better settle down." He began that day to settle down. The wedding celebration was still in progress, and his first step was to formally deny allegiance to the Catholic church. He did this in a saloon, insisting that every one present listen to him and state their objections; he was a little insistent on there being objections, though there were none; not, that is, up to the time when he was led away by friends. The next day he said that he meant it, anyhow; that he would not belong to a church full of frogeating slaveholders. That was in Saint Louis. He bought a home there, and a year later he was a father. He said then that he had denied the Catholic church a year ago for the sake of his son's soul; almost as soon as the boy was born, he set about to imbue the child with the religion of his New England forbears. There was no Unitarian meetinghouse available, and Burden could not read the English bible. But he had learned to read in Spanish from the priests in California, and as soon as the child could walk Burden (he pronounced it Burden now, since he could not spell it at all and the priests had taught him to write it laboriously so with a hand more apt for a rope or a gunbutt or a knife than a pen) began to read to the child in Spanish from the book which he had brought with him from California, interspersing the fine, sonorous flowing of mysticism in a foreign tongue with harsh, extemporised dissertations composed half of the bleak and bloodless logic which he remembered from his father on interminable New England Sundays, and half of immediate hellfire and tangible brimstone of which any country Methodist circuit rider would have been proud. The two of them would be alone in the room: the tall, gaunt, Nordic man, and the small, dark, vivid child who had inherited his mother's build and coloring, like people of two different races. When the boy was about five, Burden killed a man in an argument over slavery and had to take his family and move, leave Saint Louis. He moved westward, "to get away from Democrats," he said.

The settlement to which he moved consisted of a store, a blacksmith shop, a church and two saloons. Here Burden spent much of his time talking politics and in his harsh loud voice cursing slavery and slaveholders. His reputation had come with him and he was known to carry a pistol, and his opinions were received without comment, at least. At times, especially on Saturday nights, he came home, still full of straight whiskey and the sound of his own ranting. Then he would wake his son (the mother was dead now and there were three daughters, all with blue eyes) with his hard hand. "I'll learn you to hate two things," he would say, "or I'll frail the tar out of you. And those things are hell and slaveholders. Do you hear me?"

"Yes," the boy would say. "I cant help but hear you. Get on to bed and let me sleep."

He was no proselyter, missionary. Save for an occasional minor episode with pistols, none of which resulted fatally, he confined himself to his own blood. "Let them all go to their own benighted hell," he said to his children. "But I'll beat the loving God into the four of you as long as I can raise my arm." That would be on Sunday, each Sunday when, washed and clean, the children in calico or denim, the father in his broadcloth frockcoat bulging over the pistol in his hip pocket, and the collarless plaited shirt which the oldest girl laundered each Saturday as well as the dead mother ever had, they gathered in the clean crude parlor while Burden read from the once gilt and blazoned book in that language which none of them understood. He continued to do that up to the time when his son ran away from home.

The son's name was Nathaniel. He ran away at fourteen and did not return for sixteen years, though they heard from him twice in that time by word-of-mouth messenger. The first time was from Colorado, the second time from Old Mexico. He did not say what he was doing in either place. "He was all right when I left him," the messenger said. This was the second messenger; it was in 1863, and the messenger was eating breakfast in the kitchen, bolting his food with decorous celerity. The three girls, the two oldest almost grown now, were serving him, standing with arrested dishes and softly open mouths in their full, coarse, clean dresses, about the crude table, the father sitting opposite the messenger across the table, his head propped on his single hand. The other arm he had lost two years ago while a member of a troop of partisan guerilla horse in the Kansas fighting, and his head and beard were grizzled now. But he was still vigorous, and his frockcoat still bulged behind over the butt of the heavy pistol. "He got into a little trouble," the messenger said. "But he was still all right the last I heard."

"Trouble?" the father said.

"He killed a Mexican that claimed he stole his horse. You know how them Spanish are about white men, even when they dont kill Mexicans." The messenger drank some coffee. "But I reckon they have to be kind of strict, with the country filling up with tenderfeet and all.——Thank you kindly," he said, as the oldest girl slid a fresh stack of corn cakes onto his plate; "yessum, I can reach the sweetening fine.——Folks claim it wasn't the Mexican's horse noways. Claim the Mexican never owned no horse. But I reckon even them Spanish have got to be strict, with these Easterners already giving the West such a bad name."

The father grunted. "I'll be bound. If there was trouble there, I'll be bound he was in it. You tell him," he said violently, "if he lets them yellowbellied priests bamboozle him, I'll shoot him myself quick as I would a Reb."

"You tell him to come on back home," the oldest girl said. "That's what you tell him."

"Yessum," the messenger said. "I'll shore tell him. I'm going east to Indianny for a spell. But I'll see him soon as I get back. I'll shore tell him. O yes; I nigh forgot. He said to tell you the woman and kid was fine."

"Whose woman and kid?" the father said.

"His," the messenger said. "I thank you kindly again. And goodbye all."

They heard from the son a third time before they saw him again. They heard him shouting one day out in front of the house, though still some distance away. It was in 1866. The family had moved again, a hundred miles further west, and it had taken the son two months to find them, riding back and forth across Kansas and Missouri in a buckboard with two leather sacks of gold dust and minted coins and crude jewels thrown under the seat like a pair of old shoes, before he found the sod cabin and drove up to it, shouting. Sitting in a chair before the cabin door was a man. "There's father," Nathaniel said to the woman on the buckboard seat beside him. "See?" Though the father was only in his late fifties, his sight had begun to fail. He did not distinguish his son's face until the buckboard had stopped and the sisters had billowed shrieking through the door. Then Calvin rose; he gave a long, booming shout. "Well," Nathaniel said; "here we are."

Calvin was not speaking sentences at all. He was just yelling, cursing. "I'm going to frail the tar out of you!" he roared. "Girls! Vangie! Beck! Sarah!" The sisters had already emerged. They seemed to boil through the door in their full skirts like balloons on a torrent, with shrill cries, above which the father's voice boomed and roared. His coat—the frock-coat of Sunday or the wealthy or the retired—was open now and he was tugging at something near his waist with the same gesture and attitude with which he might be drawing the pistol. But he was merely dragging from about his waist with his single hand a leather strap, and flourishing it he now thrust and shoved through the shrill and birdlike hovering of the women. "I'll learn you yet!" he roared. "I'll learn you to run away!" The strap fell twice across Nathaniel's shoulders. It fell twice before the two men locked.

It was in play, in a sense: a kind of deadly play and smiling seriousness: the play of two lions that might or might not leave marks. They locked, the strap arrested: face to face and breast to breast they stood: the old man with his gaunt, grizzled face and his pale New England eyes, and the young one who bore no resemblance to him at all, with his beaked nose and his white teeth smiling. "Stop it," Nathaniel said. "Dont you see who's watching yonder in the buckboard?"

They had none of them looked at the buckboard until now. Sitting on the seat was a woman and a boy of about twelve. The father looked once at the woman; he did not even need to see the boy. He just looked at the woman, his jaw slacked as if he had seen a ghost. "Evangeline!" he said. She looked enough like his dead wife to have been her sister. The boy who could hardly remember his mother at all, had taken for wife a woman who looked almost exactly like her.

"That's Juana," he said. "That's Calvin with her. We come home to get married."

After supper that night, with the woman and child in bed, Nathaniel told them. They sat about the lamp: the father, the sisters, the returned son. There were no ministers out there where he had been, he explained; just priests and Catholics. "So when we found that the chico was on the way, she begun to talk about a priest. But I wasn't going to have any Burden born a heathen. So I begun to look around, to humor her. But first one thing and then another come up and I couldn't get away to meet a minister; and then the boy came and so it wasn't any rush anymore. But she kept on worrying, about priests and such, and so in a couple of years I heard how there was to be a white minister in Santa Fe on a certain day. So we packed up and started out and got to Santa Fe just in time to see the dust of the stage that was carrying the minister on away. So we waited there and in a couple more years we had another chance, in Texas. Only this time I got kind of mixed up with helping some Rangers that were cleaning up some kind of a mess where some folks had a deputy treed in a dance hall. So when that was over we just decided to come on home and get married right. And here we are."

The father sat, gaunt, grizzled, and austere, beneath the lamp. He had been listening, but his expression was brooding, with a kind of violently slumbering contemplativeness and bewildered outrage. "Another damn black Burden," he said. "Folks will think I bred to a damn slaver. And now he's got to breed to one, too." The son listened quietly, not even attempting to tell his father that the woman was Spanish and not Rebel. "Damn, lowbuilt black folks: lowbuilt because of the weight of the wrath of God, black because of the sin of human bondage staining their blood and flesh." His gaze was vague, fanatical, and convinced. "But we done freed them now, both black and white alike. They'll bleach out now. In a hundred years they will be white folks again. Then maybe we'll let them come back into America." He mused, smoldering, immobile. "By God," he said suddenly, "he's got a man's build, anyway, for all his black look. By God, he's going to be as big a man as his grandpappy; not a runt like his pa. For all his black dam and his black look, he will."

She told Christmas this while they sat on the cot in the darkening cabin. They had not moved for over an hour. He could not see her face at all now; he seemed to swing faintly, as though in a drifting boat, upon the sound of her voice as upon some immeasurable and drowsing peace evocative of nothing of any moment, scarce listening. "His name was Calvin, like grandpa's, and he was as big as grandpa, even if he was dark like father's mother's people and like his mother. She was not my mother: he was just my halfbrother. Grandpa was the last of ten, and father was the last of two, and Calvin was the last of all." He had just turned twenty when he was killed in the town two miles away by an ex-slaveholder and Confederate soldier named Sartoris, over a question of negro voting.

She told Christmas about the graves—the brother's, the grandfather's, the father's and his two wives—on a cedar knoll in the pasture a half mile from the house; listening quietly, Christmas thought, 'Ah. She'll take me to see them. I will have to go.' But she did not. She never mentioned the graves to him again after that night when she told him where they were and that he could go and see them for himself if he wished. "You probably cant find them, anyway," she said. "Because when they brought grandfather and Calvin home that evening, father waited until after dark and buried them and hid the graves, levelled the mounds and put brush and things over them."

"Hid them?" Christmas said.

There was nothing soft, feminine, mournful and retrospective, in her voice. "So they would not find them. Dig them up. Maybe butcher them." She went on, her voice a little impatient, explanatory: "They hated us here. We were Yankees. Foreigners. Worse than foreigners: enemies. Carpet baggers. And it—the War—still too close for even the ones that got whipped to be very sensible. Stirring up the negroes to murder and rape, they called it. Threatening white supremacy. So I suppose that Colonel Sartoris was a town hero because he killed with two shots from the same pistol an old onearmed man and a boy who had never even cast his first vote. Maybe they were right. I dont know."

"Oh," Christmas said. "They might have done that? dug them up after they were already killed, dead? Just when do men that have different blood in them stop hating one another?"

"When do they?" Her voice ceased. She went on: "I dont know. I dont know whether they would have dug them up or not. I wasn't alive then. I was not born until fourteen years after Calvin was killed. I dont know what men might have done then. But father thought they might have. So he hid the graves. And then Calvin's mother died and he buried her there, with Calvin and grandpa. And so it sort of got to be our burying ground before we knew it. Maybe father hadn't planned to bury her there. I remember how my mother (father sent for her up to New Hampshire where some of our kin people still live, soon after Calvin's mother died. He was alone here, you see. I suppose if it hadn't been for Calvin and grandpa buried out yonder, he would have gone away) told me that father started once to move away, when Calvin's mother died. But she died in the summer, and it would have been too hot then to take her back to Mexico, to her people. So he buried her here. Maybe that's why he decided to stay here. Or maybe it was because he was getting old too then, and all the men who had fought in the War were getting old and the negroes hadn't raped or murdered anybody to speak of. Anyway, he buried her here. He had to hide that grave too, because he thought that someone might see it and happen to remember Calvin and grandfather. He couldn't take the risk, even if it was all over and past and done then. And the next year he wrote to our cousin in New Hampshire. He said, 'I am fifty years old. I have all she will ever need. Send me a good woman for a wife. I dont care who she is, just so she is a good housekeeper and is at least thirtyfive years old.' He sent the railroad fare in the letter. Two months later my mother got here and they were married that day. That was quick marrying, for him. The other time it took him over twelve years to get married, that time back in Kansas when he and Calvin and Calvin's mother finally caught up with grandfather. They got home in the middle of the week, but they waited until Sunday to have the wedding. They had it outdoors, down by the creek, with a barbecued steer and a keg of whiskey and everybody that they could get word to or that heard about it, came. They began to get there Saturday morning, and on Saturday night the preacher came. All that day father's sisters worked, making Calvin's mother a wedding gown and a veil. They made the gown out of flour sacks and the veil out of some mosquito netting that a saloon keeper had nailed over a picture behind the bar. They borrowed it from him. They even made some kind of a suit for

Calvin to wear. He was twelve then, and they wanted him to be the ringbearer. He didn't want to. He found out the night before what they intended to make him do, and the next day (they had intended to have the wedding about six or seven oclock the next morning) after everybody had got up and eaten breakfast, they had to put off the ceremony until they could find Calvin. At last they found him and made him put on the suit and they had the wedding, with Calvin's mother in the homemade gown and the mosquito veil and father with his hair slicked with bear's grease and the carved Spanish boots he had brought back from Mexico. Grandfather gave the bride away. Only he had been going back to the keg of whiskey every now and then while they were hunting for Calvin, and so when his time came to give the bride away he made a speech instead. He got off on Lincoln and slavery and dared any man there to deny that Lincoln and the negro and Moses and the children of Israel were the same, and that the Red Sea was just the blood that had to be spilled in order that the black race might cross into the Promised Land. It took them some time to make him stop so the wedding could go on. After the wedding they stayed about a month. Then one day father and grandfather went east, to Washington, and got a commission from the government to come down here, to help with the freed negroes. They came to Jefferson, all except father's sisters. Two of them got married, and the youngest one went to live with one of the others, and grandfather and father and Calvin and his mother came here and bought the house. And then what they probably knew all the time was going to happen did happen, and father was alone until my mother came from New Hampshire. They had never even seen one another before, not even a picture. They got married the day she got here and two years later I was born and father named me Joanna after Calvin's mother. I dont think he even wanted another son at all. I cant remember him very well. The only time I can remember him as somebody, a person, was when he took me and showed me Calvin's and grandpa's graves. It was a bright day, in the spring. I remember how I didn't want to go, without even knowing where it was that we were going. I didn't want to go into the cedars. I dont know why I didn't want to. I couldn't have known

what was in there; I was just four then. And even if I had
known, that should not have frightened a child. I think it was
something about father, something that came from the cedar
grove to me, through him. A something that I felt that he
had put on the cedar grove, and that when I went into it,
the grove would put on me so that I would never be able to
forget it. I dont know. But he made me go in, and the two
of us standing there, and he said, 'Remember this. Your
grandfather and brother are lying there, murdered not by
one white man but by the curse which God put on a whole
race before your grandfather or your brother or me or you
were even thought of. A race doomed and cursed to be forever and ever a part of the white race's doom and curse for
its sins. Remember that. His doom and his curse. Forever
and ever. Mine. Your mother's. Yours, even though you are
a child. The curse of every white child that ever was born
and that ever will be born. None can escape it.' And I said,
'Not even me?' and he said, 'Not even you. Least of all,
you.' I had seen and known negroes since I could remember.
I just looked at them as I did at rain, or furniture, or food
or sleep. But after that I seemed to see them for the first
time not as people, but as a thing, a shadow in which I
lived, we lived, all white people, all other people. I thought
of all the children coming forever and ever into the world,
white, with the black shadow already falling upon them before they drew breath. And I seemed to see the black
shadow in the shape of a cross. And it seemed like the white
babies were struggling, even before they drew breath, to escape from the shadow that was not only upon them but beneath them too, flung out like their arms were flung out, as
if they were nailed to the cross. I saw all the little babies that
would ever be in the world, the ones not yet even born—a
long line of them with their arms spread, on the black
crosses. I couldn't tell then whether I saw it or dreamed it.
But it was terrible to me. I cried at night. At last I told father, tried to tell him. What I wanted to tell him was that I
must escape, get away from under the shadow, or I would
die. 'You cannot,' he said. 'You must struggle, rise. But in
order to rise, you must raise the shadow with you. But you
can never lift it to your level. I see that now, which I did

not see until I came down here. But escape it you cannot. The curse of the black race is God's curse. But the curse of the white race is the black man who will be forever God's chosen own because He once cursed him'." Her voice ceased. Across the vague oblong of open door fireflies drifted. At last Christmas said:

"There was something I was going to ask you. But I guess I know the answer myself, now."

She did not stir. Her voice was quiet. "What?"

"Why your father never killed that fellow——what's his name? Sartoris."

"Oh," she said. Then there was silence again. Across the door the fireflies drifted and drifted. "You would have. Wouldn't you?"

"Yes," he said, at once, immediately. Then he knew that she was looking toward his voice almost as if she could see him. Her voice was almost gentle now, it was so quiet, so still.

"You dont have any idea who your parents were?"

If she could have seen his face she would have found it sullen, brooding. "Except that one of them was part nigger. Like I told you before."

She was still looking at him; her voice told him that. It was quiet, impersonal, interested without being curious. "How do you know that?"

He didn't answer for some time. Then he said: "I dont know it." Again his voice ceased; by its sound she knew that he was looking away, toward the door. His face was sullen, quite still. Then he spoke again, moving; his voice now had an overtone, unmirthful yet quizzical, at once humorless and sardonic: "If I'm not, damned if I haven't wasted a lot of time."

She in turn seemed to muse now, quiet, scarcebreathing, yet still with nothing of selfpity or retrospect: "I had thought of that. Why father didn't shoot Colonel Sartoris. I think that it was because of his French blood."

"French blood?" Christmas said. "Dont even Frenchmen get mad when a man kills his father and his son on the same day? I guess your father must have got religion. Turned preacher, maybe."

She did not answer for a time. The fireflies drifted; somewhere a dog barked, mellow, sad, faraway. "I thought about that," she said. "It was all over then. The killing in uniform and with flags, and the killing without uniforms and flags. And none of it doing or did any good. None of it. And we were foreigners, strangers, that thought differently from the people whose country we had come into without being asked or wanted. And he was French, half of him. Enough French to respect anybody's love for the land where he and his people were born and to understand that a man would have to act as the land where he was born had trained him to act. I think that was it."

XII

IN THIS WAY the second phase began. It was as though he had fallen into a sewer. As upon another life he looked back upon that first hard and manlike surrender, that surrender terrific and hard, like the breaking down of a spiritual skeleton the very sound of whose snapping fibers could be heard almost by the physical ear, so that the act of capitulation was anticlimax, as when a defeated general on the day after the last battle, shaved overnight and with his boots cleaned of the mud of combat, surrenders his sword to a committee.

The sewer ran only by night. The days were the same as they had ever been. He went to work at half past six in the morning. He would leave the cabin without looking toward the house at all. At six in the evening he returned, again without even looking toward the house. He washed and changed to the white shirt and the dark creased trousers and went to the kitchen and found his supper waiting on the table and he sat and ate it, still without having seen her at all. But he knew that she was in the house and that the coming of dark within the old walls was breaking down something and leaving it corrupt with waiting. He knew how she had spent the day; that her days also were no different from what they had always been, as if in her case too another person had lived them. All day long he would imagine her, going about her housework, sitting for that unvarying period at the scarred desk, or talking, listening, to the negro women who came to the house from both directions up and down the road, following paths which had been years in the wearing and which radiated from the house like wheelspokes. What they talked about to her he did not know, though he had watched them approaching the house in a manner not exactly secret, yet purposeful, entering usually singly though sometimes in twos and threes, in their aprons and headrags and now and then with a man's coat thrown about their shoulders, emerging again and returning down the radiating paths not fast and yet not loitering. They would be brief in his mind, thinking *Now she is doing this. Now she is doing that* not thinking much about her. He believed that during the day she thought no more about him than he did about her, too. Even when at night, in her dark bedroom, she insisted on telling him in tedious detail the trivial matters of her day and insisted on his telling her of his day in turn, it was in the fashion of lovers: that imperious and insatiable demand that the trivial details of both days be put into words, without any need to listen to the telling. Then he would finish his supper and go to her where she waited. Often he would not hurry. As time went on and the novelty of the second phase began to wear off and become habit, he would stand in the kitchen door and look out across the dusk and see, perhaps with foreboding and premonition, the savage and lonely street which he had chosen of his own will, waiting for him, thinking *This is not my life. I dont belong here*

At first it shocked him: the abject fury of the New England glacier exposed suddenly to the fire of the New England biblical hell. Perhaps he was aware of the abnegation in it: the imperious and fierce urgency that concealed an actual despair at frustrate and irrevocable years, which she appeared to attempt to compensate each night as if she believed that it would be the last night on earth by damning herself forever to the hell of her forefathers, by living not alone in sin but in filth. She had an avidity for the forbidden wordsymbols; an insatiable appetite for the sound of them on his tongue and on her own. She revealed the terrible and impersonal curiosity of a child about forbidden subjects and objects; that rapt and tireless and detached interest of a surgeon in the physical body and its possibilities. And by day he would see the calm, coldfaced, almost manlike, almost middleaged woman who had lived for twenty years alone, without any feminine fears at all, in a lonely house in a neighborhood populated, when at all, by negroes, who spent a certain portion of each day sitting tranquilly at a desk and writing tranquilly for the eyes of both youth and age the practical advice of a combined priest and banker and trained nurse.

During that period (it could not be called a honeymoon) Christmas watched her pass through every avatar of a woman in love. Soon she more than shocked him: she astonished and bewildered him. She surprised and took him unawares with fits of jealous rage. She could have had no such experience at all, and there was neither reason for the scene nor any possible protagonist: he knew that she knew that. It was as if she had invented the whole thing deliberately, for the purpose of playing it out like a play. Yet she did it with such fury, with such convincingness and such conviction, that on the first occasion he thought that she was under a delusion and the third time he thought that she was mad. She revealed an unexpected and infallible instinct for intrigue. She insisted on a place for concealing notes, letters. It was in a hollow fence post below the rotting stable. He never saw her put a note there, yet she insisted on his visiting it daily; when he did so, the letter would be there. When he did not and lied to her, he would find that she had already set traps to catch him in the lie; she cried, wept.

Sometimes the notes would tell him not to come until a certain hour, to that house which no white person save himself had entered in years and in which for twenty years now she had been all night alone; for a whole week she forced him to climb into a window to come to her. He would do so and sometimes he would have to seek her about the dark house until he found her, hidden, in closets, in empty rooms, waiting, panting, her eyes in the dark glowing like the eyes of cats. Now and then she appointed trysts beneath certain shrubs about the grounds, where he would find her naked, or with her clothing half torn to ribbons upon her, in the wild throes of nymphomania, her body gleaming in the slow shifting from one to another of such formally erotic attitudes and gestures as a Beardsley of the time of Petronius might have drawn. She would be wild then, in the close, breathing half-dark without walls, with her wild hair, each strand of which would seem to come alive like octopus tentacles, and her wild hands and her breathing: "Negro! Negro! Negro!"

Within six months she was completely corrupted. It could not be said that he corrupted her. His own life, for all its anonymous promiscuity, had been conventional enough, as a life of healthy and normal sin usually is. The corruption came from a source even more inexplicable to him than to her. In fact, it was as though with the corruption which she seemed to gather from the air itself, she began to corrupt him. He began to be afraid. He could not have said of what. But he began to see himself as from a distance, like a man being sucked down into a bottomless morass. He had not exactly thought that yet. What he was now seeing was the street lonely, savage, and cool. That was it: cool; he was thinking, saying aloud to himself sometimes, "I better move. I better get away from here."

But something held him, as the fatalist can always be held: by curiosity, pessimism, by sheer inertia. Meanwhile the affair went on, submerging him more and more by the imperious and overriding fury of those nights. Perhaps he realised that he could not escape. Anyway, he stayed, watching the two creatures that struggled in the one body like two moon-gleamed shapes struggling drowning in alternate throes upon the surface of a black thick pool beneath the last moon. Now it would be that still, cold, contained figure of the first phase who, even though lost and damned, remained somehow impervious and impregnable; then it would be the other, the second one, who in furious denial of that impregnability strove to drown in the black abyss of its own creating that physical purity which had been preserved too long now even to be lost. Now and then they would come to the black surface, locked like sisters; the black waters would drain away. Then the world would rush back: the room, the walls, the peaceful myriad sound of insects from beyond the summer windows where insects had whirred for forty years. She would stare at him then with the wild, despairing face of a stranger; looking at her then he paraphrased himself: "She wants to pray, but she dont know how to do that either."

She had begun to get fat.

The end of this phase was not sharp, not a climax, like the first. It merged into the third phase so gradually that he could not have said where one stopped and the other began. It was summer becoming fall, with already, like shadows before a westering sun, the chill and implacable import of autumn cast ahead upon summer; something of dying summer spurting again like a dying coal, in the fall. This was over a period of two years. He still worked at the planing mill, and in the meantime he had begun to sell a little whiskey, very judiciously, restricting himself to a few discreet customers none of whom knew the others. She did not know this, although he kept his stock hidden on the place and met his clients in the woods beyond the pasture. Very likely she would not have objected. But neither would Mrs McEachern have objected to the hidden rope; perhaps he did not tell her for the same reason that he did not tell Mrs McEachern. Thinking of Mrs McEachern and the rope, and of the waitress whom he had never told where the money came from which he gave to her, and now of his present mistress and the whiskey, he could almost believe that it was not to make money that he sold the whiskey but because he was doomed to conceal always something from the women who surrounded him. Meanwhile he would see her from a distance now and then in the daytime, about the rear premises, where moved articulate beneath the clean, austere garments which she wore that rotten richness ready to flow into putrefaction at a touch, like something growing in a swamp, not once looking toward the cabin or toward him. And when he thought of that other personality that seemed to exist somewhere in physical darkness itself, it seemed to him that what he now saw by daylight was a phantom of someone whom the night sister had murdered and which now moved purposeless about the scenes of old peace, robbed even of the power of lamenting.

Of course the first fury of the second phase could not last. At first it had been a torrent; now it was a tide, with a flow and ebb. During its flood she could almost fool them both. It was as if out of her knowledge that it was just a flow that must presently react was born a wilder fury, a fierce denial that could flag itself and him into physical experimentation that transcended imagining, carried them as though by momentum alone, bearing them without volition or plan. It was as if she knew somehow that time was short, that autumn was almost upon her, without knowing yet the exact significance of autumn. It seemed to be instinct alone: instinct physical and instinctive denial of the wasted years. Then the tide would ebb. Then they would be stranded as behind a dying mistral, upon a spent and satiate beach, looking at one another like strangers, with hopeless and reproachful (on his part with weary: on hers with despairing) eyes.

But the shadow of autumn was upon her. She began to talk about a child, as though instinct had warned her that now was the time when she must either justify or expiate. She talked about it in the ebb periods. At first the beginning of the night was always a flood, as if the hours of light and of separation had dammed up enough of the wasting stream to simulate torrent for a moment at least. But after a while the stream became too thin for that: he would go to her now with reluctance, a stranger, already backlooking; a stranger he would leave her after having sat with her in the dark bedroom, talking of still a third stranger. He noticed now how, as though by premeditation, they met always in the bedroom, as though they were married. No more did he have to seek her through the house; the nights when he must seek her, hidden and panting and naked, about the dark house or among the shrubbery of the ruined park were as dead now as the hollow fencepost below the barn.

That was all dead: the scenes, the faultlessly played scenes of secret and monstrous delight and of jealousy. Though if she had but known it now, she had reason for jealousy. He made trips every week or so, on business, he told her. She did not know that the business took him to Memphis, where he betrayed her with other women, women bought for a price. She did not know it. Perhaps in the phase in which she now was she could not have been convinced, would not have listened to proof, would not have cared. Because she had taken to lying sleepless most of the night, making up the sleep in the afternoons. She was not sick; it was not her body. She had never been better; her appetite was enormous and she weighed thirty pounds more than she had ever weighed in her life. It was not that that kept her awake. It was something out of the darkness, the earth, the dying summer itself: something threatful and terrible to her because instinct assured her that it would not harm her; that it would overtake and betray her completely, but she would not be harmed: that on the contrary, she would be saved, that life would go on the same and even better, even less terrible. What was terrible was that she did not want to be saved. "I'm not ready to pray yet," she said aloud, quietly, rigid, soundless, her eyes wide open, while the moon poured and poured into the window, filling the room with something cold and irrevocable and wild with regret. "Dont make me have to pray yet. Dear God, let me be damned a little longer, a little while." She seemed to see her whole past life, the starved years, like a gray tunnel, at the far and irrevocable end of which, as unfading as a reproach, her naked breast of three short years ago ached as though in agony, virgin and crucified; "Not yet, dear God. Not yet, dear God."

So when he now came to her, after the passive and cold and seemly transports of sheer habit she began to speak of a child. She talked about it impersonally at first, discussing children. Perhaps it was sheer and instinctive feminine cunning and indirection, perhaps not. Anyway, it was some time before he discovered with a kind of shock that she was discussing it as a possibility, a practical thought. He said No at once.

"Why not?" she said. She looked at him, speculative. He was thinking fast, thinking *She wants to be married. That's it. She wants a child no more than I do* 'It's just a trick,' he thought. 'I should have known it, expected it. I should have cleared out of here a year ago.' But he was afraid to tell her this, to let the word marriage come between them, come aloud, thinking, 'She may not have thought of it, and I will just put the notion in her head.' She was watching him. "Why not?" she said. And then something in him flashed *Why not? It would mean ease, security, for the rest of your life. You would never have to move again. And you might as well be married to her as this* thinking 'No. If I give in now, I will deny all the thirty years that I have lived to make me what I chose to be.' He said:

"If we were going to have one, I guess we would have had one two years ago."

"We didn't want one then."

"We dont want one now, either," he said.

That was in September. Just after Christmas she told him that she was pregnant. Almost before she ceased to speak, he believed that she was lying. He discovered now that he had been expecting her to tell him that for three months. But when he looked at her face, he knew that she was not. He believed that she also knew that she was not. He thought, 'Here it comes. She will say it now: marry. But I can at least get out of the house first.'

But she did not. She was sitting quite still on the bed, her hands on her lap, her still New England face (it was still the face of a spinster: prominently boned, long, a little thin, almost manlike: in contrast to it her plump body was more richly and softly animal than ever) lowered. She said, in a tone musing, detached, impersonal: "A full measure. Even to a bastard negro child. I would like to see father's and Calvin's faces. This will be a good time for you to run, if that's what you want to do." But it was as though she were not listening to her own voice, did not intend for the words to have any actual meaning: that final upflare of stubborn and dying summer upon which autumn, the dawning of halfdeath, had come unawares. 'It's over now,' she thought quietly; 'finished.' Except the waiting, for one month more to pass, to be sure; she had learned that from the negro women, that you could not always tell until after two months. She would have to wait another month, watching the calendar. She made a mark on the calendar to be sure, so there would be no mistake; through the bedroom window she watched that month accomplish. A frost had come, and some of the leaves were beginning to turn. The marked day on the calendar came and passed; she gave herself another week, to be doubly sure. She was not elated, since she was not surprised. "I am with child," she said, quietly, aloud.

'I'll go tomorrow,' he told himself, that same day. 'I'll go Sunday,' he thought. 'I'll wait and get this week's pay, and then I am gone.' He began to look forward to Saturday, planning where he would go. He did not see her all that week. He expected her to send for him. When he entered or left the cabin he would find himself avoiding looking toward the house, as he had during the first week he was there. He did not see her at all. Now and then he would see the negro women, in nondescript garments against the autumn chill, coming or going along the worn paths, entering or leaving the house. But that was all. When Saturday came, he did not go. 'Might as well have all the jack I can get,' he thought. 'If she aint anxious for me to clear out, no reason why I should be. I'll go next Saturday.'

He stayed on. The weather remained cold, bright and cold. When he went to bed now in his cotton blanket, in the draughty cabin, he would think of the bedroom in the house, with its fire, its ample, quilted, lintpadded covers. He was nearer to selfpity than he had ever been. 'She might at least send me another blanket,' he thought. So might he have bought one. But he did not. Neither did she. He waited. He waited what he thought was a long time. Then one evening in February he returned home and found a note from her on his cot. It was brief; it was an order almost, directing him to come to the house that night. He was not surprised. He had never yet known a woman who, without another man available, would not come around in time. And he knew now that tomorrow he would go. 'This must be what I have been waiting for,' he thought; 'I have just been waiting to be vindicated.' When he changed his clothes, he shaved also. He prepared himself like a bridegroom, unaware of it. He found the table set for him in the kitchen, as usual; during all the time that he had not seen her, that had never failed. He ate and went up stairs. He did not hurry. 'We got all night,' he thought. 'It'll be something for her to think about tomorrow night and the next one, when she finds that cabin empty.' She was sitting before the fire. She did not even turn her head when he entered. "Bring that chair up with you," she said.

This was how the third phase began. It puzzled him for a while, even more than the other two. He had expected eagerness, a kind of tacit apology; or lacking that, an acquiescence that wanted only to be wooed. He was prepared to go that length, even. What he found was a stranger who put aside with the calm firmness of a man his hand when at last and in a kind of baffled desperation he went and touched her. "Come on," he said. "If you have something to tell me. We always talk better afterward. It wont hurt the kid, if that's what you have been afraid of."

She stayed him with a single word; for the first time he looked at her face: he looked upon a face cold, remote, and fanatic. "Do you realise," she said, "that you are wasting your life?" And he sat looking at her like a stone, as if he could not believe his own ears.

It took him some time to comprehend what she meant. She did not look at him at all. She sat looking into the fire, her face cold, still, brooding, talking to him as if he were a stranger, while he listened in outraged amazement. She wanted him to take over all her business affairs—the correspondence and the periodical visits—with the negro schools. She had the plan all elaborated. She recited it to him in detail while he listened in mounting rage and amazement. He was to have complete charge, and she would be his secretary, assistant: they would travel to the schools together, visit in the negro homes together; listening, even with his anger, he knew that the plan was mad. And all the while her calm profile in the peaceful firelight was as grave and tranquil as a portrait in a frame. When he left, he remembered that she had not once mentioned the expected child.

He did not yet believe that she was mad. He thought that it was because she was pregnant, as he believed that was why she would not let him touch her. He tried to argue with her. But it was like trying to argue with a tree: she did not even rouse herself to deny, she just listened quietly and then talked again in that level, cold tone as if he had never spoken. When he rose at last and went out he did not even know if she was aware that he had gone.

He saw her but once more within the next two months. He followed his daily routine, save that he did not approach the house at all now, taking his meals downtown again, as when he had first gone to work at the mill. But then, when he first went to work, he would not need to think of her during the day; he hardly ever thought about her. Now he could not help himself. She was in his mind so constantly that it was almost as if he were looking at her, there in the house, patient, waiting, inescapable, crazy. During the first phase it had been as though he were outside a house where snow was on the ground, trying to get into the house; during the second phase he was at the bottom of a pit in the hot wild darkness; now he was in the middle of a plain where there was no house, not even snow, not even wind.

He began now to be afraid, whose feeling up to now had been bewilderment and perhaps foreboding and fatality. He now had a partner in his whiskey business: a stranger named Brown who had appeared at the mill one day early in the spring, seeking work. He knew that the man was a fool, but at first he thought, 'At least he will have sense enough to do what I tell him to do. He wont have to think himself at all'; it was not until later that he said to himself: 'I know now that what makes a fool is an inability to take even his own good advice'. He took Brown because Brown was a stranger and had a certain cheerful and unscrupulous readiness about him, and not overmuch personal courage, knowing that in the hands of a judicious man, a coward within his own limitations can be made fairly useful to anyone except himself.

His fear was that Brown might learn about the woman in the house and do something irrevocable out of his own unpredictable folly. He was afraid that the woman, since he had avoided her, might take it into her head to come to the cabin some night. He had not seen her but once since February. That was when he sought her to tell her that Brown was coming to live with him in the cabin. It was on Sunday. He called her, and she came out to where he stood on the back porch and listened quietly. "You didn't have to do that," she said. He didn't understand then what she meant. It was not until later that thinking again flashed, complete, like a printed sentence: *She thinks that I brought him out here to keep her off. She believes that I think that with him there, she wont dare come down to the cabin; that she will have to let me alone*

Thus he put his belief, his fear of what she might do, into his own mind by believing that he had put it into hers. He believed that, since she had thought that, that Brown's presence would not only not deter her: it would be an incentive for her to come to the cabin. Because of the fact that for over a month now she had done nothing at all, made no move at all, he believed that she might do anything. Now he too lay awake at night. But he was thinking, 'I have got to do something. There is something that I am going to do.'

So he would trick and avoid Brown in order to reach the cabin first. He expected each time to find her waiting. When he would reach the cabin and find it empty, he would think in a kind of impotent rage of the urgency, the lying and the haste, and of her alone and idle in the house all day, with nothing to do save to decide whether to betray him at once or torture him a little longer. By ordinary he would not have minded whether Brown knew about their relations or not. He had nothing in his nature of reticence or of chivalry toward women. It was practical, material. He would have been indifferent if all Jefferson knew he was her lover: it was that he wanted no one to begin to speculate on what his private life out there was because of the hidden whiskey which was netting him thirty or forty dollars a week. That was one reason. Another reason was vanity. He would have died or murdered rather than have anyone, another man, learn what their relations had now become. That not only had she changed her life completely, but that she was trying to change his too and make of him something between a hermit and a missionary to negroes. He believed that if Brown learned the one, he must inevitably learn the other. So he would reach the cabin at last, after the lying and the hurry, and as he put his hand on the door, remembering the haste and thinking that in a moment he would find that it had not been necessary at all and yet to neglect which precaution he dared not, he would hate her with a fierce revulsion of dread and impotent rage. Then one evening he opened the door and found the note on the cot.

He saw it as soon as he entered, lying square and white and profoundly inscrutable against the dark blanket. He did not even stop to think that he believed he knew what the message would be, would promise. He felt no eagerness; he felt relief. 'It's over now,' he thought, not yet taking up the folded paper. 'It will be like it was before now. No more talking about niggers and babies. She has come around. She has worn the other out, seen that she was getting nowhere. She sees now that what she wants, needs, is a man. She wants a man by night; what he does by daylight does not matter.' He should have realised then the reason why he had not gone away. He should have seen that he was bound just as tightly by that small square of still undivulging paper as though it were a lock and chain. He did not think of that. He saw only himself once again on the verge of promise and delight. It would be quieter though, now. They would both want it so; besides the whiphand which he would now have. 'All that foolishness,' he thought, holding the yet unopened paper in his hands; 'all that damn foolishness. She is still she and I am still I. And now, after all this damn foolishness'; thinking how they would both laugh over it tonight, later, afterward, when the time for quiet talking and quiet laughing came: at the whole thing, at one another, at themselves.

He did not open the note at all. He put it away and washed and shaved and changed his clothes, whistling while he did so. He had not finished when Brown came in. "Well, well, well," Brown said. Christmas said nothing. He was facing the shard of mirror nailed to the wall, knotting his tie. Brown had stopped in the center of the floor: a tall, lean, young man in dirty overalls, with a dark, weakly handsome face and curious eyes. Beside his mouth there was a narrow scar as white as a thread of spittle. After a while Brown said: "Looks like you are going somewhere."

"Does it?" Christmas said. He did not look around. He whistled monotonously but truely: something in minor, plaintive and negroid.

"I reckon I wont bother to clean up none," Brown said, "seeing as you are almost ready."

Christmas looked back at him. "Ready for what?"

"Aint you going to town?"

"Did I ever say I was?" Christmas said. He turned back to the glass.

"Oh," Brown said. He watched the back of Christmas' head. "Well, I reckon from that that you're going on private business." He watched Christmas. "This here's a cold night to be laying around on the wet ground without nothing under you but a thin gal."

"Aint it, though?" Christmas said, whistling, preoccupied and unhurried. He turned and picked up his coat and put it on, Brown still watching him. He went to the door. "See you in the morning," he said. The door did not close behind him. He knew that Brown was standing in it, looking after him.

But he did not attempt to conceal his purpose. He went on toward the house. 'Let him watch,' he thought. 'Let him follow me if he wants to.'

The table was set for him in the kitchen. Before sitting down he took the unopened note from his pocket and laid it beside his plate. It was not enclosed, not sealed; it sprang open of its own accord, as though inviting him, insisting. But he did not look at it. He began to eat. He ate without haste. He had almost finished when he raised his head suddenly, listening. Then he rose and went to the door through which he had entered, with the noiselessness of a cat, and jerked the door open suddenly. Brown stood just outside, his face leaned to the door, or where the door had been. The light fell upon his face and upon it was an expression of intent and infantile interest which became surprise while Christmas looked at it, then it recovered, falling back a little. Brown's voice was gleeful though quiet, cautious, conspiratorial, as if he had already established his alliance and sympathy with Christmas, unasked, and without waiting to know what was going on, out of loyalty to his partner or perhaps to abstract man as opposed to all woman. "Well, well, well," he said. "So this is where you tomcat to every night. Right at our front door, you might say——"

Without saying a word Christmas struck him. The blow did not fall hard, because Brown was already in innocent and gleeful backmotion, in midsnicker as it were. The blow cut his voice short off; moving, springing backward, he vanished from the fall of light, into the darkness, from which his voice came, still not loud, as if even now he would not jeopardise his partner's business, but tense now with alarm, astonishment: "Dont you hit me!" He was the taller of the two: a gangling shape already in a ludicrous diffusion of escape as if he were on the point of clattering to earth in complete disintegration as he stumbled backward before the steady and still silent advance of the other. Again Brown's voice came, high, full of alarm and spurious threat: "Dont you hit me!" This time the blow struck his shoulder as he turned. He was running now. He ran for a hundred yards before he slowed, looking back. Then he stopped and turned. "You durn yellowbellied wop," he said, in a tentative tone, jerking his head immediately, as if his voice had made more noise, sounded louder, than he had intended. There was no sound from the house; the kitchen door was dark again, closed again. He raised his voice a little: "You durn yellowbellied wop! I'll learn you who you are monkeying with." There came no sound anywhere. It was chilly. He turned and went back to the cabin, mumbling to himself.

When Christmas reentered the kitchen he did not even look back at the table on which lay the note which he had not yet read. He went on through the door which led into the house and on to the stairs. He began to mount, not fast. He mounted steadily; he could now see the bedroom door, a crack of light, firelight, beneath it. He went steadily on and put his hand upon the door. Then he opened it and he stopped dead still. She was sitting at a table, beneath the lamp. He saw a figure that he knew, in a severe garment that he knew—a garment that looked as if it had been made for and worn by a careless man. Above it he saw a head with hair just beginning to gray drawn gauntly back to a knot as savage and ugly as a wart on a diseased bough. Then she looked up at him and he saw that she wore steelrimmed spectacles which he had never seen before. He stood in the door, his hand still on the knob, quite motionless. It seemed to him that he could actually hear the words inside him: *You should have read that note. You should have read that note* thinking, 'I am going to do something. Going to do something.'

He was still hearing that while he stood beside the table on which papers were scattered and from which she had not risen, and listened to the calm enormity which her cold, still voice unfolded, his mouth repeating the words after her while he looked down at the scattered and enigmatic papers and documents and thinking fled smooth and idle, wondering what this paper meant and what that paper meant. "To school," his mouth said.

"Yes," she said. "They will take you. Any of them will. On my account. You can choose any one you want among them. We wont even have to pay."

"To school," his mouth said. "A nigger school. Me."

"Yes. Then you can go to Memphis. You can read law in Peebles' office. He will teach you law. Then you can take charge of all the legal business. All this, all that he does, Peebles does."

"And then learn law in the office of a nigger lawyer," his mouth said.

"Yes. Then I will turn over all the business to you, all the money. All of it. So that when you need money for yourself you could. . . . . . .you would know how; lawyers know how to do it so that it. . . . . . . You would be helping them up out of darkness and none could accuse or blame you even if they found out. . . . . . .even if you did not replace. . . . . . .but you could replace the money and none would ever know. . . . . . ."

"But a nigger college, a nigger lawyer," his voice said, quiet, not even argumentative; just promptive. They were not looking at one another; she had not looked up since he entered.

"Tell them," she said.

"Tell niggers that I am a nigger too?" She now looked at him. Her face was quite calm. It was the face of an old woman now.

"Yes. You'll have to do that. So they wont charge you anything. On my account."

Then it was as if he said suddenly to his mouth: 'Shut up. Shut up that drivel. Let me talk.' He leaned down. She did not move. Their faces were not a foot apart: the one cold, dead white, fanatical, mad; the other parchmentcolored, the lip lifted into the shape of a soundless and rigid snarl. He said quietly: "You're old. I never noticed that before. An old woman. You've got gray in your hair." She struck him, at once, with her flat hand, the rest of her body not moving at all. Her blow made a flat sound; his blow as close upon it as echo. He struck with his fist, then in that long blowing wind he jerked her up from the chair and held her, facing him, motionless, not a flicker upon her still face, while the long wind of knowing rushed down upon him. "You haven't got any baby," he said. "You never had one. There is not anything the matter with you except being old. You just got old and it happened to you and now you are not any good anymore. That's all that's wrong with you." He released her and struck her again. She fell huddled onto the bed, looking up at him, and he struck her in the face again and standing over her he spoke to her the words which she had once loved to hear on his tongue, which she used to say that she could taste there, murmurous, obscene, caressing. "That's all. You're just worn out. You're not any good anymore. That's all."

She lay on the bed, on her side, her head turned and looking up at him across her bleeding mouth. "Maybe it would be better if we both were dead," she said.

He could see the note lying on the blanket as soon as he opened the door. Then he would go and take it up and open it. He would now remember the hollow fencepost as something of which he had heard told, as having taken place in another life from any that he had ever lived. Because the paper, the ink, the form and shape, were the same. They had never been long; they were not long now. But now there was nothing evocative of unspoken promise, of rich and unmentionable delights, in them. They were now briefer than epitaphs and more terse than commands.

His first impulse would be to not go. He believed that he dared not go. Then he knew that he dared not fail to go. He would not change his clothes now. In his sweatstained overalls he would traverse the late twilight of May and enter the kitchen. The table was never set with food for him now. Sometimes he would look at it as he passed and he would think, 'My God. When have I sat down in peace to eat.' And he could not remember.

He would go on into the house and mount the stairs. Already he would be hearing her voice. It would increase as he mounted and until he reached the door to the bedroom. The door would be shut, locked; from beyond it the monotonous steady voice came. He could not distinguish the words; only the ceaseless monotone. He dared not try to distinguish the words. He did not dare let himself know what she was at. So he would stand there and wait, and after a while the voice would cease and she would open the door and he would enter. As he passed the bed he would look down at the floor beside it and it would seem to him that he could distinguish the prints of knees and he would jerk his eyes away as if it were death that they had looked at.

Likely the lamp would not yet be lighted. They did not sit down. Again they stood to talk, as they used to do two years ago; standing in the dusk while her voice repeated its tale: ". . . . . . .not to school, then, if you dont want to go. . . . Do without that. . . . . . . Your soul. Expiation of. . . . . ." And he waiting, cold, still, until she had finished: ". . . . . .hell. . . . . .forever and ever and ever. . . . . ."

"No," he said. And she would listen as quietly, and he knew that she was not convinced and she knew that he was not. Yet neither surrendered; worse: they would not let one another alone; he would not even go away. And they would stand for a while longer in the quiet dusk peopled, as though from their loins, by a myriad ghosts of dead sins and delights, looking at one another's still and fading face, weary, spent, and indomitable.

Then he would leave. And before the door had shut and the bolt had shot to behind him, he would hear the voice again, monotonous, calm, and despairing, saying what and to what or whom he dared not learn nor suspect. And so as he sat in the shadows of the ruined garden on that August night three months later and heard the clock in the courthouse two miles away strike ten and then eleven, he believed with calm paradox that he was the volitionless servant of the fatality in which he believed that he did not believe. He was saying to himself *I had to do it* already in the past tense; *I had to do it. She said so herself*

She had said it two nights ago. He found the note and went to her. As he mounted the stairs the monotonous voice grew louder, sounded louder and clearer than usual. When he reached the top of the stairs he saw why. The door was open this time, and she did not rise from where she knelt beside the bed when he entered. She did not stir; her voice did not cease. Her head was not bowed. Her face was lifted, almost with pride, her attitude of formal abjectness a part of the pride, her voice calm and tranquil and abnegant in the twilight. She did not seem to be aware that he had entered until she finished a period. Then she turned her head. "Kneel with me," she said.

"No," he said.

"Kneel," she said. "You wont even need to speak to Him yourself. Just kneel. Just make the first move."

"No," he said. "I'm going."

She didn't move, looking back and up at him. "Joe," she said. "Will you stay? Will you do that much?"

"Yes," he said. "I'll stay. But make it fast."

She prayed again. She spoke quietly, with that abjectness of pride. When it was necessary to use the symbolwords which he had taught her, she used them, spoke them forthright and without hesitation, talking to God as if He were a man in the room with two other men. She spoke of herself and of him as of two other people, her voice still, monotonous, sexless. Then she ceased. She rose quietly. They stood in the twilight, facing one another. This time she did not even ask the question; he did not even need to reply. After a time she said quietly:

"Then there's just one other thing to do."

"There's just one other thing to do," he said.

'So now it's all done, all finished,' he thought quietly, sitting in the dense shadow of the shrubbery, hearing the last stroke of the far clock cease and die away. It was a spot where he had overtaken her, found her on one of the wild nights two years ago. But that was in another time, another life. Now it was still, quiet, the fecund earth now coolly suspirant. The dark was filled with the voices, myriad, out of all time that he had known, as though all the past was a flat pattern. And going on: tomorrow night, all the tomorrows, to be a part of the flat pattern, going on. He thought of that with quiet astonishment: going on, myriad, familiar, since all that had ever been was the same as all that was to be, since tomorrow to-be and had-been would be the same. Then it was time.

He rose. He moved from the shadow and went around the house and entered the kitchen. The house was dark. He had not been to the cabin since early morning and he did not know if she had left a note for him or not, expected him or not. Yet he did not try for silence. It was as if he were not thinking of sleep, of whether she would be asleep or not. He mounted the stairs steadily and entered the bedroom. Almost at once she spoke from the bed. "Light the lamp," she said.

"It wont need any light," he said.

"Light the lamp."

"No," he said. He stood over the bed. He held the razor in his hand. But it was not open yet. But she did not speak again and then his body seemed to walk away from him. It went to the table and his hands laid the razor on the table and found the lamp and struck the match. She was sitting up in the bed, her back against the headboard. Over her nightdress she wore a shawl drawn down across her breast. Her arms were folded upon the shawl, her hands hidden from sight. He stood at the table. They looked at one another.

"Will you kneel with me?" she said. "I dont ask it."

"No," he said.

"I dont ask it. It's not I who ask it. Kneel with me."

"No."

They looked at one another. "Joe," she said. "For the last time. I dont ask it. Remember that. Kneel with me."

"No," he said. Then he saw her arms unfold and her right hand come forth from beneath the shawl. It held an old style, single action, cap-and-ball revolver almost as long and heavier than a small rifle. But the shadow of it and of her arm and hand on the wall did not waver at all, the shadow of both monstrous, the cocked hammer monstrous, backhooked and viciously poised like the arched head of a snake; it did not waver at all. And her eyes did not waver at all. They were as still as the round black ring of the pistol muzzle. But there was no heat in them, no fury. They were calm and still as all pity and all despair and all conviction. But he was not watching them. He was watching the shadowed pistol on the wall; he was watching when the cocked shadow of the hammer flicked away.

Standing in the middle of the road, with his right hand lifted full in the glare of the approaching car, he had not actually expected it to stop. Yet it did, with a squealing and sprawling suddenness that was almost ludicrous. It was a small car, battered and old. When he approached it, in the reflected glare of the headlights two young faces seemed to float like two softcolored and aghast balloons, the nearer one, the girl's, backshrunk in a soft, wide horror. But Christmas did not notice this at the time. "How about riding with you, as far as you go?" he said. They said nothing at all, looking at him with that still and curious horror which he did not notice. So he opened the door to enter the rear seat.

When he did so, the girl began to make a choked wailing sound which would be much louder in a moment, as fear gained courage as it were. Already the car was in motion; it seemed to leap forward, and the boy, without moving his hands from the wheel or turning his head toward the girl hissed: "Shut up! Hush! It's our only chance! Will you hush now?" Christmas did not hear this either. He was sitting back now, completely unaware that he was riding directly behind desperate terror. He only thought with momentary interest that the small car was travelling at a pretty reckless speed for a narrow country road.

"How far does this road go?" he said.

The boy told him, naming the same town which the negro boy had named to him on that afternoon three years ago, when he had first seen Jefferson. The boy's voice had a dry, light quality. "Do you want to go there, cap'm?"

"All right," Christmas said. "Yes. Yes. That will do. That will suit me. Are you going there?"

"Sure," the boy said, in that light, flat tone. "Wherever you say." Again the girl beside him began that choked, murmurous, small-animallike moaning; again the boy hissed at her, his face still rigidly front, the little car rushing and bouncing onward: "Hush! Shhhhhhhhhhhh. Hush! Hush!" But again Christmas did not notice. He saw only the two young, rigidly forwardlooking heads against the light glare, into which the ribbon of the road rushed swaying and fleeing. But he remarked both them and the fleeing road without curiosity; he was not even paying attention when he found that the boy had apparently been speaking to him for some time; how far they had come or where they were he did not know. The boy's diction was slow now, recapitulant, each word as though chosen simply and carefully and spoken slowly and clearly for the ear of a foreigner: "Listen, cap'm. When I turn off up here. It's just a short cut. A short cutoff to a better road. I am going to take the cutoff. When I come to the short cut. To the better road. So we can get there quicker. See?"

"All right," Christmas said. The car bounced and rushed on, swaying on the curves and up the hills and fleeing down again as if the earth had dropped from under them. Mail boxes on posts beside the road rushed into the lights and flicked past. Now and then they passed a dark house. Again the boy was speaking:

"Now, this here cutoff I was telling you about. It's right down here. I'm going to turn into it. But it dont mean I am leaving the road. I am just going a little way across to a better road. See?"

"All right," Christmas said. Then for no reason he said: "You must live around here somewhere."

Now it was the girl who spoke. She turned in the seat, whirling, her small face wan with suspense and terror and blind and ratlike desperation: "We do!" she cried. "We both do! Right up yonder! And when my pappy and brothers——" Her voice ceased, cut short off; Christmas saw the boy's hand clapped upon her lower face and her hands tugging at the wrist while beneath the hand itself her smothered voice choked and bubbled. Christmas sat forward.

"Here," he said. "I'll get out here. You can let me out here."

"Now you've done it!" the boy cried, too, thinly, with desperate rage too. "If you'd just kept quiet——"

"Stop the car," Christmas said. "I aint going to hurt either of you. I just want to get out." Again the car stopped with sprawling suddenness. But the engine still raced, and the car leaped forward again before he was clear of the step; he had to leap forward running for a few steps to recover his balance. As he did so, something heavy and hard struck him on the flank. The car rushed on, fading at top speed. From it floated back the girl's shrill wailing. Then it was gone; the darkness, the now impalpable dust, came down again, and the silence beneath the summer stars. The object which had struck him had delivered an appreciable blow; then he discovered that the object was attached to his right hand. Raising the hand, he found that it held the ancient heavy pistol. He did not know that he had it; he did not remember having picked it up at all, nor why. But there it was. 'And I flagged that car with my right hand,' he thought. 'No wonder she . . . . . . .they. . . . . . .' He drew his right hand back to throw, the pistol balanced upon it. Then he paused, and he struck a match and examined the pistol in the puny dying glare. The match burned down and went out, yet he still seemed to see the ancient thing with its two loaded chambers: the one upon which the hammer had already fallen and which had not exploded, and the other upon which no hammer had yet fallen but upon which a hammer had been planned to fall. 'For her and for me,' he said. His arm came back, and threw. He heard the pistol crash once through undergrowth. Then there was no sound again. 'For her and for me.'

XIII

WITHIN FIVE MINUTES after the countryman found the fire, the people began to gather. Some of them, also on the way to town in wagons to spend Saturday, also stopped. Some came afoot from the immediate neighborhood. This was a region of negro cabins and gutted and outworn fields out of which a corporal's guard of detectives could not have combed ten people, man woman or child, yet which now within thirty minutes produced, as though out of thin air, parties and groups ranging from single individuals to entire families. Still others came out from town in racing and blatting cars. Among these came the sheriff of the county—a fat, comfortable man with a hard, canny head and a benevolent aspect—who thrust away those who crowded to look down at the body on the sheet with that static and childlike amaze with which adults contemplate their own inescapable portraits. Among them the casual Yankees and the poor whites and even the southerners who had lived for a while in the north, who believed aloud that it was an anonymous negro crime committed not by a negro but by Negro and who knew, believed, and hoped that she had been ravished too: at least once before her throat was cut and at least once afterward. The sheriff came up and looked himself once and then sent the body away, hiding the poor thing from the eyes.

Then there was nothing for them to look at except the place where the body had lain and the fire. And soon nobody could remember exactly where the sheet had rested, what earth it had covered, and so then there was only the fire to look at. So they looked at the fire, with that same dull and static amaze which they had brought down from the old fetid caves where knowing began, as though, like death, they had never seen fire before. Presently the fire truck came up gallantly, with noise, with whistles and bells. It was new, painted red, with gilt trim and a handpower siren and a bell gold in color and in tone serene, arrogant, and proud. About it hatless men and youths clung with the astonishing disregard of physical laws that flies possess. It had mechanical ladders that sprang to prodigious heights at the touch of a hand, like opera hats; only there was now nothing for them to spring to. It had neat and virgin coils of hose evocative of telephone trust advertisements in the popular magazines; but there was nothing to hook them to and nothing to flow through them. So the hatless men, who had deserted counters and desks, swung down, even including the one who ground the siren. They came too and were shown several different places where the sheet had lain, and some of them with pistols already in their pockets began to canvass about for someone to crucify.

But there wasn't anybody. She had lived such a quiet life, attended so to her own affairs, that she bequeathed to the town in which she had been born and lived and died a foreigner, an outlander, a kind of heritage of astonishment and outrage, for which, even though she had supplied them at last with an emotional barbecue, a Roman holiday almost, they would never forgive her and let her be dead in peace and quiet. Not that. Peace is not that often. So they moiled and clotted, believing that the flames, the blood, the body that had died three years ago and had just now begun to live again, cried out for vengeance, not believing that the rapt infury of the flames and the immobility of the body were both affirmations of an attained bourne beyond the hurt and harm of man. Not that. Because the other made nice believing. Better than the shelves and the counters filled with longfamiliar objects bought, not because the owner desired them or admired them, could take any pleasure in the owning of them, but in order to cajole or trick other men into buying them at a profit; and who must now and then contemplate both the objects which had not yet sold and the men who could buy them but had not yet done so, with anger and maybe outrage and maybe despair too. Better than the musty offices where the lawyers waited lurking among ghosts of old lusts and lies, or where the doctors waited with sharp knives and sharp drugs, telling man, believing that he should believe, without resorting to printed admonishments, that they labored for that end whose ultimate attainment would leave them with nothing whatever to do. And the women came too, the idle ones in bright and sometimes hurried garments, with secret and passionate and glittering looks and with secret frustrated breasts (who have ever loved death better than peace) to print with a myriad small hard heels to the constant murmur *Who did it? Who did it?* periods such as perhaps *Is he still free? Ah. Is he? Is he?*

The sheriff also stared at the flames with exasperation and astonishment, since there was no scene to investigate. He was not yet thinking of himself as having been frustrated by a human agent. It was the fire. It seemed to him that the fire had been selfborn for that end and purpose. It seemed to him that that by and because of which he had had ancestors long enough to come himself to be, had allied itself with crime. So he continued to walk in a baffled and fretted manner about that heedless monument of the color of both hope and catastrophe until a deputy came up and told how he had discovered in a cabin beyond the house, traces of recent occupation. And immediately the countryman who had discovered the fire (he had not yet got to town; his wagon had not progressed one inch since he descended from it two hours ago, and he now moved among the people, wildhaired, gesticulant, with on his face a dulled, spent, glaring expression and his voice hoarsed almost to a whisper) remembered that he had seen a man in the house when he broke in the door.

"A white man?" the sheriff said.

"Yes, sir. Blumping around in the hall like he had just finished falling down the stairs. Tried to keep me from going upstairs at all. Told me how he had already been up there and it wasn't nobody up there. And when I come back down, he was gone."

The sheriff looked about at them. "Who lived in that cabin?"

"I didn't know anybody did," the deputy said. "Niggers, I reckon. She might have had niggers living in the house with her, from what I have heard. What I am surprised at is that it was this long before one of them done for her."

"Get me a nigger," the sheriff said. The deputy and two or three others got him a nigger. "Who's been living in that cabin?" the sheriff said.

"I dont know, Mr Watt," the negro said. "I aint never paid it no mind. I aint even knowed anybody lived in it."

"Bring him on down here," the sheriff said.

They were gathering now about the sheriff and the deputy

and the negro, with avid eyes upon which the sheer prolongation of empty flames had begun to pall, with faces identical one with another. It was as if all their individual five senses had become one organ of looking, like an apotheosis, the words that flew among them wind- or airengendered *Is that him? Is that the one that did it? Sheriff's got him. Sheriff has already caught him* The sheriff looked at them. "Go away," he said. "All of you. Go look at the fire. If I need any help, I can send for you. Go on away." He turned and led his party down to the cabin. Behind him the repulsed ones stood in a clump and watched the three white men and the negro enter the cabin and close the door. Behind them in turn the dying fire roared, filling the air though not louder than the voices and much more unsourceless *By God, if that's him, what are we doing, standing around here? Murdering a white woman the black son of a* None of them had ever entered the house. While she was alive they would not have allowed their wives to call on her. When they were younger, children (some of their fathers had done it too) they had called after her on the street, "Nigger lover! Nigger lover!"

In the cabin the sheriff sat down on one of the cots, heavily. He sighed: a tub of a man, with the complete and rocklike inertia of a tub. "Now, I want to know who lives in this cabin," he said.

"I done told you I dont know," the negro said. His voice was a little sullen, quite alert, covertly alert. He watched the sheriff. The other two white men were behind him, where he could not see them. He did not look back at them, not so much as a glance. He was watching the sheriff's face as a man watches a mirror. Perhaps he saw it, as in a mirror, before it came. Perhaps he did not, since if change, flicker, there was in the sheriff's face it was no more than a flicker. But the negro did not look back; there came only into his face when the strap fell across his back a wince, sudden, sharp, fleet, jerking up the corners of his mouth and exposing his momentary teeth like smiling. Then his face smoothed again, inscrutable.

"I reckon you aint tried hard enough to remember," the sheriff said.

"I cant remember because I cant know," the negro said. "I

dont even live nowhere near here. You ought to know where I stay at, white folks."

"Mr Buford says you live right down the road yonder," the sheriff said.

"Lots of folks live down that road. Mr Buford ought to know where I stay at."

"He's lying," the deputy said. His name was Buford. He was the one who wielded the strap, buckle end outward. He held it poised. He was watching the sheriff's face. He looked like a spaniel waiting to be told to spring into the water.

"Maybe so; maybe not," the sheriff said. He mused upon the negro. He was still, huge, inert, sagging the cot springs. "I think he just dont realise yet that I aint playing. Let alone them folks out there that aint got no jail to put him into if anything he wouldn't like should come up. That wouldn't bother to put him into a jail if they had one." Perhaps there was a sign, a signal, in his eyes again; perhaps not. Perhaps the negro saw it; perhaps not. The strap fell again, the buckle raking across the negro's back. "You remember yet?" the sheriff said.

"It's two white men," the negro said. His voice was cold, not sullen, not anything. "I dont know who they is nor what they does. It aint none of my business. I aint never seed them. I just heard talk about how two white men lived here. I didn't care who they was. And that's all I know. You can whup the blood outen me. But that's all I know."

Again the sheriff sighed. "That'll do. I reckon that's right."

"It's that fellow Christmas, that used to work at the mill, and another fellow named Brown," the third man said. "You could have picked out any man in Jefferson that his breath smelled right and he could have told you that much."

"I reckon that's right, too," the sheriff said.

He returned to town. When the crowd realised that the sheriff was departing, a general exodus began. It was as if there were nothing left to look at now. The body had gone, and now the sheriff was going. It was as though he carried within him, somewhere within that inert and sighing mass of flesh, the secret itself: that which moved and evoked them as with a promise of something beyond the sluttishness of stuffed entrails and monotonous days. So there was nothing left to look at now but the fire; they had now been watching it for three hours. They were now used to it, accustomed to it; now it had become a permanent part of their lives as well as of their experiences, standing beneath its windless column of smoke taller than and impregnable as a monument which could be returned to at any time. So when the caravan reached town it had something of that arrogant decorum of a procession behind a catafalque, the sheriff's car in the lead, the other cars honking and blatting behind in the sheriff's and their own compounded dust. It was held up momentarily at a street intersection near the square by a country wagon which had stopped to let a passenger descend. Looking out, the sheriff saw a young woman climbing slowly and carefully down from the wagon, with that careful awkwardness of advanced pregnancy. Then the wagon pulled aside; the caravan went on, crossing the square, where already the cashier of the bank had taken from the vault the envelope which the dead woman had deposited with him and which bore the inscription *To be opened at my death. Joanna Burden* The cashier was waiting at the sheriff's office when the sheriff came in, with the envelope and its contents. This was a single sheet of paper on which was written, by the same hand which inscribed the envelope *Notify E. E. Peebles, Attorney, —— Beale St., Memphis, Tenn., and Nathaniel Burrington, —— St., Exeter, N. H.* That was all.

"This Peebles is a nigger lawyer," the cashier said.

"Is that so?" the sheriff said.

"Yes. What do you want me to do?"

"I reckon you better do what the paper says," the sheriff said. "I reckon maybe I better do it myself." He sent two wires. He received the Memphis reply in thirty minutes. The other came two hours later; within ten minutes afterward the word had gone through the town that Miss Burden's nephew in New Hampshire offered a thousand dollars reward for the capture of her murderer. At nine oclock that evening the man whom the countryman had found in the burning house when he broke in the front door, appeared. They did not know then that he was the man. He did not tell them so. All they knew was that a man who had resided for a short time in the town and whom they knew as a bootlegger named Brown, and not much of a bootlegger at that, appeared on the square in a state of excitement, seeking the sheriff. Then it began to piece together. The sheriff knew that Brown was associated somehow with another man, another stranger named Christmas about whom, despite the fact that he had lived in Jefferson for three years, even less was known than about Brown; it was only now that the sheriff learned that Christmas had been living in the cabin behind Miss Burden's house for three years. Brown wanted to talk; he insisted on talking, loud, urgent; it appeared at once that what he was doing was claiming the thousand dollars reward.

"You want to turn state's evidence?" the sheriff asked him.

"I dont want to turn nothing," Brown said, harsh, hoarse, a little wild in the face. "I know who done it and when I get my reward, I'll tell."

"You catch the fellow that done it, and you'll get the reward," the sheriff said. So they took Brown to the jail for safekeeping. "Only I reckon it aint no actual need of that," the sheriff said. "I reckon as long as that thousand dollars is where he can smell it, you couldn't run him away from here." When Brown was taken away, still hoarse, still gesticulant and outraged, the sheriff telephoned to a neighboring town, where there was a pair of bloodhounds. The dogs would arrive on the early morning train.

About the bleak platform, in the sad dawn of that Sunday morning, thirty or forty men were waiting when the train came in, the lighted windows fleeing and jarring to a momentary stop. It was a fast train and it did not always stop at Jefferson. It halted only long enough to disgorge the two dogs: a thousand costly tons of intricate and curious metal glaring and crashing up and into an almost shocking silence filled with the puny sounds of men, to vomit two gaunt and cringing phantoms whose droopeared and mild faces gazed with sad abjectness about at the weary, pale faces of men who had not slept very much since night before last, ringing them about with something terrible and eager and impotent. It was as if the very initial outrage of the murder carried in its wake and made of all subsequent actions something monstrous and paradoxical and wrong, in themselves against both reason and nature.

It was just sunrise when the posse reached the cabin behind the charred and now cold embers of the house. The dogs, either gaining courage from the light and warmth of the sun or catching the strained and tense excitement from the men, began to surge and yap about the cabin. Snuffing loudly and as one beast they took a course, dragging the man who held the leashes. They ran side by side for a hundred yards, where they stopped and began to dig furiously into the earth and exposed a pit where someone had buried recently emptied food tins. They dragged the dogs away by main strength. They dragged them some distance from the cabin and made another cast. For a short time the dogs moiled, whimpering, then they set off again, fulltongued, drooling, and dragged and carried the running and cursing men at top speed back to the cabin, where, feet planted and with backflung heads and backrolled eyeballs, they bayed the empty doorway with the passionate abandon of two baritones singing Italian opera. The men took the dogs back to town, in cars, and fed them. When they crossed the square the church bells were ringing, slow and peaceful, and along the streets the decorous people moved sedately beneath parasols, carrying bibles and prayer-books.

That night a youth, a countryboy, and his father came in to see the sheriff. The boy told of having been on the way home in a car late Friday night, and of a man who stopped him a mile or two beyond the scene of the murder, with a pistol. The boy believed that he was about to be robbed and even killed, and he told how he was about to trick the man into permitting him to drive right up into his own front yard, where he intended to stop the car and spring out and shout for help, but that the man suspected something and forced him to stop the car and let him out. The father wanted to know how much of the thousand dollars would become theirs.

"You catch him and we'll see," the sheriff said. So they waked the dogs and put them into another car and the youth showed them where the man had got out, and they cast the dogs, who charged immediately into the woods and with their apparent infallibility for metal in any form, found the old pistol with its two loaded chambers almost at once.

"It's one of them old Civil War, cap-and-ball pistols," the deputy said. "One of the caps has been snapped, but it never went off. What do you reckon he was doing with that?"

"Turn them dogs loose," the sheriff said. "Maybe them leashes worry them." They did so. The dogs were free now; thirty minutes later they were lost. Not the men lost the dogs; the dogs lost the men. They were just across a small creek and a ridge, and the men could hear them plainly. They were not baying now, with pride and assurance and perhaps pleasure. The sound which they now made was a longdrawn and hopeless wailing, while steadily the men shouted at them. But apparently the animals could not hear either. Both voices were distinguishable, yet the belllike and abject wailing seemed to come from a single throat, as though the two beasts crouched flank to flank. After a while the men found them so, crouched in a ditch. By that time their voices sounded almost like the voices of children. The men squatted there until it was light enough to find their way back to the cars. Then it was Monday morning.

The temperature began to rise Monday. On Tuesday, the night, the darkness after the hot day, is close, still, oppressive; as soon as Byron enters the house he feels the corners of his nostrils whiten and tauten with the thick smell of the stale, mankept house. And when Hightower approaches, the smell of plump unwashed flesh and unfresh clothing—that odor of unfastidious sedentation, of static overflesh not often enough bathed—is well nigh overpowering. Entering, Byron thinks as he has thought before: 'That is his right. It may not be my way, but it is his way and his right.' And he remembers how once he had seemed to find the answer, as though by inspiration, divination: 'It is the odor of goodness. Of course it would smell bad to us that are bad and sinful.'

They sit again opposite one another in the study, the desk, the lighted lamp, between. Byron sits again on the hard chair, his face lowered, still. His voice is sober, stubborn: the voice of a man saying something which will be not only unpleasing, but will not be believed. "I am going to find another place for her. A place where it will be more private. Where she can. . . . . . ."

Hightower watches his lowered face. "Why must she move? When she is comfortable there, with a woman at hand if she should need one?" Byron does not answer. He sits motionless, downlooking; his face is stubborn, still; looking at it, Hightower thinks 'It is because so much happens. Too much happens. That's it. Man performs, engenders, so much more than he can or should have to bear. That's how he finds that he can bear anything. That's it. That's what is so terrible. That he can bear anything, anything.' He watches Byron. "Is Mrs Beard the only reason why she is going to move?"

Still Byron does not look up, speaking in that still, stubborn voice: "She needs a place where it will be kind of home to her. She aint got a whole lot more time, and in a boarding house, where it's mostly just men. . . . . . A room where it will be quiet when her time comes, and not every durn horsetrader or courtjury that passes through the hallway. . . . . . ."

"I see," Hightower says. He watches Byron's face. "And you want me to take her in here." Byron makes to speak, but the other goes on: his tone too is cold, level: "It wont do, Byron. If there were another woman here, living in the house. It's a shame too, with all the room here, the quiet. I'm thinking of her, you see. Not myself. I would not care what was said, thought."

"I am not asking that." Byron does not look up. He can feel the other watching him. He thinks *He knows that is not what I meant, too. He knows. He just said that. I know what he is thinking. I reckon I expected it. I reckon it is not any reason for him to think different from other folks, even about me* "I reckon you ought to know that." Perhaps he does know it. But Byron does not look up to see. He talks on, in that dull, flat voice, downlooking, while beyond the desk Hightower, sitting a little more than erect, looks at the thin, weatherhardened, laborpurged face of the man opposite him. "I aint going to get you mixed up in it when it aint none of your trouble. You haven't even seen her, and I dont reckon you ever will. I reckon likely you have never seen him to know it either. It's just that I thought maybe. . . . . . ." His voice ceases. Across the desk the unbending minister looks at him, waiting, not offering to help him. "When it's a matter of not-do, I reckon a man can trust himself for advice. But when it comes to a matter of doing, I reckon a fellow had better listen to all the advice he can get. But I aint going to mix you up in it. I dont want you to worry about that."

"I think I know that," Hightower says. He watches the other's downlooking face. 'I am not in life anymore,' he thinks. 'That's why there is no use in even trying to meddle, interfere. He could hear me no more than that man and that woman (ay, and that child) would hear or heed me if I tried to come back into life.' "But you told me she knows that he is here."

"Yes," Byron says, brooding. "Out there where I thought the chance to harm ere a man or woman or child could not have found me. And she hadn't hardly got there before I had to go and blab the whole thing."

"I dont mean that. You didn't know yourself, then. I mean, the rest of it. About him and the——that. . . . . . . It has been three days. She must know, whether you told her or not. She must have heard by now."

"Christmas." Byron does not look up. "I never said any more, after she asked about that little white scar by his mouth. All the time we were coming to town that evening I was afraid she would ask. I would try to think up things to talk to her about so she would not have a chance to ask me any more. And all the time I thought I was keeping her from finding out that he had not only run off and left her in trouble, he had changed his name to keep her from finding him, and that now when she found him at last, what she had found was a bootlegger, she already knew it. Already knew that he was a nogood." He says now, with a kind of musing astonishment: "I never even had any need to keep it from her, to lie it smooth. It was like she knew beforehand what I would say, that I was going to lie to her. Like she had already thought of that herself, and that she already didn't believe it before I even said it, and that was all right too. But the part of her that knew the truth, that I could not have fooled anyway. . . . . . ." He fumbles, gropes, the unbending man beyond the desk watching him, not offering to help. "It's like she was in two parts, and one of them knows that he is a scoundrel. But the other part believes that when a man and a woman are going to have a child, that the Lord will see that they are all together when the right time comes. Like it was God that looks after women, to protect them from men. And if the Lord dont see fit to let them two parts meet and kind of compare, then I aint going to do it either."

"Nonsense," Hightower says. He looks across the desk at the other's still, stubborn, ascetic face: the face of a hermit who has lived for a long time in an empty place where sand blows. "The thing, the only thing, for her to do is to go back to Alabama. To her people."

"I reckon not," Byron says. He says it immediately, with immediate finality, as if he has been waiting all the while for this to be said. "She wont need to do that. I reckon she wont need to do that." But he does not look up. He can feel the other looking at him.

"Does Bu—Brown know that she is in Jefferson?"

For an instant Byron almost smiles. His lip lifts: a thin movement almost a shadow, without mirth. "He's been too busy. After that thousand dollars. It's right funny to watch him. Like a man that cant play a tune, blowing a horn right loud, hoping that in a minute it will begin to make music. Being drug across the square on a handcuff every twelve or fifteen hours, when likely they couldn't run him away if they was to sic them bloodhounds on him. He spent Saturday night in jail, still talking about how they were trying to beat him out of his thousand dollars by trying to make out that he helped Christmas do the killing, until at last Buck Conner went up to his cell and told him he would put a gag in his mouth if he didn't shut up and let the other prisoners sleep. And he shut up, and Sunday night they went out with the dogs and he raised so much racket that they had to take him out of jail and let him go too. But the dogs never got started. And him hollering and cussing the dogs and wanting to beat them because they never struck a trail, telling everybody again how it was him that reported Christmas first and that all he wanted was fair justice, until the sheriff took him aside and talked to him. They didn't know what the sheriff said to him. Maybe he threatened to lock him back up in jail and not let him go with them next time. Anyway, he calmed down some, and they went on. They never got back to town until late Monday night. He was still quiet. Maybe he was wore out. He hadn't slept none in some time, and they said how he was trying to outrun the dogs so that the sheriff finally threatened to handcuff him to a deputy to keep him back so the dogs could smell something beside him. He needed a shave already when they locked him up Saturday night, and he needed one bad by now. I reckon he must have looked more like a murderer than even Christmas. And he was cussing Christmas now, like Christmas had done hid out just for meanness, to spite him and keep him from getting that thousand dollars. And they brought him back to jail and locked him up that night. And this morning they went and took him out again and they all went off with the dogs, on a new scent. Folks said they could hear him hollering and talking until they were clean out of town."

"And she doesn't know that, you say. You say you have kept that from her. You had rather that she knew him to be a scoundrel than a fool: is that it?"

Byron's face is still again, not smiling now; it is quite sober. "I dont know. It was last Sunday night, after I came out to talk to you and went back home. I thought she would be asleep in bed, but she was still sitting up in the parlor, and she said 'What is it? What has happened here?' And I didn't look at her and I could feel her looking at me. I told her it was a nigger killed a white woman. I didn't lie then. I reckon I was so glad I never had to lie then. Because before I thought, I had done said 'and set the house afire'. And then it was too late. I had pointed out the smoke, and I had told her about the two fellows named Brown and Christmas that lived out there. And I could feel her watching me the same as I can you now, and she said 'What was the nigger's name?' It's like God sees that they find out what they need to know out of men's lying, without needing to ask. And that they dont find out what they dont need to know, without even knowing they have not found it out. And so I dont know for sure what she knows and what she dont know. Except that I have kept it from her that it was the man she is hunting for that told on the murderer and that he is in jail now except when he is out running with dogs the man that took him up and befriended him. I have kept that from her."

"And what are you going to do now? Where does she want to move?"

"She wants to go out there and wait for him. I told her that he is away on business for the sheriff. So I didn't lie altogether. She had already asked me where he lived and I had already told her. And she said that was the place where she belonged until he come back, because that is his house. She said that's what he would want her to do. And I couldn't tell her different, that that cabin is the last place in the world he would want her to ever see. She wanted to go out there as soon as I got home from the mill this evening. She had her bundle all tied up and her bonnet on, waiting for me to get home. 'I started once to go on by myself,' she said. 'But I wasn't sho I knowed the way.' And I said Yes; only it was too late today and we would go out there tomorrow, and she said 'It's a hour till dark yet. It aint but two miles, is it?' and I said to let's wait because I would have to ask first, and she said 'Ask who? Aint it Lucas' house?' and I could feel her watching me and she said 'I thought you said that that was where Lucas lived' and she was watching me and she said 'Who is this preacher you keep on going to talk to about me?' "

"And you are going to let her go out there to live."

"It might be best. She would be private out there, and she would be away from all the talking until this business is over."

"You mean, she has got her mind set on it, and you wont stop her. You dont want to stop her."

Byron does not look up. "In a way, it is his house. The nighest thing to a home of his own he will ever own, I reckon. And he is her. . . . . . ."

"Out there alone, with a child coming. The nearest house a few negro cabins a half mile away." He watches Byron's face.

"I have thought of that. There are ways, things that can be done. . . . . . ."

"What things? What can you do to protect her out there?"

Byron does not answer at once; he does not look up. When

he speaks his voice is dogged. "There are secret things a man can do without being evil, Reverend. No matter how they might look to folks."

"I dont think that you could do anything that would be very evil, Byron, no matter how it looked to folks. But are you going to undertake to say just how far evil extends into the appearance of evil? just where between doing and appearing evil stops?"

"No," Byron says. Then he moves slightly; he speaks as if he too were waking: "I hope not. I reckon I am trying to do the right thing by my lights."—'And that,' Hightower thinks, 'is the first lie he ever told me. Ever told anyone, man or woman, perhaps including himself.' He looks across the desk at the stubborn, dogged, sober face that has not yet looked at him. 'Or maybe it is not lie yet because he does not know himself that it is so.' He says:

"Well." He speaks now with a kind of spurious brusqueness which, flabbyjowled and darkcaverneyed, his face belies. "That is settled, then. You'll take her out there, to his house, and you'll see that she is comfortable and you'll see that she is not disturbed until this is over. And then you'll tell that man—Burch, Brown—that she is here."

"And he'll run," Byron says. He does not look up, yet through him there seems to go a wave, of exultation, of triumph, before he can curb and hide it, when it is too late to try. For the moment he does not attempt to curb it; backthrust too in his hard chair, looking for the first time at the minister, with a face confident and bold and suffused. The other meets his gaze steadily.

"Is that what you want him to do?" Hightower says. They sit so in the lamplight. Through the open window comes the hot, myriad silence of the breathless night. "Think what you are doing. You are attempting to come between man and wife."

Byron has caught himself. His face is no longer triumphant. But he looks steadily at the older man. Perhaps he tried to catch his voice too. But he cannot yet. "They aint man and wife yet," he says.

"Does she think that? Do you believe that she will say that?" They look at one another. "Ah, Byron, Byron. What

are a few mumbled words before God, before the steadfast-
ness of a woman's nature? Before that child?"

"Well, he may not run. If he gets that reward, that money.
Like enough he will be drunk enough on a thousand dollars
to do anything, even marry."

"Ah, Byron, Byron."

"Then what do you think we—I ought to do? What do
you advise?"

"Go away. Leave Jefferson." They look at one another.
"No," Hightower says. "You dont need my help. You are already being helped by someone stronger than I am."

For a moment Byron does not speak. They look at one
another, steadily. "Helped by who?"

"By the devil," Hightower says.

'And the devil is looking after *him*, too,' Hightower thinks.
He is in midstride, halfway home, his laden small market basket on his arm. 'Him, too. Him, too,' he thinks, walking. It
is hot. He is in his shirt sleeves, tall, with thin blackclad legs
and spare, gaunt arms and shoulders, and with that flabby
and obese stomach like some monstrous pregnancy. The shirt
is white, but it is not fresh; his collar is soiled, as is the white
lawn cravat carelessly knotted, and he has not shaved for two
or three days. His panama hat is soiled, and beneath it, between hat and skull against the heat, the edge and corners of
a soiled handkerchief protrude. He has been to town to do
his semiweekly marketing, where, gaunt, misshapen, with his
gray stubble and his dark spectacleblurred eyes and his blackrimmed hands and the rank manodor of his sedentary and
unwashed flesh, he entered the one odorous and cluttered
store which he patronised and paid with cash for what he
bought.

"Well, they found that nigger's trail at last," the proprietor
said.

"Negro?" Hightower said. He became utterly still, in the
act of putting into his pocket the change from his purchases.

"That bah—fellow; the murderer. I said all the time that
he wasn't right. Wasn't a white man. That there was some-

thing funny about him. But you cant tell folks nothing until——"

"Found him?" Hightower said.

"You durn right they did. Why, the fool never even had sense enough to get out of the county. Here the sheriff has been telephoning all over the country for him, and the black son—uh was right here under his durn nose all the time."

"And they have. . . . . . ." He leaned forward against the counter, above his laden basket. He could feel the counter edge against his stomach. It felt solid, stable enough; it was more like the earth itself were rocking faintly, preparing to move. Then it seemed to move, like something released slowly and without haste, in an augmenting swoop, and cleverly, since the eye was tricked into believing that the dingy shelves ranked with flyspecked tins, and the merchant himself behind the counter, had not moved; outraging, tricking sense. And he thinking, 'I wont! I wont! I have bought immunity. I have paid. I have paid.'

"They aint caught him yet," the proprietor said. "But they will. The sheriff taken the dogs out to the church before daylight this morning. They aint six hours behind him. To think that the durn fool never had no better sense. . . . . . .show he is a nigger, even if nothing else. . . . . . ." Then the proprietor was saying, "Was that all today?"

"What?" Hightower said. "What?"

"Was that all you wanted?"

"Yes. Yes. That was. . . . . . ." He began to fumble in his pocket, the proprietor watching him. His hand came forth, still fumbling. It blundered upon the counter, shedding coins. The proprietor stopped two or three of them as they were about to roll off the counter.

"What's this for?" the proprietor said.

"For the. . . . . . ." Hightower's hand fumbled at the laden basket. "For——"

"You already paid." The proprietor was watching him, curious. "That's your change here, that I just gave you. For the dollar bill."

"Oh," Hightower said. "Yes. I. . . . . . I just——" The merchant was gathering up the coins. He handed them back. When the customer's hand touched his it felt like ice.

"It's this hot weather," the proprietor said. "It does wear a man out. Do you want to set down a spell before you start home?" But Hightower apparently did not hear him. He was moving now, toward the door, while the merchant watched him. He passed through the door and into the street, the basket on his arm, walking stiffly and carefully, like a man on ice. It was hot; heat quivered up from the asphalt, giving to the familiar buildings about the square a nimbus quality, a quality of living and palpitant chiaroscuro. Someone spoke to him in passing; he did not even know it. He went on, thinking *And him too. And him too* walking fast now, so that when he turned the corner at last and entered that dead and empty little street where his dead and empty small house waited, he was almost panting. 'It's the heat,' the top of his mind was saying to him, reiterant, explanatory. But still, even in the quiet street where scarce anyone ever paused now to look at, remember, the sign, and his house, his sanctuary, already in sight, it goes on beneath the top of his mind that would cozen and soothe him: 'I wont. I wont. I have bought immunity.' It is like words spoken aloud now: reiterative, patient, justificative: 'I paid for it. I didn't quibble about the price. No man can say that. I just wanted peace; I paid them their price without quibbling.' The street shimmers and swims; he has been sweating, but now even the air of noon feels cool upon him. Then sweat, heat, mirage, all, rush fused into a finality which abrogates all logic and justification and obliterates it like fire would: I *will* not! I *will* not!

When, sitting in the study window in the first dark, he saw Byron pass into and then out of the street lamp, he sat suddenly forward in his chair. It was not that he was surprised to see Byron there, at that hour. At first, when he first recognised the figure, he thought *Ah. I had an idea he would come tonight. It is not in him to support even the semblance of evil* It was while he was thinking that that he started, sat forward: for an instant after recognising the approaching figure in the full glare of the light he believed that he was mistaken, knowing all the while that he could not be, that it could be no one except Byron, since he was already turning in to the gate.

Tonight Byron is completely changed. It shows in his walk, his carriage; leaning forward Hightower says to himself *As though he has learned pride, or defiance* Byron's head is erect, he walks fast and erect; suddenly Hightower says, almost aloud: 'He has done something. He has taken a step.' He makes a clicking sound with his tongue, leaning in the dark window, watching the figure pass swiftly from sight beyond the window and in the direction of the porch, the entrance, and where in the next moment Hightower hears his feet and then his knock. 'And he didn't offer to tell me,' he thinks. 'I would have listened, let him think aloud to me.' He is already crossing the room, pausing at the desk to turn on the light. He goes to the front door.

"It's me, Reverend," Byron says.

"I recognised you," Hightower says. "Even though you didn't stumble on the bottom step this time. You have entered this house on Sunday night, but until tonight you have never entered it without stumbling on the bottom step, Byron." This was the note upon which Byron's calls usually opened: this faintly overbearing note of levity and warmth to put the other at his ease, and on the part of the caller that slow and countrybred diffidence which is courtesy. Sometimes it would seem to Hightower that he would actually hale Byron into the house by a judicious application of pure breath, as though Byron wore a sail.

But this time Byron is already entering, before Hightower has finished his sentence. He enters immediately, with that new air born somewhere between assurance and defiance. "And I reckon you are going to find that you hate it worse when I dont stumble than when I do," Byron says.

"Is that a hope, or is it a threat, Byron?"

"Well, I dont mean it to be a threat," Byron says.

"Ah," Hightower says. "In other words, you can offer no hope. Well, I am forewarned, at least. I was forewarned as soon as I saw you in the street light. But at least you are going to tell me about it. What you have already done, even if you didn't see fit to talk about it before hand." They are moving toward the study door. Byron stops; he looks back and up at the taller face.

"Then you know," he says. "You have already heard." Then, though his head has not moved, he is no longer looking at the other. "Well," he says. He says: "Well, any man has got a free tongue. Woman too. But I would like to know who told you. Not that I am ashamed. Not that I aimed to keep it from you. I come to tell you myself, when I could."

They stand just without the door to the lighted room. Hightower sees now that Byron's arms are laden with bundles, parcels that look like they might contain groceries. "What?" Hightower says. "What have you come to tell me?——But come in. Maybe I do know what it is already. But I want to see your face when you tell me. I forewarn you too, Byron." They enter the lighted room. The bundles are groceries: he has bought and carried too many like them himself not to know. "Sit down," he says.

"No," Byron says. "I aint going to stay that long." He stands, sober, contained, with that air compassionate still, but decisive without being assured, confident without being assertive: that air of a man about to do something which someone dear to him will not understand and approve, yet which he himself knows to be right just as he knows that the friend will never see it so. He says: "You aint going to like it. But there aint anything else to do. I wish you could see it so. But I reckon you cant. And I reckon that's all there is to it."

Across the desk, seated again, Hightower watches him gravely. "What have you done, Byron?"

Byron speaks in that new voice: that voice brief, terse, each word definite of meaning, not fumbling. "I took her out there this evening. I had already fixed up the cabin, cleaned it good. She is settled now. She wanted it so. It was the nearest thing to a home he ever had and ever will have, so I reckon she is entitled to use it, especially as the owner aint using it now. Being detained elsewhere, you might say. I know you aint going to like it. You can name lots of reasons, good ones. You'll say it aint his cabin to give to her. All right. Maybe it aint. But it aint any living man or woman in this country or state to say she cant use it. You'll say that in her shape she ought to have a woman with her. All right. There is a nigger

woman, one old enough to be sensible, that dont live over
two hundred yards away. She can call to her without getting
up from the chair or the bed. You'll say, but that aint a white
woman. And I'll ask you what will she be getting from the
white women in Jefferson about the time that baby is due,
when here she aint been in Jefferson but a week and already
she cant talk to a woman ten minutes before that woman
knows she aint married yet, and as long as that durn scoundrel stays above ground where she can hear of him now and
then, she aint going to be married. How much help will she
be getting from the white ladies about that time? They'll see
that she has a bed to lay on and walls to hide her from the
street alright. I dont mean that. And I reckon a man would
be justified in saying she dont deserve no more than that,
being as it wasn't behind no walls that she got in the shape
she is in. But that baby never done the choosing. And even if
it had, I be durn if any poor little tyke, having to face what
it will have to face in this world, deserves——deserves more
than——better than——But I reckon you know what I
mean. I reckon you can even say it." Beyond the desk Hightower watches him while he talks in that level, restrained
tone, not once at a loss for words until he came to something
still too new and nebulous for him to more than feel. "And
for the third reason. A white woman out there alone. You aint
going to like that. You will like that least of all."

"Ah, Byron, Byron."

Byron's voice is now dogged. Yet he holds his head up still.
"I aint in the house with her. I got a tent. It aint close, neither. Just where I can hear her at need. And I fixed a bolt on
the door. Any of them can come out, at any time, and see me
in the tent."

"Ah, Byron, Byron."

"I know you aint thinking what most of them think. Are
thinking. I know you would know better, even if she
wasn't——if it wasn't for——I know you said that because
of what you know that the others will think."

Hightower sits again in the attitude of the eastern idol, between his parallel arms on the armrests of the chair. "Go
away, Byron. Go away. Now. At once. Leave this place forever, this terrible place, this terrible, terrible place. I can read

you. You will tell me that you have just learned love; I will tell you that you have just learned hope. That's all; hope. The object does not matter, not to the hope, not even to you. There is but one end to this, to the road that you are taking: sin or marriage. And you would refuse the sin. That's it, God forgive me. It will, must be, marriage or nothing with you. And you will insist that it be marriage. You will convince her; perhaps you already have, if she but knew it, would admit it: else, why is she content to stay here and yet make no effort to see the man whom she has come to find? I cannot say to you, Choose the sin, because you would not only hate me: you would carry that hatred straight to her. So I say, Go away. Now. At once. Turn your face now, and dont look back. But not this, Byron."

They look at one another. "I knew you would not like it," Byron says. "I reckon I done right not to make myself a guest by sitting down. But I did not expect this. That you too would turn against a woman wronged and betrayed——"

"No woman who has a child is ever betrayed; the husband of a mother, whether he be the father or not, is already a cuckold. Give yourself at least the one chance in ten, Byron. If you must marry, there are single women, girls, virgins. It's not fair that you should sacrifice yourself to a woman who has chosen once and now wishes to renege that choice. It's not right. It's not just. God didn't intend it so when He made marriage. Made it? Women made marriage."

"Sacrifice? Me the sacrifice? It seems to me the sacrifice——"

"Not to her. For the Lena Groves there are always two men in the world and their number is legion: Lucas Burches and Byron Bunches. But no Lena, no woman, deserves more than one of them. No woman. There have been good women who were martyrs to brutes, in their cups and such. But what woman, good or bad, has ever suffered from any brute as men have suffered from good women? Tell me that, Byron."

They speak quietly, without heat, giving pause to weigh one another's words, as two men already impregnable each in his own conviction will. "I reckon you are right," Byron says. "Anyway, it aint for me to say that you are wrong. And I dont reckon it's for you to say that I am wrong, even if I am."

"No," Hightower says.

"Even if I am," Byron says. "So I reckon I'll say good-night." He says, quietly: "It's a good long walk out there."

"Yes," Hightower says. "I used to walk it myself, now and then. It must be about three miles."

"Two miles," Byron says. "Well." He turns. Hightower does not move. Byron shifts the parcels which he has not put down. "I'll say goodnight," he says, moving toward the door. "I reckon I'll see you, sometime soon."

"Yes," Hightower says. "Is there anything I can do? Anything you need? bedclothes and such?"

"I'm obliged. I reckon she has a plenty. There was some already there. I'm obliged."

"And you will let me know? If anything comes up. If the child——Have you arranged for a doctor?"

"I'll get that attended to."

"But have you seen one yet? Have you engaged one?"

"I aim to see to all that. And I'll let you know."

Then he is gone. From the window again Hightower watches him pass and go on up the street, toward the edge of town and his two mile walk, carrying his paperwrapped packages of food. He passes from sight walking erect and at a good gait; such a gait as an old man already gone to flesh and short wind, an old man who has already spent too much time sitting down, could not have kept up with. And Hightower leans there in the window, in the August heat, oblivious of the odor in which he lives—that smell of people who no longer live in life: that odor of overplump desiccation and stale linen as though a precursor of the tomb—listening to the feet which he seems to hear still long after he knows that he cannot, thinking, 'God bless him. God help him'; thinking *To be young. To be young. There is nothing else like it: there is nothing else in the world* He is thinking quietly: 'I should not have got out of the habit of prayer.' Then he hears the feet no longer. He hears now only the myriad and interminable insects, leaning in the window, breathing the hot still rich maculate smell of the earth, thinking of how when he was young, a youth, he had loved darkness, of walking or sitting alone among trees at night. Then the ground, the bark of trees, became actual, savage, filled with, evocative of, strange and baleful half delights and half terrors. He was afraid of it. He feared; he loved in being afraid. Then one day while at the seminary he realised that he was no longer afraid. It was as though a door had shut somewhere. He was no longer afraid of darkness. He just hated it; he would flee from it, to walls, to artificial light. 'Yes,' he thinks. 'I should never have let myself get out of the habit of prayer.' He turns from the window. One wall of the study is lined with books. He pauses before them, seeking, until he finds the one which he wants. It is Tennyson. It is dogeared. He has had it ever since the seminary. He sits beneath the lamp and opens it. It does not take long. Soon the fine galloping language, the gutless swooning full of sapless trees and dehydrated lusts begins to swim smooth and swift and peaceful. It is better than praying without having to bother to think aloud. It is like listening in a cathedral to a eunuch chanting in a language which he does not even need to not understand.

XIV

"THERE's SOMEBODY out there in that cabin," the deputy told the sheriff. "Not hiding: living in it."

"Go and see," the sheriff said.

The deputy went and returned.

"It's a woman. A young woman. And she's all fixed up to live there a good spell, it looks like. And Byron Bunch is camped in a tent about as far from the cabin as from here to the postoffice."

"Byron Bunch?" the sheriff says. "Who is the woman?"

"I dont know. She is a stranger. A young woman. She told me all about it. She begun telling me almost before I got inside the cabin, like it was a speech. Like she had done got used to telling it, done got into the habit. And I reckon she has, coming here from over in Alabama somewhere, looking for her husband. He had done come on ahead of her to find work, it seems like, and after a while she started out after him and folks told her on the road that he was here. And about that time Byron come in and he said he could tell me about it. Said he aimed to tell you."

"Byron Bunch," the sheriff says.

"Yes," the deputy says. He says: "She's fixing to have a kid. It aint going to be long, neither."

"A kid?" the sheriff says. He looks at the deputy. "And from Alabama. From anywhere. You cant tell me that about Byron Bunch."

"No more am I trying to," the deputy says. "I aint saying it's Byron's. Leastways, Byron aint saying it's his. I'm just telling you what he told me."

"Oh," the sheriff says. "I see. Why she is out there. So it's one of them fellows. It's Christmas, is it?"

"No. This is what Byron told me. He took me outside and told me, where she couldn't hear. He said he aimed to come and tell you. It's Brown's. Only his name aint Brown. It's Lucas Burch. Byron told me. About how Brown or Burch left her over in Alabama. Told her he was just coming to find work and fix up a home and then send for her. But her time come nigh and she hadn't heard from him, where he was at or anything, so she just decided to not wait any longer. She started out afoot, asking along the road if anybody knowed a fellow named Lucas Burch, getting a ride here and there, asking everybody she met if they knew him. And so after a while somebody told her how there was a fellow named Burch or Bunch or something working at the planing mill in Jefferson, and she come on here. She got here Saturday, on a wagon, while we were all out at the murder, and she come out to the mill and found it was Bunch instead of Burch. And Byron said he told her that her husband was in Jefferson before he knew it. And then he said she had him pinned down and he had to tell her where Brown lived. But he aint told her that Brown or Burch is mixed up with Christmas in this killing. He just told her that Brown was away on business. And I reckon you can call it business. Work, anyway. I never saw a man want a thousand dollars badder and suffer more to get it, than him. And so she said that Brown's house was bound to be the one that Lucas Burch had promised to get ready for her to live in, and so she moved out to wait until Brown come back from this here business he is away on. Byron said he couldn't stop her because he didn't want to tell her the truth about Brown after he had already lied to her in a way of speaking. He said he aimed to come and tell you about it before now, only you found it out too quick, before he had got her settled down good."

"Lucas Burch?" the sheriff says.

"I was some surprised, myself," the deputy says. "What do you aim to do about it?"

"Nothing," the sheriff says. "I reckon they wont do no harm out there. And it aint none of my house to tell her to get out of it. And like Byron told her, Burch or Brown or whatever his name is, is going to be right busy for a while longer yet."

"Do you aim to tell Brown about her?"

"I reckon not," the sheriff says. "It aint any of my business. I aint interested in the wives he left in Alabama, or anywhere else. What I am interested in is the husband he seems to have had since he come to Jefferson."

The deputy guffaws. "I reckon that's a fact," he says. He

sobers, muses. "If he dont get that thousand dollars, I reckon he will just die."

"I reckon he wont," the sheriff says.

At three oclock Wednesday morning a negro rode into town on a saddleless mule. He went to the sheriff's home and waked him. He had come direct from a negro church twenty miles away, where a revival meeting was in nightly progress. On the evening before, in the middle of a hymn, there had come a tremendous noise from the rear of the church, and turning the congregation saw a man standing in the door. The door had not been locked or even shut yet the man had apparently grasped it by the knob and hurled it back into the wall so that the sound crashed into the blended voices like a pistol shot. Then the man came swiftly up the aisle, where the singing had stopped short off, toward the pulpit where the preacher leaned, his hands still raised, his mouth still open. Then they saw that the man was white. In the thick, cavelike gloom which the two oil lamps but served to increase, they could not tell at once what he was until he was halfway up the aisle. Then they saw that his face was not black, and a woman began to shriek, and people in the rear sprang up and began to run toward the door; and another woman on the mourners' bench, already in a semihysterical state, sprang up and whirled and glared at him for an instant with whiterolling eyes and screamed "It's the devil! It's Satan himself!" Then she ran, quite blind. She ran straight toward him and he knocked her down without stopping and stepped over her and went on, with the faces gaped for screaming falling away before him, straight to the pulpit and put his hand on the minister.

"Wasn't nobody bothering him, even then," the messenger said. "It was all happening so fast, and nobody knowed him, who he was or what he wanted or nothing. And the women hollering and screeching and him done retch into the pulpit and caught Brother Bedenberry by the throat, trying to snatch him outen the pulpit. We could see Brother Bedenberry talking to him, trying to pacify him quiet, and him

jerking at Brother Bedenberry and slapping his face with his
hand. And the womenfolks screeching and hollering so you
couldn't hear what Brother Bedenberry was saying, cep he
never tried to hit back nor nothing, and then some of the old
men, the deacons, went up to him and tried to talk to him
and he let Brother Bedenberry go and he whirled and he
knocked seventy year old Pappy Thompson clean down into
the mourners' pew and then he retch down and caught up a
chair and whirled and made a pass at the others until they
give back. And the folks still yelling and screeching and trying
to get out. Then he turned and clumb into the pulpit, where
Brother Bedenberry had done clumb out the other side, and
he stood there—he was all muddy, his pants and his shirt,
and his jaw black with whiskers—with his hands raised like a
preacher. And he begun to curse, hollering it out, at the folks,
and he cursed God louder than the women screeching, and
some of the men trying to hold Roz Thompson, Pappy
Thompson's daughter's boy, that was six foot tall and had a
razor nekkid in his hand, hollering 'I'll kill him. Lemme go,
folks. He hit my grandpappy. I'll kill him. Lemme go. Please
lemme go' and the folks trying to get out, rushing and trom-
pling in the aisle and through the door, and him in the pulpit
cursing God and the men dragging Roz Thompson out back-
wards and Roz still begging them to let him go. But they got
Roz out and we went back into the bushes and him still hollering and cursing back there in the pulpit. Then he quit after
a while and we seed him come to the door and stand there.
And they had to hold Roz again. He must have heard the
racket they made holding Roz, because he begun to laugh.
He stood there in the door, with the light behind him, laughing loud, and then he begun to curse again and we could see
him snatch up a bench leg and swing it back. And we heard
the first lamp bust, and it got dim in the church, and then we
heard the other lamp bust and then it was dark and we
couldn't see him no more. And where they was trying to hold
Roz a terrible racket set up, with them hollerwhispering
'Hold him! Hold him! Ketch him! Ketch him!' Then somebody hollered 'He's done got loose' and we could hear Roz
running back toward the church and Deacon Vines says to
me 'Roz will kill him. Jump on a mule and ride for the sheriff.

Tell him just what you seen.' And wasn't nobody bothering him, captain," the negro said. "We never even knowed him to call his name. Never even seed him before. And we tried to hold Roz back. But Roz a big man, and him done knocked down Roz' seventy year old grandpappy and Roz with that nekkid razor in his hand, not caring much who else he had to cut to carve his path back to the church where that white man was. But fore God we tried to hold Roz."

That was what he told, because that was what he knew. He had departed immediately: he did not know that at the time he was telling it, the negro Roz was lying unconscious in a neighboring cabin, with his skull fractured where Christmas, just inside the now dark door, had struck him with the bench leg when Roz plunged into the church. Christmas struck just once, hard, savagely, at the sound of running feet, the thick shape which rushed headlong through the doorway, and heard it without pause plunge on crashing among the overturned benches and become still. Also without pausing Christmas sprang out and to the earth, where he stood lightly, poised, still grasping the bench leg, cool, not even breathing hard. He was quite cool, no sweat; the darkness cool upon him. The churchyard was a pallid crescent of trampled and beaten earth, shaped and enclosed by undergrowth and trees. He knew that the undergrowth was full of negroes: he could feel the eyes. 'Looking and looking,' he thought. 'Dont even know they cant see me.' He breathed deeply; he found that he was hefting the bench leg, curiously, as though trying its balance, as if he had never touched it before. 'I'll cut a notch in it tomorrow,' he thought. He leaned the leg carefully against the wall beside him and took from his shirt a cigarette and a match. As he struck the match he paused, and with the yellow flame spurting punily into life he stood, his head turned a little. It was hooves which he heard. He heard them come alive and grow swift, diminishing. "A mule," he said aloud, not loud. "Bound for town with the good news." He lit the cigarette and flipped the match away and he stood there, smoking, feeling the negro eyes upon the tiny living coal. Though he stood there until the cigarette was smoked down, he was quite alert. He had set his back against the wall and he held the bench leg in his right hand again.

He smoked the cigarette completely down, then he flipped it, twinkling, as far as he could toward the undergrowth where he could feel the negroes crouching. "Have a butt, boys," he said, his voice sudden and loud in the silence. In the undergrowth where they crouched they watched the cigarette twinkle toward the earth and glow there for a time. But they could not see him when he departed, nor which way he went.

At eight oclock the next morning the sheriff arrived, with his posse and the bloodhounds. They made one capture immediately, though the dogs had nothing to do with it. The church was deserted; there was not a negro in sight. The posse entered the church and looked quietly about at the wreckage. Then they emerged. The dogs had struck something immediately, but before they set out a deputy found, wedged into a split plank on the side of the church, a scrap of paper. It had been obviously put there by the hand of man, and opened, it proved to be an empty cigarette container torn open and spread smooth, and on the white inner side was a pencilled message. It was raggedly written, as though by an unpractised hand or perhaps in the dark, and it was not long. It was addressed to the sheriff by name and it was unprintable—a single phrase—and it was unsigned. "Didn't I tell you?" one of the party said. He was unshaven too and muddy, like the quarry which they had not yet even seen, and his face looked strained and a little mad, with frustration, outrage, and his voice was hoarse, as though he had been doing a good deal of unheeded shouting or talking recently. "I told you all the time! I told you!"

"Told me what?" the sheriff said, in a cold, level voice, bearing upon the other a gaze cold and level, the pencilled message in his hand. "What did you tell me when?" The other looked at the sheriff, outraged, desperate, frayed almost to endurance's limit; looking at him, the deputy thought, 'If he dont get that reward, he will just die.' His mouth was open though voiceless as he glared at the sheriff with a kind of baffled and unbelieving amaze. "And I done told you, too," the sheriff said, in his bleak, quiet voice. "If you dont like the way I am running this, you can wait back in town. There's a good place there for you to wait in. Cool, where you wont stay so heated up like out here in the sun. Aint I told you, now? Talk up."

The other closed his mouth. He looked away, as though with a tremendous effort; as though with a tremendous effort he said "Yes" in a dry, suffocated voice.

The sheriff turned heavily, crumpling the message. "You try to keep that from slipping your mind again, then," he said. "If you got any mind to even slip on you." They were ringed about with quiet, interested faces in the early sunlight. "About which I got the Lord's own doubts, if you or anybody else wants to know." Someone guffawed, once. "Shet up that noise," the sheriff said. "Let's get going. Get them dogs started, Bufe."

The dogs were cast, still on leash. They struck immediately. The trail was good, easily followed because of the dew. The fugitive had apparently made no effort whatever to hide it. They could even see the prints of his knees and hands where he had knelt to drink from a spring. "I never yet knew a murderer that had more sense than that about the folks that would chase him," the deputy said. "But this durn fool dont even suspect that we might use dogs."

"We been putting dogs on him once a day ever since Sunday," the sheriff said. "And we aint caught him yet."

"Them were cold trails. We aint had a good hot trail until today. But he's made his mistake at last. We'll get him today. Before noon, maybe."

"I'll wait and see, I reckon," the sheriff said.

"You'll see," the deputy said. "This trail is running straight as a railroad. I could follow it, myself almost. Look here. You can even see his footprints. The durn fool aint even got enough sense to get into the road, in the dust, where other folks have walked and where the dogs cant scent him. Them dogs will find the end of them footprints before ten oclock."

Which the dogs did. Presently the trail bent sharply at right angles. They followed it and came onto a road, which they followed behind the lowheaded and eager dogs who, after a short distance, swung to the roadside where a path came down from a cotton house in a nearby field. They began to bay, milling, tugging, their voices loud, mellow, ringing;

whining and surging with excitement. "Why, the durn fool!" the deputy said. "He set down here and rested: here's his footmarks: them same rubber heels. He aint a mile ahead right now! Come on, boys!" They went on, the leashes taut, the dogs baying, the men moving now at a trot. The sheriff turned to the unshaven man.

"Now's your chance to run ahead and catch him and get that thousand dollars," he said. "Why dont you do it?"

The man did not answer; none of them had much breath for talking, particularly when after about a mile the dogs, still straining and baying, turned from the road and followed a path which went quartering up a hill and into a corn field. Here they stopped baying, but if anything their eagerness seemed to increase; the men were running now. Beyond the headtall corn was a negro cabin. "He's in there," the sheriff said, drawing his pistol. "Watch yourselves now, boys. He'll have a gun now."

It was done with finesse and skill: the house surrounded by concealed men with drawn pistols, and the sheriff, followed by the deputy, getting himself for all his bulk swiftly and smartly flat against the cabin wall, out of range of any window. Still flat to the wall he ran around the corner and kicked open the door and sprang, pistol first, into the cabin. It contained a negro child. The child was stark naked and it sat in the cold ashes on the hearth, eating something. It was apparently alone, though an instant later a woman appeared in an inner door, her mouth open, in the act of dropping an iron skillet. She was wearing a pair of man's shoes, which a member of the posse identified as having belonged to the fugitive. She told them about the white man on the road about daylight and how he had swapped shoes with her, taking in exchange a pair of her husband's brogans which she was wearing at the time. The sheriff listened. "That happened right by a cotton house, didn't it?" he said. She told him Yes. He returned to his men, to the leashed and eager dogs. He looked down at the dogs while the men asked questions and then ceased, watching him. They watched him put the pistol back into his pocket and then turn and kick the dogs, once each, heavily. "Get them durn eggsuckers on back to town," he said.

But the sheriff was a good officer. He knew as well as his men that he would return to the cottonhouse, where he believed that Christmas had been hidden all the while, though he knew now that Christmas would not be there when they returned. They had some trouble getting the dogs away from the cabin, so that it was in the hot brilliance of ten oclock that they surrounded the cotton house carefully and skilfully and quietly and surprised it with pistols, quite by the rules and without any particular hope; and found one astonished and terrified field rat. Nevertheless the sheriff had the dogs— they had refused to approach the cotton house at all; they refused to leave the road, leaning and straining against the collars with simultaneous and reverted heads pointed back down the road toward the cabin from which they had been recently dragged away—brought up. It took two men by main strength to fetch them up, where as soon as the leashes were slacked, they sprang as one and rushed around the cotton house and through the very marks which the fugitive's legs had left in the tall and still dewed weeds in the house's shadow, and rushed leaping and straining back toward the road, dragging the two men for fifty yards before they succeeded in passing the leashes about a sapling and snubbing the dogs up. This time the sheriff did not even kick them.

At last the noise and the alarms, the sound and fury of the hunt, dies away, dies out of his hearing. He was not in the cottonhouse when the man and the dogs passed, as the sheriff believed. He paused there only long enough to lace up the brogans: the black shoes, the black shoes smelling of negro. They looked like they had been chopped out of iron ore with a dull axe. Looking down at the harsh, crude, clumsy shapelessness of them, he said "Hah" through his teeth. It seemed to him that he could see himself being hunted by white men at last into the black abyss which had been waiting, trying, for thirty years to drown him and into which now and at last he had actually entered, bearing now upon his ankles the definite and ineradicable gauge of its upward moving.

It is just dawn, daylight: that gray and lonely suspension

filled with the peaceful and tentative waking of birds. The air, inbreathed, is like spring water. He breathes deep and slow, feeling with each breath himself diffuse in the neutral grayness, becoming one with loneliness and quiet that has never known fury or despair. 'That was all I wanted,' he thinks, in a quiet and slow amazement. 'That was all, for thirty years. That didn't seem to be a whole lot to ask in thirty years.'

He has not slept very much since Wednesday, and now Wednesday has come and gone again, though he does not know it. When he thinks about time, it seems to him now that for thirty years he has lived inside an orderly parade of named and numbered days like fence pickets, and that one night he went to sleep and when he waked up he was outside of them. For a time after he fled on that Friday night he tried to keep up with the days, after the old habit. Once, after lying all night in a haystack, he was awake in time to watch the farm house wake. He saw before daylight a lamp come yellowly alive in the kitchen, and then in the gray yetdark he heard the slow, clapping sound of an axe, and movement, manmovement, among the waking cattlesounds in the nearby barn. Then he could smell smoke, and food, the hot fierce food, and he began to say over and over to himself *I have not eaten since I have not eaten since* trying to remember how many days it had been since Friday in Jefferson, in the restaurant where he had eaten his supper, until after a while, in the lying still with waiting until the men should have eaten and gone to the field, the name of the day of the week seemed more important than the food. Because when the men were gone at last and he descended, emerged, into the level, jonquil-colored sun and went to the kitchen door, he didn't ask for food at all. He had intended to. He could feel the harsh words marshalling in his mind, just behind his mouth. And then the gaunt, leatherhard woman come to the door and looked at him and he could see shock and recognition and fear in her eyes and while he was thinking *She knows me. She has got the word too* he heard his mouth saying quietly: "Can you tell me what day this is? I just want to know what day this is."

"What day it is?" Her face was gaunt as his, her body as gaunt and as tireless and as driven. She said: "You get away from here! It's Tuesday! You get away from here! I'll call my man!"

He said "Thank you" quietly as the door banged. Then he was running. He did not remember starting to run. He thought for a while that he ran because of and toward some destination that the running had suddenly remembered and hence his mind did not need to bother to remember why he was running, since the running was not difficult. It was quite easy, in fact. He felt quite light, weightless. Even in full stride his feet seemed to stray slowly and lightly and at deliberate random across an earth without solidity, until he fell. Nothing tripped him. He just fell full length, believing for a while that he was still on his feet and still running. But he was down, lying on his face in a shallow ditch at the edge of a plowed field. Then he said suddenly, "I reckon I better get up." When he sat up he found that the sun, halfway up the sky, now shone upon him from the opposite direction. At first he believed that he was merely turned around. Then he realised that it was now evening. That it was morning when he fell running and that, though it seemed to him that he had sat up at once, it was now evening. 'I have been asleep,' he thought. 'I have slept more than six hours. I must have gone to sleep running without knowing it. That is what I did.'

He felt no surprise. Time, the spaces of light and dark, had long since lost orderliness. It would be either one now, seemingly at an instant, between two movements of the eyelids, without warning. He could never know when he would pass from one to the other, when he would find that he had been asleep without remembering having lain down, or find himself walking without remembering having waked. Sometimes it would seem to him that a night of sleep, in hay, in a ditch, beneath an abandoned roof, would be followed immediately by another night without interval of day, without light between to see to flee by; that a day would be followed by another day filled with fleeing and urgency, without any night between or any interval for rest, as if the sun had not set but instead had turned in the sky before reaching the horizon and retraced its way. When he went to sleep walking or even kneeling in the act of drinking from a spring, he could never

know if his eyes would open next upon sunlight or upon
stars.

For a while he had been hungry all the time. He gathered
and ate rotting and wormriddled fruit; now and then he crept
into fields and dragged down and gnawed ripened ears of
corn as hard as potato graters. He thought of eating all the
time, imagining dishes, food. He would think of that meal set
for him on the kitchen table three years ago and he would
live again through the steady and deliberate backswinging of
his arm as he hurled the dishes into the wall, with a kind of
writhing and excruciating agony of regret and remorse and
rage. Then one day he was no longer hungry. It came sudden
and peaceful. He felt cool, quiet. Yet he knew that he had to
eat. He would make himself eat the rotten fruit, the hard
corn, chewing it slowly, tasting nothing. He would eat enormous quantities of it, with resultant crises of bleeding flux.
Yet immediately afterward he would be obsessed anew with
the need and the urge to eat. It was not with food that he
was obsessed now, but with the necessity to eat. He would
try to remember when he had eaten last of cooked, of decent
food. He could feel, remember, somewhere a house, a cabin.
House or cabin, white or black: he could not remember
which. Then, as he sat quite still, with on his gaunt, sick,
stubbled face an expression of rapt bemusement, he smelled
negro. Motionless (he was sitting against a tree beside a
spring, his head back, his hands upon his lap, his face worn
and peaceful) he smelled and saw negro dishes, negro food.
It was in a room. He did not remember how he got there.
But the room was filled with flight and abrupt consternation,
as though people had fled it recently and suddenly and in fear.
He was sitting at a table, waiting, thinking of nothing in an
emptiness, a silence filled with flight. Then there was food
before him, appearing suddenly between long, limber black
hands fleeing too in the act of setting down the dishes. It
seemed to him that he could hear without hearing them wails
of terror and distress quieter than sighs all about him, with
the sound of the chewing and the swallowing. 'It was a cabin
that time,' he thought. 'And they were afraid. Of their
brother afraid.'

That night a strange thing came into his mind. He lay

ready for sleep, without sleeping, without seeming to need the sleep, as he would place his stomach acquiescent for food which it did not seem to desire or need. It was strange in the sense that he could discover neither derivation nor motivation nor explanation for it. He found that he was trying to calculate the day of the week. It was as though now and at last he had an actual and urgent need to strike off the accomplished days toward some purpose, some definite day or act, without either falling short or overshooting. He entered the coma state which sleeping had now become with the need in his mind. When he waked in the dewgray of dawn, it was so crystallised that the need did not seem strange anymore.

It is just dawn, daylight. He rises and descends to the spring and takes from his pocket the razor, the brush, the soap. But it is still too dim to see his face clearly in the water, so he sits beside the spring and waits until he can see better. Then he lathers his face with the hard, cold water, patiently. His hand trembles, despite the urgency he feels a lassitude so that he must drive himself. The razor is dull; he tries to whet it upon the side of one brogan, but the leather is ironhard and wet with dew. He shaves, after a fashion. His hand trembles; it is not a very good job, and he cuts himself three or four times, stanching the blood with the cold water until it stops. He puts the shaving tools away and begins to walk. He follows a straight line, disregarding the easier walking of the ridges. After a short distance he comes out upon a road and sits down beside it. It is a quiet road, appearing and vanishing quietly, the pale dust marked only by narrow and infrequent wheels and by the hooves of horses and mules and now and then by the print of human feet. He sits beside it, coatless, the once white shirt and the once creased trousers muddy and stained, his gaunt face blotched with patches of stubble and with dried blood, shaking slowly with weariness and cold as the sun rises and warms him. After a time two negro children appear around the curve, approaching. They do not see him until he speaks; they halt, dead, looking at him with white-rolling eyes. "What day of the week is it?" he repeats. They say nothing at all, staring at him. He moves his head a little. "Go on," he says. They go on. He does not watch them. He sits, apparently musing upon the place where they had stood, as though to him they had in moving merely walked out of two shells. He does not see that they are running.

Then, sitting there, the sun warming him slowly, he goes to sleep without knowing it, because the next thing of which he is conscious is a terrific clatter of jangling and rattling wood and metal and trotting hooves. He opens his eyes in time to see the wagon whirl slewing around the curve beyond and so out of sight, its occupants looking back at him over their shoulders, the whiphand of the driver rising and falling. 'They recognised me too,' he thinks. 'Them, and that white woman. And the negroes where I ate that day. Any of them could have captured me, if that's what they want. Since that's what they all want: for me to be captured. But they all run first. They all want me to be captured, and then when I come up ready to say Here I am *Yes I would say Here I am I am tired I am tired of running of having to carry my life like it was a basket of eggs* they all run away. Like there is a rule to catch me by, and to capture me that way would not be like the rule says.'

So he moves back into the bushes. This time he is alert and he hears the wagon before it comes into sight. He does not show himself until the wagon is abreast of him. Then he steps forth and says "Hey." The wagon stops, jerked up. The negro driver's head jerks also; into his face also comes the astonishment, then the recognition and the terror. "What day is this?" Christmas says.

The negro glares at him, slackjawed. "W—what you say?"

"What day of the week is this? Thursday? Friday? What? What day? I am not going to hurt you."

"It's Friday," the negro says. "O Lawd God, it's Friday."

"Friday," Christmas says. Again he jerks his head. "Get on." The whip falls, the mules surge forward. This wagon too whirls from sight at a dead run, the whip rising and falling. But Christmas has already turned and entered the woods again.

Again his direction is straight as a surveyor's line, disregarding hill and valley and bog. Yet he is not hurrying. He is like a man who knows where he is and where he wants to go and how much time to the exact minute he has to get there in. It is as though he desires to see his native earth in all its phases for the first or the last time. He had grown to manhood in the country, where like the unswimming sailor his physical shape and his thought had been molded by its compulsions without his learning anything about its actual shape and feel. For a week now he has lurked and crept among its secret places, yet he remained a foreigner to the very immutable laws which earth must obey. For some time as he walks steadily on, he thinks that this is what it is—the looking and seeing—which gives him peace and unhaste and quiet, until suddenly the true answer comes to him. He feels dry and light. 'I dont have to bother about having to eat anymore,' he thinks. 'That's what it is.'

By noon he has walked eight miles. He comes now to a broad gravelled road, a highway. This time the wagon stops quietly at his raised hand. On the face of the negro youth who drives it there is neither astonishment nor recognition. "Where does this road go?" Christmas says.

"Mottstown. Whar I gwine."

"Mottstown. You going to Jefferson too?"

The youth rubs his head. "Dont know whar that is. I gwine to Mottstown."

"Oh," Christmas says. "I see. You dont live around here, then."

"Naw, sir. I stays two counties back yonder. Been on the road three days. I gwine to Mottstown to get a yellin calf pappy bought. You wanter go to Mottstown?"

"Yes," Christmas says. He mounts to the seat beside the youth. The wagon moves on. 'Mottstown,' he thinks. Jefferson is only twenty miles away. 'Now I can let go for a while,' he thinks. 'I haven't let go for seven days, so I guess I'll let go for a while.' He thinks that perhaps, sitting, with the wagon's motion to lull him, he will sleep. But he does not sleep. He is not sleepy or hungry or even tired. He is somewhere between and among them, suspended, swaying to the motion of the wagon without thought, without feeling. He has lost account of time and distance; perhaps it is an hour later, perhaps three. The youth says:

"Mottstown. Dar tis."

Looking, he can see the smoke low on the sky, beyond an imperceptible corner; he is entering it again, the street which ran for thirty years. It had been a paved street, where going should be fast. It had made a circle and he is still inside of it. Though during the last seven days he has had no paved street, yet he has travelled further than in all the thirty years before. And yet he is still inside the circle. 'And yet I have been further in these seven days than in all the thirty years,' he thinks. 'But I have never got outside that circle. I have never broken out of the ring of what I have already done and cannot ever undo,' he thinks quietly, sitting on the seat, with planted on the dashboard before him the shoes, the black shoes smelling of negro: that mark on his ankles the gauge definite and ineradicable of the black tide creeping up his legs, moving from his feet upward as death moves.

XV

ON THAT FRIDAY when Christmas was captured in Mottstown, there lived in the town an old couple named Hines. They were quite old. They lived in a small bungalow in a neighborhood of negroes; how, upon what, the town in general did not know since they appeared to live in filthy poverty and complete idleness, Hines, as far as the town knew, not having done any work, steady work, in twentyfive years.

They came to Mottstown thirty years ago. One day the town found the woman established in the small house where they had lived ever since, though for the next five years Hines was at home only once a month, over the weekend. Soon it became known that he held some kind of a position in Memphis. Exactly what, was not known, since even at that time he was a secret man who could have been either thirtyfive or fifty, with something in his glance coldly and violently fanatical and a little crazed, precluding questioning, curiosity. The town looked upon them both as being a little touched— lonely, gray in color, a little smaller than most other men and women, as if they belonged to a different race, species—even though for the next five or six years after the man appeared to have come to Mottstown to settle down for good in the small house where his wife lived, people hired him to do various odd jobs which they considered within his strength. But in time he stopped this, too. The town wondered for a while, how they would live now, then it forgot to speculate about this just as later when the town learned that Hines went on foot about the county, holding revival services in negro churches, and that now and then negro women carrying what were obviously dishes of food would be seen entering from the rear the house where the couple lived, and emerging emptyhanded, it wondered about this for a time and then forgot it. In time the town either forgot or condoned, because Hines was an old man and harmless, that which in a young man it would have crucified. It just said, "They are crazy; crazy on the subject of negroes. Maybe they are Yankees", and let it go at that. Or perhaps what it condoned was not the man's selfdedication to the saving of Negro souls, but the public ignoring of the fact of that charity which they received from negro hands, since it is a happy faculty of the mind to slough that which conscience refuses to assimilate.

So for twentyfive years the old couple had had no visible means of support, the town blinding its collective eye to the negro women and the covered dishes and pans, particularly as some of the dishes and pans had in all likelihood been borne intact from white kitchens where the women cooked. Perhaps this was a part of the mind's sloughing. Anyway the town did not look, and for twentyfive years now the couple had lived in the slack backwater of their lonely isolation, like they might have been two muskoxen strayed from the north pole, or two homeless and belated beasts from beyond the glacial period.

The woman was hardly ever seen at all, though the man— he was known as Uncle Doc—was a fixture about the square: a dirty little old man with a face which had once been either courageous or violent—either a visionary or a supreme ego- ist—collarless, in dirty blue jean clothes and with a heavy piece of handpeeled hickory worn about the grip dark as wal- nut and smooth as glass. At first, while he held the Memphis position, on his monthly visits he had talked a little about himself, with a selfconfidence not alone of the independent man, but with a further quality, as though at one time in his life he had been better than independent, and that not long ago. There was nothing beaten about him. It was rather that confidence of a man who has had the controlling of lesser men and who had voluntarily and for a reason which he be- lieved that no other man could question or comprehend, changed his life. But what he told about himself and his pres- ent occupation did not make sense, for all its apparent coher- ence. So they believed that he was a little crazy, even then. It was not that he seemed to be trying to conceal one thing by telling another. It was that his words, his telling, just did not synchronise with what his hearers believed would (and must) be the scope of a single individual. Sometimes they decided that he had once been a minister. Then he would talk about Memphis, the city, in a vague and splendid way, as though all his life he had been incumbent there of some important though still nameless municipal office. "Sure," the men in Mottstown said behind his back; "he was railroad superintendent there. Standing in the middle of the street crossing with a red flag every time a train passed" or "He's a big newspaper-man. Gathers up the papers from under the park benches." They did not say this to his face, not the boldest among them, not the ones with the most precariously nourished reputations for wit.

Then he lost the Memphis job, or quit it. One weekend he came home, and when Monday came he did not go away. After that he was down town all day long, about the square, untalkative, dirty, with that furious and preclusive expression about the eyes which the people took for insanity: that quality of outworn violence like a scent, an odor; that fanaticism like a fading and almost extinct ember, of some kind of two-fisted evangelism which had been one quarter violent conviction and three quarters physical hardihood. So they were not so surprised when they learned that he was going about the county, usually on foot, preaching in negro churches; not even when a year later they learned what his subject was. That this white man who very nearly depended on the bounty and charity of negroes for sustenance was going singlehanded into remote negro churches and interrupting the service to enter the pulpit and in his harsh, dead voice and at times with violent obscenity, preach to them humility before all skins lighter than theirs, preaching the superiority of the white race, himself his own exhibit A, in fanatic and unconscious paradox. The negroes believed that he was crazy, touched by God, or having once touched Him. They probably did not listen to, could not understand much of, what he said. Perhaps they took him to be God Himself, since God to them was a white man too and His doings also a little inexplicable.

He was downtown that afternoon when Christmas' name first flew up and down the street, and the boys and men—the merchants, the clerks, the idle and the curious, with countrymen in overalls predominating—began to run. Hines ran too. But he could not run fast and he was not tall enough to see over the clotted shoulders when he did arrive. Nevertheless he tried, as brutal and intent as any there, to force his way into the loud surging group as though in a resurgence of the old violence which had marked his face, clawing at the backs and at last striking at them with the stick until men turned and recognised him and held him, struggling, striking at them with the heavy stick. "Christmas?" he shouted. "Did they say Christmas?"

"Christmas!" one of the men who held him cried back, his face too strained, glaring. "Christmas! That white nigger that did that killing up at Jefferson last week!"

Hines glared at the man, his toothless mouth lightly foamed with spittle. Then he struggled again, violent, cursing: a frail little old man with the light, frail bones of a child, trying to fight free with the stick, trying to club his way into the center where the captive stood bleeding about the face. "Now, Uncle Doc!" they said, holding him; "now, Uncle Doc. They got him. He cant get away. Here, now."

But he struggled and fought, cursing, his voice cracked, thin, his mouth slavering, they who held him struggling too like men trying to hold a small threshing hose in which the pressure is too great for its size. Of the entire group the captive was the only calm one. They held Hines, cursing, his old frail bones and his stringlike muscles for the time inherent with the fluid and supple fury of a weasel. He broke free of them and sprang forward, burrowing, and broke through and came face to face with the captive. Here he paused for an instant, glaring at the captive's face. It was a full pause, but before they could grasp him again he had raised the stick and struck the captive once and he was trying to strike again when they caught him at last and held him impotent and raging, with that light, thin foam about his lips. They had not stopped his mouth. "Kill the bastard!" he cried. "Kill him. Kill him."

Thirty minutes later two men brought him home in a car. One of them drove while the other held Hines up in the back seat. His face was pale now beneath the stubble and the dirt, and his eyes were closed. They lifted him bodily from the car and carried him through the gate and up the walk of rotting bricks and shards of concrete, to the steps. His eyes were open now, but they were quite empty, rolled back into his skull until the dirty, bluish whites alone showed. But he was still quite limp and helpless. Just before they reached the porch the front door opened and his wife came out and closed the door behind her and stood there, watching them.

They knew that it was his wife because she came out of the house where he was known to live. One of the men, though a resident of the town, had never seen her before. "What is it?" she said.

"He's all right," the first man said. "We just been having a right smart of excitement down town a while ago, and with this hot weather and all, it was a little too much for him." She stood before the door as if she were barring them from the house——a dumpy, fat little woman with a round face like dirty and unovened dough, and a tight screw of scant hair. "They just caught that nigger Christmas that killed that lady up at Jefferson last week," the man said. "Uncle Doc just got a little upset over it."

Mrs Hines was already turning back, as though to open the door. As the first man said later to his companion, she halted in the act of turning, as if someone had hit her lightly with a thrown pebble. "Caught who?" she said.

"Christmas," the man said. "That nigger murderer. Christmas."

She stood at the edge of the porch, looking down at them with her gray, still face. "As if she already knew what I would tell her," the man said to his companion as they returned to the car. "Like she wanted all at the same time for me to tell her it was him and it wasn't him."

"What does he look like?" she said.

"I never noticed much," the man said. "They had to bloody him up some, catching him. Young fellow. He dont look no more like a nigger than I do, either." The woman looked at them, down at them. Between the two men Hines stood on his own legs now, muttering a little now as if he were waking from sleep. "What do you want us to do with Uncle Doc?" the man said.

She did not answer that at all. It was as though she had not even recognised her husband, the man told his companion later. "What are they going to do with him?" she said.

"Him?" the man said. "Oh. The nigger. That's for Jefferson to say. He belongs to them up there."

She looked down at them, gray, still, remote. "Are they going to wait on Jefferson?"

"They?" the man said. "Oh," he said. "Well, if Jefferson aint too long about it." He shifted his grip on the old man's arm. "Where do you want us to put him?" The woman moved then. She descended the steps and approached. "We'll tote him into the house for you," the man said.

"I can tote him," she said. She and Hines were about the same height, though she was the heavier. She grasped him beneath the arms. "Eupheus," she said, not loud; "Eupheus." She said to the two men, quietly: "Let go. I got him." They released him. He walked a little now. They watched her help him up the steps and into the door. She did not look back.

"She never even thanked us," the second man said. "Maybe we ought to take him back and put him in jail with the nigger, since he seemed to know him so well."

"Eupheus," the first man said. "Eupheus. I been wondering for fifteen years what his name might be. Eupheus."

"Come on. Let's get on back. We might miss some of it."

The first man looked at the house, at the closed door through which the two people had vanished. "She knowed him too."

"Knowed who?"

"That nigger. Christmas."

"Come on." They returned to the car. "What do you think about that durn fellow, coming right into town here, within twenty miles of where he done it, walking up and down the main street until somebody recognised him. I wish it had been me that recognised him. I could have used that thousand dollars. But I never do have any luck." The car moved on. The first man was still looking back at the blank door through which the two people had disappeared.

In the hall of that little house dark and small and rankly-odored as a cave, the old couple stood. The old man's spent condition was still little better than coma, and when his wife led him to a chair and helped him into it, it seemed a matter of expediency and concern. But there was no need to return and lock the front door, which she did. She came and stood over him for a while. At first it seemed as if she were just watching him, with concern and solicitude. Then a third person would have seen that she was trembling violently and that she had lowered him into the chair either before she dropped him to the floor or in order to hold him prisoner until she could speak. She leaned above him: dumpy, obese, gray in color, with a face like that of a drowned corpse. When she spoke her voice shook and she strove with it, shaking, her hands clenched upon the arms of the chair in which he half lay, her voice shaking, restrained: "Eupheus. You listen to me. You got to listen to me. I aint worried you before. In thirty years I aint worried you. But now I am going to. I am going to know and you got to tell me. What did you do with Milly's baby?"

Through the long afternoon they clotted about the square and before the jail—the clerks, the idle, the countrymen in overalls; the talk. It went here and there about the town, dying and borning again like a wind or a fire until in the lengthening shadows the country people began to depart in wagons and dusty cars and the townspeople began to move supperward. Then the talk flared again, momentarily revived, to wives and families about supper tables in electrically lighted rooms and in remote hill cabins with kerosene lamps. And on the next day, the slow, pleasant country Sunday while they squatted in their clean shirts and decorated suspenders, with peaceful pipes about country churches or about the shady dooryards of houses where the visiting teams and cars were tethered and parked along the fence and the womenfolks were in the kitchen, getting dinner, they told it again: "He dont look any more like a nigger than I do. But it must have been the nigger blood in him. It looked like he had set out to get himself caught like a man might set out to get married. He had got clean away for a whole week. If he had not set fire to the house, they might not have found out about the murder for a month. And they would not have suspected him then if it hadn't been for a fellow named Brown, that the nigger used to sell whiskey while he was pretending to be a white man and tried to lay the whiskey and the killing both on Brown and Brown told the truth.

"Then yesterday morning he come into Mottstown in broad daylight, on a Saturday with the town full of folks. He

went into a white barbershop like a white man, and because
he looked like a white man they never suspected him. Even
when the bootblack saw how he had on a pair of second hand
brogans that were too big for him, they never suspected.
They shaved him and cut his hair and he payed them and
walked out and went right into a store and bought a new
shirt and a tie and a straw hat, with some of the very money
he stole from the woman he murdered. And then he walked
the streets in broad daylight, like he owned the town, walking
back and forth with people passing him a dozen times and
not knowing it, until Halliday saw him and ran up and
grabbed him and said, 'Aint your name Christmas?' and the
nigger said that it was. He never denied it. He never did anything. He never acted like either a nigger or a white man.
That was it. That was what made the folks so mad. For him
to be a murderer and all dressed up and walking the town like
he dared them to touch him, when he ought to have been
skulking and hiding in the woods, muddy and dirty and running. It was like he never even knew he was a murderer, let
alone a nigger too.

"And so Halliday (he was excited, thinking about that
thousand dollars, and he had already hit the nigger a couple
of times in the face, and the nigger acting like a nigger for
the first time and taking it, not saying anything: just bleeding
sullen and quiet)—Halliday was hollering and holding him
when the old man they call Uncle Doc Hines come up and
begun to hit the nigger with his walking stick until at last
two men had to hold Uncle Doc quiet and took him home in
a car. Nobody knew if he really did know the nigger or not.
He just come hobbling up, screeching 'Is his name Christmas?
Did you say Christmas?' and shoved up and took one look at
the nigger and then begun to beat him with the walking stick.
He acted like he was hypnotised or something. They had to
hold him, and his eyes rolling blue into his head and slobbering at the mouth and cutting with that stick at everything that
come into reach, until all of a sudden he kind of flopped.
Then two fellows carried him home in a car and his wife
come out and took him into the house, and the two fellows
come on back to town. They didn't know what was wrong
with him, to get so excited after the nigger was caught, but

anyway they thought that he would be all right now. But here it was not a half an hour before he was back down town again. He was pure crazy by now, standing on the corner and yelling at whoever would pass, calling them cowards because they wouldn't take the nigger out of jail and hang him right then and there, Jefferson or no Jefferson. He looked crazy in the face, like somebody that had done slipped away from a crazy house and that knew he wouldn't have much time before they come and got him again. Folks say that he used to be a preacher, too.

"He said that he had a right to kill the nigger. He never said why, and he was too worked up and crazy to make sense even when somebody would stop him long enough to ask a question. There was a right good crowd around him by then, and him yelling about how it was his right to say first whether the nigger should live or should die. And folks were beginning to think that maybe the place for him was in the jail with the nigger, when here his wife come up.

"There are folks that have lived in Mottstown for thirty years and haven't ever seen her. They didn't know who she was then until she spoke to him, because the ones that had seen her, she was always around that little house in Niggertown where they live, in a mother hubbard and one of his woreout hats. But she was dressed up now. She had on a purple silk dress and a hat with a plume on it and she was carrying a umbrella and she come up to the crowd where he was hollering and yelling and she said, 'Eupheus.' He stopped yelling then and he looked at her, with that stick still raised in his hand and it kind of shaking, and his jaw dropped slack, slobbering. She took him by the arm. A lot of folks had been scared to come nigh him because of that stick; he looked like he might hit anybody at any minute and not even knowed it or intended it. But she walked right up under the stick and took him by the arm and led him across to where there was a chair in front of a store and she set him down in the chair and she said, 'You stay here till I come back. Dont you move, now. And you quit that yelling.'

"And he did. He sho did. He set right there where she put him, and she never looked back, neither. They all noticed that. Maybe it was because folks never saw her except around home, staying at home. And him being a kind of fierce little old man that a man wouldn't cross without he thought about it first. Anyhow they were surprised. They hadn't even thought of him taking orders from anybody. It was like she had got something on him and he had to mind her. Because he sat down when she told him to, in that chair, not hollering and talking big now, but with his head bent down and his hands shaking on that big walking stick and a little slobber still running out of his mouth, onto his shirt.

"She went straight to the jail. There was a big crowd in front of it, because Jefferson had sent word that they were on the way down to get the nigger. She walked right through them and into the jail and she said to Metcalf, 'I want to see that man they caught.'

" 'What do you want to see him for?' Metcalf said.

" 'I aint going to bother him,' she said. 'I just want to look at him.'

"Metcalf told her there was a right smart of other folks that wanted to do that, and that he knew she didn't aim to help him escape, but that he was just the jailor and he couldn't let anybody in without he had permission from the sheriff. And her standing there, in that purple dress and the plume not even nodding and bending, she was that still. 'Where is the sheriff?' she said.

" 'He might be in his office,' Metcalf said. 'You find him and get permission from him. Then you can see the nigger.' Metcalf thought that that would finish it. So he watched her turn and go out and walk through the crowd in front of the jail and go back up the street toward the square. The plume was nodding now. He could see it nodding along above the fence. And then he saw her go across the square and in to the courthouse. The folks didn't know what she was doing, because Metcalf hadn't had time to tell them what happened at the jail. They just watched her go on into the courthouse, and then Russell said how he was in the office and he happened to look up and there that hat was with the plume on it just beyond the window across the counter. He didn't know how long she had been standing there, waiting for him to look up. He said she was just tall enough to see over the counter, so that she didn't look like she had any body at all. It just looked like somebody had sneaked up and set a toy balloon with a face painted on it and a comic hat set on top of it, like the Katzenjammer kids in the funny paper. 'I want to see the sheriff,' she says.

" 'He aint here,' Russell says. 'I'm his deputy. What can I do for you?'

"He said she didn't answer for a while, standing there. Then she said, 'Where can I find him?'

" 'He might be at home,' Russell says. 'He's been right busy, this week. Up at night some, helping those Jefferson officers. He might be home taking a nap. But maybe I can——' But he said that she was already gone. He said he looked out the window and watched her go on across the square and turn the corner toward where the sheriff lived. He said he was still trying to place her, to think who she was.

"She never found the sheriff. But it was too late then, anyway. Because the sheriff was already at the jail, only Metcalf hadn't told her, and besides she hadn't got good away from the jail before the Jefferson officers came up in two cars and went into the jail. They came up quick and went in quick. But the word had already got around that they were there, and there must have been two hundred men and boys and women too in front of the jail when the two sheriffs come out onto the porch and our sheriff made a speech, asking the folks to respect the law and that him and the Jefferson sheriff both promised that the nigger would get a quick and fair trial; and then somebody in the crowd says, 'Fair, hell. Did he give that white woman a fair trial?' And they hollered then, crowding up, like they were hollering for one another to the dead woman and not to the sheriffs. But the sheriff kept on talking quiet to them, about how it was his sworn word given to them on the day they elected him that he was trying to keep. 'I have no more sympathy with nigger murderers than any other white man here,' he says. 'But it is my sworn oath, and by God I aim to keep it. I dont want no trouble, but I aint going to dodge it. You better smoke that for a while.' And Halliday was there too, with the sheriffs. He was the foremost one about reason and not making trouble. 'Yaaah,' somebody hollers; 'we reckon you dont want him lynched. But he aint worth any thousand dollars to us. He aint worth

a thousand dead matches to us.' And then the sheriff says
quick: 'What if Halliday dont want him killed? Dont we all
want the same thing? Here it's a local citizen that will get the
reward: the money will be spent right here in Mottstown.
Just suppose it was a Jefferson man was going to get it. Aint
that right, men? Aint that sensible?' His voice sounded little,
like a doll's voice, like even a big man's voice will sound when
he is talking not against folks' listening but against their already half-made-up minds.

"Anyway, that seemed to convince them, even if folks did
know that Mottstown or nowhere else was going to see
enough of that thousand dollars to fat a calf, if Halliday was
the one that had the spending of it. But that did it. Folks are
funny. They cant stick to one way of thinking or doing anything unless they get a new reason for doing it ever so often.
And then when they do get a new reason, they are liable to
change anyhow. So they didn't give back exactly; it was like
when before that the crowd had kind of milled from the inside out, now it begun to mill from the outside in. And the
sheriffs knew it, the same as they knew that it might not last
very long, because they went back into the jail quick and then
come out again, almost before they had time to turn around,
with the nigger between them and five or six deputies following. They must have had him ready just inside the jail door
all the time, because they come out almost at once, with the
nigger between them with his face sulled up and his wrists
handcuffed to the Jefferson sheriff; and the crowd kind of
says, 'Ahhhhhhhhhhhhhh.'

"They made a kind of lane down to the street, where the
first Jefferson car was waiting with the engine running and a
man behind the wheel, and the sheriffs were coming along
without wasting any time, when she come up again, the
woman, Mrs Hines. She was shoving up through the crowd.
She was so lowbuilt that all the folks could see was that
plume kind of bumping along slow, like something that could
not have moved very fast even if there wasn't anything in the
way, and that couldn't anything stop, like a tractor. She
shoved right on through and out into the lane the folks had
made, right out in front of the two sheriffs with the nigger
between them, so that they had to stop to keep from running

over her. Her face looked like a big hunk of putty and her
hat had got knocked sideways so the plume hung down in
front of her face and she had to push it back to see. But she
didn't do anything. She just stopped them dead for a minute
while she stood there and looked at the nigger. She never said
a word, like that was all she had wanted and had been worrying folks for, like that was the reason she had dressed up
and come to town: just to look that nigger in the face once.
Because she turned and begun to burrow back into the crowd
again, and when the cars drove off with the nigger and the
Jefferson law and the folks looked around, she was gone. And
they went back to the square then, and Uncle Doc was gone
too from the chair where she had set him and told him to
wait. But all of the folks didn't go straight back to the square.
A lot of them stayed there, looking at the jail like it might
have been just the nigger's shadow that had come out.

"They thought that she had taken Uncle Doc home. It was
in front of Dollar's store and Dollar told about how he saw
her come back up the street ahead of the crowd. He said that
Uncle Doc had not moved, that he was still sitting in the
chair where she had left him like he was hypnotised, until she
come up and touched his shoulder and he got up and they
went on together with Dollar watching him. And Dollar said
that from the look on Uncle Doc's face, home was where he
ought to be.

"Only she never took him home. After a while folks saw
that she wasn't having to take him anywhere. It was like they
both wanted to do the same thing. The same thing but for
different reasons, and each one knew that the other's reason
was different and that whichever of them got his way, it
would be serious for the other one. Like they both knew it
without saying it and that each was watching the other, and
that they both knew that she would have the most sense
about getting them started.

"They went straight to the garage where Salmon keeps his
rent car. She did all the talking. She said they wanted to go
to Jefferson. Maybe they never dreamed that Salmon would
charge them more than a quarter apiece, because when he
said three dollars she asked him again, like maybe she could
not believe her ears. 'Three dollars,' Salmon says. 'I couldn't

do it for no less.' And them standing there and Uncle Doc
not taking any part, like he was waiting, like it wasn't any
concern of his, like he knew that he wouldn't need to bother:
that she would get them there.

"'I cant pay that,' she says.

"'You wont get it done no cheaper,' Salmon says. 'Unless
by the railroad. They'll take you for fiftytwo cents apiece.' But
she was already going away, with Uncle Doc following her
like a dog would.

"That was about four oclock. Until six oclock the folks saw
them sitting on a bench in the courthouse yard. They were
not talking: it was like each one never even knew the other
one was there. They just set there side by side, with her all
dressed up in her Sunday clothes. Maybe she was enjoying
herself, all dressed up and downtown all Saturday evening.
Maybe it was to her what being in Memphis all day would be
to other folks.

"They set there until the clock struck six. Then they got up.
Folks that saw it said she never said a word to him; that they
just got up at the same time, like two birds do from a limb
and a man cant tell which one of them give the signal. When
they walked, Uncle Doc walked a little behind her. They
crossed the square this way and turned into the street toward
the depot. And the folks knew that there wasn't any train due
for three hours and they wondered if they actually were going
somewhere on the train, before they found out that they were
going to do something that surprised the folks more than
that, even. They went to that little café down by the depot
and ate supper, that hadn't ever been seen together on the
street before, let alone eating in a café, since they come to
Mottstown. But that's where she took him; maybe they were
afraid they would miss the train if they ate downtown. Because they were there before half past six oclock, sitting on
two of them little stools at the counter, eating what she had
ordered without asking Uncle Doc about it at all. She asked
the café man about the train to Jefferson and he told her it
went at two a.m. 'Lots of excitement in Jefferson tonight,' he
says. 'You can get a car downtown and be in Jefferson in
fortyfive minutes. You dont need to wait until two oclock on

that train.' He thought they were strangers maybe; he told her which way town was.

"But she didn't say anything and they finished eating and she paid him, a nickel and a dime at a time out of a tiedup rag that she took out of the umbrella, with Uncle Doc setting there and waiting with that dazed look in his face like he was walking in his sleep. Then they left, and the café man thought they were going to take his advice and go to town and get that car when he looked out and saw them going on across the switch tracks, toward the depot. Once he started to call, but he didn't. 'I reckon I misunderstood her,' he says he thought. 'Maybe it's the nine oclock southbound they want.'

"They were sitting on the bench in the waiting room when the folks, the drummers and loafers and such, begun to come in and buy tickets for the southbound. The agent said how he noticed there was some folks in the waiting room when he come in after supper at half past seven, but that he never noticed particular until she come to the ticket window and asked what time the train left for Jefferson. He said he was busy at the time and that he just glanced up and says 'Tomorrow' without stopping what he was doing. Then he said that after a while something made him look up, and there was that round face watching him and that plume still in the window, and she says,

" 'I want two tickets on it.'

" 'That train is not due until two oclock in the morning,' the agent says. He didn't recognise her either. 'If you want to get to Jefferson anytime soon, you'd better go to town and hire a car. Do you know which way town is?' But he said she just stood there, counting nickels and dimes out of that knotted rag, and he came and gave her the two tickets and then he looked past her through the window and saw Uncle Doc and he knew who she was. And he said how they sat there and the folks for the southbound come in and the train come and left and they still set there. He said how Uncle Doc still looked like he was asleep, or doped or something. And then the train went, but some of the folks didn't go back to town. They stayed there, looking in the window, and now and then they would come in and look at Uncle Doc and his wife setting on the bench, until the agent turned off the lights in the waitingroom.

"Some of the folks stayed, even after that. They could look in the window and see them setting there in the dark. Maybe they could see the plume, and the white of Uncle Doc's head. And then Uncle Doc begun to wake up. It wasn't like he was surprised to find where he was, nor that he was where he didn't want to be. He just roused up, like he had been coasting for a long time now, and now was the time to put on the power again. They could hear her saying 'Shhhhhhh. Shhhhhhhhhh.' to him, and then his voice would break out. They were still setting there when the agent turned on the lights and told them that the two oclock train was coming, with her saying 'Shhhhhhh. Shhhhhhhhhhhh' like to a baby, and Uncle Doc hollering 'Bitchery and abomination! Abomination and bitchery!' "

XVI

WHEN HIS KNOCK gets no response, Byron leaves the porch and goes around the house and enters the small, enclosed back yard. He sees the chair at once beneath the mulberry tree. It is a canvas deck chair, mended and faded and sagged so long to the shape of Hightower's body that even when empty it seems to hold still in ghostly embrace the owner's obese shapelessness; approaching, Byron thinks how the mute chair evocative of disuse and supineness and shabby remoteness from the world, is somehow the symbol and the being too of the man himself. 'That I am going to disturb again,' he thinks, with that faint lift of lip, thinking *Again? The disturbing I have done him, even he will see that that disturbing is nothing now. And on Sunday again. But then I reckon Sunday would want to take revenge on him too, being as Sunday was invented by folks*

He comes up behind the chair and looks down into it. Hightower is asleep. Upon the swell of his paunch, where the white shirt (it is a clean and fresh one now) balloons out of the worn black trousers, an open book lies face down. Upon the book Hightower's hands are folded, peaceful, benignant, almost pontifical. The shirt is made after an old fashion, with a pleated though carelessly ironed bosom, and he wears no collar. His mouth is open, the loose and flabby flesh sagging away from the round orifice in which the stained lower teeth show, and from the still fine nose which alone age, the defeat of sheer years, has not changed. Looking down at the unconscious face, it seems to Byron as though the whole man were fleeing away from the nose which holds invincibly to something yet of pride and courage above the sluttishness of vanquishment like a forgotten flag above a ruined fortress. Again light, the reflection of sky beyond the mulberry leaves, glints and glares upon the spectacle lenses, so that Byron cannot tell just when Hightower's eyes open. He sees only the mouth shut, and a movement of the folded hands as Hightower sits up. "Yes," he says; "yes? Who is——Oh, Byron."

Byron looks down at him, his face quite grave. But it is not compassionate now. It is not anything: it is just quite sober and quite determined. He says, without any inflection at all: "They caught him yesterday. I dont reckon you have heard that any more than you heard about the killing."

"Caught him?"

"Christmas. In Mottstown. He came to town, and near as I can learn, he stood around on the street until somebody recognised him."

"Caught him." Hightower is sitting up in the chair now. "And you have come to tell me that he is——that they have. . . ."

"No. Aint anybody done anything to him yet. He aint dead yet. He's in the jail. He's all right."

"All right. You say that he is all right. Byron says that he is all right——Byron Bunch has helped the woman's paramour sell his friend for a thousand dollars, and Byron says that it is all right. Has kept the woman hidden from the father of her child, while that——Shall I say, other paramour, Byron? Shall I say that? Shall I refrain from the truth because Byron Bunch hides it?"

"If public talking makes truth, then I reckon that is truth. Especially when they find out that I have got both of them locked up in jail."

"Both of them?"

"Brown too. Though I reckon most folks have about decided that Brown wasn't anymore capable of doing that killing or helping in it than he was in catching the man that did do it or helping in that. But they can all say that Byron Bunch has now got him locked up safe in jail."

"Ah yes." Hightower's voice shakes a little, high and thin. "Byron Bunch, the guardian of public weal and morality. The gainer, the inheritor of rewards, since it will now descend upon the morganatic wife of——Shall I say that too? Shall I read Byron there too?" Then he begins to cry, sitting huge and lax in the sagging chair. "I dont mean that. You know I dont. But it is not right to bother me, to worry me, when I have——when I have taught myself to stay——have been taught by them to stay—— That this should come to me, taking me after I am old, and reconciled to what they deemed——" Once before Byron saw him sit while sweat ran down his face like tears; now he sees the tears themselves run down the flabby cheeks like sweat.

"I know. It's a poor thing. A poor thing to worry you. I didn't know. I didn't know, when I first got into it. Or I would have. . . . . . . But you are a man of God. You cant dodge that."

"I am not a man of God. And not through my own desire. Remember that. Not of my own choice that I am no longer a man of God. It was by the will, the more than behest, of them like you and like her and like him in the jail yonder and like them who put him there to do their will upon, as they did upon me, with insult and violence upon those who like them were created by the same God and were driven by them to do that which they now turn and rend them for having done it. It was not my choice. Remember that."

"I know that. Because a man aint given that many choices. You made your choice before that." Hightower looks at him. "You were given your choice before I was born, and you took it before I or her or him either was born. That was your choice. And I reckon them that are good must suffer for it the same as them that are bad. The same as her, and him, and me. And the same as them others, that other woman."

"That other woman? Another woman? Must my life after fifty years be violated and my peace destroyed by two lost women, Byron?"

"This other one aint lost now. She has been lost for thirty years. But she is found now. She's his grandmother."

"Whose grandmother?"

"Christmas'," Byron says.

Waiting, watching the street and the gate from the dark study window, Hightower hears the distant music when it first begins. He does not know that he expects it, that on each Wednesday and Sunday night, sitting in the dark window, he waits for it to begin. He knows almost to the second when he should begin to hear it, without recourse to watch or clock. He uses neither, has needed neither for twentyfive years now. He lives dissociated from mechanical time. Yet for that reason he has never lost it. It is as though out of his subconscious he produces without volition the few crystallizations of stated instances by which his dead life in the actual world had been governed and ordered once. Without recourse to clock he could know immediately upon the thought just where, in his old life, he would be and what doing between the two fixed moments which marked the beginning and the end of Sunday morning service and Sunday evening service and prayer service on Wednesday night; just when he would have been entering the church, just when he would have been bringing to a calculated close prayer or sermon. So before twilight has completely faded he is saying to himself *Now they are gathering, approaching along the street slowly and turning in, greeting one another: the groups, the couples, the single ones. There is a little informal talking in the church itself, low-toned, the ladies constant and a little sibilant with fans, nodding to arriving friends as they pass in the aisle. Miss Carruthers* (she was his organist and she has been dead almost twenty years) *is among them; soon she will rise and enter the organloft* Sunday evening prayer meeting. It has seemed to him always that at that hour man approaches nearest of all to God, nearer than at any other hour of all the seven days. Then alone, of all church gatherings, is there something of that peace which is the promise and the end of the Church. The mind and the heart purged then, if it is ever to be; the week and its whatever disasters finished and summed and expiated by the stern and formal fury of the morning service; the next week and its whatever disasters not yet born, the heart quiet now for a little while beneath the cool soft blowing of faith and hope.

Sitting in the dark window he seems to see them *Now they are gathering, entering the door. They are nearly all there now* And then he begins to say, "Now. Now" leaning a little forward; and then, as though it had waited for his signal, the music begins. The organ strains come rich and resonant through the summer night, blended, sonorous, with that quality of abjectness and sublimation, as if the freed voices themselves were assuming the shapes and attitudes of crucifixions, ecstatic, solemn, and profound in gathering volume. Yet even then the music has still a quality stern and implacable, deliberate and without passion so much as immolation, pleading, asking, for not love, not life, forbidding it to others, demanding in sonorous tones death as though death were the boon, like all Protestant music. It was as though they who accepted it and raised voices to praise it within praise, having been made what they were by that which the music praised and symbolised, they took revenge upon that which made them so by means of the praise itself. Listening, he seems to hear within it the apotheosis of his own history, his own land, his own environed blood: that people from which he sprang and among whom he lives who can never take either pleasure or catastrophe or escape from either, without brawling over it. Pleasure, ecstasy, they cannot seem to bear: their escape from it is in violence, in drinking and fighting and praying; catastrophe too, the violence identical and apparently inescapable *And so why should not their religion drive them to crucifixion of themselves and one another?* he thinks. It seems to him that he can hear within the music the declaration and dedication of that which they know that on the morrow they will have to do. It seems to him that the past week has rushed like a torrent and that the week to come, which will begin tomorrow, is the abyss, and that now on the brink of cataract the stream has raised a single blended and sonorous and austere cry, not for justification but as a dying salute before its own plunge, and not to any god but to the doomed man in the barred cell within hearing of them and of two other churches, and in whose crucifixion they too will raise a cross. 'And they will do it gladly,' he says, in the dark window. He feels his mouth and jaw muscles tauten with something premonitory, something more terrible than laughing even. 'Since to pity him would be to admit selfdoubt and to hope for and need pity themselves. They will do it gladly, gladly. That's why it is so terrible, terrible, terrible.' Then, leaning forward, he sees three people approach and turn into the gate, in silhouette now against the street lamp, among the shadows. He has already recognised Byron and he looks at the two who follow him. A woman and a man he knows them to be, yet save for the skirt which one of them wears they are almost interchangeable: of a height, and of a width which is twice that of ordinary man or woman, like two bears. He begins to laugh before he can prepare to stop it.

'If Byron just had a handkerchief about his head, and ear-rings,' he thinks, laughing and laughing, making no sound, trying to prepare to stop it in order to go to the door when Byron will knock.

Byron leads them into the study—a dumpy woman in a purple dress and a plume and carrying an umbrella, with a perfectly immobile face, and a man incredibly dirty and apparently incredibly old, with a tobaccostained goat's beard and mad eyes. They enter not with diffidence, but with something puppetlike about them, as if they were operated by clumsy springwork. The woman appears to be the more assured, or at least the more conscious, of the two of them. It is as though, for all her frozen and mechanically moved inertia, she had come for some definite purpose or at least with some vague hope. But he sees at once that the man is in something like coma, as though oblivious and utterly indifferent to his whereabouts, and yet withal a quality latent and explosive, paradoxically rapt and alert at the same time. "This is her," Byron says quietly. "This is Mrs Hines."

They stand there, motionless: the woman as though she had reached the end of a long journey and now among strange faces and surroundings waits, quiet, glacierlike, like something made of stone and painted, and the calm, rapt yet latently furious and dirty old man. It is as though neither of them had so much as looked at him, with curiosity or without. He indicates chairs. Byron guides the woman, who lowers herself carefully, clutching the umbrella. The man sits at once. Hightower takes his chair beyond the desk. "What is it she wants to talk to me about?" he says.

The woman does not move. Apparently she has not heard. She is like someone who has performed an arduous journey on the strength of a promise and who now ceases completely and waits. "This is him," Byron says. "This is Reverend Hightower. Tell him. Tell him what you want him to know." She looks at Byron when he speaks, her face quite blank. If there is inarticulateness behind it, articulateness is nullified by the immobility of the face itself; if hope or yearning, neither hope nor yearning show. "Tell him," Byron says. "Tell him why you came. What you came to Jefferson for."

"It was because——" she says. Her voice is sudden and deep, almost harsh, though not loud. It is as though she had not expected to make so much noise when she spoke; she ceases in a sort of astonishment as though at the sound of her own voice, looking from one to the other of the two faces.

"Tell me," Hightower says. "Try to tell me."

"It's because I. . . . . . ." Again the voice ceases, dies harshly though still not raised, as though of its own astonishment. It is as if the three words were some automatic impediment which her voice cannot pass; they can almost watch her marshalling herself to go around them. "I aint never seen him when he could walk," she says. "Not for thirty years I never saw him. Never once walking on his own feet and calling his own name——"

"Bitchery and abomination!" the man says suddenly. His voice is high, shrill, strong. "Bitchery and abomination!" Then he ceases. Out of his immediate and dreamlike state he shouts the three words with outrageous and prophetlike suddenness, and that is all. Hightower looks at him, and then at Byron. Byron says quietly:

"He is their daughter's child. He——" with a slight movement of the head he indicates the old man, who is now watching Hightower with his bright, mad glare "——he took it right after it was born and carried it away. She didn't know what he did with it. She never even knew if it was still alive or not until——"

The old man interrupts again, with that startling suddenness. But he does not shout this time: his voice now is as calm and logical as Byron's own. He talks clearly, just a little jerkily: "Yes. Old Doc Hines took him. God give old Doc Hines his chance and so old Doc Hines give God His chance too. So out of the mouths of little children God used His will. The little children hollering Nigger! Nigger! at him in the hearing of God and man both, showing God's will. And old Doc Hines said to God 'But that aint enough. Them children call one another worse than nigger' and God said 'You wait and you watch, because I aint got the time to waste neither with this world's sluttishness and bitchery. I have put the mark on him and now I am going to put the knowledge. And I have set you there to watch and guard My will. It will be yours to tend to it and oversee'." His voice ceases; his tone does not drop at all. His voice just stops, exactly like when the needle is lifted from a phonograph record by the hand of someone who is not listening to the record. Hightower looks from him to Byron, also almost glaring.

"What's this? What's this?" he says.

"I wanted to fix it so she could come and talk to you without him being along," Byron says. "But there wasn't anywhere to leave him. She says she has to watch him. He was trying down in Mottstown yesterday to get the folks worked up to lynch him, before he even knew what he had done."

"Lynch him?" Hightower says. "Lynch his own grandson?"

"That's what she says," Byron says levelly. "She says that's what he come up here for. And she had to come with him to keep him from doing it."

The woman speaks again. Perhaps she has been listening. But there is no more expression on her face now than when she entered; woodenfaced, she speaks again in her dead voice, with almost the suddenness of the man. "For fifty years he has been like that. For more than fifty years, but for fifty years I have suffered it. Even before we were married, he was always fighting. On the very night that Milly was born, he was locked up in jail for fighting. That's what I have bore and suffered. He said he had to fight because he is littler than most men and so folks would try to put on him. That was his vanity and his pride. But I told him it was because the devil was in him. And that some day the devil was going to come on him and him not know it until too late, and the devil was going to say 'Eupheus Hines, I have come to collect my toll.' That's what I told him, the next day after Milly was born and me still too weak to raise my head, and him just out of jail again. I told him so: how right then God had given him a sign and a warning: that him being locked up in a jail on the very hour and minute of his daughter's birth was the Lord's own token that heaven never thought him fitten to raise a daughter. A sign from God above that town (he was a brakeman then, on the railroad) was not doing him anything but harm. And he took it so himself then, because it was a sign, and we moved away from the town then and after a while he got to be foreman at the sawmill, doing well because he hadn't begun then to take God's name in vain and in pride to justify and excuse the devil that was in him. So when Lem Bush's wagon passed that night coming home from the circus and never stopped to let Milly out and Eupheus come back into the house and flung the things out of the drawer until he come to the pistol, I said 'Eupheus, it's the devil. It's not Milly's safety that's quicking you now' and he said 'Devil or no devil. Devil or no devil' and he hit me with his hand and I laid across the bed and watched him——" She ceases. But hers is on a falling inflection, as if the machine had run down in midrecord. Again Hightower looks from her to Byron with that expression of glaring amazement.

"That's how I heard it too," Byron says. "It was hard for me to get it straight too, at first. They were living at a sawmill that he was foreman of, over in Arkansas. The gal was about eighteen then. One night a circus passed the mill, on the way to town. It was December and there had been a lot of rain, and one of the wagons broke through a bridge close to the mill and the men come to their house to wake him up and borrow some log tackle to get the wagon out——"

"It's God's abomination of womanflesh!" the old man cries suddenly. Then his voice drops, lowers; it is as though he were merely gaining attention. He talks again rapidly, his tone plausible, vague, fanatic, speaking of himself again in the third person. "He knowed. Old Doc Hines knowed. He had seen the womansign of God's abomination already on her, under her clothes. So when he went and put on his raincoat and lit the lantern and come back, she was already at the door, with a raincoat on too and he said 'You get on back to bed' and she said 'I want to go too' and he said 'You get on back inside that room' and she went back and he went down and got the big tackle from the mill and got the wagon out. Till nigh daybreak he worked, believing she had obeyed the command of the father the Lord had given her. But he ought to knowed. He ought to knowed God's abomination of womanflesh; he should have knowed the walking shape of bitchery and abomination already stinking in God's sight. Telling old Doc Hines, that knowed better, that he was a Mexican.

When old Doc Hines could see in his face the black curse of God Almighty. Telling him—"

"What?" Hightower says. He speaks loudly, as if he had anticipated having to drown the other's voice by sheer volume. "What is this?"

"It was a fellow with the circus," Byron says. "She told him that the man was a Mexican, the daughter told him when he caught her. Maybe that's what the fellow told the gal. But he——" again he indicates the old man "——knew somehow that the fellow had nigger blood. Maybe the circus folks told him. I dont know. He aint never said how he found out, like that never made any difference. And I reckon it didn't, after the next night."

"The next night?"

"I reckon she slipped out that night when the circus was stuck. He says she did. Anyway, he acted like it, and what he did could not have happened if he hadn't known and she hadn't slipped out. Because the next day she went in to the circus with some neighbors. He let her go, because he didn't know then that she had slipped out the night before. He didn't suspect anything even when she came out to get into the neighbor's wagon with her Sunday dress on. But he was waiting for the wagon when it came back that night, listening for it, when it came up the road and passed the house like it was not going to stop to let her out. And he ran out and called, and the neighbor stopped the wagon and the gal wasn't in it. The neighbor said that she had left them on the circus lot, to spend the night with another girl that lived about six miles away, and the neighbor wondered how Hines didn't know about it, because he said that the gal had her grip with her when she got into the wagon. Hines hadn't seen the grip. And she——" this time he indicates the stonefaced woman; she may or may not be listening to what he is saying "——she says it was the devil that guided him. She says he could not have known anymore than she did, where the gal was then, and yet he come into the house and got his pistol and knocked her down across the bed when she tried to stop him and saddled his horse and rode off. And she said he took the only short cut he could possibly have taken, choosing it in the dark, out of a half a dozen of them, that would ever have caught up with them. And yet it wasn't any possible way that he could have known which road they had taken. But he did. He found them like he had known all the time just where they would be, like him and the man that his gal told him was a Mexican had made a date to meet there. It was like he knew. It was pitch dark, and even when he caught up with a buggy, there wasn't any way he could have told it was the one he wanted. But he rode right up behind the buggy, the first buggy he had seen that night. He rode up on the right side of it and he leaned down, still in the pitch dark and without saying a word and without stopping his horse, and grabbed the man that might have been a stranger or a neighbor for all he could have known by sight or hearing. Grabbed him by one hand and held the pistol against him with the other and shot him dead and brought the gal back home behind him on the horse. He left the buggy and the man both there in the road. It was raining again, too."

He ceases. At once the woman begins to speak, as though she has been waiting with rigid impatience for Byron to cease. She speaks in the same dead, level tone: the two voices in monotonous strophe and antistrophe: two bodiless voices recounting dreamily something performed in a region without dimension by people without blood: "I laid across the bed and I heard him go out and then I heard the horse come up from the barn and pass the house, already galloping. And I laid there without undressing, watching the lamp. The oil was getting low and after a while I got up and took it back to the kitchen and filled it and cleaned the wick and then I undressed and laid down, with the lamp burning. It was still raining and it was cold too and after a while I heard the horse come back into the yard and stop at the porch and I got up and put on my shawl and I heard them come into the house. I could hear Eupheus' feet and then Milly's feet, and they come on down the hall to the door and Milly stood there with the rain on her face and her hair and her new dress all muddy and her eyes shut and then Eupheus hit her and she fell to the floor and laid there and she didn't look any different in the face than when she was standing up. And Eupheus standing in the door wet and muddy too and he said 'You said I was at the devil's work. Well, I have brought you back the devil's laidby crop. Ask her what she is toting now inside her. Ask her.' And I was that tired, and it was cold, and I said 'What happened?' and he said 'Go back yonder and look down in the mud and you will see. He might have fooled her that he was a Mexican. But he never fooled me. And he never fooled her. He never had to. Because you said once that someday the devil would come down on me for his toll. Well, he has. My wife has bore me a whore. But at least he done what he could when the time come to collect. He showed me the right road and he held the pistol steady.'

"And so sometimes I would think how the devil had conquered God. Because we found out Milly was going to have a child and Eupheus started out to find a doctor that would fix it. I believed that he would find one, and sometimes I thought it would be better so, if human man and woman was to live in the world. And sometimes I hoped he would, me being that tired and all when the trial was over and the circus owner come back and said how the man really was a part nigger instead of Mexican, like Eupheus said all the time he was, like the devil had told Eupheus he was a nigger. And Eupheus would take the pistol again and say he would find a doctor or kill one, and he would go away and be gone a week at a time, and all the folks knowing it and me trying to get Eupheus to let's move away because it was just that circus man that said he was a nigger and maybe he never knew for certain, and besides he was gone too and we likely wouldn't ever see him again. But Eupheus wouldn't move, and Milly's time coming and Eupheus with that pistol, trying to find a doctor that would do it. And then I heard how he was in jail again; how he had been going to church and to prayer meeting at the different places where he would be trying to find a doctor, and how one night he got up during prayer meeting and went to the pulpit and begun to preach himself, yelling against niggers, for the white folks to turn out and kill them all, and the folks in the church made him quit and come down from the pulpit and he threatened them with the pistol, there in the church, until the law came and arrested him and him like a crazy man for a while. And they found out how he had beat up a doctor in another town and run away before they could catch him. So when he got out of jail and got back home Milly's time was about on her. And I thought then that he had give up, had seen God's will at last, because he was quiet about the house, and one day he found the clothes me and Milly had been getting ready and kept hid from him, and he never said nothing except to ask when it would be. Every day he would ask, and we thought that he had give up, that maybe going to them churches or being in jail again had reconciled him like it had on that night when Milly was born. And so the time come and one night Milly waked me and told me it had started and I dressed and told Eupheus to go for the doctor and he dressed and went out. And I got everything ready and we waited and the time when Eupheus and the doctor should have got back come and passed and Eupheus wasn't back neither and I waited until the doctor would have to get there pretty soon and then I went out to the front porch to look and I saw Eupheus setting on the top step with the shotgun across his lap and he said 'Get back into that house, whore's dam' and I said 'Eupheus' and he raised the shotgun and said 'Get back into that house. Let the devil gather his own crop: he was the one that laid it by.' And I tried to get out the back way and he heard me and run around the house with the gun and he hit me with the barrel of it and I went back to Milly and he stood outside the hall door where he could see Milly until she died. And then he come in to the bed and looked at the baby and he picked it up and held it up, higher than the lamp, like he was waiting to see if the devil or the Lord would win. And I was that tired, setting by the bed, looking at his shadow on the wall and the shadow of his arms and the bundle high up on the wall. And then I thought that the Lord had won. But now I dont know. Because he laid the baby back on the bed by Milly and he went out. I heard him go out the front door and then I got up and built up the fire in the stove and heated some milk." She ceases; her harsh, droning voice dies. Across the desk Hightower watches her: the still, stonefaced woman in the purple dress, who has not moved since she entered the room. Then she begins to speak again, without moving, almost without lipmovement, as if she were a puppet and the voice that of a ventriloquist in the next room.

"And Eupheus was gone. The man that owned the mill

didn't know where he had gone to. And he got a new foreman, but he let me stay in the house a while longer because
we didn't know where Eupheus was, and it coming winter
and me with the baby to take care of. And I didn't know
where Eupheus was any more than Mr Gillman did, until the
letter came. It was from Memphis and it had a postoffice
moneypaper in it, and that was all. So I still didn't know. And
then in November another moneypaper came, without any
letter or anything. And I was that tired, and then two days
before Christmas I was out in the back yard, chopping wood,
and I come back into the house and the baby was gone. I
hadn't been out of the house an hour, and it looked like
I could have seen him when he come and went. But I didn't.
I just found the letter where Eupheus had left it on the pillow
that I would put between the baby and the edge of the bed
so he couldn't roll off, and I was that tired. And I waited, and
after Christmas Eupheus come home, and he wouldn't tell
me. He just said that we were going to move, and I thought
that he had already took the baby there and he had come back
for me. And he wouldn't tell me where we were going to
move to but it didn't take long and I was worried nigh crazy
how the baby would get along until we got there and he still
wouldn't tell me and it was like we wouldn't ever get there.
Then we got there and the baby wasn't there and I said 'You
tell me what you have done with Joey. You got to tell me'
and he looked at me like he looked at Milly that night when
she laid on the bed and died and he said 'It's the Lord God's
abomination, and I am the instrument of His will.' And he
went away the next day and I didn't know where he had
gone, and another moneypaper came, and the next month
Eupheus come home and said he was working in Memphis.
And I knew he had Joey hid somewhere in Memphis and I
thought that that was something because he could be there to
see to Joey even if I wasn't. And I knew that I would have to
wait on Eupheus' will to know, and each time I would think
that maybe next time he will take me with him to Memphis.
And so I waited. I sewed and made clothes for Joey and I
would have them all ready when Eupheus would come home
and I would try to get him to tell me if the clothes fit Joey
and if he was alright and Eupheus wouldn't tell me. He

would sit and read out of the Bible, loud, without nobody there to hear it but me, reading and hollering loud out of the Bible like he believed I didn't believe what it said. But he would not tell me for five years and I never knew whether he took Joey the clothes I made or not. And I was afraid to ask, to worry at him, because it was something that he was there where Joey was, even if I wasn't. And then after five years he came home one day and he said 'We are going to move' and I thought that now it would be, I will see him again now; if it was a sin, I reckon we have all paid it out now, and I even forgave Eupheus. Because I thought that we were going to Memphis this time, at last. But it was not to Memphis. We come to Mottstown. We had to pass through Memphis, and I begged him. It was the first time I had ever begged him. But I did then, just for a minute, a second; not to touch him or talk to him or nothing. But Eupheus wouldn't. We never even left the depot. We got off of one train and we waited seven hours without even leaving the depot, until the other train come, and we come to Mottstown. And Eupheus never went back to Memphis to work anymore, and after a while I said 'Eupheus' and he looked at me and I said 'I done waited five years and I aint never bothered you. Cant you tell me just once if he is dead or not?' and he said 'He is dead' and I said 'Dead to the living world, or just dead to me? If he is just dead to me, even. Tell me that much, because in five years I have not bothered you' and he said 'He is dead to you and to me and to God and to all God's world forever and ever more'."

She ceases again. Beyond the desk Hightower watches her with that quiet and desperate amazement. Byron too is motionless, his head bent a little. The three of them are like three rocks above a beach, above ebbtide, save the old man. He has been listening now, almost attentively, with that ability of his to flux instantaneously between complete attention that does not seem to hear, and that comalike bemusement in which the stare of his apparently inverted eye is as uncomfortable as though he held them with his hand. He cackles, suddenly, bright, loud, mad; he speaks, incredibly old, incredibly dirty. "It was the Lord. *He* was there. Old Doc Hines give God His chance too. The Lord told old Doc Hines what to do and old Doc Hines done it. Then the Lord said to old Doc

Hines 'You watch, now. Watch My will a-working.' And old
Doc Hines watched and heard the mouths of little children,
of God's own fatherless and motherless, putting His words
and knowledge into their mouths even when they couldn't
know it since they were without sin yet, even the girl ones
without sin and bitchery yet: Nigger! Nigger! in the innocent
mouths of little children. 'What did I tell you?' God said to
old Doc Hines. 'And now I've set My will to working and
now I'm gone. There aint enough sin here to keep Me busy
because what do I care for the fornications of a slut, since
that is a part of My purpose too' and old Doc Hines said
'How is the fornications of a slut a part of Your purpose too?'
and God said 'You wait and see. Do you think it is just
chanceso that I sent that young doctor to be the one that
found My abomination laying wrapped in that blanket on
that doorstep that Christmas night? Do you think it was just
chanceso that the Madam should have been away that night
and give them young sluts the chance and call to name him
Christmas in sacrilege of My son? So I am gone now, because
I have set My will a-working and I can leave you here to
watch it.' So old Doc Hines he watched and he waited. From
God's own boiler room he watched them children, and the
devil's walking seed unbeknownst among them, polluting the
earth with the working of that word on him. Because he
didn't play with the other children no more now. He stayed
by himself, standing still, and then old Doc Hines knew that
he was listening to the hidden warning of God's doom, and
old Doc Hines said to him 'Why dont you play with them
other children like you used to?' and he didn't say nothing
and old Doc Hines said 'Is it because they call you nigger?'
and he didn't say nothing and old Doc Hines said 'Do you
think you are a nigger because God has marked your face?'
and he said 'Is God a nigger too?' and old Doc Hines said
'He is the Lord God of wrathful hosts, His will be done. Not
yours and not mine, because you and me are both a part of
His purpose and His vengeance.' And he went away and old
Doc Hines watched him hearing and listening to the vengeful
will of the Lord, until old Doc Hines found out how he was
watching the nigger working in the yard, following him
around the yard while he worked, until at last the nigger said

'What you watching me for, boy?' and he said 'How come you are a nigger?' and the nigger said 'Who told you I am a nigger, you little white trash bastard?' and he says 'I aint a nigger' and the nigger says 'You are worse than that. You dont know what you are. And more than that, you wont never know. You'll live and you'll die and you wont never know' and he says 'God aint no nigger' and the nigger says 'I reckon you ought to know what God is, because dont nobody but God know what you is.' But God wasn't there to say, because He had set His will to working and left old Doc Hines to watch it. From that very first night, when He had chose His own Son's sacred anniversary to set it a-working on, He set old Doc Hines to watch it. It was cold that night, and old Doc Hines standing in the dark just behind the corner where he could see the doorstep and the accomplishment of the Lord's will, and he saw that young doctor coming in lechery and fornication stop and stoop down and raise the Lord's abomination and tote it into the house. And old Doc Hines he followed and he seen and heard. He watched them young sluts that was desecrating the Lord's sacred anniversary with eggnog and whiskey in the Madam's absence, open the blanket. And it was her, the Jezebel of the doctor, that was the Lord's instrument, that said 'We'll name him Christmas' and another one said 'What Christmas. Christmas what' and God said to old Doc Hines 'Tell them' and they all looked at old Doc Hines with the reek of pollution on them, hollering 'Why, it's Uncle Doc. Look what Santa Claus brought us and left on the doorstep, Uncle Doc' and old Doc Hines said 'His name is Joseph' and they quit laughing and they looked at old Doc Hines and the Jezebel said 'How do you know' and old Doc Hines said 'The Lord says so' and then they laughed again, hollering 'It is so in the Book: Christmas, the son of Joe. Joe, the son of Joe. Joe Christmas' they said 'To Joe Christmas' and they tried to make old Doc Hines drink too, to the Lord's abomination, but he struck the cup aside. And he just had to watch and to wait, and he did and it was in the Lord's good time, for evil to come from evil. And the doctor's Jezebel come running from her lustful bed, still astink with sin and fear. 'He was hid behind the bed' she says, and old Doc Hines said 'You used that perfumed soap that

tempted your own undoing, for the Lord's abomination and
outrage. Suffer it' and she said 'You can talk to him. I have
seen you. You could persuade him' and old Doc Hines said 'I
care no more for your fornications than God does' and she
said 'He will tell and I will be fired. I will be disgraced'. Stinking with her lust and lechery she was then, standing before
old Doc Hines with the working of God's will on her at that
minute, who had outraged the house where God housed His
fatherless and motherless. 'You aint nothing' old Doc Hines
said 'You and all sluts. You are a instrument of God's wrathful
purpose that nere a sparrow can fall to earth. You are a instrument of God, the same as Joe Christmas and old Doc Hines'.
And she went away and old Doc Hines he waited and he
watched and it wasn't long before she come back and her face
was like the face of a ravening beast of the desert. 'I fixed him'
she said and old Doc Hines said 'How fixed him' because it
was not anything that old Doc Hines didn't know because
the Lord did not keep His purpose hid from His chosen instrument, and old Doc Hines said 'You have served the fore-
ordained will of God. You can go now and abominate Him
in peace until the Day' and her face looked like the ravening
beast of the desert, laughing out of her rotten colored dirt at
God. And they come and took him away. Old Doc Hines saw
him go away in the buggy and he went back to wait for God
and God come and He said to old Doc Hines 'You can go
too now. You have done My work. There is no more evil here
now but womanevil, not worthy for My chosen instrument
to watch.' And old Doc Hines went when God told him to
go. But he kept in touch with God and at night he said 'That
bastard, Lord' and God said 'He is still walking My earth' and
old Doc Hines kept in touch with God and at night he said
'That bastard, Lord' and God said 'He is still walking My
earth' and old Doc Hines kept in touch with God and one
night he wrestled and he strove and he cried aloud 'That bastard, Lord! I feel! I feel the teeth and the fangs of evil!' and
God said 'It's that bastard. Your work is not done yet. He's a
pollution and a abomination on My earth'."

The sound of music from the distant church has long since ceased. Through the open window there comes now only the peaceful and myriad sounds of the summer night. Beyond the desk Hightower sits, looking more than ever like an awkward beast tricked and befooled of the need for flight, brought now to bay by those who tricked and fooled it. The other three sit facing him; almost like a jury. Two of them are also motionless, the woman with that stonevisaged patience of a waiting rock, the old man with a spent quality like the charred wick of a candle from which the flame has been violently blown away. Byron alone seems to possess life. His face is lowered. He seems to muse upon one hand which lies upon his lap, the thumb and forefinger of which rub slowly together with a kneading motion while he appears to watch with musing absorption. When Hightower speaks, Byron knows that he is not addressing him, not addressing anyone in the room at all. "What do they want me to do?" he says. "What do they think, hope, believe, that I can do?"

Then there is no sound. Neither the man nor the woman have heard, apparently. Byron does not expect the man to hear. 'He dont need any help,' he thinks. 'Not him. It's hindrance he needs'; thinking remembering the comastate of dreamy yet maniacal suspension in which the old man had moved from place to place a little behind the woman since he had met them twelve hours ago. 'It's hindrance he needs. I reckon it's a good thing for more folks than her that he is wellnigh helpless.' He is watching the woman. He says quietly, almost gently: "Go on. Tell him what you want. He wants to know what you want him to do. Tell him."

"I thought maybe——" she says. She speaks without stirring. Her voice is not tentative so much as rusty, as if it were being forced to try to say something outside the province of being said aloud, of being anything save felt, known. "Mr Bunch said that maybe——"

"What?" Hightower says. He speaks sharply, impatiently, his voice a little high; he too has not moved, sitting back in the chair, his hands upon the armrests. "What? That what?"

"I thought. . . . . . ." The voice dies again. Beyond the window the steady insects whirr. Then the voice goes on, flat, toneless, she sitting also with her head bent a little, as if she

too listened to the voice with the same quiet intentness: "He
is my grandson, my girl's little boy. I just thought that if
I . . . . . .if he. . . . . ." Byron listens quietly, thinking
It's right funny. You'd think they had done got swapped some-
where. Like it was him that had a nigger grandson waiting to be
hung The voice goes on. "I know it aint right to bother a
stranger. But you are lucky. A bachelor, a single man that
could grow old without the despair of love. But I reckon you
couldn't never see it even if I could tell it right. I just thought
that maybe if it could be for one day like it hadn't happened. Like folks never knew him as a man that had
killed. . . . . . ." The voice ceases again. She has not
stirred. It is as though she listened to it cease as she listened
to it begin, with the same interest, the same quiet unas-
tonishment.

"Go on," Hightower says, in that high impatient voice; "go
on."

"I never saw him when he could walk and talk. Not for
thirty years I never saw him. I am not saying he never did
what they say he did. Ought not to suffer for it like he made
them that loved and lost suffer. But if folks could maybe just
let him for one day. Like it hadn't happened yet. Like the
world never had anything against him yet. Then it could be
like he had just went on a trip and grew mangrown and
come back. If it could be like that for just one day. After that
I would not interfere. If he done it, I would not be the one to
come between him and what he must suffer. Just for one day,
you see. Like he had been on a trip and come back, telling
me about the trip, without any living earth against him yet."

"Oh," Hightower says, in his shrill, high voice. Though he
has not moved, though the knuckles of the hands which grip
the chairarms are taut and white, there begins to emerge from
beneath his clothing a slow and repressed quivering. "Ah
yes," he says. "That's all. That's simple. Simple. Simple." Apparently he cannot stop saying it. "Simple. Simple." He has
been speaking in a low tone; now his voice rises. "What is it
they want me to do? What must I do now? Byron! Byron?
What is it? What are they asking of me now?" Byron has
risen. He now stands beside the desk, his hands on the desk,
facing Hightower. Still Hightower does not move save for

that steadily increasing quivering of his flabby body. "Ah yes. I should have known. It will be Byron who will ask it. I should have known. That will be reserved for Byron and for me. Come, come. Out with it. Why do you hesitate now?"

Byron looks down at the desk, at his hands upon the desk. "It's a poor thing. A poor thing."

"Ah. Commiseration? After this long time? Commiseration for me, or for Byron? Come; out with it. What do you want me to do? For it is you: I know that. I have known that all along. Ah Byron, Byron. What a dramatist you would have made."

"Or maybe you mean a drummer, a agent, a salesman," Byron says. "It's a poor thing. I know that. You dont need to tell me."

"But I am not clairvoyant, like you. You seem to know already what I could tell you, yet you will not tell me what you intend for me to know. What is it you want me to do? Shall I go plead guilty to the murder? Is that it?"

Byron's face cracks with that grimace faint, fleeting, sardonic, weary, without mirth. "It's next to that, I reckon." Then his face sobers; it is quite grave. "It's a poor thing to ask. God knows I know that." He watches his slow hand where it moves, preoccupied and trivial, upon the desk top. "I mind how I said to you once that there is a price for being good the same as for being bad; a cost to pay. And it's the good men that cant deny the bill when it comes around. They cant deny it for the reason that there aint any way to make them pay it, like a honest man that gambles. The bad men can deny it; that's why dont anybody expect them to pay on sight or any other time. But the good cant. Maybe it takes longer to pay for being good than for being bad. And it wont be like you haven't done it before, haven't already paid a bill like it once before. It oughtn't to be so bad now as it was then."

"Go on. Go on. What is it I am to do?"

Byron watches his slow and ceaseless hand, musing. "He aint never admitted that he killed her. And all the evidence they got against him is Brown's word, which is next to none. You could say he was here with you that night. Every night when Brown said he watched him go up to the big house and go in it. Folks would believe you. They would believe that, anyway. They would rather believe that about you than to believe that he lived with her like a husband and then killed her. And you are old now. They wouldn't do anything to you about it that would hurt you now. And I reckon you are used to everything else they can do."

"Oh," Hightower says. "Ah. Yes. Yes. They would believe it. That would be very simple, very good. Good for all. Then he will be restored to them who have suffered because of him, and Brown without the reward could be scared into making her child legitimate and then into fleeing again and forever this time. And then it would be just her and Byron. Since I am just an old man who has been fortunate enough to grow old without having to learn the despair of love." He is shaking, steadily; he looks up now. In the lamplight his face looks slick, as if it had been oiled. Wrung and twisted, it gleams in the lamplight; the yellowed, oftwashed shirt which was fresh this morning is damp with sweat. "It's not because I cant, dont dare to," he says; "it's because I wont! I wont! do you hear?" He raises his hands from the chair arms. "It's because I wont do it!" Byron does not move. His hand on the desk top has ceased; he watches the other, thinking *It aint me he is shouting at. It's like he knows there is something nearer him than me to convince of that* Because now Hightower is shouting "I wont do it! I wont!" with his hands raised and clenched, his face sweating, his lip lifted upon his clenched and rotting teeth from about which the long sagging of flabby and puttycolored flesh falls away. Suddenly his voice rises higher yet. "Get out!" he screams. "Get out of my house! Get out of my house!" Then he falls forward, onto the desk, his face between his extended arms and his clenched fists. As, the two old people moving ahead of him, Byron looks back from the door, he sees that Hightower has not moved, his bald head and his extended and clenchfisted arms lying full in the pool of light from the shaded lamp. Beyond the open window the sound of insects has not ceased, not faltered.

XVII

THAT WAS Sunday night. Lena's child was born the next morning. It was just dawn when Byron stopped his galloping mule before the house which he had quitted not six hours ago. He sprang to the ground already running, and ran up the narrow walk toward the dark porch. He seemed to stand aloof and watch himself, for all his haste, thinking with a kind of grim unsurprise: 'Byron Bunch borning a baby. If I could have seen myself now two weeks ago, I would not have believed my own eyes. I would have told them that they lied.'

The window was dark now beyond which six hours ago he had left the minister. Running, he thought of the bald head, the clenched hands, the prone flabby body sprawled across the desk. 'But I reckon he has not slept much,' he thought. 'Even if he aint playing——playing——' He could not think of the word midwife, which he knew that Hightower would use. 'I reckon I dont have to think of it,' he thought. 'Like a fellow running from or toward a gun aint got time to worry whether the word for what he is doing is courage or cowardice.'

The door was not locked. Apparently he knew that it would not be. He felt his way into the hall, not quiet, not attempting to be. He had never been deeper into the house than the room where he had last seen the owner of it sprawled across the desk in the full downglare of the lamp. Yet he went almost as straight to the right door as if he knew, or could see, or were being led. 'That's what he'd call it,' he thought, in the fumbling and hurried dark. 'And she would too.' He meant Lena, lying yonder in the cabin, already beginning to labor. 'Only they would both have a different name for whoever did the leading.' He could hear Hightower snoring now, before he entered the room. 'Like he aint so much upset, after all,' he thought. Then he thought immediately: 'No. That aint right. That aint just. Because I dont believe that. I know that the reason he is asleep and I aint asleep is that he is an old man and he cant stand as much as I can stand.'

He approached the bed. The still invisible occupant snored profoundly. There was a quality of profound and complete

surrender in it. Not of exhaustion, but surrender, as though
he had given over and relinquished completely that grip upon
that blending of pride and hope and vanity and fear, that
strength to cling to either defeat or victory, which is the
I-Am, and the relinquishment of which is usually death.
Standing beside the bed Byron thought again *A poor thing.*
A poor thing It seemed to him now that to wake the man
from that sleep would be the sorest injury which he had ever
done him. 'But it aint me that's waiting,' he thought. 'God
knows that. Because I reckon He has been watching me too
lately, like the rest of them, to see what I will do next.'

He touched the sleeper, not roughly, but firmly. Hightower ceased in midsnore; beneath Byron's hand he surged
hugely and suddenly up. "Yes?" he said. "What? Who is it?
Who is there?"

"It's me," Byron said. "It's Byron again. Are you awake
now?"

"Yes. What———"

"Yes," Byron said. "She says it's about due now. That the
time has come."

"She?"

"Tell me where the light———Mrs Hines. She is out there.
I am going on for the doctor. But it may take some time. So
you can take my mule. I reckon you can ride that far. Have
you still got your book?"

The bed creaked as Hightower moved. "Book? My book?"

"The book you used when that nigger baby came. I just
wanted to remind you in case you would need to take it with
you. In case I dont get back with the doctor in time. The
mule is out at the gate. He knows the way. I will walk on to
town and get the doctor. I'll get back out there as soon as I
can." He turned and recrossed the room. He could hear, feel,
the other sitting up in the bed. He paused in the middle of
the floor long enough to find the suspended light and turn it
on. When it came on he was already moving on toward the
door. He did not look back. Behind him he heard Hightower's voice:

"Byron! Byron!" He didn't pause, didn't answer.

Dawn was increasing. He walked rapidly along the empty
street, beneath the spaced and failing street lamps about

which bugs still whirled and blundered. But day was growing; when he reached the square the façade of its eastern side
was in sharp relief against the sky. He was thinking rapidly.
He had made no arrangement with a doctor. Now as he
walked he was cursing himself in all the mixed terror and rage
of any actual young father for what he now believed to have
been crass and criminal negligence. Yet it was not exactly the
solicitude of an incipient father. There was something else
behind it, which he was not to recognise until later. It was as
though there lurked in his mind, still obscured by the need
for haste, something which was about to spring full clawed
upon him. But what he was thinking was, 'I got to decide
quick. He delivered that nigger baby all right, they said. But
this is different. I ought to done it last week, seen ahead
about a doctor instead of waiting, having to explain now, at
the last minute, hunt from house to house until I find one
that will come, that will believe the lies that I will have to tell.
I be dog if it dont look like a man that has done as much
lying lately as I have could tell a lie now that anybody would
believe, man or woman. But it dont look like I can. I reckon
it just aint in me to tell a good lie and do it well.' He walked
rapidly, his footsteps hollow and lonely in the empty street;
already his decision was made, without his even being aware
of it. To him there was nothing either of paradox or of comedy about it. It had entered his mind too quickly and was too
firmly established there when he became aware of it; his feet
were already obeying it. They were taking him to the home
of the same doctor who had arrived too late at the delivery of
the negro child at which Hightower had officiated with his
razor and his book.

The doctor arrived too late this time, also. Byron had to
wait for him to dress. He was an oldish man now, and fussy,
and somewhat disgruntled at having been wakened at this
hour. Then he had to hunt for the switch key to his car,
which he kept in a small metal strong box, the key to which
in turn he could not find at once. Neither would he allow
Byron to break the lock. So when they reached the cabin at
last the east was primrosecolor and there was already a hint
of the swift sun of summer. And again the two men, both
older now, met at the door of a one-room cabin, the profes-

sional having lost again to the amateur, for as he entered the
door, the doctor heard the infant cry. The doctor blinked at
the minister, fretfully. "Well, doctor," he said. "I wish Byron
had told me he had already called you in. I'd still be in bed."
He thrust past the minister, entering. "You seem to have had
better luck this time than you did the last time we consulted.
Only you look about like you need a doctor yourself. Or
maybe it's a cup of coffee you need." Hightower said something, but the doctor had gone on, without stopping to listen. He entered the room, where a young woman whom he
had never seen before lay wan and spent on a narrow army
cot, and an old woman in a purple dress whom he had also
never seen before, held the child upon her lap. There was an
old man asleep on a second cot in the shadow. When the
doctor noticed him, he said to himself that the man looked
like he was dead, so profoundly and peacefully did he sleep.
But the doctor did not notice the old man at once. He went
to the old woman who held the child. "Well, well," he said.
"Byron must have been excited. He never told me the whole
family would be on hand, grandpa and grandma too." The
woman looked up at him. He thought, 'She looks about as
much alive as he does, for all she is sitting up. Dont look like
she has got enough gumption to know she is even a parent,
let alone a grandparent.'

"Yes," the woman said. She looked up at him, crouching
over the child. Then he saw that her face was not stupid,
vacuous. He saw that at the same time it was both peaceful
and terrible, as though the peace and the terror had both died
long ago and come to live again at the same time. But he
remarked mainly her attitude at once like a rock and like a
crouching beast. She jerked her head at the man; for the first
time the doctor looked full at him where he lay sleeping upon
the other cot. She said in a whisper at once cunning and tense
with fading terror: "I fooled him. I told him you would come
in the back way this time. I fooled him. But now you are
here. You can see to Milly now. I'll take care of Joey." Then
this faded. While he watched, the life, the vividness, faded,
fled suddenly from a face that looked too still, too dull to ever
have harbored it; now the eyes questioned him with a gaze
dumb, inarticulate, baffled as she crouched over the child as

if he had offered to drag it from her. Her movement roused it perhaps; it cried once. Then the bafflement too flowed away. It fled as smoothly as a shadow; she looked down at the child, musing, woodenfaced, ludicrous. "It's Joey," she said. "It's my Milly's little boy."

And Byron, outside the door where he had stopped as the doctor entered, heard that cry and something terrible happened to him. Mrs Hines had called him from his tent. There was something in her voice so that he put on his trousers as he ran almost, and he passed Mrs Hines, who had not undressed at all, in the cabin door and ran into the room. Then he saw her and it stopped him dead as a wall. Mrs Hines was at his elbow, talking to him; perhaps he answered, talked back. Anyway he had saddled the mule and was already galloping toward town while he still seemed to be looking at her, at her face as she lay raised on her propped arms on the cot, looking down at the shape of her body beneath the sheet with wailing and hopeless terror. He saw that all the time he was waking Hightower, all the time he was getting the doctor started, while somewhere in him the clawed thing lurked and waited and thought was going too fast to give him time to think. That was it. Thought too swift for thinking, until he and the doctor returned to the cabin. And then, just outside the cabin door where he had stopped, he heard the child cry once and something terrible happened to him.

He knew now what it was that seemed to lurk clawed and waiting while he crossed the empty square, seeking the doctor whom he had neglected to engage. He knew now why he neglected to engage a doctor beforehand. It is because he did not believe until Mrs Hines called him from his tent that he (she) would need one, would have the need. It was like for a week now his eyes had accepted her belly without his mind believing. 'Yet I did know, believe,' he thought. 'I must have knowed, to have done what I have done: the running and the lying and the worrying at folks.' But he saw now that he did not believe until he passed Mrs Hines and looked into the cabin. When Mrs Hines' voice first came into his sleeping, he knew what it was, what had happened; he rose and put on, like a pair of hurried overalls, the need for haste, knowing why, knowing that for five nights now he had been expecting it. Yet still he did not believe. He knew now that when he ran to the cabin and looked in, he expected to see her sitting up; perhaps to be met by her at the door, placid, unchanged, timeless. But even as he touched the door with his hand he heard something which he had never heard before. It was a moaning wail, loud, with a quality at once passionate and abject, that seemed to be speaking clearly to something in a tongue which he knew was not his tongue nor that of any man. Then he passed Mrs Hines in the door and he saw her lying on the cot. He had never seen her in bed before and he believed that when or if he ever did, she would be tense, alert, maybe smiling a little, and completely aware of him. But when he entered she did not even look at him. She did not even seem to be aware that the door had opened, that there was anyone or anything in the room save herself and whatever it was that she had spoken to with that wailing cry in a tongue unknown to man. She was covered to the chin, yet her upper body was raised upon her arms and her head was bent. Her hair was loose and her eyes looked like two holes and her mouth was as bloodless now as the pillow behind her, and as she seemed in that attitude of alarm and surprise to contemplate with a kind of outraged unbelief the shape of her body beneath the covers, she gave again that loud, abject, wailing cry. Mrs Hines was now bending over her. She turned her head, that wooden face, across her purple shoulder. "Get," she said. "Get for the doctor. It's come now."

He did not remember going to the stable at all. Yet there he was, catching his mule, dragging the saddle out and clapping it on. He was working fast, yet thinking went slow enough. He knew why now. He knew now that thinking went slow and smooth with calculation, as oil is spread slowly upon a surface above a brewing storm. 'If I had known then,' he thought. 'If I had known then. If it had got through then.' He thought this quietly, in aghast despair, regret. 'Yes. I would have turned my back and rode the other way. Beyond the knowing and memory of man forever and ever I reckon I would have rode.' But he did not. He passed the cabin at a gallop, with thinking going smooth and steady, he not yet knowing why. 'If I can just get past and out of hearing before she hollers again,' he thought. 'If I can just get past before I

have to hear her again.' That carried him for a while, into the
road, the hardmuscled small beast going fast now, thinking,
the oil, spreading steady and smooth: '*I'll go to Hightower
first. I'll leave the mule for him. I must remember to remind
him about his doctor book. I mustn't forget that,*' the oil said,
getting him that far, to where he sprang from the still running mule and into Hightower's house. Then he had something else. 'Now that's done' thinking *Even if I cant get a
regular doctor* That got him to the square and then betrayed
him; he could feel it, clawed with lurking, thinking *Even if
I dont get a regular doctor. Because I have never believed that I
would need one. I didn't believe* It was in his mind, galloping
in yoked and headlong paradox with the need for haste while
he helped the old doctor hunt for the key to the strongbox in
order to get the switch key for the car. They found it at last,
and for a time the need for haste went hand in hand with
movement, speed, along the empty road beneath the empty
dawn—that, or he had surrendered all reality, all dread and
fear, to the doctor beside him, as people do. Anyway it got
him back to the cabin, where the two of them left the car and
approached the cabin door, beyond which the lamp still
burned: for that interval he ran in the final hiatus of peace
before the blow fell and the clawed thing overtook him from
behind. Then he heard the child cry. Then he knew. Dawn
was making fast. He stood quietly in the chill peace, the waking quiet—small, nondescript, whom no man or woman had
ever turned to look at twice anywhere. He knew now that
there had been something all the while which had protected
him against believing, with the believing protected him. With
stern and austere astonishment he thought *It was like it was
not until Mrs Hines called me and I heard her and saw her face
and knew that Byron Bunch was nothing in this world to her right
then, that I found out that she is not a virgin* And he thought
that that was terrible, but that was not all. There was something else. His head was not bowed. He stood quite still in
the augmenting dawn, while thinking went quietly *And this
too is reserved for me, as Reverend Hightower says. I'll have to tell
him now. I'll have to tell Lucas Burch* It was not unsurprise
now. It was something like the terrible and irremediable despair of adolescence. *Why, I didn't even believe until now that*

he was so. It was like me, and her, and all the other folks that I had to get mixed up in it, were just a lot of words that never even stood for anything, were not even us, while all the time what was us was going on and going on without even missing the lack of words. Yes. It aint until now that I ever believed that he is Lucas Burch. That there ever was a Lucas Burch

---

'Luck,' Hightower says; 'luck. I dont know whether I had it or not.' But the doctor has gone on into the cabin. Looking back for another moment, Hightower watches the group about the cot, hearing still the doctor's cheery voice. The old woman now sits quietly, yet looking back at her it seems but a moment ago that he was struggling with her for the child, lest she drop it in her dumb and furious terror. But no less furious for being dumb it was as, the child snatched almost from the mother's body, she held it high aloft, her heavy, bearlike body crouching as she glared at the old man asleep on the cot. He was sleeping so when Hightower arrived. He did not seem to breathe at all, and beside the cot the woman was crouching in a chair when he entered. She looked exactly like a rock poised to plunge over a precipice, and for an instant Hightower thought *She has already killed him. She has taken her precautions well beforehand this time* Then he was quite busy; the old woman was at his elbow without his being aware of it until she snatched the still unbreathing child and held it aloft, glaring at the old sleeping man on the other cot with the face of a tiger. Then the child breathed and cried, and the woman seemed to answer it, also in no known tongue, savage and triumphant. Her face was almost maniacal as he struggled with her and took the child from her before she dropped it. "See," he said. "Look! He's quiet. He's not going to take it away this time." Still she glared at him, dumb, beastlike, as though she did not understand English. But the fury, the triumph, had gone from her face: she made a hoarse, whimpering noise, trying to take the child from him. "Careful, now," he said. "Will you be careful?" She nodded, whimpering, pawing lightly at the child. But her hands were steady, and he let her have it. And she now sits with it upon her lap while the doctor who had arrived too late stands beside the cot, talking in his cheerful, testy voice while his hands are busy. Hightower turns and goes out, lowering himself carefully down the broken step, to the earth like an old man, as if there were something in his flabby paunch fatal and highly keyed, like dynamite. It is now more than dawn; it is morning: already the sun. He looks about, pausing; he calls: "Byron." There is no answer. Then he sees that the mule, which he had tethered to a fence post nearby, is also gone. He sighs. 'Well,' he thinks. 'So I have reached the point where the crowning indignity which I am to suffer at Byron's hands is a two-mile walk back home. That's not worthy of Byron, of hatred. But so often our deeds are not. Nor we of our deeds.'

He walks back to town slowly—a gaunt, paunched man in a soiled panama hat and the tail of a coarse cotton nightshirt thrust into his black trousers. 'Luckily I did take time to put on my shoes,' he thinks. 'I am tired,' he thinks, fretfully. 'I am tired, and I shall not be able to sleep.' He is thinking it fretfully, wearily, keeping time to his feet when he turns into his gate. The sun is now high, the town has wakened; he smells the smoke here and there of cooking breakfasts. 'The least thing he could have done,' he thinks, 'since he would not leave me the mule, would have been to ride ahead and start a fire in my stove for me. Since he thinks it better for my appetite to take a two-mile stroll before eating.'

He goes to the kitchen and builds a fire in the stove, slowly, clumsily; as clumsily after twentyfive years as on the first day he had ever attempted it, and puts coffee on. 'Then I'll go back to bed,' he thinks. 'But I know I shall not sleep.' But he notices that his thinking sounds querulous, like the peaceful whining of a querulous woman who is not even listening to herself; then he finds that he is preparing his usual hearty breakfast, and he stops quite still, clicking his tongue as though in displeasure. 'I ought to feel worse than I do,' he thinks. But he has to admit that he does not. And as he stands, tall, misshapen, lonely in his lonely and illkept kitchen, holding in his hand an iron skillet in which yesterday's old grease is bleakly caked, there goes through him a glow, a wave, a surge of something almost hot, almost triumphant. 'I

showed them!' he thinks. 'Life comes to the old man yet,
while they get there too late. They get there for his leavings,
as Byron would say.' But this is vanity and empty pride. Yet
the slow and fading glow disregards it, impervious to repri-
mand. He thinks, 'What if I do? What if I do feel it? triumph
and pride? What if I do?' But the warmth, the glow, evidently
does not regard or need buttressing either; neither is it
quenched by the actuality of an orange and eggs and toast.
And he looks down at the soiled and empty dishes on the
table and he says, aloud now: "Bless my soul. I'm not even
going to wash them now." Neither does he go to his bedroom to try to sleep. He goes to the door and looks in, with
that glow of purpose and pride, thinking, 'If I were a woman,
now. That's what a woman would do: go back to bed to rest.'
He goes to the study. He moves like a man with a purpose
now, who for twentyfive years has been doing nothing at all
between the time to wake and the time to sleep again. Neither
is the book which he now chooses the Tennyson: this time
also he chooses food for a man. It is Henry IV and he goes
out into the back yard and lies down in the sagging deck chair
beneath the mulberry tree, plumping solidly and heavily into
it. 'But I shant be able to sleep,' he thinks, 'because Byron
will be in soon to wake me. But to learn just what else he can
think of to want me to do, will be almost worth the waking.'

He goes to sleep soon, almost immediately, snoring. Anyone pausing to look down into the chair would have seen,
beneath the twin glares of sky in the spectacles, a face innocent, peaceful, and assured. But no one comes, though when
he wakes almost six hours later, he seems to believe that
someone has called him. He sits up abruptly, the chair creaking beneath him. "Yes?" he says. "Yes? What is it?" But there
is no one there, though for a moment longer he looks about,
seeming to listen and to wait, with that air forceful and assured. And the glow is not gone either. 'Though I had hoped
to sleep it off,' he thinks, thinking at once, 'No. I dont mean
hoped. What is in my thought is *feared*. And so I have surrendered too,' he thinks, quiet, still. He begins to rub his hands,
gently at first, a little guiltily. 'I have surrendered too. And I
will permit myself. Yes. Perhaps this too is reserved for me.
And so I shall permit myself.' And then he says it, thinks it

That child that I delivered. I have no namesake. But I have known them before this to be named by a grateful mother for the doctor who officiated. But then, there is Byron. Byron of course will take the pas *of me. She will have to have others, more* remembering the young strong body from out whose travail even there shone something tranquil and unafraid. *More of them. Many more. That will be her life, her destiny. The good stock peopling in tranquil obedience to it the good earth; from these hearty loins without hurry or haste descending mother and daughter. But by Byron engendered next. Poor boy. Even though he did let me walk back home*

He enters the house. He shaves and removes the nightshirt and puts on the shirt which he had worn yesterday, and a collar and the lawn tie and the panama hat. The walk out to the cabin does not take him as long as the walk home did, even though he goes now through the woods where the walking is harder. 'I must do this more often,' he thinks, feeling the intermittent sun, the heat, smelling the savage and fecund odor of the earth, the woods, the loud silence. 'I should never have lost this habit, too. But perhaps they will both come back to me, if this itself be not the same as prayer.'

He emerges from the woods at the far side of the pasture behind the cabin. Beyond the cabin he can see the clump of trees in which the house had stood and burned, though from here he cannot see the charred and mute embers of what were once planks and beams. 'Poor woman,' he thinks. 'Poor, barren woman. To have not lived only a week longer, until luck returned to this place. Until luck and life returned to these barren and ruined acres.' It seems to him that he can see, feel, about him the ghosts of rich fields, and of the rich fecund black life of the quarters, the mellow shouts, the presence of fecund women, the prolific naked children in the dust before the doors; and the big house again, noisy, loud with the treble shouts of the generations. He reaches the cabin. He does not knock; with his hand already opening the door he calls in a hearty voice that almost booms: "Can the doctor come in?"

The cabin is empty save for the mother and child. She is propped up on the cot, the child at breast. As Hightower enters, she is in the act of drawing the sheet up over her bared bosom, watching the door not with alarm at all, but with alertness, her face fixed in an expression serene and warm, as though she were about to smile. He sees this fade. "I thought——" she says.

"Who did you think?" he says, booms. He comes to the cot and looks down at her, at the tiny, weazened, terracotta face of the child which seems to hang suspended without body and still asleep, from the breast. Again she draws the sheet closer, modest and tranquil, while above her the gaunt, paunched, bald man stands with an expression on his face gentle, beaming, and triumphant. She is looking down at the child.

"It looks like he just cant get caught up. I think he is asleep again and I lay him down and then he hollers and I have to put him back again."

"You ought not to be here alone," he says. He looks about the room. "Where——"

"She's gone, too. To town. She didn't say, but that's where she has gone. He slipped out, and when she woke up she asked me where he was and I told her he went out, and she followed him."

"To town? Slipped out?" Then he says "Oh" quietly. His face is grave now.

"She watched him all day. And he was watching her. I could tell it. He was making out like he was asleep. She thought that he was asleep. And so after dinner she gave out. She hadn't rested any last night, and after dinner she set in the chair and dozed. And he was watching her, and he got up from the other cot, careful, winking and squinching his face at me. He went to the door, still winking and squinting back at me over his shoulder, and tiptoed out. And I never tried to stop him nor wake her, neither." She looks at Hightower, her eyes grave, wide. "I was scared to. He talks funny. And the way he was looking at me. Like all the winking and squinching was not for me to not wake her up, but to tell me what would happen to me if I did. And I was scared to. And so I laid here with the baby and pretty soon she jerked awake. And then I knew she hadn't aimed to go to sleep. It was like she come awake already running to the cot where he had been, touching it like she couldn't believe he had done got away. Because she stood there at the cot, pawing at the

blanket like maybe she thought he was mislaid inside the blanket somewhere. And then she looked at me, once. And she
wasn't winking and squinting, but I nigh wished she was.
And she asked me and I told her and she put on her hat and
went out." She looks at Hightower. "I'm glad she's gone. I
reckon I ought not to say it, after all she done for me.
But. . . . . . ."

Hightower stands over the cot. He does not seem to see
her. His face is very grave; it is almost like it had grown ten
years older while he stood there. Or like his face looks now
as it should look and that when he entered the room, it had
been a stranger to itself. "To town," he says. Then his eyes
wake, seeing again. "Well. It cant be helped now," he says.
"Besides, the men downtown, the sane. . . . . . .there will
be a few of them.——Why are you glad they are gone?"

She looks down. Her hand moves about the baby's head,
not touching it: a gesture instinctive, unneeded, apparently
unconscious of itself. "She has been kind. More than kind.
Holding the baby so I could rest. She wants to hold him all
the time, setting there in that chair——You'll have to excuse
me. I aint once invited you to set." She watches him as he
draws the chair up to the cot and sits down. "——setting
there where she could watch him on the cot, making out that
he was asleep." She looks at Hightower; her eyes are questioning, intent. "She keeps on calling him Joey. When his
name aint Joey. And she keeps on. . . ." She watches
Hightower. Her eyes are puzzled now, questioning, doubtful.
"She keeps on talking about——She is mixed up someway. And sometimes I get mixed up too, listening, having
to. . . . . . ." Her eyes, her words, grope, fumble.

"Mixed up?"

"She keeps on talking about him like his pa was that——
the one in jail, that Mr Christmas. She keeps on, and then I
get mixed up and it's like sometimes I cant——like I am
mixed up too and I think that his pa is that Mr——Mr
Christmas too——" She watches him; it is as though she
makes a tremendous effort of some kind. "But I know that
aint so. I know that's foolish. It's because she keeps on saying
it and saying it, and maybe I aint strong good yet, and I get
mixed up too. But I am afraid. . . . . . ."

"Of what?"

"I dont like to get mixed up. And I am afraid she might get me mixed up, like they say how you might cross your eyes and then you cant uncross. . . . . . ." She stops looking at him. She does not move. She can feel him watching her.

"You say the baby's name is not Joe. What is his name?"

For a moment longer she does not look at Hightower. Then she looks up. She says, too immediately, too easily: "I aint named him yet."

And he knows why. It is as though he sees her for the first time since he entered. He notices for the first time that her hair has been recently combed and that she has freshened her face too, and he sees, half hidden by the sheet, as if she had thrust them hurriedly there when he entered, a comb and a shard of broken mirror. "When I came in, you were expecting someone. And it was not me. Who were you expecting?"

She does not look away. Her face is neither innocent nor dissimulating. Neither is it placid and serene. "Expecting?"

"Was it Byron Bunch you expected?" Still she does not look away. Hightower's face is sober, firm, gentle. Yet in it is that ruthlessness which she has seen in the faces of a few good people, men usually, whom she has known. He leans forward and lays his hand on hers where it supports the child's body. "Byron is a good man," he says.

"I reckon I know that, well as anybody. Better than most."

"And you are a good woman. Will be. I dont mean——" he says quickly. Then he ceases. "I didn't mean——"

"I reckon I know," she says.

"No. Not this. This does not matter. This is not anything yet. It all depends on what you do with it, afterward. With yourself. With others." He looks at her; she does not look away. "Let him go. Send him away from you." They look at one another. "Send him away, daughter. You are probably not much more than half his age. But you have already out- lived him twice over. He will never overtake you, catch up with you, because he has wasted too much time. And that too, his nothing, is as irremediable as your all. He can no more ever cast back and do, than you can cast back and undo. You have a manchild that is not his, by a man that is not him. You will be forcing into his life two men and only the third part of a woman, who deserves at the least that the nothing with which he has lived for thirtyfive years be violated, if violated it must be, without two witnesses. Send him away."

"That aint for me to do. He is free. Ask him. I have not tried once to hold him."

"That's it. You probably could not have held him, if you had tried to. That's it. If you had known how to try. But then, if you had known that, you would not be here in this cot, with this child at your breast. And you wont send him away? You wont say the word?"

"I can say no more than I have said. And I said No to him five days ago."

"No?"

"He said for me to marry him. To not wait. And I said No."

"Would you say No now?"

She looks at him steadily. "Yes. I would say it now."

He sighs, huge, shapeless; his face is again slack, weary. "I believe you. You will continue to say it until after you have seen——" He looks at her again; again his gaze is intent, hard. "Where is he? Byron?"

She looks at him. After a while she says quietly: "I dont know." She looks at him; suddenly her face is quite empty, as though something which gave it actual solidity and firmness were beginning to drain out of it. Now there is nothing of dissimulation nor alertness nor caution in it. "This morning about ten oclock he came back. He didn't come in. He just came to the door and he stood there and he just looked at me. And I hadn't seen him since last night and he hadn't seen the baby and I said 'Come and see him' and he looked at me, standing there in the door, and he said 'I come to find out when you want to see him' and I said 'See who?' and he said 'They may have to send a deputy with him but I can persuade Kennedy to let him come' and I said 'Let who come?' and he said 'Lucas. Burch' and I said 'Yes' and he said 'This evening? Will that do?' and I said 'Yes' and he went away. He just stood there, and then he went away." While he watches her with that despair of all men in the presence of female tears, she begins to cry. She sits upright, the child at her breast, crying, not loud and not hard, but with a patient and hopeless abjectness, not hiding her face. "And you worry me about if I said No or not and I already said No and you worry me and worry me and now he is already gone. I will never see him again." And he sits there, and she bows her head at last, and he rises and stands over her with his hand on her bowed head, thinking *Thank God, God help me. Thank God, God help me*

He found Christmas' old path through the woods to the mill. He did not know that it was there, but when he found in which direction it ran, it seemed like an omen to him in his exultation. He believes her, but he wants to corroborate the information for the sheer pleasure of hearing it again. It is just four oclock when he reaches the mill. He inquires at the office.

"Bunch?" the bookkeeper says. "You wont find him here. He quit this morning."

"I know, I know," Hightower says.

"Been with the company for seven years, Saturday evenings too. Then this morning he walked in and said he was quitting. No reason. But that's the way these hillbillies do."

"Yes, yes," Hightower says. "They are fine people, though. Fine men and women." He leaves the office. The road to town passes the planer shed, where Byron worked. He knows Mooney, the foreman. "I hear Byron Bunch is not with you anymore," he says, pausing.

"Yes," Mooney says. "He quit this morning." But Hightower is not listening; the overalled men watch the shabby, queershaped, not-quite-familiar figure looking with a kind of exultant interest at the walls, the planks, the cryptic machinery whose very being and purpose he could not have understood or even learned. "If you want to see him," Mooney says, "I reckon you'll find him downtown at the courthouse."

"At the courthouse?"

"Yes, sir. Grand Jury meets today. Special call. To indict that murderer."

"Yes, yes," Hightower says. "So he is gone. Yes. A fine young man. Goodday, goodday, gentlemen. Goodday to you." He goes on, while the men in overalls look after him for a time. His hands are clasped behind him. He paces on, thinking quietly, peacefully, sadly: 'Poor man. Poor fellow. No man is, can be, justified in taking human life; least of all, a warranted officer, a sworn servant of his fellowman. When it is sanctioned publicly in the person of an elected officer who knows that he has not himself suffered at the hands of his victim, call that victim by what name you will, how can we expect an individual to refrain when he believes that he has suffered at the hands of *his* victim?' He walks on; he is now in his own street. Soon he can see his fence, the signboard; then the house beyond the rich foliage of August. 'So he departed without coming to tell me goodbye. After all he has done for me. Fetched to me. Ay; given, restored, to me. It would seem that this too was reserved for me. And this must be all.'

But it is not all. There is one thing more reserved for him.

XVIII

WHEN BYRON reached town he found that he could not see the sheriff until noon, since the sheriff would be engaged all morning with the special Grand Jury. "You'll have to wait," they told him.

"Yes," Byron said. "I know how."

"Know how what?" But he did not answer. He left the sheriff's office and stood beneath the portico which faced the south side of the square. From the shallow, flagged terrace the stone columns rose, arching, weathered, stained with generations of casual tobacco. Beneath them, steady and constant and with a grave purposelessness (and with here and there, standing motionless or talking to one another from the sides of their mouths, some youngish men, townsmen, some of whom Byron knew as clerks and young lawyers and even merchants, who had a generally identical authoritative air, like policemen in disguise and not especially caring if the disguise hid the policeman or not) countrymen in overalls moved, with almost the air of monks in a cloister, speaking quietly among themselves of money and crops, looking quietly now and then upward at the ceiling beyond which the Grand Jury was preparing behind locked doors to take the life of a man whom few of them had ever seen to know, for having taken the life of a woman whom even fewer of them had known to see. The wagons and the dusty cars in which they had come to town were ranked about the square, and along the streets and in and out of the stores the wives and daughters who had come to town with them moved in clumps, slowly and also aimlessly as cattle or clouds. Byron stood there for quite a while, motionless, not leaning against anything—a small man who had lived in the town seven years yet whom even fewer of the country people than knew either the murderer or the murdered, knew by name or habit.

Byron was not conscious of this. He did not care now, though a week ago it would have been different. Then he would not have stood here, where any man could look at him and perhaps recognise him: *Byron Bunch, that weeded another man's laidby crop, without any halvers. The fellow that took care*

*of another man's whore while the other fellow was busy making a
thousand dollars. And got nothing for it. Byron Bunch that protected her good name when the woman that owned the good name
and the man she had given it to had both thrown it away, that
got the other fellow's bastard born in peace and quiet and at Byron
Bunch's expense, and heard a baby cry once for his pay. Got nothing for it except permission to fetch the other fellow back to her soon
as he got done collecting the thousand dollars and Byron wasn't
needed any more. Byron Bunch* 'And now I can go away,' he
thought. He began to breathe deep. He could feel himself
breathing deep, as if each time his insides were afraid that
next breath they would not be able to give far enough and
that something terrible would happen, and that all the time
he could look down at himself breathing, at his chest, and see
no movement at all, like when dynamite first begins, gathers
itself for the now Now NOW, the shape of the outside of the
stick does not change; that the people who passed and looked
at him could see no change: a small man you would not look
at twice, that you would never believe he had done what he
had done and felt what he had felt, who had believed that out
there at the mill on a Saturday afternoon, alone, the chance
to be hurt could not have found him.

He was walking, among the people. 'I got to go somewhere,' he thought. He could walk in time to that: 'I got to
go somewhere.' That would get him along. He was still saying it when he reached the boardinghouse. His room faced
the street. Before he realised that he had begun to look toward it, he was looking away. 'I might see somebody reading
or smoking in the window,' he thought. He entered the hall.
After the bright morning, he could not see at once. He could
smell wet linoleum, soap. 'It's still Monday,' he thought. 'I
had forgot that. Maybe it's next Monday. That's what it
seems like it ought to be.' He did not call. After a while he
could see better. He could hear the mop in the back of the
hall or maybe the kitchen. Then against the rectangle of light
which was the rear door, also open, he saw Mrs Beard's head
leaning out, then her body in full silhouette, advancing up
the hall.

"Well," she said. "It's Mister Byron Bunch. Mister Byron
Bunch."

"Yessum," he said, thinking, 'Only a fat lady that never had much more trouble than a mopping pail would hold ought not to try to be. . . . . . .' Again he could not think of the word that Hightower would know, would use without having to think of it. 'It's like I not only cant do anything without getting him mixed up in it, I cant even think without him to help me out.'——"Yessum," he said. And then he stood there, not even able to tell her that he had come to say goodbye. 'Maybe I aint,' he thought. 'I reckon when a fellow has lived in one room for seven years, he aint going to get moved in one day. Only I reckon that aint going to interfere with her renting out his room.'——"I reckon I owe you a little room rent," he said.

She looked at him: a hard, comfortable face, not unkind either. "Rent for what?" she said. "I thought you was settled. Decided to tent for the summer." She looked at him. Then she told him. She did it gently, delicately, considering. "I done already collected the rent for that room."

"Oh," he said. "Yes. I see. Yes." He looked quietly up the scoured, linoleumstripped stairway, scuffed bare by the aid of his own feet. When the new linoleum was put down three years ago, he had been the first of the boarders to mount upon it. "Oh," he said. "Well, I reckon I better——"

She answered that too, immediately, not unkind. "I tended to that. I put everything you left in your grip. It's back in my room. If you want to go up and look for yourself, though?"

"No. I reckon you got every. . . . . . Well, I reckon I. . . . . . ."

She was watching him. "You men," she said. "It aint a wonder womenfolks get impatient with you. You cant even know your own limits for devilment. Which aint more than I can measure on a pin, at that. I reckon if it wasn't for getting some woman mixed up in it to help you, you'd ever one of you be drug hollering into heaven before you was ten years old."

"I reckon you aint got any call to say anything against her," he said.

"No more I aint. I dont need to. Dont no other woman need to that is going to. I aint saying that it aint been women that has done most of the talking. But if you had more than mansense you would know that women dont mean anything when they talk. It's menfolks that take talking serious. It aint any woman that believes hard against you and her. Because it aint any woman but knows that she aint had any reason to have to be bad with you, even discounting that baby. Or any other man right now. She never had to. Aint you and that preacher and ever other man that knows about her, already done everything for her that she could think to want? What does she need to be bad for? Tell me that."

"Yes," Byron says. He was not looking at her now. "I just come. . . . . . ."

She answered that too, before it was spoken. "I reckon you'll be leaving us soon." She was watching him. "What have they done this morning? at the courthouse?"

"I dont know. They aint finished yet."

"I bound that, too. They'll take as much time and trouble and county money as they can cleaning up what us women could have cleaned up in ten minutes Saturday night. For being such a fool. Not that Jefferson will miss him. Cant get along without him. But being fool enough to believe that killing a woman will do a man anymore good than killing a man would a woman. . . . I reckon they'll let the other one go, now."

"Yessum. I reckon so."

"And they believed for a while that he helped do it. And so they will give him that thousand dollars to show it aint any hard feelings. And then they can get married. That's about right, aint it?"

"Yessum." He could feel her watching him, not unkindly.

"And so I reckon you'll be leaving us. I reckon you kind of feel like you have wore out Jefferson, dont you?"

"Something like that. I reckon I'll move on."

"Well, Jefferson's a good town. But it aint so good but what a footloose man like you can find in another one enough devilment and trouble to keep him occupied too. . . . You can leave your grip here until you are ready for it, if you want."

He waited until noon and after. He waited until he believed that the sheriff had finished his dinner. Then he went to the sheriff's home. He would not come in. He waited at the door until the sheriff came out—the fat man, with little wise eyes like bits of mica embedded in his fat, still face. They

went aside, into the shade of a tree in the yard. There was no
seat there; neither did they squat on their heels, as by ordinary (they were both countrybred) they would have done. The
sheriff listened quietly to the man, the quiet little man who for
seven years had been a minor mystery to the town and who
had been for seven days wellnigh a public outrage and affront.

"I see," the sheriff said. "You think the time has come to
get them married."

"I dont know. That's his business and hers. I reckon he
better go out and see her, though. I reckon now is the time
for that. You can send a deputy with him. I told her he would
come out there this evening. What they do then is her business and hisn. It aint mine."

"Sho," the sheriff said. "It aint yourn." He was looking at
the other's profile. "What do you aim to do now, Byron?"

"I dont know." His foot moved slowly upon the earth; he
was watching it. "I been thinking about going up to Memphis. Been thinking about it for a couple of years. I might do
that. There aint nothing in these little towns."

"Sho. Memphis aint a bad town, for them that like city life.
Of course, you aint got any family to have to drag around
and hamper you. I reckon if I had been a single man ten years
ago I'd have done that too. Been better off, maybe. You're
figuring on leaving right away, I reckon."

"Soon, I reckon." He looked up, then down again. He
said: "I quit out at the mill this morning."

"Sho," the sheriff said. "I figured you hadn't walked all the
way in since twelve and aimed to get back out there by one
oclock. Well, it looks like——" He ceased. He knew that by
night the Grand Jury would have indicted Christmas, and
Brown—or Burch—would be a free agent save for his bond
to appear as a witness at next month's court. But even his
presence would not be absolutely essential, since Christmas
had made no denial and the sheriff believed that he would
plead guilty in order to save his neck. 'And it wont do no
harm, anyway, to throw the scare of God into that durn fellow, once in his life,' he thought. He said: "I reckon that can
be fixed. Of course, like you say, I will have to send a deputy
with him. Even if he aint going to run so long as he has any

hope of getting some of that reward money. And provided he dont know what he is going to meet when he gets there. He dont know that yet."

"No," Byron said. "He dont know that. He dont know that she is in Jefferson."

"So I reckon I'll just send him out there with a deputy. Not tell him why: just send him out there. Unless you want to take him yourself."

"No," Byron said. "No. No." But he did not move.

"I'll just do that. You'll be gone by that time, I reckon. I'll just send a deputy with him. Will four oclock do?"

"It'll be fine. It'll be kind of you. It'll be a kindness."

"Sho. Lots of folks beside me has been good to her since she come to Jefferson. Well, I aint going to say goodbye. I reckon Jefferson will see you again someday. Never knowed a man yet to live here a while and then leave it for good. Except maybe that fellow in the jail yonder. But he'll plead guilty, I reckon. Save his neck. Take it out of Jefferson though, anyway. It's right hard on that old lady that thinks she is his grandmother. The old man was downtown when I come home, hollering and ranting, calling folks cowards because they wouldn't take him out of jail right then and there and lynch him." He began to chuckle, heavily. "He better be careful, or Percy Grimm'll get him with that army of his." He sobered. "It's right hard on her. On women." He looked at Byron's profile. "It's been right hard on a lot of us. Well, you come back some day soon. Maybe Jefferson will treat you better next time."

At four oclock that afternoon, hidden, he sees the car come up and stop, and the deputy and the man whom he knew by the name of Brown get out and approach the cabin. Brown is not handcuffed now, and Byron watches them reach the cabin and sees the deputy push Brown forward and into the door. Then the door closes behind Brown, and the deputy sits on the step and takes a sack of tobacco from his pocket. Byron rises to his feet. 'I can go now,' he thinks. 'Now I can go.' His hiding place is a clump of shrubbery on the lawn where the house once stood. On the opposite side of the clump, hidden from the cabin and the road both, the mule is tethered. Lashed behind the worn saddle is a battered yellow suitcase which is not leather. He mounts the mule and turns it into the road. He does not look back.

The mild red road goes on beneath the slanting and peaceful afternoon, mounting a hill. 'Well, I can bear a hill,' he thinks. 'I can bear a hill, a man can.' It is peaceful and still, familiar with seven years. 'It seems like a man can just about bear anything. He can even bear what he never done. He can even bear the thinking how some things is just more than he can bear. He can even bear it that if he could just give down and cry, he wouldn't do it. He can even bear it to not look back, even when he knows that looking back or not looking back wont do him any good.'

The hill rises, cresting. He has never seen the sea, and so he thinks, 'It is like the edge of nothing. Like once I passed it I would just ride right off into nothing. Where trees would look like and be called by something else except trees, and men would look like and be called by something else except folks. And Byron Bunch he wouldn't even have to be or not be Byron Bunch. Byron Bunch and his mule not anything with falling fast, until they would take fire like the Reverend Hightower says about them rocks running so fast in space that they take fire and burn up and there aint even a cinder to have to hit the ground.'

But then from beyond the hill crest there begins to rise that which he knows is there: the trees which are trees, the terrific and tedious distance which, being moved by blood, he must compass forever and ever between two inescapable horizons of the implacable earth. Steadily they rise, not portentous, not threatful. That's it. They are oblivious of him. 'Dont know and dont care,' he thinks. 'Like they were saying *All right. You say you suffer. All right. But in the first place, all we got is your naked word for it. And in the second place, you just say that you are Byron Bunch. And in the third place, you are just the one that calls yourself Byron Bunch today, now, this minute.* . . . . . . Well,' he thinks, 'if that's all it is, I reckon I might as well have the pleasure of not being able to bear looking back too.' He halts the mule and turns in the saddle.

He did not realise that he has come so far and that the crest is so high. Like a shallow bowl the once broad domain of

what was seventy years ago a plantation house lies beneath
him, between him and the opposite ridge upon which is Jefferson. But the plantation is broken now by random negro
cabins and garden patches and dead fields erosiongutted and
choked with blackjack and sassafras and persimmon and brier.
But in the exact center the clump of oaks still stand as they
stood when the house was built, though now there is no
house among them. From here he cannot even see the scars
of the fire; he could not even tell where it used to stand if it
were not for the oaks and the position of the ruined stable
and the cabin beyond, the cabin toward which he is looking.
It stands full and quiet in the afternoon sun, almost toylike;
like a toy the deputy sits on the step. Then, as Byron watches,
a man appears as though by magic at the rear of it, already
running, in the act of running out from the rear of the cabin
while the unsuspecting deputy sits quiet and motionless on
the front step. For a while longer Byron too sits motionless,
half turned in the saddle, and watches the tiny figure flee on
across the barren slope behind the cabin, toward the woods.

Then a cold, hard wind seems to blow through him. It is
at once violent and peaceful, blowing hard away like chaff or
trash or dead leaves all the desire and the despair and the
hopelessness and the tragic and vain imagining too. With the
very blast of it he seems to feel himself rush back and empty
again, without anything in him now which had not been
there two weeks ago, before he ever saw her. The desire of
this moment is more than desire: it is conviction quiet and
assured; before he is aware that his brain has telegraphed his
hand he has turned the mule from the road and is galloping
along the ridge which parallels the running man's course
when he entered the woods. He has not even named the
man's name to himself. He does not speculate at all upon
where the man is going, and why. It does not once enter his
head that Brown is fleeing again, as he himself had predicted.
If he thought about it at all, he probably believed that Brown
was engaged, after his own peculiar fashion, in some thoroughly legitimate business having to do with his and Lena's
departure. But he was not thinking about that at all; he was
not thinking about Lena at all; she was as completely out of
his mind as if he had never seen her face nor heard her name.

He is thinking: 'I took care of his woman for him and I borned his child for him. And now there is one more thing I can do for him. I cant marry them, because I aint a minister. And I may not can catch him, because he's got a start on me. And I may not can whip him if I do, because he is bigger than me. But I can try it. I can try to do it.'

When the deputy called for him at the jail, Brown asked at once where they were going. Visiting, the deputy told him. Brown held back, watching the deputy with his handsome, spuriously bold face. "I dont want to visit nobody here. I'm a stranger here."

"You'd be strange anywhere you was at," the deputy said. "Even at home. Come on."

"I'm a American citizen," Brown said. "I reckon I got my rights, even if I dont wear no tin star on my galluses."

"Sho," the deputy said. "That's what I am doing now: helping you get your rights."

Brown's face lighted: it was a flash. "Have they——Are they going to pay——"

"That reward? Sho. I'm going to take you to the place myself right now, where if you are going to get any reward, you'll get it."

Brown sobered. But he moved, though he still watched the deputy suspiciously. "This here is a funny way to go about it," he said. "Keeping me shut up in jail while them bastards tries to beat me out of it."

"I reckon the bastard aint been whelped yet that can beat you at anything," the deputy said. "Come on. They're waiting on us."

They emerged from the jail. In the sunlight Brown blinked, looking this way and that, then he jerked his head up, looking back over his shoulder with that horselike movement. The car was waiting at the curb. Brown looked at the car and then at the deputy, quite sober, quite wary. "Where are we going in a car?" he said. "It wasn't too far for me to walk to the courthouse this morning."

"Watt sent the car to help bring back the reward in," the deputy said. "Get in."

Brown grunted. "He's done got mighty particular about my comfort all of a sudden. A car to ride in, and no handcuffs. And just one durn fellow to keep me from running away."

"I aint keeping you from running," the deputy said. He paused in the act of starting the car. "You want to run now?"

Brown looked at him, glaring, sullen, outraged, suspicious. "I see," he said. "That's his trick. Trick me into running and then collect that thousand dollars himself. How much of it did he promise you?"

"Me? I'm going to get the same as you, to a cent."

For a moment longer Brown glared at the deputy. He cursed, pointless, in a weak, violent way. "Come on," he said. "Let's go if we are going."

They drove out to the scene of the fire and the murder. At steady, almost timed intervals Brown jerked his head up and back with that movement of a free mule running in front of a car in a narrow road. "What are we going out here for?"

"To get your reward," the deputy said.

"Where am I going to get it?"

"In that cabin yonder. It's waiting for you there."

Brown looked about, at the blackened embers which had once been a house, at the blank cabin in which he had lived for four months sitting weathered and quiet in the sunlight. His face was quite grave, quite alert. "There's something funny about this. If Kennedy thinks he can tromple on my rights, just because he wears a durn little tin star. . . ."

"Get on," the deputy said. "If you dont like the reward, I'll be waiting to take you back to jail any time you want. Just any time you want." He pushed Brown on, opening the cabin door and pushing him into it and closing the door behind him and sitting on the step.

Brown heard the door close behind him. He was still moving forward. Then, in the midst of one of those quick, jerking, allembracing looks, as if his eyes could not wait to take in the room, he stopped dead still. Lena on the cot watched the white scar beside his mouth vanish completely, as if the

ebb of blood behind it had snatched the scar in passing like a
rag from a clothesline. She did not speak at all. She just lay
there, propped on the pillows, watching him with her sober
eyes in which there was nothing at all—joy, surprise, reproach, love—while over his face passed shock, astonishment, outrage, and then downright terror, each one mocking
in turn at the telltale little white scar, while ceaselessly here
and there about the empty room went his harried and desperate eyes. She watched him herd them by will, like two terrified beasts, and drive them up to meet her own. "Well, well,"
he said. "Well, well, well. It's Lena." She watched him holding his eyes up to hers like two beasts about to break, as if he
knew that when they broke this time he would never catch
them, turn them again, and that he himself would be lost. She
could almost watch his mind casting this way and that, ceaseless, harried, terrified, seeking words which his voice, his
tongue, could speak. "If it aint Lena. Yes, sir. So you got my
message. Soon as I got here I sent you a message last month
as soon as I got settled down and I thought it had got
lost——It was a fellow I didn't know what his name was but
he said he would take——He didn't look reliable but I had
to trust him but I thought when I gave him the ten dollars
for you to travel on that he. . . . . . ." His voice died
somewhere behind his desperate eyes. Yet still she could
watch his mind darting and darting as without pity, without
anything at all, she watched him with her grave, unwinking,
unbearable gaze, watched him fumble and flee and tack until
at last all that remained in him of pride, of what sorry pride
the desire for justification was, fled from him and left him
naked. Then for the first time she spoke. Her voice was quiet,
unruffled, cool.

"Come over here," she said. "Come on. I aint going to let
him bite you." When he moved he approached on tiptoe. She
saw that, though she was now no longer watching him. She
knew that just as she knew that he was now standing with a
kind of clumsy and diffident awe above her and the sleeping child. But she knew that it was not at and because of the
child. She knew that in that sense he had not even seen the
child. She could still see, feel, his mind darting and darting.
He is going to make out like he was not afraid she thought. *He*

*will have no more shame than to lie about being afraid, just as he
had no more shame than to be afraid because he lied*

"Well, well," he said. "So there it is, sho enough."

"Yes," she said. "Will you set down?" The chair which
Hightower had drawn up was still beside the cot. He had already remarked it. *She had it all ready for me* he thought. Again
he cursed, soundless, badgered, furious. *Them bastards. Them
bastards* But his face was quite smooth when he sat down.

"Yes, sir. Here we are again. Same as I had planned it. I
would have had it all fixed up ready for you, only I have been
so busy lately. Which reminds me——" Again he made that
abrupt, mulelike, backlooking movement of the head. She
was not looking at him. She said:

"There is a preacher here. That has already come to see
me."

"That's fine," he said. His voice was loud, hearty. Yet the
heartiness, like the timbre, seemed to be as impermanent as
the sound of the words, vanishing, leaving nothing, not even
a definitely stated thought in the ear or the belief. "That's just
fine. Soon as I get caught up with all this business——" He
jerked his arm in a gesture vague, embracing, looking at her.
His face was smooth and blank. His eyes were bland, alert,
secret, yet behind them there lurked still that quality harried
and desperate. But she was not looking at him.

"What kind of work are you doing now? At the planing
mill?"

He watched her. "No. I quit that." His eyes watched her.
It was as though they were not his eyes, had no relation to
the rest of him, what he did and what he said. "Slaving like a
durn nigger ten hours a day. I got something on the string
now that means money. Not no little piddling fifteen cents a
hour. And when I get it, soon as I get a few little details
cleared up, then you and me will. . . . . . ." Hard, intent,
secret, the eyes watched her, her lowered face in profile.
Again she heard that faint, abrupt sound as he jerked his head
up and back. "And that reminds me——"

She had not moved. She said: "When will it be, Lucas?"
Then she could hear, feel, utter stillness, utter silence.

"When will what be?"

"You know. Like you said. Back home. It was alright for

just me. I never minded. But it's different now. I reckon I
got a right to worry now."

"Oh, that," he said. "That. Dont you worry about that. Just
let me get this here business cleaned up and get my hands on
that money. It's mine by right. There cant nere a bastard one
of them——" He stopped. His voice had begun to rise, as
though he had forgot where he was and had been thinking
aloud. He lowered it; he said: "You just leave it to me. Dont
you worry none. I aint never give you no reason yet to worry,
have I? Tell me that."

"No. I never worried. I knowed I could depend on you."

"Sho you knowed it. And these here bastards——these
here——" He had risen from the chair. "Which reminds
me——" She neither looked up nor spoke while he stood
above her with those eyes harried, desperate, and importunate. It was as if she held him there and that she knew it. And
that she released him by her own will, deliberately.

"I reckon you are right busy now, then."

"For a fact, I am. With all I got to bother me, and them
bastards——" She was looking at him now. She watched him
as he looked at the window in the rear wall. Then he looked
back at the closed door behind him. Then he looked at her,
at her grave face which had either nothing in it, or everything, all knowledge. He lowered his voice. "I got enemies
here. Folks that dont want me to get what I done earned. So
I am going to——" Again it was as though she held him,
forcing him to, trying him with, that final lie at which even
his sorry dregs of pride revolted; held him neither with rods
nor cords but with something against which his lying blew
trivial as leaves or trash. But she said nothing at all. She just
watched him as he went on tiptoe to the window and opened
it without a sound. Then he looked at her. Perhaps he
thought that he was safe then, that he could get out the window before she could touch him with a physical hand. Or
perhaps it was some sorry tagend of shame, as a while ago it
had been pride. Because he looked at her, stripped naked for
the instant of verbiage and deceit. His voice was not much
louder than a whisper: "It's a man outside. In front, waiting
for me." Then he was gone, through the window, without a
sound, in a single motion almost like a long snake. From be-

yond the window she heard a single faint sound as he began to run. Then only did she move, and then but to sigh once, profoundly.

"Now I got to get up again," she said, aloud.

When Brown emerges from the woods, onto the railroad right-of-way, he is panting. It is not with fatigue, though the distance which he has covered in the last twenty minutes is almost two miles and the going was not smooth. Rather, it is the snarling and malevolent breathing of a fleeing animal: while he stands looking both ways along the empty track his face, his expression, is that of an animal fleeing alone, desiring no fellowaid, clinging to its solitary dependence upon its own muscles alone and which, in the pause to renew breath, hates every tree and grassblade in sight as if it were a live enemy, hates the very earth it rests upon and the very air it needs to renew breathing.

He has struck the railroad within a few hundred yards of the point at which he aimed. This is the crest of a grade where the northbound freights slow to a terrific and crawling gait of almost less than that of a walking man. A short distance ahead of him the twin bright threads appear to have been cut short off as though with scissors.

For a while he stands just within the screen of woods beside the right-of-way, still hidden. He stands like a man in brooding and desperate calculation, as if he sought in his mind for some last desperate cast in a game already lost. After standing for a moment longer in an attitude of listening, he turns and runs again, through the woods and parallelling the track. He seems to know exactly where he is going; he comes presently upon a path and follows it, still running, and emerges into a clearing in which a negro cabin sits. He approaches the front, walking now. On the porch an old negro woman is sitting, smoking a pipe, her head wrapped in a white cloth. Brown is not running, but he is breathing fast, heavily. He quiets it to speak. "Hi, Aunty," he says. "Who's here?"

The old negress removes the pipe. "Ise here. Who wanter know?"

"I got to send a message back to town. In a hurry." He
holds his breathing down to talk. "I'll pay. Aint there somebody here that can take it?"

"If it's all that rush, you better tend to it yourself."

"I'll pay, I tell you!" he says. He speaks with a kind of
raging patience, holding his voice, his breathing, down. "A
dollar, if he just goes quick enough. Aint there somebody
here that wants to make a dollar? Some of the boys?"

The old woman smokes, watching him. With an aged and
inscrutable midnight face she seems to contemplate him with
a detachment almost godlike but not at all benign. "A dollar
cash?"

He makes a gesture indescribable, of hurry and leashed rage
and something like despair. He is about to turn away when
the negress speaks again. "Aint nobody here but me and the
two little uns. I reckon they'd be too little for you."

Brown turns back. "How little? I just want somebody that
can take a note to the sheriff in a hurry and——"

"The sheriff? Then you come to the wrong place. I aint
ghy have none of mine monkeying around no sheriff. I done
had one nigger that thought he knowed a sheriff well enough
to go and visit with him. He aint never come back, neither.
You look somewhere else."

But Brown is already moving away. He does not run at
once. He has not yet thought about running again; for the
moment he cannot think at all. His rage and impotence is
now almost ecstatic. He seems to muse now upon a sort of
timeless and beautiful infallibility in his unpredictable frustra-
tions. As though somehow the very fact that he should be so
consistently supplied with them elevates him somehow above
the petty human hopes and desires which they abrogate
and negative. Hence the negress has to shout twice at him
before he hears and turns. She has said nothing, she has not
moved: she merely shouted. She says, "Here one will take it
for you."

Standing beside the porch now, materialised apparently
from thin air, is a negro who may be either a grown imbecile
or a hulking youth. His face is black, still, also quite inscrutable. They stand looking at one another. Or rather, Brown
looks at the negro. He cannot tell if the negro is looking at

him or not. And that too seems somehow right and fine and in keeping: that his final hope and resort should be a beast that does not appear to have enough ratiocinative power to find the town, let alone any given individual in it. Again Brown makes an indescribable gesture. He is almost running now, back toward the porch, pawing at his shirt pocket. "I want you to take a note to town and bring me back an answer," he says. "Can you do it?" But he does not listen for a reply. He has taken from his shirt a scrap of soiled paper and a chewed pencil stub, and bending over the edge of the porch, he writes, laborious and hurried, while the negress watches him:

Mr Wat Kenedy Dear sir please give barer My reward Money for captain Murder Xmas rapp it up in Paper 4 given it toe barer yrs truly

He does not sign it. He snatches it up, glaring at it, while the negress watches him. He glares at the dingy and innocent paper, at the labored and hurried pencilling in which he had succeeded for an instant in snaring his whole soul and life too. Then he claps it down and writes   *not Sined but All rigt You no who*   and folds it and gives it to the negro. "Take it to the sheriff. Not to nobody else. You reckon you can find him?"

"If the sheriff dont find him first," the old negress says. "Give it to him. He'll find him, if he is above ground. Git your dollar and go on, boy."

The negro had started away. He stops. He just stands there, saying nothing, looking at nothing. On the porch the negress sits, smoking, looking down at the white man's weak, wolflike face: a face handsome, plausible, but drawn now by a fatigue more than physical, into a spent and vulpine mask. "I thought you was in a hurry," she says.

"Yes," Brown says. He takes a coin from his pocket. "Here. And if you bring me back the answer to that inside of an hour, I'll give you five more like it."

"Git on, nigger," the woman says. "You aint got all day. You want the answer brought back here?"

For a moment longer Brown looks at her. Then again caution, shame, all flee from him. "No. Not here. Bring it to the top of the grade yonder. Walk up the track until I call to you. I'll be watching you all the time too. Dont you forget that. Do you hear?"

"You needn't to worry," the negress says. "He'll git there with it and git back with the answer, if dont nothing stop him. Git on, boy."

The negro goes on. But something does stop him, before he has gone a half mile. It is another white man, leading a mule.

"Where?" Byron says. "Where did you see him?"

"Just now. Up yon at de house." The white man goes on, leading the mule. The negro looks after him. He did not show the white man the note because the white man did not ask to see it. Perhaps the reason the white man did not ask to see the note was that the white man did not know that he had a note; perhaps the negro is thinking this, because for a while his face mirrors something terrific and subterraneous. Then it clears. He shouts. The white man turns, halting. "He aint dar now," the negro shouts. "He say he gwine up ter de railroad grade to wait."

"Much obliged," the white man says. The negro goes on.

Brown returned to the track. He was not running now. He was saying to himself, 'He wont do it. He cant do it. I know he cant find him, cant get it, bring it back.' He called no names, thought no names. It seemed to him now that they were all just shapes like chessmen—the negro, the sheriff, the money, all—unpredictable and without reason moved here and there by an Opponent who could read his moves before he made them and who created spontaneous rules which he and not the Opponent, must follow. He was for the time being even beyond despair as he turned from the rails and entered the underbrush near the crest of the grade. He moved now without haste, gauging his distance as though there were nothing else in the world or in his life at least, save that. He chose his place and sat down, hidden from the track but where he himself could see it.

'Only I know he wont do it,' he thinks. 'I dont even expect

it. If I was to see him coming back with the money in his hand, I would not believe it. It wouldn't be for me. I would know that. I would know that it was a mistake. I would say to him *You go on. You are looking for somebody else beside me. You aint looking for Lucas Burch. No, sir, Lucas Burch dont deserve that money, that reward. He never done nothing to get it. No, sir*' He begins to laugh, squatting, motionless, his spent face bent, laughing. 'Yes, sir. All Lucas Burch wanted was justice. Just justice. Not that he told them bastards the murderer's name and where to find him only they wouldn't try. They never tried because they would have had to give Lucas Burch the money. Justice.' Then he says aloud, in a harsh, tearful voice: "Justice. That was all. Just my rights. And them bastards with their little tin stars, all sworn everyone of them on oath, to protect a American citizen." He says it harshly, almost crying with rage and despair and fatigue: "I be dog if it aint enough to make a man turn downright bowlsheyvick." Thus he hears no sound at all until Byron speaks directly behind him:

"Get up onto your feet."

It does not last long. Byron knew that it was not going to. But he did not hesitate. He just crept up until he could see the other, where he stopped, looking at the crouching and unwarned figure. 'You're bigger than me,' Byron thought. 'But I dont care. You've had every other advantage of me. And I dont care about that neither. You've done throwed away twice inside of nine months what I aint had in thirtyfive years. And now I'm going to get the hell beat out of me and I dont care about that, neither.'

It does not last long. Brown, whirling, takes advantage of his astonishment even. He did not believe that any man, catching his enemy sitting, would give him a chance to get on his feet, even if the enemy were not the larger of the two. He would not have done it himself. And the fact that the smaller man did do it when he would not have, was worse than insult: it was ridicule. So he fought with even a more savage fury than he would have if Byron had sprung upon his back without warning: with the blind and desperate valor of a starved and cornered rat he fought.

It lasted less than two minutes. Then Byron was lying

quietly among the broken and trampled undergrowth, bleeding quietly about the face, hearing the underbrush crashing on, ceasing, fading into silence. Then he is alone. He feels no particular pain now, but better than that, he feels no haste, no urgency, to do anything or go anywhere. He just lies bleeding and quiet, knowing that after a while will be time enough to reenter the world and time.

He does not even wonder where Brown has gone. He does not have to think about Brown now. Again his mind is filled with still shapes like discarded and fragmentary toys of childhood piled indiscriminate and gathering quiet dust in a forgotten closet—Brown. Lena Grove. Hightower. Byron Bunch—all like small objects which had never been alive, which he had played with in childhood and then broken and forgot. He is lying so when he hears the train whistle for a crossing a half mile away.

This rouses him; this is the world and time too. He sits up, slowly, tentatively. 'Anyway, I aint broke anything,' he thinks. 'I mean, he aint broke anything that belongs to me.' It is getting late: it is time now, with distance, moving, in it. 'Yes. I'll have to be moving. I'll have to get on so I can find me something else to meddle with.' The train is coming nearer. Already the stroke of the engine has shortened and become heavier as it begins to feel the grade; presently he can see the smoke. He seeks in his pocket for a handkerchief. He has none, so he tears the tail from his shirt and dabs at his face gingerly, listening to the short, blasting reports of the locomotive exhaust just over the grade. He moves to the edge of the undergrowth, where he can see the track. The engine is in sight now, almost headon to him beneath the spaced, heavy blasts of black smoke. It has an effect of terrific nomotion. Yet it does move, creeping terrifically up and over the crest of the grade. Standing now in the fringe of bushes he watches the engine approach and pass him, laboring, crawling, with the rapt and boylike absorption (and perhaps yearning) of his country raising. It passes; his eye moves on, watching the cars as they in turn crawl up and over the crest, when for the second time that afternoon he sees a man materialise apparently out of air, in the act of running.

Even then he does not realise what Brown is about. He has

progressed too far into peace and solitude to wonder. He just stands there and watches Brown run to the train, stooping, fleeing, and grasp the iron ladder at the end of a car and leap upward and vanish from sight as though sucked into a vacuum. The train is beginning to increase its speed; he watches the approach of the car where Brown vanished. It passes; clinging to the rear of it, between it and the next car, Brown stands, his face leaned out and watching the bushes. They see one another at the same moment: the two faces, the mild, nondescript, bloody one and the lean, harried, desperate one contorted now in a soundless shouting above the noise of the train, passing one another as though on opposite orbits and with an effect as of phantoms or apparitions. Still Byron is not thinking. "Great God in the mountain," he says, with childlike and almost ecstatic astonishment; "he sho knows how to jump a train. He's sho done that before." He is not thinking at all. It is as though the moving wall of dingy cars were a dyke beyond which the world, time, hope unbelievable and certainty incontrovertible, waited, giving him yet a little more of peace. Anyway, when the last car passes, moving fast now, the world rushes down on him like a flood, a tidal wave.

It is too huge and fast for distance and time; hence no path to be retraced, leading the mule for a good way before he remembers to get on it and ride. It is as though he has already and long since outstripped himself, already waiting at the cabin until he can catch up and enter. *And then I will stand there and I will. . . . . . .* He tries it again: *Then I will stand there and I will. . . . . . .* But he can get no further than that. He is in the road again now, approaching a wagon homeward bound from town. It is about six oclock. He does not give up, however. *Even if I cant seem to get any further than that: when I will open the door and come in and stand there. And then I will. Look at her. Look at her. Look at her—— * The voice speaks again:

"——excitement, I reckon."

"What?" Byron says. The wagon has halted. He is right beside it, the mule stopped too. On the wagon seat the man speaks again, in his flat, complaining voice:

"Durn the luck. Just when I had to get started for home. I'm already late."

"Excitement?" Byron says. "What excitement?"

The man is looking at him. "From your face, a man would say you had been in some excitement yourself."

"I fell down," Byron says. "What excitement in town this evening?"

"I thought maybe you hadn't heard. About an hour ago. That nigger, Christmas. They killed him."

XIX

ABOUT THE SUPPERTABLES on that Monday night, what the town wondered at was not so much how Christmas had escaped but why when free, he had taken refuge in the place which he did, where he must have known he would be certainly run to earth, and why when that occurred he neither surrendered nor resisted. It was as though he had set out and made his plans to passively commit suicide.

There were many reasons, opinions, as to why he had fled to Hightower's house at the last. "Like to like," the easy, the immediate, ones said, remembering the old tales about the minister. Some believed it to have been sheer chance; others said that the man had shown wisdom, since he would not have been suspected of being in the minister's house at all if someone had not seen him run across the back yard and run into the kitchen.

Gavin Stevens though had a different theory. He is the District Attorney, a Harvard graduate, a Phi Beta Kappa: a tall, loosejointed man with a constant cob pipe, with an untidy mop of irongray hair, wearing always loose and unpressed dark gray clothes. His family is old in Jefferson; his ancestors owned slaves there and his grandfather knew (and also hated, and publicly congratulated Colonel Sartoris when they died) Miss Burden's grandfather and brother. He has an easy quiet way with country people, with the voters and the juries; he can be seen now and then squatting among the overalls on the porches of country stores for a whole summer afternoon, talking to them in their own idiom about nothing at all.

On this Monday night there descended from the nine oclock southbound train a college professor from the neighboring State University, a schoolmate of Stevens' at Harvard, come to spend a few days of the vacation with his friend. When he descended from the train he saw his friend at once. He believed that Stevens had come down to meet him until he saw that Stevens was engaged with a queerlooking old couple whom he was putting on the train. Looking at them, the professor saw a little, dirty old man with a short goat's beard who seemed to be in a state like catalepsy, and an old woman who must have been his wife—a dumpy creature with a face like dough beneath a nodding and soiled white plume, shapeless in a silk dress of an outmoded shape and in color regal and moribund. For an instant the professor paused in a sort of astonished interest, watching Stevens putting into the woman's hand, as into the hand of a child, two railroad tickets; moving again and approaching and still unseen by his friend, he overheard Stevens' final words as the flagman helped the old people into the vestibule: "Yes, yes," Stevens was saying, in a tone soothing and recapitulant; "he'll be on the train tomorrow morning. I'll see to it. All you'll have to do is to arrange for the funeral, the cemetery. You take Granddad on home and put him to bed. I'll see that the boy is on the train in the morning."

Then the train began to move and Stevens turned and saw the professor. He began the story as they rode to town and finished it as they sat on the veranda of Stevens' home, and there recapitulated. "I think I know why it was, why he ran into Hightower's house for refuge at the last. I think it was his grandmother. She had just been with him in his cell when they took him back to the courthouse again; she and the grandfather—that little crazed old man who wanted to lynch him, who came up here from Mottstown for that purpose. I dont think that the old lady had any hope of saving him when she came, any actual hope. I believe that all she wanted was that he die 'decent', as she put it. Decently hung by a Force, a principle; not burned or hacked or dragged dead by a Thing. I think she came here just to watch that old man, lest he be the straw that started the hurricane, because she did not dare let him out of her sight. Not that she doubted that Christmas was her grandchild, you understand. She just didn't hope. Didn't know how to begin to hope. I imagine that after thirty years the machinery for hoping requires more than twentyfour hours to get started, to get into motion again.

"But I believe that, having got started physically by the tide of the old man's insanity and conviction, before she knew it she had been swept away too. So they came here. They got here on the early train, about three oclock Sunday morning. She made no attempt to see Christmas. Perhaps she was watching the old man. But I dont think so. I dont think that the hoping machine had got started then, either. I dont think that it ever did start until that baby was born out there this morning, born right in her face, you might say; a boy too. And she had never seen the mother before, and the father at all, and that grandson whom she had never seen as a man; so to her those thirty years just were not. Obliterated when that child cried. No longer existed.

"It was all coming down on her too fast. There was too much reality that her hands and eyes could not deny, and too much that must be taken for granted that her hands and eyes could not prove; too much of the inexplicable that hands and eyes were asked too suddenly to accept and believe without proof. After the thirty years it must have been like a person in solitary blundering suddenly into a room full of strange people all talking at once, and she casting desperately about for anything that would hold sanity together by choosing some logical course of action which would be within her limitations, which she could have some assurance of being able to perform. Until that baby was born and she found some means by which she could stand alone, as it were, she had been like an effigy with a mechanical voice being hauled about on a cart by that fellow Bunch and made to speak when he gave the signal, as when he took her last night to tell her story to Doctor Hightower.

"And she was still groping, you see. She was still trying to find something which that mind which had apparently not run very much in thirty years, could believe in, admit to be actual, real. And I think that she found it there, at Hightower's, for the first time: someone to whom she could tell it, who would listen to her. Very likely that was the first time she had ever told it. And very likely she learned it herself then for the first time, actually saw it whole and real at the same time with Hightower. So I dont think it is so strange that for the time she got not only the child but his parentage as well mixed up, since in that cabin those thirty years did not exist—the child and its father whom she had never seen, and her grandson whom she had not seen since he was a baby like the other, and whose father likewise to her had never existed, all confused. And that, when hope did begin to move in her, she should have turned at once, with that sublime and bound-less faith of her kind in those who are the voluntary slaves and the sworn bondsmen of prayer, to the minister.

"That's what she was telling Christmas in the jail today, when the old man, watching his chance, had slipped away from her and she followed him to town and found him on the street corner again, mad as a hatter and completely hoarse, preaching lynching, telling the people how he had grandfathered the devil's spawn and had kept it in trust for this day. Or perhaps she was on her way to see him in the jail when she left the cabin. Anyway she left the old man alone as soon as she saw that his audience was more interested than moved, and went on to the sheriff. He had just got back from dinner and for a while he could not understand what she wanted. She must have sounded quite crazy to him, with that story of hers, in that hopelessly respectable Sunday dress, planning a jailbreak. But he let her go to the jail, with a dep-uty. And there, in the cell with him, I believe she told him about Hightower, that Hightower would save him, was going to save him.

"But of course I dont know what she told him. I dont be-lieve that any man could reconstruct that scene. I dont think that she knew herself, planned at all what she would say, be-cause it had already been written and worded for her on the night when she bore his mother, and that was now so long ago that she had learned it beyond all forgetting and then forgot the words. Perhaps that's why he believed her at once, without question. I mean, because she did not worry about what to say, about plausibility or the possibility of incredulity on his part: that somewhere, somehow, in the shape or pres-ence or whatever of that old outcast minister was a sanctuary which would be inviolable not only to officers and mobs, but to the very irrevocable past; to whatever crimes had molded and shaped him and left him at last high and dry in a barred cell with the shape of an incipient executioner everywhere he looked.

"And he believed her. I think that is what gave him not the courage so much as the passive patience to endure and recog-nise and accept the one opportunity which he had to break in the middle of that crowded square, manacled, and run. But there was too much running with him, stride for stride with him. Not pursuers: but himself: years, acts, deeds omitted and committed, keeping pace with him, stride for stride, breath for breath, thud for thud of the heart, using a single heart. It was not alone all those thirty years which she did not know, but all those successions of thirty years before that which had put that stain either on his white blood or his black blood, whichever you will, and which killed him. But he must have run with believing for a while; anyway, with hope. But his blood would not be quiet, let him save it. It would not be either one or the other and let his body save itself. Because the black blood drove him first to the negro cabin. And then the white blood drove him out of there, as it was the black blood which snatched up the pistol and the white blood which would not let him fire it. And it was the white blood which sent him to the minister, which rising in him for the last and final time, sent him against all reason and all reality, into the embrace of a chimaera, a blind faith in something read in a printed Book. Then I believe that the white blood deserted him for the moment. Just a second, a flicker, allowing the black to rise in its final moment and make him turn upon that on which he had postulated his hope of salvation. It was the black blood which swept him by his own desire beyond the aid of any man, swept him up into that ecstasy out of a black jungle where life has already ceased before the heart stops and death is desire and fulfillment. And then the black blood failed him again, as it must have in crises all his life. He did not kill the minister. He merely struck him with the pistol and ran on and crouched behind that table and defied the black blood for the last time, as he had been defying it for thirty years. He crouched behind that overturned table and let them shoot him to death, with that loaded and unfired pistol in his hand."

In the town on that day lived a young man named Percy Grimm. He was about twentyfive and a captain in the State national guard. He had been born in the town and had lived there all his life save for the periods of the summer encamp-

ments. He was too young to have been in the European War,
though it was not until 1921 or '22 that he realised that he
would never forgive his parents for that fact. His father, a
hardware merchant, did not understand this. He thought that
the boy was just lazy and in a fair way to become perfectly
worthless, when in reality the boy was suffering the terrible
tragedy of having been born not alone too late but not late
enough to have escaped first hand knowledge of the lost time
when he should have been a man instead of a child. And now,
with the hysteria passed away and the ones who had been
loudest in the hysteria and even the ones, the heroes who had
suffered and served, beginning to look at one another a little
askance, he had no one to tell it, to open his heart to. In fact,
his first serious fight was with an exsoldier who made some
remark to the effect that if he had to do it again, he would
fight this time on the German side and against France. At
once Grimm took him up. "Against America too?" he said.

"If America's fool enough to help France out again," the
soldier said. Grimm struck him at once; he was smaller than
the soldier, still in his teens. The result was foregone; even
Grimm doubtless knew that. But he took his punishment
until even the soldier begged the bystanders to hold the boy
back. And he wore the scars of that battle as proudly as he
was later to wear the uniform itself for which he had blindly
fought.

It was the new civilian-military act which saved him. He
was like a man who had been for a long time in a swamp, in
the dark. It was as though he not only could see no path
ahead of him, he knew that there was none. Then suddenly
his life opened definite and clear. The wasted years in which
he had shown no ability in school, in which he had been
known as lazy, recalcitrant, without ambition, were behind
him, forgotten. He could now see his life opening before
him, uncomplex and inescapable as a barren corridor, completely freed now of ever again having to think or decide, the
burden which he now assumed and carried as bright and
weightless and martial as his insignatory brass: a sublime and
implicit faith in physical courage and blind obedience, and a
belief that the white race is superior to any and all other races
and that the American is superior to all other white races and

that the American uniform is superior to all men, and that all that would ever be required of him in payment for this belief, this privilege, would be his own life. On each national holiday that had any martial flavor whatever he dressed in his captain's uniform and came down town. And those who saw him remembered him again on the day of the fight with the exsoldier as, glittering, with his marksman's badge (he was a fine shot) and his bars, grave, erect, he walked among the civilians with about him an air half belligerent and half the selfconscious pride of a boy.

He was not a member of the American Legion, but that was his parents' fault and not his. But when Christmas was fetched back from Mottstown on that Saturday afternoon, he had already been to the commander of the local Post. His idea, his words, were quite simple and direct. "We got to preserve order," he said. "We must let the law take its course. The law, the nation. It is the right of no civilian to sentence a man to death. And we, the soldiers in Jefferson, are the ones to see to that."

"How do you know that anybody is planning anything different?" the legion commander said. "Have you heard any talk?"

"I dont know. I haven't listened." He didn't lie. It was as though he did not attach enough importance to what might or might not have been said by the civilian citizens to lie about it. "That's not the question. It's whether or not we, as soldiers, that have worn the uniform, are going to be the first to state where we stand. To show these people right off just where the government of the country stands on such things. That there wont be any need for them even to talk." His plan was quite simple. It was to form the legion Post into a platoon, with himself in command vide his active commission. "But if they dont want me to command, that's all right too. I'll be second, if they say. Or a sergeant or a corporal." And he meant it. It was not vainglory that he wanted. He was too sincere. So sincere, so humorless, that the legion commander withheld the flippant refusal he was about to make.

"I still dont think that there is any need of it. And if there was, we would all have to act as civilians. I couldn't use the

Post like that. After all, we are not soldiers now. I dont think I would, if I could."

Grimm looked at him, without anger, but rather as if he were some kind of bug. "Yet you wore the uniform once," he said, with a kind of patience. He said: "I suppose you wont use your authority to keep me from talking to them, will you? As individuals?"

"No. I haven't any authority to do that, anyway. But just as individuals, mind. You mustn't use my name at all."

Then Grimm gave him a shot on his own account. "I am not likely to do that," he said. Then he was gone. That was Saturday, about four oclock. For the rest of that afternoon he circulated about the stores and offices where the legion members worked, so that by nightfall he had enough of them also worked up to his own pitch to compose a fair platoon. He was indefatiguable, restrained yet forceful; there was something about him irresistible and prophetlike. Yet the recruits were with the commander in one thing: the official designation of the legion must be kept out of it——whereupon and without deliberate intent, he had gained his original end: he was now in command. He got them all together just before suppertime and divided them into squads and appointed officers and a staff; the younger ones, the ones who had not gone to France, taking proper fire by now. He addressed them, briefly, coldly: ". . . . . . .order. . . . . . .course of justice. . . . . .let the people see that we who have worn the uniform of the United States. . . . . . And one thing more." For the moment now he had descended to familiarity: the regimental commander who knows his men by their first names. "I'll leave this to you fellows. I'll do what you say. I thought it might be a good thing if I wear my uniform until this business is settled. So they can see that Uncle Sam is present in more than spirit."

"But he's not," one said quickly, immediately; he was of the same cut as the commander, who by the way was not present. "This is not government trouble yet. Kennedy might not like it. This is Jefferson's trouble, not Washington's."

"Make him like it," Grimm said. "What does your legion stand for, if not for the protection of America and Americans?"

"No," the other said. "I reckon we better not make a parade out of this. We can do what we want without that. Better. Aint that right, boys?"

"All right," Grimm said. "I'll do as you say. But every man will want a pistol. We'll have a small arms' inspection here in one hour. Every man will report here."

"What's Kennedy going to say about pistols?" one said.

"I'll see to that," Grimm said. "Report here in one hour exactly, with side arms." He dismissed them. He crossed the quiet square to the sheriff's office. The sheriff was at home, they told him. "At home?" he repeated. "Now? What's he doing at home now?"

"Eating, I reckon. A man as big as him has got to eat several times a day."

"At home," Grimm repeated. He did not glare; it was again that cold and detached expression with which he had looked at the legion commander. "Eating," he said. He went out, already walking fast. He recrossed the empty square, the quiet square empty of people peacefully at suppertables about that peaceful town and that peaceful country. He went to the sheriff's home. The sheriff said No at once.

"Fifteen or twenty folks milling around the square with pistols in their pants? No, no. That wont do. I cant have that. That wont do. You let me run this."

For a moment longer Grimm looked at the sheriff. Then he turned, already walking fast again. "All right," he said. "If that's the way you want it. I dont interfere with you and you dont interfere with me, then." It didn't sound like a threat. It was too flat, too final, too without heat. He went on, rapidly. The sheriff watched him; then he called. Grimm turned.

"You leave yours at home, too," the sheriff said. "You hear me?" Grimm didn't answer. He went on. The sheriff watched him out of sight, frowning.

That evening after supper the sheriff went back downtown—something he had not done for years save when urgent and inescapable business called. He found a picket of Grimm's men at the jail, and another in the courthouse, and a third patrolling the square and the adjacent streets. The others, the relief, they told the sheriff, were in the cotton office where Grimm was employed, which they were using for an orderly room, a P.C. The sheriff met Grimm on the street, making a round of inspection. "Come here, boy," the sheriff said. Grimm halted. He did not approach; the sheriff went to him. He patted Grimm's hip with a fat hand. "I told you to leave that at home," he said. Grimm said nothing. He watched the sheriff levelly. The sheriff sighed. "Well, if you wont, I reckon I'll have to make you a special deputy. But you aint to even show that gun unless I tell you to. You hear me?"

"Certainly not," Grimm said. "You certainly wouldn't want me to draw it if I didn't see any need to."

"I mean, not till I tell you to."

"Certainly," Grimm said, without heat, patiently, immediately. "That's what we both said. Dont you worry. I'll be there."

Later, as the town quieted for the night, as the picture show emptied and the drug stores closed one by one, Grimm's platoon began to drop off too. He did not protest, watching them coldly; they became a little sheepish, defensive. Again without knowing it he had played a trump card. Because of the fact that they felt sheepish, feeling that somehow they had fallen short of his own cold ardor, they would return tomorrow if just to show him. A few remained; it was Saturday night anyhow, and someone got more chairs from somewhere and they started a poker game. It ran all night, though from time to time Grimm (he was not in the game; neither would he permit his second in command, the only other there who held the equivalent of commissioned rank, to engage) sent a squad out to make a patrol of the square. By this time the night marshal was one of them, though he too did not take a hand in the game.

Sunday was quiet. The poker game ran quietly through that day, broken by the periodical patrols, while the quiet church bells rang and the congregations gathered in decorous clumps of summer colors. About the square it was already known that the special Grand Jury would meet tomorrow. Somehow the very sound of the two words with their evocation secret and irrevocable and something of a hidden and unsleeping and omnipotent eye watching the doings of men, began to reassure Grimm's men in their own makebelieve. So quickly is man unwittingly and unpredictably moved that without knowing that they were thinking it, the town had suddenly accepted Grimm with respect and perhaps a little awe and a deal of actual faith and confidence, as though somehow his vision and patriotism and pride in the town, the occasion, had been quicker and truer than theirs. His men anyway assumed and accepted this; after the sleepless night, the tenseness, the holiday, the suttee of volition's surrender, they were almost at the pitch where they might die for him, if occasion rose. They now moved in a grave and slightly awe-inspiring reflected light which was almost as palpable as the khaki would have been which Grimm wished them to wear, wished that they wore, as though each time they returned to the orderly room they dressed themselves anew in suave and austerely splendid scraps of his dream.

This lasted through Sunday night. The poker game ran. The caution, the surreptitiousness, which had clothed it was now gone. There was something about it too assured and serenely confident to be braggadocio; tonight when they heard the marshal's feet on the stairs, one said, "Ware M.P.'s" and for an instant they glanced at one another with hard, bright, daredevil eyes; then one said, quite loud: "Throw the son of a bitch out" and another through pursed lips made the immemorial sound. And so the next morning, Monday, when the first country cars and wagons began to gather, the platoon was again intact. And they now wore uniforms. It was their faces. Most of them were of an age, a generation, an experience. But it was more than that. They now had a profound and bleak gravity as they stood where crowds milled, grave, austere, detached, looking with blank, bleak eyes at the slow throngs who, feeling, sensing without knowing, drifted before them, slowing, staring, so that they would be ringed with faces rapt and empty and immobile as the faces of cows, approaching and drifting on, to be replaced. And all morning the voices came and went, in quiet question and answer: "There he goes. That young fellow with the automatic pistol. He's the captain of them. Special officer sent by the governor. He's the head of the whole thing. Sheriff aint got no say in it today."

Later, when it was too late, Grimm told the sheriff: "If you had just listened to me. Let me bring him out of that cell in a squad of men, instead of sending him across the square with one deputy and not even handcuffed to him, in all that crowd where that damned Buford didn't dare shoot, even if he could hit a barn door."

"How did I know he aimed to break, would think of trying it right then and there?" the sheriff said. "When Stevens had done told me he would plead guilty and take a life sentence."

But it was too late then. It was all over then. It happened in the middle of the square, halfway between the sidewalk and the courthouse, in the midst of a throng of people thick as on Fair Day, though the first that Grimm knew of it was when he heard the deputy's pistol twice, fired into the air. He knew at once what had happened, though he was at the time inside the courthouse. His reaction was definite and immediate. He was already running toward the shots when he shouted back over his shoulder at the man who had tagged him now for almost fortyeight hours as half aide and half orderly: "Turn in the fire alarm!"

"The fire alarm?" the aide said. "What——"

"Turn in the fire alarm!" Grimm shouted back. "It dont matter what folks think, just so they know that something. . . . . ." He did not finish; he was gone.

He ran among running people, overtaking and passing them, since he had an objective and they did not; they were just running, the black, blunt, huge automatic opening a way for him like a plow. They looked at his tense, hard, young face with faces blanched and gaped, with round, toothed orifices; they made one long sound like a murmuring sigh: "There. . . . . .went that way. . . . . ." But already Grimm had seen the deputy, running, his pistol aloft in his hand. Grimm glanced once about and sprang forward again; in the throng which had evidently been pacing the deputy and the prisoner across the square was the inevitable hulking youth in the uniform of the Western Union, leading his bicycle by the horns like a docile cow. Grimm rammed the pistol back into the holster and flung the boy aside and sprang onto the bicycle, with never a break in motion.

The bicycle possessed neither horn nor bell. Yet they sensed him somehow and made way; in this too he seemed to be served by certitude, the blind and untroubled faith in the rightness and infallibility of his actions. When he overtook the running deputy he slowed the bicycle. The deputy turned upon him a face sweating, gaped with shouting and running. "He turned," the deputy screamed. "Into that alley by——"

"I know," Grimm said. "Was he handcuffed?"

"Yes!" the deputy said. The bicycle leaped on.

'Then he cant run very fast,' Grimm thought. 'He'll have to hole up soon. Get out of the open, anyway.' He turned into the alley, fast. It ran back between two houses, with a board fence on one side. At that moment the fire siren sounded for the first time, beginning and mounting to a slow and sustained scream that seemed at last to pass beyond the realm of hearing, into that of sense, like soundless vibration. Grimm wheeled on, thinking swiftly, logically, with a kind of fierce and constrained joy. 'The first thing he will want is to get out of sight,' he thought, looking about. On one hand the lane was open, on the other stood the board fence six feet high. At the end it was cut short off by a wooden gate, beyond which was a pasture and then a deep ditch which was a town landmark. The tops of tall trees which grew in it just showed above the rim; a regiment could hide and deploy in it. "Ah," he said, aloud. Without stopping or slowing he swept the bicycle around and pedalled back down the lane toward the street which he had just quitted. The wail of the siren was dying now, descending back into hearing again, and as he slewed the bicycle into the street he saw briefly the running people and a car bearing down upon him. For all his pedalling the car overtook him; its occupants leaned shouting toward his set, forwardlooking face. "Get in here!" they shouted. "In here!" He did not answer. He did not look at them. The car had overshot him, slowing; now he passed it at his swift, silent, steady pace; again the car speeded up and passed him, the men leaning out and looking ahead. He was going fast too, silent, with the delicate swiftness of an apparition, the implacable undeviation of Juggernaut or Fate. Behind him the siren began again its rising wail. When next the men in the car looked back for him, he had vanished completely.

He had turned full speed into another lane. His face was

rocklike, calm, still bright with that expression of fulfillment, of grave and reckless joy. This lane was more rutted than the other, and deeper. It came out at last upon a barren knoll where, springing to earth while the bicycle shot on, falling, he could see the full span of the ravine along the edge of town, his view of it broken by two or three negro cabins which lined the edge of it. He was quite motionless, still, alone, fateful, like a landmark almost. Again from the town behind him the scream of the siren began to fall.

Then he saw Christmas. He saw the man, small with distance, appear up out of the ditch, his hands close together. As Grimm watched he saw the fugitive's hands glint once like the flash of a heliograph as the sun struck the handcuffs, and it seemed to him that even from here he could hear the panting and desperate breath of the man who even now was not free. Then the tiny figure ran again and vanished beyond the nearest negro cabin.

Grimm ran too now. He ran swiftly, yet there was no haste about him, no effort. There was nothing vengeful about him either, no fury, no outrage. Christmas saw that, himself. Because for an instant they looked at one another almost face to face. That was when Grimm, running, was in the act of passing beyond the corner of the cabin. At that instant Christmas leaped from the rear window of it, with an effect as of magic, his manacled hands high and now glinting as if they were on fire. For an instant they glared at one another, the one stopped in the act of crouching from the leap, the other in midstride of running, before Grimm's momentum carried him past the corner. In that instant he saw that Christmas now carried a heavy nickelplated pistol. Grimm whirled and turned and sprang back past the corner, drawing the automatic.

He was thinking swiftly, calmly, with that quiet joy: 'He can do two things. He can try for the ditch again, or he can dodge around the house until one of us gets a shot. And the ditch is on his side of the house.' He reacted immediately. He ran at full speed around the corner which he had just turned. He did it as though under the protection of a magic or a providence, or as if he knew that Christmas would not be waiting there with the pistol. He ran on past the next corner without pausing.

He was beside the ditch now. He stopped, motionless in midstride. Above the blunt, cold rake of the automatic his face had that serene, unearthly luminousness of angels in church windows. He was moving again almost before he had stopped, with that lean, swift, blind obedience to whatever Player moved him on the Board. He ran to the ditch. But in the beginning of his plunge downward into the brush that choked the steep descent he turned, clawing. He saw now that the cabin sat some two feet above the earth. He had not noticed it before, in his haste. He knew now that he had lost a point. That Christmas had been watching his legs all the time beneath the house. He said, "Good man."

His plunge carried him some distance before he could stop himself and climb back out. He seemed indefatiguable, not flesh and blood, as if the Player who moved him for pawn likewise found him breath. Without a pause, in the same surge that carried him up out of the ditch again, he was running again. He ran around the cabin in time to see Christmas fling himself over a fence three hundred yards away. He did not fire, because Christmas was now running through a small garden and straight toward a house. Running, he saw Christmas leap up the back steps and enter the house. "Hah," Grimm said. "The preacher's house. Hightower's house."

He did not slow, though he swerved and ran around the house and to the street. The car which had passed him and lost him and then returned was just where it should have been, just where the Player had desired it to be. It stopped without signal from him and three men got out. Without a word Grimm turned and ran across the yard and into the house where the old disgraced minister lived alone, and the three men followed, rushing into the hall, pausing, bringing with them into its stale and cloistral dimness something of the savage summer sunlight which they had just left.

It was upon them, of them: its shameless savageness. Out of it their faces seemed to glare with bodiless suspension as though from haloes as they stooped and raised Hightower, his face bleeding, from the floor where Christmas, running up the hall, his raised and armed and manacled hands full of glare and glitter like lightning bolts, so that he resembled a vengeful and furious god pronouncing a doom, had struck him down. They held the old man on his feet.

"Which room?" Grimm said, shaking him. "Which room, old man?"

"Gentlemen!" Hightower said. Then he said: "Men! Men!"

"Which room, old man?" Grimm shouted.

They held Hightower on his feet; in the gloomy hall, after the sunlight, he too with his bald head and his big pale face streaked with blood, was terrible. "Men!" he cried. "Listen to me. He was here that night. He was with me the night of the murder. I swear to God——"

"Jesus Christ!" Grimm cried, his young voice clear and outraged like that of a young priest. "Has every preacher and old maid in Jefferson taken their pants down to the yellowbellied son of a bitch?" He flung the old man aside and ran on.

It was as though he had been merely waiting for the Player to move him again, because with that unfailing certitude he ran straight to the kitchen and into the doorway, already firing, almost before he could have seen the table overturned and standing on its edge across the corner of the room, and the bright and glittering hands of the man who crouched behind it, resting upon the upper edge. Grimm emptied the automatic's magazine into the table; later someone covered all five shots with a folded handkerchief.

But the Player was not done yet. When the others reached the kitchen they saw the table flung aside now and Grimm stooping over the body. When they approached to see what he was about, they saw that the man was not dead yet, and when they saw what Grimm was doing one of the men gave a choked cry and stumbled back into the wall and began to vomit. Then Grimm too sprang back, flinging behind him the bloody butcher knife. "Now you'll let white women alone, even in hell," he said. But the man on the floor had not moved. He just lay there, with his eyes open and empty of everything save consciousness, and with something, a shadow, about his mouth. For a long moment he looked up at them with peaceful and unfathomable and unbearable eyes.

Then his face, body, all, seemed to collapse, to fall in upon itself, and from out the slashed garments about his hips and loins the pent black blood seemed to rush like a released breath. It seemed to rush out of his pale body like the rush of sparks from a rising rocket; upon that black blast the man seemed to rise soaring into their memories forever and ever. They are not to lose it, in whatever peaceful valleys, beside whatever placid and reassuring streams of old age, in the mirroring faces of whatever children they will contemplate old disasters and newer hopes. It will be there, musing, quiet, steadfast, not fading and not particularly threatful, but of itself alone serene, of itself alone triumphant. Again from the town, deadened a little by the walls, the scream of the siren mounted toward its unbelievable crescendo, passing out of the realm of hearing.

XX

NOW THE FINAL copper light of afternoon fades; now the street beyond the low maples and the low signboard is prepared and empty, framed by the study window like a stage.

He can remember how when he was young, after he first came to Jefferson from the seminary, how that fading copper light would seem almost audible, like a dying yellow fall of trumpets dying into an interval of silence and waiting, out of which they would presently come. Already, even before the falling horns had ceased, it would seem to him that he could hear the beginning thunder not yet louder than a whisper, a rumor, in the air.

But he had never told anyone that. Not even her. Not even her in the days when they were still the night's lovers, and shame and division had not come and she knew and had not forgot with division and regret and then despair, why he would sit here at this window and wait for nightfall, for the instant of night. Not even to her, to woman. *The* woman. Woman (not the seminary, as he had once believed): the Passive and Anonymous whom God had created to be not alone the recipient and receptacle of the seed of his body but of his spirit too, which is truth or as near truth as he dare approach.

He was an only child. When he was born his father was fifty years old, and his mother had been an invalid for almost twenty years. He grew up to believe that this was the result of the food which she had had to subsist on during the last year of the Civil War. Perhaps this was the reason. His father had owned no slaves, though he was the son of a man who did own slaves at the time. He could have owned them. But though born and bred and dwelling in an age and land where to own slaves was less expensive than to not own them, he would neither eat food grown and cooked by, nor sleep in a bed prepared by, a negro slave. Hence during the war and while he was absent from home, his wife had no garden save what she could make herself or with the infrequent aid of neighbors. And this aid the husband would not allow her to accept for the reason that it could not be repaid in kind. "God will provide," he said.

"Provide what? Dandelions and ditch weeds?"

"Then He will give us the bowels to digest them."

He was a minister. For a year he had been leaving home early each Sunday morning before his father (this was before the son's marriage) who though a member in good standing of the Episcopal church had not entered any church since the son could remember, discovered where he went. He found that the son, then just turned twentyone, was riding sixteen miles each Sunday to preach in a small Presbyterian chapel back in the hills. The father laughed. The son listened to the laughter as he would if it had been shouts or curses: with a cold and respectful detachment, saying nothing. The next Sunday he went back to his congregation.

When the war began, the son was not among the first to go. Neither was he among the last. And he stayed with the troops for four years, though he fired no musket and wore instead of uniform the somber frock coat which he had purchased to be married in and which he had used to preach in. When he returned home in '65 he still wore it, though he never put it on again after that day when the wagon stopped at the front steps and two men lifted him down and carried him into the house and laid him on the bed. His wife removed the coat and put it away in a trunk in the attic. It stayed there for twentyfive years, until one day his son opened the trunk and took it out and spread out the careful folds in which it had been arranged by hands that were now dead.

He remembers it now, sitting in the dark window in the quiet study, waiting for twilight to cease, for night and the galloping hooves. The copper light has completely gone now; the world hangs in a green suspension in color and texture like light through colored glass. Soon it will be time to begin to say *Soon now. Now soon* 'I was eight then,' he thinks. 'It was raining.' It seems to him that he can still smell the rain, the moist grieving of the October earth, and the musty yawn as the lid of the trunk went back. Then the garment, the neat folds. He did not know what it was, because at first he was almost overpowered by the evocation of his dead mother's hands which lingered among the folds. Then it opened, tumbling slowly. To him, the child, it seemed unbelievably huge, as though made for a giant; as though merely from having been worn by one of them, the cloth itself had assumed the properties of those phantoms who loomed heroic and tremendous against a background of thunder and smoke and torn flags which now filled his waking and sleeping life.

The garment was almost unrecognisable with patches. Patches of leather, mansewn and crude, patches of Confederate grey weathered leafbrown now, and one that stopped his very heart: it was blue, dark blue; the blue of the United States. Looking at this patch, at the mute and anonymous cloth, the boy, the child born into the autumn of his mother's and father's lives, whose organs already required the unflagging care of a Swiss watch, would experience a kind of hushed and triumphant terror which left him a little sick.

That evening at supper he would be unable to eat. Looking up, the father, now a man nearing sixty, would find the child staring at him with terror and awe and with something else. Then the man would say, "What have you been into now?" and the child could not answer, could not speak, staring at his father with on his child's face an expression as of the Pit itself. That night in bed he would not be able to sleep. He would lie rigid, not even trembling, in his dark bed while the man who was his father and his only remaining relative, and between whom and himself there was so much of distance in time that not even the decades of years could measure, that there was not even any physical resemblance, slept walls and floors away. And the next day the child would suffer one of his intestinal fits. But he would not tell what it was, not even to the negro woman who ran the household and who was his mother too and nurse. Gradually his strength would return. And then one day he would steal again to the attic and open the trunk and take out the coat and touch the blue patch with that horrified triumph and sick joy and wonder if his father had killed the man from whose blue coat the patch came, wondering with still more horror yet at the depth and strength of his desire and dread to know. Yet on the very next day, when he knew that his father had gone to call upon one of his country patients and would not possibly return before dark, he would go to the kitchen and say to the negro woman: "Tell again about grandpa. How many Yankees did he kill?" And when he listened now it was without terror. It was not even triumph: it was pride.

This grandfather was the single thorn in his son's side. The son would no more have said that than he would have thought it, anymore than it would ever have occurred to either of them to wish mutually that he had been given a different son or a different father. Their relations were peaceable enough, being on the son's part a cold, humorless, automatically respectful reserve, and on the father's a bluff, direct, coarsely vivid humor which lacked less of purport than wit. They lived amicably enough in the two-storey house in town, though for some time now the son had refused, quiet and firm, to eat any food prepared by the slave woman who had raised him from babyhood. He cooked his own food in the kitchen, to the negress' outraged indignation, and put it on the table himself and ate it face to face with his father, who saluted him punctiliously and unfailingly with a glass of bourbon whiskey: this too the son did not touch and had never tasted.

On the son's wedding day the father surrendered the house. He was waiting on the porch, with the key to the house in his hand, when the bride and groom arrived. He wore his hat and cloak. About him was piled his personal luggage and behind him stood the two slaves which he owned: the negro woman who cooked, and his 'boy', a man older than himself and who did not have one remaining hair, who was the cook's husband. He was not a planter: he was a lawyer, who had learned law somewhat as his son was to learn medicine, "by main strength and the devil's grace and luck" as he put it. He had already bought for himself a small house two miles in the country, and his surrey and his matched team stood before the porch waiting while he too stood, his hat tilted back and his legs apart—a hale, bluff, rednosed man with the moustache of a brigand chief—while the son, and the daughter-in-law whom he had never seen before, came up the path from the gate. When he stooped and saluted her, she smelled whiskey and cigars. "I reckon you'll do," he said. His eyes were bluff and bold, but kind. "All the sanctimonious cuss wants anyway is somebody that can sing alto out of a Presbyterian hymnbook, where even the good Lord Himself couldn't squeeze in any music."

He drove away in the tasselled surrey, with his personal belongings about him—his clothes, his demijohn, his slaves. The slave cook did not even remain to prepare the first meal. She was not offered, and so not refused. The father never entered the house again alive. He would have been welcome. He and the son both knew this, without it ever being said. And the wife—she was one of many children of a genteel couple who had never got ahead and who seemed to find in the church some substitute for that which lacked upon the dinnertable—liked him, admired him in a hushed, alarmed, secret way: his swagger, his bluff and simple adherence to a simple code. They would hear of his doings though, of how in the next summer after he removed to the country he invaded a protracted al fresco church revival being held in a nearby grove and turned it into a week of amateur horse racing while to a dwindling congregation gaunt, fanaticfaced country preachers thundered anathema from the rustic pulpit at his oblivious and unregenerate head. His reason for not visiting his son and his daughter-in-law was apparently frank: "You'd find me dull and I'd find you dull. And who knows? the cuss might corrupt me. Might corrupt me in my old age into heaven." But that was not the reason. The son knew that it was not, who would have been first to fight the aspersion were it to come from another: that there was delicacy of behavior and thought in the old man.

The son was an abolitionist almost before the sentiment had become a word to percolate down from the North. Though when he learned that the Republicans did have a name for it, he completely changed the name of his conviction without abating his principles or behavior one jot. Even then, not yet thirty, he was a man of spartan sobriety beyond his years, as the offspring of a not overly particular servant of Chance and the bottle often is. Perhaps that accounted for the fact that he had no child until after the war, from which he returned a changed man, 'deodorised,' as his dead father would have put it, of sanctity somewhat. Although during those four years he had never fired a gun, his service was not alone that of praying and preaching to troops on Sunday mornings. When he returned home with his wound and re-covered and established himself as a doctor, he was only prac-tising the surgery and the pharmacy which he had practised and learned on the bodies of friend and foe alike while help-ing the doctors at the front. This probably of all the son's doings the father would have enjoyed the most: that the son had taught himself a profession on the invader and devastator of his country.

'But sanctity is not the word for him,' the son's son in turn thinks, sitting at the dark window while outside the world hangs in that green suspension beyond the faded trumpets. 'Grandfather himself would have been the first to confront any man that employed that term.' It was some throwback to the austere and not dim times not so long passed, when a man in that country had little of himself to waste and little time to do it in, and had to guard and protect that little not only from nature but from man too, by means of a sheer for-titude that did not offer, in his lifetime anyway, physical ease for reward. That was where his disapproval of slavery lay, and of his lusty and sacrilegious father. The very fact that he could and did see no paradox in the fact that he took an active part in a partisan war and on the very side whose principles op-posed his own, was proof enough that he was two separate and complete people, one of whom dwelled by serene rules in a world where reality did not exist.

But the other part of him, which lived in the actual world, did as well as any and better than most. He lived by his prin-ciples in peace, and when war came he carried them into war and lived by them there; when there was preaching on peace-ful Sundays in quiet groves to be done, he had done it, with-out any particular equipment for it other than his will and his convictions and what he could pick up as he went along; when there was the saving of wounded men under fire and the curing of them without proper tools, he did that too, again without other equipment save his strength and courage and what he could pick up as he went along. And when the war was lost and the other men returned home with their eyes stubbornly reverted toward what they refused to believe was dead, he looked forward and made what he could of defeat by making practical use of that which he had learned in it.

He turned doctor. One of his first patients was his wife. Possibly he kept her alive. At least, he enabled her to produce life, though he was fifty and she past forty when the son was born. That son grew to manhood among phantoms, and side by side with a ghost.

The phantoms were his father, his mother, and an old negro woman. The father who had been a minister without a church and a soldier without an enemy, and who in defeat had combined the two and become a doctor, a surgeon. It was as though the very cold and uncompromising conviction which propped him upright, as it were, between puritan and cavalier, had become not defeated and not discouraged, but wiser. As though it had seen in the smoke of cannon as in a vision that the layingon of hands meant literally that. As if he came suddenly to believe that Christ had meant that him whose spirit alone required healing, was not worth the having, the saving. That was one phantom. The second was the mother whom he remembers first and last as a thin face and tremendous eyes and a spread of dark hair on a pillow, with blue, still, almost skeleton hands. If on the day of her death he had been told that he had ever seen her otherwise than in bed, he would not have believed it. Later he remembered differently: he did remember her moving, about the house, attending to household affairs. But at eight and nine and ten he thought of her as without legs, feet; as being only that thin face and the two eyes which seemed daily to grow bigger and bigger, as though about to embrace all seeing, all life, with one last terrible glare of frustration and suffering and foreknowledge, and that when that finally happened, he would hear it: it would be a sound, like a cry. Already, before she died, he could feel them through all walls. They were the house: he dwelled within them, within their dark and allembracing and patient aftermath of physical betrayal. He and she both lived in them like two small, weak beasts in a den, a cavern, into which now and then the father entered—that man who was a stranger to them both, a foreigner, almost a threat: so quickly does the body's wellbeing alter and change the spirit. He was more than a stranger: he was an enemy. He smelled differently from them. He spoke with a different voice, almost in different words, as though he dwelled by

ordinary among different surroundings and in a different
world; crouching beside the bed the child could feel the man
fill the room with rude health and unconscious contempt, he
too as helpless and frustrated as they.

The third phantom was the negro woman, the slave, who
had ridden away in the surrey that morning when the son and
his bride came home. She rode away a slave; she returned in
'66 still a slave, on foot now—a huge woman, with a face
both irascible and calm: the mask of a black tragedy between
scenes. After her master's death and until she was convinced
at last that she would never more see either him or her husband,—the 'boy', who had followed the master to the war
and who also did not return—she refused to leave the house
in the country to which her master had moved and of which
he had left in her charge when he rode away. After the father's death the son went out, to close the house and remove
his father's private possessions, and he offered to make pro-
vision for her. She refused. She also refused to leave. She
made her own small kitchen garden and she lived there, alone,
waiting for her husband to return, the rumor of whose death
she refused to believe. It was just rumor, vague: how, following his master's death in Van Dorn's cavalry raid to destroy
Grant's stores in Jefferson, the negro had been inconsolable.
One night he disappeared from the bivouac. Presently there
began to come back tales of a crazy negro who had been
halted by Confederate pickets close to the enemy's front, who
told the same garbled story about a missing master who was
being held for ransom by the Yankees. They could not make
him even entertain for a moment the idea that the master
might be dead. "No, suh," he would say. "Not Marse Gail.
Not him. Dey wouldn't *dare* to kill a Hightower. Dey
wouldn't *dare*. Dey got im hid somewhar, tryin to sweat
outen him whar me and him hid Mistis' coffee pot and de
gole waiter. Dat's all dey wants." Each time he would escape.
Then one day word came back from the Federal lines of a
negro who had attacked a Yankee officer with a shovel, forcing the officer to shoot him to protect his own life.

The woman would not believe this for a long time. "Not
dat he aint fool enough to done it," she said. "He jest aint
got ernough sense to know a Yankee to hit at wid a shovel if

he wuz to see um." She said that for over a year. Then one day she appeared at the son's home, the house which she had quitted ten years ago and had not entered since, carrying her possessions in a handkerchief. She walked into the house and said: "Here I is. You got ernough wood in de box ter cook supper wid?"

"You're free, now," the son told her.

"Free?" she said. She spoke with still and brooding scorn. "Free? Whut's freedom done except git Marse Gail killed and made a bigger fool outen Pawmp den even de Lawd Hisself could do? Free? Dont talk ter me erbout freedom."

This was the third phantom. With this phantom the child ('and he little better than a phantom too, then,' that same child now thinks beside the fading window) talked about the ghost. They never tired: the child with rapt, wide, half dread and half delight, and the old woman with musing and savage sorrow and pride. But this to the child was just peaceful shuddering, of delight. He found no terror in the knowledge that his grandfather on the contrary had killed men 'by the hundreds' as he was told and believed, or in the fact that the negro Pomp had been trying to kill a man when he died. No horror here because they were just ghosts, never seen in the flesh, heroic, simple, warm; while the father which he knew and feared was a phantom which would never die. 'So it's no wonder,' he thinks, 'that I skipped a generation. It's no wonder that I had no father and that I had already died one night twenty years before I saw light. And that my only salvation must be to return to the place to die where my life had already ceased before it began.'

While at the seminary, after he first came there, he often thought how he would tell them, the elders, the high and sanctified men who were the destiny of the church to which he had willingly surrendered. How he would go to them and say, "Listen. God must call me to Jefferson because my life died there, was shot from the saddle of a galloping horse in a Jefferson street one night twenty years before it was ever born." He thought that he could say that, at first. He believed that they would comprehend. He went there, chose that as his vocation, with that as his purpose. But he believed in more than that. He had believed in the church too, in all that it ramified and evoked. He believed with a calm joy that if ever there was shelter, it would be the Church; that if ever truth could walk naked and without shame or fear, it would be in the seminary. When he believed that he had heard the call it seemed to him that he could see his future, his life, intact and on all sides complete and inviolable, like a classic and serene vase, where the spirit could be born anew sheltered from the harsh gale of living and die so, peacefully, with only the far sound of the circumvented wind, with scarce even a handful of rotting dust to be disposed of. That was what the word seminary meant: quiet and safe walls within which the hampered and garmentworried spirit could learn anew serenity to contemplate without horror or alarm its own nakedness.

'But there are more things in heaven and earth too than truth,' he thinks, paraphrases, quietly, not quizzical, not humorous; not unquizzical and not humorless too. Sitting in the failing dusk, his head in its white bandage looming bigger and more ghostly than ever, he thinks, 'More things indeed', thinking how ingenuity was apparently given man in order that he may supply himself in crises with shapes and sounds with which to guard himself from truth. He had at least one thing to not repent: that he had not made the mistake of telling the elders what he had planned to say. He had not needed to live in the seminary a year before he learned better than that. And more, worse: that with the learning of it, instead of losing something he had gained, had escaped from something. And that that gain had colored the very face and shape of love.

She was the daughter of one of the ministers, the teachers, in the college. Like himself, she was an only child. He believed at once that she was beautiful, because he had heard of her before he ever saw her and when he did see her he did not see her at all because of the face which he had already created in his mind. He did not believe that she could have lived there all her life and not be beautiful. He did not see the face itself for three years. By that time there had already been for two years a hollow tree in which they left notes for one another. If he believed about that at all, he believed that the idea had sprung spontaneously between them, regardless of whichever one thought of it, said it, first. But in reality he had got the idea not from her or from himself, but from a book. But he did not see her face at all. He did not see a small oval narrowing too sharply to chin and passionate with discontent (she was a year or two or three older than he was, and he did not know it, was never to know it). He did not see that for three years her eyes had watched him with almost desperate calculation, like those of a harassed gambler.

Then one night he saw her, looked at her. She spoke suddenly and savagely of marriage. It was without preamble or warning. It had never been mentioned between them. He had not even ever thought of it, thought the word. He had accepted it because most of the faculty were married. But to him it was not men and women in sanctified and living physical intimacy, but a dead state carried over into and existing still among the living like two shadows chained together with the shadow of a chain. He was used to that; he had grown up with a ghost. Then one evening she talked suddenly, savagely. When he found out at last what she meant by escape from her present life, he felt no surprise. He was too innocent. "Escape?" he said. "Escape from what?"

"This!" she said. He saw her face for the first time as a living face, as a mask before desire and hatred: wrung, blind, headlong with passion. Not stupid: just blind, reckless, desperate. "All of it! All! All!"

He was not surprised. He believed at once that she was right, and that he just had not known better. He believed at once that his own belief about the seminary had been wrong all the while. Not seriously wrong, but false, incorrect. Perhaps he had already begun to doubt himself, without knowing it until now. Perhaps that was why he had not yet told them why he must go to Jefferson. He had told her, a year ago, why he wanted to, must, go there, and that he intended to tell them the reason, she watching him with those eyes which he had not yet seen. "You mean," he said, "that they would not send me? arrange for me to go? That that would not be reason enough?"

"Certainly it wouldn't," she said.

"But why? That's the truth. Foolish, maybe. But true. And what is the church for, if not to help those who are foolish but who want truth? Why wouldn't they let me go?"

"Why, I wouldn't let you go myself, if I were them and you gave me that as your reason."

"Oh," he said. "I see." But he did not see, exactly, though he believed that he could have been wrong and that she was right. And so when a year later she talked to him suddenly of marriage and escape in the same words, he was not surprised, not hurt. He just thought quietly, 'So this is love. I see. I was wrong about it too', thinking as he had thought before and would think again and as every other man has thought: how false the most profound book turns out to be when applied to life.

He changed completely. They planned to be married. He knew now that he had seen all the while that desperate calculation in her eyes. 'Perhaps they were right in putting love into books,' he thought quietly. 'Perhaps it could not live anywhere else.' The desperation was still in them, but now that there were definite plans, a day set, it was quieter, mostly calculation. They talked now of his ordination, of how he could get Jefferson as his call. "We'd better go to work right away," she said. He told her that he had been working for that since he was four years old; perhaps he was being humorous, whimsical. She brushed it aside with that passionate and leashed humorlessness, almost inattention, talking as though to herself of men, names, to see, to grovel to or threaten, outlining to him a campaign of abasement and plotting. He listened. Even the faint smile, whimsical, quizzical, perhaps of despair, did not leave his face. He said, "Yes. Yes. I see. I understand" as she talked. It was as if he were saying *Yes. I see. I see now. That's how they do such, gain such. That's the rule. I see now*

At first, when the demagoguery, the abasement, the small lying had its reverberation in other small lies and ultimate threats in the form of requests and suggestions among the hierarchate of the Church and he received the call to Jefferson, he forgot how he had got it for the time. He did not remember until after he was settled in Jefferson; certainly not while the train of the journey's last stage fled toward the consummation of his life across a land similar to that where he had been born. But it looked different, though he knew that the difference lay not outside but inside the car window against which his face was almost pressed like that of a child, while his wife beside him had also now something of eagerness in her face, beside hunger and desperation. They had been married now not quite six months. They had married directly after his graduation. Not once since then had he seen the desperation naked in her face. But neither had he seen passion again. And again he thought quietly, without much surprise and perhaps without hurt: *I see. That's the way it is. Marriage. Yes. I see now*

The train rushed on. Leaning to the window, watching the fleeing countryside, he talked in the bright, happy voice of a child: "I could have come to Jefferson before, at almost any time. But I didn't. I could have come at any time. There is a difference, you know, between civilian and military casualness. Military casualness? Ah, it was the casualness of desperation. A handfull of men (he was not an officer: I think that was the only point on which father and old Cinthy were ever in accord: that grandfather wore no sword, galloped with no sword waving in front of the rest of them) performing with the grim levity of schoolboys a prank so foolhardy that the troops who had opposed them for four years did not believe that even they would have attempted it. Riding for a hundred miles through a country where every grove and hamlet had its Yankee bivouac, and into a garrisoned town—I know the very street that they rode into town upon and then out again. I have never seen it, but I know exactly how it will look. I know exactly how the house that we will someday own and live in upon the street will look. It wont be at first, for a while. We will have to live in the parsonage at first. But soon, as soon as we can, where we can look out the window and see the street, maybe even the hoofmarks or their shapes in the air, because the same air will be there even if the dust, the mud, is gone——Hungry, gaunt, yelling, setting fire to the store depots of a whole carefully planned campaign and riding out again. No looting at all: no stopping for even shoes, tobacco. I tell you, they were not men after spoils and glory; they were boys riding the sheer tremendous tidal wave of desperate living. Boys. Because this. This is beautiful. Listen. Try to see it. Here is that fine shape of eternal youth and virginal desire which makes heroes. That makes the doings of heroes

border so close upon the unbelievable that it is no wonder
that their doings must emerge now and then like gunflashes
in the smoke, and that their very physical passing becomes
rumor with a thousand faces before breath is out of them, lest
paradoxical truth outrage itself. Now this is what Cinthy told
me. And I believe. I know. It's too fine to doubt. It's too
fine, too simple, ever to have been invented by white thinking. A negro might have invented it. And if Cinthy did, I still
believe. Because even fact cannot stand with it. I dont know
whether grandfather's squadron were lost or not. I dont think
so. I think that they did it deliberately, as boys who had set
fire to an enemy's barn, without taking so much as a shingle
or a door hasp, might pause in flight to steal a few apples
from a neighbor, a friend. Mind you, they were hungry. They
had been hungry for three years. Perhaps they were used to
that. Anyway, they had just set fire to tons of food and clothing and tobacco and liquors, taking nothing though there had
not been issued any order against looting, and they turn now,
with all that for background, backdrop: the consternation, the
conflagration; the sky itself must have been on fire. You can
see it, hear it: the shouts, the shots, the shouting of triumph
and terror, the drumming hooves, the trees uprearing against
that red glare as though fixed too in terror, the sharp gables
of houses like the jagged edge of the exploding and ultimate
earth. Now it is a close place: you can feel, hear in the darkness horses pulled short up, plunging; clashes of arms; whispers overloud, hard breathing, the voices still triumphant;
behind them the rest of the troops galloping past toward the
rallying bugles. That you must hear, feel: then you see. You
see before the crash, in the abrupt red glare the horses with
wide eyes and nostrils in tossing heads, sweatstained; the
gleam of metal, the white gaunt faces of living scarecrows
who have not eaten all they wanted at one time since they
could remember; perhaps some of them had already dismounted, perhaps one or two had already entered the hen-
house. All this you see before the crash of the shotgun
comes: then blackness again. It was just the one shot. 'And
of course he would be right in de way of hit,' Cinthy said.
'Stealin chickens. A man growed, wid a married son, gone to
a war whar his business was killin Yankees, killed in some-

body else's henhouse wid a han'full of feathers.' Stealing
chickens." His voice was high, childlike, exalted. Already his
wife was clutching his arm: *Shhhhhhh! Shhhhhhhhh! People
are looking at you!* But he did not seem to hear her at all. His
thin, sick face, his eyes, seemed to exude a kind of glow.
"That was it. They didn't know who fired the shot. They
never did know. They didn't try to find out. It may have
been a woman, likely enough the wife of a Confederate soldier. I like to think so. It's fine so. Any soldier can be killed
by the enemy in the heat of battle, by a weapon approved by
the arbiters and rulemakers of warfare. Or by a woman in a
bedroom. But not with a shotgun, a fowling piece, in a hen-
house. And so is it any wonder that this world is peopled
principally by the dead? Surely, when God looks about at
their successors, He cannot be loath to share His own with
us."

"Hush! Shhhhhhhhh! They are looking at us!"

Then the train was slowing into the town; the dingy purlieus slid vanishing past the window. He still looked out—a
thin, vaguely untidy man with still upon him something yet
of the undimmed glow of his calling, his vocation—quietly
surrounding and enclosing and guarding his urgent heart,
thinking quietly how surely heaven must have something of
the color and shape of whatever village or hill or cottage of
which the believer says, This is my own. The train stopped:
the slow aisle, still interrupted with outlooking, then the descent among faces grave, decorous, and judicial: the voices,
the murmurs, the broken phrases kindly yet still reserved of
judgment, not yet giving and (let us say it) prejudicial. 'I admitted that,' he thinks. 'I believe that I accepted it. But perhaps that was all I did do, God forgive me.' The earth has
almost faded from sight. It is almost night now. His bandage-
distorted head has no depth, no solidity; immobile, it seems
to hang suspended above the twin pale blobs which are his
hands lying upon the ledge of the open window. He leans
forward. Already he can feel the two instants about to touch:
the one which is the sum of his life, which renews itself between each dark and dusk, and the suspended instant out of
which the *soon* will presently begin. When he was younger,
when his net was still too fine for waiting, at this moment he

would sometimes trick himself and believe that he heard them before he knew that it was time.

'Perhaps that is all I ever did, have ever done,' he thinks, thinking of the faces: the faces of old men naturally dubious of his youth and jealous of the church which they were putting into his hands almost as a father surrenders a bride: the faces of old men lined by that sheer accumulation of frustration and doubt which is so often the other side of the picture of hale and respected full years—the side, by the way, which the subject and proprietor of the picture has to look at, cannot escape looking at. 'They did their part; they played by the rules,' he thinks. 'I was the one who failed, who infringed. Perhaps that is the greatest social sin of all; ay, perhaps moral sin.' Thinking goes quietly, tranquilly, flowing on, falling into shapes quiet, not assertive, not reproachful, not particularly regretful. He sees himself a shadowy figure among shadows, paradoxical, with a kind of false optimism and egoism believing that he would find in that part of the Church which most blunders, dreamrecovering, among the blind passions and the lifted hands and voices of men, that which he had failed to find in the Church's cloistered apotheosis upon earth. It seems to him that he has seen it all the while: that that which is destroying the Church is not the outward groping of those within it nor the inward groping of those without, but the professionals who control it and who have removed the bells from its steeples. He seems to see them, endless, without order, empty, symbolical, bleak, skypointed not with ecstasy or passion but in adjuration, threat, and doom. He seems to see the churches of the world like a rampart, like one of those barricades of the middleages planted with dead and sharpened stakes, against truth and against that peace in which to sin and be forgiven which is the life of man.

'And I accepted that,' he thinks. 'I acquiesced. Nay, I did worse: I served it. I served it by using it to forward my own desire. I came here where faces full of bafflement and hunger and eagerness waited for me, waiting to believe; I did not see them. Where hands were raised for what they believed that I would bring them; I did not see them. I brought with me one trust, perhaps the first trust of man, which I had accepted of my own will before God; I considered that promise and trust of so little worth that I did not know that I had even accepted it. And if that was all I did for her, what could I have expected? what could I have expected save disgrace and despair and the face of God turned away in very shame? Perhaps in the moment when I revealed to her not only the depth of my hunger but the fact that never and never would she have any part in the assuaging of it; perhaps at that moment I became her seducer and her murderer, author and instrument of her shame and death. After all, there must be some things for which God cannot be accused by man and held responsible. There must be'. Thinking begins to slow now. It slows like a wheel beginning to run in sand, the axle, the vehicle, the power which propels it not yet aware.

He seems to watch himself among faces, always among, enclosed and surrounded by, faces, as though he watched himself in his own pulpit, from the rear of the church, or as though he were a fish in a bowl. And more than that: the faces seem to be mirrors in which he watches himself. He knows them all; he can read his doings in them. He seems to see reflected in them a figure antic as a showman, a little wild: a charlatan preaching worse than heresy, in utter disregard of that whose very stage he preempted, offering instead of the crucified shape of pity and love, a swaggering and unchastened bravo killed with a shotgun in a peaceful henhouse, in a temporary hiatus of his own avocation of killing. The wheel of thinking slows; the axle knows it now but the vehicle itself is still unaware.

He sees the faces which surround him mirror astonishment, puzzlement, then outrage, then fear, as if they looked beyond his wild antics and saw behind him and looking down upon him, in his turn unaware, the final and supreme Face Itself, cold, terrible because of Its omniscient detachment. He knows that they see more than that: that they see the trust of which he proved himself unworthy, being used now for his chastisement; it seems to him now that he talks to the Face: "Perhaps I accepted more than I could perform. But is that criminal? Shall I be punished for that? Shall I be held responsible for that which was beyond my power?" And the Face:

"It was not to accomplish that that you accepted her. You took her as a means toward your own selfishness. As an instrument to be called to Jefferson; not for My ends, but for your own."

'Is that true?' he thinks. 'Could that have been true?' He sees himself again as when the shame came. He remembers that which he had sensed before it was born, hiding it from his own thinking. He sees himself offer as a sop fortitude and forbearance and dignity, making it appear that he resigned his pulpit for a martyr's reasons, when at the very instant there was within him a leaping and triumphant surge of denial behind a face which had betrayed him, believing itself safe behind the lifted hymnbook, when the photographer pressed his bulb.

He seems to watch himself, alert, patient, skillful, playing his cards well, making it appear that he was being driven, uncomplaining, into that which he did not even then admit had been his desire since before he entered the seminary. And still casting his sops as though he were flinging rotten fruit before a drove of hogs: the meagre income from his father which he continued to divide with the Memphis institution; allowing himself to be persecuted, to be dragged from his bed at night and carried into the woods and beaten with sticks, he all the while bearing in the town's sight and hearing, without shame, with that patient and voluptuous ego of the martyr, the air, the behavior, the *How long, O Lord* until, inside his house again and the door locked, he lifted the mask with voluptuous and triumphant glee: *Ah. That's done now. That's past now. That's bought and paid for now*

'But I was young then,' he thinks. 'I too had to do, not what I could, but what I knew.' Thinking is running too heavily now; he should know it, sense it. Still the vehicle is unaware of what it is approaching. 'And after all, I have paid. I have bought my ghost, even though I did pay for it with my life. And who can forbid me doing that? It is any man's privilege to destroy himself, so long as he does not injure anyone else, so long as he lives to and of himself——' He stops suddenly. Motionless, unbreathing, there comes upon him a consternation which is about to be actual horror. He is aware of the sand now; with the realization of it he feels within himself a gathering as though for some tremendous effort. Progress now is still progress, yet it is now indistinguishable from the recent past like the already traversed inches of sand which cling to the turning wheel, raining back with a dry hiss that before this should have warned him: '. . . . . . .revealed to my wife my hunger, my ego . . . . . . .instrument of her despair and shame. . . . . . .' and without his having thought it at all, a sentence seems to stand fullsprung across his skull, behind his eyes: *I dont want to think this. I must not think this. I dare not think this* As he sits in the window, leaning forward above his motionless hands, sweat begins to pour from him, springing out like blood, and pouring. Out of the instant the sandclutched wheel of thinking turns on with the slow implacability of a mediaeval torture instrument, beneath the wrenched and broken sockets of his spirit, his life: 'Then, if this is so, if I am the instrument of her despair and death, then I am in turn instrument of someone outside myself. And I know that for fifty years I have not even been clay: I have been a single instant of darkness in which a horse galloped and a gun crashed. And if I am my dead grandfather on the instant of his death, then my wife, his grandson's wife. . . . . . .the debaucher and murderer of my grandson's wife, since I could neither let my grandson live or die. . . . . . .'

The wheel, released, seems to rush on with a long sighing sound. He sits motionless in its aftermath, in his cooling sweat, while the sweat pours and pours. The wheel whirls on. It is going fast and smooth now, because it is freed now of burden, of vehicle, axle, all. In the lambent suspension of August into which night is about to fully come, it seems to engender and surround itself with a faint glow like a halo. The halo is full of faces. The faces are not shaped with suffering, not shaped with anything: not horror, pain, not even reproach. They are peaceful, as though they have escaped into an apotheosis; his own is among them. In fact, they all look a little alike, composite of all the faces which he has ever seen. But he can distinguish them one from another: his wife's; townspeople, members of that congregation which denied him, which had met him at the station that day with eagerness and hunger; Byron Bunch's; the woman with the child;

and that of the man called Christmas. This face alone is not clear. It is confused more than any other, as though in the now peaceful throes of a more recent, a more inextricable, compositeness. Then he can see that it is two faces which seem to strive (but not of themselves striving or desiring it: he knows that, but because of the motion and desire of the wheel itself) in turn to free themselves one from the other, then fade and blend again. But he has seen now, the other face, the one that is not Christmas. 'Why, it's. . . . . . .' he thinks. 'I have seen it, recently. . . . Why, it's that. . . . . . .boy. With that black pistol, automatic they call them. The one who. . . . . . .into the kitchen where. . . . . . .killed, who fired the——' Then it seems to him that some ultimate dammed flood within him breaks and rushes away. He seems to watch it, feeling himself losing contact with earth, lighter and lighter, emptying, floating. 'I am dying,' he thinks. 'I should pray. I should try to pray.' But he does not. He does not try. 'With all air, all heaven, filled with the lost and unheeded crying of all the living who ever lived, wailing still like lost children among the cold and terrible stars. . . . I wanted so little. I asked so little. It would seem. . . . . . .' The wheel turns on. It spins now, fading, without progress, as though turned by that final flood which had rushed out of him, leaving his body empty and lighter than a forgotten leaf and even more trivial than flotsam lying spent and still upon the window ledge which has no solidity beneath hands that have no weight; so that it can be now Now

It is as though they had merely waited until he could find something to pant with, to be reaffirmed in triumph and desire with, with this last left of honor and pride and life. He hears above his heart the thunder increase, myriad and drumming. Like a long sighing of wind in trees it begins, then they sweep into sight, borne now upon a cloud of phantom dust. They rush past, forwardleaning in the saddles, with brandished arms, beneath whipping ribbons from slanted and eager lances; with tumult and soundless yelling they sweep past like a tide whose crest is jagged with the wild heads of horses and the brandished arms of men like the crater of the world in explosion. They rush past, are gone; the dust swirls skyward sucking, fades away into the night which has fully come. Yet, leaning forward in the window, his bandaged head huge and without depth above the twin blobs of his hands upon the ledge, it seems to him that he still hears them: the wild bugles and the clashing sabres and the dying thunder of hooves.

XXI

THERE LIVES in the eastern part of the state a furniture repairer and dealer who recently made a trip into Tennessee to get some old pieces of furniture which he had bought by correspondence. He made the journey in his truck, carrying with him, since the truck (it had a housedin body with a door at the rear) was new and he did not intend to drive it faster than fifteen miles an hour, camping equipment to save hotels. On his return home he told his wife of an experience which he had had on the road, which interested him at the time and which he considered amusing enough to repeat. Perhaps the reason why he found it interesting and that he felt that he could make it interesting in the retelling is that he and his wife are not old either, besides his having been away from home (due to the very moderate speed which he felt it wise to restrict himself to) for more than a week. The story has to do with two people, passengers whom he picked up; he names the town, in Mississippi, before he entered Tennessee:

"I had done decided to get some gas and I was already slowing into the station when I saw this kind of young, pleasantfaced gal standing on the corner, like she was waiting for somebody to come along and offer her a ride. She was holding something in her arms. I didn't see what it was at first, and I didn't see the fellow that was with her at all until he come up and spoke to me. I thought at first that I didn't see him before because he wasn't standing where she was. Then I saw that he was the kind of fellow you wouldn't see the first glance if he was alone by himself in the bottom of a empty concrete swimming pool.

"So he come up and I said, quick like: 'I aint going to Memphis, if that's what you want. I am going up past Jackson, Tennessee.' And he says,

" 'That'll be fine. That would just suit us. It would be a accommodation.' And I says,

" 'Where do you all want to go to?' And he looked at me, like a fellow that aint used to lying will try to think up one quick when he already knows that he likely aint going to be believed. 'You're just looking around, are you?' I says.

" 'Yes,' he says. 'That's it. We're just travelling. Wherever you could take us, it would be a big accommodation.'

"So I told him to get in. 'I reckon you aint going to rob and murder me.' He went and got her and come back. Then I saw that what she was carrying was a baby, a critter not yearling size. He made to help her into the back of the truck and I says, 'Whyn't one of you ride up here on the seat?' and they talked some and then she come and got on the seat and he went back into the filling station and got one of these leatherlooking paper suit cases and put it into the bed and got in too. And here we went, with her on the seat, holding the baby and looking back now and then to see if he hadn't maybe fell out or something.

"I thought they was husband and wife at first. I just never thought anything about it, except to wonder how a young, strapping gal like her ever come to take up with him. It wasn't anything wrong with him. He looked like a good fellow, the kind that would hold a job steady and work at the same job a long time, without bothering anybody about a raise neither, long as they let him keep on working. That was what he looked like. He looked like except when he was at work, he would just be something around. I just couldn't imagine anybody, any woman, knowing that they had ever slept with him, let alone having anything to show folks to prove it."

Aint you shamed? his wife says. *Talking that way before a lady* They are talking in the dark.

Anyway, I cant see you blushing any he says. He continues: "I never thought anything about it until that night when we camped. She was sitting up on the seat by me, and I was talking to her, like a fellow would, and after a while it begun to come out how they had come from Alabama. She kept on saying 'We come' and so I thought she meant her and the fellow in the back. About how they had been on the road nigh eight weeks now. 'You aint had that chap no eight weeks,' I says. 'Not if I know color' and she said it was just born three weeks ago, down at Jefferson, and I said, 'Oh. Where they lynched that nigger. You must have been there then' and she clammed up. Like he had done told her not to talk about it. I knowed that's what it was. So we rode on and then it was coming toward night and I said, 'We'll be in a town soon. I aint going to sleep in town. But if you all want to go on with me tomorrow, I'll come back to the hotel for you in the morning about six oclock' and she sat right still, like she was waiting for him to say, and after a while he says,

" 'I reckon with this here truck house you dont need to worry about hotels' and I never said anything and we was coming into the town and he said, 'Is this here any size town?'

" 'I dont know,' I says. 'I reckon they'll have a boarding house or something here though.' And he says,

" 'I was wondering if they would have a tourist camp.' And I never said anything and he said, 'With tents for hire. These here hotels are high, and with folks that have a long piece to go.' They hadn't never yet said where they was going. It was like they didn't even know themselves, like they was just waiting to see where they could get to. But I didn't know that, then. But I knowed what he wanted me to say, and that he wasn't going to come right out and ask me himself. Like if the Lord aimed for me to say it, I would say it, and if the Lord aimed for him to go to a hotel and pay maybe three dollars for a room, he would do that too. So I says,

" 'Well, it's a warm night. And if you folks dont mind a few mosquitoes and sleeping on them bare boards in the truck.' And he says,

" 'Sho. It will be fine. It'll be mighty fine for you to let her.' I noticed then how he said *her*. And I begun to notice how there was something funny and kind of strained about him. Like when a man is determined to work himself up to where he will do something he wants to do and that he is scared to do. I dont mean it was like he was scared of what might happen to him, but like it was something that he would die before he would even think about doing it if he hadn't just tried everything else until he was desperate. That was before I knew. I just couldn't understand what in the world it could be then. And if it hadn't been for that night and what happened, I reckon I would not have known at all when they left me at Jackson."

What was it he aimed to do? the wife says.

You wait till I come to that part. Maybe I'll show you, too He continues: "So we stopped in front of the store. He was already jumping out before the truck had stopped. Like he was afraid I would beat him to it, with his face all shined up like a kid trying to do something for you before you change your mind about something you promised to do for him. He went into the store on a trot and came back with so many bags and sacks he couldn't see over them, so that I says to myself, 'Look a here, fellow. If you are aiming to settle down permanent in this truck and set up housekeeping.' Then we drove on and came pretty soon to a likely place where I could drive the truck off the road, into some trees, and he jumps down and runs up and helps her down like she and the kid were made out of glass or eggs. And he still had that look on his face like he pretty near had his mind made up to do whatever it was he was desperated up to do, if only nothing I did or she did before hand would prevent it, and if she only didn't notice in his face that he was desperated up to something. But even then I didn't know what it was."

What was it? the wife says.

I just showed you once. You aint ready to be showed again, are you?

I reckon I dont mind if you dont. But I still dont see anything funny in that. How come it took him all that time and trouble, anyway?

It was because they were not married the husband says. *It wasn't even his child. I didn't know it then, though. I didn't find that out until I heard them talking that night by the fire, when they didn't know I heard, I reckon. Before he had done got himself desperated up all the way. But I reckon he was desperate enough, all right. I reckon he was just giving her one more chance* He continues: "So there he was skirmishing around, getting camp ready, until he got me right nervous: him trying to do everything and not knowing just where to begin or something. So I told him to go rustle up some firewood, and I took my blankets and spread them out in the truck. I was a little mad, then, at myself about how I had got into it now and I would have to sleep on the ground with my feet to the fire and nothing under me. So I reckon I was short and grumpy maybe, moving around, getting things fixed, and her sitting with her back to a tree, giving the kid his supper under a shawl and saying ever so often how she was ashamed to inconvenience me and that she aimed to sit up by the fire because she wasn't tired noway, just riding all day long and not doing anything. Then he came back, with enough wood to barbecue a steer, and she began to tell him and he went to the truck and taken out that suitcase and opened it and taken out a blanket. Then we had it, sho enough. It was like those two fellows that used to be in the funny papers, those two Frenchmen that were always bowing and scraping at the other one to go first, making out like we had all come away from home just for the privilege of sleeping on the ground, each one trying to lie faster and bigger than the next. For a while I was a mind to say, 'All right. If you want to sleep on the ground, do it. Because be durned if I want to.' But I reckon you might say that I won. Or that me and him won. Because it wound up by him fixing their blanket in the truck, like we all might have known all the time it would be, and me and him spreading mine out before the fire. I reckon he knew that would be the way of it, anyhow. If they had come all the way from south Alabama like she claimed. I reckon that was why he brought in all that firewood just to make a pot of coffee with and heat up some tin cans. Then we ate, and then I found out."

Found out what? What it was he wanted to do?

Not right then. I reckon she had a little more patience than you He continues: "So we had eaten and I was lying down on the blanket. I was tired, and getting stretched out felt good. I wasn't aiming to listen, anymore than I was aiming to look like I was asleep when I wasn't. But they had asked me to give them a ride; it wasn't me that insisted on them getting in my truck. And if they seen fit to go on and talk without making sho nobody could hear them, it wasn't any of my business. And that's how I found out that they were hunting for somebody, following him, or trying to. Or she was, that is. And so all of a sudden I says to myself, 'Ah-ah. Here's another gal that thought she could learn on Saturday night what her mammy waited until Sunday to ask the minister.' They never called his name. And they didn't know just which way he had run. And I knew that if they had known where he went, it wouldn't be by any fault of the fellow that was doing the running. I learned that quick. And so I heard him talking to her, about how they might travel on like this from one truck to another and one state to another for the rest of their lives and not find any trace of him, and her sitting there on the log, holding the chap and listening quiet as a stone and pleasant as a stone and just about as nigh to being moved or persuaded. And I says to myself, 'Well, old fellow, I reckon it aint only since she has been riding on the seat of my truck while you rode with your feet hanging out the back end of it that she has travelled out in front on this trip.' But I never said anything. I just lay there and them talking, or him talking, not loud. He hadn't even mentioned marriage, neither. But that's what he was talking about, and her listening placid and calm, like she had heard it before and she knew that she never even had to bother to say either yes or no to him. Smiling a little she was. But he couldn't see that.

"Then he give up. He got up from the log and walked away. But I saw his face when he turned and I knew that he hadn't give up. He knew that he had just give her one more chance and that now he had got himself desperated up to risking all. I could have told him that he was just deciding now to do what he should have done in the first place. But I reckon he had his own reasons. Anyway he walked off into the dark and left her sitting there, with her face kind of bent down a little and that smile still on it. She never looked after him, neither. Maybe she knew he had just gone off by himself to get himself worked up good to what she might have been advising him to do all the time, herself, without saying it in out and out words, which a lady naturally couldn't do; not even a lady with a Saturday night family.

"Only I dont reckon that was it either. Or maybe the time and place didn't suit her, let alone a audience. After a while she got up and looked at me, but I never moved, and then she went and climbed into the truck and after a while I heard her quit moving around and I knew that she had done got fixed to sleep. And I lay there—I had done got kind of waked up myself, now—and it was a right smart while. But I knew that he was somewhere close, waiting maybe for the fire to die down or for me to get good to sleep. Because, sho enough, just about the time the fire had died down good, I heard him come up, quiet as a cat, and stand over me, looking down at me, listening. I never made a sound; I dont know but I might have fetched a snore or two for him. Anyway, he goes on toward the truck, walking like he had eggs under his feet, and I lay there and watched him and I says to myself, 'Old boy, if you'd a just done this last night, you'd a been sixty miles further south than you are now, to my knowledge. And if you'd a done it two nights ago, I reckon I wouldn't ever have laid eyes on either one of you.' Then I got a little worried. I wasn't worried about him doing her any harm she didn't want done to her. In fact, I was pulling for the little cuss. That was it. I couldn't decide what I had better do when she would begin to holler. I knew that she would holler, and if I jumped up and run to the truck, it would scare him off, and if I didn't come running, he would know that I was awake and watching him all the time, and he'd be scared off faster than ever. But I ought not to worried. I ought to have known that from the first look I taken at her and at him."

I reckon the reason you knew you never had to worry was that you had already found out just what she would do in a case like that the wife says.

Sho the husband says. *I didn't aim for you to find that out. Yes, sir. I thought I had covered my tracks this time*

Well, go on. What happened?

What do you reckon happened, with a big strong gal like that, without any warning that it was just him, and a durn little cuss that already looked like he had reached the point where he could bust out crying like another baby? He continues: "There wasn't any hollering or anything. I just watched him climb slow and easy into the truck and disappear and then didn't anything happen for about while you could count maybe fifteen slow, and then I heard one kind of astonished sound she made when she woke up, like she was just surprised and then a little put out without being scared at all, and she says, not loud neither: 'Why, Mr Bunch. Aint you ashamed. You might have woke the baby, too.' Then he come out the back door of the truck. Not fast, and not climbing down on his own legs at all. I be dog if I dont believe she picked him up and set him back outside on the ground like she would that baby if it had been about six years old, say, and she says, 'You go and lay down now, and get some sleep. We got another fur piece to go tomorrow.'

"Well, I was downright ashamed to look at him, to let him know that any human man had seen and heard what happened. I be dog if I didn't want to find the hole and crawl into it with him. I did for a fact. And him standing there where she had set him down. The fire had burned down good now and I couldn't hardly see him at all. But I knew about how I would have been standing and feeling if I was him. And that would have been with my head bowed, waiting for the Judge to say, 'Take him out of here and hang him quick.' And I didn't make a sound, and after a while I heard him go on off. I could hear the bushes popping, like he had just struck off blind through the woods. And when daylight came he hadn't got back.

"Well, I didn't say anything. I didn't know what to say. I kept on believing that he would show up, would come walking up out of the bushes, face or no face. So I built up the fire and got breakfast started, and after a while I heard her climbing out of the truck. I never looked around. But I could hear her standing there like she was looking around, like maybe she was trying to tell by the way the fire or my blanket looked if he was there or not. But I never said anything and she never said anything. I wanted to pack up and get started. And I knew I couldn't leave her in the middle of the road. And that if my wife was to hear about me travelling the country with a goodlooking country gal and a three weeks' old baby, even if she did claim she was hunting for her husband. Or both husbands now. So we ate and then I said, 'Well, I got a long road and I reckon I better get started.' And she never said nothing at all. And when I looked at her I saw that her face was just as quiet and calm as it had ever been. I be dog if she was even surprised or anything. And there I was, not knowing what to do with her, and she done already packed up her things and even swept the truck out with a gum branch before she put in that paper suitcase and made a kind of cushion with the folded blanket at the back end of the truck; and I says to myself, 'It aint any wonder you get along. When they up and run away on you, you just pick up whatever they left and go on.'——'I reckon I'll ride back here,' she says.

" 'It'll be kind of rough on the baby,' I says.

" 'I reckon I can hold him up,' she says.

" 'Suit yourself,' I says. And we drove off, with me hanging out the seat to look back, hoping that he would show up before we got around the curve. But he never. Talk about a fellow being caught in the depot with a strange baby on his hands. Here I was with a strange woman and a baby too, expecting every car that come up from behind and passed us to be full of husbands and wives too, let alone sheriffs. We were getting close to the Tennessee line then and I had my mind all fixed how I would either burn that new truck up or get to a town big enough to have one of these ladies' welfare societies in it that I could turn her over to. And now and then I would look back, hoping that maybe he had struck out afoot after us, and I would see her sitting there with her face as calm as church, holding that baby up so it could eat and ride the bumps at the same time. You cant beat them." He lies in the bed, laughing. "Yes, sir. I be dog if you can beat them."

Then what? What did she do then?

Nothing. Just sitting there, riding, looking out like she hadn't ever seen country—roads and trees and fields and telephone poles—before in her life. She never saw him at all until he come around to the back door of the truck. She never had to. All she needed to do was wait. And she knew that

Him?

Sho. He was standing at the side of the road when we come around the curve. Standing there, face and no face, hangdog and determined and calm too, like he had done desperated himself up for the last time, to take the last chance, and that now he knew he wouldn't ever have to desperate himself again He continues: "He never looked at me at all. I just stopped the truck and him already running back to go around to the door where she was sitting. And he come around the back of it and he stood there, and her not even surprised. 'I done come too far now,' he says. 'I be dog if I'm going to quit now.' And her looking at him like she had known all the time what he was going to do before he even knew himself that he was going to, and that whatever he done, he wasn't going to mean it.

" 'Aint nobody never said for you to quit,' she says." He laughs, lying in the bed, laughing. "Yes, sir. You cant beat a woman. Because do you know what I think? I think she was just travelling. I dont think she had any idea of finding whoever it was she was following. I dont think she had ever aimed to, only she hadn't told him yet. I reckon this was the first time she had ever been further away from home than she could walk back before sundown in her life. And that she had got along all right this far, with folks taking good care of her. And so I think she had just made up her mind to travel a little further and see as much as she could, since I reckon she knew that when she settled down this time, it would likely be for the rest of her life. That's what I think. Setting back there in that truck, with him by her now and the baby that hadn't never stopped eating, that had been eating breakfast now for about ten miles, like one of these dining cars on the train, and her looking out and watching the telephone poles and the fences passing like it was a circus parade. Because after a while I says, 'Here comes Saulsbury' and she says,

" 'What?' and I says,

" 'Saulsbury, Tennessee' and I looked back and saw her face. And it was like it was already fixed and waiting to be surprised, and that she knew that when the surprise come, she was going to enjoy it. And it did come and it did suit her. Because she said,

" 'My, my. A body does get around. Here we aint been coming from Alabama but two months, and now it's already Tennessee.' "

PYLON

Contents

Dedication of an Airport

F OR A FULL MINUTE Jiggs stood before the window in a
light spatter of last night's confetti lying against the win-
dowbase like spent dirty foam, lightpoised on the balls of his
greasestained tennis shoes, looking at the boots. Slantshim-
mered by the intervening plate they sat upon their wooden
pedestal in unblemished and inviolate implication of horse
and spur, of the posed countrylife photographs in the magazine advertisements, beside the easelwise cardboard placard
with which the town had bloomed overnight as it had with
the purple-and-gold tissue bunting and the trodden confetti
and broken serpentine—the same lettering, the same photographs of the trim vicious fragile aeroplanes and the pilots
leaning upon them in gargantuan irrelation as if the aeroplanes were a species of esoteric and fatal animals not trained
or tamed but just for the instant inert, above the neat brief
legend of name and accomplishment or perhaps just hope.

He entered the store, his rubber soles falling in quick hissing thuds on pavement and iron sill and then upon the tile
floor of that museum of glass cases lighted suave and sourceless by an unearthly daycolored substance in which the hats
and ties and shirts, the beltbuckles and cufflinks and handkerchiefs, the pipes shaped like golfclubs and the drinking tools
shaped like boots and barnyard fowls and the minute im-
pedimenta for wear on ties and vestchains shaped like bits
and spurs, resembled biologic specimens put into the inviolate preservative before they had ever been breathed
into. "Boots?" the clerk said. "The pair in the window?"

"Yair," Jiggs said. "How much?" But the clerk did not
even move. He leaned back on the counter, looking down at
the hard tough shortchinned face, blueshaven, with a long
threadlike and recentlystanched razorcut on it and in which
the hot brown eyes seemed to snap and glare like a boy's
approaching for the first time the aerial wheels and stars and
serpents of a nighttime carnival; at the filthy raked swaggering peaked cap, the short thick musclebound body like the
photographs of the one who two years before was lightmid-
dleweight champion of the army or Marine Corps or navy;

the cheap breeches overcut to begin with and now skintight
like both they and their wearer had been recently and hopelessly rained on and enclosing a pair of short stocky thick fast
legs like a polo pony's, which descended into the tops of a
pair of boots footless now and secured by two rivetted straps
beneath the insteps of the tennis shoes.

"They are twenty-two and a half," the clerk said.

"All right. I'll take them. How late do you keep open at
night?"

"Until six."

"Hell. I'll be out at the airport then. I wont get back to
town until seven. How about getting them then?" Another
clerk came up: the manager, the floorwalker.

"You mean you dont want them now?" the first said.

"No," Jiggs said. "How about getting them at seven?"

"What is it?" the second clerk said.

"Says he wants a pair of boots. Says he cant get back from
the airport before seven oclock."

The second looked at Jiggs. "You a flyer?"

"Yair," Jiggs said. "Listen. Leave a guy here. I'll be back by
seven. I'll need them tonight."

The second also looked down at Jiggs' feet. "Why not take
them now?"

Jiggs didn't answer at all. He just said, "So I'll have to wait
until tomorrow."

"Unless you can get back before six," the second said.

"O.K.," Jiggs said. "All right, mister. How much do you
want down?" Now they both looked at him: at the face, the
hot eyes: the appearance entire articulate and complete, badge
regalia and passport, of an oblivious and incorrigible insolvency. "To keep them for me. That pair in the window."

The second looked at the first. "Do you know his size?"

"That's all right about that," Jiggs said. "How much?"

The second looked at Jiggs. "You pay ten dollars and we
will hold them for you until tomorrow."

"Ten dollars? Jesus, mister. You mean ten percent. I could
pay ten percent. down and buy an airplane."

"You want to pay ten percent. down?"

"Yair. Ten percent. Call for them this afternoon if I can get
back from the airport in time."

"That will be two and a quarter," the second said. When Jiggs put his hand into his pocket they could follow it, finger-nail and knuckle, the entire length of the pocket like watching the ostrich in the movie cartoon swallow the alarm clock. It emerged a fist and opened upon a wadded dollar bill and coins of all sizes. He put the bill into the first clerk's hand and began to count the coins onto the bill.

"There's fifty," he said. "Seventy-five. And fifteen's ninety, and twenty-five is. . . . . . ." His voice stopped; he became motionless, with the twenty-five cent piece in his left hand and a half dollar and four nickels on his right palm. The clerks watched him put the quarter back into his right hand and take up the four nickels. "Let's see," he said. "We had ninety, and twenty will be——"

"Two dollars and ten cents," the second said. "Take back two nickels and give him the quarter."

"Two and a dime," Jiggs said. "How about taking that down?"

"You were the one who suggested ten percent."

"I cant help that. How about two and a dime?"

"Take it," the second said. The first took the money and went away. Again the second watched Jiggs' hand move downward along his leg, and then he could even see the two coins at the end of the pocket, through the soiled cloth.

"Where do you get this bus to the airport?" Jiggs said. The other told him. Now the first returned, with the cryptic scribbled duplicate of the sale; and now they both looked into the hot interrogation of the eyes.

"They will be ready for you when you call," the second said.

"Yair; sure," Jiggs said. "But get them out of the window."

"You want to examine them?"

"No. I just want to see them come out of that window." So again outside the window, his rubber soles resting upon that light confettispatter more forlorn than spattered paint since it had neither inherent weight nor cohesiveness to hold it anywhere, which even during the time that Jiggs was in the store had decreased, thinned, vanishing particle by particle into nothing like foam does, he stood until the hand came into the window and drew the boots out. Then he went on, walking fast with his short bouncing curiously stiffkneed gait. When he turned into Grandlieu Street he could see a clock, though he was already hurrying or rather walking at his fast stiff hard gait like a mechanical toy that has but one speed and though the clock's face was still in the shadow of the opposite streetside and what sunlight there was was still high, diffused, suspended in soft refraction by the heavy damp bayou-and-swampsuspired air. There was confetti here too, and broken serpentine, in neat narrow swept windrows against wallangles and lightly vulcanised along the gutterrims by the flushing fireplugs of the past dawn, while, upcaught and pinned by the cryptic significant shields to doorfront and lamppost, the purple-and-gold bunting looped unbroken as a trolley wire above his head as he walked, turning at last at right angles to cross the street itself and meet that one on the opposite side making its angle too, to join over the center of the street as though to form an aerial and bottomless regalcolored cattlechute suspended at first floor level above the earth, and suspending beneath itself in turn, the outwardfacing cheeseclothlettered interdiction which Jiggs, passing, slowed looking back to read: *Grandlieu Street CLOSED To Traffic 8:00 P.M. – Midnight*

Now he could see the bus at the curb, where they had told him it would be, with its cloth banner fastened by the four corners across its broad stern to ripple and flap in motion, and the wooden sandwich board at the curb too: *Bluehound to Feinman Airport. 75¢* The driver stood beside the open door; he too watched Jiggs' knuckles travel the length of the pocket. "Airport?" Jiggs said.

"Yes," the driver said. "You got a ticket?"

"I got seventy-five cents. Wont that do?"

"A ticket into the airport. Or a workman's pass. The passenger busses dont begin to run until noon." Jiggs looked at the driver with that hot pleasant interrogation, holding his breeches by one hand while he drew the other out of the pocket. "Are you working out there?" the driver said.

"Oh," Jiggs said. "Sure. I'm Roger Shumann's mechanic. You want to see my license?"

"That'll be all right," the driver said. "Get aboard." In the driver's seat there lay folded a paper: one of the colored ones, the pink or the green editions of the diurnal dogwatches, with a thick heavy typesplattered front page filled with ejaculations and pictures. Jiggs paused, stooped, turning.

"Have a look at your paper, cap," he said. But the driver did not answer. Jiggs took up the paper and sat in the next seat and took from his shirt pocket a crumpled cigarette pack and upended and shook into his other palm from it two cigarette stubs and put the longer one back into the crumpled paper and into his shirt again and lit the shorter one, pursing it away from his face and slanting his head aside to keep the matchflame from his nose. Three more men entered the bus, two of them in overalls and the third in a kind of porter's cap made of or covered by purple-and-gold cloth in alternate stripes, and then the driver came and sat sideways in his seat.

"You got a ship in the race today, have you?" he said.

"Yair," Jiggs said. "In the three-seventy-five cubic inch."

"How does it look to you? Do you think you will have a chance?"

"We might if they would let us fly it in the two hundred cubic inch," Jiggs said. He took three quick draws from the cigarette stub like darting a stick at a snake and snapped it through the stillopen door as though it were the snake, or maybe a spider, and opened the paper. "Ship's obsolete. It was fast two years ago, but that's two years ago. We'd be O.K. now if they had just quit building racers when they finished the one we got. There aint another pilot out there except Shumann that could have even qualified it."

"Shumann's good, is he?"

"They're all good," Jiggs said, looking at the paper. It spread its pale green surface: heavy, blacksplotched, staccato: *Airport Dedication Special*; in the exact middle the photograph of a plump, bland, innocently sensual Levantine face beneath a raked fedora hat; the upper part of a thick body buttoned tight and soft into a peaked lightcolored doublebreasted suit with a carnation in the lapel: the photograph inletted like a medallion into a drawing full of scrolled wings and propeller symbols which enclosed a shieldshaped penand-ink reproduction of something apparently cast in metal and obviously in existence somewhere and lettered in gothic relief:

Feinman Airport
New Valois, Franciana
Dedicated to
The Aviators of America
and
Colonel H. I. Feinman, Chairman, Sewage Board

Through Whose Undeviating Vision and Unflagging Effort This Airport was Raised Up and Created out of the Waste Land at the Bottom of Lake Rambaud at a Cost of One Million Dollars

"This Feinman," Jiggs said. "He must be a big son of a bitch."

"He's a son of a bitch all right," the driver said. "I guess you'd call him big too."

"He gave you guys a nice airport, anyway," Jiggs said.

"Yair," the driver said. "Somebody did."

"Yair," Jiggs said. "It must have been him. I notice he's got his name on it here and there."

"Here and there; yair," the driver said. "In electric lights on both hangars and on the floor and the ceiling of the lobby and four times on each lamppost and a guy told me the beacon spells it too but I dont know about that because I dont know the Morse code."

"For Christ's sake," Jiggs said. Now a fair crowd of men, in the overalls or the purple-and-gold caps, appeared suddenly and began to enter the bus, so that for the time the scene began to resemble that comic stage one where the entire army enters one taxicab and drives away. But there was room for all of them and then the door swung in and the bus moved away and Jiggs sat back, looking out; the bus swung immediately away from Grandlieu Street and Jiggs watched himself plunging between iron balconies, catching fleeting glimpses of dirty paved courts as the bus seemed to rush with tremendous clatter and speed through cobbled streets which did not look wide enough to admit it, between low brick walls which seemed to sweat a rich slow overfecund smell of fish and coffee and sugar, and another odor profound faint and distinctive as a musty priest's robe: of some spartan effluvium of mediaeval convents.

Then the bus ran out of this and began to run, faster still, through a long avenue between palmbordered bearded live-oak groves and then suddenly Jiggs saw that the liveoaks stood not in earth but in water so motionless and thick as to make no reflection, as if it had been poured about the trunks and allowed to set; the bus ran suddenly past a row of flimsy cabins whose fronts rested upon the shell foundation of the road itself and whose rears rested upon stilts to which row-boats were tied and between which nets hung drying, and he saw that the roofs were thatched with the smokecolored growth which hung from the trees, before they flicked away and the bus ran again overarched by the oak boughs from which the moss hung straight and windless as the beards of old men sitting in the sun. "Jesus," Jiggs said. "If a man dont own a boat here he cant even go to the can, can he?"

"Your first visit down here?" the driver said. "Where you from?"

"Anywhere," Jiggs said. "The place I'm staying away from right now is Kansas."

"Family there, huh?"

"Yair. I got two kids there; I guess I still got the wife too."

"So you pulled out."

"Yair. Jesus, I couldn't even keep back enough to have my shoes halfsoled. Everytime I did a job her or the sheriff would catch the guy and get the money before I could tell him I was through; I would make a parachute jump and one of them would have the jack and be on the way back to town before I even pulled the ripcord."

"For Christ's sake," the driver said.

"Yair," Jiggs said, looking out at the backrushing trees. "This guy Feinman could spend some more of the money giving these trees a haircut, couldn't he?" Now the bus, the road, ran out of the swamp though without mounting, with no hill to elevate it; it ran now upon a flat plain of sawgrass and of cypress and oak stumps—a pocked desolation of some terrific and apparently purposeless reclamation across which the shell road ran ribbonblanched toward something low and dead ahead of it—something low, unnatural: a chimaera

quality which for the moment prevented one from compre-
hending that it had been built by man and for a purpose. The
thick heavy air was full now of a smell thicker, heavier,
though there was yet no water in sight: there was only the
soft pale sharp chimaerashape above which pennons floated
against a further drowsy immensity which the mind knew
must be water, apparently separated from the flat earth by a
mirageline so that, taking shape now as a doublewinged
building, it seemed to float lightly like the apocryphal tur-
reted and battlemented cities in the colored Sunday sections,
where beneath sillless and floorless arches people with yellow
and blue flesh pass and repass: myriad, purposeless, and free
from gravity. Now the bus, swinging, presented in broadside
the low broad main building with its two hangarwings, mod-
ernistic, crenelated, with its façade faintly Moorish or Califor-
nian beneath the gold-and-purple pennons whipping in a
breeze definitely from water and giving to it an air both aerial
and aquatic like a mammoth terminal for some species of machine of a yet unvisioned tomorrow, to which air earth and
water will be as one: and viewed from the bus across a plaza
of beautiful and incredible grass labyrinthed by concrete
driveways which Jiggs will not for two or three days yet recognise to be miniature replicas of the concrete runways on
the field itself—a mathematic monogram of two capital Fs
laid by compass to all the winds. The bus ran into one of
these, slowing between the bloodless grapes of lampglobes on
bronze poles; as Jiggs got out he stopped to look at the four
Fs cast into the quadrants of the base before going on.

He went around the main building and followed a narrow
alley like a gutter, ending in a blank and knobless door; he
put his hand too among the handprints in oil or grease on
the door and pushed through it and into a narrow alcove
walled by neatly ranked and numbered tools from a sound, a
faint and cavernous murmur. The alcove contained a lavatory,
a row of hooks from which depended garments—civilian
shirts and coats, one pair of trousers with dangling braces,
the rest greasy dungarees, one of which Jiggs took down and
stepped into and bounced them lightly up and around his
shoulders all in one motion, already moving toward a second
door built mostly of chickenwire and through which he could

now see the hangar itself, the glass-and-steel cavern, the aeroplanes, the racers. Waspwaisted, wasplight, still, trim, vicious,
small and immobile, they seemed to poise without weight, as
though made of paper for the sole purpose of resting upon
the shoulders of the dungareeclad men about them. With
their soft bright paint tempered somewhat by the steelfiltered
light of the hangar they rested for the most part complete and
intact, with whatever it was that the mechanics were doing to
them of such a subtle and technical nature as to be invisible
to the lay eye, save for one. Unbonneted, its spare entrails
revealed as serrated top-and-bottomlines of delicate rockerarms and rods inferential in their very myriad delicacy of a
weightless and terrific speed any momentary faltering of
which would be the irreparable difference between motion
and mere matter, it appeared more profoundly derelict than
the halfeaten carcass of a deer come suddenly upon in a forest.
Jiggs paused, still fastening the coverall's throat, and looked
across the hangar at the three people busy about it—two of
a size and one taller, all in dungarees although one of the two
shorter ones was topped by a blob of savage mealcolored hair
which even from here did not look like man's hair. He did
not approach at once; still fastening the coverall he looked on
and saw, in another clump of dungarees beside another aeroplane, a small towheaded boy in khaki miniature of the men,
even to the grease. "Jesus Christ," Jiggs thought. "He's done
smeared oil on them already. Laverne will give him hell." He
approached on his short bouncing legs; already he could hear
the boy talking in the loud assured carrying voice of a spoiled
middlewestern child. He came up and put out his blunt hard
greasegrained hand and scoured the boy's head.

"Look out," the boy said. Then he said, "Where you been?
Laverne and Roger——" Jiggs scoured the boy's head again
and then crouched, his fists up, his head drawn down into his
shoulders in burlesque pantomime. But the boy just looked
at him. "Laverne and Roger——" he said again.

"Who's your old man today, kid?" Jiggs said. Now the boy
moved. With absolutely no change of expression he lowered
his head and rushed at Jiggs, his fists flailing at the man. Jiggs
ducked, taking the blows while the boy hammered at him
with puny and deadly purpose; now the other men had all

turned to watch, with wrenches and tools and engineparts in their suspended hands. "Who's your old man, huh?" Jiggs said, holding the boy off and then lifting and holding him away while he still hammered at Jiggs' head with that grim and puny purpose. "All right!" Jiggs cried. He set the boy down and held him off, still ducking and dodging and now blind since the peaked cap was jammed over his face and the boy's hard light little fists hammering upon the cap. "Oke! Oke!" Jiggs cried. "I quit! I take it back!" He stood back and tugged the cap off his face and then he found why the boy had ceased: that he and the men too with their arrested tools and safety wire and engineparts were now looking at something which had apparently crept from a doctor's cupboard and, in the snatched garments of an etherised patient in a charity ward, escaped into the living world. He saw a creature which, erect, would be better than six feet tall and which would weigh about ninetyfive pounds, in a suit of no age nor color, as though made of air and doped like an aeroplane wing with the incrusted excretion of all articulate life's contact with the passing earth, which ballooned light and impedimentless about a skeleton frame as though suit and wearer both hung from a flapping clothesline;—a creature with the leashed, eager loosejointed air of a halfgrown highbred setter puppy, crouched facing the boy with its hands up too in more profound burlesque than Jiggs' because it was obviously not intended to be burlesque.

"Come on, Dempsey," the man said. "How about taking me on for an icecream cone? Hey?" The boy did not move. He was not more than six, yet he looked at the apparition before him with the amazed quiet immobility of the grown men. "How about it, huh?" the man said.

Still the boy did not move. "Ask him who's his old man," Jiggs said.

The man looked at Jiggs. "So's his old man?"

"No. Who's his old man."

Now it was the apparition who looked at Jiggs in a kind of shocked immobility. "Who's his old man?" he repeated. He was still looking at Jiggs when the boy rushed upon him with his fists flailing again and his small face grimly and soberly homicidal; the man was still stooping, looking at Jiggs; it seemed to Jiggs and the other men that the boy's fists made

a light woodensounding tattoo as though the man's skin and
the suit too hung on a chair while the man ducked and
dodged too, trying to guard his face while still glaring at Jiggs
with that skulllike amazement, repeating, "Who's his old
man? *Who's his old man?*"

When Jiggs at last reached the unbonneted aeroplane the
two men had the supercharger already off and dismantled.
"Been to your grandmother's funeral or something?" the
taller one said.

"I been over there playing with Jack," Jiggs said. "You just
never saw me because there aint any women around here to
be looking at yet."

"Yair?" the other said.

"Yair," Jiggs said. "Where's that crescent wrench we
bought in Kansas City?" The woman had it in her hand; she
gave it to him and drew the back of her hand across her forehead, leaving a smudge of grease up and into the mealcolored, the strong pallid Iowacorncolored, hair. So he was
busy then, though he looked back once and saw the apparition with the boy now riding on his shoulder, leaning into
the heads and greasy backs busy again about the other aeroplane, and when he and Shumann lifted the supercharger
back onto the engine he looked again and saw them, the boy
still riding on the man's shoulder, going out the hangar door
and toward the apron. Then they put the cowling back on
and Shumann set the propeller horizontal and Jiggs raised the
aeroplane's tail, easily, already swinging it to pass through the
door, the woman stepping back to let the wing pass her, looking back herself into the hangar now.

"Where did Jack go?" she said.

"Out toward the apron," Jiggs said. "With that guy."

"With what guy?"

"Tall guy. Says he is a reporter. That looks like they locked
the graveyard up before he got in last night." The aeroplane
passed her, swinging again into the thin sunshine, the tail
high and apparently without weight on Jiggs' shoulder, his
thick legs beneath it moving with tense stout pistonlike
thrusts, Shumann and the taller man pushing the wings.

"Wait a minute," the woman said. But they did not pause
and she overtook and passed the moving tailgroup and

reached down past the uptilted cockpit hatch and stepped clear, holding a bundle wrapped tightly in a dark sweater. The aeroplane went on; already the guards in the purple-and-gold porter caps were lowering the barrier cable onto the apron; and now the band had begun to play, heard twice: once the faint light almost airy thump-thump-thump from where the sun glinted on the actual hornmouths on the platform facing the reserved section of the stands, and once where the disembodied noise blared brazen, metallic, and loud from the amplifyer which faced the barrier. She turned and reentered the hangar, stepping aside to let another aeroplane and its crew pass; she spoke to one of the men: "Who was that Jack went out with, Art?"

"The skeleton?" the man said. "They went to get an ice-cream cone. He says he is a reporter." She went on, across the hangar and through the chickenwire door and into the toolroom with its row of hooks from which depended the coats and shirts and now one stiff linen collar and tie such as might be seen on a barbershop hook where a preacher was being shaved and which she recognised as belonging to the circuitriderlooking man in steel spectacles who won the Graves Trophy race at Miami two months ago. There was neither lock nor hook on this door, and the other, the one through which Jiggs had entered, hung perfectly blank too save for the greaseprints of hands; for less than a second she stood perfectly still, looking at the second door while her hand made a single quick stroking movement about the doorjamb where hook or lock would have been. It was less than a second, then she went on to the corner where the lavatory was—the greasestreaked bowl, the cake of what looked like lava, the metal case for paper towels—and laid the bundle carefully on the floor next the wall where the floor was cleanest and rose and looked at the door again for a pause that was less than a second—a woman not tall and not thin, looking almost like a man in the greasy coverall, with the pale strong rough ragged hair actually darker where it was sunburned, a tanned heavyjawed face in which the eyes looked like pieces of china. It was hardly a pause; she rolled her sleeves back, shaking the folds free and loose, and opened the coverall at the throat and freed it about her shoulders too like she had the sleeves, obviously and apparently arranging it so she would not need to touch the foul garment any more than necessary again. Then she scrubbed face neck and forearms with the harsh soap and rinsed and dried herself and, stooping, keeping her arms well away from the coverall, she opened the rolled sweater on the floor. It contained a comb, a cheap metal vanity and a pair of stockings rolled in turn into a man's clean white shirt and a worn wool skirt. She used the comb and the vanity's mirror, stopping to scrub again at the grease-smudge on her forehead. Then she unbuttoned the shirt and shook out the skirt and spread paper towels on the lavatory and laid the garments on them, openings upward and facing her and, holding the open edges of the coverall's front between two more paper towels, she paused and looked again at the door: a single still cold glance empty of either hesitation, concern, or regret while even here the faint beat of the band came in mute thuds and blares. Then she turned her back slightly toward the door and in the same motion with which she reached for the skirt she stepped out of the coverall in a pair of brown walking shoes not new now and which had not cost very much when they had been, and a man's thin cotton undershorts and nothing else.

Now the first starting bomb went—a jarring thud followed by a vicious light repercussion as if the bomb had set off another smaller one in the now empty hangar and in the rotundra too. Within the domed steel vacuum the single report became myriad, high and everywhere about the concave ceiling like invisible unearthly winged creatures of that yet unvisioned tomorrow, mechanical instead of blood bone and meat, speaking to one another in vicious highpitched ejaculations as though concerting an attack on something below. There was an amplifyer in the rotundra too and through it the sound of the aeroplanes turning the field pylon on each lap filled the rotundra and the restaurant where the woman and the reporter sat while the little boy finished the second dish of icecream. The amplifyer filled rotundra and restaurant even above the sound of feet as the crowd moiled and milled and trickled through the gates onto the field, with the announcer's voice harsh masculine and disembodied; then at the end of each lap would come the mounting and then fading snarl and snore of engines as the aeroplanes came up and zoomed and banked away, leaving once more the scuffle and murmur of feet on tile and the voice of the announcer reverberant and sonorous within the domed shell of glass and steel in a running commentation to which apparently none listened, as if the voice were merely some unavoidable and inexplicable phenomenon of nature like the sound of wind or of erosion. Then the band would begin to play again, though faint and almost trivial behind and below the voice, as if the voice actually were that natural phenomenon against which all man-made sounds and noises blew and vanished like leaves. Then the bomb again, the faint fierce thwack-thwack-thwack, and the sound of engines again too and trivial and meaningless as the band, as though like the band mere insignificant properties which the voice used for emphasis as the magician uses his wand or handkerchief: "——ending the second event, the two hundred cubic inch class dash, the correct time of the winner of which will be given you as soon as the judges report. Meanwhile while we are waiting for it to come in I will run briefly over the afternoon's program of events for the benefit of those who have come in late or have not purchased a program which by the way may be purchased for twenty-five cents from any of the attendants in the purple-and-gold Mardi Gras caps——"

"I got one here," the reporter said. He produced it, along with a mass of blank yellow copy and a folded newspaper of the morning, from the same pocket of his disreputable coat— a pamphlet already opened and creased back upon the faint mimeographed letters of the first page:

Thursday (Dedication Day)

2:30 P.M.	Spot Parachute Jump. Purse $25.00
3:00 P.M.	200 cu. in. Dash. Qualifying Speed 100 mph. Purse $150.00 (1) 45%. (2) 30%. (3) 15% (4) 10%
3:30 P.M.	Aerial Acrobatics. Jules Despleins, France. Lieut. Frank Burnham, United States
4:30 P.M.	Scull Dash. 375 cu.in. Qualifying Speed 160 m.p.h. (1, 2, 3, 4)
5:00 P.M.	Delayed Parachute Drop

———————

8:00 P.M.   Special Mardi Gras Evening Event. Rocket Plane.
             Lieut. Frank Burnham

"Keep it," the reporter said. "I dont need it."

"Thanks," the woman said. "I know the setup." She looked
at the boy. "Hurry and finish it," she said. "You have already
eaten more than you can hold." The reporter looked at the
boy too, with that expression leashed, eager, cadaverous; sitting forward on the flimsy chair in that attitude at once inert
yet precarious and lightpoised as though for violent and complete departure like a scarecrow in a winter field. "All I can
do for him is buy him something to eat," he said. "To take
him to see an air race would be like taking a colt out to Washington Park for the day. You are from Iowa and Shumann
was born in Ohio and he was born in California and he has
been across the United States four times, let alone Canada
and Mexico. Jesus. He could take me and show me, couldn't
he?" But the woman was looking at the boy; she did not seem
to have heard at all.

"Go on," she said. "Finish it or leave it."

"And then we'll eat some candy," the reporter said. "Hey,
Dempsey?"

"No," the woman said. "He's had enough."

"But maybe for later?" the reporter said. She looked at him
now: the pale stare without curiosity, perfectly grave, perfectly blank, as he rose, moved, dry loose weightless and sudden and longer than a lath, the disreputable suit ballooning
even in this windless conditioned air as he went toward the
candy counter. Above the shuffle and murmur of feet in the
lobby and above the clash and clatter of crockery in the restaurant the amplified voice still spoke, profound and effortless, as though it were the voice of the steel-and-chromium
mausoleum itself talking of creatures imbued with motion
though not with life and incomprehensible to the puny crawling painwebbed globe, incapable of suffering, wombed and
born complete and instantaneous, cunning intricate and
deadly, from out some blind iron batcave of the earth's prime
foundation:

"——dedication meet, Feinman million dollar airport,
New Valois, Franciana, held under the official auspices of the

American Aeronautical Association. And here is the official clocking of the winners of the two hundred cubic inch race which you just witnessed——" Now they had to breast the slow current; the gatemen (these wore tunics of purple-and-gold as well as caps) would not let them pass because the woman and the child had no tickets. So they had to go back and out and around through the hangar to reach the apron. And here the voice met them again—or rather it had never ceased; they had merely walked in it without hearing or feeling it like in the sunshine; the voice too almost as sourceless as light. Now, on the apron, the third bomb went and looking up the apron from where he stood among the other mechanics about the aeroplanes waiting for the next race, Jiggs saw the three of them—the woman in an attitude of inattentive hearing without listening, the scarecrow man who even from here Jiggs could discern to be talking steadily and even now and then gesticulating, the small khaki spot of the little boy's dungarees riding high on his shoulder and the small hand holding a scarcetasted chocolate bar in a kind of static surfeit. They went on, though Jiggs saw them twice more, the second time the shadow of the man's and the little boy's heads falling for an incredible distance eastward along the apron. Then the taller man began to beckon him and already the five aeroplanes entered for the race were moving, the tails high on the shoulders of their crews, out toward the starting line.

When he and the taller man returned to the apron the band was still playing. Faced by the bright stands with their whipping skyline of purple-and-gold pennons the amplifyers at regular intervals along the apronedge erupted snatched blares of ghostlike and ubiquitous sound which, as Jiggs and the other passed them, died each into the next without loss of beat or particular gain in sense or tune. Beyond the amplifyers and the apron lay the flat triangle of reclaimed and tortured earth dragged with slow mechanical violence into air and alterations of light—the oyster-and-shrimpfossil bed notched into the ceaseless surface of the outraged lake and upon which the immaculate concrete runways lay in the attitude of two stiffly embracing capital Fs, on one of which the six aeroplanes rested like six motionless wasps, the slanting sun glinting on their soft bright paint and on the faint propellerblurs. Now the band ceased; the bomb bloomed again on the pale sky and had already begun to fade even before the jarring thud, the thin vicious crack of reverberation; and now the voice again, amplified and ubiquitous, louder even than the spatter and snarl of the engines as the six aeroplanes rose raggedly and dissolved, converging, coveying, toward the scattering pylon out in the lake: "—fourth event, Scull Speed Dash, three hundred and seventy-five cubic inch, twenty-five miles, five times around, purse three hundred and twenty-five dollars. I'll give you the names of the contestants as the boys, the other pilots on the apron here, figure they will come in. First and second will be Al Myers and Bob Bullitt, in number thirty-two and number five. You can take your choice, your guess is as good as ours; they are both good pilots—Bullitt won the Graves Trophy against a hot field in Miami in December—and they are both flying Chance Specials. It will be the pilot, and I'm not going to make anybody mad by making a guess——Vas you dere, Sharlie? I mean Mrs Bullitt. The other boys are good too, but Myers and Bullitt have the ships. So I'll say third will be Jimmy Ott, and Roger Shumann and Joe Grant last, because as I said, the other boys have the ships——There they are, coming in from the scattering pylon, and it's——Yes, it's Myers or Bullitt out front and Ott close behind, and Shumann and Grant pretty well back. And here they are coming in for the first pylon." The voice was firm, pleasant, assured; it had an American reputation for announcing air meets as other voices had for football or music or prizefights. A pilot himself, the announcer stood hiphigh among the caps and horns of the bandstand below the reserved seats, bareheaded, in a tweed jacket even a little oversmart, reminiscent a trifle more of Hollywood Avenue than of Madison, with the modest winged badge of a good solid pilots' fraternity in the lapel and turned a little to face the box seats while he spoke into the microphone as the aeroplanes roared up and banked around the field pylon and faded again in irregular order.

"There's Feinman," Jiggs said. "In the yellow-and-blue pulpit. The one in the gray suit and the flower. The one with the women. Yair; he'd make lard, now."

"Yes," the taller man said. "Look yonder. Roger is going to take that guy on this next pylon." Although Jiggs did not look at once, the voice did, almost before the taller man spoke, as if it possessed some quality of omniscience beyond even vision:

"Well, well, folks, here's a race that wasn't advertised. It looks like Roger Shumann is going to try to upset the boys' dope. That's him that went up into third place on that pylon then; he has just taken Ott on the lake pylon. Let's watch him now; Mrs Shumann's here in the crowd somewhere: maybe she knows what Roger's got up his sleeve today. A poor fourth on the first pylon and now coming in third on the third lap——oh oh oh, look at him take that pylon! If we were all back on the farm now I would say somebody has put a cockleburr under Roger's—well, you know where: maybe it was Mrs Shumann did it. Good boy, Roger! If you can just hold Ott now because Ott's got the ship on him, folks; I wouldn't try to fool you about that—No; wait, w-a-i-t——Folks, he's trying to catch Bullitt oh oh did he take that pylon! Folks, he gained three hundred feet on Bullitt on that turn—Watch now, he's going to try to take Bullitt on the next pylon—there there there—watch him WATCH him. He's beating them on the pylons, folks, because he knows that on the straightaway he hasn't got a chance oh oh oh watch him now, up there from fourth place in four and a half laps and now he is going to pass Bullitt unless he pulls his wings off on this next——Here they come in now oh oh oh, Mrs Shumann's somewhere in the crowd here; maybe she told Roger if he dont come in on the money he needn't come in at all——There it is, folks; here it is: Myers gets the flag *and* now it's Shumann or Bullitt, Shumann or——It's Shumann, folks, in as pretty a flown race as you ever watched——"

"There it is," Jiggs said. "Jesus, he better had come in on somebody's money or we'd a all set up in the depot tonight with our bellies thinking our throats was cut. Come on. I'll help you put the 'chutes on." But the taller man was looking up the apron. Jiggs paused too and saw the boy's khaki garment riding high above the heads below the bandstand, though he could not actually see the woman. The six aeroplanes which for six minutes had followed one another around the course at one altitude and in almost undeviating order like so many beads on a string, were now scattered about the adjacent sky for a radius of two or three miles as if the last pylon had exploded them like so many scraps of paper, jockeying in to land.

"Who's that guy?" the taller man said. "Hanging around Laverne?"

"Lazarus?" Jiggs said. "Jesus, if I was him I would be afraid to use myself. I would be even afraid to take myself out of bed, like I was a cutglass monkeywrench or something. Come on. Your guy is already warmed up and waiting for you."

For a moment longer the taller man looked up the apron, bleakly. Then he turned. "Go and get the 'chutes and find somebody to bring the sack; I will meet——"

"They are already at the ship," Jiggs said. "I done already carried them over. Come on."

The other, moving, stopped dead still. He looked down at Jiggs with a bleak handsome face whose features were regular, brutally courageous, the expression quick if not particularly intelligent, not particularly strong. Under his eyes the faint smudges of dissipation appeared to have been put there by a makeup expert. He wore a narrow moustache above a mouth much more delicate and even feminine than that of the woman whom he and Jiggs called Laverne. "What?" he said. "*You* carried the 'chutes and that sack of flour over to the ship? *You* did?"

Jiggs did not stop. "You're next, aint you? You're ready to go, aint you? And it's getting late, aint it? What are you waiting on? for them to turn on the boundary lights and maybe the floods? or maybe to have the beacon to come in on to land?"

The other walked again, following Jiggs along the apron toward where an aeroplane, a commercial type, stood just without the barrier, its engine running. "I guess you have been to the office and collected my twenty-five bucks and saved me some more time too," he said.

"All right; I'll attend to that too," Jiggs said. "Come on. The guy's burning gas; he'll be trying to charge you six bucks instead of five if you dont snap it up." They went on to where the aeroplane waited, the pilot already in his cockpit, the already low sun, refracted by the invisible propeller blades, shimmering about the nose of it in a faint coppercolored nimbus. The two parachutes and the sack of flour lay on the ground beside it. Jiggs held them up one at a time while the other backed into the harness, then he stooped and darted about the straps and buckles like a squirrel, still talking. "Yair, he come in on the money. I guess I will get my hooks on a little jack myself tonight. Jesus, I wont know how to count higher than two bucks."

"But dont try to learn again on my twenty-five," the other said. "Just get it and hold it until I get back."

"What would I want with your twenty-five?" Jiggs said. "With Roger just won thirty percent. of three hundred and twenty-five, whatever that is. How do you think twenty-five bucks will look beside that?"

"I can tell you a bigger difference still," the other said. "The money Roger won aint mine but this twenty-five is. Maybe you better not even collect it. I'll attend to that, too."

"Yair," Jiggs said, busy, bouncing on his short strong legs, snapping the buckles of the emergency parachute. "Yair, we're jake now. We can eat and sleep again tonight. . . . . . . O.K." He stood back and the other waddled stiffly toward the aeroplane. The checker came up with his pad and took their names and the aeroplane's number and went away.

"Where you want to land?" the pilot said.

"I dont care," the jumper said. "Anywhere in the United States except that lake."

"If you see you're going to hit the lake," Jiggs said, "turn around and go back up and jump again."

They paid no attention to him. They were both looking back and upward toward where in the high drowsy azure there was already a definite alteration toward night. "Should be about dead up there now," the pilot said. "What say I spot you for the hangar roofs and you can slip either way you want."

"All right," the jumper said. "Let's get away from here." With Jiggs shoving at him he climbed onto the wing and into the front cockpit and Jiggs handed up the sack of flour and the jumper took it onto his lap like it was a child; with his bleak humorless handsome face he looked exactly like the comedy young bachelor caught by his girl while holding a strange infant on a street corner. The aeroplane began to move; Jiggs stepped back as the jumper leaned out, shouting: "Leave that money alone, you hear?"

"Okey doke," Jiggs said. The aeroplane waddled out and onto the runway and turned and stopped; again the bomb, the soft slow bulb of cotton batting flowered against the soft indefinite lakehaze where for a little while still evening seemed to wait before moving in; again the report, the thud and jar twice reverberant against the stands as if the report bounced once before becoming echo: and now Jiggs turned as if he had waited for that signal too and almost parallel he and the aeroplane began to move—the stocky purposeful man, and the machine already changing angle and then lifting, banking in a long climbing turn. It was two thousand feet high when Jiggs shoved past the purple-and-gold guards at the main gate and through the throng huddled in the narrow underpass beneath the reserved seats, one of whom plucked at his sleeve:

"When's the guy going to jump out of the parachute?"

"Not until he gets back down here," Jiggs said, butting on past the other purple-and-gold guards and so into the rotundra itself and likewise not into the amplified voice again for the reason that he had never moved out of it:

"—still gaining altitude now; the ship has a long way to go yet. And then you will see a living man, a man like yourselves—a man like half of yourselves and that the other half of yourselves like, I should say—hurl himself into space and fall for almost four miles before pulling the ripcord of the parachute; by ripcord we mean the trigger that——" Once inside, Jiggs paused, looking swiftly about, breasting now with very immobility the now comparatively thin tide which still set toward the apron and talking to itself with one another in voices forlorn, baffled, and amazed:

"What is it now? What are they doing out there now?"

"Fella going to jump ten miles out of a parachute."

"Better hurry too," Jiggs said. "It may open before he can jump out of it." The rotundra, filled with dusk, was lighted now, with a soft sourceless wash of no earthly color or substance and which cast no shadow: spacious, suave, sonorous

and monastic, wherein relief or murallimning or bronze and
chromium skilfully shadowlurked presented the furious, still,
and legendary tale of what man has come to call his conquer-
ing of the infinite and impervious air. High overhead the
dome of azure glass repeated the mosaiced twin Fsymbols of
the runways to the brass twin Fs let into the tile floor and
which, brightpolished, gleaming, seemed to reflect and find
soundless and fading echo in turn monogrammed into the
bronze grilling above the ticket-and-information windows
and inletted friezelike into baseboard and cornice of the synthetic stone. "Yair," Jiggs said. "It must have set them back
that million.—Say, mister, where's the office?" The guard
told him; he went to the small discreet door almost hidden in
an alcove and entered it and for a time he walked out of the
voice though it was waiting for him when, a minute later, he
emerged:

"——still gaining altitude. The boys down here cant tell
just how high he is but he looks about right. It might be any
time now; you'll see the flour first and then you will know
there is a living man falling at the end of it, a living man
falling through space at the rate of four hundred feet a second——" When Jiggs reached the apron again (he too had
no ticket and so though he could pass from the apron into
the rotunda as often as he pleased, he could not pass from
the rotunda to the apron save by going around through the
hangar) the aeroplane was no more than a trivial and insignificant blemish against the sky which was now definitely that
of evening, seeming to hang there without sound or motion.
But Jiggs did not look at it. He thrust on among the upgaz-
ing motionless bodies and reached the barrier just as one of
the racers was being wheeled in from the field. He stopped
one of the crew; the bill was already in his hand. "Monk, give
this to Jackson, will you? For flying that parachute jump.
He'll know."

He went back into the hangar, walking fast now and already unfastening his coverall before he pushed through the
chickenwire door. He removed the coverall and hung it up
and only for a second glanced at his hands. "I'll wash them
when I get to town," he said. Now the first port lights came
on; he crossed the plaza, passing the bloomed bloodless

grapes on their cast stalks on the quadrate bases of which the four Fs were discernible even in twilight. The bus was lighted too. It had its quota of passengers though they were not inside. Including the driver they stood beside it, looking up, while the voice of the amplifyer, apocryphal, sourceless, inhuman, ubiquitous and beyond weariness or fatigue, went on:

"——in position now; it will be any time now—There. There. There goes the wing down; he has throttled back now now Now——There he is, folks; the flour, the flour——" The flour was a faint stain unrolling ribbonlike, light, lazy, against the sky, and then they could see the falling dot at the head of it which, puny, increasing, became the tiny figure of a man plunging without movement toward a single long suspiration of human breath, until at last the parachute bloomed. It unfolded swaying against the accomplished and ineradicable evening; beneath it the jumper oscillated slowly, settling slowly now toward the field. The boundary and obstruction lights were on too now; he floated down as though out of a soundless and breathless void, toward the bright necklace of field lights and the electrified name on each hangarroof; at the moment the green light above the beacon on the signal tower began to wink and flash too: dot-dot-dash-dot. dot-dot-dash-dot. dot-dot-dash-dot. across the nightbound lake. Jiggs touched the driver's arm.

"Come on, Jack," he said. "I got to be at Grandlieu Street before six oclock."

An Evening in New Valois

THE DOWNFUNNELLED LIGHT from the desklamp struck the reporter across the hips; to the city editor sitting behind the desk the reporter loomed from the hips upward for an incredible distance to where the cadaverface hung against the dusty gloom of the city room's upper spaces, in a green corpseglare as appropriate as water to fish—the raked disreputable hat, the suit that looked as if someone else had just finished sleeping in it and with one coat pocket sagging with yellow copy paper and from the other protruding, folded, the cold violent stilldamp black

ALITY OF
BURNED

—the entire air and appearance of a last and cheerful stage of what old people call galloping consumption—the man whom the editor believed (certainly hoped) to be unmarried, though not through any knowledge or report but because of something which the man's living being emanated—a creature who apparently never had any parents either and who will not be old and never was a child, who apparently sprang full-grown and irrevocably mature out of some violent and instantaneous transition like the stories of dead steamboatmen and mules: if it were learned that he had a brother for instance it would create neither warmth nor surprise anymore than finding the mate to a discarded shoe in a trashbin—of whom the editor had heard how a girl in a Barricade Street crib said that it would be like assessing the invoked spirit at a seance held in a rented restaurant room with a covercharge.

Upon the desk, in the full target of the lamp's glare, it lay too: the black bold stilldamp **FIRST FATALITY OF AIR MEET. PILOT BURNED ALIVE.** beyond it, backflung, shirtsleeved, his bald head above the green eyeshade corpseglared too, the city editor looked at the reporter fretfully. "You have an instinct for events," he said. "If you were turned into a room with a hundred people you never saw before and two of them were destined to enact a homicide, you would go straight to them as crow to carrion; you would be there from the very first:

you would be the one to run out and borrow a pistol from the nearest policeman for them to use. Yet you never seem to bring back anything but information. Oh you have that, all right, because we seem to get everything that the other papers do and we haven't been sued yet and so doubtless it's all that anyone should expect for five cents and doubtless more than they deserve. But it's not the living breath of news. It's just information. It's dead before you even get back here with it." Immobile beyond the lamp's hard radius the reporter stood, watching the editor with an air leashed, attentive, and alert. "It's like trying to read something in a foreign language. You know it ought to be there; maybe you know by God it is there. But that's all. Can it be by some horrible mischance that without knowing it you listen and see in one language and then do what you call writing in another? How does it sound to you when you read it yourself?"

"When I read what?" the reporter said. Then he sat down in the opposite chair while the editor cursed him. He collapsed upon the chair with a loose dry scarecrowlike clatter as though of his own skeleton and the wooden chair's in contact, and leaned forward across the desk, eager, apparently not only on the verge of the grave itself but in actual sight of the other side of Styx: of the saloons which have never sounded with cashregister or till; of that golden District where gleam with frankincense and scented oils the celestial anonymous bosoms of eternal and subsidised delight. "Why didn't you tell me this before?" he cried. "Why didn't you tell me before that this is what you want? Here I have been running my ass ragged eight days a week trying to find something worth telling and then telling it so it wont make eight thousand different advertisers and subscribers. . . . . . . But no matter now. Because listen." He jerked off his hat and flung it onto the desk; as quickly the editor snatched it up as if it had been a crust of antladen bread on a picnic tablecloth and jerked it back into the reporter's lap. "Listen," the reporter said. "She's out there at the airport. She's got a little boy, only it's two of them, that fly those little ships that look like mosquitoes. No: just one of them flies the ship; the other makes the delayed parachute jump—you know, with the fifty pound sack of flour and coming down like the haunt of Yuletide or something. Yair; they've got a little boy, about the size of this telephone, in dungarees like they w——"

"What?" the editor cried. "Who have a little boy?"

"Yair. They dont know.——in dungarees like they wear; when I come into the hangar this morning they were clean, maybe because the first day of a meet is the one they call Monday, and he had a stick and he was swabbing grease up off the floor and smearing it onto himself so he would look like they look.——Yair, two of them: this guy Shumann that took second money this afternoon, that come up from fourth in a crate that all the guys out there that are supposed to know said couldn't even show. She's his wife, that is her name's Shumann and the kid's is Shumann too: out there in the hangar this morning in dungarees like the rest of them, with her hands full of wrenches and machinery and a gob of cotter keys in her mouth like they tell how women used to do with the pins and needles before General Motors begun to make their clothes for them, with this Harlowcolored hair that they would pay her money for it in Hollywood and a smear of grease where she had swiped it back with her wrist; she's his wife: they have been married almost ever since the kid was born six years ago in a hangar in California; yair, this day Shumann comes down at whatever town it was in Iowa or Indiana or wherever it was that she was a sophomore in the highschool back before they had the airmail for farmers to quit plowing and look up at; in the highschool at recess, and so maybe that was why she come out without a hat even and got into the front seat of one of those Jennies the army used to sell them for cancelled stamps or whatever it was. And maybe she sent a postcard back from the next cowpasture to the aunt or whoever it was that was expecting her to come home to dinner, granted that they have kinfolks or are descended from human beings, and he taught her to jump parachutes. Because they aint human like us; they couldn't turn those pylons like they do if they had human blood and senses and they wouldn't want to or dare to if they just had human brains. Burn them like this one tonight and they dont even holler in the fire; crash one and it aint even blood when you haul him out: it's cylinder oil the same as in the crankcase. And listen: it's both of them; this morning I walk into the hangar where they are getting the ships ready and I see the kid and a guy that looks like a little horse squared off with their fists up and the rest of them watching with wrenches and things in their hands and the kid rushes in flailing his arms and the guy holding him off and the others watching and the guy put the kid down and I come up and square off too with my fists up too and I says 'Come on, Dempsey; how about taking me on next' and the kid dont move, he just looks at me and then the guy says 'Ask him who's his old man' only I thought he said 'So's his old man' and I said 'So's his old man?' and the guy says 'No. *Who's* his old man' and I said it, and here the kid comes with his fists flailing, and if he had just been half as big as he wanted to be right then he would have beat hell out of me. And so I asked them and they told me." He stopped; he ran out of speech or perhaps out of breath not as a vessel runs empty but with the instantaneous cessation of some weightless winddriven toy, say a celluloid pinwheel. Behind the desk, still backflung, clutching the chairarms, the editor glared at him with outraged amazement.

"What?" he cried. "Two men, with one wife and child between them?"

"Yair. The third guy, the horse one, is just the mechanic; he aint even a husband, let alone a flyer. Yair. Shumann and the airplane landing at Iowa or Indiana or wherever it is, and her coming out of the schoolhouse without even arranging to have her books took home, and they went off maybe with a canopener and a blanket to sleep on under the wing of the airplane when it rained hard, and then the other guy, the parachute guy, dropping in, falling the couple or three miles with his sack of flour before pulling the ripcord. They aint human, you see. No ties; no place where you were born and have to go back to it now and then even if it's just only to hate the damn place good and comfortable for a day or two. From coast to coast and Canada in summer and Mexico in winter, with one suitcase and the same canopener because three can live on one canopener as easy as one or twelve,— wherever they can find enough folks in one place to advance them enough money to get there and pay for the gasoline afterward. Because they dont need money; it aint money they

are after anymore than it's glory because the glory cant only
last until the next race and so maybe it aint even until tomorrow. And they dont need money except only now and then
when they come in contact with the human race like in a
hotel to sleep or eat now and then or maybe to buy a pair of
pants or a skirt to keep the police off of them. Because money
aint that hard to make: it aint up there fourteen and a half
feet off the ground in a vertical bank around a steel post at
two or three hundred miles an hour in a damn gnat built like
a Swiss watch that the top speed of it aint a number on a
little dial but it's where you burn the engine up or fly out
from between the wings and the undercarriage. Around the
home pylon on one wingtip and the fabric trembling like a
bride and the crate cost four thousand dollars and good for
maybe fifty hours if one ever lasted that long and five of them
in the race and the top money at least two-hundred-thirtyeight-
fiftytwo less fines fees commissions and gratuities. And the
rest of them, the wives and children and mechanics, standing
on the apron and watching like they might have been stole
out of a department store window and dressed in greasy khaki
coveralls and not even thinking about the hotel bill over in
town or where we are going to eat if we dont win and how
we are going to get to the next meet if the engine melts and
runs backward out of the exhaust pipe. And Shumann dont
even own a ship; she told me about how they want Vic
Chance to build one for them and how Vic Chance wants to
build one for Shumann to fly only neither Vic Chance nor
them have managed to save up enough jack yet. So he just
flies whatever he can get that they will qualify. This one he
copped with today he is flying on a commission; it was next
to the slowest one in the race and they all said he never had
a chance with it and he beat them on the pylons. So when he
dont cop they eat on the parachute guy, which is O.K. because the parachute guy makes almost as much as the guy at
the microphone does, besides the mike guy having to work
all afternoon for his while it dont only take the parachute guy
a few seconds to fall the ten or twelve thousand feet with the
flour blowing back in his face before pulling the ripcord. And
so the kid was born on an unrolled parachute in a hangar in
California; he got dropped already running like a colt or a

calf from the fuselage of an airplane, onto something because it happened to be big enough to land on and then takeoff again. And I thought about him having ancestors and hell and heaven like we have, and birthpangs to rise up out of and walk the earth with your arm crooked over your head to dodge until you finally get the old blackjack at last and can lay back down again;—all of a sudden I thought about him with a couple or three sets of grandparents and uncles and aunts and cousins somewhere, and I like to died. I had to stop and lean against the hangarwall and laugh. Talk about your immaculate conceptions: born on a unrolled parachute in a California hangar and the doc went to the door and called Shumann and the parachute guy. And the parachute guy got out the dice and says to her 'Do you want to catch these?' and she said 'Roll them' and the dice come out and Shumann rolled high, and that afternoon they fetched the J.P. out on the gasoline truck and so hers and the kid's name is Shumann. And they told me how it wasn't them that started saying Who's your old man? to the kid; it was her, and the kid flailing away at her and her stooping that hard boy's face that looks like any one of the four of them might cut her hair for her with a pocket knife when it needs it, down to where he can reach it and saying 'Hit me. Hit me hard. Harder. Harder.' And what do you think of that?" He stopped again. The editor sat back in the swivel chair and drew a deep, full, deliberate breath while the reporter leaned above the desk like a dissolute and eager skeleton, with that air of worn and dreamy fury which Don Quixote must have had.

"I think you ought to write it," the editor said. The reporter looked at him for almost half a minute without moving.

"Ought to write. . . . . . ." He murmured. "Ought to write. . . . . . ." His voice died away in ecstasy; he glared down at the editor in bonelight exultation while the editor watched him in turn with cold and vindictive waiting.

"Yes. Go home and write it."

"Go home and. . . . . . . Home, where I wont be dis— where I can——O pal o pal o pal! Chief, where have I been all your life or where have you been all mine?"

"Yes," the editor said. He had not moved. "Go home and

lock yourself in and throw the key out the window and write it." He watched the gaunt ecstatic face before him in the dim corpseglare of the green shade. "And then set fire to the room." The reporter's face sank slowly back, like a Halloween mask on a boy's stick being slowly withdrawn. Then for a long time he too did not move save for a faint working of the lips as if he were tasting something either very good or very bad. Then he rose slowly, the editor watching him; he seemed to collect and visibly reassemble himself bone by bone and socket by socket. On the desk lay a pack of cigarettes. He reached his hand toward it; as quickly as when he had flung back the hat and without removing his gaze from the reporter's face, the editor snatched the pack away. The reporter lifted from the floor his disreputable hat and stood gazing into it with musing attention, as though about to draw a lot from it. "Listen," the editor said; he spoke patiently, almost kindly: "The people who own this paper or who direct its policies or anyway who pay the salaries, fortunately or unfortunately I shant attempt to say, have no Lewises or Hemingways or even Tchekovs on the staff: one very good reason doubtless being that they do not want them, since what they want is not fiction, not even Nobel Prize fiction, but news."

"You mean you dont believe this?" the reporter said. "About h—these guys?"

"I'll go you better than that: I dont even care. Why should I find news in this woman's supposed bedhabits as long as her legal (so you tell me) husband does not?"

"I thought that women's bedhabits were always news," the reporter said.

"You thought? You thought? You listen to me a minute. If one of them takes his airplane or his parachute and murders her and the child in front of the grandstand, then it will be news. But until they do, what I am paying you to bring back here is not what you think about somebody out there nor what you heard about somebody out there nor even what you saw: I expect you to come in here tomorrow night with an accurate account of everything that occurs out there tomorrow that creates any reaction excitement or irritation on any human retina; if you have to be twins or triplets or even a regiment to do this, be so. Now you go on home and go to bed. And remember. Remember. There will be someone out there to report to me personally at my home the exact moment at which you enter the gates. And if that report comes to me one minute after ten oclock, you will need a racing airplane to catch your job Monday morning. Go home. Do you hear me?" The reporter looked at him, without heat, perfectly blank, as if he had ceased several moments ago not alone to listen but even to hear, as though he were now watching the editor's lips courteously to tell when he had finished.

"O.K., chief," he said. "If that's the way you feel about it."

"That's exactly the way I feel about it. Do you understand?"

"Yair; sure. Good night."

"Good night," the editor said. The reporter turned away; he turned away quietly, putting the hat on his head exactly as he had laid it on the editor's desk before the editor flung it off, and took from the pocket containing the folded newspaper a crumpled cigarettepack; the editor watched him put the cigarette into his mouth and then tug the incredible hat to a raked dissolute angle as he passed out the door, raking the match across the frame as he disappeared. But the first match broke; the second one he struck on the bellplate while the elevator was rising. The door opened and clashed behind him; already his hand was reaching into his pocket while with the other he lifted the top paper from the shallow stack on the second stool beside the one on which the elevator man sat, sliding the facedown dollar watch which weighted it onto the next one, the same, the identical: black harsh and restrained:

FIRST FATALITY OF AIR MEET: PILOT BURNED ALIVE
Lieut. Frank Burnham in Crash of Rocket Plane

He held the paper off, his face tilted aside, his eyes squinted against the smoke. " 'Shumann surprises spectators by beating

Bullitt for second place'," he read. "What do you think of that, now?"

"I think they are all crazy," the elevator man said. He had not looked at the reporter again. He received the coin into the same hand which clutched a dead stained cob pipe, not looking at the other. "Them that do it and them that pay money to see it." Neither did the reporter look at him.

"Yair; surprised," the reporter said, looking at the paper. Then he folded it and tried to thrust it into the pocket with the other folded one just like it. "Yair. And in one more lap he would have surprised them still more by beating Myers for first place." The cage stopped. "Yair; surprised. . . . . . What time is it?" With the hand which now held both the coin and the pipe the elevator man lifted the facedown watch and held it out. He said nothing, he didn't even look at the reporter; he just sat there, waiting, holding the watch out with a kind of weary patience like a houseguest showing his watch to the last of several children. "Two minutes past ten?" the reporter said. "Just two minutes past ten? Hell."

"Get out of the door," the elevator man said. "There's a draft in here." It clashed behind the reporter again; as he crossed the lobby he tried again to thrust the paper into the pocket with the other one; antic, repetitive, his reflection in the glass street doors glared and flicked away. The street was empty, though even here, fourteen minutes afoot from Grandlieu Street, the February darkness was murmurous with faint uproar, with faint and ordered pandemonium; overhead, beyond the palmtufts, the overcast sky reflected that interdict and lightglared canyon now adrift with serpentine and confetti, through which the floats, bearing grimacing and antic mimes dwarfed chalkwhite and forlorn and contemplated by static curbmass of amazed confettifaces, passed as though through steady rain. He walked, not fast exactly but with a kind of loose and purposeless celerity, as though it were not exactly faces that he sought but solitude that he was escaping, or even as if he actually were going home like the editor had told him, thinking already of Grandlieu Street which he would have to cross somehow in order to do so. "Yah," he thought, "he should have sent me home by airmail." As he passed from light to light his shadow in midstride resolved, pacing him, on pavement and wall. In a dark plate window, sidelooking, he walked beside himself; stopping and turning so that for the moment shadow and reflection superposed he stared full at himself as though he still saw the actual shoulder sagging beneath the dead afternoon's phantom burden, and saw reflected beside him yet the sweater and the skirt and the harsh pallid hair as, bearing upon his shoulder the arch-fathered, he walked beside the oblivious and archadultress.

"Yah," he thought, "the damn little yellowheaded bastard. . . . . . . Yair, going to bed now, to sleep; the three of them in one bed or maybe they take it night about or maybe you just put your hat down on it first like in a barbershop." He faced himself in the dark glass, long and light and untidy as a bundle of laths dressed in human garments. "Yah," he thought, "the poor little towheaded son of a bitch." When he moved it was to recoil from an old man almost over-walked—a face, a stick, a suit filthier even than his own. He extended the two folded papers along with the coin. "Here, pop," he said. "Maybe you can get another dime for these. You can buy a big beer then."

When he reached Grandlieu Street he discovered that by air would be the only way he could cross it, though even now he had not actually paused to decide whether he were really going home or not. And this not alone because of police regulations but because of the physical curbmass of heads and shoulders in moiling silhouette against the lightglare, the serpentine and confettidrift, the antic passing floats. But even before he reached the corner he was assailed by a gust of screaming newsboys apparently as oblivious to the moment's significance as birds are aware yet oblivious to the human doings which their wings brush and their droppings fall upon. They swirled about him, screaming: in the reflected light of the passing torches the familiar black thick type and the raucous cries seemed to glare and merge faster than the mind could distinguish the sense through which each had been received: "Boinum boins!" **FIRST FATALITY OF AIR** "Read about it! Foist Moidigror foitality!" **LIEUT. BURN-HAM KILLED IN AIR CRASH** "Boinum boins!"

"Naw!" the reporter cried. "Beat it! Should I throw away a nickel like it was into the ocean because another lunatic has fried himself?—Yah," he thought, vicious, savage, "even they will have to sleep some of the time just to pass that much of the dark half of being alive. Not to rest because they have to race again tomorrow, but because like now air and space aint passing them fast enough and time is passing them too fast to rest in except during the six and a half minutes it takes to go the twenty-five miles, and the rest of them standing there on the apron like that many window dummies because the rest of them aint even there, like in the girls' school where one of them is gone off first with all the fine clothes. Yair, alive only for six and a half minutes a day in one aeroplane. And so every night they sleep in one bed and why shouldn't the either of them or the both of them at once come drowsing unawake in one womandrowsing and none of the three of them know which one nor care?—Yah," he thought, "maybe I was going home, after all." Then he saw Jiggs, the pony man, the manpony of the afternoon, recoiled now into the center of a small violent backwater of motionless back-turned faces.

"Why dont you use your own feet to walk on?" Jiggs snarled.

"Excuse me," one of the faces said. "I didn't mean——"

"Well, watch yourself," Jiggs cried. "Mine have got to last me to the end of my life. And likely even then I will have to walk a ways before I can catch a ride." The reporter watched him stand on alternate legs and scrub at his feet in turn with his cap, presenting to the smoky glare of the passing torches a bald spot neat as a tonsure and the color of saddleleather. As they stood side by side and looked at one another they resembled the tall and the short man of the orthodox and unfailing comic team—the one looking like a cadaver out of a medical school vat and dressed for the moment in garments out of a floodrefugee warehouse; the other filling his clothing without any fraction of surplus cloth which might be pinched between two fingers, with that trim vicious economy of wrestlers' tights; again Jiggs thought, since it had been good the first time, "Jesus. Dont they open the graveyards until midnight either?" About the two of them now the newsboys hovered and screamed:

"Globe Stoytsman! Boinum boins!"

"Yair," Jiggs said. "Burn to death on Thursday night or starve to death on Friday morning. So this is Moddy Graw. Why aint I where I have been all my life." But the reporter continued to glare down at him in bright amazement.

"At the Terrebonne?" he said. "She told me this afternoon you all had some rooms down in French town. You mean to tell me that just because he won a little money this afternoon he has got to pick up and move over to the hotel this time of night when he ought to been in bed an hour ago so he can fly tomorrow?"

"I dont mean nothing, mister," Jiggs said. "I just said I saw Roger and Laverne go into that hotel up the street a minute ago. I never asked them what for.—How about that cigarette?" The reporter gave it to him from the crumpled pack. Beyond the barricade of heads and shoulders, in the ceaseless rain of confetti, the floats moved past with an air esoteric, almost apocryphal, without inference of motion, like an inhabited archipelago putting out to sea on a floodtide. And now another newsboy, a new face, young, ageless, the teeth gaped raggedly as though he had found them one by one over a period of years about the streets, shrieked at them a new sentence like a kind of desperate ace:

"Laughing Boy in fit at Woishndon Poik!"

"Yair!" the reporter cried, glaring down at Jiggs. "Because you guys dont need to sleep. You aint human. I reckon the way he trains for a meet is to stay out on the town all the night before. Besides that—what was it?—thirty percent. of three hundred and twenty-five dollars he won this afternoon.—Come on," he said. "We wont have to cross the street."

"I thought you were going home so fast," Jiggs said.

"Yair," the reporter cried back over his shoulder, seeming not to penetrate the static human mass but to filter through it like a phantom, without alteration or diminution of bulk; now, turned sideways to cry back at Jiggs, passing between the individual bodies like a playingcard, he cried, "I have to sleep at night. I aint a racing pilot; I aint got an airplane to sleep in; I cant concentrate twenty-five miles of space at three miles an hour into six and a half minutes. Come on." The hotel was not far and the side, the carriage, entrance was com-

paratively clear in the outfalling of light beneath a suave canopy with its lettered frieze: Hotel Terrebonne. Above this
from a jackstaff hung an oilcloth painted tabard: Headquarters, American Aeronautical Association. Dedication
Meet, Feinman Airport. "Yair," the reporter cried, "they'll be
here. Here's where to find guys that dont aim to sleep at the
hotel. Yair; tiered identical cubicles of one thousand rented
sleepings. And if you just got jack enough to last out the
night you dont even have to go to bed."

"Did what?" Jiggs said, already working over toward the
wall beside the entrance. "Oh. Teared Q pickles. Yair; teared
Q pickles of one thousand rented cunts if you got the jack
too. I got the Q pickle all right. I got enough Q pickle for
one thousand. And if I just had the jack too it wouldn't be
teared. How about another cigarette?" The reporter gave him
another one from the crumpled pack. Jiggs now stood against
the wall. "I'll wait here," he said.

"Come on in," the reporter said. "They are bound to be
here. It will be after midnight before they even find out that
Grandlieu Street has been closed. . . . . . . That's a snappy
pair of boots you got on there."

"Yair," Jiggs said. He looked down at his right foot again.
"At least he wasn't a football player or maybe driving a
truck.—I'll wait here. You can give me a call if Roger wants
me." The reporter went on; Jiggs stood again on his left leg
and scrubbed at his right instep with his cap. "What a town,"
he thought. "Where you got to wear a street closed sign on
your back to walk around in it."

"Because at least I am a reporter until one minute past ten
tomorrow," the reporter thought, mounting the shallow steps
toward the lobby; "he said so himself. I reckon I will have to
keep on being one until then. Because even if I am fired now,
at this minute while I walk here, there wont be anybody for
him to tell to take my name off the payroll until noon tomorrow. So I can tell him it was my conscience. I can call him
from the hotel here and tell him my conscience would not let
me go home and go to sleep." He recoiled, avoiding here also
the paperplumage, the parrotmask, a mixed party, whiskey-
and-ginreeking, and then gone, leaving behind them the draggled cumulant hillocks of trampled confetti minching across

the tile floor before the minching pans and brooms of paid monkeymen who for three nights now will do little else; they vanished, leaving the reporter for the instant marooned beside the same easelplat with which the town bloomed—the photographs of man and machine each above its neat legend:

Matt Ord, New Valois. Holder, World's Land
           Plane Speed Record
Al Myers. Calexco
Jimmy Ott. Calexco
R.Q. Bullitt. Winner Graves Trophy, Miami, Fla
Lieut. Frank Burnham

And here also the cryptic shieldcaught (i n r i) loops of bunting giving an appearance temporary and tentlike to the interminable long corridor of machine plush and gilded synthetic plaster running between anonymous and rentable spaces or alcoves from sunrise to sunset across America, between the nameless faience womanface behind the phallic ranks of cigars and the stuffed chairs sentineled each by its spittoon and potted palm;—the congruous stripe of Turkeyred beneath the recentgleamed and homeless shoes running, on into an interval of implacable circumspection: a silent and discreet inference of lysol and a bath—billboard stage and vehicle for what in the old lusty days called themselves drummers: among the brass spittoons of elegance and the potted palms of decorum, legion homeless and symbolic: the immemorial flying buttresses of ten million American Saturday nights, with shrewd heads filled with tomorrow's cosmic alterations in the form of pricelists and the telephone numbers of discontented wives and highschool girls. "Until time to take the elevator up and telephone the bellhop for gals," the reporter thought. "Yair," he thought, "tiered Q pickles of one thousand worn oftcarried phoenixbastions of rented cunts." But the lobby tonight was crowded with more than these; already he saw them fallen definitely into two distinct categories: the one in Madison Avenue jackets, who perhaps once held transport ratings and perhaps still hold them, like the manufacturer who once wrote himself mechanic or clerk retains in the new chromiumGeddes sanctuary the ancient primary die or mimeograph machine with which he started out, and perhaps have

now only the modest Q.B. wings which clip to the odorous
lapel the temperate silk ribbon stencilled Judge or Official
without the transport rating and perhaps the ribbon and the
tweed but not even the wings; and the other with faces both
sober and silent because they cannot drink tonight and fly
tomorrow and have never learned to talk at any time, in blue
serge cut apparently not only from the same bolt but folded
at the same crease on the same shelf, who hold the severe
transport rating and are here tonight by virtue of painfully-
drummed chartertrips from a hundred little nameless bases
known only to the Federal Department of Commerce, about
the land and whose equipment consists of themselves and a
mechanic and one aeroplane which is not new. The reporter
thrust on among them, with that semblance of filtering rather
than passing. "Yair," he thought, "you dont need to look. It's
the smell, you can tell the bastards because they smell like
pressingclubs instead of Harris tweed." Then he saw her,
standing beside a Spanish jar filled with sand pocked by chew-
inggum and cigarettes and burnt matches, in a brown worn
hat and a stained trenchcoat from whose pocket protruded a
folded newspaper. "Yah," he thought, "because a trenchcoat
will fit anybody and so they can have two of them and then
somebody can always stay at home with the kid." When he
approached her she looked full at him for a moment, with
pale blank complete unrecognition, so that while he crossed
the crowded lobby toward her and during the subsequent
three hours while at first he and she and Shumann and Jiggs,
and later the little boy and the parachute jumper too, sat
crowded in the taxicab while he watched the implacable
meterfigures compound, he seemed to walk solitary and chill
and without progress down a steel corridor like a fly in a
gunbarrel, thinking "Yah, Hagood told me to go home and I
never did know whether I intended to go or not. But Jiggs
told me she would be at the hotel but I didn't believe that at
all"; thinking (while the irrevocable figures clicked and clicked
beneath the dim insistent bulb and the child slept on his bony
lap and the other four smoked the cigarettes which he had
bought for them and the cab spun along the dark swamp-
smelling shell road out to the airport and then back to town
again)—thinking how he had not expected to see her again

because tomorrow and tomorrow do not count because that will be at the field, with air and earth full of snarling and they not even alive out there because they are not human. But not like this, in clad decorous attitudes that the police will not even look once at, in the human nightworld of halfpast ten oclock and then eleven and then twelve: and then behind a million separate secret closed doors we will slack ourselves profoundly defenseless on our backs, opened for the profound unsleeping, the inescapable and compelling flesh. Standing there beside the Pyrenæan chamberpot at twenty-two minutes past ten because one of her husbands flew this afternoon in a crate that three years ago was all right, that three years ago was so all right that ever since all the others have had to conjoin as one in order to keep it so that the word 'race' would still apply, so that now they cannot quit because if they once slow down they will be overreached and destroyed by their own spawning, like the Bornean whatsits-name that has to spawn running to keep from being devoured by its own litter. "Yah," he thought, "standing there waiting so he can circulate in his blue serge suit and the other trench-coat among the whiskey and the tweed when he ought to be at what they call home in bed except they aint human and dont have to sleep"; thinking how it seems that he can bear either of them, either one of them alone. "Yair," he thought, "teared Q pickles of one thousand cuntless nights. They will have to hurry before anybody can go to bed with her", walk-ing straight into the pale cold blank gaze which waked only when he reached his hand and drew the folded paper from the trenchcoat's pocket.

"Dempsey asleep, huh?" he said, opening the paper, the page which he could have recited offhand before he even looked at it:

B U R N H A M   B U R N S
VALOISIAN CLAIMS LOVENEST FRAMEUP
Myers Easy Winner in Opener at Feinman Airport
Laughing Boy in Fifth at Washington Park

"No news is good newspaper news," he said, folding the pa-per again. "Dempsey in bed, huh?"

"Yes," she said. "Keep it. I've seen it." Perhaps it was his face. "Oh, I remember. You work on a paper yourself. Is it this one? or did you tell me?"

"Yair," he said. "I told you. No, it aint this one." Then he turned too, though she had already spoken.

"This is the one that bought Jack the icecream today," she said. Shumann wore the blue serge, but there was no trenchcoat. He wore a new gray homburg hat, not raked like in the department store cuts but set square on the back of his head so that (not tall, with blue eyes in a square thin profoundly sober face) he looked out not from beneath it but from within it with open and fatal humorlessness, like an early Briton who has been assured that the Roman governor will not receive him without he wear the borrowed centurion's helmet; he looked at the reporter for a single unwinking moment even blanker than the woman's had been.

"Nice race you flew in there today," the reporter said.

"Yair?" Shumann said. Then he looked at the woman. The reporter looked at her too. She had not moved, yet she now stood in a more complete and somehow terrific immobility, in the stained trenchcoat, a cigarette burning in the grained and blackrimmed fingers of one hand, looking at Shumann with naked and urgent concentration. "Come on," Shumann said. "Let's go." But she did not move.

"You didn't get it," she said. "You couldn't——"

"No. They dont pay off until Saturday night," Shumann said. ("Yah," the reporter thought, clashing the tight hermetic door behind him as the automatic domelight came on; "ranked coffincubicles of dead tail; the Great American in one billion printings slavepostchained and scribblescrawled: annotations of eternal electrodeitch and bottomhope.")

"Deposit five cents for three minutes please," the bland machinevoice chanted. The metal stalk sweatclutched, the guttapercha bloom cupping his breathing back at him, he listened, fumbled, counting as the discreet click and cling died into wirehum.

"That's five," he bawled. "Hear them? Five nickels. Now dont cut me off in three hundred and eighty-one seconds and tell me to——Hello," he bawled, crouching, clutching the metal stalk as if he hung by it from the edge of a swimmingpool; "listen. Get this——Yair. At the Terrebonne——Yair, after midnight; I know. Listen. Chance for the goddamn paper to do something at last beside run our ass ragged between what Grandlieu Street kikes tell us to print in their half of the paper and tell you what you cant print in our half and still find something to fill the blank spaces under Connotator of the World's Doings and Moulder of the Peoples' Thought ha ha ha ha——"

"What?" the editor cried. "Terrebonne Hotel? I told you when you left here three hours ago to——"

"Yair," the reporter said. "Almost three hours, that's all. Just a taxi ride to get to the other side of Grandlieu Street first, and then out to the airport and back because they dont have but a hundred beds for visiting pilots out there and General Behindman needs all of them for his reception and so we come on back to the hotel because this is where they all are to tell him to come back Saturday night provided the bastard dont kill him tomorrow or Saturday. And you can thank whatever tutelary assscratcher you consider presides over the fate destiny and blunders of that office that me or somebody happened to come in here despite the fact that this is the logical place to find what we laughingly call news at ten oclock at night, what with half the airmeet proprietors getting drunk here and all of Mardi Gras done already got drunk here. And him that ought to been in bed three hours ago because he's got to race again tomorrow only he cant race tomorrow because he cant go to bed yet because he hasn't got any bed to go to bed in because they haven't got any money to hire a place with a floor in it with because he only won thirty percent. of three hundred and twenty-five dollars this afternoon and to the guys that own an airmeet that aint no more than a borrowed umbrella and the parachute guy cant do them any good now because Jiggs collected his twenty bucks and——"

"What? What? Are you drunk?"

"No. Listen. Just stop talking a minute and listen. When I saw her out at the airport today they were all fixed up for the night like I tried to tell you but you said it was not news; yair, like you said, whether a man sleeps or not or why he cant sleep aint news but only what he does while he aint asleep, provided of course that what he does is what the guys that are ordained to pick and choose it consider news; yair, I tried to tell you but I'm just a poor bastard of an ambulance-chaser: I aint supposed to know news when I see it at thirty-five bucks a week or I'd be getting more——Where was I? O yair.——had a room for tonight because they have been here since Wednesday and so they must have had somewhere that they could lock the door and take off some of their clothes or at least put the trenchcoat down and lay down themselves, because they had shaved somewhere: Jiggs has got a slash on his jaw that even at a barber college you dont get one like it; so they were all fixed up, only I never asked them what hotel because I knew it would not have a name, just a sign on the gallery post that the old man made on Saturday when his sciatica felt good enough for him to go down town only she wouldn't let him leave until he made the sign and nailed it up: and so what was the use in me having to say 'What street did you say? Where is that?' because I aint a racing pilot, I am a reporter ha ha ha and so I would not know where these places are, Yair, all fixed up, and so he come in on the money this afternoon and I was standing there holding the kid and she says, 'There.' just like that: 'There.' and then I know that she has not moved during the whole six and a half minutes or maybe six and forty-nine-fifty-two ten thousandths or whatever the time was; she just says 'There.' like that and so it was o.k. even when he come in from the field with the ship and we couldn't find Jiggs to help roll the ship into the hangar and he just says 'Chasing a skirt, I guess' and we put the ship away and he went to the office to get his one-O-seven-fifty and we stayed there waiting for the parachute guy to come down and he did and wiped the flour out of his eyes and says, 'Where's Jiggs?' 'Why?' she says. 'Why?' he says. 'He went to collect my money.' and she says, 'My God'——"

"Listen! Listen to me!" the editor cried. "Listen!"

"Yair, the mechanic. In a pair of britches that must have zippers so he can take them off at night like you would peel two bananas, and the tops of a pair of boots this afternoon, because tonight I dont get it, even when I see them;—rivetted under the insteps of a pair of tennis shoes. He collected the parachute guy's twenty-five bucks for him while the parachute guy was still on the way back from work because the parachute guy gets twenty-five berries for the few seconds it takes except for the five bucks he has to pay the transport pilot to take him to the office you might say, and the eight cents a pound for the flour only today the flour was already paid for and so the whole twenty bucks was velvet. And Jiggs collected it and beat it because they owed him some jack and he thought that since Shumann had won the race that he would win the actual money too like the program said and not only be able to pay last night's bill at the whore house where they——"

"Will you listen to me? Will you? Will you?"

"Yair; sure. I'm listening. So I come on to Grandlieu Street thinking about how you had told me to go home and wr— go home, and wondering how in hell you expected me to get across Grandlieu between then and midnight and all of a sudden I hear this excitement and cursing and it is Jiggs where some guy has stepped on his foot and put a scratch on one of them new boots, only I dont get it then. He just tells me he saw her and Shumann going into the Terrebonne because that was all he knew himself; I dont reckon he stayed to hear much when he beat it back to town with the parachute guy's jack and bought the boots and then walked in with them on where they had just got in from the field where Shumann had tried to collect his one-O-seven-fifty and they wouldn't pay him. So I couldn't cross Grandlieu and so we walked on to the Terrebonne even though this is the last place in town a reporter's got any business being at halfpast ten at night, what with all the airmeet getting drunk here, and half of Mardi Gras already——but never mind; I already told you that. So we come on over and Jiggs wont come in and still I dont get it, even though I had noticed the boots. So I come in and there she is, standing by this greaser chamberpot and the lobby full of drunk guys with ribbon badges and these kind of coats that look like they need a shave bad, and the guys all congratulating one another about how the airport cost a million dollars and how maybe in the three days more they could find out how to spend another million and make it balance; and he come up, Shumann come up, and her stiller than the pot even and looking at him and he says they

dont pay off until Saturday and she says 'Did you try? Did
you try?' Yair, trying to collect an installment on the hundred
and seven bucks so they can go to bed, with the kid already
asleep on the sofa in the madam's room and the parachute
guy waiting with him if he happened to wake up, and so they
walked up to the hotel from Amboise Street because it aint
far, they are both inside the city limits, to collect something
on the money he was under the delusion he had won and I
said 'Amboise Street?' because in the afternoon she just said
they had a room down in French Town and she said 'Amboise
Street' looking at me without batting an eye and if you dont
know what kind of beddinghouses they have on Amboise
Street your son or somebody ought to tell you: yair, you rent
the bed and the two towels and furnish your own cover. So
they went to Amboise Street and got a room; they always do
that because in the Amboise Streets you can sleep tonight and
pay tomorrow because a whore will leave a kid sleep on
credit. Only they hadn't paid for last night yet and so tonight
they dont want to take up the bed again for nothing, what
with the airmeet in town, let alone the natural course of
Mardi Gras. So they left the kid asleep on the madam's sofa
and they come on to the hotel and Shumann said they dont
pay off until Saturday and I said 'Never mind; I got Jiggs
outside' and they never even looked at me. Because I hadn't
got it then that Jiggs had spent the money, you see: and so
we went out to the taxi and Jiggs was still standing there
against the wall and Shumann looked at him and says 'You
can come on too. If I could eat them I would have done it at
dinnertime' and Jiggs comes and gets in too, kind of sidling
over and then ducking into the cab like it was a henhouse and
hunkering down on the little seat with his feet under him and
I still dont get it even yet, not even when Shumann says to
him 'You better find a manhole to stand in until Jack gets into
the cab.' So we got in and Shumann says 'We can walk' and
I says 'Where? Out to Lanier Avenue to get across Grandlieu?' and so that was the first dollar-eighty and we eased up
as soon as the door got unclogged a little; yair, they were
having a rush; and we went in and there the kid was, awake
now and eating a sandwich the madam had sent out for him,
and the madam and a little young whore and the whore's fat

guy in his shirtsleeves and his galluses down, playing with the
kid and the fat guy wanting to buy the kid a beer and the kid
setting there and telling them how his old man flew the best
pylon in America and Jiggs hanging back in the hall and jerking at my elbow until I could hear what he was whispering:
'Say, listen. Find my bag and open it and you will find a pair
of tennis shoes and a paper package that feels like it's got a—
a—well, a bootjack in it and hand them out to me, will you?'
and I says 'What? A what in it?' and then the parachute guy
in the room says 'Who's that out there? Jiggs?' and nobody
answered and the parachute guy says 'Come in here' and Jiggs
kind of edged into the door where the parachute guy could
just see his face and the guy says 'Come on' and Jiggs edges a
little further in and the guy says 'Come on' and Jiggs edges
into the light then, with his chin between his shirt pockets
and his head turned to one side and the guy looking him slow
from feet to his head and then back again and says 'The son
of a bitch' and the madam says 'I think so myself. The idea of
them dirty bastard kikes holding him up on a purchase of that
size for just forty cents' and the parachute guy says 'Forty
cents?' Yair, it was like this. The boots was twenty-two-fifty.
Jiggs paid down two dollars and a dime on them and he had
to pay the parachute guy's pilot five bucks and so he never
had but twenty bucks left even when he beat the bus, and so
he borrowed the forty cents from the madam; yair, he left the
airport at five-thirty and did all that before the store closed at
six; he got there just in time to stick one of the tennis shoes
into the door before it shut. So we paid the madam and that
was the next five-forty because the room for last night she just
charged them three bucks for it because they set in her room
so she could use the other one for business until midnight
when the rush slacked up and so she just charged them three
bucks just to use the room to sleep in and the other two
bucks was busfare. And we had the kid and the parachute guy
too now but the driver said it would be o.k. because it would
be a long haul out to the airport, because the program said
there was accommodations for a hundred visiting pilots out
there and if there was more than two or three missing from
the lobby of the Terrebonne it was because they was just lost
and hadn't come in yet, and besides you had told me you

would fire me if I wasn't out there at daylight tomorrow
morning—no; today now—and it was eleven then, almost
tomorrow then, and besides it would save the paper the
cabfare for me back to town. Yair, that's how I figured too
because it seems like I aint used to airmeets either and so we
took all the baggage, both of them and Jiggs' mealsack too,
and went out there and that was the next two dollars and
thirty-five cents, only the kid was asleep again by that time
and so maybe one of the dollars was Pullman extra fare. And
there was a big crowd still there, standing around and looking
at the air where this guy Burnham had flew in it and at the
scorched hole in the field where he had flew in that too, and
we couldn't stay out there because they aint only got beds for
a hundred visiting pilots and Colonel Feinman is using all of
them for his reception. Yair, reception. You build the airport
and you get some receptive women and some booze and you
lock the entrances and the information and ticket windows
and if they dont put any money into the tops of their stockings, it's a reception. So they cant sleep out there and so we
come on back to town and that's the next two dollars and
sixty-five cents because we left the first cab go and we had to
telephone for another one and the telephone was a dime and
the extra twenty cents was because we didn't stop at Amboise
Street, we come on to the hotel because they are still here and
he can still ask them for his jack, still believing that air racing
is a kind of sport or something run by men that have got
time to stop at almost one oclock in the morning and count
up what thirty percent. of three hundred and twenty-five dollars is and give it to him for no other reason than that
they told him they would if he would do something first.
And so now is the chance for this connotator of the world's
doings and molder of the people's thought to——"

"Deposit five cents for three minutes please," the bland
machinevoice said. In the airless cuddy the reporter coinfum-
bled, sweatclutching the telephone; again the discreet click
and cling died into dead wirehum.

"Hello! Hello!" he bawled. "You cut me off; gimme
my——" But now the buzzing on the editor's desk had
sounded again; now the interval out of outraged and apoplec-

tic waiting: the wirehum clicked fullvoiced before the ava-
lanched, the undammed:

"Fired! Fired! Fired! Fired!" the editor screamed. He
leaned halfway across the desk beneath the greenshaded light,
telephone and receiver clutched to him like a tackled halfback
lying half across the goalline, as he had caught the instrument
up; as, sitting bolt upright in the chair, his knuckles white on
the arms and his teeth glinting under his lip while he glared
at the telephone in fixed and waiting fury, he had sat during
the five minutes since putting the receiver carefully back and
waiting for the buzzer to sound again. "Do you hear me?" he
screamed.

"Yair," the reporter said. "Listen. I wouldn't even bother
with that son of a bitch Feinman at all; you can have the right
guy paged right here in the lobby. Or listen. You dont even
need to do that. All they need is just a few dollars to eat and
sleep on until tomorrow; just call the desk and tell them to
let me draw on the paper; I will just add the eleven-eighty I
had to spend to——"

"WILL you listen to me?" the editor said. "Please! Will
you?"

"——to ride out there and——. . . . . . . Huh? Sure. Sure,
chief. Shoot."

The editor gathered himself again; he seemed to extend and
lie a little further and flatter across the desk even as the back
with the goal safe, tries for an extra inch while already
downed; now he even ceased to tremble. "No," he said; he
said it slowly and distinctly. "No. Do you understand? NO."
Now he too heard only dead wirehum, as if the other end of
it extended beyond atmosphere, into cold space; as though he
listened now to the profound sound of infinity, of void itself
filled with the cold unceasing murmur of aeonweary and unflagging stars. Into the round target of light a hand slid the
first tomorrow's galley: the stilldamp neat row of boxes
which in the paper's natural order had no scarehead, containing, since there was nothing new in them since time began,
likewise no alarm:—that crosssection out of timespace as
though of a lightray caught by a speed lens for a second's
fraction between infinity and furious and trivial dust:

FARMERS REFUSE   BANKERS DENY
STRIKERS DEMAND   PRESIDENT'S YACHT
ACREAGE REDUCTION   QUINTUPLETS GAIN
EX-SENATOR RENAUD CELEBRATES TENTH
ANNIVERSARY AS RESTAURATEUR

Now the wirehum came to life.

"You mean you wont——" the reporter said. "You aint going to——"

"No. No. I wont even attempt to explain to you why I will not or cannot. Now listen. Listen carefully. You are fired. Do you understand? You dont work for this paper. You dont work for anyone this paper knows. If I should learn tomorrow that you do, so help me God I will tear their advertisement out with my own hands. Have you a telephone at home?"

"No. But there's one at the corner; I co——"

"Then go home. And if you call this office or this building again tonight I will have you arrested for vagrancy. Go home."

"All right, chief. If that's how you feel about it, O.K. We'll go home; we got a race to fly tomorrow, see?—Chief! Chief!"

"Yes?"

"What about my eleven-eighty? I was still working for you when I sp——"

Night in the Vieux Carré

N OW THEY could cross Grandlieu Street; there was traffic
in it now; to clash and clang of light and bell trolley
and automobile crashed and glared across the intersection,
rushing in a light curbchanneled spindrift of tortured and
draggled serpentine and trodden confetti pending the dawn's
whitewings—spent tinseldung of Momus' Nilebarge clatterfalque; ordered and marked by light and bell and carrying the
two imitationleather bags and the drill mealsack they could
now cross, the four others watching the reporter who, the
little boy still asleep on his shoulder, stood at the extreme of
the curbedge's channelbrim, in poised and swooping immobility like a scarecrow weathered gradually out of the earth
which had supported it erect and intact and now poised for
the first light vagrant air to blow it into utter dissolution. He
translated himself into a kind of flapping gallop, gaining fifteen or twenty feet on the others before they could move,
passing athwart the confronting glares of automobiles apparently without contact with earth like one of those apocryphal
nighttime batcreatures whose nest or home no man ever saw,
which are seen only in midswoop caught for a second in a
lightbeam between nothing and nowhere. "Somebody take
Jack from him," the woman said. "I am afr——"

"Of him?" the parachute jumper said, carrying one of the
bags, his other hand under her elbow. "A guy would no more
hit him than he would a glass barberpole. Or a paper sack of
empty beerbottles in the street."

"He might fall down though and cut the kid all to pieces,"
Jiggs said. Then he said (it was still good, it pleased him no
less even though this was the third time): "When he gets to
the other side he might find out that they have opened the
cemetery too and that would not be so good for Jack." He
handed the sack to Shumann and passed the woman and the
jumper, stepping quick on his short bouncing legs, the boots
twinkling in the aligned tense immobility of the headlights,
and overtook the reporter and reached up for the boy.
"Gimme," he said. The reporter glared down at him without

stopping, with a curious glazed expression like that of one who has not slept much lately.

"I got him," he said. "He aint heavy."

"Yair; sure," Jiggs said, dragging the still sleeping boy down from the other's shoulder like a bolt of wingfabric from a shelf as they stepped together onto the other curb. "But you want to have your mind free to find the way home."

"Yair," the reporter cried. They paused, turning, waiting for the others; the reporter glared down with that curious dazed look at Jiggs who carried the boy now with no more apparent effort than he had carried the aeroplane's tail, half-turned also, balanced like a short pair of tailor's shears stuck lightly upright into the tabletop, leaning a little forward like a dropped bowieknife. The other three still walked in the street—the woman who somehow even contrived to wear the skirt beneath the sexless trenchcoat as any one of the three men would; the tall parachute jumper with his handsome face now wearing an expression of sullen speculation; and Shumann behind them, in the neat serge suit and the new hat which even yet had the appearance of resting exactly as the machine stamped and molded it, on the hatblock in the store—the three of them with that same air which in Jiggs was merely oblivious and lightlyworn insolvency but which in them was that irrevocable homelessness of three immigrants walking down the steerage gangplank of a ship. As the woman and the parachute jumper stepped onto the curb light and bell clanged again and merged into the rising gearwhine as the traffic moved; Shumann sprang forward and onto the curb with a stiff light movement of unbelievable and rigid celerity, without a hair's abatement of expression or hatangle; again, behind them now, the light harried spindrift of tortured confetti and serpentine rose from the gutter in sucking gusts. The reporter glared at them all now with his dazed, strained and urgent face. "The bastards!" he cried. "The son of a bitches!"

"Yair," Jiggs said. "Which way now?" For an instant longer the reporter glared at them. Then he turned, as though put into motion not by any spoken word but by the sheer solid weight of their patient and homeless passivity, into the dark mouth of the street now so narrow of curb that they followed in single file, walking beneath a shallow overhang of iron-grilled balconies. The street was empty, unlighted save by the reflection from Grandlieu Street behind them, smelling of mud and of something else richly anonymous somewhere between coffeegrounds and bananas. Looking back Jiggs tried to spell out the name, the letters inletted into the curbedge in tileblurred mosaic, unable to discern at once that it was not only a word, a name which he had neither seen nor heard in his life, but that he was looking at it upside down. "Jesus," he thought, "it must have took a Frenchman to be polite enough to call this a street, let alone name it" carrying the sleeping boy on his shoulder and followed in turn by the three others and the four of them hurrying quietly after the hurrying reporter as though Grandlieu Street and its light and movement were Lethe itself just behind them and they four shades this moment out of the living world and being hurried, grave quiet and unalarmed, on toward complete oblivion by one not only apparently long enough in residence to have become a citizen of the shadows, but who from all outward appearances had been born there too. The reporter was still talking, but they did not appear to hear him, as though they had arrived too recently to have yet unclogged their ears of human speech in order to even hear the tongue in which the guide spoke. Now he stopped again, turning upon them again his wild urgent face. It was another intersection: two narrow roofless tunnels like exposed mine-galleries marked by two pale oneway arrows which seemed to have drawn to themselves and to hold in faint suspension what light there was. Then Jiggs saw that to the left the street ran into something of light and life—a line of cars along the curb beneath an electric sign, a name, against which the shallow dark grillwork of the eternal balconies hung in weightless and lacelike silhouette. This time Jiggs stepped from the curb and spelled out the street's name. "Toulouse," he spelled. "Too loose," he thought. "Yair. Swell. Our house last night must have got lost on the way home." So at first he was not listening to the reporter, who now held them immobile in a tableau reminiscent (save for his hat) of the cartoon pictures of city anarchists; Jiggs looked up only to see him rushing away toward the lighted sign; they all looked, watching the thin long batlike shape as it fled on.

"I dont want anything to drink," Shumann said. "I want to go to bed." The parachute jumper put his hand into the pocket of the woman's trenchcoat and drew out a pack of cigarettes, the third of those which the reporter had bought before they left the hotel the first time. He lit one and jetted smoke viciously from his nostrils.

"I heard you tell him that," he said.

"Booze?" Jiggs said. "Jesus, is that what he was trying to tell us?" They watched the reporter, the gangling figure in the flapping suit running loosely toward the parked cars; they saw the newsboy emerge from somewhere, the paper already extended and then surrendered, the reporter scarcely pausing to take it and pay.

"That's the second one he has bought tonight since we met him," Shumann said. "I thought he worked on one." The parachute jumper inhaled and jetted the vicious smoke again.

"Maybe he cant read his own writing," he said. The woman moved abruptly; she came to Jiggs and reached for the little boy.

"I'll take him a while," she said. "You and whatever his name is have carried him all evening." But before Jiggs could even release the boy the parachute jumper came and took hold of the boy too. The woman looked at him. "Get away, Jack," she said.

"Get away yourself," the jumper said. He lifted the boy from both of them, not gentle and not rough. "I'll take him. I can do this much for my board and keep." He and the woman looked at one another across the sleeping boy.

"Laverne," Shumann said, "give me one of the cigarettes." The woman and the jumper looked at one another.

"What do you want?" she said. "Do you want to walk the streets tonight? Do you want Roger to sit in the railroad station tonight and then expect to win a race tomorrow? Do you want Jack to——"

"Did I say anything?" the jumper said. "I dont like his face. But all right about that. That's my business. But did I say anything? Did I?"

"Laverne," Shumann said, "give me that cigarette." But it was Jiggs who moved; he went to the jumper and took the child from him.

"Jesus, gimme," he said. "You never have learned how to carry him." From somewhere among the dark dead narrow streets there came a sudden burst of sound, of revelry: shrill, turgid, wallmuted, as though emerging from beyond a low doorway or from a cave—some place airless and filled with smoke. Then they saw the reporter. He appeared from beneath the electric sign, emerging too from out a tilefloored and -walled cavern containing nothing like an incomplete gymnasium showerroom, and lined with two rows of discreet and curtained booths from one of which a faunfaced waiter with a few stumps of rotting teeth had emerged and recognised him.

"Listen," the reporter had said. "I want a gallon of absinth. You know what kind. I want it for some friends but I am going to drink it too and besides they aint Mardi Gras tourists. You tell Pete that. You know what I mean?"

"Sure mike," the waiter said. He turned and went on to the rear and so into a kitchen, where at a zinccovered table a man in a silk shirt, with a shock of black curls, eating from a single huge dish, looked up at the waiter with a pair of eyes like two topazes while the waiter repeated the reporter's name. "He says he wants it good," the waiter said in Italian. "He has friends with him. I guess I will have to give him gin."

"Absinth?" the other said, also in Italian. "Fix him up. Why not?"

"He said he wanted the good."

"Sure. Fix him up. Call mamma." He went back to eating. The waiter went out a second door; a moment later he returned with a gallon jug of something without color and followed by a decent withered old lady in an immaculate apron. The waiter set the jug on the sink and the old lady took from the apron's pocket a small phial. "Look and see if it's the paregoric she has," the man at the table said without looking up or ceasing to chew. The waiter leaned and looked at the phial from which the old lady was pouring into the jug. She poured about an ounce; the waiter shook the jug and held it to the light.

"A trifle more, madonna," he said. "The color is not quite right." He carried the jug out; the reporter emerged from beneath the sign, carrying it; the four at the corner watched him approach at his loose gallop, as though on the verge not of falling down but of completely disintegrating at the next stride.

"Absinth!" he cried. "New Valois absinth! I told you I knew them. Absinth! We will go home and I will make you some real New Valois drinks and then to hell with them!" He faced them, glaring, with the actual jug now gesticulant. "The bastards!" he cried. "The son of a bitches!"

"Watch out!" Jiggs cried. "Jesus, you nearly hit that post with it!" He shoved the little boy at Shumann. "Here; take him," he said. He sprang forward, reaching for the jug. "Let me carry it," he said.

"Yair; home!" the reporter cried. He and Jiggs both clung to the jug while he glared at them all with his wild bright face. "Hagood didn't know he would have to fire me to make me go there. And get this, listen! I dont work for him now and so he never will know whether I went there or not!"

As the cage door clashed behind him, the editor himself reached down and lifted the facedown watch from the stack of papers, from that cryptic staccato crosssection of an instant crystallised and now dead two hours, though only the moment, the instant: the substance itself not only not dead, not complete, but in its very insoluble enigma of human folly and blundering possessing a futile and tragic immortality:

FARMERS   BANKERS   STRIKERS   ACREAGE   WEATHER POPULATION

Now it was the elevator man who asked the time. "Half past two," the editor said. He put the watch back, placing it without apparent pause or calculation in the finicking exact center of the line of caps, so that now, in the shape of a cheap metal disc, the cryptic stripe was parted neatly in the exact center by the blank backside of the greatest and most inescapable enigma of all. The cage stopped, the door slid back. "Good night," the editor said.

"Good night, Mr Hagood," the other said. The door clashed behind him again; now in the glass street doors into which the reporter had watched himself walk five hours ago, the editor watched his reflection—a shortish sedentary man in worn cheap neartweed knickers and rubbersoled golfshoes, a silk muffler, a shetland jacket which unmistakably represented money and from one pocket of which protruded the collar and tie which he had removed probably on a second or third tee sometime during the afternoon, topped by a bare bald head and the horn glasses—the face of an intelligent betrayed asceticism, the face of a Yale or perhaps a Cornell senior outrageously surprised and overwhelmed by a sudden and vicious double decade—which marched steadily upon him as he crossed the lobby until just at the point where either he or it must give way, when it too flicked and glared away and he descended the two shallow steps and so into the chill and laggard predawn of winter. His roadster stood at the curb, the hostler from the allnight garage beside it, the neatgleamed and vaguely obstetrical shapes of golfclubheads projecting, raked slightly, above the lowered top and repeating the glint and gleam of other chromium about the car's dullsilver body. The hostler opened the door but Hagood gestured him in first.

"I've got to go down to French Town," he said. "You drive on to your corner." The hostler slid, lean and fast, past the golfbag and the gears and under the wheel. Hagood entered stiffly, like an old man, letting himself down into the low seat, whereupon without sound or warning the golfbag struck him across the head and shoulder with an apparently calculated and lurking viciousness, emitting a series of dry clicks as though produced by the jaws of a beast domesticated though not tamed, half in fun and half in deadly seriousness, like a pet shark. Hagood flung the bag back and then caught it just before it clashed at him again. "Why in hell didn't you put it into the rumble?" he said.

"I'll do it now," the hostler said, opening the door.

"Never mind now," Hagood said. "Let's get on. I have to go clear across town before I can go home."

"Yair, I guess we will all be glad when Moddy Graw is over," the hostler said. The car moved; it accelerated smoothly and on its fading gearwhine it drifted down the alley, poising without actually pausing; then it swung into the

Avenue, gaining speed—a machine expensive, complex, delicate and intrinsically useless, created for some obscure psychic
need of the species if not the race, from the virgin resources
of a continent, to be the individual muscles bones and flesh
of a new and legless kind—into the empty avenue between
the purple-and-yellow paper bunting caught from post to
post by cryptic shields symbolic of laughter and mirth now
vanished and departed. It rushed along the dark lonely street,
its displacement and the sum of money it represented concentrated and reduced to a single suavely illuminated dial on
which numerals without significance increased steadily toward
some yet unrevealed crescendo of ultimate triumph whose
only witnesses were waifs. It slowed and stopped as smoothly
and skilfully as it had started; the hostler slid out before it
came to a halt. "O.K., Mr Hagood," he said. "Good
night."

"Good night," Hagood said. As he slid across to the wheel
the golfbag feinted silently at him. This time he slammed it
over and down into the other corner. The car moved again,
though now it was a different machine. It got into motion
with a savage overpowered lurch as if something of it besides
the other and younger man had quitted it when it stopped; it
rolled on and into Grandlieu Street unchallenged now by
light or bell. Instead, only the middle eye on each post stared
dimly and steadily yellow, the four corners of the intersection
marked now by four milkcolored jets from the fireplugs and
standing one beside each plug, motionless and identical, four
men in white like burlesqued internes in comedies, while
upon each gutterplaited stream now drifted the flotsam and
jetsam of the dead evening's serpentine and confetti. The car
drifted on across the intersection and into that quarter of narrow canyons, the exposed minegalleries hung with iron lace,
going faster now, floored now with cobbles and roofed by
the low overcast sky and walled by a thick and tremendous
uproar as though all reverberation hung like invisible fog in
the narrow streets, to be waked into outrageous and monstrous sound even by streamlining and airwheels. He slowed
into the curb at the mouth of an alley in which even as he got
out of the car he could see the shape of a lighted second
storey window printing upon the flag paving the balcony's

shadow, and then in the window's rectangle the shadow of an arm which even from here he could see holding the shadow of a drinkingglass as, closing the car door, he turned upon the curb's chipped mosaic inlet *The Drowned* and walked up the alley in outrage but not surprise. When he came opposite the window he could see the living arm itself, though long before that he had begun to hear the reporter's voice. Now he could hear nothing else, scarcely his own voice as he stood beneath the balcony, shouting, beginning to scream, until without warning a short trimlegged man bounced suddenly to the balustrade and leaned outward a blunt face and a tonsure like a priest's as Hagood glared up at him and thought with raging impotence, "He told me they had a horse too. Damn damn damn!"

"Looking for somebody up here, doc?" the man on the balcony said.

"Yes!" Hagood screamed, shouting the reporter's name again.

"Who?" the man on the balcony said, cupping his ear downward. Again Hagood screamed the name. "Nobody up here by that name that I know of," the man on the balcony said; then he said, "Wait a minute." Perhaps it was Hagood's amazed outraged face; the other turned his head and he too bawled the name into the room behind him. "Anybody here named that?" he said. The reporter's voice ceased for a second, no more, then it shouted in the same tone which Hagood had been able to hear even from the end of the alley:

"Who wants to know?" But before the man on the balcony could answer, it shouted again: "Tell him he aint here. Tell him he's moved away. He's married. He's dead." then the voice, for its type timbre and volume, roared: "Tell him he's gone to work!" The man on the balcony looked down again.

"Well, mister," he said, "I guess you heard him about as plain as I did."

"No matter," Hagood said. "You come down."

"Me?"

"Yes!" Hagood shouted. "You!" So he stood in the alley and watched the other go back into the room which he himself had never seen. He had never before been closer to what the reporter who had worked directly under him for twenty

months now called home than the file form which the reporter had filled out on the day he joined the paper. That
room, that apartment which the reporter called bohemian, he
had hunted down in this section of New Valois's vieux carré
and then hunted down piece by piece the furniture which
cluttered it, with the eager and deluded absorption of a child
hunting colored easter eggs. It was a gaunt cavern roofed like
a barn, with scuffed and worn and even rotted floorboards
and scrofulous walls and cut into two uneven halves, bedroom and studio, by an old theatre curtain and cluttered with
slovenlymended and useless tables draped with imitation batik
bearing precarious lamps made of liquorbottles, and other objects of oxidised metal made for what original purpose no
man knew, and hung with more batik and machinemade
Indian blankets and indecipherable basrelief plaques vaguely
religio-Italian primitive. It was filled with objects whose
desiccated and fragile inutility bore a kinship to their owner's
own physical being as though he and they were all conceived
in one womb and spawned in one litter—objects which possessed that quality of veteran prostitutes: of being overlaid by
the ghosts of so many anonymous proprietors that even the
present titleholder held merely rights but no actual possession—a room apparently exhumed from a theatrical morgue
and rented intact from one month to the next.

One day, it was about two months after the reporter had
joined the paper without credentials or any past, documentary
or hearsay, at all, with his appearance of some creature
evolved by forced draft in a laboratory and both beyond and
incapable of any need for artificial sustenance, like a tumble-
weed, with his eager doglike air and his child's aptitude for
being not so much where news happened exactly but for
being wherever were the most people at any given time rushing about the vieux carré for his apartment and his furniture
and the decorations—the blankets and batik and the objects
which he would buy and fetch into the office and then listen
with incorrigible shocked amazement while Hagood would
prove to him patiently how he had paid two or three prices
for them;—one day Hagood looked up and watched a
woman whom he had never seen before enter the city room.
"She looked like a locomotive," he told the paper's owner

later with bitter outrage. "You know: when the board has
been devilled and harried by the newsreels of Diesel trains
and by the reporters that ask them about the future of rail-
roading until at last the board takes the old engine, the one
that set the record back in nineteen-two or nineteen-ten or
somewhere and sends it to the shops and one day they unveil
it (with the newsreels and the reporters all there, too) with
horseshoe rose wreaths and congressmen and thirty-six highschool girls out of the beauty show in bathing suits, and it is
a new engine on the outside only, because everyone is glad
and proud that inside it is still the old fast one of nineteen-
two or -ten. The same number is on the tender and the old
fine, sound, timeproved workingparts, only the cab and the
boiler are painted robin'segg blue and the rods and the bell
look more like gold than gold does and even the supercharger
dont look so very noticeable except in a hard light, and the
number is in neon now: the first number in the world to be
in neon?" He looked up from his desk and saw her enter on
a blast of scent as arresting as mustard gas and followed by
the reporter looking more than ever like a shadow whose pro-
jector had eluded it weeks and weeks ago—the fine big
bosom like one of the walled impervious towns of the
middleages whose origin antedates writing, which have been
taken and retaken in uncountable fierce assaults which overran
them in the brief fury of a moment and vanished, leaving no
trace, the broad tomatocolored mouth, the eyes pleasant
shrewd and beyond mere disillusion, the hair of that diamond-
hard and imperviously recent luster of a gilt service in a
shopwindow, the goldstudded teeth square and white and big
like those of a horse—all seen beneath a plump rich billowing
of pink plumes so that Hagood thought of himself as looking
at a canvas out of the vernal equinox of pigment when they
could not always write to sign their names to them—a canvas
conceived in and executed out of that fine innocence of sleep
and open bowels capable of crowning the rich foul unchaste
earth with rosy cloud where lurk and sport oblivious and in-
congruous cherubim. "I just dropped into town to see who
he really works for," she said. "May I—Thanks." She took
the cigarette from the pack on the desk before he could move,
though she did wait for him to strike and hold the match.

"And to ask you to sort of look out for him. Because he is a fool, you see. I dont know whether he is a newspaperman or not. Maybe you dont know yet, yourself. But he is the baby." Then she was gone—the scent, the plumes; the room which had been full of pink vapor and golden teeth darkened again, became niggard—and Hagood thought, "Baby of what?" because the reporter had told him before and now assured him again that he had neither brothers nor sisters, that he had no ties at all save the woman who had passed through the city room and apparently through New Valois too without stopping, with something of that aura of dwarfed distances and selfsufficient bulk of a light cruiser passing through a canal-lock, and the incredible name. "Only the name is right," the reporter told him. "Folks dont always believe it at first, but it's correct as far as I know."—"But I thought she said her name was—" and Hagood repeated the name the woman had given. "Yair," the reporter said. "It is now."—"You mean she has—" Hagood said. "Yair," the reporter said. "She's changed it twice since I can remember. They were both good guys, too." So then Hagood believed that he saw the picture—the woman not voracious, not rapacious; just omnivorous like the locomotive's maw of his late symbology; he told himself with savage disillusion, Yes. Come here to see just who he really worked for. What she meant was she came here to see that he really had a job and whether or not he was going to keep it. He believed now that he knew why the reporter cashed his paycheck before leaving the building each Saturday night; he could almost see the reporter, running now to reach the postoffice station before it closed—or perhaps the telegraph office; in the one case the flimsy blue strip of money order, in the other the yellow duplicate receipt—so that on that first midweek night when the reporter opened the subject diffidently, Hagood set a precedent out of his own pocket which he did not break for almost a year, cursing the big woman whom he had seen but once, who had passed across the horizon of his life without stopping yet forever after disarranging it, like the airblast of the oblivious locomotive crossing a remote and trashfilled suburban street. But he said nothing until the reporter came and requested a loan twice the size of an entire week's pay, and even then he did not open the matter; it was his face which caused the reporter to explain; it was for a weddingpresent. "A weddingpresent?" Hagood said. "Yair," the reporter said. "She's been good to me. I reckon I better send her something, even if she wont need it."—"Wont need it?" Hagood cried. "No. She wont need what I could send her. She's always been lucky that way."—"Wait," Hagood said. "Let me get this straight. You want to buy a weddingpresent. I thought you told me you didn't have any sisters or br——"—"No," the reporter said. "It's for mamma."—"Oh," Hagood said after a time, though perhaps it did not seem very long to the reporter; perhaps it did not seem long before Hagood spoke again: "I see. Yes. Am I to congratulate you?"—"Thanks," the reporter said. "I dont know the guy. But the two I did know were o.k."—"I see," Hagood said. "Yes. Well. Married. The two you did know. Was one of them your——But no matter. Dont tell me. Dont tell me!" he cried. "At least it is something. Anyway, she did what she could for you!" Now it was the reporter looking at Hagood with courteous interrogation. "It will change your life some now," Hagood said. "Well, I hope not," the reporter said. "I dont reckon she has done any worse this time than she used to. You saw yourself she's still a finelooking old gal and a good goer still, even if she aint any longer one of the ones you will find in the dance marathons at six a.m. So I guess it's o.k. still. She always has been lucky that way."—"You hope. . . . . ." Hagood said. "You. . . . . . . Wait," he said. He took a cigarette from the pack on the desk, though at last the reporter himself leaned and struck the match for him and held it. "Let me get this straight. You mean you haven't been. . . . . . .that that money you borrowed from me, that you send. . . . . . ."— "Send what where?" the reporter said after a moment. "Oh, I see. No. I aint sent her money. She sends me money. And I dont reckon that just getting married again will——" Hagood did not even sit back in the chair. "Get out of here!" he screamed. "Get out! Out!" For a moment longer the reporter looked down at him with that startled interrogation, then he turned and retreated. But before he had cleared the railing around the desk Hagood was calling him back in a voice hoarse and restrained; he returned to the desk and watched the editor snatch from a drawer a pad of note forms and scrawl on the top one and thrust pad and pen toward him. "What's this, chief?" the reporter said. "It's a hundred and eighty dollars," Hagood said in that tense careful voice, as though speaking to a child. "With interest at six percent. per annum and payable at sight. Not even on demand: on sight. Sign it."—"Jesus," the reporter said. "Is it that much already?"—"Sign it," Hagood said. "Sure, chief," the reporter said. "I never did mean to try to beat you out of it."

"So that's his name," Jiggs said. "That what?"

"That nothing!" Hagood said. They stood side by side on the old uneven flags which the New Valoisians claim rang more than once to the feet of the pirate Lafitte, looking up toward the window and the loud drunken voice beyond it. "It's his last name. Or the only name he has except the one initial as far as I or anyone else in this town knows. But it must be his; I never heard of anyone else named that and so no one intelligent enough to have anything to hide from would deliberately assume it. You see? Anyone, even a child, would know it is false."

"Yair," Jiggs said. "Even a kid wouldn't be fooled by it." They looked up at the window.

"I know his mother," Hagood said. "Oh, I know what you are thinking. I thought the same thing myself when I first saw him: what anyone would think if he were to begin to explain where and when and why he came into the world, like what you think about a bug or a worm: 'All right! All right! For God's sake, all right!' And now he has doubtless been trying ever since, I think it was about half past twelve, to get drunk and I daresay successfully."

"Yair," Jiggs said. "You're safe there. He's telling Jack how to fly, about how Matt Ord gave him an hour's dual once. About how when you takeoff and land on them concrete Fs out at the airport he says it's like flying in and out of a, organization maybe; he said organization or organasm but maybe he never knew himself what he was trying to say; something about a couple of gnats hanging around a couple of married elephants in bed together like they say it takes them days and days and even weeks to get finished. Yair, him and Jack both, because Laverne and Roger have gone to bed in the bed with the kid and so maybe him and Jack are trying to get boiled enough to sleep on the floor, because Jesus, he spent enough on that taxi to have taken us all to the hotel. But nothing would do but we must come home with him; yair, he called it a house too; and on the way he rushes into this dive and rushes out with a gallon of something that he is hollering is absinth only I never drank any absinth but I could have made him all he wanted of it with a bathtub and enough grain alcohol and a bottle of paregoric or maybe it's laudanum. But you can come up and try it yourself. Besides, I better get on back; I am kind of keeping an eye on him and Jack, see?"

"Watching them?" Hagood said.

"Yair. It wont be no fight though; like I told Jack, it would be like pushing over your grandmother. It happened that Jack kept on seeing him and Laverne this afternoon standing around on the apron or coming out of the——" Hagood turned upon Jiggs.

"Do I," Hagood cried with thin outrage, "do I have to spend half my life listening to him telling me about you people and the other half listening to you telling me about him?" Jiggs' mouth was still open; he closed it slowly; he looked at Hagood steadily with his hot bright regard, his hands on his hips, lightpoised on his bronco legs, leaning a little forward.

"You dont have to listen to anything I can tell you if you dont want to, mister," he said. "You called me down here. I never called you. What is it you want with me or him?"

"Nothing!" Hagood said. "I only came here in the faint hope that he would be in bed, or at least sober enough to come to work tomorrow."

"He says he dont work for you. He says you fired him."

"He lied!" Hagood cried. "I told him to be there at ten oclock tomorrow morning. That's what I told him."

"Is that what you want me to tell him, then?"

"Yes! Not tonight. Dont try to tell him tonight. Wait until tomorrow, when he. . . . . . You can do that much for your night's lodging, cant you?" Again Jiggs looked at him with that hot steady speculation.

"Yair. I'll tell him. But it wont be just because I am trying to pay him back for what he done for us tonight. See what I mean?"

"I apologise," Hagood said. "But tell him. Do it anyway you want to, but just tell him, see that he is told before he leaves here tomorrow. Will you?"

"O.K.," Jiggs said. He watched the other turn and go back down the alley, then he turned too and entered the house, the corridor, and mounted the cramped dark treacherous stairs and into the drunken voice again. The parachute jumper sat on an iron cot disguised thinly by another Indian blanket and piled with bright faded pillows about which dust seemed to lurk in a thin nimbuscloud even at the end of the couch which the jumper had not disturbed. The reporter stood beside a slopped table on which the gallon jug sat and a dishpan containing now mostly dirty icewater, though a few fragments of the actual ice still floated in it. He was in his shirtsleeves, his collar open and the knot of his tie slipped downward and the ends of the tie darkly wet, as if he had leaned them downward into the dishpan; against the bright vivid even though machinedyed blanket on the wall behind him he resembled some slain curious trophy of a western vacation half finished by a taxidermist and then forgotten and then salvaged again.

"Who was it?" he said. "Did he look like if you would want to see him right after supper on Friday night you would have to go around to the church annex where the boy scouts are tripping one another up from behind?"

"What?" Jiggs said. "I guess so." Then he said, "Yair. That's him." The reporter looked at him, holding in his hand a glass such as chainstore jam comes in.

"Did you tell him I was married? Did you tell him I got two husbands now?"

"Yair," Jiggs said. "How about going to bed?"

"Bed?" the reporter cried. "Bed? When I got a widowed guest in the house that the least thing I can do for him is to get drunk with him because I cant do anything else because I am in the same fix he is only I am in this fix all the time and not just tonight?"

"Sure," Jiggs said. "Let's go to bed." The reporter leaned

against the table and with his bright reckless face he watched Jiggs go to the bags in the corner and take from the stained canvas sack a paperwrapped parcel and open it and take out a brandnew bootjack; he watched Jiggs sit on one of the chairs and try to remove the right boot; then at the sound he turned and looked with that bright speculation at the parachute jumper completely relaxed on the cot, his long legs crossed and extended, laughing at Jiggs with vicious and humorless steadiness. Jiggs sat on the floor and extended his leg toward the reporter. "Give it a yank," he said.

"Sure," the jumper said. "We'll give it a yank for you." The reporter had already taken hold of the boot; the jumper struck him aside with a backhanded blow. The reporter staggered back into the wall and watched the jumper, his handsome face tense and savage in the lamplight, his teeth showing beneath the slender moustache, take hold of the boot and then lift his foot suddenly toward Jiggs' groin before Jiggs could move. The reporter half fell into the jumper, jolting him away so that the jumper's foot only struck Jiggs' turned flank.

"Here!" he cried. "You aint playing!"

"Playing?" the jumper said. "Sure I'm playing. That's all I do—like this." The reporter did not see Jiggs rise from the floor at all; he just saw Jiggs in midbounce, as though he had risen with no recourse to his legs at all, and Jiggs' and the jumper's hands flick and lock as with the other hand Jiggs now hurled the reporter back into the wall.

"Quit it, now," Jiggs said. "Look at him. What's the fun in that, huh?" He looked back over his shoulder at the reporter. "Go to bed," he said. "Go on, now. You got to be at work at ten oclock. Go on." The reporter did not move. He leaned back against the wall, his face fixed in a thin grimace of smiling as though glazed. Jiggs sat on the floor again, his right leg extended again, holding it extended between his hands. "Come on," he said. "Give them a yank." The reporter took hold of the boot and pulled; abruptly he too was sitting on the floor facing Jiggs, listening to himself laughing. "Hush," Jiggs said. "Do you want to wake up Roger and Laverne and the kid? Hush now. Hush."

"Yair," the reporter whispered. "I'm trying to quit. But I cant. See? Just listen at me."

"Sure you can quit," Jiggs said. "Look. You done already quit. Aint you? See now?"

"Yair," the reporter said. "But maybe it's just freewheeling." He began to laugh again, and then Jiggs was leaning forward, slapping his thigh with the flat of the bootjack until he stopped.

"Now," Jiggs said. "Pull." The boot loosened, since it had already been worked at; Jiggs slipped it off. But when the left one came it gave way so suddenly that the reporter went over on his back, though this time he did not laugh; he lay there saying,

"It's o.k. I aint going to laugh," then he was looking up at Jiggs standing over him in a pair of cotton socks which, like the homemade putties of the morning, consisted of legs and insteps only.

"Get up," Jiggs said, lifting the reporter.

"All right," the reporter said. "Just make the room stop." He began to struggle to stay down, but Jiggs hauled him up and he leaned outward against the arms which held him on his feet, toward the couch, the cot. "Wait till it comes around again," he cried; then he lunged violently, sprawling onto the cot and then he could feel someone tumbling him onto the cot and he struggled again to be free, saying thickly through a sudden hot violent liquid mass in his mouth, "Look out! Look out! I'm on now. Let go!" Then he was free, though he could not move yet. Then he saw Jiggs lying on the floor next the wall, his back to the room and his head pillowed on the canvas sack and the parachute jumper at the slopped table, pouring from the jug. The reporter got up, unsteadily, though he spoke quite distinctly: "Yair. That's the old idea. Little drink, hey?" He moved toward the table, walking carefully, his face wearing again the expression of bright and desperate recklessness, speaking apparently in soliloquy to an empty room: "But nobody to drink with now. Jiggs gone to bed and Roger gone to bed and Laverne cant drink tonight because Roger wont let her drink. See?" Now he looked at the jumper across the table, above the jug, the jam glasses, the dishpan, with that bright dissolute desperation though he still seemed to speak into an empty room: "Yair. It was Roger, see. Roger was the one that wouldn't let her have anything to drink tonight, that took the glass out of her hand after a friend gave it to her. And so she and Roger have gone to bed. See?" They looked at one another.

"Maybe you wanted to go to bed with her yourself?" the jumper said. For a moment longer they looked at one another. The reporter's face had changed. The bright recklessness was still there, but now it was overlaid with that abject desperation which, lacking anything better, is courage.

"Yes!" he cried. "Yes!" flinging himself backward and crossing his arms before his face at the same time; at first he did not even realise that it was only the floor which had struck him until he lay prone again, his arms above his face and head and looking between them at the feet of the parachute jumper who had not moved. He watched the jumper's hand go out and strike the lamp from the table and then when the crash died he could see nothing and hear nothing, lying on the floor perfectly and completely passive and waiting. "Jesus," he said quietly, "for a minute I thought you were trying to knock the jug off." But there was no reply, and again his insides had set up that fierce maelstrom to which there was no focalpoint, not even himself. He lay motionless and waiting and felt the quick faint airblast and then the foot, the shoe, striking him hard in the side, once, and then he heard the jumper's voice from above him speaking apparently from somewhere within the thick instability of the room, the darkness, whirling and whirling away, in a tone of quiet detachment saying the same words and in the same tone in which he had spoken them to Jiggs in the brothel six hours ago. They seemed to continue, to keep on speaking, clapping quietly down at him even after he knew by sound that the jumper had gone to the cot and stretched out on it; he could hear the quiet savage movements as the other arranged the dusty pillows and drew the blanket up. "That must be at least twelve times," the reporter thought. "He must have called me a son of a bitch at least eight times after he went to sleep.— Yair," he thought, "I told you. I'll go, all right. But you will have to give me time, until I can get up and move.—Yair," he thought, while the long vertiginous darkness completed a swirl more profound than any yet; now he felt the thick cold oil start and spring from his pores and which, when his dead hand found his dead face, did not sop up nor wipe away beneath the hand but merely doubled as though each drop were the atom which instantaneously divides not only into two equal parts but into two parts each of which is equal to the recent whole; "yesterday I talked myself out of a job, but tonight I seem to have talked myself out of my own house." But at last he began to see: it was the dim shape of the window abruptly against some outer lightcolored space or air; vision caught, snagged and clung desperately and blindly like the pinafore of a child falling from a fence or a tree. On his hands and knees and still holding to the window by vision he found the table and got to his feet. He remembered exactly where he had put the key, carefully beneath the edge of the lamp, but now with the lamp gone his still nerveless hand did not feel the key at all when he knocked it from the table: it was hearing alone: the forlorn faint clink. He got down and found it at last and rose again, carefully, and wiped the key on the end of his necktie and laid it in the center of the table, putting it down with infinite care as though it were a dynamite cap, and found one of the sticky glasses and poured from the jug by sound and feel and raised the glass, gulping, while the icy almost pure alcohol channeled fiercely down his chin and seemed to blaze through his cold wet shirt and onto and into his flesh. It tried to come back at once; he groped to the stairs and down them, swallowing and swallowing the vomit which tried to fill his throat; and there was something else that he had intended to do which he remembered only when the door clicked irrevocably behind him and the cold thick predawn breathed against his damp shirt which had no coat to cover it and warm it. And now he could not recall at once what he had intended to do, where he had intended to go, as though destination and purpose were some theoretical point like latitude or time which he had passed in the hall, or something like a stamped and forgotten letter in the coat which he had failed to bring. Then he remembered; he stood on the cold flags, shaking with slow and helpless violence inside his wet shirt, remembering that he had started for the newspaper to spend the rest of the night on the floor of the now empty city room (he had done it before), having for the time forgotten that he was now fired. If he had been sober he would have tried the door, as people will, out of that vague hope for even though not belief in, miracles. But, drunk, he did not. He just began to move carefully away, steadying himself along the wall until he should get into motion good, waiting to begin again to try to keep the vomit swallowed, thinking quietly out of peaceful and profound and detached desolation and amazement: "Four hours ago they were out and I was in, and now it's turned around exactly backward. It's like there was a kind of cosmic rule for poverty like there is for water-level, like there has to be a certain weight of bums on park benches or in railroad waitingrooms waiting for morning to come or the world will tilt up and spill all of us wild and shrieking and grabbing like so many shooting stars, off into nothing." But it would have to be a station, walls, even though he had long since surrendered to the shaking and felt no cold at all anymore. There were two stations, but he had never walked to either of them and he could not decide nor remember which was the nearer, when he stopped abruptly, remembering the Market, thinking of coffee. "Coffee," he said. "Coffee. When I have had some coffee, it will be tomorrow. Yair. When you have had coffee, then it is already tomorrow and so you dont have to wait for it."

He walked pretty well now, breathing with his mouth wide open as if he hoped (or were actually doing it) to soothe and quiet his stomach with the damp and dark and the cold. Now he could see the Market—a broad low brilliant wallless cavern filled with ranked vegetables as bright and impervious in appearance as artificial flowers, among which men in sweaters and women in men's sweaters and hats too sometimes, with Latin faces still swollen with sleep and vapored faintly about the mouth and nostrils by breathing still warm from slumber, paused and looked at the man in shirtsleeves and loosened collar, with a face looking more than ever like that of a corpse roused and outraged out of what should have been the irrevocable and final sleep. He went on toward the coffee stall; he felt fine now. "Yair, I'm all right now," he thought, because almost at once he had quit trembling and shaking, and when at last the cup of hot pale liquid was set before him he told himself again that he felt fine; indeed, the very fact of his insistence to himself should have been intimation enough that things were not all right. And then he sat perfectly motionless, looking down at the cup in that rapt concern with which one listens to his own insides. "Jesus," he thought. "Maybe I tried it too quick. Maybe I should have walked around a while longer." But he was here, the coffee waited before him; already the counterman was watching him coldly. "And Jesus, I'm right; after a man has had his coffee it's tomorrow: it has to be!" he cried, with no sound, with that cunning selfdeluding logic of a child. "And tomorrow it's just a hangover; you aint still drunk tomorrow; tomorrow you cant feel this bad." So he raised the cup as he had the final glass before he left home; he felt the hot liquid channeling down his chin too and striking through his shirt against his flesh; with his throat surging and trying to gag and his gaze holding desperately to the low cornice above the coffeeurn he thought of the cup exploding from his mouth, shooting upward and without trajectory like a champagnecork; he put the cup down, already moving though not quite running, out of the stall and between the bright tables, passing from one to another by his hands like a monkey runs until he brought up against a table of strawberry boxes, holding to it without knowing why he had stopped nor when, while a woman in a black shawl behind the table repeated,

"How many, mister?" After a while he heard his mouth saying something, trying to.

"Qu'est-ce qu'il voulait?" a man's voice said from the end of the table.

"D' journal d' matin," the woman said.

"Donne-t-il," the man said. The woman stooped and reappeared with a paper, folded back upon an inner sheet, and handed it to the reporter.

"Yair," he said. "That's it." But when he tried to take it he missed it; it floated down between his and the woman's hands, opening onto the first page. She folded it right now and he took it, swaying, holding to the table with the other hand, reading from the page in a loud declamatory voice: "Bankers strike! Farmers yacht! Quintuplets acreage! Reduction gains!——No; wait." He swayed, staring at the shawled woman with gaunt concentration. He fumbled in his pocket; the coins rang on the floor with the same sound which the key made, but now as he began to stoop the cold floor struck him a shocking blow on the face and then hands were holding him again while he struggled to rise. Now he was plunging toward the entrance; he caromed from the last table without even feeling it, the hot corrupted coffee gathering inside him like a big heavy bird beginning to fly as he plunged out the door and struck a lamppost and clung to it and surrendered as life, sense, all, seemed to burst out of his mouth as though his entire body were trying in one fierce orgasm to turn itself wrongsideout.

Now it was dawn. It had come unremarked; he merely realised suddenly that he could now discern faintly the words on the paper and that he now stood in a gray palpable substance without weight or light, leaning against the wall which he had not yet tried to leave. "Because I dont know whether I can make it yet or not," he thought, with peaceful and curious interest as if he were engaged in a polite parlor game for no stakes; when he did move at last he seemed to blow leaflight along the graying wall to which he did not cling exactly but rather moved in some form of light slow attrition, like the leaf without quite enough wind to keep it in motion. The light grew steadily, without seeming to come from any one source or direction; now he could read the words, the print, quite well though they still had a tendency to shift and flow in smooth elusion of sense, meaning while he read them aloud: "Quintuplets bank. . . . No; there aint any pylon— Wait. Wait. . . . Yair, it was a pylon only it was pointed down and buried at the time and they were not quintuplets yet when they banked around it.——Farmers bank. Yair. Farmer's boy, two farmers' boys, at least one from Ohio anyway she told me. And the ground they plow from Iowa; yair, two farmers' boys downbanked; yair, two buried pylons in the one Iowadrowsing womandrowsing pylondrowsing. . . . . . No; wait." He had reached the alley now and he would have to cross it since his doorway was in the opposite wall: so that now the paper was in the hand on the side which now clung creeping to the wall and he held the page up into the gray dawn as though for one last effort, concentrating sight, the vision without mind or thought, on the symmetrical line of boxheads: **FARMERS REFUSE BANKERS DENY   STRIKERS DEMAND   PRESIDENT'S YACHT   ACREAGE REDUCTION   QUINTUPLETS GAIN EX-SENATOR RENAUD CELEBRATES TENTH ANNIVERSARY AS RESTAURATEUR**—the fragile web of ink and paper, assertive, proclamative; profound and irrevocable if only in the sense of being profoundly and irrevocably unimportant—the dead instant's fruit of forty tons of machinery and an entire nation's antic delusion. The eye, the organ without thought speculation or amaze, ran off the last word and then, ceasing again, vision went on ahead and gained the door beneath the balcony and clung and completely ceased. "Yair," the reporter thought. "I'm almost there but still I dont know if I am going to make it or not."

Tomorrow

IT WAS a foot in his back prodding him that waked Jiggs. He rolled over to face the room and the daylight and saw Shumann standing over him, dressed save for his shirt, and the parachute jumper awake too, lying on his side on the couch with the Indian blanket drawn to his chin and across his feet the rug which last night had been on the floor beside the cot. "It's half past eight," Shumann said. "Where's what's his name?"

"Where's who?" Jiggs said. Then he sat up, bounced up into sitting, his feet in the socklegs projecting before him as he looked about the room in surprised recollection. "Jesus, where is he?" he said. "I left him and Jack—Jesus, his boss came down here about three oclock and said for him to be somewhere at work at ten oclock." He looked at the parachute jumper, who might have been asleep save for his open eyes. "What became of him?" he said.

"How should I know?" the jumper said. "I left him lying there on the floor, about where you are standing," he said to Shumann. Shumann looked at the jumper too.

"Were you picking on him again?" he said.

"Yair he was," Jiggs said. "So that's what you were staying awake until I went to sleep for." The jumper did not answer. They watched him throw the blanket and the rug back and rise, dressed as he had been the night before—coat vest and tie—save for his shoes; they watched him put the shoes on and stand erect again and contemplate his now wrinkled trousers in bleak and savage immobility for a moment, then turn toward the faded theatre curtain.

"Going to wash," he said. Shumann watched Jiggs, seated now, delve into the canvas sack and take out the tennis shoes and the bootlegs which he had worn yesterday and put his feet into the shoes. The new boots sat neatly, just the least bit wrinkled about the ankles, against the wall where Jiggs' head had been. Shumann looked at the boots and then at the worn tennis shoes which Jiggs was lacing, but he said nothing: he just said,

"What happened last night? Did Jack——"

"Nah," Jiggs said. "They were all right. Just drinking. Now and then Jack would try to ride him a little, but I told him to let him alone. And Jesus, his boss said for him to be at work at ten oclock. Have you looked down stairs? Did you look under the bed in there? Maybe he——"

"Yair," Shumann said. "He aint here." He watched Jiggs now forcing the tennis shoes slowly and terrifically through the bootlegs, grunting and cursing. "How do you expect them to go on over the shoes?"

"How in hell would I get the strap on the outside of the shoes if I didn't?" Jiggs said. "You ought to know what become of him; you wasn't drunk last night, were you? I told his boss I would——"

"Yair," Shumann said. "Go back and wash." With his legs drawn under him to rise Jiggs paused and glanced at his hands for an instant.

"I washed good at the hotel last night," he said. He began to rise, then he stopped and took from the floor a halfsmoked cigarette and bounced up, already reaching into his shirt pocket as he came up facing the table. With the stub in his mouth and the match in his hand, he paused. On the table, amid the stained litter of glasses and matches burnt and not burnt and ashes which surrounded the jug and the dishpan, lay a pack of cigarettes, another of those which the reporter had bought last night. Jiggs put the stub into his shirt pocket and reached for the pack. "Jesus," he said, "during the last couple months I have got to where a whole cigarette aint got any kick to it." Then his hand paused again, but for less than a watchtick, and Shumann watched it go on to the jug's neck while the other hand broke free from the table's sticky top the glass, the same from which the reporter had drunk in the darkness.

"Leave that stuff alone," Shumann said. He looked at the blunt watch on his naked wrist. "It's twenty to nine. Let's get out of here."

"Yair," Jiggs said, pouring into the glass. "Get your clothes on; let's go check them valves. Jesus, I told the guy's boss I would——Say, I found out last night what his name is. Jesus, you wouldn't never guess in. . . . . . ." He stopped; he and Shumann looked at one another.

"Off again, huh?" Shumann said.

"I'm going to take one drink, that I saved out from last night to take this morning. Didn't you just say let's get out to the field? How in hell am I going to get anything to drink out there, even if I wanted it, when for Christ's sake the only money I have had in three months I was accused of stealing it? When the only guy that's offered me a drink in three months we took both his beds away from him and left him the floor to sleep on and now we never even kept up with him enough to deliver a message from his boss where he is to go to work——"

"One drink, huh?" Shumann said. "There's a slop jar back there; why not get it and empty the jug into it and take a good bath?" He turned away. Jiggs watched him lift the curtain aside and pass beyond it. Then Jiggs began to raise the glass, making already the preliminary grimace and shudder, when he paused again. This time it was the key where the reporter had carefully placed it and beside which Shumann had set the broken lamp which he had raised from the floor. Touching the key, Jiggs found it too vulcanised lightly to the table's top by spilt liquor.

"He must be here, then," he said. "But for Christ's sake where?" He looked about the room again; suddenly he went to the couch and lifted the tumbled blanket and looked under the cot. "He must be somewheres though," he thought. "Maybe behind the baseboard. Jesus, he wouldn't make no more bulge behind it than a snake would." He went back to the table and raised the glass again; this time it was the woman and the little boy. She was dressed, the trenchcoat belted; she gave the room a single pale comprehensive glance, then she looked at him, brief, instantaneous, blank. "Drinking a little breakfast," he said.

"You mean supper," she said. "You'll be asleep in two hours."

"Did Roger tell you we have mislaid the guy?" he said.

"Go on and drink it," she said. "It's almost nine oclock. We have got to pull all those valves today." But again he did not get the glass to his mouth. Shumann was also dressed now; across the arrested glass Jiggs watched the jumper go to the bags and jerk them and then the boots out into the floor and then turn upon Jiggs, snarling,

"Go on. Drink it."

"Dont either of them know where he went?" the woman said.

"I dont know," Shumann said. "They say they dont."

"I told you No," the jumper said. "I didn't do anything to him. He flopped down there on the floor and I put the light out and went to bed and Roger woke me up and he was gone and it's damned high time we were doing the same thing if we are going to get those valves miked and back in the engine before three oclock."

"Yair," Shumann said, "he can find us if he wants us. We are easier for him to find than he is for us to find." He took one of the bags; the jumper already had the other. "Go on," he said, without looking at Jiggs. "Drink it and come on."

"Yair," Jiggs said. "Let's get started." He drank now and set the glass down while the others moved toward the stairs and began to descend. Then he looked at his hands; he looked at them as if he had just discovered he had them and had not yet puzzled out what they were for. "Jesus, I had better wash," he said. "You all go ahead; I'll catch you before you get to the bus stop."

"Sure; tomorrow," the jumper said. "Take the jug too. No; leave it. If he's going to lay around drunk all day long too, better here than out there in the way." He was last; he kicked the boots savagely out of his path. "What are you going to do with these? carry them in your hands?"

"Yair," Jiggs said. "Until I get them paid for."

"Paid for? I thought you did that yesterday, with my——"

"Yair," Jiggs said. "So did I."

"Come on, come on," Shumann said from the stairs. "Go on, Laverne." The jumper went on to the stairs. Shumann now herded them all before him. Then he paused and looked back at Jiggs, dressed, neat, profoundly serious beneath the new hat which Jiggs might still have been looking at through plate glass. "Listen," he said. "Are you starting out on a bat today? I aint trying to stop you because I know I cant, I have tried that before. I just want you to tell me so I can get some-body else to help Jack and me pull those valves."

"Dont you worry about me," Jiggs said. "Jesus, dont I know we are in a jam as well as you do? You all go on; I'll

wash up and catch you before you get to Main Street." They
went on; Shumann's hat sank from sight. Then Jiggs moved
with rubbersoled and light celerity. He caught up the boots
and passed on beyond the curtain and into a cramped alcove
hung with still more blankets and pieces of frayed and faded
dyed or painted cloth enigmatic of significance and inscrutable of purpose, and containing a chair, a table, a washstand,
a chest of drawers bearing a celluloid comb and two ties such
as might be salvaged from a trashbin but for the fact that
anyone who would have salvaged them would not wear ties,
and a bed neatly madeup, so neatly restored that it shouted
the fact that it had been recently occupied by a woman who
did not live there. Jiggs went to the washstand but it was not
his hands and face that he bathed. It was the boots, examining with grim concern a long scratch across the instep of the
right one where he believed that he could even discern the reversed trademark of the assaulting heeltap, scrubbing at the
mark with the damp towel. "Maybe it wont show through a
shine," he thought. "Anyway I can be glad the bastard wasn't
a football player." It did not improve any now, however, so
he wiped both the boots, upper and sole, and hung the now
filthy towel carefully and neatly back and returned to the
other room. He may have looked at the jug in passing but
first he put the boots carefully into the canvas sack before
going to the table. He could have heard sounds, even voices,
from the alley beneath the window if he had been listening.
But he was not. All he heard now was that thunderous silence
and solitude in which man's spirit crosses the eternal repetitive rubicon of his vice in the instant after the terror and before the triumph becomes dismay—the moral and spiritual
waif shrieking his feeble I-am-I into the desert of chance and
disaster. He raised the jug; his hot bright eyes watched the
sticky glass run almost half full; he gulped it, raw, scooping
blindly the stale and trashladen water from the dishpan and
gulping that too; for one fierce and immolated instant he
thought about hunting and finding a bottle which he could
fill and carry with him in the bag along with the boots, the
soiled shirt, the sweater, the cigarbox containing a cake of
laundry soap and a cheap straight razor and a pair of pliers
and a spool of safetywire, but he did not. "Be damned if I

will," he cried silently, even while his now ruthless inside was telling him that within the hour he would regret it; "be damned if I will steal any man's whiskey behind his back," he cried, catching up the sack and hurrying down the stairs, fleeing at least from temptation's protagonist, even if it was rather that virtue which is desire's temporary assuagement than permanent annealment, since he did not want the drink right now and so when he did begin to want it, he would be at least fifteen miles away from that particular jug. It was not the present need for another drink that he was running from. "I aint running from that," he told himself, hurrying down the corridor toward the street door. "It's because even if I am a bum there is some crap I will not eat," he cried out of the still white glare of honor and even pride, jerking the door open and then leaping up and outward as the reporter, the last night's missing host, tumbled slowly into the corridor at Jiggs' feet as he had at the feet of the others when the parachute jumper opened the door five minutes before and Shumann dragged the reporter up and the door of its own weight swung to behind them and the reporter half lay again in the frame of it, his nondescript hair broken down about his brow and his eyes closed and peaceful and his shirt and awry tie stiff and sour with vomit until Jiggs in turn jerked open the door and once more the reporter tumbled slowly sideways into the corridor as Shumann caught him and Jiggs hurdled them both as the door swung to with its own weight and locked itself. Whereupon something curious and unpresaged happened to Jiggs. It was not that his purpose had flagged or intention and resolution had reversed, switched back on him. It was as though the entire stable world across which he hurried from temptation, victorious and in good faith and unwarned, had reversed ends while he was in midair above the two men in the doorway; that his own body had become corrupt too and without consulting him at all had made that catlike turn in midair and presented to him the blank and now irrevocable panel upon which like on the screen he saw the jug sitting on the table in the empty room above plain enough to have touched it. "Catch that door!" he cried; he seemed to bounce back to it before even touching the flags, scrabbling at its blank surface with his hands. "Why didn't

somebody catch it?" he cried. "Why in hell didn't you holler?" But they were not even looking at him; now the
parachute jumper stooped with Shumann over the reporter.
"What?" Jiggs said. "Breakfast, huh?" They did not even look
at him.

"Go on," the jumper said. "See what he's got or get away
and let me do it."

"Wait," Jiggs said. "Let's find some way to get him back
into the house first." He leaned across them and tried the
door again. He could even see the key now, still on the table
beside the jug—an object trivial in size, that a man could
almost swallow without it hurting him much probably and
which now, even more than the jug, symbolised taunting and
fierce regret since it postulated frustration not in miles but in
inches; the gambit itself had refused, confounding him and
leaving him hung up on a son of a bitch who couldn't even
get into his own house.

"Come on," the jumper said to Shumann. "See what he's
got—unless somebody has already beat us to him."

"Yair," Jiggs said, putting his hand on the reporter's flank.
"But if we could just find some way to get him back into the
house——" The jumper caught him by the shoulder and
jerked him backward; again Jiggs caught balance, bouncing
back, and saw the woman catch the jumper's arm as the
jumper reached toward the reporter's pocket.

"Get away yourself," she said. The jumper rose; he and the
woman glared at one another—the one cold, hard, calm; the
other tense, furious, restrained. Shumann had risen too; Jiggs
looked quietly and intently from him to the others and back
again.

"So you're going to do it yourself," the jumper said.

"Yes. I'm going to do it myself." They stared at one another for an instant longer, then they began to curse each
other in short hard staccato syllables that sounded like slaps
while Jiggs, his hands on his hips and leaning a little forward
on his lightpoised rubber soles, looked from them to Shumann and back again.

"All right," Shumann said. "That'll do now." He stepped
between them, shoving the jumper a little. Then the woman
stooped and while Jiggs turned the reporter's inert body from

thigh to thigh she took from his pockets a few crumpled bills
and a handfull of silver.

"There's a five and four ones," Jiggs said. "Let me count
that change."

"Three will pay the bus," Shumann said. "Just take three
more."

"Yair," Jiggs said. "Seven or eight will be a plenty. Look.
Leave him the five and one of the ones for change." He took
the five and one of the ones from the woman's hand and
folded them and thrust them into the reporter's fob pocket
and was about to rise when he saw the reporter looking at
him, lying sprawled in the door with his eyes open and quiet
and profoundly empty—that vision without contact yet with
mind or thought, like two dead electric bulbs set into his
skull. "Look," Jiggs said, "he's——" He sprang up, then he
saw the jumper's face for the second before the jumper
caught the woman's wrist and wrenched the money from her
hand and flung it like a handfull of gravel against the reporter's peaceful and openeyed and sightless face and said in a
tone of thin and despairing fury,

"I will eat and sleep on Roger and I will eat and sleep on
you. But I wont eat and sleep on your ass, see?" He took up
his bag and turned; he walked fast; Jiggs and the little boy
watched him turn the alley mouth and vanish. Then Jiggs
looked back at the woman who had not moved and at Shumann kneeling and gathering up the scattered coins and bills
from about the reporter's motionless legs.

"Now we got to find some way to get him into the house,"
Jiggs said. They did not answer. But then he did not seem to
expect or desire any answer. He knelt too and began to pick
up the scattered coins. "Jesus," he said. "Jack sure threw them
away. We'll be lucky to find half of them." But still they
seemed to pay him no heed.

"How much was it?" Shumann said to the woman, extending his palm toward Jiggs.

"Six dollars and seventy cents," the woman said. Jiggs put
the coins into Shumann's hand; as motionless as Shumann,
Jiggs' hot eyes watched Shumann count the coins by sight.

"All right," Shumann said. "That other half."

"I'll just pick up some cigarettes with it," Jiggs said. Now

Shumann didn't say anything at all; he just knelt with his hand out. After a moment Jiggs put the last coin into it. "O.K.," Jiggs said. His hot bright eyes were now completely unreadable; he did not even watch Shumann put the money into his pocket, he just took up his canvas bag. "Too bad we aint got any way to get him off the street," he said.

"Yair," Shumann said, taking up the other bag. "We aint, though. So let's go." He went on; he didn't even look back. "It's a valvestem has stretched," he said. "I'll bet a quarter. That must be why she ran hot yesterday. We'll have to pull them all."

"Yair," Jiggs said. He walked behind the others, carrying the canvas bag. He didn't look back either yet; he stared at the back of Shumann's head with intent secret speculation blank and even tranquil; he spoke to himself out of a sardonic reserve almost of humor: "Yair. I knew I would be sorry. Jesus, you would think I would have learned by now to save being honest for Sunday. Because I was all right until. . . . . .and now to be hung up on a bastard that. . . . . ." He looked back. The reporter still lay propped in the doorway; the quiet thoughtful empty eyes seemed still to watch them gravely, without either surprise or reproach. "Jesus," Jiggs said aloud, "I told that guy last night it wasn't paregoric: it was laudanum or some-thing. . . . . ." because for a little while now he had for-got the jug, he was thinking about the reporter and not about the jug, until now. "And it wont be long now," he thought, with a sort of desperate outrage, his face perfectly calm, the boots striking through the canvas sack, against his legs at each step as he walked behind the other three, his eyes hot blank and dead as if they had been reversed in his skull and only the blank backsides showed while sight contemplated the hot wild secret coiling of drink netted and snared by the fragile web of flesh and nerves in which he lived, resided. "I will call the paper and tell them he is sick," he said out of that spe-cious delusion of need and desire which even in this inviola-ble privacy brushed ruthlessly aside all admission of or awareness of lying or truth: "Maybe some of them will know some way to get in. I will tell him and Laverne that they asked me to wait and show them where. . . . . ." They

reached the alley's mouth. Without pausing Shumann craned
and peered up the street where the jumper had vanished. "Get
on," Jiggs said. "We'll find him at the bus stop. He
aint going to walk out there no matter how much his feelings are hurt." But the jumper was not at the bus stop. The bus
was about to depart but the jumper was not in it. Another
had gone ten minutes before and Shumann and the woman
described the jumper to the starter and he had not been in
that one either. "He must have decided to walk out, after all,"
Jiggs said, moving toward the step. "Let's grab a seat."

"We might as well eat now," Shumann said. "Maybe he will
come along before the next bus leaves."

"Sure," Jiggs said. "We could ask the bus driver to start
taking off the overhead."

"Yes," the woman said, suddenly. "We can eat out there."

"We might miss him," Shumann said. "And he hasn't——"

"All right," she said; she spoke in a cold harsh tone, without looking at Jiggs. "Do you think that Jack will need more
watching this morning than he will?" Now Jiggs could feel
Shumann looking at him too, thoughtfully from within the
machinesymmetry of the new hat. But he did not move; he
stood immobile, like one of the dummy figures which are
wheeled out of slumdistrict stores and pawnshops at eight
a.m., quiet waiting and tranquil; and bemused too, the in-
turned vision watching something which was not even
thought supplying him out of an inextricable whirl of half-
caught pictures, like a roulette wheel bearing printed sentences in place of numbers, with furious tagends of plans and
alternatives—telling them he had heard the jumper say he
was going back to the place on Amboise street and that he,
Jiggs, would go there and fetch him—of escaping even for
five minutes and striking the first person he met and then the
next and the next and the next until he got a half dollar; and
lastly and this steadily, with a desperate conviction of truth
and regret, that if Shumann would just hand him the coin
and say go get a shot, he would not even take it, or lacking
that, would take the one drink and then no more out of sheer
gratitude for having been permitted to escape from impotence
and need and thinking and calculation by means of which he
must even now keep his tone casual and innocent.

"Who, me?" he said. "Hell, I drank enough last night to do me a long time. Let's get on; he must have deadheaded out somehow."

"Yair," Shumann said, still watching him with that open and deadly seriousness. "We got to pull those valves and mike them. Listen. If things break right today, tonight I'll get you a bottle. O.K.?"

"Jesus," Jiggs said. "Have I got to get drunk again? Is that it? Come on; let's get a seat." They got in. The bus moved. It was better then, because even if he had the half dollar he could not buy a drink with it until the bus either stopped or reached the airport, and also he was moving toward it at last; he thought again out of the thunder of solitude, the instant of exultation between the terror and the dismay: "They cant stop me. There aint enough of them to stop me. All I got to do is wait."—"Yair," he said, leaning forward between Shumann's and the woman's heads above the seatback in front of the one on which he and the boy sat, "he's probably already on the ship. I'll go right over and get on those valves and I can send him back to the restaurant." But they did not find the jumper at once at the airport either, though Shumann stood for a while and looked about the forenoon's deserted plaza as though he had expected to see the parachute jumper still in the succeeding elapsed second from that in which he had walked out of sight beyond the alley's mouth. "I'll go on and get started," Jiggs said. "If he's in the hangar I'll send him on to the restaurant."

"We'll eat first," Shumann said. "You wait."

"I aint hungry," Jiggs said. "I'll eat later. I want to get started——"

"No," the woman said; "Roger, dont——"

"Come on and eat some breakfast," Shumann said. It seemed to Jiggs that he stood a long time in the bright hazy sunlight with his jaws and the shape of his mouth aching a little, but it was not long probably, and anyway his voice seemed to sound all right too.

"O.K.," he said. "Let's go. They aint my valves. I aint going to have to ride behind them at three oclock this afternoon." The rotundra was empty, the restaurant empty too save for themselves. "I just want some coffee," he said.

"Eat some breakfast," Shumann said. "Come on, now."

"I aint any hungrier now than I was out there by that lamp-post two minutes ago," Jiggs said. But his voice was still all right. "I just said I would come in, see," he said. "I never said I would eat, see." Shumann watched him bleakly.

"Listen," he said. "You have had—was it two or three drinks this morning? Eat something. And tonight I will see that you have a couple or three drinks if you want. You can even get tight if you want. But now let's get those valves out." Jiggs sat perfectly still, looking at his hands on the table and then at the waitress' arm propped beside him with waiting, wristnestled by four woolworth bracelets, the fingernails five spots of crimson glitter as if they had been bought and clipped onto the fingerends too.

"All right," he said. "Listen too. What do you want? A guy with two or three drinks in him helping you pull valves, or a guy with a gut full of food on top of the drinks, asleep in a corner somewhere? Just tell me what you want, see? I'll see you get it. Because listen. I just want coffee. I aint even telling you; I'm just asking you. Jesus, would please do any good?"

"All right," Shumann said. "Just three breakfasts then," he said to the waitress. "And two extra coffees.——Damn Jack," he said. "He ought to eat too."

"We'll find him at the hangar," Jiggs said. They found him there, though not at once; when Shumann and Jiggs emerged from the toolroom in their dungarees and waited outside the chickenwire door for the woman to change and join them, they saw first five or six other dungaree figures gathered about a sandwich board which had not been there yesterday, set in the exact center of the hangar entrance—a big board lettered heavily by hand and possessing a quality cryptic and peremptory and for the time incomprehensible as though the amplifyer had spoken the words:

NOTICE

All contestants, all pilots and parachute jumpers and all others eligible to win cash prizes during this meet, are requested to meet in Superintendent's office at 12 noon today. All absentees will be considered to acquiesce and submit to the action and discretion of the race committee.

The others watched quietly while Shumann and the woman read it.

"Submit to what?" one of the others said. "What is it? Do you know?"

"I dont know," Shumann said. "Is Jack Holmes on the field yet? Has anybody seen him this morning?"

"There he is," Jiggs said. "Over at the ship, like I told you." Shumann looked across the hangar. "He's already got the cowling off. See?"

"Yair," Shumann said. He moved at once. Jiggs spoke to the man beside whom he stood, almost without moving his lips:

"Lend me half a buck," he said. "I'll hand it back tonight. Quick." He took the coin; he snatched it; when Shumann reached the aeroplane Jiggs was right behind him. The jumper, crouched beneath the engine, looked up at them, briefly and without stopping, as he might have glanced up at the shadow of a passing cloud.

"You had some breakfast?" Shumann said.

"Yes," the jumper said, not looking up again.

"On what?" Shumann said. The other did not seem to have heard. Shumann took the money from his pocket—the remaining dollar bill, three quarters and some nickels, and laid two of the quarters on the engine mount at the jumper's elbow. "Go and get some coffee," he said. The other did not seem to hear, busy beneath the engine. Shumann stood watching the back of his head. Then the jumper's elbow struck the engine mount. The coins rang on the concrete floor and Jiggs stooped, ducking, and rose again, extending the coins before Shumann could speak or move.

"There they are," Jiggs said, not loud; he could not have been heard ten feet away: the fierceness, the triumph. "There you are. Count them. Count both sides so you will be sure." After that they did not talk anymore. They worked quiet and fast, like a circus team, with the trained team's economy of motion, while the woman passed them the tools as needed; they did not even have to speak to her, to name the tool. It was easy now, like in the bus; all he had to do was to wait as the valves came out one by one and grew in a long neat line on the workbench and then, sure enough, it came.

"It must be nearly twelve," the woman said. Shumann finished what he was doing. Then he looked at his watch and stood up, flexing his back and legs. He looked at the jumper.

"You ready?" he said.

"You are not going to wash up and change?" the woman said.

"I guess not," Shumann said. "It will be that much more time wasted." He took the money again from his pocket and gave the woman the three quarters. "You and Jiggs can get a bite when Jiggs gets the rest of the valves out. And, say—" he looked at Jiggs "—dont bother about trying to put the micrometer on them yourself. I'll do that when I get back. You can clean out the supercharger; that ought to hold you until we get back." He looked at Jiggs. "You ought to be hungry now."

"Yair," Jiggs said. He had not stopped; he did not watch them go out. He just squatted beneath the engine with the spraddled tenseness of an umbrellarib, feeling the woman looking at the back of his head. He spoke now without fury, without triumph, to himself: without sound: "Yair, beat it. You cant stop me. You couldn't stop me but for a minute even if you tried to hold me between your legs." He was not thinking of the woman as Laverne, as anyone: she was just the last and now swiftlyfading residuum of the *it*, the *they*, watching the back of his head as he removed the supercharger without even knowing that she was already defeated.

"Do you want to eat now?" she said. He didn't answer. "Do you want me to bring you a sandwich?" He didn't answer. "Jiggs," she said. He looked up and back, his eyebrows rising and vanishing beyond the cap's peak, the hot bright eyes blank, interrogatory, arrested.

"What? How was that?" he said. "Did you call me?"

"Yes. Do you want to go and eat now or do you want me to bring you something?"

"No. I aint hungry yet. I want to get done with this supercharger before I wash my hands. You go on." But she didn't move yet; she stood looking at him.

"I'll leave you some money and you can go when you are ready, then."

"Money?" he said. "What do I need with money up to my elbows in this engine?" She turned away then. He watched her pause and call the little boy, who came out of a group across the hangar and joined her; they went on toward the apron and disappeared. Then Jiggs rose; he laid the tool down carefully, touching the coin in his pocket through the cloth, though he did not need to since he had never ceased to feel it; he was not thinking about her, not talking to her; he spoke without triumph or exultation, quietly: "Goodbye, you snooping bitch," he said.

But they had not been able to tell if the reporter had seen them or not, though he probably could neither see nor hear; certainly the thin youngish lightcolored negress who came up the alley about half past nine, in a modish though not new hat and coat and carrying a wicker marketbasket covered neatly with a clean napkin, decided almost immediately that he could not. She looked down at him for perhaps ten seconds with complete and impersonal speculation, then she waggled one hand before his face and called him by name: and when she reached into his pockets she did not move or shift his body at all; her hand reached in and drew out the two folded bills where Jiggs had put them with a single motion limber and boneless and softly rapacious as that of an octopus, then the hand made a second limber swift motion, inside her coat now, and emerged empty. It was her racial and sex's nature to have taken but one of the bills, no matter how many there might have been—either the five or the one, depending upon her own need or desire of the moment or upon the situation itself—but now she took them both and stood again, looking down at the man in the doorway with a kind of grim though still impersonal sanctimoniousness. "If he found any of hit left hit wouldn't learn him no lesson," she said, aloud. "Laying out here in the street, drunk. Aint no telling where he been at, but hit couldn't a been much for them to let him git back out and that much money in his pocket." She took a key from somewhere beneath the coat and unlocked the door and caught him back in her turn as he began to tumble slowly and deliberately into the corridor, and entered herself. She was not gone long and now she carried the dishpan of dirty water, which she flung suddenly into his face and caught him again as he gasped and started. "I hopes you had sense enough to left your pocketbook in the house fo you decided to take a nap out here," she cried, shaking him. "If you didn't, I bound all you got left now is the pocketbook." She carried him up the cramped stairs almost bodily, like that much firehose, and left him apparently unconscious again on the cot and went beyond the curtain and looked once with a perfectly inscrutable face at the neat bed which but one glance told her was not her handiwork. From the basket she took an apron and a bright handkerchief; when she returned to the reporter she wore the apron and the handkerchief about her head in place of the hat and coat, and she carried the dishpan filled now with fresh water, and soap and towels; she had done this before too, apparently, stripping the fouled shirt from the man who was her employer for this half hour of the six weekdays, and both washing him off and slapping him awake during the process until he could see and hear again. "It's past ten oclock," she said. "I done lit the gas so you can shave."

"Shave?" he said. "Didn't you know? I dont have to ever shave again. I'm fired."

"The more reason for you to git up from here and try to look like something." His hair, soaked, was plastered to his skull, yet it fitted no closer to the bones and ridges and joints than the flesh of his face did, and now his eyes did indeed look like holes burned with a poker in a parchment diploma, some postgraduate certificate of excess; naked from the waist up, it seemed as if you not only saw his ribs front and side and rear but that you saw the entire ribcage complete from any angle like you can see both warp and woof of screen wire from either side. He swayed laxly beneath her limber soft and ungentle hands, articulate and even collected though moving for a while yet in the twilight between the delusion of drunkenness and the delusion of sobriety.

"Are they gone?" he said. The negress' face and manner did not change at all.

"Is who gone?" she said.

"Yair," he said, drowsily. "She was here last night. She slept yonder in the bed last night. There was just one of them slept with her and there could have been both of them. But she was here. And it was him himself that wouldn't let her drink, that took the glass out of her hand. Yair. I could hear all the long soft waiting sound of all womanmeat in bed beyond the curtain." At first, for the moment, the negress did not even realise what it was touching her thigh until she looked down and saw the sticklike arm, the brittle light and apparently senseless hand like a bundle of dried twigs too, blundering and fumbling stiffly at her while in the gaunt eyesockets the eyes looked like two spots of dying daylight caught by water at the bottom of abandoned wells. The negress did not become coy nor outraged; she avoided the apparently blind or possibly just still insensible hand with a single supple shift of her hips, speaking to him, calling him by name, pronouncing the m.i.s.t.e.r. in full, in the flat lingering way of negroes, like it had two sets of two or three syllables each.

"Now then," she said, "if you feel like doing something yourself, take a holt of this towel. Or see how much of whatever money you think you had folks is left you, besides leaving you asleep on the street."

"Money?" he said. He waked completely now, his mind did, though even yet his hands fumbled for a while before finding the pocket while the negress watched him, standing now with her hands on her hips. She said nothing else, she just watched his quiet bemused and intent face as he plumbed his empty pockets one by one. She did not mention company again; it was he who cried, "I was out there, asleep in the alley. You know that, you found me. I left here, I was out there asleep because I forgot the key and I couldn't get in again; I was out there a long time even before daylight. You know I was." Still she said nothing, watching him. "I remember just when I quit remembering!"

"How much did you have when you quit remembering?"

"Nothing!" he said. "Nothing. I spent it all. See?" When he got up he offered to help him back to the bedroom, but he refused. He walked unsteadily still, but well enough, and when after a time she followed him she could hear him through the beaverboard wall of the alcove somewhat larger than a clothescloset and which she entered too and set water to heat on the gas plate beside which he was shaving, and prepared to make coffee. She gave the undisturbed bedroom

another cold inscrutable look and returned to the front room
and restored the tumbled cot, spreading the blanket and the
pillows and picked up the soiled shirt and the towel from the
floor and paused, laying the shirt on the couch but still carrying the towel, and went to the table and looked at the jug
now with that bemused inscrutable expression. She wiped
one of the sticky glasses with finicking care and poured into
it from the jug almost what a thimble would have held and
drank it, the smallest finger of that hand crooked delicately,
in a series of birdlike and apparently extremely distasteful sips.
Then she gathered up what she could conveniently carry of
the night's misplaced litter and returned beyond the curtain,
though when she went to where she had set the basket on the
floor against the wall with the hat and coat lying upon it, you
could not hear her cross the floor at all nor stoop and take
from the basket an empty pint bottle sparklingly clean as a
sterilised milkbottle. By ordinary she would not have filled
the flask at any single establishment of her morning round,
on the contrary filling the bottle little by little with a sort of
niggard and foresighted husbandry and arriving at home in
midafternoon with a pint of liquid weird, potent, anonymous
and strange, but once more she seemed to find the situation
its own warrant, returning and putting the filled flask back
into the basket still without any sound. The reporter heard
only the broom for a time, and other muted sounds as though
the room were putting itself to rights by means of some
ghostly and invisible power of its own, until she came at last
to the alcove's doorway, where he stood tying his tie, with
the hat and coat on again and the basket beneath its neat
napkin again on her arm.

"I'm through," she said. "The coffee's ready, but you better
not waste no time over drinking hit."

"All right," he said. "I'll have to make another loan from
you."

"You wont need but a dime to get to the paper. Aint you
got even that much left?"

"I aint going to the paper. I'm fired, I tell you. I want two
dollars."

"I has to work for my money. Last time I lent you hit took
you three weeks to start paying me back."

"I know. But I have to have it. Come on, Leonora. I'll pay you back Saturday." She reached inside her coat; one of the bills was his own.

"The key's on the table," she said. "I washed hit off too." It lay there, on the table clean and empty save for the key; he took it up and mused upon it with that face which the few hours of violent excess had altered from that of one brightly and peacefully dead to that of one coming back from, or looking out of, hell itself.

"But it's all right," he said. "It dont matter. It aint anything." He stood in the clean empty room where there was not even a cigarettestub or a burned match to show any trace. "Yair. She didn't even leave a hair pin," he thought. "Or maybe she dont use them. Or maybe I was drunk and they were not even here"; looking down at the key with a grimace faint and tragic which might have been called smiling while he talked to himself, giving himself the advice which he knew he was not going to take when he insisted on borrowing the two dollars. "Because I had thirty before I spent the eleven-eighty and then the five for the absinth. That left about thirteen." Then he cried, not loud, not moving: "Besides, maybe she will tell me. Maybe she intended to all the time but they couldn't wait for me to come to", without even bothering to tell himself that he knew he was lying, just saying quietly and stubbornly, "All right. But I'm going anyway. Even if I dont do anything but walk up where she can see me and stand there for a minute." He held the key in his hand now while the door clicked behind him, standing for a moment longer with his eyes shut against the impact of light, of the thin sun, and then opening them, steadying himself against the doorframe where he had slept, remembering the coffee which the negress had made and he had forgot about until now, while the alley swam away into mirageshapes, tilting like the sea or say the lakesurface, against which the ordeal of destination, of hope and dread, shaped among the outraged nerves of vision the bright vague pavilionglitter beneath the whipping purple-and-gold pennons. "It's all right," he said. "It aint nothing but money. It dont matter." It was not two when he reached the airport, but already the parkinglots along the boulevard were filling, with the young men paid doubtless out of some wearily initialled national fund, in the purple-and-gold caps lent or perhaps compulsory, clinging to runningboards, moving head-and-shoulders above the continuous topline of alreadyparked cars as though they consisted of torsos alone and ran on wires for no purpose and toward no discernible destination. A steady stream of people flowed along the concrete gutters, converging toward the entrances, but the reporter did not follow. To the left was the hangar where they would be now, but he did not go there either; he just stood in the bright hazy dampfilled sunlight, with the pennons whipping stiffly overhead and the wind which blew them seeming to blow through him too, not cold, not unpleasant: just whipping his clothing about him as if it blew unimpeded save by the garment, through his ribcage and among his bones. "I ought to eat," he thought. "I ought to", not moving yet as though he hung static in a promise made to someone which he did not believe even yet that he was going to break. The restaurant was not far; already it seemed to him that he could hear the clash and clatter and the voices and smell the food, thinking of the three of them yesterday while the little boy burrowed with flagging determination into the second plate of icecream. Then he could hear the sounds, the noise, and smell the food itself as he stood looking at the table where they had sat yesterday, where a family group from a grandmother to an infant in arms now sat. He went to the counter. "Breakfast," he said.

"What do you want to eat?" the waitress said.

"What do people eat for breakfast?" he said, looking at her—a porcelainfaced woman whose hair complexion and uniform appeared to have been made of various shades of that material which oldtime bookkeepers used to protect their sleeves with—and smiling: or he would have called it smiling. "That's right. It aint breakfast now, is it?"

"What do you want to eat?"

"Roast beef," his mind said at last. "Potatoes," he said. "It dont matter."

"Sandwich or lunch?"

"Yes," he said.

"Yes what? You wanna order dont you wanna?"

"Sandwich," he said.

"Mash one!" the waitress cried.

"And that's that," he thought, as though he had discharged the promise; as though by ordering, acquiescing to the idea, he had eaten the food too. "And then I will. . . . . . ." Only the hangar was not the mirage but the restaurant, the counter, the clash and clatter, the sound of food and of eating; it seemed to him that he could see the group: the aeroplane, the four dungaree figures, the little boy in dungarees too, himself approaching: *I hope you found everything you wanted before you left? Yes, thank you. It was thirteen dollars. Just till Saturday—No matter; it dont matter; dont even think of it* Now suddenly he heard the amplifyer too in the rotunda; it had been speaking for some time but he had just noticed it:

"——second day of the Feinman Airport dedication invitation meet held under the official rules of the American Aeronautical Association and through the courtesy of the city of New Valois and of Colonel H.I. Feinman, Chairman of the Sewage Board of New Valois. Events for the afternoon as follows——" He quit listening to it then, drawing from his pocket the pamphlet program of yesterday and opening it at the second fading imprint of the mimeograph:

Friday

2:30 P.M.	Spot Parachute Jump. Purse $25.00
3:00 P.M.	Scull Speed Dash. 375 cu. in. Qualifying speed 180 m.p.h. Purse $325.00 (1, 2, 3, 4)
3:30 P.M.	Aerial Acrobatics. Jules Despleins, France. Lieut. Frank Burnham, United States.
4:30 P.M.	Scull Speed Dash. 575 cu.in. Qualifying speed, 200 m.p.h. Purse $650.00 (1, 2, 3, 4)
5:00 P.M.	Delayed Parachute Drop.
8:00 P.M.	Special Mardi Gras Evening Event. Rocket Plane. Lieut. Frank Burnham

He continued to look at the page long after the initial impact of optical surprise had faded. "That's all," he said. "That's all she would have to do. Just tell me they. . . . . . . It aint the money. She knows it aint that. It aint the money with me anymore than it is with them," he said; the man had to speak to him twice before the reporter knew he was there. "Hello," he said.

"So you got out here after all," the other said. Behind the man stood another, a short man with a morose face, carrying a newspaper camera.

"Yes," the reporter said. "Hi, Jug," he said to the second man. The first looked at him, curiously.

"You look like you have been dragged through hell by the heels," he said. "You going to cover this today too?"

"Not that I know of," the reporter said. "I understand I am fired. Why?"

"I was about to ask you. Hagood phoned me at four this morning, out of bed. He told me to come out today and if you were not here, to cover it. But mostly to watch out for you if you came and to tell you to call him at this number." He took a folded strip of paper from his vest and gave it to the reporter. "It's the country club. He said to call him as soon as I found you."

"Thanks," the reporter said. But he did not move. The other looked at him.

"Well, what do you want to do? You want to cover it or you want me to?"

"No. I mean, yes. You take it. It dont matter. Jug knows better what Hagood wants than you or I either."

"O.K.," the other said. "Better call Hagood right away, though."

"I will," the reporter said. Now the food came: the heaped indestructible plate and the hand scrubbed, with vicious coral nails, the hand too looking like it had been conceived formed and baked in the kitchen, or perhaps back in town and sent out by light and speedy truck along with the scrolled squares of pastry beneath the plate glass counter; he looked at both the food and the hand from the crest of a wave of pure almost physical flight. "Jesus, sister," he said, "I was joking with the wrong man, wasn't I?" But he drank the coffee and ate some of the food; he seemed to watch himself creeping slowly and terrifically across the plate like a mole, blind to all else and deaf now even to the amplifyer; he ate a good deal of it, sweating, seeming to chew forever and ever before getting each mouthful in position to be swallowed. "I guess that'll be

enough," he said at last. "Jesus, it will have to be," he said.
He was in the rotundra now and moving toward the gates
into the stands before he remembered and turned and
breasted the stream toward the entrance and so outside and
into the bright soft hazy sunlight with its quality of having
been recently taken out of water and not yet thoroughly dried
and full of the people, the faces, the cars coming up and discharging and moving on. Across the plaza the hangarwing
seemed to sway and quiver like a grounded balloon. "But I
feel better," he thought. "I must. They would not have let me
eat all that and not feel better because I cant possibly feel as
bad as I still think I do." He could hear the voice again now
from the amplifyer above the entrance:

"——wish to announce that due to the tragic death of
Lieutenant Frank Burnham last night, the airport race committee has discontinued the evening events. . . . The time
is now one-forty-two. The first event on today's program
will. . . . . . ." The reporter stopped.

"One-forty-two," he thought. Now he could feel something which must have been the food he had just eaten beating slow and steady against his skull which up to this time
had been empty, had hardly troubled him at all except for the
sensation of being about to float off like one of the small
balloons escaped from the hand of a child at a circus, trying
to remember what hour the program had allotted to the three
hundred and seventy-five cubic inch race, thinking that perhaps when he got into the shade he could bear to look at the
program again. "Since it seems I am bound to offer her the
chance to tell me that they stole. . . . . . .not the money.
It's not the money. It's not that." Now the shade of the hangar fell upon him and he could see the program again, the
faint mimeographed letters beating and pulsing against his
cringing eyeballs and steadying at last so that he could read
his watch. It would be an hour still before he could expect to
find her alone. He turned and followed the hangarwall and
passed beyond it. Across the way the parkinglot was almost
full and there was another stream here, moving toward the
bleachers, though he stood on the edge of it while his eyeballs
still throbbed and watched the other fringe of them slowing
and clotting before one of the temporary wooden refreshment

booths which had sprung up about the borders of the airport
property as the photographs of the pilots and machines had
bloomed in the shopwindows downtown for some time before he began to realise that something besides the spectacle
(still comparatively new) of outdoors drinking must be drawing them. Then he thought he recognised the voice and then
he did recognise the raked filthy swagger of the cap and
moved, pressing, filtering, on and into the crowd and so came
between Jiggs' drunken belligerent face and the Italian face of
the booth's proprietor who was leaning across the counter
and shouting,

"Bastard, huh? You theenk bastard, hey?"

"What is it?" the reporter said. Jiggs turned and looked at
him for a moment of hot blurred concentration without recognition; it was the Italian who answered.

"For me, nothing!" he shouted. "He come here, he have
one drink, two drink; he no need either one of them but o.k.;
he pay; that o.k. for me. Then he say he wait for friend, that
he have one more drink to surprise friend. That not so good
but my wife she give it to him and that maka three drink he
dont need and I say, You pay and go, eh? Beat it. And he say,
O.K., goodbye and I say Why you no pay, eh? and he say
That drink to surprise friend; looka like it surprise you too,
eh? and I grab to hold and call policaman because I dont
want for trouble with drunk and he say bastard to me before
my wife——" Still Jiggs did not move. Even while holding
himself upright by the counter he gave that illusion of tautly
sprung steel set delicately on a hair trigger.

"Yair," he said. "Three drinks, and just look what they
done to me!" on a rising note which stopped before it became
idiotic laughter; whereupon he stared again at the reporter
with that blurred gravity, watching while the reporter took
the second of the two dollar bills which the negress had
loaned him and gave it to the Italian. "There you are, Colum-
bus," Jiggs said. "Yair. I told him. Jesus, I even tried to tell
him your name, only I couldn't remember it." He looked at
the reporter with hot intensity, like an astonished child. "Say,
that guy last night told me your name. Is that it, sure enough?
you swear to Christ, no kidding?"

"Yair," the reporter said. He put his hand on Jiggs' arm.

"Come on. Let's go." The spectators had moved on now. Behind the counter the Italian and his wife seemed to pay them no more attention. "Come on," the reporter said. "It must be after two. Let's go help get the ship ready and then I'll buy another drink." But Jiggs did not move, and then the reporter found Jiggs watching him with something curious, calculating and intent, behind the hot eyes; they were not blurred now at all, and suddenly Jiggs stood erect before the reporter could steady him.

"I was looking for you," Jiggs said.

"I came along at the right time, didn't I, for once in my life. Come on. Let's go to the hangar. I imagine they are waiting for you there. Then I will buy a——"

"I dont mean that," Jiggs said. "I was kidding the guy. I had the quarter, all right. I've had all I want. Come on." He led the way, walking a little carefully yet still with the light springlike steps, bumping and butting through the gateward stream of people, the reporter following, until they were beyond it and clear; anyone who approached them now would have to do so deliberately and should have been visible a hundred yards away, though neither of them saw the parachute jumper who was doing just that.

"You mean the ship's all ready?" the reporter said.

"Sure," Jiggs said. "Roger and Jack aint even there. They have gone to the meeting."

"Meeting?"

"Sure. Contestants' meeting. To strike, see? But listen——"

"To strike?"

"Sure. For more jack. It aint the money: it's the principle of the thing. Jesus, what do we need with money?" Jiggs began to laugh again on that harsh note which stopped just as it became laughing and started before it was mirth. "But that aint it. I was looking for you." Again the reporter looked at the hot unreadable eyes. "Laverne sent me. She said to give me five dollars for her." The reporter's face did not change at all. Neither did Jiggs': the hot impenetrable eyes, the membrane and fiber netting and webbing the unrecking and the undismayed. "Roger was in the money yesterday; you'll get it back Saturday. Only if it was me, I wouldn't even wait for that. Just let her underwrite you, see?"

"Underwrite me?"

"Sure. Then you wouldn't even have to bother to put anything back into your pocket. All you would have to do would
be to button up your pants." Still the reporter's face did not
change, his voice did not change, not loud, without amazement, anything.

"Do you reckon I could?"

"I dont know," Jiggs said. "Didn't you ever try it? It's done
every night somewhere, so I hear. Probably done right here
in New Valois, even. And if you cant, she can show you how."
The reporter's face did not change; he was just looking at
Jiggs and then suddenly Jiggs moved, sudden and complete;
the reporter saw the hot secret eyes come violently alive and,
turning, the reporter also saw the parachute jumper's face.
That was a little after two oclock; Shumann and the jumper
had been in the Superintendent's office from twelve until fifteen to one. They passed through the same discreet door
which Jiggs had used the afternoon before and went on
through the anteroom and into a place like a board room in
a bank—a long table with a row of comfortable chairs behind
it, in which perhaps a dozen men who might have been found
about any such table back in town sat, and another group of
chairs made out of steel and painted to resemble wood, in
which with a curious gravity something like that of the older
and better behaved boys in a reform school on Christmas eve,
sat the other men who by ordinary at this hour would have
been working over the aeroplanes in the hangar—the pilots
and parachute jumpers, in greasy dungarees or leather jackets
almost as foul, the quiet sober faces looking back as Shumann
and the jumper entered. Just as the blue serge of last night
was absent, so were the tweed coats and the ribbon badges
with one exception. This was the microphone's personified
voice. He sat with neither group, his chair that which should
have been at the end of the table but which he had drawn
several feet away as though preparing to tip it back against
the wall. But he was as grave as either group; the scene was
exactly that of the conventional conference between the mill-
owners and the delegation from the shops, the announcer
representing the labor lawyer—that man who was once a laborer himself but from whose hands now the callouses have

softened and whitened away so that, save for something nameless and ineradicable—a quality incorrigibly dissentive and perhaps even bizarre—about his clothing which distinguishes him forever from the men behind the table as well as from the men before it as the badge of the labor organization in his lapel establishes him forever as one of them, he might actually sit behind the table too. But he did not. But the very slightness of the distance between him and the table postulated a gap more unbridgable even than that between the table and the second group, as if he had been stopped in the midst of a violent movement, if not of protest at least of dissent, by the entrance into the room of the men in whose absent names he dissented. He nodded to Shumann and the jumper as they found chairs, then he turned to the thickfaced man at the center of the table.

"They're all here now," he said. The men behind the table murmured to one another.

"We must wait for him," the thickfaced man said. He raised his voice. "We are waiting for Colonel Feinman, men," he said. He took a watch from his vest; three or four others looked at their watches. "He instructed us to have everyone present at twelve oclock. He has been delayed. You can smoke, if you like." Some of the second group began to smoke, passing lighted matches, speaking quietly like a school class which has been told that it can talk for a moment:

"What is it?"

"I dont know. Maybe something about Burnham."

"Oh, yair. Probably that's it."

"Hell, they dont need all of us to——"

"Say, what do you suppose happened?"

"Blinded, probably."

"Yair. Blinded."

"Yair. Probably couldn't read his altimeter at all. Or maybe forgot to watch it. Flew it right into the ground."

"Yair. Jesus, I remember one time I was. . . . . . ." They smoked. Sometimes they held the cigarettes like dynamite caps so as not to spill the ash, looking quietly about the clean new floor; sometimes they spilled the ashes discreetly down their legs. But finally the stubs were too short to hold. One of them rose; the whole room watched him cross to the table and take up an ashtray made to resemble a radial engine and bring it back and start it passing along the three rows of chairs like a church collection plate. Shumann looked at his watch and it was twenty-five minutes past twelve. He spoke quietly, to the announcer, as though they were alone in the room:

"Listen, Hank. I've got all my valves out. I have got to put the micrometer on them before I——"

"Yair," the announcer said. He turned to the table. "Listen," he said. "They are all here now. And they have got to get the ships ready for the race at three; Mr Shumann there has got all his valves out. So cant you tell them without waiting for F——Colonel Feinman? They will agree, all right. I told you that. There aint anything else they can—I mean they will agree."

"Agree to what?" the man beside Shumann said. But the chairman, the thickfaced man, was already speaking.

"Colonel Feinman said——"

"Yair." The announcer spoke patiently. "But these boys have got to get their ships ready. We've got to be ready to give these people that are buying the tickets out there something to look at." The men behind the table murmured again, the others watching them quietly.

"Of course we can take a straw vote now," the chairman said. Now he looked at them and cleared his throat. "Gentlemen, the committee representing the business men of New Valois who have sponsored this meet and offered you the opportunity to win these cash prizes——" The announcer turned to him.

"Wait," he said. "Let me tell them." He turned now to the grave almost identical faces of the men in the hard chairs; he spoke quietly too. "It's about the programs. The printed ones—you know. With the setup for each day. They were all printed last week and so they have still got Frank's name on them——" The chairman interrupted him now:

"And the committee wants to express here and now to you other pilots who were con——" Now he was interrupted by one of the men beside him:

"—and on behalf of Colonel Feinman."

"Yes.—and on behalf of Colonel Feinman.—contemporaries and friends of Lieutenant Burnham, its sincere regret at last night's unfortunate accident."

"Yair," the announcer said; he had not even looked toward the speaker, he just waited until he had got through. "So they—the committee—feel that they are advertising something they cant produce. They feel that Frank's name should come off the program. I agree with them there and I know you will too."

"Why not take it off, then?" one of the second group said.

"Yes," the announcer said. "They are going to. But the only way they can do that is to have new programs printed, you see." But they did not see yet. They just looked at him, waiting. The chairman cleared his throat, though at the moment there was nothing for him to interrupt.

"We had these programs printed for your benefit and convenience as contestants, as well as that of the spectators, without whom I dont have to remind you there would be no cash prizes for you to win. So you see, in a sense you contestants are the real benefactors of these printed programs. Not us; the schedule of these events can be neither information nor surprise to us, since we were privy to the arranging of them even if we are not to the winning—since we have been given to understand (and I may add, have seen for ourselves) that air racing has not yet reached the, ah, scientific heights of horse racing——" He cleared his throat again; a thin polite murmur of laughter rose from about the table and died away. "We had these programs printed at considerable expense, none of which devolved on you, yet they were planned and executed for your—I wont say profit, but convenience and benefit. We had them printed in good faith that what we guaranteed in them would be performed; we knew no more than you did that that unfortunate ac——"

"Yes," the announcer said. "It's like this. Somebody has got to pay to have new programs printed. These g—this . . . . . . .they say w—the contestants and announcers and everybody drawing jack from the meet, should do it." They did not make a sound, the still faces did not change expression; it was the announcer himself, speaking now in a tone urgent, almost pleading, where no dissent had been offered or intimated: "It's just two and a half percent. We're all in it;

I'm in it too. Just two and a half percent.; when it comes out of prizemoney, like they say you wont notice it because you haven't got it anyway until after the cut is taken out. Just two and a half percent., and——" The man in the second group spoke for the second time:

"Or else?" he said. The announcer did not answer. After a moment Shumann said,

"Is that all?"

"Yes," the announcer said. Shumann rose.

"I better get back on my valves," he said. Now when he and the jumper crossed the rotunda the crowd was trickling steadily through the gates. They worked into line and shuffled up to the gates too before they learned that they would have to have grandstand tickets to pass. So they turned and worked back out of the crowd and went out and around toward the hangar, walking now in a thin deep drone from somewhere up in the sun, though presently they could see them—a flight of army pursuit singleseaters circling the field in formation to land and then coming in, fast, bluntnosed, fiercelyraked, viciously powerful. "They're oversouped," Shumann said. "They will kill you if you dont watch them. I wouldn't want to do that for two-fifty-six a month."

"You wouldn't be cut two and a half percent. while you were out to lunch though," the jumper said savagely. "What's two and a half percent. of twenty-five bucks?"

"It aint the whole twenty-five," Shumann said. "I hope Jiggs has got that supercharger ready to go back." So they had almost reached the aeroplane before they discovered that it was the woman and not Jiggs at work on it and that she had put the supercharger back on with the engine head still off and the valves still out. She rose and brushed her hair back with the flat of her wrist, though they had asked no question.

"Yes," she said. "I thought he was all right. I went out to eat and left him here."

"Have you seen him since?" Shumann said. "Do you know where he is now?"

"What the hell does that matter?" the jumper said in a tense furious voice. "Let's get the damned supercharger off and put the valves in." He looked at the woman, furious, restrained. "What has this guy done to you? give you a dose of faith in mankind like he would syphilis or consumption or whatever it is, that will even make you trust Jiggs?"

"Come on," Shumann said. "Let's get the supercharger off. I guess he didn't check the valve stems either, did he?"

"I dont know," she said.

"Well, no matter. They lasted out yesterday. And we haven't time now. But maybe we can get on the line by three if we dont stop to check them." They were ready before that; they had the aeroplane on the apron and the engine running before three, and then the jumper who had worked in grim fury turned away, walking fast even though Shumann called after him. He went straight to where Jiggs and the reporter stood. He could not have known where to find them yet he went straight to them as though led by some blind instinct out of fury; he walked into Jiggs' vision and struck him on the jaw so that the surprise the alarm and the shock were almost simultaneous, hitting him again before he finished falling and then whirled as the reporter caught his arm.

"Here! here!" the reporter cried. "He's drunk! You cant hit a——" But the jumper didn't say a word; the reporter saw the continuation of the turning become the blow of the fist. He didn't feel the blow at all. "I'm too light to be knocked down or even hit hard," he thought; he was still telling himself that while he was being raised up again and while the hands held him upright on his now boneless legs and while he looked at Jiggs sitting up now in a small stockade of legs and a policeman shaking him. "Hello, Leblanc," the reporter said. The policeman looked at him now.

"So it's you, hey?" the policeman said. "You got some news this time, aint you? Something to put in the paper that people will like to read. Reporter knocked down by irate victim, hey? That's news." He began to prod Jiggs with the side of his shoe. "Who's this? Your substitute? Get up. On your feet now."

"Wait," the reporter said. "It's all right. He wasn't in it. He's one of the mechanics here. An aviator."

"I see," the policeman said, hauling at Jiggs' arm. "Aviator, hey? He dont look very high to me. Or maybe it was a cloud hit him in the jaw, hey?"

"Yes. He's just drunk. I'll be responsible; I tell you he

wasn't even in it; the guy hit him by mistake. Leave him be, Leblanc."

"What do I want with him?" the policeman said. "So you're responsible, are you? Get him up out of the street, then." He turned and began to shove at the ring of people. "Go; beat it; get on, now," he said. "The race is about to start. Go on, now." So presently they were alone again, the reporter standing carefully, balancing, on his weightless legs ("Jesus," he thought, "I'm glad now I am light enough to float"), feeling gingerly his jaw, thinking with peaceful astonishment, "I never felt it at all. Jesus, I didn't think I was solid enough to be hit that hard but I must have been wrong." He stooped, still gingerly, and began to pull at Jiggs' arm until after a time Jiggs looked up at him blankly.

"Come on," the reporter said. "Let's get up."

"Yair," Jiggs said. "Yair. Get up."

"Yes," the reporter said. "Come on, now." Jiggs rose slowly, the reporter steadying him; he stood blinking at the reporter.

"Jesus," he said. "What happened?"

"Yes," the reporter said. "But it's all right now. It's all over now. Come on. Where do you want to go?" Jiggs moved, the reporter beside him, supporting him; suddenly Jiggs recoiled; looking up the reporter also saw the hangar door a short distance away.

"Not there," Jiggs said.

"Yes," the reporter said. "We dont want to go there." They turned; the reporter led the way now, working them clear again of the people passing toward the stands. He could feel his jaw beginning now, and looking back and upward he watched the aeroplanes come into position one by one as beneath them each dropping body bloomed into parachute. "And I never even heard the bomb," he thought. "Or maybe that was what I thought hit me." He looked at Jiggs walking stiffly beside him, as though the spring steel of his legs had been reft by enchantment of temper and were now mere dead iron. "Listen," he said. He stopped and stopped Jiggs too, looking at him and speaking to him tediously and carefully as though Jiggs were a child. "I've got to go to town. To the paper. The boss sent for me to come in, see? Now you tell me where you want to go. You want to go somewhere and lie down a while? Maybe I can find a car where you can——"

"No," Jiggs said. "I'm all right. Go on."

"Yes. Sure. But you ought. . . . . . ." Now all the parachutes were open; the sunny afternoon was filled with down-cupped blooms like inverted water hyacinths; the reporter shook Jiggs a little. "Come on, now. What's next now? after the chute jumps?"

"What?" Jiggs said. "Next? What next?"

"Yes. What? Cant you remember?"

"Yair," Jiggs said. "Next." For a full moment the reporter looked down at Jiggs with a faint lift of one side of his mouth as though favoring his jaw, not of concern nor regret nor even hopelessness so much as of faint and quizzical fore-knowledge.

"Yes," he said. He took the key from his pocket. "Can you remember this, then?" Jiggs looked at the key, blinking. Then he stopped blinking.

"Yair," he said. "It was on the table right by the jug. And then we got hung up on the bastard laying there in the door and I let the door shut behind. . . . . . ." He looked at the reporter, peering at him, blinking again. "For Christ's sake," he said. "Did you bring it too?"

"No," the reporter said.

"Hell. Gimme the key; I will go and——"

"No," the reporter said. He put the key back into his pocket and took out the change which the Italian had given him, the three quarters. "You said five dollars. But I haven't got that much. This is all I have. But that will be all right because if it was a hundred it would be the same; it would not be enough because all I have never is, you see? Here." He put the three quarters into Jiggs' hand. For a moment Jiggs looked at his hand without moving. Then the hand closed; he looked at the reporter while his face seemed to collect, to become sentient.

"Yair," he said. "Thanks. It's o.k. You'll get it back Saturday. We're in the money now; Roger and Jack and the others struck this afternoon, see. Not for the money: for the principle of the thing, see?"

"Yes," the reporter said. He turned and went on. Now he

could feel his jaw quite distinctly through the faint grimace of smiling, the grimace thin bitter and wrung. "Yes. It aint the money. That aint it. That dont matter." He heard the bomb this time and saw the five aeroplanes dart upward, diminishing, as he reached the apron, beginning to pass the spaced amplifyers and the rich voice:

"——second event. Three-seventy-five cubic inch class. Some of the same boys that gave you a good race yesterday, except Myers, who is out of this race to save up for the five-fifty later this afternoon. But Ott and Bullitt are out there, and Roger Shumann who surprised us all yesterday by taking second in a field that——" He found her almost at once; she had not changed from the dungarees this time. He extended the key, feeling his jaw plainer and plainer through his face's grimace.

"Make yourselves at home," he said. "As long as you want to. I'm going to be out of town for a few days. So I may not even see you again. But you can just drop the key in an envelope and address it to the paper. And make yourselves at home; there is a woman comes every morning but Sunday to clean up. . . . . . ." The five aeroplanes came in on the first lap: the snarl, the roar banking into a series of downwind scuttering pops as each one turned the pylon and went on.

"You mean you're not going to need the place yourself at all?" she said.

"No. I wont be there. I am going out of town on an assignment."

"I see. Well, thanks. I wanted to thank you for last night, but——"

"Yair," he said. "So I'll beat it. You can say goodbye to the others for me."

"Yes. But are you sure it wont——"

"Sure. It's all right. You make yourselves at home." He turned; he began to walk fast, thinking fast, "Now if I only can just——" He heard her call him twice; he thought of trying to run on his boneless legs and knew that he would fall, hearing her feet just behind him now, thinking, "No. No. Dont. That's all I ask. No. No." Then she was beside him; he stopped and turned, looking down at her.

"Listen," she said. "We took some money out of your——"

"Yes. I knew. It's o.k. You can hand it back. Put it in the envelope with the——"

"I intended to tell you as soon as I saw you today. It was——"

"Yair; sure." He spoke loudly now, turning again, fleeing before yet beginning to move. "Anytime. Goodbye now."

"——it was six-seventy. We left. . . . . . ." Her voice died away; she stared at him, at the thin rigid grimace which could hardly have been called smiling but which could have been called nothing else. "How much did you find in your pocket this morning?"

"It was all there," he said. "Just the six-seventy was missing. It was all right." He began to walk. The aeroplanes came in and turned the field pylon again as he was passing through the gate and into the rotundra. When he entered the bar the first face he saw was that of the photographer whom he had called Jug.

"I aint going to offer you a drink," the photographer said, "because I never buy them for nobody. I wouldn't even buy Hagood one."

"I dont want a drink," the reporter said. "I just want a dime."

"A dime? Hell, that's damn near the same as a drink."

"It's to call Hagood with. That will look better on your expense account than a drink would." There was a booth in the corner; he called the number from the slip which the substitute had given him. After a while Hagood answered. "Yair, I'm out here," the reporter said. "Yair, I feel o.k. . . . . Yair, I want to come in. Take something else, another assignment. . . . . . . Yair, out of town if you got anything, for a day or so if you——Yair. Thanks, chief. I'll come right on in." He had to walk through the voice again to pass through the rotundra, and again it met him outside though for the moment he did not listen to it for listening to himself: "It's all the same! I did the same thing myself! I dont intend to pay Hagood either! I lied to him about money too!" and the answer, loud too: "You lie, you bastard. You're lying, you son of a bitch." So he was hearing the amplifyer before he knew that he was listening, just as he had stopped and halfturned before he knew that he had stopped, in the bright thin sunlight filled with mirageshapes which pulsed against his painful eyelids: so that when two uniformed policemen appeared suddenly from beyond the hangar with Jiggs struggling between them, his cap in one hand and one eye completely closed now and a long smear of blood on his jaw, the reporter did not even recognise him; he was now staring at the amplifyer above the door as though he were actually seeing in it what he merely heard:

"——Shumann's in trouble; he's out of the race; he's turning out to. . . . . . He's cut his switch and he's going to land; I dont know what it is but he's swinging wide; he's trying to keep clear of the other ships and he's pretty wide and that lake's pretty wet to be out there without any motor——Come on, Roger; get back into the airport, guy!—— He's in now; he's trying to get back onto the runway to land and it looks like he'll make it all right but the sun is right in his eyes and he swung mightywide to keep clear of——I dont know about this——I dont. . . . . . Hold her head up, Roger! Hold her head up! Hold——" The reporter began to run; it was not the crash that he heard: it was a single long exhalation of human breath as though the microphone had reached out and caught that too out of all the air which people had ever breathed. He ran back through the rotunda and through the suddenly clamorous mob at the gate, already tugging out his policecard; it was as though all the faces, all the past twenty-four hours' victories and defeats and hopes and renunciations and despairs, had been blasted completely out of his life as if they had actually been the random sheets of that organ to which he dedicated his days, caught momentarily upon one senseless member of the scarecrow which he resembled, and then blown away. A moment later, above the heads streaming up the apron and beyond the ambulance and the firetruck and the motorcycle squad rushing across the field, he saw the aeroplane lying on its back, the undercarriage projecting into the air rigid and delicate and motionless as the legs of a dead bird. Two hours later, at the bus stop on the Grandlieu Street corner, from where she and Shumann stood

a few feet away, the woman could see the reporter standing
quietly as he had emerged from the bus and surrendered the
four tickets for which he had paid. She could not tell who or
what he was looking at: his face was just peaceful, waiting,
apparently inattentive even when the parachute jumper
limped over to him, dragging savagely the leg which even
through the cloth of the trousers appeared thick stiff and un-
gainly with the emergency dressing from the airport's surgery, result of having been drifted by an unforeseen windgust
over the stands and then slammed into one of the jerrybuilt
refreshment booths when landing his parachute.

"Look here," he said. "This afternoon. I was mad at Jiggs.
I never meant to sock you. I was worried and mad. I even
thought it was still Jiggs' face until too late."

"It's all right," the reporter said. It was not smiling: it was
just peaceful and serene. "I guess I just got in the way."

"I didn't plan to. If you want any satisfaction——"

"It's all right," the reporter said. They didn't shake hands;
the jumper just turned after a moment and dragged his leg
back to where he had been standing, leaving the reporter as
before, in that attitude of peaceful waiting. The woman
looked at Shumann again.

"Then if the ship's all right, why wont Ord fly it himself,
race it himself?" she said.

"Maybe he dont have to," Shumann said. "If I had his
Ninety-Two I wouldn't need this ship either. I guess Ord
would do the same. Besides, I—we haven't got it yet. So
there aint anything to worry about. Because if it is a bum,
Ord wont let us have it. Yair, you see? if we can get it, that's
proof that it's o.k. because Ord wouldn't——" She was looking down now, motionless save for her hands, with the heel
of one of which she was striking lightly the other's palm. Her
voice was flat, hard, and low, not carrying three feet:

"We. We. He has boarded and fed us for a day and
night now, and now he is even going to get us another ship
to fly. And all I want is just a house, a room; a cabin will do,
a coalshed where I can know that next Monday and the Monday after that and the Monday after that——. . . . . . . Do
you suppose he would have something like that he could give
to me?" She turned; she said, "We better get on and get that

stuff for Jack's leg." The reporter had not heard her, he had not been listening; now he found that he had not even been watching; his first intimation was when he saw her walking toward him. "We're going on to your house," she said. "I guess we'll see you and Roger when we see you. You have changed your plan about leaving town, I imagine?"

"Yes," the reporter said. "I mean no. I'm going home with a guy on the paper to sleep. Dont you bother about me." He looked at her, his face gaunt, serene, peaceful. "Dont you worry. I'll be o.k."

"Yes," she said. "About that money. That was the truth. You can ask Roger and Jack."

"It's all right," he said. "I would believe you even if I knew you had lied."

And Tomorrow

S O YOU SEE how it is," the reporter said. He looked down at Ord too, as he seemed doomed to look down at everyone with whom he seemed perennially and perpetually compelled either to plead or just to endure: perhaps enduring and passing the time until that day when time and age would have thinned still more what blood he had and so permit him to see himself actually as the friendly and lonely ghost peering timidly down from the hayloft at the other children playing below. "The valves went bad and then he and Holmes had to go to that meeting so they could tell them that thirty percent. exceeded the code or something: and then Jiggs went and then they didn't have time to check the valvestems and take out the bad ones and then the whole engine went and the rudderpost and a couple of longerons and tomorrow's the last day. That's tough luck, aint it?"

"Yes," Ord said. They all three still stood. Ord had probably invited them to sit out of habit, courtesy, when they first came in though probably he did not remember now doing so any more than the reporter and Shumann could remember declining if they had declined. But probably neither invitation nor refusal had passed at all, that the reporter had brought into the house, the room, with him that atmosphere of a fifteenth century Florentine stage scene—an evening call with formal courteous words in the mouth and naked rapiers under the cloaks. In the impregnably new glow of two rose-shaded lamps which looked like the ones that burn for three hours each night in a livingroom suite in the storewindows dressed by a junior manclerk, they all stood now as they had come from the airport, the reporter in that single suit which apparently composed his wardrobe, and Shumann and Ord in greasestained suede jackets which a third person could not have told apart, standing in the livingroom of Ord's new neat little flowercluttered house built with the compact economy of an aeroplane itself, with the new matched divan and chairs and tables and lamps arranged about it with the myriad compactness of the dials and knobs of an instrument panel. From somewhere toward the rear they could hear a dinnertable being set, and a woman's voice singing obviously to a small child. "All right," Ord said. He did not move; his eyes seemed to watch them both without looking at either, as though they actually were armed invaders. "What do you want me to do?"

"Listen," the reporter said. "It's not the money, the prize; I dont have to tell you that. You were one too, not so long ago, before you met Atkinson and got a break. Hell, look at you now, even when you got Atkinson and all you have to do is just build them without even seeing a pylon closer to it than the grandstand, without ever taking your other foot off the ground except to get into bed. But do you? Yair; maybe it was somebody else pulling that Ninety-Two around those pylons at Chicago last summer that day; maybe that wasn't Matt Ord at all. So you know it aint the money, the damn cash: Jesus Christ, he aint got the jack he won yesterday yet. Because if it was just the money, if he just had to have it and he come to you and told you, you would lend it to him. Yair, I know. I dont have to tell you. Jesus, I dont have to tell anybody that after today, after up there in that office at noon. Yair; listen. Suppose instead of them up there on those damn hard chairs today it had been a gang of men hired to go down into a mine say, not to do anything special down there but just to see if the mine would cave in on top of them, and five minutes before they went down the bigbellied guys that own the mine would tell them that everybody's pay had been cut two and a half percent. to print a notice how the elevator or something had fell on one of them the night before: would they go down? Naw. But did these guys refuse to fly that race? Maybe it was not a valve that Shumann's ship swallowed but a peanut somebody in the grandstand threw down on the apron. Yair; they could have kept back the ninety-seven and a half and give them the two and a half and it would——"

"No," Ord said. He spoke with complete and utter finality. "I wouldn't even let Shumann make a field hop in it. I wouldn't let any man, let alone fly it around a closed course. Even if it was qualified." Now it was as though with a word Ord had cut through the circumlocution like through a light net and that the reporter, without breaking stride, had followed him onto new ground as bleak and forthright as a prizering.

"But you have flown it. I dont mean that Shumann can fly as good as you can; I dont believe anybody can do that even though I know mine aint even an opinion: it's just that hour's dual you give me talking. But Shumann can fly anything that will fly. I believe that. And we will get it qualified; the license is still o.k."

"Yes. The license is o.k. But the reason it hasn't been revoked yet is the Department knows I aint going to let it off the ground again. Only to revoke it would not be enough: it ought to be broken up and then burned, like you would kill a maddog. Hell, no. I wont do it. I feel sorry for Shumann but not as sorry as I would feel tomorrow night if that ship was over at Feinman Airport tomorrow afternoon."

"But listen, Matt," the reporter said. Then he stopped. He did not speak loud, and with no especial urgency, yet he emanated the illusion still of having longsince collapsed yet being still intact of his own weightlessness like a dandelion burr moving where there is no wind; in the soft pink glow his face appeared gaunter than ever, as though following the excess of the past night, his vital spark now fed on the inner side of the actual skin itself, paring it steadily thinner and more and more transparent, as parchment is made. Now his face was completely inscrutable. "So even if we could get it qualified, you wouldn't let Shumann fly it."

"Right," Ord said. "It's tough on him. I know that. But he dont want to commit suicide."

"Yair," the reporter said. "He aint quite got to where wont nothing else content him. Well, I guess we better get on back to town."

"Stay and eat some dinner," Ord said. "I told Mrs Ord you fellows——"

"I reckon we better get on back," the reporter said. "It looks like we will have all day tomorrow with nothing to do but eat."

"We could eat and then drive over to the hangar and I will show you the ship and try to explain——"

"Yair," the reporter said pleasantly. "But what we want is one that Shumann can look at from inside the cockpit three

oclock tomorrow afternoon. Well, sorry we troubled you."
The station was not far; they followed a quiet graveled village
street in the darkness, the Franciana February darkness already heavy with spring—the Franciana spring which
emerges out of the Indian summer of fall almost, like a mis-
timed stage resurrection which takes the curtain even before
rigor mortis has made its bow, where the decade's phenomenon of ice occurs simultaneous with bloomed stalk and bud-
ded leaf. They walked quietly; even the reporter was not
talking now—the two of them who could have had nothing
in common save the silence which for the moment the reporter permitted them—the one volatile, irrational, with his
ghostlike quality of being beyond all mere restrictions of flesh
and time, of possessing no intrinsic weight or bulk himself
and hence being everywhere to supply that final straw's mod-
icum of surprise and even disaster to the otherwise calculable
doings of calculable people; the other singlepurposed, fatally
and grimly without any trace of introversion or any ability to
objectivate or ratiocinate as though like the engine, the machine for which he apparently existed, he functioned, moved,
only in the vapor of gasoline and the filmslick of oil—the two
of them taken in conjunction and because of this dissimilarity
capable of almost anything; walking, they seemed to communicate by some means or agency of the purpose, the disaster, toward which without yet being conscious of it apparently, they moved. "Well," the reporter said. "That's about
what we expected."

"Yair," Shumann said. They walked on in silence again; it
was as though the silence were the dialogue and the actual
speech the soliloquy, the marshalling of thought:

"Are you afraid of it?" the reporter said. "Let's get that
settled; we can do that right now."

"Tell me about it again," Shumann said.

"Yes. The guy brought it down here from Saint Louis for
Matt to rebuild it; it wouldn't go fast enough for him. He
had it all doped out, about how they would pull the engine
and change the body a little and put in a big engine and Matt
told him he didn't think that was so good, that the ship had
all the engine then it had any business with and the guy asked

Matt whose ship it was and Matt said it was the guy's and the guy asked Matt whose money it was and so Matt said o.k. Only Matt thought they ought to change the body more than the guy thought they ought to and at last Matt refused to have anything to do with it unless the guy compromised with him and even then Matt didn't think so much of it, he didn't want to butcher it up because it was a good ship, even I can tell that by looking at it. And so they compromised because Matt told him he would not test it otherwise, besides getting the license back on it and the guy saying how he seemed to have been misinformed in what he had heard about Matt and so Matt told him o.k., if he wanted to take the ship to some-body else he would put it back together and not even charge the guy storage space on it. So finally the guy agreed to let Matt make the changes he absolutely insisted on and then he wanted Matt to guarantee the ship and Matt told the guy his guarantee would be when Matt got into the cockpit and took it off and the guy said he meant to turn a pylon with it and Matt told the guy maybe he had been misinformed about him and maybe he had better take the ship to somebody else and so the guy cooled down and Matt made the changes and put in the big engine and he brought Sales, the inspector, out there and they stressed it and Sales o.k.'d the job and then Matt told the guy he was ready to test it. The guy had been kind of quiet for some time now, he said o.k., he would go into town and get the money while Matt was testing it, flying it in, and so Matt took it off." They didn't stop walking, the reporter talking quietly: "Because I dont know much; I just had an hour's dual with Matt because he gave it to me one day: I dont know why he did it and I reckon he dont either. So I dont know: only what I could understand about what Matt said, that it flew o.k. because Sales passed it; it flew o.k. and it stalled o.k. and did everything it was supposed to do up in the air, because Matt wasn't even expecting it when it happened: he was coming in to land, he said how he was getting the stick back and the ship coming in fine and then all of a sudden his belt caught him and he saw the ground up in front of his nose instead of down under it where it ought to been, and how he never took time to think, he just jammed

the stick forward like he was trying to dive it into the ground
and sure enough the nose came up just in time; he said the
slipstream on the tailgroup made a—a———"

"Burble," Shumann said.

"Yair. Burble. He dont know if it was going slow to land
or being close to the ground that changed the slipstream, he
just levelled it off with the stick jammed against the firewall until it lost speed and the burble went away and he got the stick
back and blasted the nose up with the gun and he managed to
stay inside the field by groundlooping it. And so they waited
a while for the guy to get back from town with the money and
after a while Matt put the ship back in the hangar and it's
still there. So you say now if you think you better not."

"Yair," Shumann said. "Maybe it's weight distribution."

"Yair. That may be it. Maybe we will find out right away
it's just that, maybe as soon as you see the ship you will
know." They came to the quiet little station lighted by a single bulb, almost hidden in a mass of oleander and vines and
palmettos. In either direction the steady green eye of a
switchlamp gleamed faintly on the rails where they ran,
sparsely strung with the lighted windows of houses, through
a dark canyon of mosshung liveoaks. To the south, on the low
night overcast, lay the glare of the city itself. They had about
ten minutes to wait.

"Where you going to sleep tonight?" Shumann said.

"I got to go to the office for a while. I'll go home with one
of the guys there."

"You better come on home. You got enough rugs and
things for us all to sleep. It wouldn't be the first time Jiggs
and Jack and me have slept on the floor."

"Yes," the reporter said. He looked down at the other; they
were little better than blurs to one another; the reporter said
in a tone of hushed quiet amazement: "You see, it dont matter where I would be. I could be ten miles away or just on
the other side of that curtain, and it would be the same. Jesus,
it's funny: Holmes is the one that aint married to her and if
I said anything like that to him I would have to dodge—if I
had time. And you are married to her, and I can. . . . . .
Yair. You can go on and hit me too. Because maybe if I was

to even sleep with her, it would be the same. Sometimes I think about how it's you and him and how maybe sometimes she dont even know the difference, one from another, and I would think how maybe if it was me too she wouldn't even know I was there at all."

"Here, for Christ's sake," Shumann said. "You'll have me thinking you are ribbing me up in this crate of Ord's so you can marry her maybe."

"Yair," the reporter said; "all right. I'd be the one. Yair. Because listen. I dont want anything. Maybe it's because I just want what I am going to get, only I dont think it's just that. Yair, I'd just be the name, my name, you see: the house and the beds and what we would need to eat. Because, Jesus, I'd just be walking: it would still be the same: you and him, and I'd just be walking, on the ground; I would maybe keep up with Jiggs and that's all. Because it's thinking about the day after tomorrow and the day after that and after that and me smelling the same burnt coffee and dead shrimp and oysters and waiting for the same light to change like me and the red light worked on the same clock so I could cross and get home and go to bed so I could get up and start smelling the coffee and fish and waiting for the light to change again; yair, smelling the paper and the ink too where it says how among those who beat or got beat at Omaha or Miami or Cleveland or Los Angeles was Roger Shumann and family. Yes. I would be the name; I could anyway buy her the pants and the nightgowns and it would be my sheets on the bed and even my towels.—Well, come on. Aint you going to sock me?" Now the far end of the canyon of liveoaks sprang into more profound impenetrability yet as the headlight of the train fell upon it and then swept down the canyon itself. Now Shumann could see the other's face.

"Does this guy you are going to stay with tonight expect you?" he said.

"Yes. I'll be all right. And listen. We better catch the eight-twenty back here."

"All right," Shumann said. "Listen. About that money——"

"It's all right," the reporter said. "It was all there."

"We put a five and a one back into your pocket. But if it

was gone, I'll make it good Saturday, along with the other. It was our fault for leaving it there. But we couldn't get in; the door had locked when it shut."

"It dont matter," the reporter said. "It's just money. It dont matter if you dont ever pay it back." The train came up, slowing, the lighted windows jarred to a halt. The car was full, since it was not yet eight oclock, but they found two seats at last, in tandem, so they could not talk anymore until they got out in the station. The reporter still had a dollar of the borrowed five; they took a cab. "We'll go by the paper first," he said. "Jiggs ought to be almost sober now." The cab, even at the station, ran at once into confetti, emerging beneath dingy gouts of the purple-and-gold bunting three days old now dropped across the smokegrimed façade of the station like flotsam left by a spent and falling tide and murmuring even yet of the chalkwhite, the forlorn, the glare and pulse of Grandlieu Street miles away. Now the cab began to run between loops of it from post to post of lamps; the cab ran now between the lofty and urbane palms and turned slowing and then drew up at the twin glass doors. "I wont be but a minute," the reporter said. "You can stay here in the cab."

"We can walk from here," Shumann said. "The police station aint far."

"We'll need the cab to get around Grandlieu," the reporter said. "I wont be long." He walked into no reflection now, since darkness was behind him; the doors swung to. The elevator door was slightly ajar and he could see the stack of papers beneath the facedown watch and he could smell the stinking pipe but he did not pause, taking the steps two at a time, and on into the cityroom; beneath his green eyeshade Hagood looked up and saw the reporter. But this time the reporter neither sat down nor removed his hat: he stood, loomed, into the green diffusion above the desklamp, looking down at Hagood with gaunt and quiet immobility as though he had been blown for a second against the desk by a wind and would in another second be blown onward once more.

"Go home and go to bed," Hagood said. "The story you phoned in is already set up."

"Yes," the reporter said. "I must have fifty dollars, chief." After a while Hagood said,

"Must, do you?" He did not move at all. "Must, eh?" he said. The reporter did not move either.

"I cant help it. I know that I. . . . . . .yesterday, whenever it was. When I thought I was fired. I got the message, all right. I ran into Cooper about noon and I didn't call you until after three. And I didn't report in here, like I said. But I did phone in the story; I will come back in about an hour and clean it. . . . . . . But I got to have fifty dollars."

"It's because you know I wont fire you," Hagood said. "Is that it?" The reporter said nothing. "All right. Come on. What is it this time? I know, all right. But I want to hear it from you—or are you still married or moved away or dead?" The reporter did not move; he spoke quietly, apparently into the green lampshade like it was a microphone:

"The cops got him. It happened just about the time Shumann nosed over, and so I. . . . . So he's in the can. And they will need some jack too until Shumann gets his money tomorrow night."

"So," Hagood said. He looked up at the still face above him which for the time had that calm sightless contemplation of a statue. "Why dont you let these people alone?" he said. Now the blank eyes waked; the reporter looked at Hagood for a full minute. His voice was as quiet as Hagood's.

"I cant," he said.

"You cant?" Hagood said. "Did you ever try to?"

"Yes," the reporter said in his dead flat voice, looking at the lamp again; that is, Hagood knew that the reporter was not looking at him. "I tried." After a moment Hagood turned, heavily. His coat hung on the back of his chair. He took his wallet from it and counted fifty dollars onto the desk and pushed it over to the reporter and saw the bony, clawlike hand come into the lamp's glare and take up the money. "Do you want me to sign anything now?" the reporter said.

"No," Hagood said without looking up. "Go home and go to bed. That's all I want."

"I'll come in later and clean up the story."

"It's already in galley," Hagood said. "You go home." The reporter moved away from the desk quietly enough, but as he entered the corridor it was as though the wind which had blown him against Hagood's desk and left him there had now begun to blow him again; he was passing the elevator shaft toward the stairs with only a glance at it when the door clashed back and someone got out, whereupon he turned and entered, reaching with one hand into his pocket as with the other he lifted the top paper beneath the sliding facedown watch. But he did not even glance at it now; he thrust it, folded, into his pocket as the cage stopped and the door clashed open.

"Well, I see where another of them tried to make a headline out of himself this afternoon," the elevator man said.

"Is that so?" the reporter said. "Better close that door; I think you got a draft in there." He ran into the swinging reflection in the glass doors this time, on his long loose legs, with the long loose body which had had no food since noon and little enough before that but which, weightless anyway, had the less to carry now. Shumann opened the cab door for him. "Bayou Street police station," the reporter told the driver. "Make it snappy."

"We could walk," Shumann said.

"Hell, I got fifty bucks now," the reporter said. They traveled crosstown now; the cab could rush fast down each block of the continuous alley, pausing only at the intersections where, to the right, canyonniched, the rumor of Grandlieu Street swelled and then faded in repetitive and indistinguishable turmoil, flicking on and past as though the cab ran along the rimless periphery of a ghostly wheel spoked with light and sound. "Yair," the reporter said, "I reckon they took Jiggs to the only quiet place in New Valois for a man to sober up in. He'll be sober now." He was sober; a turnkey fetched him in to where the reporter and Shumann waited at the desk. His eye was closed now and his lip swollen though the blood had been cleaned away except where it had dried on his shirt.

"Got enough for a while?" Shumann said.

"Yair," Jiggs said. "Give me a cigarette, for God's sake." The reporter gave him the cigarette and held the match while Jiggs tried to bring the cigarette into the flame, jerking and twitching until at last the reporter grasped Jiggs' hand and steadied it to make the contact.

"We'll get a piece of steak and put it on your eye," the reporter said.

"You better put it inside of him," the desk man said.

"How about that?" the reporter said. "You want to eat?" Jiggs held the cigarette in both shaking hands.

"All right," Jiggs said.

"What?" the reporter said. "Would you feel better if you ate something?"

"All right," Jiggs said. "Do we go now or do I go back in there?"

"No, we're going right now," the reporter said. He said to Shumann, "You take him on to the cab; I'll be right out." He turned to the desk. "What's it, Mac? Drunk or vag?"

"You springing him, or the paper?"

"I am."

"Call it vag," the desk man said. The reporter took out Hagood's money and laid ten dollars on the desk.

"O.K.," he said. "Will you give the other five to Leblanc? I borrowed it off of him out at the airport this afternoon." He went out too. Shumann and Jiggs waited beside the cab. The reporter saw now the once raked and swaggering cap crumpled and thrust into Jiggs' hip pocket and that the absence of the raked and filthy object from Jiggs' silhouette was like the dropped flag from the shot buck's—the body still ran, still retained a similitude of power and even speed, would even run on for yards and even perhaps miles, and then for years in a gnawing burrowing of worms, but that which tasted air and drank the sun was dead. "The poor bastard," the reporter thought; he still carried the mass of bills as he had thrust them into and withdrawn them from his pocket. "You're o.k. now," he said, loudly, heartily. "Roger can stop somewhere and get you something to eat and then you will be all right. Here." He nudged his hand at Shumann.

"I wont need it," Shumann said. "Jack collected his eighteen-fifty for the jump this afternoon."

"Yair; I forgot," the reporter said. Then he said, "But what about tomorrow? We'll be gone all day, see? Here, take it; you can leave it with her in case. . . . . . . You can just keep it and pay it all back, then."

"Yair," Shumann said. "Thanks then." He took the crumpled wad without looking at it and put it into his pocket and pushed Jiggs into the cab.

"Besides, you can pay the cab, too," the reporter said. "We forgot about that.—I told him where to go. See you in the morning." He leaned to the window; beyond Shumann Jiggs sat in the other corner, smoking the cigarette out of both shaking hands. The reporter spoke in a tone repressed, conspiratorial: "Train leaves at eight-twenty-two. O.K.?"

"O.K.," Shumann said.

"I'll have everything fixed up and meet you at the station."

"O.K.," Shumann said. The cab moved on. Through the back window Shumann saw the reporter standing at the curb in the glare of the two unmistakable pariahgreen globes on either side of the entrance, still, gaunt, the garments which hung from the skeleton frame seeming to stir faintly and steadily even when and where there was no wind, as though having chosen that one spot out of the entire sprawled and myriad city he stood there without impatience or design: patron (even if no guardian) saint of all waifs, all the homeless the desperate and the starved. Now the cab turned its back on Grandlieu Street, though presently it turned parallel to it or to where it must be now, since now there was no rumor, no sound, save the lightglare on the sky which held to their right even after the cab turned and now ran toward where the street should be; Shumann did not know they had crossed it until they plunged suddenly into the region of narrow gashes between balconies, crossing intersections marked by the ghostly oneway arrows. "We must be almost there," he said. "You want to stop and eat?"

"All right," Jiggs said.

"Do you or dont you?"

"Yair," Jiggs said. "Whatever you want me to do." Then Shumann looked at him and saw him trying to hold the cigarette to his mouth with both hands, and that the cigarette was dead.

"What do you want?" Shumann said.

"I want a drink," Jiggs said quietly.

"Do you have to have one?"

"I guess I dont if I cant get one." Shumann watched him holding the dead cigarette to his mouth, drawing at it.

"If I give you a drink, will you eat something?"

"Yair. I'll do anything." Shumann leaned forward and tapped on the glass. The driver turned his head.

"Where can I get something to eat?" Shumann said. "A bowl of soup?"

"You'll have to go back up toward Grandlieu for that."

"Aint there any place close around here?"

"You can get a ham sandwich at these wop stores, if you can find one open."

"All right. Stop at the next one you see, will you?" It was not far; Shumann recognised the corner, though he asked to be sure as they got out. "Noy-dees Street aint far from here, is it?"

"Noyades?" the driver said. "That's it in the next block there. On the right."

"We'll get out here then," Shumann said. He drew out the crumpled money which the reporter had given him, glancing down at the plump neat figure five in the corner. "That makes eleven-seventy," he thought, then he discovered a second bill crumpled into the first one; he passed it to the driver, still looking at the compact "5" on the one in his hand. "Damn," he thought. "That's seventeen dollars", as the driver spoke to him:

"It's just two-fifteen. Aint you got anything smaller than this?"

"Smaller?" Shumann said. He looked at the bill in the driver's hand, held so that the light from the meter fell upon it. It was a ten. "No," he thought; he didn't even swear now. "It's twenty-two dollars." The store was a room the size shape and temperature of a bankvault. It was illuminated by one kerosene lamp which seemed to cast not light but shadows, out of whose brown Rembrandtgloom the hushed bellies of ranked cans gleamed behind a counter massed with an unbelievable quantity of indistinguishable objects which the proprietor must vend by feel alone to distinguish not only object from object but object from chiaroscuro. It smelled of cheese and garlic and of heated metal; sitting on either side of a small fiercelyburning kerosene heater a man and a woman, both wrapped in shawls and distinguishable by gender only because the man wore a cap and whom Shumann had not

seen until now, looked up at him. The sandwich was the end
of a hard French loaf, with ham and cheese. He gave it to
Jiggs and followed him out, where Jiggs stopped again and
stood looking at the object in his hand with a sort of oxlike
despair.

"Could I have the drink first?" he said.

"You eat while we walk home," Shumann said. "I'll give
you the drink later."

"It would be better if I had the drink first," Jiggs said.

"Yes," Shumann said. "You thought that this morning
too."

"Yair," Jiggs said. "That's right." He became motionless
again, looking at the sandwich.

"Go on," Shumann said. "Eat it."

"All right," Jiggs said. He began to eat; Shumann watched
him bring the sandwich to his mouth with both hands and
turn his face sideways to bite into it; he could see Jiggs shaking and jerking all over now as he worried the bite off and
began to chew; chewing, Jiggs looked full at Shumann,
holding the bitten sandwich in both grimed hands before his
breast as though it were a crucifix, chewing with his mouth
open, looking full at Shumann until Shumann realised that
Jiggs was not looking at him at all, that the one good eye
was merely open and filled with a profound and hopeless
abnegation as if the despair which both eyes should have
divided between them had now to be concentrated
and contained in one alone, and that Jiggs' face was now
slicked over with something which in the faint light resembled oil in the instant before Jiggs began to vomit. Shumann
held him up, holding the sandwich clear with the other
hand, while Jiggs' stomach continued to go through the
motions of refusal long after there was nothing left to
abdicate.

"Try to stop it now," Shumann said.

"Yair," Jiggs said. He dragged his sleeve across his mouth.

"Here," Shumann said. He extended his handkerchief. Jiggs
took it, but at once he reached his hand again, groping.
"What?" Shumann said.

"The sandwich."

"Could you hold it down if you had a drink?"

"I could do anything if I had a drink," Jiggs said.

"Come on," Shumann said. When they entered the alley they could see the outfall of light from the window beyond the balcony as Hagood had seen it last night, though there was now no armshadow, no voice. Shumann halted beneath the balcony. "Jack," he said. "Laverne." But still there was nothing to see: just the parachute jumper's voice from beyond the window:

"It's off the latch. Lock it when you come in." When they came up the stairs the jumper was sitting on the cot, in his underclothes, his clothing arranged neatly on a chair and his foot on the chair too while with a stained wad of cotton he swabbed liquid from a bottle into the long raw abrasion like a paintsmear from his ankle to his thigh. On the floor lay the bandage and tape which he had worn in from the airport. He had already arranged the cot for the night; the blanket was turned neatly back and the rug from the floor spread over the foot.

"You better sleep in the bed tonight," Shumann said. "That blanket will give that skinned place hell." The jumper did not answer, bent over his leg, swabbing the medicine in with a sort of savage concentration. Shumann turned; he seemed to notice for the first time the sandwich in his hand and then to remember Jiggs who now stood quietly beside his canvas bag, watching Shumann quietly and patiently with the one eye, with that patient inarticulate quality of a dog. "Oh yes," Shumann said, turning on toward the table. The jug still sat there, though the glasses and the dishpan were gone and the jug itself appeared to have been washed. "Get a glass and some water," he said. When the curtain fell behind Jiggs Shumann laid the sandwich on the table and looked at the jumper again. After a moment the jumper looked up at him.

"Well?" the jumper said. "What about it?"

"I guess I can get it," Shumann said.

"You mean you didn't see Ord?"

"Yair. We found him."

"Suppose you do get it. How are you going to get it qualified in time to race tomorrow?"

"I dont know," Shumann said. He lit a cigarette. "He said he could get that fixed up. I dont know, myself."

"How? Does the race committee think he is Jesus too, the same as the rest of you do?"

"I said I dont know," Shumann said. "If we cant get it qualified, that's all there is to it. But if we can. . . . . . ." He smoked. The jumper swabbed carefully and viciously at his leg. "There's two things I could do," Shumann said. "It will qualify under five hundred and seventy-five cubic inches. I could enter it in that and loaf back on half throttle and take third without having to make a vertical turn, and the purse tomorrow is eight-ninety. Or I could enter the other, the Trophy. It will be the only thing out there that will even stay in sight of Ord. And Ord is just in it so his home folks can see him fly; I dont believe he would beat that Ninety-Two to death just to win two thousand dollars. Not on a five mile course. Because it must be fast. We would be fixed then."

"Yes; fixed. She'd owe Ord about five thousand for the crate and the motor. What's wrong with it?"

"I dont know. I didn't ask Ord. All I know is what Ord told him—" he made a brief indescribable motion with his head as though to indicate the room but which indicated the reporter as plainly as if Shumann had spoken his name—"he said the controls cross when it lands. Whether it's slowing up or whether it's the air off the ground. Because he said that Ord stalled it out when he. . . . . . Or maybe a different weight distribution, a couple of sandbags in the——"

"Yair. Or maybe when he gets it qualified tomorrow he will have them move the pylons up to around four thousand feet and hold the race up there instead of at General Behindman's country club." He ceased and bent over his leg again, then Shumann also saw Jiggs. He had apparently been in the room for some time, standing beside the table with two of the jam glasses, one of them containing water, in his hands. Shumann went to the table and poured into the empty glass and looked at Jiggs who now mused upon the drink.

"Aint that enough?" Shumann said.

"Yair," Jiggs said, rousing; "yair." When he poured water from the other glass into the drink the two rims clicked together with a faint chattering; Shumann watched him set the water glass down, where it chattered again on the table before he released it, and then with both hands attempt to raise the other one to his lips. As the glass approached Jiggs' whole head began to jerk so that he could not make contact with his mouth, the rim of the glass clicking against his teeth while he tried to still it. "Jesus," he said quietly, "Jesus. I tried for two hours to sit on the bed because when I would walk up and down the guy would come and holler at me through the bars."

"Here," Shumann said. He put his hand on the glass and stopped it and tilted it; he could watch Jiggs swallowing now and the liquid trickling down his bluestubbled chin from each corner of his mouth and splotching dark on his shirt until Jiggs pushed the glass away, panting.

"Wait," he said. "It's wasting. Maybe if you wont look at me I can drink it."

"And then get on the sandwich again," Shumann said. He took the jug from the table and looked back at the jumper again. "Go on and take the bed tonight," he said. "You'll have that leg infected under a blanket. Are you going to put the bandage back on?"

"I'll sleep in a cuckold's bed but not in a pimp's," the jumper said. "Go on. Get yourself a piece to take to hell with you tomorrow."

"I can take third in the five-seventy-five without even crossing the airport," Shumann said. "Anyway, by the time it is qualified I'll know whether I can land it or not.—How about putting that bandage back on?" But the jumper did not answer nor even look at him. The blanket was already turned back; with the injured leg swinging stiffly he turned on the ball of his buttocks and swung into the cot and drew the blanket up in one motion; for a while longer Shumann looked at him, the jug against his leg. Then he realised that for some time he had been hearing Jiggs chewing and he looked at him and saw Jiggs squatting on the floor beside the canvas bag, chewing, holding the sandwich in both hands. "You, too," Shumann said. "You going to sleep there?" Jiggs looked up at him with the one eye. His whole face was swollen and puffed now; he chewed slowly and gingerly, looking up at Shumann with that doglike quality abject, sad, and at peace. "Go on," Shumann said. "Get settled. I'm going to turn out the light." Without ceasing to chew Jiggs disengaged one hand and dragged the canvas sack over and lay down, his head upon it. Shumann could still hear him chewing as he groped in the darkness toward the curtain and lifted it and passed beyond it and groped on to the lamp beside the bed, moving quietly now, and snapped it on and found the woman, the boy asleep beside her, watching him. She lay in the middle of the bed with the boy between her and the wall. Her clothes were laid neatly too on a chair and then Shumann saw the nightgown, the only silk one she had, lying across the chair too; and stooping to set the jug beneath the bed he paused and then lifted from the floor the cotton shorts which she wore, or had worn, from where they had either been dropped or flung, and put them on the chair too and removed his jacket and began to unbutton his shirt while she watched him, the bedclothes huddled to her chin.

"So you got the ship," she said.

"I dont know. We're going to try." He removed the watch from his wrist and wound it carefully and put it on the table; when the faint clicking ceased he could hear again from beyond the curtain the sound of Jiggs chewing. He set his feet in turn on the corner of the chair and unlaced his shoes, feeling her watching him. "I can take at least third in the five-seventy-five without passing the pylons close enough for anybody on them to read the ship's number. And that's fifteen percent. of eight-ninety. Or there's two thousand in the Trophy and I dont believe Ord will——"

"Yes. I heard you through the curtain. But why?" He set the shoes neatly side by side and stepped out of his trousers and shook them into crease by the cuffs and folded them and put them on the chest of drawers beside the celluloid comb and brush and the cravat and stood also in shorts. "And the ship is all right except you wont know until you are in the air whether or not you can take it off and you wont know until you are back on the ground and standing up again whether or not you can land it."

"I guess I can land it, all right." He lit a cigarette and then stood with his hand on the light switch, looking at her. She had not moved, lying with the covers drawn smooth and nun-like up to her chin; again from beyond the curtain he could hear Jiggs chewing, mouthing at the hard sandwich with that painful patience.

"You're lying," she said. "We got along before."

"Because we had to. This time we dont have to."

"But it's seven months yet."

"Yair. Just seven months. And one more meet, and the only ship we have with a shot engine and two wrenched longerons." He looked at her a moment longer; at last she opened the covers; as he snapped off the light his retina carried into the darkness the imprint of one bare shoulder and breast down to the waist. "Want to move Jack to the middle?" he said. She did not answer, though it was not until he drew the covers up himself that he discovered that she was lying rigid, her flank tense and hard with rigid muscles where his own touched it as he settled himself. He withdrew the cigarette and held it suspended above his mouth, hearing Jiggs chewing beyond the curtain and then the jumper's voice: "Jesus God, stop eating that! You sound just like a dog!"

"Here, take it easy," Shumann said. "I haven't got it qualified yet, even."

"You bastard," she said in a tense rigid whisper. "You rotten pilot, you bastard rotten pilot. Hanging off there with a dead stick so you wouldn't interfere in their damn race and then mushing in over that seawall and you wouldn't even hold its head up! you wouldn't even hold——" Her hand shot out and snatched the cigarette from him; he felt his own fingers wrench and bend and then saw the red coal twinkle and arc across the dark and strike the invisible floor.

"Here," he whispered. "Let me pick it up off the——" But now the hard hand struck his cheek, clutching and scrabbling about his jaw and throat and shoulder until he caught it and held it, wrenching and jerking.

"You bastard rotten, you rotten——" she panted.

"All right," he said. "Steady, now." She ceased, breathing hard and fast. But he still held the wrist, wary and without gentleness too. "All right, now.—You want to take your pants off?"

"They're already off."

"Oh yair," he said. "I forgot." When she made her first

parachute jump they had not been together very long. She was the one who suggested that he teach her to jump, and he already had a parachute, the exhibition kind; when he used it he either flew the aeroplane or made the jump, depending on whether the casual partner with whom he would join forces for a day or a week or a season were a pilot himself or not. She made the suggestion herself and he showed her, drilled her, in the simple mechanics of climbing out onto the wing with the parachute harness buckled on and then dropping off and letting her own weight pull the parachute from the case attached to the wing. The act was billed for a Saturday afternoon in a small Kansas town and he did not know that she was frightened until they were in the air and the money collected and the crowd waiting and she had begun to climb out along the wing. She wore skirts; they had decided that her exposed legs would not only be a drawing card but that in the skirt no one would doubt that she was a woman, and now she was clinging to the inner bay strut and looking back at him with an expression that he was later to realise was not at all fear of death but on the contrary a wild and now mindless repudiation of bereavement as if it were he who was the one about to die and not her. He sat in the back cockpit with the aeroplane in position, holding the wing up under her weight, gesturing her on out toward the wingtip, almost angrily, when he saw her leave the strut and with that blind and completely irrational expression of protest and wild denial on her face and the hem of the skirt whipping out of the parachute harness about her loins climb, not back into the front seat which she had left but on toward the one in which he sat holding the aeroplane level, scrambling and sprawling into the cockpit (he saw her knuckles perfectly white where she gripped the cockpit's edge) astride his legs and facing him. In the same instant of realising (as with one hand she ripped her skirthem free of the safetywire with which they had fastened it bloomerfashion between her legs) that she was clawing blindly and furiously not at the belt across his thighs but at the fly of his trousers he realised that she had on no undergarment, pants. She told him later that the reason was that she was afraid that from fear she might soil one of the few undergarments which she now possessed. So he tried to fight

her off for a while, but he had to fly the aeroplane, keep it in
position over the field, and besides (they had been together
only a few months then) soon he had two opponents; he was
outnumbered, he now bore in his own lap, between himself
and her wild and frenzied body, the perennially undefeated,
the victorious; it was some blind instinct out of the long
swoon while he waited for his backbone's fluid marrow to
congeal again that he remembered to roll the aeroplane toward the wing to which the parachute case was attached because the next that he remembered was the belt catching him
across the legs as, looking up he saw the parachute floating
between him and the ground, and looking down he saw the
bereaved, the upthrust, the stalk: the annealed rapacious
heartshaped crimson bud. He had to land the aeroplane, the
rest he learned later: how she had come down with the dress,
pulled or blown free of the parachute harness, up about her
armpits and had been dragged along the ground until overtaken by a yelling mob of men and youths, in the center of
which she now lay dressed from the waist down in dirt and
parachute straps and stockings. When he fought through the
mob to where she was she had been arrested by three village
officers one of whose faces Shumann remarked even then with
a violent foreboding—a youngish man with a hard handsome
face sadistic rather than vicious, who was using the butt of a
pistol to keep the mob back and who struck at Shumann with
it with the same blind fury. They carried her to jail, the younger one threatening her with the pistol now; already Shumann realised that in the two other officers he had only
bigotry and greed to contend with, it was the younger one
that he had to fear—a man besotted and satiated by his
triumphs over abased human flesh which his corrupt and pic-
ayune office supplied him, seeing now and without forewarn-
ing the ultimate shape of his jaded desires fall upon him out
of the sky, not merely naked but clothed in the very traditional symbology—the ruined dress with which she was
trying wildly to cover her loins, and the parachute harness—
of female bondage. They would neither arrest Shumann too
nor allow him access to her. After he was driven back along
with the mob by the younger officer's pistol from the jail
door—a square building of fierce new brick into which he

saw her, struggling still, vanish—a single glimpse of her indomitable and terrified face beyond the younger officer's
shoulder as the now alarmed older officers hurried her inside—for the time he became one of the mob though even
then, mad with rage and terror, he knew that it was merely
because his and the mob's immediate object happened to be
the same—to see, touch her, again. He knew too that the
two older craven officers were at least neutral, pulled to his
side by their own physical fear of the mob, and that actually
the younger one had for support only his dispensation for
impunitive violence with which the dingy cadaver of the law
invested him. But it seemed to be enough. It was for the next
hour anyway, during which, followed by his ragamuffin train
of boys and youths and drunken men, he accomplished his
nightmare's orbit about the town, from mayor to lawyer to
lawyer to lawyer and back again. They were at supper, or
about to sit down to it or just finishing; he would have to tell
his story with the round eyes of children and the grim implacable faces of wives and aunts watching him while the em-
powered men from whom he sought what he sincerely
believed to be justice and no more forced him step by step to
name what he feared, whereupon one of them threatened to
have him arrested for criminal insinuations against the town's
civil structure. It was a minister (and two hours after dark)
who finally telephoned to the mayor. Shumann learned only
from the overheard conversation that the authorities were apparently seeking him now; five minutes later a car called for
him, with one of the two older officers in it and two others
whom he had not seen yet. "Am I under arrest too?" he said.
"You can try to get out and run if you want to," the officer
said. That was all. The car stopped at the jail and the officer
and one of the others got out. "Hold him," the officer said.
"I'll hold him, all right," the second deputy said. So Shumann
sat in the car with the deputy's shoulder jammed into his and
watched the two others hurry up the bricked walk; the door
of the jail opened for them and closed; then it opened again
and he saw her. She wore a raincoat now; he saw her for an
instant as the two men hurried her out and the door closed
again; it was not until the next day that she showed him the
dress now in shreds and the scratches and bruises on the in-

sides of her legs and on her jaw and face and the cut in her
lip. They thrust her into the car, beside him. The officer was
about to follow when the second deputy shoved him roughly
away. "Ride in front," the deputy said. "I'll ride back here."
There were now four in the back seat; Shumann sat rigid with
the first deputy's shoulder jammed into his and Laverne's
rigid flank and side jammed against him so that it seemed to
him that he could feel through her rigidity the second deputy
crowding and dragging his flank against Laverne's other side.
"All right," the officer said. "Let's get away from here while
we can."—"Where are we going?" Shumann asked. The officer did not answer. He leaned out, looking back at the jail as
the car gathered speed, going fast now. "Go on," he said.
"Them boys may not can hold him and there's been too much
whore's hell here already." The car rushed on, out of the village; Shumann realised that they were going in the direction
of the field, the airport. The car swung in from the road; its
headlights fell upon the aeroplane standing as he had jumped
out of it, already running, in the afternoon; as the car stopped
the lights of a second one came into sight, coming fast down
the road. The officer began to curse. "Durn him. Durn them
boys. I knew they couldn't——" He turned to Shumann.
"There's your airship. You and her get out of here."—"What
do you want us to do?" Shumann said. "You're going to
crank up that flying machine and get out of this town. And
you do it quick; I was afraid them boys couldn't hold
him."—"Tonight?" Shumann said. "I haven't got any
lights."—"Aint nothing going to run into you up there, I
guess," the officer said. "You get her into it and get away
from here and dont you never come back." Now the second
car slewed from the road, the lights swung full upon them; it
rushed up, slewing again, with men already jumping out of it
before it had stopped. "Hurry!" the officer cried. "We'll try to
hold him."—"Get into the ship," Shumann told her. At first
he thought that the man was drunk. He watched Laverne,
holding the raincoat about her, run down the long tunnel of
the cars' lights and climb into the aeroplane and vanish, then
he turned and saw the man struggling while the others held
him. But he was not drunk, he was mad, he was insane for
the time; he struggled toward Shumann who saw in his face

not rage, not even lust, but almost a counterpart of that terror
and wild protest against bereavement and division which he
had seen in Laverne's face while she clung to the strut and
looked back at him. "I'll pay you!" the man screamed. "I'll
pay her! I'll pay either of you! Name it! Let me fuck her once
and you can cut me if you want!"—"Go on, I tell you!" the
older officer panted at him. He ran too; for an instant the
man ceased to struggle; perhaps for the instant he believed
that Shumann had gone to fetch her back. Then he began to
struggle and scream again, cursing now, screaming at Laverne, calling her whore and bitch and pervert in a tone wild
with despair until the engine blotted it. But Shumann could
still see him struggling with the men who held him, the
group silhouetted by the lights of the two cars, while he sat
and warmed the engine as long as he dared. But he had to
take it off cold after all; he could hear the shouts now and
against the headlights he saw the man running toward him,
toward the aeroplane; he took it off from where it stood, with
nothing to see ahead but the blue flames at the exhaust ports,
into a night without moon; thirty minutes later, using a
dimlyseen windmill to check his altitude and making a fast
blind landing in an alfalfa field, he struck an object which he
found the next morning, fifty feet from the overturned aeroplane, to be a cow.

It was now about nine-thirty. The reporter thought for a
moment of walking on over to Grandlieu Street and its celluloid and confettirained uproar and down it to Saint Jules
and so back to the paper that way, but he did not. When he
moved it was to turn back into the dark cross street out of
which the cab had emerged a half hour before. There was no
reason for him to do this anymore than there would have
been any reason to return by Grandlieu Street: it was as
though the grim Spectator himself had so ordained and arranged that when the reporter entered the twin glass doors
and the elevator cage clashed behind him this time, stooping
to lift the facedown watch alone and look at it he would contemplate unwitting and unawares peace's ultimate morato-
rium in the exact second of the cycle's completion—the
inexplicable and fading fury of the past twenty-four hours circled back to itself and become whole and intact and objective

and already vanishing slowly like the damp print of a lifted glass on a bar. Because he was not thinking about time, about any postulated angle of clockhands on a dial; he had even less reason to do that than he had to choose either of the two directions, since the one moment out of all the future which he could see where his body would need to coincide with time or dial would not occur for almost twelve hours yet; he was not even to recognise at once the cycle's neat completion toward which he walked steadily, not fast, from block to block of the narrow cross street notched out of the blunt and now slumbering backends of commerce while at each intersection where he waited during the trafficdammed moment or while there reached him, as in the cab previously, the faint rumor, the sound felt rather than heard, of Grandlieu Street: the tonight's Nilebarge clatterfalque—the furious faint butterflyspawn, substanceless oblivious and doomed, against the choraldrop of the dawn's biding white wings—and at last Saint Jules Avenue itself running broad and suave between the austere palms springing full immobile and monstrous like burlesqued bunches of country broomsedge set on scabby posts, and then the twin doors and the elevator cage where the elevator man, glancing up at him from beneath shaggy pepper-and-salt brows that looked like his moustache had had twins suddenly, said with grim and vindictive unction, "Well, I see how this afternoon another of them tried to make the front page, only he never quite——"

"Is that so," the reporter said pleasantly, laying the watch back. "Two past ten, huh? That's a fine hour for a man not to have nothing to do until tomorrow but go to work, aint it?"

"That ought not to be much hardship on a man that dont only work except when he aint got nothing else to do," the elevator man said.

"Is that so too," the reporter said pleasantly. "You better close that door; I think I felt a——" It clashed behind him. "Two minutes past ten," he thought. "That leaves . . . ." But that fled before he had begun to think it; he hung in a slow long backwash of peaceful and serene waiting, thinking *Now she will be.* . . . Just above the button on the bellplate the faintly oxidised streak of last night's match still

showed; the match now, without calculation, without sight
to guide it, almost followed the mark. The washroom was the
last door: a single opaque sheet of glass stencilled GENTLE-
MEN in a frame without knob ("Maybe that's why only gentlemen," the reporter thought) inswinging into eternal
creosote. He removed even his shirt to wash, fingering gingerly the left side of his face, leaning to the blunt wavering
mirror the replica of his gingerly grimace as he moved his jaw
back and forth as he contemplated the bluish autograph of
violence upon his diplomacolored flesh like tattooing, thinking quietly, "Yair. Now she will be. . . . . . ." Now the
cityroom (he scratched this match on the door itself) the
barncavern, looming: the copydesk like a cluttered island, the
other single desks beneath the single greenshaded bulbs had
that quality of profound and lonely isolation of buoymarked
shoals in an untravelled and forgotten sea, his own among
them. He had not seen it in twenty-four hours it is true, yet
as he stood beside it he looked down at its cluttered surface—
the edgenotching of countless vanished cigarettes, the half-
filled sheet of yellow copy in the typewriter—with slow and
quiet amaze as though not only at finding anything of his
own on the desk but at finding the desk itself still in its old
place, thinking how he could not possibly have got that
drunk and got that sober in just that time. There was someone else at Hagood's desk when he passed and so Hagood
had not seen him yet; he had been at his desk for almost an
hour while yellow sheet after yellow sheet passed steadily
through the typewriter when the copyboy came.

"He wants you," the boy said.

"Thanks," the reporter said. In his shirt sleeves and with
his tie loose again though still wearing his hat, he stopped at
the desk and looked down at Hagood with pleasant and courteous interrogation. "You wanted me, chief?" he said.

"I thought you went home. It's eleven oclock. What are
you doing?"

"Buggering up a Sunday feature for Smitty. He asked me
to do it."

"Asked you to?"

"Yair. I had caught up. I was all through."

"What is it?"

"It's all right. It's about how the loves of Antony and Cleopatra had been prophesied all the time in Egyptian architecture only they never knew what it meant; maybe they had to wait on the Roman papers. But it's all right. Smitty's got some books and a couple or three cuts to run, and all you have to do is try to translate the books so that any guy with a dime can understand what it means, and when you dont know yourself you just put it down like the book says it and that makes it better still because even the censors dont know what it says they were doing." But Hagood was not listening.

"You mean you are not going home tonight?" The reporter looked down at Hagood, gravely and quietly. "They are still down yonder at your place, are they?" The reporter looked at him. "What are you going to do tonight?"

"I'm going home with Smitty. Sleep on his sofa."

"He's not even here," Hagood said.

"Yair. He's at home. I told him I would finish this for him first."

"All right," Hagood said. The reporter returned to his desk.

"And now it's eleven oclock," he thought. "And that leaves . . . . *Yair. She will be.* . . . . . ." There were three or four others at the single desks, but by midnight they had snapped off their lights and gone; now there was only the group about the copydesk and now the whole building began to tremble to the remote travail of the presses; now about the copydesk the six or seven men, coatless and collarless, in their green eyeshades like a uniform, seemed to concentrate toward a subterranean crisis, like so many puny humans conducting the lyingin of a mastodon. At half past one Hagood himself departed; he looked across the room toward the desk where the reporter sat immobile now, his hands still on the keyboard and his lowered face shaded and so hidden by his hatbrim; it was at two oclock that one of the proofreaders approached the desk and found that the reporter was not thinking but asleep, sitting bolt upright, his bony wrists and his thin hands projecting from his frayed clean tooshort cuffs and lying peaceful and inert on the typewriter before him.

"We're going over to Joe's," the proofreader said. "Want to come?"

"I'm on the wagon," the reporter said. "I aint through here, anyway."

"So I noticed," the other said. "Only you better finish it in bed.—What do you mean, on the wagon? That you are going to start buying your own? You can do that with us; maybe Joe wont drop dead."

"No," the reporter said. "On the wagon."

"Since when, for Christ's sake?"

"I dont know. Some time this morning.—Yair, I got to finish this. Dont you guys wait on me." So they went out, putting on their coats, though almost at once two charwomen came in. But the reporter did not heed them. He removed the sheet from the typewriter and laid it on the stack and evened them meticulously, his face peaceful. "Yair," he thought. "It aint the money. It aint that.——Yair. And now she will be. . . . . . ." The women did not pay him any mind either as he went to Hagood's desk and turned on the light above it. He chose the right drawer at once and took out the pad of blank note forms and tore off the top one and put the pad back into the drawer. He did not return to his own desk, neither did he pause at the nearest one because one of the women was busy there. So he snapped on the light above the next one and sat down and racked the note form into the typewriter and began to fill it in, carefully—the neat convenient flimsy scrap of paper which by a few marks became transposed into an implement sharper than steel and more enduring than stone and by means of which the final and fatal step became anesthetised out of the realm not only of dread but of intelligence too, into that of delusion and mindless hope like the superscription on a loveletter: . . . . . . *February 16, 1935* . . . . *February 16, 1936 we* . . . . *The Ord-Atkinson Aircraft Corp., Blaisedell, Franciana* . . . .—— He did not pause at all, his fingers did not falter; he wrote in the sum exactly as though he were writing two words of a column head: *Five Thousand Dollars ($5000.00)* . . . .——Now he did pause, his fingers poised, thinking swiftly while the charwoman did something in the wastebasket beside the desk in front of him, producing a mute deliberate scratching like a huge rat: "There's one of them is against the law, only if I put in the other one it might look fishy." So he wrote again, striking the keys clean and firm, spelling out the *e-i-g-h-t* and flipping the note out; now he went to the copydesk itself, since he did not own a fountain pen, and turned on the light there and signed the note on the first signature line and blotted it and sat looking at it quietly for a moment, thinking, "Yair. In bed now. And now he will. . . . . . Yair," he said aloud, quietly, "that looks o.k." He turned, speaking to either of the two women: "You all know what time it is?" One of them leaned her mop against a desk and began to draw from the front of her dress an apparently interminable length of shoestring, though at last the watch—a heavy oldfashioned gold one made for a man to carry—came up.

"Twenty-six minutes to three," she said.

"Thanks," the reporter said. "Dont neither of you smoke cigarettes, do you?"

"Here's one I found on the floor," the second one said. "It dont look like much. It's been walked on." Nevertheless some of the tobacco remained in it, though it burned fast; at each draw the reporter received a sensation precarious and lightly temporary, as though at a breath tobacco fire and all would evacuate the paper tube and stop only when it struck the back of his throat or the end of his lungs; three draws consumed it.

"Thanks," he said. "If you find any more, will you put them on that desk back there where the coat is? Thanks.— Twenty-two to three," he thought. "That dont even leave six hours."—*Yair*, he thought, then it blew out of his mind, vanished, again into the long peaceful slack nothope, notjoy: just waiting, thinking how he ought to eat, then he thought how the elevator would not be running now, so that should settle that. "Only I could get some cigarettes," he thought. "Jesus, I ought to eat something." There was no light now in the corridor, but there would be one in the washroom; he returned to his desk and took the folded paper from his coat and went out again; and now, leaning against the carbolised wall he opened the paper upon the same boxheadings, the identical from day to day—the bankers the farmers the strikers, the foolish the unlucky and the merely criminal—distinguishable from one day to another not by what they did but by the single brief typeline beneath the paper's registered name. He could stand easily so, without apparent need to shift his weight in rotation among the members which bore it; now with mere inertia and not gravity to contend with he had even less of bulk and mass to support than he had carried running up the stairs at eight oclock, so that he moved only when he said to himself, "It must be after three now." He folded the paper neatly and returned to the corridor, where one glance into the dark cityroom showed him that the women were done. "Yair. It's making toward four," he thought, thinking, wondering if it were actually dawn which he felt, or that anyway the dark globe on which people lived had passed the dead point at which the ill and the weary were supposed to be prone to die and now it was beginning to turn again, soon beginning to spin again out of the last laggard reluctance of darkness—the garblement which was the city: the scabby hoppoles which elevated the ragged palmcrests like the monstrous broomsage out of an old country thought, the spent stage of last night's clatterfalque Nilebarge supine now beneath today's white wings treadling, the hydrantgouts gutterplaited with the trodden tinseldung of stars. "And at Alphonse's and Renaud's the waiters that can not only understand Mississippi Valley French but they can even fetch back from the kitchen what you were not so sure yourself you told them to," he thought, passing among the desks by feel now and rolling the paper into his coat for pillow before stretching out on the floor. "Yair," he thought, "in bed now, and he will come in and she will say *Did you get it?* and he will say *What? Get what? Oh, you mean the ship. Yair, we got it. That's what we went over there for.*"

It was not the sun that waked him, nor what would have been the sun save for the usual winter morning's overcast: he just waked, regardless of the fact that during the past forty-eight hours he had slept but little more than he had eaten, like so many people who, living always on the outside of the mechanical regimentation of hours, seem able at need to coincide with a given moment with a sort of unflagging instinctive facility. But the train would be ordered by mechanical postulation though, and there would be no watch or clock in the building yet; gaunt, worn (he had not even paused to wash his face) he ran down the stairs and along the street itself, still running, and turned in this side of the window and the immemorial grapefruit halves which apparently each morning at the same moment at which the street lamps went out would be set, age- and timeproved for intactness and imperviousness like the peasant vases exhumed from Greek and Roman ruins, between the paper poinsettias and the easel bearing the names of food printed upon interchangeable metal strips. In the cityroom they called it the dirty spoon: one of ten thousand narrow tunnels furnished with a counter, a row of buttockpolished backless stools, a coffeeurn and a Greek proprietor resembling a retired wrestler adjacent to ten thousand newspapers and dubbed by ten thousand variations about the land; the same thickbodied Greek in the same soiled drill jacket might have looked at him across the same glass coffin filled with bowls of cereal and oranges and plates of buns apparently exhumed along with the grapefruit in the window, only just this moment varnished. Then the reporter was able to see the clock on the rear wall; it was only fifteen past seven. "Well, for Christ's sake," he said.

"Coffee?" the Greek said.

"Yair," the reporter said. "I ought to eat too," he thought, looking down into the glasswalled and -topped gutter beneath his hands, not with any revulsion now, but with a kind of delicate distasteful abstemiousness like the old novel women. And not from impatience, hurry: just as last night he seemed to see his blind furious course circling implacably back to the point where he had lost control of it like a kind of spiritual groundloop, now he seemed to feel it straighten out at last, already lifting him steadily and as implacably and undeviatingly onward so that now he need make no effort to move with it; all he had to do now was to remember to carry along with him everything which he was likely to need because this time he was not coming back. "Gimme one of these," he said, tapping the glass with one hand while with the other he touched, felt, the folded slip of paper in his watchpocket. He ate the bun along with his coffee, tasting neither, feeling only the coffee's warmth; it was now twenty-five past seven. "I can walk," he thought. The overcast would burn away later. But it still lay overhead when he entered the station where Shumann rose from the bench. "Had some breakfast yet?" the reporter said.

"Yes," Shumann said. The reporter looked at the other with a kind of bright grave intensity.

"Come on," he said. "We can get on now." The lights still burned in the trainshed; the skylight was the same color of the sky outside. "It will be gone soon though," the reporter said. "Maybe by the time we get there; you will probably fly the ship back in the sun. Just think of that." But it was gone before that; it was gone when they ran clear of the city; the car (they had the entire end of it to themselves) ran almost at once in thin sunlight. "I told you you would fly back in the sunshine," the reporter said. "I guess we had better fix this up now, too." He took out the note; he watched with that grave bright intensity while Shumann read it and then seemed to muse upon it soberly.

"Five thousand," Shumann said. "That's. . . . . . ."

"High?" the reporter said. "Yair. I didn't want there to be any hitch until we got into the air with it, got back to the airport with it. To look like a price that even Marchand wouldn't dare refuse to. . . . . . ." He watched Shumann, bright, quiet, grave.

"Yair," Shumann said. "I see." He reached into his coat. Then perhaps it was the fountain pen, though the reporter did not move yet and the brightness and intensity and gravity had not altered yet as he watched the deliberate, unhurried, slightly awkward movement of the pen across the blank signature line beneath the one where he had signed, watching the letters emerge: *Roger Shumann* But he did not move even yet; it was not until the pen without stopping dropped down to the third line and was writing again that he leaned and stopped it with his hand, looking at the half finished third name: *Dr Carl S*

"Wait," he said. "What's that?"

"It's my father's name."

"Would he let you sign it on this?"

"He'd have to, after it was done. Yes. He would help you out on it."

"Help me out on it?"

"I wouldn't be worth even five hundred unless I managed to finish that race first." A trainman passed, swinging from seatback to seatback, pausing above them for a moment.

"Blaisedell," he said. "Blaisedell."

"Wait," the reporter said. "Maybe I didn't understand. I aint a flyer; all I know is that hour's dual Matt gave me that time. I thought maybe what Matt meant was he didn't want to risk having the undercarriage busted or the propeller bent or maybe a wingtip——" He looked at Shumann, bright, grave, his hand still holding Shumann's wrist.

"I guess I can land it all right," Shumann said. But the reporter did not move, looking at Shumann.

"Then it will be all right? it'll just be landing it, like what Matt said about the time he landed it?"

"I guess so," Shumann said. The train began to slow; the oleander bushes, the mosshung liveoaks in which light threads of mistsnared gossamer glinted in the sun; the vineshrouded station flowed up, slowing; it would not quite pass.

"Because, Jesus, it's just the money prize; it's just one afternoon. And Matt will help you build your ship back and you will be all set with it for the next meet——" They looked at one another.

"I guess I can get it back down," Shumann said.

"Yair. But listen——"

"I can land it," Shumann said.

"All right," the reporter said. He released the other's wrist; the pen moved again, completing the signature steadily: *Dr Carl Shumann, by Roger Shumann* The reporter took the note, rising.

"All right," he said. "Let's go." They walked again; it was about a mile; presently the road ran beside the field beyond which they could see the buildings—the detached office, the shop, the hangar with a broad legend above the open doors: ORD-ATKINSON AIRCRAFT CORPORATION—all of pale brick, as neat as and apparently contemporaneous with Ord's new house. Sitting on the ground a little back from the road they watched two mechanics wheel out the red-and-white monoplane with which Ord had set his record and start it and warm it, and then they saw Ord himself come out of the office and get into the racer and taxi to the end of the field and turn and takeoff straight over their heads, already travelling a hundred feet ahead of his own sound. "It's forty miles over to Feinman from here," the reporter said. "He flies it in ten minutes. Come on. You let me do the talking. Jesus," he cried, in a kind of light amazed exultation, "I never told a lie in my life that anybody believed; maybe this is what I have been needing all the time!" When they reached the hangar the doors were now closed to a crack just large enough for a man to enter. Shumann entered, already looking about, until he found the aeroplane—a lowwing monoplane with a big nose and a tubular fuselage ending in a curiously flattened tail-group which gave it the appearance of having been drawn lightly and steadily through a huge lightlyclosed gloved fist. "There it is," the reporter said.

"Yair," Shumann said. "I see.—Yes," he thought, looking quietly at the queer empennage, the blunt short cylindrical body; "I guess Ord wasn't so surprised, at that." Then he heard the reporter speaking to someone and he turned and saw a squat man with a shrewd Cajun face above a scrupulously clean coverall.

"This is Mr Shumann," the reporter said, saying in a tone of bright amazement: "You mean Matt never told you? We have bought that ship." Shumann did not wait. For a moment he watched Marchand, the note in both hands, looking at it with that baffled immobility behind which the mind flicks and darts like a terrier inside a fence.

"Yair," Shumann thought, without grimness, "he cant pass five thousand dollars anymore than I could. Not without warning, anyway." He went on to the aeroplane, though once or twice he looked back and saw Marchand and the reporter, the Cajun still emanating that stubborn and slowly crystallising bewilderment while the reporter talked, flapped, before him with an illusion of being held together only by the clothes he wore; once he even heard the reporter:

"Sure, you could telephone to Feinman and catch him. But for God's sake dont let anybody overhear how Matt stuck us for five thousand bucks for the damn crate. He promised he wouldn't tell." But there was no telephoning done apparently, because almost at once (or so it seemed to Shumann) the reporter and Marchand were beside him, the reporter quiet now, watching him now with that bright attention.

"Let's get it out where we can look at it," Shumann said. They rolled it out onto the apron, where it squatted again, seemed to. It had none of the waspwaisted trimness of the ones at the airport. It was blunt, a little thickbodied, almost sluggish looking; its lightness when moved by hand seemed curiously paradoxical. For a good minute the reporter and Marchand watched Shumann stand looking at it with thoughtful gravity. "All right," he said at last. "Let's wind her up." Now the reporter spoke, leaning lightly and slightly just off balance like a ragged penstaff dropped pointfirst into the composition apron:

"Listen. You said last night maybe it was the distribution of the weight; you said how maybe if we could shift the weight somehow while it was in the air that maybe you could find——" Later (almost as soon as Shumann was out of sight the reporter and Marchand were in Marchand's car on the road to the village, where the reporter hired a cab, scrambling into it even before he had asked the price and yelling out of his gaunt and glarefixed face, "Hell, no! Not New Valois! Feinman Airport!") he lived and relived the blind timeless period during which he lay on his stomach in the barrel, clutching the two bodymembers, with nothing to see but Shumann's feet on the rudderpedals and the movement of the aileron balancerod and nothing to feel but terrific motion— not speed and not progress—just blind furious motion like a sealed force trying to explode the monococque barrel in which he lay from the waist down on his stomach, leaving him clinging to the bodymembers in space; he was still thinking, "Jesus, maybe we are going to die and all it is is a taste like sour hot salt in your mouth" even while looking out the car window at the speeding marsh and swamp through which they skirted the city, thinking with a fierce and triumphant conviction of immortality, "We flew it! We flew it!" Now the airport, the forty miles accomplished before he knew it, what with his skull still cloudy with the light tagends of velocity and speed like the drifting feathers from a shot bird so that he had never become conscious of the sheer inertia of dimension, space, distance through which he had had to travel. He was thrusting the five dollar bill at the driver before the car began to turn into the plaza and he was out of it before it had stopped, running toward the hangar, probably not even aware that the first race was in progress. Wildfaced, gaunt and sunkeneyed from lack of sleep and from strain, his clothes ballooning about him, he ran into the hangar and on to where Jiggs stood at the workbench with a new bottle of polish and a new tin of paste open before him, shining the boots, working now with tedious and intent concern at the scar on the instep of the right one. "Did he——" the reporter cried.

"Yair, he landed it, all right," Jiggs said. "He used all the field, though. Jesus, I thought for a while he was going to run out of airport before he even cut the gun; when he stopped you couldn't have dropped a match between the prop and the seawall. They are all upstairs now, holding the caucus."

"It'll qualify itself!" the reporter cried. "I told him that. I may not know airplanes but I know sewage board Jews!"

"Yair," Jiggs said. "Anyway, he wont have to make but two landings with it. And he's already made one of them."

"Two?" the reporter cried; now he glared at Jiggs with more than exultation: with ecstasy. "He's already made two! We made one before he left Ord's!"

"We?" Jiggs said. With the boot and the rag poised he blinked painfully at the reporter with the one good hot bright eye. "We?"

"Yair; him and me! He said how it was the weight, that maybe if we could just shift the weight somehow while it was in the air, and he said Are you afraid? and I said Hell yes. But not if you aint, because Matt gave me an hour once, or maybe if I had had more than an hour I wouldn't have been. So Marchand helped us take the seat out and we rigged another one so there would be room under it for me and I slid back into the fuselage because it aint got any crossbracing, it's mon—mon—"

"Monococque," Jiggs said. "Jesus Christ, do you mean——"

"Yair. And him and Marchand rigged the seat again and he showed me where to hold on and I could just see his heels and that was all; I couldn't tell; yair, after a while I knew we were flying but I couldn't tell forward nor backward or anything because, Jesus, I just had one hour with Matt and then he cut the gun and then I could hear him, he said quiet, Jesus, we might have been standing on the ground; he said 'Now slide back. Easy. But hold tight.' And then I was hanging just by my hands; I wasn't even touching the floor of it at all; Jesus, I was thinking 'Well, here it is then; it will be tough about that race this afternoon'; I didn't even know we were on the ground again until I found out it was him and Marchand lifting the seat out and Marchand saying 'Goddamn. Goddamn. Goddamn' and him looking at me and the bastard crate standing there quiet as one of them photographs on Grandlieu Street, and him looking at me and then he says, 'Would you go up again?' and I said 'Yes. You want to go now?' and he said, 'Let's get her on over to the field and qualify'."

"Sweet Jesus Christ," Jiggs said.

"Yair," the reporter cried. "It was just weight distribution: him and Marchand rigged up a truck inner tube full of sand on a pulley so he can——And put the seat back and even if they see the end of the cable they wouldn't——Because the only ship in it that can beat him is Ord and the purse aint but two thousand and Ord dont need it, he is only in it so New Valois folks can see him fly the Ninety-Two once and he aint going to beat that fifteen-thousand-dollar ship to death just to——"

"Here; here," Jiggs said. "You're going to blow all to pieces in a minute. Smoke a cigarette; aint you got some?" The reporter fumbled the cigarettes out at last, though it was Jiggs who took two from the pack and struck the match while the reporter stooped to it, trembling. The dazed spent wild look was still on his face but he was quieter now.

"So they were all out to meet him, were they?"

"Jesus, did they," Jiggs said. "And Ord out in front; he recognised the ship as soon as it come in sight; Jesus, I bet he recognised it before Roger even recognised the airport, and by the time he landed you would have thought he was Lindbergh. And him sitting there in the cockpit and looking at them and Ord hollering at him and then they all come back up the apron like Roger was a kidnapper or something and went into the administration building and a minute later the microphone begun to holler for the inspector, what's his—"

"Sales," the reporter said. "It's licensed; they cant stop him."

"Sales can ground it, though," Jiggs said.

"Yair." The reporter was already turning, moving. "But Sales aint nothing but a Federal officer; Feinman is a Jew and on the sewage board."

"What's that got to do with it?"

"What?" the reporter cried, glaring, gaunt, apparently having already rushed on and out of his precarious body so that only the shell glared back at Jiggs. "What? What's he holding this meet for? What did he——do you think maybe he built this airport just for a smooth place for airplanes to land on?" He went on, not running yet but fast; as he hurried up the apron the aeroplanes overtook and passed him and banked around the field pylon and faded on; he did not even look at them. Then suddenly he saw her, leading the little boy by the hand, emerge from the crowd about the gate to intercept him, wearing now a clean linen dress under the trenchcoat, and a hat, the brown hat of the first evening. He stopped. His hand went into his pocket and into his face came the expression bright, quiet, almost smiling as she walked fast up to him, staring at him with pale and urgent intensity.

"What is it?" she said. "What is this you have got him into?" He looked down at her with that expression not yearning nor despair but profound tragic and serene like in the eyes of bird dogs.

"It's all right," he said. "My signature is on the note too. It will hold. I am going in right now to testify; that's all that's holding them; that's all that Ord has to——" He drew out the nickel and gave it to the boy.

"What?" she said. "Note? Note? The ship, you idiot!"

"Oh." He smiled down at her. "The ship. We flew it, tested it over there. We made a field hop before we——"

"We?"

"Yes. I went with him. I laid on the floor in the tail, so we could find out where the weight ought to be to pass the burble. That's all it was. We have a sandbag rigged now on a cable so he can let it slide back. It's all right."

"All right?" she said. "Good God, what can you know about it? Did he say it was all right?"

"Yes. He said last night he could land it. I knew he could. And now he wont need to make but one more——" She stared at him, the eyes pale cold and urgent, at the face worn, dreamy, and peaceful in the soft bright sun; again the aeroplanes came in and snored on and away. Then he was interrupted; it was the amplifyer; all the amplifyers up and down the apron began to call his name, telling the stands, the field, the land and lake and air, that he was wanted in the superintendent's office at once. "There it is," he said. "Yair. I knew that the note would be the only thing that Ord could . . . . That was why I signed it too. And dont you worry; all I need to do is walk in and say Yes, that's my signature. And dont you worry. He can fly it. He can fly anything. I used to think that Matt Ord was the best pilot alive, but now I——" The amplifyer began to repeat itself. It faced him; it seemed to stare straight at him while it roared his name deliberately as though he had to be summoned not out of the living world of population but evoked peremptory and repetitive out of the air itself; the one in the rotunda was just beginning again when he entered; the sound followed him through the door and across the anteroom, though beyond that it did not reach, not into the board room of yesterday where now Ord and Shumann alone occupied the hard chairs since they were ushered in a half hour ago and sat down and faced the men behind the table and Shumann saw Feinman for the first time, sitting not in the center but at one end of the table where the announcer had sat yesterday, his suit, doublebreasted still, tan instead of gray beneath the bright splash of the carnation. He alone wore his hat; it appeared to be the smallest object about him; from beneath it his dark smooth face began at once to droop into folds of flesh which, constricted for the instant by his collar, swelled and rolled again beneath the tight creases of his coat. On the table one hand bearing a goldclamped ruby held a burning cigar. He did not even glance at Shumann and Ord; he was looking at Sales, the inspector—a square bald man with a blunt face which by ordinary would be quite pleasant, though not now—who was saying bluntly:

"Because I can ground it. I can forbid it to fly."

"You mean, you can forbid anybody to fly it, dont you?" Feinman said.

"Put it that way if you want to," Sales said.

"Let's say, put it that way for the record," another voice said—a young man, sleek, in horn rim glasses, sitting just back of Feinman. He was Feinman's secretary; he spoke now with a kind of silken insolence, like the pampered intelligent hateridden eunuchmountebank of an eastern despot: "Colonel Feinman is, even before a public servant, a lawyer."

"Yair; lawyer," Feinman said. "Maybe country lawyer to Washington. Let me get this straight. You're a government agent. All right. We have had our crops regimented and our fisheries regimented and even our money in the bank regimented. All right. I still dont see how they did it but they did, and so we are used to that. If he was trying to make his living out of the ground and Washington come in and regimented him, all right. We might not understand it any more than he did, but we would say all right. And if he was trying to make his living out of the river and the government come in and regimented him, we would say all right too. But do you mean to tell me that Washington can come in and regiment a man that's trying to make his living out of the air? Is there a crop reduction in the air too?" They—the others about the table (three of them were reporters)—laughed. They laughed with a kind of sudden and loud relief, as though they had been waiting all the time to find out just how they were supposed to listen and now they knew. Only Sales and Shumann and Ord did not laugh; then they noticed that the secretary was not laughing either and that he was already speaking, seeming to slide his silken voice into the laughter and stop it as abruptly as a cocaine needle in a nerve:

"Yes. Colonel Feinman is lawyer enough (perhaps Mr Sales will add, country enough) to ask even a government official to show cause. As the colonel understands it, this airplane bears a license which Mr Sales approved himself. Is that true, Mr Sales?" For a moment Sales did not answer. He just looked at the secretary grimly.

"Because I dont believe it is safe to fly," he said. "That's the cause."

"Ah," the secretary said. "For a moment I almost expected Mr Sales to tell us that it would not fly; that it had perhaps walked over here from Blaisedell. Then all we would need to say would be 'Good; we will not make it fly; we will just let it walk around the pylons during the race this afternoon'——" Now they did laugh, the three reporters scribbling furiously. But it was not for the secretary: it was for Feinman. The secretary seemed to know this; while he waited for it to subside his unsmiling insolent contempt touched them all face by face. Then he spoke to Sales again. "You admit that it is licensed, that you approved it yourself—meaning, I take it, that it is registered at Washington as being fit and capable of discharging the function of an airplane, which is to fly. Yet you later state that you will not permit it to fly because it is not capable of discharging the function for which you yourself admit having approved it—in simple language for us lawyers, that it cannot fly. Yet Mr Ord has just told us that he flew it in your presence. And Mr——" he glanced down; the pause was less than pause—"Shumann states that he flew it once at Blaisedell before witnesses, and we know that he flew it here because we saw him. We all know that Mr Ord is one of the best (we New Valoisians believe *the* best) pilots in the world, but dont you think it barely possible, barely I say, that the man who has flown it twice where Mr Ord has flown it but once. . . . . . . Wouldn't this almost lead one to think that Mr Ord has some other motive for not wanting this airplane to compete in this race——"

"Yair," Feinman said. He turned to look at Ord. "What's the matter? Aint this airport good enough for your ships? Or aint this race important enough for you? Or do you just think he might beat you? Aint you going to use the airplane you broke the record in? Then what are you afraid of?" Ord glared from face to face about the table, then at Feinman again.

"Why do you want this ship in there this afternoon? What is it? I'd lend him the money, if that's all it is."

"Why?" Feinman said. "Aint we promised these folks out there—" he made a jerking sweep with the cigar—"a series of races? Aint they paying their money in here to see them? And aint it the more airplanes they will have to look at the better they will think they got for the money? And why should he want to borrow money from you when he can maybe earn it at his job where he wont have to pay it back or even the interest? Now, let's settle this business." He turned to Sales. "The ship is licensed, aint it?" After a moment Sales said,

"Yes." Feinman turned to Ord.

"And it will fly, wont it?" Ord looked at him for a long moment too.

"Yes," he said. Now Feinman turned to Shumann.

"Is it dangerous to fly?" he said.

"They all are," Shumann said.

"Well, are you afraid to fly it?" Shumann looked at him. "Do you expect it to fall with you this afternoon?"

"If I did I wouldn't take it up," Shumann said. Suddenly Ord rose; he was looking at Sales.

"Mac," he said, "this aint getting anywhere. I will ground the ship myself." He turned to Shumann. "Listen, Roger——"

"On what grounds, Mr Ord?" the secretary said.

"Because it belongs to me. Is that grounds enough for you?"

"When an authorised agent of your corporation has accepted a legal monetary equivalent for it and surrendered the machine?"

"But they are not good for the note. I know that. I was a damn stickstraddler myself until I got a break. Why, damn it, one of the names on it is admitted to not be signed by the owner of it. And listen; yair; I dont even know whether Shumann did the actual signing; whoever signed it signed it before I saw it or even before Marchand saw it. See?" He glared at the secretary, who looked at him in turn with his veiled contemptuous glance.

"I see," the secretary said pleasantly. "I was waiting for you to bring that up. You seem to have forgotten that the note has a third signer." Ord stared at him for a minute.

"But he aint good for it either," he said.

"Possibly not, alone. But Mr Shumann tells us that his father is and that his father will honor this signature. So by your own token, the question seems to resolve to whether or not Mr Shumann did or did not sign his and his father's name to the note. And we seem to have a witness to that. It is not exactly legal, I grant you. But this other signer is known to some of us here; you know him yourself, you tell us, to be a person of unassailable veracity. We will have him in." Then it was that the amplifyers began to call the reporter's name; he entered; he came forward while they watched him. The secretary extended the note toward him. ("Jesus," the reporter thought, "they must have sent a ship over for Marchand.")

"Will you examine this?" the secretary said.

"I know it," the reporter said.

"Will you state whether or not you and Mr Shumann signed it in each other's presence and in good faith?" The reporter looked about, at the faces behind the table, at Shumann sitting with his head bent a little and at Ord halfrisen, glaring at him. After a moment Shumann turned his head and looked quietly at him.

"Yes," the reporter said. "We signed it."

"There you are," Feinman said. He rose. "That's all. Shumann has possession; if Ord wants anymore to be stubborn about it we will just let him run to town and see if he can get back with a writ of replevin before time for the race."

"But he cant enter it!" Ord said. "It aint qualified." Feinman paused long enough to look at Ord for a second with impersonal inscrutability.

"Speaking for the citizens of Franciana who donated the ground and for the citizens of New Valois that built the airport the race is going to be run on, I will waive qualification."

"You cant waive the A.A.A.," Ord said. "You cant make it official if he wins the whole damn meet."

"Then he will not need to rush back to town to pawn a silver cup," Feinman said. He went out; the others rose from the table and followed. After a moment Ord turned quietly to Shumann.

"Come on," he said. "We'd better check her over."

The reporter did not see them again. He followed them through the rotundra, through the amplifyer's voice and through the throng at the gates, or so he thought because his policecard had passed him before he remembered that they would have had to go around to reach the apron. But he could see the aeroplane with a crowd standing around it, and then the woman had forgot too that Shumann and Ord would have to go around and through the hangar; she emerged again from the crowd beneath the bandstand. "So they did it," she said. "They let him."

"Yes. It was all right. Like I told you."

"They did it," she said, staring at him yet speaking as though in amazed soliloquy. "Yes. You fixed it."

"Yes. I knew that's all it would be. I wasn't worried. And dont you——" But she was gone; she didn't move for a moment; there was nothing of distraction especially; he just seemed to hang substanceless in the long peaceful backwash of waiting, saying quietly out of the dreamy smiling, "Yair. Ord talking about how he would be disqualified for the cup, the prize, like that would stop him, like that was what. . . ." not even aware that it was only the shell of her speaking quietly back to him, asking him if he would mind the boy.

"Since you seem to be caught up for the time."

"Yair," he said. "Of course." Then she was gone, the white dress and the trenchcoat lost in the crowd—the ones with ribbon badges and the ones in dungarees—which streamed suddenly down the apron toward the darkhorse, the sensation. As he stood so, holding the little boy by one damp sticky hand, the Frenchman Despleins passed again down the runway which parallelled the stands, on one wheel; the reporter watched him takeoff and half roll, climbing upside down: now he heard the voice; he had not heard it since it called his own name despite the fact that it had never ceased, perhaps because of the fact:

"——oh oh oh mister, dont, dont! Oh, mister! Please get up high enough so your parachute can try to open! Now, now; now, now——Oh, Mac! Oh, Mr Sales! Make him stop!" The reporter looked down at the boy.

"I bet you a dime you haven't spent that nickel," he said.

"Naw," the boy said. "I aint had a chance to. She wouldn't let me."

"Well, my goodness!" the reporter said. "I owe you twenty cents then, dont I? Come——" He paused, turning; it was the photographer, the man whom he had called Jug, laden again with the enigmatic and faintly macabre utensils of his calling so that he resembled vaguely a trained dog belonging to a country doctor.

"Where in hell you been?" the photographer said. "Hagood told me to find you at ten oclock."

"Here I am," the reporter said. "We're just going inside to spend twenty cents. Want to come?" Now the Frenchman came up the runway about twenty feet high and on his back, his head and face beneath the cockpitrim motionless and alert like that of a roach or a rat immobile behind a crack in a wainscoat, his neat short beard unstirred by any wind as though cast in one piece of bronze.

"Yair," the photographer said; perhaps it was the bilious aspect of an inverted world seen through a hooded lens or emerging in grimacing and attitudinal miniature from stinking trays in a celibate and stygian cell lighted by a red lamp: "and have that guy come down on his whiskers and me not here to get it?"

"All right," the reporter said. "Stay and get it." He turned to go on.

"Yair; but Hagood told me——" the photographer said. The reporter turned back.

"All right," he said. "But hurry up."

"Hurry up what?"

"Snap me. You can show it to Hagood when you go in." He and the boy went on; he did not walk back into the voice, he had never walked out of it:

"——an in-ver-ted spin, folks; he's going into it still upside down—oh oh oh oh——" The reporter stooped suddenly and lifted the boy to his shoulder.

"We can make better time," he said. "We will want to get back in a few minutes." They passed through the gate, among the gaped and upturned faces which choked the gangway. "That's it," he thought quietly, with that faint quiet grimace almost like smiling; "they aint human. It aint adultery; you cant anymore imagine two of them making love than you can two of them aeroplanes back in the corner of the hangar, coupled." With one hand he supported the boy on his shoulder, feeling through the harsh khaki the young brief living flesh. "Yair; cut him and it's cylinder oil; dissect him and it aint bones: it's little rockerarms and connecting rods——" The restaurant was crowded; they did not wait to eat the icecream there on a plate; with one cone in his hand and one in the boy's and the two chocolate bars in his pocket they were working back through the crowded gangway when the bomb went and then the voice:

"—fourth event: unlimited free-for-all, Vaughn Trophy race, prize two thousand dollars. You will not only have a chance to see Matt Ord in his famous Ninety-Two Ord-Atkinson Special in which he set a new land plane speed record, but as a surprise entry through the courtesy of the American Aeronautical Association and the Feinman Airport Commission, Roger Shumann who yesterday nosed over in a forced landing, in a special rebuilt job that Matt Ord rebuilt himself. Two horses from the same stable, folks, and two pilots both of whom are so good that it is a pleasure to give the citizens of New Valois and Franciana the chance to see them pitted against each other——" He and the boy watched the takeoff, then they went on; presently he found her—the brown hat and the coat—and he came up and stood a little behind her steadying the boy on his shoulder and carrying the second melting cone in his other hand as the four aeroplanes came in on the first lap—the red-and-white monoplane in front and two more side by side and some distance back, so that at first he did not even see Shumann. Then he saw him, higher than the others and well outside, though the voice now was not from the amplifyer but from a mechanic:

"Jesus, look at Shumann! It must be fast: he's flying twice as far as the rest of them—or maybe Ord aint trying. . . . . . . Why in hell dont he bring it on in?" Then the voice was drowned in the roar, the snarl, as the aeroplanes turned the field pylon and, followed by the turning heads along the apron as if the faces were geared to the sound, diminished singly out and over the lake again, Shumann still quite wide, making a turn that was almost a skid yet holding his position. They converged toward the second pylon, the lake one; in slightly irregular order and tiny now with distance and with Shumann still cautiously high and outside they wafted lightly upward and around the pylon. Now the reporter could hear the mechanic again: "He's coming in now, watch him. Jesus, he's second—he's diving in—Jesus, he's going to be right behind Ord on this pylon; maybe he was just feeling it out—" The noise was faint now and disseminated; the drowsy afternoon was domed with it and the four machines seemed to hover like dragonflies silently in vacuum, in various distance-softened shades of pastel against the ineffable blue, with now a quality trivial, random, almost like notes of music—a harp, say—as the sun glinted and lost them. The reporter leaned down to the woman who was not yet aware of his presence, crying,

"Watch him! Oh, can he fly! Can he fly! And Ord aint going to beat the Ninety-Two to——Second money Thursday, and if Ord aint going to——Oh, watch him! Watch him!" She turned: the jaw, the pale eyes, the voice which he did not even listen to:

"Yes. The money will be fine." Then he even stopped looking at her, staring down the runway as the four aeroplanes, now in two distinct pairs, came in toward the field, increasing fast. The mechanic was talking again:

"He's in! Jesus, he's going to try Ord here! And look at Ord giving him room——" The two in front began to bank at the same time, side by side, the droning roar drawing down and in as though sucked down out of the sky by them in place of being produced by them. The reporter's mouth was still open; he knew that by the needling of nerves in his sore jaw; later he was to remember seeing the icecream cone crush in his fist and begin to ooze between his fingers as he let the little boy slide to the ground and took his hand, though not now; now the two aeroplanes, side by side and Shumann outside and now above, banked into the pylon as though bolted together, when the reporter suddenly saw something like a light scattering of burnt paper or feathers floating in the air above the pylontip. He was watching this, his mouth still open, when a voice somewhere said, "Ahhhhhhh!" and he saw Shumann now shooting almost straight upward and then a whole wastebasketful of the light trash blew out of the aeroplane; they said later about the apron that he used the last of his control before the fuselage broke to zoom out of the path of the two aeroplanes behind while he looked down at the closepeopled land and the empty lake, and made a choice before the tailgroup came completely free. But most of them were busy saying how his wife took it, how she did not scream nor faint (she was standing quite near the microphone, near enough for it to have caught the scream) but instead she just stood there and watched the fuselage break in two and said, "Oh damn you, Roger! Oh damn you! damn you!" and turned and snatched the little boy's hand and ran toward the seawall, the little boy dangling vainly on his short legs between her and the reporter who, holding the little boy's other hand, ran at his loose lightly-clattering gallop like a scarecrow in a gale, after the bright plain shape of love. Perhaps it was the added weight because she turned, still running, and gave him a single pale cold terrible look, crying,

"God damn you to hell! Get away from me!"

Lovesong of J. A. Prufrock

O̶N THE SHELL BEACH between the boulevard and the seaplane slip one of the electric company's trucks stood while its crew set up a searchlight at the water's edge. When the photographer called Jug saw the reporter he was standing beside the empty truck, in the backwash which it created between the faces beyond the policeline, and the men—police and newspapermen and airport officials and the others, the ones without authority or object who manage to pass policelines at all scenes of public violence—gathered along the beach. The photographer approached at a flagging trot, the camera banging against his flank. "Christ Almighty," he said. "I got that, all right. Only Jesus, I near vomited into the box while I was changing plates." Beyond the crowd at the water-edge and just beyond the outer markers of the seaplane basin a police launch was scattering the fleet of small boats which, like most of the people on the beach itself, had appeared as though by magic from nowhere like crows, to make room for the dredgeboat to anchor over the spot where the aeroplane was supposed to have sunk. The seaplane slip, dredged out, was protected from the sluggish encroachment of the lake's muddy bottom by a sunken mole composed of various refuse from the city itself—shards of condemned paving and masses of fallen walls and even discarded automobile bodies—any and all the refuse of man's twentieth century clotting into communities large enough to pay a mayor's salary—dumped into the lake. Either directly above or just outside of this mass the aeroplane was believed, from the accounts of three oyster-men in a dory who were about two hundred yards away, to have struck the water. The three versions varied as to the ex-act spot, despite the fact that both wings had reappeared on the surface almost immediately and were towed ashore, but then one of the oystermen (from the field, the apron, Shu-mann could be seen struggling to open the cockpit hatch as though to jump, as though with the intention of trying to open his parachute despite his lack of height)—one of the oystermen claimed that the body had fallen free of the ma-chine, having either extricated itself or been flung out. But

the three agreed that the body and the machine were both
either upon or beside the mole from whose vicinity the police
launch was now harrying the small boats. It was after sunset.
Upon the mirrorsmooth water even the little foul skiffs—the
weathered and stinking dories and dinghys of oyster- and
shrimpmen—had a depthless and fairylight quality as they
scattered like butterflies or moths before a mechanical reaper,
just ahead of the trim low martialcolored police launch, onto
which at the moment the photographer saw being transferred
from one of the skiffs two people whom he recognised as
being the dead pilot's wife and child; among them the dredge
looked like something antediluvian crawled for the first time
into light, roused but not alarmed by the object or creature
out of the world of light and air which had plunged without
warning into the watery fastness where it had been asleep.
"Jesus," the photographer said. "Why wasn't I standing right
here: Hagood would have had to raise me then. Jesus God,"
he said in a hoarse tone of hushed and unbelieving amazement, "how's it now for being a poor bastard that never even
learned to rollerskate?" The reporter looked at him, for the
first time. The reporter's face was perfectly calm; he looked
down at the photographer, turning carefully as though he
were made of glass and knew it, blinking a little, and spoke
in a peaceful dreamy voice such as might be heard where a
child is sick—not sick for a day or even two days, but for so
long that even wasting anxiety has become mere surface
habit:

"She told me to go away. I mean, to go clean away, like to
another town."

"She did?" the photographer said. "To what town?"

"You dont understand," the reporter said, in that peaceful
baffled voice. "Let me explain to you."

"Yair; sure," the photographer said. "I still feel like vomiting too. But I got to get on in with these plates. And I bet
you aint even phoned in. Have you?"

"What?" the reporter said. "Yes. I phoned in. But listen.
She didn't understand. She told me——"

"Come on, now," the other said. "You will have to call in
with the buildup on it. Jesus, I tell you I feel bad too. Here,
smoke a cigarette. Yair. I could vomit too. But what the hell?

He aint our brother. Come on, now." He took the cigarettes from the reporter's coat and took two from the pack and struck a match. The reporter roused somewhat; he took the burning match himself and held it to the two cigarettes. But then at once the photographer seemed to watch him sink back into that state of peaceful physical anesthesia as though the reporter actually were sinking slowly away from him into clear and limpid water out of which the calm, slightly distorted face looked and the eyes blinked at the photographer with that myopic earnestness while the voice repeated patiently,

"But you dont understand. Let me explain it to——"

"Yair; sure," the other said. "You can explain it to Hagood while we are getting a drink." The reporter moved obediently. But before they had gone very far the photographer realised that they had reassumed their customary mutual physical complementing when working together: the reporter striding on in front and the photographer trotting to keep up. "That's the good thing about being him," the photographer thought. "He dont have to move very far to go nuts in the first place and so he dont have so far to come back."

"Yair," the reporter said. "Let's move. We got to eat, and the rest of them have got to read. And if they ever abolish fornication and blood, where in hell will we all be?—Yair. You get on in with what you got; if they get it up right away it will be too dark to get anything. I'll stay out here and cover it. You can tell Hagood."

"Yair; sure," the photographer said, trotting, the camera bouncing against his flank. "We'll have a shot and we'll feel better. For Christ's sake, we never made him go up in it." Before they reached the rotunda the sunset had faded; even while they walked up the apron the boundary lights came on, and now the flat swordlike sweep of the beacon swung in across the lake and vanished for an instant in a long *flick!* as the turning eye faced them full, and then reappeared again as it swung now over the land to complete its arc. The field, the apron, was empty, but the rotunda was full of people and with a cavernous murmuring sound which seemed to linger not about the mouths which uttered it but to float somewhere about the high serene shadowy dome overhead; as they

entered a newsboy screamed at them, flapping the paper, the
headline: **PILOT KILLED. Shumann Crashes Into Lake. SEC-
OND FATALITY OF AIRMEET.** as it too flicked away. The bar
was crowded too, warm with lights and with human bodies.
The photographer led the way now, shouldering into the rail,
making room for the reporter beside him. "Rye, huh?" he
said, then to the bartender, loudly: "Two ryes."

"Yair; rye," the reporter said. Then he thought quietly, "I
cant. I cannot." He felt no revulsion from his insides; it was
as though his throat and the organs of swallowing had experienced some irrevocable alteration of purpose from which he
would suffer no inconvenience whatever but which would
forever more mark the exchange of an old psychic as well as
physical state for a new one, like the surrendering of a maid-
enhead. He felt profoundly and peacefully empty inside, as
though he had vomited and very emptiness had supplied into
his mouth or somewhere about his palate like a lubricant a
faint thin taste of salt which was really pleasant: the taste not
of despair but of Nothing. "I'll go and call in now," he
said.

"Wait," the photographer said. "Here comes your drink."

"Hold it for me," the reporter said. "It wont take but a
minute." There was a booth in the corner, the same from
which he had called Hagood yesterday. As he dropped the
coin in he closed the door behind him. The automatic dome
light came on; he opened the door until the light went off
again; he spoke not loud, his voice murmuring back from the
close walls as he recapitulated at need with succinct and patient care as though reading into the telephone in a foreign
tongue: "—yes, f-u-s-e-l-a-g-e. The body of the airplane,
broke off at the tail. . . . . . No, he couldn't have landed
it. The pilots here said he used up what control he had left
getting out of the way of the others and to head toward the
lake instead of the grandst. . . . . . No, they say not. He
wasn't high enough for the chute to have opened even if he
had got out of the ship. . . . . . .yair, dredgeboat was just
getting into position when I. . . . . . .they say probably
right against the mole; it may have struck the rocks and slid
down. . . . . . Yair, if he should be close enough to all
that muck the dredgeboat cant. . . . . . .yair, probably a

diver tomorrow, unless sometime during the night. And by
that time the crabs and gars will have. . . . . . .yair, I'll stay
out here and flash you at midnight." When he came out of
the booth, back into the light, he began to blink again like he
might have a little sand in his eyes, trying to recall exactly
what eyemoisture tasted like, wondering if perhaps the thin
moist salt in his mouth might not somehow have got misplaced from where it belonged. The photographer still held
his place at the bar and the drink was waiting, though this
time he only looked down at the photographer, blinking, almost smiling. "You go on and drink it," he said. "I forgot I
went on the wagon yesterday." When they went out to the
cab, it was dark; the photographer, ducking, the camera
jouncing on its strap, scuttled into the cab, turning a face
likewise amazed and spent.

"It's cold out here," he said. "Jesus, I'm going to lock the
damn door and turn on both them red lamps and fill me a
good big tray to smell and I'm going to just sit there and get
warm. I'll tell Hagood you are on the job." The face vanished,
the cab went on, curbing away toward the boulevard where
beyond and apparently just behind the ranked palms which
lined it the glare of the city was visible even from here upon
the overcast. People were still moiling back and forth across
the plaza and in and out of the rotundra, and the nightly
overcast had already moved in from the lake; against it the
measured and regular swordsweep of the beacon was quite
distinct, and there was some wind in it too; a long breath of
it at the moment came down over the building and across the
plaza and the palms along the boulevard began to clash and
hiss with a dry wild sound. The reporter began to inhale the
dark chill wind; it seemed to him that he could taste the lake,
water, and he began to pant, drawing the air in by lungsfull
and expelling it and snatching another lungfull of it as if he
were locked inside a burning room and were hunting handfull
by handfull through a mass of cotton batting for the doorkey,
ducking his head and hurrying past the lighted entrance and
the myriad eyes his face which for the time had frozen like a
piece of unoiled machinery freezes, into a twisted grimace
which filled his sore jaw with what felt like icy needles so that
Ord had to call him twice before he turned and saw the other

getting out of his roadster, still in the suede jacket and the hind-part-before cap in which he flew.

"I was looking for you," Ord said, taking something from his pocket—the narrow strip of paper folded again as it had lain in the reporter's fob pocket this morning before he gave it to Marchand. "Wait; dont tear it," Ord said. "Hold it a minute." The reporter held it while Ord struck the match. "Go on," Ord said. "Look at it." With his other hand he opened the note out, holding the match so that the reporter could see it, identify it, waiting while the reporter stood with the note in his hand long enough to have examined it anyway. "That's it, aint it?" Ord said.

"Yes," the reporter said.

"All right. Stick it to the match. I want you to do it yourself. . . . . . . Damn it, drop it! Do you want to . . . ." As it floated down the flame seemed to turn back and upward, to climb up the falling scrap and on into space, vanishing; the charred carbon leaf drifted on without weight or sound and Ord ground his foot on it. "You bastard," he said. "You bastard."

"God, yes," the reporter said, as quietly. "I'll make out another one tomorrow. You will just have to take me alone——"

"Like hell. What are they going to do now?"

"I dont know," the reporter said. Then at once he began to speak in that tone of peaceful and bemused incomprehensibility. "You see, she didn't understand. She told me to go away. I mean, away. Let me ex——" But he stopped, thinking quietly, "Wait. I mustn't start that. I might not be able to stop it next time." He said: "They dont know yet, of course, until after the dredge. . . . . . . I'll be here. I'll see to them."

"Bring her on over home if you want to. But you better go yourself and take a couple of drinks. You dont look so good either."

"Yair," the reporter said. "Only I quit yesterday. I got mixed up and went on the wagon."

"Yes?" Ord said. "Well, I'm going home. You better get in touch with her right away. Get her away from here. Just put her in a car and come on over home. If it's where they say it is, it will take a diver to get him out." He returned to the roadster; the reporter had already turned on too, back toward the entrance before he was aware of it, stopping again; he could not do it—the lights and the faces, not even for the warmth of lights and human suspirations, thinking, "Jesus, if I was to go in there I would drown." He could go around the opposite hangar and reach the apron and be on his way back to the seaplane slip. But when he moved it was toward the first hangar, the one in which it seemed to him that he had spent enough of breathing's incomprehensible and unpredictable frenzy and travail to have been born and raised there, walking away from the lights and sound and faces, walking in solitude where despair and regret could sweep down over the building and across the plaza and on into the harsh thin hissing of the palms and so at least he could breathe it, at least endure. It was as though some sixth sense, some economy out of profound inattention guided him, on through the blank door and the tool room and into the hangar itself where in the hard light of the overhead clusters the motionless aeroplanes squatted in fierce and depthless relief among one another's monstrous shadows, and on to where Jiggs sat on the tongue of a dolly, the shined boots rigid and fiercely highlighted on his outthrust feet, gnawing painfully at a sandwich with one side of his face, his head turned parallel to the earth like a dog eats while the one good eye rolled, painful and bloodshot, up at the reporter.

"What is it you want me to do?" Jiggs said. The reporter blinked down at him with quiet and myopic intensity.

"You see, she didn't understand," he said. "She told me to go away. To let her alone. And so I cant——"

"Yair," Jiggs said. He drew the boots under him and prepared to get up, but he stopped and sat so for a moment, his head bent and the sandwich in one hand, looking at what the reporter did not know, because at once the single eye was looking at him again. "Will you look behind that junk over in the corner there and get my bag?" Jiggs said. The reporter found the canvas bag hidden carefully beneath a rubbishheap of empty oil cans and boxes and such; when he returned with it Jiggs was already holding one foot out. "Would you mind giving it a pull?" The reporter took hold of the boot. "Pull it easy."

"Have they made your feet sore?" the reporter said.

"No. Pull it easy." The boots came off easier than they did two nights ago; the reporter watched Jiggs take from the sack a shirt not soiled but filthy, and wipe the boots carefully, with an air thoughtful, intent, bemused, upper sole and all, and wrap them in the shirt and put them into the sack and, again in the tennis shoes and the makeshift leggings, hide the sack once more in the corner, the reporter following him to the corner and then back as if it were now the reporter who was the dog.

"You see," he said (even as he spoke it seemed to him to be not himself speaking but something inside him which insisted on preempting his tongue)—"you see, I keep on trying to explain to somebody that she didn't understand. Only she understands exactly, dont she? He's out there in the lake and I cant think of anything plainer than that. Can you?" The main doors were locked now; they had to return through the tool room as the reporter had entered. As they emerged the beacon's beam swept overhead again with its illusion of powerful and slow acceleration. "So they gave you all a bed this time," he said.

"Yair," Jiggs said. "The kid went to sleep on the police boat. Jack brought him in and they let them have a bed this time. She didn't come in. She aint going to leave now, anyway. I'll try if you want to, though."

"Yes," the reporter said. "I guess you are right. I didn't mean to try to make——I just wanted to. . . . . . ." He began to think *now. now. NOW.* and it came: the long nebulous swordstroke sweeping steadily up from beyond the other hangar until almost overhead and then accelerating with that illusion of terrific strength and speed which should have left a sound, a swish, behind it but did not. "You see, I dont know about these things. I keep on thinking about fixing it up so that a woman, another woman——"

"All right," Jiggs said. "I'll try."

"Just so she can see you and call you if she needs—wants. . . . . . .if. . . . . . . She wont even need to know I am——but if she should. . . . . . ."

"Yair. I'll fix it if I can." They went on around the other hangar. Now they could see half of the beacon's entire arc;

the reporter could watch it now as it swung across the lake, watching the skeletonlattice of the empty bleachers come into relief against it, and the parapet of staffs from which the purple-and-gold pennons, black now, streamed rigid in the rising wind from the lake as the beam picked them up one by one and discarded them in swift and accelerating succession as it swept in and overhead and on, and they could see the looped bunting too tossing and laboring and even here and there blown out of the careful loops of three days ago and whipping in forlorn and ceaseless shreds as though, sentient itself, it had anticipated the midnight bells from town which would signal the beginning of Lent. And now, beyond the black rampart of the seawall the searchlight beside whose truck the photographer had found the reporter was burning—a fierce white downwardglaring beam brighter though smaller than the beacon—and they saw presently another one on the tower of the dredgeboat itself. In fact it was as though when they reached the seawall they would look down into a pit filled not by one steady source of light but by a luminous diffusion as though from the airparticles, beyond which the shoreline curved twinkling faintly away into darkness. But it was not until they reached the wall that they saw that the light came not from the searchlight on the shore nor the one on the dredgeboat nor the one on the slowly cruising police launch engaged still in harrying away the little skiffs from some of which puny flashlights winked but in most of which burned the weak turgid flame of kerosene, but from a line of automobiles drawn up along the boulevard. Extending for almost a mile along the shore and facing the water, their concerted refulgence, broken at short intervals by the buttons and shields of policemen and now by the sidearms and putties of a national guard company, glared down upon the disturbed and ceaseless dark water which seemed to surge and fall and surge and fall as though in travail of amazement and outrage. There was a skiff just landing from the dredgeboat; while the reporter waited for Jiggs to return the dark steady chill wind pushed hard against him, through his thin clothes; it seemed to have passed through the lights, the faint human sounds and movement, without gaining anything of warmth or light; after a while he believed that he could discern the faint hissing plaint of the ground and powdered oystershells on which he stood even above the deep steady humming of the searchlight not far away. The men from the skiff came up and passed him, Jiggs following. "It's like they said," Jiggs said. "It's right up against the rocks. I asked the guy if they had hooked anything yet and he said hooked, hell; they had hooked something the first throw with one hook and aint even got the hook loose yet. But the other hook came up with a piece of that damn monocococque plywood, and he said there was oil on it." He looked at the reporter. "So that will be from the belly."

"Yes," the reporter said.

"So it's bottomupwards. The guy says they think out there that it is fouled on some of them old automobiles and junk they throwed in to build it with.—Yair," he said, though the reporter had not spoken, but had only looked at him: "I asked that too. She's up yonder at that lunchwagon getting——" The reporter turned; like the photographer Jiggs now had to trot to keep up, scrabbling up the shelving beach toward the ranked automobiles until he bumped into the reporter who had paused in the headlights' glare with his head lowered and one arm raised before his face. "Over this way," Jiggs said, "I can see." He took the reporter's arm and guided him on to the gap in the cars where the steps led up from the beach and through the gap to where, across the boulevard, they could see the heads and shoulders against the broad low dingy window. Jiggs could hear the reporter breathing, panting, though the climb up from the beach had not been that hard. When the reporter's fumbling hand touched his own it felt like ice.

"She hasn't got any money," the reporter said. "Hurry. Hurry." Jiggs went on. Then the reporter could still see them (for the instant he made one as he pushed through them and went around the end of the lunchwagon to the smaller window)—the faces pressed to the glass and looking in at her where she sat on one of the backless stools at the counter between a policeman and one of the mechanics whom the reporter had seen about the hangar. The trenchcoat was open and there was a long smear either of oil or mud across the upper part of her white dress and she was eating, a sandwich,

wolfing it and talking to the two men; he watched her drop
the fragments back into the plate and wipe her hand across
her mouth and lift the thick mug of coffee and drink, wolfing
the coffee too, the coffee running down her chin from the
toofast swallowing like the food had done. At last Jiggs finally
found him, still standing there though now the counter was
vacant and the faces had gone away too, followed back to the
beach.

"Even the proprietor wanted to washout the check, but I
got there in time," Jiggs said. "She was glad to get it, too;
you were right, she never had any money with her. Yair. She's
like a man about not bumming from just any guy. Always
was. So it's o.k." But he was still looking at the reporter with
an expression which a more observing person than the reporter could not have read now in the tough face to which
the blue and swollen eye and lip lent no quality evoking compassion or warmth but on the contrary merely increased a
little the face's brutality. When he spoke again it was not in a
rambling way exactly but with a certain curious alertness as
of imminent and irrevocable dispersion; the reporter thought
of a man trying to herd a half dozen blind sheep through a
passage a little wider than he could span with his extended
arms. Jiggs now had one hand in his pocket but the reporter
did not notice it. "So she's going to have to be out here all
night, in case they begin to—And the kid's already asleep;
yair, no need to wake him up, and maybe tomorrow we will
all know better where we—Yair, a night or two to sleep on
it makes a lot of difference about anything, no matter how bad
you think you h—I mean. . . . . . ." He stopped. ("He
aint only not held the sheep, he aint even holding out his
arms anymore," the reporter thought) The hand came out of
his pocket, opening; the doorkey glinted faintly on the grained
palm. "She told me to give it back to you when I saw you,"
Jiggs said. "You come on and eat something yourself, now."

"Yes," the reporter said. "It will be a good chance to,
wont it. Besides, we will be in out of the cold for a little
while."

"Sure," Jiggs said. "Come on." It was warm inside the
lunchwagon; the reporter stopped shaking even before the
food came. He ate a good deal of it, then he realised that he

was going to eat all of it, without taste or enjoyment especially but with a growing conviction of imminent satisfaction
like when a tooth cavity that has not been either pleasant or
unpleasant is about to be filled without pain. The faces were
gone from the window now, following her doubtless back to
the beach, or as near to it as the police and soldiers would let
them, where they now gazed no doubt at the police boat or
whatever other boat she had reembarked in; nevertheless he
and Jiggs still sat in it, breathed and chewed it along with the
stale hot air and the hot rancid food—the breathing, the exhalation, the variations of the remark which the photographer
had made; the ten thousand different smug and gratulant be-
hindsighted forms of *I might be a bum and a bastard but I am
not out there in that lake*. But he did not see her again. During
the next three hours until midnight he did not leave the
beach, while the ranked cars glared steadily downward and
the searchlights hummed and the police launch cruised in
slow circles while the little boats moved outward before its
bows and inward again behind its stern like so many min-
nows in the presence of a kind of harmless and vegetarian
whale, and steadily, with clocklike and deliberate precision,
the long sicklebar of the beacon swept inward from the lake,
to vanish at the instant when the yellow eye came broadside
on and apparently halting there with only a slow and terrific
centrifugal movement within the eye itself until with that gi-
gantic and soundless *flick!* the beam shot incredibly outward
across the dark sky. But he did not see her, though presently
one of the little skiffs came in and beached to take on another
bootleg cargo of twenty-five-cent passengers and Jiggs got
out. "They are still fast to it," he said. "They thought they
had it started once but something happened down there and
when they hauled up all they had was the cable; they were
even short the hook. They say now it must have hit on one
of those big blocks of concrete and broke it loose and they
both went down together only the ship got there first.
They're going to send the diver down at daylight to see what
to do. Only they dont want to use dynamite because even if
it starts him back up it will bust the mole all to pieces. But
they'll know tomorrow.—Didn't you want to call the paper
at midnight or something?" There was a paystation in the

lunchwagon, on the wall. Since there was no booth he had to talk into the telephone with his other ear plugged with his hand against the noise and again spending most of the time answering questions; when he turned away he saw that Jiggs was asleep on the backless stool, his arms folded on the counter and his forehead resting on them. It was quite warm inside, what with the constant frying of meat and with the human bodies with which the room was filled now long after its usual closing hour; the window facing the lake was fogged over so that the lighted scene beyond was one diffused glow such as might be shining behind falling snow; looking at it the reporter began to shake again, slowly and steadily inside the suit to which there was apparently no waistcoat, while there grew within him the first active sensation or impulse which he could remember since he watched Shumann begin to bank into the field pylon for the last time—a profound reluctance to go out which acted not on his will but on his very muscles. He went to the counter; presently the proprietor saw him and took up one of the thick cups.

"Coffee?"

"No," the reporter said. "I want a coat. Overcoat. Have you got one you could lend me or rent me? I'm a reporter," he added. "I got to stick around down there at the beach until they get through."

"I aint got a coat," the proprietor said. "But I got a piece of tarpaulin I keep my car under. You can use that if you will bring it back."

"All right," the reporter said. He did not disturb Jiggs; when he emerged into the cold and the dark this time he resembled a soiled and carelessly setup tent. The tarpaulin was stiff and heavy to hold and presently heavy to carry too, but inside it he ceased to shake. It was well after midnight now and he had expected to find that the cars drawn up along the boulevard to face the lake would have thinned somewhat, but they had not. Individually they might have changed, but the ranked line was still intact—a silhouetted row of oval rear-windows framing the motionless heads whose eyes, along with the headlights, stared with immobile and unmurmuring patience down upon the scene in which they were not even aware that nothing was happening—that the dredge squatted inactive now, attached as though by one steel umbilical cord not to one disaster but to the prime oblivious mother of all living and derelict too. Steady and unflagging the long single spoke of the beacon swept its arc across the lake and vanished into the full broadside of the yellow eye and, already out-shooting, swept on again, leaving that slow terrific vacuum in mind or sense which should have been filled with the flick and the swish which never came. The sightseeing skiff had ceased to ply, perhaps having milked the business or perhaps having been stopped by authority; the next boat to land came direct from the dredge, one of the passengers the mechanic who had sat beside the woman in the lunchwagon. This time the reporter did his own asking.

"No," the other said. "She went back to the field about an hour ago, when they found out they would have to wait for the diver. I'm going to turn in, myself. I guess you can knock off now yourself, cant you?"

"Yes," the reporter said. "I can knock off now too." At first he thought that perhaps he was going in, walking in the dry light treacherous shellpowder, holding the harsh stiff tarpaulin with both hands to ease the dead weight of it on his neck and shoulders; it was the weight, the cold rasp of it on his fingers and palms. "I'll have to take it back first, like I prom-ised," he thought. "If I dont now, I wont do it at all." The ramp of the boulevard rose here, so that the carlights passed over his head and he walked now in comparative darkness to where the seawall made its right angle with the boulevard. The wind did not reach here and since he could sit on the edge of the tarpaulin and fold it about him knees and all and so soon his body heated it inside like a tent. Now he did not have to watch the beacon sweep in from across the lake in its full arc but only when the beam materialised slicing across the pieshaped quarter of sky framed by the right angle of wall and ramp. It was the warmth; all of a sudden he had been telling Shumann for some time that she did not understand. And he knew that that was not right; all the while that he was telling Shumann he was also telling himself that that was not right; his cramped chin came up from the bony peaks of his knees; his feet were cold too or were probably cold be-cause at first he did not feel them at all until they filled sud-

denly with the cold needles; now (the searchlight on the
shore was black and only the one on the dredge stared as
before downward into the water) the police boat layto and
there was not one of the small boats in sight at all and he saw
that most of the cars were gone too from the ramp overhead
even while he was thinking that it could not possibly have
been that long. But it had; the steady clocklike sweep flick!
sweep. sweep flick! sweep of the beacon had accomplished
something apparently, it had checked something off; as he
looked upward the dark seawall overhead came into abrupt
sharp relief and then simultaneous with the recognition of the
glow as floodlights he heard the displacing of air and then
saw the navigation lights of the transport as it slid, quite low,
across the black angle and onto the field. "That means it's
after four oclock," he thought. "That means it's tomorrow."
It was not dawn yet though; before that he was trying to
draw himself back as though by the arm while he was saying
again to Shumann, "You see, it looks like I have just got to
try to explain to somebody that she——" and jerked himself
upward (he had not even leaned his head down to his knees
this time and so had nowhere to jerk back to), the needles
not needles now but actual ice and his mouth open as though
it were not large enough to accommodate the air which his
lungs required or the lungs not large enough to accommodate
the air which his body had to have, and the long arm of the
beacon sweeping athwart his gaze with a motion peremptory
ruthless and unhurried and already fading and it some time
even yet before he realised that it was not the beacon fading
but the brightening sky. The sun had risen before the diver
went down and came up, and most of the cars were back by
then too, ranked into the ubiquitous blue-and-drab rampart.
The reporter had returned the tarpaulin; relieved of its stiff
and chafing weight he now shook steadily in the pink chill of
the first morning of the entire four days to be ushered in by
no overcast. But he did not see her again at all. There was a
somewhat larger crowd than there had been the evening before (It was Sunday, and there were now two police launches
and the number of skiffs and dories had trebled as though the
first lot had spawned somewhere during the night) yet he had
daylight to assist him now. But he did not see her. He saw

Jiggs from a distance several times, but he did not see her; he
did not even know that she had been to the beach again until
after the diver came up and reported and he (the reporter)
was climbing back toward the boulevard and the telephone
and the parachute jumper called to him. The jumper came
down the beach, not from the water but from the direction
of the field, jerking the injured leg from which he had burst
the dressing and the fresh scab in making his jump yesterday
savagely after him, as though in raging contempt of the leg
itself.

"I was looking for you," he said. From his pocket he took
a neatlyfolded sheaf of bills. "Roger said he owed you twenty-
two dollars. Is that right?"

"Yes," the reporter said. The jumper held the money
clipped between two fingers and folded over under his thumb.

"You got time to attend to some business for us or are you
going to be busy?" he said.

"Busy?" the reporter said.

"Yes. Busy. If you are, say so so I can find somebody else
to do it."

"Yes," the reporter said. "I'll do it."

"You sure? If not, say so. It wont be much trouble; anybody can do it. I just thought of you because you seem to
have already got yourself pretty well mixed up with us, and
you will be here."

"Yes," the reporter said. "I'll do it."

"All right, then. We're going to get away today. No use
hanging around here. Those bastards out there—" he jerked
his head toward the lake, the clump of boats on the rosy water "—aint going to get him out from under all that muck
with just a handfull of ropes. So we're going. What I want to
do is leave some money with you in case they do fuck around
out there and finally get him up."

"Yes," the reporter said. "I see." The jumper stared at him
with that bleak tense quiet.

"Dont think I like to ask this anymore than you like to hear
it. But maybe you never sent for us to come here, and maybe
we never asked you to move in on us; you'll have to admit
that. Anyway, it's all done now; I cant help it anymore than
you can." The jumper's other hand came to the money; the

reporter saw how the bills had already been separated carefully into two parts and that the part which the jumper extended toward him was clipped neatly with two paper clips beneath a strip of paper bearing a neatly printed address, a name which the reporter read at a glance because he had seen it before when he watched Shumann write it on the note. "Here's seventy-five bucks, and that's the address. I dont know what it will cost to ship him. But if it is enough to ship him and still pay you your twenty-two bucks, do it. And if it aint enough to pay you your twenty-two and still ship him, ship him and write me and I will send you the difference." This time the slip of paper came, folded, from his pocket. "This is mine. I kept them separate so you wouldn't get them mixed. Do you understand? Send him to the first address, the one with the money. And if there aint enough left to pay you your twenty-two, write to me at the second one and I will send it to you. It may take some time for the letter to catch up with me, but I will get it sooner or later and I will send you the money. Understand?"

"Yes," the reporter said.

"All right. I asked you if you would attend to it and you said you would. But I didn't say anything about promise. Did I?"

"I promise," the reporter said.

"I dont want you to promise that. What I want you to promise is another thing. Something else. Dont think I want to ask it; I told you that; I dont want to ask it anymore than you want to hear it. What I want you to promise is, dont send him collect."

"I promise," the reporter said.

"All right. Call it a gamble on your twenty-two dollars, if you want to. But not collect. The seventy-five may not be enough. But all we got now is my nineteen-fifty from yesterday and the prize money from Thursday. That was a hundred and four. So I cant spare more than seventy-five. You'll have to chance it. If the seventy-five wont ship him ho—to that address I gave you, you can do either of two things. You can pay the difference yourself and write me and I will send you the difference and your twenty-two. Or if you dont want to take a chance on me, use the seventy-five to bury him here;

there must be some way you can do it so they can find him later if they want to. But dont send him collect. I am not asking you to promise to put out any money of your own to send him back; I am just asking you to promise not to leave it so they will have to pay him out of the freight or the express office. Will you?"

"Yes," the reporter said. "I promise."

"All right," the jumper said. He put the money into the reporter's hand. "Thanks. I guess we will leave today. So I guess I will tell you goodbye." He looked at the reporter, bleak, his face spent with sleeplessness too, standing with the injured leg propped stiffly in the shelldust. "She took a couple of big drinks and she is asleep now." He looked at the reporter with that bleak speculation which seemed to be almost clairvoyant. "Dont take it too hard. You never made him try to fly that crate anymore than you could have kept him from it. No man will hold that against you, and what she might hold against you wont hurt you because you wont ever see her again, see?"

"Yes," the reporter said. "That's true."

"Yair. So sometime when she is feeling better about it I will tell her how you attended to this and she will be obliged to you, and for the rest of it too. Only take a tip from me and stick to the kind of people you are used to after this."

"Yes," the reporter said.

"Yair." The jumper moved, shifting stiffly the injured leg to turn, then he paused again, looking back. "You got my address; it may take some time for the letter to catch up with me. But you will get your money. Well——" He extended his hand; it was hard, not clammy, just absolutely without warmth. "Thanks for attending to this and for trying to help us out. Be good to yourself." Then he was gone, limping savagely away. The reporter did not watch him; after a while it was one of the soldiers who called him and showed him the gap.

"Better put that stuff into your pocket, doc," the soldier said. "Some of these guys will be cutting your wrist off." The cab, the taxi, ran with the sun, yet a ray of it fell through the back window and glinted on a chromium fitting on the collapsible seat and though after a while the reporter gave up trying to move the seat and finally thought of laying his hat over the lightpoint, he still continued to try to blink away that sensation of light fine sand inside his lids. It didn't matter whether he watched the backwardstreaming wall of moss and liveoaks above the dark waterglints or whether he tried to keep vision, sight, inside the cab. As soon as he closed them he would find himself, out of some attenuation of weariness, sleeplessness, confusing both the living and the dead without concern now, with profound conviction of the complete unimportance of either or of the confusion itself, trying with that mindless and unflagging optimism to explain to someone that she did not understand and now without bothering to decide or care whether or not and why or not he was asleep. The cab did not have to go as far up as Grandlieu Street and so he did not see a clock, though by the position of the balcony's shadow across the door beneath it he guessed it to be about nine. In the corridor he quit blinking, and on the stairs too; but no sooner had he entered the room with the sun coming into the windows and falling across the bright savage bars of the blanket on the cot (even the other blankets on the walls, which the sun did not reach, seemed to have confiscated light into their harsh red-white-and-black lightnings and which they released slowly into the room as other blankets might have soaked up and then emitted the smell of horses) he began to blink again, with that intent myopic bemusement. He seemed to await the office of something outside himself before he moved and closed the jalousies before the windows. It was better then because for a while he could not see at all; he just stood there in some ultimate distillation of the savage bright neartropical day, not knowing now whether he was still blinking or not, in an implacable infiltration which not even walls could stop, from the circumambient breathing of fish and coffee and sugar and fruit and hemp and swampland dyked away from the stream because of which they came to exist, so that the very commercebearing units of their breath and life came and went not beside or among them but above them like straying skyscrapers putting in from and out to the sea. There was even less light beyond the curtain, though it was not completely dark. "How could it be," he thought, standing quietly with his coat in one hand

and the other already slipping the knot of his tie, thinking how no place where a man has lived for almost two years or even two weeks or even two days is completely dark to him without he has got so fat in the senses that he is already dead walking and breathing and all places are dark to him even in sunlight; not completely dark but just enough so that now the room's last long instant of illimitable unforgetting seemed to draw in quietly in a long immobility of fleeing, with a quality poised and imminent but which could not be called waiting and which contained nothing in particular of farewell, but just paused inbreathing and without impatience and incurious, for him to make the move. His hand was already on the light, the switch.

He had just finished shaving when Jiggs began to call his name from the alley. He took from the bed in passing the fresh shirt which he had laid out, and went to the window and opened the jalousie. "It's on the latch," he said. "Come on in." He was buttoning the shirt when Jiggs mounted the stairs, carrying the canvas sack, wearing the tennis shoes and the bootlegs.

"Well, I guess you have heard the news," Jiggs said.

"Yes. I saw Holmes before I came to town. So I guess you'll all be moving now."

"Yair," Jiggs said. "I'm going with Art Jackson. He's been after me a good while. He's got the chutes, see, and I have done some exhibition jumping and so it wont take me long to pick up free jumping, delayed. . . . . . Then we can split the whole twenty-five bucks between ourselves. But Jesus, it wont be like racing. Maybe I'll go back to racing after a while, after I have. . . . . . ." He stood motionless in the center of the room, holding the dragging canvas bag, the battered brutal face lowered and sober and painfully bemused. Then the reporter discovered what he was looking at. "Jesus," Jiggs said, "I tried again to put them on this morning and I couldn't even seem to open the bag and take them out." That was about ten oclock because almost immediately the negress Leonora came in, in the coat and hat and carrying the neat basket beneath its neat cloth so fresh that the ironed creases were still visible. But the reporter only allowed her to put the basket down.

"A bottle of wood alcohol and a can of that stuff you take grease out of clothes with," he told her, giving her the bill; then to Jiggs: "What do you want to fix that scratch with?"

"I got something for that," Jiggs said. "I brought that with me." He took it from the bag—a coca cola bottle stoppered with paper and containing wingdope. The negress left the basket and went out and returned with the two bottles, and made a pot of coffee and set it with cups and sugar on the table and looked again about the untouched, unused rooms, and took up the basket and stood for a while and watched what they were doing with prim and grim inscrutability before departing for good. And the reporter too, sitting on the couch and blowing quietly into his cup to cool it, watched Jiggs squatting before the two gleaming boots, in the tight soiled clothes and the tennis shoes now upturned behind him, and he thought how never before had he ever heard of rubber soles wearing through. "Because what the hell do I need with a pair of new boots for Christ's sake, when probably this time next month I wont even have on anything to stuff into the tops of them?" Jiggs said. That was toward eleven. By noon, still holding the cold stale cup between his hands, the reporter had watched Jiggs remove the polish from the boots, first with the alcohol, watching the cold dark flowing of the liquid move, already fading, up the length of each boot like the shadow of a cloud travelling along a road, and then by scraping them with the back of a knifeblade, so that at last the boots had returned to the mere shape of what they were like the blank gunstocks manufactured for sale to firearms amateurs. He watched Jiggs, sitting on the couch now and with the soiled shirt for padding and the inverted boot clamped between his knees, with sandpaper remove delicately from the sole all trace of contact with the earth; and last of all, intent, his blunt grained hands moving with minute and incredible lightness and care, with the wingdope begin to fill in the heel-mark on the right boot's instep so that presently it was invisible to the casual glance of anyone who did not know that it had been there. "Jesus," Jiggs said, "if I only hadn't walked in them. Just hadn't creased them at the ankle. But maybe after I get them rubbed smooth again——" But when the cathedral clock struck one they had not accomplished that.

Rubbing only smoothed them and left them without life; the reporter suggested floorwax and went out and got it, and it had to be removed.

"Wait," he said, looking at Jiggs—the gaunt, the worn, the face worn with fatigue and lack of sleep and filled with a spent unflagging expression of quiet endurance like a hypnotised person. "Listen. That magazine with the pictures of what you wish you could get your white American servants to wear so you could think they were English butlers, and what if you wore yourself maybe the horse would think he was in England too unless the fox happened to run under a billboard or something. . . . . . . About how a fox's tail is the only. . . . ." He stared at Jiggs, who stared back at him with blinking and oneeyed attention. "Wait. No. It's the horse's bone. Not the fox; the horse's shin bone. That's what we need."

"A horse's shinbone?"

"For the boots. That's what you use."

"All right. But where——"

"I know where. We can pick it up on the way out to see Hagood. We can rent a car." They had to walk up to Grandlieu Street to rent the car.

"Want me to drive?" Jiggs said.

"Can you?"

"Sure."

"Then I guess you will have to," the reporter said. "I cant." It was a bright soft sunny day, quite warm, the air filled, breathing, with a faint suspiration which made the reporter think of organs and bells—of mortification and peace and shadowy kneeling—though he heard neither. The streets were crowded though the throngs were quiet, not only with ordinary Sunday decorum but with a certain slow tranquillity as though the very brick and stone had just recovered from fever. Now and then, in the lees of walls and gutters as they left downtown behind them the reporter saw little drifts of the spent confetti but soiled and stained now until it resembled more dingy sawdust or even dead leaves. Once or twice he saw tattered loops of the purple-and-gold bunting and once at a corner a little boy darted almost beneath the wheels with a tattered streamer of it whipping behind him. Then the city dissolved into swamp and marsh again; presently the road ran into a broad expanse of saltmarsh broken by the dazzling sunblanched dyke of a canal; presently a rutted lane turned off into the saltgrass. "Here we are," the reporter said. The car turned into the lane and they began to pass the debris, the silent imperishable monument tranquil in the bright sun—the old carbodies without engines or wheels, the old engines and wheels without bodies; the rusted scraps and sections of iron machinery and standpipes and culverts rising halfburied out of the blanched sand and shelldust which was so white itself that for a time Jiggs saw no bones at all. "Can you tell a horse from a cow?" the reporter said.

"I dont know," Jiggs said. "I aint very certain whether I can even tell a shinbone or not."

"We'll get some of everything and try them all," the reporter said. So they did; moving about, stooping (the reporter was blinking again now between the fierce quiet glare of the pigmentless sand and the ineffable and cloudless blue) they gathered up about thirty pounds of bones. They had two complete forelegs both of which were horses' though they did not know it, and a set of shoulderblades from a mule and Jiggs came up with a full set of ribs which he insisted belonged to a colt but which were actually those of a big dog, and the reporter had one object which turned out not to be bone at all but the forearm from a piece of statuary. "We ought to have something in here that will do," he said.

"Yair," Jiggs said. "Now which way?" They did not need to return through the city. They skirted it, leaving the saltmarsh behind and now, crossing no actual boundary or demarcation and challenged by no sentry, they entered a region where even the sunlight seemed different, where it filtered among the ordered liveoaks and fell suavely upon parked expanses and vistas beyond which the homes of the rich oblivious and secure presided above clipped lawns and terraces, with a quality of having itself been passed by appointment through a walled gate by a watchman. Presently they ran along a picketline of palmtrunks beyond which a clipped fairway

stretched, broken only by sedate groups of apparently armed
men and boys all moving in one direction like a kind of
decorouslyembattled skirmish advance.

"It aint four yet," the reporter said. "We can wait for him
right here, at number fifteen." So after a time Hagood, preparing to drive with his foursome, his ball teed and addressed,
looked up and saw them standing quietly just inside the club's
grounds, the car waiting in the road behind them, watching
him—the indefatiguable and now ubiquitous cadaver and
the other, the vicious halfmetamorphosis between thug and
horse—the tough hard blunt face to which the blue swollen
eye lent no quality of pity or suffering, made it look not at all
like a victim or one deserving compassion, but merely like a
pirate. Hagood stepped down from the tee.

"A message from the office," he said quietly. "You fellows
drive and play on; I'll catch you." He approached Jiggs and
the reporter. "How much do you want this time?" he said.

"Whatever you will let me have," the reporter said.

"So," Hagood said quietly. "It's that bad this time, is it?"
The reporter said nothing; they watched Hagood take his
wallet from his hip pocket and open it. "This is the last, this
time, I suppose?" he said.

"Yes," the reporter said. "They're leaving tonight." From
the wallet Hagood took a thin sheaf of check blanks.

"So you wont suggest a sum yourself," Hagood said. "You
are using psychology on me."

"Whatever you can. Will. I know I have borrowed more
from you than I have paid back. But this time maybe I
can. . . . . . ." He drew something from his coat now and
extended it—a postcard, a colored lithograph; Hagood read
the legend: *Hotel Vista del Mar, Santa Monica, California*,
the plump arrow drawn by a hotel pen and pointing to a
window.

"What?" Hagood said.

"Read it," the reporter said. "It's from mamma. Where
they are spending their honeymoon, her and Mr Hurtz. She
said how she has told him about me and he seems to like me
all right and that maybe when my birthday comes on the first
of April. . . . . . ."

"Ah," Hagood said. "That will be very nice, wont it?" He took a short fountain pen from his shirt and glanced about; now the second man, the cartoon comedy centaur who had been watching him quietly and steadily with the one bright hot eye, spoke for the first time.

"Write on my back if you want to, mister," he said, turning and stooping, presenting a broad skintight expanse of soiled shirt, apparently as hard as a section of concrete, to Hagood.

"And get the hell kicked out of me and serve me right," Hagood thought viciously. He spread the blank on Jiggs' back and wrote the check and waved it dry and folded it and handed it to the reporter.

"Do you want me to sign anyth——" the reporter began.

"No. But will you let me ask a favor of you?"

"Yes, chief. Of course."

"Go to town and look in the book and find where Doctor Legendre lives and go out there. Dont telephone; go out there; tell him I sent you, tell him I said to give you some pills that will put you to sleep for about twenty-four hours, and go home and take them. Will you?"

"Yes, chief," the reporter said. "Tomorrow when you fix the note for me to sign you can pin the postcard to it. It wont be legal, but it will be——"

"Yes," Hagood said. "Go on, now. Please go on."

"Yes, chief," the reporter said. They went on. When they reached home it was almost five oclock. They unloaded the bones and now they both worked, each with a boot, fast. It seemed to be slow work, nevertheless the boots were taking on a patina deeper and less brilliant than wax or polish.

"Jesus," Jiggs said. "If I just hadn't creased the ankles, and if I just had kept the box and paper when I unwrapped them. . . . . . ." Because he had forgot that it was Sunday. He knew it; he and the reporter had known it was Sunday all day but they had both forgotten it; they did not remember it until, at halfpast five, Jiggs halted the car before the window into which he had looked four days ago—the window from which now both boots and photographs were missing. They looked at the locked door quietly for a good while. "So we didn't need to hurry after all," he said. "Well, maybe I

couldn't have fooled them, anyway. Maybe I'd a had to went
to the pawnshop just the same anyway.—We might as well
take the car back."

"Let's go to the paper and cash the check first," the reporter said. He had not yet looked at it; while Jiggs waited
in the car he went in and returned. "It was for a hundred,"
he said. "He's a good guy. He's been white to me, Jesus." He
got into the car.

"Now where?" Jiggs said.

"Now we got to decide how. We might as well take the car
back while we are deciding." The lights were on now; when
they emerged from the garage, walking, they moved in red-
green-and-white glare and flicker, crossing the outfall from
the theatre entrances and the eating places, passing athwart
the hour's rich resurgence of fish and coffee. "You cant give
it to her yourself," the reporter said. "They would know you
never had that much."

"Yair," Jiggs said. "All I could risk would have been that
twenty bucks. But I'll have room for some of it, though. If I
get as much as ten from Uncle Isaac I will want to pinch
myself."

"And if we slipped it to the kid, it would be the. . . . . . .
Wait," he said; he stopped and looked at Jiggs. "I got it. Yair.
Come on." Now he was almost running, weaving on through
the slow Sunday evening throng, Jiggs following. They tried
five drugstores before they found it—a blue-and-yellow toy
hanging by a piece of cord before a rotary ventilator in similitude of flight. It had not been for sale; Jiggs and the reporter
fetched the stepladder from the rear of the store in order to
take it down. "You said the train leaves at eight," the reporter
said. "We got to hurry some." It was half past six now as they
left Grandlieu Street; when they reached the corner where
Shumann and Jiggs had bought the sandwich two nights ago,
they parted.

"I can see the balls from here," Jiggs said. "Aint any need
of you going with me; I guess I wont have any trouble carrying what they will give me for them. You get the sandwiches and leave the door unlocked for me." He went on, the
newspaperwrapped boots under his arm; even now as each
foot flicked backward with that motion like a horse's hock,

the reporter believed that he could see the coinshaped patch
of blackened flesh in each pale sole: so that when he entered
the corridor and set the door ajar and mounted the stairs and
turned on the light, he did not open the sandwiches at once.
He put them and the toy aeroplane on the table and went
beyond the curtain. When he emerged he carried in one hand
the gallon jug (it contained now about three pints) and in the
other a pair of shoes which looked as much like him as his
hair or hands looked. He was sitting on the cot, smoking,
when Jiggs entered, carrying now a biggish bundle, a bundle
bigger even though shorter than the boots had been. "He
gave me five bucks for them," Jiggs said. "I give twenty-two
and a half and wear them twice and he gives me five. Yair. He
throws it away." He laid the bundle on the couch. "So I decided that wasn't even worth the trouble of handing to her.
So I just got some presents for all of them." He opened the
parcel. It contained a box or chest of candy about the size of
a suitcase and resembling a miniature bale of cotton and lettered heavily by some pyrographic process: *Souvenir of New
Valois. Come back again* and three magazines—Boy's Life,
The Ladies' Home Journal, and one of the pulp magazines of
war stories in the air. Jiggs' blunt grained hands riffled them
and evened the edges again, his brutal battered face was curiously serene. "It will give them something to do on the train,
see? Now let me get my pliers and we will fix that ship." Then
he saw the jug on the table as he turned. But he did not go
to it; he just stopped, looking at it, and the reporter saw the
good eye rush sudden and inarticulate and hot. But he did
not move. It was the reporter who went and poured the first
drink and gave it to him, and then the second one. "You need
one too," Jiggs said.

"Yes," the reporter said. "I will in a minute." But he didn't
for a while, though he took one of the sandwiches when Jiggs
opened them and then watched Jiggs, his jaw bulged by a
huge bite, stoop and take from the canvas sack the cigarbox
and from the box produced a pair of pliers; not beginning yet
to eat his own sandwich the reporter watched Jiggs raise the
metal clamps which held the toy aeroplane's tin body together
and open it. The reporter produced the money—the seventy-
five which the jumper had given him and the hundred from

Hagood—and they wedged it into the toy and Jiggs clamped it to again.

"Yair, he'll find it, all right," Jiggs said. "Every toy he gets he plays with it a couple of days and then he takes it apart. To fix it, he says. But Jesus, he came by that natural; Roger's old man is a doctor, see. A little country town where it's mostly Swede farmers and the old man gets up at any hour of the night and rides twenty or thirty miles in a sleigh and borns the babies and cuts off arms and legs and a lot of them even pay him; sometimes it aint but a couple or three years before they will bring him in a ham or a bedspread or something on the installment. So the old man wanted Roger to be a doctor too, see, and he was hammering that at Roger all the time Roger was a kid and watching Roger's grades in school and all: so that Roger would have to doctor up his report cards for the old man but the old man never found it out; he would see Roger start off for school every morning (they lived in a kind of big place, half farm, a little ways out of town that never nobody tried to farm much Roger said, but his old man kept it because it was where his old man, his father's old man, had settled when he come into the country) over in town and he never found it out until one day he found out how Roger hadn't even been inside the school in six months because he hadn't never been off the place any further than out of sight down the road where he could turn and come back through the woods to an old mill his grandfather had built and Roger had built him a motorcycle in it out of scraps saved up from mowing machines and clocks and such, and it run, see. That's what saved him. When his old man saw that it would run he let Roger go then and quit worrying him to be a doctor; he bought Roger the first ship, the Hisso Standard, with the money he had been saving up to send Roger to the medical school, but when he saw that the motorcycle would run, I guess he knew he was whipped. And then one night Roger had to make a landing without any lights and he run over a cow and cracked it up and the old man paid for having it rebuilt; Roger told me once the old man must have borrowed the jack to do it with on the farm and that he aimed to pay his old man back the first thing as soon as he could but I guess it's o.k. because a farm with-

out a mortgage on it would probably be against the law or
something. Or maybe the old man didn't have to mortgage
the farm but he just told Roger that so Roger would pick out
a vacant field next time." The cathedral clock had struck seven
shortly after Jiggs came in with his bundle; it must be about
half past seven now. Jiggs squatted now, holding one of the
shoes in his hand. "Jesus," he said. "I sure wont say I dont
need them. But what about you?"

"I couldn't wear but one pair of them, no matter how many
I had," the reporter said. "You better go ahead and try them
on."

"They'll fit, all right. There are two garments that will fit
anybody: a handkerchief when your nose is running and a
pair of shoes when your feet are on the ground."

"Yes," the reporter said. "That was the same ship that he
and Laverne——"

"Yair. Jesus, they were a pair. She was glad to see him when
he come into town that day in it. One day she told me something about it. She was a orphan, see; her older sister that
was married sent for her to come live with them when her
folks died. The sister was about twenty years older than Laverne and the sister's husband was about six or eight years
younger than the sister and Laverne was about fourteen or
fifteen; she hadn't had much fun at home with a couple of
old people like her father and mother, and she never had
much with her sister neither, being that much younger; yair,
I dont guess the sister had a whole lot of fun either with the
kind of guy the husband seemed to be. So when the husband
started teaching Laverne how to slip out and meet him and
they would drive to some town forty or fifty miles away when
the husband was supposed to be at work or something and
he would buy her a glass of soda water or maybe stop at a
dive where the husband was sure nobody he knowed would
see them and dance, I guess she thought that was all the fun
there was in the world and that since he would tell her it was
all right to twotime the sister that way, that it was all right
for her to do the rest of it he wanted. Because he was the big
guy, see, the one that paid for what she wore and what she
ate. Or maybe she didn't think it was all right so much as she
just thought that that was the way it was—that you was

either married and wore down with housework to where your husband was just the guy that twotimed you and you knew it and all you could do about it was nag at him while he was awake and go through his clothes while he was asleep to see if you found any hairpins or letters or rubbers in his pockets, and then cry and moan about him to your younger sister while he was gone; or you were the one that somebody else's husband was easing out with and that all the choice you had was the dirty dishes to wash against the nickel sodas and a half an hour of dancing to a backalley orchestra in a dive where nobody give his right name and then being wallowed around on the back seat of a car and then go home and slip in and lie to your sister and when it got too close, having the guy jump on you too to save his own face and then make it up by buying you two sodas next time. Or maybe at fifteen she just never saw any way of doing better because for a while she never even knowed that the guy was holding her down himself, see, that he was hiding her out at the cheap dives not so they would not be recognised but so he would not have any competition from anybody but guys like himself; no young guys for her to see or to see her. Only the competition come; somehow she found out there was sodas that cost more than even a dime and that all the music never had to be played in a back room with the shades down. Or maybe it was just him, because one night she had used him for a stalking horse and he hunted her down and the guy she was with this time finally had to beat him up and so he went back home and told the sister on her——" The reporter rose, quickly. Jiggs watched him go to the table and pour into the glass, splashing the liquor onto the table. "That's right," Jiggs said. "Take a good one." The reporter lifted the glass, gulping, his throat filled with swallowing and the liquor cascading down his chin; Jiggs sprang up quickly too but the other passed him, running toward the window and onto the balcony where Jiggs, following, caught him by the arms as he lunged outward as the liquor, hardly warmed, burst from his mouth. The cathedral clock struck the half hour; the sound followed them back into the room and seemed to die away too, like the light, into the harsh bright savage zigzags of color on the blankethung walls. "Let me get you some water," Jiggs said. "You sit down now, and I will——"

"I'm all right now," the reporter said. "You put on your shoes. That was half past seven then."

"Yair. But you better——"

"No. Sit down; I'll pull your leggings for you."

"You sure you feel like it?"

"Yes. I'm all right now." They sat facing one another on the floor again as they had sat the first night, while the reporter took hold of the rivetted strap of the right bootleg. Then he began to laugh. "You see, it got all mixed up," he said, laughing, not loud yet. "It started out to be a tragedy. A good orthodox Italian tragedy. You know: one Florentine falls in love with another Florentine's wife and he spends three acts fixing it up to put the bee on the second Florentine and so just as the curtain falls on the third act the Florentine and the wife crawl down the fire escape and you know that the second Florentine's brother wont catch them until daylight and they will be asleep in the monk's bed in the monastery? But it went wrong. When he come climbing up to the window to tell her the horses was ready, she refused to speak to him. It turned into a comedy, see?" He looked at Jiggs, laughing, not laughing louder yet but just faster.

"Here, fellow!" Jiggs said. "Here now! Quit it!"

"Yes," the reporter said. "It's not that funny. I'm trying to quit it. I'm trying to. But I cant quit. See? See how I cant quit?" he said, still holding to the strap, his face twisted with laughing, which as Jiggs looked, burst suddenly with drops of moisture running down the cadaverous grimace which for an instant Jiggs thought was sweat until he saw the reporter's eyes.

It was after half past seven; they would have to hurry now. But they found a cab at once and they got the green light at once at Grandlieu Street even before the cab began to slow, shooting athwart the glare of neon, the pulse and glitter of electrics which bathed the idle slow Sunday pavementthrong as it drifted from window to window beyond which the immaculate, the unbelievable wax men and women gazed back at them with expressions inscrutable and delphic. Then the palms in Saint Jules Avenue began to swim and flee past—

the scabby picket posts, the sage dusters out of the old Southern country thought; the lighted clock in the station façade said six minutes to eight.

"They are probably already on the train," Jiggs said.

"Yes," the reporter said. "They'll let you through the gate, though."

"Yair," Jiggs said, taking up the toy aeroplane and the package which he had rewrapped. "Dont you want to come inside?"

"I'll just wait here," the reporter said. He watched Jiggs enter the waitingroom and vanish. He could hear the announcer calling another train; moving toward the doors he could see passengers begin to rise and take up bags and bundles and move toward the numbered gates, though quite a few still remained for other trains. "But not long," the reporter thought. "Because they can go home now"; thinking of all the names of places which railroads go to, fanning out from the River's mouth to all of America; of the cold February names: Minnesota and Dakota and Michigan, the high iceclad riverreaches and the long dependable snow; "yair, home now, knowing that they have got almost a whole year before they will have to get drunk and celebrate the fact that they will have more than eleven months before they will have to wear masks and get drunk and blow horns again." Now the clock said two minutes to eight; they had probably got off the car to talk to Jiggs, perhaps standing now on the platform, smoking maybe; he could cross the waitingroom and doubtless even see them, standing beside the hissing train while the other passengers and the redcaps hurried past; she would carry the bundle and the magazines and the little boy would have the aeroplane already, probably performing wingovers or vertical turns by hand. "Maybe I will go and look," he thought, waiting to see if he were until suddenly he realised that now, opposite from when he had stood in the bedroom before turning on the light, it was himself who was the nebulous and quiet ragtag and bobend of touching and breath and experience without visible scars, the waiting incurious unbreathing and without impatience, and another save him this time to make the move. There was a second hand on the clock too—a thin spidery splash; he watched it now as it

moved too fast to follow save between the intervals of motion
when it became instantaneously immobile as though drawn
across the clock's face by a pen and a ruler—9. 8. 7. 6. 5. 4.
3. 2. and done; it was now the twenty-first hour, and that was
all. No sound, as though it had not been a steam train which
quitted the station two seconds ago but rather the shadow of
one on a magic lantern screen until the child's vagrant and
restless hand came and removed the slide.

"Well," Jiggs said, "I guess you'll be wanting to get home
and catch some shuteye."

"Yair," the reporter said, "we might as well be moving."
They got into the cab, though this time Jiggs lifted the canvas
sack from the floor and sat with it on his lap.

"Yair," Jiggs said. "He'll find it. He already dropped it a
couple of times trying to make it spin on the platform.—You
told him to stop at Main Street, didn't you?"

"I'll take you on to the hotel," the reporter said.

"No, I'll get out at Main. Jesus, it's a good thing I dont
live here; I never would get back home unless somebody took
me; I couldn't even remember the name of the street I lived
on even if I could pronounce it to ask where it was."

"Grandlieu," the reporter said. "I will take you——" The
cab slowed into the corner and stopped; Jiggs gathered up
the canvas bag and opened the door.

"This'll be fine. It aint but eight-fifteen; I aint to meet Art
until nine. I'll just walk up the street a ways and get a little
air."

"I wish you'd let me——Or if you'd like to come on back
home and——"

"No; you get on home and go to bed; we have kept you
up enough, I guess." He leaned into the cab, the cap raked
above his hard blue face and the violent plumcolored eye;
suddenly the light changed to green and the bell clanged and
shrilled. Jiggs stuck out his hand; for an instant the hot hard
limp rough palm sweated against the reporter's as if the
reporter had touched a piece of machinery belting. "Much
obliged. And thanks for the drinks. I'll be seeing you." The
cab moved; Jiggs banged the door; his face fled backward
past the window; the green and red and white electrics waned
and pulsed and flicked away too as through the rear window

the reporter watched Jiggs swing the now limp dirty sack over his shoulder and turn on into the crowd. The reporter leaned forward and tapped on the glass.

"Out to the airport," he said.

"Airport?" the driver said. "I thought the other fellow said you wanted to go to Noyades street."

"No; airport," the reporter said. The driver looked forward again; he seemed to settle himself, to shape his limbs for comfort for the long haul even while the one-way arrows of the old constricted city flicked past. But presently the old quarter gave way to outraveling and shabby purlieus, mostly lightless now, and the cab went faster; presently the street straightened and became the ribbonstraight road running across the terraqueous plain and the cab was going quite fast, and now the illusion began, the sense of being suspended in a small airtight glass box clinging by two puny fingers of light in the silent and rushing immensity of space. By looking back he could still see the city, the glare of it, no further away; if he were moving, regardless at what terrific speed and in what loneliness, so was it, parallelling him. He was not escaping it; symbolic and encompassing, it outlay all gasolinespanned distances and all clock- or sunstipulated destinations. It would be there—the eternal smell of the coffee the sugar the hemp sweating slow iron plates above the forked deliberate brown water and lost lost lost all ultimate blue of latitude and horizon; the hot rain gutterfull plaiting the eaten heads of shrimp; the ten thousand inescapable mornings wherein ten thousand airplants swinging stippleprop the soft scrofulous soaring of sweating brick and ten thousand pairs of splayed brown hired Leonorafeet tigerbarred by jaloused armistice with the invincible sun: the thin black coffee, the myriad fish stewed in a myriad oil—tomorrow and tomorrow and tomorrow; not only not to hope, not even to wait: just to endure.

The Scavengers

A T MIDNIGHT—one of the group of newspapermen on the
beach claimed to have watched the mate of the dredgeboat and the sergeant of the police launch holding flashlights
on their watches for fifteen minutes—the dredge upped anchor and stood offshore and steamed away while the police
launch, faster, had taken its white bone beyond the seawall
almost before the dredge had got enough offing to turn. Then
the five newspapermen—four in overcoats with upturned collars—turned too and mounted the beach toward where the
ranked glaring cars were beginning to disperse while the policemen—there were not so many of them now—tried to
forestall the inevitable jam. There was no wind tonight, neither was there any overcast. The necklace of lights along the
lakeshore curved away faint and clear, with that illusion of
tremulous wavering which distance and clarity gave them, like
bright not-quite-settled roosting birds, as did the boundary
lights along the seawall; and now the steady and measured
rake of the beacon seemed not to travel so much as to murmur like a moving forefoot of wind across water, among the
thick faint stars. They mounted the beach to where a policeman, hands on hips, stood as though silhouetted not against
the crisscrossing of headlights but against the blatting and
honking uproar as well, as though contemplating without any
emotion whatever the consummation of that which he had
been waiting on for twenty hours now. "Aint you talking to
us too, sergeant?" the first newspaperman said. The policeman looked back over his shoulder, squinting down at the
group from under his raked cap.

"Who are you?" he said.

"We are the press," the other said in a smirking affected
voice.

"Get on, get on," a second said behind him. "Let's get in-
doors somewhere." The policeman had already turned back
to the cars, the racing engines, the honking and blatting.

"Come, come, sergeant," the first said. "Come come come
come. Aint you going to send us back to town too?" The
policeman did not even look back. "Well, wont you at least

call my wife and tell her you wont make me come home, since
you wear the dark blue of honor integrity and purity——"
The policeman spoke without turning his head.

"Do you want to finish this wake out here or do you really
want to finish it in the wagon?"

"Ex-actly. You have got the idea at last. Boys, he's even
com——"

"Get on, get on," the second said. "Let him buy a paper
and read it." They went on, the reporter (he was the one
without an overcoat) last, threading their way between the
blatting and honking, the whining and clashing of gears, the
glare of backbouncing and crossing headlight beams and
reached the boulevard and crossed it toward the lunchstand.
The first led the way in, his hatbrim crumpled on one side
and his overcoat caught one button awry and a bottleneck
protruding from one pocket. The proprietor looked up at
them with no especial pleasure; he was about to close up.

"That fellow out there kept me up all last night and I am
about wore out," he said.

"You would think we were from the District Attorney's
office and trying to padlock him instead of a press delegation
trying to persuade him to stay open and accept our pittances,"
the first said. "You are going to miss the big show at daylight,
let alone all the country trade that never heard about it until
the noon train got in with the papers."

"How about coming to the back room and letting me lock
the door and turn out the lights up here, then?" the proprietor said.

"Sure," they told him. So he locked up and turned off the
lights and led them to the back, to the kitchen—a stove, a
zinc table encrusted with weekend after weekend of slain meat
and fish—and supplied them with glasses and bottles of coca
cola and a deck of cards and beercases to sit on and a barrel-
head for table, and prepared to retire.

"If anybody knocks, just sit quiet," he said. "And you can
beat on that wall there when they get ready to begin; I'll wake
up."

"Sure," they told him. He went out. The first opened the
bottle and began to pour into the five glasses. The reporter
stopped him.

"None for me. I'm not drinking."

"What?" the first said. He set the bottle carefully down and took out his handkerchief and went through the pantomime of removing his glasses and polishing them and replacing them and staring at the reporter, though before he had finished the fourth took up the bottle and finished pouring the drinks. "You what?" the first said. "Did I hear my ears, or was it just blind hope I heard?"

"Yes," the reporter said; his face wore that faint, spent, aching expression which a man might wear toward the end of a private babyshow. "I've quit for a while."

"Thank God for that," the first breathed, then he turned and began to scream at the one who now held the bottle, with that burlesque outrage and despair of the spontaneous amateur buffoon. But he ceased at once and then the four of them (again the reporter declined) sat about the barrel and began to deal blackjack. The reporter did not join them. He drew his beercase aside, whereupon the first, the habitual opportunist who must depend upon all unrehearsed blundering and recalcitrant circumstance to be his stooge, noticed at once that he had set his beercase beside the now cold stove. "If you aint going to take the drink yourself maybe you better give the stove one," he said.

"I'll begin to warm up in a minute," the reporter said. They played; the fourth had the deal; their voices came quiet and brisk and impersonal above the faint slapping of the cards.

"That's what I call a guy putting himself away for keeps," he said.

"What do you suppose he was thinking about while he was sitting up there waiting for that water to smack him?" the first said.

"Nothing," the second said shortly. "If he had been a man that thought, he would not have been up there in the first place."

"Meaning he would have had a good job on a newspaper, huh?" the first said.

"Yes," the second said. "That's what I mean." The reporter rose quietly. He lit a cigarette, his back turned a little to them, and dropped the match carefully into the cold stove and sat down again. None of the others appeared to have noticed him.

"While you are supposing," the fourth said, " what do you suppose his wife was thinking about?"

"That's easy," the first said. "She was thinking, 'Thank God I carry a spare'." They did not laugh; the reporter heard no sound of laughter, sitting quiet and immobile on his beercase while the cigarette smoke lifted in the unwinded stale air and broke about his face, streaming on, and the voices spoke back and forth with a sort of brisk dead slap-slap-slap like that of the cards.

"Do you suppose it's a fact that they were both laying her?" the third said.

"That's not news," the first said. "But how about the fact that Shumann knew it too? Some of these mechanics that have known them for some time say they dont even know who the kid belongs to."

"Maybe both," the fourth said. "A dual personality: the flying Jekyll and Hyde brother, who flies the ship and makes the parachute jump all at once."

"Unless he cant ever tell which one of him it is that's getting the insertion into the ship," the third said.

"Well, that will be all right too," the first said. "Just so it's one of them and actually inserted, the ship wont care which one it is." The reporter did not move, only his hand, the arm bending at the elbow which rested upon his knee, rose with the cigarette to his mouth and became motionless again while he drew in the smoke with an outward aspect of intense bemused concentration, trembling quietly and steadily and apparently not only untroubled by it but not even aware of it, like a man who has had palsy for years and years; the voices might have indeed been the sound of the cards or perhaps leaves blowing past him.

"You bastards," the second said. "You dirtymouthed bastards. Why dont you let the guy rest? Let them all rest. They were trying to do what they had to do, with what they had to do it with, the same as all of us only maybe a little better than us. At least without squealing and bellyaching."

"Sure," the first said. "You get the point exactly. What they could do, with what they had to do it with: that's just what we were talking about when you called us dirtyminded bastards."

"Yes," the third said. "Grady's right. Let him rest; that's what she seems to have done herself. But what the hell: probably nowhere to send him, even if she had him out of there. So it would be the same whether she stayed any longer or not, besides the cost. Where do you suppose they are going?"

"Where do people like that go?" the second said. "Where do mules and vaudeville acts go? You see a wagon broken down in the ditch or you see one of those trick bicycles with one wheel and the seat fourteen feet from the earth in a pawnshop. But do you wonder whatever became of whatever it was that used to make them move?"

"Do you mean you think she cleared out just to keep from having to pay out some jack to bury him if they get him up?" the fourth said.

"Why not?" the second said. "People like that dont have money to spend on corpses because they dont use money. It dont take money especially to live; it's only when you die that you or somebody has got to have something put away in the sock. A man can eat and sleep and keep the purity squad off of him for six months on what the undertaker will make you believe you cant possibly be planted for a cent less and preserve your selfrespect. So what would they have to bury him with even if they had him to bury?"

"You talk like he didn't kill himself taking a chance to win two thousand dollars," the third said.

"That's correct. Oh, he would have taken the money, all right. But that wasn't why he was flying that ship up there. He would have entered it if he hadn't had anything but a bicycle, just so it would have got off the ground. But it aint for money. It's because they have got to do it, like some women have got to be whores. They cant help themselves. Ord knew that the ship was dangerous, and Shumann must have known it as well as Ord did—dont you remember how for the first lap he stayed so far away he didn't even look like he was in the same race, until he forgot and came in and tried to catch Ord? If it had just been the money, do you think he could have thought about money hard enough to have decided to risk his life to get it in a machine that he knew was

unsafe, and then have forgot about the money for a whole lap
of the race while he hung back there not half as close to
the pylons as the judges were, just riding around? Dont kid
yourself."

"And dont kid yourself," the first said. "It was the money.
Those guys like money as well as you and me. What would
he have done with it? Hell, what would any other three people do with two thousand bucks? She would have bought
herself a batch of new clothes and they would have moved to
the hotel from wherever it was they were staying, and they
would have taken a couple of days and blowed it out good.
That's what they would have done. But they didn't get it and
so you are right, by God: what she did was the sensible thing:
when a game blows up in your face you dont sit down on the
pocketbook that used to make a bump on your ass and cry
about it, you get out and hustle up another roll and go on
and find another game that maybe you can beat. Yes. They
want money, all right. But it aint to sweat just to have something in the sock when the snow flies, or to be buried with
either. So I dont know anymore than you guys do but if somebody told me that Shumann had some folks somewhere and
then they told me the name of the town she bought hers and
the kid's tickets to, I would tell you where Shumann used to
live. And then I would bet a quarter maybe that the next time
you see them, the kid wont be there. Because why? Because
that's what I would do if I were her. And so would you
guys."

"No," the second said.

"You mean you wouldn't or she wouldn't?" the first said.
The reporter sat motionless, the cigarette's windless upstream
breaking upon his face. "Yes," the first said. "Before, they
might not have known whose the kid was, but it was Shumann's name he went under and so in comparison to the
whole mess they must have lived in, who had actually fa-
thered the kid didn't matter. But now Shumann's gone; you
asked a while ago what she was thinking about while he was
sitting up there waiting for that water to hit him. I'll tell you
what she and the other guy were both thinking about: that
now that Shumann was gone, they would never get rid of

him. Maybe they took it night about: I dont know. But now they couldn't even get him out of the room; even turning off the light wont do any good, and all the time they would be awake and moving there he will be, watching them right out of the mixedup name, Jack Shumann, that the kid has. It used to be the guy had one competitor; now he will have to compete with every breath the kid draws and be cuckolded by every ghost that walks and refuses to give his name. So if you will tell me that Shumann has some folks in a certain town, I will tell you where she and the kid——" The reporter did not move. He sat quite still while the voice ceased on that note of abrupt transition, hearing out of the altered silence the voices talking at him and the eyes talking at him while he held himself rigid, watching the calculated hand flick the ash carefully from the cigarette. "You hung around them a lot," the first said. "Did you ever hear any of them mention any kin that Shumann or she had?" The reporter did not move; he let the voice repeat the question; he even raised the cigarette again and flicked the ash off, or what would have been ash if he had not flicked it only a second ago. Then he started; he sat up, looking at them with an expression of startled interrogation.

"What?" he said. "What was that? I wasn't listening."

"Did you ever hear any mention of Shumann having any kinfolks, mother and father and such?" the first said. The reporter's face did not alter.

"No," he said. "I dont believe I did. I believe his mechanic told me that he was an orphan."

It was two oclock then but the cab went fast, so it was just past two-thirty when the cab reached the Terrebonne and the reporter entered and leaned his gaunt desperate face across the desk while he spoke to the clerk. "Dont you call yourselves the headquarters of the American Aeronautical Association?" he said. "You mean you didn't keep any registration of contestants and such? that the committee just let them scatter to hell and gone over New Valois without——"

"Who is it you want to find?" the clerk said.

"Art Jackson. A stunt flyer."

"I'll see if there is any record. The meet was over yesterday." The clerk left the window. The reporter leaned in it, not panting, just completely motionless until the clerk returned.

"There is an Arthur Jackson registered as staying at the Bienville Hotel yesterday. But whether or not he is——" But the reporter was gone, not running, but fast, back toward the entrance; a porter with a longhandled brush sweeping the floor jerked it back just before the reporter was about to walk through the brushhandle like it was a spiderweb. The taxi driver did not know exactly where the Bienville was, but at last they found it—a side street, a sign reading mostly Turkish Bath, then a narrow entrance, a corridor dimly lighted and containing a few chairs and a few palms and more spittoons than either and a desk beside which a negro in no uniform slept—a place ambiguous, redolent of hard Saturday nights, whose customers seldom had any baggage and beyond the turnings of whose dim and threadbare corridors there seemed to whisk forever bright tawdry kimonos in a kind of hopeful nostalgic convocation of all the bought female flesh which ever breathed and perished. The negro waked; there was no elevator; the reporter was directed to the room from his description of Jiggs and knocked beneath the ghost of two numbers attached to the door's surface by the ghost of four tacks until the door opened and Jiggs blinked at him with the good eye and the injured one, wearing now only the shirt. The reporter held in his hand the slip of paper which had been clipped to the money the jumper gave him. He did not blink, himself: he just stared at Jiggs with that desperate urgency.

"The tickets," he said. "Where——"

"Oh," Jiggs said. "Myron, Ohio. Yair, that's it on the paper. Roger's old man. They're going to leave the kid there. I thought you knew. You said you saw Jack at the——Here, doc! What is it?" He opened the door wider and put out his hand, but the reporter had already caught the doorjamb. "You come on in and set down a——"

"Myron, Ohio," the reporter said. His face wore again that faint wrung quiet grimace as with the other hand he continued to try to put Jiggs' hand aside even after Jiggs was no longer offering to touch him. He began to apologise to Jiggs for having disturbed him, talking through that thin wash over his wasted gaunt face which would have been called smiling for lack of anything better.

"It's all right, doc," Jiggs said, watching him, blinking still with a sort of brutal concern. "Jesus, aint you been to bed yet? Here; you better come in here; me and Art can make room——"

"Yes, I'll be getting on." He pushed himself carefully back from the door as though he were balancing himself before turning the door loose, feeling Jiggs watching him. "I just happened to drop in. To say goodbye." He looked at Jiggs with that thin fixed grimace while Jiggs blinked at him.

"Goodbye, doc. Only you better——"

"And good luck to you. Or do you say happy landings to a parachute jumper?"

"Jesus," Jiggs said. "I hope so."

"Then happy landings too."

"Yair. Thanks. The same to you, doc." The reporter turned away. Jiggs watched him go down the corridor, walking with that curious light stiff care, and turn the corner and vanish. The light was even dimmer on the stairs than it had been in the corridor, though the brass strips which bound the rubber tread to each step glinted bright and still in the center where the heels had kept it polished. The negro was already asleep again in the chair beside the desk; he did not stir as the reporter passed him and went on and got into the cab, stumbling a little on the step.

"Back to the airport," he said. "You needn't hurry. We got until daylight." He was back on the beach before daylight, though it was dawn before the other four saw him again, before they came out of the dark lunchstand and passed again through another barricade of parked cars though not so many this time since it was now Monday, and descended to the beach. They saw him then. The smooth water was a pale rose color from the waxing east, so that the reporter in silhouette against it resembled a tatting Christmas gift made by a little girl and supposed to represent a sleeping crane.

"Good Lord," the third said. "You suppose he has been down here by himself all the time?" But they did not have much time to wonder about it; they were barely on time themselves; they heard the aeroplane taking off before they reached the beach and then they watched it circling; it came over into what they thought was position and the sound of the engine died for a time and then began again and the aeroplane went on, though nothing else happened. They saw nothing fall from it at all, they just saw three gulls converge suddenly from nowhere and begin to slant and tilt and scream above a spot on the water some distance away, making a sound like rusty shutters in a wind. "So that's that," the third said. "Let's go to town." Again the fourth one spoke the reporter's name.

"Are we going to wait for him?" he said. They looked back, but the reporter was gone.

"He must have got a ride with somebody," the third said. "Come on. Let's go."

When the reporter got out of the car at the Saint Jules Avenue corner the clock beyond the restaurant's window said eight oclock. He did not look at the clock; he was looking at nothing for the time, shaking slowly and steadily. It was going to be another bright vivid day; the sunlight, the streets and walls themselves emanated that brisk up-and-doing sobriety of Monday morning. But he was not looking at that either; he was not looking at anything; when he began to see it was as if the letters were beginning to emerge from the back of his skull—the broad page under a rusting horseshoe, the quality of grateful astonishment which Monday headlines have like when you learn that the uncle whom you believed to have perished two years ago in a poorhouse fire died yesterday in Tucson, Arizona and left you five hundred dollars: **AVIATOR'S BODY RESIGNED TO LAKE GRAVE.** Then he quit seeing it. He had not moved; his pupils would still have repeated the page in inverted miniature, but he was not seeing it at all, shaking quietly and steadily in the bright warm sun until he turned and looked into the window with an expression of quiet and bemused despair—the notflies or wereflies, the two grapefruit halves, the printed names of food like the printed stations in a train schedule and set on an easel like a family portrait—and experienced that profound and unshakable not only reluctance but actual absolute refusal of his entire organism. "All right," he said. "If I wont eat, then

I am going to take a drink. If I wont go in here then I am going to Joe's." It was not far: just down an alley and through a barred door—one of the places where for fifteen years the United States had tried to keep them from selling whiskey and where for one year now it had been trying to make them sell it. The porter let him in and poured him a drink in the empty bar while starting the cork in the bottle itself. "Yair," the reporter said. "I was on the wagon for an entire day. Would you believe that?"

"Not about you," the porter said.

"Neither would I. It surprised me. It surprised the hell out of me until I found out it was two other guys. See?" He laughed too; it wasn't loud; it still didn't seem loud even after the porter was holding him up, calling him by name too, mister too, like Leonora, saying,

"Come on, now; try to quit now."

"All right," the reporter said. "I've quit now. If you ever saw any man quitter than me right now I will buy you an airplane."

"O.K.," the porter said. "Only make it a taxi cab and you go on home."

"Home? I just come from home. I'm going to work now. I'm o.k. now. Give me another shot and just point me toward the door and I will be all right. All right, see? Then I learned by mistake that it was two other guys——" But he stopped himself, this time; he held himself fine while the porter poured the other drink and brought it to him; he had himself in hand fine now; he did not feel at all now: just the liquor flowing slow down him, fiery, dead, and cold; soon he would even quit shaking, soon he did quit; walking now with the bright unsoiled morning falling upon him he did not have anything to shake with. "So I feel better," he said. Then he began to say it fast: "Oh God, I feel better! I feel better! I feel! I feel!" until he quit that too and said quietly, looking at the familiar wall, the familiar twin door through which he was about to pass, with tragic and passive clairvoyance: "Something is going to happen to me. I have got myself stretched out too far and too thin and something is going to bust." He mounted the quiet stairs; in the empty corridor he drank from the bottle, though this time it was merely cold and felt like water. But when he entered the deserted city room he remembered that he could have drunk here just as well, and so he did. "I see so little of it," he said. "I dont know the family's habits yet." But it was empty, or comparatively so, because he kept on making that vertical reverse without any rudder or flippers and looking down on the closepeopled land and the empty lake and deciding, and the dredgeboat hanging over him for twenty hours and then having to lie there too and look up at the wreath dissolving faintly rocking and stared at by gulls away, and trying to explain that he did not know. "I didn't think that!" he cried. "I just thought they were all going. I dont know where, but I thought that all three of them, that maybe the hundred and seventy-five would be enough until Holmes could . . . . . . .and that then he would be big enough and I would be there; I would maybe see her first and she would not look different even though he was out there around the pylon and so I wouldn't be either even if it was forty-two instead of twenty-eight and he would come on in off the pylons and we would go up and she maybe holding my arm and him looking at us over the cockpit and she would say, 'This is the one back in New Valois that time. That used to buy you the ice-cream'." Then he had to hurry, saying, "Wait. Stop now. Stop" until he did stop, tall, humped a little, moving his mouth faintly as if he were tasting, blinking fast now and now stretching his eyelids to their full extent like a man trying to keep himself awake while driving a car; again it tasted, felt, like so much dead icy water, that cold and heavy and lifeless in his stomach; when he moved he could both hear and feel it sluggish and dead within him as he removed his coat and hung it on the chairback and sat down and racked a sheet of yellow paper into the machine. He could not feel his fingers on the keys either: he just watched the letters materialise out of thin air, black sharp and fast, along the creeping yellow.

During the night the little boy slept on the seat facing the woman and the parachute jumper, the toy aeroplane clutched to his chest; when daylight came the train was running in snow. They changed trains in snow too, and when in mid-afternoon the trainman called the town and looking out the window the woman read the name on the little station, it was snowing hard. They got out and crossed the platform, among the milkcans and the fowlcrates, and entered the waitingroom where a porter was putting coal into the stove. "Can we get a cab here?" the jumper asked him.

"There's one outside now," the porter said. "I'll call him."

"Thanks," the jumper said. The jumper looked at the woman; she was buttoning the trenchcoat. "I'll wait here," he said.

"Yes," she said. "All right. I dont know how——"

"I'll wait. No use standing around anywhere else."

"Aint he coming with us?" the little boy said. He looked at the jumper, the toy aeroplane under his arm now, though he still spoke to the woman. "Dont he want to see Roger's old man too?"

"No," the woman said. "You tell him goodbye now."

"Goodbye?" the boy said. He looked from one to the other. "Aint we coming back?" He looked from one to the other. "I'll stay here with him until you get back. I'll see Roger's old man some other time."

"No," the woman said. "Now." The boy looked from one to the other. Suddenly the jumper said,

"So long, kid. I'll be seeing you."

"You're going to wait? You aint going off?"

"No. I'll wait. You and Laverne go on." The porter came in.

"He's waiting for you folks," he said.

"The cab's waiting," the woman said. "Tell Jack so long."

"O.K.," the boy said. "You wait here for us. Soon as we get back we'll eat."

"Yair; sure," the jumper said. Suddenly he set the bag down and stooped and picked the boy up.

"No," the woman said; "you wait here out of the——" But the jumper went on, carrying the little boy, swinging his stiff leg along. The woman followed him, into the snow again. The cab was a small touring car with a lettered sign on the windshield and a blanket over the hood and driven by a man with a scraggly grayish moustache. The driver opened the door; the jumper swung the boy in and stepped back and helped the woman in and leaned again into the door; now his face wore an expression which anyone who had seen very much of the reporter lately would have recognised—that faint grimace (in this instance savage too) which would have been called smiling for lack of anything better.

"So long, old fellow," he said. "Be good now."

"O.K.," the boy said. "You be looking around for somewhere to eat before we get back."

"O.K.," the jumper said.

"All right, mister," the woman said. "Let's go." The car moved, swinging away from the station; the woman was still leaning forward. "Do you know where Doctor Carl Shumann lives?" she said. For an instant the driver did not move. The car still swung on, gaining speed, and there was little possible moving for the driver to do. Yet during that moment he seemed to have become caught in that sort of instantaneous immobility like when a sudden light surprises a man or an animal out of darkness. Then it was gone.

"Doctor Shumann? Sure. You want to go there?"

"Yes," the woman said. It was not far; the town was not large; it seemed to the woman that almost at once the car had stopped and looking out through the falling snow she saw a kind of cenotaph, penurious and without majesty or dignity, of forlorn and victorious desolation—a bungalow, a tight flimsy mass of stoops and porte-cochères and flat gables and bays not five years old and built in that colored mud-and-chickenwire tradition which California moving picture films have scattered across North America as if the celluloid carried germs, not five years old yet wearing already an air of dilapidation and rot; a quality furious and recent as if immediate disintegration had been included in the architect's blueprints and inherent in the wood and plaster and sand of its mushroom growth. Then she found the driver looking at her.

"This is it," he said. "Or maybe you were thinking about his old place? or are you acquainted with him that well?"

"No," the woman said. "This is it." He made no move to open the door; he just sat halfturned, watching her struggling with the doorhandle.

"He used to have a big old place out in the country until he lost it a few years back. His son took up av-aytion and he mortgaged the place to buy his son a flying machine and then his son wrecked the machine and so the doctor had to borrow some more money on the place to fix the machine up. I guess the boy aimed to pay it back but he just never got around to it maybe. So he lost the old place and built this one. Probly this one suits him just as well, though; womenfolks usually like to live close to town——" But she had got the door open now and she and the boy got out.

"Do you mind waiting?" she said. "I dont know how long I'll be. I'll pay you for the time."

"Sure," he said. "That's my business. What you do with the car while you are hiring it is yours, not mine." He watched them enter the gate and go on up the narrow concrete walk in the snow. "So that's her," he thought. "Only she dont look a whole lot like a widow. But then I hear tell she never acted a whole lot like a wife." He had a robe, another horseblanket, in the seat beside him. He bundled himself into it, which was just as well because dark had come and the snow drifted and whirled, funneled now by the downglare of a streetlamp nearby before the door opened and he recognised against the light the silhouette of the trenchcoat and then that of Doctor Shumann as they came out and the door shut behind them. He threw the robe off and started the engine. But after a while he cut the switch and drew the robe about him again though it was too dark and the snow was falling too fast for him to see the two people standing on the stoop before the entrance of the house.

"You are going to leave him like this?" Dr Shumann said. "You are going to leave him asleep and go away?"

"Can you think of any better way?" she said.

"No. That's true." He was speaking loudly, too loudly. "Let us understand one another. You leave him here of your own free will; we are to make a home for him until we die: that is understood."

"Yes. I agreed to that inside," she said patiently.

"No; but let us understand. I. . . . . . ." He talked in that curious loud wild rushing manner, as though she were still moving away and were at some distance now: "We are old; you cannot understand that, that you will or can ever reach a time when you can bear so much and no more; that nothing else is worth the bearing; that you not only cannot, you will not; that nothing is worth anything but peace, peace, peace, even with bereavement and grief—nothing! nothing! But we have reached that stage. When you came here with Roger that day before the boy was born, you and I talked and I talked different to you. I was different then; I meant it when you told me you did not know whether or not Roger was the father of your unborn child and that you would never know, and I told you, do you remember? I said 'Then make Roger his father from now on'. And you told me the truth, that you would not promise, that you were born bad and could not help it or did not think you were going to try to help it; and I told you nobody is born anything, bad or good God help us, anymore than anybody can do anything save what they must: do you remember? I meant that then. But I was younger then. And now I am not young. And now I cant—I cannot——I——"

"I know. If I leave him with you, I must not try to see him again until you and she are dead."

"Yes. I must; I cannot help it. I just want peace now. I dont want equity or justice, I dont want happiness; I just want peace. We wont live very much longer, and then. . . . . . ."

She laughed, short, mirthless, not moving. "And then he will have forgotten me."

"That's your risk. Because, remember," he cried; "remember! I dont ask this. I did not ask you to leave him, to bring him to us. You can go up now and wake him and take him with you. But if you do not, if you leave him with us and turn your back on this house and go away——Think well. If you like, take him with you tonight, to the hotel or wherever and think about it and make up your mind and bring him back tomorrow or come yourself and tell me what you have decided."

"I have decided now," she said.

"That you leave him here of your own free will. That we give him the home and care and affection which is his right both as a helpless child and as our gra—grand——and that in return for this, you are to make no attempt to see him or communicate with him as long as we live. That is your understanding, your agreement? Think well."

"Yes," she said. "I have to do it."

"But you do not. You can take him with you now; all this tonight can be as if it had never happened. You are his mother; I still believe that any mother is better—better than. . . . . . . How do you have to?"

"Because I dont know whether I can buy him enough food to eat and enough clothes to keep him warm and medicine if he is sick," she said. "Do you understand that?"

"I understand that this—your——this other man does not earn as much in his line as Roger did in his. But you tell me that Roger did not always earn enough for the four of you: nevertheless you never thought while Roger was alive of leaving the boy with us. And now, with one less mouth to feed, you try to tell me that you——"

"I'll tell you, if you will listen a minute," she said. "I'm going to have another child." Now he did not speak at all; his unfinished sentence seemed to hang between them. They stood face to face but they could not see one another: just the two vague shapes with the snow falling between them and upon them, though since her back was to the streetlamp she could see him the better of the two. After a while he said quietly,

"I see. Yes. And you know that this other child is——is not——"

"Not Roger's. Yes. Roger and I were——But no matter. I know, this time. Roger and I both know. So we will need money and that's what Roger was trying to do in that meet. The ship he won a prize with the first day was too slow, obsolete. But that was all we could get and he outflew them, beat them on the pylons, by turning the pylons closer than the others dared for that little money. Then Saturday he had a chance to fly a ship that was dangerous, but he had a chance to win two thousand dollars in the race. That would have fixed us up. But the ship came to pieces in the air. Maybe I could have stopped him. I dont know. But maybe I could have. But I didn't. I didn't try, anyhow. So now we didn't get that money, and we left most of the first day's prize to send his body here when they get it out of the lake."

"Ah," Dr Shumann said. "I see. Yes. So you are giving us the chance to—the opportunity to. . . . . ." Suddenly he cried: "If I just knew that he is Roger's! If I just knew! Cant you tell me? Cant you give me some sign, some little sign? Any little sign?" She didn't move. The light came through the snow, across her shoulder, and she could see him a little—a small thin man with untidy thin irongray hair and the snow whispering in it, standing with his face turned aside and his hand not before it exactly but held palmout between his face and hers. After a while she said,

"Maybe you would rather take a little time to think about it. To decide." She could not see his face now: only the lifted hand; she seemed to be speaking to the hand: "Suppose I wait at the hotel until tomorrow, so——" The hand moved, a faint motion from the wrist as though it were trying to push her voice away. But she repeated, once more, as though for a record: "You mean you dont want me to wait?" But only the hand moved again, replied; she turned quietly and went down the steps, feeling for each step beneath the snow, and went on down the walk, vanishing into the drowsing pantomime of the snow, not fast. She did not look back. Dr Shumann did not watch her. He heard the engine of the car start, but he was already turning, entering the house, fumbling at the door for a moment before he found the knob and entered, his hair and shoulders (he was in his shirtsleeves) powdered with snow. He went on down the hall; his wife, sitting beside the bed in the darkened room where the boy was asleep, heard him blunder against something in the hall and then saw him come into the door, framed so against the lighted hall, holding to the doorframe, the light glinting in the melting snow in his untidy hair.

"If we just had a sign," he said. He entered, stumbling again. She rose and approached him but he pushed her aside, entering. "Let me be," he said.

"Shhhhhh," she said. "Dont wake him. You come on and eat your supper."

"Let me alone," he said, pushing with his hand at the empty air now since she stood back now, watching him approach the bed, fumbling at the footboard. But his voice was quiet enough. "Go out," he said. "Leave me be. Go away and leave me be."

"You come on and eat your supper and lay down."

"Go on. I'm all right, I tell you." She obeyed; he stood holding to the bed's footboard and heard her feet move slowly up the hall and cease. Then he moved, fumbling until he found the lightcord, the bulb, and turned it on. The little boy stirred, turning his face from the light. The garment in which he slept was a man's shirt, an oldfashioned garment with a onceglazed bosom, soft now from many washings, pinned about his throat with a gold brooch and with the sleeves cut recently off at his wrists. On the pillow beside him the toy aeroplane rested. Suddenly Dr Shumann stooped and took the boy by the shoulder and began to shake him. The toy aeroplane slid from the pillow; with his other hand Dr Shumann flipped it to the floor, still shaking the little boy. "Roger," he said, "wake up. Wake up, Roger." The boy waked; without moving he blinked up at the man's face bending over him.

"Laverne," he said. "Jack. Where's Laverne? Where'm I at?"

"Laverne's gone," Dr Shumann said, still shaking the boy as though he had forgot to tell his muscles to desist. "You're at home, but Laverne is gone. Gone, I tell you. Are you going to cry? Hey?" The boy blinked up at him, then he turned and put out his hand toward the pillow beside him.

"Where's my new job?" he said. "Where's my ship?"

"Your ship, hey?" Dr Shumann said. "Your ship, hey?" He stooped and caught up the toy and held it up, his face twisted into a grimace of gnomelike rage, and whirled and hurled the toy at the wall and, while the boy watched him, ran to it and began to stamp upon it with blind maniac fury. The little boy made one sharp sound: then, silent, raised on one elbow, his eyes a little wide as though with curious interest alone, he watched the shabby wildhaired old man jumping up and down upon the shapeless trivial mass of blue-and-yellow tin in maniacal ludicrosity. Then the little boy saw him pause, stoop, take up the ruined toy and apparently begin to try to tear it to pieces with his hands. His wife, sitting beside the livingroom stove, heard his feet too through the flimsy walls, feeling the floor shake too, then she heard him approaching up the hall, fast now. She was small too—a faded woman with faded eyes and a quiet faded face sitting in the stuffy room containing a worn divan and fumed oak chairs and a fumed oak revolving bookcase racked neatly with battered medical books from whose bindings the gilt embossed titles had long since vanished, and a table littered with medical magazines and on which lay at the moment a thick cap with earmuffs, a pair of mittens and a small scuffed black bag. She did not move: she was sitting there watching the door when Dr Shumann came in, holding one hand out before him; she did not stir even then: she just looked quietly at the mass of money. "It was in that airplane!" he said. "He even had to hide his money from her!"

"No," the wife said. "She hid it from him."

"No!" he shouted. "He hid it from her. For the boy. Do you think a woman would ever hide money and or anything else and then forget where she put it? And where would she get a hundred and seventy-five dollars, anyway?"

"Yes," the wife said, the faded eyes filled with immeasurable and implacable unforgiving; " where would she get a hundred and seventy-five dollars that she would have to hide from both of them in a child's toy?" He looked at her for a long moment.

"Ah," he said. He said it quietly: "Oh. Yes. I see." Then he cried, "But no matter! It dont matter now!" He stooped and swung open the door of the stove and shut it again; she did not move, not even when, glancing past him as he stooped, she saw in the door and looking in at them, the little boy in the man's shirt and carrying the battered mass of the toy in one hand and the clothes which he had worn wadded in the other, against his chest and his cap already on. Dr Shumann had not seen him yet; he rose from the stove; it was the draft of course, from the opening and closing of the door, but it did seem as though it were the money itself passing in flame and fire up the pipe with a deep faint roar into nothing as Dr Shumann stood again, looking down at her. "It's our boy," he said; then he shouted: "It's our boy, I tell you!" Then he collapsed; he seemed to let go all at once though not hard because of his spareness, onto his knees beside the chair, his head in her lap, crying.

When the city room began to fill that evening a copyboy noticed the overturned wastebasket beside the reporter's desk and the astonishing amount of savagely defaced and torn copy which littered the adjacent floor. The copyboy was a bright lad, about to graduate from highschool; he had not only ambitions but dreams too. He gathered up all the sheets, whole and in fragments, from the floor and emptied the wastebasket and, sitting at the reporter's desk he began to sort them, discarding and fitting and resorting at the last to paste; and then, his eyes big with excitement and exultation and then downright triumph, he regarded what he had salvaged and restored to order and coherence—the sentences and paragraphs which he believed to be not only news but the beginning of literature:

> On Thursday Roger Shumann flew a race against four competitors, and won. On Saturday he flew against but one competitor. But that competitor was Death, and Roger Shumann lost. And so today a lone aeroplane flew out over the lake on the wings of dawn and circled the spot where Roger Shumann got the Last Checkered Flag, and vanished back into the dawn from whence it came.

> Thus two friends told him farewell. Two friends, yet two competitors too, whom he had met in fair contest and conquered in the lonely sky from which he fell, dropping a simple wreath to mark his Last Pylon

It stopped there, but the copyboy did not. "O Jesus," he whispered. "Maybe Hagood will let me finish it!" already moving toward the desk where Hagood now sat though the copyboy had not seen him enter. Hagood had just sat down; the copyboy, his mouth already open, paused behind Hagood. Then he became more complete vassal to surprise than ever, for lying on Hagood's desk and weighted neatly down by an empty whiskey bottle was another sheet of copy which Hagood and the copyboy read together:

> At midnight last night the search for the body of Roger Shumann, racing pilot who plunged into the lake Saturday p.m. was finally abandoned by a threeplace biplane of about eighty horsepower which managed to fly out over the water and return without falling to pieces and dropping a wreath of flowers into the water approximately three quarters of a mile away from where Shumann's body is generally supposed to be since they were precision pilots and so did not miss the entire lake. Mrs Shumann departed

with her husband and children for Ohio, where it is understood that their six year old son will spend an indefinite time with some of his grandparents and where any and all finders of Roger Shumann are kindly requested to forward any and all of same.

and beneath this, savagely in pencil: *I guess this is what you want you bastard and now I am going down to Amboise st. and get drunk a while and if you dont know where Amboise st. is ask your son to tell you and if you dont know what drunk is come down there and look at me and when you come bring some jack because I am on a credit*

Chronology

1897   Born William Cuthbert Falkner, September 25, in New Albany, northeast Mississippi, first child of Maud Butler Falkner and Murry Cuthbert Falkner. Father was eldest son of John Wesley Thompson Falkner, eldest son of William Clark Falkner. (Great-grandfather William Clark Falkner, born in Tennessee in 1825, had come to Ripley, Mississippi, in his teens and become a lawyer, slave-owning planter, and colonel in Confederate Army. He changed his name, according to family legend, from Faulkner to Falkner to avoid confusion with "some no-account folks," wrote several books, including a successful romance, *The White Rose of Memphis*, built a short, narrow-gauge railroad, and was elected to the state legislature. Shot to death by an embittered former partner in 1889.) Grandfather John Wesley (banker, lawyer, and politician) controls Gulf & Ship Island Railroad where father Murry Cuthbert is employed.

1898–1901 Father becomes treasurer of railroad (renamed Gulf & Chicago); family moves to Ripley. Brothers Murry C. Falkner, Jr. (nicknamed "Jack"), born June 26, 1899, and John Wesley Thompson Falkner III, born September 24, 1901. William and Murry are dangerously ill with scarlet fever.

1902   Grandfather sells railroad and father loses his job. Family moves in September forty miles southwest to Oxford, seat of Lafayette County, where grandfather is influential resident of seventeen years. Father begins series of small business ventures. Maternal grandmother, Lelia Dean Swift Butler ("Damuddy"), moves into family home. Caroline Barr ("Mammy Callie"), born in slavery, is hired to take care of children. She tells them stories and takes them on long walks in the woods, teaching them to recognize different birds.

1905   Enters first grade.

1906   Skips to third grade. Grandmother Sallie Murry Falkner dies December 21.

1907   Grandmother Lelia Butler dies June 1. Third brother, Dean Swift Falkner, born August 15.

1909–13 Works in father's livery stable beginning in June. ("Being the eldest of four boys, I escaped my mother's influence pretty easy, since my father thought it was fine for me to apprentice to the business.") Athletic activities are curtailed for several years when he is put in a tight canvas brace to correct shoulder stoop in winter 1910. Draws, writes stories and poems, and starts to play hooky. ("I never did like to go to school and I stopped going as soon as I got big enough to play hooky and not be caught at it.") Increasingly attracted to Estelle Oldham (b. 1896), daughter of Republican political appointee Lemuel E. Oldham; shows her his poems. Reads *The Arkansas Traveller*, *Pilgrim's Progress*, and *Moby-Dick*, telling his brother Murry, "It's one of the best books ever written." Reads Mark Twain, Joel Chandler Harris, Shakespeare, Fielding, Conrad, Balzac, and Hugo, among others. Shoots his dog accidentally while hunting rabbits in the fall of 1911 and does not hunt again for several years. Becomes active Boy Scout and begins to play high school football in fall 1913.

1914–15 Shows his poetry to Phil Stone, four years his senior. Stone becomes close friend, gives him books to read ("Swinburne, Keats and a number of the then moderns, such as Conrad Aiken, and the Imagists in verse and Sherwood Anderson and the others in prose") and introduces him to writer and fellow townsman Stark Young. Enters eleventh and final grade at Oxford High School. Helps plan yearbook and does sketches for it. Pitches and plays shortstop on baseball team. Returns to school briefly in fall 1915 to play football, then drops out completely. Hunts deer and bear at camp of "General" James Stone, Phil's father, thirty miles west of Oxford, near Batesville.

1916–17 Begins work early in year as clerk at grandfather's bank, the First National, and hates it. Drinks his grandfather's liquor. ("Grandfather thought it was the janitor. Hard on the janitor.") By end of year spends much of his time on nearby campus of University of Mississippi, where he meets Ben Wasson. Contributes drawings to "Social Activities" section of university yearbook, *Ole Miss*. Continues to write verse influenced by Swinburne and A. E. Housman, among others.

1918   Estelle Oldham tells Falkner she is "ready to elope" with him, despite her engagement to Cornell Franklin, a successful lawyer practicing in Hawaii and much favored by her family. Falkner insists on asking the Oldhams' consent, but both families oppose marriage, and Estelle's wedding to Franklin is set for April 18. Tries to enlist for pilot training in U.S. Army but is rejected for being under regulation height and weight. Joins Phil Stone, then studying law at Yale, in New Haven early in April. Meets poets Stephen Vincent Benét and Robert Hillyer. Reads Yeats. Works as ledger clerk at Winchester Repeating Arms Co., where name is recorded "Faulkner." Determined to join British forces, he and Stone practice English accents and mannerisms. Accepted by Royal Air Force in mid-June, reports to Toronto Recruits' Depot on July 9, listing birthplace as Middlesex, England, birthdate as May 25, 1898, and spelling his name "Faulkner." Brother Murry enlists in Marines and is wounded in the Argonne. Faulkner's experience is limited to 179 days of ground school. ("The war quit on us before we could do anything about it.") Discharged in December, returns to Oxford wearing officer's uniform and RAF wings, suffering, he claims, from effects of crashing a plane.

1919   Continues to work on poetry; drinks with friends in Clarksdale and Charleston, Mississippi, Memphis, and New Orleans. Composes long cycle of poems influenced by classic pastoral tradition and modern poets, especially T. S. Eliot. Sees Estelle frequently during her four-month visit home from Hawaii with daughter Victoria. "L'Après-Midi d'un Faune," forty-line poem, appears in *The New Republic* August 6. Other poems are not accepted. Registers as a special student at University of Mississippi in September, where father is now Assistant Secretary of university. Studies French, Spanish, and English; publishes poems in campus paper, *The Mississippian*, and Oxford *Eagle*. In December, agrees to be initiated into Sigma Alpha Epsilon fraternity because of family tradition. Given nickname "Count No 'Count" by fellow students, who consider him aloof and affected.

1920   Translates and publishes four poems by Paul Verlaine in
            The Mississippian, February to March. Contributes draw-
            ings to the yearbook. Awarded $10 poetry prize by Pro-
            fessor Calvin S. Brown in June. Does odd jobs and assists
            with Boy Scout troop. Helps build clay tennis court be-
            side Falkners' university-owned home; becomes a good
            player. Joins the Marionettes, a new university drama
            group; finishes one-act play (not produced) and works on
            stage props and set design. Withdraws from university in
            November during crackdown on fraternities. Receives
            commission as honorary second lieutenant in RAF; wears
            uniform on various occasions. Writes *The Marionettes*, an
            experimental verse play; hand-letters several copies of its
            fifty-five pages, adding illustrations influenced by Aubrey
            Beardsley. Wasson sells four at $5 apiece. The Marionettes
            decline to produce it.

1921   Presents Estelle Franklin with eighty-eight-page bound
            typescript volume of poems entitled *Vision in Spring* dur-
            ing one of her visits home. Accepts invitation of Stark
            Young to visit him in New York City in the fall. Rents
            room in Greenwich Village and works as clerk in Lord &
            Taylor bookstore managed by Elizabeth Prall. Returns
            home in December to become postmaster at university
            post office.

1922   Writes while on duty at the post office, neglects custom-
            ers, is reluctant to sort mail, does not always forward it,
            and keeps patrons' magazines and periodicals in the office
            until he and his friends have read them. Grandfather Falk-
            ner dies in March. Does last drawing for yearbook *Ole
            Miss*. Plays golf. Writes poems, stories, and criticism. *The
            Double Dealer*, a New Orleans magazine, publishes his
            short poem "Portrait." Continues to read widely. Receives
            through Stone books ordered from New Haven, including
            works by Conrad Aiken, Eugene O'Neill, and Elinor
            Wylie.

1923   The Four Seas Company of Boston agrees to publish
            Orpheus, and Other Poems if Faulkner will pay manufactur-
            ing costs; Faulkner declines, saying, "on re-reading some
            of the things, I see that they aren't particularly signifi-
            cant." Becomes scoutmaster.

1924   Receives gift of James Joyce's *Ulysses* from Phil Stone.
        Reads Voltaire and Thomas Beer, whose stories appeared
        in magazines at this time. (Faulkner later said he "influ-
        enced me a lot.") In May, Four Seas agrees to publish
        cycle of pastoral poems, *The Marble Faun*, and Faulkner
        sends $400 to cover publication costs. Phil Stone writes
        preface and takes active role in negotiations. Continues to
        write stories and verse, compiling gift volumes for friends.
        Removed as scoutmaster for drinking. Complaints of neg-
        ligence investigated by postal authorities and Faulkner re-
        signs October 31. ("I reckon I'll be at the beck and call of
        folks with money all my life, but thank God I won't ever
        again have to be at the beck and call of every son of a
        bitch who's got two cents to buy a stamp.") Visits Eliza-
        beth Prall in New Orleans and meets her husband, Sher-
        wood Anderson, whose work he admires. *The Marble
        Faun* published in December.

1925   Leaves for New Orleans in January, intending to work his
        way to Europe. Accepts Elizabeth Prall Anderson's invi-
        tation to stay in spare room while Sherwood Anderson is
        away on a lecture tour. By February moves into quarters
        rented from artist William Spratling and begins contrib-
        uting essays, poems, stories, and sketches to the New Or-
        leans *Times-Picayune* and *The Double Dealer*. Begins work
        on manuscript of novel then called *Mayday*, praised by
        Sherwood Anderson, now a close friend. ("We would
        meet in the afternoons . . . we'd walk and he'd talk and
        I'd listen, we'd meet in the evenings and we'd go to a
        drinking place and we'd sit around till one or two o'clock
        drinking.") Offended when Anderson, now busy with his
        own work, tells his wife he will do anything for Faulkner,
        "so long as I don't have to read his damn manu-
        script." Anderson recommends Faulkner's novel to pub-
        lisher, Boni & Liveright. Meets Anita Loos. Visits Stone
        family at Pascagoula on Gulf Coast in June; falls in love
        with Helen Baird, a sculptor he had met in New Orleans.
        Sails on a freighter from New Orleans to Genoa with Wil-
        liam Spratling July 7; throws mass of manuscript over-
        board en route. Travels through Italy and Switzerland to
        Paris, settling on Left Bank. Goes to Louvre and various
        galleries; writes to mother in August, ". . . went to a very
        modern exhibition the other day—futurist and vorticist. I
        was talking to a painter, a real one. He wont go to the

exhibitions at all. He says its all right to paint the damn things, but as far as looking at them, he'd rather go to the Luxembourg gardens and watch the children sail their boats. And I agree with him." In September writes, "I have spent afternoon after afternoon in the Louvre . . . I have seen Rodin's museum, and 2 private collections of Matissse and Picasso (who are yet alive and painting) as well as numberless young and struggling moderns. And Cezanne! That man dipped his brush in light." Years later, says of James Joyce in Paris: "I would go to some effort to go to the café that he inhabited to look at him. But that was the only literary man that I remember seeing in Europe in those days." Works on articles, poems, and fiction, including two novels, *Mosquito* and *Elmer* (never finished). Grows beard. Travels in France on foot and by train. Visits England briefly, writes of Kent countryside: "Quietest most restful country under the sun. No wonder that Joseph Conrad could write such fine books here." Finds England too expensive and returns to France. Writes his mother, "I am expecting to hear from Liveright when I reach Paris. I waked up yesterday with such a grand feeling that something out of the ordinary has happened to me that I am firmly expecting news of some sort—either very good or very bad." Hears on return that novel *Mayday*, retitled *Soldiers' Pay*, accepted for publication. Sails home for Christmas.

1926   Presents a hand-lettered, illustrated tale (giving it the same title originally given novel—*Mayday*) to Helen Baird in January. Moves in with Spratling at 632 St. Peter Street, New Orleans, in February, going back to Oxford for brief visits. *Soldiers' Pay* published by Boni & Liveright February 25. Mother, shocked by sexual material in the novel, says that the best thing he could do is leave the country; father refuses to read it. Reviews are generally favorable— one reviewer notes its "hard intelligence as well as consummate pity." Hand-letters a sequence of poems called *Helen: A Courtship* for Helen Baird in June. Vacations in Pascagoula, then returns to New Orleans. Collaborates with Spratling on a book of drawings, *Sherwood Anderson & Other Famous Creoles*, which they publish themselves in an edition of 400 copies that sells out in a week at $1.50 a copy. Book includes Faulkner's parody of Sherwood Anderson, which widens the breach between them.

1927   Gives Estelle's daughter, Victoria, a forty-seven-page tale,
            The Wishing Tree, typed and bound in varicolored paper,
            as a present for her eighth birthday. Helen Baird marries
            Guy C. Lyman in March. *Mosquitoes* published April 30.
            Begins to concentrate on Mississippi material. Works on
            novel he calls *Father Abraham*, about an avaricious family
            named Snopes, but puts it aside in favor of another manu-
            script, *Flags in the Dust*, depicting four generations of Sar-
            toris family, based on Southern and family lore. Horace
            Liveright rejects *Flags in the Dust* and advises Faulkner not
            to offer it elsewhere.

1928   *Flags in the Dust* submitted to more than twelve publish-
            ers, all of whom reject it. Early in the year, begins "Twi-
            light," story about the Compson family. ("One day I
            seemed to shut a door, between me and all publishers'
            addresses and book lists. I said to myself, Now I can
            write.") Centered on Caddie Compson, it becomes *The
            Sound and the Fury*. ("I loved her so much I couldn't de-
            cide to give her life just for the duration of a short story.
            She deserved more than that. So my novel was created,
            almost in spite of myself.") Sends *Flags in the Dust*, exten-
            sively revised, and group of short stories to Ben Wasson,
            now New York literary agent. Continues to work on new
            novel. In September, Harcourt, Brace and Company
            agrees to publish *Flags in the Dust* on condition that it be
            cut. Faulkner uses advance to go to New York to work on
            it. Dismayed at the cuts Wasson says are necessary, allows
            him to do most of the cutting. (" 'The trouble is,' he said,
            'is that you had about 6 books in here. You were trying
            to write them all at once.' He showed me what he meant,
            what he had done, and I realized for the first time that I
            had done better than I knew . . .") Tries unsuccessfully
            to sell short stories. Rents a small furnished flat and re-
            vises and types manuscript of *The Sound and the Fury*. Fin-
            ishes; drinks heavily; found unconscious by friends Eric J.
            (Jim) Devine and Leon Scales, who take care of him in
            their apartment. Returns home in December.

1929   *Sartoris* (the cut and retitled *Flags in the Dust*) published
            by Harcourt, Brace and Company January 21. Starts writ-
            ing *Sanctuary* in January and finishes it in May. *The Sound
            and the Fury* accepted by new firm of Jonathan Cape and
            Harrison Smith in February, but Smith says *Sanctuary* is

too shocking to publish. Marries Estelle (divorced from Cornell Franklin, April 29), in Presbyterian Church in nearby College Hill, June 20. They honeymoon at Pascagoula, where Faulkner reads proofs of *The Sound and the Fury* (published October 7). Returns to Oxford and takes job on nightshift at the university power plant. Writes *As I Lay Dying* while at work, beginning October 29 and finishing December 11. ("I am going to write a book by which, at a pinch, I can stand or fall if I never touch ink again.") Visits mother daily. Reviews of *The Sound and the Fury* are enthusiastic, sales disappointing.

1930   Begins publishing stories in national magazines in April when "A Rose for Emily" appears in *Forum*. Achieves mass-market success when *The Saturday Evening Post* accepts "Thrift." Later "Red Leaves" and "Lizards in Jamshyd's Courtyard" sell for $750 apiece (a better price than he had received for any novel). *Scribner's* accepts "Dry September" (published January 1931). Purchases rundown antebellum house, names it Rowan Oak, and begins renovation, doing much of the work himself. Moves into it in June with Estelle and her two children, Victoria (born 1919) and Malcolm (born 1923) Franklin. Chatto & Windus publishes *Soldiers' Pay*, with introduction by Richard Hughes, June 20, first of Faulkner's works to appear in England. *As I Lay Dying*, where for the first time in print the Mississippi locale is identified as Yoknapatawpha County, published October 6 by Cape & Smith. Harrison Smith now thinks *Sanctuary* may make money for ailing publishing firm, and sends galley proofs in November. Though the resetting costs Faulkner $270, he revises extensively "to make out of it something which would not shame *The Sound and the Fury* and *As I Lay Dying*." Finishes revision in December.

1931   Daughter, born January 11, named for Faulkner's great-aunt Alabama, dies after nine days; Faulkner is grief-stricken. *Sanctuary*, published February 9 by Cape & Smith, sells 3,519 copies by March 4—more than combined sales of *The Sound and the Fury* and *As I Lay Dying*; elicits high praise and increasing attention for Faulkner abroad. Maurice Coindreau writes to ask if he can be Faulkner's French translator. Gallimard acquires the rights to *As I Lay Dying* and *Sanctuary*. Many in Oxford are shocked by

Sanctuary; father Murry Falkner tells a coed carrying *Sanctuary* that it isn't fit for a nice girl to read. Mother Maud Falkner defends her son. Chatto & Windus publishes *The Sound and the Fury* in April. "Spotted Horses" appears in *Scribner's* in June. Begins work on novel tentatively titled *Dark House*. *These 13*, a collection of stories, published by Cape & Smith September 21; sells better than any of his works except *Sanctuary*. Attends Southern Writers' Conference at University of Virginia in Charlottesville on his way to New York in October. Drinks heavily. Wooed by publishers Bennett Cerf and Donald Klopfer of Random House, Harold Guinzburg and George Oppenheimer of Viking, and Alfred A. Knopf. To keep him away from other publishers, Harrison Smith has Milton Abernethy take Faulkner on ship cruise to Jacksonville, Florida, and back to New York. Firm of Cape & Smith fails, owing him royalties that will eventually amount to over $4,000. Signs with new firm, Harrison Smith, Inc. Meets Dorothy Parker, Robert Lovett, H. L. Mencken, Robert Benchley, John O'Hara, John Dos Passos, Frank Sullivan, and Corey Ford (will continue to see some of them on later trips). Spends hours talking and drinking with Dashiell Hammett and Lillian Hellman. Meets Nathanael West. Works on new novel and stories, one of them—"Turn About"—based on tale told by Lovett (finished in Oxford and published in *The Saturday Evening Post*, March 1932). Finishes introduction to Random House's Modern Library edition of *Sanctuary*. Makes contacts with film studios and writes film treatments. Earns enough money during stay in New York to pay bills at home. Drinks heavily; friends contact Estelle. She arrives early in December, and they return to Oxford before the middle of the month.

1932   Finishes novel now called *Light in August* (earlier *Dark House*) in February. Goes to work May 7 at Metro-Goldwyn-Mayer studio in Culver City, California, on six-week, $500-per-week contract. Leaves the studio almost immediately, not returning for a week. ("When they took me into a projection room and kept assuring me that it was all going to be very, very easy, I got flustered.") Takes $30-a-month cottage on Jackson Street near studio and works unsuccessfully on series of scripts. At the end of contract makes plans to return home, but director-producer Howard Hawks hires him as scriptwriter for

movie *Today We Live*, based on "Turn About," beginning
his longest Hollywood association. Father Murry Falkner
dies August 6, and Faulkner returns home as head of
family. "Dad left mother solvent for only about 1 year,"
he writes Ben Wasson. "Then it is me." Agreement with
Hawks allows him to work in Oxford. Takes stepson
Malcolm on walks through woods and bottoms, teaching
him to distinguish dangerous from harmless snakes. Returns to Hollywood in October for three weeks, taking
mother and brother Dean with him. *Light in August*
published October 6 by new firm of Harrison Smith and
Robert Haas. Paramount buys film rights to *Sanctuary*
(released as *The Story of Temple Drake*, May 12, 1933).
Faulkner receives $6,000 from sale. Continues working
for MGM in Oxford. Spends part of Hollywood earnings
on renovation of Rowan Oak.

1933   Begins flying lessons with Captain Vernon Omlie in February and soon flies regularly. Solos in April. *A Green
Bough*, poems, published April 20 by Smith & Haas. *Today
We Live* premieres in Oxford. Travels to New Orleans in
May to work on film script, *Louisiana Lou*, but refuses to
return to Hollywood for revisions, and studio terminates
contract May 13. Daughter Jill born June 24. Buys more
land adjoining Rowan Oak. Works on stories and plans
two novels, *The Peasants* (with Snopes characters) and *Requiem for a Nun*. Prepares a three-color marked copy (now
lost) for a projected Random House limited edition of
The Sound and the Fury (never published) and writes an
introduction. ("I wrote this book and learned to
read. . . . I discovered that there is actually something to
which the shabby term Art not only can, but must, be
applied.") Buys Omlie's Waco C cabin biplane in fall.
Concerned about brother Dean's future, arranges to have
Omlie train Dean as a pilot. Flies with Omlie and Dean
to New York City to meet with publishers early in November. Returns in time to go hunting. Earns pilot's
license December 14.

1934   Begins new novel (reusing title *Dark House*). Flies with
Omlie to New Orleans for dedication of Shushan Airport
February 15; participates in air shows with Omlie, Dean,
and others, billed as "William Faulkner's (Famous Author)

Air Circus." *Doctor Martino and Other Stories* published April 16 by Smith & Haas. Pressed for money, writes a series of Civil War stories centering on Bayard Sartoris and black companion Ringo, hoping to sell them to *The Saturday Evening Post*. Goes back to work with Hawks in Hollywood for $1,000 a week, from the end of June to late July. Finishes script *Sutter's Gold* in Oxford. Brother Murry is member of FBI team that kills John Dillinger in Chicago, July 22. Dissatisfied with lack of progress on *Dark House*. Writes Smith that novel "is not quite ripe yet," but "I have a title for it which I like, by the way: ABSALOM, ABSALOM; the story is of a man who wanted a son through pride, and got too many of them and they destroyed him." Puts it aside and converts unpublished story "This Kind of Courage" into novel, *Pylon*. Sends first chapter to Harrison Smith in November and finishes it by end of December.

1935 Forms Okatoba Hunting and Fishing Club with R. L. Sullivan and Whitson Cook, receiving hunting and fishing rights to General Stone's land, several thousand acres near Batesville, Mississippi, at eastern edge of Mississippi Delta. *Pylon* published by Smith & Haas, March 25. Pressed for money, works intensively at writing stories meant to sell. Writes his agent in April: "What I really need is $10,000. With that I could pay my debt, and insurance for two years and really write. I mean write." Returns to *Absalom, Absalom!*. Resumes occasional flying, though the Waco now belongs to Dean. Goes to New York September 23 to negotiate a better contract with Smith & Haas and sell stories to magazines. Returns home October 13, without gaining much from the trip. Brother Dean is killed when the Waco crashes November 10. Distraught and guilt-ridden, Faulkner assumes responsibility for Dean's pregnant wife, Louise, and stays for several weeks with her and his grieving mother, who feels suicidal. On December 10, goes to Hollywood for five-week, $1,000-per-week assignment with Hawks for Twentieth Century-Fox, taking *Absalom, Absalom!* with him. Begins intermittent and sometimes intense fifteen-year relationship with Hawks's 28-year-old secretary and later scriptgirl, Mississippi divorcee Meta Doherty Carpenter.

1936   With successful completion of script (*The Road to Glory*),
            begins to drink heavily. Goes home on sick leave January
            13. Finishes final draft of *Absalom, Absalom!* January 31.
            Needs money, and does not want to stop making final
            revisions of novel to write stories. Signs new contract with
            Twentieth Century-Fox (again for $1,000 a week until
            "employment shall be terminated by either party"); re-
            turns to Hollywood February 26, moving into the Beverly
            Hills Hotel. Works on several scripts, sees old friends.
            Goes boar hunting with Nathanael West in April. Returns
            to Oxford early in June and writes to agent when his sto-
            ries don't sell: "Since last summer I seem to have got out
            of the habit of writing trash." Goes back to Hollywood in
            mid-July (for six-month, $750-per-week contract), taking
            Estelle and Jill with him, and moves into a large house
            just north of Santa Monica. Captain Omlie dies in crash
            as passenger on commercial flight August 6. Sees Meta,
            who has decided to marry pianist Wolfgang Rebner. Es-
            telle and Faulkner both drink heavily. *Absalom, Absalom!*,
            published October 26 by Random House (which has ab-
            sorbed the firm of Smith & Haas), receives critical praise,
            though sales are not enough to allow freedom from script-
            writing. Proposes to convert Bayard Sartoris–Ringo sto-
            ries into novel and is encouraged by Bennett Cerf and
            Robert Haas. Harrison Smith leaves Random House.
            Laid off from Twentieth Century-Fox in December after
            earning almost $20,000. Makes final payment on Rowan
            Oak.

1937   Returns to studio from layoff February 26 at salary of
            $1,000 a week. Family moves closer to studio. Unhappi-
            ness at work and home exacerbates Faulkner's drinking.
            March to June, works on *Drums Along the Mohawk*, di-
            rected by John Ford. Estelle and Jill return to Oxford in
            late May. Maurice Coindreau stays with Faulkner for week
            in June to discuss French translation of *The Sound and the
            Fury*. Returns to Rowan Oak in late August, having
            earned over $21,000 for the year working for Twentieth
            Century-Fox. Begins the story "The Wild Palms." Goes to
            New York in mid-October to prepare the Bayard–Ringo
            stories for publication with new Random House editor,
            Saxe Commins. Stays at Algonquin Hotel; sees old
            friends, including Harrison Smith, Joel Sayre, Eric J. De-
            vine, and Meta Rebner. Renews friendship with Sherwood

Anderson ("a giant . . . in an earth populated . . . by pygmies"). Drinks heavily, collapses, and burns back severely on Algonquin steam pipe. Treated by doctor, then cared for by Eric J. Devine. Sherwood Anderson visits him. Returns to Oxford accompanied by Devine. Resumes work on novel, *If I Forget Thee, Jerusalem* (to be published as *The Wild Palms* at his editor's insistence); says the theme of the book is: "Between grief and nothing I will take grief." Reads poetry aloud and does crossword puzzles with stepdaughter Victoria after breakup of her first marriage ("He kept me alive," she later says). Intense pain from burn makes sleeping difficult.

1938   *The Unvanquished*, Bayard–Ringo stories, reworked with new material into novel, published February 15 by Random House. MGM buys screen rights for $25,000, of which Faulkner receives $19,000 after payment of commissions. Buys 320-acre farm seventeen miles northeast of Oxford and names it Greenfield Farm; insists on raising mules despite brother John's (who is tenant manager) preference for more profitable cattle. Still suffering from burn; despite skin-graft infection at the end of February, continues work on *If I Forget Thee, Jerusalem*; writes to Haas in July: "To me it was written just as if I had sat on the one side of a wall and the paper was on the other and my hand with the pen thrust through the wall and writing not only on invisible paper but in pitch darkness too . . ." Returns to work on Snopes book, working title *The Peasants*, and plots out two more volumes to form trilogy. Goes to New York to read proof of novel now titled *The Wild Palms* in late September. Takes Harold Ober as literary agent.

1939   Elected to National Institute of Arts and Letters in January. *The Wild Palms* published January 19, reviewed in *Time* cover story, sells more than 1,000 copies a week and tops sales of *Sanctuary* by late March. Raises $6,000 (by cashing in life insurance policy and obtaining advance from Random House) to save Phil Stone from financial disaster. Works on Snopes trilogy and writes stories. Helps brother John at Greenfield Farm, sometimes serving tenants in commissary. Retitles Snopes trilogy *The Hamlet*, *The Town*, and *The Mansion*. Takes short holidays in New York City in October and December after testifying in Washington, D.C., in plagiarism suit brought against Twentieth Century-Fox by writer who claims (wrongly) to have written *The Road to Glory*. Donates manuscript of *Absalom, Absalom!* to relief fund for Spanish loyalists. "Barn Burning" wins first O. Henry Memorial Award ($300 prize) for best short story published in an American magazine.

1940   Works on proofs of *The Hamlet*. Caroline Barr, in her mid-nineties, suffers stroke and dies January 31. Faulkner gives eulogy in parlor of Rowan Oak. ("She was born in bondage and with a dark skin and most of her early maturity was passed in a dark and tragic time for the land of her birth. She went through vicissitudes which she had not caused; she assumed cares and griefs which were not even her cares and griefs. She was paid wages for this, but pay is still just money. And she never received very much of that . . .") Writes stories about black families. *The Hamlet*, published by Random House April 1, is reviewed favorably, but sales fall below those of *The Wild Palms*. Expenses (debts and taxes) are large because of property— "It's probably vanity as much as anything else which makes me want to hold onto it. I own a larger parcel of it than anybody else in town and nobody gave me any of it or loaned me a nickel to buy any of it with and all my relations and fellow townsmen including the borrowers and frank spongers, all prophesied I'd never be more than a bum." Tries to get a job in Hollywood. Works on a series of stories about related black and white families which can form a novel. Appeals to Random House for higher advances against royalties. After unsatisfactory negotiations, goes to New York late in June to negotiate with Harold Guinzburg of The Viking Press, but Viking cannot substantially improve on Random House offer. Resumes writing stories (five published in the year). Drinking at annual deer hunt in November causes near-fatal hemorrhage.

1941   Wires literary agent Harold Ober on January 16 asking for $100; uses it to pay light bill. Organizes Lafayette County aircraft warning system in late June. Wishing to do more in anticipation of U.S. entry into W.W. II, thinks about securing military commission. "The Bear" accepted by *The Saturday Evening Post* for $1,000 in November.

Finishes work on series of stories forming novel *Go Down, Moses* in December.

1942   Goes to Washington, D.C., in unsuccessful attempt to secure military commission. *Go Down, Moses and Other Stories*, dedicated to Caroline Barr, published by Random House May 11. Faulkner considers it a novel; "and Other Stories" added by publisher. Unable to sell enough stories to remain solvent, and deeply in debt, seeks Hollywood work through publishers, agents, and friends. Reports for five-month segment of low-paying ($300 a week), long-term Warner Bros. contract in July. Moves into Highland Hotel. Works with producer Robert Buckner on projected film about Charles de Gaulle until project is dropped. Resumes relationship with Meta Carpenter (now divorced from Rebner). Sees other old friends, including Ruth Ford (University of Mississippi alumna who had once dated brother Dean) and Clark Gable and Howard Hawks, with whom he goes fishing and hunting. Becomes friends with writers A. I. ("Buzz") Bezzerides and Jo Pagano. Eats often at favorite restaurant in Hollywood, Musso & Frank Grill. Gets month's leave to return to Oxford for Christmas while remaining on payroll.

1943   Returns to Warner Bros. January 16 on a 26-week, $350-per-week contract. Works with Hawks on *Battle Cry*. Sends one of his RAF pips to nephew James M. ("Jimmy") Faulkner, training to become Marine Corps fighter pilot. Warner Bros. picks up 52-week option at $400 a week beginning in August; Faulkner then takes leave of absence without pay to return to Oxford. Receives $1,000 advance from producer William Bacher to work at home on screenplay—"a fable, an indictment of war perhaps."

1944   Reports back to Warner Bros. February 14, and moves in with Bezzerides family on Saltair Street, just north of Santa Monica. Begins work for Hawks on film version of Ernest Hemingway's *To Have and Have Not*. Estelle and Jill join him in June. Depression, drinking, and periods of hospitalization follow their departure in September. Critic Malcolm Cowley writes the first of several essays on Faulkner to "redress the balance between his worth and his reputation," comparing him to Balzac and noting that nearly all his works are out of print. Writes to Cowley that "life is the same frantic steeplechase toward nothing everywhere and man stinks the same stink no matter where in time." Does some work on *Mildred Pierce*. Requests leave without pay and returns home December 15, taking with him the script for *The Big Sleep*, another Hawks film. Offered $5,000 advance to write a nonfiction book on the Mississippi River by Doubleday. Provisionally turns it down, saying: "I am 47. I have three more books of my own I want to write. I am like an aging mare, who has three more gestations in her before her time is over, and doesn't want to spend one of them breeding what she considers . . . a mule."

1945   Works on what he calls a "fable" ("writing and rewriting, weighing every word"). Returns to Hollywood and Warner Bros. in June, now at $500 a week. Cowley obtains publishers' approval in August to edit a collection of Faulkner's works for the Viking Portable Library series; Faulkner advises him. Works on scripts for *Stallion Road* and briefly with Jean Renoir on *The Southerner*. Continues work on the "fable," rising at 4:00 A.M. and working until 8:00 A.M. before going to the studio. Hollywood agent William Herndon refuses to release him from agent-client agreement and Warner Bros. refuses to release him from exclusive contract. Writes: "I dont like this damn place any better than I ever did. There is one comfort: at least I cant be any sicker tomorrow for Mississippi than I was yesterday." Refusing to assign Warner Bros. film rights to his own writings (including the "fable"), leaves studio without permission September 21. Returns to Rowan Oak, bringing with him Lady, the mare Jill rode during her stay in California. Draws map of Yoknapatawpha County and writes "1699–1945 The Compsons" to go with excerpt from *The Sound and the Fury* in Cowley's *Portable Faulkner*; says, "I should have done this when I wrote the book. Then the whole thing would have fallen into pattern like a jigsaw puzzle when the magician's wand touched it." Takes part in annual hunt in November. Short story, "An Error in Chemistry," wins second prize ($250) in *Ellery Queen's Mystery Magazine* contest in December.

1946   Feels trapped and depressed, drinks heavily. Cerf, Haas, and Ober persuade Jack Warner to give Faulkner leave of absence and release from rights assignment so he can finish his novel. Random House pays immediate advance of $1,000 and $500 a month after that. Faulkner worries that novel will take longer to complete than advances can cover. *The Portable Faulkner* published by Viking April 29. Tells class at University of Mississippi in May that the four greatest influences on his work were the Old Testament, Melville, Dostoevski, and Conrad. European reputation, especially in France, grows as works are translated. Jean-Paul Sartre writes of Faulkner's significance in "American Novelists in French Eyes" in September *Atlantic Monthly*. Sells film rights for stories "A Death Drag" and "Honor" to RKO, and "Two Soldiers" to Cagney Productions, for combined net of $6,600. Random House issues *The Sound and the Fury* (with "1699–1945 The Compsons" retitled "Appendix/Compson: 1699–1945" added as first part) and *As I Lay Dying* together in Modern Library edition in October. Works secretly on film script (unidentified) at home. Continues work on "fable" ("I dont write as fast as I used to").

1947   Meets with six literature classes at University of Mississippi on condition no notes be taken. Ranks Hemingway among top contemporaries, but says: "he has no courage, has never gone out on a limb." Quote appears in wire-service account, deeply offending Hemingway. Faulkner writes apology ("I have believed for years that the human voice has caused all human ills and I thought I had broken myself of talking. Maybe this will be my valedictory lesson"). In October *Partisan Review* refuses excerpt about a horse race from the "fable."

1948   Returns in January to mystery story mentioned to Haas seven years earlier; calls it *Intruder in the Dust*, and finishes it in April. MGM buys film rights for $50,000 before publication. Published by Random House September 27, it is his most commercially successful book. Feels free of financial pressure for the first time. Turns down Hamilton Basso's proposal of *New Yorker* profile: ". . . no piece in any paper about me as I am working tooth and nail at my lifetime ambition to be the last private individual on earth & expect every success since apparently there is no competition for the place." Eager to visit friends, goes to New York for holiday in October, but collapses after few days and recuperates at Cowley's home in Connecticut. Discusses collection of stories arranged by cycles with publisher, an idea first suggested by Cowley. Elected to the American Academy of Arts and Letters November 23.

1949   Director Clarence Brown brings MGM company to Oxford to film *Intruder in the Dust*. Faulkner works on film but is not given credit because of legal complications with Warner Bros. Buys and sails sloop, the *Ring Dove*, on Sardis Reservoir during spring and summer. Eudora Welty visits and Faulkner takes her sailing. In August is sought out by twenty-year-old Joan Williams, Bard College student and aspiring writer from Memphis, who admires his work. Reluctantly attends world premiere of *Intruder in the Dust* on October 9 at refurbished Lyric Theatre, owned by cousin Sallie Murry Williams and husband. Event causes the most excitement since Union General Smith burned Oxford in Civil War. "A Courtship" wins O. Henry Award for 1949. Random House publishes *Knight's Gambit*, volume of detective stories, November 27.

1950   Writes to Joan Williams in January, offering help as mentor: he will give her notes to write from, material he thinks will be a play. Goes to New York for ten days in February, staying at Algonquin; sees publishers, old friends actress Ruth Ford, Joel Sayre, and others, and Joan Williams. Receives American Academy's William Dean Howells Medal for Fiction in May; does not attend ceremony. Personal involvement with Joan Williams deepens when she returns to Memphis for summer. Gives her manuscript of *The Sound and the Fury*. Collaboration with her on play, *Requiem for a Nun*, becomes increasingly complicated. *Collected Stories of William Faulkner* published August 2 by Random House and adopted by Book-of-the-Month Club as alternate fiction selection, receiving generally good reviews. Informed November 10 he will receive 1949 (delayed until 1950) Nobel Prize for Literature. Reluctant to attend, drinks heavily at annual hunt, contracts bad cold, but finally agrees to go to Stockholm with Jill to receive award in December. Gives address, widely quoted. ("I believe that man will not merely endure: he will prevail.") Afterwards, writes to friend, "I fear that some of my fellow Mississippians will never forgive that 30,000$ that durn foreign country gave me for just sitting on my ass writing stuff that makes my own state ashamed to own me." Taking $5,000 for his own use, establishes "Faulkner Memorial" trust fund with rest of money for scholarships and other educational purposes.

1951   Goes to Hollywood in February for five weeks scriptwriting on *The Left Hand of God* for Hawks; given star treatment. Earns $14,000, including bonus for finishing script one day before deadline. Sees Meta Carpenter for last time. The Levee Press of Greenville, Mississippi, publishes horse-race piece as *Notes on a Horsethief* February 10. *Collected Stories* receives National Book Award for Fiction March 6. Page One Award given by Newspaper Guild of New York April 13. Releases statement to Memphis *Commercial Appeal* to correct earlier reports and to declare his belief that Willie McGee, a black man accused of raping a white woman, is innocent (McGee later executed). Takes three-week trip in April to New York, England, and France, visiting Verdun battlefield, which figures in "fable." Gives short commencement address at Jill's high school graduation May 28. Hears from Ruth Ford that Lemuel Ayers would like to produce *Requiem for a Nun* on stage, and goes to New York for week in July to work on it. *Requiem for a Nun*, with long prose introductions to its three acts, published by Random House October 2. Drives Jill to school at Pine Manor Junior College in Wellesley, Massachusetts, with Estelle. Goes to Cambridge, Massachusetts, in October and November to continue work on stage version of *Requiem for a Nun*. Receives Legion of Honor of the Republic of France at French Consulate in New Orleans October 26.

1952   Works on "fable" and trains horse; has two falls in February and March, injuring his back. Work now widely taught in colleges, but turns down honorary degree of Doctor of Letters from Tulane University, writing: "I feel that for one who did not even graduate from grammar school, to accept an honorary degree representative not only of higher learning but of post-graduate labor in it, would debase and nullify the whole aim of learning." (Later declines all other attempts to award him honorary degrees, often using this same reply.) Attacks " welfare and other bureaus of economic or industrial regimentation" in address delivered May 15 to Delta Council in Cleveland, Mississippi. Takes one-month trip to Europe, though plans to produce his play during Paris cultural festival had fallen through. Collapses in severe pain in Paris; doctors discover two old spinal compression fractures, possibly riding injuries, and advise spinal operation. Faulkner refuses and visits Harold Raymond of Chatto & Windus in England, still suffering severe pain. Treated near Oslo, Norway, by masseur on advice of Else Jonsson, friend working for his Swedish publisher, Bonniers ("he relaxed the muscles and with his hand, set the bad vertebra back into place"). Returns home feeling better than he has in years, but is not allowed to ride. Helps Joan Williams with her writing, but relationship is increasingly troubled. Injures back in boating accident in August. Hospitalized in Memphis in September for convulsive seizure brought on by drinking and back pain, and again in October after fall down stairs. Wears back brace. Helps Ford Foundation prepare *Omnibus* production of "The Faulkner Story" for television in November. Accepts editor and friend Saxe Commins' invitation to write at his Princeton home. Depression and drinking precipitate collapse and is admitted to private hospital in New York. After discharge stays in New York, working on "fable"; sees Joan Williams. Returns home for Christmas.

1953   Stays in Oxford until Estelle recovers from cataract operation. Returns to New York January 31 for indefinite stay. Hopes to finish the "fable." Medical problems continue; has extensive physiological and neurological examinations to determine cause of memory lapses, but nothing new is discovered. Returns to Oxford with Jill when Estelle is hospitalized for severe hemorrhage. Returns to New York May 9, when danger is over. Estelle accompanies him when he gives commencement address at Jill's graduation from Pine Manor. Jill enters University of Mexico in fall, and Estelle goes with her. Faulkner stays at Rowan Oak, working on "fable." Hospitalized in September in Memphis and in Wright's Sanitarium, small private hospital in Byhalia, fifty miles north of Oxford. *Life* magazine publishes two articles on him in October. Writes Phil Mullen: "Sweden gave me the Nobel Prize. France gave me the Legion d'Honneur. All my native land did for me was to invade my privacy over my protest and my plea." Drives to New York with Joan Williams in October; they see Dylan Thomas (whose earlier poetry-reading Faulkner had found moving) shortly before Thomas's death in November. Finishes *A Fable*. Leaves for Paris to work with Hawks on film, *Land of the Pharaohs*. Meets nineteen-year-old admirer, Jean Stein, in St. Moritz on Christmas Eve. Spends Christmas holidays in Stockholm.

1954   Returns to Kent, England, for a short stay, and then goes to Switzerland, Paris, and Rome, visiting friends and working on film. Joins Hawks near Cairo in mid-February. Arrives very ill with back pain and drinking and is taken to Anglo-American hospital. Works with veteran screenwriter Harry Kurnitz; produces largely unusable script. Joan Williams marries Ezra Bowen on March 6. Leaves Egypt March 29. Stays three weeks in Paris, spending one night in hospital. Returns home late April, after short stay in New York. Works on farm most of May; sells livestock and then rents farm out for a year. *A Fable* published by Random House, August 2. At request of U.S. State Department, attends International Writers' Conference in São Paulo, Brazil, stopping off on the way at Lima, Peru. Offers his services again on return home, writing, "I became suddenly interested in what I was trying to do . . ." Jill marries Paul D. Summers, Jr., August 21, and moves to Charlottesville, Virginia, where Paul attends law school. Checks into Algonquin Hotel, New York, September 10; divides time between New York and Oxford for next six months. Makes spoken record for Caedmon Records, works on stories and magazine pieces, and feels reassured of ability to earn money. Sees Jean Stein often.

1955   Writes article on hockey game at Madison Square Garden, "An Innocent at Rinkside," for *Sports Illustrated*. Accepts National Book Award for Fiction for *A Fable*, January 25. Works on script for *The Era of Fear*, ABC program about McCarthy hearings, but angrily rejects contract in March which includes morals clause and requires membership in the unions ABC deals with. Becomes increasingly involved in civil rights crisis; writes letters to editors advocating school integration; receives abusive letters and phone calls. Gives lecture "On Privacy. The American

Dream: What Happened to It" at the University of Oregon and University of Montana in April. *A Fable* wins Pulitzer Prize in May. Writes article on eighty-first running of Kentucky Derby for *Sports Illustrated*. Helps publicize *Land of the Pharaohs*; at Memphis preview in June says: "It's *Red River* all over again. The Pharaoh is the cattle baron, his jewels are the cattle, and the Nile is the Red River. But the thing about Howard is, he knows it's the same movie and he knows how to make it." July 29, leaves on State Department trip; spends three weeks in Japan, delighting Japanese hosts (remarks from colloquia published as *Faulkner at Nagano*, 1956). Returns to New York by way of Philippines (to visit stepdaughter and family), Italy, France, and Iceland, combining State Department appearances and vacation. *Big Woods*, collection of hunting stories with linking material, illustrated by Edward Shenton, published by Random House, October 14. Rushes to Oxford October 23 when mother, almost eighty-five, suffers cerebral hemorrhage; remains while she recuperates. Speaks against discrimination to integrated audience at Memphis meeting of Southern Historical Association, November 10; receives more threatening letters and phone calls. When Jean Stein visits the South, shows her New Orleans and Gulf Coast; they encounter Helen Baird Lyman on Pascagoula beach. Begins second Snopes volume (*The Town*) in early December.

1956   Columbia Pictures takes option on *The Sound and the Fury* for $3,500, and Universal buys *Pylon* for $50,000 (released in 1958 as *The Tarnished Angels*). Goes to New York February 8 to discuss finances with Ober: "what to do with money I have, where my kin and friends cant borrow it, against my old age." Worried about imminent violence, writes two articles urging voluntary integration in South to prevent Northern intervention: "On Fear: The South in Labor" (*Harper's*, June) and "A Letter to the North" (*Life*, March). Increasingly alarmed by rising tensions over court-ordered integration of University of Alabama, agrees to magazine interview; desperate and drinking, says if South were pushed too hard there would be civil war. Interviewer quotes him as saying that "if it came to fighting I'd fight for Mississippi against the United States even if it meant . . . shooting Negroes." (Later repudiates interview: "They are statements which no sober man would make, nor it seems to me, any sane man be-lieve.") On return to Oxford, injures back again when he is thrown by horse. Begins vomiting blood March 18; hos-pitalized in Memphis. By early April feels well enough to go with Estelle to Charlottesville, Virginia, where first grandson, Paul D. Summers III, is born April 15. Travels between New York, Charlottesville, and Oxford. Works on *The Town*. With P. D. East, starts semi-annual paper for Southern moderates consisting of political satire, entitled *The Southern Reposure*. First and only issue appears in mid-summer. Writes essay for *Ebony*, appealing for modera-tion. Albert Camus' adaptation of *Requiem for a Nun* suc-cessfully staged in Paris. Goes to Washington, D.C., for four days in September as chairman of writers' group in Eisenhower Administration's People-to-People Program. Chooses Harvey Breit of *The New York Times* as co-chair-man; attends meeting at Breit's home November 29.

1957　　Continues chairman's work into early February. Refuses Estelle's offer of a divorce. Depressed by changing rela-tionship with Jean Stein, suffers collapse. Goes to Char-lottesville as University of Virginia's first writer-in-residence February 15; moves into house on Rugby Road. Meets Professors Frederick L. Gwynn and Joseph Blotner, who assist him in setting schedules. Goes to Athens March 18 for two weeks at invitation of State Department; sees Greek adaptation of *Requiem for a Nun*. Cruises four days on private yacht in the Aegean. Accepts Silver Medal from Greek Academy. *The Town*, published May 1 by Ran-dom House, receives mixed reviews. Presents National In-stitute of Arts and Letters' Gold Medal for Fiction to John Dos Passos May 22. Concludes successful university se-mester of classroom and public appearances. Rides with friends and in the Farmington Hunt. Film *The Long Hot Summer*, based on *The Hamlet*, released. Returns to Row-an Oak for summer, tends farm and boat, visits mother. Goes to Charlottesville in November, intending to ride and fox-hunt, but falls ill with strep throat. Hunts quail near Oxford in December.

1958　　Begins to type first draft of *The Mansion*, third and last of the Snopes Trilogy, at Rowan Oak in early January. Re-turns to Charlottesville for second term as writer-in-resi-dence, January 30, meeting classes and public groups. At one session presents "A Word to Virginians," an appeal to Virginia to provide moderate leadership in the civil rights struggle. Goes to Princeton for two weeks, March 1, meeting with students individually and in groups. Declines invitation to visit Soviet Union with group of writers. Returns to Oxford in May. Saxe Commins dies July 17. Gives away niece Dean Falkner, daughter of brother Dean, at her wedding November 5, and hosts large reception for her at Rowan Oak. Goes to Princeton for another week of student sessions, and then to New York to work on *The Mansion* with Random House editor Albert Erskine. Returns to Charlottesville and rides in the Keswick and Farmington Hunts. Second grandchild, William Cuthbert Faulkner Summers, born December 2.

1959   *Requiem for a Nun*, version written for Ruth Ford, opens on Broadway January 30 after successful London run; closes after forty-three performances. Though not reappointed as writer-in-residence for the year, takes position as consultant on contemporary literature to Alderman Library at University of Virginia, and is assigned library study and typewriter. Accepted as outside member in Farmington Hunt; rides also with Keswick Hunt. Fractures collarbone when horse falls at Farmington hunter trials March 14. Rides again in May at Rowan Oak despite slow and painful recovery; another accident causes additional injuries, necessitating use of crutches for two weeks. Completes purchase of Charlottesville home on Rugby Road, August 21. Attends four-day UNESCO conference in Denver late September. Harold Ober, long-time agent and good friend, dies October 31. *The Mansion* published by Random House, November 13. Continues riding and hunting, suffering occasional falls.

1960   Divides time between Oxford and Charlottesville. Hospitalized briefly at Byhalia for collapse brought on by bourbon administered for self-diagnosed pleurisy. Accepts appointment as Balch Lecturer in American Literature at University of Virginia with minimal duties (salary $250 a year) in August. Mother Maud Butler Falkner suffers cerebral hemorrhage, dies October 16. Sees Charlottesville friends often, including Joseph and Yvonne Blotner. Becomes full member of Farmington Hunt; writes to Albert Erskine, "I have been awarded a pink coat, a splendor worthy of being photographed in." Establishes William Faulkner Foundation December 28, providing scholarships for Mississippi blacks and prize for first novels; wills Foundation manuscripts deposited in Alderman Library.

1961   Hunts quail in Oxford in January. Reluctantly leaves on two-week State Department trip to Venezuela April 1. Receives the Order of Andrés Bello, Venezuela's highest civilian award, gives speech expressing gratitude in Spanish. Third grandson, A. Burks Summers, born May 30. Shocked by news of Hemingway's suicide, July 2. Returns to Rowan Oak. Begins writing *The Horse Stealers: A Reminiscence*, conceived years earlier as novel about "a sort of Huck Finn"; enjoys work and finishes first draft August 21. Returns to Charlottesville in mid-October. Novel, re-titled *The Reivers*, taken by Book-of-the-Month Club eight months before publication. Checks into Algonquin Hotel to work on book with editor Albert Erskine, November 27. Hospitalized in Charlottesville, December 18, suffering from acute respiratory infection, back trouble, and drinking. Leaves after several days, but soon has relapse and is treated at Tucker Neurological and Psychiatric Hospital in Richmond until December 29.

1962   Still weak, injured in fall from horse, January 3. Readmitted to Tucker suffering from chest pain, fever, and drinking, January 8. Returns to Rowan Oak to recuperate in mid-January. Goes hunting with nephew James Faulkner. Returns to Charlottesville in early April; intends to make move permanent. Travels to West Point with Estelle, Jill, and Paul, April 19, and reads from *The Reivers*. Turns down President John F. Kennedy's invitation to attend White House dinner for American Nobel Prize winners. Accepts Gold Medal for Fiction of National Institute of Arts and Letters, presented by Eudora Welty, May 24. *The Reivers* published by Random House, June 4. Returns to Oxford, and on June 17 thrown by horse near Rowan Oak. Endures much pain, but continues to go for walks, and negotiates purchase of Red Acres, $200,000 estate outside Charlottesville. Pain and drinking increase; taken by Estelle and nephew James Faulkner to Wright's Sanitarium at Byhalia, July 5. Dies of heart attack, 1:30 A.M. on July 6. After service at Rowan Oak is buried in St. Peter's Cemetery, Oxford, Mississippi.

Note on the Texts

This volume reproduces the texts of *As I Lay Dying, Sanctuary, Light in August,* and *Pylon* that have been established by Noel Polk for publication by Faulkner's publisher. All texts are based upon Faulkner's own typescripts, which have been emended to account for his revisions in proof, his indisputable typing errors, and certain other errors and inconsistencies which clearly demand correction. The underlying holograph manuscript for each work has been consulted regularly throughout the editorial process; indeed, comparison has been made of all extant forms of these titles, published and unpublished, to determine what variants exist among the texts and why they exist. The goal of these labors, to discover the form of these works that Faulkner wanted in print at the time of their original publication, is frequently elusive. Although thousands of pages of typescript and manuscript and proof are available to the editor, it is not always clear what Faulkner's final intentions were, or even whether Faulkner had any "final" intentions regarding the individual component parts of his novels.

Copy-texts for these four novels are his own ribbon typescript setting copies. Faulkner typed and proofread these documents himself, with varying degrees of care; all of them bear his own holograph corrections and revisions. They also bear alterations of varying degrees of seriousness by his editors. Faulkner was in some ways an extremely consistent writer. He never included apostrophes in the words "dont," "wont," "aint," "cant," or "oclock," and very seldom used an apostrophe to indicate a dropped letter at the beginning or end of a spoken dialect word, such as "bout" or "runnin." He never used a period after the titles "Mr," "Mrs," or "Dr". The original editors generally accepted these practices (though the editor of *Light in August* did not accept "oclock" and the editor of *Pylon* did not accept "cant"), but the compositors often made mistakes and many apostrophes slipped in. A more serious problem was the editors' treatment of punctuation. The editors of *Pylon*, for example, made all of Faulkner's dashes into ellipses. They also frequently inserted commas into monologues where Faulkner was deliberately attempting to give the effect of spoken language. The occasionally broke up long sentences, and combined short sentences. Faulkner's compound words were also often changed—for example "oftenbrushed" and "flatvoiced" might become "often brushed" and "flat-voiced"—and some words he left separate were joined—"before hand" might become "beforehand," "down stream" become "downstream." Most of the editorial alterations in *As I Lay Dying*, *Sanctuary*, and *Light in August* are of these relatively minor types. Editorial intervention in *Pylon*, however, might well be called wholesale revision.

Faulkner's attitude toward such intervention is neither consistent nor entirely clear, though one might say, to put it oversimply, that he seems to have appreciated it when editors did something he liked and resented it when they did something he did not like. Almost from the beginning of his career, Faulkner was a supremely confident craftsman; he was at the same time also aware of the complexity of the demands his work would make not merely on the reader but also on publisher and editor and proofreader. His response to Ben Wasson's tampering with the Benjy section of *The Sound and the Fury*—that he would rewrite it if publishing were not grown up enough to publish it as he wanted it—reflects a very complex combination in his attitude of flexibility toward the realities of publication and of impatience with those mechanical processes of publication beyond his control that might thwart the accomplishment of his high artistic goals. His response also very specifically displays an irritation with the editors of this period who failed to understand what he was trying to do. He seems to have been indifferent to some types of editorial changes, and so he acquiesced to them: he sometimes simply did not care whether a semicolon became a full stop, or a long sentence or paragraph were shortened; he seems not to have cared whether certain words were spelled consistently or not, whether certain of his archaisms were modernized or not; and he seems to have expected his editor to divine from his typing whether each sentence was punctuated exactly as he wanted it—that is, whether or not a variation from an apparent pattern was in fact a deliberate variation or merely an inadvertency an editor should correct. Thus while some of his marks on galley and page proofs were genuine revisions of his own, many others were attempts to repair damage of one sort or another made by another hand on the typescript setting copy.

With the benefit of hindsight and decades of intense scholarship, we are now in a better position to understand Faulkner's intentions than the original editors were, although clearly many of the original editorial problems remain. The Polk texts attempt to reproduce Faulkner's typescripts as he presented them to his publishers, before editorial intervention. They accept only those revisions on typescript or proof that Faulkner seems to have initiated himself as a response to his own text, not those he made in response to a revision or a correction suggested by an editor; this is a very conservative policy which rejects many of Faulkner's proof revisions in favor of his original typescript.

While every effort has been made to preserve Faulkner's idiosyncrasies in spelling and punctuation, certain corrections of the typescript have been necessary. Unmistakable typing errors and other demonstrable errors have been corrected. Faulkner's punctuation has been regularized in two cases: except for using three hyphens (---) to indicate a one-em dash, Faulkner was inconsistent throughout his career in the number of hyphens he typed to indicate a dash longer than one em, and in the number of dots he typed to indicate ellipses; he frequently typed as many as twelve or thirteen hyphens or dots. In the Polk texts, three or four hyphens become a one-em dash, five or more become a two-em dash; up to six dots of ellipses are regularized to three or four according to traditional usage, seven or more become seven. Accent marks have been added to foreign words where appropriate.

According to Faulkner's sarcastic testimony in his notorious introduction to the Modern Library *Sanctuary* in 1932, he wrote *As I Lay Dying* "in six weeks, without changing a word." The manuscript and typescript reveal that he did not, of course, write it "without changing a word," although the dates on the manuscript indicate that he did indeed complete the holograph version in about eight weeks, between October 25 and December 29, 1929. "I set out deliberately to write a tour-de-force," he claimed later. "Before I ever put pen to paper and set down the first words I knew what the last word would be. . . . Before I began I said, I am going to write a book by which, at a pinch, I can stand or fall if I never touch ink again." He wrote *As I Lay Dying* at the University of Mississippi power plant, where he was employed as fireman and night watchman, mostly in the early morning, after everybody had gone to bed and power needs had diminished. He finished the typing, according to the date on the carbon typescript, on January 12, 1930, and sent it to Harrison Smith, who published it with very few editorial changes on October 6, 1930.

Extant documents relevant to the editing of *As I Lay Dying* are the holograph manuscript and the carbon typescript, at the Alderman Library of the University of Virginia, and the ribbon typesetting copy, at the Humanities Research Center of the University of Texas. No proof is known to survive; this is unfortunate, since there are a number of differences between the typescript and published book that must have occurred in proof. Copy-text for the Polk edition is the ribbon setting copy.

Sanctuary is a problematic novel in the Faulkner canon, partly because his introduction to it for its 1932 appearance in the Modern Library stresses its deliberate sensationalism and exploitation of "current trends" in literature for financial gain. After four novels which did not make him any money, he wrote: "I began to think of books in terms of possible money. I decided I might just as well make some of it myself. I took a little time out, and speculated what a person in Mississippi would believe to be current trends, chose what I thought was the right answer and invented the most horrific tale I could imagine and wrote it in about three weeks and sent it to Smith." Evidence from the holograph manuscript, however, completely refutes Faulkner's claim of haste and carelessness. This manuscript, among the two or three most complex documents in the Faulkner archive, preserves the painstaking effort, the thousands of revisions, the hundreds of shifts of large bodies of material and small that went into the composition of *Sanctuary*. We also know, despite his claim that he "took a little time out" and "speculated" about what to write, that the materials of *Sanctuary* reach further back into Faulkner's life (he had heard a story about a gangster named Popeye from some bootlegging friends), and that as early as 1925 while in Paris he wrote a long passage that was to become part of the novel's ending. Thus Faulkner's introduction to the Modern Library *Sanctuary* should properly be taken as a sardonic response to critics' charges that his work was sloppy and undisciplined—a response in particular to reviewers of *Sanctuary* who could not see past its sensational elements into its seriousness.

As Faulkner and legend would have it, Smith, upon reading *Sanctuary*, responded, "Good God, I can't publish this. We'd both be in jail." Faulkner then worked on *As I Lay Dying* and numerous short stories and was surprised some months later when Smith sent him galleys. "Then I saw that it was so terrible that there were but two things to do: tear it up or rewrite it. I thought again, 'It might sell; maybe 10,000 of them will buy it.' So I tore the galleys down and rewrote the book." Like other elements of Faulkner's account of *Sanctuary*, this one also begs a number of questions and does not tell the complete truth. Although it is not at this point clear what the complete truth is—why, that is, Smith originally delayed publication—we may assume, from information provided by Joseph Blotner's one-volume *Faulkner: A Biography* (New York: Random House, 1984), that Smith and Faulkner's agreement about its publication and that of *As I Lay Dying* were tied up with money that Smith lent Faulkner as an advance so that he could get married. Whether he revised the novel because he thought it was "terrible," as he claimed, or if there were perhaps other reasons for the revision, and whether he improved the novel in revision, are questions scholars are just now beginning to investigate.

Faulkner's revision of *Sanctuary*, like the original writing, was a very complex process: some large bodies of material he retyped and pasted to the existing galleys in appropriate places; he shifted material already set in type from one galley to another; other portions of the galleys he simply corrected in ink. As a major example of the kinds of revisions Faulkner made, one may note that the novel's opening scene, the long confrontation between Horace Benbow and Popeye across the spring, was originally tucked away in chapter II; Faulkner retyped the scene, changed its point of view from Horace's to Popeye's, and moved it to the beginning of the novel. The novel's original opening, Horace's meditation on the Negro murderer in the Jefferson jail, became chapter XVI of the revised version.

Extant documents relevant to the editing of *Sanctuary* are the holograph manuscript, the carbon typescript, and a set of the original uncorrected galley proofs, all at the Alderman Library of the University of Virginia; the ribbon typescript setting copy, at the University of Mississippi; and the corrected galleys, at the Humanities Research Center of the University of Texas. The manuscript of *Sanctuary* bears the dates January–May 1929; the carbon typescript is dated, on the final page, May 25, 1929. The revisions in galley took place in the late summer of 1930. Jonathan Cape and Harrison Smith published the novel on February 9, 1931.

Copy-text for the Polk edition of *Sanctuary* consists of the new typescript appended to the old galleys and the original typescript underlying those portions of the galley text which he allowed to stand as set or as revised by hand. Typescript of the original version is used wherever possible in order to avoid editorial and compositorial errors that may have crept into the original typesetting. Differences between the published book and the revised galleys imply that someone made further changes on a second set of galleys, now missing, pulled after the revisions had been set; all of these additions are complete sentences and seem clearly to be Faulkner's additions. Some regularizing has been necessary; Faulkner's usage changed somewhat over the eighteen months between the original writing and the revision: he was very explicit, for example, in altering the original's "suitcase" to "suit case" several times, though he did not catch them all; he invariably typed "whisky" in the original typescript, "whiskey" in the new. Such simple alterations have been regularized in favor of the newer version. Other cases are more complicated: Tommy's dialect, for example, is noticeably different in the later version; these inconsistencies have been allowed to stand except in one passage (p. 193) where the final "g" has been deleted from several "ing" words so as not to have Tommy's use of "ing" in some words and of "in" in others distort the reader's sense of Tommy's dialect pronunciation.

According to the dates on the manuscript, Faulkner began a novel called *Dark House* on August 17, 1931; the finished manuscript, completed February 19, 1932, was called *Light in August*. The typescript was only minimally marked by editors. Faulkner made several minor changes in proof. The novel was published on October 6, 1932. Extant documents relevant to the editing of *Light in August* include the holograph manuscript and the larger portion of the typescript setting copy (pp. 1–470), at the Alderman Library of the University of Virginia; the final pages (471–527) of the setting copy and the corrected galleys are in the Humanities Research Center of the University of Texas. Copy-text for the Polk edition is Faulkner's typescript.

In October 1934 Faulkner began writing *Pylon*, as a respite, he said, from his work on *Absalom, Absalom!*, which had grown "inchoate." He wrote *Pylon* very rapidly, sending chapters to Hal Smith as he typed them, between November 25 and December 15, 1934; he did a good deal of revising in galleys. Smith and Haas published it on March 25, 1935. The editors at Smith and Haas made many changes in this text: they bowdlerized; they shortened sentences and paragraphs and clarified and simplified whenever they thought appropriate; sometimes they queried Faulkner, sometimes not; sometimes he replied to their inquiries and changes, sometimes he did not. The galleys of this novel are thus extremely interesting, in that they are full of Faulkner's and his editors' revisions and exchanges. Many of Faulkner's changes on these galleys are efforts to repair damage done to the typescript by these editors. For example, the long paragraph beginning on page 836 (ending on page 840), a flashback detailing an encounter between Hagood and the reporter's mother and a related encounter between Hagood and the reporter, was typed by Faulkner as a single paragraph; Faulkner did this to separate it typographically and visually from the rest of the text. It occurs abruptly in the middle of a conversation between Hagood and Jiggs; the text reverts to that same conversation at the end of the flashback with no other signal than Faulkner's paragraph break. The editors at Smith and Haas, however, broke the long paragraph into numerous smaller, conventional ones, destroying the visual effect Faulkner intended. When confronted with the reparagraphing in galleys, Faulkner, at least as far as available evidence would indicate, did not try to restore the passage to its original form, but noted instead some confusion about the transition from the flashback into present time, and so rewrote the first paragraph following the flashback, adding, "But that was eighteen months ago, now Hagood and Jiggs stood side by side . . ." The Polk text does not take Faulkner's acquiescence to the reparagraphing to indicate his full approval of it, but rather to indicate his professional willingness to recognize that there might be more than one way to accomplish his general aims. Because this was not an original inspiration, but rather a simple and efficient repair of damage the editors had done, the Polk text restores the typescript's long paragraph and rejects Faulkner's revision of the succeeding paragraph. The typescript and galleys present numerous such problems. Many other changes were generated by Faulkner's response to the text as he saw it set in type for the first time. The Polk text tries to distinguish the latter from those caused by editorial intervention, although it is not always easy to do so. The reader familiar with the first edition of *Pylon* will find the Polk text considerably different in a number of significant respects.

Extant documents relevant to the editing of *Pylon* are the typescript setting copy at the University of Virginia's Alderman Library and the corrected galleys at the Humanities Research Center of the University of Texas. The holograph manuscript, at the University of Mississippi, is incomplete. Polk's copy-text is Faulkner's typescript setting copy.

American English continues to fluctuate; for example, a word may be spelled in more than one way, even in the same work. Commas are sometimes used expressively to suggest the movements of voice, and capitals are sometimes meant to give significances to a word beyond those it might have in its uncapitalized form. Since standardization would remove such effects, this volume preserves the spelling, punctuation, capitalization, and wording of the texts established by Noel Polk, which strive to be as faithful to Faulkner's usage as surviving evidence permits. In this volume the reader has the results of the most detailed scholarly efforts thus far made to establish the texts of *As I Lay Dying*, *Sanctuary*, *Light in August*, and *Pylon*.

Notes

In the notes below, numbers refer to page and line of the present volume (the line count includes chapter headings). For further information on *As I Lay Dying*, consult Calvin S. Brown, *A Glossary of Faulkner's South* (New Haven: Yale University Press, 1976); Jessie McGuire Coffee, *Faulkner's Un-Christlike Christians: Biblical Allusions in the Novels* (Ann Arbor: UMI Research Press, 1983); André Bleikasten, *Faulkner's As I Lay Dying* (Bloomington: Indiana University Press, rev. ed., 1973); and *William Faulkner's "As I Lay Dying,"* ed. by Dianne L. Cox (New York: Garland Publishing, 1984). For further information on *Sanctuary*, consult *Sanctuary: The Original Text*, edited, with an Afterword and Notes, by Noel Polk (New York: Random House, 1981); Gerald Langford, *Faulkner's Revision of "Sanctuary": A Collation of the Unrevised Galleys and the Published Book* (Austin: University of Texas Press, 1972); and *Twentieth Century Interpretations of Sanctuary: A Collection of Critical Essays*, ed. by J. Douglas Canfield (Englewood Cliffs, N.J.: Prentice-Hall, 1982). For further information on *Light in August*, consult *Twentieth Century Interpretations of Light in August: A Collection of Critical Essays*, ed. by David L. Minter (Englewood Cliffs, N.J.: Prentice-Hall, 1969); François Pitavy, *Faulkner's "Light in August"* (Bloomington: Indiana University Press, rev. ed., 1973); Regina K. Fadiman, *Faulkner's "Light in August": A Description and Interpretation of the Revisions* (Charlottesville: University Press of Virginia, 1975); and *William Faulkner's "Light in August,"* ed. by François L. Pitavy (New York: Garland Publishing, 1981). For further information on *Pylon*, consult the appropriate portions of Joseph Blotner, *Faulkner: A Biography* (New York: Random House, 1974); Cleanth Brooks, *William Faulkner: Toward Yoknapatawpha and Beyond* (New Haven: Yale University Press, 1978); and Michael Millgate, *The Achievement of William Faulkner* (New York: Random House, 1965).

AS I LAY DYING

1.1   AS I LAY DYING]   When asked the source of his title, Faulkner would sometimes quote from memory the speech of Agamemnon to Odysseus in the *Odyssey*, Book XI: "As I lay dying the woman with the dog's eyes would not close my eyes for me as I descended into Hades."

3.8   laidby cotton]   A cultivated crop that will require no further attention until it is picked at harvest time.

10.9   pussel-gutted]   Faulkner defined this to mean "bloated."

15.10   frailed]   Variant of flailed. To whip or beat.

22.37   laid-by]   See note 3.8.

26.1–2   I . . . falls.]   See Matt. 10:29.

48.7   Christmas masts]   According to Faulkner, comic masks worn by children at Christmas and Halloween.

71.3–12   sweat . . . Lord.]   Cf. Gen. 3:19 and Matt. 13:12.

71.19–20   I . . . chastiseth.]   Anse's garbled recollection of Heb. 12:6.

83.36   busted out]   Plowed or harrowed in preparation for planting.

87.24–28   It . . . away.]   Book Four of *The Hamlet* (1940) tells the story of the incursion of these "spotted horses" into Yoknapatawpha County in the first decade of the twentieth century.

112.12–14 there . . . sinned]   See Jesus' parable of the lost sheep in Luke 15:7.

124.32   Inverness]   A town about ninety miles southwest of Oxford.

126.27   aguer]   An ague, a malarial fever.

136.37   Yoknapatawpha county]   The first appearance of the name of what Faulkner would call "my apocryphal county." Mississippi's Lafayette County, where Faulkner spent most of his life, is bounded on the south by the Yocona River. Some early maps transliterated the river's Chickasaw name as Yockney-Patafa. According to Faulkner, it meant "water runs slow through flat land."

SANCTUARY

179.1   SANCTUARY]   Faulkner wrote the following misleading, but often quoted introduction to *Sanctuary* when the Modern Library reprinted it in 1932. He did not want it included in later printings by Random House.

"This book was written three years ago. To me it is a cheap idea, because it was deliberately conceived to make money. I had been writing books for about five years, which got published and not bought. But that was all right. I was young then and hard-bellied. I had never lived among nor known people who wrote novels and stories and I suppose I did not know that people got money for them. I was not very much annoyed when publishers refused the mss. now and then. Because I was hard-gutted then. I could do a lot of things that could earn what little money I needed, thanks to my father's unfailing kindness which supplied me with bread at need despite the outrage to his principles at having been of a bum progenitive.

"Then I began to get a little soft. I could still paint houses and do carpenter work, but I got soft. I began to think about making money by writing. I began to be concerned when magazine editors turned down short stories, concerned enough to tell them that they would buy these stories later any-way, and hence why not now. Meanwhile, with one novel completed and consistently refused for two years, I had just written my guts into *The Sound and the Fury* though I was not aware until the book was published that I had done so, because I had done it for pleasure. I believed then that I would never be published again. I had stopped thinking of myself in publishing terms.

"But when the third mss., *Sartoris*, was taken by a publisher and (he having refused *The Sound and the Fury*) it was taken by still another publisher, who warned me at the time that it would not sell, I began to think of myself again as a printed object. I began to think of books in terms of possible money. I decided I might just as well make some of it myself. I took a little time out, and speculated what a person in Mississippi would believe to be current trends, chose what I thought was the right answer and invented the most horrific tale I could imagine and wrote it in about three weeks and sent it to Smith, who had done *The Sound and the Fury* and who wrote me immedi-ately, 'Good God, I can't publish this. We'd both be in jail.' So I told Faulk-ner, 'You're damned. You'll have to work now and then for the rest of your life.' That was in the summer of 1929. I got a job in the power plant, on the night shift, from 6 P.M. to 6 A.M., as a coal passer. I shoveled coal from the bunker into a wheelbarrow and wheeled it in and dumped it where the fire-man could put it into the boiler. About 11 o'clock the people would be going to bed, and so it did not take so much steam. Then we could rest, the fireman and I. He would sit in a chair and doze. I had invented a table out of a wheelbarrow in the coal bunker, just beyond a wall from where a dynamo ran. It made a deep, constant humming noise. There was no more work to do until about 4 A.M., when we would have to clean the fires and get up steam again. On these nights, between 12 and 4, I wrote *As I Lay Dying* in six weeks, without changing a word. I sent it to Smith and wrote him that by it I would stand or fall.

"I think I had forgotten about *Sanctuary*, just as you might forget about anything made for an immediate purpose, which did not come off. *As I Lay Dying* was published and I didn't remember the mss. of *Sanctuary* until Smith sent me the galleys. Then I saw that it was so terrible that there were but two things to do: tear it up or rewrite it. I thought again, 'It might sell; maybe 10,000 of them will buy it.' So I tore the galleys down and rewrote the book. It had been already set up once, so I had to pay for the privilege of rewriting it, trying to make out of it something which would not shame *The Sound and the Fury* and *As I Lay Dying* too much and I made a fair job and I hope you will buy it and tell your friends and I hope they will buy it too."

182.30–31   Kinston]   A fictional town in the Mississippi Delta (that part of the river's flood plain extending roughly from Memphis, Tenn., to Vicks-burg, Miss.) about twenty miles west of Water Valley, not Kingston, Miss., which is southeast of Natchez.

182.31   Jefferson]   The seat of Faulkner's Yoknapatawpha County, resembling Oxford of Lafayette County. See note 136.37.

184.5–6   that . . . mouth]   In Gustave Flaubert's *Madame Bovary* (1856), Emma Bovary kills herself by taking arsenic. When her head is momentarily raised in her coffin, a black liquid flows from her mouth. (Part III, Ch. 9.)

189.40   Delta]   See note 182.30–31.

192.15   orange stick]   A pointed stick of orange-wood, used in manicuring.

195.33   F.F.V.]   A member of one of the "First Families of Virginia."

197.30   Starkville]   A town seventy miles southeast of Oxford, the seat of what was then Mississippi Agricultural and Mechanical College, traditional athletic rival of the University of Mississippi.

201.23   "The Shack'll be open,"]   The Shack was operated at one time by Faulkner's lifelong friend, Miss Ella Somerville.

226.10   use in]   To live in, or stay in.

258.17   heaven-tree]   The princess tree, or royal paulownia (*Paulownia tomentosa*).

263.40   loblollies]   Mud-puddles.

267.8   Yoknapatawpha county]   See note 136.37.

279.23   was hael]   An archaic drinking toast, meaning literally "be in good health," that became associated with Christmas, particularly Twelfth Night festivities. Now generally spelled "wassail."

296.31   Gordon hall]   The men's dining hall at the University of Mississippi when Faulkner worked at the post office there.

309.36   The Gayoso hotel]   At this time Memphis's most notable hotel.

328.36   kissing your elbow]   That if you could actually do it, you could change your sex.

336.5   John Gilbert]   A popular leading man who scored his greatest success in romantic silent films.

357.34   monkey glands]   Dr. Eugen Steinach experimented with the transplantation of sex glands to produce rejuvenation.

366.2–3   Delsarte-ish]   François Delsarte invented a system to produce graceful speech and elocution.

370.17–18   O tempora! O mores!]   "Oh what times! Oh what standards!" Marcus Tullius Cicero, *In Catilinam*, I, 1.

386.39   Less oft is peace.]   From Percy Bysshe Shelley, "To Jane: The Recollection" (1822).

395.32   "Ed Pinaud."]   A line of toilet preparations were marketed under this name.

LIGHT IN AUGUST

402.21   mixed train]   A train composed of passenger cars and freight cars.

443.6–7   General . . . Jefferson]   On December 20, 1862, Confederate Major General Earl Van Dorn carried out a daring raid on General Ulysses S. Grant's stores at Holly Springs, thirty miles north of Oxford.

493.23   Out . . . children]   See Psalms 8:22; Matt. 21:16.

534.3   Hiram]   A derisive term for a country man: yokel or bumpkin.

535.24–25   hands . . . beast]   Cf. Rev. 7:14.

549.3   Michael Himself]   The Archangel (cf. Rev. 12:7).

549.28   wrathful . . . Throne.]   Cf. Rev. 20:11–12.

578.3   frail]   See note 15.10.

607.24   single action]   The hammer must be cocked by hand before the trigger can be pulled.

612.17   Not . . . often]   See note 386.39.

649.18   Mottstown]   This spelling also appears in *The Hamlet* (1940), although in *As I Lay Dying* Faulkner spelled the name of what is apparently the same town as Mottson.

670.23   that peace]   See John 14:27.

673.34   out . . . children]   See note 493.23.

673.40–674.1   I have . . . him]   Cf. God's mark on Cain in Gen. 4:11–12, 15.

684.11   nere . . . earth]   Matt. 10:29.

684.14–15   her . . . desert]   See Isa. 13:21 and 35:9.

684.30   'He . . . earth']   Cf. Job 1:7.

684.33–34   one . . . strove]   Cf. Gen. 32:24–26.

706.38   *halvers*]   Claim to a half share of the crop.

736.1   P.C.]   Post of command, command post.

769.8–9   those two Frenchmen]   Alphonse and Gaston, excessively polite to each other, as in giving precedence in going through doors.

774.19   Saulsbury]   A town about seventy-five miles east of Memphis.

PYLON

784.1–10   **FEINMAN . . . Dollars**]   On February 9, 1934, New Orleans'
Shushan Airport, constructed on land reclaimed from Lake Pontchartrain,
was officially dedicated. It was named after Colonel A. L. Shushan, president
of the Levee Board. Beginning on February 14, several days of aerial competition and exhibitions followed. The events of the air meet, postponed because of bad weather, coincided with the Mardi Gras festivities. In December
1934, Faulkner wrote his publisher about his use of New Orleans and Shushan Airport and added, "But there all actual resemblance stops . . . the
incidents in Pylon are all fiction and Feinman is fiction so far as I know, the
only more or less deliberate copying of fact, or the nearest to it, is the character 'Matt Ord,' who is Jimmy Weddell."

792.34   Jules Despleins]   One of the Shushan competitors was Michael de
Troyat, billed as the "European acrobatic champion."

795.19   Vas . . . Sharlie?]   The frequent refrain of a radio comedian of
the 1930s who called himself the Baron Munchausen.

795.33–34   modest . . . lapel]   Faulkner occasionally wore on his lapel a
small pair of silver wings bearing the initials QB, which stood for Quiet
Birdmen, an organization of pilots formed after World War I for charitable
purposes, later a purely social group.

801.22   dot-dot-dash-dot]   The Morse code signal for F identifies Feinman Airport.

809.33–36   **FIRST . . . Plane**]   The night Faulkner and Omlie arrived at
Shushan Airport, Capt. W. Merle Nelson died in the crash of his "Comet
plane."

813.23   "Laughing . . . Poik!"]   Here reporting a race result, the newsboy employs one variety of New Orleans dialect, one of several in the novel.

815.12   (i n r i)]   This abbreviation stands for *Iesus Nazarenus, Rex Iudaeo-
rum*, which Pilate ordered placed above Jesus' head on the cross. (John 19:19)

817.1   tomorrow and tomorrow]   From the passage in Shakespeare's *Mac-
beth*, V, v, 19–28; also used for the titles of the fourth and fifth chapters and
the title of *The Sound and the Fury*.

827.1   *the Vieux Carré*]   The old square, the site of the original city of
New Orleans, later called the French Quarter, the hundred-odd square blocks
stretching from Canal Street on the south to Esplanade on the north, and
from North Rampart Street to the Mississippi River.

827.7–8   spent . . . clatterfalque;]   The debris left after the passage in the
Mardi Gras parade of one of the ornate floats built by particular social groups
("Krewes") according to a dominant theme. Cf. ll. 77–78 of *The Waste Land*,
by T. S. Eliot, and the passage from which these lines are derived in Shakespeare's *Antony and Cleopatra*, II, ii, 196–97.

829.35 "Toulouse,"] Street in the French Quarter. The following fictional streets are apparently derived from real ones in New Orleans: Grand-lieu St. from Canal St., St. Jules Ave. from St. Charles Ave., Barricade St. from Rampart St., and perhaps Lanier Ave. from Claiborne Ave. Alphonse's Restaurant is probably based on Antoine's, and Renaud's upon Arnaud's.

854.9 miked] Used a micrometer to measure the valves in the airplane engine to ensure that they are within the proper tolerance for efficient operation.

856.13–14 there . . . eat] Cf. "i sing of olaf glad and big," by E. E. Cummings.

916.34 *The . . . Franciana*] This corporation is probably modeled on that of Jimmy Weddell and Harry T. Williams, The Weddell-Williams Air Corporation at Patterson, Louisiana, on which the Blaisdell of the novel is based.

928.13–15 We . . . regimented.] Feinman is referring to regulatory agencies of the Roosevelt administration such as the A.A.A., the Agricultural Adjustment Administration.

937.1 *Lovesong of J. A. Prufrock*] From the poem by T. S. Eliot.

CATALOGING INFORMATION

Faulkner, William, 1897–1962.
    Novels 1930–1935: As I lay dying; Sanctuary;
    Light in August; Pylon.
    Ed. by Joseph Blotner and Noel Polk.

    (The Library of America ; 25)
I. Title. II. As I lay dying. III. Sanctuary. IV. Light
in August. V. Pylon. VI. Series.
PS3511.A86A6   1985   813'.52
ISBN 0-940450-26-7

This book is set in 10 point Linotron Galliard,
a face designed for photocomposition by Matthew Carter
and based on the sixteenth-century face Granjon. The paper
is acid-free Olin Nyalite and meets the requirements for perma-
nence of the American National Standards Institute. The binding
material is Brillianta, a 100% woven rayon cloth made by
Van Heek-Scholco Textielfabrieken, Holland. The com-
position is by Haddon Craftsmen, Inc., and The
Clarinda Company. Printing and binding
by R. R. Donnelley & Sons Company.
Designed by Bruce Campbell.